THE LYRIC THEORY READER

The Lyric Theory Reader

A Critical Anthology

Edited by Virginia Jackson and Yopie Prins

JOHNS HOPKINS UNIVERSITY PRESS BALTIMORE

Printed in the United States of America on acid-free paper
9 8 7 6 5 4 3 2

Johns Hopkins University Press
2715 North Charles Street
Baltimore, Maryland 21218-4363
www.press.jhu.edu

Library of Congress Cataloging-in-Publication Data

The lyric theory reader : a critical anthology / edited by Virginia Jackson and Yopie Prins.
pages cm
Includes index.
ISBN 978-1-4214-1199-6 (hardcover : acid-free paper) — ISBN 978-1-4214-1200-9 (pbk. : acid-free paper) — ISBN 1-4214-1199-7 (hardcover : acid-free paper) — ISBN 1-4214-1200-4 (pbk. : acid-free paper) 1. Lyric poetry—History and criticism—Theory, etc. I. Jackson, Virginia Walker, editor of compilation. II. Prins, Yopie, editor of compilation.
PN1356.L98 2013
809.1'4—dc23 2013016725

A catalog record for this book is available from the British Library.

Special discounts are available for bulk purchases of this book. For more information, please contact Special Sales at 410-516-6936 or specialsales@press.jhu.edu.

Johns Hopkins University Press uses environmentally friendly book materials, including recycled text paper that is composed of at least 30 percent post-consumer waste, whenever possible.

CONTENTS

PART TWO: TWENTIETH-CENTURY LYRIC READERS

PART THREE: LYRIC DEPARTURES

ACKNOWLEDGMENTS

The Lyric Theory Reader is a collaborative project in every sense. It would not be possible without the deep and lifelong collaboration of the editors, so we begin by thanking one another. Our research assistants—Leif Eckstrom, Rachel Feder, and Sara Grewal—deserve co-editorial credit. Their wizardry in transcribing, proofing, filing, and gathering permissions for the essays included here literally made this book possible. Generous research funding from Tufts University, the University of Michigan, and the University of California, Irvine, supported these collaborations. The editors at Johns Hopkins University Press have also been extraordinarily supportive of our collective editorial efforts at every step in this long process. We thank them and the Press's insightful outside reader for believing in this book.

The graduate students in our lyric theory seminars at Rutgers, New York University, Tufts, Irvine, and Michigan have each and all contributed to making this a better book. They test drove the anthology at high speeds and with great skill, and they did us the great favor of figuring out what worked and what slowed them down. There are also colleagues across many universities who have helped to shape the ongoing conversation surrounding this project. At institutions and conferences, the agreements, disagreements, celebrations, and discoveries we have been fortunate enough to encounter with other thinkers about poetry and poetics are the living foundation of this book. And like all long intellectual labors, this anthology has required not only enormous institutional and intellectual support but also the patience and help of our friends and family, including Martin Harries and Michael Daugherty. We are grateful to all our interlocutors, near and far.

Finally, we would like to thank the lyric theorists whose essays appear in this volume. This anthology is about them, and it is for the readers who continue to think about poetry in the ways these theorists have imagined they might—and in ways neither the editors nor the contributors could have foreseen.

THE LYRIC THEORY READER

General Introduction

We take it for granted that we know what a lyric is. As a term derived from ancient Greek to designate a song accompanied by the lyre, its association with musical performance persists today in popular "song lyrics" with instrumental accompaniment, but "lyric poetry" is also invoked more abstractly as a literary production that is read, not sung. Often a poem is considered lyric when it represents an utterance in the first person, an expression of personal feeling, according to a model of modern lyric reading that diverges from the way poems were performed (and read) in antiquity. Or as an alternative to expressive reading, a poem may be called lyric when it foregrounds the musicality of language by appeal to the ear or to the eye. Sometimes poems are called lyrics simply because they are short; sometimes lyric is defined in opposition to narrative, assuming a modern binary in literary modes; increasingly, lyric is a way to describe the essence of poetry, a poem at its most poetic. Whether we think about the lyric as ancient origin or modern imaginary, on the page or in the air, we need to have some idea of what a lyric is (or was) in the first place. Yet it has become as notoriously difficult to define the lyric as it is impossible to define poetry itself.[1] How is it possible that almost all poetry has come to be read as essentially lyric and at the same time we do not seem to know how to define the lyric? Since assumptions widely shared are usually the ideas least and last investigated, it may be the case that because we have come to think of all poetry as lyric, we have not really wanted a concise definition of lyric. Perhaps the lyric has become so difficult to define because we need it to be blurry around the edges, to remain capacious enough to include all kinds of verse and all kinds of ideas about what poetry is or should be.

Yet such problems of definition are also always invitations to theorists. This anthology traces a critical genealogy of the modern idea of lyric as it has emerged in Anglo-American literary criticism of the past century. To say that the lyric is a modern idea or theory rather than an ancient genre might surprise readers accustomed to thinking about lyric poetry as a given in the Western tradition—indeed, as the oldest form in that tradition, the origin of literature and civilization. It is true that if we think of choral hymns or Sappho's odes or even tribal chants or popular song as the roots of lyric, a critical genealogy of lyric as a modern theory does not make much sense. But the concept of lyric as the oldest form of poetic expression is actually a relatively recent notion; specifically, it is a post-Enlightenment idea, developed steadily over the course of the nineteenth and twentieth centuries. *The Lyric Theory Reader* traces only the past century's consolidation of our current thinking about the lyric, though the history of that idea is a much longer story, and whoever "we" are is subject to change. By "our current thinking" we mean primarily literary criticism that has proven influential for Anglo-American readers and poets both inside and outside the academy in the past century. Although the critics included in this anthology did not invent the lyric, we can trace the sources and direction of their influence by gathering the recent history of critical thought about the lyric. The purpose of this volume is to demonstrate how a reading of poetry as lyric that emerged by fits and starts in the nineteenth century became mainstream practice in the development of modern literary criticism in the twentieth century. The majority of the essays selected for this volume were written after the middle of the twentieth century; we think that by examining the most recent chapter of the critical history of the lyric, we may be able to see not only where our ideas have come from but also where they might be going.

The history of lyric reading is the history of thinking about poetry as more and more abstract and ineffable. A resistance to definition may be the best basis for definition of the lyric—and of poetry—we currently have. While it is still common to cite the definition of lyric in "official verse culture" (as described by Charles Bernstein in his 1992 manifesto, *A Poetics*)[2] in terms of a record of the voice or the mind speaking to itself (as in T. S. Eliot's understanding of the "first voice" of poetry, for which see section 3), in practice the lyric is whatever we think poetry is. Sometimes we think that the lyric is what contemporary poetry reacts against, as in recent avant-garde or conceptual thinking about poetics that views lyric as a mummified remnant of Romanticism, for example.[3] And sometimes we think that the lyric is the most fundamental and unchanging poetic form, as when Helen Vendler writes, "the lyric remains the genre that directs its *mimesis* toward the performance of the mind in *solitary* speech" (see section 2). These may seem like competing definitions of the lyric in our contemporary moment, but their difference is only apparent inasmuch as they share a general sense that the lyric is the genre of personal expression, a sense assumed whenever we talk about "the lyric I." What they disagree about is the value to attribute to that general sense.

The survey of twentieth- and twenty-first-century criticism offered here shows that this general definition of the lyric (whether valued or devalued) now seems to us a given only because twentieth-century literary criticism made it up. Reuben Brower (see section 3) was enormously influential in creating the dramatic model of "the mind in *solitary* speech" that Vendler (his student) expanded, but that was not the model for many of the other critics included here. The many overlapping models of the lyric in the twentieth and twenty-first centuries contribute to making our current sense of lyric poetry very large, so large that we think we know what we mean when we refer to poems as *lyric* (whether we think that is a good or a bad thing), but also too large to mean anything in particular.

This is not to say that the twentieth century invented the lyric out of whole cloth. The modern invention of the lyric has usually been attributed to Romanticism. Mary Poovey has gone so far as to claim that "contemporary literary criticism is organized around the romantic lyric—both in the sense that it treats its analytic objects as if they were lyrics and in the sense that it contains features that perform lyric functions."[4] But it does not make much sense to talk about "the romantic lyric" as if the lyric was in fact one genre in the nineteenth century and ever after—whether a contemporary revision of the genre does or does not now organize literary criticism as such. It seems more accurate to describe the lyric as a project modern literary criticism took from the nineteenth century and made its own. In the late eighteenth century, neoclassical and popular verse genres began to merge into larger categories, eventuating in what in 1819 Johann Wolfgang von Goethe called "the three natural forms of poetry": the narrative, the lyric, and the dramatic. Goethe suggested that all poetry could be fit into these three major categories and that if one put the "three main elements on a circle, equidistant from one another" one could see how these broad categories formed a system of genres, the system of literature itself.[5]

This way of thinking indicated a shift not only in the fortunes of the lyric but also in the conception of the form and function of literary genres—in many ways, it marked the invention not simply of the modern lyric but of literature as we know it. Before that, William Wordsworth and Samuel Taylor Coleridge had signaled the movement of popular genres with particular social functions toward the abstract literary lyric in their *Lyrical Ballads* (1798), but the term remained adjectival rather than nominal. In the 1820s and 1830s, G. W. F. Hegel famously elevated the name of the lyric to one of the highest places in his *Aesthetics*, considering it the pure representation of subjectivity and therefore a form likely to further the spirit of the age. Hegel cast the lyric as the most difficult of modern genres because in it the poet must become "the centre which holds the whole lyric work of art together," and in order to do so he must achieve a "specific mood" and "must identify *himself* with this particularization of himself as with himself, so that in it he feels and envisages *himself*."[6] Hegel repeated these assertions because he saw no less than the achievement of subjectivity at stake in the lyric: "In this way alone does [the poet] then become a self-bounded subjective entity (*Totalität*)." That attainment of subjective wholeness would in turn represent both perfect expression and the dialectical accomplishment of historical progress, for in his expression the poet moves us all forward toward enlightenment. Hegel's was an idealized version of the lyric indeed, especially in comparison to the enormous variety of verse genres in active circulation in the nineteenth century: epistles and hymns, ballads and elegies, drinking songs and odes. The immense social currency of so many verse genres seems to have inspired nineteenth-century thinkers to imagine a transcendent poetic genre ever more abstracted from that currency, a genre ever more a perfect idea rather than an imperfect practice.

In 1833, John Stuart Mill paralleled Hegel in claiming that lyric poetry is "more eminently and peculiarly poetry than any other," yet he sought in vain for an adequate representative of a lyric poet among his British contemporaries.[7] Though he praised Wordsworth and Percy Bysshe Shelley, he lamented that "the genius of Wordsworth is essentially unlyrical," and that Shelley "is the reverse" in the sense that he had immense lyrical gifts but "had not, at the period of his deplorably early death, reached sufficiently far that intellectual progression of which he was capable" (35–38). If for Hegel the ideal lyric poet would move civilization forward in his perfect self-expression, for Mill the ideal lyric poet would have to be the representative of both original nature and acquired culture, something no one yet had done perfectly. For such idealized accounts, the lyric poet could only be an imagined figure, a hero of a poetry yet to appear (as indeed the poet became rather explicitly for Ralph Waldo Emerson, until Walt Whitman volunteered for the job).

It is a bit ironic that the nineteenth-century definition of the lyric as "utterance overheard"—the construction that appears most often in twentieth-century literary criticism—is taken from an essay in which Mill failed to find any poet who could be called truly lyric, who could represent the "lyric" essence of poetry. Actually, in Mill's argument the idea that "eloquence is *heard*, poetry is *overheard*" (12) is not so much a definition of the essence of lyric as it is a distinction between discursive modes of direct and indirect address. Popular verse such as the *Corn-Law Ballads* could not fit his definition of poetry because such verse directly addressed its readers for political purposes. In contrast, "the peculiarity of poetry appears to us to lie in the poet's utter unconsciousness of a listener," as Mill famously declared: "Poetry is feeling confessing itself to itself, in moments of solitude" (12). But of course the solitude of the lyric poet is a solitude we witness, a solitude exhibited in public. Mill ventured various metaphors for that predicament when he wrote that lyric song "has always seemed to us like the lament of a prisoner in a solitary cell, ourselves listening, unseen in the next" or that "it may be said that poetry that is printed on hot-pressed paper, and sold at a bookseller's shop, is a soliloquy in full dress, and on the stage" (12). Such extravagant metaphors testify to the peculiar pressures on the notion of the lyric ideal in the nineteenth century, yet they also indicate that even a writer like Mill, who thought of the lyric as poetry's utopian horizon, knew that his requirement that the lyric poet be unconscious of the audience always already posed a problem.

If nineteenth-century thinking about poetry sought to distinguish a transcendent version of lyric from contemporary cultures of circulation and at the same time imagined an ideal (and perhaps impossible) new culture of circulation, the twentieth-century criticism that inherited these ambitions for the lyric tended to embrace it not as an ideal to be aspired toward but as the given poetic genre already in circulation. When in 1957 Northrop Frye (see section 1) defined the lyric as "preeminently the utterance that is overheard," he went so far as to say that there is "no word for the audience of the lyric" because "the poet, so to speak, turns his back on his listeners." Over a century after Mill and Hegel, the self-absorption of the lyric poet ceased to be a utopian horizon or a problem to be metaphorically solved and was assumed as a normative practice. Turning away from listeners became what the modern lyric poet did for a living.

Thus what began in the nineteenth century as an aspiration became in the twentieth century a real genre—indeed, became not only the genre to which poetry aspired but the genre so identified with poetry that poetry became another name for it. In this progression, the lyric first became an abstraction that could include various verse genres, then poetry became a genre that could include lyric. In the second half of the nineteenth century, there was an uneven progression toward that exchange of terms, but in this anthology we gather a range of criticism that inherits those terms. In many of the essays included in this anthology, critics struggle with this lyricized idea of poetry, working to reconcile the theoretical self-enclosure of the lyric with the ways lyric poems are or were or could be read. Jonathan Culler, one of the foremost contemporary theorists of the lyric, suggests that "observing particular shifts in the lyric does not . . . prevent one from maintaining a broad conception of lyric as genre" (see section 1). Yet even if we embrace such a broad conception (as indeed the twentieth century did) how do we account for the historical shifts that brought it about? As Culler observes, our answer to that question will depend on what we think a literary genre is in the first place. While Culler favors an account of genre as "a set of norms or structural possibilities," this anthology presents a critical history of how such a broad conception of the lyric as a genre became the norm.

It has become common to credit the Anglo-American New Criticism of the middle of the twentieth century with the elevation of the self-enclosed lyric to paradigmatic status, but the history of twentieth-century thinking about poetry is not that simple. The late-twentieth-century demand for a theory of *Lyric Poetry: Beyond New Criticism* (as the title of an important 1985 anthology of criticism phrased it) made New Criticism seem more monumental than it was. The New Critics were hardly a coherent group, and there were many differences among them. While it is possible to say that I. A. Richards, Cleanth Brooks, Robert Penn Warren, T. S. Eliot, W. K. Wimsatt, Monroe Beardsley, and Reuben Brower (the critics included here in section 3), along with John Crowe Ransom, Yvor Winters, R. P. Blackmur, Allen Tate, William Empson, and many others shared a lyricized view of poetry, precisely for that reason midcentury critics did not tend to think about "the lyric" but rather assumed that most poetry conforms to lyric protocols. As Brooks and Warren wrote in the first edition of *Understanding Poetry: An Anthology for College Students* in 1938 (see section 3), "classifications such as 'lyrics of meditation,' and 'religious lyrics' and 'poems of patriotism,' or 'the sonnet,' 'the Ode,' 'the song,' etc. are arbitrary and irrational classifications" that should give way to "poetry as a thing in itself worthy of study." The emphasis on "poetry as a thing in itself" was an emphasis shared by many critics in the twentieth century, but as this anthology demonstrates, what it meant for poetry to be "a thing in itself" varied dramatically from critic to critic. We think it is more productive to view New Criticism as part of a longer history of abstraction in which various verse genres (as in Brooks and Warren's list) were collapsed into a large, lyricized idea of poetry as such. This "super-sizing" of the lyric remained in place after the New Criticism, and in fact critics were struggling with it before the New Criticism. It is not an idea created and promoted by a particular school of thought but an ongoing historical process of thinking about poetry in which we are still very much engaged.

What did characterize the New Criticism was a focus on making poetry available to all kinds of readers. As the subtitle of Brooks and Warren's anthology suggests, in the middle of the twentieth century (with the rise of a university system broadly accessible to the middle class) the college classroom became the community of readers ideally positioned to resolve the contradictions evident in Mill's metaphors. Students were addressed by poems precisely because they were taught that they could all "overhear" the poet speaking to herself. Robert Lowell complained later in the twentieth century that "the modern world has destroyed the intelligent poet's audience and given him students."[8] Whether or not an audience for poetry deteriorated in this period, the audience for what in classroom practice came to be referred to as "the lyric I" could be generated by teaching students to read poetry from all periods "as a thing in itself." In the middle of the century, that first-person subject of the poem came to be called "the speaker," a dramatic persona considered a fiction made for the purposes of the poem. As Barbara Herrnstein Smith has pointed out, the advantage of thinking about (and teaching) "the lyric I" as a speaker or a dramatic fiction is that "the context of a fictive utterance . . . is understood to be *historically indeterminate*."[9] A fictional person of all times and all places, the first-person speaker of the lyric could speak to no one in particular and thus to all of us.

No wonder this way of reading was so widespread in the middle of the twentieth century if it made the teaching of such a variety of poems to such a variety of student "listeners" possible. At the same time, the suspension of that fiction over any particular historical context or sociality beyond the classroom created problems for critics like René Wellek, who tried to place this lyricized version of poetry in literary history, or for later critics like Stanley Fish, who realized that such fictions were products of the special interpretive community of the classroom. Other critics tried to provide a context for this lyric fiction in earlier poetic models or to posit it as an essential (perhaps even universal) experience embedded in the phenomenology of lyric reading. Earlier in the century, Frankfurt School literary theory had argued that the lyric fiction was itself a product of a decadent capitalist society in which poems had become commodities, and this line of thought has produced a critical discourse worried about the investments of New Criticism. After the middle of the century, structuralist critics focused on how poetic fictions worked in everyday discourse and in the formal world of the poem itself; post-structuralist readers attended to the ways in which these fictions did not work or broke down under sustained attention; post-Heideggerian phenomenological readers explored the interior worlds of thought and feeling in lyric fictions. But since the late twentieth century, critics have also pushed back against the fiction of the lyric, whether in the interest of post-lyric textual or conceptual poetics or in the interest of sexual politics or in the interest of challenging the Western inheritance of the lyric with other models. We have given some representative examples of these approaches both to give readers a survey of their diversity and to think about the general sense of the lyric *as* fictional that such diverse approaches continue to share. Precisely because it has been shared for so long by such a range of readers, it is a fiction that has remained unexamined.

The Lyric Theory Reader is neither a defense of nor an attack on lyric. How can we defend or attack a moving target? Because what a lyric is or was keeps changing, this volume invites readers to examine moments in the intellectual history of a received idea over the past century. It is therefore both an anthology of criticism and a critical anthology that makes an argument about the history of reading. A longer history would ideally include earlier critics who have proven influential for twentieth-century criticism (classical treatises by Aristotle and Horace and Longinus, or apologias penned by poets like Sir Philip Sidney and Alexander Pope and Shelley, or often-quoted passages from Coleridge's *Biographia Literaria* and meditations from William Hazlitt's essay "On Poetry in General," or Mill's "Thoughts on Poetry and Its Varieties," or Edgar Allan Poe's "Philosophy of Composition," or Matthew Arnold's "The Study of Poetry," just to name a few obvious examples). But such a sampling of classic writing on poetry is already available in other anthologies, while our focus is on twentieth-century literary criticism, where the reworking of familiar quotations about poetry also draws attention to discontinuities and divergences within only apparently continuous histories of interpretation. Rather than proposing or pursuing a straightforward line of influence or progressive development in discourses about lyric, we emphasize a loopier logic that attributes later ideas about lyric to earlier moments in literary history and discovers in these historical moments the latent possibilities of later ideas. Thus reading lyric, where *lyric* is the object of interpretation, necessarily involves lyric reading, where *lyric* is part of the interpretive process to be called into question. Our aim is to provoke debate about theoretical questions that remain unsettled: where, when, how, and why do we discover theories of lyric, and what are the critical genealogies of such theories?

This anthology is divided into three parts, containing multiple sections, with an introduction to each section explaining the critical context and theoretical implications of essays we have selected and (in some cases) excerpted for inclusion. Part One draws a large circle around the history of lyric reading in the twentieth century by asking an apparently simple question: "How does lyric become a genre?" Rather than assuming that the lyric is (or has always been) a genre, we present examples of modern genre theory that take up the question of lyric, demonstrating how changing ideas about the form and functions of literary genres made it possible to imagine lyric as a modern idea. A brief introduction to genre theory (section 1) is followed by critical essays that project this idea back into literary history by identifying particular poets or poems as "models of lyric" (section 2). These two sections offer complementary "macro" and "micro" perspectives (one broadly generic, the other specifically historical) on the logic by which lyric has come to be identified with poetry as such. To lay the theoretical groundwork for the anthology as a whole, the first section is best read in sequence (especially for teaching purposes); after this first section, readers may select from essays in the remaining sections according to historical and critical interests.

Part Two is dedicated to twentieth-century lyric readers, featuring five major critical trends or schools of criticism that consolidated modern thinking about poetry as lyric, albeit with different critical investments. The techniques of close reading developed by Anglo-American New Criticism (section 3) paved the way for structuralist and post-structuralist readings of lyric (sections 4 and 5). In these various approaches to formalist analysis, lyric serves as an exemplary literary artefact for critics who want to demonstrate the construction of a text as organic unity or linguistic pattern or to demonstrate its deconstruction. Meanwhile, critics associated with the legacy of Frankfurt School thought (section 6) have pursued a Marxist reading of lyric as exemplifying the social contradictions of modernity. Other critics have been more interested in tracing a phenomenology of lyric reading (section 7) to describe an experience of lyric not as an object of thought but as a mode of perception and an instrument for thinking. What these different approaches to lyric reading have in common is the idea that lyric is an important category for modern critical thought. For all of these critics, for all sorts of different reasons, the lyric is a fiction in which they find ways to believe.

Given the ambitious claims for lyric made by critics in the first two parts of the anthology, Part Three explores a series of critical disclaimers that we call "lyric departures." Here we present critics who depart, in both senses, from an idea of lyric that they seek to call into question. The essays included in section 8 mark a radical break from an expressive model of lyric in order to explore avant-garde poetics that do not revolve around the assumption of lyric subjectivity or the figure of voice. By placing this argument within, rather than outside, a history of lyric reading that it seems to reject, our anthology makes it possible to see how readers and writers committed to this strain of anti-lyricism are part of the very tradition they critique. The essays included in the last two sections challenge traditional lyric reading in another way, not through refusal of history but through an insistence on alternate histories. We include several examples of gender criticism and queer theory that generate different histories of lyric reading by foregrounding questions of sexual difference (section 9). These histories are further expanded by critical explorations in comparative poetics, where modern lyric reading is brought into dialogue with poetry from non-Western traditions (section 10). Looking ahead to more diverse modes of lyric reading necessarily involves looking back on a critical framework that has been consolidated in the course of the twentieth century, a framework that continues to serve many different purposes.

Our anthology provides an overview of the modern consolidation of lyric as a genre of critical reading; our central argument is that the lyricization of poetry is a product of twentieth-century critical thought, and our purpose is to make available some exemplary instances of that thought and its many variations. In this respect, *The Lyric Theory Reader* is a companion to *Theory of the Novel*, edited by Michael McKeon and also published by The Johns Hopkins University Press (2000). In his anthology, McKeon argues that "modernity conjoins several, seemingly contradictory elements: the emergence of the novel genre, the decay of the genre system, and the movement to replace the historical theory of the novel by the transhistorical theory of narrative" (71). The same may be said, *mutatis mutandis*, of the modern emergence of lyric as a genre, the decay of the genre system, and the movement to replace historical poetic genres by a transhistorical theory of lyric. Like McKeon's anthology, our anthology highlights these only apparently contradictory elements. The introductory essays provide an interpretive framework for the selected readings in each section and together make a sustained argument about the gradual lyricization of poetry that reached its culmination in twentieth-century criticism.

The essays gathered here are not comprehensive, but we think they are representative. What they represent is not a developmental narrative, exactly, and they also do not constitute an influence study. Rather, our anthology presents an intellectual history of a theory of lyric reading that has circulated both within and beyond the classroom, wherever poetry is being taught and read and discussed and debated today. Such an intellectual history offers a timely critical perspective at a moment when all kinds of claims are being made for poetry as a way of redeeming a decadent culture, of restoring literariness to literary studies, of making personal expression possible in public, of bestowing creative freedom on poet, critic, and reader alike. Those deep investments in what poetry can do for us have a history as poetic practice but also as critical construction. *The Lyric Theory Reader* encourages the next generation of lyric theory readers—students, teachers, scholars, critics, poets—to reflect further on the paths by which we have reached the point of such idealization of the potential function of poetry in our time. Histories of poetic practices often establish poetry as a stable term that then takes various forms or is used in a range of ways at different places at different times. This volume instead surveys the idea of poetry as lyric that emerged at a particular place and time (the twentieth century in Anglo-America); once we see the outlines of that idea, that notion of poetry may not seem so stable or appropriate for other places and other times, and from that insight other histories of reading—and other ideas of poetry and its possibilities—may appear.

NOTES

1. There have of course been many attempts to define *lyric* in Anglo-American criticism over the past century. See suggested readings listed at the end of section 1 on the general idea of lyric and at the end of section 2 on particular models of lyric. See also the different entries on "lyric" in *The Princeton Encyclopedia of Poetry and Poetics* by James William Johnson (1st, 2nd, and 3rd eds., Princeton, NJ: Princeton University Press, 1965–93) and by Virginia Jackson (4th ed., 2012), and differing perspectives in contributions to "The New Lyric Studies" in *PMLA* 123:1 (Jan. 2008): 181–234.

2. See Charles Bernstein, *A Poetics* (Cambridge, MA: Harvard University Press, 1992).

3. See, for example, Craig Dworkin's introduction to the Anthology of Conceptual Writing on the UbuWeb: www.ubu.com/concept/.

4. Mary Poovey, "The Model System of Contemporary Literary Criticism," *Critical Inquiry* 27.3 (Spring 2001): 408–38.

5. Johann Wolfgang von Goethe, "Noten und Abhandlungen zu besserem Verstandnis des West-ostichen Diwans," in *Goethes Werke*, Hamburger Ausgabe (Munich: C. H. Beck, 1981) 2:187–89.

6. G. W. Hegel, *Aesthetics: Lectures on Fine Art*, trans. T. M. Knox (Oxford: Clarendon Press, 1975), 2:971.

7. John Stuart Mill, *Essays on Poetry*, ed. F. Parvin Sharpless (Columbia: University of South Carolina Press, 1976), 36. Mill's essays most often quoted by critics ("What Is Poetry?" and "The Two Kinds of Poetry") both date from 1833 and are reprinted as "Thoughts on Poetry and Its Varieties," revised in 1859.

8. Robert Lowell, 1960 National Book Award Acceptance Speech: www.nationalbook.org/nbaacceptspeech_rlowell.html#.T61PnRw71Ew.

9. Barbara Herrnstein Smith, *On the Margins of Discourse: The Relation of Literature to Language* (Chicago: University of Chicago Press, 1978), 33.

PART ONE

How Does Lyric Become a Genre?

SECTION 1

Genre Theory

How did the lyric become a genre? This may seem an odd question, especially to those readers who think of the lyric as the most fundamental kind of poetry, or who think of lyricism as poetry's essence.[1] Yet the idea that lyric poetry has always been a primary form of literary—indeed, of human—expression is surprisingly modern. In the early romantic period, literature began to be divided into three large categories, culminating in Goethe's idea of the three "natural forms of poetry": lyric, epic, and drama.[2] Those categories were then cast as ancient distinctions, but in fact (as Gérard Genette argues in his essay included in this section), while epic and drama had various theories attached to them before the seventeenth century, *lyric* was a third term added to literary description by eighteenth- and nineteenth-century literary criticism. This is not to say that there were no ancient or medieval or early modern or seventeenth- or eighteenth-century lyric poems; rather, these poems were not understood as *lyric* in our current sense of the term. Alistair Fowler puts the observation succinctly when he warns that *lyric* in literary theory from Cicero through Dryden is "not to be confused with the modern term."[3] The important distinction between the modern term and its antecedents is the way in which lyric has been considered a genre, since in the eighteenth century the conception of genre itself changed. As the essays in this section attest, the way we read the lyric (which is to say the way we think about poetry) has everything to do with what we think literary genres are or do.

In *The Architext*, Genette demonstrates that the relationship between theories of the lyric and theories of genre is intimate in modernity. Observing the near ubiquitous invocation of "the three major genres" (lyric, epic, and dramatic) in twentieth-century literary criticism, Genette notices that this tripartite system is almost always attributed to the ancients, specifically to Plato and Aristotle. Yet in his reading of Plato and Aristotle, Genette does not find any theory of these three major genres—in fact, he cannot find any mention at all of "the lyric" as such. Where did the lyric come from, or how did "the retrospective illusion" that the lyric has always been a major genre become so "deeply rooted in our conscious, or unconscious, literary minds" that it could be referred to as self-evident by twentieth-century critics as different from one another as Austin Warren, Northrop Frye, and Mikhail Bakhtin? The search for an answer to this question leads Genette through an elaborate meditation on the history of genre theory. If for Plato "there is no poem except a representative one" and Aristotle "also excludes non-imitative verse," then it begins to seem as if the shift from classical to modern poetics entailed a shift in the work that genres were expected to do. While "lyric" was used as a name for various sorts of poetry before the eighteenth century, toward the end of that century Genette finds that the lyric began to be understood as a representative or imitative genre because literary thinkers decided that "it imitates feelings" and thus could finally be "integrated into classical poetics." In order to achieve this integration, the lyric poem had to be understood as a fiction, as a representation of feeling rather than as feeling itself. Modern poetics required the reconstruction of the lyric as something it had never been before: not a mode of enunciation but "a real genre" with its own thematic content, the expression of an essentially fictive individual subject. In that reconstruction, the idea of the lyric, epic, and dramatic as what Genette calls "*archigenres*" emerged: "*Archi-*, because each of them is supposed to overarch and include, ranked by degree of importance, a certain number of empirical genres that—whatever their amplitude, longevity, or potential for recurrence—are apparently phenomena of culture and history." In order to make the three "archigenres" apparently natural forms (in Goethe's phrase), or not simply effects of culture and history (as, for example, ballads or epistles or elegies could be said to be), critics began to attribute the romantic tripartite division to the ancients. As a structuralist, Genette is most interested in what that attribution means for the large structures we have come to think of as literary genres. In the context of the *Lyric Theory Reader*, Genette's insight also means that a shift in the conception of genre gave birth to the modern theory of the lyric.

In *The Anatomy of Criticism* (1957), Northrop Frye, the Canadian literary critic who proved highly influential for Anglo-American genre theory, dramatically demonstrated and elaborated the modern theory of genre that Genette later identified as "a retrospective illusion." Invested in his own version of natural literary forms, Frye declared that in the mid-twentieth century it was "time for criticism to leap to a new ground from which it [could] discover what the organizing or containing forms of its conceptual framework are." Like Genette, Frye's approach was essentially structuralist, but his structures were large literary categories he called "archetypes" rather than "archigenres." Taking his cue from Aristotle, Frye developed a systematic theory of literature that assumed and built upon the tripartite division of major genres, but Frye elaborated the work of these genres by suggesting that "the basis of generic distinctions in literature appears to be the radical of presentation." What Frye means by "the radical of presentation" is the mode of performance, "the distinctions of acted, spoken, and written word" or "the relationship between a poet and his public." Frye essentially made genres back into modes of enunciation, a shift from modern genre theory toward the classical sense of rhetorical performance. Frye is thus able to think of the lyric as one of the "spoken genres" even when it is printed, since its "radical of presentation" remains a particular kind of performance; the lyric is always, according to Frye, "utterance that is overheard." This famous aphorism—taken out of the context of J. S. Mill's "Thoughts on Poetry and Its Varieties" (1833)—was abstracted by Frye (and, as we shall see, by other literary critics of the 1950s) and transformed into a model for reading the lyric, so often quoted that it has become a normative claim rather than a theoretical proposition. The fiction of overhearing an utterance (whether spoken or written) leads Frye to claim not just that the lyric is an imitation of feeling but that "the lyric is an internal mimesis of sound and imagery," a representation he analyzes at length in terms of *melos* and *opsis*, or "babble" and "doodle." Through the rhetorical dynamics of sight and sound, Frye traces a history of variations on the dimensions of lyric performance.

Between Genette, who, late in the twentieth century, wondered when our modern idea of the lyric began, and Frye, who had already embraced and extended that modern idea in the middle of the twentieth century, René Wellek suggested in 1967 that literary criticism recognize that "genres exist as institutions exist"—that is, that criticism might want to accept genres as social fictions with particular uses and give up on writing about the grand idea of the lyric. Through a reading of two contemporary German literary critics (Emil Staiger and Käte Hamburger), Wellek argues (in this sense agreeing with Genette) that twentieth-century theories of lyric can be traced to German romanticism and specifically to Schlegel and Hegel, who, with Goethe, outlined a dialectical system of genre. In that system, the lyric was associated with *erlebnis*, or the lived experience of the subject—that is, with a nineteenth-century elevation of the eighteenth-century notion that the lyric imitates feeling. Wellek's essay demonstrates how persistent that association has been for modern criticism, but then it turns to point out how many different literary works from different periods could be said to represent *erlebnis*: "If everything in poetry is *Erlebnis*," then "the term loses its original relation to something given in life. It is simply a term for the artist's activity. It is so broad as to be meaningless." According to this modern definition, *all* poetry is lyric poetry. What is the alternative to the post-romantic tradition of lyric theory founded on such a capacious idea of lyric experience? For Wellek, "lyrical theory . . . seems to have arrived at a complete impasse" by the time of his writing; he thus concludes that we should "abandon attempts to define the general nature of the lyric or the lyrical . . . It seems much more profitable to turn to a study of the variety of poetry and to the history and thus the description of genres which can be grasped in their concrete conventions and traditions." In this way, Wellek moved in the opposite direction to Frye; while Frye sought broad categories that could transcend historical contingency, Wellek urged criticism to return to such contingencies. The question left hanging at the end of Wellek's essay is what such a historical description of the lyric would look like.

As the editor of *New Literary History*, Ralph Cohen had an interest in Wellek's question, though while Wellek was one of the creators of the modern version of comparative literature, Cohen's historical focus was very much on British literary history. Cohen's 1986 essay "History and Genre" agrees with Wellek by acknowledging that (as Fredric Jameson put it) genre criticism has been "thoroughly discredited by modern literary theory and practice" but suggests that rather than abandoning genre (if that were possible), critics might want to acknowledge "that genre concepts in theory and practice arise, change, and decline for historical reasons."[4] As Cohen writes, "If Frye were a historical critic concerned with actual texts, he would proceed to illustrate the kind of interrelations that empirical critics develop, interrelations that show the choral chanting, riddling, and other oral devices in works acted in front of a spectator. He would undertake to explain how his genres interrelate historically with earlier genres as well as with each other. His efforts, however, are directed at traditions and affinities rather than the actualities of changing traditions and changing affinities." For Cohen, Frye typifies the problem with modern genre theory, which depends on the abstract grouping of particular traits or (in Jameson's variation) on an implied contract between the writer and the reader. But what if critics were to give up such categories and instead were to trace the history of "generic transformations as [when], for example, the 'ballad' and the 'lyric' are joined by Wordsworth to form 'Lyrical Ballads.' Still another generic inquiry is to examine a single narrative as it undergoes generic variations, becoming, in turn, a ballad, a prose fiction, a tragedy, a memoir, as well as a member of other genres." The latter tack is the one Cohen takes in his essay here through the variety of "genres" assumed by what was originally

"The Excellent Ballad of George Barnwel" over the course of the seventeenth and eighteenth centuries. By the time that the Barnwel ballad was included in Percy's *Reliques of Ancient English Poetry* in 1765, we might call it a "lyric," but doing so would obscure all of the other genres (from various kinds of ballads to prose narrative to tragedy to news or memoir) it had been along the way. Cohen urges us to understand the ways in which genres shift over time as one source for a possible "regeneration of genre theory." In that theory, the historical process of generic transformation would take precedence over a theory of any one genre, since the latter supposes that a genre remains stable while history changes. But what does Cohen's method of literary history mean for the theory of the lyric? Could there be a history of the transformation of the lyric that could match Cohen's account of the transformation of the ballad? What would we have to understand a lyric to be in order to write such a history?

Jonathan Culler, one of the primary contemporary theorists of the lyric, has an answer to this question. As a literary theorist committed to the comparative study of poetics, Culler approaches the lyric as a "particularly interesting generic problem" that invites us to articulate historical continuities as well as discontinuities. In response to Cohen, Culler argues that "it would be wrong merely to accept as empirical fact every ascription and description of genre"; instead, he emphasizes that literary critics should "reflect on what makes something count as a genre" and pursue "a claim about fundamental structures that may be at work even when not manifest." Thus Culler counters Cohen's descriptive approach in favor of a normative concept of lyric, one that seeks "an account of a set of norms or structural possibilities" instead of particular uses and instances. For Culler, it is not enough to study what critics and poets of a particular period thought about lyric; we need to recognize the mutual implication of historical and theoretical conceptions of generic categories within a longer "lyric tradition" that allows for continual transformation while assuming that there is a genre there to be transformed. While Culler accepts both Genette's point that lyric was not made into one of three fundamental genres until the romantic period and Wellek's critique of romantic theories of the lyric, he concludes that focusing on particular historical verse genres (such as the ode or elegy as proposed by Wellek or on the ballad as analyzed by Cohen) is "not a very promising strategy for nineteenth- and twentieth-century poetry, where many of the most interesting lyrics do not seem to belong to those particular genres or subgenres." Of course much depends here on Culler's assumption that the most interesting poems of the last two centuries are essentially lyric. Here he takes up the "lyricization" argument proposed by Virginia Jackson, who traces the historical process by which different poetic genres began to be collapsed into an abstract idea of lyric in the course of the nineteenth century. Jackson argues that various historical verse genres gradually became "lyric" as reading practices shifted over the nineteenth century and were consolidated in the twentieth century. Whether or not such a process took place is of less interest to Culler than the fact that by the nineteenth and twentieth centuries, poets wrote and people read lyrics—and they knew how to do so because that is what they had already been doing in one way or another for centuries before.

Thus the critical debate about the lyric as a genre comes down to a basic question: how do we know a lyric when we see one? Whether the lyric as we know it was invented in the eighteenth century or is as old as human expression, whether the lyric is "utterance that is overheard" or is any representation of our essential, lived experience, whether the lyric is historically contingent and ephemeral or is dependent on norms and structures continuous across periods and cultures, you need to have some idea of what you think a lyric poem is in order to know that you are reading (or hearing, or overhearing, or experiencing) one. In the final essay included in this section, Stanley Fish brings this fundamental premise of generic recognition into relief by performing a classroom experiment. In his class on seventeenth-century religious poetry in 1971, Fish's students learned to recognize a particular variety of lyric in seventeenth-century religious poetry. One day, the students entered the classroom to discover a text written on the blackboard, a list of linguistic textbooks left over from Fish's previous class. Fish asked the students to read the list as if it were a seventeenth-century religious lyric. Fish's point in tricking his class was not only to prove that his students were so well versed in the genre they had studied that they could construct what in the specialized discourse of literary studies is called "a reading"; the interest of this particular reading is that the students were capable of recognizing a poem that they had actually created themselves. That point leads Fish to conclude that "acts of recognition, rather than being triggered by formal characteristics, are their source. It is not that the presence of poetic qualities compels a certain kind of attention but that the paying of a certain kind of attention results in the emergence of poetic qualities." On this view, the debates over the status of the lyric as a genre—and over what a literary genre is or does—might be reduced to kinds of attention to the problem.

All of the essays in this section agree that there is such a thing as the lyric, but none can agree on the work that the lyric as a genre performs for its readers. What if Fish is right that this set of disagreements has approached the question from the wrong direction? What if we turn the question around to ask instead what kind of work readers perform in order to make poems into lyrics? As Fish writes, "If the understandings of the people in question are informed by the same notions of what counts as a fact, of what is central, peripheral, and worthy of being noticed, in short, by the same interpretive principles—then agreement between them will be assured, and its source will not be a text that enforces its own perception but a way of perceiving that results in the emergence to those who share it (or those whom it shares) of the same text." Of course, Fish's experiment was rigged to produce this conclusion as inevitable, and it was not designed as a theory of the lyric. We include Fish's essay at the conclusion of this section in order to frame the central issues in contemporary lyric theory as questions about what a genre—or a text—is in the first place. *The Lyric Theory Reader* presents the interpretive principles that have assured agreement in classrooms over the last seventy-five years among readers who have produced the genre that now counts as lyric poetry. As those ways of perceiving begin to change, not only our ways of reading but our ways of recognizing a lyric when we see one will change as well.

NOTES

1. For recent examples of such arguments, see Blasing (2006), Brewster (2009), Stewart (2002 and 2011) and von Hallberg (2008).

2. Johann Wolfgang von Goethe, "Noten und Abhandlungen zu besserem Verständnis des West-östlichen Diwans," in *Goethes Werke*, Hamburger Ausgabe (Munich: C. H. Beck, 1981), 2:187–89. On the three-genre system as critical norm, see Rogers (1983) and Guillén (1971).

3. See Fowler (1982), 220.

4. For an extension of Cohen's contention that genre concepts—and particularly the concept of the lyric—shift for historical reasons, see Clifford Siskin, *The Historicity of Romantic Discourse* (Oxford: Oxford University Press, 1988). In his later work, Siskin has pursued Cohen's logic into the history of media shift and the eighteenth-century invention of the system of genres.

FURTHER READING

Bahti, Timothy. *Ends of the Lyric: Direction and Consequence in Western Poetry.* Baltimore: Johns Hopkins University Press, 1996.

Beebee, Thomas. *The Ideology of Genre: A Comparative Study of Generic Instability.* University Park: Pennsylvania State University Press, 1994.

Blasing, Mutlu Konuk. *Lyric Poetry: The Pain and Pleasure of Words.* Princeton, NJ: Princeton University Press, 2006.

Brewster, Scott. *Lyric*. New York: Routledge, 2009.

Burke, Kenneth. *The Philosophy of Literary Form*. Baton Rouge: Louisiana State University Press, 1941. 3rd rev. ed., Berkeley: University of California Press, 1973.

Cameron, Sharon. *Lyric Time: Dickinson and the Limits of Genre*. Baltimore: Johns Hopkins University Press, 1979.

Cavitch, Max. "Genre." In *The Princeton Encyclopedia of Poetry and Poetics*, 4th ed., edited by R. Greene, S. Cushman, C. Cavanagh, J. Ramazani, and P. Rouzer. Princeton, NJ: Princeton University Press, 2012.

Culler, Jonathan. "Genre: Lyric." In *The Work of Genre: Collected Essays from the English Institute*, edited by Robin Warhol. Cambridge, MA: English Institute in collaboration with the American Council of Learned Societies, 2011. http://hdl.handle.net/2027/heb.90055.0001.001.

Dimock, W. C. and Robbins, Bruce, eds. "Remapping *Genre*." Special issue of *PMLA* 122.5 (2007).

Dubrow, Heather. *Genre*. London: Methuen, 1982.

Duff, David, ed. *Modern Genre Theory*. Essex: Longman, 2000.

Fowler, Alastair. *Kinds of Literature: An Introduction to the Theory of Genres and Modes*. Cambridge: Cambridge University Press, 1982.

Guillén, Claudio. *Literature as System: Essays toward a Theory of Literary History*. Princeton, NJ: Princeton University Press, 1971.

Hernadi, Paul. *Beyond Genre: New Directions in Literary Classification*. Ithaca, NY: Cornell University Press, 1972.

Hošek, Chaviva, and Patricia Parker, eds. *Lyric Poetry: Beyond New Criticism*. Ithaca, NY: Cornell University Press, 1985.

Jackson, Virginia. *Dickinson's Misery: A Theory of Lyric Reading*. Princeton, NJ: Princeton University Press, 2005.

———. "Lyric." In *The Princeton Encyclopedia of Poetry and Poetics*, 4th ed., ed. R. Greene, S. Cushman, C. Cavanagh, J. Ramazani, and P. Rouzer. Princeton, NJ: Princeton University Press, 2012.

Jameson, Fredric. *The Political Unconscious: Narrative as a Socially Symbolic Act*. Ithaca, NY: Cornell University Press, 1981.

Jeffreys, Mark, ed. *New Definitions of Lyric: Theory, Technology, and Culture*. New York: Garland, 1998.

Johnson, James William. "Lyric." In *The New Princeton Encyclopedia of Poetry and Poetics*, ed. A. Preminger, T. Brogan, and F. Warnke. Princeton, NJ: Princeton University Press, 1993.

Lewis, C. Day. *The Lyric Impulse*. London: Chatto and Windus, 1965.

Lindley, David. *Lyric*. New York: Methuen, 1985.

Miller, Paul Allen. *Lyric Texts and Lyric Consciousness: The Birth of a Genre from Archaic Greece to Augustan Rome*. London: Routledge, 1994.

Olson, Elder. "The Lyric." *PMMLA* 1 (1969): 59–66.

Poovey, Mary. "The Model System of Contemporary Literary Criticism." *Critical Inquiry* 27.3 (Spring 2001): 408–38.

———. *Genres of the Credit Economy*. Chicago: University of Chicago Press, 2008.

Rhys, Ernest. *Lyric Poetry*. New York: E. P. Dutton, 1913.

Rogers, William Elford. *The Three Genres and the Interpretation of Lyric*. Princeton, NJ: Princeton University Press, 1983.

Rosmarin, Adena. *The Power of Genre*. Minneapolis: University of Minnesota Press, 1985.

Schelling, Felix E. *The English Lyric*. London: Constable, 1913.

Tiffany, Daniel. *Toy Medium: Materialism and Modern Lyric*. Berkeley: University of California Press, 2000.

Todorov, Tzvetan. *Genres in Discourse*. Trans. Catherine Porter. Cambridge: Cambridge University Press, 1990.

Von Hallberg, Robert. *Lyric Powers*. Chicago: University of Chicago Press, 2011.

Wellek, René, and Austin Warren. *Theory of Literature*. New York: Harcourt, Brace, 1942.

Waters, William. *Poetry's Touch: On Lyric Address*. Ithaca, NY: Cornell University Press, 2003.

The Architext (1979; trans. 1992) 1.1

GÉRARD GENETTE Translated by Jane E. Lewin[1]

1.

We are all familiar with that passage in *A Portrait of the Artist as a Young Man* in which Stephen explains to his friend Lynch "his" theory of the three major aesthetic forms: "The lyrical form, the form wherein the artist presents his image in immediate relation to himself; the epical form, the form wherein he presents his image in mediate relation to himself and to others; the dramatic form, the form wherein he presents his image in immediate relation to others."[2] This tripartition in itself is not especially original, as Joyce was well aware, for in the first version of the episode he added ironically that Stephen was expressing himself "with a naïf air of discovering novelties," even though "his Esthetic was in the main 'applied Aquinas.'"[3]

I don't know whether Saint Thomas ever proposed such a tripartition—or even whether Joyce was really suggesting he did—but I have noted here and there that, for some time, the tripartition has been readily attributed to Aristotle, even to Plato. In her study of the history of the division into genres, Irene Behrens cited an example of the attribution from the pen of Ernest Bovet ("Aristotle having distinguished among the lyric, epic, and dramatic genres . . .") and immediately refuted it, while asserting that it was already very widespread.[4] But, as we will see, her clarification did not keep others from repeating the offense—undoubtedly in part because the error (or, rather, the retrospective illusion that is in question here) is deeply rooted in our conscious, or unconscious, literary minds. Besides, her clarification itself was not entirely untainted by the tradition she was denouncing, for she wondered in all seriousness how it came about that the traditional tripartition did not appear in Aristotle, and she found one possible reason in the fact that Greek lyricism was too closely associated with music to be included within poetics. But tragedy was just as closely associated with music; and lyric is absent from Aristotle's *Poetics* for a much more basic reason—a reason that needs only to be perceived for the question itself to lose any kind of relevance.

But not, apparently, any raison d'être; we do not easily forgo projecting onto the founding text of classical poetics a fundamental tenet of "modern" poetics (which actually, as we will often see, really means *romantic* poetics), and perhaps the theoretical consequences of the projection are unfortunate. For by usurping that remote ancestry, the relatively recent theory of the "three major genres" not only lays claim to ancientness, and thus to an appearance or presumption of being eternal and therefore self-evident; it also misappropriates for the benefit of its three generic institutions a natural foundation that Aristotle, and Plato before him, had established, perhaps more legitimately, for something very different. This knot of confusions, quid pro quos, and unnoticed substitutions that has lain at the heart of Western poetics for several centuries is what I want to try to untangle a bit.

But first, not for the pedantic pleasure of finding fault with some very bright minds but to illustrate, by their examples, the pervasiveness of this *lectio facilior*, here are a few other, more recent occurrences of it. In Austin Warren:

> Aristotle and Horace are our classical texts for genre theory. From them, we think of tragedy and epic as the characteristic (as well as the two major) kinds. But Aristotle at least is also aware of other and more fundamental distinctions—between drama, epic, and lyric. . . . The three major kinds are already, by Plato and Aristotle, distinguished according to "manner of imitation" (or "representation"): lyric poetry is the poet's own *persona*; in epic poetry (or the novel) the poet partly speaks in his own person, as narrator, and partly makes his characters speak in direct discourse (mixed narrative); in drama, the poet disappears behind his cast of characters. . . . Aristotle's *Poetics* . . . roughly nominates epic, drama, and lyric ("melic") poetry as the basic kinds of poetry.

Northrop Frye, more vague or more prudent: "We have the three generic terms drama, epic, and lyric, derived from *the Greeks*." More circumspect still, or more evasive, Philippe Lejeune assumes that the point of departure for the theory was "the threefold division by *the Ancients* among the epical, the dramatic, and the lyrical." Not so, though, Robert Scholes, who specifies that Frye's system "begins with his acceptance of the basic *Aristotelian* division into lyric, epic, and dramatic forms." And even less so Hélène Cixous, who, commenting on Stephen's speech, pinpoints its source thus: "A classical tripartite division derived from Aristotle's *Poetics*, 1447a, b, 1456–62a and b." As for Tzvetan Todorov, he has the triad go back to Plato and to Diomedes' definitive systematization of Plato:

> From Plato to Goethe and Jakobson to Emil Staiger, attempts have been made to divide literature into three categories and to consider these as the fundamental or even the natural forms of literature. . . . Systematizing Plato in the fourth century, Diomedes defined three basic genres: one including the works in which only the author speaks, another including the works in which only the characters speak, and a third including the works in which both author and characters speak.

In 1938 Mikhail Bakhtin, without formulating the attribution in question quite so precisely, asserted that the theory of genres "has not, up to our own time, been able to add anything substantial to what Aristotle had already done. His poetics remains the immutable foundation of the theory of genres, although sometimes this foundation is so deeply buried that we no longer discern it."[5]

Evidently Bakhtin is unaware of the massive silence the *Poetics* maintains on the subject of lyric genres, and paradoxically his mistake demonstrates the very ignorance of the foundation of the theory of genres that he thinks he is denouncing. For what is important, as we will see, is the retrospective illusion by which modern (preromantic, romantic, and postromantic) literary theorists blindly project their own contributions onto Aristotle, or Plato, and thus "bury" their own difference—their own modernity.

That attribution, so widespread today, is not entirely an invention of the twentieth century. We find it as early as the eighteenth century, in a chapter that Abbé Batteux added to his essay *Les Beaux-Arts réduits à un même principe* (The Fine Arts Obeying One Law). The title of this chapter is almost more than we could have hoped for: "Que cette doctrine est conforme à celle d'Aristote" (That This Doctrine Is in Keeping with Aristotle's).[6] The doctrine in question is Batteux's general theory on "the imitation of fair nature" as the sole "law" of the fine arts, including poetry; but for the most part the chapter concentrates on demonstrating that Aristotle divides the art of poetry into three genres or, as Batteux called them, borrowing a term from Horace, three basic *colors*. "These three colors are those of the dithyramb, or lyric poetry; the epic, or narrative poetry; and finally the drama, or tragedy and comedy." The abbé himself quotes the passage in the *Poetics* on which he bases his claim, and the quotation is worth repeating, in his own translation: "Les mots composés de plusieurs mots conviennent plus spécialement aux dithyrambes, les mots inusités aux épopées, et les tropes aux drames" (The words made up of several words are more especially appropriate to dithyrambs, rare words to epics, and tropes to dramas). This comes at the end of chapter 22, which focuses on questions of *lexis* or, as we would say, style. As one can see, at issue here is the appropriate linkage between genres and stylistic methods—although Batteux stretches Aristotle's terms a bit in that direction by translating *ta héroika* (heroic verses, that is, dactylic hexameter) as "epic" and *ta iambeia* (iambic verses, and more particularly, no doubt, the trimeters of tragic or comic dialogue) as "drama."

Let us overlook this slight accentuation: here Aristotle indeed seems to apportion three stylistic features among three genres or forms (dithyramb, epic, dramatic dialogue). What we still need to evaluate is the equivalence Batteux establishes between dithyramb and lyric poetry. Today the dithyramb is not a well-known form, for almost no examples of it remain; but scholars generally describe it as a "choral song in honor of Dionysus" and thus readily classify it among the "lyric forms."[7] They do not, however, go as far as Batteux, who says that "nothing corresponds better to our lyric poetry," an assertion that gives short shrift to, for example, the odes of Pindar or Sappho. But as it happens, Aristotle does not mention the dithyramb anywhere else in the *Poetics*, except to refer to it as a forerunner of tragedy.[8] In the *Homeric Problems*, he specifies that the form was originally narrative and later became "mimetic"—that is, dramatic.[9] As for Plato, he mentions the dithyramb as the consummate example of poetry that is . . . purely narrative.[10]

Nothing there, then, authorizes us to claim that *in Aristotle* (*or Plato*) the dithyramb illustrates the lyric "genre"—quite the contrary. The passage Batteux cites is the only one in all the *Poetics* he could have invoked to give Aristotle's sanction to the illustrious triad. The distortion is flagrant, and the point at which it is applied is significant. To appreciate the significance more fully, we must once again return to the source—that is, to the system of genres that Plato conceived and Aristotle developed. I say "system of genres" as a provisional concession to the vulgate, but we will soon see that the term is incorrect and that something entirely different is involved.

2.

In the third book of the *Republic*, Plato justifies his well-known decision to expel poets from the state with two sets of considerations. The first bears on the content (*logos*) of the poets' works, which basically should be moralizing (though all too often it is not): the poet should not represent shortcomings, especially in gods and heroes, and should certainly not promote shortcomings by representing virtue as miserable or vice as triumphant. The second bears on the "form" (*lexis*), meaning the *mode of representation*.[11] Every poem is a narrative (*diègèsis*) of past, present, or future events; narrative in this broad sense can take three forms: it can be purely narrative (*haplè diègèsis*), it can be mimetic (*dia mimèséôs*—in other words, as in the theater, by way of dialogue between characters), or it can be "mixed" (in other words, in reality alternating—sometimes narrative and sometimes dialogue, as in Homer). Here I will not go back over the details of Plato's demonstration[12] or his well-known devaluing of the mimetic and mixed modes, which is one of his main grounds for indicting poets (the other, of course, is the immorality of their subjects). I simply wish to point out the correspondence between the three modes of *lexis* distinguished by Plato and what will later be called the poetic "genres": the pure mimetic corresponds to tragedy and comedy, the mixed to epic, and the pure narrative to—"especially" (*malista pou*)—*dithyramb* (the only illustration). The whole "system" comes down to that. Clearly, Plato here is considering only the forms of poetry that is "narrative" in the broad sense—poetry that the subsequent tradition, after Aristotle, will more readily call (inverting the terms) "mimetic" or *representational*:

poetry that "reports" events, real or fictive. Plato deliberately, leaves out all nonrepresentational poetry—and thus, above all, what we call lyric poetry—and a fortiori all other forms of literature (including, of course, any possible "representation" in prose, like our novel or modern theater). An exclusion not only in fact but indeed in principle, for again, the representation of events is here the very definition of poetry: there is no poem except a representational one. Plato obviously was not unaware of lyric poetry, but he excludes it here with a deliberately restrictive definition—a restriction perhaps ad hoc, since it facilitates the banning of poets (except lyric poets?), but a restriction that, via Aristotle, will become—and for centuries will remain—the basic tenet of classical poetics.

Indeed, the first page of the *Poetics* clearly defines poetry as the art of imitation in verse (more exactly, "by rhythm, language, or 'harmony'" [1447 a]), explicitly excluding imitation in prose (the mimes of Sophron, the Socratic dialogues) and nonimitative verse—and making no mention at all of nonimitative prose, such as oratory, on which the *Rhetoric*, for its part, focuses.[13] To illustrate nonimitative verse Aristotle selects the work of Empedocles, and more generally any "treatise on medicine or natural science . . . brought out in verse" (1447 b)—in other words, didactic poetry, which he rejects despite what he calls a widespread opinion ("the name of poet is by custom given to the author"). To Aristotle, as we know, "it would be right to call . . . [Empedocles] physicist rather than poet," even though Empedocles uses the same meter as Homer. As for the poems that we would call lyric (for example, those of Sappho or Pindar), neither here nor elsewhere in the *Poetics* does Aristotle mention them; they are plainly outside his field, as they were outside Plato's. The subsequent subdivisions will thus be brought to bear only within the strictly circumscribed area of representational poetry.

Their basis is an intersecting of categories that are directly connected to the very fact of representation: the object imitated (the question *what?*) and the manner of imitation (the question *how?*). The object imitated—here we have a new restriction—consists solely of human actions, or more precisely of human beings in action, who can be represented as superior to (*beltionas*), equal to (*kat'hèmas*), or inferior to (*kheironas*) "us" (1448 a)[14]—that is, no doubt, to ordinary people. The middle group will receive very little attention, so the criterion of content (the object imitated) comes down to the contrast between superior and inferior heroes. As for the manner of imitation, it consists either of telling (the Platonic *haplè diègèsis*) or of "present[ing] all [the] characters as living and moving before us" (1448 a)—that is, setting them on stage moving about and speaking (the Platonic *mimèsis*, or dramatic representation). Here again we see that an intermediate class—the Platonic mixed class—has disappeared, at least as a taxonomic principle. Apart from that disappearance, what Aristotle calls "the manner . . . of imitation" (1447 a) is exactly equivalent to what Plato called *lexis*. This is not yet a system of genres; the most exact term for designating this category is undoubtedly the term—used in the [Butcher] translation—*mode*. Strictly speaking, we are dealing not with "form" in the traditional sense, as in the contrast between verse and prose or between different types of verse, but with *situations of enunciating*. To use Plato's terms, in the narrative mode the poet speaks in his own name, whereas in the dramatic mode the characters themselves speak—or, more precisely, the poet speaks disguised as so many characters.

[. . .]

4.

For several centuries, the Platonic-Aristotelian restriction of poetics to the representative will weigh heavily on the theory of genres and keep the theory's adherents in a state of malaise or confusion.[15] The idea of lyric poetry is obviously not unknown to the Alexandrian critics, but it is not made part of the paradigm alongside the ideas of epic and dramatic poetry, and its definition is still purely technical (poems with lyre accompaniment) and restrictive. Aristarchus, in the third to second century B.C., draws up a list of nine lyric poets (including Alcaeus, Sappho, Anacreon, and Pindar), which will long remain canonical and excludes, for example, the iambic and the elegiac distich. Horace, although himself a lyricist and satirist, limits the *Art of Poetry*, in terms of genre, to praising Homer and setting forth the rules of dramatic poetry. In the list of readings in Greek and Latin that Quintilian recommends to the future orator, he mentions, besides history, philosophy, and of course rhetoric, seven poetic genres: epic (which here comprises all kinds of narrative, descriptive, or didactic poems, including those of Hesiod, Theocritus, and Lucretius), tragedy, comedy, elegy (Callimachus, the Latin elegists), iambic (Archilochus, Horace), satire ("tota nostra": Lucilius and Horace), and lyric poetry—this last illustrated by, among others, Pindar, Alcaeus, and Horace. In other words, here the lyric is simply one of several nonnarrative and nondramatic genres and comes down in fact to one form, which is the ode.

But Quintilian's list is obviously not an *art of poetry*, since it includes works in prose. The later attempts at systematization, at the end of antiquity and in the Middle Ages, make great efforts to integrate lyric poetry into the systems of Plato or Aristotle without modifying their categories. Thus Diomedes (late fourth century) rechristens the three Platonic modes "genres" (*genera*) and, after a fashion, apportions among them the "species" (*species*) that we would call genres: the *genus imitativum* (dramatic), in which only the characters speak, comprises the tragic, comic, and satiric species (the last-named is the satiric drama of the early Greek tetralogies, not mentioned by Plato or Aristotle); the *genus ennarativum* (narrative), in which only the poet speaks, comprises the properly narrative, the sententious (gnomic?), and the didactic species; the *genus commune* (mixed), in which poet and characters speak in turn, comprises the species that are heroic (the epic) and . . . lyric (Archilochus and Horace). Proclus (fifth century) omits the mixed category, as Aristotle did, and in the narrative genre he puts—alongside epic—iambic, elegy, and *mélos* (lyricism). John of Garland (thirteenth century) goes back to Diomedes' system.

The sixteenth-century authors of arts of poetry generally forgo constructing systems and are content instead simply to juxtapose species. Thus Peletier du Mans (1555): epigram, sonnet, ode, epistle, elegy, satire, comedy, tragedy, "heroic work"; or Vauquelin de La Fresnaye (1605): epic, elegy, sonnet, iambic, song, ode, comedy, tragedy, satire, idyll, pastoral; or Sir Philip Sidney (*An Apologie for Poetrie*, about 1580): heroic, lyric, tragic, comic, satiric, iambic, elegiac, pastoral, etc. The main arts of poetry of the classical tradition, from Vida to Rapin, are basically, as we know, commentaries on Aristotle, in which the inexhaustible debate about the comparative merits of tragedy and epic goes on and on, while the emergence in the sixteenth century of new genres (like the heroical-romantic poem, the pastoral novel, the dramatic pastoral, or the tragicomedy, each too easily reducible to the narrative or the dramatic mode) never really alters the picture. In the classical vulgate, the de facto recognition of the various nonrepresentational forms is reconciled, after a fashion, with the maintenance of Aristotelian orthodoxy by means of a convenient distinction between "the major genres" and . . . the others—a distinction to which the arrangement of Boileau's *Art poétique* (1674) perfectly (albeit implicitly) attests: canto 3 deals with tragedy, epic, and comedy, while canto 2, like its sixteenth-century predecessors, strings together idyll, elegy, ode, sonnet, epigram, rondeau, madrigal, ballad, satire, vaudeville, and song, without any comprehensive classification.[16] In the same year, Rapin speaks openly of the distinction and pushes it further:

> Poetics as a whole can be divided into three different species of perfect Poem—Epic, Tragedy, and Comedy—and these three species can be reduced to only two, one of which consists of action and the other of narration. All the other species that Aristotle mentions [?] can be reduced to those two: Comedy to dramatic Poetry, Satire to Comedy, Ode and Eclogue to heroic Poetry. The Sonnet, the Madrigal, the Epigram, the Rondeau, and the Ballad are but species of imperfect Poetry.[17]

In short, the nonrepresentational genres may choose only between an annexation that enhances their value (satire annexed to comedy and thus to dramatic poetry, ode and eclogue to epic) or a dismissal to outer darkness or, if one prefers, to the limbo of "imperfection." There is undoubtedly no better comment on this segregative assessment than the discouraged avowal René Bray makes when, having studied the classical theories of the "major genres" and then tried to bring together some information on bucolic poetry, elegy, ode, epigram, and satire, he abruptly breaks off: "But let us stop sifting through so barren a doctrine. The theorists were too contemptuous of everything outside the major genres. Tragedy and the heroic poem were all they paid attention to."[18]

Beside—or rather, therefore, beneath—the major narrative and dramatic genres is a cloud of small forms, whose inferiority or lack of poetic status is due somewhat to their littleness (real in the case of their dimensions, alleged in the case of their subjects) and much more to the centuries-old exclusion applied to everything that is not "an imitation of men in action." Odes, elegies, sonnets, etc., "imitate" no action, because theoretically all they do, like a speech or a prayer, is express their authors' ideas or feelings, real or fictitious. Consequently, there are only two conceivable ways of promoting them to poetic dignity. The first way is to uphold, while somewhat expanding, the classical dogma of *mimèsis* and strive to show that that type of statement is still, in its own fashion, an "imitation." The second and more radical way is to break with the dogma and proclaim the equal poetic dignity of a nonrepresentational utterance. Today those two movements seem antithetical and logically incompatible. But in fact one will succeed the other and link up with it almost unnoticeably, the former paving the way for the latter while cloaking it, as reforms sometimes break the ground for revolutions.

5.

The idea of federating all the kinds of nonmimetic poetry to establish them as a third party under the common name of lyric poetry is not wholly unknown to the classical period: it is merely marginal and, so to speak, heterodox. The first occurrence of it that Irene Behrens noted is in the work of the Italian Minturno, for whom "poetry is divided into three parts, one of which is called theatrical, the second lyrical, the third epical." Cervantes, in chapter 47 of *Don Quixote*, has his Canon speak of a fourfold division, with dramatic poetry split into two parts: "The unrestricted range [of books of chivalry] enables the author to show his powers, epic, lyric, tragic, or comic." Milton claims to find in Aristotle, Horace, "and the Italian commentaries of Castelvetro, Tasso, Mazzoni, and others . . . the laws . . . of a true epic . . . , dramatic . . . , [or] lyric" poem—the earliest example, to my knowledge, of our improper attribution. Dryden distinguishes three "ways": dramatic, epic, lyric. Gravina devotes one chapter of his *Ragion poetica* (1708) to epic and dramatic poetry and the next chapter to lyric poetry. Houdar de la Motte, a "modern" in the context of the Quarrel of the Ancients and Moderns, compares the three categories and describes himself as "at once an epic, dramatic, and lyric poet." Finally, Baumgarten, in a 1735 text that outlines or prefigures his *Aesthetica*, evokes "the lyrical, the epical, the dramatic and their generic subdivisions."[19] And my enumeration lays no claim to exhaustiveness.

But none of those propositions is truly well grounded and well explained. The earliest effort in that direction seems to have been made by the Spaniard Francisco Cascales, in his *Tablas poeticas* (1617) and *Cartas philologicas* (1634): lyric poetry, says Cascales apropos of the sonnet, has for its "plot" not an action, as epic and dramatic poetry do, but a thought (*concepto*). This distortion of orthodoxy is significant: the term *plot* (*fábula*) is Aristotelian, and the term *thought* could correspond to the equally Aristotelian term *dianoia*. But the idea that a thought can serve as the plot of anything whatsoever is totally alien to the spirit of the *Poetics*, which explicitly defines plot (*muthos*) as "the arrangement of the incidents" (1450 a)[20] and in which *dianoia* ("the faculty of saying what is possible and pertinent in given circumstances," 1450 b) covers scarcely more than the characters' techniques of argumentation; very logically, therefore, Aristotle dismisses the topic, referring to his study of it in "the Rhetoric, to which inquiry the subject more strictly belongs" (1456 a). Even though some critics, like Northrop Frye,[21] extend the definition to include the thought of the poet himself, obviously all of that cannot constitute a plot in the Aristotelian sense. Cascales is using a vocabulary that is still orthodox to cover an idea that is already as far from orthodox as possible, namely, the idea that a poem, like a discourse or a letter, may have as its subject a thought or feeling that it simply exposes or expresses. Utterly banal today, for centuries this idea remained not unthought of, surely (no literary theorist could be unaware of the immense corpus it covers), but almost systematically repressed because it could not be integrated into the system of a poetics founded on the dogma of "imitation."

Batteux's effort—the last effort classical poetics makes to survive by opening itself up to what it has never managed either to ignore or to acknowledge—therefore consists of attempting the impossible: retaining imitation as the sole law of all poetry (as of all the arts) but extending this law to lyric poetry itself. That is his aim in chapter 13, "Sur la poésie lyrique." Batteux begins by admitting that, looked at superficially, lyric poetry "seems to lend itself less than the other species to the general law that reduces everything to imitation." Thus, it is said, the psalms of David, the odes of Pindar and Horace are only "fire, emotion, intoxication, . . . a song inspired by joy, admiration, thankfulness . . . a cri de coeur, an outburst in which nature does everything and art nothing." The poet, therefore, is expressing his feelings and imitating nothing. "Which makes two things true: first, that lyric poems are true poems; second, that these poems are not characterized by imitation." But actually, answers Batteux, this pure expression, this true poetry without imitation, is found only in the biblical hymns. God himself dictated them, and God "has no need to imitate; he creates." Poets, on the contrary, who are only human beings,

> have nowhere to turn but to their natural gift, an imagination excited by art, a feigned rapture. That they may have really felt gladness is something to sing about, but for only one or two couplets. If something more extensive is wanted, it is up to art to stitch to that first cloth new feelings resembling the earlier ones. Let nature light the fire; art must at least nourish and sustain it. So the example of the prophets, who sang without imitating, proves nothing against poets as imitators.

At least in part, therefore, the feelings expressed by poets are feelings pretended through art, and this part carries the whole, since it shows the *possibility* of expressing fictitious feelings—which, moreover, drama and epic have done right from the start:

> So long as the action [in epic or drama] moves forward, the poetry is epic or dramatic; when the action stops and the poetry portrays nothing except the unique state of the soul, the pure feeling it is experiencing, the poetry in itself is lyric; to be set to song, it need only be given the appropriate form. The monologues of Polyeucte, Camille, and Chimène are lyric

> fragments; and in that case, why should feeling, which is susceptible of imitation in a drama, not be susceptible of it in an ode? Why can passion be imitated on a stage but not in a song? So there is no exception. All poets have the same object, which is to imitate nature, and all have to proceed in the same manner to imitate it.

Therefore lyric poetry, too, is imitation: it imitates feelings.

> One could consider [it] a species apart, without violating the law that governs the other species. But there is no need to separate them; lyric poetry enters naturally and even necessarily into imitation, with but one difference to characterize and distinguish it: its particular object. The main object of the other species of poetry is actions; lyric poetry focuses completely on feelings: they are its theme, its chief object.

So now lyric poetry is integrated into classical poetics. But, as readers may have observed, that integration entailed two very noticeable distortions in opposite directions. On the one hand, Batteux had to slip silently from a mere *possibility* of fictitious expression to an *essential* fictitiousness of the feelings expressed, had to reduce all lyric poetry to the reassuring model of the tragic monologue, so that he could admit into the heart of all lyric creation that screen of fiction without which the idea of imitation could not be applied to lyric. On the other hand, he had to slip, as Cascales had already done, from the orthodox term *imitation of actions* to a broader term: *imitation*, period. As Batteux himself says, "In epic and dramatic poetry, one imitates actions and customs; in the lyric, one sings of imitated feelings or passions."[22] The asymmetry remains obvious, and with it the surreptitious betrayal of Aristotle. Thus, a supplementary guarantee (or precaution) is indeed necessary in this direction, and that is what lies behind Batteux's addition of the chapter entitled "Que cette doctrine est conforme à celle d'Aristote."

The principle of the operation is simple and already familiar to us: it consists first of deriving from a fairly marginal stylistic comment a tripartition of the poetic genres into dithyramb, epic, and drama, which brings Aristotle to the Platonic point of departure; then of interpreting dithyramb as an example of the lyric genre, which allows one to attribute to the *Poetics* a triad that neither Plato nor Aristotle had ever considered. But we must immediately add that this generic misappropriation has something to be said for it on the level of mode: the initial definition of the pure narrative mode, we should remember, was that the poet constitutes the only enunciating subject, monopolizing speech without ever turning it over to any of his characters. In principle this is what happens in the lyric poem also, except that in lyric, the speech in question is not inherently narrative. If we overlook this proviso and go on to define the three Platonic modes purely in terms of enunciation, we get the following tripartition:

enunciation reserved for the poet	alternating enunciation	enunciation reserved for the characters

Defined in this way, the first position can equally well be purely narrative or purely "expressive" or can blend the two functions in any proportion at all. Since, as we noted earlier, no purely narrative genre exists, the first position is just the right place for any kind of genre devoted chiefly to expressing, sincerely or not, ideas or feelings: it is a negative catchall (for everything that is neither narrative nor dramatic),[23] on which the name *lyric* will bestow its hegemony and its prestige. Hence the expected chart:

lyrical	epical	dramatic

One will rightly object to such an "accommodation" by pointing out that this modal definition of lyric cannot be applied to the so-called lyric monologues in the theater, in the style of Rodrigue's celebrated "stances,"[24] to which Batteux attributes so much importance for the reason we have seen and in which the enunciating subject is not the poet. But we must remember that this modal definition is not Batteux's doing, for he pays no attention to modes (any more than his romantic successors do). That (trans)historic compromise, continuing to slither along, so to speak, comes out into the open only in the twentieth century, when the enunciating situation again gains prominence for the more general reasons we are all aware of. In the interim, the ticklish matter of the "lyric monologue" receded into the background. It remains intact, of course, and demonstrates, if nothing else, that modal and generic definitions do not always coincide: modally, it is always Rodrigue who speaks, whether to sing of his love or to provoke Don Gormas; generically, the provoking is "dramatic," whereas the love song (with or without the formal markers of meter or strophe) is "lyric," and the distinction, once again, is (partly) thematic in nature: not every monologue is perceived as lyric (Auguste's in the fifth act of *Cinna* is not, although it is no more integrated dramatically than Rodrigue's, both of which indeed lead to a decision), and conversely, a dialogue on love ("O miracle of love! / O crowning woe! . . .")[25] can easily be so perceived.

[. . .]

9.

I have tried to show how and why theorists reached the point of devising, and then (as a supplementary consideration) of attributing to Plato and Aristotle, a division of the "literary genres" that the whole "unconscious poetics" of both philosophers rejects. To get a firmer grip on the historical reality, we should no doubt make clear that the attribution passed through two periods and stemmed from two very distinct motives. At the end of classicism, it stemmed from a still deepseated respect for orthodoxy and a need to treat it with care. In the twentieth century, a better reason for the attribution is retrospective illusion (the vulgate is so well established that imagining a time when it did not exist is very difficult) and also (as is evident in Frye, for example) the legitimate renewal of interest in a modal interpretation of the phenomena of genre—that is, an interpretation based on the enunciating situation. Between the two periods, the romantics and postromantics were not overly concerned about dragging Plato and Aristotle into all these matters. But the present telescoping of these various positions—the fact, for example, that authority is claimed to derive at one and the same time from Aristotle, Batteux, Schlegel (or, as we will see, Goethe), Jakobson, Benveniste, and Anglo-American analytical philosophy—aggravates the theoretical drawbacks of this erroneous attribution, or (to define the error itself in theoretical terms) this confusion between modes and genres.

In Plato, and again in Aristotle, as we have seen, the basic division had a clearly defined status, for it bore explicitly on a text's *mode of enunciation*. To the extent that genres in the proper sense of the term were taken into consideration (very little in Plato, more so in Aristotle), they were allocated among modes inasmuch as they came under one enunciating stance or another: dithyramb under pure narration, epic under mixed narration, tragedy and comedy under dramatic imitation. But this inclusive relationship did not prevent the generic and modal criteria from being absolutely dissimilar, as well as radically different in status: each genre was defined essentially by a specification of content that was in no way prescribed by the definition of its mode. The romantic and postromantic division, in contrast, views the lyrical, the epical, and the dramatic no longer simply as modes of enunciation but as real genres, whose definitions already inevitably include thematic elements, however vague. We see this in Hegel, among others: for him there exists an epic *world* defined by a specific type of social aggregate and human relationship; a lyric *content* ("the individual subject"); a dramatic *milieu* "made up of conflicts and collisions." We also see it in Hugo, for whom real drama, for example, is inseparable from the Christian message (separation of body and soul). We see it, as well, in Karl Viëtor, for whom the three major genres express three "basic attitudes": the lyrical expresses feeling; the epical, knowledge; the dramatic, will and action.[26] Viëtor thus resurrects the distribution Hölderlin ventured at the end of the eighteenth century, but modifies it by transposing epic and dramatic.

The transition from one status to the other is clearly, if not intentionally, illustrated by a well-known text of Goethe's, which we have mentioned in passing and must now consider on its own account.[27] Here Goethe contrasts the ordinary "poetic species" (*Dichtarten*)—particular genres, such as the novel, the ballad, or satire—with the "three genuine natural forms" (*drei echte Naturformen*) of poetry: the epic, defined as pure narration (*klar erzählende*); the lyric, as a burst of rapture (*enthusiastisch aufgeregte*); and the drama, as lifelike representation (*persönlich handelnde*).[28] "These three poetic modes [*Dichtweisen*]," he adds, "can function either jointly or separately." The contrast between *Dichtarten* and *Dichtweisen* clearly encompasses the distinction between genres and modes, and it is reinforced by the purely modal definitions of epic and drama. The definition of lyric, however, is thematic, making the term *Dichtweisen* irrelevant and sending us to the vaguer idea of *Naturform*, which covers all interpretations and is for that reason, no doubt, the term commentators have most frequently used.

But the whole point is, precisely, to know whether the term *natural forms* can still be legitimately applied to the triad *lyrical/epical/dramatic* once that triad has been redefined in generic terms. The modes of enunciation can, in a pinch, be termed "natural forms," at least in the sense in which we speak of "natural languages." Except when using language for literary purposes, the language user is constantly required—even (or especially) if unconsciously—to choose between forms of utterance such as discourse and story (in Benveniste's sense), direct quotation and indirect style, etc. Therein lies the essential difference of status between genres and modes: genres are properly literary categories,[29] whereas modes are categories that belong to linguistics, or (more exactly) to what we now call *pragmatics*. They are "natural forms," therefore, in this wholly relative sense and only to the extent that language and its use appear as facts of nature vis-à-vis the conscious and deliberate elaboration of aesthetic forms. But the romantic triad and its subsequent derivatives no longer occupy that terrain: lyrical, epical, and dramatic contrast with *Dichtarten* no longer as modes of verbal enunciation that precede and are external to any literary definition but, rather, as kinds of *archigenres*. *Archi-*, because each of them is supposed to overarch and include, ranked by degree of importance, a certain number of empirical genres that—whatever their amplitude, longevity, or potential for recurrence—are apparently phenomena of culture and history; but still (or already) *-genres*, because (as we have seen) their defining criteria always involve a thematic element that eludes purely formal or linguistic description. This dual status is not peculiar to them, for a "genre" like the novel or comedy may also be subdivided into more specific "species"—tale of chivalry, picaresque novel, etc.; comedy of humours, farce, vaudeville, etc.—with no limit set a priori to this series of inclusions. We all know, for example, that the species *detective novel* may in turn be divided into several varieties (police procedural, thriller, "realistic" detective story à la Simenon, etc.), that with a little ingenuity one can always multiply the positions between the species and the individual, and that no one can set a limit on this proliferation of species (the spy story would, I suppose, have been completely unforeseeable to a literary theorist of the eighteenth century, and many species yet to come are still unimaginable to us today). In short, any genre can always contain several genres, and in that respect the archigenres of the romantic triad are distinguished by no natural privilege. At most they can be described as the highest—the most capacious—positions of the classification then in use. But the example of Käte Hamburger shows us that a new reduction is not to be ruled out a priori (and it would not be unreasonable—quite the contrary—to envisage a fusion that would be the reverse of hers, a fusion between the lyrical and the epical that would leave the dramatic as the only form with a rigorously "objective" enunciation). And the example of W. V. Ruttkowski shows that one can always, and just as reasonably, propose another ultimate position, in this case the *didactic*.[30] And so on. In the classification of literary species as in the classification of genres, no position is essentially more "natural" or more "ideal"—unless we abandon the literary criteria themselves, as the ancients did implicitly with the modal position. There is no generic level that can be decreed more "theoretical," or that can be attained by a more "deductive" method, than the others: all species and all subgenres, genres, or supergenres are empirical classes, established by observation of the historical facts or, if need be, by extrapolation from those facts—that is, by a deductive activity superimposed on an initial activity that is always inductive and analytical, as we have seen in the charts (whether explicit or implicit) of Aristotle and Frye, where the existence of an empty compartment (comic narrative; extroverted-intellectual) helps one discover a genre ("parody," "anatomy") otherwise condemned to invisibility. The major ideal "types" that, since Goethe, have so often been contrasted with the minor forms and intermediate genres[31] are simply more capacious, less precisely defined classes; for that reason they are more likely to have a broader cultural reach, but their principle is neither more ahistorical nor less. The "epic type" is neither more ideal nor more natural than the genres of novel and epic that it supposedly encompasses—unless we define it as the ensemble of basically *narrative* genres, which immediately brings us back to the division by mode. For narrative, like dramatic dialogue, is a basic stance of enunciation—which cannot be said of the epical or the dramatic or, of course, the lyrical, in the romantic sense of these terms.

NOTES

1. [Translator's Note]: In English, the words *epic*, *lyric*, and *narrative* function both as nouns and as adjectives; unless the context provides a decisive "adjectivity" cue, the reader processes each of those words as a noun. In this book, however, it is essential for the reader to recognize when the noun is meant and when the adjective. (French makes the distinction *l'épopée/épique*, *le lyrique / lyrique*, *le récit / narratif*.) Thus, whenever the adjectival form is meant but the context lacks a strong adjectivity cue (a cue that leads the reader to process the word instantaneously as an adjective), I have used *epical* instead of *epic*, *lyrical* instead of *lyric*, and have placed "[*narratif*]" immediately after narrative. [In a few places the context makes it appropriate to modify this practice in one direction or another. For the English translation, the author modified the original French text in a handful of places.]

2. James Joyce, *A Portrait of the Artist as a Young Man* (1916; rpt. New York: Viking, 1966), 214.

3. *Stephen Hero* (New York: New Directions, 1944), 77.

4. Ernest Bovet, *Lyrisme, épopée, drame: une loi de l'évolution littéraire expliquée par l'évolution générale* (Paris: Colin,1911), 12; Irene Behrens, *Die Lehre von der Einteilung der Dichtkunst, vornehmlich vom 16. bis 19. Jahrhundert: Studien zur Geschichte der poetischen Gattungen*, Beihefte zur Zeitschrift für romanische Philologie, no. 92 (Halle: Niemeyer, 1940).

5. "Literary Genres," in René Wellek and Austin Warren, *Theory of Literature* (New York: Harcourt, Brace, 1956), 217, 223; Northrop Frye, *Anatomy of Criticism: Four Essays* (1957; rpt. New York: Atheneum, 1967), 246; Philippe Lejeune, *Le Pacte autobiographique* (Paris: Seuil, 1975), 330; Robert Scholes, *Structuralism in Literature* (New Haven: Yale University Press, 1974), 124; Hélène Cixous, *The Exile of James Joyce*, trans. Sally A. J. Purcell (New York: David Lewis, 1972), 625;

Oswald Ducrot and Tzvetan Todorov, *Encyclopedic Dictionary of the Sciences of Language*, trans. Catherine Porter (Baltimore: Johns Hopkins University Press, 1979), 153; Mikhail Bakhtin, *Esthétique et théorie du roman*, trans. Daria Olivier (Paris: Gallimard, 1978), 445. All emphases on attributions are mine.

6. This chapter first appeared in the 1764 reprint of the essay (originally published in 1746) in the first volume of *Les Principes de littérature*. At that time it was only the end of a chapter, "La Poésie des vers," that was added on. In the posthumous edition of 1824, this ending was made into a separate chapter, with a title taken from the text of the material added in 1764.

7. Jacqueline de Romilly, *La Tragédie grecque* (Paris: Presses universitaires de France, 1970), 12.

8. 1449 a.

9. 19.918 b–919.

10. *Republic* 394 c. "It seems that at the beginning of the fifth century, the lyric song in honor of Dionysus may have dealt with sacred or heroic subjects more or less associated with the god; thus, according to the fragments of Pindar that have been preserved, the dithyramb appears to have been a piece of heroic narration, sung by a choir, without dialogue, and leading into an invocation to Dionysus or sometimes even to other divinities. Plato must be alluding to this type of composition rather than to the dithyramb of the fourth century, which was profoundly modified by the mixing of musical modes and the introduction of lyric solos" (Roselyne Dupont-Roc, "Mimesis et énonciation," in *Ecriture et théorie poétiques: lectures d'Homère, Eschyle, Platon, Aristote* [Paris: Presses de l'Ecole normale supérieure, 1976], 8). Cf. Arthur Wallace Pickard-Cambridge, *Dithyramb, Tragedy, and Comedy* (Oxford: Clarendon, 1927).

11. Of course the terms *logos* and *lexis* do not a priori have this antithetical value; out of context, the most faithful translations would be "discourse" and "diction." It is Plato himself who constructs the opposition (392 c) and glosses it as *ha lekteon* ("the matter of speech") and *hós lekteon* ("the manner of speech"). Subsequently, as we know, rhetoric limits *lexis* to the meaning "style." [Translator's note: Translations of Plato are from the Loeb edition.]

12. I discuss them in *Figures of Literary Discourse*, trans. Alan Sheridan (New York: Columbia University Press, 1982), 128–33; and *Narrative Discourse*, trans. Jane E. Lewin (Ithaca: Cornell University Press, 1980), 162–70.

13. [Translator's note.] Throughout, translations of the *Poetics* are S. H. Butcher's (1895; rev. 1911; rpt. in *Criticism: The Major Texts*, ed. Walter Jackson Bate [New York: Harcourt, Brace, 1952]). All references to the *Poetics* are given in the text.

14. The translation and therefore the interpretation of these terms obviously involve the entire interpretation of this aspect of the *Poetics*. Their usual meaning is clearly moral, as is the context of their first appearance in this chapter: characters are distinguished by vice (*kakia*) and virtue (*arètè*). The later classical tradition tends rather to interpret them in social terms, with tragedy (and epic) portraying characters of high rank and comedy characters of low rank; and it is certainly true that the Aristotelian theory of the tragic hero, which we will come upon later, is not consistent with a purely moral definition of the hero's excellence. "Superior"/"inferior" is a prudent compromise, perhaps too prudent, but one hesitates to have Aristotle rank an Oedipus or a Medea with heroes who are "better" than the average person. As for Hardy's [French] translation (Paris: Les Belles Lettres), it gets enmeshed in incoherence from the start by trying both renderings within fifteen lines of each other.

15. For the most part, the historical information that follows is taken from Edmond Faral, *Les Arts poétiques du XIIe et du XIIIe siècle: recherches et documents sur la technique littéraire du moyen âge* (Paris: Champion, 1924); Behrens, *Lehre von der Einteilung*; Wellek and Warren, *Theory of Literature*; M. H. Abrams, *The Mirror and the Lamp: Romantic Theory and the Critical Tradition* (Oxford: Oxford University Press, 1953); Mario Fubini, "Genesi e storia dei generi litterari" (1951), in *Critica e poesia: saggi e discorsi di teoria letteraria* (Bari: Laterza, 1966); René Wellek, "Genre Theory, the Lyric, and Erlebnis" (1967), in *Discriminations: Further Concepts of Criticism* (New Haven: Yale University Press, 1970); Peter Szondi, "La Théorie des genres poétiques chez F. Schlegel" (1968), in *Poésie et poétique de l'idéalisme allemand*, trans. Jean Bollack, Barbara Cassin, et al. (Paris: Minuit, 1975); Wolfgang V. Ruttkowski, *Die literarischen Gattungen: Reflexionen über eine modifizierte Fundamentalpoetik* (Bern: Francke, 1968); Claudio Guillén, "Literature as System" (1970), in *Literature as System: Essays toward the Theory of Literary History* (Princeton: Princeton University Press, 1971).

16. We should remember that cantos 1 and 4 are devoted to transgeneric considerations. And, in passing, that certain misunderstandings, not to say misinterpretations, of "classical doctrine" are due to an improper generalization of specific "precepts" that have become proverbs without

context and thus without relevance. For example, everyone knows that "un beau désordre est un effet de l'art" (a fine disorder is an effect of art), but this is a five-foot alexandrine that people readily complete with a "Souvent" (ofttimes) as apocryphal as it is evasive. The real beginning of the line is "Chez elle" (with her). With whom? The answer is in canto 2, lines 58–72.

17. *Réflexions sur la poétique* (Paris, 1674); part 2, chapter 1.

18. *La Formation de la doctrine classique en France* (1927; rpt. Paris: Nizet, 1966), 354.

19. Minturno, *De Poeta* (Venice, 1559); his *Arte poetica* of 1563, in Italian, has the same division. Miguel de Cervantes, *Don Quixote*, trans. John Ormsby (New York: W. W. Norton and Co., Norton Critical Editions, 1981), 375. John Milton, *Of Education* (1644), in *Complete Poems and Major Prose*, ed. Merritt Y. Hughes (Indianapolis: Bobbs-Merrill Co., Odyssey Press, 1957), 637. John Dryden, *An Essay of Dramatic Poesy* (1668), in *Selected Works of John Dryden*, ed. William Frost (New York: Holt, Rinehart and Winston, 1953), 326. Houdar de la Motte, *Réflexions sur la critique*, 2d ed. (Paris: Du Puis, 1716), 166. Baumgarten, *Meditationes philosophicae de nonnullis ad poema pertinentibus* (1735), section 106.

20. Cf. 1451 b: "The poet or 'maker' should be the maker of plots rather than of verses; since he is a poet because he imitates, and what he imitates are actions."

21. *Anatomy*, 52–53.

22. The chapter "Sur la poésie lyrique," at the end. Incidentally, the change from the *concepto* (thought) of Cascales to the *sentiments* (feelings) of Batteux—skipping over the classical silence—is a good measure of the distance between baroque intellectualism and preromantic sentimentalism.

23. Mario Fubini, "Genesi e storia," quotes this revealing sentence from an Italian adaptation of Hugh Blair's *Lectures on Rhetoric and Belles Lettres* (1783; compendiate dal P. Soave, Parma, 1835, 211): "People commonly distinguish three genres of poetry: epic, dramatic, and lyric, with the latter including everything that does not belong to the first two." Unless I am mistaken, that reduction does not appear in the work of Blair himself, who, being closer to classical orthodoxy, distinguished poetry as dramatic, epic, lyric, pastoral, didactic, descriptive, and . . . Hebraic.

24. [Translator's note.] Corneille, *Le Cid*, 1.6. The *Petit Robert dictionnaire de la langue française* defines *stances* as "the name given since the sixteenth century to lyric poems of serious inspiration (religious, moral, elegiac) composed in a variable number of strophes customarily of the same type."

25. *Le Cid*, in *Pierre Corneille: The Cid, Cinna, The Theatrical Illusion*, trans. John Cairncross (Harmondsworth: Penguin, 1975), 3.4.985–86.

26. "Die Geschichte literarischer Gattungen" (1931), in vol. 9 of *Deutscher Vierteljahrsschrift für Literaturwissenschaft und Geistesgeschichte* (rpt. in *Geist und Form* [Bern: Francke, 1952], 292–309); French translation in *Poétique* 8, no. 32 (1977): 490–506. We have seen the same term (*Grundhaltung*) in Kayser and the same concept in Bovet, who spoke of "basic ways of viewing life and the universe."

27. I am referring to two notes (*Dichtarten* and *Naturformen der Dichtung*) that were made part of the 1819 *Divan*.

28. The list of *Dichtarten*, deliberately put in [German] alphabetical order, is allegory, ballad, cantata, drama, elegy, epigram, epistle, epic, narrative (*Erzählung*) fable, heroic verse, idyll, didactic poem, ode, parody, novel, romance, satire. In Lichtenberger's bilingual edition of the *Divan*, which does not include the German text of the notes, the translations (377–78) of *klar erzählende* and *persönlich handelnde* ("qui raconte clairement" [who recounts clearly] and "qui agit personnellement" [who acts in person]) are more cautious or evasive than my translations ("narration pure" [pure narration] and "représentation vivante" [lifelike representation]). Nevertheless, it seems to me that two other statements in that note confirm the modal interpretation. First, "In French tragedy, the exposition is epical, the middle part dramatic"; and then, with a strictly Aristotelian criterion, "The Homeric epic [*Heldengedicht*] is purely epical: the rhapsodist is always in the foreground to recount the events; no one may utter a word unless the rhapsodist first gives him the floor." In both cases "epical" clearly means *narrative* [*narratif*].

29. To be more precise, we should say "properly aesthetic," for, as we know, the fact of genre is common to all the arts. Here, therefore, "properly literary" means proper to the aesthetic level of literature, the level literature shares with the other arts, as opposed to the linguistic level, which literature shares with the other types of discourse.

30. *Die literarischen Gattungen*, chapter 6, "Schlussforderungen: eine modifizierte Gattungspoetik."

31. *Type* is sometimes one term of the opposition (Lämmert, Todorov in the *Dictionary*); other terminological couples that have been used are *kind/genre* (Wellek and Warren), *mode/genre*

(Scholes), *theoretical genre / historical genre* (Todorov in *The Fantastic: A Structural Approach to a Literary Genre*, trans. Richard Howard [Ithaca: Cornell University Press, 1975]), *basic attitude / genre* (Viëtor), *basic genre* or *basic type / genre* (Petersen), or even, with some slight differences, *simple form / real form* in Jolles. Todorov's current position is closer to the one I am upholding here:

> In the past, attempts have been made to distinguish "natural" forms of poetry (for example, lyric, epic, or dramatic poetry) from its conventional forms (sonnets, ballads, odes), or even to oppose [the "natural" and the conventional]. We need to try to see on what level such an assertion may still have some meaning. One possibility is that lyric poetry, epic poetry, and so on, are universal categories and *thus belong to discourse*. . . . The other possibility is that such terms are used with regard to historical phenomena: thus the epic is what Homer's *Iliad* embodies. In the second case, we are indeed dealing with genres, but these are not qualitatively different on the discursive level from a genre like the sonnet (which for its part is based on constraints: thematic, verbal, and so on). ("L'origine des genres" [1976], in *Les Genres du discours* [Paris: Seuil, 1978], 50; tr. *Genres in Discourse*, trans. Catherine Porter [New York: Cambridge University Press, 1990], 18. Emphasis mine.)

1.2 Theory of Genres (1957)

Northrop Frye

We complained in our introduction that the theory of genres was an undeveloped subject in criticism. We have the three generic terms drama, epic, and lyric, derived from the Greeks, but we use the latter two chiefly as jargon or trade slang for long and short (or shorter) poems respectively. The middle-sized poem does not even have a jargon term to describe it, and any long poem gets to be called an epic, especially if it is divided into a dozen or so parts, like Browning's *Ring and the Book*. This poem takes a dramatic structure, a triangle of jealous husband, patient wife, and chivalrous lover involved in a murder trial with courtroom and death-house scenes, and works it all out through the soliloquies of the characters. It is an astounding *tour de force*, but we can fully appreciate this only when we see it as a generic experiment in drama, a drama turned inside out, as it were. Similarly, we call Shelley's *Ode to the West Wind* a lyric, perhaps because it is a lyric; if we hesitate to call *Epipsychidion* a lyric, and have no idea what it is, we can always call it the product of an essentially lyrical genius. It is shorter than the *Iliad*, and there's an end of it.

However, the origin of the words drama, epic, and lyric suggests that the central principle of genre is simple enough. The basis of generic distinctions in literature appears to be the radical of presentation. Words may be acted in front of a spectator; they may be spoken in front of a listener; they may be sung or chanted; or they may be written for a reader. Criticism, we note resignedly in passing, has no word for the individual member of an author's audience, and the word "audience" itself does not really cover all genres, as it is slightly illogical to describe the readers of a book as an audience. The basis of generic criticism in any case is rhetorical, in the sense that the genre is determined by the conditions established between the poet and his public.

We have to speak of the *radical* of presentation if the distinctions of acted, spoken, and written word are to mean anything in the age of the printing press. One may print a lyric or read a novel aloud, but such incidental changes are not enough in themselves to alter the genre. For all the loving care that is rightfully expended on the printed texts of Shakespeare's plays, they are still radically acting scripts, and belong to the genre of drama. If a Romantic poet gives his poem a dramatic form, he may not expect or even want any stage representation; he may think entirely in terms of print and readers; he may even believe, like many Romantics, that the stage drama is an impure form because of the limitations it puts on individual expression. Yet the poem is still being referred back to some kind of theatre, however much of a castle in the air. A novel is written, but when Conrad employs a narrator to help him tell his story, the genre of the written word is being assimilated to that of the spoken one.

The question of how we are to classify such a novel is less important than the recognition of the fact that two different radicals of presentation exist in it. It might be thought simpler, instead of using the term radical, to say that the generic distinctions are among the ways in which literary works are *ideally* presented, whatever the actualities are. But Milton, for example, seems to have no ideal of reciter and audience in mind for *Paradise Lost*; he seems content to leave it, in practice, a poem to be read in a book. When he uses the convention of invocation, thus bringing the poem into the genre of the spoken word, the significance of the convention is to indicate what tradition his work primarily belongs to and what its closest affinities are with. The purpose of criticism by genres is not so much to classify as to clarify such traditions and affinities, thereby bringing out a large number of literary relationships that would not be noticed as long as there were no context established for them.

The genre of the spoken word and the listener is very difficult to describe in English, but part of it is what the Greeks meant by the phrase *ta epe*, poems intended to be recited, not necessarily epics of the conventional jumbo size. Such "epic" material does not have to be in metre, as the prose tale and the prose oration are important spoken forms. The difference between metre and prose is evidently not in itself a generic difference, as the example of drama shows, though it tends to become one. In this essay I use the word "*epos*" to describe works in which the radical of presentation is oral address, keeping the word epic for its customary use as the name of the form of the *Iliad*, *Odyssey*, *Aeneid*, and *Paradise Lost*. *Epos* thus takes in all literature, in verse or prose, which makes some attempt to preserve the convention of recitation and a listening audience.

The Greeks gave us the names of three of our four genres: they did not give us a word for the genre that addresses a reader through a book, and naturally we have not invented one of our own. The nearest to it is "history," but this word, in spite of *Tom Jones*, has gone outside literature, and the Latin "scripture" is too specialized in meaning. As I have to have some word, I shall make an arbitrary choice of "fiction" to describe the genre of the printed page. I know that I used this word in the first essay in a different context, but it seems better to compromise with the present confused terminology than to increase the difficulties of this book by introducing too many new terms. The analogy of the keyboard in music may illustrate the difference between fiction and other genres which for practical purposes exist in books. A book, like a keyboard, is a mechanical device for bringing an entire artistic structure under the interpretive control of a single person. But just as it is possible to distinguish genuine piano music from the piano score of an opera or symphony, so we may distinguish genuine "book literature" from books containing the reduced textual scores of recited or acted pieces.

The connection between a speaking poet and a listening audience, which may be actual in Homer or Chaucer, soon becomes increasingly theoretical, and as it does so *epos* passes insensibly into fiction. One may even suggest, not quite seriously, that the legendary figure of the blind bard, which is used so effectively by Milton, indicates that the drift toward an unseen audience sets in very early. But whenever the same material does duty for both genres, the distinction between the genres becomes immediately apparent. The chief distinction, though not a simple one of length, is involved with the fact that *epos* is episodic and fiction continuous. The novels of Dickens are, as books, fiction; as serial publications in a magazine designed for family reading, they are still fundamentally fiction, though closer to *epos*. But when Dickens began to give readings from his own works, the genre changed wholly to *epos*; the emphasis was then thrown on immediacy of effect before a visible audience.

In drama, the hypothetical or internal characters of the story confront the audience directly, hence the drama is marked by the concealment of the author from his audience. In very spectacular drama, such as we get in many movies, the author is of relatively little importance. Drama, like music, is an ensemble performance for an audience, and music and drama are most likely to flourish in a society with a strong consciousness of itself as a society, like Elizabethan England. When a society becomes individualized and competitive, like Victorian England, music and drama suffer accordingly, and the written word almost monopolizes literature. In *epos*, the author confronts his audience directly, and the hypothetical characters of his story are concealed. The author is still theoretically there when he is being represented by a rhapsode or minstrel, for the latter speaks as the poet, not as a character in the poem. In written literature both the author and his characters are concealed from the reader.

The fourth possible arrangement, the concealment of the poet's audience from the poet, is presented in the lyric. There is, as usual, no word for the audience of the lyric: what is wanted is something analogous to "chorus" which does not suggest simultaneous presence or dramatic context. The lyric is, to go back to Mill's aphorism referred to at the beginning of this book, preeminently the utterance that is overheard. The lyric poet normally pretends to be talking to himself or to someone else: a spirit of nature, a Muse (note the distinction from *epos*, where the Muse speaks *through* the poet), a personal friend, a lover, a god, a personified abstraction, or a natural object. The lyric is, as Stephen Dedalus says in Joyce's *Portrait*, the poet presenting the image in relation to himself: it is to *epos*, rhetorically, as prayer is to sermon. The radical of presentation in the lyric is the hypothetical form of what in religion is called the "I-Thou" relationship. The poet, so to speak, turns his back on his listeners, though he may speak for them, and though they may repeat some of his words after him.

Epos and fiction make up the central area of literature, and are flanked by the drama on one side and by the lyric on the other. Drama has a peculiarly intimate connection with ritual, and lyric with dream or vision, the individual communing with himself. We said at the beginning of this book that there is no such thing as direct address in literature, but direct address is natural communication, and literature may imitate it as it may imitate anything else in nature. In *epos*, where the poet faces his audience, we have a *mimesis* of direct address. Epos and fiction first take the form of scripture and myth, then of traditional tales, then of narrative and didactic poetry, including the epic proper, and of oratorical prose, then of novels and other written forms. As we progress historically through the five modes, fiction increasingly overshadows *epos*, and as it does, the mimesis of direct address changes to a mimesis of assertive writing. This in its turn, with the extremes of documentary or didactic prose, becomes actual assertion, and so passes out of literature.

The lyric is an internal mimesis of sound and imagery, and stands opposite the external mimesis, or outward representation of sound and imagery, which is drama. Both forms avoid the mimesis of direct address. The characters in a play talk to each other, and are theoretically talking to themselves in an aside or soliloquy. Even if they are conscious of an audience, they are not speaking for the poet, except in special cases like the parabasis of Old Comedy or the prologues and epilogues of the rococo theatre, where there is an actual generic change from drama to *epos*. In Bernard Shaw the comic parabasis is transferred from the middle of the play to a separate prose preface, which is a change from drama to fiction.

In *epos* some kind of comparatively regular metre tends to predominate: even oratorical prose shows many metrical features, both in its syntax and in its punctuation. In fiction prose tends to predominate, because only prose has the continuous rhythm appropriate for the continuous form of the book. Drama has no controlling rhythm peculiar to itself, but it is most closely related to *epos* in the earlier modes and to fiction in the later ones. In the lyric a rhythm which is poetic but not necessarily metrical tends to predominate. We proceed to examine each genre in turn with a view to discovering what its chief features are. As in what immediately follows we are largely concerned with diction and linguistic elements, we must limit our survey mainly to a specific language, which will be English: this means that a good deal of what we say will be true only of English, but it is hoped that the main principles can be adapted to other languages as well.

[. . .]

The Rhythm of Association: Lyric

In the historical sequence of modes, each genre in turn seems to rise to some degree of ascendancy. Myth and romance express themselves mainly in *epos*, and in the high mimetic the rise of a new national consciousness and an increase of secular rhetoric bring the drama of the settled theatre into the foreground. The low mimetic brings fiction and an increasing use of prose, the rhythm of which finally begins to influence verse. Wordsworth's theory that apart from metre the *lexis* of poetry and of prose are identical is a low mimetic manifesto. The lyric is the genre in which the poet, like the ironic writer, turns his back on his audience. It is also the genre which most clearly shows the hypothetical core of literature, narrative and meaning in their literal aspects as word-order and word-pattern. It looks as though the lyric genre has some peculiarly close connection with the ironic mode and the literal level of meaning.

Let us take a line of poetry at random, say the beginning of Claudio's great speech in *Measure for Measure*:

> Ay, but to die, and go we know not where:

We can hear of course the metrical rhythm, an iambic pentameter spoken as a four-stress line. We can hear the semantic or prose rhythm, and we hear what we may call the rhythm of decorum, the verbal representation of the horror of a man facing death. But we can also, if we listen to the line very attentively, make out still another rhythm in it, an oracular, meditative, irregular, unpredictable, and essentially discontinuous rhythm, emerging from the coincidences of the sound-pattern:

> Ay:
> But to die . . .
> and go
> we know
> not where . . .

Just as the semantic rhythm is the initiative of prose, and as the metrical rhythm is the initiative of *epos*, so this oracular rhythm seems to be the predominating initiative of lyric. The initiative of prose normally has its center of gravity in the conscious mind: the discursive writer writes deliberately, and the literary prose writer imitates a deliberative process. In verse *epos* the choice of a metre prescribes the form of rhetorical organization: the poet develops an unconscious habitual skill in thinking in this metre, and is thereby set free to do other things, such as tell stories, expound ideas, or make the various modifications demanded by decorum. Neither of these by itself seems quite to get down to what we think of as typically the poetic creation, which is an associative rhetorical process, most of it below the threshold of consciousness, a chaos of paronomasia, sound-links, ambiguous sense-links, and memory-links very like that of the dream. Out of this the distinctively lyrical union of sound and sense emerges. Like the dream, verbal association is subject to a censor, which (or whom) we may call the "plausibility-principle," the necessity of shaping itself into a form acceptable to the poet's and his reader's waking consciousness, and of adapting itself to the sign-meanings of assertive language well enough to be communicable to that consciousness. But associative rhythm seems to retain a connection with dream corresponding to the drama's connection with ritual. The associative rhythm, no less than the others, can be found in all writing: Yeats's typographical rearrangement of Pater which begins *The Oxford Book of Modern Verse* illustrates how it may be extracted from prose.

The most natural unit of the lyric is the discontinuous unit of the stanza, and in earlier periods most lyrics tended to be fairly regular strophic patterns, reflecting the ascendancy of *epos*. Stanzaic *epos*, such as we find in medieval romance, is usually much closer to the atmosphere of a dream world than linear *epos*. With the Romantic movement a sense that the "true voice of feeling" was unpredictable and irregular in its rhythm began to increase. Poe's *Poetic Principle* maintains that poetry is *essentially* oracular and discontinuous, that the poetic *is* the lyrical, and that verse *epos* consists really of lyrical passages stuck together with versified prose. This is a manifesto of the ironic age, as Wordsworth's preface was a low mimetic one, and announces the arrival of a third period of technical experiment in English literature, in which the object is to liberate the distinctive rhythm of lyric. The aim of "free" verse is not simply revolt against metre and *epos* conventions, but the articulation of an independent rhythm equally distinct from metre and from prose. If we do not recognize this third rhythm, we shall have no answer for the naive objection that when poetry loses regular metre it becomes prose.

The loosening of rhyme in Emily Dickinson and of stanzaic structure in Yeats are intended, not to make the metrical pattern more irregular, but to make the lyric rhythm more precise. Hopkins's term "sprung rhythm," too, has as close an affinity with lyric as running rhythm has with *epos*. Pound's theories and techniques, from his early imagism to the discontinuous pastiche of the *Cantos* (preceded by a half-century of French and English experiment in the "fragmentation" or lyricizing of *epos*), are lyric-centered theories and techniques. The rhetorical analysis founded on ambiguity in new criticism is a lyric-centered criticism which tends, often explicitly, to extract the lyrical rhythm from all the genres. The most admired and advanced poets of the twentieth century are chiefly those who have most fully mastered the elusive, meditative, resonant, centripetal word-magic of the emancipated lyrical rhythm. In the course of this development the associative rhythm has become more flexible, and has consequently moved from its Romantic basis in style to a new kind of subjectivized decorum.

The traditional associations of lyric are chiefly with music. The Greeks spoke of lyrics as *ta mele*, usually translated as "poems to be sung"; in the Renaissance, lyric was constantly associated with the lyre and the lute, and Poe's essay just referred to lays an emphasis on the importance of music in poetry which makes up in strength what it lacks in precision. We should remember, however, that when a poem is "sung," at least in the modern musical sense, its rhythmical organization has been taken over by music. The words of a "singable" lyric are generally neutral and conventional words, and modern song has the stress accent of music, with little if anything left of the pitch accent that marks the domination of music by poetry. We should therefore get a clearer impression of the lyric if we translated *ta mele* as "poems to be chanted," for chanting, or what Yeats called cantillation, is an emphasis on words as words. Modern poets who, like Yeats, want their poems chanted are often precisely those who are most suspicious of musical settings.

The history of music shows a recurrent tendency to develop elaborate contrapuntal structures which, in vocal music, almost annihilate the words. There has also been a recurrent tendency to reform and simplify musical structures in order to give the words more prominence. This has sometimes been the result of religious pressure, but literary influences have been at work too. We may take the madrigal, perhaps, as representing something close to a limit of the subservience of poetry to music. In the madrigal the poetic rhythm disappears as the words are tossed from voice to voice, and the imagery in the words is expressed by the devices of what is usually called program music. We may find long passages filled up with nonsense words, or the whole collection may bear the subtitle "apt for voices or viols," indicating that the words can be dispensed with altogether. The dislike of poets for this trituration of their words can be seen in the support they gave to the seventeenth-century style of isolating the words on a single melodic line, the style which made the opera possible. This certainly brings us closer to poetry, though music still predominates in the rhythm. But the closer the composer moves toward emphasizing the verbal rhythm of the poem, the closer he comes to the chanting which is the real rhythmical basis of lyric. Henry Lawes made some experiments in this direction which won the applause of Milton, and the admiration that so many *symbolistes* expressed for Wagner was evidently based on the notion (if so erroneous a notion can be said to be a base) that he was also trying to identify, or at least closely associate, the rhythm of music and the rhythm of poetry.

But now that we have music on one boundary of lyric, and the purely verbal emphasis of cantillation in the center, we can see that lyric has a relation to the pictorial on the other side which is equally important. Something of this is present in the typographical appearance of a lyric on a printed page, where it is, so to speak, overseen as well as overheard. The arrangement of stanzas and indentations gives a visible pattern to a lyric which is quite distinct from *epos*, where the lines have approximately the same length, as well as of course from prose. In any case there are thousands of lyrics so intently focussed on visual imagery that they are, as we may say, set to pictures. In the emblem an actual picture appears, and the poet-painter Blake, whose engraved lyrics are in the emblem tradition, has a role in the lyric analogous to that of the poet-composers Campion and Dowland on the musical side. The movement called imagism made a great deal of the pictorial element in the lyric, and many imagistic poems could almost be described as a series of captions to invisible pictures.

In such emblems as Herbert's *The Altar* and *Easter Wings*, where the pictorial shape of the subject is suggested in the shape of the lines of the poem, we begin to approach the pictorial boundary of the lyric. The absorption of words by pictures, corresponding to the madrigal's absorption of words by music, is picture-writing, of the kind most familiar to us in comic strips, captioned cartoons, posters, and other emblematic forms. A further stage of absorption is represented by Hogarth's *Rake's Progress* and similar narrative sequences of pictures, in the scroll pictures of the Orient, or in the novels in woodcuts that occasionally appear. Pictorial arrangements of the visible basis of literature, which is alphabetical writing, have had a more fitful and sporadic existence, ranging from capitals in illuminated manuscripts to surrealist experiments in collage, and have not had much specifically literary importance. They would have had more, of course, if our writing had remained in the hieroglyphic stage, as in hieroglyphics writing and drawing are much the same art. We have previously glanced at Pound's comparison of the imagistic lyric to the Chinese ideogram.

We should expect that during the last century there would have been a good deal said about the relation of poetry to music on the one hand, and to painting on the other. In fact the attempts to bring words as near as possible to the more repetitive and emphatic rhythm of music or the more concentrated stasis of painting make up the main body of what is usually called experimental writing. It would make for clearer thinking if these developments were regarded as lateral explorations of a single phase of rhetoric, not, through a false analogy with science, as "new directions" portending a general advance of literary technique on all fronts. The reverse movement of the same progressive fallacy gives us the moral indignation that talks about "decadence." A question on which little has yet been said is the extent to which poetry may, so to speak, disappear into painting or music and come back with a different rhythm. This happened for example in the emergence of the "prosa" out of the sequence in medieval music, and it happens in a different way when a song becomes a kind of rhythmical reservoir for a number of different lyrics.

The two elements of subconscious association which form the basis for lyrical *melos* and *opsis* respectively have never been given names. We may call them, if the terms are thought dignified enough, babble and doodle. In babble, rhyme, assonance, alliteration, and puns develop out of sound-associations. The thing that gives shape to the associating is what we have been calling the rhythmical initiative, though in a free verse poem it would be rather a sense of the oscillations of rhythm within an area which gradually becomes defined as the containing form. We can see from the revisions poets make that the rhythm is usually prior, either in inspiration or in importance or both, to the selection of words to fill it up. This phenomenon is not confined to poetry: in Beethoven's notebooks, too, we often see how he knows that he wants a cadence at a certain bar before he has worked out any melodic sequence to reach it. One can see a similar evolution in children, who start with rhythmical babble and fill in the appropriate words as they go along. The process is also reflected in nursery rhymes, college yells, work songs, and the like, where rhythm is a physical pulsation close to the dance, and is often filled up with nonsense words. An obvious priority of rhythm to sense is a regular feature of popular poetry, and verse, like music, is called "light" whenever it has the rhythmical accentuation of a railway coach with a flat wheel.

When babble cannot rise into consciousness, it remains on the level of uncontrolled association. This latter is often a literary way of representing insanity, and Smart's *Jubilate Agno*, parts of which are usually considered mentally unbalanced, shows the creative process in an interesting formative stage:

> For the power of some animal is predominant in every language.
> For the power and spirit of a CAT is in the Greek.
> For the sound of a cat is in the most useful preposition κατ' εὐ-χεν . . .
> For the Mouse (Mus) prevails in the Latin.
> For edi-mus, bibi-mus, vivi-mus—ore-mus . . .
> For two creatures the Bull & the Dog prevail in the English,
> For all the words ending in ble are in the creature.
> Invisi-ble, Incomprehensi-ble, ineffa-ble, A-ble . . .

For there are many words under Bull . . .
For Brook is under Bull. God be gracious to Lord Bolingbroke.

It is possible that similar sputters and sparks of the fusing intellect take place in all poetic thinking. The puns in this passage impress the reader as both outrageous and humorous, which is consistent with Freud's view of wit as the escape of impulse from the control of the censor. In creation the impulse is the creative energy itself, and the censor is what we have called the plausibility-principle. Paronomasia is one of the essential elements of verbal creation, but a pun introduced into a conversation turns its back on the sense of the conversation and sets up a self-contained verbal sound-sense pattern in its place.

There is a perilous balance in paronomasia between verbal wit and hypnotic incantation. In Poe's line "the viol, the violet and the vine," we have a fusion of two opposed qualities. Wit makes us laugh, and is addressed to the awakened intelligence; incantation by itself is humorlessly impressive. Wit detaches the reader; the oracle absorbs him. In dream-poems like Arthur Benson's *The Phoenix*, or in poems intended to represent dreaming or drowsy states, like the medieval *Pearl* and many passages in Spenser and Tennyson, we notice a similar insistence on hypnotically recurrent sound-patterns. If we were to laugh at the wit in such a line as Poe's, we should break the spell of his poem, yet the line is witty, just as *Finnegans Wake* is a very funny book, although it never leaves the oracular solemnity of the dream world. In the latter, of course, the researches of Freud and Jung into the mechanisms of both dream and wit have been extensively drawn upon. There may well be buried in it some such word as "vinolent," intended to express everything in Poe's line at once. In fiction the associative process ordinarily shows itself chiefly in the names the author invents for his characters. Thus "Lilliputian" and "Ebenezer Scrooge" are associative names for midgets and misers respectively, because one suggests "little" and "puny" and the other "squeeze," "screw" and perhaps "geezer." Spenser says that a character of his has been named Malfont:

Eyther for th' euill, which he did therein,
Or that he likened was to a welhed,

which implies that the second syllable of his name is to be derived both from *fons* and from *facere*. We may call this kind of associative process poetic etymology, and we shall say more about it later.

The characteristics of babble are again present in doggerel, which is also a creative process left unfinished through lack of skill or patience, though the psychological conditions are of the opposite kind from those of *Jubilate Agno*. Doggerel is not necessarily stupid poetry; it is poetry that begins in the conscious mind and has never gone through the associative process. It has a prose initiative, but tries to make itself associative by an act of will, and it reveals the same difficulties that great poetry has overcome at a subconscious level. We can see in doggerel how words are dragged in because they rhyme or scan, how ideas are dragged in because they are suggested by a rhyme-word, and so on. Deliberate doggerel, as we have it in *Hudibras* or German *knittelvers*, can be a source of brilliant rhetorical satire, and one which involves a kind of parody of poetic creation itself, just as malapropism is a parody of poetic etymology. The difficulties in the way of giving prose itself something of the associative concentration of poetry are enormous, and not many prose writers, apart from Flaubert and Joyce, have consistently and resolutely faced them.

The first rough sketches of verbal design ("doodle") in the creative process are hardly separable from associative babble. Phrases are scribbled in notebooks to be used later; a first stanza may suddenly "come" and then other stanzas of the same shape have to be designed to go with it, and all the ingenuity that Freud has traced in the dream has to be employed in putting words into patterns. The elaborateness of conventional forms—the sonnet and its less versatile congeners the ballade, villanelle, sestina, and the like, together with all the other conventions that the individual lyric poet invents for himself—indicates how far removed the lyrical initiative really is from whatever a *cri de coeur* is supposed to be. Poe's essay on his own *The Raven* is a perfectly accurate account of what he did in that poem, whether he did it on the conscious mental level that the essay suggests or not, and this essay, like *The Poetic Principle*, anticipates the critical techniques of a new mode.

We may note that although of course lyrics in all ages are addressed to the ear, the rise of fiction and the printing press develops an increasing tendency to address the ear through the eye. The visual patterns of E. E. Cummings are obvious examples, but do not by any means stand alone. A poem of Marianne Moore's, *Camellia Sabina*, employs an eight-line stanza in which the rhyming words are at the end of the first line, at the end of the eighth line, and at the third syllable of the seventh line. I doubt if the most attentive listener could pick this last rhyme up merely from hearing the poem read aloud: one sees it first on the page, and then translates the visual structural pattern to the ear.

We are now in a position to find more acceptable words for babble and doodle, the radicals of lyrical *melos* and *opsis* respectively. The radical of *melos* is *charm*: the hypnotic incantation that, through its pulsing dance rhythm, appeals to involuntary physical response, and is hence not far from the sense of magic, or physically compelling power. The etymological descent of charm from *carmen*, song, may be noted. Actual charms have a quality that is imitated in popular literature by work songs of various kinds, especially lullabies, where the drowsy sleep-inducing repetition shows the underlying oracular or dream pattern very clearly. Invective or flyting, the literary imitation of the spell-binding curse, uses similar incantatory devices for opposite reasons, as in Dunbar's *Flyting with Kennedy*:

> Mauch mutton, byt buttoun, peilit gluttoun, air to Hilhous;
> Rank beggar, ostir dregar, foule fleggar in the flet;
> Chittirlilling, ruch rilling, like schilling in the milhous;
> Baird rehator, theif of natour, fals tratour, feyindis gett . . .

From here the line of descent is easy to the *melos* of physical absorption in sound and rhythm, the pounding movement and clashing noise which the heavy accentuation of English makes possible. Lindsay's *The Congo* and *Sweeney Agonistes* are modern examples of a tendency to ragtime in English poetry that can be traced back through Poe's *Bells* and Dryden's *Alexander's Feast* to Skelton and to Dunbar's *Ane Ballat of our Lady*. A more refined aspect of *melos* is exhibited in lyrics which combine accentual repetition with variations in speed. Thus Wyatt's sonnet:

> I abide and abide and better abide,
> And, after the olde proverbe, the happie daye:
> And ever my ladye to me dothe saye,
> "Let me alone and I will provyde."
> I abide and abide and tarrye the tyde
> And with abiding spede well ye maye:
> Thus do I abide I wott allwaye,
> Nother obtayning nor yet denied.

Aye me! this long abidyng
Semithe to me as who sayethe
A prolonging of a dieng dethe,
Or a refusing of a desyred thing.
Moche ware it bettre for to be playne,
Then to saye abide and yet shall not obtayne.

This lovely sonnet is intensely musical in its conception: there is the repeated clang of "abide" and the musical, though poetically very audacious, sequential repetition of the first line in the fifth. Then as hope follows expectancy, doubt hope, and despair doubt, the lively rhythm gradually slows down and collapses. On the other hand, Skelton, like Scarlatti after him, gets fidgety in a slow rhythm and is more inclined to speed up. Here is an *accelerando* in a rhyme royal stanza from *The Garland of Laurell*:

That long tyme blew a full tymorous blaste,
Like to the Boriall wyndes, whan they blowe,
That towres and tounes and trees downe cast,
Drove clouds together like dryftes of snowe;
The dredful dinne drove all the route on a row;
Som trembled, som girned, som gasped, som gased,
As people half pevissh or men that were mased.

In the same poem there is a curious coincidental link with music: the verses to Margery Wentworth, Margaret Hussey, and Gertrude Statham are miniature musical rondos of the *abaca* type.

We have several times noticed the close relation between the visual and the conceptual in poetry, and the radical of *opsis* in the lyric is *riddle*, which is characteristically a fusion of sensation and reflection, the use of an object of sense experience to stimulate a mental activity in connection with it. Riddle was originally the cognate object of read, and the riddle seems intimately involved with the whole process of reducing language to visible form, a process which runs through such by-forms of riddle as hieroglyphic and ideogram. The actual riddle-poems of Old English include some of its finest lyrics, and belong to a culture in which such a phrase as "curiously inwrought" is a favorite aesthetic judgement. Just as the charm is not far from a sense of magical compulsion, so the curiously wrought object, whether sword-hilt or illuminated manuscript, is not far from a sense of enchantment or magical imprisonment. Closely parallel to the riddle in Old English is the figure of speech known as the kenning or oblique description which calls the body the bone-house and the sea the whale-road.

1.3 Genre Theory, the Lyric, and *Erlebnis* (1967)

René Wellek

The theory of genres has not been at the center of literary study and reflection in this century. Clearly this is due to the fact that in the practice of almost all writers of our time genre distinctions matter little: boundaries are being constantly transgressed, genres combined or fused, old genres discarded or transformed, new genres created, to such an extent that the very concept has been called in doubt. Benedetto Croce, in his *Estetica* (1902), launched an attack on the concept from which it has not recovered in spite of many attempts to defend it or to restate it in different terms. In my and Austin Warren's *Theory of Literature* (1949), in a chapter on "Literary Genres" written by Mr. Warren, some of these attempts at renovation of the concept are surveyed and endorsed. Genre exists as an institution exists. "One can work through, express oneself through, existing institutions, create new ones . . . one can also join, but then reshape, institutions." Genres are aesthetic (stylistic and thematic) conventions which have molded individual works of art importantly. Genres can be observed even in the apparently anarchic welter of twentieth-century literary activity. Yet Mr. Warren was frankly dubious whether the division of poetry into three basic kinds, the epic, the drama, and the lyric, can be upheld and whether these three kinds can have "ultimate status."[1]

Since our book was written (in 1944–46), Emil Staiger's *Grundbegriffe der Poetik* (1946) and Käte Hamburger's *Logik der Dichtung* (1957) have presented theories which make impressive efforts to arrive at basic distinctions of poetry with new arguments in different philosophical contexts. Miss Hamburger appeals to phenomenology, Emil Staiger to Heideggerian existentialism. Miss Hamburger defends a dichotomy, Staiger a threefold division. In both theories the lyric or the lyrical presents the crux of the matter and thus will be the focus of our discussion.

Miss Hamburger draws the main distinction between two kinds of poetry: fictional or mimetic and lyrical or existential. Lyrical poetry is a "real utterance" (*Wirklichkeitsaussage*) of the same status as a letter or a historical narrative, while epic and drama are "fiction," the invention of actions and characters. The dividing criterion is the speaker: in the lyric the poet himself speaks, in the epic and drama he makes others speak. The novel in the first person (*Ich-Roman*) is resolutely grouped with lyrical poetry, as the author speaks there himself. Miss Hamburger's observations on the novel and the narrator in a novel have attracted much attention. Her thesis that the past tense in the novel loses its temporal function and becomes a present tense is stated persuasively. She buttresses this view by the observation that adverbs of time can be used in fictional contexts in disregard of the past meaning of the verbs. Without denying her thesis that, in some narrative contexts, the past verb loses its pastness, one may, however, object that combinations such as "he was coming to her party to-night," which she quotes from Virginia Woolf's *Mrs. Dalloway*,[2] can only occur in narrated monologue (*Erlebte Rede*) and do not set off all fiction. Still, her reflections on the narrator and the narrative function are ingenious and stimulating.

Miss Hamburger's other side of the bifurcation has, however, not aroused much discussion. Her attempt to prove the lyric to be "real utterance," undistinguishable from a passage in a letter if we dissolve a poem into prose, has gone unchallenged. In many variations she asserts the thesis that a lyrical poem is a real utterance with its origin in an "I" (*Ich-Origo*) in which the object must be understood to be experienced (*erlebt*) by the speaker. She rejects the idea of a "fictive I," a "persona" or mask, propounded in our *Theory of Literature* as "falser and more misleading than the older naïve conception that a lyrical poem betrays much of the experience of the poet."[3] Still, she constantly appeals to a criterion of "subjektive Erlebnisechtheit," even though she may not believe in a literal transcription of actual events in the poet's life. But the criterion of "genuineness," "sincerity," "intensity," etc., is a psychological criterion which puts the onus on a completely unprovable and elusive past experience of the poet. It is of course also not in any way peculiar to lyrical poetry. Miss Hamburger, in her psychologism, even arrives at a formula which divorces the inner act from the outward expression. A lyrical poem, she says, is a "secondary phenomenon" since it is only "the expression, and proclamation of the will of the subject." She argues that "the lyrical intensity of the lyrical I may be stronger than the expression, the form." Thus any bad love poem by a schoolboy is "constituted by the lyrical I."[4] She does not see that the very same problem raised by the sincere rhyming schoolboy occurs also in fiction. We can imagine a charming yarn-spinning "raconteur" inventing conversations and characters in a real life situation. The boundary between art and nonart, art and life, disappears in Miss Hamburger's scheme, because she believes in the possibility of a purely phenomenological description of art apart from value judgment, from criticism.[5] But it is a contradiction to speak of art as nonvalue or even disvalue. It is value-charged by definition.

Miss Hamburger not only considers "lived experience," intensity, *Erlebnis* the criterion of lyrical poetry, she also endorses the view that a lyrical poem can have a function in reality. She quotes a hysterical passage from a letter by Rahel Varnhagen commenting on a charming gallant poem by Goethe, "Mit einem gemalten Band," addressed to Friederike Brion: "Es musste sie vergiften. Dem hätte sie nicht glauben sollen? . . . Und zum ersten Male war Goethe feindlich für mich da."[6] Moreover, Miss Hamburger endorses Staiger's in its sexual metaphor, embarrassing characterization of the contemporary "Mailied" addressed to the same woman. "Friederike ist zugegen. Goethe ist durchdrungen von ihr, wie ihn seinerseits das Gefühl beglückt, dass sie von ihm durchdrungen sei."[7] But soberly examined, all these high-flown phrases mean little more than that Goethe expressed his feelings of love and happiness successfully in fine poetry and that he addressed his poems, as other poets before and after him, to real persons in a concrete situation, a fact which has never been doubted. But the purpose, the aim of persuasion to love, can not constitute value and will not set the poem off from any other utterance, a letter, a speech, a treatise, even a fable or a fiction invented to serve a practical purpose. The poem remains the same even if we should discover that the poet changed the addressee, as Ronsard and Lamartine did with some of their love poems, or that we were mistaken in identifying the woman addressed as Minna Herzlieb or Marianne von Willemer.

But Miss Hamburger is too sophisticated and subtle not to notice the difficulties raised with her insistence on "real utterance." She has to account for lyrical poetry, which is simply a descriptive statement about some natural object. She quotes some German verses of this kind and then draws from Hermann Amman's *Die menschliche Rede* the view that in such poetry we encounter sentences "which have no proper place in human intercourse"—e.g. "Der Bach rauscht, der Wind weht." She endorses Amman's view that such a statement is "ein Stück Leben . . . es sind die Dinge selbst, die hier zu Worte kommen," "the utterance about the things has no function in a reality nexus: they are seized, animated and hence transformed." But why could a statement such as "der Bach rauscht" not be made about a rushing brook outside a poetic context? How could one distinguish such a pronouncement, which she calls "meaningless in isolation," or "aufeinander zugeordnet," from any speech-situation comprehensible only in a context? The phrase about "the things speaking for themselves," "the piece of life," seem to me only farfetched metaphors for romantic animism. The conclusion that a lyrical poem is a "real utterance which still has no function in a reality nexus"[8] is not only a flat contradiction to the discussion about the Friederike poems but is simply an attempt to describe aesthetic distance, *Schein*, illusion—what I would call fiction—in such a way that the thesis of "real utterance" and "nonfiction" is preserved, at least verbally.

Usually, however, Miss Hamburger argues that we "must use external, even biographical investigations" for the explanation of a lyrical poem, considering this a "categorical distinction" between the lyric and fiction. It is, however, hard to see why biographical evidence is not as relevant to the study of Tolstoy, Dante, Proust, or Gide as to a lyrical poet like Mallarmé or Valéry, or what can be the justification for her view—exactly inverting the contrast between the "loose baggy monsters" of Tolstoy and the tight-closed realm of a poem by Hopkins—in asserting that drama and novel are "closed structures" while "every lyrical poem is an open structure." She argues that every lyrical poem eludes complete explanation while even the most obscure surrealistic symbolic novel is explainable in principle. All fiction, in her view, is through and through rational and hence knowable: a lyrical poem is open to the experience of the uttering "I," "toward the irrational life of the poet."[9] She thinks it an argument for her view that biographical research has been most intense on the lives of poets, as if Napoleon, Tolstoy, Voltaire, or Dr. Johnson had not as much or more attention than Hölderlin or Keats. She admits that "how far the lyrical I is the poet-I can never be settled and the poet himself would hardly be able to do so,"[10] a concession she should have extended to fictional characters such as Pierre Bezukhov or Konstantin Levin, to give examples from an author particularly dear to Miss Hamburger.

One difficulty of her theory worries her: the use of lyrical poems in the novel. Are the poems fiction, utterances of the characters, or are they "real utterances"? She draws a justifiable distinction between Goethe's use in *Wilhelm Meister* and that of Eichendorff in his novels and stories. The Mignon and Harper songs are clearly more closely related to the fictional speakers than those of Eichendorff's shadowy and often interchangeable characters. But the conclusion drawn by Miss Hamburger that Eichendorff's poems remain "Wirklichkeitsaussage," while Goethe's are part of his fiction construes an untenable contrast.[11] Goethe, after all, reprinted these poems among his collections of lyrical poetry, and they have been read and sung by many who have never read *Wilhelm Meister*; and Eichendorff's poems have also a characterizing function: the singing makes these men the carefree, melancholy, nature-loving, wandering, musical fellows that they are. The distinction simply does not hold. It seems impossible to exclude from the lyric cycles such as Petrarch's Canzoniere, Shakespeare's Sonnets, or Donne's Songs and Sonnets, which imply some thread of a story or progression or vary their speakers, and to assign them to "fiction" in Miss Hamburger's scheme.

This is the same difficulty raised by the "Rollenlyrik," which Miss Hamburger quite wrongly dismisses as "eine an sich unbedeutende Erscheinung."[12] Half the world's lyrical poetry could be described as such. It is ubiquitous in folk poetry: the oldest Romance lyrics recently discovered, the eleventh-century Mozarabic poems, put into the mouths of women, and certainly much of English poetry, often misnamed "dramatic monologue" or even "poetry of experience" (Robert Langbaum), from Donne to Browning and Eliot would have to be classed here. Its history is completely distorted when Miss Hamburger explains the "Rollengedicht" as derived from the ancient picture inscription and considers it "as the germ for the formation of the ballad form."[13] Neither the popular women's poem nor the medieval ballad has anything to do with the Alexandrian *ekphrasis*. Nor can she convince by dismissing the ballad as "a museum piece," if we think, for instance, of recent American and Russian examples. Finally she seems to admit some ambiguity and complains "of a betrayal of the lyric" to fiction in the ballad,[14] a telltale phrase for her annoyance with the breakdown of her scheme. In order to save it, she has recourse to an obscure distinction between "fictiv" and "fingiert." Mörike's poem "Früh, wann die Hähne krähn," put into the mouth of a girl, is "fingiert," while "Nur wer die Sehnsucht kennt," spoken by Mignon, is apparently "fiktiv." Miss Hamburger knows that a man, Eduard Mörike, wrote the first poem and that Mignon, a fictional figure, sings the second poem in a novel, but as texts the two poems do not differ in their status: they are both spoken by a "persona," a fictive speaker, a young girl. As a matter of fact, "Das verlassene Mägdlein" occurs also first in Mörike's novel, *Maler Nolten*. Miss Hamburger can thus complain that the ballad (and she includes the "Rollenlyrik" as a subdivision) is "ein struktureller Fremdling im lyrischen Raum."[15]

She has to treat the first person narrative as an analogous stranger in the epic-fictional space. She still insists that the first person narrative is nonfiction, a form of real utterance, though she admits that in an "Ich-Roman" the fixed teller who makes persons in the past engage in dialogue comes very near the epic "I," the narrative function.[16] But she has again recourse to her concept of "Fingiertsein," which she once admits would require further analysis,[17] to account for the obvious fact that the "I" of a first person narrative may be very different from the poet's. She speaks of this difference as containing a "factor of uncertainty," though there seems no doubt, for instance, in what specific way Felix Krull is not Thomas Mann, or the judge in *La Chute* not Albert Camus. She parallels this uncertainty with the uncertainty about the lyrical speaker, though the speaker in a lyric may be clearly identified and distinguished from the poet (as in Browning's "Cavalier Tunes"), and though a third-person narrative may raise the same doubts about the relationship of the teller to the writer as a first-person story.

Miss Hamburger also does not properly face the question of the ease and frequency of the switch from first person to third person and the other way round. Joyce, in some sections of Ulysses, shifts in almost every other sentence. Dostoevsky transcribed the original first person confession of Raskolnikov into the third person, often changing only the inflectional endings. Miss Hamburger herself refers to the two versions of Gottfried Keller's *Grüner Heinrich*, the later with a part rewritten from the original third person into the first. What would she say to a novel like Michel Butor's *La Modification*, written throughout in the second person? What can she do with Caesar's *Commentaries* or *The Education of Henry Adams*, both told by their authors in the third person? At one point she seems to admit that the "form does not guarantee the reality content," but she insists that a third-person narrative, however close to empirical reality, will always be fiction, while a first-person narrative, however fantastically unreal, will still be nonfiction, *Wirklichkeitsaussage*. "It is the form of the I utterance which preserves the character of a reality utterance even for the most extreme unreality utterance."[18] One must quote such an awkward sentence to see that Miss Hamburger throughout the book simply reiterates one undoubted fact: many poems and novels use "I" as the speaker, while other novels and some poems use "he" and have characters speak for themselves. All the talk about the "logic of poetry," all the ingenuity spent in relating her observations to a theory of knowledge lead only to a meager result: a grammar of poetry, the description of stylistic devices, a restatement of the ancient division of poetry by speaker.

Miss Hamburger herself appeals to historical precedence: she recognizes that she revives Aristotle's concept of mimesis, which she oddly enough thinks was first "restored to honor" by Erich Auerbach. As if the Neo-Thomists, the Marxists, and the Chicago Aristotelians had not honored it long before 1946! Actually, her division descends from Plato's *Republic*[19] and was codified by the fourth-century grammarian Diomedes. Plato distinguishes three kinds of imitation: pure narrative, in which the poet speaks in his own person; narrative by means of imitation, in which the poet speaks in the person of his characters; and mixed narrative, in which he speaks now in his own person and now by means of imitation. The epic would be the mixed kind; what we call lyric would appear under first-person narrative. The theory has been restated many times since: in Germany, for instance, in Johann Joachim Eschenburg's *Entwurf einer Theorie und Litteratur der schönen Wissenschaften* (1783), where the lyric, ode, elegy, and even satire, allegory, and epigram consistently appear under epic. Also, the well-known common scheme drawn up by Goethe and Schiller, "Über epische und dramatische Dichtung" (1797), distinguishes the two kinds in terms of the speaker: "the rhapsode who as a higher being ought not to appear in the poem, so that we may separate everything personal from his work, and may believe that we are hearing only the voice of the Muses in general," while "the *mime*, the actor, constitutes the opposite. He presents himself as a distinct individuality."[20] The lyric is completely ignored, but Goethe's later scheme, "Die Naturformen der Dichtung"(1819), finds a place for the lyric distinguished from the "clearly telling epic" and the "personally acting drama" by being "enthusiastically excited."[21] Goethe, one sees, introduced the totally different criterion of tone, excitement, enthusiasm, in order to accommodate the third kind.

The division was restated most strikingly in Jean Paul's *Vorschule der Ästhetik* (1804), in a discussion of the lyric added in the second edition (1813). Jean Paul apologizes for having ignored the lyric in the first edition and then restates Eschenburg's dichotomy: one can look at the poet like philosophers arguing about God's relation to the world, as either "extramundane" or "intramundane." But Jean Paul asks then:

> could there be a more fluid division right in the middle of the poetic sea? For neither the intrusion nor the concealment of the poet decides what form a poem may take . . . How easy it would be—if the trivialities of speaking and letting speak made the division—to fuse forms with forms. The same dithyramb e.g. would become quickly epical if the poet were to say or chant at the outset that he is going to chant about another poet; or it would be quickly lyrical with a few words saying that he is to sing himself; or quickly dramatic if he were to insert him, without himself saying a word, in a dramatic soliloquy. But mere formalities, at least in poetry, are not forms.[22]

Here, 144 years before Miss Hamburger's *Logik der Dichtung*, her theory is cogently refuted.

Miss Hamburger arrives at a dichotomy splitting the realm of poetry: telling versus saying, fiction versus real utterance, "he" versus "I". Many other genre theories arrive at a triad, in defense of the three established kinds: lyric, epic, tragedy. Emil Staiger's *Grundbegriffe der Poetik* (1946) is the most influential attempt to reformulate the triad on new grounds: to replace the kinds by categories which he calls "the lyrical," "the epical," "the dramatic." Every piece of poetry is conceived as located somewhere between these three extremes, since only very few works embody or fulfill the idea of the lyrical, the epical, or the dramatic. Staiger's examples, which he analyzes sensitively—Brentano for the lyrical, Homer for the epical, Kleist for the dramatic—are not meant to be normative. The three attitudes (not kinds) are coordinated mainly with the three dimensions of time: the past with the lyrical, the present with the epical, the future with the dramatic, and these time dimensions are interpreted in terms of Heidegger's conception: the past implies recollection ("Er-innerung," in Heidegger's punning term); the present "Vorstellung," presentation; the future, "Spannung," tension. "Stimmung" for the lyrical, "Verfallen" for the epical, "Verstehen" for the dramatic mode is another series of coordinates drawn from Heidegger; it corresponds to the three ages of man: the lyrical to childhood, the epical to youth, the dramatic to maturity. The triad of man's faculties is introduced by calling the lyrical "emotional" or "sinnlich," the epical "bildlich" or "anschauend," the dramatic "logical" or "begrifflich," and the activities of "fühlen, zeigen, beweisen" correspond closely. Finally, we are told the three modes are correlated with the series: syllable, word, and sentence. Cassirer's theories provided the terminology here.

The crux of the scheme lies in the coordination of the "lyrical" with the "past," which seems to contradict all the usual analyses of lyrical presence or immediacy. But the Heideggerian use of "Erinnerung" allows the term to mean a lack of distance between subject and object: "Gegenwärtiges, Vergangenes, ja sogar Zukünftiges kann in lyrischer Dichtung erinnert werden."[23] The time scheme is abolished for the lyrical mode, permitting gestures toward the mystical and ineffable. We are told that "lyrisches Dichten ist jenes an sich unmögliche Sprechen der Seele." A contradiction between the lyrical and the nature of language is asserted.[24] Lyrical poetry somehow happens: "der lyrische Dichter leistet nichts," and even the relation of man and nature is reversed. I do not understand what is meant by saying "die Natur erinnert den Dichter"[25] or what the meaning of the last sentence of the chapter could be: "Ein ungeheuerliches Dasein, das die Beseligungen der Gnade mit einer erschütternden Hilflosigkeit in allem, was Verdienst ist, erkauft, das Glück der Übereinstimmung mit einer im Alltag blutenden Wunde, für die auf Erden kein Heilkraut blüht."[26] One need not be a rationalist to doubt whether anybody could coincide with a wound bleeding on a sober day. Quite seriously Staiger calls the lyrical "the liquid element," or speaks of the soul as being "the fluidity [*die Flüssigkeit*] of a landscape in recollection," an attempt to use distinctions from Franz Baader's theosophic speculations to which Staiger alludes with apparent approval.[27]

The trouble with the scheme is primarily its lack of relation to actual poetry. It could be arrived at without any literary evidence, as Staiger admits when he says that the "ideal meaning" of the lyrical can be experienced in front of a landscape, of the epical, in front of a stream of refugees (an example suggested by *Hermann und Dorothea*), the dramatic from a quarrel.[28] The terms which are, after all, derived from and devised for poetics become names for human attitudes in an existential "anthropology." Nor can one imagine a poem made out of syllables and not of words or sentences, as even Dada poetry uses words (and of course syllables are often words, particularly in monosyllabic languages). The examples on which Staiger demonstrates his concept of the "lyrical" are all German romantic "Stimmungsgedichte," private moody musings for which even the admired "Über allen Gipfeln" is too rational, too pointed. "Warte nur, balde Ruhest du auch" is not completely lyrical in Staiger's sense. The poem, after all, was written with an eye to the point: it was conceived because of that point. Staiger asserts "im Augenblick des Verstehens aber hört das lyrische Dasein auf."[29] In practice, we are sent off to the grossest irrationalism, to an "inwardness" which cannot be expressed in words and hence cannot be art or poetry. Staiger had disclaimed that his scheme has anything to do with valuation and he even makes the admission which, one would think, questions the validity of the whole enterprise when he says that "in English or the Romance languages everything looks different." "The Italian when he speaks of *lirica* thinks of Petrarch's 'Canzoniere.' For us Petrarch's work is no prototype of the lyrical style."[30] But these differences are dismissed as merely "annoying" (*ärgerlich*), and in the postscript to the second edition (1952) the claim to practical application to concrete literature is asserted much more clearly. Staiger recognizes somewhat cautiously that his scheme has to do with traditional kinds, though he should like to interpret them freely, with a "Spielraum" around them. He even allows the possibility of a "Musterpoetik" of the ode, the elegy, the novel, and the comedy, though he disclaims any intention of furnishing it. But he does make value judgments according to his assumed genre scheme on Klopstock's *Messias* and on Keller's lyrical poetry. He recognizes, however, that his "Fundamentalpoetik" is not an appropriate instrument to grasp the type of poetry represented by Horace, in which the echo, the artistic game, share in the nature and value of the verse.[31]

Fortunately, Staiger's practice of interpretation always eludes his theory. The three volumes on Goethe successfully combine narrative and interpretation as well as judgment and use only occasionally the scheme of the *Grundbegriffe*. Staiger introduces the more general concept of a "rhythm" of Goethe's life and work which he constantly tries to characterize as the achievement of a moment, "Augenblick," a metaphor for harmony, "erfüllte Gegenwart," suggested by Faust and interpreted in Heideggerian terms. But "rhythm" remains a hieroglyph, a gesture toward something felt, even though Staiger appeals to Gustav Becking's completely fanciful idea of "Schlagfiguren." He wisely decided at last that he will not demonstrate Goethe's "Schlagfigur" (he could not anyhow) and is content to speak vaguely of the structure of his imagination or the rhythm of his life.[32]

The peculiarity of Staiger's genre theory is the adaptation of the Heideggerian time scheme, with the paradoxical result of assigning the lyric (or rather in Staiger "the lyrical") to the past, the epic to the present, the drama to the future. In contrast to other theories, Staiger's does not appeal to the speaker as a criterion. With his Heideggerian assumptions, the subjective-objective dichotomy is abolished: the lyrical poem is described in terms of such a mystical fusion.[33] The account of Goethe's Strassburg lyrics, in the Goethe book, plays another variation on the theme of the subject-object identity often phrased pantheistically or sentimentally. Goethe's feeling that "his heart is the heart of creation and the heart of creation his heart" is proclaimed the main accomplishment of the whole German literary revival![34]

In the history of genre theories the triadic division is a leading theme. In a well documented thesis, *Die Lehre von der Einteilung der Dichtkunst* (1940), Miss Irene Behrens tried to show that the triad is only the result of eighteenth-century theorizing. She considers Charles Batteux's *Les Beaux Arts réduits à un même principe* (1746) the crucial document and traces its codification and general acceptance to the later German critics. Her own book contains many examples of the triads used in earlier centuries often quite casually. Many Italian examples could also be given from other sources.[35] Two of the greatest English poets, Milton and Dryden, use the distinction casually. Milton speaks of the "laws of a true Epic poem, of a Dramatic and a Lyric,"[36] and Dryden, in the Preface to the *Essay of Dramatic Poetry*, speaks of "the English poets who have written either in this, the epic, or the lyric way."[37] The lyric is here used not, as often in earlier times, as some minor genre but as the alternative to epic and drama exhausting all possibilities. One can find other examples: for instance, in Muratori, who includes even satire under lyric.[38]

But the mere number three means little. All depends on the principle of division. The rediscovery of dialectics with Kant and Fichte is obviously the crucial event. Genre theory was resolutely connected with a theory of knowledge in Schiller's *Über naive and senti-*

mentalische Dichtung (1795), which arrives at a scheme of the relationship between man and nature which is at the same time a historical scheme and a genre theory. But Schiller discarded the traditional kinds and devised, within "sentimental" poetry, a triad of genres: satire, elegy, and idyll, which he himself emphasizes have nothing to do with the original names: they are determined by "Empfindungsweisen."[39]

The innovator was Friedrich Schlegel, whose originality and speculative boldness is becoming more widely appreciated since the publication of his early notebooks and manuscripts. In a note dated 1797 Schlegel makes the coordination with subjective-objective still very much within the scheme of the voice categories. "Lyrical [form] is merely subjective; dramatic merely objective. As form the epic has apparently precedence. It is subjective-objective." Two years later he changed the coordination: "epic is objective poetry; lyric, subjective; drama, objective-subjective." But he reverts again to the older coordination in 1800: "the epic is subjective- objective, the drama objective, the lyric subjective." Later notes, "Zur Poesie und Literatur" (1808), reassert that "the epic is the root of the whole and the exact middle between the wholly interior lyrical and the wholly external dramatic poetry."[40] But curiously enough, in Friedrich Schlegel's published writings such a genre theory plays no role. In his histories of Greek literature a sequence, epic (Homer), lyric (Sappho, etc.), drama (Aeschylus, etc.) is traced, and in the Preface to *Über das Studium der griechischen Poesie* (1797) a historical typology is worked out in which "objective" is associated with Greek poetry, while modern poetry is "interesting" or "characteristic." Goethe is considered the hope for a revival of objective poetry in the very same manner Schiller considered Goethe the naïve poet surviving in the modern sentimental age.[41] In the sketch of the phases of Goethe's evolution in *Gespräch über die Poesie* (1800) Goethe's early manner is considered mixed subjective-objective, while the second epoch is "objective to the highest degree."[42] "Objectivity" is here not a genre distinction, as Goethe wrote in all genres, but an attitude, implying aesthetic distance, detachment, classicism.

August Wilhelm Schlegel probably picked up the idea of relating the genres to the dialectics from his younger brother. In notes preserved for the continuation of the Berlin lectures (1803), he remarks: "Episch, lyrisch, dramatisch als These, Antithese, Synthese. Das Epische das rein objektive im menschlichen Geiste. Das lyrische das rein subjektive. Das Drama die Durchdringung der beiden."[43] At about the same time Schelling, in his lectures on *Philosophie der Kunst* (1803), for which he had access to Schlegel's manuscript lectures, uses the dialectics again: the lyric is characterized by the predominance of the subject of the poet; it is the most individualized, particular genre. In the epic the poet rises to objectivity, the drama represents the union of the lyric and the epic, of the subjective and objective, as in tragedy necessity is objective (i.e. in the order of the universe) and freedom subjective (i.e. in the moral revolt of the hero). In comedy the relation is reversed.[44] Schelling, if I understand him correctly, means that comic characters are somehow fixed and fated, while the world and its order is treated with freedom and irony. A puzzling question of the history of genre theories is raised, however, by the circumstance that neither August Wilhelm Schlegel's nor Schelling's lectures were published in their time.[45] One would have to examine the numerous German books on poetics during the first decades of the century to make sure who formulated the dialectical scheme for the first time in print.

One new motif emerges: the coordination of the main kinds with the dimensions of time. I find it in Wilhelm von Humboldt's *Über Goethes Hermann und Dorothea* (1799), which does not propound a triadic scheme but rather develops Schiller's theories. Humboldt divides all poetry into "plastic" and "lyrical," and plastic poetry, in its turn, into epical and dramatic. Humboldt then makes the suggestion that the simplest distinction between epic and tragedy is "indisputably" (*unstreitig*) that between past and present time.[46]

Here apparently a coordination between the genres and time is asserted for the first time, but the specific coordination was and is far from "indisputable." Humboldt makes no effort to relate the future to a genre, and the lyric would, presumably, belong to the present. In Schelling's *Philosophie der Kunst* the epic is referred to the past, the lyrical poem to the present, but later Schelling speaks of the epic as indifferent to time, as "beyond time" or timeless.[47] The coordination with all three times is carried out expressly in Jean Paul's *Vorschule der Ästhetik*, in the second edition of 1813. The epic represents the event which develops from the past, the drama the action which extends toward the future, the lyric the emotion confined to the present.[48]

All these motifs meet in Hegel's *Vorlesungen über Ästhetik*, which were given in the twenties but published in 1835. There the genres are worked into a dialectical scheme which is also historical. The objective epic, the thesis, is contradicted by the subjective lyric and synthesized by the drama. Hegel also speaks of the relation to time: "the lyrical effusion has a much nearer relation to time than epical narration, which places real phenomena into the past, and puts them or combines them next to each other in a more spatial unfolding, while the lyric represents the momentary emergence of feelings and images in the temporal succession of their genesis and formation and thus has to shape artistically the diverse temporal motion itself."[49] The Hegelian scheme is developed and, in the theory of the lyric, refined in Friedrich Theodor Vischer's *Ästhetik*. The fifth volume on poetry (1857) repeats the subjective-objective scheme and relates the genres to time: "the epic considers the object from the point of view of the past, in lyrical poetry everything becomes present in feeling, in drama the present tends toward the future as the action develops." In developing a theory of the lyric which distinguishes many subgenres, Vischer makes much of the immediacy, the momentariness of the lyric in relation to time. He speaks of its character of "Punctualität: sie ist ein punktuelles Zünden der Welt im Subjecte." Though the detailed discussion brings in much historical knowledge and thus modifies the initial statements, Vischer radically limits the lyric to the overflow of feeling, even passive feeling, suffering. "Erleben, erfahren, heisst durch Leiden gehn."[50]

These theories had some echo also among English and American critics. They could not leave the coordination between the genres and the tenses alone. In Eneas Sweetland Dallas' *Poetics* (1852), for instance, the play is coordinated with the present, the tale with the past, and the song, mysteriously, with the future.[51] John Erskine, in *The Kinds of Poetry* (1920), finds the lyric expresses present time, the drama past, and the epic future. This odd reversal is defended by interpreting tragedy in Ibsen's words as a judgment day on the hero's past, while the epic predicts and projects the destiny of a nation or of the race.[52]

One need not argue any specific influence to see how Staiger's and Miss Hamburger's schemes grow out of a long tradition with roots in the great period of German aesthetic speculation. Their theories of the lyric all have one common feature: the lyric is subjective; it is the expression of feeling, of experience, *Erlebnis*. This in itself is not new at all. It is an error to consider the idea of personal poetry, of poetry as autobiography, an innovation of romanticism or more particularly of the German *Sturm und Drang*. No doubt, the reaction against formal neoclassicism was then particularly vocal. It is easy to collect passages from Bürger, Stolberg, and others to prove that they thought of poetry as emotional overflow. It is sufficient to quote Franz in *Götz von Berlichingen* (1771): "'So fühl' ich denn in dem Augenblick, was den Dichter macht, ein volles, ganz von Einer Empfindung volles Herz!"[53] But such pronouncements could be paralleled all over Europe at that time. They are common in the earlier English accounts of original poetry: in 1763 John Brown calls it "a kind of rapturous exclamations, of joy, grief, triumph, or exultation."[54] Robert Burns speaks of his poetry as "the spontaneous language of my heart."[55] Much of this is simply good classical doctrine. It can appeal to Horace: "Si vis me flere, dolendum est / Primum ipsi tibi" (*De art. poet.*, vv. 102 ff), which, in the context, applies to the actor but was constantly quoted as a precept for all rhetoric. It is the demand for sincerity which has been discussed throughout history, not only in the context of lyrical poetry. The troubadour Bernart de Ventadour knows that "the song must come from the heart,"[56] and Sir Philip Sidney says: "Look into thy heart and write."[57] Much poetry even in older times was definitely and concretely autobiographical. It is hard to imagine that a poem like Sir Thomas Wyatt's "They Flee from Me That Sometimes Did Me Seek" (before 1542) does not refer to an intimate personal experience. Such a surmise cannot be refuted in spite of all arguments about the conventionality of many devices, the universalizing of feelings in much older poetry, and the general weight of traditional "topoi" and motifs. But what matters in criticism is the claim that sincerity, emotion, *Erlebnis* is a guarantee of good art. As I have said before, "the volumes of agonizingly felt love poetry by adolescents and the dreary (however fervently felt) religious verse which fills libraries, are sufficient proof" that it is not.[58] Yeats has said this memorably, referring to men in general:

> The best lack all conviction, while the worst
> Are full of passionate intensity.[59]

But lived experience, intense, private experience, became precisely the central value criterion in German lyrical (and not only lyrical) theories. *Erlebnis* became the term around which they crystallize. It makes one reflect that the term cannot be readily matched in other languages and that it is a neologism of the early nineteenth century. Hans Georg Gadamer, in *Wahrheit und Methode* (1960), is, so far as I know, the only writer who has tried to trace the history of the term. He has had information from the German Academy in Berlin which supplied him with the earliest example from a casual letter of Hegel's in 1827 and with isolated occurrences of the word in the thirties and forties, in Tieck, Alexis, and Gutzkow.[60] My own very limited research confirms these findings. The word does not occur in Herder and Goethe, Novalis and Schleiermacher, who would seem to be the natural antecedents for Dilthey. Gervinus, in his discussion of what today would be called "Erlebnislyrik," never uses the term.[61] Nor do Jean Paul and Schopenhauer. The novelty of the word is indicated also by the fact that Hegel makes *Erlebnis* feminine, saying: "Das ist meine ganze Erlebnis,"[62] the kind of vacillation which later afflicted another literary term in German: Baroque.[63]

Gadamer notes that Goethe comes near the term in his very late advice to young poets: "Fragt euch nur bei jedem Gedicht, ob es ein Erlebtes enthalte, und ob dieses Erlebte euch gefördert habe."[64] Thus it seems appropriate that *Erlebnis* occurs in one of Heinrich Laube's *Reisenovellen* (2nd ed. 1847), where it is put in the mouth of Goethe discussing *Die Wahlverwandtschaften*: "Das Benutzen des Erlebnisses ist mir alles gewesen; das Erfinden aus der Luft war nie meine Sache."[65] Laube, however, has no independent source for this pronouncement. He rephrases what Goethe had said to Eckermann about the novel: "Darin ist kein Strich enthalten, der nicht erlebt, aber kein Strich wie er erlebt worden,"[66] and he might have remembered similar pronouncements and known even the advice to the young poets.

Erlebnis occurs in early statements by Theodor Storm which bring the meaning nearer to recent usage, though these passages could hardly have been noticed widely. In 1854, in a review of one M. A. Niendorf's *Lieder der Liebe*, Storm asserts that "bei einem lyrischen Gedicht muss nicht allein . . . das Leben, nein da muss geradezu das Erlebnis das Fundament desselben bilden"; and he complains in a review of Julius von Rodenberg's *Lieder*: "Es fehlt überall der Hintergrund des inneren Erlebnisses." In a later preface to his anthology

Deutsche Liebeslieder (1859) he criticizes J. G. Jacobi for not having written "aus dem Drange ein inneres Erlebnis zu fixieren."[67] Hermann Lotze, in his *Geschichte der Ästhetik in Deutschland* (1868), uses the term in the standard context: "so grossen Werth Göthe und Schiller darauf legen, dass das lyrische Gedicht einem innern Erlebnisse entspringe, die blosse Darestellung der subjectiven Erschütterung galt ihnen doch nicht für genügend."[68]

This passage is about contemporaneous with Dilthey's earliest specific uses. In his *Leben Schleiermachers* (1870), on the very first page of the Introduction *Erlebnis* is used three times most emphatically. Dilthey defines Schleiermacher's importance in the development of European religiosity. "In ihm vollzog sich das grosse Erlebnis einer aus den Tiefen unseres Verhältnisses zum Universum entspringenden Religion," and on the same page he speaks of "dieses Erlebnis seiner Jugend" and again of "dieses Erlebnis." But in the whole long book we hear only once about his "religiös-sittliche Erlebnisse."[69] Surprisingly, in the articles which Dilthey wrote in the sixties and which he eventually used, in a revised and expanded form, in *Das Erlebnis und die Dichtung* (1905), the word does not occur at all. It is never used in the Novalis essay (1865) and not until the 1905 revision was it introduced into the essays on Lessing (1867) and Hölderlin (1867).[70] Only in the article "Goethe und die dichterische Phantasie" (1877) does the term become central to Dilthey's poetics. There *Erlebnis* reveals a quality of life: it may come from the world of ideas or may be suggested by trivial circumstances, a chance meeting, the reading of a book, etc. One cannot thus accuse Dilthey of simple "biographism," of a reduction of experience to private events or feelings, but the concept, with him, remains psychological. It means an experience, of whatever origin, intense enough to become the stimulus to creation. In one passage, however, the dualism of life and poetry is denied. Dilthey speaks of a "Strukturzusammenhang zwischen dem Erleben und dem Ausdruck des Erlebten; das Erlebte geht hier voll und ganz in den Ausdruck ein."[71] An identification is made which seems the same as Croce's between intuition and expression: an equation which was anticipated also by Dilthey's own revered Schleiermacher. But in general, *Erlebnis* in Dilthey remained another term for intense personal experience, for involvement, or for what in different contexts has been called sincerity, "engagement," and even "belief."[72] Later in his life, in notes which Dilthey wrote for a revision of his *Poetik* (1907–08), he recognized the failure of his psychologistic conception: he speaks of the detachment of the imaginative process from the personal and admits that the "subject with which literary history and poetics have to deal primarily is totally distinct from psychic events in the poet or his hearers."[73] But these notes were not published then and the damage was done: *Erlebnis* became the shibboleth of German poetic theory.

Most often it was used simply as a new term for the old biographical fallacy which found here a less literal-minded formula for the study of the life, its incidents, the models in life, the emotional states preceding a work of art, without having to commit the student to a one-to-one relationship. In Gundolf's distinction between "Urerlebnis" and "Bildungserlebnis" (suggested first by Herman Nohl[74] in 1908) a terminology is established which allows the grading of experiences according to their presumed immediacy, and in Ermatinger's *Das dichterische Kunstwerk* (1921) *Erlebnis* becomes the overriding term, which is then subdivided into "Gedankenerlebnis," "Stofferlebnis," and "Formerlebnis." Everything in poetry is *Erlebnis*: with Ermatinger the term loses its original relation to something given in life. It is simply a term for the artist's activity. It is so broad as to be meaningless.[75]

Certainly the relationship to the lyric or even to biography has been completely lost sight of. Lyrical theory—at least with the terms which we have discussed, *Erlebnis*, subjective, presence, *Stimmung*—seems to have arrived at a complete impasse. These terms cannot take care of the enormous variety, in history and in the different literatures, of lyrical forms and constantly lead into an insoluble psychological cul-de-sac: the supposed intensity, inwardness, immediacy of an experience which can never be demonstrated as certain and can never be shown to be relevant to the quality of art. Miss Hamburger, Staiger, Ermatinger, Dilthey and their predecessors, in their different ways, lead all to this central mystery, which remains a mystery to them and possibly to all of us.

The way out is obvious. One must abandon attempts to define the general nature of the lyric or the lyrical. Nothing beyond generalities of the tritest kind can result from it. It seems much more profitable to turn to a study of the variety of poetry and to the history and thus the description of genres which can be grasped in their concrete conventions and traditions. Several German books have shown the way, though some have suffered from confusion with general "Geistesgeschichte." I think of Karl Viëtor's *Geschichte der deutschen Ode* (1923), Gunther Müller's *Geschichte des deutschen Liedes* (1925), Friedrich Beissner's *Geschichte der deutschen Elegie* (1941), or of Kurt Schlüter's *Die englische Ode* (1964) all of which show an awareness of the paradoxical task: How can we arrive at a genre description from history without knowing beforehand what the genre is like, and how can we know a genre without its history, without a knowledge of its particular instances?[76] This is obviously a case of the logical circle which Schleiermacher, Dilthey, and Leo Spitzer have taught us not to consider "vicious." It can be solved in the concrete dialectics of past and present, fact and idea, history and aesthetics. Psychological and existential categories such as *Erlebnis*, subjectivity, and *Stimmung* accomplish nothing for poetics.

NOTES

1. New York, 1949, pp. 235, 238.

2. *Die Logik der Dichtung* (Stuttgart, 1957), pp. 9, 35. See also her defense: "Noch einmal: Vom Erzählen," *Euphorion*, 59 (1965), 46–71.

3. *Logik*, pp. 183 (referring to *Theory of Literature*, p. 15), 186 (for quotation).

4. Ibid., pp. 202 ff.

5. Ibid., p. 5.

6. Ibid., p. 183.

7. *Goethe*, *1*(3 vols. Zürich, 1952), 56.

8. *Logik*, pp. 176 ff., 180.

9. Ibid., p. 187.

10. Ibid., pp. 190, 186.

11. Ibid., pp. 204 ff.

12. Ibid., p. 220.

13. Ibid., p. 214.

14. Ibid., p. 217.

15. Ibid., p. 220.

16. Ibid., p. 231.

17. Ibid., p. 233.

18. Ibid., p. 235: "Es ist die Form der Ichaussage, die auch der extremsten Unwirklichkeitsaussage noch den Charakter der Wirklichkeitsaussage belässt."

19. III 392 D–394 C.

20. Cf. Goethe, *Sämtliche Werke, Jubiläumsausgabe*, *36* (40 vols. Stuttgart, 1962–07), 149–52.

21. Ibid., 5, 223.

22. *Sämtliche Werke*, ed. E. Berend, I, *11* (Weimar, 1935), 254: "Gibt es dann aber eine flüssigere Abtheilung und Abscheidung mitten im poetischen Meere? Denn weder die Einmengung, noch die Versteckung des Dichters entscheidet zwischen zwei Formen des Gedichts . . . Wie leicht wären, falls nur die Kleinigkeiten des Sprechens und des Sprechenlassens abtheilten, Formen in Formen einzuschmelzen, und derselbe Dithyrambus würde, z. B. bald episch, wenn der Dichter vorher sagte und sänge, er wolle einen fremden singen, bald lyrisch durch die Worte, er wolle seinen eignen singen, bald dramatisch, wenn er ihn ohne ein Wort von sich in ein tragisches Selbstgespräch einschöbe. Aber blosse Förmlichkeiten sind—in der Poesie wenigstens—keine Formen."

23. *Grundbegriffe* (Zürich, 1946), p. 67.

24. Ibid., pp. 83, 82.

25. Ibid., p. 67.

26. Ibid., p. 88.

27. Ibid., pp. 223, 227 ff, 231.

28. Ibid., p. 9.

29. Ibid., p. 79.

30. Ibid., pp. 246, 245.

31. *Grundbegriffe* (5th ed. Zürich, 1961), pp. 248, 246.

32. *Goethe*, *3* (3 vols. Zürich, 1959), 474, 478 ff.

33. *Grundbegriffe* (1946), p. 64.

34. *Goethe*, *1*, 59.

35. See, e.g., Antonio Possevino (1593), cited in Bernard Weinberg, *A History of Literary Criticism*

in the Italian Renaissance (Chicago, 1961), p. 336, or Gregorio Led (1667), cited in Ciro Trabalza, *La Critica letteraria* (Milano, 1915), p. 239.

36. *Treatise of Education* (1644).

37. *Essay of Dramatic Poetry* (1668), Preface to the Reader.

38. *Della Perfetta Poesia italiana, 3* (4 vols. Modena, 1706), 3 ff.

39. See note at beginning of section: "Idylle."

40. *Literary Notebooks 1797–1801*, ed. H. Eichner (Toronto, 1957), pp. 48, 175, 204, 238.

41. *Kritische Schriften*, ed. W. Rasch (München, 1956), pp. 105–12.

42. Ibid., p. 334.

43. *Die Kunstlehre*, ed. E. Lohner (Stuttgart, 1963), p. 306.

44. *Werke*, ed. O. Weiss, *3* (3 vols. Leipzig, 1907), 287, 296, 335, 341; cf. also p. 19.

45. Schlegel's lectures in 1884 by J. Minor, Schelling's in 1859 in *Sämtliche Werke*.

46. *Werke*, ed. A. Flitner and K. Giel, *2* (4 vols. Stuttgart, 1961), 272; corresponds to 2, 246, of the Prussian Academy edition.

47. *Werke, 3*, 291, 298.

48. *Werke, 11*, 254.

49. *Sämtliche Werke*, ed. H. Glockner, *14* (Stuttgart, 1928), 451.

50. *Ästhetik, 5* (5 vols. Stuttgart, 1857), 1260, 1331.

51. London, 1852, pp. 81, 91, 105.

52. New York, 1920, p. 12. The essay was originally published in 1912.

53. Goethe, *Werke, 10*, 39; cf. p. 161. Cf., e.g. *Sturm und Drang. Kritische Schriften*, ed. E. Löwenthal (Heidelberg, 1949), pp. 805–11, 798.

54. *Dissertation on the Rise, Union and Power, the Progressions, Separations and Corruptions of Poetry and Music* (London, 1763).

55. *Scrapbook*, No. 434.

56. *Anthology of Provençal Troubadours*, ed. Hill-Bergin (New Haven 1941), No. 26.

57. *Astrophel and Stella* (published 1591), the first sonnet.

58. *Theory of Literature* (2nd ed. New York, 1956), p. 56.

59. "The Second Coming." Yeats, *The Variorum Edition of the Poems*, ed. P. Allt and R. K. Alspach (New York, 1957), p. 402.

60. Tübingen, 1960, pp. 56–60.

61. *Geschichte der poetischen Nationalliteratur der Deutschen, 4* (5 vols. Leipzig 1835–42; 2nd ed. 1843), 126, 130, 133, 504.

62. *Briefe von und an Hegel*, ed. J. Hoffmeister 3, (3 vols. Hamburg, 1954), 179. To his wife from Kassel, Aug. 19, 1827.

63. Johann Willibald Nagel and Jakob Zeidler, in *Deutsch-österreichische Literaturgeschichte* (Wien, 1899), use "die Barocke." "Der Barock" seems to have won out over "das Barock."

64. *Werke, 38*, 326. First published in 1833.

65. 2nd ed. Mannheim, 1847, p. 36.

66. *Gespräche mit Goethe*, ed. H. H. Houben (23rd ed. Leipzig, 1948), p. 315, Feb. 17, 1830. Cf. pp. 498, 583.

67. *Werke*, ed. F. Böhme, *8* (9 vols. Leipzig, 1936), 63, 69, 112.

68. München, 1868, p. 643.

69. H. Mulert, ed. (2nd ed. Berlin, 1922), p. XXIII; cf. p. 333.

70. Novalis, in *Preussische Jahrbücher, 15* (1865), 650–81. Lessing, ibid. *19* (1867), 117–61, 271–94. Hölderlin, in *Westermanns Monatshefte, 20* (1867), 156–65.

71. *Das Erlebnis und die Dichtung* (9th ed. Leipzig 1924), p. 236.

72. Cf. e.g., Hofmannsthal's use in "Der Dichter und diese Zeit" (1906) in *Gesammelte Werke in Einzelausgaben*, ed. H. Steiner, *Prosa* II (Frankfurt/M., 1951), pp. 294, 296.

73. *Gesammelte Schriften, 7* (12 vols. Stuttgart, 1913–58), 85. Cf. my discussion in *A History of Modern Criticism, 4* (4 vols. New Haven, 1965), 323.

74. Die Weltanschauungen der Malerei (Jena, 1908).

75. Cf. Charlotte Bühler, "Der Erlebnisbegriff in der modernen Kunstwissenschaft," in *Vom Geiste neuerer Literaturforschung, Festschrift für Oskar Walzel*, ed. J. Wahle and V. Klemperer (Wildpark-Potsdam, 1924), pp. 195–209, for more examples.

76. A good discussion in Karl Viëtor's "Probleme der literarischen Gattungsgeschichte," in *Deutsche Vierteljahrschrift für Literaturwissenschaft und Geistesgeschichte, 9* (1931) 425–47; reprinted in his *Geist und Form* (Bern, 1952), pp. 292–309.

History and Genre (1986)

1.4

RALPH COHEN

1.

I call this paper "History and Genre" though history is a genre and genre has a history. It is this interweaving between history and genre that I seek to describe. In *The Political Unconscious* Fredric Jameson wrote that genre criticism has been "thoroughly discredited by modern literary theory and practice."[1] There are at least three reasons for this. First, the very notion that texts compose classes has been questioned. Secondly, the assumption that members of a genre share a common trait or traits has been questioned, and thirdly, the function of a genre as an interpretative guide has been questioned.

But what is this genre that has been discredited? The term "genre" is relatively recent in critical discourse. Previous to the nineteenth century the terms used for it were "kinds" or "species." Genre has its source in the Latin *genus* which refers in some cases to "kind" or "sort" or "class" or "species." But in others, "species" is considered a subclass of "genus." Its root terms are *genre, gignere*—to beget and (in the passive) to be born. In this latter sense it refers both to a class and an individual. And it is, of course, derived from the same root terms as *gender.* The connection of "genre" to "gender" suggests that an early use of the term was based on division or classification. Two genders are necessary in order to define one and sexual genders implied not merely classification but a hierarchy or dominance of one gender over the other. Genres included, in the Attic age, poems written in a distinctive meter like elegiac or satiric poetry. With regard to the number of genres, critics have suggested that every work is its own genre, that there are two genres—literature and nonliterature; that there are three genres—lyric, epic, and drama; that there are four genres—lyric, epic, drama, and prose fiction—and, finally, that genres are any group of texts selected by readers to establish continuities that distinguish this group from others. As one critic puts it, genre is "any group of works selected on the basis of some shared features."[2] Genre has been defined in terms of meter, inner form, intrinsic form, radical of presentation, single traits, family traits, institutions, conventions, contracts, and these have been considered either as universals or as empirical historical groupings.

In recognition of this multiplicity of definitions, I wish to argue that genre concepts in theory and practice arise, change, and decline for historical reasons. And since each genre is composed of texts that accrue, the grouping is a process, not a determinate category. Genres are open categories. Each member alters the genre by adding, contradicting, or changing constituents, especially those of members most closely related to it. The process by which genres are established always involves the human need for distinction and interrelation. Since the purposes of critics who establish genres vary, it is self-evident that the same texts can belong to different groupings or genres and serve different generic purposes.

Have all the theories of genre from Menander to Morson been discredited? Contemporary critics continue to invest in genre, and I shall urge that there are critical tasks that can best be undertaken by genre. But it is necessary to understand what aspects, what assumptions of genre theory are being attacked. The first is that the classes or groupings that are called genres are no longer acceptable because we cannot be sure how to understand the texts as a class.

Michel Foucault states the general objection that dividing genre into groups like literature or philosophy is not useful since users of such distinctions no longer agree on how to take them. "We are not even sure of ourselves when we use these distinctions in our own world of discourse, let alone when we are analysing groups of statements which, when first formulated, were distributed, divided, and characterized in a quite different way."[3]

Jacques Derrida argues, characteristically, for the need and futility of genre designation. He points out that any generic classification system is untenable because individual texts although participating in it cannot belong to it. Individual texts resist classification because they are interpretatively indeterminate. He asks: "Can one identify a work of art, of whatever sort, but especially a work of discursive art, if it does not bear the mark of a genre, if it does not signal or mention it or make it remarkable in any way?"[4]

In putting the question in this manner Derrida wishes to confront all possible definitions of genre. For example, "literature" can be considered a genre which includes novel, elegy, tragedy, and so forth. It is a genre that includes other genres that define it; again, a genre can intermix genres—as a novel can contain poems, proverbs, sermons, letters, and so forth. The mark of belonging to a class need not be conscious (to author or reader) though it obviously is conscious to the critic who notes it. Indeed, a work can refer to itself even in its title, as *The History of Tom Jones a Foundling* does, although subsequent critics and readers distinguish "history" from "novel." Or a text can refer to itself as a travel description when it is, like *Travels into Several Remote Nations of the World* by Lemuel Gulliver, an imagined prose fiction. For Derrida, no generic trait completely or absolutely confines a text to a genre or class because such belonging falsifies the constituents of a text. He writes: "If . . . such a [generic] trait is remarkable, that is, noticeable, in every aesthetic, poetic, or literary corpus, then consider this paradox, consider the irony . . . this supplementary and distinctive trait, a mark of belonging or inclusion, does not properly pertain to any genre or class. The re-mark of belonging does not belong. It belongs without belonging . . ." (pp. 64–65).

Belonging without belonging. With it but not of it. Why should an author, reader, or critic wish to classify a work or to identify it as belonging with other works of a similar kind? What acts and assumptions are concealed in the infinitive *to identify*? After all, classifications are undertaken for specific purposes. Derrida assumes that such classes are determinate and thus fix a text within them—even though a text may be "fixed" in several different genres. But if one considers genres as processes, this criticism does not hold. Considerations of purposes are historical; different authors, readers, critics have different reasons for identifying texts as they do. The reasons for identifying texts differently do not interest Derrida; the identifications themselves do. He wishes to demonstrate that generic traits cannot *belong* to genres: "this supplementary and distinctive trait, a mark of belonging or inclusion, does not properly pertain to any genre or class." And not because a text is "an abundant overflowing or a free, anarchic, and unclassifiable productivity, but because of the *trait* of participation itself, because of the effect of the code and of the generic mark" (p. 65). No text which is denominated "novel," for example, has traits that will identify all texts within the class.

Derrida both affirms and denies genre, and the basis for this inclusion and exclusion is the manner in which the individual text *participates* in the class and denies the class. Derrida does not pursue the historical inquiry of the types of "participation" involved in specific works; he assumes that all such participations are to be distinguished from "belonging." Indeed, for him, the individual text has so many contrary markings that participations undo belonging.

Derrida wishes to lead us away from the analysis of a class to an analysis of a text; textual interpretation will then support the paradox of belonging and not belonging. How persuasive is his undoing of a class? He does not deny the necessity for grouping texts, for showing that a text participates in a group. But he points out that "at the very moment that a genre or a literature is broached, at that very moment, degenerescence has begun, the end begins" (p. 66). No sooner is a genre stipulated, than it proceeds to be ungenerated. But it must be noted that this is a historical procedure—both the broaching of a genre and the beginning of its end. For in order for the end to have a beginning we must be in time; temporal history, however, insofar as it pertains to the process of undoing, is not what Derrida examines. By failing to do so, he takes a road that leads not to a history of generic purposes in a study of individual texts, but to a study of individual texts as distinct from genre. He creates a Herculean dilemma where none exists. Thus, to understand the aims and purposes of genre, to understand beginnings and endings it is necessary to take the road Derrida has not taken.

2.

Francis Cairns points out that genres are as old as organized societies and that early genres were classifications in terms of content. The functions of these were to aid the listener in making logical connections and distinctions; generic distinctions aided him in following oral communications from the poet. Genre markers served to distinguish one type of communication from another since such communications shared many secondary elements. Oral communication demanded primary markers. Members of the same oral genre shared at least one primary trait for purposes of recognition by hearers.[5] From these early beginnings of communication between poet and audience, we can note that genres possessed social purposes in a community, and that genres arose to contrast, complement, define each other's aims.

When an oral society is replaced by a literate one, the reasons for generic classification undergo change. The functions of markers or traits become the bases for value distinctions as well as for artistic distinctions and interrelations. When Aristotle deals with tragedy, for example, he lists plot as the primary marker within tragedy; he suggests the proper model for tragedy and he compares tragedy with epic in terms of generic value. He continues to note the interrelation of genres by showing the similarities and differences in qualitative elements and quantitative parts of tragedy and epic. "Again, tragedy has everything that epic has (it can even use its metre), and moreover has a considerable addition in the music and the spectacle, which produce pleasure in a most vividly perceptible way. . . . So much for tragedy and epic, their nature, the number and differences of their qualitative parts, the reasons for success and failure in them, and criticisms of them and how to answer them."[6]

Even for Aristotle generic markers are not absolutes; they indicate stages through which a genre passes. Moreover, the traits that are shared do not necessarily share the same function. Trait sharing may be, but need not be, the way to characterize a genre. A genre does not exist independently; it arises to compete or to contrast with other genres, to complement, augment, interrelate with other genres. Genres do not exist by themselves; they are named and placed within hierarchies or systems of genres, and each is defined by reference to the system and its members. A genre, therefore, is to be understood in relation to other genres, so that its aims and purposes at a particular time are defined by its interrelation with and differentiation from others. Thus critics can classify a Shakespearean "tragedy" not merely as a tragedy, but as a poem, a performance, a narrative, and so forth, depending on the points a critic wishes to make. What is at stake is not some single trait that would place it in each of these classes, but the purpose for so classifying it within a generic system. Only if one dehistoricizes genre does the notion of classification with one or more traits shared by each member become a problem; such a claim would make it impossible for a class to undergo change since its traits would be essential rather than existential.

Contemporary critics do not find classification to be the purpose of genres, nor do they find that classifications serve evaluative purposes. When Northrop Frye sets up four genres based on the radical of presentation, he returns to the view that genres are rhetorical "in the sense that the genre is determined by the conditions established between the poet and his public."[7]

The trait called "radical of presentation" is the marker of a genre: "Words may be acted in front of a spectator; they may be spoken in front of a listener; they may be sung or chanted; or they may be written for a reader" (p. 247). It is apparent that, given this single trait, Frye has to provide numerous qualifications and interrelations in the texts he consults. If Frye were a historical critic concerned with actual texts, he would proceed to illustrate the kind of interrelations that empirical critics develop, interrelations that show the choral chanting, riddling, and other oral devices in works acted in front of a spectator. He would undertake to explain how his genres interrelate historically with earlier genres as well as with each other. His efforts, however, are directed at traditions and affinities rather than the actualities of changing traditions and changing affinities. He knows that genre is determined by conditions that vary between poet and public, and that the terms "conditions" and "public" are both problematic. Generic distinctions, he points out, "are among the ways in which literary works are ideally presented, whatever the actualities are" (p. 247). "Milton, for example, seems to have no ideal of reciter and audience in mind for *Paradise Lost*; he seems content to leave it, in practice, a poem to be read in a book" (p. 247). "The purpose of criticism by genres [writes Frye] is not so much to classify as to clarify . . . traditions and affinities, thereby bringing out a large number of literary relationships that would not be noticed as long as there were no context established for them" (pp. 247–48).

Frye's approach accepts the ideal of markers even though he has reservations about their use in practice. But he desists, in the *Anatomy*, from attributing the weakness of markers to different historical situations. The attempt to "recuperate" Frye's approach by historicizing it was undertaken by Fredric Jameson. He set out to convert aspects of Frye's approach to a Marxist theory of genres which coordinates "immanent formal analysis of the individual text with the twin diachronic perspective of the history of forms and the evolution of social life" (p. 105). Jameson sees genre as a literary institution, as a social contract between a writer and a particular public "whose function is to specify the proper use of a particular cultural artifact" (p. 106). Like Frye, he argues that genres exist in performance situations, but he notes that genres do undergo changes: "as texts free themselves more and more from an immediate performance situation, it becomes ever more difficult to enforce a given generic rule on their readers" (p. 106). The generic contract can indeed be broken. "The generic contract and institution itself, . . . along with so many other institutions and traditional practices, falls casualty to the gradual penetration of a market system and a money economy. . . . The older generic categories do not, for all that, die out, but persist in the half-life of the subliterary genres of mass culture, transformed into the drugstore and airport paperback lines of gothics, mysteries, romances, bestsellers, and popular biographies, where they await the resurrection of their immemorial, archetypal resonance at the hands of a Frye or a Bloch" (p. 107).

The contract theory of genre avoids the concept of specific markers; it rests on an agreement between a writer and a particular public that specifies the proper use of a cultural artifact. But is there only one public that specifies "proper" use? And how can such a contract negotiate for the present, let alone for the future? Each new text that critics join to the genre results in interrelations with other genres. How does a contract come to be established and how is it abrogated? How many contracts exist for the same text at any given time? Jameson claims that each genre is "immanently and intrinsically an ideology in its own right," but insofar as a genre retains past elements in a text, and insofar as different texts become members of a genre, how is this ideology determined?

Jameson's contract theory of genre presupposes a devolution of genres that follow the economic pattern, "the gradual penetration of a market system and a money economy." But the homology between genre and Marxist economic history disregards the contrasting aims of contemporary readers, as witness the diverse views about genre. Moreover, the reconceptualization of one genre often coincides with the initiation or restancing of others because of the process of interrelation. Thus a genre like tragedy continues despite the fact that it is reconceptualized by "domestic" tragedy; it is not abandoned despite serious changes in the economy. It seems a logical misstep to compare a kind of writing with an economic system rather than with the writings about an economic system. When such writings intersect with those of different genres they do not trivialize or dispose of such genres; they establish combinations that can make their contributions subservient rather than dominant in the genres that include them. As for genres possessing immanent ideologies, it would appear that such an assumption disregards the differences among the members of a genre. This is not to deny that texts—as generic members—can be interpreted as possessing ideologies, but rather that these cannot be deduced from generalizations about the genre.

For example, the characters, narrative, language—indeed all aesthetic strategies of *Lord Jim*—form, for Jameson, one specific instance of the symbolic act of the end of capitalist expansion. In the history of forms, *Lord Jim* "may be described as a structural breakdown of the older realisms, from which emerges not modernism alone, but rather two literary and cultural structures, dialectically interrelated and necessarily presupposing each other for any adequate analysis: these now find themselves positioned in the distinct and generally incompatible spaces of the institutions of high literature and what the Frankfurt School conveniently termed the 'culture industry,' that is, the apparatuses for the production of 'popular' or mass culture" (p. 207). Jameson argues that *Lord Jim* represents in its structure the breakdown of the novel as a genre in terms of what he calls "older realisms." From this breakdown emerge two literary or cultural structures that are interrelated—"necessarily presupposing each other for any adequate analysis"—institutions of high literature and the apparatuses for the production of "popular" or mass culture. Since my concern is with genre theory and how a member of the genre "novel"—*Lord Jim*, for example—alters the genre while remaining a member of the class, the question arises, How are we to understand the persistence of a classification without charting the processes of classification change? It is, after all, through interrelation and competition with other genres, alterations or omissions of generic traits, and so forth that a modernist text begins to replace an "older realism."

My argument about text classes or genres can be summarized as follows: Classifications are empirical, not logical. They are historical assumptions constructed by authors, audiences, and critics in order to serve communicative and aesthetic purposes. Such groupings are always in terms of distinctions and interrelations, and they form a system or community of genres. The purposes they serve are social and aesthetic. Groupings arise at particular historical moments, and as they include more and more members, they are subject to repeated redefinitions or abandonment.

Genres are open systems; they are groupings of texts by critics to fulfill certain ends. And each genre is related to and defined by others to which it is related. Such relations change based on internal contraction, expansion, interweaving. Members of a genre need not have a single trait in common since to do so would presuppose that the trait has the same function for each of the member texts. Rather the members of a generic classification have multiple relational possibilities with each other, relationships that are discovered only in the process of adding members to a class. Thus the claim that genre study should be abandoned because members of a genre do not share a single trait or traits can be seen not as undermining genre but as offering an argument for its study. Aimed as an attack against an essentialist theory, this claim fails to address those theories that begin by denying essential generic traits altogether.

3.

Finally there is the attack on genre as an interpretative guide. The attack rests on two premises: that of genre and that of the text. With regard to genre, the argument is that a class generalization cannot help to interpret a specific member of the class; with regard to text, the argument is that a specific text is indeterminate; thus no determinate statements are useful in its interpretation. Genre defenders have at least two important answers: genres provide expectations for interpretations, and, a variant of this, genres provide conventions for interpretation. Elizabeth Bruss, for example, writes: "The genre does not tell us the style or construction of a text as much as how we should expect to 'take' that style or mode of construction—what force it should have for us. And this force is derived from the kind of action that text is taken to be."[8] A knowledge of genre, says another critic, provides "invaluable clues about how to interpret" a poem,[9] and the strongest argument for generic expectations is made by Hans Robert Jauss. In his essay on theory of genres and medieval vernacular literature, he writes: "The new text evokes for the reader (listener) the horizon of expectations and 'rules of the game' familiar to him from earlier texts, which as such can then be varied, extended, corrected, but also transformed, crossed out, or simply reproduced. Variation, extension, and correction determine the latitude of a generic structure; a break with the convention on the one hand and mere reproduction on the other determines its boundaries."[10] Jauss offers as an explanation of genre the view that "the relationship between the individual text and the series of texts formative of a genre presents itself as a process of the continual founding and altering of horizons" (p. 88). Jauss deals with the individual text as well as with a group of texts; yet it is difficult to see how a single text can fuse its horizons with a body of texts each of which has its own individual fusions.

The assumption of generic expectations makes or implies the claim that generalizations about a class can help interpret any particular instance of that class. What kind of expectations does *Oedipus Rex* or *Hamlet* or the genre tragedy offer us in understanding *Death of a Salesman* that we couldn't achieve without them? Such a conclusion does Jauss an injustice since the aim of his genre theory is to trace the succession of responses to a text and to explain its relation to society, author, and reader. He thus pursues history, in Jameson's terms, as a history of forms and as a history to be compared with histories of other genres and disciplines. Jauss seems minimally interested in how a text as a member of a genre is constituted. But such a procedure is necessary for an interpretative theory.

Jauss realizes that readers extend beyond the original responders to a text, and it is to the continuity or succession of responders that he turns in order to explain the responses a text elicits. One might, therefore, point out that whereas Frye directs his generic inquiry toward traditions and affinities that a writer has, Jauss directs his to the historical responses of readers who are governed by "rules of the game." But both, it should be noticed, are concerned with the changing responses toward a text and with textual affinities.

"Rules of the game" are but another name for "conventions," and some genre theorists argue for the interpretative importance of genre conventions. "Texts are . . . classified according to what I shall call their 'semiotic nature,' [writes Gary Morson] which is to say, the conventions acknowledged to be appropriate for interpreting them. . . . Readers can and do disagree about conventions for interpreting a work; when they do, I shall say they disagree about its genre. Strictly speaking, therefore, I shall not be stating that given works belong to certain genres. I shall, rather, describe the hermeneutic consequences entailed by classifying a work as one of a particular semiotic type."[11] This genre theory substitutes "reading conventions" for "genre," thus avoiding the problem of generic consistency or constituents by placing them upon "conventions." The notion of convention as a basis for interpreting works within a class refers to "conventions acknowledged to be appropriate for interpreting them." But conventions of interpretation are themselves writings (or genre members) that control readings, and thus they are subject to the same kind of changes that genres undergo. For example, conventions about treating a work as literature are not conventions applicable to one genre but to all genres included under the genre "literature." Moreover, the notion of "convention" is clearly not shared by informed readers of the same time since interpretative disagreements do indeed arise. My point is not that interpretative conventions do not exist, but that they exist within literary criticism and literary theory and that the attempt to define such conventions merely leads—as the examples of Wolfgang Iser, Stanley Fish, and Jacques Derrida illustrate—to different views of reading conventions. If reading conventions fall within the genres of criticism and theory, are we not involved in a circular argument? Genres are identified by reading conventions. But reading conventions are themselves parts of genres or genres. Thus reading conventions are themselves involved in the problem of generic specification.

The difficulty with this semiotic approach to interpretation is that the critics assume "interpretation" exists nongenerically. If they considered interpretation as text- and genre-bound, as I have suggested, they would be dealing with the changes in and transformation of texts. They would thus be led to reconsider the function of textual constituents and to analyze "conventions" in the same manner that they analyze other generic texts.

Consider Eric Havelock's discussion of the interpenetration of oral procedures in written tragedy. Discussing orality as a genre that includes many oral genres, he illustrates that a number of the practices characteristic of oral genres enter into Attic tragedy, and the example he chooses for illustration is *Oedipus Rex*. "The *Oedipus* therefore is, under one aspect, a personally produced product embodying a degree of personal creativity. Nevertheless its composition, like that of all Greek drama, involves a partnership between the oral and the written, the acoustic and the visual, a dichotomy which can also be rendered in terms of tradition versus design, generic versus specific, communal versus personal. It is a combination which lies at the heart of all high classic Greek 'literature' from Homer to Euripides."[12]

The point to be made here is that an individual instance of a genre—*Oedipus Rex*—can reveal its individuality only by comparison with other tragedies within the genre and within the oeuvre of Sophocles, but also by comparison with older oral genres. The conceptual change brought about by literacy permits us to identify a historical process of change. This process includes the absorption of elements from nontragic forms to tragedy, and, in particular, to Sophoclean tragedy. If, in other words, we wish to study literature as an interrelated system of texts and society, generic distinctions offer us a procedure to accomplish this.

Havelock outlines the interpenetration of one type of orality in the plays of Sophocles. I quote: "The riddling of the *Oedipus*, then, while giving to this particular play a peculiar degree of dramatic tension, can be seen as a revival of a traditional device, mnemonic in character and having its roots in the habits of primary orality" (p. 190). Here a constituent of oral performance enters into a later form, and in doing so we can come to understand how a text is multitemporal. *Oedipus Rex* has sedimented in it elements from older genres or elements from earlier examples of the same genre. In this respect generic composition expresses diverse communal (or ideological) values.

Some defenders of genre theory find no inconsistency between the claim that texts are indeterminate and their own assumption that a text can have diverse interpretations. The expectations of readers change and the conventions of readings change and both these hypotheses are advanced by genre critics. I have indicated that these hypotheses can be made more adequate, but I do not find that they have been discredited. Critics who assume that every text is self-contradictory still have to grant that types of contradiction exist and that such types, including their own writings, presuppose generic groupings. The view of genre that I have been advocating has considerable potential for interpretation and literary history, and I shall indicate some of this in my final section.

4.

It is unfortunate that one of the difficulties with genre is that we have the same term to describe a genre like novel or a particular novel like *Finnegans Wake*. One designation for a whole and for parts of the whole creates the impression of an organic linkage. But knowledge of the relation between the genre "novel" and members such as Austen's *Emma* and Faulkner's *The Sound and the Fury* is useful for literary study only if we can explain how they are continuous, how discontinuous. What inquiries can a genre study undertake to explain changes in individual texts or genres and literary and historical reasons for them? One is to examine the different genres an author undertakes; Joyce, for example, writes short stories, poems, a play, novels, letters. What is involved in these generic variations? Another is to relate generic changes to changes in the writing of history, granting that there are special and general histories, Marxist and other approaches to history. Another is to analyze the reasons for generic omissions or neglect of genres that can be but are not written, as the neglect of the sonnet after Milton until the end of the eighteenth century. Another is to analyze generic transformations as, for example, the "ballad" and the "lyric" are joined by Wordsworth to form "Lyrical Ballads." Still another generic inquiry is to examine a single narrative as it undergoes generic variations, becoming, in turn, a ballad, a prose fiction, a tragedy, a memoir, as well as a member of other genres. This is the inquiry I shall offer in order to consider the potentialities of generic criticism. My assumption is that an author in making a generic choice involves himself in an ideological choice, and that the critic in reconsidering the generic choices he attributes to a text involves himself in certain ideological, social, and literary commitments.

There is an early seventeenth-century ballad (ca. 1600–1624) called—in short—"The Excellent Ballad of George Barnwel." Like most ballads, it was sung in the streets, and the sheets on which it was printed—broadsides—usually wound up on the bottom of baking dishes or in the fireplace. The ballad is a confession addressed to the youths of London, and it serves as a moral warning at the same time that it notes the erotic pleasures of immorality. Its subject matter undergoes numerous generic transformations, indicating the persistent audience appeal of sexual seduction, criminal licentiousness, and parricide while paradoxically invoking the need for morality. The action of the ballad is as follows:

1. George Barnwel, a youth apprenticed to a merchant, is accosted by a woman.
2. She is an experienced harlot and seduces him.
3. As a result of his infatuation and incapacity to resist sexual pleasures, she persuades him to embezzle his master's money. He does so and flees to her when his exposure is imminent.
4. She instigates him to murder and rob his rich uncle, and he does so.
5. When the money is spent, she betrays him to the authorities.
6. He escapes and betrays her to the authorities in turn and she is hanged.
7. He flees to Poland and is hanged for an unrelated murder.

This ballad was republished several times during the seventeenth century and at the end of the century there appeared a prose fiction chapbook based on the poem and to which was appended a version of the ballad. The poetic song with its first person narrative was converted into a third person prose narrative. The prose version has a different generic history from the ballad. It is modeled upon criminal biographies with quotations from Proverbs, a life history in outline, with episodes from fabliaux. Why should a popular form be rewritten in another popular form? (1) The rewriting is addressed to a more literate audience than the original since it goes into detail about the effects of the reading of classical romances. (2) It seeks to mitigate the criminality of Barnwel by making him an innocent who can't distinguish between an angel and a whore. (3) It makes the narrative more erotic while becoming more didactically religious. (4) It is an attack upon the dangers of reading pagan texts. The change of form nevertheless continues a narrative that is recognizably that of the original ballad. What we have, therefore, is a generic change that expands upon the narrative of the ballad, but selects certain features—like the character of the harlot—to concentrate upon. There is an antifeminism that surfaces in the prose version, and a structure that resembles other criminal biographies.

In 1731 the ballad was rewritten as a tragedy, called *The London Merchant*. Here we have an elevation of a low genre into a high one: a tragedy about common people addressed to common people, altering the genre of tragedy that characteristically was about kings and aristocrats and dealt with affairs of state. The subject matter and characters altered the constituents of the tragedy. In his introduction, the author, George Lillo, argued for the need to extend the characters and subject matter of tragedy to include common people and the events in which they were involved. What this implied was a conceptual change in tragedy. The genre was now a model for what critics called "domestic" tragedy. The question for the genre critic is why and how such a subgenre is initiated. The most obvious explanation is ideological: the plot of a known popular form becomes the subject of a traditionally elite one. The intermingling of the two suggests an elevation of the merchant's role that is one of the tragedy's themes. It also indicates a reshifting of the hierarchy of generic kinds. It will not do to talk here about a reader's contract or reading conventions, since key sections of the "contract" are abrogated and conventions disregarded. This classification shift of ballad from subliterature to high literature involves generic procedures of transformation and incorporation too complicated to discuss here. But I can point out that the claim for the elevation of the ballad was made by Joseph Addison in a new genre, the periodical essay, a "newspaper" genre; it justified, by analogy, the periodical essay itself as a literary form. Moreover, ballad elevation was made analogous to the class elevation of the merchant. Generic consciousness is not, in the early eighteenth century, separated from social consciousness. It does not matter that critics parodied Addison's interest in ballads; what does matter is that his argument for genre elevation offered a procedure for treating class elevation. In this respect, generic considerations do indeed suggest that they can shape how critics look at social life rather than merely reflect it.

Some of the problems that such a genre theory invites includes the interrelation of forms; for example, in the ballad opera individual ballads become interrelated with music, dialogue, spectacle, and comedy. Then again, there is the phenomenon in which a single sonnet is joined to others to form a sequence. Or a single prose narrative or short story joined to form a series of stories.

In Bishop Percy's *Reliques of Ancient English Poetry* (1765), which became the central transmission agency by which the ballad genre entered English literature, there was published a version of the Barnwel ballad. Percy rationalized ballads as literature by claiming they were individual compositions; he consciously sought to identify them with a national tradition and he sought to illustrate them as "literature" by including in his collection a number of esteemed contemporary poems. But an important aspect of this effort at gaining establishment acceptance of the popular genre was his editing of them. He imposed on Barnwel the standards of decorum and correctness practiced by established eighteenth-century poets, standards that he found consistent with the needs of his audience. He deliberately revised the ballad of George Barnwel, therefore, to meet their assumed social and literary criteria.

What conclusions can one draw about history and genre from this limited example? Most obviously, genres have popular and polite functions and statuses. Generic transformation can be a social act. Generic transformation reveals the social changes in audiences and the interpenetration of popular and polite literature. Within a common audience different genres complement or contrast with one another. Some processes of generic alteration—for example, of the single text leading to a collective text (sonnet to sonnet sequence)—tend to repeat themselves regardless of cultural change. The success of one genre—for example, *The London Merchant*—can lead to ideological changes in an earlier genre—the ballad—now prepared for an audience familiar with the tragedy. Generic differentiation serves different ends, but each new rewriting of the ballad involves a selection from the original narrative. The ballad dealt with the mercenary, the economic behavior of the prostitute, but the tragedy dealt with the noble behavior of the merchant who had no role in the poem. The elements selected thus provide a clue to the social and cultural implications of genre. The process of sedimentation involves, in the different genres, elements from other genres that preceded them. Some of the ballad repetitions interpenetrate the prose fiction, and others are explored in greater detail. Since genres are understood in terms of their interrelation they can be seen as renewing a distance which earlier genres sought to erase, to renew a justification for separating once again popular and polite literature, once ballads are established as polite literature. Narrative can function to establish an element of continuity among different genres and thus provide a guide for historical continuity while making possible the recognition of historical changes in attitude—to merchant, merchant's apprentice, and harlot.

In this paper I have sought to answer three types of discreditation of genre theory and to offer an alternative theory. The claim that generic classes are indecipherable or indeterminate I have answered by showing how to decipher them and how a process theory can explain their transformability. The claim that members of a genre share a common element or elements in consequence of which genre is an essentialist study, I have answered by showing the historical naiveté of this argument and by illustrating that genre theory is not dependent on such essentialist assumptions. The claim that genre cannot be a guide to interpretation I have answered by showing how a process theory of genre explains the constituents of texts that it seeks historically to explain. The whole direction of my paper may thus be seen as a contribution to the regeneration of genre theory.

NOTES

1. Fredric Jameson, *The Political Unconscious* (Ithaca, 1981), p. 105; hereafter cited in text.

2. John Reichert, "More than Kin and Less than Kind: The Limits of Genre Theory," in *Theories of Literary Genre*, ed. Joseph P. Strelka (University Park, Pa., 1978), p. 57.

3. Michel Foucault, *The Archaeology of Knowledge*, tr. A. M. Sheridan Smith (New York, 1972), p. 22.

4. Jacques Derrida, "The Law of Genre," *Critical Inquiry*, 7, No. 1 (Autumn 1980), 64; hereafter cited in text. This essay also appeared in *Glyph* 7 (Baltimore, 1980), 176–232.

5. Francis Cairns, *Generic Composition in Greek and Roman Poetry* (Edinburgh, 1972), pp. 6–7, 34.

6. Aristotle, *Poetics* 26 1462a–1462b.

7. Northrop Frye, *Anatomy of Criticism* (Princeton, 1957), p. 247; hereafter cited in text.

8. Elizabeth Bruss, *Autobiographical Acts* (Baltimore, 1976), p. 4.

9. Heather Dubrow, *Genre* (London, 1982), p. 135.

10. Hans Robert Jauss, *Toward an Aesthetics of Reception*, tr. Timothy Bahti (Minneapolis, 1982), p. 88.

11. Gary Saul Morson, *The Boundaries of Genre: Dostoevsky's "Diary of a Writer" and the Traditions of Literary Utopia* (Austin, 1981), pp. viii–ix.

12. Eric Havelock, "Oral Composition in the *Oedipus Tyrannus* of Sophocles," *New Literary History*, 16, No. 1 (Autumn 1984), 186.

Lyric, History, and Genre (2009) 1.5

Jonathan Culler

In an article entitled "History and Genre," Cohen quotes Fredric Jameson's claim in *The Political Unconscious* that genre criticism has been "thoroughly discredited by modern literary theory and practice," and he sets about efficiently and systematically to consider reasons for the disparagement of the idea of genre and to elucidate a conception of genre that can be defended against common criticisms.[1] Though skepticism about the idea of genre has remained powerful in literary studies, I believe there are signs of a growing recognition of the importance of generic categories. In 2007, *PMLA* devoted a special issue to "Remapping Genre"; the subject of the September 2009 meeting of The English Institute was simply "Genre"; and the so-called "new lyric studies" has sparked a lively debate about the validity and bearing of the notion of the lyric as a genre.[2] It seems timely to take up the sort of argument offered by Ralph Cohen's discussion of the category of genre, its relation to history and importance to literary studies.

Traditionally, theorists say there are two sorts of theories of genres, empirical and theoretical; the latter is based on some claim about elementary possibilities of thought, representation, or discourse. Aristotle distinguishes literary types according to the possible modes and objects of representation. Northrop Frye bases genre categories on "radicals [root forms] of presentation": "words may be acted in front of a spectator, they may be spoken in front of a listener, they may be sung or chanted, and they may be written for a reader"—fundamental possibilities, which for him yield drama, epic, lyric, and narrative fiction.[3] Goethe spoke of the "drei echte Naturformen der Dichtung" (three pure natural forms of poetry): epic, dramatic, and lyric, which he distinguished from the variety of *Dichtarten*, which one might translate as empirical genres: ballads, drama, epistles, fables, ode, novel, parody, romance, et cetera.[4] The alternative to theories of genres based on logical divisions of a sphere of possibilities would be such empirical genres, groupings that are observed or practiced, based on principles other than theoretical. Empirical genres would be lists of whatever genres people believe exist, some based on form, others on content—classifications that do not seem very logical—like the categories we find in bookstores.

Now these do seem to be two different conceptions of genre, which we could call theoretical and historical, but I believe that in separating the two conceptions one obscures fundamental aspects of genre and creates the sort of confusion that contributes to the tendency to dismiss genres. On the one hand, theories of genre have indeed usually attempted to find a logical basis for taxonomies but use these to situate historically-attested genres. They do not derive categories that do not correspond to historically-attested forms of literary practice. The attempt to posit genres based on fundamental features of language or communication always draws on historically existing genres, as Gérard Genette argues in his fine little book about genre, *Introduction à l'Architexte*, even if, as in the case of the romantic division into subjective, objective, and mixed, theorists disagree about whether it is epic that is objective and drama mixed, or vice versa. Insofar as genres are literary categories, the projection of naturalness onto them is fallacious, Genette argues: "in the classification of genres no position is essentially more natural or more ideal than any other."[5] They are all historical categories.

This is important because our historicist age has tended to be suspicious of generic categories that previous theorists have claimed to base on some fundamental aspect of language, communication, or representation, as if these were eternal, atemporal categories, which of course they are not. If, on the other hand, genres are seen as merely contingent empirical groupings, categories that people have for various reasons found it convenient to use in dealing with literature, then it is easy to dismiss them as mere conveniences of classification—as in a bookstore or catalogue—with no critical purchase or function. But the notion of genres as merely empirical categories is very dubious—classification schemes are never without a theoretical or ideological basis of some sort, even the most heterogeneous, which might be based on marketing schemes and ideas about distinct target audiences. And a great many supposedly empirical generic categories do play a constitutive role in reading and writing, whether independently, when writers compose a detective story or readers consume a romance novel, or in combination, as when a writer deploys the conventions of one genre while ostensibly working in another. If one avoids the temptation to separate generic categories into the theoretical and the empirical but insists that genres are always historical yet based on some sort of theoretical rationale, they are more defensible as critical categories, essential to the understanding both of literature as a social institution and of the individual works that take on meaning through their relations to generic categories.

Generic categories frame both reading and writing—writers write in relation to other texts and textual traditions, both consciously and unconsciously, imitating, misreading, and rejecting, and readers approach works differently according to how they conceive them, even if those expectations are going to be disappointed. It was crucial to the effect of the French *nouveau roman*, for example, that these texts were approached as novels, with the framework of expectations governing plot, character, and meaning. The concept of the novel in its capaciousness has proved a very fruitful one for thinking about literature, perhaps especially for productions that seem to lie on its margins.

In "History and Genre," Ralph Cohen critiques essentialist theories of genre, which presume that genres are defined by necessary features that all examples of the genre share, and describes genres as open systems, defined in relation to one another. He summarizes his argument as follows:

> Classifications are empirical, not logical. They are historical assumptions constructed by authors, audiences, and critics in order to serve communicative and aesthetic purposes. Such groupings are always in terms of distinctions and interrelations, and they form a system or community of genres. The purposes they serve are social and aesthetic. Groupings arise at particular historical moments, and as they include more and more members, they are subject to repeated redefinitions or abandonment.[6]

And he concludes "History and Genre" with the splendid example of "The Excellent Ballad of George Barnwel," which began as a broadside ballad in the early seventeenth century, was transformed into a prose fiction chapbook in the late seventeenth century, then in 1731 was rewritten as a tragedy, *The London Merchant*, and finally was incorporated as a ballad in Bishop Percy's *Reliques of English Poetry* in 1765 but was revised in accordance with the standards of decorum thought appropriate to a form newly promoted as literary. These generic transformations involve the negotiation of social meanings, drawing upon the social and cultural implications of genres, but also using popular material to enrich and modify existing genres, such as tragedy. The rewritings highlight different narrative elements and play up or play down the possible moral of the story. Asking what one can learn about history and genre from this briefly sketched example, Cohen concludes, "Most obviously, genres have popular and polite functions and statuses. Generic transformation can be a social act. Generic transformation reveals the social changes in audiences and the interpenetration of popular and polite literature. Within a common audience different genres complement or contrast with one another," and in general what he calls "a process theory of genre"—seeing genres as open-ended and in a constant process of historical transformation—"explains the constituents of texts that it seeks historically to explain" (216–17).

In explicitly treating genres as historical rather than logical, Cohen sometimes appears to assume that genres are whatever critics of a particular period say they are (genres "are groupings of texts by critics to fulfill certain ends" [210]). But since, as he says in a passage I quoted earlier, genre study analyzes our procedures for acquiring and accumulating knowledge, it would be wrong merely to accept as empirical fact every ascription and description of genre. We need to evaluate such claims, and to do so, we need to reflect on what makes something count as a genre, posing the question of the relation of the groupings posited by later critics, including ourselves, to those posited by critics of an earlier era. And as soon as we take up this problem, genres are no longer merely empirical categories with no theoretical standing. Given the historicizing inclinations of criticism these days, it is important to stress that conceptions of genres are not just accounts of what people of a particular period thought; it is crucial to the notion of genre as model that people might have been wrong about them, unaware of affinities or ignoring continuities in favor of more striking novelties, or recognizing only an attenuated version of a larger tradition. Genre study cannot be just a matter, for instance, of looking at what Renaissance critics say about genres and using only those categories for thinking about Renaissance literature, though of course one should try them out, while keeping in mind the possibility that more capacious and historically informed categories may be essential to grasping the full import and deepest resources of literary productions.

In my own work on the Western lyric tradition, for example, I find myself needing to say that poets and critics have had erroneous conceptions of the lyric, which are undermined by the functioning of the poems themselves, when they are viewed in the context of a longer or broader lyric tradition. This desire to correct, which drives much academic research on subjects like this, presumes that lyric is more than a construction of the moment, that the weight of tradition helps make there be something to be right or wrong about, and in particular that a given historical construction of or notion of the lyric can neglect or obscure crucial aspects of the nature and function even of the poems to which the construction is supposed most directly to apply. The theory of a genre is an abstract model, an account of a set of norms or structural possibilities that underlie and enable the production and reception of literature: reading something as an epic or as a novel involves sets of conventions and expectations even when the text is contesting or undermining them. A claim about a generic model is not an assertion about some property that all works that might be attached to this genre possess. It is a claim about fundamental structures that may be at work even when not manifest, a claim which directs attention to certain aspects of a work, which mark a tradition and an evolution, that is to say, dimensions of transformation. The test of generic categories is how far they help relate a work to others and activate aspects of works that make them rich, dynamic, and revealing, though it is crucial to stress that interpretation of individual works is not the goal of poetics, which seeks to understand how systems of literary discourse work.

What about lyric, then, which constitutes a particularly interesting generic problem? Aristotle has little to say about it. Lyric was an important literary mode of his day but, perhaps because it is fundamentally nonmimetic, it is not taken up in the *Poetics*. Lyric was finally made one of three fundamental genres during the romantic period, when a more vigorous conception of the individual subject made it possible to conceive of lyric as mimetic: mimetic of the experience of the subject. Distinguished by its mode of enunciation, where the poet speaks *in propria persona*, lyric becomes the subjective form, with drama and epic as alternately the objective and the mixed, depending on the theorist. Hegel gives the fullest expression to the romantic theory of the lyric, whose distinguishing feature is the centrality of subjectivity coming to consciousness of itself through experience and reflection.[7] The lyric poet absorbs into himself the external world and stamps it with inner consciousness, and the unity of the poem is provided by this subjectivity.

This conception of the lyric no longer has great currency in the academic world. In a notorious article, "Genre Theory, the Lyric and *Erlebnis*," René Wellek concludes that the idea of lyric, at least in the conception inherited from the poetic theory of German romanticism as an expression of intense subjective experience, does not work. "These terms cannot take care of the enormous variety, in history and different literatures, of lyrical forms and constantly lead into an insoluble psychological cul de sac: the supposed intensity, inwardness and immediacy of an experience which can never be demonstrated as certain and can never be shown to be relevant to the quality of art. . . . The way out is obvious," he continues; "One must abandon attempts to define the general nature of the lyric or the lyrical. Nothing beyond generalities of the tritest kind can result from it."[8] Wellek proposes that we focus instead on describing particular genres, such as the ode, elegy, and song, their conventions and traditions—a not very promising strategy for nineteenth- and twentieth-century poetry, certainly, where many of the most interesting lyrics do not seem to belong to those particular genres or subgenres. It would be a major theoretical and practical failure to ignore a vast group of poems, which in fact depend upon a conceptual frame for their effect.

A more recent critique of "lyric" ends up with a surprisingly similar conclusion. What some have called "the new lyric studies" is best observed in Virginia Jackson's book, *Dickinson's Misery* and in a set of short papers in *PMLA* of January 2008, of which the introduction by Jackson and Rei Terada's contribution are the most significant. In *Dickinson's*

Misery, Jackson describes the process of lyricization or lyrical reading whereby the various kinds of writing in which Emily Dickinson engaged were made by editors and critics into lyric poems. She argues that it is criticism that has made Dickinson into a lyric poet, according to a particular model of lyric, as expression of the attitudes of a lyric persona, whereas for her producing this verse was continuous with other mundane activities such as writing letters to friends, working in the garden, et cetera. Extending M. H. Abrams' argument in *The Mirror and the Lamp* concerning the lyric as poetic norm and Paul de Man's conception of "lyrical reading," Jackson explores the process whereby the lyric takes form during the nineteenth century "through the development of various reading practices . . . that eventually become the practice of literary criticism."[9] In the process, as "poetic subgenres collapsed into the expressive romantic lyric of the nineteenth century, the various modes of poetic circulation—scrolls, manuscript books, song cycles, miscellanies, broadsides, hornbooks, libretti, quartos, chapbooks, recitation manuals, annuals, gift books, newspapers, anthologies—tended to disappear behind an idealized scene of reading progressively identified with an idealized mode of expression."[10]

Jackson argues for a critical history of this process of lyricization, a project I am happy to endorse. Where we disagree is that she seems to want to dissolve the category of lyric in order to return us to a variety of particular historical practices—though this is not entirely clear. She does not tell us how she thinks we should treat Dickinson's verse if we do not approach it as lyric; whereas I think that a critical history of lyricization should lead us to a more capacious understanding of the lyric tradition that is not restricted either to the idea of the decontextualized expression of subjectivity or what I take to be its successor, the model of the dramatic monologue with a speakers whose situation, attitude, and goals we should novelistically reconstruct. A process theory of genre, such as Ralph Cohen's, enables us to study historically the transformations of a genre, as the system of literary genres undergoes immense changes, while appreciating continuities.

I would add that the historical construction of lyric is carried out by poets as well as critics, so we can study the struggle between William Wordsworth's move to constructing lyrical ballads, attaching lyric to the modest anecdote rather than taking the ode as paradigmatic for lyric, and John Keats and Percy Bysshe Shelley's exploitation of that latter strain in new and powerful ways. Observing particular shifts in the lyric does not, though, prevent one from maintaining a broad conception of lyric as genre and its historical tradition. Conceiving of a broad range of possibilities for lyric in many periods and languages can help prevent a certain narrowing of the conception of lyric and a tendency, understandable given the realities of literary education today, to treat lyric on the model of narrative, so that the dramatic monologue becomes the model of lyric.[11] A broadly historical and, I would add, transnational conception of lyric enhances critical understanding.

But let me narrow my inquiry to exploration of some historical continuities and discontinuities that make the concept of a lyric genre valuable. Northrop Frye, in arguing that the basis of genre distinctions is what he calls the radical of presentation, identifies an underlying structure of lyric:

> The lyric poet normally pretends to be talking to himself or to someone else: a spirit of nature, a muse, a personal friend, a lover, a god, a personified abstraction, or a natural object. . . . The radical of presentation in the lyric is the hypothetical form of what in religion is called the "I-Thou" relationship. The poet, so to speak, turns his back on his listeners, though he may speak for them and though they may repeat some of his words after him.[12]

One way in which lyrics may hyperbolically mark this combination of indirection and address is through the figure of apostrophe, a turning aside from supposedly real listeners to address to someone or something that is not an ordinary, empirical listener, such as a nightingale, an urn, or one's own poem. I have been interested in the neglect of this rather striking figure by most accounts of lyric, even discussions of the ode, where it is of course endemic, and have speculated that this absence of critical attention indicates that apostrophe represents what is most embarrassing in lyric: the pretension to vatic action that critics prefer to evade, as they discuss instead, for instance, the theme of the power of poetic imagination—a serious matter that ought not to be linked to an empty "o" of address: "O Wild West Wind . . ."[13]

Apostrophe works to constitute a poetic speaker taking up an active relationship to a world or element of the world constructed as addressee, an addressee which is often asked to respond in some way, as if the burden of this apostrophic event were to make something happen, as in Shelley's address to the wild west wind,

> Be thou spirit fierce, my spirit,
> Be thou me, impetuous one . . .
> Be through my lips to unawakened earth
> The trumpet of a prophecy . . .[14]

The wind should respond, in the terms the verse suggests.

The fundamental characteristic of lyric, in this account, is not the description and interpretation of a past event but the performance of an event in the lyric present, a time of enunciation. What lyrics demand of the world is often something to be accomplished by the performativity of lyric itself. With Charles Baudelaire's "Sois sage, o ma douleur," *douleur* is to be assuaged by this familiar address, which constructs it as a child through the familiar, chiding address, "sois sage!" Rainer Maria Rilke's lines from the ninth Duino Elegy address the earth:

> Erde, ist es nicht dies, was du willst, *unsichtbar*
> in uns erstehn?—Ist es dein Traum nicht,
> Einmal unsichtbar zu sein?[15]
> [Earth, isn't this what you want, to arise invisible within us? Is it not your dream to be, one day, invisible?]

The claim is that the things of the world, addressed as subjects, would desire, like all subjects, to transcend a purely material condition and become spirit. If earth can be addressed and have desires, it must want to be a spirit, to be invisible, and the speaker boldly agrees to help:

> Erde, unsichtbar!
> Was, wenn Verwandlung nicht, ist dein drangender Auftrag?
> Erde, du liebe, ich will.
> [Earth, invisible!
> What is your urgent command if not transformation.
> Earth, you darling, I will.]

The speaker agrees to attempt this transformation willed by earth, which the poem hopes to accomplish, constructing Earth as addressee.

In locating lyric value in a certain performativity, I have essentially treated it as an active form of naming, which performatively seeks to create what it names, and may fail or succeed in this extraordinarily arrogant ambition.

Apostrophe, which in this account can be identified with the ambitions of lyric, is not just one trope among others but a troping on the circuit of communication or situation of address, a turning aside from whatever is taken to be the real or normal addressee (in forensic oratory, the judge) to some other entity which is not an ordinary, present addressee. Apostrophes foreground the act of address, lift it out of ordinary empirical contexts, and thus at some level identify the poetic act as ritualistic, hortatory, a special sort of linguistic event.

So, William Blake's "The Sick Rose," addressing the rose, "O rose, thou art sick," constitutes it as addressee:

O rose, thou art sick;
The invisible worm
That flies in the night
In the howling storm

Has found out thy bed
Of crimson joy,
And his dark secret love
Does thy life destroy.[16]

This is a poem that has provoked a good deal of critical discussion, especially because other texts of Blake's do *not* treat sexuality as a dark, destructive secret—except insofar as a perverted religious and social order constrains and represses it. Critics argue about this poem's take on beauty and human sexuality: is this a poem of beauty destroyed by evil, or a critique of the myth of female flight and male pursuit, or a representation of a puritanical, misogynistic male speaker who imputes sickness to any rose or woman whose bed is a site of sexual pleasure? We seem to have a scenario in which a phallic force has invaded the rose's bed. But Blake in one draft changed "his dark secret love" to "her dark secret love," making the invisible worm feminine, before changing it back again, suggesting that, for him at least, this is not a straightforward male-female scenario, with the rose as the woman and the worm as male sexuality.[17] Blake himself seems to have been convinced that social and religious structures which keep fantasies from leading to action were a source of illness: "He who desires and acts not breeds pestilence," he wrote. And there is a highly relevant sequence in Shakespeare's *Twelfth Night*: "She never told her love, / But let concealment, like a worm i' the bud, / feed on her damask cheek" (and, of course *damask* is a rose).[18]

But I am interested in the function of the address to the rose, which in this version of lyric works to constitute it as a sentient creature, a potential listener, or rather, such address *presupposes* an animate listener, as in Alphonse de Lamartine's apostrophic question, "Objets inanimés, avez vous donc une âme?"[19] [You inanimate objects, have you a soul?] The difference between asking "Do inanimate objects have a soul" and asking *them* whether they have a soul is that the latter presupposes the animicity by the act of addressing the question to them and constitutes the first person speaker who is reciprocally implied by the you as a visionary. The energy of poetic address creates a surprisingly strong sense of prophetic revelation and marks this speech act as poetic discourse. If one has trouble figuring out what the speaker is doing in saying "O Rose, thou art sick," it is because this statement does not correspond to any everyday speech act, and the simplest answer to what the speaker is doing is something like "waxing poetical." Address to the rose, which personifies it as sentient creature with a life of its own, creating an I-thou relation between poetic subject and natural object, works to create the subject as bardic, visionary voice, and can be inscribed in the tradition of poetry that seeks to make things happen by acts of naming. Paradoxically, the more such poetry addresses natural or inanimate objects, the more it proffers *figures* of voice, the more it reveals itself at another level as not spoken, but as writing that through its personification engenders an image of voice, for the readers to whom it presents itself again and again. By addressing the flower or other nonempirical listeners the poet works to constitute him- or herself as poet, in the tradition not just of epic, with its address to the muse, but of lyric.

Whether we think of apostrophic poems as establishing an I-thou relation with the universe, whose elements they constitute as addressees, or whether we see them as acts of radical solipsism, constituting a world with projections of the self, the apostrophic act works to constitute the poetic voice as vatic agent and thus to foreground the poetic act itself. Paul de Man, in a notoriously difficult paper, "Anthropomorphism and Trope in the Lyric," analyzes Baudelaire's apostrophic poem "Obsession"—"Grands bois, vous m'effrayez comme des cathédrales!"—as a translation of the celebrated "Correspondances" into lyric intelligibility. De Man treats the lyric genre as a "defensive motion of the understanding," designed to make the world intelligible if oppressive (by contrast with what he sees as the ultimate unintelligibility of the pre-text that "Obsession" transforms, "Correspondances.")[20] His analysis tempts readers to prefer the enumeration of the end of "Correspondances" (which he calls a "stutter") to the lyrical operation set in motion by apostrophic address, but his implicit disparagement of the lyric only strengthens my inclination to explore the generic tradition of the lyric and the relation of apostrophic address to it.

The notion of the lyric as a genre which undergoes historical transformations leads one to consider the historicity of this lyrical function of address, as an aspect of that generic history. So we might compare Blake's address to the rose with Edmund Waller's "Go, lovely Rose" of a century earlier.[21]

Go, lovely rose!
Tell her that wastes her time and me
That now she knows
When I resemble her to thee,
How sweet and fair she seems to be.

Tell her that's young,
And shuns to have her graces spied,
That hadst thou sprung
In deserts where no men abide,
Thou must have uncommended died.

Small is the worth
Of beauty from the light retired;
Bid her come forth,
Suffer herself to be desired,
And not blush so to be admired.

Then die, that she
The common fate of all things rare
May read in thee;
How small a part of time they share,
That are so wondrous sweet and fair![22]

Addressing the rose and urging it to speak and then to die seems a different sort of gesture here, for though it is certainly a distinctively poetic act it has a social dimension missing in the Blake: the rose is lovely like the lady, asked to serve as a concrete instantiation of the poetic act of comparison, but it is also the messenger, the go-between, a metonymical extension of the speaker. By invoking the rose, this speaker does not so much constitute himself as bardic voice as engage in social indirection. By apostrophizing the rose rather than addressing the beloved directly, and telling the rose what to say to the beloved, the speaker makes the argument about virginity more gracious, less aggressive and self-serving, than it would be if he directly told the imagined beloved, "suffer yourself to be desired." This apostrophic poem does indeed involve a turning away from a possible empirical listener, the lady, to another addressee, which is animated by this poetic address, but the animation is not an intensification or an instantiation of bardic power so much as gracious and witty indirection, a social gesture. Though there is a certain poetic extravagance in willing the rose to speak, giving it lines to utter, and directing it to die, the trope of apostrophe seems here to install us in a social situation rather than extract us from it, as so often happens in the apostrophic lyrics of the romantic period.

Frye's model of lyric as address overheard (following John Stuart Mill's initial formulation) makes apostrophic address one possibility, but it also allows for others, such as poems explicitly addressed to no one or nothing, which are generally taken as meditative, as if we were overhearing the poet speaking to himself or herself, and poems addressed to persons, living or dead, real or imaginary, which modern criticism has tended to treat as miniature dramas that we overhear. One modern theoretical model takes literary works as fictional imitations of real world speech acts—the novel as fictional history or fictional biography, for example—and in this account, the lyric is a fictional representation of a personal utterance. It is as if every poem began, "For example, I or someone might say . . . ."[23] Confronted with a lyric, we interpret it by asking what is the situation of the speaker (not to be identified with the poet) and attempt to work out what would lead someone to speak thus and feel thus. I would argue that the dominant modern notion of the lyric—at least in Anglo-American criticism, and especially in textbooks for the study of poetry—is the dramatic monologue, in which we overhear a speaker responding to a situation.

Criticism of the modern lyric, or modern criticism of the lyric in general, has challenged the romantic conception of lyric as the direct or sincere expression of emotion, but in so doing, it has allowed emphasis to fall on the importance of thinking of the speaker of lyric as a persona created by the poet rather than as the poet him- or herself. If the speaker is a persona, then interpretation of the poem is a characterization of the persona, as if he or she were a character in a novel, and of the situation in which the event of speech occurs. Though there is separation of the discourse of the lyric from the life of the poet as historical-biographical figure, emphasis falls on the lyric as a representation of consciousness, and ideally of a drama of consciousness.[24] Some of the reasons for the dominance of this model are, very schematically, (1) the post-Enlightenment assumption of the priority of experience over reflection,[25] (2) the increasing priority in literary education of the model of prose fiction, where narrators and point of view are central, (3) modernism's claim to objectivity, and the consequent stress on the poem as artifact rather than statement by the poet, and (4) the New Criticism's insistence that interpretation focus on the words on the page rather than the intentions of the author, so that it became a point of doctrine that the speaker of a lyric is to be treated as a *persona*, not the poet him- or herself. William Wimsatt and Cleanth Brooks write in their history of criticism, "Once we have dissociated the speaker of the lyric from the personality of the poet, even the tiniest lyric reveals itself as drama."[26]

There are numerous reasons to resist this normative model of lyric as dramatic monologue: it pushes lyric in the direction of the novel by adopting a mimetic model and focusing on the speaker as character, and it neglects all those elements of lyric—including rhyme, meter, refrain—not drawn from ordinary speech acts. But an alternative model of lyric emerges from Greek and Roman literature, illustrating the importance of treating lyric as a continuing genre that undergoes historical transformations. In *The Idea of the Lyric*, Ralph Johnson writes, "Lyric as inherited from the Greeks was sung to an audience, so that there is a *you* as well as an *I*, 'a speaker, or a singer,' talking to, singing to, another person or persons."[27] Modern conceptions of the lyric, he complains, have led us to imagine that the lyric in general is to be understood as the solipsistic meditation of an individual, expressing or working out personal feelings, if not the impersonal statement of someone unable to communicate, whereas in the classical model, "I" and "you," speaker and listener, are, according to Johnson, directly related to one another in a community.

Now a lot could be said about the familiar move that opposes public to private, speech to writing, integrated to alienated, but Johnson's argument at least alerts us to the potential importance of address, though it does lead us to ask whether the forms of address in the classical lyric do really indicate an integrated community. Though there are many second-person pronouns in Greek and Latin lyrics, they very rarely designate a community the poet could be said to address directly. Sappho's only complete poem is a complex invocation of Aphrodite where the discourse addressed to Aphrodite quotes how the Goddess herself on previous occasions invoked Sappho: "What is it now? Who, O Sappho is wronging you?"[28] This configuration is very striking and unusual, giving concrete form to what for later poets could only be wished for: that the figures invoked would actually respond. And Sappho's most famous poem—"He seems to me equal to the Gods, that man who sits opposite you and listens close to your sweet speaking. . . ."—addresses the girl whose sweet speaking and laughing "puts the heart in my chest on wings." "When I look at you, even a moment, no speaking is left in me, no: my tongue breaks and thin fire races under the skin. . . ."[29] Critics trying to imagine directness here have suggested that this might have been sung at a wedding celebration, praising the bridegroom as a god while describing a powerful erotic reaction to the bride, but this is certainly a stretch (and of course the poem is incomplete). What we have is both extremely powerful and hard to imagine spoken directly to the *you* as its audience. We find here a structure of triangulated address fundamental to lyric.

If we look to Horace and Catullus for models of lyric, we find, first, that they do not address the Roman people, the most obvious possible community. Of eighty-seven poems in the first three books of Horace's *Odes*, only nine are addressed to no one and twenty-three to nonhuman addressees (including gods and goddesses), but the address to human *you*'s, I argue, does not function in a radically different way from apostrophic address. The pronouns do not designate the true audience for the poems. Even the poems addressed to historical individuals seem designed to honor them (as a dedication would today) rather than to tell them something they need to know, but the real test case is the corpus of poems addressed to people regarded as fictional (many of them given Greek names). How do these work? One of the most famous, the fifth ode of Book One, is addressed to Pyrrha.

Quis multa gracilis te puer in rosa
perfusus liquidis urget odoribus
  grato, Pyrrha, sub antro?
    cui flavam religas comam,
simplex munditiis? heu, quotiens fidem
mutatosque deos flebit, et aspera
  nigris aequora ventis
    emirabitur insolens,

qui nunc te fruitur credulus aurea;
qui semper vacuam, semper amabilem
  sperat, nescius aurae
  fallacis! miseri, quibus
intemptata nites! me tabula sacer
votiva paries indicat uvida.
  suspendisse potenti . . .
    vestimenta maris deo.

What slim youngster soaked in perfumes
is hugging you now, Pyrrha, on a bed of roses
  deep in your lovely cave? For whom
    are you tying up your blonde hair?
You're so elegant and simple. Many's the time
he'll weep at your faithlessness and the changing gods,
  and be amazed at seas
    roughened by black winds,
but now in all innocence he enjoys your golden beauty
and imagines you always available, always loveable,
  not knowing about treacherous breezes—
    I pity poor devils who have no experience of you
and are dazzled by your radiance. As for me,
the tablet on the temple wall announces
  that I have dedicated my dripping clothes
    to the god who rules the sea.[30]

Classicists, influenced by modern critical practice, have now begun to treat this poem as a dramatic monologue. One writes that the speaker "is addressing Pyrrha and as we read we gradually come to understand their story and their characters."[31] To understand the poem, then, would be to read it as the fictional representation of a real world speech act of address and thus to try to reconstruct the situation of utterance, the relation of speaker and hearer to one another (with as much of their history as is relevant and inferable), and the aim or purpose of the speaker's utterance. To read the poem in this way certainly gives readers something to do, but it involves a great deal of speculation, and many simple questions are hard to answer. Where does this speech act take place, for instance? And why would the speaker say this to Pyrrha? Is the speaker supposed to have stumbled upon Pyrrha in a cave, being amorously pressed by a gracile youth unknown to him? Presumably not—we don't imagine he interrupts the love scene to put the question—but if we posit that he encounters Pyrrha elsewhere, in the street, for instance, it is hard to imagine the motivation for the question, "What slim youngster is pressing you now?" Or if we take this as a wittily hyperbolic version of "so who are you seeing these days?" then it is hard to imagine the circumstances or rationale for the comments that follow, which would be better addressed to a young man. This is especially true, given the order of the comments about this young lover: one might imagine someone saying, "I'm sure he is dazzled by your radiance now, not realizing that the future will bring storms," but the converse—"Many's the time that he will weep at your faithlessness. . . . though he is dazzled now"—seems much more like musing about the vicissitudes of love than an utterance to the woman on a specific occasion.

If we try to imagine lines five to thirteen addressed to Pyrrha, it makes the poem obscure rather than clarifies it, whereas if we think of the poem as a disquisition on the vicissitudes of love directed at an imagined Pyrrha, apostrophized in the lyric present, the poem makes much more sense. And the final lines come to emphasize the speaker's position as worldly wise, not jealous of the youth who may have supplanted him (as the one might suppose he was if the poem were really spoken to Pyrrha). The speaker announces that he is no longer engaged in such matters, which he can now view with wry amusement. Rather than a dramatic monologue representing a real world speech act addressed to Pyrrha, we have an addressee imagined for rhetorical purposes. Why not take the ode as an act of *poetic address*: writing which imagines the addressee as it imagines the gracile youth, with his present excitement and his future disappointments, and whose act of addressing, precisely because it does not seem focused on the referent of the pronoun, is more likely to attain the reader?

We could say, in fact, that the key question is, whom is the poem seeking to persuade? In ancient Greece, poetry was a form of epideictic discourse, a rhetorical transaction and instrument of ethical *paideia*. The audience was expected to make observations (*theôros*), about what is praiseworthy, worthy of belief. In Plato's *Protagoras*, where the protagonists discuss the arguments of a poem by Simonides in order to reach conclusions about the world, everyone takes it for granted that, as Protagoras says, the most important part of a man's *paideia* is to be capable concerning verses—capable of judging which sayings of poets are well-crafted and valuable and to give reasons when questioned. (Socrates argues, against the received view, that people ought to discuss dialectic rather than poetry).[32]

So, whom does this poem seek to persuade, and of what? Not Pyrrha—she is not addressed so as to be persuaded to act differently, for her behavior is compared to the natural changeableness of the sea. More plausibly, the gracile youth, or rather, since he is not addressed at all, but pitied, as one of many "Miseri," perhaps all those "poor devils" who don't anticipate the storms that will come. One could certainly argue that it is the audience of the poem that is to be persuaded to adopt the attitude that the speaking voice projects of knowledgeable wariness, accepting what comes. Pyrrha is elegant and not to be shunned; the youth should enjoy himself now, but not get too involved, for reversals will occur, suffering will follow. There is a time for everything, says the wise man, retiring from the amorous fray.

Now there are a few of Horace's odes that *should* be read as dramatic monologues (such as *Natis in usum*, I.27)—where to make sense of the poem we really do have to imagine a context of utterance and work out why in these circumstances someone would say just these words. But they are rare, whereas this sort of structure—address to a *you* in a situation better left indeterminate—is extremely common. The second person address functions above all to place the act of lyric speech in the lyric present and to accentuate the paradox of poetry, that evokes immediacy while adopting a temporality of deferral, as it repeats itself for readers in a future not even imagined, and articulates an attitude whose appropriateness future audiences of readers are to judge.

In a strange article entitled "The View from Halicarnassus," Jeffrey Walker argues that Pindar's encomiastic verse provides the proper model for lyric—lyric is the original form of epideictic rhetoric—and that because of a "brilliant mistake" by Aristotle, who failed to honor the Greek notion of lyric, criticism has ever since possessed only a model for minor poetry, what he calls the "apostrophic lyric," where lyric discourse is not public, argumentative discourse, but private ejaculation.[33] It is ironic that Walker seeks to trivialize the modern lyric by calling it "apostrophic," since until recently critics universally treated apostrophe, when it occurs in modern lyrics, as a purely conventional element inherited from the classical tradition. But Walker is right to emphasize that the classical model helps us towards a more capacious and apposite notion of lyric. (Whether Pindar, as opposed to, say, Horace, is really a good model for the lyric tradition is a different question.) Only a broad concept of lyric, with its sweep across eras and languages, provides the scope to activate possibilities occluded by narrower conceptions, such as that of the ode or elegy, useful though they may be.

In particular, the classical example reminds us that the model of the dramatic monologue—a speaker-character whose situation and aims need to be reconstructed novelistically—forecloses important traditional aspects and potentials of lyric—especially those features, from rhythm and sound patterning to performative address, by which it differentiates itself from narrative fiction and mimetic modes generally.

In an afterword to the *PMLA* issue on genre, Bruce Robbins compares notions of genre to the norms in the socioeconomic realm that allow, for instance, transnational comparison of living standards and argues that the case of genre in a nutshell is that of historical comparison.[34] Genre, he maintains, is a crucial instrument combatting the professional inclination to focus on a literary period—which he calls "a sort of pseudo-anthropocentric norm that has been adopted for a long time out of laziness. It is one level of magnification among others, no less valid than any other but also no less arbitrary." Genre, he insists, offers us "versions of history that take us beyond the period-by-period agenda of our ordinary studies." Foregrounding the generic cateogry of lyric, for instance, helps promote the possibility of comparisons with other traditions, and allows us, for example, to see that it is perhaps only because the greatest systematic philosopher of the west, Aristotle, wrote a treatise on mimetic literature and did not include lyric that lyric has not been seen as a foundational genre in Western culture until the romantic era, whereas it is in other cultures, whose literature did not originate in epic or tragedy.[35] "Why," Robbins concludes, "would criticism voluntarily deprive itself of this additional scale of transperiodic vision and the aggregations it brings into view?"[36] Whether or not notions of genre are what make possible a literary history, as Ralph Cohen's work suggests, they certainly can connect various narrower modes of reading and interpretation and enlarge our vision of historical discursive possibilities.

A. R. Ammons, in a posthumously published poem, "Aubade," evokes the "you" of poetic address and its history:

> that "you" has
> moved out of the woods and rocks and streams

and now is elusive, "nowhere to / be found or congratulated."[37] When one writes "you," the poem suggests, "one lifts up one's voice to the / lineations of singing." The "you" of lyric address "dwells in our heads now as a bit of / yearning, maybe vestigial." Perhaps there is always a *you* in the lyric, whether expressed or not, whatever its variations, as lyrics strive to be an event in the special temporality of the lyric present. Often that you is expressed—the *you* of the beloved, or the wind, a flower, a yearning. But the lyric "you" is also a bit of language, a trope, and Ammons concludes that this "nearly reachable presence" is also "something / we can push aside as we get up to rustle up a / little breakfast." It is through preserving the notion of lyric as a genre, an open process of generic negotiation, that such historical variations in function and effect can be registered and analyzed.

NOTES

1. Ralph Cohen, "History and Genre," *NLH* 17, no. 2 (1986): 203.

2. "Remapping Genre," *PMLA* 122, no. 5 (October 2007). See the section "The New Lyric Studies" in *PMLA* 123, no. 1 (January 2008). The original manifesto for this movement is Virginia Jackson and Yopie Prins, "Lyrical Studies," *Victorian Literature and Culture* (1999), 521–30.

3. Northrop Frye, *Anatomy of Criticism* (Princeton, NJ: Princeton Univ. Press, 1957), 247.

4. The Dichtarten are listed alphabetically: "Allegorie, Ballade, Cantate, Drama, Elegie, Epigramm, Epistel, Epopee, Erzählung, Fabel, Heroide, Idylle, Lehrgedicht, Ode, Parodie, Roman, Romanze, Satyre." Johann Wolfgang von Goethe, "Noten und Abhandlungen zu besserem Verständnis des West-östlichen Diwans," in *Goethes Werke*, Hamburger Ausgabe (Munich: C. H. Beck, 1981), 2:187–89.

5. Gérard Genette, *The Architext, An Introduction* (Berkeley and Los Angeles: Univ. of California Press, 1992), 65–6.

6. Cohen, "History and Genre," 210 (hereafter cited in text).

7. G. W. F. Hegel, *Aesthetics* (Oxford: Oxford Univ. Press, 1975), 2:1113.

8. René Wellek, "Genre Theory, the Lyric and *Erlebnis*," *Discriminations* (New Haven, CT: Yale Univ. Press, 1970), 251–2.

9. M. H. Abrams, *The Mirror and the Lamp* (New York: Oxford Univ. Press, 1953), 84–8; Paul de Man, "Anthropomorphism and Trope in the Lyric," *The Rhetoric of Romanticism* (New York: Columbia Univ. Press, 1984); Virginia Jackson, *Dickinson's Misery: A Theory of Lyric Reading* (Princeton, NJ: Princeton Univ. Press, 2005), 7.

10. Virginia Jackson and Yopie Prins, "Lyrical Studies," *Victorian Literature and Culture* (1999), 521–30.

11. See Jonathan Culler, "Why Lyric?" *PMLA* 123, no. 1 (January 2008).

12. Northrop Frye, *Anatomy of Criticism*, 250.

13. Jonathan Culler, "Apostrophe," *The Pursuit of Signs* (Ithaca, NY: Cornell Univ. Press, 1981), 135–54.

14. Percy Bysshe Shelley, "Ode to the West Wind," *Poetical Works* (Boston: Cambridge Riverside Press, 1957), 377–9.

15. Rainer Maria Rilke, *Duino Elegies* (Einseideln, Switzerland: Daimon Verlag, 1992), 90.

16. William Blake, *Complete Works*, ed. Geoffrey Keynes (London: Clarendon Press, 1969), 213.

17. Blake, *Complete Works*, 175.

18. William Shakespeare, *Twelfth Night*, Act 2, scene 4.

19. Alphonse de Lamartine, *Oeuvres poétiques* (Paris: Gallimard, 1966), 392.

20. De Man, "Anthropomorphism and Trope in the Lyric," 261.

21. See Paul Alpers, "Apostrophe and the Rhetoric of Renaissance Lyric," forthcoming.

22. Edmund Waller, "Go, Lovely Rose," *Oxford Anthology of English Poetry* (New York: Oxford Univ. Press, 1956), 322.

23. Barbara Herrnstein Smith, *On the Margins of Discourse* (Chicago: Univ. of Chicago Press, 1978), 142.

24. See Culler, "Changes in the Study of the Lyric," and Herbert Tucker, "Dramatic Monologue and the Overhearing of Lyric," both in *Lyric Poetry: Beyond the New Criticism*, ed. C. Hošek and P. Parker (Ithaca, NY: Cornell Univ. Press, 1985).

25. An influential book in the Anglo-American tradition, Robert Langbaum's *The Poetry of Experience* (New York: Random House, 1957), argues that the desire to overcome subjectivity and achieve objectivity has determined poetic developments since the end of the Enlightenment, and that the central idea of the nineteenth century is the doctrine that the imaginative apprehension gained through immediate experience is primary and certain, whereas the analytical reflection that follows upon it is secondary and problematical. Thus the poem comes to be above all the representation of the experience of consciousness as it senses, investigates, recollects, and so on—not an idea distilled from past experience but the drama of consciousness as it engages some aspect of the human condition, and it offers the reader an experience rather than a truth. Langbaum goes on to describe an important nineteenth century form, the dramatic monologue, but does caution against the inclination to treat as dramatic monologue every poem where there seems to be a speaker other than the poet. For a shrewd discussion see Herbert Tucker, "Dramatic Monologue and the Overhearing of Lyric" in *Lyric Poetry: Beyond the New Criticism*, ed. C. Hošek and P. Parker.

26. W. K. Wimsatt and Cleanth Brooks, *Literary Criticism: A Short History* (New York: 1957), 675.

27. W. R. Johnson, *The Idea of Lyric: Lyric Modes in Ancient and Modern Poetry* (Berkeley and Los Angeles: Univ. of California Press, 1982), 3.

28. Sappho #1 in Anne Carson, *If Not Winter: Fragments of Sappho* (New York: Virago Press, 2003), 1.

29. Sappho #31, *If Not Winter*, 63.

30. Horace, *The Complete Odes and Epodes*, trans. David West (Oxford: Oxford Univ. Press, 1997), 30.

31. David West, *Horace Odes* I, Carpe Diem (Oxford: Oxford Univ. Press, 1995), 40.

32. See Jeffrey Walker, *Rhetoric and Poetics in Antiquity* (Oxford: Oxford Univ. Press, 2000), 9, 149; (Plato's Protagoras, 339–47) Epideictic rhetoric, which Walker argues derives from archaic lyric, includes panegyric, and unlike pragmatic rhetoric, which is directed towards decision, is directed to an audience that does not make decisions, *kritês*, but forms opinions in

response to the discourse, which thus "shapes and cultivates the basic codes of value and belief by which a society or culture lives." This holds, he argues, for the audience of Thucydides, Plato, and Sappho. And of course Horace aspires to revive the Greek lyric tradition of Sappho and Alcaeus.

33. Jeffrey Walker, "The View from Halicarnassus: Aristotelianism and the Rhetoric of Epideictic Song," in *New Definitions of Lyric*, ed. Mark Jeffreys (New York: Routledge, 1998), 19–21.

34. Bruce Robbins, "Afterword," *PMLA* 12, no. 5 (October 2007): 1648.

35. Earl Miner, an eminent comparatist of Asian literatures as well as English, observes: "Lyric is the foundation genre for the poetics or literary assumptions of cultures throughout the world. Only Western poetics differs. Even the major civilizations that have not shown a need to develop a systematic poetics (the Islamic, for instance) have demonstrably based their ideas of literature on lyric assumptions." "Why Lyric?" in *The Renewal of Song: Renovation in Lyric Conception and Practice*, ed. Earl Miner and Amiya Dev (Calcutta: Seagull Books, 2000). And he adds, "The first thing to be said of lyric poetic systems is that they are not mimetic."

36. Robbins, "Afterword," 1650.

37. A. R. Ammons, *Bosh and Flapdoodle* (New York: Norton, 2005), 22–4.

How to Recognize a Poem When You See One (1980) 1.6

STANLEY FISH

Last time I sketched out an argument by which meanings are the property neither of fixed and stable texts nor of free and independent readers but of interpretive communities that are responsible both for the shape of a reader's activities and for the texts those activities produce. In this lecture I propose to extend that argument so as to account not only for the meanings a poem might be said to have but for the fact of its being recognized as a poem in the first place. And once again I would like to begin with an anecdote.

In the summer of 1971 I was teaching two courses under the joint auspices of the Linguistic Institute of America and the English Department of the State University of New York at Buffalo. I taught these courses in the morning and in the same room. At 9:30 I would meet a group of students who were interested in the relationship between linguistics and literary criticism. Our nominal subject was stylistics but our concerns were finally theoretical and extended to the presuppositions and assumptions which underlie both linguistic and literary practice. At 11:00 these students were replaced by another group whose concerns were exclusively literary and were in fact confined to English religious poetry of the seventeenth century. These students had been learning how to identify Christian symbols and how to recognize typological patterns and how to move from the observation of these symbols and patterns to the specification of a poetic intention that was usually didactic or homiletic. On the day I am thinking about, the only connection between the two classes was an assignment given to the first which was still on the blackboard at the beginning of the second. It read:

Jacobs-Rosenbaum
Levin
Thorne
Hayes
Ohman (?)

I am sure that many of you will already have recognized the names on this list, but for the sake of the record, allow me to identify them. Roderick Jacobs and Peter Rosenbaum are two linguists who have coauthored a number of textbooks and coedited a number of anthologies. Samuel Levin is a linguist who was one of the first to apply the operations of transformational grammar to literary texts. J. P. Thorne is a linguist at Edinburgh who, like Levin, was attempting to extend the rules of transformational grammar to the notorious irregularities of poetic language. Curtis Hayes is a linguist who was then using transformational grammar in order to establish an objective basis for his intuitive impression that the language of Gibbon's *Rise and Fall of the Roman Empire* is more complex than the language of Hemingway's novels. And Richard Ohmann is the literary critic who, more than any other, was responsible for introducing the vocabulary of transformational grammar to the literary community. Ohmann's name was spelled as you see it here because I could not remember whether it contained one or two n's. In other words, the question mark in parenthesis signified nothing more than a faulty memory and a desire on my part to appear scrupulous. The fact that the names appeared in a list that was arranged vertically, and that Levin, Thorne, and Hayes formed a column that was more or less centered in relation to the paired names of Jacobs and Rosenbaum, was similarly accidental and was evidence only of a certain compulsiveness if, indeed, it was evidence of anything at all.

In the time between the two classes I made only one change. I drew a frame around the assignment and wrote on the top of that frame "p. 43." When the members of the second class filed in I told them that what they saw on the blackboard was a religious poem of the kind they had been studying and I asked them to interpret it. Immediately they began to perform in a manner that, for reasons which will become clear, was more or less predictable. The first student to speak pointed out that the poem was probably a hieroglyph, although he was not sure whether it was in the shape of a cross or an altar. This question was set aside as the other students, following his lead, began to concentrate on individual words, interrupting each other with suggestions that came so quickly that they seemed spontaneous. The first line of the poem (the very order of events assumed the already constituted status of the object) received the most attention: Jacobs was explicated as a reference to Jacob's ladder, traditionally allegorized as a figure for the Christian ascent to heaven. In this poem, however, or so my students told me, the means of ascent is not a ladder but a tree, a rose tree or rosenbaum. This was seen to be an obvious reference to the Virgin Mary who was often characterized as a rose without thorns, itself an emblem of the immaculate conception. At this point the poem appeared to the students to be operating in the familiar manner of an iconographic riddle. It at once posed the question, "How is it that a man can climb to heaven by means of a rose tree?" and directed the reader to the inevitable answer: by the fruit of that tree, the fruit of Mary's womb, Jesus. Once this interpretation was established it received support from, and conferred significance on, the word "thorne," which could only be an allusion to the crown of thorns, a symbol of the trial suffered by Jesus and of the price he paid to save us all. It was only a short step (really no step at all) from this insight to the recognition of Levin as a double reference, first to the tribe of Levi, of whose priestly function Christ was the fulfillment, and second to the unleavened bread carried by the children of Israel on their exodus from Egypt, the place of sin, and in response to the call of Moses, perhaps the most familiar of the old testament types of Christ. The final word of the poem was given at least three complementary readings: it could be "omen," especially since so much of the poem is concerned with foreshadowing and prophecy; it could be Oh Man, since it is man's story as it intersects with the divine plan that is the poem's subject; and it could, of course, be simply "amen," the proper conclusion to a poem celebrating the love and mercy shown by a God who gave his only begotten son so that we may live.

In addition to specifying significances for the words of the poem and relating those significances to one another, the students began to discern larger structural patterns. It was noted that of the six names in the poem three—Jacobs, Rosenbaum, and Levin—are Hebrew, two—Thorne and Hayes—are Christian, and one—Ohman—is ambiguous, the ambiguity being marked in the poem itself (as the phrase goes) by the question mark in parenthesis. This division was seen as a reflection of the basic distinction between the old dispensation and the new, the law of sin and the law of love. That distinction, however, is blurred and finally dissolved by the typological perspective which invests the old testament events and heroes with new testament meanings. The structure of the poem, my students concluded, is therefore a double one, establishing and undermining its basic pattern (Hebrew vs. Christian) at the same time. In this context there is finally no pressure to resolve the ambiguity of Ohman since the two possible readings—the name is Hebrew, the name is Christian—are both authorized by the reconciling presence in the poem of Jesus Christ. Finally, I must report that one student took to counting letters and found, to no one's surprise, that the most prominent letters in the poem were S, O, N.

Some of you will have noticed that I have not yet said anything about Hayes. This is because of all the words in the poem it proved the most recalcitrant to interpretation, a fact not without consequence, but one which I will set aside for the moment since I am less interested in the details of the exercise than in the ability of my students to perform it. What is the source of that ability? How is it that they were able to do what they did? What is it that they did? These questions are important because they bear directly on a question often asked in literary theory, What are the distinguishing features of literary language? Or, to put the matter more colloquially, How do you recognize a poem when you see one? The commonsense answer, to which many literary critics and linguists are committed, is that the act of recognition is triggered by the observable presence of distinguishing features. That is, you know a poem when you see one because its language displays the characteristics that you know to be proper to poems. This, however, is a model that quite obviously does not fit the present example. My students did not proceed from the noting of distinguishing features to the recognition that they were confronted by a poem; rather, it was the act of recognition that came first—they knew in advance that they were dealing with a poem and the distinguishing features then followed.

In other words, acts of recognition, rather than being triggered by formal characteristics, are their source. It is not that the presence of poetic qualities compels a certain kind of attention but that the paying of a certain kind of attention results in the emergence of poetic qualities. As soon as my students were aware that it was poetry they were seeing, they began to look with poetry-seeing eyes, that is, with eyes that saw everything in relation to the properties they knew poems to possess. They knew, for example (because they were told by their teachers), that poems are (or are supposed to be) more densely and intricately organized than ordinary communications; and that knowledge translated itself into a willingness—one might even say a determination—to see connections between one word and another and between every word and the poem's central insight. Moreover, the assumption that there *is* a central insight is itself poetry-specific, and presided over its own realization. Having assumed that the collection of words before them was unified by an informing purpose (because unifying purposes are what poems have), my students proceeded to find one and to formulate it. It was in the light of that purpose (now assumed) that significances for the individual words began to suggest themselves, significances which then flesh out the assumption that had generated them in the first place. Thus the meanings of the words and the interpretation in which those words were seen to be embedded emerged together, as a consequence of the operations my students began to perform once they were told that this was a poem.

It was almost as if they were following a recipe—if it's a poem do this, if it's a poem, see it that way—and indeed definitions of poetry *are* recipes, for by directing readers as to what to look for in a poem, they instruct them in ways of looking that will produce what they expect to see. If your definition of poetry tells you that the language of poetry is complex, you will scrutinize the language of something identified as a poem in such a way as to bring out the complexity you know to be "there." You will, for example, be on the look-out for latent ambiguities: you will attend to the presence of alliterative and consonantal patterns (there will always be some), and you will try to make something of them (you will always succeed); you will search for meanings that subvert, or exist in a tension with the meanings that first present themselves; and if these operations fail to produce the anticipated complexity, you will even propose a significance for the words that are *not* there, because, as everyone knows, everything about a poem, including its omissions, is significant. Nor, as you do these things, will you have any sense of performing in a willful manner, for you will only be doing what you learned to do in the course of becoming a skilled reader of poetry. Skilled reading is usually thought to be a matter of discerning what is there, but if the example of my students can be generalized, it is a matter of knowing how to *produce* what can thereafter be said to be there. Interpretation is not the art of construing but the art of constructing. Interpreters do not decode poems; they make them.

To many, this will be a distressing conclusion, and there are a number of arguments that could be mounted in order to forestall it. One might point out that the circumstances of my students' performance were special. After all, they had been concerned exclusively with religious poetry for some weeks, and therefore would be uniquely vulnerable to the deception I had practiced on them and uniquely equipped to impose religious themes and patterns on words innocent of either. I must report, however, that I have duplicated this experiment any number of times at nine or ten universities in three countries, and the results were always the same, even when the participants know from the beginning that what they are looking at was originally an assignment. Of course this very fact could itself be turned into an objection: doesn't the reproducibility of the exercise prove that there is something about these words that leads everyone to perform in the same way? Isn't it just a happy accident that names like Thorne and Jacobs have counterparts or near counterparts in biblical names and symbols? And wouldn't my students have been unable to do what they did if the assignment I gave to the first class had been made up of different names? The answer to all of these questions is no. Given a firm belief that they were confronted by a religious poem, my students would have been able to turn any list of names into the kind of poem we have before us now, because they would have read the names within the assumption that they were informed with Christian significances. (This is nothing more than a literary analogue to Augustine's rule of faith.) You can test this assertion by replacing Jacobs-Rosenbaum, Levin, Thorne, Hayes, and Ohman with names drawn from the faculty of Kenyon College—Temple, Jordan, Seymour, Daniels, Star, Church. I will not exhaust my time or your patience by performing a full-dress analysis, which would involve, of course, the relation between those who saw the River Jordan and those who saw *more* by seeing the Star of Bethlehem, thus fulfilling the prophecy by which the temple of Jerusalem was replaced by the inner temple or church built up in the heart of every Christian. Suffice it to say that it could easily be done (you can take the poem home and do it yourself) and that the shape of its doing would be constrained not by the names but by the interpretive assumptions that gave them a significance even before they were seen. This would be true even if there were no names on the list, if the paper or blackboard were blank; the blankness would present no problem to the interpreter, who would immediately see in it the void out of which God created the earth, or the abyss into which unregenerate sinners fall, or, in the best of all possible poems, both.

Even so, one might reply, all you've done is demonstrate how an interpretation, if it is prosecuted with sufficient vigor, can impose itself on material which has its own proper shape. Basically, at the ground level, in the first place, when all is said and done, "Jacobs-Rosenbaum Levin Thorne Hayes Ohman(?)" is an assignment; it is only a trick that allows you to transform it into a poem, and when the effects of the trick have worn off, it will return to its natural form and be seen as an assignment once again. This is a powerful argument because it seems at once to give interpretation its due (as an act of the will) and to maintain the independence of that on which interpretation works. It allows us, in short, to preserve our commonsense intuition that interpretation must be interpretation of *something*. Unfortunately, the argument will not hold because the assignment we all see is no less the product of interpretation than the poem into which it was turned. That is, it requires just as much work, and work of the same kind, to see this as an assignment as it does to see it as a poem. If this seems counterintuitive, it is only because the work required to see it as an assignment is work we have already done, in the course of acquiring the huge amount of background knowledge that enables you and me to function in the academic world. In order to know what an assignment is, that is, in order to know what to do with something identified as an assignment, you must first know what a class is (know that it isn't an economic grouping) and know that classes meet at specified times for so many weeks, and that one's performance in a class is largely a matter of performing between classes.

Think for a moment of how you would explain this last to someone who did not already know it. "Well," you might say, "a class is a group situation in which a number of people are instructed by an informed person in a particular subject." (Of course the notion of "subject" will itself require explication.) "An assignment is something you do when you're not in class." "Oh, I see," your interlocutor might respond, "an assignment is something you do to take your mind off what you've been doing in class." "No, an assignment is a part of a class." "But how can that be if you only do it when the class is not meeting?" Now it would be possible, finally, to answer that question, but only by enlarging the horizons of your explanation to include the very concept of a university, what it is one might be doing there, why one might be doing it instead of doing a thousand other things, and so on. For most of us these matters do not require explanation, and indeed, it is hard for us to imagine someone for whom they do; but that is because our tacit knowledge of what it means to move around in academic life was acquired so gradually and so long ago that it doesn't seem like knowledge at all (and therefore something someone else might *not* know) but a part of the world. You might think that when you're on campus (a phrase that itself requires volumes) that you are simply walking around on the two legs God gave you; but your walking is informed by an internalized awareness of institutional goals and practices, of norms of behavior, of lists of do's and don't's, of invisible lines and the dangers of crossing them; and, as a result, you see everything as *already* organized in relation to those same goals and practices. It would never occur to you, for example, to wonder if the people pouring out of that building are fleeing from a fire; you *know* that they are exiting from a class (what could be more obvious?) and you know that because your perception of their action occurs within a knowledge of what people in a university could possibly be doing and the reasons they could have for doing it (going to the next class, going back to the dorm, meeting someone in the student union). It is within that same knowledge that an assignment becomes intelligible so that it appears to you immediately as an obligation, as a set of directions, as something with parts, some of which may be more significant than others. That is, it is a proper question to ask of an assignment whether some of its parts might be omitted or slighted, whereas readers of poetry know that no part of a poem can be slighted (the rule is "everything counts") and they do not rest until every part has been given a significance.

In a way this amounts to no more than saying what everyone already knows: poems and assignments are different, but my point is that the differences are a result of the different interpretive operations we perform and not of something inherent in one or the other. An assignment no more compels its own recognition than does a poem; rather, as in the case of a poem, the shape of an assignment emerges when someone looks at something identified as one with assignment-seeing eyes, that is, with eyes which are capable of seeing the words as already embedded within the institutional structure that makes it possible for assignments to have a sense. The ability to see, and therefore to make, an assignment is no less a learned ability than the ability to see, and therefore to make, a poem. Both are constructed artifacts, the products and not the producers of interpretation, and while the differences between them are real, they are interpretive and do not have their source in some bedrock level of objectivity.

Of course one might want to argue that there is a bedrock level at which these names constitute neither an assignment or a poem but are merely a list. But that argument too fails because a list is no more a natural object—one that wears its meaning on its face and can be recognized by anyone—than an assignment or a poem. In order to see a list, one must already be equipped with the concepts of seriality, hierarchy, subordination, and so on, and while these are by no mean esoteric concepts and seem available to almost everyone, they are nonetheless learned, and if there were someone who had not learned them, he or she would not be able to see a list. The next recourse is to descend still lower (in the direction of atoms) and to claim objectivity for letters, paper, graphite, black marks on white spaces, and so on; but these entities too have palpability and shape only because of the assumption of some or other system of intelligibility, and they are therefore just as available to a deconstructive dissolution as are poems, assignments, and lists.

The conclusion, therefore, is that all objects are made and not found, and that they are made by the interpretive strategies we set in motion. This does not, however, commit me to subjectivity because the means by which they are made are social and conventional. That is, the "you" who does the interpretative work that puts poems and assignments and lists into the world is a communal you and not an isolated individual. No one of us wakes up in the morning and (in French fashion) reinvents poetry or thinks up a new educational system or decides to reject seriality in favor of some other, wholly original, form of organization. We do not do these things because we could not do them, because the mental operations we can perform are limited by the institutions in which we are *already* embedded. These institutions precede us, and it is only by inhabiting them, or being inhabited by them, that we have access to the public and conventional senses they make. Thus while it is true to say that we create poetry (and assignments and lists), we create it through interpretive strategies that are finally not our own but have their source in a publicly available system of intelligibility. Insofar as the system (in this case a literary system) constrains us, it also fashions us, furnishing us with categories of understanding, with which we in turn fashion the entities to which we can then point. In short, to the list of made or constructed objects we must add ourselves, for we no less than the poems and assignments we see are the products of social and cultural patterns of thought.

To put the matter in this way is to see that the opposition between objectivity and subjectivity is a false one because neither exists in the pure form that would give the opposition its point. This is precisely illustrated by my anecdote in which we do *not* have free-standing readers in a relationship of perceptual adequacy or inadequacy to an equally free-standing text. Rather, we have readers whose consciousnesses are constituted by a set of conventional notions which when put into operation constitute in turn a conventional, and conventionally seen, object. My students could do what they did, and do it in unison, because as members of a literary community they knew what a poem was (their knowledge was public), and that knowledge led them to look in such a way as to populate the landscape with what they knew to be poems.

Of course poems are not the only objects that are constituted in unison by shared ways of seeing. Every object or event that becomes available within an institutional setting can be so characterized. I am thinking, for example, of something that happened in my classroom just the other day. While I was in the course of vigorously making a point, one of my students, William Newlin by name, was just as vigorously waving his hand. When I asked the other members of the class what it was that Mr. Newlin was doing, they all answered that he was seeking permission to speak. I then asked them how they knew that. The immediate reply was that it was obvious; what else could he be thought to be doing? The meaning of his gesture, in other words, was right there on its surface, available for reading by anyone who had the eyes to see. That meaning, however, would not have been available to someone without any knowledge of what was involved in being a student. Such a person might have thought that Mr. Newlin was pointing to the fluorescent lights hanging from the ceiling, or calling our attention to some object that was about to fall ("the sky is falling," "the sky is falling"). And if the someone in question were a child of elementary or middle-school age, Mr. Newlin might well have been seen as seeking permission not to speak but to go to the bathroom, an interpretation or reading that would never occur to a student at Johns Hopkins or any other institution of "higher learning" (and how would we explain to the uninitiated the meaning of *that* phrase).

The point is the one I have made so many times before: it is neither the case that the significance of Mr. Newlin's gesture is imprinted on its surface where it need only be read off, or that the construction put on the gesture by everyone in the room was individual and idiosyncratic. Rather, the source of our interpretive unanimity was a structure of interests and understood goals, a structure whose categories so filled our individual consciousnesses that they were rendered as one, immediately investing phenomena with the significance they *must* have, given the already-in-place assumptions about what someone could possibly be intending (by word or gesture) in a classroom. By seeing Mr. Newlin's raised hand with a single shaping eye, we were demonstrating what Harvey Sacks has characterized as "the fine power of a culture. It does not, so to speak, merely fill brains in roughly the same way, it fills them so that they are alike in fine detail."[1] The occasion of Sacks's observation was the ability of his hearers to understand a sequence of two sentences—"The baby cried. The mommy picked it up."—exactly as he did (assuming, for example that "the 'mommy' who picks up the 'baby' is the mommy of that baby"), despite the fact that alternative ways of understanding were demonstrably possible. That is, the mommy of the second sentence could well have been the mommy of some other baby, and it need not even have been a baby that this "floating" mommy was picking up. One is tempted to say that in the absence of a specific context we are authorized to take the words literally, which is what Sacks's hearers do; but as Sacks observes, it is within the assumption of a context—one so deeply assumed that we are unaware of it—that the words acquire what seems to be their literal meaning. There is nothing *in the words* that tells Sacks and his hearers how to relate the mommy and the baby of this story, just as there is nothing *in the form* of Mr. Newlin's gesture that tells his fellow students how to determine its significance. In both cases the determination (of relation and significance) is the work of categories of organization—the family, being a student—that are from the very first giving shape and value to what is heard and seen.

Indeed, these categories are the very shape of seeing itself, in that we are not to imagine a perceptual ground more basic than the one they afford. That is, we are not to imagine a moment when my students "simply see" a physical configuration of atoms and *then* assign that configuration a significance, according to the situation they happen to be in. To be in the situation (this or any other) is to "see" with the eyes of its interests, its goals, its understood practices, values, and norms, and so to be conferring significance *by* seeing, not after it. The categories of my students' vision are the categories by which they understand themselves to be functioning as students (what Sacks might term "doing studenting"), and objects will appear to them in forms related to that way of functioning rather than in some objective or preinterpretive form. (This is true even when an object is seen as not related, since nonrelation is not a pure but a differential category—the specification of something by enumerating what it is not; in short, nonrelation is merely one form of relation, and its perception is always situation-specific.)

Of course, if someone who was not functioning as a student was to walk into my classroom, he might very well see Mr. Newlin's raised hand (and "raised hand" is already an interpretation-laden description) in some other way, as evidence of a disease, as the salute of a political follower, as a muscle-improving exercise, as an attempt to kill flies; but he would always see it in *some* way, and never as purely physical data waiting for his interpretation. And, moreover, the way of seeing, whatever it was, would never be individual or idiosyncratic, since its source would always be the institutional structure of which the "see-er" was an extending agent. This is what Sacks means when he says that a culture fills brains "so that they are alike in fine detail"; it fills them so that no one's interpretive acts are exclusively his own but fall to him by virtue of his position in some socially organized environment and are therefore always shared and public. It follows, then, that the fear of solipsism, of the imposition by the unconstrained self of its own prejudices, is unfounded because the self does not exist apart from the communal or conventional categories of thought that enable its operations (of thinking, seeing, reading). Once one realizes that the conceptions that fill consciousness, including any conception of its own status, are culturally derived, the very notion of an unconstrained self, of a consciousness wholly and dangerously free, becomes incomprehensible.

But without the notion of the unconstrained self, the arguments of Hirsch, Abrams, and the other proponents of objective interpretation are deprived of their urgency. They are afraid that in the absence of the controls afforded by a normative system of meanings, the self will simply substitute its own meanings for the meanings (usually identified with the intentions of the author) that texts bring with them, the meanings that texts "*have*"; however, if the self is conceived of not as an independent entity but as a social construct whose operations are delimited by the systems of intelligibility that inform it, then the meanings it confers on texts are not its own but have their source in the interpretive community (or communities) of which it is a function. Moreover, these meanings will be neither subjective nor objective, at least in the terms assumed by those who argue within the traditional framework: they will not be objective because they will always have been the product of a point of view rather than having been simply "read off"; and they will not be subjective because that point of view will always be social or institutional. Or by the same reasoning one could say that they are *both* subjective and objective: they are subjective because they inhere in a particular point of view and are therefore not universal; and they are objective because the point of view that delivers them is public and conventional rather than individual or unique.

To put the matter in either way is to see how unhelpful the terms "subjective" and "objective" finally are. Rather than facilitating inquiry, they close it down, by deciding in advance what shape inquiry can possibly take. Specifically, they assume, without being aware that it is an assumption and therefore open to challenge, the very distinction I have been putting into question, the distinction between interpreters and the objects they interpret. That distinction in turn assumes that interpreters and their objects are two different kinds of *a*contextual entities, and within these twin assumptions the issue can only be one of control: will texts be allowed to constrain their own interpretation or will irresponsible interpreters be allowed to obscure and overwhelm texts. In the spectacle that ensues, the spectacle of Anglo-American critical controversy, texts and selves fight it out in the persons of their respective champions, Abrams, Hirsch, Reichert, Graff on the one hand, Holland, Bleich, Slatoff, and (in some characterizations of him) Barthes on the other. But if selves are constituted by the ways of thinking and seeing that inhere in social organizations, and if these constituted selves in turn constitute texts according to these same ways, then there can be no adversary relationship between text and self because they are the necessarily related products of the same cognitive possibilities. A text cannot be overwhelmed by an irresponsible reader and one need not worry about protecting the purity of a text from a reader's idiosyncrasies. It is only the distinction between subject and object that gives rise to these urgencies, and once the distinction is blurred they simply fall away. One can respond with a cheerful yes to the question "Do readers make meanings?" and commit oneself to very little because it would be equally true to say that meanings, in the form of culturally derived interpretive categories, make readers.

Indeed, many things look rather different once the subject-object dichotomy is eliminated as the assumed framework within which critical discussion occurs. Problems disappear, not because they have been solved but because they are shown never to have been problems in the first place. Abrams, for example, wonders how, in the absence of a normative system of stable meanings, two people could ever agree on the interpretation of a work or even of a sentence; but the difficulty is only a difficulty if the two (or more) people are thought of as isolated individuals whose agreement must be compelled by something external to them. (There is something of the police state in Abrams's vision, complete with posted rules and boundaries, watchdogs to enforce them, procedures for identifying their violators as criminals.) But if the understandings of the people in question are informed by the same notions of what counts as a fact, of what is central, peripheral, and worthy of being noticed—in short, by the same interpretive principles—then agreement between them will be assured, and its source will not be a text that enforces its own perception but a way of perceiving that results in the emergence to those who share it (or those whom it shares) of the same text. That text might be a poem, as it was in the case of those who first "saw" "Jacobs-Rosenbaum Levin Hayes Thorne Ohman(?)," or a hand, as it is every day in a thousand classrooms; but whatever it is, the shape and meaning it appears immediately to have will be the "ongoing accomplishment"[2] of those who agree to produce it.

NOTES

1. "On the Analysability of Stories by Children," in *Ethnomethodology*, ed. Roy Turner (Baltimore: Penguin, 1974), p. 218.

2. A phrase used by the ethnomethodologists to characterize the interpretive activities that create and maintain the features of everyday life. See, for example, Don H. Zimmerman, "Fact as a Practical Accomplishment," in *Ethnomethodology*, pp. 128–143.

SECTION 2

Models of Lyric

Focusing on "models of lyric" borrowed from earlier centuries, the essays collected in this section offer exemplary rather than generic approaches; that is to say, they generalize from particular historical examples of poets or poems in order to make broad claims about lyric as it may be found (or found missing) in other literary periods. For some critics, an earlier model may serve as prototype for a transhistorical idea of lyric, or as an imagined origin for a continually self-transforming lyric tradition; for other critics, an earlier model may serve as a contrast case to demonstrate historical differences and discontinuities in ideas about lyric. But on both ends of this critical spectrum, lyric is already assumed to be a generic category that exists across history. Thus, while the previous section of *The Lyric Theory Reader* showed the consolidation of lyric as a genre through twentieth-century genre theory, this section demonstrates how that idea has been projected back into literary history. The essays are arranged chronologically according to the models to which they refer (drawn from classical, medieval, and early modern periods, and extending to the late nineteenth century). Such a chronological arrangement is itself reminiscent of early-twentieth-century studies on the history of lyric, such as *Lyric Poetry* by Ernest Rhys and *The English Lyric* by Felix Schelling, both published in 1913 as surveys of Western poetics that chronicled the evolution or devolution of lyric from one literary period to the next. However, our purpose in juxtaposing different historical models of lyric (just a few among many possible examples) is not to suggest that this story really is the history of lyric but rather to emphasize the continual reinvention of that history by Anglo-American critics for the purposes of modern lyric reading.

We include W. R. Johnson as one example of a critic who (in a longer tradition of literary criticism) looks back to classical antiquity to discover the origins of lyric. In *The Idea of Lyric*, Johnson announces that the theoretical project of his book is to advance an idea of "this genre as immutable and universal" (2), and he refers to classical poets like Sappho and Catullus to define the "typical lyric form" in terms of direct address: "The most usual mode in Greek lyric (probably) and in Latin lyric (certainly) was to address the poem (in Greek, the song) to another person or to other persons" (4). By contrast, the modern lyric (according to Johnson, in a reformulation of Mill) is characterized by the conversion of direct to indirect address, leading to the loss of "the lyric You" and the dissolution of "the lyric I." Johnson is in this sense working in a long tradition of literary criticism that seeks to describe the modern lyric "I" by way of ancient Greek poetry. In that tradition of tracing the modern lyric back to its classical origin, Sappho in particular becomes the site of lyric invention and lyric possibility. As Yopie Prins has argued in *Victorian Sappho*, this idealization of Sappho has a long and varied history, culminating in nineteenth-century personifications of the poetess as an exemplary lyric figure precisely because her song is always already lost. But for Johnson, the late Victorian context for the reception of the Sapphic fragments has become a background assumption: Sappho and classical lyric simply do represent the source for the poetry we recognize in modernity as lyric.

Yet the disappearance (or death) of classical lyric is also the beginning of its afterlife in theory, as Johnson goes on to argue in "On the Absence of Ancient Lyric Theory." He discovers the critical invention of modern lyric in ancient literary criticism, exemplified by Hellenistic scholar-librarians who "lived in a world of books rather than performed poems, in a world where music, had for the most part, separated from poetry and where the occasions for and the function of the old lyric poetry had either disappeared or had been altered beyond recognition." In Johnson's account, Aristophanes of Byzantium (who arranged the poems of Pindar into seventeen books) was a pivotal figure for generating an Alexandrian theory of lyric genre that was further elaborated by Horace, the Latin poet and critic "who was to serve as the essential link in the chain of Western lyrical tradition." According to Johnson, "largely because of the work and genius of Horace, it is this rhetorical theory of lyric poetry that dominates European poetry from the late Middle Ages until very recent times." Into this longer history Johnson projects another essential feature of lyric that can only become explicit (and fully explicated) in modern lyric theory, as he writes: "One thing about the nature of poetry that moderns have steadily recognized and that ancients could not recognize is the significance, the importance, of the inner stories that personal lyric imitates." Assuming the continuity of a longer Western tradition, Johnson's approach to lyric theory is both retrospective (looking back on classical lyric) and prospective (looking ahead to modern lyric); indeed, it is only in the presence of this modern idea that we discover what was always implicit or "absent" in ancient lyric theory.

Moving from classical to medieval models of lyric, we excerpt an article by Seth Lerer, who explores the transition from Old to Middle English poetry, before and after the Norman conquest of England. He revisits a commonplace of twentieth-century criticism, where "to speak of the origins of Middle English lyric is to speak about the idea of the lyric voice itself and, furthermore, about the birth of subjectivity in the vernacular." But Lerer argues that this birth also marks the afterlife of Old English idioms and genres, as he goes on to trace the historical process by which older genres like the poem on the grave are embedded (or entombed) in later Middle English lyrics. He exhumes an elegiac strain in these poems (in a more detailed analysis, not included in the excerpt below) and also in a reading of "The Owl and the Nightingale," as an early Middle English poem in which "we may discern not just the outpouring of a lyric voice but an assessment of the idea of lyricality itself." While emphasizing that "the lyric, as we have been taught to think of it, is foreign to pre-conquest England," Lerer also assumes a normative lyric reading in order to analyze how "the Nightingale, traditionally a figure for the secular, the lyrical, the felt, the emotive, makes a case not just for a particular approach to life or love but for a lyric subjectivity." In his reading, "The Owl and the Nightingale" exemplifies the emergence of "the idea of the lyric voice and of the literary as a function of the speaking subject," albeit in "a placement of the speaking self at moments of decline, nostalgia, or internal exile." From a moment in which the lyric seemed not to exist, Lerer thus moves to the moment at which he claims what we now think of as the modern lyric subject began to emerge.

Yet such moments of modern lyric emergence tend to repeat themselves. Identifying the 1590s as another critical turning point in the history of English poetry, Heather Dubrow's essay surveys the proliferation of "many types of lyric" in order to ask, "Why did the Renaissance lyric develop when and how?" Dubrow argues that definitions and descriptions of the lyric should be historically specific because "the variety lyric manifests even within a single historical period, such as the early modern one, offers further caveats about generalizations." Despite the difficulty of extrapolating a general idea of lyric from early modern miscellanies and hierarchies of genre, (Dubrow notes that "the lyric does not win the lottery" in that revolving wheel of fortune), she does connect the characterization of the poet "with his well-tuned lyre and well-accorded voice" (in Sidney's 1595 "Defence of Poetrie") to the emergence of a lyric mode that can be found in a variety of poetic genres. According to Dubrow, "genre provides the best perspective on the sixteenth-century lyric," glimpsed in various generic classifications including epithalamium, complaint, elegy, hymn, love song, sonnet, and pastoral, the last of these being "a strikingly reflexive genre" that may be understood as "metalyric" insofar as it demonstrates how "the workings of poetry itself are at the core of the lyric mode." Hovering between genre and mode, Dubrow's definition understands later ideas about lyric as already embedded in Renaissance lyric, yet she does note that "One can also assert with confidence that Renaissance lyrics variously qualify and challenge definitions that emphasize an isolated speaker overheard rather than participate in social interactions." For Dubrow, early modern lyric made the modern lyric possible, but remains distinguished by its temporalizing adjective—it was not yet everything we now take a lyric to be.

By contrast, Helen Vendler insists that "lyric, though it may *refer* to the social, remains the genre that directs its mimesis toward the performance of the mind in *solitary* speech," whether that mimesis is in the modern or in the early modern period. For Vendler, the lyric always was what it now is. She begins her commentary on Shakespeare's sonnets with a general introduction that explains and defends her approach to lyric reading as a radically privatized, internalized, and transhistorical activity. Going beyond Mill's formulation, Vendler argues that "the act of the lyric is to offer its reader a script to say," not as if the poem were "overheard" or as if the poet were "speaking to himself," but as an "utterance for us to utter as ours." What is understood to be "as if" by Mill is literalized and dramatized by Vendler in her reading of Shakespeare's sonnets, which she declares "new in Western lyric" and indeed the very model of lyric because the sonnets demonstrate most perfectly how "the lyric gives us the mind alone with itself." As a supplement to critical and scholarly editions of Shakespeare, the pedagogical purpose of Vendler's book is to teach the reader to inhabit the structure of the sonnet stanza (often figured as a room) as a space for private reading, where "lyric can present no 'other' as alive and listening or responding in the same room as the solitary speaker." Writing in the tradition of Anglo-American New Criticism, and especially of her teacher Reuben Brower (further discussed in section 3 of *The Lyric Theory Reader*), Vendler explicates the formal structures and patterns of Shakespeare's sonnets in order to demonstrate "the strategies that create a credible speaker with a complex and imaginative mind (a mind which we take on as our own when stepping into the voice)." On the one hand, Vendler attributes the invention of the speaker to the poet, as she proclaims, "Shakespeare's speaker, alone with his thoughts, is the greatest achievement, imaginatively speaking, of the sequence." On the other hand, the speaker is a critical invention that is predicated on—and according to Vendler, predicted by—a voice that is found in Shakespeare's sonnets as the fulfillment of modern assumptions about reading lyric as a genre. Following this logic of lyric reading, the "mind which we take on as our own" is indeed our own. Thus it may come as no surprise that the original publication of Vendler's book on Shakespeare included a recording of the sonnets recited by Vendler herself, whose greatest achievement, imaginatively speaking, is to produce a reading of the sequence that imagines the convergence of speaker, reader, and author in her own voice. Vendler's radically performative approach to the history of lyric reading makes the lyric always a creature of the present tense, a living vehicle of readerly expectation and experience.

As an influential literary critic in the study of Romanticism in the mid-twentieth century, M. H. Abrams turned to a later moment in literary history to discover the origins of an expressive model of lyric. In "The Lyric as Poetic Norm," Abrams describes how "the lyric form . . . connected by critics to the state of mind of the author" increasingly became a "poetic norm" in the course of the eighteenth century, leading toward its apotheosis in high Romanticism. In part, this literary historical narrative draws on the work of Norman Maclean, who traced shifting theories of the lyric in the eighteenth century by demonstrating how the greater ode (associated with the Longinian sublime and English imitations of the Pindaric Ode) gave way to the increased versification and diversification of the lesser ode (included among "minor" poetic genres like the sonnet, song, epitaph, elegy, and so on). For Maclean and Abrams alike, a more abstract idea of lyric as poetic norm thus emerged through a gradual lyricization of the ode. Abrams further builds on this idea by looking for its origins not only in biblical and classical prototypes for eighteenth-century ideas about lyric, but in the translations and imitations of Sanskrit and Persian poems published by Sir William Jones in 1772. According to Abrams, "Jones employs the lyric not only as the original poetic form, but as the prototype for poetry as a whole, and thereby expands what had occasionally been proposed as the differentia of one poetic species into the defining attribute of the genus." Through the example of Jones, the late-eighteenth-century Orientalist who proclaimed the primitive origins of lyric as expression of the passions, Abrams makes a powerful claim for a reorientation of lyric reading in nineteenth-century England, leading to "its climax in the theory of John Mill." But what Abrams attributes to Jones—namely, the expansion of one poetic species into the defining attribute of the genre—may in fact be definitive for twentieth-century lyric theory, in its progressive expansion of all poetry into an abstract idea of lyric. In the process of historicizing the emergence of the lyric as poetic norm, Abrams assumes the existence of that norm then as well as now.

The modern critical investment in the lyric as poetic norm is evident as well in another essay by Abrams, "Structure and Style in the Greater Romantic Lyric," not reprinted here but worth mentioning because of its influence on twentieth-century ideas about Romantic poetry. Abrams identifies a certain kind of descriptive-meditative Romantic poem that presents "a determinate speaker in a particularized, and usually a localized, outdoor setting, whom we overhear as he carries on, in a fluent vernacular which rises easily to a more formal speech, a sustained colloquy, sometimes with himself or with the outer scene but more frequently with a silent human auditor, present or absent" (76–77). Emerging from various descriptive poetic genres in the seventeenth and eighteenth centuries, this Romantic genre is (according to Abrams) "of great interest because it was the earliest Romantic formal invention, and at once demonstrated the stability of organization and the capacity to engender successors which define a distinct lyric species. New lyric forms are not as plentiful as blackberries, and when one turns up, it is worth critical attention" (79). Here again, a "distinct lyric species" has been expanded into a defining attribute of the genus. What Abrams calls the "greater Romantic Lyric" is not just another lyric form but the very form of lyric that twentieth-century readers have retrospectively identified with Romanticism, as a critical turning point from "the greater ode" celebrated by neoclassical criticism to the expressive lyric celebrated by modern criticism.

The greater Romantic lyric canonized by Abrams looks somewhat different, however, from the perspective of the Victorian dramatic monologue, as Herbert Tucker argues in "Dramatic Monologue and the Overhearing of Lyric." In a canny rereading of Mill, Tucker suggests that Mill's lyricism was "overheard" in the sense of being "heard too much" and "overdone" by poets like Browning and Tennyson, whose invention of the dramatic monologue played out "a *reductio ad absurdum* of the very lyric premises staked out in Mill's essays." The dramatic monologue is a hybrid genre constituted by "narrative" and "lyrical" elements, according to Tucker, and best understood as a further elaboration of the greater Romantic lyric that "may help us save it from assimilation to orthodox lyricism by reminding us that the genre Abrams called 'greater' was not more-lyrical-than-lyric but rather more-than-lyrical." Demonstrating in delicate detail how to read between the lines of poems like "My Last Duchess" and "Fra Lippo Lippi," Tucker argues that the orthodoxies of modern lyric reading (the critical fiction of a speaker, the assumption of a voice, the intersubjective confirmation of a self) were both anticipated and disrupted by the dramatic monologue. It is an ironic twist that the dramatic monologue, seemingly resistant to lyric, became the abstract paradigm for reading lyric in the twentieth century. Or perhaps not ironic but overdetermined, since Tucker's argument depends on the opposition between dramatic monologue and an undifferentiated lyric terrain: "Lyric, in dramatic monologue, is what you cannot have and what you cannot forget." This binary is part of a revisionist history of poetry astutely described by Tucker himself as "a lyrically normed historiography," when nostalgia for lyric among fin-de-siècle purists produced a "generic backformation . . . from the dramatic monologue and related nineteenth-century forms": the purification of lyric from a hybrid to a singular form.

Of course this nostalgia for lyric at the end of the nineteenth century is, from the historical and theoretical perspective of *The Lyric Theory Reader*, also the invention of lyric. Like the other critics presented in this section, Tucker projects a modern problem back into an earlier moment in literary history. Where to locate the origin of lyric is a recurring question, the answer to which keeps shifting according to the scholarly preference and historical expertise of each critic. Does lyric originate in antiquity or in modernity, in primitive or advanced cultures, as a function of classical or medieval or early modern or neoclassical or romantic or Victorian or modernist aesthetics? It is possible to find many historical models for lyric reading, each time with different historical implications for the study of lyric; at the same time, it remains impossible to claim a definitive history of lyric, precisely because its origins keep changing.

FURTHER READING

Abrams, M. H. "Structure and Style in the Greater Romantic Lyric," in *The Correspondent Breeze: Essays in British Romanticism*. New York: W. W. Norton, 1984.

Albright, Daniel. *Lyricality in English Literature*. Lincoln: University of Nebraska Press, 1985.

Biester, James. *Lyric Wonder: Rhetoric and Wit in Renaissance English Poetry*. Ithaca, NY: Cornell University Press, 1997.

Brower, Reuben, ed. *Forms of Lyric: Selected Papers from the English Institute*. New York: Columbia University Press, 1970.

Clausen, Christopher. *The Place of Poetry: Two Centuries of an Art in Crisis*. Lexington: University Press of Kentucky, 1981.

Cohen, J. M. *The Baroque Lyric*. London: Hutchinson, 1963.

Dronke, Peter. *The Medieval Lyric*. London: Hutchinson, 1968. 3rd ed., London: Boydell and Brewer, 1996.

Dubrow, Heather. *The Challenges of Orpheus: Lyric Poetry and Early Modern England*. Baltimore, MD: Johns Hopkins University Press, 2008.

Duff, David. *Romanticism and the Uses of Genre*. Oxford: Oxford University Press, 2009.

Fineman, Joel. *Shakespeare's Perjured Eye: The Invention of Poetic Subjectivity in the Sonnets*. Berkeley: University of California Press, 1986.

Fry, Paul H. *The Poet's Calling in the English Ode*. New Haven, CT: Yale University Press, 1980.

Greene, Roland. *Post-Petrarchism: Origins and Innovations of the Western Lyric Sequence.* Princeton, NJ: Princeton University Press, 1991.

Greene, Thomas M. *The Light in Troy: Imitation and Discovery in Renaissance Poetry.* New Haven, CT: Yale University Press, 1982.

Hardy, Barbara. *The Advantage of Lyric: Essays on Feeling in Poetry.* Bloomington: Indiana University Press, 1977.

Harman, William, ed. *Classic Writings on Poetry.* New York: Columbia University Press, 2003.

Huot, Sylvia. *From Song to Book: The Poetics of Writing in Old French Lyric and Lyrical Narrative Poetry.* Ithaca, NY: Cornell University Press, 1987.

Langbaum, Robert. *The Poetry of Experience: The Dramatic Monologue in Modern Literary Tradition.* Chicago: University of Chicago Press, 1986.

Levinson, Marjorie. *Keats's Life of Allegory: The Origins of a Style.* Oxford: Blackwell, 1988.

———. *The Romantic Fragment Poem: A Critique of a Form.* Chapel Hill: University of North Carolina Press, 1986.

Lowrie, Michele. *Horace's Narrative Odes.* Oxford: Clarendon Press, 1997.

Maclean, Norman. "From Action to Image: Theories of the Lyric in the Eighteenth Century." In *Critics and Criticism: Ancient and Modern*, edited by R. S. Crane, 408–60. Chicago: University of Chicago Press, 1955.

Prins, Yopie. *Victorian Sappho.* Princeton, NJ: Princeton University Press, 1999.

Rader, Ralph. "The Dramatic Monologue and Related Lyric Forms." *Critical Inquiry* 3 (1976): 131–51.

Rowlinson, Matthew. "Lyric." In *A Companion to Victorian Poetry*, edited by R. Cronin, A. Chapman, H. A. Harrison, 59–79. Malden, MA: Blackwell, 2002.

Scodel, Joshua. "Lyric Forms." In *The Cambridge Companion to English Literature 1650–1740*, edited by Steven N. Zwicker, 148–52. Cambridge: Cambridge University Press, 1998.

Siskin, Clifford. *The Historicity of Romantic Discourse.* London: Oxford University Press, 1988.

Thain, Marion, ed. *The Lyric Poem: Formation of a Genre.* Cambridge: Cambridge University Press, forthcoming.

Vendler, Helen. *Invisible Listeners: Lyric Intimacy in Herbert, Whitman and Ashbery.* Princeton, NJ: Princeton University Press, 2007.

———. *The Odes of John Keats.* Cambridge, MA: Harvard University Press, 1985.

Walker, Jeffrey. *Rhetoric and Poetics in Antiquity.* Oxford: Oxford University Press, 2000.

Welsh, Andrew. *Roots of Lyric: Primitive Poetry and Modern Poetics.* Princeton, NJ: Princeton University Press, 1972.

On the Absence of Ancient Lyric Theory (1982)

2.1

W. R. Johnson

> Cicero said that even if his lifetime were to be doubled he would still not have time to waste on reading the lyric poets . . . .
>
> Seneca, *Epistles* 49.5

Though exacerbated by the new vogue for Alexandrian frivolity that contributed its share to the irritations of his declining years, Cicero's judgment is not unrepresentative of the received, established position toward lyric in the ancient world after the decline of the Greek city-state. Some of this hostile indifference to lyric we may ascribe to the misease with emotion that is common to schoolmasters, politicians, and military men in any age, to their vague anxiety that the young, and even the middle-aged and the elderly, may somewhere be ignoring their duties or even be having fun. But more crucial to this contempt for lyric poetry is the fact that the kind of lyrical poetry we have just examined was not composed and performed with any real vigor or success after the collapse of the civilization of classical Greece. Even the surviving memorials to that poetry, having been increasingly replaced by epic, drama, oratory, and popular philosophy in the schools,[1] became the private preserve of literary scholars and of connoisseurs of poetry; and because of their difficulties and what seemed their obscurities, the old lyrics were misunderstood, ignored, and finally all but abandoned by the common reader, who is, after all, the final arbiter of what literature lives and does not live. Hymns and victory songs, of course, continued to be esteemed for their legends of law and order and for their unequivocal moral utterance and were therefore sharply distinguished from the immoral, amoral poems that Cicero had consciously in mind when he dismissed lyric poetry from the attention of serious grownups. But even this moral, acceptable variety of lyric suffered a general neglect, for the moral functions it performed had been taken over by epic and by tragedy, high comedy, history, and oratory. As we shall see in the next chapter, the living lyric of this period did not deeply engage the serious attention of most ancient readers,[2] and even the frequent and amazing *tours de force* of Horace could not quite invest lyric poetry at Rome with anything like the dignity and the popularity it had enjoyed in Greece for well over two centuries.

If we take into consideration these attitudes to lyric poetry and keep in mind that by the time attempts to theorize about the nature of lyric began its composition and performance had all but ceased, we shall not be surprised when we discover how relatively unimpressive ancient theories of this most protean and complex literary genre seem to have been.[3] The ancients' efforts to grapple with the ideas of epic, tragedy, history, and oratory were as persistent as they were, in various ways at various times, successful; but lyric was curiously unsuited to the major categories of ancient literary theory. Ancient classical Greek lyric was, as we have seen, essentially concerned with worlds that were at once inner and shared, with the ceremonies and the habits of feeling of small, closed communities; it was musical and performed; and it transcended the morality of classical humanism as it transcended reason, logic, and rhetoric. The theorists of lyric lived in worlds where the social patterns that shaped and sustained Greek lyric were dying or dead, where the convictions about human nature and human destiny were radically different from the convictions that had informed Greek lyric and the communities that it had educated, solaced, and entertained. In ancient lyric theory, the dominant critical categories center on ideas of imitating the visible, outer world; on a rhetoric devoted to analyzing the structure and the effects of the spoken, as against the sung, word; on the strict moral functions of poetry (literature as the handmaiden, not the mother, of philosophy and politics); and on the autonomy both of artistic creation and of the enjoyment of art—at Alexandria and later at Rome the concept of art for art's sake naturally flourished in cosmopolitan societies which were too large and too complex to allow much scope for the older lyric poetry and its profound, eccentric commitment to *communitas*.[4]

I am not, of course, suggesting that ancient critics of lyric did not know far more facts about ancient lyric than its modern students, but it is clear that they interpreted the old lyrics and the idea of lyric according to their own critical categories and their own patterns of aesthetic enjoyment and that in so doing they tended to misinterpret the function and the nature of a kind of poetry that was essentially alien to their interests, their expectations, and their experience. This is, of course, a perennial, inescapable, necessary problem in literary criticism, but if we consider that ancient literary critics were less prone to err in theorizing about other major literary genres than they were when handling lyric, we may perhaps gain a better sense both of the peculiarities of Greek lyric poetry and the difficulties of lyric theory in general.

> There is one kind of poetry and fable which entirely consists of imitation: this is tragedy and comedy, and there's another kind consisting of the poet's own report—you find this particularly in dithyrambs; while the mixture of the two exists in epic and in many other places. . . . (*Republic* 3.394B–C)

> What shall we do then? Shall we admit all these patterns into the city, or one or the other unmixed, or the mixed one? If my vote is to prevail, the imitator of the good, unmixed. (*Republic* 3.397D)

In the passage quoted here from his attack on mimesis in general and the epic and tragedy in particular, Plato seems to be stating his approval of lyric poetry, but we quickly see that the only kind of lyric poetry he deigns to sanction is the most ancient, the most conservative, and the least lyrical form of lyric poetry: the other, later and richer, forms are utterly ignored as if they did not exist; and indeed in Plato's city of the soul they do not and must not. For Plato, as for Aristotle, the object of poetic mimesis is the human being and his behavior,[5] and if there must be mimesis in the city of the soul, it can only be an imitation of "the brave, the self-controlled, the righteous, the free" (3.395C) that promotes the growth toward goodness that is the goal of Platonic man. Pure imitation (tragedy and comedy, where the poet disappears into his creatures and thus apes them freely and irresponsibly) and mixed imitation (epic, where the poet mingles direct narrative with pure imitation) are inevitably drawn to imitate men and even gods in their passions, their weakness, and their degradation; and the result of such imitation—consider Emma Bovary leafing ruthlessly through her penny dreadful—is spiritual ruin, in which the illusory fruit of such imitation becomes the evil reality. The seductive power of such artifice first instills a desire for the illusions it imitates, then convinces that the intense, disgraceful illusions and passions are the only realities, that they alone are proper models for our lives. Only the poet who does not need to hide behind his personae because he has nothing to hide, who can tell his story straight because his story is straight[6] (*haple diegesis*—"pure, direct, simple narration") may be permitted to remain within the walls of the soul's city because only he is a good man imitating (or rather, pointing to) the good.

In his usual manner, Plato has taken a fundamental concept of Greek civilization—here, the concept of mimesis, the belief that reality can be understood by being re-created and reordered through metaphors, through imagination, by being sculpted, drawn, danced—and radically redefined it. For Plato the object of poetic mimesis is no longer humans and their behavior. And the agent of poetic mimesis is no longer any poet, whatever the mode of his narration, whatever his persona as a storyteller; it is always and only the good man telling his story about goodness candidly, without artifice:

> So when you find admirers of Homer saying that he educated Greece and that for human management and education one ought to take him up and learn his lesson and direct one's whole life on his principles, you must be kind and polite to them—they are as good as they are able to be—and concede that Homer is foremost and the most poetical of the tragic poets; but you must be clear in your mind that the only poetry admissible in our city is hymns to the gods and encomia to good men. If you accept the "sweetened Muse" in lyric or epic, pleasure and pain will be enthroned in your city instead of law and the principle which the community accepts in any given situation. (*Republic* 10.607A)

In this closing attack on "bad" mimesis and irresponsible, destructive poetry, the kinds of lyric poetry that Plato had carefully ignored in his earlier argument are banished from the city along with epic (tragedy and comedy have long since been bundled off); it is Pindar[7] and his holy predecessors who remain to foster the imitation that instills righteousness and prepares the soul for the journey into goodness and the really real.

This is not the place to argue the wisdom or folly of Plato's moral and ontological aesthetics. For our present purposes, it is enough to point out that in the course of his argument Plato succeeds in establishing the classic triad of genres (lyric, epic, and drama) that continues, even today, to exert a strong influence on generic theory and that he distinguishes among these genres by examining them in terms of their characteristic agents of mimesis. If he ignores Sappho, Anacreon, and Simonides in this discussion, it is perhaps because narrative lyric provides him with the clearest foil to the drama and the epic that he is anxious to reject; but it is also possible that neither he nor his audience would think of the various kinds of personal lyric as vehicles of stories. In any case, it is certain that whatever it was that Plato may have thought Sappho and Anacreon to be imitating, both the objects and the agents of this imitation could do the city of the soul no possible good and could do it endless harm. Such dismissal of this considerable portion of lyric poetry does not advance investigation of the idea of lyric very far, but in raising these issues about the nature of lyric in order to conduct his ethical debate, Plato nevertheless fastened on problems that are central to any discussion of lyric genre: the primacy of the object and the agent of mimesis, of story and of lyric voice, in discussions of lyric as a genre.

This Platonic formulation of generic distinctions in poetry is recalled and, of course, reformulated by Aristotle at the opening of his *Poetics*:

> Epic and tragic poetry, comedy and dithyrambic, and most music for the flute or lyre are all, generally considered, varieties of mimesis, differing from each other in three respects, the media, the objects, and the mode of mimesis. (1447a)

In addition to agent (mode) of mimesis, Aristotle also posits medium of mimesis (rhythm, harmony, verse) and object of mimesis (people performing actions: people as they are in life, or better or worse than they are in life) as elements to be considered when we are attempting to distinguish among genres, but he gives agent or mode of mimesis pride of place in his listing of generic differentiae, and much of what he goes on to say about Homer and tragedy turns on this final element:

> There is still a third difference, the mode in which one presents each of these objects. For one can represent the same objects in the same media
>
> 1. sometimes in narration and sometimes becoming someone else, as Homer does, or
> 2. speaking in one's own person without change, or
> 3. with all the people engaged in the mimesis actually doing things. (1448a)

At first glance, it might appear that Aristotle has done nothing more than rephrase Plato's description of the agents of mimesis and their particular genres (mixed agency, epic; pure narrative, lyric; pure imitation, drama), but Aristotle, for all his passion for both Homer and tragedy, at first seems to play no favorites with one of the three possible agents of mimesis: all are equally necessary, all are equally valid—in theory. In practice, Aristotle's bias in favor of drama requires that he prefer the mode of pure imitation of drama (not incorrectly, Aristotle recognizes Homer as a forerunner of dramatic sensibility and technique, and it is the dramatic Homer that he reveres). In drama the biologist discovers a concentration of plot and action, a unity, a tidiness, and an immanent intelligibility that neither pure nor mixed narrative can achieve. After his balanced and objective analysis and description of possible narrative agents, he tacitly opts for the supremacy of the narrative mode that Plato had specifically condemned, the pure imitation of drama, partly because it was natural to him (and perhaps fun for him) to disagree with Plato and partly because the controlled dynamism and the concrete lucidity of drama were as welcome to him as narrative sweep (when untempered by Homeric drama) was alien to him.

But why is lyric not even in the running here?[8] It is possible, of course, that in lost portions of the *Poetics* Aristotle did examine lyric in some detail and gave to it the appreciation that he lavishes on tragedy and grudgingly allows to epic. But when the superiority of tragedy over epic has been so elaborately and so cunningly demonstrated (1461a–1462b), it is unlikely that lyric could have garnered anything but the crumbs of his praise. Although it is idle to speculate about the reasons for Aristotle's prejudices here, it may yet be worthwhile to indulge in such speculation because what I take to be the possible prejudices of Aristotle against lyric suggest the real prejudices of later ancient literary critics who were inevitably influenced in some degree by his formulations and who also show only the faintest interest in the theory of lyric. What follows then, is sheer fiction, but I hope it may be useful fiction. First, as against Plato, Aristotle believes that mimesis is a way of learning about truth (1448b) and that poetry is a form of knowledge (1451b); therefore, though Aristotle is wholly lacking in Plato's rage for perfection and is everywhere charitable to natural aberrations from the ideal in space and time, he has his own hierarchies of moral grandeur, and it is not likely that Sappho, let alone Anacreon, would stand any chance against Homer or Sophocles in Aristotle's ordering of degrees of poetic truth. In his own way, Aristotle is as much a proponent of moral aesthetics as Plato, which is not strange because all ancient literary critics were, and wisely so, essentially moral in their aesthetic orientations.

Second, just as Aristotle may have found Sappho's "He is a god in my eyes" either frivolous or immoral or purely artistic (and therefore relatively deficient in valid general truth), so he may very well have failed to see that Sappho is in fact engaged in telling a story (in a lyric manner) whose plot and action (*muthos-praxis*—"story-action") are, in their own way, for all their brevity, as valid, as significant, as true as the story of Achilles and Hector and the story of Oedipus. In other words, judged by the categories of Aristotle's criticism, the object of Sappho's mimesis may seem, in comparison with Homer and Sophocles, so fragile as to appear almost insignificant. (It may also seem lacking in amplitude [1450b–1451b]: after Callimachus' defense of brevity, it will not be until the romantics in general and Edgar Allan Poe in particular that champions of the short personal lyric will dare, without qualification, to assert its superiority over epic and drama and "short" will become not only beautiful but also the only beautiful.)

One thing about the nature of poetry that moderns have steadily recognized and that ancients could not recognize is the significance, the importance, of the inner stories that personal lyric imitates. Aristotle, perhaps, did not see that Sappho also is imitating a human action, or he thought that the action she imitated (whether her own or that of an imagined person—"When I state myself," said Dickinson, "as the Representative of the Verse—it does not mean—me—but a supposed person")[9] was too insignificant, too "merely personal," to be the vehicle of the *anagnorisis* ("recognition") and the *peripeteia* ("sudden change in fortune") that make manifest *hoia an genoito* ("what may be")—such things as may possibly occur any place, any time. But "He is a god in my eyes," fragile and ephemeral as the action it imitates might seem, catches and holds the light of things as they are, everywhere, always, as surely as does the *Iliad* or the *Antigone*. It differs from an epic or a tragedy in its dimensions and range; but it needs offer no apologies for its intensity or its profundity or its own moral grandeur. Aristotle's passion for order led him, it seems, to prefer the concentration of drama to the (to him) uncontrolled sprawl of epic; but, so far as one can judge, his earnestness precluded his appreciating both the earnestness and the concentration of personal lyric. It would not be until the romantics taught us that any inner story, precisely imitated (imagined), can reveal general truth that the real seriousness of lyric could be seen and understood. These hindrances to lyrical theory—exaggerated and misdirected emphasis on the morality of art and inability to grasp and appreciate the kinds of stories, that is, emotional actions, that lyric has to tell—exert their force throughout antiquity. They are both serious hindrances, but the more serious is the ancients' inability to make proper use of their favorite and precise aesthetic concept, mimesis, in their efforts to investigate the genre of lyric.

After Aristotle, the Alexandrian critics worked hard and well to define the forms and subgenres of lyric poetry, and this effort implies a theory of lyric that has not, unfortunately, come down to us. The beginnings of serious literary scholarship in Athens of the late fourth century B.C. might easily have been aborted or have dwindled into fruitless word games had the structure and dynamics of Alexander's empire not caused its diffusion throughout the new Greek world of the third century B.C. But it was at Alexandria, with the founding of the museum and its library, that the study of literature in the West came to its first flowering, for in gathering literary texts and scholars to edit and order them, the Ptolemies both assured the survival of the literature of classical Greece and promoted an atmosphere in which the work of sorting out and interpreting that literature could be vigorously and profitably pursued. To suppose, as it has sometimes been, that this endless chore of collecting manuscripts, sorting them, correcting them, cataloguing them, and arranging them was somehow dull and simple-minded is to fail in performing the act of historical imagination. Imagine all of English literature from Chaucer to Tennyson, long circulated in manuscripts indifferent and bad, suddenly dumped helter-skelter in your lap. The task that confronted the Alexandrian scholar-librarians was herculean, and they performed it for the benefit of all posterity magnificently, their imagination and ingenuity as ruthlessly tested as their erudition and industry.

None of the sorting and editing can have been easy, but lyric presented special problems. In its linguistic variety, its antiquity, its metrical difficulties, and its bewildering profusion of similar, sometimes nearly identical subgenres, lyric poetry required all the talent and all the tools of scholarship and criticism that the museum had been able to assemble. The immediate practical result of the long and arduous labor of editing Greek lyric of the archaic and classical ages was the survival of this poetry (much of it down through the life of Byzantium) in accurate and readable editions, but what matters here is that in performing this labor, the scholar-critics of Alexandria were forced to shape theoretical categories that remain invaluable to the study and enjoyment of lyric poetry. With Aristophanes of Byzantium we encounter the first serious and successful theorist of lyric genre in Western literature, for it is he, who, confronted with the jungle of the Pindaric corpus, invented the strategem of sorting them, not only on the basis of their musical modes or metrical schemes but also on the basis of their themes and concerns.[10]

Aristophanes arranged the Pindaric corpus into seventeen books: hymns and paeans in one book each; dithyrambs, processionals, maiden songs, and poems for dancing in two books each (with perhaps an added book for purely secular maiden songs); four books of victory songs; and a book each of encomia and threnoi.[11] It is not a question here of Aristophanes's having invented these terms and the categories they denote since at least some of them go all the way hack to Homer and most likely precede him.[12] What Aristophanes did, what he had to do in order to make adequate use of these old, vague categories, was to study their formal properties, the meters, the topoi and rhetorical stratagems, the formulae and themes that were characteristic of them; on the basis of this study he was prepared to formulate descriptive definitions of the categories that were superior both in precision and in flexibility to the traditional, uncertain definitions that he had inherited; and on the basis of his improved definitions he was able to assign the jumble of poems he had confronted to their proper categories.

Beyond his immediate purpose—the ordering of chaotic bodies of poetry, the making of intelligible, enjoyable collections—the method he devised and refined had and continues to have major importance for the theory and practice of the lyric genre. The idea behind Aristophanes's method (this is a modern inference for which we have no hard evidence) is the idea of decorum, and the method itself is the analysis of particular instances of decorum. The kinds of questions he seems to have asked himself, both in devising and refining the method itself and in applying it to the actual sorting of poems into their proper categories, would seem to have been something like this. What are the essential elements in a paean? What is the natural (or conventional) order of these elements? What metrical or rhetorical patterns tend to appear in the paean? What instruments accompanied it and what were the conditions of its performance? What elements can possibly be omitted from a paean without its ceasing to be a paean, and what elements cannot under any circumstances be neglected or altered? How does a paean differ from a dithyramb or a hymn?

The concept of decorum, its uses and its limitations, is so familiar as to seem to us perhaps obvious, if not simple-minded. But to ignore the realities of decorum in the study of literature is usually to invite confusion and error. In concentrating on the contents of lyric poems and the surfaces of their content, in systematically collecting and synthesizing his observations on the conventional and formal appearance of lyric poems, Aristophanes made it possible for later critics and common readers to see the substance of the poems through their surfaces ("It is only shallow people," remarked Wilde, "who do not judge by appearances"). Once it became habitual for critics and readers to look for and recognize the conventional features in a poem that would tell them what kind of poem it was (and the looking for and the recognizing quickly become almost automatic and largely unconscious), it became easier to understand and to enjoy the special artistry and the special sensibility—the originality—of its poet. What are the usual, what are the suitable, things to say in a love poem? What sort of person is the proper person to say these things? Once a spectrum of conventions has been established and the reader's expectations have been properly defined, it is then possible to notice how a particular poet distorts conventions even as he makes use of them, defeats expectations even as he satisfies them. Guided by an understanding of decorum (what is proper for a given kind of poem), we can respond accurately to wide varieties of feeling, to a given poet's new, unfamiliar attitudes toward his material—life, his chosen form, the conventions that obtain in that form. We can, in other words, hear precisely the distinctive voice of a particular poet because we hear it against, magnified by, the standard patterns that he uses and transforms. But until that standard pattern is isolated and defined, the artifice and the integrity of the poet's voice in a given poem will not be available to the reader.

It goes without saying that Sappho's audience did not consciously consider what species of poem they were listening to when they watched and heard her perform it—because they did not need to. When conventions are living, when both poets and their listeners respond to poetic conventions they have grown up with as naturally as they breathe air or drink water, there is of course no need for critics to distinguish among kinds of poems and to list the characteristic formal elements of different species of lyric.[13] In general, it is only when artistic conventions are dead or dying or when they have been so transformed as to be unrecognizable that critics want or are required to attempt to recover them, to distinguish them, stabilize them, arrange them. There was, for example, very little effort to describe and codify the formal conventions of modernist poetry until it began to be vaguely sensed that the great modernist poets had all disappeared and that the music of their epigones sounded not quite right; while the great modernists were writing, though there was plenty of propaganda, controversy, and explications, there was not and could not be much in the way of formal analysis. The living contemporaries of the great modernists did not need to be instructed in conventions that they lived in and shared with their poets—they needed only to read the poetry, experience and enjoy it. We who live when modernism is exhausted can only experience and enjoy its poetry by trying to understand it, and to do this, we need all the help we can get from critics who can recover and describe its formal conventions, its special hybrid genres, and the sensibilities that created them.

Aristophanes of Byzantium and the readers he helped lived in a world of books rather than of performed poems, in a world where music had become, for the most part, separated from poetry and where the occasions for and the function of the old lyric poetry had either disappeared or had been altered beyond recognition. Thus, as the circumstances in which old lyric poetry was experienced changed, as its conventions became unintelligible or blurred through the passage of time and the hybridization of genres and subgenres, the services of Aristophanes and his successors became indispensable to ancient readers, who, without these scholar-critics, would have had neither adequate texts nor notions of literary convention and generic forms that were and are necessary for enjoyable reading of these poems. But it was not merely readers of the postclassical age who were indebted to the Alexandrian critics. All lyric poets in the classical tradition of Europe, whether they are directly or indirectly in that tradition, whether they are consciously or unconsciously influenced by it, depend on Aristophanes and his school for their understanding of the possibilities of lyric poetry, of its various kinds, and of the various voices and combinations of voices that are suitable to its various kinds. It goes without saying that good lyricists could grasp the generic forms and the voices they need by direct imitation of their predecessors, by the intuitions proper to their talents, without the help of critics. But the fact is that they seldom do this, that they "find their own voices," their particular attitudes toward their materials and their artistry within the tradition of lyrical categories that critics (many of whom are poets) redefine after each of the poetry's major renewals.[14] What Aristophanes found and sanctioned—it was not exactly what he intended to find and the way I define his discovery is not the way he would have defined it—was the range of voices, styles, and attitudes that are appropriate to the varieties of lyric poetry; and he found this spectrum of lyric voices by studying the outward forms of classical lyric poems.

It was the poet-critic who was to serve as the essential link in the chain of Western lyrical tradition who saw and acknowledged the prime importance of this Alexandrian theory of lyric genre. In discussing the importance of metrical decorum and metrical tradition, Horace turns from epic, elegiacs, and iambics to lyric poetry and remarks:

> To praise the gods and the children of gods,
> to honor the triumphant boxer,
> to tell of young lovers and their sufferings,
> to commend the solace of wine—
> these offices the Muse conferred upon the lyre.
> If I am unable or unwilling

to preserve the distinctive patterns,
the special shades of the several genres,
why should I expect to be hailed as poet? (*Art of Poetry*, lines 83–88)

Though "the distinctive patterns" and "special shades"[15] refer to epic and the other genres mentioned before lyric, it is possible that Horace discusses lyric last not only because it has become his own special preserve and the source of his greatest pride but also because the "shifts and shades" of lyric poetry needed far more care in their analysis than the other, larger and simpler genres.[16] In its metrical variety, in its subtle differences in content, function and form, and, above all, in its varieties and combinations of voices, the practice as well as the theory of lyric poetry had benefited and would continue to benefit from Aristophanes's analysis of lyric content, from his emphasis on the crucial importance of lyric categories.

The successors of Aristophanes continued to be engaged in refining the lyrical categories that he established, but so far as we can tell from the meagre and often obscure information that has survived, their interest in these categories and their manner of dealing with them gradually shifted direction and focus. If the résumé of Proclus's work on lyric by the Byzantine Photius can be trusted,[17] it would seem that some time soon after the beginning of the Christian era, lyrical theory has completely abandoned (or taken as resolved) the question of the essential nature of lyric, has come to treat the musical nature of ancient Greek lyric as something approaching antiquarian curiosity, and has begun to busy itself primarily with rhetorical analysis of lyric and with definition of the purely secular, purely literary varieties of poetry that had replaced ancient lyric in Hellenistic literature. Given the overwhelming importance of rhetoric in education (throughout this period and until the end of antiquity), combined with the failure of music in poetry, this change—one is tempted to say, this trivialization—of emphasis is natural enough, indeed, is all but inevitable, but it betokens not only the death of ancient lyric but also, incredibly, a lack of any awareness that lyric had died. As we shall see in the next chapter, the lyric spirit had, of course, survived, had emigrated into and hidden itself in other kinds of poetry, but Greek lyric, this musical, ontological, social, performed poetry, had vanished as a living art.

Proclus, apparently, divided lyric poetry into four major categories: (1) lyrics addressed to the gods, (2) lyrics addressed to men, (3) lyrics addressed to both gods and men (a confusing, uncertain category), and (4) verse for occasions (*prospiptousai peristaseis*). Proclus himself protested that this final category should not properly be classed with the others, which are traditional.[18] That he finally and grudgingly does admit this category is an index to its extreme popularity in late Hellenistic times, and to the fact that this occasional verse had almost completely replaced the older lyric forms.[19] Religious poetry continued to be written (and the old religious poetry continued to be performed) for cults and festivals; and royal personages and wealthy men continued to commission celebrations of themselves, but the remnants of this poetry show why it perished rapidly. Love songs, dirges, victory celebrations, semiphilosophical drinking songs, marriage songs, the poems that comprise Proclus's second category, tend to find themselves transformed into elegiac epigram. Since there was in fact little real, or at least little good, lyric poetry during the centuries in which Proclus's sources were theorizing, it is no wonder that the lyric categories were expanded (padded out) to include prosaic doodling in metrical disguise that concerns itself with impressions of travelers, advice to friends in epistolary form, suggestions about farming, musings on Life , and reflections on destiny—Polonius poetasting.

But why did Polonius take to writing verse? How did he learn to do it? And why did he think anyone would be interested if he attempted to subject his earnest ponderings to the discipline of verse?—because he had been to school and there learned to read poetry rhetorically, as had the readers he wrote for. Reading poetry for its rhetoric and for its moral platitudes was, of course, no worse than reading it for its ironies and ambiguities or for its criticism of life or for any other modern reductive function of poetry we might recall here—indeed, to read poetry for its rhetoric is hardly the worst way to read poetry. Nor was much harm done by the little rhetoricians who grew up to be soldiers, businessmen, teachers, and government officials and who scribbled verselets in their spare time on subjects dear to their hearts—money, connections, prospects, status. The harm was—well, but there was no harm. These poets and their readers were apparently content with this versifying, and the lyric spirit, while waiting its reincarnations into Horace, into Latin and Greek Christian hymns, and into the songs of Provence and Sicily, masqueraded as epic, as epigram, as pastoral. It is a world of rhetoricians, professional and amateur, active and passive, that unites to produce the categories of Proclus, in which occasional verse, prosaic thoughts woven into mechanical verse and mechanical rhetoric, hobnobs with Pindaric *epinicia* ("victory songs") and Sapphic *erotica* ("love songs"). A strange poetic world—emptied of the lyric spirit, filled with busy poets with their dull, correct rhythms, their rhetorical commonplaces and their commonplace notions—a million miles from the passions and paradoxes of great lyric poetry; yet if it is boring, it is civilized, and if it is safe, complacent, tidy, it is not wholly unattractive. There are worse poetic worlds than this.

Nor, moreover, were its virtues merely negative or neutral. Schoolmasters and the students who were obsessed with rhetoric and occasional verse perfected the discipline of poetic rhetoric that in the hands of Horace, Joachim du Bellay, and Ben Jonson would kindle into incomparable glories. Francis Cairns has reminded us, indeed has retaught us, that each of the varieties of lyric (he calls them genres)

> can be thought of as having a set of primary or logically necessary elements which in combination distinguish that genre from every other genre. For example, the primary elements of the propemtikon are in these terms someone departing, another person bidding him farewell, and a relationship of affection between the two, plus an appropriate setting. . . . As well as containing the primary elements of its genre every generic example contains some secondary elements (topoi). These topoi are the smallest divisions of the material of any genre useful for analytical purposes. Their usefulness lies in the fact that they are the commonplaces which recur in different forms in different examples of the same genre. They help, in combination with the primary elements, to identify a generic example. But the primary elements are the only final arbiters of generic identity since any particular individual topos (secondary element) can be found in several different genres.[20]

The poet who inherited and submitted himself to the strict yet flexible system of these primary and secondary elements was possessed of an enormous poetic freedom, the freedom to use and to alter the system that he preserved. Poetic rhetoric, at least by the beginning of the Christian era, was the common, living poetic language just as oratorical rhetoric was the common language of history and moral philosophy as well as of the forum and the courtroom.

In a very real sense, it was his reader's mastery of poetic rhetoric that assured the poet his complete poetic freedom. And if the modern reader shudders as he glances through Cairns's invaluable discussion of this poetic rhetoric, if he pities the ancients who troubled themselves with the endless, ugly jargon that denotes varieties of lyric poems and who learned by heart the lists of decorous clichés (topoi) that structured these lyric poems—*tant pis pour lui* ("that is his problem")—and the problem of the contemporary poets he reads. The lyrical theorists of later and late antiquity completed the work begun by Aristophanes of Byzantium by systematically subdividing the varieties of lyric, by rigorously defining the elements of lyrical poetry, and by collecting, distinguishing, sorting out the commonplaces and the combinations of commonplaces that are typical of particular kinds of lyric poems.[21] Much of the poetry that grew out of and depended on this theory of lyrical poetry was evidently (and, naturally) not very good, but largely because of the work and genius of Horace, it is this rhetorical theory of lyric poetry that dominates European poetry from the late Middle Ages until very recent times, and it is this rhetorical tradition that is largely responsible for Petrarch's, Herbert's, Goethe's, and Valéry's having been able to do with lyric poetry what they could do with it. In this sense, the patient labors of Aristophanes and his followers were and remain crucial to lyric and the idea of lyric.

Not the least surprising thing about lyric theory in antiquity is that one of the greatest lyricists, himself a literary theorist of the first rank, did not bother to theorize formally about the idea of lyric. Horace's theory of lyric is implicit, of course, in his lyric composition, that careful, systematic re-creation of as much of ancient Greek lyric as a Roman poet, writing in Latin in the second half of the first century B.C., could succeed in recreating. Still, it is puzzling that this poet who had given so much of his time and talent to reviving the dead genre, transplanting it into a culture and language that were alien to it, should refrain from a precise and extended statement of his theory of lyric. Perhaps he eschewed such a statement because he found, at last, that it was unnecessary—his poems, in which the old Greek voices spoke again, in another language, in the modern world, needed neither explanation nor defense. Perhaps that is what he thought, but he did defend them, rankled apparently by their tepid reception outside the charmed circle of the best people, the happy few who recognized his lyric genius and his lyric achievement. *Epistles* 1.19 is a ferocious answer to the stupid critics and semiliterate readers who had no notion of Greek lyric and could therefore have no notion of how hard his task had been or how brilliantly, how completely, he had performed it: "I have set my footprints in open country/where none before me dared venture" (lines 21–22). That is a favorite topos among both Greek and Roman Alexandrians, but the next statement, which introduces his claim to have imported Archilochus and Alcaeus into Roman literature undamaged and (perhaps) improved, has none of the ironic modesty, almost the coyness, of similar claims elsewhere (see particularly *Odes* 2.20 and 3.30): "He who trusts himself will rule the swarm" (lines 22–23). The poet who has confidence in his own powers, the poet with guts, is the "king" bee who dominates the hive. He had dared much and won everything. If he seems merely an imitator (lines 26–31), he must seem so only to the uneducated who misunderstand tradition and do not see that Sappho and Alcaeus had imitated Archilochus even as Horace has imitated all three. But especially Alcaeus:

> His verse forms, attempted by none before,
> I, the Latin lyricist, have given the world.
> It pleases me to be read by the eyes,
> to be held in the hands,
> of the happy few. (lines 33–34)

Latinus fidicen, "*the* Latin lyricist"! It is more than a boast, more than a challenge: it is a full-voiced, ruthless statement of fact, a fact that the *ingratus lector* (the "thankless reader," the Philistines, the stupid public) cannot begin to grasp. It is the eyes of the happy few (*ingenuis oculis*) that will read his poems, and it is their hands that will hold the book.

Yet if the ignorant herd cannot appreciate the blessed miracle of a Horace in their midst, an emperor can:

The poet is usually a lazy, a terrible soldier.
Yet if you'll admit
that greatness can he served by what is humble—
he has his uses to the City. (*Epistles* 2.1.124–25)

The ironic humility returns as he addresses Augustus in one of his greatest, perhaps one of his last, poems. The Latin lyricist serves his community even if it cannot appreciate who he is and what he is doing for it:

The poet shapes the child's stammering mouth,
diverts his ear from vulgar speech,
then forms his heart with cordial lessons,
redeeming it from harshness, from envy and rage.
He sings of good deeds and he furnishes
those flowering years with famous models,
he comforts the poor and the sick.
Where could the unmarried girl or the pure young man
discover a teacher of their prayers,
had the muse not sent them a sacred poet?
Their chorus begs his assistance,
then, feeling the divine presence,
persuading with the prayer he taught,
it asks for rain from heaven,
it wards off plague and banishes war,
it wins peace for the city and rich harvest.
The heavenly gods and the gods below
yield to its incantation. (*Epistles* 2.1.126–38)

Musa dedit fidibus ("the Muse gave to the lyre") (AP 83) recalls *vatem ni Musa dedisset* ("had the muse not sent"). Though Horace seems to slight lyric poetry in his theoretical criticism, here, in his most subtle and most powerful defense of poetry, he places lyric even above epic and tragedy. A poet of many voices, Horace deliberately avoids mention of his favorite voices (Archilochus, Alcaeus, Anacreon, Simonides) in this passage in order to elevate lyric poetry by focusing on its most exalted figure—the vatic Pindar. The satirist, the epicurean dialectical poet, and the dandified hedonist are temporarily and ironically sequestered because this is no moment for the paradoxes, the ironies, and the eccentric orbits that this configuration of voices recalls. What is needed here is the shaman, the figure of Pindar, "to purify the language of the tribe," to preside over the city's *paideia* ("education"), to define and to instill *sophrosyne* ("prudence"), to recall the grand origins of courage and morality, to evoke eternity (*praesentia numina*), and to win divine blessings for the community. The image of the chorus recalls Horace's own *Carmen Saeculare*, and this image is, in the modern Rome of Horace and Augustus, as anachronistic as that poem and its performance had been. Yet it is the image that Horace wants and needs here, for since the question he is asking in this poem is, "What are the uses of poetry?" and since the answer he gives Augustus is, "Not primarily, not really, to immortalize emperors," he does well to exclude from his definition of lyric all varieties of lyric except the one that manifests clearly the most ancient and most vital lyrical form and function. By this strategem he answers Augustus with a fair amount of tact, and he also reminds the vulgar throng of their ignorance of the essence of lyric poetry, a long vanished, long dead art that he had succeeded in resuscitating almost single-handedly. Himself an ironic Pindarist, a spoiled shaman-turned-epicurean humanist, he ironically and sincerely recalls, defines eloquently and for good in the classical tradition, the religious origin, the religious function, and the religious power of lyric poetry. Having put away his feathers and his drum, having relapsed once more into Simonidean humanism and modern times, he had still the taste and the judgment to praise his betters—the forgotten authentic *vates* ("seer") with whom the evocation of eternal moments had begun. This is not perhaps a theory of lyric, but it is good to find Horace in his humility reminding a world that had lost all memory of great lyric what the idea of great lyric must be.

NOTES

1. For a reasoned statement of the attitudes behind this sad mistake, see Quintillian, *Institutes* 1.8.6.

2. See C. O. Brink, *Horace on Poetry* (Cambridge: Cambridge University Press, 1963), 1:182.

3. See Joel E. Springarn, *The History of Literary Criticism in the Renaissance* (New York: Columbia University Press, 1924), pp. 27–99.

4. Brink, *Horace on Poetry*, 1:169–70.

5. See Hans Färber, *Die Lyrik in der Kunsttheorie der Antike* (Munich: Neue Filser, 1936), pp. 3ff. The translations of Plato are by M. E. Hubbard, those of Aristotle by D. A. Russell, in *Ancient Literary Criticism: The Principal Texts in New Translations*, ed. D. A. Russell and Michael Winterbottom (Oxford: Oxford University Press, 1972).

6. Färber, *Die Lyrik*, pp. 23–4.

7. See Paul Vicaire, *Platon, Critique Littéraire* (Paris: Klincksieck, 1960), p. 146; see also Plato, *The Laws* 799b.

8. What Aristotle does, in fact, is to reduce the means of literary mimesis to narrative (mixed and unmixed being fused) and dramatic. See Färber, *Die Lyrik*, pp. 4ff.; and P. Steinmetz, "Gattungen und Epochen der griechischen Literatur in der Sicht Quintilians," *Hermes* 92 (1964): 461. For his apparent neglect of lyric, see Gerald Else, *Aristotle's Poetics: The Argument* (Cambridge, Mass: Harvard University Press, 1957), pp. 567–68; Luigi E. Rossi, "I generi letterari e le loro leggi scritte e non scritte nelle letterature classiche," *Institute of Classical Studies, University of London Bulletin* 18 (1971): 78. For the difficulties with the triad of modes, see Claudio Guillen, *Literature as System* (Princeton: Princeton University Press, 1971), pp. 383–405.

9. Emily Dickinson, *Selected Letters*, ed. Thomas H. Johnson (Cambridge, Mass.: Harvard University Press, 1971), letter 268, p. 176. For lyric mimesis of an action, see Charles Batteux, *Principes de la littérature* (Paris: Nyons, 1775; reprt., Geneva: Slatkin Reprints, 1967), 1:316–28. For an elegant criticism of antimimetic theories, see Gerald Graff, *Literature Against Itself* (Chicago: University of Chicago Press, 1979), pp. 179–205.

10. See Francis Cairns, *Generic Composition in Greek and Roman Poetry* (Edinburgh: Edinburgh University Press, 1972), p. 6.

11. See Plato, *The Laws* 700a–b. For useful descriptions of the species of Greek lyric, see Herbert W. Smyth, *Greek Melic Poets* (London: Macmillan, 1900), pp. xxiii–cxxxiv; Calame, "Réflexions sur les genres," pp. 116–120; Steinmetz, "Gattungen und Epochen," pp. 458ff.

12. See Cairns, *Generic Composition*, p. 14. For the possible influence of Callimachus, see Pfeiffer, *History of Classical Scholarship*, p. 130. See also P. M. Fraser, *Ptolemaic Alexandria* (Oxford: Oxford University Press, 1972), 1:459–63.

13. See Cairns, *Generic Composition*, pp. 71–72, 75.

14. See Stanley Edgar Hyman, *Poetry and Criticism* (New York: Atheneum, 1961), passim.

15. See C. O. Brink, *Horace on Poetry* (*Ars Poetica*) (Cambridge: Cambridge University Press, 1971), 2: 172–73.

16. See Cairns, *Generic Composition*, p. 138.

17. Calame, "Réflexions sur les genres," pp. 114–5, shows clearly why we should not; see also Douglas E. Gerber, "Studies in Greek Lyric Poetry," *Classical World* 70 (October 1976): 69. If, as seems likely, this Proclus is the neoplatonist (fifth century A.D.), we are here assuming, and it is a large assumption, that Proclus recapitulates the entire late tradition from Didymus to his own time. See Pfeiffer, *History of Classical Scholarship*, pp. 182–84, 277; and Rossi, "I generi litterari," pp. 74–75.

18. See Albert Severyns, *Recherches sur la Chrestomatie de Proclus, Bibliotheque de la Faculté de Philosophie et Lettres de l'Université de Liège* 79 (1938): 33–40, 115. See also Färber, *Die Lyrik*, pp. 31ff.; and Pfeiffer, *History of Classical Scholarship*, p. 184.

19. Much of Statius's *Silvae* and some of Martial may be thought to represent this category adequately.

20. See Cairns, *Generic Composition*, p. 6.

21. Ibid., pp. 10, 75.

2.2 The Genre of the Grave and the Origins of the Middle English Lyric (1997)

Seth Lerer

Written along the top margin of a late-twelfth-century theological manuscript, penciled as continuous prose in a hand now only barely legible, is the following brief text. Lineated by modern editors, the uneven marginalia in the manuscript become a supple stanza of personal poetry.

ic an̄ witles fuli wis
of worldles blisse nabbe ic nout
for a lafdi þet is pris
of alle þet in bure goð
seþen furst þe heo was his
iloken in castel wal of stan
nes ic hol ne bliþe iwis
ne þriuiinde mon
lif þ mon non bildes me
abiden ⁊ bliþe for to bee
ned efter mi deað me longgeþ
I mai siggen wel by me
herde þet wo hongeþ

[I am completely without sense,
of the world's bliss have I nothing,
on account of a lady who is valued
above all others who walk in the bower.
Since first she was his,
locked up inside a castle wall of stone,
I have been neither whole nor happy,
nor a thriving man.
There is not a man alive who does not advise me
to wait and be happy,
but it is my death that I long for;
I can say truthfully that on me,
woes hang terribly.]

Since its publication by Carleton Brown over sixty years ago, this poem has been understood to represent the "earliest example of the secular lyric" in Middle English (xii). With its arresting first-person declaratives, its masterful command of a complex rhyme scheme, and its seemingly effortless blend of personal desire and literary convention, the poem speaks directly to our modern critical appreciations of the medieval lyric. Brown himself queried its marginal status, wondering if it recorded the "actual human experience" of its author (xii), and his original impressions have informed all subsequent readings of the text. It remains, as far as anyone can tell, the earliest piece of Middle English lyric poetry and thus appears to anticipate the individual voiced feelings of the famous Harley Lyrics and the verities of such familiar anthology pieces as "Foweles in the frith." There is, as Peter Dronke puts it in a highly influential formulation, a shared "underlying innocence" to these early poems, a compression of events into "concreteness and dramatic power" that defines our "first encounter" with the Middle English lyric (*Medieval Lyric*, 145).

But what precisely does it mean to speak of first encounters with the Middle English lyric or to locate its beginnings in such verses? On the one hand, it implies formal and linguistic standards. The emergence of Middle English has long been traced to the mix of imported Norman vocabulary and domestic grammatical change that characterizes the immense diversity of vernacular writing from the late eleventh to the early thirteenth centuries.[2] Quantitative meter and patterns of rhyme (as opposed to Old English prosody, based on a four-stress line and alliteration) take over as the organizing principles of verse making, and the genres of this poetry are often understood to follow Continental, rather than Insular, models.[3] Thus Middle English poetry is found to consist of "lyrics," "romances," and "fables," rather than of the epics, elegies, and gnomic sayings of the Anglo-Saxon tradition. It offers *pastourelles* and *ballades*, treatments of the themes of *carpe diem*, *contemptus mundi*, and *memento mori*.[4]

On the other hand, to speak of the origins of Middle English lyric is to speak about the idea of the lyric voice itself and, furthermore, about the birth of subjectivity in the vernacular.[5] Few modern readers would find in the corpus of Old English the expected personal identity we seek in lyric poetry.[6] The very names that modern scholars have bequeathed to Anglo-Saxon shorter verse—the riddle, the gnome, the elegy—place these texts outside the expectations of truly lyric utterance.[7] First-person texts in Old English are rarely considered as anything but examples of a speaking object or narrativized versions of Christian doctrine. Even such seemingly felt utterances as *Deor* and *Widsith* are largely understood to stand along the axes of Germanic lament or Indo-European blame-and-praise verse: depersonalized forms that seek not the recovery of individuated voices but the verities of social statement and the ventriloquizings of the bardic.[8] In short, the lyric, as we have been taught to think of it, is foreign to pre-Conquest England, an invention of the continental European consciousness and an importation from the Latin schools or Romance courts (Woolf, 1–2; Pearsall, 126–7).

Although they have long dominated criticism of the early English lyric, such approaches to post-Conquest literary history are themselves curiously ahistoricist. Modern readings of the poems, in fact, have often valorized their anonymity, their lack of context, their free-standing status and survival. The lack of identifiable authors or audiences—celebrated in the title of one critical anthology, *Poems without Names*—made them the delight of both New Critical formalists and patristic exegetes, the former commending their structure, imagery, and drama, the latter detailing their doctrinal message or biblical idiom.[9] The survival of many early Middle English texts in flyleaves, marginalia, or *disjecta membra* does not deprive them of a recoverable context. Rather, it provokes a reassessment of the historical conditions in which they were written down and read. It makes them products of reception and transmission: documents in the history of reading in the English past.

This essay seeks to understand such documents in the changing linguistic, aesthetic, and political conditions of post-Conquest England, in particular in the sustained interest in an Old English literary culture that established small but highly active communities of scholarly antiquarianism in the twelfth and thirteenth centuries. Early Middle English verse, I argue, shares not the "underlying innocence" of the first forays into a form but the complex and multilayered ambiguities of a literary tradition. Its "concreteness and dramatic power" issue from the matrix of Old English elegy, religious polemic, and vernacular chronicle. Such verse gives voice not just to a loving, longing self but to a community beset by the loss of language, landscape, and national institutions.

Much has been made, of late, of the emergent "nationhood" of English literary culture: its self-consciousness of vernacular expression, its explicit topicality, its political agendas, its satiric mien, its penchant for precise topographical description.[10] Thorlac Turville-Petre, reappraising the national identity articulated in the early Middle English period, suggests that "concepts of nationhood become dominant when the nation is perceived to be under threat from outside attack or influence, for it is national identity that distinguishes the English from the feared French or the despised Scots." Writing in English is "a statement about belonging," a claim for cultural uniqueness in an age when French rulers had measured out the land, built strange fortifications, and replaced familiar leaders of the Church and local communities with foreigners (*England the Nation*, 4, 11). "Anglia exterorum facta est habitatio et alienigenarum dominatio" [England has become the dwelling place of foreigners and the property of strangers], wrote William of Malmesbury in the early 1120s. His sentiments were echoed in 1237 by Matthew of Paris: "Vae Angliae, quae quondam princeps provinciarum . . . nunc facta est sub tributo, conculcaverunt eam ignobiles, et facta est in praedam degeneribus" [Alas, England, once first among regions . . . now she is placed under tribute, low-born men have trodden her down, and she has been plundered by degenerates].[11]

The literary culture of the century bracketed by these remarks has come under renewed scrutiny. Recent accounts of Insular romance, of the epic antiquarianism of Laȝamon's *Brut*, and of the theories of history behind the burst of local and official annalistic writing have all, to varying degrees, attended to the blend of poetics and politics in post-Conquest writing.[12] My goal is to bring critical discussion of Middle English lyrics into the ambit defined by this cultural historiography,[13] as well as to call attention to a set of tropes and idioms controlling the making and reception of late Old and early Middle English writing. Central to both purposes is a preoccupation with architectural form and topographical manipulation, a response to the new Norman projects of castle building, cathedral reorganization, and forest management but also to the older Anglo-Saxon philosophical concerns with the transitoriness of human works and with death and burial. My title therefore evokes an important genre of Old English verse, the poem on the grave, to find in early Middle English a poetics of the entombed body and an inhumed past. By focusing on architectural control, the lyric seeks analogies between the artifacts of engineering and the structures of society. By drawing on naturalistic description, it illustrates the dislocated English voice, lost in a landscape changed by castle, church, and royal forest. I survey a poetry of enclosed spaces: not the privacy of the domestic but the confines of the coffin. In the longer poems and the manuscript assemblies of the age—most notably the witty bird debate known as *The Owl and the Nightingale* and the mid-thirteenth-century anthologies in which it survives—we may discern not just the outpourings of a lyric voice but an assessment of the idea of lyricality itself. There is, even in this most celebratory of early Middle English poems, a pervasive elegiac cast, and when we see the text anew in its manuscript contexts, we witness how compilations shape a sense of English literary history in the post-Conquest age. What Turville-Petre dubs "England the nation" lies, I propose, in the act not only of making new vernacular expressions but of reading older English texts, maintaining older English ecclesiastical foundations, and keeping local memories and human bodies secure in the face of alien encroachment.

[. . .]

These bits and pieces of post-Conquest verse have long been seen as sharing in a teleology of literary history, a trajectory from early-thirteenth-century folk song to the powerful sophistications of the early-fourteenth-century Harley Lyrics. Yet, according to standard literary histories, there is little in these early verses to prepare us for the poignancy of Harley. Pearsall sees in them "no evidence of a tradition of courtly love lyrics"; but for the Harley collection, our understanding of the early Middle English secular lyric would be confined to "cryptic love songs, a fly-leaf fragment of a popular dance-song with refrain . . . [and] some casually preserved jottings of strange poignant individuality" (101). Similarly, Thomas C. Moser Jr. finds in "Foweles in the frith" and its kin "a tiny, enigmatic fragment of an intellectual world that we can only see in scattered parts and whose parts are held together by a wild sort of meditational-exegetical glue" (334).

I wish to redirect our notions of this literature from scholarly laments and dismissals of scattered fossils to a new, historically minded understanding of the fragments *as fragments*. Post-Conquest writing is a collocation of images commensurate with the broken quality of an Anglo-Saxon afterlife. Like the stones piled up by Wulfstan's flock, the reminiscences of an Alfredian education, and the grave sites and cells of distant saints, these stanzas of early Middle English lyric are the pieces of a world, the objects of linguistic and literary study by the Worcester antiquarians. They are verse examples of a vernacular culture shoring itself up against the claims of other languages and other readers. They are the English versions of what Maria Rosa Menocal calls "shards of love," expressions of the alienation that provokes the lyric statement and, in historical terms, locates the speaking subject in a landscape of displacement:

> The medieval—and thus what we call the modern and the postmodern—lyric is invented in bitter exile. And not just the normal and conventional and essentially metaphoric exile that is, perhaps, the condition of all poetry and its reading. No, here the poet must finally face the harsh winter night when he knows, in that full solitude, that he will never again see the lovely terra-cotta rooftops of Florence, that he will never be buried in the barren but olive-fragrant soil outside Granada. In that cold and darkness, the solitary voice asks what he will do about it. Among the thousands of answers that have come with the morning, one singular and unexpected one, the love lyric, has been a powerful and charming defense, a form of resistance commonly taken for retreat. (91–2)

For early Middle English lyricists, the sense of exile is not conditioned by physical removal to a place of punishment or pathos. Rather, it remains the product of a country stripped of its familiarities, an exile now internal and the product of a language and a landscape taken over. To live as English speakers in a newly French land, to pile up stones against the monumentalism of the Conquest, is to live in the *regio dissimilitudinis* at the heart of all exilics. The very images of Menocal's review vibrate with the reflections of the Middle English lyric: the harsh winter night, the architecture of desire, cold and darkness. Early Middle English lyric, I have argued, is a form of resistance, a defense of the vernacular against the impositions of the foreign. "When is a song of love . . . about a city and not a woman?" Menocal asks (92). The longings of the lyric she finds in medieval and modern traditions are themselves longings not just for persons but for places, and in her account the city and the woman become interchangeable counters in the poetry of loss. So, too, in early Middle English verse, it is the place that is estranged. The "lafdi þet is pris" of "Ic an̄ witles," locked in the Norman "castel wal of stan," is England itself. The association is not as fanciful as it might seem, when we reread the poem against the full text of

Matthew of Paris's lament: "Alas, England, once first among regions, mistress of peoples *[domina gentium]*, mirror of the Church and a pattern of religion: now she is placed under tribute, low-born men have trodden her down, and she has been plundered by degenerates." To recall Matthew's words now is to see their gender made explicit, to see the historian transformed into a lyricist. Such sentiments are those of the speaker of "Foweles in the frith," whose madness comes as a consequence of seeing the familiar seasons change in a demesne now scripted by the Domesday Book. So, too, for the others. "Ej! ej! what þis nicht is long." "Dureleas is þæt hus and dearc hit is wiðinnen."

If the first century and a half after the Conquest saw the emergence of "shards of love" in scribal ephemera, the following century witnessed attempts to bring together the examples of Middle English lyric into compilations of pedagogical or thematic value. A manuscript such as Trinity College Cambridge MS 323—with its interlarding of the English, French, and Latin—illustrates the range of languages and literary forms that occupied monastic readers, as does British Library MS Harley 2253, the famous compilation containing the Harley Lyrics, the early-fourteenth-century collection of secular English verse, Latin religious prose, and Anglo-Norman fabliaux and saints' lives. Perhaps nowhere is such multilingualism so palpable as in the macaronic lyric from that manuscript, "Dum ludis floribus," in which Latin and French lines alternate until the final stanza proceeds, in all three languages, from schoolroom notes through Parisian wanderings to English love and loss:

Scripsi hec carmina in tabulis;
mon ostel est en mi la vile de Paris;
may y sugge namore, so wel me is;
ȝef hi deȝe for loue of hire, duel hit ys.
[I have written this song on tablets (of wax);
my dwelling is in the middle of the city of Paris;
may I say no more, to keep me happy;
if I die for love of her, it would be a grievous thing.][14]

Such poetry bears witness not just to the multilingualism of contemporary culture but to the growing sense, in the late thirteenth and early fourteenth centuries, of retrospection and review. Scribal assembly of lyrics often older than their compilation preserves a tradition and anthologizes the exemplars of vernacular expression.

Such acts of preservation are politically thematized in two related manuscripts from the mid- to late thirteenth century. British Library MS Cotton Caligula A.ix and Jesus College Oxford MS 29 are best known for *The Owl and the Nightingale*, but they also contain religious verse, secular lyric, and metrical history.[15] The Caligula manuscript begins with a copy of Laȝamon's *Brut*, while Jesus preserves a text of the versified *Proverbs of Alfred*. They share copies of *The Latemest Day*, *Domesday*, and *Death's Wither-Clench*, all securely in the late Old English tradition of elegiac mournfulness, while offering texts in Anglo-Norman French. They have long been studied for their similarities of content and order as well as for their representativeness in the history of Insular paleography.[16] In tandem, they constitute an anthology of English literary history: Latin *altercatio* and French fable, proverbs attributed to Alfred and the poems of the grave, fit together here and also in the omnivorous purview of *The Owl and the Nightingale*'s avian disputants. The manuscripts mime something of the world distilled, half a century later, into the macaronic Harley stanza quoted above: its inhabitants pass from the text to the home, from Paris to England, from scholarship to longing and loss.

While displaying the capacity of English verse to mime the patterns of the Latin school or the matter of Marie de France, *The Owl and the Nightingale* is also about the idea of lyricality and thus the relations between vernacular language and the speaking voice. The Nightingale, traditionally a figure for the secular, the lyrical, the felt, and the emotive, makes a case not just for a particular approach to life or love but for a lyric subjectivity. Hers is the world of love song and desire, of seasonal change and emotional response.[17] She is the "bryd one brere," whose announcements mark not only the occasions of desire but the moments of desiring individuals, in a voice from which another, human, lyric "I" may speak.

At stake in the Nightingale's arguments, and at the heart of her rebuttal to the Owl's claims that her songs lead women into adultery (1045–66), are the nature of individual will and, consequently, the relations between authorial utterance and reader response. The Nightingale claims that she does not "teache wif breke spuse" (1334) but sings of an idealized love that can exist in marriage. She is not responsible for women of "nesche mode" (1349) who misunderstand her:

Þat heo, for sume sottes lore
Þe ȝeorne bit & sikeþ sore,
Misrempe & misdo summe stunde,
Schal ich þaruore beon ibunde?
ȝif wimmen luuieþ unrede,
Hwi witistu me hore misdede? (1351–6)

[That these women, on account of some foolish learning,
Eagerly pray and sigh sorrowfully,
Go astray and sometimes act wrongly,
Should I therefore be held responsible?
If women live ill-advisedly,
Why do you blame me for their misdeeds?]

Such women may well turn the song amiss (1364):

Alswa hit is bi mine songe:
Þah he beo god, me hine mai misfonge
An drahe hine to sothede
And to oþre uuele dede. (1373–6)

[Likewise, the same is true about my song:
If it is good, one may misapply it
And drag oneself down into folly
And to other evil actions.]

Here, as elsewhere, *The Owl and the Nightingale* remains a poem about understanding and intention. Its central claim, voiced throughout myriad disputations on secular and religious issues, is that language often does go amiss: the gap between intention and expression is a feature of linguistic competence, and the speaker need not be blamed for what the listener hears. The linguistic epistemology of the poem recalls many disputes on language and understanding that pre-occupied English and French intellectuals in the late twelfth century. The poem's notion of intention, for example, resonates strongly with Abelard's conception of *intentio* and responsibility in his *Ethics* and *De dialectica*. Its pre-occupations with perception and impression similarly recall John of Salisbury's academic skepticism in the *Metalogicon* and, in turn, his understanding of the ambience of debate as the realm of the verisimilar, rather than of the absolutely true (Murphy, "Rhetoric and

Dialectic"; Reed, 255–60). *The Owl and the Nightingale* marries these philosophical concerns with an interest in the idea of the lyric voice and of the literary as a function of the speaking subject and its understandings. The poem is, at this level, an essay in the arts of subjectivity: a playful exercise in how words go well or awry, a meditation on the power of the lyric to convey and sway emotion.

Like the poem's philosophy, its appearance is Continental. In both manuscripts it is written out in lineated couplets. Unlike the *Brut*, which, in spite of its scribes' pointing of its half lines, remains written out as continuous prose, *The Owl and the Nightingale* is visually indistinguishable from verse in Latin or the Romance vernaculars. Both of its manuscripts offer short lines in double columns, and both punctuate line endings. In the Jesus manuscript the poem comes with a Latin title (*Incipit altercacio inter filomenam et bubonem*), and each line's initial letter is set off from the others. In Caligula the text is written in a "professional" gothic hand, more usual for works of the learned Latin tradition, such as the *Historia scholastica* in British Museum MS Royal 3 D.vi (c. 1283–1300). In these texts *The Owl and the Nightingale* looks for all the world like a European rather than an English poem, and it may have been as striking to a reader of the mid-thirteenth century as to one of the late twentieth (Ker, xvi).

Indeed, perhaps the poem is not a translation, in the narrow sense, but a formally and generically Continental work. Throughout the texts I have surveyed it has been apparent that the Englishness of English verse is less a function of vocabulary, theme, or genre than a product of the scribes. Regardless of its metrical form or subject matter—be it the heroics of the *Brut*; the lyric voicings of "Ic añ witles"; the homiletics of *The Soul's Address*, *The Grave*, or the *First Worcester Fragment*; or the encomiums of *Durham* or the *Rime of King William*—all verse of this period is inscribed as continuous prose. The visual appearance of *The Owl and the Nightingale* thus announces a vernacularity more Continental than Insular, a métier more in tune with Latin schooling and the Ile de France than with the antiquarianism of Worcester Cathedral.

Yet it remains an English poem. *The Proverbs of Alfred* takes precedence over material drawn from the fables of Marie de France. The English Nicholas of Guildford (whoever he may be) is the final judge of the birds' argument, in spite of earlier appeals to canon law and the pope of Rome.[18] For all its scribal trappings of European literacy, the *altercatio* transpires in a landscape unique to the British Isles.

Ich was in one sumere dale;
In one suþe diȝele hale
Iherde ich holde grete tale
An Hule and one Niȝtingale. (1–4)

[I was in a summer valley;
In a secret, hidden nook,
I heard a great debate held
Between an Owl and a Nightingale.]

Though arranged in precise octosyllabics and perfect rhymes, the words descend directly from Old English. And if the *locus amoenus* seems universally familiar from a range of literary disputations, the bird's setting should remind the reader that it is still England: "Þe Niȝtingale bigon þe spece / In one hurne of one breche" [The Nightingale began the plea / In a corner of a fallow field] (13–4).[19] Such fields, broken up for cultivation, were the product of the domestication of the forest that began under William the Conqueror and continued through the thirteenth century. New clearings took on new names—Gilibertesbreche,

Parkeresbreche, Brechehurne—and with them came new castles. As the Nightingale puts it, in an early disclaimer to the Owl's accusations of her weakness, "I habbe on brede & eck on lengþe / Castel god on mine rise" [I have in the length and breadth of my bough / A castle, good in every respect] (174–5). Alive to a political landscape manipulated by castellation, she equates her own strength with that of the Conqueror, of whom it is said, in the *Peterborough Chronicle*'s memorable phrase, that "castelas . . . he let wyrcean." Closer to the date of the poem's composition, the Nightingale's references would recall, too, the massive castle building—and castle besieging—that marked the anarchy under King Stephen.

> Mid lutle strengþe þurȝ ginne
> Castel & burȝ me mai iwinne;
> Mid liste me mai walles felle
> And worpe of horsse kniȝtes snelle. (765–8)
>
> [With only a little strength, but through ingenuity,
> One may conquer castle and town;
> One may bring down walls with deceit
> And throw bold knights off their horses.]

The lesson of the Nightingale is also that of King Stephen. Both the *Peterborough Chronicle* and the Latin *Gesta Stephani* tell stories of castle building and besieging. In the *Chronicle* the king's enemies "fylden þe land ful of castles" after having deprived the people of it (Clark, 55). In the *Gesta* Stephen himself works through guile and stealth, as well as brute force, to retake the castles of the towns held by his rebels.[20] Castle building, the nexus of political control and dynastic establishment under Stephen, continued as the mode of rule until the reign of Henry II (the late "king Henri" of one of the Nightingale's stories [1091], whose death in 1189 has been taken as the *terminus post quem* for the poem's composition).[21] It was for the twelfth century what it had been for the age of the Conqueror: "one of the consequences of the suspension of the juridical protection of property rights," in other words, the way kings made themselves kings (Coulson, 68).

Yet the castle falls before the Nightingale's "ginne." This Middle English word, together with its semantic pair *liste*, translates the Old French *engin*, the ingenuity and guile of romance that topple castle, burg, and wall.[22] Not only a claim for philomenal strength against bubonic pressure but a large set of linguistic and historical references is advanced in these lines. In an English landscape full of both newer castles and older burgs, what is left in the aftermath of conquest and anarchy is not so much brute strength as it is craft and skill. Subtly the nature of the poem's landscape shifts, locating the Nightingale's sense of bodily strength in terms of built, controlled, or crafted things—or their destruction.

From this poem, as from the short lyrics that are its literary contemporaries, emerges the speaking voice, set or enhoused within a landscape. The opening words of this unmistakably urbane Middle English poem take us back to the rough couplets of the *Rime of King William* and the little stanzas of the early lyrics, and for all its delicacy of diction and easy wit, *The Owl and the Nightingale* offers tensions as deep as those of the other poems written in the first centuries of Norman rule. For the first readers of the Caligula manuscript, such tensions would have been felt immediately, as the text segues without break or *explicit* into the lyric known as *Death's Wither-Clench*.[23] Coming after the battle of the birds, it presents a somber commentary on their vigor and wit. "Þat plait was sif ⁊ starc ⁊ strong," the narrator told us (5), but *Death's Wither-Clench* reminds us, "Nis non so stronge ne sterche ne kene / þat mai ago deaþes wither clench" [There is no one so strong or stark or keen / who may withstand death's wither clench] (11–2).

As the coda to a debate poem full of misdoings and misunderstandings (where *misded*, *misdon*, and other *mis-* words appear over twenty times),[24] *Death's Wither-Clench* invites the reader to recall the teachings of Solomon, in order that "þenne ne schal þu never mis do" [then you shall never do wrong] (22). What the poem calls "salemones rede" [Solomon's counsel] (21) now replaces as present, unambiguous advice the deferred judgment of the absent Nicholas of Guildford, to whom the Owl and the Nightingale will fly. "Ah wa schal unker speche rede, / An telle touore unker deme?" [Who shall advise us in our speech, / And render therefore our judgment?] (1782–3), asks the Nightingale—and the scribe of the Caligula manuscript offers, in effect, an answer. *Death's Wither-Clench* is a poem about *deme*, about judgment and decision. Indeed, after a poem in which one bird has accused the other of subsisting on a diet of "attercroppe & fule ugliȝe / & wormes" [spiders and foul flies / And worms] (601–2), *Death's Wither-Clench* reiterates the inescapable fact that in the end, all of us "wormes fode . . . shald beo" [shall be food for worms] (34).

To read *The Owl and the Nightingale* in its historical, political, codicological, and literary contexts is to move past appreciations of its innovation or its ease to see the darkness of its past and present. Through its vocabulary and its manuscript environment, it locates itself in the late Old English traditions of a subjective geography: a placement of the speaking self at moments of decline, nostalgia, or internal exile. The voices that emerge from castles and from graves remind the reader of conquest's "wither-clench" and of the afterlife of Old English idioms and genres in later lyrics. If the Nightingale seeks to upset the world of power through her verbal "liste" and "ginne," then so, perhaps, do the first Middle English lyricists as their tiny verses find their places in landscapes of desire and release the "lafdi þet is pris," the *domina gentium*, from a "castel wal of stan."

NOTES

1. The text appears in British Library MS Royal 8.D.xiii, fol. 25r. It was first edited by Carleton Brown, *English Lyrics of the Thirteenth Century* (Oxford: Clarendon, 1932), xii. The manuscript was reexamined and reedited by Theo Stemmler, who also reproduced a photograph of the manuscript folio ("Textologische Probleme mittelenglischen Dichtungen," *Mannheimer Berichte aus Forschung und Lehre* 8 [1974]: 245–8). Peter Dronke reviewed Stemmler's edition and offered new readings and emendations of his own, together with a modern translation (*The Medieval Lyric*, 2d ed. [London: Hutchinson, 1978], 144, 280). My edition is based (with slight modifications) on that of Dronke. The translation is mine (as are all further unattributed translations).

2. J. A. W. Bennett, G. V. Smithers, and Norman Davis, eds., *Early Middle English Verse and Prose*, 2d ed. (Oxford: Clarendon, 1968), xxi–lxi; J. A. Burrow and Thorlac Turville-Petre, *A Book of Middle English*, 2d ed. (Oxford: Blackwell, 1996), 3–65; for technical details see Fernand Mossé, *A Handbook of Middle English*, trans. James A. Walker (Baltimore, Md.: Johns Hopkins University Press, 1952), 1–130.

3. Burrow and Turville-Peyre, 57–62; Derek Pearsall, *Old and Middle English Poetry* (London: Routledge and Kegan Paul, 1977), 57–118. Specialized studies of the metrical shifts at work in the period include N. F. Blake, "Rhythmical Alliteration," *Modern Philology* 67 (1969): 118–24; S. K Brehe, "Reassembling *The First Worcester Fragment*," *Speculum* 65 (1990): 521–36; and Daniel Donoghue, "Laȝamon's Ambivalence," *Speculum* 65 (1990): 537–63. For discussions of generic affiliations along the lines of Romance verse forms see Rosemary Woolf, *The English Religious Lyric in the Middle Ages* (Oxford: Clarendon, 1968), 1–15.

4. Woolf, 67–85; Raymond Oliver, *Poems without Names: The English Lyric, 1200–1500* (Berkeley: University of California Press, 1970), 74–85.

5. Peter Dronke, *Medieval Latin and the Rise of the European Love Lyric*, 2d ed., 2 vols. (Oxford: Oxford University Press, 1968); Dronke, *Poetic Individuality in the Middle Ages* (Oxford: Clarendon, 1970); Andrew Welsh, *Roots of Lyric* (Princeton, N.J.: Princeton University Press, 1972); Lois Bragg, *The Lyric Speakers of Old English Poetry* (Cranbury, N.J.: Associated University Presses, 1991); Maria Rosa Menocal, *Shards of Love: Exile and the Origins of the Lyric* (Durham, N.C.: Duke University Press, 1994).

6. Though Bragg clearly does (she defines Old English poetry not on formal or metrical grounds

but on the basis of a "taxonomy of Old English lyric speakers" [39]).

7. For attempts to frame shorter Old English verse generically see Martin Green, ed., *The Old English Elegies: New Essays in Criticism and Research* (London: Associated University Presses, 1983); and Anne L. Klinck, *The Old English Elegies* (Montreal: McGill-Queen's University Press, 1992).

8. See Kemp Malone, ed., *Widsith* (Copenhagen: Rosenkilde and Bagge, 1962); and Joseph Harris, "*Deor* and Its Refrain: Preliminaries to an Interpretation," *Traditio* 43 (1987): 23–53.

9. See G. L. Brook, ed., *The Harley Lyrics* (Manchester: Manchester University Press, 1956); Oliver (n. 4 above), whose critical inheritance actually lies in the judgmental formalism of Yvor Winters; and Maxwell S. Luria and Richard L. Hoffman, eds., *Middle English Lyrics*, Norton Critical Edition (New York: Norton, 1974), an anthology with a distinctively Robertsonian exegetical bias (for a review of competing opinions along New Critical / exegetical lines see 309–50). For the ideological and institutional tensions between New Criticism and exegesis in American medieval studies generally see Lee Patterson, *Negotiating the Past: The Historical Study of Medieval Literature* (Madison: University of Wisconsin Press, 1987), 3–39.

10. See, e.g., Richard Helgerson, *Forms of Nationhood: The Elizabethan Writing of England* (Chicago: University of Chicago Press, 1992); Larry Scanlon, *Narrative, Authority, and Power: The Medieval Exemplum and the Chaucerian Tradition* (Cambridge: Cambridge University Press, 1994); and Thorlac Turville-Petre, *England the Nation: Language, Literature, and National Identity, 1290–1340* (Oxford: Clarendon, 1996). Behind them all, to varying degrees, stands Benedict Anderson, *Imagined Communities: Reflections on the Origin and Spread of Nationalism*, 2d ed. (London: Verso, 1991).

11. William Stubbs, ed., *Willelmi Malmesbiriensis Monachi De Gestis Regum Anglorum*, 2 vols. (London: Rolls Series, 1887–89), 1:278; Henry Richards Luard, ed., *Matthaei Parisiensis: Chronica Majora*, 7 vols. (London: Rolls Series, 1872–87), 3:390. Quoted and translated in Turville-Petre, *England the Nation*, 41, 22.

12. Susan Crane, *Insular Romance* (Berkeley: University of California Press, 1986); Donoghue (n. 3 above); M. T. Clanchy, *From Memory to Written Record, England, 1066–1307* (Cambridge, Mass.: Harvard University Press, 1979); James Campbell, "Some Twelfth-Century Views of the Anglo-Saxon Past," *Peritia* 3 (1984): 131–50.

13. Some gestures have been made in this direction by Pearsall, 85–118; and Turville-Petre, *England the Nation*, 181–221.

14. Harley Lyrics, no. 19, ll. 17–20, in Brook, 55. For trilingual literary culture in England and its impact on the making of lyric anthologies see Turville-Petre, *England the Nation*, 181–221.

15. Eric Gerald Stanley, ed., *The Owl and the Nightingale*, 2d ed. (Manchester: Manchester University Press, 1972). All quotations and references to the poem are from this edition. The studies most relevant to my discussion are Kathryn D. Hume, *"The Owl and the Nightingale" and Its Critics* (Toronto: University of Toronto Press, 1977); J. J. Murphy, "Rhetoric and Dialectic in the *Owl and the Nightingale*," in *Medieval Eloquence*, ed. J. J. Murphy (Berkeley: University of California Press, 1978), 198–230; and Thomas L. Reed Jr., *Middle English Debate Poetry and the Aesthetics of Irresolution* (Columbia: University of Missouri Press, 1990), 219–60. Some of the interpretations I advance here are developed from my dissertation, "Classical Skepticism and English Poetry in the Twelfth Century" (University of Chicago, 1981).

16. See N. R. Ker, *"The Owl and the Nightingale": Facsimile of the Jesus and Cotton Manuscripts*, Early English Text Society, 251 (London: Oxford University Press, 1963).

17. See Thomas A. Shippey, "Listening to the Nightingale," *Comparative Literature* 22 (1970): 46–60.

18. For the poem's appeal to these sources, and the likely fictionality of Nicholas of Guildford, see Stanley's introduction to his edition (19–35).

19. See Stanley's note to l. 14 (105) and his glossary entry for the word. See, too, *MED*, s.v. "breche," sense 6, for the information concerning the place-names quoted below.

20. K. R. Potter, ed. and trans., *Gesta Stephani* (London: Thomas Nelson, 1955), 45–7.

21. Stanley convincingly dates the poem between Henry II's death and Henry III's ascension in 1216 (19).

22. See Robert W. Hanning, *The Individual in Twelfth-Century Romance* (New Haven, Conn.: Yale University Press, 1977), 108–11; and Geraldine Barnes, "Cunning and Ingenuity in the Middle English *Floris and Blaunchefleur*," *Medium/Ævum* 53 (1984): 10–25.

23. *Death's Wither-Clench* is titled and edited by Brown (15–8). The poem survives in two different versions in four manuscripts: Maidstone Museum MS A.13; British Museum MS Laud Miscell.471; and the two manuscripts of *The Owl and the Nightingale* (see Ker, x–xi). The quotation of the

 poem in several later compilations, prose works, and personal anthologies testifies to its wide popularity (Brown, 170–1). Brown printed the texts from Maidstone and Laud. The Caligula text (fol. 246r), from which I quote, was printed by Richard Morris, *An Old English Miscellany*, Early English Text Society, o.s., 49 (London: Trench, 1872), 156–9.

24. See Stanley's glossary (188–9).

2.3 Lyric Forms (2000)

Heather Dubrow

Definitions and Distinctions

Students with a keen sense of curiosity—or possibly merely a keen sense of mischief—could fruitfully exercise either predilection by asking their teachers for a brief definition of lyric. The complexities of responding to that demand, like the problems a similar query about tragedy would generate, demonstrate the complexities of the literary types in question. But despite the difficulty of defining lyric, exploring the forms it took during the English Renaissance can illuminate this mode as a whole, some of its most challenging and exciting texts, and the workings of the early modern era.

Aristotle posits an apparently clear-cut division of all literature into lyric, epic, and drama, basing the distinctions on the mode of presentation: lyric is sung, epic recited, and drama staged. This division remains influential, lying behind the work of Northrop Frye and many other modern theorists. Yet certain successors to Aristotle devise more elaborate subdivisions of poetry, adducing criteria that narrow the concept of lyric and lead to withholding that label from some forms of poetry. Thus, for example, in Book I, Chapter II of his *Arte of English Poesie* (1589), George Puttenham distinguishes heroic, lyric, elegaic, and epigrammatic verse and nods toward the presence of other types as well; this list shows the influence of classical writers like Horace.

When they attempt to define and describe lyric, twentieth-century critics replicate the problems earlier writers confronted. Some try to categorize it through formal qualities; lyrics are generally considered to be short, though of course that criterion is frustratingly relative and imprecise. Some argue that stanzaic form is typical of lyric though not necessarily present in all poems deserving that title. Other definitions emphasize the connection between lyric and song, variously citing direct allusions to songs, such as *Carmina* (a title of Horace's poems), the presence of such characteristics as the refrain, and references to musicality like Keats' famous address to a nightingale.

Another approach is defining lyric in terms of its relationship to time. The claim that it rejects or ignores temporality, though common, is less persuasive than more subtle attempts to anatomize the complex and varied ways the lyric engages with time. Thus, for example, Sharon Cameron's trenchant study *Lyric Time: Dickinson and the Limits of Genre* suggests that the mode in question fears time, associating it with death, and works out ways of redefining that potential antagonist. But how does this imputed fear relate to the indubitable presence of history in many lyrics?

Yet another avenue toward a definition is characterizing the lyric speaker. Some argue that this form allows the poet to express his real feelings, but recently most critics have instead asserted that this, like virtually all types of writing, is mediated in so many ways that the concept of actual emotions risks naivete. It is common to claim that the lyric speaker is isolated; yet, as we will see, early modern pastorals, like many other lyrics of the period, not only celebrate community as a value but also are typically situated in a community of shepherds. One group of critics maintains that lyric speakers express universal feelings and represent all of us rather than individualized, historically situated people; another group, however, retorts that such speakers are often, or even necessarily, historicized.

Certain commentators in turn focus on the relationship between the speaker and his audience, with John Stuart Mill delivering the highly influential observation that the lyric speaker is overheard. Similarly, in opposition to the suggestion that lyric is fundamentally a social mode, Helen Vendler defends the isolation and universality of its speaker. The reader is present, she insists, as a kind of mirror: "a lyric is *a role offered to a reader*; the reader is to be the voice speaking the poem."[1]

Northrop Frye offers another seminal approach when he discusses lyric in terms of what he playfully terms "babble" and "doodle." Associated with sound or *melos*, the former, he suggests, signals its connections with the charm and is manifest in rhythm, alliteration, and puns. "Doodle," in contrast, is the realm of verbal pattern or *opsis*, and Frye connects it to another blood relative of lyric, the riddle.[2]

Influenced by the importation of influential Continental theorists such as Derrida, Foucault, and Lacan and by the emphasis on the instability of language that characterizes and arguably defines poststructuralism, in the final three decades of the twentieth century critics have challenged many preconceptions lying behind earlier descriptions of the lyric.[3] One of the most common moves of poststructuralist criticism, the dismissal of older conceptions of the autonomous individual as tainted products of humanist ideology, is manifest in focusing on the rhetoric and performativity of lyric in lieu of the experience of the speaker or author.

Feminism has also informed reconsiderations of the mode in question, with critics variously endorsing and questioning the frequently cited gendering of the lyric as female and of narrative as male. In addition, love lyrics pivot on gender more immediately in the relationship between speaker and object, the first generally male and the second female. Hence many critics have read the lyric as both source and symptom of its culture's suppression of women, pointing to the ways its addresses to the woman may silence her and its descriptions dismember and disempower her; in particular, the blazon, a part-by-part celebration of the female body based on the French *blason*, is seen as an assertion of control under the guise of praise. And the concern for the historical and political that characterizes many critical movements at the end of the twentieth century has variously produced both distaste for the lyric's imputed tendency to suppress historical imperatives and issues rather than merely ignoring them, and demonstrations of its putative participation in historical discourses despite assumptions to the contrary.

Finally, however, the controversies surrounding these and other attempts to define lyric mandate distinctions based on both historical periods and genres. David Lindley, the author of an excellent short overview entitled *Lyric*, brackets his attempts at definition by insisting on historical specificity.[4] As he and others have pointed out, many discussions of the mode are shaped—and misshaped—by their positing the Romantic lyric as the normative model. How and why, then, do sixteenth-century poets approach that protean form, the lyric?

Principal Poets and Styles of the Sixteenth Century

Even a brief and preliminary chronological survey of major developments and authors of the period provides some answers to that question—but in so doing generates yet more questions. Though born in the fifteenth century, John Skelton composed most of his important poetry in the sixteenth. His output is varied, encompassing spiritual meditations on death and salvation, a portrait of an alehouse, and a dream vision; one of his best-known poems is *Philip Sparrow*, a thought-provoking example of lyric lament. Equally thought-provoking is Skelton's approach to metrics; his short lines, so idiosyncratic that they are aptly termed "Skeltonics," may well be based on church music, especially plainsong.[5]

Sir Thomas Wyatt, who lived between 1503 and 1542, is not only one of the earliest poets of the period but also one of the most intriguing. His canon includes several forms that were to be popular throughout the period, such as satires and metrical translations of the Psalms; his love poetry is especially impressive for its often colloquial diction and its intensity. Adapting sonnets by his Italian predecessor Francis Petrarch, he variously fashions poems that are virtually translations and others that reformat Petrarch's lines in a darker, more bitter font. Henry Howard, Earl of Surrey, who was born fourteen years after Wyatt, also contributed to the development of the sonnet, working out the rhyme scheme discussed below that came to be called "Shakespearean." In contrast to the irregular metrics and tangled emotions of Wyatt's sonnets, those of Surrey are typically limpid and graceful.

George Gascoigne, indubitably among the most significant writers in the early years of Elizabeth's reign though he is often neglected, includes among his varied canon, *A Hundred Sundry Flowers* (1573) and *The Posies* (1575). These volumes contain skillfully crafted love poetry, some of which is reminiscent of Wyatt's bitterness and wryness, as well as instances of such forms as the epitaph and satire. Among his most moving lyrics is "Lullaby of a Lover," which plays the soothing reassurances associated with the lullaby against its own caustic reflections on aging and desire. Gascoigne's contemporaries in this period experimented with a number of forms that were to become very popular later in the century; George Turberville, for example, translates the pastorals of the Italian monk Battista Spagnoli, often known as Mantuan. These decades also saw the publication of several collections of lyrics, notably the popular book known as *Tottel's Miscellany* (1557); this volume includes love poetry, pastoral, and satire and represents a wide range of authors, including Wyatt and Surrey.

Edmund Spenser's collection of pastorals entitled *The Shepheardes Calender* (1579), a text to which I will return in more detail, is often seen as inaugurating the extraordinarily rich production of poetry that characterizes the final decades of the sixteenth century. Certainly it manifests many characteristics that were to recur in its author's later poetry, such as his self-conscious and complex relationship to his literary predecessors, his engagement with the controversies surrounding English Protestantism, and his delight in stylistic experimentation, which in this instance is especially manifest in his range of verse forms and his use of archaic language. In his sonnet collection *Amoretti* (1595), Spenser laments the tension between working on *The Faerie Queene* (1590; 1596) and pursuing other types of writing; but he continued to produce lyric poetry throughout his career.

Often described as a seventeenth-century poet in order to substantiate a clear-cut break between the Elizabethan and Jacobean periods, John Donne in fact probably wrote many of his love lyrics and elegies during the 1590s. The rapid variations in tone and style from poem to poem, as well as within a single text, render his work as difficult to encapsulate as it is intriguing to read. The approaches commonly associated with him—the argumentative stance, the conversational voice, the witty playfulness, the intellectual knottiness—are famously present in such poems as "The Canonization" and "The Ecstasy," among many others. Such lyrics thus exemplify certain characteristics generally associated with metaphysical poetry: its philosophical speculations, its interest in abstract ratiocinations, and its so-called metaphysical conceits, startling images that typically link apparent opposites, such as sexuality and spirituality. Yet Donne's secular verse encompasses many other registers as well, including the lyric simplicity of songs like "Sweetest love, I do not go," a poem we would not be surprised to find in any Elizabethan miscellany. As such texts as "The Bait" and "The Funeral" demonstrate, Donne's canon also swerves from bitterly misogynistic poems, notably some graphically bawdy elegies, to ones that celebrate the beloved (or, as some readers claim, in appearing to do so primarily celebrate the speaker's power over her). (Some critics attempt to negotiate the infinite variety of Donne's lyrics by positing a chronological movement from the conventional language and eroticism of Petrarchism, a movement discussed in more detail below, to the refined spirituality of Neo-Platonism; but in fact these and other strains coexist in his work.)

The 1590s was a decade of not only extraordinary richness but also extraordinary variety in English poetry; remembering that John Donne may well have written many of his acerbic love poems during the period and that it also saw the development of formal verse satire provides a salutary qualification to generalizations about the lush, graceful verse conventionally associated with these ten years. Love poetry of many types flourished during the decade, drawing particularly on the erotic lyrics of Ovid and the sonnets of Petrarch. In particular, the sonnet tradition enjoyed a great vogue in the 1590s, inspired by the posthumous publication in 1591 of Sir Philip Sidney's collection *Astrophil and Stella*, which is discussed in more detail in the section on the sonnet below. Contributions to this genre during the 1590s range in tone and subject matter from the predictable but gracefully melodic verse in Samuel Daniel's *Delia* (1592) to the iconoclasm of Barnabe Barnes's *Parthenophil and Parthenophe* (1593), which ends in a startling fantasy of a rape.

In addition to love poetry, the 1590s saw the appearance of many other types of lyric. Witness, for example, the career of Michael Drayton, who during that decade alone published scriptural paraphrases, sonnets, pastorals, historical complaints, and historical epistles based on Ovid's *Heroides*. Indeed, some of the most intriguing lyric poems in the English language—variously intriguing in the ways they challenge their readers intellectually, impress them aesthetically, and woo them ideologically—date from the 1590s.

Literary and Cultural Conditions

Why, then, did the Renaissance lyric develop when and how it did? Literary, social, and cultural conditions in the early modern period inform it, and are in turn informed by it. To begin with, during that era the mode in question enjoyed, or more accurately endured, a lower status than certain other types of writing. Not only the problems of defining lyric but the imbricated challenges of evaluating and justifying it emerge with particular force in Sidney's *Defence of Poetrie* (1595), a treatise manifesting the defensiveness about the mode that recurs throughout the Tudor period. Sidney offers an impassioned justification of lyric: "who with his tuned lyre and well-accorded voice, giveth praise, the reward of virtue, to virtuous acts; who gives moral precepts, and natural problems; who sometimes raiseth up his voice to the height of the heavens, in singing the lauds of the immortal God."[6] Thus Sidney elevates and justifies the lyric by encompassing didactic poetry, the poetry of praise, and religious verse within the category in question. The text nervously proceeds, however, to answer the charge that lyric poetry includes amoral love poetry by suggesting such texts are an abuse of the potentials of the genre.

Other literary theories in the early modern period further complicated evaluations of lyric. A medieval formulation that remains popular during the Renaissance, the concept of the Vergilian wheel, states that Vergil moves chronologically from pastoral to georgic (literature about agricultural practice) to epic. This model encouraged later poets to define their careers in similar terms, thus spurring the writing of pastoral; yet the widely cited if historically inaccurate trajectory of the Vergilian wheel clearly privileges narrative forms over lyric. We encounter the same preference for narrativity when Aristotle posits a hierarchy of genres with tragedy at the pinnacle, a judgment adopted by many other writers as well; some Renaissance rhetoricians, including Sidney himself, offer an alternative ranking that privileges epic, reflecting the nationalistic aspirations of their era. But whichever of those systems one adopts, lyric does not win the lottery.

As I have already suggested, gender and gendering offer additional explanations for its dubious status. Love has been the subject of lyric poetry in many different eras, and in the early modern period in particular the connection between the two was intensified by the vogue the sonnet enjoyed in England in the 1590s, as well as by the popularity of love songs throughout the era. But the credo that love, including the activity of writing about it, is effeminate and effeminizing recurs throughout early modern texts. Or, to put it another way, one might say that in Renaissance aesthetics lyric adopts a female subject position to the male one of epic—not only inferior but also in some way threatening, much as female characters in both classical and Renaissance epics threaten the city that must be built, the nation that must be founded.

Yet sixteenth-century culture also offered many justifications for composing lyrics, even ones about love. Nationalism encouraged demonstrations that English poetry could rival the achievements of classical and Continental writers, including those of sonneteers. Attending to the commonplace that the Bible is a compendium of all genres, Renaissance lyricists could claim as their predecessor no less a figure than David, considered the author of the Psalms. Similarly, pastoral writers could dignify their work by adducing the revered Vergil as a forebear, as Spenser insistently does in his *Shepheardes Calender* (1579).

Prosodic developments and disagreements also shaped the aesthetics of the early modern lyric. Essentially English poets inherited two principal possibilities, accentual-syllabic and quantitative verse. The first, the main form of English poetry, grounds its metrical schemes both in where stresses fall and in the number of syllables. In contrast to these patterns, quantitative verse, practiced by Greek and Latin writers, ignores stress, relying instead on the length or quantity of its syllables. It is common—and broadly speaking accurate—to map the history of prosody in the sixteenth century as a movement from rough and unsuccessful experiments with iambic pentameter, the form of accentual-syllabic verse based on a pattern of five units that are typically iambic, to its triumphant execution in the mellifluous poetry of the 1590s. But this schema, while providing a sound overview, resembles the parallel assumption that the English sonnet was gradually moving from less successful rhyme schemes toward its natural form, the so-called Shakespearean sonnet; both trajectories have tempted critics to express a xenophobic nationalism, and both encompass as well the threat of underestimating the achievements of material that does not fit the pattern. Writers who do not achieve smooth iambic pentameter might be marching to, or rather composing for, a different drummer. Witness the debates about the decasyllabic (ten-syllable) lines of Sir Thomas Wyatt. Some read them as instances of crude early sorties into iambic pentameter; alternatively, critics have proposed a whole series of different systems that Wyatt might be successfully shaping, such as the skillful combination of the versification of Lydgate and Italianate hendecasyllabic (eleven-syllable) patterns that George T. Wright identifies as the drummer in Wyatt's hauntingly irregular lines.[7]

A more extreme alternative to iambic pentameter was the possibility of importing a system of quantitative verse into English. Impelled by their respect for Latin and Greek verse, a number of poets in the period debated and experimented with this option.

Edmund Spenser and an academic with whom he was friendly, Gabriel Harvey, exchanged a series of letters, published in 1580, about quantitative verse. Sir Philip Sidney, who delighted in experimenting with verse forms as well as with meter, also wrote some quantitative lyrics.

Debates about alternative metrical systems are closely related to controversies about whether rhyme is an appropriate ornament or a lamentable barbarism, since here too one central issue is whether English verse could and should imitate its classical predecessors. Despite his own success with rhyme, Thomas Campion, associating it with a lamentable neglect of classical principles of meter, mocks it in his *Observations in the Art of English Poesie* (1602): "the facilitie and popularitie of Rime creates as many Poets, as a hot sommer flies";[8] yet other sixteenth-century poets, notably Samuel Daniel, as vigorously defend rhyme.

Whatever their position on such debates, in practice sixteenth-century poets enthusiastically experimented with a range of stanzaic patterns. Courtly forms popular in the fifteenth century such as the rondeau, a French stanza in which the opening words recur, survive and flourish in the work of Sir Thomas Wyatt in particular—yet another warning of the dangers of stressing the modernity of the period at the expense of acknowledging its continuing affiliations with the past. Later in the century, poets, reveling in virtuoso performance, adopted a number of other difficult forms. For example, both Sidney and Spenser composed sestinas, a devilishly complex system of six six-line stanzas plus envoi that they inherited from Italian writers. The technical triumphs achieved in such challenging stanzaic patterns in turn pose challenges for us as critics: how can we most incisively reconcile—or perhaps most illuminatingly juxtapose—contemporary interpretations of the early modern writer as passive vehicle for cultural anxieties with the recognition that such poets were also agents effecting pyrotechnics of prosody?

The early modern lyric was, of course, shaped not only by rhythm in the literal sense but also by the rhythms of court life. Although the profound impact of the literary movement New Historicism and its English cousin cultural materialism have intensified critical interest in that environment, it was investigated from different perspectives by earlier students of the lyric. In particular, in *Music and Poetry in the Early Tudor Court*, a study published in 1961, John Stevens relates Renaissance poetry to conditions at the Tudor court, emphasizing in particular practices of setting poems to music and of passing lyrics among a circle of friends in what he terms "the game of love." Such connections between the Renaissance lyric and courtly music clarify debates about the workings of lyric in general, reminding us that in some important instances it is indeed linked with song—and, more significantly, linked as well with performance and courtly ritual, thus further calling into question generalizations about lyric as a spontaneous overflow of emotion.

The connections between lyric and song manifest the fascination with music that characterizes the English Renaissance, like its Continental counterparts. Philosophical treatises deploy music as a symbol for cosmic orders; the Renaissance schoolmaster Richard Mulcaster movingly advocates teaching it; poetic texts frequently fashion musical imagery. But this sibling art affected early modern poetry more immediately and directly as well. Songbooks were published throughout the sixteenth century, though they became especially popular and prevalent around the turn of the century. Songs ranged in form from the simple monophonic type called an "air," a form to which Thomas Campion and John Dowland contributed significantly, to the elaborately polyphonic madrigal, a form with Continental antecedents that was developed in England by William Byrd.

Musical settings survive for some well-known Renaissance lyrics, including the songs that were frequently incorporated into plays by Shakespeare and his contemporaries. A manuscript heading reminds us that no fewer than six of Donne's love poems were set to airs. Other poems allude to musical performance, as Wyatt famously does in "Blame not my lute" and "My lute, awake." Indeed, among the significant authors of Renaissance lyrics should be listed the composer Campion.

The second question Stevens had raised, the use of the lyric within social interactions, has been pursued from different perspectives by critics at the end of the twentieth century. Exemplifying the New Historicist privileging of politics in its many senses over the private spheres, Arthur F. Marotti's article "'Love is not love': Elizabethan Sonnet Sequences and the Social Order" (*ELH*, 49 [1982]: 396–428) impelled a revisionary redefinition of the functions of lyric. Sonnets that appear to be about love, Marotti argues, should really be read as statements about the author's struggle for patronage, a link encouraged by that supreme patroness Elizabeth's predilection for presenting herself as the mistress of sonnets. Marotti's assertion that struggles for place in the patronage system inform the more overt struggles for the affections of a disdainful mistress is persuasive. Yet, like many revisionist readings, this essay overstates its case: the insistence that poems that appear to be about love instead encode their primary concern with patronage is far less convincing than the alternative formulation that love lyrics, while centrally and often primarily concerned with romantic relationships, play love against courtly politics in ways that comment on both arenas.

Marotti and others have recently repositioned the Renaissance lyric in a different type of social context. Impelled by the materialist concern for the conditions of production, many critics have been tracing the consequences of the form in which Renaissance lyrics appeared. In particular, extensive and often exciting scholarship has illuminated the consequences of the movement from a manuscript to a print culture, with critics positing a radical change in conceptions of authorship.[9] As these studies indicate, numerous early modern lyrics were in fact circulated in manuscript, often in collections that included a range of poets and did not identify the authors; others appeared within popular collections such as *Tottel's Miscellany*; and yet others were published in single-author books, the format enjoyed by the posthumous volume of Sidney's *Astrophil and Stella*. All these patterns were complicated by the appearance of lyrics in commonplace books, collections compiled by an individual that might, for example, juxtapose poetry and recipes or scurrilous verse with more elevated poetry. Manuscript culture, according to the critics studying it, virtually erases the autonomy of the individual writer: a given poem might be significantly changed a number of times in transmission, and texts are seen as amorphous and permeable in ways that minimize the poet's identification with or control over his work. Print culture, in contrast, both impels and is impelled by a greater emphasis on the individual author, a perspective that such analyses see as tellingly parallel to the development of bourgeois conceptions of subjectivity.

Such arguments carry with them many intriguing implications about not only authorship but also content and style. For example, it is likely that the juxtaposition of disparate texts within a given manuscript both encouraged and was encouraged by the lyric's tendency to explore meaning relationally. That is, lyrics often comment explicitly or implicitly on alternative generic possibilities, which come to represent different perspectives and ideologies; for example, as Rosalie L. Colie demonstrates, the sonnet is on one level the opposite of epigram and on the other a host that welcomes epigrammatic couplets.[10] Moreover, the juxtapositions of texts in the practices of manuscript culture arguably encouraged as well an equally revealing phenomenon in the print culture of the period, the habit of publishing related but significantly different texts together in ways that invite comparison and contrast. Thus Spenser's *Amoretti* appears with his "Epithalamion" and some short lyrics in the form known as anacreontic.

Yet, despite these and many other important implications of the research that compares manuscript and print cultures, arguments about it need to be nuanced more than is sometimes the case. We have to recognize the coexistence of several models of authorship throughout the period, including very early versions of characteristics attributed to print culture. For example, the elaborate revisions visible on Wyatt's manuscripts suggest a pride in and concern for details of the text not usually associated with manuscript culture even though his poems were circulated in that form and, indeed, the kinds of laborious revision involved in crafting forms like the sonnet also suggest a model of authorship sometimes associated largely or even exclusively with a later period.

Lyric Genres

The significance of literary form in the period—a significance as paradoxical as it was profound—helps to explain why genre provides the best perspective on the sixteenth-century lyric. In England as on the Continent, generic classifications were at once studied sedulously and violated repeatedly. Forms not sanctioned by Aristotle, such as the romance, and so-called mixed genres or *genera mista* such as tragicomedy were variously condemned and pursued. Not coincidentally, in this combination of firmly established divisions and frequent violations of them the genre systems of the early modern period resemble its systems of social class and gender.

A wide range of literary types flourished during the sixteenth century. Given its intimate relationship to the sonnet, the epigram should also be read in relation to lyric. The epithalamium or wedding poem tradition, very popular in the seventeenth century, produced only a few sixteenth-century examples; but this select company includes Spenser's *Epithalamion* (1595) and his cognate poem the *Prothalamion* (1596), the latter celebrating nuptials of sisters rather than a marriage. The complaint, a type of poem whose speaker delivers a lament, often though not invariably about love, also proved popular in the period, encompassing such texts as Daniel's *Complaint of Rosamond* (1592). In 1591 Spenser published a group of poems, including "Prosopopoia," "Muiopotmos," and "Visions of the Worlds Vanitie" under the title *Complaints*; they demonstrate the variety in the genre, with the first a fable; the second a description, sometimes read allegorically, of a butterfly's capture; and the third visionary sonnets influenced by Du Bellay and Petrarch.

The elegy is another sixteenth-century form with complex valences. In classical literature, the term refers to a particular meter, the alternation of hexameter and pentameter lines. In sixteenth-century England, however, the label "elegy" was used loosely for a range of literary types, generally lyric—in particular, funeral poetry and solemn meditations on many different subjects, including love. Hence instances range from Spenser's funeral lament *Daphnaida* (1591) to a series of Ovidian poems by Donne. The popularity of the elegy in the early modern period and the recurrent, in fact obsessive, references to loss in many other genres signal the intimate relationship between lyric and loss. Although this relationship occurs in many periods, it is particularly marked in the English Renaissance because both the sonnet and pastoral are genres of loss. The versions of repetition—the recurrence of a refrain, a word, an action—that are so characteristic of lyric may be a way of negotiating loss and recovery: subsequent versions of the repeated element remind us of the absence of the original one and yet offer the hope of recovery via substitution.

Although the category of religious poetry is too loose clearly to constitute a genre, it represents another important type of sixteenth-century poetry. It is no accident that the sixteenth-century flowering of the English lyric coincided with the development of Protestantism, for the Reformation's emphasis on interior states and meditation is clearly very congenial to lyric poetry; tellingly, medieval religious poems often celebrate Mary or Christ rather than scrutinize the soul of the speaker. Protestantism also, of course, informed religious poetry more directly. Thus it generated an outpouring of hymns, the genre to which that deeply Protestant poet Sidney repeatedly alludes in his *Defence of Poetrie*; their influence is manifest, when, for example, Donne deploys the term in three of his divine poems, "A Hymne to Christ, at the Authors Last Going into Germany," "Hymne to God my God, in my Sicknesse," and "A Hymne to God the Father." This is not to deny, however, that the period also encompasses significant religious lyrics by Catholics, notably Robert Southwell.

Like the hymn, the sonnet form attracted many poets writing about religion and spirituality. Some critics have even suggested that a rejection of secular for spiritual love is central to the sonnet, although it is in fact present more intermittently and ambivalently. In any event it is clear that the struggles between the Augustinian concepts of *caritas* and *cupiditas*, which may roughly be rendered as the attraction of the soul toward God and its pull toward the corporeal, were sometimes enacted in the implicit or explicit juxtaposition of religious and spiritual poems; thus Barnabe Barnes published *Parthenophil and Parthenophe*, a highly eroticized collection of sonnets, in 1593, and two years later brought out what was virtually a palinode, *A Divine Centurie of Spirituall Sonnets*. Another type of religious poetry, metrical translations of the Psalms, was so common in the period that composing such texts has been described as a virtual initiation rite for fledgling poets. Sidney's sister Mary, Countess of Pembroke, participated in that vogue, while another woman writer, Anne Lok, wrote a collection of sonnets based on the fifty-first Psalm.

As such instances demonstrate, while women such as Louise Labé composed sonnets and other types of verse on the Continent, the principal mode of writing for sixteenth-century Englishwomen was religious verse, whether they translated it or, as in the case of Lok, composed it themselves. The argument that this was a less threatening arena for women's voices is persuasive; Lok not only writes spiritual poetry but also quite literally locates her voice within patriarchal strictures by appending her poetry to her translation of Calvin. But equally persuasive is the assertion that such poems demonstrate at least some measure of resistance to and even subversion of patriarchy; female poets were turning to a form whose value was unassailable and in so doing arguably implying as well that a higher audience would attend to their words even if their contemporaries did not.

The Sonnet

Love poetry was of course composed in a range of forms, including that broad category generally called "song." Even—or especially—collections of poems termed "sonnet sequences" frequently encompass a number of other stanzaic forms; *Astrophil and Stella*, for example, incorporates eleven songs. But arguably the sonnet and pastoral were the two most popular and characteristic lyric forms of the period. Hence exploring these two genres in greater depth than others can help us to address many questions about the workings of lyric in the sixteenth century.

One of the few instances in which a genre is defined in terms of a verse form, the sonnet can most safely be categorized as a fourteen-line poem that often, although not invariably, follows one of a handful of specified rhyme schemes and often, although not invariably, concerns love. One mark of the variety and experimentation that characterized the lyric during the early modern period, however, is the instability of even that loose a definition. In 1582, Thomas Watson published *Hecatompathia*, a collection of eighteen-line sonnets, and throughout the period other writers occasionally deviated from the fourteen-line pattern; moreover, the term "sonnet" was sometimes used loosely for love poetry, so that Donne's lyrics were termed *Songs and Sonnets* even though few of them have anything like the length or rhyme scheme usually associated with the term.

But normative models were also available and frequently imitated. Thus the so-called Petrarchan sonnet may rhyme *abba abba cde edc*; the first eight lines, the octet or octave, are fixed in their rhyme scheme, while the final three, the sestet, can assume a range of other shapes, such as *cdecde* or *cdcdee*. The sonnet labeled Shakespearean consists of three four-line units known as quatrains and a couplet, so it assumes the form: *abab cdcd efef gg*. All these versions of the sonnet play subdivisions against each other, the octet versus the sestet in the Petrarchan form and the quatrains versus the couplet in its English cousins; in addition, patterns of rhyme and meaning create further subdivisions, so that English sonnets, like their Italian predecessors, often include a significant break after line eight as well as the secondary shifts between quatrains. In the English sonnet these relationships among prosodic and semantic units tend to be varied and unstable. For example, while the Shakespearean sonnet often effects closure on a reassuring note of epigrammatic finality, couplets may undercut what has come before, or they may undercut the apparent neatness of their own unit, as when Shakespeare's Sonnet 35, a poem engaged throughout with the loss of comfortingly predictable patterns, begins its final statement in the twelfth, not thirteenth, line. Thus the form itself may enact an imperiled and often unsuccessful attempt at resolution.

Sidney's *Astrophil and Stella*, which signals both the speaker's connection with and distance from the author by naming him "Astrophil" or "star-lover," demonstrates the dramatic immediacy and psychological complexity the form could achieve. The sequence also demonstrates its author's delight in experimenting with verse form, rhyme, and rhetorical devices such as complex patterns of repetition. These poems, whose author attained a virtually mythic status after his early death, enjoyed an extraordinary popularity, as did many of Sidney's other writings. Spenser's *Amoretti* (1595) is sometimes contrasted with Sidney's collection as more melodious and descriptive in its style and less troubled in its responses to love and desire, though Spenser does in fact include some extraordinarily bitter invective as well as soaring praise of his lady. Similarly, it is customary to contrast the graceful lyricism of Samuel Daniel's *Delia* with the Sidneyan drama of Michael Drayton's sonnets, but such generalizations also need qualifications. Many of the poems in the first edition of Drayton's *Ideas Mirrour* (1594) are indistinguishable from Daniel's work; some of the putative distinctions in question gradually emerged as Drayton saw the volume through eleven editions, including three significant revisions in the seventeenth century, but the collection remained varied in tone and style. Other poets of the period produced not only some impressive sonnet sequences but also enough indifferent or truly dreadful ones to inspire Sir John Davies' witty parodies entitled "gullinge sonnets" (appearing only in a manuscript miscellany, not in printed form, during the early modern period and speculatively dated 1594). Although many of the other poems in the tradition were indeed as humdrum as Davies' mockery suggests, some distinguished themselves in significant ways. Richard Barnfield, for example, writes homoerotic sonnets. The sonnet became less popular around the turn of the century, though the first English sonnet sequence by a woman, Lady Mary Wroth's *Pamphilia to Amphilanthus*, appeared in 1621.

English sonnets have multiple and intertwined roots, including the poetry of the troubadours, the idealized visionary love poems in Dante's *Vita nuova*, and Neo-Platonic philosophy. The Italian poet Petrarch's collection, variously known by the revealing titles *Rime sparse* ("scattered rhymes") and *Canzoniere* ("songs"), is, however, the principal source of the English sonnet tradition. Although the *Rime sparse* encompasses a range of verse forms and subjects, most of its poems are sonnets concerning the speaker's relationship to Laura, a woman who may or may not have been fictive. These lyrics model several characteristics that English sonneteers were to imitate: a typically unhappy relationship with a woman who is often idealized but sometimes demonized (feminism has trenchantly glossed the reactive dynamic that structures that paradox), a preoccupation with representation itself, a struggle between a commitment to secular love and an attempt to disavow it, whether in the name of its spiritual counterpart or simply common sense and self-protection. Petrarch contributed as well a number of formal characteristics that recur in English sonnets. From him English poets borrowed the signature trope of the genre, the oxymoron, which combines opposites, generally in the form of an adjective-noun phrase such as "icy fire" or "sweet warrior." They adapted as well images for love that appeared in Petrarch and his predecessors, such as references to a hunt or a careening ship. Their interaction with the author of the *Rime sparse* was, however, mediated not only by his own commentators (his immense popularity generated ten major commentaries, so that his poems often appeared with elaborate and lengthy glosses) but also by the later Italian and French poets who themselves imitated him and thus implicitly commented on him. Four poems Daniel published in *Delia* derive from Du Bellay, for example, and Lodge bases several of his poems on sonnets by Ronsard, sometimes virtually plagiarizing them.

Indeed, nationalism, so central to the English early modern period in England in other ways, shapes its sonneteering as well, with an impulse to appropriate, nationalize, and surpass Continental models among its principal motivations. But, as I have already suggested, this is only one of several explanations for the extraordinary popularity of sonneteering. The sonnet attracted poets and readers in part because it enacted many of the central struggles of the age, often distancing them through transposition: its swings between power and powerlessness, for example, staged contemporary concerns about the uncertainties of social status.[11] Above all, though, Petrarchism served variously to intensify and resolve early modern negotiations about gender. As many critics have demonstrated, the genre provides reassuring scenarios for controlling the threats associated with the female body and female subjectivity; for example, the blazon, that part-by-part description of the female body, can provide an instance of divide and conquer. And yet such generalizations, though widely accepted, risk over-simplification: despite the conventional wisdom about the silencing of women in early modern culture, Petrarchan mistresses not only speak but are praised for their voices, and in fact the sequences most often manifest not the power of the male speaker but an unresolved struggle between power and powerlessness. Indeed, the Petrarchan sonnet models gender relations elsewhere in the culture above all in its complexities, contradictions, and ambivalences.

Pastoral

Pastoral was also especially popular in and characteristic of early modern English literature. But whereas the sonnet enjoyed a relatively brief but extraordinarily intense vogue during the sixteenth century, pastoral poetry was written virtually throughout the period, being variously deployed for love poetry, funeral elegies, meditations on religious and ethical problems, and satire, especially of the church; Spenser's *Shepheardes Calender* includes all of these approaches to the mode. Important and highly influential precedents to the English tradition include the *Eclogues* of Vergil (which attracted interest in part because the fourth poem was interpreted as prophesying the birth of Christ) and the lyrics of the Greek poets Theocritus, Bion, and Moschus. English poets were also familiar with their Continental predecessors in the genre; for example, Mantuan provided a significant precedent for using pastoral to discuss religion.

Probably the most famous pastoral of the period is Spenser's *Shepheardes Calender*; his choice of this form for his virtual poetic debut (he had previously published some translations) reflects both the continuing power of the model of the Vergilian wheel and the significance of this genre for his culture. Twelve eclogues comprise this collection, each accompanied by a woodcut, a motto, and elaborate notes by one "E.K.," who may or may not be Spenser himself. Among the many pastorals included in Sidney's prose romance, the *Arcadia* (1590), is "Ye goteherd gods"; the poet here skillfully deploys the repeated rhymes of the sestina to stage the obsessiveness of mourning. Another influential and revealing version of the genre is Christopher Marlowe's "Passionate Shepherd to his Love," a poem whose speaker attempts to seduce a lady by promising her the delights of the countryside; this lyric inspired a number of retorts in its own day, notably Sir Walter Ralegh's "Nymph's Reply to the Shepherd" and Donne's "Bait." In our own century Marlowe's text was turned into a cabaret song in Ian McKellan's cinematic version of *Richard III*, thus figuring the destruction and deformation of the values the poem ostensibly celebrates.

Once one moves beyond the obvious generalization that pastoral concerns the countryside, engaging with the values it represents and playing them against those of court or city, it becomes more complicated to define and describe the form. Certain conventionalized situations and formats do recur in the pastorals of many periods: shepherds often participate in singing contests, and they lament the sorrows of love. Often, too, pastorals describe invasions into the pastoral world, though this characteristic of the genre has not received the attention it deserves; whether effected by the intruders on whose threatened arrival Vergil tellingly opens his collection or by death, such intrusions mime and comment on the presence of other genres within pastoral, such as references to epic and satiric rebukes. Dialogues are common within pastoral, as is the Chinese-box effect of a frame story within which other stories are told. And pastoral, a strikingly reflexive genre, characteristically incorporates commentaries on its own practices, such as the act of writing poetry. Indeed, it is not only metapastoral but also metalyric in that the questions it raises about temporality, loss, and the workings of poetry itself are at the core of the lyric mode.

But what values and ideologies characterize pastoral? Some assert that it focuses on the relationship between man and nature, while others instead draw attention to its eroticism. Some claim pastoral is simple and idyllic, while others stress the complexities and ambivalences exemplified by the statement attributed to death in pastoral, *Et in Arcadia ego* ("I am even in Arcadia"). Some associate it with detachment, while others trace the ways pastoral allegorizes political, social, and religious controversies, as Spenser famously does in his *Shepheardes Calender*. In a major study of the genre, *What Is Pastoral?*, Paul Alpers negotiates a number of these debates, incisively arguing, for example, that pastoral typically neither denies nor drowns in the threats it engages but rather suspends them. And pastoral is, he suggests, often concerned primarily with the interactions in human communities.[12]

To understand the workings of pastoral in the early modern period, one needs to look more closely at additional characteristics and predilections as well. Its emphasis on the contrast between the *here* of the country and the *there* of city or court is the spatial analogue to its recurrent temporal preoccupation with *then* and *now*; the former is generally represented as the idyllic time before the pastoral world is threatened, whether by the new inhabitants who displace the shepherds in Vergil's first eclogue, by love, or by that figure who is both enemy and sibling of love in pastoral, death. This contrast between *then* and *now* is sometimes figured in the combination of narrative and lyric elements in pastoral. Pastoral is also typically concerned with the unstable relationship between loss and recovery. Thus, for example, in a sense the pastoral landscape is a second Eden, and yet it too is under threat (a pattern that recurs in dramatic pastorals such as Shakespeare's *As You Like It* as well as their lyric counterparts); and when a shepherd sings a song associated with another shepherd, he both recuperates that lyric and signals the absence of its original author. Pastoral, the genre that on some level represents a lost home, is also deeply concerned with threats to an abode; witness Vergil's telling decision to open his eclogues on a story of a shepherd being dispossessed.

Although these characteristics recur throughout the history of pastoral, they would have been especially appealing in the early modern period. Its interest in time and change attracted an era that was fascinated with history and historicity. Its emphasis on both the loss and restoration of home interested a culture that mythologized itself as a second Troy—and that feared that that Troy, like the first one, was subject to invasions, notably from the Catholic powers in Europe. Seamus Heaney, whose own poems are so often written within, about, and in defiance of history, observes, "A poem floats adjacent to, parallel to, the historical moment."[13] Even when pastoral does not comment directly on history and politics, it may trope them, floating adjacent to and thus variously refracting, redefining, and reinterpreting them.

But pastoral is often more directly connected with its culture as well, and this too helps to explain its appeal. Two of the most significant rhetorical treatises of the sixteenth century emphasize its congeniality to allegorical treatments of political and social issues. Although pastoral was seen as a low form during the Renaissance, involving both language and speakers less elevated than their counterparts in, say, epic, Sidney stresses that it could perform an important social function. "Is the poor pipe disdained, which sometime out of Meliboeus' mouth can show the misery of people under hard lords or ravening soldiers? . . . sometimes, under the pretty tales of wolves and sheep, can include the whole considerations of wrongdoing and patience" (*Defence of Poetrie*, p. 116). Sidney does precisely what he describes in his romance, the *Arcadia*. And in Book 1, Chapter 18 of his *Arte of English Poesie*, Puttenham asserts that the impetus behind pastoral was not in fact the exploration of love "but under the veil of homely persons, and in rude speeches to insinuate and glance at greater matters."[14] Exploring and expanding the commentaries by Sidney and Puttenham, recent studies have trenchantly traced how pastoral glances at "greater matters" of English Renaisssance politics and culture. Thus Annabel Patterson traces references to patronage, while Louis Montrose demonstrates the ways this genre explores, often in safely allegorical form, questions about power, status, and patronage.[15]

Conclusion

But much as Shakespeare's sonnets end on ostensible summaries that often instead challenge what has come before, so a survey of the genres of lyric poetry should terminate on an acknowledgment of the instability of that category. Some genres regularly encompass both lyric and narrative modes: witness the range of poems in Spenser's *Complaints*. The so-called lyric epithalamium dovetails both modes, insistently temporal in its chronicle of the events of the wedding day and lyric in its meditations on them. Similarly, the nymphs' song in Spenser's "Prothalamion" signals a change of mode through a change of speakers. But one of the best examples of the interplay between lyric and narrative is the sonnet tradition. Individual sonnets often tell stories; witness the whole host of mythological tales so popular in the genre, such as the seventeenth poem in Sidney's *Astrophil and Stella*. The tension between the attempt to find a plot in a collection of sonnets published by a given poet and the insistence that the poems in question reject narrativity is manifest in the terms used for such collections: "sonnet sequence" versus "sonnet cycle." The soundest approach to these debates moderates (in both senses of that verb) the extreme arguments on both sides: we need to recognize that the balance between lyric and narrative elements differs significantly from one group of sonnets to the next, but often a single author's collection of sonnets will juxtapose poems that are discrete meditations and might as plausibly be arranged in a different order with groups of sonnets that appear to tell a story. In any event, however one resolves the disagreements about the presence of narrative plots, in the sonnet as in many other genres the interaction among lyric, narrative, and dramatic elements stages the tensions among differing visions of problems ranging from temporality to gender.

We are now in a position briefly to return to my initial questions about the problems of defining lyric and relating it to sixteenth-century culture. Not only should definitions and descriptions be historically specific; the variety lyric manifests even within a single historical period, such as the early modern one, offers further caveats about generalizations. One can, however, say that in the Renaissance the connection between lyric and song is central. One can also assert with confidence that Renaissance lyrics variously qualify and challenge definitions that emphasize an isolated speaker overheard rather than participate in social interactions. To be sure, some poems, notably in the sonnet tradition, are indeed internalized meditations, and often their so-called plots are far more amorphous than critics more accustomed to reading narrative and drama like to acknowledge. But many other Renaissance lyrics evoke a social situation, whether it be that of the shepherd communicating with other shepherds or of the elegiac poet addressing the dead person or other mourners. And even the poems that involve internalized reflection often presume as well an audience who is not simply overhearing private thoughts but rather being indirectly addressed. The lament in a sonnet, for example, may present itself as a private outpouring of sorrow but also function as implicit pressure on the lady and an implicit complaint about her behavior to a male audience. Thus, though this predilection has not received the attention it deserves, Renaissance lyrics frequently address not just a single audience but rather multiple and different audiences.[16] In an age fascinated by rhetoric, the lyric poet is typically a consummate rhetorician, adorned with the literary skills and shadowed with the ethical dangers of that role.

The presence of multiple audiences aptly figures the ways contemporary critics can most fruitfully read the sixteenth-century lyric. We need to eschew generalizations that neglect its own multiplicity, and we need to approach it from many critical perspectives, alert to both technical virtuosity and ideological imperatives and thus to the complex interplay between formal potentialities and cultural history.

NOTES

1. Helen Vendler, "*Tintern Abbey*: Two Assaults," in *Wordsworth in Context*, ed. Pauline Fletcher and John Murphy (Lewisburg and London: Bucknell University Press and Associated University Presses, 1991), p. 184.

2. Northrop Frye, *Anatomy of Criticism: Four Essays* (Princeton: Princeton University Press, 1957), pp. 275–80.

3. For a useful overview of these changes, see Chaviva Hošek and Patricia Parker, "Introduction," in *Lyric Poetry: Beyond New Criticism*, ed. Hošek and Parker (Ithaca, NY: Cornell University Press, 1985).

4. David Lindley, *Lyric* (London: Methuen, 1985), pp. 22–24.

5. For this explanation of Skelton's prosody, see Arthur F. Kinney, *John Skelton; Priest as Poet: Seasons of Discovery* (Chapel Hill: University of North Carolina Press, 1987), esp. pp. 46–51.

6. The reference is to Sidney, *An Apologie for Poetrie*, ed. Geoffrey Shepherd (London: Nelson, 1965), p. 118.

7. George T. Wright, *Shakespeare's Metrical Art* (Berkeley: University of California Press, 1988), pp. 27–37.

8. The citation is to Campion, *Observations in the Art of English Poesie* (London, 1602), p. 4.

9. See esp. Arthur F. Marotti, *Manuscript, Print, and the English Renaissance Lyric* (Ithaca, NY: Cornell University Press, 1995); Wendy Wall, *The Imprint of Gender: Authorship and Publication in the English Renaissance* (Ithaca, NY: Cornell University Press, 1993).

10. Rosalie L. Colie, *Shakespeare's Living Art* (Princeton: Princeton University Press, 1974), ch. 2.

11. For a more detailed discussion of this and cognate explanations for its popularity, see my study *Echoes of Desire: English Petrarchism and Its Counterdiscourses* (Ithaca, NY: Cornell University Press, 1995).

12. On suspension see Paul Alpers, *What Is Pastoral?* (Chicago: University of Chicago Press, 1996), pp. 68–69, 173; he discusses community in a number of places, but see esp. pp. 81–82.

13. Heaney, *The Government of the Tongue: Selected Prose 1978–1987* (New York: Farrar, Straus and Giroux, 1989), p. 121.

14. I cite Puttenham, *The Arte of English Poesie*, ed. Baxter Hathaway (Kent, OH: Kent State University Press, 1970), p. 53.

15. See two essays by Montrose: "'Eliza, Queene of shepheardes,' and the Pastoral of Power," *English Literary Renaissance* 10 (1980): 153–82; "Of Gentlemen and Shepherds: The Politics of Elizabethan Pastoral Form," *English Literary History* 50 (1983): 415–59; Patterson, *Pastoral and Ideology: Virgil to Valéry* (Berkeley: University of California Press, 1987).

16. Multiple audiences are also common in love poetry in particular, a point Christopher Martin demonstrates, though from perspectives different from mine, in *Policy in Love: Lyric and Public in Ovid, Petrarch and Shakespeare* (Pittsburgh, PA: Duquesne University Press, 1994).

2.4 Introduction to *The Art of Shakespeare's Sonnets* (1997)

HELEN VENDLER

> There are indeed a sort of underlying auxiliars to the difficulty of work, call'd Commentators and Critics, who wou'd frighten many people by their number and bulk, and perplex our progress under pretense of fortifying their author.
>
> Alexander Pope to Joseph Addison, 1714

> In fact, every poem has the right to ask for a new poetics. This is created only once to express the contents, also given only once, of a poem.
>
> Anna Swir, quoted by Czeslaw Milosz in his introduction to *Talking to My Body*, by Anna Swir

Writing on the Sonnets

Before I begin to describe my own intentions in commenting on Shakespeare's *Sonnets*, I must say a few prefatory words. I intend this work for those who already know the *Sonnets*, or who have beside them the sort of lexical annotation found in the current editions (for example, those of Booth, Kerrigan, or Evans). A brief account of the reception history of the *Sonnets* can be found in these editions, as well as a more comprehensive bibliography than I can offer here. The older reception history in Hyder Rollins' *Variorum Sonnets* is still the most complete—and the most sobering to anyone hazarding a new addition to that history. Perhaps total immersion in the *Sonnets*—that is to say, in Shakespeare's mind—is a mildly deranging experience to anyone, and I cannot hope, I suppose, to escape the obsessive features characterizing Shakespearean sonnet criticism.

How are the *Sonnets* being written about nowadays? And why should I add another book to those already available? I want to do so because I admire the *Sonnets*, and wish to defend the high value I put on them, since they are being written about these days with considerable jaundice.[1] The spheres from which most of the current criticisms are generated are social and psychological ones. Contemporary emphasis on the participation of literature in a social matrix balks at acknowledging how lyric, though it may *refer to* the social, remains the genre that directs its *mimesis* toward the performance of the mind in *solitary* speech. Because lyric is intended to be voiceable by anyone reading it, in its normative form it deliberately strips away most social specification (age, regional location, sex, class, even race). A social reading is better directed at a novel or a play: the abstraction desired by the writer of, and the willing reader of, normative lyric frustrates the mind that wants social fictions or biographical revelations.

Even the best sociopsychological critic to write on the *Sonnets*, Eve Sedgwick, says "Shakespeare's Sonnets seem to offer a single, discursive, deeply felt *narrative* of the dangers and vicissitudes of one male homosocial adventure" [49]; "It is here that *one most wishes the Sonnets were a novel, that readers have most treated it as a novel*, and that we are, instead, going to bring the Sonnets' preoccupation to bear on *real novels*" [46] (italics mine). The persistent wish to turn the sequence into a novel (or a drama) speaks to the interests of the sociopsychological critic, whose aim is less to inquire into the successful carrying-out of a literary project than to investigate the representation of gender relations. It is perhaps a tribute to Shakespeare's "reality-effect" that "one most wishes the Sonnets were a novel," but it does no good to act as if these lyrics were either a novel or a documentary of a lived life.

Other critics (Barrell, Marotti, Kernan) have brought the *Sonnets* into the realm of the social by drawing analogies between the language of the poetry and the language of solicitations addressed to patrons and requesting patronage. This is a reasonable semantic (if not poetic) investigation, and reminds us that lyric language in any given epoch draws on all available sociolects of that epoch. The *Sonnets*, however (as Kernan makes clear), go far outside the originating discourse: no patron was ever addressed *qua* patron in language like that of sonnet 20 (*A woman's face with Nature's own hand painted*). Aesthetically speaking, it is what a lyric *does with* its borrowed social languages—i.e., how it casts them into new permutational and combinatorial forms—that is important. Shakespeare is unusually rich in his borrowings of diction and formulas from patronage, from religion, from law, from courtship, from diplomacy, from astronomy, and so on; hut he tends to be a blasphemer in all of these realms. He was a master subverter of the languages he borrowed, and the point of *literary* interest is not the fact of his borrowings but how he turned them inside out. (See, in the commentary, sonnets 20, 33, 105, 135, or 144.)[2] One of Shakespeare's most frequent means of subversion is the total redefinition, within a single sonnet, of a word initially borrowed from a defined social realm (such as *state* in sonnet 33); there is no social discourse which he does not interrogate and ironize.

The sonnets have also been investigated by psychoanalytically minded critics, of whom the most formidable was the late Joel Fineman. Fineman, fundamentally disappointed by the Young Man sonnets, much preferred the Dark Lady sequence, where "difference" (read: the Lacanian Symbolic) replaces "sameness" (read: the Lacanian Imaginary).[3] Anyone who prizes drama above other genres delights in conflict, the structural principle of drama; and for Shakespeareans the Dark Lady sequence is, give or take a few details, a proto-sketch for a drama rather like *Othello*, with its jealousy, its sexuality, its ambiguous "darkness," its betrayals, and so on. It is much harder to imagine the Young Man sequence as a play. Yet, if one judges not by the criteria proper to drama but by those appropriate to lyric—"How well does the structure of this poem mimic the structure of thinking?" and "How well does the linguistic play of the poem embody that structural mimesis?"—Shakespeare's first subsequence is at least as good as (and in my view better than) the second. A psychological view of the *Sonnets* (whether psychoanalytically oriented or not) stresses motivation, will, and other characterological features, and above all needs a story on which to hang motivation. The "story" of the *Sonnets* continues to fascinate readers, but lyric is both more and less than story. And, in any case, the story of the *Sonnets* will always exhibit those "gaps" and that "indeterminacy" intrinsic to the sonnet sequence as a genre [Kuin, 251][4]. A coherent psychological account of the *Sonnets* is what the *Sonnets* exist to frustrate. They do not fully reward psychological criticism (or gender criticism, motivated by many of the same characterological aims) any more than they do political criticism. Too much of their activity escapes the large sieves of both psychology and politics, disciplines not much concerned to examine the basic means of lyric: subgenre, structure, syntax, and linguistic play.

The true "actors" in lyric are words, not "dramatic persons"; and the drama of any lyric is constituted by the successive entrances of new sets of words, or new stylistic arrangements (grammatic, syntactical, phonetic) which are visibly in conflict with previous arrangements used with reference to the "same" situation. (See, for example, my comments on sonnet 73 or sonnet 116.) Thus, the introduction of a new linguistic strategy is, in a sonnet, as interruptive and interesting as the entrance of a new character in a play. And any internal change in topic (from autumn to twilight to glowing fire in sonnet 73, for instance) or any change in syntactic structure (say, from parallel placement of items to chiastic placement) are among the strategies which—because they mimic changes of mind—constitute vivid drama within the lyric genre. Read in the light of these lyric criteria, the first subsequence is fully as dramatic (in the form proper to lyric) as the second. The art of seeing drama in linguistic action proper (action that may be as simple as the grammatical change in a given passage from nouns to verbals and back again—see sonnet 129) is an art that has lapsed, even in interpreters whose criteria appear to be literary rather than political or psychological.[5]

What, then, am I attempting in the Commentary below? Chiefly, a supplement to the accounts of the *Sonnets* in current editions (Ingram and Redpath, Booth,[6] Kerrigan, Evans) and in the books of the last thirty years (notably those by Leishman, Melchiori, Trousdale, Booth, Dubrow, Fineman, Vickers, de Grazia, Roche, Pequigney, Sedgwick, Weiser, and Martin). These editorial and critical accounts do not, to my mind, pay enough attention to the sonnets as poems—that is, as a writer's projects invented to amuse and challenge his own capacity for inventing artworks. Formal mimeses of the mind and heart in action are of course representative of human reality, but it is not enough to show that the moves of their language "chart . . . the ways we may be affected, morally and emotionally, by our own rhetoric" [Dubrow, 213].[7] A poem must be beautiful, too, exhibiting the double beauty that Stevens called "the poetry of the idea" and "the poetry of the words." That is, the theme must be freshly imagined, the genre must be renewed, and the words must surprise and satisfy from the point of view of proportion, musicality, and lexical vivacity.

[...]

Evidence and Import

This Commentary consists primarily of what might be called "evidential" criticism: that is, I wanted to write down remarks for which I attempt to supply instant and sufficient linguistic evidence. This, like all Platonic aims, must be imperfectly achieved, but I've tried to remember it at every point. There must of course be conjecture and speculation in divining the poetic laws which are being obeyed by a particular series of words, but I have given the reasons for my conjectures in as plain a way as I could find. One can write convincing evidential criticism only on fairly short texts (in longer texts, the permutations become too numerous). The *Sonnets* are ideal for such a purpose; and they deserve detailed and particular commentary because they comprise a virtual anthology of lyric possibility—in the poet's choice of subgenres, in arrangements of words, in tone, in dramatic modeling of the inner life, in speech-acts. In every case, I wanted to delineate whatever the given sonnet offered that seemed aesthetically most provocative: if there is an interesting change of address, it will be remarked, while a predictable change of address may not be commented on at all. The presence of unexpected (or inexplicable) words will be dwelt on; other words may go unnoticed. I have tried to point out problems that I have not been able to solve to my own satisfaction.

I come to Shakespeare's *Sonnets* as a critic of lyric poetry, interested in how successful poems are put together, ideationally, structurally, and linguistically; or, to put it another way, what ideational and structural and linguistic acts by a poet result in a successful poem. The brilliant beginnings in this direction by William Empson (on individual words and images), Winifred Nowottny (on formal arrangement), Stephen Booth (on overlapping structures), and Brian Vickers and Heather Dubrow (on rhetorical figuration) suggest that such efforts are particularly rewarding. Inevitably, rather few sonnets have been examined in detail, since critics tend to dwell on the most famous ten or fifteen out of the total 154; in fact, the *Sonnets* represent the largest tract of unexamined Shakespearean lines left open to scrutiny. As A. Nejgebauer remarked in his recapitulation (in the 1962 *Shakespeare Survey*) of work on the *Sonnets*: "Criticism of the sonnets will not stand comparison with that of the plays. . . . It has largely been amateurish and misplaced. . . . As regards the use of language, stanzaic structure, metre, tropes, and imagery, these demand the full tilth and husbandry of criticism" [18]. Nejgebauer's complaint could not be made with quite the same vehemence today, largely because of Stephen Booth's massive intervention with his *Essay on Shakespeare's Sonnets* (1969) and his provocative edition of the *Sonnets* (1977). Yet Booth's critical stance—that the critic, helpless before the plurisignification of language and overlapping of multiple structures visible in a Shakespearean sonnet, must be satisfied with irresolution with respect to its fundamental gestalt—seems to me too ready a surrender to hermeneutic suspicion.

On the other hand, the wish of interpreters of poems to arrive at something they call "meaning" seems to me misguided. However important "meaning" may be to a theological hermeneutic practice eager to convey accurately the Word of God, it cannot have that importance in lyric. Lyric poetry, especially highly conventionalized lyric of the sort represented by the *Sonnets*, has almost no significant freight of "meaning" at all, in our ordinary sense of the word. "I have insomnia because I am far away from you" is the gist of one sonnet; "Even though Nature wishes to prolong your life, Time will eventually demand that she render you to death" is the "meaning" of another. These are not taxing or original ideas, any more than other lyric "meanings" ("My love is like a rose," "London in the quiet of dawn is as beautiful as any rural scene," etc.). Very few lyrics offer the sort of philosophical depth that stimulates meaning-seekers in long, complex, and self-contradicting texts like Shakespeare's plays or Dostoevsky's novels. In an effort to make lyrics more meaning-full, even linguistically minded critics try to load every rift with ore, inventing and multiplying ambiguities, plural meanings, and puns as if in a desperate attempt to add adult interest to what they would otherwise regard as banal sentiment. This is Booth's path, and it is also that of Joseph Pequigney, who would read the words of the *Sonnets* as an elaborate code referring to homosexual activity. Somehow, Shakespeare's words and images (most of the latter, taken singly, fully conventional) do not seem interesting enough as "meaning" to scholarly critics; and so an argument for additional "ambiguous" import is presented, if only to prop up Shakespeare's reputation. The poet Frank O'Hara had a better sense for the essential semantic emptiness of love lyrics when he represented them (in his poem "Blocks") as "saying" "I need you, you need me, yum yum." The appeal of lyric lies elsewhere than in its paraphrasable statement. Where, then, does the charm of lyric lie? The answers given in this Commentary are as various as the sonnets examined, since Shakespeare almost never repeats a strategy. However, they can be summed up in the phrase "the arrangement of statement." Form is content-as-arranged; content is form-as-deployed.

[. . .]

The Art of the Sonnets, and the Speaker They Create

With respect to the *Sonnets*—a text now almost four hundred years old—what can a commentary offer that is new? It can, I think, approach the sonnets, as I have chosen to do, from the vantage point of the poet who wrote them, asking the questions that a poet would ask about any poem. What was the aesthetic challenge for Shakespeare in writing these poems, of confining himself (with a few exceptions) to a single architectural form? (I set aside, as not of essential importance, the money or privileges he may have earned from his writing.) A writer of Shakespeare's seriousness writes from internal necessity—to do the best he can under his commission (if he was commissioned) and to perfect his art. What is the inner agenda of the *Sonnets*? What are their compositional motivations? What does a writer gain from working, over and over, in one subgenre? My brief answer is that Shakespeare learned to find strategies to enact feeling in form, feelings in forms, multiplying both to a superlative degree through 154 poems. No poet has ever found more linguistic forms by which to replicate human responses than Shakespeare in the *Sonnets*.

Shakespeare comes late in the sonnet tradition, and he is challenged by that very fact to a display of virtuosity, since he is competing against great predecessors. His thematic originality in his *dramatis personae* makes the sequence new in Western lyric. Though the sharing of the speaker by the young man and the lady, and the sharing of the young man by the lady and the rival poet, could in other hands become the material of farce, the "plot" is treated by Shakespeare elegiacally, sardonically, ironically, and tragically, making the *Sonnets* a repository of relationships and moods wholly without peer in the sonnet tradition. However, thematic originality alone never yet made a memorable artwork. Nor did psychological depth—though that is at least a prerequisite for lyric profundity.

No sufficient description exists in the critical literature of how Shakespeare makes his speaker "real." (The speaker is the only "person" interiorized in the *Sonnets*, though there are other *dramatis personae*.) The act of the lyric is to offer its reader a script to say. The words of a poem are not "overheard" (as in the formulations of J. S. Mill and T. S. Eliot);

this would make the reader an eavesdropping voyeur of the writer's sensations. Nor is the poet "speaking to himself" without reference to a reader (if so, there would he no need to write the poem down, and all communicative action would be absent). While the social genres "build in" the reader either as listener (to a narrator of a novel) or as audience (to a play), the private literary genres—such as the Psalms, or prayers printed in prayer books, or secular lyrics—are scripted for repeated personal recitation. One is to utter them as one's own words, not as the words of another. Shakespeare's sonnets, with their unequaled idiomatic language-contours (written, after all, by a master in dramatic speech who shaped that speech into what C. S. Lewis called their lyric *cantabile*), are preeminently utterances for us to utter as ours. It is indispensable, then, if we are to be made to want to enter the lyric script, that the voice offered for our use be "believable" to us, resembling a "real voice" coming from a "real mind" like our own.

It is hard to achieve such "realness." Many lyrics are content with a very generalized and transient voice, one of no determinate length of life or depth of memory. In a drama, the passage of time and the interlocking of the web of events in which a character participates allow for a gradual deepening of the constructed personality of even minor characters. But Shakespeare must render his sonnet-speaker convincing in a mere fourteen lines. He is helped, to this end, by the fact that a "thick description" of his speaker accretes as the sequence progresses; but since few readers read the sequence straight through, the demand for evident "realness" in each poem, even were it to stand alone in an anthology, remains. The *Sonnets* cannot be "dramatic" in the ordinary sense because in them, as in every lyric of a normative sort, there is only one authorized voice. True drama requires at least two voices (so that even Beckett's monologues often include an offstage voice, or a tape of a voice, to fulfill this requirement). Some feminist critics, mistaking lyric for a social genre, have taken offense that the women who figure as *dramatis personae* within sonnet sequences are "silenced," meaning that they are not allowed to expostulate or reply. In that (mistaken) sense one would have to see *all* addressees in lyric as "silenced" (God by George Herbert, Robert Browning by E. B. Browning) since no addressee, in normative lyric, is given a counter and equal voice responding to that of the speaker.[8] Since the person uttering a lyric is always represented as alone with his thoughts, his imagined addressee can by definition never be present. The lyric (in contrast to the dramatic monologue, where there is always a listener present in the room), gives us the mind alone with itself. Lyric can present no "other" as alive and listening or responding in the same room as the solitary speaker. (One of Herbert's witty genre-inventions, depending on this very genre-constraint, was to assert that since God is everywhere, God could be present in the room even in the speaker's "solitariness" and could thus offer a reply, as God the Father does in "The Collar" and as Jesus does in "Dialogue.")

Shakespeare's speaker, alone with his thoughts, is the greatest achievement, imaginatively speaking, of the sequence. He is given "depth" of character in each individual sonnet by several compositional strategies on Shakespeare's part. These will be more fully described and demonstrated in the individual commentaries below, but in brief they are:

1. *Temporal*. The establishment of several retreating "panels" of time, representing episodes or epochs in the speaker's past, gives him a continuous, nontransient existence and a continuity of memory. (See, for example, sonnet 30, *When to the sessions of sweet silent thought.*)

2. *Emotional.* The reflection, within the same poem, of sharply conflicting moods with respect to the same topic (see, e.g., sonnet 148, *O me! what eyes hath love put in my head*). This can be abetted by contradictory or at least nonhomogeneous discourses rendering a topic complicated (see, e.g., sonnet 125, *Wer't aught to me I bore the canopy*). The

volatility of moods in the speaker (symbolized by the famous *lark at break of day arising* of sonnet 29) suggests a flexibility—even an instability—of response verbally "guaranteeing" the presence of passion.

3. *Semantic.* The speaker's mind has a great number of compartments of discourse (theological, legal, alchemical, medicinal, political, aesthetic, etc.). These compartments are semipervious to each other, and the osmosis between them is directed by an invisible discourse-master, who stands for the intellectual imagination.

4. *Conceptual.* The speaker resorts to many incompatible models of existence (described in detail in the commentary) even within the same poem; for example, sonnet 60 first describes life as a homogeneous steady-state succession of identical waves/minutes (a stoic model); then as a sharply delineated rise-and-eclipse of a sun (a tragic model); and next as a series of incessant violent extinctions (a brutal model). These models, unreconciled, convey a disturbing cognitive dissonance, one which is, in a philosophical sense, intolerable. The alert and observant mind that constructs these models asserts the "truth" of each for a particular occasion or aspect of life, but finds no "supramodel" under which they can be intelligibly grouped, and by which they can be intelligibly contained. In this way, the mind of the speaker is represented as one in the grip of philosophical conflict.

5. *Philosophical.* The speaker is a rebel against received ideas. He is well aware of the received topoi of his culture, but he subjects them to interrogation, as he counters neo-Platonic courtly love with Pauline marital love (116), or the Christian Trinity with the Platonic Triad (105), or analogizes sacred hermeneutics to literary tradition (106). No topics are more sharply scrutinized than those we now subsume under the phrase "gender relations": the speaker interrogates androgyny of appearance by evoking a comic myth of Nature's own dissatisfaction with her creation (20); he criticizes hyperbolic praise of female beauty in 130; he condones adultery throughout the "will" sonnets and elsewhere (and sees adultery as less criminal than adulterated discourse, e.g., in 152). This is not even to mention the interrogations of "love" and "lust" in 116 and 129 (sonnets of which the moral substance has not been properly understood because they have not been described in formal terms). No received idea of sexuality goes uninvestigated; and the thoroughly unconventional sexual attachments represented in both parts of the sequence stand as profound (if sometimes unwilling) critiques of the ideals of heterosexual desire, chastity, continence, marital fidelity, and respect for the character of one's sexual partner. What "ought to be" in the way of gender relations (by Christian and civic standards) is represented as an ideal in the "marriage sonnets" with which the sequence opens, but never takes on existential or "realist" lived validation. Shakespeare's awareness of norms is as complete as his depiction, in his speaker, of experiential violation of those norms.

6. *Perceptual.* The speaker is also given depth by the things he notices, from damask roses to the odor of marjoram to a canopy of state. Though the sonnets are always openly drifting toward emblematic or allegorical language, they are plucked back (except in extreme cases like 66) into the perceptual, as their symbolic rose is distilled into "real" perfume (54) or as an emblematic April is *burned* by *hot* June (104). The speaker stands poised between a medieval emblematic tendency and a more modern empirical posture; within his moral and philosophical systems, he savors the tang of the "sensual feast."

7. *Dramatic.* The speaker indirectly quotes his antagonist. Though no one but the speaker "speaks" in a lyric, Shakespeare exploits the usefulness of having the speaker, in private, quote in indirect discourse something one or the other of the *dramatis personae* previously said. Many of the sonnets (e.g., 76 and 116) have been misunderstood because they have been thought to be free-standing statements on the speaker's part rather than replies to the antagonist's implicitly quoted words. Again, I support this statement below in detail; but one

can see what a difference it makes to interpretation whether in sonnet 76 the poet-speaker means to criticize his own verse—"Why is my verse so barren of new pride?"—or whether he is repeating, by quoting, an anterior criticism by the young man: "Why [you ask] is my verse so [in your words] 'barren of new pride'?" In the (often bitter) give-and-take of prior-criticism-answered-by-the-speaker (in such rebuttal-sonnets as 105, 117, 151, and the previously mentioned 76 and 116), we come closest, in the sonnets, to Shakespeare the dramatist.

More could be said of the strategies that create a credible speaker with a complex and imaginative mind (a mind which we take on as our own when stepping into the voice); but I want to pass on to the greatest strength of the sonnets as "contraptions," their multiple armatures. Booth sees these "overlapping structures" as a principle of irresoluble indeterminacy; I, by contrast, see them as mutually reinforcing, and therefore as principles of authorial instruction.

Organizing Structures

When lyric poems are boring, it is frequently because they possess only one organizing structure, which reveals itself unchanged each time the poem is read. *If* the poet has decided to employ a single structure (in, say, a small two-part song such as "When daisies pied and violets blue"), then the poem needs some other principle of interest to sustain rereading (in that song, a copious set of aspects—vegetative, human, and avian—of the spring). Shakespeare abounds in such discourse-variety, and that in part sustains rereadings of the sonnets; but I have found that rereading is even better sustained by his wonderful fertility in structural complexity. The Shakespearean sonnet form, though not invented by Shakespeare, is manipulated by him in ways unknown to his predecessors. Because it has four parts—three isomorphic ones (the quatrains) and one anomalous one (the couplet), it is far more flexible than the two-part Italian sonnet. The four units of the Shakespearean sonnet can be set in any number of logical relations to one another:

successive and equal;
hierarchical;
contrastive;
analogous;
logically contradictory;
successively "louder" or "softer."

This list is merely suggestive, and by no means exhaustive. The four "pieces" of any given sonnet may also be distinguished from one another by changes of agency ("I do this; you do that"), of rhetorical address ("O Muse"; "O beloved"), of grammatical form (a set of nouns in one quatrain, a set of adjectives in another), or of discursive texture (as the descriptive changes to the philosophical), or of speech act (as denunciation changes to exhortation). Each of these has its own poetic import and effect. The four "pieces" of the sonnet may be distinguished, again, by different phonemic clusters or metrical effects. Booth rightly remarks on the presence of such patternings, but he refuses to establish hierarchy among them, or to subordinate minor ones to major ones, as I think one can often do.

I take it that a Shakespearean sonnet is fundamentally structured by an evolving inner emotional dynamic, as the fictive speaker is shown to "see more," "change his mind," "pass from description to analysis," "move from negative refutation to positive refutation," and so on. There can be a surprisingly large number of such "moves" in any one sonnet. The impression of an evolving dynamic within the speaker's mind and heart is of course created by a large "law of form" obeyed by the words in each sonnet. Other observable structural patterns play a subordinate role to this largest one. In its Shakespearean incarnation, the sonnet is a system in motion, never immobile for long, and with several subsystems going their way within the whole.

The chief defect in critical readings of the *Sonnets* has been the critics' propensity to take the first line of a sonnet as a "topic sentence" which the rest of the poem merely illustrates and reiterates (a model visible in Berowne's sonnet quoted above). Only in the plays does Shakespeare write nondramatic sonnets in this expository mode. In his lyrics, he sees structure itself as motion, as a composer of music would imagine it. Once the dynamic curve of a given sonnet is perceived, the lesser structuring principles "fall into place" beneath it. See, e.g., my commentary on 129 for a textbook example of a trajectory of changing feelings in the speaker about a single topic (lust); it is the patterns and underpatterns of the sonnet that enable us to see the way those feelings change. If the feeling were unchanging, the patterns would also remain invariable. The crucial rule of thumb in understanding any lyric is that every significant change of linguistic pattern represents a motivated change in feeling in the speaker. Or, to put it differently, if we sense a change of feeling in the speaker, we must look to see whether, and how, it is stylistically "guaranteed." Unless it is deflected by some new intensity, the poem continues by inertia in its original groove.

I deliberately do not dwell in this Commentary on Shakespeare's imagery as such, since it is a topic on which good criticism has long existed. Although large allegorical images (*beauty's rose*) are relatively stable in the *Sonnets*, imagery is meaningful only in context; it cannot be assigned secure symbolic import except with respect to the poem in which it occurs. The point, e.g., of the fire in sonnet 73 (*That time of year*) is that it is a stratified image: the glowing of the fire *lies upon* the ashes of youth. The previous images in the sonnet have been linear ones (*time of year* and *twilight*) referring to an extension in time (a year, a day), rather than superposition in space. By itself, the image "fire" does not call up the notion of stratification, nor does it in the other sonnets in which it appears; but in this poem, because of the poet's desire for variance from a previously established linear structure, the fire is called upon to play this spatial role, by which youth appears as exhausted subpositioned ashes rather than as an idyllic era (*the sweet birds*; *sunset*) lost at an earlier point in a timeline. Previous thematic commentators have often missed such contextual determination of imagistic meaning.

In trying to see the chief aesthetic "game" being played in each sonnet, I depart from the isolated registering of figures—a paradox here, an antimetabole there—to which the practice of word-by-word or phrase-by-phrase commentary inevitably leads. I wish to point out instead the larger imaginative or structural patterns in which such rhetorical figures take on functional (by contrast to purely decorative) significance. I do not intend, by this procedure, to minimize the sonnets' ornamental "excess" (so reprehensible to Pound); no art is more pointedly ornamental (see Puttenham) than the Renaissance lyric. Yet Shakespeare is happiest when an ornamental flourish can be seen to have a necessary poetic function. His changes in discursive texture, and his frequent consciousness of etymological roots as he plays on Anglo-Saxon and Latin versions of the "same" meaning ("with my *extern* the *outward* honoring"), all become more striking when incorporated into a general and dynamic theory of the poem. (Rather than invoke the terms of Renaissance rhetoric, which do not convey much to the modern reader, I use ordinary language to describe Shakespeare's rhetorical figuration.)

To give an illustration; I myself find no real functional significance in Shakespeare's alliteration when the speaker says that in *the swart com**p**lexioned night, / When **sp**arkling **st**ars **tw**ire not, thou [the young man] gild**st** the even.* Such phonetic effects seem to have a purely decorative intent. But an alliterative "meaning-string"—such as sonnet 25's *favour,* *fortune, triumph, favourites, fair, frown, painful, famousèd, fight* (*an emendation*), *foiled,* and *forgot*—encapsulates the argument of the poem in little, and helps to create and sustain that argument as it unfolds. Grammar and syntax, too, can be functionally significant to argument; see, for instance, the way in which 66 uses phrases of agency, or the way in which 129 uses its many verbals. In his edition of the *Sonnets*, Booth leaves it up to the reader to construct the poem; I have hoped to help the reader actively to that construction by laying out evidence that no interpretation can afford to ignore. Any number of interpretations, guided by any number of interests, can be built on the same foundation of evidence; but an interpretation ignoring that evidence can never be a defensible one.

I believe that anyone seriously contemplating the interior structures and interrelations of these sonnets is bound to conclude that many were composed in the order in which they are arranged. However, given the poems' variation in aesthetic success, it seems probable that some sonnets—perhaps written in youth (as Andrew Gurr suggested of the tetrameter sonnet 145, with its pun on "Hathaway") or composed before the occurrence of the triangular plot—were inserted *ad libitum* for publication. (I am inclined to believe Katherine Duncan-Jones's argument that the *Sonnets* may have been an authorized printing.) The more trifling sonnets—those that place ornament above imaginative gesture, or fancifulness above depth (such as 4, 6, 7, 9, 145, 153, and 154)—do seem to be less experienced trial-pieces. The greater sonnets achieve an effortless combination of imaginative reach with high technical invention (18, 73, 124, 138), or a quintessence of grace (104, 106, 132), or a power of dramatic condensation (121, 147) that we have come to call "Shakespearean," even if, as Kent Hieatt (1991) has persuasively shown, they were composed in groups over time.

The speaker of Shakespeare's sonnets scorns the consolations of Christianity—an afterlife in heaven for himself, a Christian resurrection of his body after death—as fully as he refuses (except in a few sonnets) the learned adornment of classical references—a staple of the continental sonnet. The sonnets stand as the record of a mind working out positions without the help of any pantheon or any systematic doctrine. Shakespeare's speaker often considers, in rapid succession, any number of intellectual or ideological positions, but he does not move among them at random. To the contrary: in the first quatrain of any given sonnet he has a wide epistemological field in which to play, but in the second quatrain he generally queries or contradicts or subverts his first position (together with its discourse-field). By the third quatrain, he must (usually) advance to his subtlest or most comprehensive or most truthful position (Q_3 therefore taking on, in the Shakespearean sonnet, the role of the sestet in the Petrarchan sonnet). And the couplet—placed not as resolution (which is the function of Q_3) but as coda—can then stand in any number of relations (summarizing, ironic, expansive) to the preceding argument. The gradually straitened possibilities as the speaker advances in his considerations give the Shakespearean sonnet a funnel-shape, narrowing in Q_3 to a vortex of condensed perceptual and intellectual force, and either constricting or expanding that vortex via the couplet.

The Couplet

The Shakespearean couplet has often been a stumbling block to readers. Rosalie Colie's helpful distinction (in *Shakespeare's Living Art*) between the *mel* (honey) of love-poetry and the *sal* (salt) of epigram—a genre conventionally used for satiric purposes—represents a real insight into the mind of Shakespeare's speaker: the speaker is a person who wishes to analyze and summarize his experience as well as to describe and enact it. The distance from one's own experience necessitated by an analytic stance is symbolized most fully by the couplet, whereas the empathetic perception necessary to display one's state of mind is symbolized by the quatrains. In speaking about the relation of quatrain to couplet, one must distinguish the fictive speaker (even when he represents himself as a poet) from Shakespeare the author. The fictive speaker gradually becomes, over the course of the poem, more analytic about his situation (and therefore more distanced from his first self-pathos) until he finally reaches the couplet, in which he often expresses a self-ironizing turn:

> For thee watch I, whilst thou dust wake elsewhere,
> From me far off, with others all too near. (sonnet 61)

This we can genuinely call intrapsychic irony in the fictive speaker. But the author, who is arranging the whole poem, has from the moment of conception a relation of irony to his fictive persona. The persona lives in the "real time" of the poem, in which he feels, thinks, and changes his mind; the author has planned the whole evolution of the poem before writing the first line, and "knows" conceptually the gyrations which he plans to represent taking place over time in his fictive speaker. There is thus a perpetual ironizing of the living temporality of the speaker by the coordinating spatial overview of the author. Although the speaker seems "spontaneous" in his utterance, the cunning arrangements of the utterance belong primarily to Shakespeare (even if dramatically ascribed to the speaker). It is at the moment of the couplet that the view of the speaker and the view of the author come nearest to convergence.

NOTES

1. The most recent book considering them in some detail—Christopher Martin's *Policy in Love: Lyric and Public in Ovid, Petrarch and Shakespeare* (Pittsburgh: Duquesne University Press, 1994)—may serve to prove my assertion. Here are some quotations. On the initial seventeen sonnets: "[The poet's] rigid alignment with a legitimizing community exhausts the technical resources of his discourse as it exposes the emotional sterility of the conventions in which he invests" [134–135]. "While the procreation subsequence's tight focus insures coherence, it simultaneously threatens a monotony that has also taken its toll on the poetry's modern audience. Even Wordsworth . . . was put off by a general 'sameness,' a feature most damagingly concentrated in this introductory series" [145]. "Lars Engle is right to suggest that the initial quatrain:

> [From fairest creatures we desire increase,
> That thereby beauty's rose might never die,
> But as the riper should by time decease
> His tender heir might bear his memory . . .]

'might be the voice-over of a Sierra Club film in which California condors soar over their eggless nest'" [148]. "The poet betrays himself [in the early sonnets] as one uneager to focus on human beings in any precise manner, much less upon the potentially messy emotions which join them to one another. . . . Questions of detail make him nervous, and he would just as soon stick to the homey blur of abstracted tradition" [148]. "On sonnets 124 ("If my dear love were but the child of state") and 125 ("Were't aught to me I bore the canopy"): "Posing as sonnets about discovery and liberation, these poems are overtaken by a spirit of persecution and resentment. . . . He resorts to a fantasy isolation . . . He lapses, moreover, by the final couplet's arch renunciation ["Hence, thou suborned informer! A true soul / When most impeached stands least in thy control"], from anxious vigilance to paranoia" [175].

2. Because of Shakespeare's subversion of any discourse he adapts, it seems to me inadequate to suggest, as John Barrell does, that sonnet 29 ("When in disgrace with fortune and men's eyes") "may be actively concealing . . . a meaning that runs like this: 'when I'm pushed for money, with all the degradation that poverty involves, I sometimes remember you, and you're always good for a couple of quid'" [30]. Barrell prefers to conceive of Shakespeare as attempting the language of transcendent love, hut unable to achieve it, "because the historical moment he seeks to transcend is represented by a discourse [of patronage] whose nature and function is to contaminate the very language by which that assertion of transcendence must try to find expression. For me, the pathos of the poem—I can repeat here my earlier point—is that the narrator

can find no words to assert the transcendent power of true love, which cannot be interpreted as making a request for a couple of quid" [42].

A poet is not quite so helpless before his discourses as Barrell believes. In the first place, the very playfulness of the poem (see my comments below on the chiasmus "most enjoy contented least" and the puns on "state") prevents its being an actual speech-act of either "transcendent love" or "a request for a couple of quid." The sonnet, taken entire, is a fictional speech-act, of which the intent is to mimic the motions of the mind when it rises from low to high. In mimicking, in the octave, the movement of the mind in agitated depression and, in the sestet, the movement of the mind in relieved elation, the sonnet is fulfilling its purpose as a lyric. Shakespeare's skill in such psychological mimicry ensures the continuing power of the poem. A poet (as the contrast between octave and sestet shows) is the master of his discourses, not (as in Barrell's scenario) their helpless performer.

3. According to Fineman's theory, the object of desire as mirror image cannot generate dramatic conflict, and so the poetry of the speaker's same-sex object-relation remains mired in narcissism; but when the object of desire changes gender, and is no longer worshipfully desired but rather is abhorred, a fruitful dissonance arises that generates a new subjectivity. Fineman's more extravagant claims for the historical newness of the subject-position in the Dark Lady sequence have generally not been adopted; but his psychoanalytic criterion of value for poetry—that "difference" is better than "sameness"—has apparently gone unquestioned. It is naturally typical of Shakespeareans to prefer drama to lyric: after all, they became Shakespeareans because they were drawn to drama. And Fineman's book on the *Sonnets* was not fundamentally concerned with lyric, any more than his essay on *The Rape of Lucrece* was about complaint; both were prefatory, in their concern with character and will, to the book on Shakespeare's plays he did not live, alas, to write.

4. [Roger Kuin, "The Gaps and the Whites: Indeterminacy and Undecidability in the Sonnet Sequences of Spenser, Sidney, and Shakespeare," *Spenser Studies* 8 (1990).]

5. One editor of the *Sonnets*, John Kerrigan, betrays his restricted criterion of lyric value—chiefly, that metaphor is necessary for a good poem—as he writes of sonnet 105 that it is "scrupulously and Shakespearianly dull, but it is dull nonetheless. . . . The text is stripped of metaphor. . . . The result is a poem which, for all its charm [unspecified by Kerrigan] (and integrity), lacks the compelling excitement of a metaphoric sonnet such as 60, 'Like as the waves make toward the pebbled shore.' In so far as Shakespeare exceeds the Erasmian *copia*, shunning 'variation' for the sake of tautologous recurrence, his verse palls" [John Kerrigan, ed., "The Sonnets" and "A Lover's Complaint" (New York: Penguin, 1986), 29]. See my commentary, on sonnet 105 for a demonstration of how interesting the poem becomes once one admits criteria for lyric excellence besides the presence or absence of metaphor (though 105 is also one continued metaphor comparing erotic worship to Christian worship, and blasphemously equating them).

To take another instance of Kerrigan's misreading (springing from his lack of interest in linguistic variation), I cite his description of sonnet 129 ("Th'expense of spirit in a waste of shame"). He, like other critics preceding him, takes a single-minded expository view of the poem, as though it were a self-consistent sermon: "While 116 deals with Love complexly, however, questioning the absolute which it erects, 129 describes and enacts with single-minded, though cynically quibbling, forcefulness the distemperature of phallocentric lust. Fitful and fretting, such a passion squanders the moral powers along with the semen, committing both to a 'waste of shame' and 'shameful waist.' . . . It goads men towards satisfaction, yet, once sated in the irrational frenzy of orgasm, it is queasy, woeful, and full of remorse. . . . Lust is fixated by the moment: yearning towards emission, it lies sullied and futile in its wake, sourly foretasting hell, with nothing to hope for but further 'pursuit.' Its imaginative field is vorticose, centripetal, obsessive" [56]. Such a passage allows for no change of mind in the course of the poem—but if there is one thing the poem *does* mimic, it is successive changes of mind in the cycle of desire, changes of mind impossible in a homiletic diatribe such as Kerrigan represents the sonnet to be (see my comments on 129).

6. Every writer on the *Sonnets* owes gratitude to Stephen Booth's giant edition, which spells out in more detail the principles guiding his critical book on the *Sonnets.* Yet in stressing the richness of implication of Shakespeare's language over the firmness of implied authorial instruction, Booth gives up on the possibility of reliable internal guides for interpretation. Of course every interpretive act brings special interests to the poem, so that a psychoanalytic interpretation foregrounds aspects that a historical interpretation

may overlook. But any respectable account of a poem ought to have considered closely its chief formal features. A set of remarks on a poem which would be equally true of a prose paraphrase of that poem is not, by my standards, interpretation at all. Commentary on the propositional content of the poem is something entirely different from the interpretation of a poem, which must take into account the poem's linguistic strategies as well as its propositional statements.

The extent of authorial instruction retrievable from a text is also disputed. Yet authorial instruction is embedded, for instance, in the mere fact that one metaphor follows another. Sonnet 73 would have to be interpreted differently if we were given the twilight in quatrain 1, the fire in quatrain 2, and the autumn in quatrain 3. Shakespeare's arrangement of his metaphors is both cognitively and morally meaningful; quatrains cannot be reordered at will. Authorial instruction is also embedded in smaller units of every sonnet. To give one instance, it can be found in the parallels drawn between one part of the poem and another. The grammatical parallel linking the four "moral nouns"—*expense, spirit, waste,* and *shame*—that open sonnet 129 to the four "emotional" nouns—*bliss, woe, joy,* and *dream*—replacing them in its sestet is an "authorial instruction" telling us to notice the contrast between the two sets, and to infer a change of mind in the speaker who is uttering them about one and the same experience.

Any account of a poem ought to contemplate such implicit authorial instructions. Booth gives up too easily on interpretation. Even in the richness of Shakespeare's language, we are not left afloat on an uninterpretable set of "ideational static," not when the formal features of the *Sonnets* are there to guide us. It was her awareness of those formal features that made the late Winifred Nowottny the best guide to the sequence; it is a matter of deep regret to me that she did not complete the Arden edition which she had undertaken, and left only a few brilliant essays as tokens of that effort. It is equally a matter for rejoicing that the new Arden *Sonnets* will soon appear, edited by Katherine Duncan-Jones.

7. [Heather Dubrow, *Captive Victors: Shakespeare's Narrative Poems and Sonnets* (Ithaca, NY: Cornell University Press, 1987).]

8. I do not include eclogues, debate-poems, etc. in the definition of normative single-speaker lyric. Such poems are constructed against the norm, and derive their originality from bringing into the public (dramatic) arena of shared speech thoughts that in normative lyric remain intrapsychic.

2.5 The Lyric as Poetic Norm (1953)

M. H. Abrams

The lyric form—used here to include elegy, song, sonnet, and ode—had long been particularly connected by critics to the state of mind of its author. Unlike the narrative and dramatic forms, most lyrics do not include such elements as characters and plot, which can be readily explained (according to the common mirror-interpretation of mimesis) as imitations of external people and events. The majority of lyrics consist of thoughts and feelings uttered in the first person, and the one readily available character to whom these sentiments may be referred is the poet himself.[1] There soon developed a decided tendency to decry, particularly in amatory and elegiac poems, the expression of feelings that lacked conviction or were obviously engineered by the poet for the lyric occasion. Sir Philip Sidney complained that many of the songs and sonnets of his day carried no persuasion of actual passion in the author. Boileau disparaged elegists "Qui s'affligent par art"—

> Il faut que le coeur seul parle dans l'élégie.

Dr. Johnson taxed the elegies and love poems of Cowley with a similar defect, and approximated the idiom of contemporary primitivists in charging that "Lycidas" "is not to be considered as the effusion of real passion."[2]

The expressive character sometimes attributed to lyric poems offered no real challenge to the mimetic and pragmatic definitions of poetry in general, so long as lyrics remained the unconsidered trifles among the poetic kinds. Their lack of magnitude and of profitable effect, and the very fact that, in lieu of representative elements, their subject matter was considered to be principally the author's own feelings, consigned them to a lowly status in the scale of the genres. In many critics, the attitude to these poems ran the narrow gamut between contempt and condescension. According to Rapin, "A Sonnet, Ode, Elegy, Epigram, and those little kind of Verses . . . are ordinarily no more than the meer productions of Imagination, a superficial wit, with a little conversation of the World, is capable of these things."[3] Temple held that among the moderns, wits who cannot succeed in heroic poetry content themselves "with the Scraps, with Songs and Sonnets, with Odes and Elegies . . ."[4]

The soaring fortunes of the lyric may be dated from 1651, the year that Cowley's Pindaric "imitations" burst over the literary horizon and inaugurated the immense vogue of the "greater Ode" in England. To account for the purported fire, impetuosity, and irregularity of these poems, critics were wont to invoke Longinus' concept of the sublime and its sources in enthusiasm and vehement passion; and to attribute this lofty quality to any poetic kind was inevitably to elevate its stature. The Pindaric and pseudo-Pindaric were soon split off from pettier lyrics and lesser odes, and assigned a place next to the greatest of the traditional forms. By 1704 John Dennis grouped together "Epick, Tragick, and the greater Lyrick poetry" as the highest literary genres, to be distinguished from the lesser Poetry of comedy, satire, "the little Ode," elegy, and pastoral; and Dennis' example was soon followed even by more traditional theorists.[5] The prestige of the greater lyric, as well as of the other lyric forms, was strongly abetted by the opinion that the poetry of the Bible was mainly lyrical, and the claim that the Psalms of David, as well as passages from the narrative books, were the Hebrew equivalent of the odes of Pindar.[6] Of course, those who believed that poetry had originated in the overflow of feeling also believed that the earliest poems were lyric—either proto-ode or proto-elegy, as the theorist assumed the religious or erotic passions to have been the more powerful and compulsive to expression. And the growing critical interest in the lyric had its counterpart in the increasing cultivation of its various kinds by the poets in the generation of the Wartons, Gray, and Collins—

> Trick'd in antique ruff and bonnet,
> Ode, and elegy, and sonnet.

All these forces showed themselves indirectly, in passing comments, and in critical judgments which merely implied the alteration of critical premises, before they resulted in a deliberate reconstruction of the bases of poetic theory. There was a conspicuous tendency, for example, to identify as 'pure poetry,' or 'the most poetical poetry,' or 'la vraie poésie,' those particular poems or passages which were thought to be peculiarly the product of passion and rapture. Because the great ode is the boldest and most rapturous by nature, Joseph Trapp said, it "is, of all kinds of Poetry, the most poetical . . . " "The ode, as it is the eldest kind of poetry, so it is more spiritous, and more remote from prose, than any other," wrote Edward Young in his Preface to *Ocean, An Ode* (1728), and enthusiasm is its "soul."[7] A similar idea of what constitutes quintessential poetry was at the heart of Joseph Warton's famous critical estimate of the writings of Pope. His finding that the "species of poetry wherein Pope Excelled . . . is not the most excellent one of the art" was one against which even the most rigorous neo-classic critic could not have demurred, but the grounds on which Warton identified the highest species of poetry plainly indicate the newer directions of critical thinking. As against the "Man of Wit" and the "Man of Sense," the "true Poet" and writer of "PURE POETRY" is stamped solely by "a creative and glowing IMAGINATION, 'acer spiritus ac vis' . . ." Warton's instances of poems that are "essentially poetical" include not only epic and drama, but an ode of Akenside, as well as Milton's "L'Allegro" and "Il Penseroso." Pope did not write "the most *poetic* species *of poetry*" because he did not "indulge" his imagination and stifled his "poetical enthusiasm." Hence Pope does not transport the reader, and although he is foremost among the second order of poets, "he has written nothing in a strain so truly sublime, as the *Bard* of *Gray*."[8]

A few writers of the latter part of the century mark themselves off from their contemporaries because they deliberately set out to revise the bases of the neo-classic theory of poetry. Sir William Jones is remembered chiefly as a liberal jurist and an Orientalist who pioneered in the study of Sanskrit. But in 1772 he published a volume of translations and 'imitations' of Arabic, Indian, and Persian poems to which he added an important "Essay on the Arts Called Imitative." There we find a conjunction of all the tendencies we have been tracing: the ideas drawn from Longinus, the old doctrine of poetic inspiration, recent theories of the emotional and imaginative origin of poetry, and a major emphasis on the lyric form and on the supposedly primitive and spontaneous poetry of Oriental nations. It was Jones's distinction, I think, to be the first writer in England to weave these threads into an explicit and orderly reformulation of the nature and criteria of poetry and of the poetic genres.

Jones opens his essay by rejecting unequivocally "the assertion of Aristotle, that all poetry consists in imitation"—one of those maxims, he thinks, "repeated a thousand times, for no other reason, than because they once dropped from the pen of a superior genius." Of the arts of poetry and music, "we cannot give a precise definition . . . till we have made a few previous remarks on their origin'; and he goes on to offer evidence "that poetry was originally no more than a strong and animated expression of the human passions."[9] Like various critics half a century later, Jones conjectures that each poetic species had its source in an appropriate emotion: religious and dramatic poetry originated in joy at the wonders of the creation, elegies in grief, moral and epic poetry in the detestation of vice, and satires in hate. There follows this definition:

> Consistently with the foregoing principles, we may define original and native poetry to be the language of the violent passions, expressed in exact measure, with strong accents and significant words.[10]

Plainly Jones employs the lyric not only as the original poetic form, but as the prototype for poetry as a whole, and thereby expands what had occasionally been proposed as the differentia of one poetic species into the defining attribute of the genus. As he says, "in defining what true poetry ought to be . . . we have described what it really was among the Hebrews, the Greeks and Romans, the Arabs and Persians." Undeniably the lyrics, the hymns, the elegies of the Greeks, like the "sacred odes, or psalms" of David, the Song of Solomon, and the prophecies of the inspired writers, "are truly and strictly poetical; but what did David or Solomon imitate in their divine poems? A man, who is really joyful or afflicted, cannot be said to imitate joy or affliction."

Jones extends the expressive concept to music and painting. Even if we admit, he says, the very dubious proposition that the descriptive elements in these forms are imitation, it remains the fact "that mere description is the meanest part of both arts." He goes on to set up a simple scale by which to measure the relative worth of the constituents of any work of art:

> If the arguments, used in this essay, have any weight, it will appear, that the finest parts of poetry, musick, and painting, are expressive of the passions . . . that the inferior parts of them are descriptive of natural objects, and affect us chiefly by substitution.[11]

Jones's theory shows that inversion of aesthetic values which reached its climax in the theory of John Stuart Mill, some sixty years later. The "imitative" elements, hitherto held to be a defining attribute of poetry or art, become inferior, if not downright unpoetic; in their place those elements in a poem that express feeling become at once its identifying characteristic and cardinal poetic value.

NOTES

1. In the attempt to subsume each species of poetry under the mimetic principle, Batteux claimed, in 1747, that even lyric poems, "the songs of the Prophets, the psalms of David, the odes of Pindar and of Horace" are only to superficial inspection "un cri du coeur, un élan, où la Nature fait tout, et l'art, rien." Like all poetry, lyric poetry is an imitation, but differs from the other forms in imitating sentiments rather than actions (*Les Beaux Arts*, Paris, 1773, pp. 316–25). Thomas Twining claimed, in 1789, that Batteux had here extended the limits of imitation beyond "all reasonable analogy," for when the lyric poet "is merely expressing his own *sentiments*, in his own *person*, we consider him not as imitating . . ." (*Aristotle's Treatise on Poetry*, pp. 139–40).

2. Sidney, *Apology for Poetry*, in *Elizabethan Critical Essays*, ed. G. Gregory Smith, I, 201; Boileau, *L'Art poétique*, II, ll. 47, 57; Johnson, *Works*, IX, 39, 43–5, 152. See also Joseph Trapp, *Lectures on Poetry* (1711–15), trans. William Bowyer (London, 1742), p. 25. For the fortunes of the lyric in England, and a discussion of the relevance of the Longinian current to the theory and practice of the Pindaric Ode, see the excellent article by Norman Maclean, "From Action to Image: Theories of the Lyric in the Eighteenth Century," *Critics and Criticism*, ed. R. S. Crane, pp. 408–60.

3. *Reflections on Aristotle's Treatise of Poesie*, tr. Rymer (London, 1694), p. 4.

4. "Of Poetry" (1690), *Critical Essays of the Seventeenth Century*, ed. Spingarn, III, 99. Cf. Hobbes, "Answer to Davenant," ibid. II, 57.

5. *The Grounds of Criticism in Poetry*, in *Critical Works*, I, 338. See also, e.g., Joseph Trapp, *Lectures on Poetry*, Lecture XII, and John Newbery, *The Art of Poetry*, I, 54. In his *Dictionary*, Dr. Johnson distinguished the "greater" from the "lesser" ode as possessing "sublimity, rapture, and quickness of transition."

6. See Lowth, *Lectures*, esp. Chaps. XXII, XXV–XXVIII. Also Sidney, *Apology for Poetry*, in *Elizabethan Critical Essays*, ed. Smith, I, 154–5; Cowley, Preface to *Pindarique Odes*, in *The Works of Mr. Abraham Cowley* (11th ed.; London, 1710), I, 184.

7. Trapp, *Lectures on Poetry*, p. 203; Young, *Poetical Works* (Boston, 1870), II, 159, 165. Cf. Hurd, *Horace's Art of Poetry* (1750), in *Works*, I, 104: "Poetry, *pure Poetry*, is the proper language of *Passion* . . ." Anna Seward, letter to Dr. Downman, 15 Mar. 1792: ". . . what should be its essence, poetry, that is, the metaphors, allusions, and imagery, are the natural product of a glowing and raised imagination" (*Letters*, Edinburgh, 1811, III, 121). J. Moir, *Gleanings* (1785), I, 27: "All true Poetry is the genuine effusion either of a glowing heart, or of an ardent fancy." And see Paul Van Tieghem, "La Notion de vraie poésie dans le préromantisme Européen," Le *Préromantisme* (Paris, 1924), I, 19ff.

8. *Essay on the Writings and Genius of Pope*, I, iv–x; II, 477–8, 481.

9. *The Works of Sir William Jones* (London, 1807), VIII, 361–4.

10. Ibid. VIII, 371. Cf. the expressive theory of the poetic species held by John Keble and Alexander Smith, as described in Chap. VI, sects. iii and iv.

11. Ibid. pp. 372–6, 379. Of the various indices to the changing directions of criticism in the last decades of the century, Thomas Barnes's paper "On the Nature and Essential Characters of Poetry" (1781) is of special interest. Like Jones, Barnes denies the validity of definitions of poetry as imitation, as fiction, or as "the art of giving pleasure"; he appeals to the fact that "the *original* language of mankind was poetical," because all perception in the infancy of the world excited passion; and he proposes a pyramid of poetic value, in which "the bursts of honest nature, the glow of animated feeling" are the properties of "the *first order* of poetic excellence." *Memoirs of the Literary and Philosophical Society of Manchester*, I (1785), pp. 55–6.

2.6 Dramatic Monologue and the Overhearing of Lyric (1985)

HERBERT F. TUCKER

His muse made increment of anything,
From the high lyric down to the low rational.

Don Juan III.1xxxv.5–6

I would say, quoting Mill, "Oratory is heard, poetry is overheard." And he would answer, his voice full of contempt, that there was always an audience; and yet, in his moments of lofty speech, he himself was alone no matter what the crowd.

The Autobiography of William Butler Yeats

1.

"Eloquence is *heard*, poetry is *overheard*. Eloquence supposes an audience; the peculiarity of poetry appears to us to lie in the poet's utter unconsciousness of a listener. Poetry is feeling confessing itself to itself, in moments of solitude." "Lyric poetry, as it was the earliest kind, is also, if the view we are now taking of poetry be correct, more eminently and peculiarly poetry than any other."[1] Thus wrote John Stuart Mill in 1833, with the wild surmise of a man who had lately nursed himself through a severe depression, thanks to published poetry and its capacity to excite intimate feeling in forms uncontaminated by rhetorical or dramatic posturing. One listener Mill's characteristically analytic eloquence is likely to have found at once was Robert Browning, who moved in London among liberal circles that touched Mill's and who in the same year published his first work, the problematically dramatic *Pauline: A Fragment of a Confession*, to which Mill drafted a response Browning saw in manuscript. Browning's entire career—most notably the generic innovation for which he is widely remembered today, the dramatic monologue—would affirm his resistance to the ideas about poetry contained in Mill's essays. Indeed, as early as *Pauline* Browning was confessing to the open secret of spontaneous lyricism, but in ways that disowned it. What follows is emphatically the depiction of a bygone state:

And first I sang as I in dream have seen
Music wait on a lyrist for some thought,
Yet singing to herself until it came. (ll. 377–79)

In this complex but typical retrospect the poet of *Pauline* figures as an eavesdropper on his own Shelleyan juvenilia, themselves relics of a dream of disengaged and thoughtless youth from which the sadder but wiser poet has on balance done well to awaken. Browning's enfolding of a lyrical interval into a narrative history sets the pattern for the establishment of character throughout his subsequent work, a pattern knowingly at odds with the subjectivist convention that governed the reading of English poetry circa 1830 and to which Mill's essay gave memorable but by no means unique voice.[2]

To the most ambitious and original young poets of the day, Browning and Alfred Tennyson, the sort of lyricism Mill admired must have seemed "overheard" in a sense quite other than Mill intended: heard overmuch, overdone, and thus in need of being done over in fresh forms. Among their other generic experiments in the lyrical drama (*Paracelsus*, *Pippa Passes*), the idyll ("Dora," "Morte d'Arthur"), and the sui generis historical epic form of *Sordello*, during the 1830s Tennyson and Browning arrived independently at the first recognizably modern dramatic monologues: "St. Simeon Stylites" (1842; written in 1833) and the paired poems of 1837 that we now know as "Johannes Agricola in Meditation" and "Porphyria's Lover." These early monologues were not only highly accomplished pieces; within the lyrical climate of the day they were implicitly polemical as well. The ascetic St. Simeon atop his pillar, exposed to the merciless assault of the elements, stands for an exalted subjectivity ironically demystified by the historical contextualization that is the generic privilege of the dramatic monologue and, I shall argue, one of its indispensable props in the construction of character. Browning's imagination was less symbolically brooding than Tennyson's and more historically alert, and he launched his dramatic monologues with speakers whose insanities were perversions, but recognizably versions, of the twin wellheads of the lyrical current that had come down to the nineteenth century from the Reformation and the Renaissance. The historical figure Johannes Agricola is an antinomian protestant lying against time as if his soul depended on it; and Porphyria's lover, though fictive, may be regarded as a gruesomely literal-minded Petrarch bent on possessing the object of his desire. Each of Browning's speakers, like St. Simeon Stylites, utters a monomaniacal manifesto that shows subjectivity up by betraying its situation in a history. The utterance of each stands revealed not as poetry, in Mill's terms, but as eloquence, a desperately concentric rhetoric whereby, to adapt Yeats's formulation from "Ego Dominus Tuus," the sentimentalist deceives himself.

What gets "overheard" in these inaugural Victorian monologues is history dramatically replayed. The charmed circle of lyric finds itself included by the kind of historical particularity that lyric genres exclude by design, and in the process readers find themselves unsettlingly historicized and contextualized as well. The extremity of each monologist's authoritative assertion awakens in us with great force the counter-authority of communal norms, through a reductio ad absurdum of the very lyric premises staked out in Mill's essays, most remarkably in a sentence that Mill deleted when republishing "What Is Poetry?": "That song has always seemed to us like the lament of a prisoner in a solitary cell, ourselves listening, unseen in the next."[3] ("Ourselves"? How many of us in that next cell? Does one eavesdrop in company? Or is that not called going to the theater, and is Mill's overheard poetry not dramatic eloquence after all?) Tennyson's and Browning's first monologues imply that Mill's position was already its own absurd reduction—a reduction not just of the options for poetry but of the prerogatives of the unimprisoned self, which ideas like Mill's have been underwriting, as teachers of undergraduate poetry classes can attest, for the better part of two centuries. Tennyson and Browning wanted to safeguard the self's prerogatives, and to that extent they shared the aims of contemporary lyrical devotees. But both poets' earliest dramatic monologues compassed those aims through a more subtle and eloquent design than the prevailing creed would admit: a design that might preserve the self on the far side of, and as a result of, a contextual dismissal of attenuated Romantic lyricism and its merely soulful claims; a design that might, as Browning was to put it in the peroration to *The Ring and the Book* (1869), "Suffice the eye and save the soul beside" (XII.863). St. Simeon, Johannes, and Porphyria's lover emerge through their monologues as characters: poorer souls than they like to fancy themselves but selves for all that, de- and re-constructed selves strung on the tensions of their texts.

2.

Both Tennyson and Browning proceeded at once to refine their generic discoveries, though they proceeded in quite different directions. While Tennyson kept the dramatic monologue in his repertoire, he turned to it relatively seldom; and with such memorable ventures as "Ulysses" and "Tithonus" he in effect relyricized the genre, running its contextualizing devices in reverse and stripping his speakers of personality in order to facilitate a lyric drive. Browning, on the other hand, moved his dramatic monologues in the direction of mimetic particularity, and the poems he went on to write continued to incorporate or "overhear" lyric in the interests of character-formation. "Johannes Agricola" and "Porphyria's Lover" had been blockbusters, comparatively single-minded exercises in the construction of a lurid character through the fissuring of an apparently monolithic ego. The gain in verisimilitude of Browning's later monologues is a function of the nerve with which he learned to reticulate the sort of pattern these strong but simple monologues had first knit. The degree of intricacy varies widely, but the generic design remains the same. Character in the Browningesque dramatic monologue emerges as an interference effect between opposed yet mutually informative discourses: between an historical, narrative, metonymic text and a symbolic, lyrical, metaphoric text that adjoins it and jockeys with it for authority. While each text urges its own priority, the ensemble works according to the paradoxical logic of the originary supplement: the alien voices of history and of feeling come to constitute and direct one another. Typically Browning's monologists tell the story of a yearning after the condition of lyric, a condition that is itself in turn unimaginable except as the object of, or pretext for, the yearning that impels the story plotted against it.[4]

What we acknowledge as the "life" of a dramatic monologue thus emerges through the interdependence of its fictive autobiography and its *élan vital*, each of which stands as the other's reason for being, and neither of which can stand alone without succumbing to one of two deconstructive ordeals that beset character in this genre (and that arguably first beset the self during the century in which this genre arose). The first ordeal lies through history and threatens to resolve the speaking self into its constituent influences, to unravel character by exposing it as merely a tissue of affiliations. At the same time, character in the dramatic monologue runs an equal but opposite risk from what certain Romantic poetics and hermeneutics would assert to be the self's very place of strength and what we have been calling, after Mill, the privacy of lyric. A kind of sublime idiocy, lyric isolation from context distempers character and robs it of contour, as Socrates said long ago in the *Ion* (lyric poets are out of their minds), and as Sharon Cameron, with an eye on Greek and earlier origins of lyric, has said again more recently: "the lyric is a departure not only from temporality but also from the finite constrictions of identity."[5] We find this lyric departure superbly dramatized in the valediction of Tennyson's Ulysses, that most marginal of characters, whose discourse poises itself at "the utmost bound of human thought" (l. 32). Insofar as we find Ulysses transgressing that bound—as for me he does in the final paragraph, with its address to a bewilderingly mythical crew of Ithacan mariners and with the concomitant evanescence of its "I"—we find Tennyson transgressing the generic boundary of dramatic monologue as well.

One good reason why the dramatic monologue is associated with Browning's name rather than with Tennyson's, who technically got to it first, is that in Browning the lyrical flight from narrative, temporality, and identity appears through a characteristic, and characterizing, resistance to its allure. Browning's Ulysses, had he invented one, would speak while bound to the mast of a ship bound elsewhere; his life would take its bearing from what he heard the Sirens sing, and their music would remain an unheard melody suffusing his monologue without rising to the surface of utterance.[6] Such a plot of lyricism resisted would mark his poem as a dramatic monologue, which we should be justified in reading as yet another allegory of the distinctive turn on Romantic lyricism that perennially recreated Browning's poetical character. "R. B. a poem" was the title he gave in advance to this allegorical testament, in the fine letter, virtually an epistolary monologue, that he addressed on the subject to Elizabeth Barrett; and by the time of "One Word More" (1855) he could proudly affirm his wife's lyricism as the privately silencing otherness his public character was to be known by.[7]

Dramatic monologue in the Browning tradition is, in a word, anything but monological. It represents modern character as a quotient, a ratio of history and desire, a function of the division of the modern mind against itself. Our apprehension of character as thus constituted is a Romantic affair; in Jerome Christensen's apt phrase for the processing of the "lyrical drama" in Romanticism, it is a matter of learning to "read the differentials." As a sampling of the dozens of poetry textbooks published in recent decades will confirm, the dramatic monologue is our genre of genres for training in how to read between the lines—a hackneyed but valuable phrase that deserves a fresh hearing.[8] In the reading of a dramatic monologue we do not so much scrutinize the ellipses and blank spaces of the text as we people those openings by attending to the overtones of the different discourses that flank them. Between the lines, we read in a no-man's-land the notes whose intervals engender character. Perhaps the poet of the dramatic monologue gave a thought to the generic framing of his own art when he had the musician Abt Vogler (1864) marvel "That out of three sounds he frame, not a fourth sound, but a star" (l. 52). The quantum leap from text to fictive persona (the dramatic "star" of a monologue) is no less miraculous for being, like Abt Vogler's structured improvisation, "framed," defined and sustained as a put-up job. That such a process of character-construction tends to elude our received means of exegesis is a contributing cause for the depression of Browning's stock among the New Critics. But one way to begin explicating a dramatic monologue in the Browning tradition is to identify a discursive shift, a moment at which either of the genre's constitutive modes—historical line or punctual lyric spot—breaks into the other.

3.

Since the premier writer of dramatic monologues was, as usual in such matters, the most ingenious, it is difficult to find uncomplicated instances in Browning that are also representative. We might sample first a passage from "Fra Lippo Lippi" (1855), a sizeable blank-verse monologue that happens to contain lyric literally in the form of *stornelli*, lyrical catches Englished in italics that Browning's artist monk emits at odd intervals during the autobiography he is improvising for the night watch. In the following lines Lippo is taking off those critics whom his new painterly realism has disturbed:

"It's art's decline, my son!
You're not of the true painters, great and old;
Brother Angelico's the man, you'll find;
Brother Lorenzo stands his single peer:
Fag on at flesh, you'll never make the third!"
Flower o' the pine,
You keep your mistr . . . manners, and I'll stick to mine!

I'm not the third, then: bless us, they must know!
Don't you think they're the likeliest to know,
They with their Latin? (ll. 233–42)

The gap for interpretation to enter is, of course, the middle of the second italicized line, marked typographically by ellipsis and prosodically by the wreckage of the embedded snatch of song. Amid Lippo's tale of the modern artist's oppression by his superiors, by religious and representational traditions, and by the Latin learning that backs up both (poetry as overseen?), the apparently spontaneous individual talent bursts forth in a rebellious chant—which is then itself interrupted by a reminder, also apparently spontaneous, of Lippo's answerability to the authorities right in front of him. Lippo's lyric flower breeds a canker: the poetry we and the police thought we were overhearing turns out to be, through versatile revision or instant overdubbing, a rhetorically canny performance. Or, if we take a larger view, it turns out to have been rhetoric all along, Lippo's premeditated means of affirming solidarity with the unlettered night watch by ruefully policing his own speech in advance and incorporating this police action into the larger speech act that is his monologue.

The passage is intensely artificial yet intensely realistic, and we should note that its success does not rely on our deciding whether the monologist has forecast his occasion or stumbled upon it. The twist of the lyrical line against itself nets a speaking subject who is tethered to circumstances and, for that very reason, is anything but tongue-tied. Here as throughout the Browningesque monologue, character is not unfolded to comprehension but enfolded in a text that draws us in. Even after nearly four hundred lines we do not grasp Lippo's character as an essence and know what he is; but if we have negotiated the text we know how he does. In the terms of the passage in question, we know his *manners*, not least his manner of covering up his *mistr* . . . Lippo's character arises, in the differentials between vitality and circumstances, as a way of life, a mazing text, a finely realized, idiosyncratic instance of a generic method.

A similarly punctuated digression from story, or transgression into lyric, occurs at the center of Browning's most famous monologue, "My Last Duchess" (1842):

She had
A heart—how shall I say?—too soon made glad,
Too easily impressed; she liked whate'er
She looked on, and her looks went everywhere.
Sir, 't was all one! My favour at her breast,
The dropping of the daylight in the West,
The bough of cherries some officious fool
Broke in the orchard for her, the white mule
She rode with round the terrace—all and each
Would draw from her alike the approving speech,
Or blush, at least. She thanked men,—good! but thanked
Somehow—I know not how—as if she ranked
My gift of a nine-hundred-years-old name
With anybody's gift. (ll. 21–34)

The framing hesitations of "How shall I say?" and "I know not how" may or may not come under the Duke's rhetorical control; but a comparable tic or stammer invades his discourse more subtly with the appositional style of the middle lines, which do here with syntax the work done otherwise in Fra Lippo's *stornelli*. Halfway through the monologue, these lines constitute a lyrical interlude around which the Duke's despotic narrative may be seen to circle, with a predatory envy that escapes his posture of condescension. Anaphora and grammatical suspension, time-honored refuges of lyric, harbor recurrent images of the daily and seasonal cycle, of natural affection, and of sexual generation that not only contradict the Duke's potent affiliation with art, culture, and domination but show these contradictions within the text to be contradictions within the Duke. Or rather, to discard the figuration of inside and outside that dramatic monologue at its best asks us to do without, it is these textual contradictions that constitute the Duke's character. The polymorphous perversity he here attributes to his last Duchess is as much an attribute of his own character as is the different, monomaniacal perversity with which he has put a stop to her egalitarian smiles. Each perversity so turns on the other as to knot the text up into that essential illusion we call character. Hence the Duke's characteristic inconsistency in objecting to the "officious fool" who, in breaking cherries for the Duchess, was not breaking ranks at all but merely executing his proper "office" in the Duke's hierarchical world. Hence, too, the undecidable ambiguity of "My favour at her breast": the phrase oscillates between suggestions of a caress naturally given and of an heirloom possessively bestowed, and its oscillation is what makes the star of dramatic character shine. Such a semantic forking of the ways, like the plotting of spontaneity against calculation in Fra Lippo's "*mistr . . . manners*" revision, blocks reference in one direction, in order to refer us to the textual production of character instead.

Because in grammatical terms it is a paratactic pocket, an insulated deviation from the syntax of narrative line, the Duke's recounting of his Duchess's easy pleasures wanders from the aims of the raconteur and foregrounds the speech impediments that make her story his monologue.[9] Moreover, the Duke's listing is also a listening, a harkening after the kind of spontaneous lyric voice that he, like the writer of dramatic monologues, comes into his own by imperfectly renouncing. Lyric, in the dramatic monologue, is what you cannot have and what you cannot forget—think of the arresting trope Browning invented for his aging poet Cleon (1855), "One lyric woman, in her crocus vest" (l. 15)—and as an organizing principle for the genre, lyric becomes present through a recurrent and partial overruling. This resisted generic nostalgia receives further figuration intertextually, in "My Last Duchess" and many another monologue, with the clustering of allusions at moments of lyric release. Here "The dropping of the daylight in the West" falls into Browning's text from major elegies, or refusals to mourn, by Milton ("Lycidas"), Wordsworth ("Tintern Abbey," "Intimations" ode), and Keats ("To Autumn"); and the Duchess on her white mule so recalls Spenser's lyrically selfless Una from the opening of *The Faerie Queene* as to cast the Duke as an archimage dubiously empowered.

Amid the Duke's eloquence the overhearing of poetry, in this literary-historical sense of allusion to prior poems, underscores the choral dissolution that lurks in lyric voice. Furthermore, it reinstates the checking of such dissolution as the mark of the individual self—of the dramatic speaker and also of the poet who, in writing him up, defines himself in opposition to lyrical orthodoxy and emerges as a distinct "I," a name to conjure with against the ominous: "This grew; I gave commands" (l. 45). Toward the end of his career, in "House" (1876) Browning would in his own voice make more explicit this engagement with the literary past and would defend literary personality, against Wordsworth on the sonnet, as just the antithesis of unmediated sincerity: "'"*With this same key / Shakespeare unlocked his heart*," once more!' / Did Shakespeare? If so, the less Shakespeare he!" (ll. 38–40). Poetry of the unlocked heart, far from displaying character in Browning's terms, undoes it: Browning reads his chief precursor in the English dramatic line as a type of the objective poet, the poetical character known through a career-long objection to the sealed intimacies of the poem à clef.

4.

In 1831 Arthur Hallam gave a promising description of the best of Tennyson's *Poems, Chiefly Lyrical* (1830) as "a graft of the lyric on the dramatic." The Victorian dramatic monologue that soon ensued from these beginnings was likewise a hybrid genre, a hardy offshoot of the earlier hybrid genre in which the first Romantics had addressed the problem of how to write the long modern poem by making modern civilization and its discontents, or longing and its impediments, into the conditions for the prolonging and further hearing of poetry: the "greater Romantic lyric." The genre M. H. Abrams thus christened some years ago has by now achieved canonical status, but a reconsideration of its given name from the standpoint of the dramatic monologue may help us save it from assimilation to orthodox lyricism by reminding us that the genre Abrams called "greater" was not more-lyrical-than-lyric but rather more-than-lyrical. Despite a still high tide of assertions to the contrary, the works of the first generations of Romantic poets were on the whole much less lyrical than otherwise.[10] Once we conceive the Romantic tradition accordingly as a perennial intermarriage, which is to say infighting, of poetic kinds, we can situate the Victorian dramatic monologue as an eminently Romantic form. In correcting the literary-historical picture we can begin, too, to see how fin-de-siècle and modernist reactions to the Browningesque monologue have conditioned the writing, reading, and teaching of poetry, literary theory, and literary history in our own time.

At the beginning of Browning's century Coleridge remarked, "A poem of any length neither can be, nor ought to be, all poetry." By the end of the century Oscar Wilde, looking askance at Browning's achievement, took up Coleridge's distinction, but with a difference: "If he can only get his music by breaking the strings of his lute, he breaks them, and they snap in discord. . . . Meredith is a prose Browning, and so is Browning. He used poetry as a medium for writing in prose."[11] The difference between Coleridge's and Wilde's ideas of what a poem should be is in large part a difference that the dramatic monologue had made in nineteenth-century poetry, a difference Browning inscribed into literary history by inscribing it into the characteristic ratios of his texts. Wilde and others at the threshold of modernism wanted Mill's pure lyricism but wanted it even purer. And through an irony of literary history that has had far-reaching consequences for our century, the Browningesque dramatic monologue gave them what they wanted. Symbolist and imagist writers could extract from such texts as *Pauline* and "Fra Lippo Lippi"—and also, to sketch in the fuller picture, from the Tennysonian idyll and most sophisticated Victorian novels—lyrical gems as finely cut as anything from the allegedly naive eras, Romantic or Elizabethan, upon which they bestowed such sentimental if creative regard. The hybrid dramatic monologue, as a result of its aim to make the world and subjectivity safe for each other in the interests of character, had proved a sturdy grafting stock for flowers of lyricism; and the governing pressures of the genre, just because they governed so firmly, had bred hothouse lyric varieties of unsurpassed intensity. These lyrical implants it was left to a new generation of rhymers, scholars, and anthologists to imitate, defend, and excerpt in a newly chastened lyric poetry, a severely purist poetics, and a surprisingly revisionist history of poetry.[12]

The fin-de-siècle purism of Wilde, Yeats, Arthur Symons, and others was polemically canted against the example of Browning; yet it remained curiously, even poignantly, in his debt. Consider, for example, Symons's resumption of a rhetoric very like Mill's, as he praises Verlaine in *The Symbolist Movement* (1899) for "getting back to nature itself":

"From the moment when his inner life may be said to have begun, he was occupied with the task of an unceasing confession, in which one seems to overhear him talking to himself."[13] The pivotally wishful "unceasing," which distinguishes Symons's formulation from Mill's, also betrays a kind of elegiac overcompensation. Mill had dissolved audience in order to overhear poetry as if from an adjacent cell; Symons, writing at an appreciable historical remove from the achievements of Verlaine, is by contrast trapped in time. Symons's overhearing of poetry resembles less Mill's eavesdropping than the belated Browningesque audition of a poignant echo, and the symbolist movement he hopes to propel is fed by an overwhelming nostalgia that creates from its own wreck the thing it contemplates. The nostalgia for lyric that throbs through the influential versions of the poetic past Symons and his contemporaries assembled sprang from a range of cultural causes we are only beginning to understand adequately.[14] But we can observe here that the rhetorical pattern into which their lyrically normed historiography fell was precisely that of the poetic genre that had preeminently confronted lyricism with history in their century: the dramatic monologue. It is as if what Symons championed as the "revolt against exteriority, against rhetoric,"[15] having repudiated the "impure" Browning tradition in principle, was condemned to reiterate its designs in writing. The symbolist and imagist schools wanted to read in their French and English antecedents an expurgated lyric that never was on page or lip. It was, rather, a generic back-formation, a textual constituent they isolated from the dramatic monologue and related nineteenth-century forms; and the featureless poems the fin-de-siècle purists produced by factoring out the historical impurities that had ballasted these forms are now fittingly, with rare exceptions, works of little more than historical interest.

Virtually each important modernist poet in English wrote such poems for a time; each became an important poet by learning to write otherwise and to exploit the internal otherness of the dramatic monologue. When the lyrical bubble burst within its bell jar, poetry became modern once again in its return to the historically responsive and dialogical mode that Browning, Tennyson, and others had brought forward from the Romantics.[16] And upon the establishment of Yeats's mask, Pound's personae, Frost's monologues and idylls, and Eliot's impersonal poetry, it became a point of dogma among sophisticated readers that every poem dramatized a speaker who was not the poet. "Once we have dissociated the speaker of the lyric from the personality of the poet, even the tiniest lyric reveals itself as drama."[17] We recognize this declaration as dogma by the simple fact that we—at least most of us—had to learn it, and had to trade for it older presuppositions about lyric sincerity that we had picked up in corners to which New Critical light had not yet pierced. The new dogma took (and in my teaching experience it takes still) with such ease that it is worth asking why it did (and does), and whether as professors of poetry we should not have second thoughts about promulgating an approach that requires so painless an adjustment of the subjectivist norms we profess to think outmoded.

The conversion educated readers now routinely undergo from lyrical to dramatic expectations about the poems they study recapitulates the history of Anglo-American literary pedagogy during our century, the middle two decades of which witnessed a great awakening from which we in our turn are trying to awaken again. Until about 1940 teachers promoted poetry appreciation in handbooks and anthologies that exalted lyric as "the supreme expression of strong emotion . . . the very real but inexplicable essence of poetry," and that throned this essential emotion in the equally essential person of the poet: "Lyrical poetry arouses emotion because it expresses the author's feeling."[18] By 1960 the end of instruction had shifted from appreciating to understanding poetry, and to this end a host of experts marched readers past the author of a poem to its dramatic speaker. John

Crowe Ransom's dictum that the dramatic situation is "almost the first head under which it is advisable to approach a poem for understanding" had by the 1960s advanced from advice to prescription. In Laurence Perrine's widely adopted *Sound and Sense* the first order of business is "to assume always that the speaker is someone other than the poet himself." For Robert Scholes in *Elements of Poetry* the speaker is the most elementary of assumptions: "In beginning our approach to a poem we must make some sort of tentative decision about who the speaker is, what his situation is, and who he seems to be addressing."[19]

That such forthright declarations conceal inconsistencies appears in the instructions of Robert W. Boynton and Maynard Mack, whose *Introduction to the Poem* promotes the familiar dramatic principle but pursues its issues to the verge of a puzzling conclusion. The authors begin dogmatically enough: "When we start looking closely at the dramatic character of poetry, we find that we have to allow for a more immediate speaker than the poet himself, one whom the poet has imagined speaking the poem, as an actor speaks a part written for him by a playwright." But then Boynton and Mack, with a candor unusual in the handbook genre, proceed to a damaging concession that dissolves the insubstantial pageant of the dramatic enterprise into thin air: "In some instances this imagined speaker is in no way definite or distinctive; he is simply a voice." (When is a speaker not a speaker? When he is a "voice," nay, an Arnoldian "lyric cry.") With this last sentence Boynton and Mack offer an all but lyrical intimation of the mystification inherent in the critical fiction of the speaker and suggest its collusion with the mysteries of the subjectivist norm it was designed to supplant.[20] It may well be easier to indicate these mysteries than to solve them; what matters is that with our New Critical guides we seem to have experienced as little difficulty in negotiating the confusions entailed by the fiction of the speaker as we have experienced in converting ourselves and our students from lyrically expressive to dramatically objective norms for reading.

Why should we have made this conversion, and why do we continue to encourage it? Why should our attempts at understanding poetry through a New Criticism rely on a fiction that baffles the understanding? These are related questions, and their answers probably lie in considerations of pedagogical expediency. One such consideration must be the sheer hard work of bringing culturally stranded students into contact with the historical particularities from which a given poem arises. Life (and courses) being short, art being long, and history being longer still, the fiction of the speaker at least brackets the larger problem of context so as to define a manageable classroom task for literary studies. To such institutional considerations as these, which have been attracting needed attention of late, I would add a consideration more metaphysical in kind. The fiction of the speaker, if it removes from the study of poetry the burden, and the dignity, of establishing contact with history, puts us in compensatory contact with the myth of unconditioned subjectivity we have inherited from Mill and Symons in spite of ourselves. Through that late ceremony of critical innocence, the readerly imagination of a self, we modern readers have abolished the poet and set up the fictive speaker; and we have done so in order to boost the higher gains of an intersubjective recognition for which, in an increasingly mechanical age that can make Mill's look positively idyllic, we seem to suffer insatiable cultural thirst. The mastery of New Critical tools may offer in this light a sort of homeopathic salve, the application of a humanistic technology to technologically induced ills.

The thirst for intersubjective confirmation of the self, which has made the overhearing of a persona our principal means of understanding a poem, would I suspect be less strong if it did not involve a kind of bad faith about which Browning's Bishop Blougram (1855) had much to say: "With me, faith means perpetual unbelief / Kept quiet like the snake 'neath Michael's foot / Who stands calm just because he feels it writhe" (ll. 666–68).

The New Criticism of lyric poetry introduced into literary study an anxiety of textuality that was its legacy from the Higher Criticism of scripture a century before: anxiety over the tendency of texts to come loose from their origins into an anarchy that the New Critics half acknowledged and half sought to curb under the regime of a now avowedly fictive self, from whom a language on parole from its author might nonetheless issue as speech. What is poetry? Textuality a speaker owns. The old king of self-expressive lyricism is dead: Long live the Speaker King! At a king's ransom we thus secure our reading against the subversive textuality of what we read; or as another handbook from the 1960s puts it with clarity: "So strong is the oral convention in poetry that, in the absence of contrary indications, we infer a voice and, though we know we are reading words on a page, create for and of ourselves an imaginary listener."[21] Imaginative recreation "for and of ourselves" here depends upon our suppressing the play of the signifier beneath the hand of a convention "so strong" as to decree the "contrary indications" of textuality absent most of the time.

Deconstructive theory and practice in the last decade have so directed our attention to the persistence of "contrary indications" that the doctrine espoused in my last citation no longer appears tenable. It seems incumbent upon us now to choose between intersubjective and intertextual modes of reading, between vindicating the self and saving the text. Worse, I fear, those of us who are both teachers and critics may have to make different choices according to the different positions in which we find ourselves—becoming by turns intertextual readers in the study and intersubjective readers in the classroom—in ways that not very fruitfully perpetuate a professional divide some latter-day Browning might well monologize upon. I wonder whether it must be so; and I am fortified in my doubts by the stubborn survival of the dramatic monologue, which began as a response to lyric isolationism, and which remains to mediate the rivalry between intersubjective appeal and intertextual rigor by situating the claims of each within the limiting context the other provides.

In its charactered life the dramatic monologue can help us put in their places critical reductions of opposite but complementary and perhaps even cognate kinds: on one hand, the transcendentally face-saving misprisions that poetry has received from Victorian romanticizers, Decadent purists, and New Critical impersonalists alike; on the other hand, the abysmal disfigurements of a deconstruction that would convert poetry's most beautiful illusion—the speaking presence—into a uniform textuality that is quite as "purist," in its own way, as anything the nineteenth century could imagine. An exemplary teaching genre, the dramatic monologue can teach us, among other things, that while texts do not absolutely lack speakers, they do not simply have them either; they invent them instead as they go. Texts do not come from speakers, speakers come from texts. *Persona fit non nascitur.* To assume in advance that a poetic text proceeds from a dramatically situated speaker is to risk missing the play of verbal implication whereby character is engendered in the first place through colliding modes of signification; it is to read so belatedly as to arrive only when the party is over. At the same time, however, the guest the party convenes to honor, the ghost conjured by the textual machine, remains the articulate phenomenon we call character: a literary effect we neglect at our peril. For to insist that textuality is all and that the play of the signifier usurps the recreative illusion of character is to turn back at the threshold of interpretation, stopping our ears to both lyric cries and historical imperatives, and from our studious cells overhearing nothing. Renewed stress upon textuality as the basis for the Western written character is a beginning as important to the study of poetry now as it has been for over a century to the writing of dramatic monologues and to the modern tradition they can illuminate in both backward and forward directions. But textuality is only the beginning.

NOTES

1. John Stuart Mill, *Essays on Poetry*, ed. F. Parvin Sharpless (Columbia, S.C., 1976), pp. 12, 36. The quotations come from two essays of 1833, "What Is Poetry?" and "The Two Kinds of Poetry."

2. Ideas like Mill's abound, for example, in Macaulay's 1825 essay "Milton," in *Critical and Historical Essays* (London, 1883): "Analysis is not the business of the poet" (p. 3); "It is the part of the lyric poet to abandon himself, without reserve, to his own emotions" (p. 6); "It is just when Milton escapes from the shackles of the dialogue, when he is discharged from the labour of uniting two incongruous styles, when he is at liberty to indulge his choral raptures without reserve, that he rises even above himself" (p. 8). Comparing Mill's writings with T. S. Eliot's "The Three Voices of Poetry" (1953), Elder Olson, *American Lyric Poems* (New York, 1964), p. 2, concludes that "the study of the question has not advanced much in over a hundred years." Olson's conclusion retains its force after two decades. See Barbara Hardy, *The Advantage of Lyric* (Bloomington and London, 1977), p. 2: "Lyric poetry thrives, then, on exclusions. It is more than usually opaque because it leaves out so much of the accustomed context and consequences of feeling that it can speak in a pure, lucid, and intense voice."

3. *Essays on Poetry*, p. 14.

4. Genre theorists have often observed this distinction, though usually in honoring the exclusivity of lyric. For Babette Deutsch, *Potable Gold* (New York, 1929), p. 21, the essential distinction lies between prose and poetry: "The one resembles a man walking toward a definite goal; the other is like a man surrendering himself to contemplation, or to the experience of walking for its own sake. Prose has intention; poetry has intensity." According to Kenneth Burke, *A Grammar of Motives* (1947; Berkeley and Los Angeles, 1969), p. 475, "The *state of arrest* in which we would situate the essence of lyric is not analogous to dramatic action at all, but is the dialectical counterpart of action." Olson, "The Lyric," *PMMLA*, 1 (1969), 65, says of lyrics that "while they may contain within themselves a considerable narrative or dramatic portion, that portion is subordinate to the lyrical whole. . . . Once expression and address and colloquy become subservient to a further end as affecting their form as complete and whole in themselves, we have gone beyond the bounds of the lyric." For a recent view of Browning opposed to that of the present essay see David Bergman, "Browning's Monologues and the Development of the Soul," *ELH*, 47 (1980), 774: "For Browning, historicity only prettifies a work. . . . History, the creation of a concrete setting, has never been a major focus for Browning." I would reply that history is indeed a major focus for Browning—one of the two foci, to speak geometrically, that define his notoriously elliptical procedures.

5. *Ion* 534; Sharon Cameron, *Lyric Time* (Baltimore and London, 1979), p. 208. See also the quirky Victorian theorist E. S. Dallas, *Poetics* (London, 1852), p. 83: "The outpourings of the lyric should spring from the law of unconsciousness. Personality or selfhood triumphs in the drama; the divine and all that is not Me triumphs in the lyric."

6. Although Browning never wrote such a monologue, he glanced at its possibility in "The Englishman in Italy" (1845), with its vision of "Those isles of the siren" (l. 199) and its audition of a song "that tells us / What life is, so clear"; "The secret they sang to Ulysses / When, ages ago, / He heard and he knew this life's secret / I hear and I know" (ll. 223–27). Life's secret, needless to add, goes untold in Browning's text.

7. Letter of 11 February 1845, in *Letters of Robert Browning and Elizabeth Barrett Barrett, 1845–1846*, ed. Elvan Kintner, 2 vols (Cambridge, Mass., 1969), 1:17.

8. Jerome Christensen, "'Thoughts That Do Often Lie Too Deep for Tears': Toward a Romantic Concept of Lyrical Drama," *Wordsworth Circle*, 12:1 (1981), 61. For an appropriately genealogical testimonial to the pedagogical virtues of the dramatic monologue see Ina Beth Sessions's postscript to "The Dramatic Monologue," *PMLA*, 62 (1947), 516 n.: "One of the most interesting comments concerning the dramatic monologue was made by Dr. J. B. Wharey of the University of Texas in a letter to the writer on January 17, 1935: 'The dramatic monologue is, I think, one of the best forms of disciplinary reading—that is, to use the words of the late Professor Genung, "reading pursued with the express purpose of feeding and stimulating inventive power."'" Among the earliest systematic students of the genre in our century were elocution teachers; their professional pedigree broadly conceived goes back at least to Quintilian, who recommended exercises in impersonation (*prosopopoeia*) as a means of imaginative discipline. See A. Dwight Culler, "Monodrama and the Dramatic Monologue," *PMLA*, 90 (1975), 368.

9. David I. Masson, "Vowel and Consonant Patterns in Poetry," in *Essays on the Language of*

Literature, ed. Seymour Chatman and Samuel R. Levin (Boston, 1967), p. 3, observes that "where lyrical feeling or sensuous description occurs in European poetry, there will usually be found patterns of vowels and consonants." For more general consideration of the linguistics of lyric, see Edward Stankiewicz, "Poetic and Non-poetic Language in Their Interrelation," in *Poetics*, ed. D. Davie et al. (Gravenhage, 1961), p. 17: "Lyrical poetry presents the most interiorized form of poetic language, in which the linguistic elements are most closely related and internally motivated." Note that Stankiewicz, following the Russian Formalists, here refers not to psychological inwardness but to the nonreferential, auto-mimetic interiority of language itself.

10. Arthur Hallam, "On Some of the Characteristics of Modern Poetry, and on the Lyrical Poems of Alfred Tennyson," in *The Writings of Arthur Hallam*, ed. T. Vail Motter (New York, 1943), p. 197; M. H. Abrams, "Structure and Style in the Greater Romantic Lyric," in *From Sensibility to Romanticism*, ed. Frederick W. Hilles and Harold Bloom (New York, 1965), pp. 527–60. On the Romantic mixture of lyric with other genres see Cameron, *Lyric Time*, p. 217; Christensen, "Thoughts," pp. 60–62; Robert Langbaum, "Wordsworth's Lyrical Characterizations," *Studies in Romanticism*, 21 (1982), 319–39. Langbaum's earlier book *The Poetry of Experience* (1957; rpt. New York, 1963), which places the dramatic monologue within Romantic tradition, should be consulted, as should two responses that appeared, almost concurrently, two decades later: Culler, "Monodrama," and Ralph W. Rader, "The Dramatic Monologue and Related Lyric Forms," *Critical Inquiry*, 3 (1976), 131–51.

11. Coleridge is quoted in Frederick A. Pottle, *The Idiom of Poetry* (Ithaca, 1941), p. 82. Wilde's comments occur in "The Critic as Artist" (1890), in *Literary Criticism of Oscar Wilde*, ed. Stanley Weintraub (Lincoln, Neb., 1968), p. 202.

12. Victorian writers were divided as to the chronological priority of lyric over other genres. For Dallas, as for Mill, "Lyrics are the first-fruits of art" (p. 245), while Walter Bagehot contends that "poetry begins in Impersonality" and that lyric represents a later refinement ("Hartley Coleridge" [1852], in *Collected Works*, ed. Norman St. John-Stevas, I [Cambridge, Mass., 1965], pp. 159–60). As to the normative status of lyric, however, the later nineteenth century had little doubt. Summaries and bibliographical aids may be found in Francis B. Gummere, *The Beginnings of Poetry* (New York, 1901), p. 147; Charles Mill Gayley and Benjamin Putnam Kurtz, *Methods and Materials of Literary Criticism* (Boston, 1920), p. 122; W. K. Wimsatt, Jr., and Cleanth Brooks, *Literary Criticism: A Short History* (New York, 1966), pp. 433, 751–52. For representative belletristic histories of poetry from a nostalgic, fin-de-siècle perspective see John Addington Symonds, *Essays Speculative and Suggestive* (London, 1893), pp. 393 ff.; Edmund Gosse, "Introduction" to *Victorian Songs: Lyrics of the Affections and Nature*, ed. E. H. Garrett (Boston, 1895); and Arthur Symons, *The Symbolist Movement in Literature* (1899; rpt. New York, 1958) and *The Romantic Movement in English Poetry* (New York, 1909). On the influence of F. T. Palgrave's *Golden Treasury* (1861; rev. 1981), an anthology that "established, retroactively and for the future, the tradition of the English lyric," see Christopher Clausen, *The Place of Poetry* (Lexington, 1981), p. 67.

13. Symons, *The Symbolist Movement*, p. 49.

14. Marxian approaches now offer the most promising and comprehensive explanations of the fortunes of lyric as a product of industrial culture, yet recently published Marxian analyses evaluate the social functions of lyric very differently. For Theodor W. Adorno, "Lyric Poetry and Society" (1957; trans. Bruce Mayo, *Telos*, 20 [Summer 1974], 56–71), "The subjective being that makes itself heard in lyric poetry is one which defines and expresses itself as something opposed to the collective and the realm of objectivity" (p. 59); in contrast, Hugh N. Grady, "Marxism and the Lyric," *Contemporary Literature*, 22 (1981), 555, argues that "the lyric has become a specialized, though not exclusive, genre of Utopian vision in the modern era."

15. Symons, *The Symbolist Movement*, p. 65.

16. Olson, "The Lyric," p. 65, in distinguishing the "verbal acts" of lyric from those of more elaborate forms, himself acts fatally on the strength of a simile: "The difference, if I may use a somewhat homely comparison, is that between a balloon inflated to its proper shape, nothing affecting it but the internal forces of the gas, and a balloon subjected to the pressure of external forces which counteract the internal." But a balloon affected only by internal forces (i.e., a balloon in a vacuum) would not inflate but explode. That the "proper shape" of a poem, as of a balloon, arises not from sheer afflatus but as a compromise between "internal" and "external" forces is precisely my point about the framing of the dramatic monologue—as it is, I think, the dramatic monologue's (deflationary) point about the lyric.

17. Wimsatt and Brooks, *Literary Criticism*, p. 675; see also Cleanth Brooks and Robert Penn Warren, *Understanding Poetry* (1938; rev. ed. New York, 1950), p. liv. Don Geiger, *The Dramatic Impulse in Modern Poetics* (Baton Rouge, 1967), pp. 85–95, provides a capable overview of the persona poetics of the New Criticism.

18. Oswald Doughty, *English Lyric in the Age of Reason* (London, 1922), p. xv; Walter Blair and W. K. Chandler, eds., *Approaches to Poetry* (New York, 1935), p. 250.

19. Ransom is quoted in William Elton, *A Glossary of the New Criticism* (Chicago, 1949), p. 38. *Sound and Sense*, 2nd ed. (New York, 1963), p. 21; *Elements of Poetry* (New York, 1969), pp. 11–12.

20. Robert W. Boynton and Maynard Mack, *Introduction to the Poem* (New York, 1965), p. 24. On p. 45, to complete the circuit, the authors equate the "voice" with "the poet." They thus return us through a backstage exit to Clement Wood's definition of lyric in *The Craft of Poetry* (New York, 1929), p. 189, as "the form in which the poet utters his own dramatic monolog." Compare the dramatic metaphor in Benedetto Croce's 1937 *Encyclopedia Britannica* article on "Aesthetic": "The lyric . . . is an objectification in which the ego sees itself on the stage, narrates itself, and dramatizes itself" (quoted in Wimsatt and Brooks, *Literary Criticism*, p. 510). For Geoffrey Crump, *Speaking Poetry* (London, 1953), p. 59, the reverse seems true: "an element of the dramatic is present in all lyrical poetry, because the speaker is to some extent impersonating the poet."

21. Jerome Beaty and William H. Matchett, *Poetry: From Statement to Meaning* (New York, 1965), p. 103.

PART TWO

Twentieth-Century Lyric Readers

SECTION 3

Anglo-American New Criticism

New Criticism did not have one way of reading the lyric. The group of critics usually assembled under that name has gradually expanded; these days, it is common to call many different kinds of critics of poetry in the twentieth century "New Critics" if they attended closely to the formal characteristics of the poem, and especially when in doing so they excluded or ignored authorial intent, historical context, or the circumstances of composition, publication, and circulation. But not all kinds of close reading (or as Reuben Brower described the practice when he coined it, of "slow reading") attended to poetic forms in the same ways or for the same reasons.[1] In the United States, the label "New Criticism" began to circulate broadly after John Crowe Ransom published a book by that title in 1941; at close range, the name was used to describe the work of Robert Penn Warren, Allen Tate, Randall Jarrell, R. P. Blackmur, W. K. Wimsatt, Monroe Beardsley, Maynard Mack, and Cleanth Brooks; at longer range, it has been used to describe the work of many others after them. In England, I. A. Richards and William Empson developed their own practices of "Practical Criticism," which anticipated and influenced the early New Critics. Though Ransom and his students Warren, Tate, and Brooks may have shared a certain ideology of the poem as self-sustaining, this was not the same ideology shared by other critics called New, nor was it the ideology of the Practical Criticism. New Critics and Practical Critics may have generally agreed that poems could be read as isolated artifacts or objects (as Wimsatt and Beardsley put it, "a poem is like a pudding or a machine," or as Richards wrote, "a book is a machine to think with"), but they did not agree on why or how poems came to be or should be considered machines or puddings that could run on their own lyric steam or contain their own lyric proof.

Within the context of *The Lyric Theory Reader*, New Criticism and the Practical Criticism may be understood as parts of a longer history of the abstraction or collapse of various verse genres into a large idea of poetry as such. That history had been going on for a century and a half before Richards's *Practical Criticism* (1929) or Ransom's *New Criticism* (1941) set the terms for the reading of poems as self-sufficient forms, for "poetry as a thing in itself," as Brooks and Warren put it in *Understanding Poetry*. The trend toward thinking of all poetry as lyrically itself had more to do with the historical shifts in readers' expectations of poetic genres than it did with whether or not critics thought poems should or should not stand on their own. Mark Jeffreys has written that "lyric became the dominant form of poetry only as poetry's authority was reduced to the cramped margins of culture,"[2] but it is also true that lyric became the dominant idea of poetry as the idea of lyric became so large that poetry became synonymous with it. That process had begun in the eighteenth century; by the middle of the twentieth century, the institutional consolidation of literary criticism in the American postwar university placed critics like Ransom and his students, Brooks and Warren, in a position to defend the marginalized authority of the lyric (Murray Krieger famously called them "The New Apologists for Poetry"; critics like John Fekete identified them as Southerners defending the marginalized authority of their own region in the name of poetry).[3] In England, Richards and his student Empson responded to the class expansion of the modern university by devising ways of reading for students from a range of backgrounds (after his dismissal from Cambridge, Empson went to China, where he tested just how far that range could expand; Richards went on to pursue the dissemination of a Basic English that could serve as a universally accessible world language).

But none of these critics wrote about "the lyric" as such. Instead, they wrote about poetry and assumed the lyric as a default genre into which all poetry could fit. Whereas elegies, odes, hymns, eclogues, ballads, and verse epistles demand that we recognize their metrical and generic histories and circumstances (if we don't know that hymns are made of alternating tetrameter and trimeter lines, usually in quatrains, we won't recognize a hymn when we see one), "poetry as a thing in itself" requires no special knowledge of the reader. By making that self-sufficient version of poetry conform to the ideas of organic unity and individual expression that had come to be associated with the lyric by the twentieth century, these critics did not so much elevate the lyric as the privileged object of critical reading as they made all poems into lyrics that everyone could (with the help of the critic) learn to read.

In the 1920s, the Cambridge critic I. A. Richards began a series of experiments: he gave poems to students and asked them to interpret them. He did not give the students any information about the poems they were to analyze. Richards's experiments had the de facto effect of removing authorial intention and historical context from the act of interpretation, since students were not given that information when asked to analyze the poem at hand. Richards published his experiments in 1929 as *Practical Criticism*, a mode of analysis that was to have wide-ranging effects on poetic pedagogy on both sides of the Atlantic. The object of Richards's experiments was to encourage students to attend to "the words on the page"; his interest was in what he called "the poetic experience," on the psychological state produced by close attention to difficult language. In reaction against his belletristic colleagues, Richards wanted to train students to develop what he called the "craft" or "technique" of reading. His exclusion of authors and historical context from his experiments were means to that end, not ideological positions in themselves. Ultimately, Richards's detailed and quirky descriptions of the experience of reading a poem positioned poetry against the distractions of mass culture, since "among all the agents by which 'the widening of the sphere of human sensibility' may be brought about, the arts are the most powerful, since it is through them that men may most cooperate and in these experiences that the mind most easily and with least interference organizes itself."

The essays we include here from Richards's 1924 *Principles of Literary Criticism* are interested in "the analysis of the experience of reading a poem." In "The Analysis of a Poem," Richards gives a rather amazing representation (he calls it a "hieroglyph") of what we might call your brain on poetry. Above the diagram, five "poetic" words appear: "Arcadia, Night, a Cloud, Pan, and the Moon." Below the words, an elaborate, spidery network of what turn out to be neurons descend toward what look like mechanical coils. On the margins of this zany line drawing, various elements of "the poetic experience" are represented by roman numerals ("visual sensations," "emotions," etc.). This bizarre schema is indebted to Richards's Cambridge colleague Sir Charles Sherrington, whose book *The Integrative Action of the Nervous System* (1906) was quite influential in its day.[4] Sherrington's theory of the "systemization of impulses" became Richards's theory of the systemization of the act of lyric reading; Richards believed that learning to read a poem well could produce "permanent modifications in the structure of the mind." Because each mind is different, "no general prescription that in great poetry there *must* always be this or that,—deep thought, superb sound or vivid imagery—is more than a piece of ignorant dogmatism." What mattered for Richards was the experience, the process through which one passes in the act of reading. The more saturated the experience, the better.

We also include here the short essay "The Definition of a Poem" to demonstrate how Richards's particular account of reading produced (or was produced by) a particular idea of poetry as lyric. Richards elaborates upon the idea that "men may most cooperate" through close attention to the work of art by distinguishing between "standard or normal criticism and erratic or eccentric criticism." If literary criticism were just a matter of whether one liked or disliked a particular poem, it would not have (and perhaps has often not had) much basis, according to Richards. But if "the only workable way of defining a poem" is as "a class of experiences which do not differ in any character more than a certain amount, varying for each character, from a standard experience," then each individual's reading experience may be valued as unique *and* as an integral part of a community of reading. Richards's student William Empson put pressure on the difficulty of maintaining that equilibrium when he insisted, in *Seven Types of Ambiguity* (1930), that a reading that focuses on single words could vary tremendously from one instance to another—indeed, that there was so much variation between possible interpretations that there may be no "standard experience" of even the smallest part of a poem.

In the United States, and particularly at Vanderbilt University in Tennessee, the potential contradictions contained in Richards's vision of a standard reading experience appeared to be resolved when Ransom and his students Cleanth Brooks and Robert Penn Warren discarded Richards's neuropsychological, pseudoscientific emphasis in favor of an antiscientific approach to reading. Like Richards, these self-described "New Critics" considered the reading of poetry exemplary for all understanding, but rather than attempting to account for the "organization of the impulses" effected by such close reading, in the many editions of *Understanding Poetry* (1937–76), Brooks and Warren created an enormously influential pedagogy of poetry as a basic form of human communication. Richards, too, had insisted that poetry was made for communication, but Brooks and Warren wanted to distinguish the kind of communication poetry is from "scientific thought . . . whose purpose, conscious or unconscious, is to give power to its possessor." In contrast, poetry "springs from the most fundamental interests that human beings have" and thus appeals equally to all of us. In order to emphasize poetry's universal appeal as human communication, Brooks and Warren also made all poems into the genre they called "poetry": rather than defining a poem as "a class of experiences," they define "*a poem as a piece of writing which gives us a certain effect in which, we discover, the 'poetry' inheres.*" This tautology—a poem is writing that contains poetry—has the benefit of erasing generic differences between poems, so that "arbitrary and irrational classifications" between sonnets, odes, elegies, eclogues, hymns, etc. can be abandoned in favor of attention to "poetry as a thing in itself worthy of study." Not incidentally, those generic differences that once marked the characters of particular reading communities could give way to the community of the postwar classroom, in which readers could be trained to recognize a generic version of "poetry as a thing in itself."

Many aspects of *Understanding Poetry* tend to lyricize this generic reading experience, but perhaps none more effectively than Brooks and Warren's conception of the "dramatic aspect of poetry." In a move Richards had not made, Brooks and Warren insist that "all poetry, including even short lyrics or descriptive pieces, involves a dramatic organization. This is clear when we reflect that every poem implies a speaker of the poem, either the poet writing in his own person or someone into whose mouth the poem is put." The use of the word "implies" here is interesting: according to this logic, all poems are essentially lyric because on some level all poems assume that there is a person at the center of the poem's organization. In place of Richards's neurons, Brooks and Warren place a fictive persona, someone "into whose mouth the poem is put." The consequences of this shift in the history of the lyricization of poetry are significant. Certainly there were dramatic monologues in the nineteenth century that prefigured the idea that poems imply fictive speakers, and one could further argue that dialect poetry at the end of the century supposed such speakers as racial, ethnic, and national types; certainly poems by Edgar Lee Masters or Robert Frost, or for that matter by Wordsworth or Tennyson or Longfellow, represented the voices of one or more central characters. But in most poetry before Brooks and Warren, those speakers were identified as such, with names or as figures. What Brooks and Warren proposed was an expansion of a poetic technique—a technique that varied from genre to genre—into a principle of reading. If "every poem implies a speaker of the poem," then all poems are equally fictional, and equally lyrical.

The New Critical fiction of the lyric speaker has become so fundamental to our teaching of poetry that it has become virtually invisible as a norm. Most readers who have had any secondary training in reading poems would be lost without the fiction of the speaker as referent. Yet T. S. Eliot, whose ideas and practices became so influential for the later New Criticism, still worried about what that fiction meant for poetry—and especially for the idea of most poetry as lyric. In "The Three Voices of Poetry" (1953), the essay we include in this section, Eliot reflected late in his career on the difference between his composition of dramatic verse for the stage and of poetry to be read on the page. In an attempt to distinguish between different sorts of fictional speakers in his poetry, Eliot wrote that "the first voice is the voice of the poet speaking to himself—or nobody. The second is the voice of the poet addressing an audience—whether large or small. The third is the voice of the poet when he attempts to create a dramatic character speaking in verse." Why did Eliot bother to make such distinctions? The essay itself foregrounds his work for the stage and comments on the difference between dramatic performance and dramatic fiction. But it also gives him the occasion to qualify the alignment of his work for the page with the emerging New Critical notion of the abstract speaker, since Eliot indulges in a long digression about what his "first voice" of poetry is *not*. "I must make the point that this poetry is not necessarily what we call loosely 'lyric poetry,' Eliot writes, insisting that "the term 'lyric' itself is unsatisfactory." After observing that the *Oxford English Dictionary* merely defines *lyric* as "the name for short poems . . . directly expressing the poet's own thoughts and sentiments," Eliot retorts, "How short does a poem have to be, to be called a 'lyric'? . . . there is no necessary relation between brevity and the expression of the poet's own thoughts and feelings. 'Come unto these yellow sands' or 'Hark! hark! the lark' are lyrics—are they not?—but what sense is there in saying that they express directly the poet's own thoughts and sentiments? *London*, *The Vanity of Human Wishes*, and *The Deserted Village* are all poems which appear to express the poet's own thoughts and sentiments, but do we ever think of such poems as 'lyrical'? They are certainly not short. Between them, all the poems I have mentioned seem to fail to qualify as lyrics, just as Mr. Daddy Longlegs and Mr. Floppy Fly failed to qualify as courtiers."

Eliot's diatribe is funny, but it is also extremely anxious that "lyric" not become the default genre for all his verse. Like Richards and Brooks and Warren, Eliot is concerned with what poetic communication can and cannot be in an era of mass communication, but he strongly resists the Practical and New Critical attempts to reduce all poetry to one generic drama of "poetic" communication. He offers the phrase "meditative verse" in place of the slippery or insufficient "lyric," but he also insists on a "second voice" of poetry not written explicitly for the stage, and under the umbrella of that second voice Eliot places all definite genres of nondramatic verse: the dramatic monologue, "all poetry, certainly, that has a conscious social purpose," including any poetry that tells a story, points to a moral, is a satire, or is an epic in ancient or modern form, since an "epic is essentially a tale told to an audience." If a mode of public address defines most verse genres, then, Eliot was at pains to define the poetry he and his contemporaries wrote as a mode of address not subject to such generic expectations but also not subject to the abstraction of one poetic "speaker"—yet still vitally engaged as a mode of communication. Essentially, Eliot wanted to resist the process of lyricization at the same time that he acknowledged that his poetry participated in it.

If some of the push and pull of Eliot's anxiety about the lyric can be traced to the New Critical lyricization of poetry, it can also be linked to an anxiety of authorship, to a worry about the poet's relation to the fictional "voice" of his poem at a time when critics were working to detach that voice from the poet. At about the same time that Eliot gave his lecture on "The Three Voices of Poetry," the American critics W. K. Wimsatt and Monroe Beardsley were writing what would come to be thought of as a manifesto severing the living poet from the voice of the poem. In "The Intentional Fallacy" (1947), Wimsatt and Beardsley famously declared that "a poem is like a pudding or a machine" in the sense that "one demands that it work": it "is detached from the author at birth and goes about the world beyond his power to intend about it or control it." Eliot's insistence on the poet's ability and responsibility to control poetic address gave way to the independence of the poem's own address in Wimsatt and Beardsley's lyricized notion of "the verbal icon." According to this notion, "even a short lyric poem is dramatic, the response of a speaker (no matter how abstractly conceived) to a situation (no matter how universalized). We ought to impute the thoughts and attitudes of the poem immediately to the dramatic speaker, and if to the author at all, only by an act of biographical inference."

While Brooks and Warren also focused their discussion of poems on speakers rather than authors, Wimsatt and Beardsley went one step further. Once all poems are rendered as the responses of fictional speakers to universal situations, then it follows that "the poem belongs to the public" and not to the poet who produced it or to the critic who interprets it. Since the poem "is embodied in language, the peculiar possession of the public, and it is about the human being, an object of public knowledge," then the speakers and their situations contained within the poem's language can only be understood in terms of the language with which they are conveyed. The tendency to attribute that language to its author is an error, according to Wimsatt and Beardsley, since the public can only have access to the author's language and never to the author himself. Thus in "The Intentional Fallacy," Eliot's infamously allusive "The Waste Land" comes in for some scrutiny, since the implication of such allusions is that the public cannot have all the knowledge needed to understand the poem. Wimsatt and Beardsley conclude that if Eliot's notes are considered as part of the poem and not as evidence of the poet's intentions, then such knowledge might be inherent in the poem itself, but they confess, "if Eliot and other contemporary poets have any characteristic fault, it may be in *planning* too much." Better by far in their view to allow the poem to speak for itself. For Wimsatt and Beardsley, all poetry should be read as lyric, and those poems-as-lyrics should be read as sharing the same mode of address. In this, as in other respects, the values the New Critics sought in poetry were the values held dear by postwar American culture.

But how or why or when can a poem speak for itself, without a poet to tell us his intention or a critic to offer us his interpretation? How can all kinds of poems—poems as full of various texts and personae as "The Waste Land," poems directed in Eliot's "second voice" in particular genres to particular audiences, poems made for particular historical circumstances or even for particular people—all speak in the same voice? Richards would not have claimed that they could, and even Brooks and Warren distinguished between various modes of address in various poems (part of the point of the many examples in *Understanding Poetry* is that not all poems can be understood in the same way). Wimsatt and Beardsley tended to assert that poems could speak for themselves but did not explore the dynamics of that fictional speech. That exploration became the project of Reuben Brower, perhaps the most influential (though seldom acknowledged) critical reader of poetry of the mid-twentieth century. When we speak these days of the poem's "speaker," or of a "close reading" of a poem, it is by and large Brower's concepts of those ideas we employ, though most readers who do so don't know how much they owe to Brower. Brower's ideas have become an invisible norm not only because his students (Helen Vendler, Paul de Man, Richard Poirier, Stephen Orgel) went on to have lots to say about how poetry could and should be read but also because his technique of "slow reading" (later, "close reading") made some of the contradictions and problems in the idea of a universally accessible poetic speaker disappear.

Whereas Eliot went to great lengths to distinguish a poem's drama from a play's drama, Brower asserted that "a poem is a dramatic fiction no less than a play, and its speaker, like a character in a play, is no less a creation of the words on the printed page." Brower took a crucial step beyond Richards, Brooks, Warren, and Wimsatt and Beardsley, as he made not only the poem's fictional speaker but the poem's actual reader characters in the drama of the poem. "'The person spoken to' is also a fictional personage," according to Brower; the object of the poem's address "is never the actual audience of 'you and me,' and only in a special abstract sense is it the literary audience of a particular time and place in history. The voice we hear in a lyric, however piercingly real, is not Keats's, or Shakespeare's; or, if it seems to be . . . we are as embarrassed and thrown off as if an actor had stopped and spoken to the audience in his own person." Thus in one fell swoop, Brower solved the riddle of poetic address that so troubled Eliot and that had complicated all thinking about lyric address since Mill, whose metaphor of the poem on stage Brower echoes. By making the poem's audience into a fiction that mirrored the fiction of the poem's speaker, Brower could read each poem as a drama sufficient unto itself. Further, he could read those poetic genres as all equally "lyric." Brower's version of all poems as dramatic lyric fictions in which the characters of speaker and auditor play twin roles marked a decisive shift in the definition of the lyric, a new chapter in the history of lyric reading.

NOTES

1. See especially Reuben Brower, "Reading in Slow Motion," in Brower and Poirier (1961), 3–21.

2. Mark Jeffreys, "Ideologies of the Lyric: A Problem of Genre in Anglophone Poetics," *PMLA* 110.2 (March 1995): 200.

3. See John Fekete, "The New Criticism: Ideological Evolution of the Right Opposition," *Telos* 20 (Summer 1974): 2–51, and Murray Krieger, *The New Apologists for Poetry* (Minneapolis: University of Minnesota Press, 1956). For a retrospective evaluation of such critiques, see Frank Lentricchia, *After the New Criticism* (Chicago: University of Chicago Press, 1980).

4. The insight about Sherrington is John Guillory's and is part of his forthcoming project on the history of close reading; see John Guillory, "How Scholars Read," *ADE Bulletin* (Modern Language Association, 2009).

FURTHER READING

Blackmur, R. P. *Language as Gesture: Essays in Poetry*. New York: Harcourt, Brace, 1952.

Brooks, Cleanth. *The Well-Wrought Urn: Studies in the Structure of Poetry*. New York: Harcourt, Brace, 1947.

Brower, Reuben. *The Fields of Light: An Experiment in Critical Reading*. New York: Oxford University Press, 1963.

Brower, Reuben, and Richard Poirier, eds. *In Defense of Reading: A Reader's Approach to Literary Criticism*. New York: Dutton, 1961.

Davis, Garrick, ed. *Praising It New: The Best of the New Criticism*. Athens, OH: Swallow Press, 2008.

Eagleton, Terry. *How to Read a Poem*. London: Wiley-Blackwell, 2006.

Empson, William. *Seven Types of Ambiguity*. London: Chatto and Windus, 1930; reprint, New York: New Directions, 1966.

———. *The Structure of Complex Words*. London: Chatto and Windus, 1951; reprint, London: Penguin Books, 1995.

Hollander, John. *Melodious Guile: Fictive Pattern in Poetic Language*. New Haven, CT: Yale University Press, 1988.

———. *Vision and Resonance: Two Senses of Poetic Form*. Oxford: Oxford University Press, 1975.

Jarrell, Randall. *Poetry and the Age*. New York: Knopf, 1952.

Jeffreys, Mark. "Ideologies of Lyric: A Problem of Genre in Contemporary Anglophone Poetics." *PMLA* 110.2 (1995): 196–205.

Krieger, Murray. *The New Apologists for Poetry*. Minneapolis: University of Minnesota Press, 1956.

Leavis, F. R. *The Common Pursuit*. London: Chatto and Windus, 1952.

Lentricchia, Frank. *After the New Criticism*. Chicago: University of Chicago Press, 1980.

Pottle, Frederick. *The Idiom of Poetry*. Ithaca, NY: Cornell University Press, 1941.

Pound, Ezra. *The ABC of Reading*. New York: New Directions, 1934.

Ransom, John Crowe, ed. *The New Criticism*. New York: New Directions, 1941.

Richards, I. A. *Practical Criticism: A Study of Literary Judgment*. London: Routledge and Paul, 1929.

Smith, Barbara Herrnstein. *Poetic Closure: A Study of How Poems End*. Chicago: University of Chicago Press, 1968.

Tate, Allen. *Reactionary Essays on Poetry and Ideas*. New York: Charles Scribner's Sons, 1936.

Wimsatt, W. K. *Days of the Leopards: Essays in Defense of Poems*. New Haven: Yale University Press, 1976.

Winters, Yvor. *In Defense of Reason*. Denver: Swallow Press, 1947.

The Analysis of a Poem and The Definition of a Poem (1924)

3.1

I. A. RICHARDS

Chapter 16: The Analysis of a Poem

Toutes choses sont dites déjà, mais comme personne n'écoute il faut toujours recommencer.

André Gide

The qualifications of a good critic are three. He must be an adept at experiencing, without eccentricities, the state of mind relevant to the work of art he is judging. Secondly, he must be able to distinguish experiences from one another as regards their less superficial features. Thirdly, he must be a sound judge of values.

Upon all these matters psychology, even in its present conjectural state, has a direct bearing. The critic is, throughout, judging of experiences, of states of mind; but too often he is needlessly ignorant of the general psychological form of the experiences with which he is concerned. He has no clear ideas as to the elements present or as to their relative importance. Thus, an outline or schema of the mental events which make up the experience of "looking at" a picture or "reading" a poem, can be of great assistance. At the very least an understanding of the probable structures of these experiences can remove certain misconceptions which tend to make the opinions of individuals of less service to other individuals than need be.

Two instances will show this. There are certain broad features in which all agree a poem of Swinburne is unlike a poem of Hardy. The use of words by the two poets is different. Their methods are dissimilar, and the proper approach for a reader differs correspondingly. An attempt to read them in the same way is unfair to one of the poets, or to both, and leads inevitably to defects in criticism which a little reflection would remove. It is absurd to read Pope as though he were Shelley, but the essential differences cannot be clearly marked out unless such an outline of the general form of a poetic experience, as is here attempted, has been provided. The psychological means employed by these poets are demonstrably different. Whether the effects are also dissimilar is a further question for which the same kind of analysis is equally required.

This separation inside the poetic experience of certain parts which are means from certain other parts which are the ends upon which the poetic value of the experience depends, leads up to our other instance. It is unquestionable that the actual experiences, which even good critics undergo when reading, as we say, *the same poem*, differ very widely. In spite of certain conventions, which endeavor to conceal these inevitable discrepancies for social purposes, there can be no doubt that the experiences of readers in connection with particular poems are rarely similar. This is unavoidable. Some differences are, however, much more important than others. Provided the ends, in which the value of the poem lies, are attained, differences in the means need not prevent critics from agreement or from mutual service. Those discrepancies alone are fatal which affect the fundamental features of experiences, the features upon which their value depends. But enough is now known of the ways in which minds work for superficial and fundamental parts of experiences to be distinguished. One of the greatest living critics praises the line:

> The fringed curtain of thine eyes advance,

for the "ravishing beauty" of the visual images excited. This common mistake of exaggerating personal accidents in the means by which a poem attains its end into the chief value of the poem is due to excessive trust in the commonplaces[1] of psychology.

In the analysis of the experience of reading a poem, a diagram, or hieroglyph, is convenient, provided that its limitations are clearly recognized. The spatial relations of the parts of the diagram, for instance, are not intended to stand for spatial relations between parts of what is represented; it is not a picture of the nervous system. Nor are temporal relations intended. Spatial metaphors, whether drawn as diagrams or merely imagined, are dangers only to the unwary. The essential service which pictures can give in abstract matters, namely, the simultaneous and compact representation of states of affairs which otherwise tend to remain indistinct and confused, is worth the slight risk of misunderstanding which they entail.

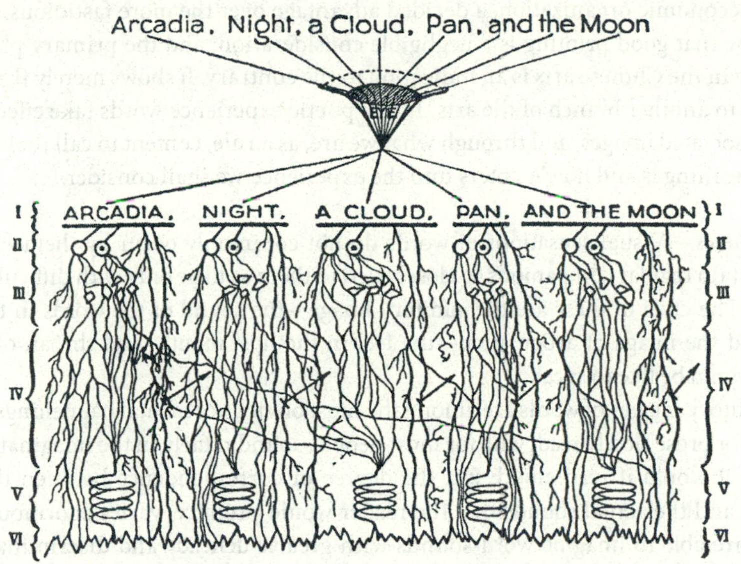

I	— VISUAL SENSATIONS	○	AUDITORY VERBAL IMAGE
II	— TIED IMAGERY	⊙	ARTICULATORY VERBAL IMAGE
III	— FREE IMAGERY		FREE IMAGERY
IV	— REFERENCES		REFERENCES
V	— EMOTIONS		EMOTIONS
VI	— ATTITUDES		ATTITUDES

We may begin then with a diagrammatic representation of the events which take place when we read a poem. Other literary experiences will only differ from this in their greater simplicity.

The eye is depicted as reading a succession of printed words. As a result there follows a stream of reaction in which six distinct kinds of events may be distinguished.

I. The visual sensations of the printed words.
II. Images very closely associated with these sensations.
III. Images relatively free.
IV. References to, or "thinkings of," various things.
V. Emotions.
VI. Affective-volitional attitudes.

Each of these kinds of occurrences requires some brief description and explanation.

Upon the visual sensations of the printed words all the rest depends (in the case of a reader not previously acquainted with the poem); but with most readers they have in themselves no great importance. The individual shapes of the letters, their size and spacing, have only a minor effect upon the whole reaction. No doubt readers differ greatly in this respect; with some, familiarity plays a great part. They find it unpleasant and disturbing to read a poem in any but the edition in which they first became acquainted with it. But the majority of readers are less exigent. Provided that the print is clear and legible, and allows the habitual eye-movements of reading to be easily performed, the full response arises equally well from widely differing sensations. Those for whom this is true have, in the present state of economic organization, a decided advantage over the more fastidious. This does not show that good printing is a negligible consideration; and the primary place of calligraphy in the Chinese arts is an indication to the contrary. It shows merely that printing belongs to another branch of the arts. In the poetic experience words take effect through their associated images, and through what we are, as a rule, content to call their meaning. What meaning is and how it enters into the experience we shall consider.

Tied Images.—Visual sensations of words do not commonly occur by themselves. They have certain regular companions so closely tied to them as to be only with difficulty disconnected. The chief of these are the auditory image—the sound of the words in the mind's ear—and the image of articulation—the feel in the lips, mouth, and throat, of what the words would be like to speak.

Auditory images of words are among the most obvious of mental happenings. Any line of verse or prose slowly read, will, for most people, sound mutely in the imagination somewhat as it would if read aloud. But the degree of correspondence between the image-sounds, and the actual sounds that the reader would produce, varies enormously. Many people are able to imagine word-sounds with greater delicacy and discrimination than they can utter them. But the reverse case is also found. What importance then is to be attached to clear, rich and delicate sound imagery in silent reading? How far must people who differ in their capacity to produce such images differ in their total reactions to poems? And what are the advantages of reading aloud? Here we reach one of the practical problems of criticism for which this analysis is required. A discussion is best postponed until the whole analysis has been given. The principal confusion which prevents a clear understanding of the point at issue does, however, concern images and may be dealt with here. It is of great importance in connection with the topic of the following section.

The sensory qualities of images, their vivacity, clearness, fullness of detail and so on, do not bear any constant relation to their effects. Images differing in these respects may have closely similar consequences. Too much importance has always been attached to the sensory qualities of images. What gives an image efficacy is less its vividness as an image than its character as a mental event peculiarly connected with sensation. It is, in a way which no one yet knows how to explain, a relict of sensation and our intellectual and emotional response to it depends far more upon its being, through this fact, a representative of a sensation, than upon its sensory resemblance to one. An image may lose almost all its sensory nature to the point of becoming scarcely an image at all, a mere skeleton, and yet represent a sensation quite as adequately as if it were flaring with hallucinatory vividity. In other words, what matters is not the sensory *resemblance* of an image to the sensation which is its prototype, but some other relation, at present hidden from us in the jungles of neurology. (Cf. Chapter 14.)

Care then should be taken to avoid the natural tendency to suppose that the more clear and vivid an image the greater will be its efficacy. There are trustworthy people who, according to their accounts, never experience any imagery at all. If certain views commonly expressed about the arts are true, by which vivid imagery is an all-important part of the experience, then these people are incapable of art experiences, a conclusion which is contrary to the facts. The views in question are overlooking the fact that *something* takes the place of vivid images in these people, and that, provided the image-substitute is efficacious, their lack of mimetic imagery is of no consequence. The efficacy required must, of course, include control over emotional as well as intellectual reactions. Needless perhaps to add that with persons of the image-producing types an increase in delicacy and vivacity in their imagery will probably be accompanied by increased subtlety in effects. Thus it is not surprising that certain great poets and critics have been remarkable for the vigour of their imagery, and dependent upon it. No one would deny the usefulness of imagery to some people; the mistake is to suppose that it is indispensable to all.

Articulatory imagery is less noticeable; yet the quality of silent speech is perhaps even more dependent upon these images than upon sound-images. Collocations of syllables which are awkward or unpleasant to utter are rarely delightful to the ear. As a rule the two sets of images are so intimately connected that it is difficult to decide which is the offender. In "Heaven, which man's generation draws," the sound doubtless is as harsh as the movements required are cramping to the lips.

The extent to which interference with one set of images will change the other may be well seen by a simple experiment. Most people, if they attempt a silent recitation while opening the mouth to its fullest stretch or holding the tongue firmly between the teeth, will notice curious transformations in the auditory images. How the experiment should be interpreted is uncertain, but it is of use in making the presence of both kinds of verbal imagery evident to those who may have overlooked them hitherto. Images of articulation should not, however, be confused with those minimal actual movements which for some people (for all, as behaviorists maintain) accompany the silent rehearsing of words.

These two forms of tied imagery might also be called verbal images, and supply the elements of what is called the "formal structure" of poetry. They differ from those to which we now proceed in being images of words, not of things words stand for, and in their very close connection with the visual sensations of printed words.

Free Imagery.—Free images, or rather one form of these, visual images, pictures in the mind's eye, occupy a prominent place in the literature of criticism, to the neglect somewhat of other forms of imagery, since, as was remarked in a preceding chapter, for every possible kind of sensation there is a corresponding possible image.

The assumption, natural before investigation, that all attentive and sensitive readers will experience the same images, vitiates most of the historical discussions from that of Longinus to that of Lessing. Even in the present day, when there is no excuse for such ignorance, the mistake still thrives, and an altogether too crude, too hasty, and too superficial form of criticism is allowed to pass unchallenged. It cannot be too clearly recognized that individuals differ not only in the type of imagery which they employ, but still more in the particular images which they produce. In their whole reactions to a poem, or to a single line of it, their free images are the point at which two readings are most likely to differ, and the fact that they differ may very well be quite immaterial. Fifty different readers will experience not one common picture but fifty different pictures. If the value of the poem derived from the value *qua* picture of the visual image excited then criticism might well despair. Those who would stress this part of the poetic reaction can have but crude views on pictures.

But if the value of the visual image in the experience is not pictorial, if the image is not to be judged as a picture, how is it to be judged? It is improbable that the many critics, some of them peculiarly well qualified in the visual arts, who have insisted upon the importance of imagery, have been entirely wasting their time. It ought to be possible to give an account of the place of free imagery in the whole poetic experience which will explain this insistence. What is required will be found if we turn our attention from the sensory qualities of the imagery to the more fundamental qualities upon which its efficacy in modifying the rest of the experience depends. It has been urged above that images which are different in their sensory qualities may have the same effects. If this were not the case the absence of glaring differences between people of different image-types would be astonishing. But since images may represent sensations without resembling them, and represent them in the sense of replacing them, as far as effects in directing thought and arousing emotion go, differences in their mimetic capacity become of minor importance. As we have seen, it is natural for those whose imagery is vivid, to suppose that vivacity and clearness go together with power over thought and feeling. It is the power of an image over these that is as a rule being praised when an intelligent and sensitive critic appears merely to be praising the picture floating before his mind's eye. To judge the image as a picture is judged, would, as we have seen, be absurd; and what is sought in poetry by those painters and others whose interest in the world is primarily visual is not pictures but records of observation, or stimuli of emotion.

Thus, provided the images (or image-substitutes for the imageless) have the due effects, deficiencies in their sensory aspect do not matter. But the proviso is important. In all forms of imagery sensory deficiencies are for many people signs and accompaniments of defective efficacy, and the habit of reading so as to allow the fullest development to imagery in its sensory aspect is likely to encourage the full development of this more essential feature, its efficacy, if the freaks and accidents of the sensory side are not taken too seriously.

Some exceptions to this general recommendation will occur to the reader. Instances in plenty may be found in which a full development of the sensory aspect of images is damaging to their effects. Meredith is a master of this peculiar kind of imagery:—

> Thus piteously Love closed what he begat
> The union of this ever diverse pair!
> These two were rapid falcons in a snare,
> Condemned to do the flitting of the bat.

The emotional as well as the intellectual effects of the various images here suggested are much impaired if we produce them vividly and distinctly.

Impulses and References.—We have now to consider those more fundamental effects upon which stress has been laid above as the true places of the values of the experience. It will be well at this point to reconsult the diagram. The vertical lines which run capriciously downwards from the visual sensations of the words, through their tied imagery and onward to the bottom of the diagram, are intended to represent, schematically, streams of impulses flowing through in the mind.

They start in the visual sensations, but the depiction of the tied imagery is intended to show how much of their further course is due to it. The placing of the free imagery in the third division is intended to suggest that while some free images may arise from visual words alone, they take their character in a large part as a consequence of the tied imagery. Thus the great importance of the tied imagery, of the formal elements, is emphasized in the diagram.

These impulses are the weft of the experience, the warp being the pre-existing systematic structure of the mind, that organized system of possible impulses. The metaphor is of course inexact, since weft and warp here are not independent. Where these impulses run, and how they develop, depends entirely upon the condition of the mind, and this depends upon the impulses which have previously been active in it. It will be seen then that impulses—their direction, their strength, how they modify one another—are the essential and fundamental things in any experience. All else, whether intellectual or emotional, arises as a consequence of their activity. The thin trickle of stimulation which comes in through the eye finds an immense hierarchy of systems of tendencies poised in the most delicate stability. It is strong enough and rightly enough directed to disturb some of these without assistance. The literal sense of a word can be grasped on the prompting of the mere sight of it, without hearing it or mentally pronouncing it. But the effects of this stimulation are immensely increased and widened when it is reinforced by fresh stimulation from tied images, and it is through these that most of the emotional effects are produced. As the agitation proceeds new reinforcement comes with every fresh system which is excited. Thus, the paradoxical fact that so trifling an irritation as the sight of marks on paper is able to arouse the whole energies of the mind becomes explicable.

To turn now to references, the only mental happenings which are as closely connected with visual words as their tied images are those mysterious events which are usually called thoughts. Thus the arrow symbol in the hieroglyph should perhaps properly be placed near the visual impression of the word. The mere sight of any familiar word is normally followed by a thought of whatever the word may stand for. This thought is sometimes said to be the "meaning," the literal or prose "meaning" of the word. It is wise, however, to avoid the use of "meaning" as a symbol altogether. The terms "thought" and "idea" are less subtle in their ambiguities, and when defined may perhaps be used without confusion.

What is essential in thought is its direction or reference to things. What is this direction or reference? How does a thought come to be "of" one thing rather than another? What is the link between a thought and what it is "of"? The outline of one answer to these questions has been suggested in Chapter 11. A further account must here be attempted. Without a fairly clear, although, of course, incomplete view, it is impossible to avoid confusion and obscurity in discussing such topics as truth in art, the intellect-*versus*-emotion *imbroglio*, the scope of science, the nature of religion and many others with which criticism must deal.

The facts upon which speculations as to the relations between thoughts and the things which they are "of" have been based, have as a rule been taken from introspection. But the facts which introspection yields are notoriously uncertain, and the special position of the observer may well preclude success. Introspection is competent, in some cases, to discover the relations between events which take place within the mind, but cannot by itself give information as to the relations of these events with the external world, and it is precisely this which we are inquiring into when we ask, What connection is there between a thought and that which it is thought of? For an answer to this question we must look further.

There is no doubt that causal relations hold between events in the mind and events outside it. Sometimes these relations are fairly simple. The striking of a clock is the cause of our thinking of its striking. In such a case the external thing is linked with the thought "of" it in a fairly direct fashion, and the view here taken is that to be a thought "of" the striking is to be merely a thought caused in this fashion by the striking. A thought of the striking is nothing else and nothing more than a thought caused by it.

But most thoughts are "of" things which are not present and not producing direct effects in the mind. This is so when we read. What is directly affecting the mind is words on paper, but the thoughts aroused are not thoughts "of" the words, but of other things which the words *stand for*. How, then, can a causal theory of thinking explain the relation between these remote things and the thoughts which are "of" them? To answer this we must look at the way in which we learn what words stand for. Without a process of learning we should only think of the words.

The process of learning to use words is not difficult to analyze. On a number of occasions the word is heard in connection with objects of a certain kind. Later the word is heard in the absence of any such object. In accordance with one of the few fundamental laws known about mental process, something then happens in the mind which is like what would happen if such an object were actually present and engaging the attention. The word has become a *sign* of an object of that kind. The word which formerly was a part of the cause of a certain effect in the mind is now followed by a similar effect in the absence of the rest of the previous cause, namely, an object of the kind in question. This kind of causation appears to be peculiar to living tissue. The relation now between the thought and what it is "of" is more indirect, the thought is "of" " something which formerly was part cause, together with the sign, of similar thoughts. It is of the missing part of the sign, or more strictly of anything which would complete the sign as a cause.

Thoughts by this account are general, they are of anything *like* such and such things, except when the object thought of and the thought are connected by direct causal relations, as, for instance, when we think of a word we are hearing. Only when these direct relations hold can we succeed in thinking simply of "That." We have to think instead of "something of a kind." By various means, however, we can contrive that there shall only be one thing of the kind, and so the need for particularity in our thoughts is satisfied. The commonest way in which we do this is by thoughts which make the kind spatial and temporal. A thought of "mosquito" becomes a thought of "mosquito there now" by combining a thought of "thing of mosquito kind" with a thought of "thing of there kind" and a thought of "thing of now kind." The awkwardness of these phrases, it may be mentioned, is irrelevant. Combined thoughts of this sort, we may notice, are capable of truth and falsity, whereas a simple thought—of "whatever is now" for instance—can only be true. Whether a thought is true or false depends simply upon whether there is anything of the kind referred to, and there must be something now. It is by no means certain that there must be anything there always. And most probably no mosquito is where we thought it was then.

The natural generality and vagueness of all reference which is not made specific by the aid of space and time is of great importance for the understanding of the senses in which poetry may be said to be true. (Cf. Chapter 35.)

In the reading of poetry the thought due simply to the words, their *sense* it may be called, comes first; but other thoughts are not of less importance. These may be due to the auditory verbal imagery, and we have onomatopoeia,[2] but this is rarely independent of the sense. More important are the further thoughts caused by the sense, the network of interpretation and conjecture which arises therefrom, with its opportunities for aberrations and misunderstanding. Poems, however, differ fundamentally in the extent to which such further interpretation is necessary. The mere sense without any further reflection is very often sufficient thought, in Swinburne, for instance, for the full response—

There glowing ghosts of flowers
Draw down, draw nigh;
And wings of swift spent hours
    Take flight and fly;
She sees by formless gleams
She hears across cold streams
    Dead mouths of many dreams that sing and sigh.

Little beyond vague thoughts of the things the words stand for is here required. They do not have to be brought into intelligible connection with one another. On the other hand, Hardy would rarely reach his full effect through sound and sense alone—

"Who's in the next room?—who?
    I seemed to see

Somebody in the dawning passing through
—Unknown to me."
—"Nay: you saw nought. He passed invisibly."

Between these and even more extreme cases, every degree of variation in the relative importance of sound, sense, and further interpretation, between form and content in short, can be found. A temptation to which few do not succumb is to suppose that there is some "proper relation" for these different parts of the experience, so that a poem whose parts are in this relation must thereby be a greater or better poem than another whose parts are differently disposed. This is another instance of the commonest of critical mistakes, the confusion of means with ends, of technique with value. There is no more a "proper place" for sound or for sense in poetry than there is one and only one "proper shape" for an animal. A dog is not a defective kind of cat, nor is Swinburne a defective kind of Hardy. But this sort of criticism is extraordinarily prevalent. The objection to Swinburne on the ground of a lack of thought is a popular specimen.

Within certain types, needless to say, some structures are more likely to be successful than others. Given some definite kind of effect as the goal, or some definite structure already being used, a good deal can of course be said as to the most probable means, or as to what may or may not be added. Lyric cannot dispense with tied imagery, it is clear, nor can we neglect the character of this imagery in reading it. A prose composition has to be longer than a lyric to produce an equal definiteness of developed effect. Poems in which there is much turmoil of emotion are likely to be strongly rhythmical and to be in meter, as we shall see when we come to discuss rhythm and meter. Drama can hardly dispense with a great deal of conjecture and further interpretation which in most forms of the novel is replaced by analysis and explanation, and in narrative poetry is commonly omitted altogether; and so on.

But no general prescription that in great poetry there *must* always be this or that,—deep thought, superb sound or vivid imagery—is more than a piece of ignorant dogmatism. Poetry may be almost devoid even of mere sense, let alone thought, or *almost* without sensory (or formal) structure, and yet reach the point than which no poem goes further. The second case, however, is very rare. Almost always, what seems structureless proves to have still a loose and tenuous (it may be an intermittent) structure. But we can for example shift the words about very often in Walt Whitman without loss, even when he is almost at his best.

It is difficult to represent diagrammatically what takes place in thought in any satisfactory fashion. The impulse coming in from the visual stimulus of the printed word must be imagined as reaching some system in the brain in which effects take place not due merely to this present stimulus, but also to past occasions on which it has been combined with other stimulations. These effects are thoughts; and they in their groupings act as signs for yet other thoughts. The little arrows are intended to symbolize these references to things outside the mind.

Emotions, and Attitudes.—Feeling or emotion is not, we have insisted above, another and a rival mode of apprehending nature. So far as a feeling or an emotion does refer to anything, it refers in the way described, through its origin. Feelings, in fact, are commonly signs, and the differences between those who "see" things by intuition, or "feel" them, and those who reason them out, is commonly only a difference between users of signs and users of symbols. Both signs and symbols are means by which our past experience assists our present responses. The advantages of symbols, due to the ease with which they are controlled and communicated, their public nature, as it were, are obvious. Their disadvantages as compared with such relatively private signs as emotions or organic sensations are perhaps less, evident. Words, when used symbolically or scientifically, not figuratively and emotively, are only capable of directing thought to a comparatively few features of the more common situations. But feeling is sometimes a more subtle way of referring, more dangerous also, because more difficult to corroborate and to control, and more liable to confusion. There is no inherent superiority, however, in feeling as opposed to thought, there is merely a difference in applicability; nor is there any opposition or clash between them except for those who are mistaken either in their thinking or in their feeling, or in both. How such mistakes arise will be discussed in Chapter 34.

As regards emotions and attitudes little need be added to what has already been said. Emotions are primarily signs of attitudes and owe their great prominence in the theory of art to this. For it is the attitudes evoked which are the all-important part of any experience. Upon the texture and form of the attitudes involved its value depends. It is not the intensity of the conscious experience, its thrill, its pleasure or its poignancy which gives it value, but the organization of its impulses for freedom and fullness of life. There are plenty of ecstatic instants which are valueless; the character of consciousness at any moment is no certain sign of the excellence of the impulses from which it arises. It is the most convenient sign that is available, but it is very ambiguous and may be very misleading. A more reliable but less accessible set of signs can be found in the readiness for this or that kind of behavior in which we find ourselves after the experience. Too great insistence upon the quality of the momentary *consciousness* which the arts occasion has in recent times been a prevalent critical blunder. The Epilogue to Pater's *Renaissance* is the *locus classicus*. The after-effects, the permanent modifications in the structure of the mind, which works of art can produce, have been overlooked. No one is ever quite the same again after any experience; his possibilities have altered in some degree. And among all the agents by which "the widening of the sphere of human sensibility" may be brought about, the arts are the most powerful, since it is through them that men may most cooperate and in these experiences that the mind most easily and with least interference organises itself.

[. . .]

Chapter 30: The Definition of a Poem

> Men take the words they find in use among their neighbors, and that they may not seem ignorant what they stand for use them confidently without much troubling their heads about a certain fixed meaning. . . . it being all one to draw these men out of their mistakes, who have no settled notions, as to dispossess a Vagrant of his habitation, who has no settled abode. This I guess to be so; and every one may observe in himself or others whether it be so or not.
>
> Locke

It may be useful to collect here some of the results of the foregoing sections and consider them from the point of view of the practicing critic. The most salient perhaps is the desirability of distinguishing clearly between the communicative and the value aspects of a work of art. We may praise or condemn a work on either ground or upon both, but if it fails entirely as a vehicle of communication we are, to say the least, not well placed for denying its value.

But, it may be said, it will then have no value for us and its value or disvalue for *us* is all that we as critics pretend or should pretend to judge. To make such a reply, however, is to abdicate as a critic. At the least a critic is concerned with the value of things for himself and for people like him. Otherwise his criticism is mere autobiography. And any critic worth attention makes a further claim, a claim to sanity. His judgment is only of general interest in so far as it is representative and reflects what happens in a mind of a certain kind, developed in a certain fashion. The services of bad critics are sometimes not less than those of good critics, but that is only because we can divine from their responses what other people's responses are likely to be.

We must distinguish between standard or normal criticism and erratic or eccentric criticism. As critics Lamb or Coleridge are very far from normal; none the less they are of extraordinary fertility in suggestion. Their responses are often erratic even when of most revelatory character. In such cases we do not take them as standards to which we endeavor to approximate, we do not attempt to see eye to eye with them. Instead we use them as means by which to make quite different approaches ourselves to the works which they have characteristically but eccentrically interpreted.

The distinction between a personal or idiosyncratic judgment and a normative is sometimes overlooked. A critic should often be in a position to say, "I don't like this but I know it is good," or "I like this and condemn it," or "This is the effect which it produces upon me, and this quite different effect is the one it should produce." For obvious reasons he rarely makes any such statements. But many people would regard praise of a work which is actually disliked by the praiser as immoral. This is a confusion of ideas. Any honest reader knows fairly well the points at which his sensibility is distorted, at which he fails as a normal critic and in what ways. It is his duty to take these into consideration in passing judgment upon the value of a work. His rank as a critic depends at least as much upon his ability to discount these personal peculiarities as upon any hypothetical impeccability of his actual responses.

So far we have been considering those cases in which the vehicle is sufficiently adequate and the critic sufficiently representative and careful for the response to be a good index of the value of the poem. But these cases are comparatively rare. The superstition which any language not intolerably prolix and uncouth encourages that there is something actual, *the poem*, which all readers have access to and upon which they pass judgment, misleads us. We naturally talk about poems (and pictures, etc.) in a way which makes it impossible for anybody to discover what it is we are talking about. Most critical discussion, in other words, is primarily emotive with only a very loose and fourfold equivocal reference. We may be talking about the artist's experience, such of it as is relevant, or about the experience of a qualified reader who made no mistakes, or about an ideal and perfect reader's possible experience, or about our own actual experience. All four in most cases will be qualitatively different. Communication is perhaps never perfect, so the first and the last will differ. The second and third differ also, from the others and from one another, the third being what we ought unrestrictedly to experience, or the best experience we could possibly undergo, whereas the second is merely what we ought to experience as things are, or the best experience that we can expect.

Which of these possible definitions of a poem shall we adopt? The question is one of convenience merely; but it is by no means easy to decide. The most usual practice is to mean by *the poem* either the first or the last; or, by forgetting what communication is, to mean both confusedly together. The last involves the personal judgment to which exception was taken on the previous page, and has the further disadvantage that there would be for every sonnet as many poems as readers. A and B, discussing *Westminster Bridge* as they thought, would unwittingly be discussing two different things. For some purposes, for the disentanglement of some misunderstandings, it is convenient to define a poem temporarily in this manner.

To define the poem as the artist's experience is a better solution. But it will not do as it stands since nobody but the artist has that experience. We must be more ingenious. We cannot take any single experience as the poem; we must have a class of more or less similar experiences instead. Let us mean by *Westminster Bridge* not the actual experience which led Wordsworth on a certain morning about a century ago to write what he did, but the class composed of all actual experiences, occasioned by the words, which do not differ within certain limits from that experience. Then anyone who has had one of the experiences comprised in the class can be said to have read the poem. The permissible ranges of variation in the class need (of course) very careful scrutiny. To work them out fully and draw up a neat formal definition of a poem would be an amusing and useful occupation for any literary logician with a knowledge of psychology. The experiences must evidently include the reading of the words with fairly close correspondence in rhythm and tune. Pitch difference would not matter, provided that pitch relations were preserved. Imagery might be allowed to vary indefinitely in its sensory aspect but would be narrowly restricted otherwise. If the reader will run over the diagram of a poetic experience given in Chapter 16 and consider in what respects his and his friends' experiences must agree if they are to be able to refer to them indifferently as though they were one and the same without confusion or misunderstanding, he will see what kind of thing a detailed definition of a poem would be.

This, although it may seem odd and complicated, is by far the most convenient, in fact it is the only workable way of defining a poem; namely, as a class of experiences which do not differ in any character more than a certain amount, varying for each character, from a standard experience. We may take as this standard experience the relevant experience of the poet when contemplating the completed composition.[3]

Anyone whose experience approximates in this degree to the standard experience will be able to judge the poem and his remarks about it will be about some experience which is included in the class. Thus we have what we want, a sense, namely, in which a critic can be said to have not read the poem or to have misread it. In this sense unrecognized failures are extremely common.

The justification for this outbreak of pedantry, as it may appear, is that it brings into prominence one of the reasons for the backwardness of critical theory. If the definition of a poem is a matter of so much difficulty and complexity, the discussion of the principles by which poetry should be judged may be expected to be confused. Critics have as yet hardly begun to ask themselves what they are doing or under what conditions they work. It is true that a recognition of the critic's predicament need not be explicit in order to be effective, but few with much experience of literary debate will underestimate the extent to which it is disregarded or the consequences which ensue from this neglect. The discussions in the foregoing chapters are intended as no more than examples of the problems which an explicit recognition of the situation will admit and of the ways in which they will be solved.

NOTES

1. The description of images belongs to the first steps in psychology, and it is often possible to judge the rank and standing of a psychologist by the degree of importance which he attaches to their peculiarities. On theoretical grounds it seems probable that they are luxury products (cf. *The Meaning of Meaning*, pp. 148–151) peculiarly connected with the reproduction of emotion. For a discussion of some experimental investigations into their utility, Spearman, *The Nature of Intelligence*, Ch. XII, may be consulted.

2. Two kinds of onomatopoeia should be distinguished. In one the sound of the words (actual or imaginal) is like some natural sound (the buzzing of bees, galloping horses, and so forth). In the other it is not like any such sound but such as

merely to call up auditory images of the sounds in question. The second case is by far the more common.

3. Difficulties even here arise, e.g. the poet may be dissatisfied without reason. Coleridge thought *Kubla Khan* merely "a psychological curiosity" without poetic merits, and may have been justified in some degree. If he was not, it is his dream experience which we should presumably have to take as our standard.

Introduction to *Understanding Poetry* (1938)

3.2

Cleanth Brooks and Robert Penn Warren

Poetry is a form of speech, or discourse, written or spoken. To the person who is not well acquainted with poetry the differences between poetic speech and other forms may seem to be more important than the similarities, but these differences should not be allowed to obscure the fundamental resemblances, for only by an understanding of the resemblances can one appreciate the meaning of the differences. Poetry, like all discourse, is a communication—the saying of something by one person to another person. But what is that "something"? We usually identify it with information. As practical people going about our affairs, we ask directions, read road signs, order a dinner from a menu, study football scores or stock market reports. It is altogether natural, therefore, that we should tend to think the important and central matter in all discourse to be information. But, after all, we may do well to ask how much of the discourse of an average man in any given day is primarily concerned with information for the sake of information. After he has transacted his business, obeyed his road signs, ordered and eaten his dinner, and read the stock market reports, he might be surprised to reflect on the number of non-practical functions speech had fulfilled for him that day. He had told the office boy a joke; he had commented on the weather to the traffic officer, who could observe the weather as well as he; he had told an old friend that he was glad to see him again; he had chatted with his wife on some subject on which there was already full knowledge and agreement. Even when he had been at lunch with some business associates with whom the talk ran on informational topics, the trend in the stock market, for instance, he had not intended to use the information for buying or selling. The interest in the conversation had not been finally practical. This practical man might discover that a large part of the business of discourse had been concerned with matters which are not ordinarily thought of as really "practical," but with his relations to other people, that is, with such elusive matters as feelings and attitudes.

That "something," then, conveyed by discourse is not necessarily information to be used for practical purposes. But even when the man in question was concerned primarily with a matter of practical interest, his discourse was colored by other considerations. If he telephoned an associate to ask the price he probably prefaced his question by saying, "How are you?" and concluded his conversation by saying, "Thank you," and "Goodbye." For even the most practical man a large part of discourse is not prompted by purely practical considerations; another "something" is present.

Moreover, even when a man is using speech for the purpose of conveying information, and how difficult it is to make speech deal only with pure and exact information. Almost always a speaker conveys not only the pure information but an attitude toward and a feeling about that information. For example, let us consider the case of a motorist who stops a man driving a hay wagon to ask about the condition of the road ahead. The man on the wagon says, "It's a tolerable good road, you won't have no trouble on it." The motorist drives on, encouraged. But after a mile or so, having experienced a few substantial jolts, he hails another motorist and asks the same question. This new man says, "It's a devil of a road, it'll jerk your teeth out." Both the man on the hay wagon and the man in the second automobile think that they are telling the truth. Both intend to be helpful and to give exact information. And both feel that they know the road. But each man's language reflects his own experience with the road. For the man with the hay wagon the road *was* tolerably good, but for the second motorist, anxious to make time on his trip, the road was devilishly bad.

If this seems to be a fairly obvious example of confusion about information in ordinary speech, let us consider an example in which a trained scholar is trying to make an exact statement.

> For sentimental pacifism is, after all, but a return to the method of the jungle. It is in the jungle that emotionalism alone determines conduct, and wherever that is true no other than the law of the jungle is possible. For the emotion of hate is sure sooner or later to follow on the emotion of love, and then there is a spring for the throat. It is altogether obvious that the only quality which really distinguishes man from the brutes is his reason.[1]

The author of this statement is Robert Andrews Millikan, the internationally famous physicist and winner of the Nobel Prize. He is making a plea for the scientific attitude in political and international affairs, but when one inspects this statement carefully one finds some propositions about human beings that cannot be proved by Mr. Millikan, or by anyone else, in the same way that he can prove certain formulae of physics in his laboratory. Furthermore, waiving this question of whether the propositions stated and implied are really true or not, one finds that a very important part of the statement consists not in information about human beings but in appeals to the reader to take a certain attitude toward the statement. The comparisons concerning the jungle and the leap of one infuriated beast at the throat of another represent the sort of comparison one finds in poetry; for the comparisons are not based on scientific analogy—the resemblance is prompted by the emotional attitude of the speaker and is calculated to incite a corresponding attitude in the reader. But the coloring of the general statement—that is, the bringing in of an implied interpretation of the statement—extends beyond the mere use of a "poetic" comparison. In the first sentence, for example, the word *pacifism* is qualified by the word *sentimental*. Presumably it is a particular sort of pacifism here defined to which Mr. Millikan's objections apply; but does the adjective *sentimental* really set off a "bad kind of pacifism" from a good kind? Could the reader determine from Mr. Millikan's statement whether or not he would consider the pacifism of Jesus Christ, the Prince of Peace, a sentimental or a non-sentimental sort? Since the only kind of pacifism that Mr. Millikan sets over against his sentimental pacifism is a scientific pacifism operating through an organization of sociologists and economists, one might conceivably assume that Jesus Christ would fall into the former classification. Or, to state the matter otherwise: is the basic argument for peace to be found in the fact that war is unprofitable or is horrible, or in the belief that it is wrong to kill one's fellowman? As a matter of fact, the adjective *sentimental* is, on logical grounds, a bogus qualification: its real function is to set up an attitude in the reader that will forbid his inspection of the basis of the statement.

Whether or not the general statement is logically sound, Mr. Millikan has not stated it with scientific precision; in Mr. Millikan's defense it may be said that *the proposition is one that cannot be stated with scientific precision by anyone*. Mr. Millikan, a scientist trying to state the virtues of a scientific method in human relationships, is forced to resort to devices which we associate with poetry. We should never find him coloring a mathematical formula by referring to a "sentimental figure four," or describing a well known chemical reaction by saying that two ferocious atoms of hydrogen spring at the throat of one defenseless atom of oxygen.

Limitations of Scientific Statement

The advantages of scientific statement are not to be had without the limitations of a scientific statement also. The primary advantage of the scientific statement is that of absolute precision. But we must remember that this precision is gained by using terms in special and previously defined sense. The scientist carefully cuts away from his technical terms all associations, emotional colorings and implications of judgment. He gives up, then, all attempts to influence the reader's attitude toward his statement. For this reason, only certain kinds of statement and certain kinds of meaning are possible to true science. Science tends, indeed, toward the condition of mathematics, and the really exact scientific statements can be expressed in mathematical formulae. The chemist describes water as H_2O—two atoms of hydrogen and one atom of oxygen. The formula, H_2O, differs tremendously from even the common word *water*, for the word water, neutral as it seems in connotation, still may possess all sorts of different associations—drinking, bathing, boating, the pull of the moon to create tides, the liquid from which the goddess Aphrodite rose, or, as Keats put it,

> The moving waters at their priestlike task
> Of pure ablution round the earth's human shores.

As with the liquid itself, so with the word: the scientist needs a distilled product.

The language of science represents an extreme degree of specialization of language in the direction of a certain kind of precision. It is unnecessary, of course, to point out that in this specialization tremendous advantages inhere, and that the man of the twentieth century is rightly proud of this achievement. But it is more often necessary to point out that scientific precision can be brought to bear only on certain kinds of materials. Literature in general—poetry in particular—also represents a specialization of language for the purpose of precision; but it aims at treating kinds of materials different from those of science.

We have already seen that science has to forego, because of its method, matters of attitude and interpretation; or that, when it does not forego them, it is so much the less science. For better or worse, certain kinds of communication are not possible to scientific statement. To return to the question raised at the beginning of this discussion, what is the "something" which is conveyed by speech? We have already seen that it is not exclusively information in the ordinary sense, and even less exclusively information in the scientific sense. The speech of that ordinary citizen in an ordinary way conveys many things, attitudes, feelings, and interpretations, that fall outside of these restrictions. These things, though they fill a large part of the speech of that ordinary citizen, are never stated very clearly or precisely by him. The specialization of speech which we find in poetry aims at clarity and precision of statement in these matters.

That the communication of attitudes, feelings, and interpretations constitutes a real problem, and indeed, in one sense, a more difficult problem than that offered by the communication of mere information, may be clearly illustrated by such an example as the following. Suppose, for instance, that a student sitting on the front row in a class room turns to his neighbor and whispers to him the information that it is ten minutes to eleven. This information might be passed from one person to another in the same manner through a whole class to the last man on the back row, and the probability is that the last man would receive correctly the message: it is ten minutes to eleven. The communication has been a relatively easy matter. But suppose that the first man on the first row, instead of whispering a mere bit of information, had made even a relatively simple statement involving a feeling or attitude: suppose he had said, for example, "John Jones is a fine fellow, but I sometimes feel that he is a little stuck-up." In all probability the last man who received the message would get an entirely different view of John's character from that intended by the original speaker. Indeed, anyone who is familiar with the distortions which often, and as a matter of fact, usually take place in the transmission of gossip will not be surprised at whatever the version has become, by the time it has been transmitted through thirty people. One of the reasons for the error is simple. The original statement about John is an interpretation. The person who hears it, naturally recognizes that it is an interpretation and not a statement of objective fact, and therefore, in turn, interprets the remark in his own fashion. For example, the last man makes an interpretation of an original interpretation which has been altered more or less by twenty-eight intervening interpretations. The "something" of the second piece of communication, unlike that of the first involves feelings which each hearer has to define for himself. In ordinary life, a hearer unconsciously bases much of his definition of such pieces of communication, not on the words themselves, but on the gestures, tone of voice, and facial expression of the speaker, and on what he knows about the speaker. For instance, every one understands how difficult it is to deal with a delicate personal matter in a letter, for the letter has nothing but words—that is, symbols written on paper and divorced from the tone of the voice, gestures, and facial expressions.

Materials of Poetry

The basic problem of communication in poetry is, therefore, one of a totally different character from that involved in communication of matters of fact, and we shall merely confuse ourselves about the meaning of any poetry if we do not realize this distinction. The specialization of language in poetry is an attempt to deal with this problem.

But the very nature of the human being, the ordinary citizen in the ordinary day speaks much of what we might call incipient poetry—he attempts to communicate attitudes, feelings, and interpretations. (Unfortunately, most of this poetry is bad poetry.) And poetry in this sense is not confined to the speech of the ordinary citizen. It appears also in editorials, sermons, political speeches, magazine articles, and advertisements. We have seen that Mr. Millikan's essay can be discussed as poetry rather than as science. This, of course, is not apparent to everybody. Many a person would regard as mere poetry the Biblical statement

> All they that take the sword shall perish by the sword.

But such a person might, during the next minute, regard Mr. Millikan's paragraph as a sober and verifiable scientific pronouncement. Or to take another case, this person might read an avowed poem:

THE MAN HE KILLED

THOMAS HARDY (1840–1928)

Had he and I but met
By some old ancient inn,
We should have sat us down to wet
Right many a nipperkin!

But ranged as infantry,
And staring face to face,
I shot at him as he at me,
And killed him in his place.

I shot him dead because—
Because he was my foe,
Just so: my foe of course he was;
That's clear enough; although

He thought he'd 'list, perhaps,
Off-hand like—just as I—
Was out of work—had sold his traps—
No other reason why.

Yes; quaint and curious war is!
You shoot a fellow down
You'd treat if met where any bar is,
Or help to half-a-crown.

He might dismiss this as mere literature, failing to see that Mr. Millikan's paragraph is "mere literature" also—and of course infinitely poorer literature. As has been indicated, Mr. Millikan's argument is not "science." And, as a matter of fact, it is possible that Hardy has, in his poem, put the case against war on a more solid basis than Mr. Millikan has done in his argument.

Mr. Millikan might or might not have been aware that he was using some of the methods of poetry to color the attitude of his readers and bring them to his own point of view; but any writer of advertising copy is perfectly aware of the fact that he is trying to persuade his readers to adopt a certain attitude.

Poetry as a Specialization of Ordinary Speech

From the examples already given we have seen that both the impulse of poetry—that is, the impulse to communicate feelings, attitudes and interpretations—and some of the methods of poetry—that is, comparisons, associations with words, etc.—appear in a great deal of our discourse that is not ordinarily considered as poetic at all. It is important to remember this fact because some people think of poetry as a thing entirely separate from ordinary life and of the matters with which poetry deals as matters with which the ordinary person is not concerned. More will have to be said about the special characteristics of formal poetry—characteristics which set it off from this "stuff of poetry" appearing in ordinary life; but it is highly important to see that both the impulse and methods of poetry are rooted very deep in human experience, and that formal poetry itself represents, not a distinction from, but a specialization of, thoroughly universal habits of human thinking and feeling.

Confusion between Scientific and Poetic Communication

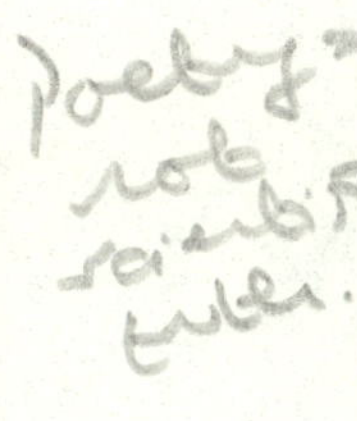

The distinction earlier mentioned between the communication of science and the communication of poetry is also an extremely important one. People, as we have seen, are constantly confusing the two sorts of communication. They will often accept as sober scientific doctrine what is essentially a poetic statement, or they will judge formal poetry as if it were aiming at scientific truth.

An example of the first type of confusion has already been indicated in the quotation from Mr. Millikan. Mr. Millikan does not rest his case on scientifically verifiable facts but also makes an emotional appeal for a certain attitude concerning those facts. Mr. Millikan is speaking, not as a professional scientist, but as a man, and he is thoroughly justified in using this kind of speech; but it is important that the reader know exactly what Mr. Millikan is doing. Even to the person who thinks that he has no interest in formal poetry an awareness of this distinction is valuable, for he cannot move through the mass of conversation, sermons, editorials, historical and sociological writings, and advertisements without encountering situations in which this distinction is fundamental to an understanding of the actual meanings involved. The case of advertising, of course, raises the question in an extreme form. Advertisers naturally are not content to rest on a statement of fact, whether such a statement is verifiable or not. They will attempt to associate the attitude toward a certain product with an attitude toward beautiful women, little children, or gray-haired mothers; they will appeal to snobbishness, vanity, patriotism, religion, and morality. In addition to these appeals to the consumer's most basic and powerful feelings, the advertiser often attempts to imply a scientific validity for his claims—a validity which may, or may not, be justified by the product—by pictures of white-robed surgeons and research experts, statements of abstruse scientific formulae, hints of recent discoveries, coy references to the research laboratories of the plant involved, and very frequent use of the phrase "science tells us." Even the man who cares nothing for "literature" will find that he constantly has to deal with literary appeals and methods while living in the hard-headed, scientific, and practical twentieth century.

The second type of confusion mentioned above—the confusion that causes people to judge formal poetry as if it were science—is the source of most of the misunderstandings of poetry and of literature in general. It is highly necessary, if one is to understand poetry, to take up some of these typical misreadings.

1. *"Message-Hunting"*

"Message-hunting"—the business of looking only for the statement of an idea which the reader thinks he can apply profitably in his own conduct—is one of the most ordinary forms of this general confusion. Here is a poem by Longfellow that has been greatly admired by many people who read poetry in this fashion:

A PSALM OF LIFE

WHAT THE HEART OF THE YOUNG MAN SAID TO THE PSALMIST

HENRY WADSWORTH LONGFELLOW (1807–1882)

Tell me not, in mournful numbers,
    Life is but an empty dream!—

For the soul is dead that slumbers,
    And things are not what they seem.

Life is real! Life is earnest!
    And the grave is not its goal;
Dust thou art, to dust returnest,
    Was not spoken of the soul.

Not enjoyment, and not sorrow,
    Is our destined end or way;
But to act, that each tomorrow
    Find us farther than today.

Art is long, and Time is fleeting,
    And our hearts, though stout and brave,
Still, like muffled drums, are beating
    Funeral marches to the grave.

In the world's broad field of battle,
    In the bivouac of Life,
Be not like dumb, driven cattle!
    Be a hero in the strife!

Trust no Future, howe'er pleasant!
    Let the dead Past bury its dead!
Act,—act in the living Present!
    Heart within, and God o'erhead!

Lives of great men all remind us
    We can make our lives sublime,
And, departing, leave behind us
    Footprints on the sands of time;

Footprints, that perhaps another,
    Sailing o'er life's solemn main,
A forlorn and shipwrecked brother,
    Seeing, shall take heart again.

Let us, then, be up and doing,
    With a heart for any fate;
Still achieving, still pursuing,
    Learning to labor and to wait.

This poem seems to give a great deal of good advice. It tells the reader not to waste his time but to be up and doing; not to be discouraged by failures but to have a heart for any fate; not to judge life by temporary standards but to look to eternal reward. There are probably few people who would quarrel with the moral value of these statements. But granting that the advice is good advice, we can still ask whether or not the poem is a good poem. If the advice is what the poem has to offer us, then we can ask why a short prose statement of the advice itself is not as good as, or even better than, the poem, itself. But even the people who say they like the poem because of its "message" will usually prefer the poem to a plain prose statement. If such people would reject the prose summary in favor of the poem, they would also reject certain other versions of the poetic statement. For instance, let us alter one of the stanzas of the poem, taking care in the alteration, however, to preserve the idea. The original stanza is:

Lives of great men all remind us
    We can make our lives sublime,
And departing, leave behind us
    Footprints on the sands of time.

An alteration might run:

Lives of all sorts of great men remind us
    That we ourselves can make our lives sublime,
And when we die we can leave behind us
    Noble recollections printed on the sands of time.

The fact that any admirer of the poem would unhesitatingly choose the first version proves that "something" aside from the mere value of the idea is involved in the choice.

The fact that we have just an idea in itself is not enough to make a poem, even when the idea may be a worthy one. The neglect of this principle causes frequent misunderstandings and misreadings of poems. But another type of misreading may result from the fact that the reader does not happen to agree with an idea expressed in a poem. We may treat this distinction by a concrete case: is an admirer of Longfellow's poem, even one who says that his admiration is based on the worth of the idea, disqualified from admiring the following poem, which states an idea rather opposed to some of the ideas in Longfellow's poem?

EXPOSTULATION AND REPLY

WILLIAM WORDSWORTH (1770–1850)

"Why, William, on that old gray stone,
    Thus for the length of half a day,
Why, William, sit you thus alone,
    And dream your time away?"

"Where are your books?—that light bequeathed
    To beings else forlorn and blind!
Up! up! And drink the spirit breathed
    From dead men to their kind.

"You look round on your Mother Earth,
    As if she for no purpose bore you;
As if you were her first-born birth,
    And none had lived before you."

One morning thus, by Esthwaite lake,
    When life was sweet, I knew not why,
To me my good friend Matthew spake,
    And thus I made reply:

"The eye—it cannot choose but see;
    We cannot bid the ear be still;
Our bodies feel, where'er they be,
    Against or with our will.

"Nor less I deem that there are Powers
Which of themselves our minds impress;
That we can feed this mind of ours
In a wise passiveness.

"Think you, 'mid all this mighty sum
Of things forever speaking,
That nothing of itself will come,
But we must still be seeking?

"—Then ask not wherefore, here, alone,
Conversing as I may,
I sit upon this old gray stone,
And dream my time away."

This poem seems to give the advice that one should neglect the "light bequeathed" by the great men of the past in favor of what one can only learn for himself; that one should not fritter away his time by being "up and doing" or by being a "hero in the strife"; and that one should learn in contemplation to cultivate that "wise passiveness" by which, only, one comes into harmony with the great powers of the universe. If the admirer of Longfellow's poem means literally what he says when he praises the poem for the "message," then he is absolutely disqualified from enjoying this poem, for its "message" is diametrically opposed to that of "The Psalm of Life." Of course, many people who describe their appreciation of poems in terms of the "messages" do not mean literally what they say; they are simply groping for some ground to justify the fact that they like poetry at all. Since they are accustomed to think of all communication as concerned with practical information, they try to put their liking on some "practical" or "scientific" basis.

As a matter of fact, the place of ideas in poetry and their relation to the goodness of a poem cannot be treated in such an over-simplified manner. We know, for example, that devout Protestants can accept the poetry of the Catholic poet Dante, or that Catholics can accept the poetry of the Protestant poet John Milton. The fact that the Protestant reader, who holds his religious beliefs seriously, may still accept the poetry of Dante does not mean that the reader regards poetry as merely trivial and unserious. This whole matter is one that cannot be dismissed in a few sentences, but requires for a satisfactory understanding the analysis of many special poems. It will suffice to say here that the "message-hunting" method of reading poetry breaks down even in the simplest cases.

2. *"Pure Realization"*

Many readers and critics of poetry, realizing the insufficiency of the "message-hunting" approach to poetry, have adopted a view that poetry does not deal with any ideas or truths all, but is an "expression of pure emotion," or "deals with emotion." This view is sometimes put in other terms, as when one critic says that a poem is the expression of "a moment of pure realization of being"—that is, it attempts merely to bring vividly to the reader some scene or sensation.

When a critic trying to point out the distinguishing marks of poetry says that poetry expresses an emotion or that poetry deals with emotion, exactly what does he mean? Does he mean that a poem, about grief, for instance, would "express" the grief a poet might feel, or have felt, in the same way as a burst of tears would express the emotion of grief? Or does he mean that the reading of a poem about grief would provoke in the reader an emotion of grief in the same way as would a personal bereavement? Quite obviously, the answer to both questions is "No." Certainly, writing of a poem would be no substitute for the relief of a burst of tears; nor would the response to the reading of a poem be as intense as the experience of a real bereavement. There is some difference. On the mere ground of emotional intensity the poem does not compete with the real experience. The justification of poetry as "pure realization," like its justification on the basis of "message-hunting," breaks down even in simple cases, for the pure realization of an experience is the experience at the moment it occurs. For instance, the taste or the smell of a real apple is always more intense than any poem describing the taste or smell of an apple. The following passage from "Ode to a Nightingale," by John Keats has sometimes been praised as a moment of "pure realization":

> O for a draught of vintage! that hath been
> Cooled a long age in the deep-delvèd earth,
> Tasting of Flora and the country green,
> Dance, and Provençal song, and sunburnt mirth!
> O for a beaker full of the warm South,
> Full of the true, the blushful Hippocrene,
> With beaded bubbles winking at the brim,
> And purple-stainèd mouth. . . .

Whatever "pure realization" there is here is certainly not the pure realization of wine as such. The stanza is obviously not a substitute for an actual glass of wine: not only does it fail to give the intensity of the sensation of actual wine-drinking but it gives an effect thoroughly different in kind from the experience of drinking a glass of wine. If there is a "pure realization" of anything it is of the poet's thinking about the wine as a thing which represents to him a certain kind of life—a warm, mirthful, carefree, healthy, pagan kind of life, which in the total context of the poem stands in contrast to his own troubled and fretful experience. As a matter of fact, when we inspect the passage we discover that it is not so much a pictorial description of a beaker of wine, or a description of the sensation of drinking wine, as it is a cluster of associations with the wine—associations which suggest the kind of life we have mentioned. The poet is not saying, actually, that he is thirsty for a drink of wine but that he wants a certain kind of life, the qualities of which he implies.

We have seen that the attempt to conceive of poetry as the "expression of emotion" or as "pure realization" represents an attempt to get away from the "message-hunting" approach to poetry. But in the case which we have just examined we have seen that experience which is "realized" or communicated to the reader is far different from the experience of a physical object (wine, in this instance), an emotional reaction, or a sensation. The experience, we have seen, really involves an interpretation by the poet, so that in so far as the term "realization" is used to imply an absence of interpretation it is thoroughly inaccurate.

3. *"Beautiful Statement of Some High Truth"*

There is another confused conception of poetry arising from the attempt to combine in a mechanical fashion the two false approaches which have just been discussed. This confused conception is variously stated. For instance, it may be expressed in a definition of poetry as "fine sentiments in fine language." Or as the "beautiful statement of some high truth." Whatever the precise manner of description may be, the basic idea may be stated as follows: poetry is a "truth" with "decorations," which may either be pleasant in themselves or dispose the reader to accept the truth.

Most often victims of this general misconception have treated poetry as a kind of "sugar-coated pill." They have justified the characteristics of poetry—rhythmical language, figures of speech, stories and dramatic situations, etc.—as a kind of bait that leads the reader to expose himself to the influence of the "truth" contained in a poem. They value these characteristics only in so far as the characteristics lead to the acceptance of the "truth." The final value of a poem for such people would depend on the value of the "truth" contained—which leads us back to the mistake of the "message hunters," which we examined with reference to Longfellow's poem.

But even if the person who regards poetry as "fine sentiments in fine language" says that he values the language as much as he values the sentiments, or "truth," he is still using a mistaken approach to poetry. For he is apparently committed to saying that the language, quite apart from its relation to some central idea or "truth," is valuable. He seems to be saying that certain words, or certain objects suggested by the words, are in themselves "poetic." He would be forced to consider a poem as simply a bundle of melodious word-combinations and pretty pictures. He would probably be embarrassed if we asked him what held these things together in any given poem, making it *a* poem rather than simply a collection of pleasing items. And he would probably be further embarrassed if we asked him to show us by what standard he would call a particular combination of sounds or a particular set of pictures poetically fine. If he should say that he took as a standard for poetical fitness the fact that any item—let us say, for instance, a rose—was pleasing in real life, he would be making a dangerous confusion. It is certainly true that in real life various combinations of word sounds and various objects and scenes, such as the rose, the moon, the ruins of a mediaeval tower, a maiden standing on a balcony, etc., are pleasing. But poetry does not consist merely in the use of objects of this sort or in the use of agreeable word combinations. Nor does the mere presence of these things make poetry. But the falsity of this conception can quickly be demonstrated by turning to great poetry from Shakespeare or Milton where we find material that in real life would be disagreeable or mean used for poetic effect. The image of a man grunting and sweating under a burden too heavy for him is not a poetic thing if judged by the above standard, but we will find it used in a passage of great poetry that is universally admired. In Hamlet's most famous speech we find these lines:

> For who would bear the whips and scorns of time,
> The oppressor's wrong, the proud man's contumely,
> The pangs of despised love, the law's delay,
> The insolence of office, and the spurns
> That patient merit of the unworthy takes,
> When he himself might his quietus make
> With a bare bodkin? who would fardels bear,
> To grunt and sweat under a weary life,
> But that the dread of something after death,
> The undiscovered country from whose bourn
> No traveller returns, puzzles the will. . . .

In fact, none of the things used in this passage would be thought of as being pleasing in itself in actual life. The passage does not give us a set of agreeable pictures that would be considered "poetic." Indeed, the more we examine good poetry the more difficult will appear the attempt to say that certain objects or situations or even ideas are in themselves poetic. *The poetic effect depends not on the things themselves but on the kind of use the poet makes of them.*

Organic Nature of Poetry

We have seen, then, that a poem is not to be thought of as merely a bundle of things which are "poetic" in themselves. Nor is it to be thought of, as the "message hunters" would seem to have it, as a kind of box, decorated or not, in which a "truth" or a "fine sentiment" is hidden. We avoid such difficulties *by thinking of a poem as a piece of writing which gives us a certain effect in which, we discover, the "poetry" inheres.*

This is very different from considering a poem as a group of mechanically combined elements—meter, rime, figurative language, idea, etc.—which are put together to make a poem as bricks are put together to make a wall. The question, then, about any element in a poem is not whether it is in itself pleasing, or agreeable, or valuable, or "poetical," but whether it works with the other elements to create the effect intended by the poet. The relationship among the elements in a poem is therefore all important, and it is not a mechanical relationship but one which is far more intimate and fundamental. If we should compare a poem to the make-up of some physical object it ought not to be a wall but to something organic like a plant.

We may investigate this general principle by looking at some particular examples. The following lines could scarcely be called melodious. Indeed, they may be thought to have a sibilant, hissing quality rather than that of melody.

> If it were done when 'tis done, then 'twere well
> It were done quickly: if the assassination
> Could trammel up the consequence, and catch,
> With his surcease, success, that but this blow
> Might be the be-all and the end-all here,
> But here, upon this bank and shoal of time,
> We'd jump the life to come.

This is the speech of Macbeth at the moment when he is debating the murder of Duncan; the passage has been considered to be great poetry by innumerable critics and readers. We are not to consider that the passage is great poetry *in spite* of its lack of ordinary melodious effects; but rather we are to see that the broken rhythms and tendency to harshness of sound are essential to the communication that Shakespeare wished. For instance, the piling up of the *s* sounds in the second, third, and fourth lines helps give an impression of desperate haste and breathless excitement. The lines give the impression of a conspiratorial whisper. The rhythm and sound effects of the passage, then, are poetic in the only sense which we have seen to be legitimate: they are poetic because of a relation to the total effect of the passage.

Or we may approach the general problem in another way. Here are two lines by Robert Burns which have been greatly admired by the poet William Butler Yeats:

> The white moon is setting behind the white wave,
> And Time is setting with me, O!

Let us suppose that the lines had been written as follows:

> The white moon is setting behind the white wave,
> And Time, O! is setting with me.

Literally considered, the two versions say exactly the same thing: they describe a scene and give an exclamation provoked by it. If one will, however, read the two versions carefully with an ear for the rhythm he will discover that the transposition of the word *O* has made a great difference in the movement.

But this difference is not finally important *merely* because the first version may be in itself more melodious than the second. The movement of the first version is superior primarily because it contributes to the total effect, or to what we might call the total interpretation, of the scene. The placing of the cry at the emphatic position of a line-end implies that the speaker had scarcely realized the full force of his own statement until he had made it. The lingering rhythm caused by the position of the exclamation at the end of the second line coincides with the fact that the poet sees in the natural scene a representation of the pathos of the passing of Time and of his own life. By placing the exclamation anywhere else we impair this relationship between the rhythm and the other elements involved—the image of the moonset and the poet's statement about the passing of Time. Yeats has summarized the general effect of the passage and the relationship of the parts as follows:

> Take from them [the lines] the whiteness of the moon and of the waves, whose relation to the setting of Time is too subtle for the intellect, and you take from them their beauty. But, when all are together, moon and wave and whiteness and setting Time and the last melancholy cry, they evoke an emotion which cannot be evoked by any other arrangement of colors and sounds and forms.[2]

The remarks by Yeats here apply, as we can see, to the elements of the scene itself as well as to the rhythm. He is not praising the lines merely because the scene of the white moon setting behind the white wave gives in itself a pretty picture. As a matter fact, a white moon may not appear as beautiful as a golden moon, but if we rewrite the lines with a golden moon we have lost something from them:

> The gold moon is setting behind the gold wave,
> And Time is setting for me, O!

The "something" that has been lost obviously depends on the relationship of the color to the other elements in the general effect. The whiteness of the moon and the wave in connection with the idea of "setting" and then more specifically in connection with the idea of the irrevocable passage of Time, suggests, even though unconsciously to most readers, a connection with the paleness of something waning or dying. The connection is not a logical connection, as Yeats intimates when he says the "relation . . . is too subtle for the intellect," but it is nonetheless a powerful one. All of this merely means that Yeats is saying that the beauty—by which he means the total poetic effect—of the lines depends on the relationship of the parts to each other.

This last point may be amply proved, as we have already hinted in discussing the passage from *Hamlet*, by considering a passage of great poetry in which the pictures used, unlike that in the lines from Burns, would be considered in ordinary life as positively ugly or at least neutral.

> Time hath, my lord, a wallet at his back,
> Wherein he puts alms for oblivion,
> A great-sized monster of ingratitudes:
> Those scraps are good deeds past; which are devoured
> As fast as they are made, forgot as soon
> As done: perseverance, dear my lord,
> Keeps honor bright: to have done, is to hang
> Quite out of fashion, like a rusty mail
> In monumental mockery. . . .
>
> (From *Troilus and Cressida*)

This is a speech which Shakespeare puts into the mouth of a character, Ulysses, who is trying to persuade Achilles to take part again in the war against the Trojans and not to rest on the reputation for valor he has already made. The pictures given here are definitely unattractive: a beggar putting alms in his sack, a monster, scraps of food, a rusty suit of armor. The poetic effect of the passage, then, cannot depend on the intrinsic prettiness of any of the objects mentioned. If we speak of the beauty of the passage, as Yeats speaks of the beauty of the lines from Burns, we must mean the relation of the objects to each other and to the idea of the passage.

Let us try to see what these relationships are. Ulysses is saying that a reputation for good deeds is quickly forgotten. Good deeds are like alms given to an ungrateful beggar, or are like scraps of food which the beggar forgets as soon as he has satisfied his appetite. The picture is poetically good because it accurately indicates the *attitude* which Ulysses wishes Achilles to take toward his past achievements. If Ulysses had merely given Achilles the general statement that the public forgets good deeds, he could not have stirred the feelings which Achilles, the hero and aristocrat, must have felt toward beggars and broken scraps of food. He plays on this contempt and disgust. The images of the first five lines, as we have seen, are closely bound together to define a certain attitude. Then, after a general statement that perseverance is necessary to keep honor bright, the image of the coat of mail is introduced: a man who bases his claim to honor merely on a deed done in the past like a suit of mail that, although it is hung up as a trophy of some great event, simply rusts. It is important to see that this is not a mere representation of the general point made about perseverance, but that it also develops and adds to the idea, for it carries with it a special urgency to immediate action. There is not only the application, as it were, of the general idea in a concrete image that can be seen as a picture, but also an application appropriate to the special situation, the need for Achilles to put on his armor and return to the battle.

The use of images in this passage, then, represents not only a close-knit organization because of the relation of the images to each other and to the intention of the passage, but also a psychological development, for the images lead from one attitude and state of mind to another. One can show the closeness of the organization of the passage even in the use of a single word. For example, take the word *monumental* in the last line. A great deal of the "meaning" of the passage is concentrated in this one word. The word *monumental* literally means, of course, the quality of something that stands as a monument. The coat of rusty mail which Ulysses uses in his comparison is one hung up as a trophy or monument to past achievement. But the word *monumental* is also used to indicate something tremendous in size. The word, then, as it appears in the present context suggests two applications to the reader: the mail is hung up as a monument and the mockery is monumental, or tremendous, in size. The fact that the word suggests to the reader these two applications gives a somewhat ironical, or sarcastic, effect to the passage—which is exactly what is intended by the speaker.

The purpose in giving the passages and comments above is to illustrate the principle that in judging the various elements of a poem or of a passage of poetry—rhythm, image, diction, etc.—one must consider not the elements taken in isolation but in relation to the total organization and intention. That is, the elements must play an organic part in the poem.

Dramatic Aspect of Poetry

It may be objected that most of the examples given above are drawn from plays and do not represent poetry as we more ordinarily find it. But the principle illustrated by these examples applies to all other poetry. It applies because all poetry, including even short lyrics or descriptive pieces, involves a dramatic organization. This is clear when we reflect that every poem implies a speaker of the poem, either the poet writing in his own person or someone into whose mouth the poem is put, and that the poem represents the reaction of such a person to a situation, a scene, or an idea. In reading poetry it is well to remember this dramatic aspect and to be sure that one sees the part it plays in any given poem.

What Good Is Poetry?

But even if one understands the principles by which poetry is to be read, one may still ask, "What good is poetry?" The value of science we all know. But we have attempted in the preceding pages to show how different the organization of poetry is from that of science, and how different are their objectives. It is only fair to admit that what makes science valuable cannot be held to make poetry valuable also. Science gives us a certain kind of description of the world—a description which is within its own terms verifiable—and gives us a basis for more effective practical achievement. Science is, as Bertrand Russell has called it, "power-knowledge."

> But scientific thought is . . . essentially power-thought—the sort of thought, that is to say, whose purpose, conscious or unconscious, is to give power to its possessor. Now power is a causal concept, and to obtain power over any given material one need only understand the causal laws to which it is subject. This is an essentially abstract matter, and the more irrelevant details we can omit from our purview, the more powerful our thoughts will become. The same sort of thing can be illustrated in the economic sphere. The cultivator, who knows every corner of his farm, has a concrete knowledge of wheat, and makes very little money; the railway which carries his wheat views it in a slightly more abstract way, and makes rather more money; the stock exchange manipulator, who knows it only in its purely abstract aspect of something which may go up or down, is, in his way, as remote from concrete reality as the physicist, and he, of all those concerned in the economic sphere, makes the most money and has the most power. So it is with science, though the power which the man of science seeks is more remote and impersonal than that which is sought on the stock exchange.[3]

But we have seen, and can see in real life every day, how much of our experience eludes the statements science can make; and how merely practical statements or statements that approximate a scientific form satisfy only a part of our interests. One does not have to look farther than the fact that this wide domain of human interests exists to find a justification for poetry. Most people are thoroughly satisfied to admit the value of any activity which satisfies a basic and healthy human interest. It may be well, however, to take a few moments to remind the reader that this interest exists, and to make plain that it is this interest which poetry seeks to satisfy.

We have already seen how often talk that is apparently practical really attempts to satisfy a non-practical interest. It is easy to point out many other aspects of our experience that testify to the fact that people—even people who think that they care nothing for poetry—really have interests which are the same as those satisfied by poetry. Very few people indeed depend for the satisfaction of these interests merely on their routine activities. Instead, they listen to speeches, go to church, listen to radio programs, read magazine stories or the gossip columns of newspapers. Such people do not see any relation between these activities and poetry, but poetry does concern the same impulses and the same interests. Why and how good poetry, and good literature in general, give a fuller satisfaction to these impulses and interests is a matter which can best be stated in connection with concrete examples before us, and the attempt in this book to state this matter will be gradually developed by the study of examples. But the fundamental point, namely, that poetry has a basis in common human interests, must not be forgotten at the beginning of any attempt to study poetry.

The question of the value of poetry, then, is to be answered by saying that it springs from a basic human impulse and fulfills a basic human interest. To answer the question finally, and not immediately, one would have to answer the question as to the value of those common impulses and interests. But that is a question which lies outside of the present concern. As we enter into a study of poetry it is only necessary to see that poetry is not an isolated and eccentric thing, but springs from the most fundamental interests which human beings have.

NOTES

1. "Science and Modern Life," *The Atlantic Monthly*, April, 1928.
2. "The Symbolism of Poetry," *Essays*, New York: Macmillan, p. 191.
3. *The Scientific Outlook*, by Bertrand Russell, London: Allen and Unwin, p. 86.

3.3 The Three Voices of Poetry[1] (1953)

T. S. ELIOT

The first voice is the voice of the poet talking to himself—or to nobody. The second is the voice of the poet addressing an audience, whether large or small. The third is the voice of the poet when he attempts to create a dramatic character speaking in verse; when he is saying, not what he would say in his own person, but only what he can say within the limits of one imaginary character addressing another imaginary character. The distinction between the first and the second voice, between the poet speaking to himself and the poet speaking to other people, points to the problem of poetic communication; the distinction between the poet addressing other people in either his own voice or an assumed voice, and the poet inventing speech in which imaginary characters address each other, points to the problem of the difference between dramatic, quasi-dramatic, and non-dramatic verse.

I wish to anticipate a question that some of you may well raise. Cannot a poem be written for the ear, or for the eye, of one person alone? You may say simply, "Isn't love poetry at times a form of communication between one person and one other, with no thought of a further audience?"

There are at least two people who might have disagreed with me on this point: Mr. and Mrs. Robert Browning. In the poem "One Word More," written as an epilogue to *Men and Women*, and addressed to Mrs. Browning, the husband makes a striking value judgment:

Rafael made a century of sonnets,
Made and wrote them in a certain volume,

Dinted with the silver-pointed pencil
Else he only used to draw Madonnas:
These, the world might view—but one, the volume.
Who that one, you ask? Your heart instructs you . . .
You and I would rather read that volume . . .
Would we not? than wonder at Madonnas . . .

Dante once prepared to paint an angel:
Whom to please? You whisper 'Beatrice' . . .
You and I would rather see that angel,
Painted by the tenderness of Dante,
Would we not?—than read a fresh Inferno.

I agree that one *Inferno*, even by Dante, is enough; and perhaps we need not too much regret the fact that Rafael did not multiply his Madonnas: but I can only say that I feel no curiosity whatever about Rafael's sonnets or Dante's angel. If Rafael wrote, or Dante painted, for the eyes of one person alone, let their privacy be respected. We know that Mr. and Mrs. Browning liked to write poems to each other, because they published them, and some of them are good poems. We know that Rossetti thought that he was writing his "House of Life" sonnets for one person, and that he was only persuaded by his friends to disinter them. Now, I do not deny that a poem may be addressed to one person: there is a well-known form, not always amatory in content, called The Epistle. We shall never have conclusive evidence: for the testimony of poets as to what they thought they were doing when they wrote a poem, cannot be taken altogether at its face value. But my opinion is, that a good love poem, though it may be addressed to one person, is always meant to be overheard by other people. Surely, the proper language of love—that is, of communication to the beloved and to no one else—is prose.

Having dismissed as an illusion the voice of the poet talking to one person only, I think that the best way for me to try to make my three voices audible, is to trace the genesis of the distinction in my own mind. The writer to whose mind the distinction is most likely to occur is probably the writer like myself, who has spent a good many years in writing poetry, before attempting to write for the stage at all. It may be, as I have read, that there is a dramatic element in much of my early work. It may be that from the beginning I aspired unconsciously to the theatre—or, unfriendly critics might say, to Shaftesbury Avenue and Broadway. I have, however, gradually come to the conclusion that in writing verse for the stage both the process and the outcome are very different from what they are in writing verse to be read or recited. Twenty years ago I was commissioned to write a pageant play to be called *The Rock*. The invitation to write the words for this spectacle—the occasion of which was an appeal for funds for church-building in new housing areas—came at a moment when I seemed to myself to have exhausted my meager poetic gifts, and to have nothing more to say. To be, at such a moment, commissioned to write something which, good or bad, must be delivered by a certain date, may have the effect that vigorous cranking sometimes has upon a motor car when the battery is run down. The task was clearly laid out: I had only to write the words of prose dialogue for scenes of the usual historical pageant pattern, for which I had been given a scenario. I had also to provide a number of choral passages in verse, the content of which was left to my own devices: except for the reasonable stipulation that all the choruses were expected to have some relevance to the purpose of the pageant, and that each chorus was to occupy a precise number of minutes of stage time. But in carrying out this second part of my task, there was nothing to call my attention to the third, or dramatic voice: it was the second voice, that of myself addressing—indeed haranguing—an audience, that was most distinctly audible. Apart from the obvious fact that writing to order is not the same thing as writing to please oneself, I learnt only that verse to be spoken by a choir should be different from verse to be spoken by one person; and that the more voices you have in your choir, the simpler and more direct the vocabulary, the syntax, and the content of your lines must be. This chorus of *The Rock* was not a dramatic voice; though many lines were distributed, the personages were unindividuated. Its members were speaking *for me*, not uttering words that really represented any supposed character of their own.

The chorus in *Murder in the Cathedral* does, I think, represent some advance in dramatic development: that is to say, I set myself the task of writing lines, not for an anonymous chorus, but for a chorus of women of Canterbury—one might almost say, charwomen of Canterbury. I had to make some effort to identify myself with these women, instead of merely identifying them with myself. But as for the dialogue of the play, the plot had the drawback (from the point of view of my own dramatic education) of presenting only one dominant character; and what dramatic conflict there is takes place within the mind of that character. The third, or dramatic voice, did not make itself audible to me until I first attacked the problem of presenting two (or more) characters, in some sort of conflict, misunderstanding, or attempt to understand each other, characters with each of whom I had to try to identify myself while writing the words for him or her to speak. You may remember that Mrs. Cluppins, in the trial of the case of Bardell *v.* Pickwick, testified that "the voices was very loud, sir, and forced themselves upon my ear." "Well, Mrs. Cluppins," said Sergeant Buzfuz, "you were not listening, but you heard the voices." It was in 1938, then, that the third voice began to force itself upon my ear.

At this point I can fancy the reader murmuring: "I'm sure he has said all this before." I will assist memory by supplying the reference. In a lecture on "Poetry and Drama," delivered exactly three years ago and subsequently published, I said:

> In writing other verse (i.e. non-dramatic verse) I think that one is writing, so to speak, in terms of one's own voice: the way it sounds when you read it to yourself is the test. For it is yourself speaking. The question of communication, of what the reader will get from it, is not paramount. . . .

There is some confusion of pronouns in this passage, but I think that the meaning is clear; so clear, as to be a glimpse of the obvious. At that stage, I rioted only the difference between speaking for oneself, and speaking for an imaginary character; and I passed on to other considerations about the nature of poetic drama. I was beginning to be aware of the difference between the first and the third voice, but gave no attention to the second voice, of which I shall say more presently. I am now trying to penetrate a little further into the problem. So, before going on to consider the other voices, I want to pursue for a few moments the complexities of the third voice.

In a verse play, you will probably have to find words for several characters differing widely from each other in background, temperament, education, and intelligence. You cannot afford to identify one of these characters with yourself, and give him (or her) all the "poetry" to speak. The poetry (I mean, the language at those dramatic moments when it reaches intensity) must be as widely distributed as characterization permits; and each of your characters, when he has words to speak which are poetry and not merely verse, must be given lines appropriate to himself. When the poetry comes, the personage on the stage must not give the impression of being merely a mouthpiece for the author. Hence the author is limited by the kind of poetry, and the degree of intensity in its kind, which can be plausibly attributed to each character in his play. And these lines of poetry must also justify themselves by their development of the situation in which they are spoken. Even if a burst of magnificent poetry is suitable enough for the character to which it is assigned, it must also convince us that it is necessary to the action; that it is helping to extract the utmost emotional intensity out of the situation. The poet writing for the theatre may, as I have found, make two mistakes: that of assigning to a personage lines of poetry not suitable to be spoken by that personage, and that of assigning lines which, however suitable to the personage, yet fail to forward the action of the play. There are, in some of the minor Elizabethan dramatists, passages of magnificent poetry which are in both respects out of place—fine enough to preserve the play for ever as literature, but yet so inappropriate as to prevent the play from being a dramatic masterpiece. The best-known instances occur in Marlowe's *Tamburlaine*.

How have the very great dramatic poets—Sophocles, or Shakespeare, or Racine—dealt with this difficulty? This is, of course, a problem which concerns all imaginative fiction—novels and prose plays—in which the characters may be said to live. I can't see, myself, any way to make a character live except to have a profound sympathy with that character. Ideally, a dramatist, who has usually far fewer characters to manipulate than a novelist, and who has only two hours or so of life to allow them, should sympathize profoundly with all of his characters: but that is a counsel of perfection, because the plot of a play with even a very small cast may require the presence of one or more characters in whose reality, apart from their contribution to the action, we are uninterested. I wonder, however, whether it is possible to make completely real a wholly villainous character one toward whom neither the author nor anyone else can feel anything but antipathy. We need an admixture of *weakness* with either heroic virtue or satanic villainy, to make character plausible. Iago frightens me more than Richard III; I am not sure that Parolles, in *All's Well That Ends Well*, does not disturb me more than Iago. (And I am quite sure that Rosamund Vincy, in *Middlemarch*, frightens me far more than Goneril or Regan.) It seems to me that what happens, when an author creates a vital character, is a sort of give-and-take. The author may put into that character, besides its other attributes, some trait of his own, some strength or weakness, some tendency to violence or to indecision, some eccentricity even, that he has found in himself. Something perhaps never realized in his own life, something of which those who know him best may be unaware, something not restricted in transmission to characters of the same temperament, the same age, and, least of all, of the same sex. Some bit of himself that the author gives to a character may be the germ from which the life of that character starts. On the other hand, a character which succeeds in interesting its author may elicit from the author latent potentialities of his own being. I believe that the author imparts something of himself to his characters, but I also believe that he is influenced by the characters he creates. It would be only too easy to lose oneself in a maze of speculation about the process by which an imaginary character can become as real for us as people we have known. I have penetrated into this maze so far only to indicate the difficulties, the limitations, the fascination, for a poet who is used to writing poetry in his own person, of the problem of making imaginary personages talk poetry. And the difference, the abyss, between writing for the first and for the third voice.

The peculiarity of my third voice, the voice of poetic drama, is brought out in another way by comparing it with the voice of the poet in non-dramatic poetry which has a dramatic element in it—and conspicuously in the dramatic monologue. Browning, in an uncritical moment, addressed himself as "Robert Browning, you writer of plays." How many of us have read a play by Browning more than once; and, if we have read it more than once, was our motive the expectation of enjoyment? What personage, in a play by Browning, remains living in our mind? On the other hand, who can forget Fra Lippo Lippi, or Andrea del Sarto, or Bishop Blougram, or the other bishop who ordered his tomb? It would seem without further examination, from Browning's mastery of the dramatic monologue, and his very moderate achievement in the drama, that the two forms must be essentially different. Is there, perhaps, another voice which I have failed to hear, the voice of the dramatic poet whose dramatic gifts are best exercised outside of the theatre? And certainly, if any poetry, not of the stage, deserves to be characterized as "dramatic," it is Browning's.

In a play, as I have said, an author must have divided loyalties; he must sympathize with characters who may be in no way sympathetic to each other. And he must allocate the 'poetry' as widely as the limitations of each imaginary character permit. This necessity to divide the poetry implies some variation of the style of the poetry according to the character to whom it is given. The fact that a number of characters in a play have claims upon the author, for their allotment of poetic speech, compels him to try to extract the poetry from the character, rather than impose his poetry upon it. Now, in the dramatic monologue we have no such check. The author is just as likely to identify the character with himself, as himself with the character: for the check is missing that will prevent him from doing so—and that check is the necessity for identifying himself with some other character replying to the first. What we normally hear, in fact, in the dramatic monologue, is the voice of the poet, who has put on the costume and make-up either of some historical character, or of one out of fiction. His personage must be identified to us—as an individual, or at least as a type—before he begins to speak. If, as frequently with Browning, the poet is speaking in the role of an historical personage, like Lippo Lippi, or in the role of a known character of fiction, like Caliban, he has taken possession of that character. And the difference is most evident in his "Caliban upon Setebos". In *The Tempest*, it is Caliban who speaks; in "Caliban upon Setebos," it is Browning's voice that we hear, Browning talking aloud through Caliban. It was Browning's greatest disciple, Mr. Ezra Pound, who adopted the term "persona" to indicate the several historical characters through whom he spoke: and the term is just.

I risk the generalization also, which may indeed be far too sweeping, that dramatic monologue cannot create a character. For character is created and made real only in an action, a communication between imaginary people. It is not irrelevant that when the dramatic monologue is not put into the mouth of some character already known to the reader—from history or from fiction—we are likely to ask the question "Who was the original?" About Bishop Blougram people have always been impelled to ask, how far was this intended to be a portrait of Cardinal Manning, or of some other ecclesiastic? The poet, speaking, as Browning does, in his own voice, cannot bring a character to life: he can only mimic a character otherwise known to us. And does not the point of mimicry lie in the recognition of the person mimicked, and in the incompleteness of the illusion? We have to be aware that the mimic and the person mimicked are different people: if we are actually deceived, mimicry becomes impersonation. When we listen to a play by Shakespeare, we listen not to Shakespeare but to his characters; when we read a dramatic monologue by Browning, we cannot suppose that we are listening to any other voice than that of Browning himself.

In the dramatic monologue, then, it is surely the second voice, the voice of the poet talking to other people, that is dominant. The mere fact that he is assuming a role, that he is speaking through a mask, implies the presence of an audience: why should a man put on fancy dress and a mask only to talk to himself? The second voice is, in fact, the voice most often and most clearly heard in poetry that is not of the theatre: in all poetry, certainly, that has a conscious social purpose—poetry intended to amuse or to instruct, poetry that tells a story, poetry that preaches or points a moral, or satire which is a form of preaching. For what is the point of a story without an audience, or of a sermon without a congregation? The voice of the poet addressing other people is the dominant voice of epic, though not the only voice. In Homer, for instance, there is heard also, from time to time, the dramatic voice: there are moments when we hear, not Homer telling us what a hero said, but the voice of the hero himself. *The Divine Comedy* is not in the exact sense an epic, but here also we hear men and women speaking to us. And we have no reason to suppose that Milton's sympathy with Satan was so exclusive as to seal him of the Devil's Party. But the epic is essentially a tale told to an audience, while drama is essentially an action exhibited to an audience.

Now, what about the poetry of the first voice—that which is not primarily an attempt to communicate with anyone at all?

I must make the point that this poetry is not necessarily what we call loosely "lyric poetry." The term "lyric" itself is unsatisfactory. We think first of verse intended to be sung—from the songs of Campion and Shakespeare and Burns, to the arias of W. S. Gilbert, or the words of the latest "musical number." But we apply it also to poetry that was never intended for a musical setting, or which we dissociate from its music: we speak of the "lyric verse" of the metaphysical poets, of Vaughan and Marvell as well as Donne and Herbert. The very definition of "lyric", in the Oxford Dictionary, indicates that the word cannot be satisfactorily defined:

> *Lyric*: Now the name for short poems, usually divided into stanzas or strophes, and directly expressing the poet's own thoughts and sentiments.

How short does a poem have to be, to be called a "lyric"? The emphasis on brevity, and the suggestion of division into stanzas, seem residual from the association of the voice with music. But there is no necessary relation between brevity and the expression of the poet's own thoughts and feelings. "Come unto these yellow sands" or "Hark! hark! the lark" are lyrics—are they not?—but what sense is there in saying that they express directly the poet's own thoughts and sentiments? *London*, *The Vanity of Human Wishes*, and *The Deserted Village* are all poems which appear to express the poet's own thoughts and sentiments, but do we ever think of such poems as "lyrical"? They are certainly not short. Between them, all the poems I have mentioned seem to fail to qualify as lyrics, just as Mr. Daddy Longlegs and Mr. Floppy Fly failed to qualify as courtiers:

> *One never more can go to court,*
> *Because his legs have grown too short;*
> *The other cannot sing a song,*
> *Because his legs have grown too long!*

It is obviously the lyric in the sense of a poem "directly expressing the poet's own thoughts and sentiments," not in the quite unrelated sense of a short poem intended to be set to music, that is relevant to my first voice—the voice of the poet talking to himself—or to nobody. It is in this sense that the German poet Gottfried Benn, in a very interesting lecture entitled *Probleme der Lyrik*, thinks of lyric as the poetry of the first voice: he includes, I feel sure, such poems as Rilke's Duinese Elegies and Valéry's *La Jeune Parque*. Where he speaks of "lyric poetry," then, I should prefer to say "meditative verse."

What, asks Herr Benn in this lecture, does the writer of such a poem, "addressed to no one," start with? There is first, he says, an inert embryo or "creative germ" (*ein dumpfer schöpferischer Keim*) and, on the other hand, the Language, the resources of the words at the poet's command. He has something germinating in him for which he must find words; but he cannot know what words he wants until he has found the words; he cannot identify this embryo until it has been transformed into an arrangement of the right words in the right order. When you have the words for it, the "thing" for which the words had to be found has disappeared, replaced by a poem. What you start from is nothing so definite as an emotion, in any ordinary sense; it is still more certainly not an idea; it is—to adapt two lines of Beddoes to a different meaning—a

> *bodiless childful of life in the gloom*
> *Crying with frog voice, 'what shall I be?'*

I agree with Gottfried Benn, and I would go a little further. In a poem which is neither didactic nor narrative, and not animated by any other social purpose, the poet may be concerned solely with expressing in verse—using all his resources of words, with their history, their connotations, their music—this obscure impulse. He does not know what he has to say until he has said it; and in the effort to say it he is not concerned with making other people understand anything. He is not concerned, at this stage, with other people at all: only with finding the right words or, anyhow, the least wrong words. He is not concerned whether anybody else will ever listen to them or not, or whether anybody else will ever understand them if he does. He is oppressed by a burden which he must bring to birth in order to obtain relief. Or, to change the figure of speech, he is haunted by a demon, a demon against which he feels powerless, because in its first manifestation it has no face, no name, nothing; and the words, the poem he makes, are a kind of form of exorcism of this demon. In other words again, he is going to all that trouble, not in order to communicate with anyone, but to gain relief from acute discomfort; and when the words are finally arranged in the right way—or in what he comes to accept as the best arrangement he can find—he may experience a moment of exhaustion, of appeasement, of absolution, and of something very near annihilation, which is in itself indescribable. And then he can say to the poem: "Go away! Find a place for your self in a book—and don't expect *me* to take any further interest in you."

I don't believe that the relation of a poem to its origins is capable of being more clearly traced. You can read the essays of Paul Valéry, who studied the workings of his own mind in the composition of a poem more perseveringly than any other poet has done. But if, either on the basis of what poets try to tell you, or by biographical research, with or without the tools of the psychologist, you attempt to explain a poem, you will probably be getting further and further away from the poem without arriving at any other destination. The attempt to explain the poem by tracing it back to its origins will distract attention from the poem, to direct it on to something else which, in the form in which it can be apprehended by the critic and his readers, has no relation to the poem and throws no light upon it. I should not like you to think that I am trying to make the writing of a poem more of a mystery than it is. What I am maintaining is, that the first effort of the poet should be to achieve clarity for himself, to assure himself that the poem is the right outcome of the process that has taken place. The most bungling form of obscurity is that of the poet who has not been able to express himself *to* himself; the shoddiest form is found when the poet is trying to persuade himself that he has something to say when he hasn't.

So far I have been speaking, for the sake of simplicity, of the three voices as if they were mutually exclusive: as if the poet, in any particular poem, was speaking *either* to himself or to others, and as if neither of the first two voices was audible in good dramatic verse. And this indeed is the conclusion to which Herr Benn's argument appears to lead him: he speaks as if the poetry of the first voice—which he considers, moreover, to be on the whole a development of our own age—was a totally different kind of poetry from that of the poet addressing an audience. But for me the voices are most often found together—the first and second, I mean, in non-dramatic poetry; and together with the third in dramatic poetry too. Even though, as I have maintained, the author of a poem may have written it primarily without thought of an audience, he will also want to know what the poem which has satisfied *him* will have to say to other people. There are, first of all, those few friends to whose criticism he may wish to submit it before considering it completed. They can be very helpful, in suggesting a word or a phrase which the author has not been able to find for himself; though their greatest service perhaps is to say simply "this passage won't do"—thus confirming a suspicion which the author had been suppressing from his own consciousness. But I am not thinking primarily of the few judicious friends whose opinion the author prizes, but of the larger and unknown audience—people to whom the author's name means only his poem which they have read. The final handing over, so to speak, of the poem to an unknown audience, for what that audience will make of it, seems to me the consummation of the process begun in solitude and without thought of the audience, the long process of gestation of the poem, because it marks the final separation of the poem from the author. Let the author, at this point, rest in peace.

So much for the poem which is primarily a poem of the first voice. I think that in every poem, from the private meditation to the epic or the drama, there is more than one voice to be heard. If the author never spoke to himself, the result would not be poetry, though it might be magnificent rhetoric; and part of our enjoyment of great poetry is the enjoyment of *overhearing* words which are not addressed to us. But if the poem were exclusively for the author, it would be a poem in a private and unknown language; and a poem which was a poem only for the author would not be a poem at all. And in poetic drama, I am inclined to believe that all three voices are audible. First, the voice of each character—an individual voice different from that of any other character: so that of each utterance we can say, that it could only have come from that character. There may be from time to time, and perhaps when we least notice it, the voices of the author and the character in unison, saying something appropriate to the character, but something which the author could say for himself also, though the words may not have quite the same meaning for both. That may be a very different thing from the ventriloquism which makes the character only a mouthpiece for the author's ideas or sentiments.

To-morrow and to-morrow and to-morrow . . .

Is not the perpetual shock and surprise of these hackneyed lines evidence that Shakespeare and Macbeth are uttering the words in unison, though perhaps with somewhat different meaning? And finally there are the lines, in plays by one of the supreme poetic dramatists, in which we hear a more impersonal voice still than that of either the character or the author.

Ripeness is all

or

Simply the thing I am
Shall make me live.

And now I should like to return for a moment to Gottfried Benn and his unknown, dark *psychic material*—we might say, the octopus or angel with which the poet struggles. I suggest that between the three kinds of poetry to which my three voices correspond there is a certain difference of process. In the poem in which the first voice, that of the poet talking to himself, dominates, the "psychic material" tends to create its own form—the eventual form will be to a greater or less degree the form for that one poem and for no other. It is misleading, of course, to speak of the material as creating or imposing its own form: what happens is a simultaneous development of form and material; for the form affects the material at every stage; and perhaps all the material does is to repeat "not that! not that!" in the face of each unsuccessful attempt at formal organization; and finally the material is identified with its form. But in poetry of the second and in that of the third voice, the form is already to some extent given. However much it may be transformed before the poem is finished, it can be represented from the start by an outline or scenario. If I choose to tell a story, I must have some notion of the plot of the story I propose to tell; if I undertake satire, moralizing, or invective, there is already something given which I can recognize and which exists for others as well as myself. And if I set out to write a play, I start by an act of choice: I settle upon a particular emotional situation, out of which characters and a plot will emerge, and I can make a plain prose outline of the play in advance—however much that outline may be altered before the play is finished, by the way in which the characters develop. It is likely, of course, that it is in the beginning the pressure of some rude unknown *psychic material* that directs the poet to tell that particular story, to develop that particular situation. And on the other hand, the frame, once chosen, within which the author has elected to work, may itself evoke other psychic material; and then, lines of poetry may come into being, not from the original impulse, but from a secondary stimulation of the unconscious mind. All that matters is, that in the end the voices should be heard in harmony; and, as I have said, I doubt whether in any real poem only one voice is audible.

The reader may well, by now, have been asking himself what I have been up to in all these speculations. Have I been toiling to weave a labored web of useless ingenuity? Well, I have been trying to talk, not to myself—as you may have been tempted to think—but to the reader of poetry. I should like to think that it might interest the reader of poetry to test my assertions in his own reading. Can you distinguish these voices in the poetry you read, or hear recited, or hear in the theatre? If you complain that a poet is obscure, and apparently ignoring you, the reader, or that he is speaking only to a limited circle of initiates from which you are excluded—remember that what he may have been trying to do, was to put something into words which could not be said in any other way, and therefore in a language which may be worth the trouble of learning. If you complain that a poet is too rhetorical, and that he addresses you as if you were a public meeting, try to listen for the moments when he is not speaking to you, but merely allowing himself to be overheard: he may be a Dryden, a Pope, or a Byron. And if you have to listen to a verse play, take it first at its face value, as entertainment, for each character speaking for himself with whatever degree of reality his author has been able to endow him. Perhaps, if it is a great play, and you do not try too hard to hear them, you may discern the other voices too. For the work of a great poetic dramatist, like Shakespeare, constitutes a world. Each character speaks for himself, but no other poet could have found those words for him to speak. If you seek for Shakespeare, you will find him only in the characters he created; for the one thing in common between the characters is that no one but Shakespeare could have created any of them. The world of a great poetic dramatist is a world in which the creator is everywhere present, and everywhere hidden.

NOTE

1. The eleventh Annual Lecture of the National Book League, delivered in 1953 and published for the N.B.L. by the Cambridge University Press.

The Intentional Fallacy (1946)

3.4

W. K. Wimsatt and Monroe Beardsley

He owns with toil he wrote the following scenes;
But, if they're naught, ne'er spare him for his pains:
Damn him the more; have no commiseration
For dullness on mature deliberation.

William Congreve, Prologue to *The Way of the World*

I

The claim of the author's "intention" upon the critic's judgment has been challenged in a number of recent discussions, notably in the debate entitled *The Personal Heresy*, between Professors Lewis and Tillyard. But it seems doubtful if this claim and most of its romantic corollaries are as yet subject to any widespread questioning. The present writers, in a short article entitled "Intention" for a *Dictionary*[1] of literary criticism, raised the issue but were unable to pursue its implications at any length. We argued that the design or intention of the author is neither available nor desirable as a standard for judging the success of a work of literary art, and it seems to us that this is a principle which goes deep into some differences in the history of critical attitudes. It is a principle which accepted or rejected points to the polar opposites of classical "imitation" and romantic expression. It entails many specific truths about inspiration, authenticity, biography, literary history and scholarship, and about some trends of contemporary poetry, especially its allusiveness. There is hardly a problem of literary criticism in which the critic's approach will not be qualified by his view of "intention."

Intention, as we shall use the term, corresponds to *what he intended* in a formula which more or less explicitly has had wide acceptance. "In order to judge the poet's performance, we must know *what he intended*." Intention is design or plan in the author's mind. Intention has obvious affinities for the author's attitude toward his work, the way he felt, what made him write.

We begin our discussion with a series of propositions summarized and abstracted to a degree where they seem to us axiomatic.

1. A poem does not come into existence by accident. The words of a poem, as Professor Stoll has remarked, come out of a head, not out of a hat. Yet to insist on the designing intellect as a cause of a poem is not to grant the design or intention as a standard by which the critic is to judge the worth of the poet's performance.
2. One must ask how a critic expects to get an answer to the question about intention. How is he to find out what the poet tried to do? If the poet succeeded in doing it, then the poem itself shows what he was trying to do. And if the poet did not succeed, then the poem is not adequate evidence, and the critic must go outside the poem—for evidence of an intention that did not become effective in the poem. "Only one caveat must be borne in mind," says an eminent intentionalist[2]

in a moment when his theory repudiates itself; "the poet's aim must be judged at the moment of the creative act, that is to say, by the art of the poem itself."

3. Judging a poem is like judging a pudding or a machine. One demands that it work. It is only because an artifact works that we infer the intention of an artificer. "A poem should not mean but be." A poem can *be* only through its *meaning*—since its medium is words—yet it *is*, simply *is*, in the sense that we have no excuse for inquiring what part is intended or meant. Poetry is a feat of style by which a complex of meaning is handled all at once. Poetry succeeds because all or most of what is said or implied is relevant; what is irrelevant has been excluded, like lumps from pudding and "bugs" from machinery. In this respect poetry differs from practical messages, which are successful if and only if we correctly infer the intention. They are more abstract than poetry.
4. The meaning of a poem may certainly be a personal one, in the sense that a poem expresses a personality or state of soul rather than a physical object like an apple. But even a short lyric poem is dramatic, the response of a speaker (no matter how abstractly conceived) to a situation (no matter how universalized). We ought to impute the thoughts and attitudes of the poem immediately to the dramatic *speaker*, and if to the author at all, only by an act of biographical inference.
5. There is a sense in which an author, by revision, may better achieve his original intention. But it is a very abstract sense. He intended to write a better work, or a better work of a certain kind, and now has done it. But it follows that his former concrete intention was not his intention. "He's the man we were in search of, that's true," says Hardy's rustic constable, "and yet he's not the man we were in search of. For the man we were in search of was not the man we wanted."

"Is not a critic," asks Professor Stoll, "a judge, who does not explore his own consciousness, but determines the author's meaning or intention, as if the poem were a will, a contract, or the constitution? The poem is not the critic's own." He has accurately diagnosed two forms of irresponsibility, one of which he prefers. Our view is yet different. The poem is not the critic's own and not the author's (it is detached from the author at birth and goes about the world beyond his power to intend about it or control it). The poem belongs to the public. It is embodied in language, the peculiar possession of the public, and it is about the human being, an object of public knowledge. What is said about the poem is subject to the same scrutiny as any statement in linguistics or in the general science of psychology.

A critic of our *Dictionary* article, Ananda K. Coomaraswamy, has argued[3] that there are two kinds of inquiry about a work of art: (1) whether the artist achieved his intentions; (2) whether the work of art "ought ever to have been undertaken at all" and so "whether it is worth preserving." Number (2), Coomaraswamy maintains, is not "criticism of any work of art *qua* work of art," but is rather moral criticism; number (1) is artistic criticism. But we maintain that (2) need not be moral criticism: that there is another way of deciding whether works of art are worth preserving and whether, in a sense, they "ought" to have been undertaken, and this is the way of objective criticism of works of art as such, the way which enables us to distinguish between a skillful murder and a skillful poem. A skillful murder is an example which Coomaraswamy uses, and in his system the difference between the murder and the poem is simply a "moral" one, not an "artistic" one, since each if carried out according to plan is "artistically" successful. We maintain that (2) is an inquiry of more worth than (1), and since (2) and not (1) is capable of distinguishing poetry from murder, the name "artistic criticism" is properly given to (2).

II

It is not so much a historical statement as a definition to say that the intentional fallacy is a Romantic one. When a rhetorician of the first century A.D. writes: "Sublimity is the echo of a great soul," or when he tells us that "Homer enters into the sublime actions of his heroes" and "shares the full inspiration of the combat," we shall not be surprised to find this rhetorician considered as a distant harbinger of romanticism and greeted in the warmest terms by Saintsbury. One may wish to argue whether Longinus should be called romantic, but there can hardly be a doubt that in one important way he is.

Goethe's three questions for "constructive criticism" are "What did the author set out to do? Was his plan reasonable and sensible, and how far did he succeed in carrying it out?" If one leaves out the middle question, one has in effect the system of Croce—the culmination and crowning philosophic expression of romanticism. The beautiful is the successful intuition-expression, and the ugly is the unsuccessful; the intuition or private part of art is the aesthetic fact, and the medium or public part is not the subject of aesthetic at all.

The Madonna of Cimabue is still in the Church of Santa Maria Novella; but does she speak to the visitor of today as to the Florentines of the thirteenth century?

> *Historical interpretation* labors . . . to reintegrate in us the psychological conditions which have changed in the course of history. It . . . enables us to see a work of art (a physical object) as its *author saw it* in the moment of production.[4]

The first italics are Croce's, the second ours. The upshot of Croce's system is an ambiguous emphasis on history. With such passages as a point of departure a critic may write a nice analysis of the meaning or "spirit" of a play by Shakespeare or Corneille—a process that involves close historical study but remains aesthetic criticism—or he may, with equal plausibility, produce an essay in sociology, biography, or other kinds of nonaesthetic history.

III

> I went to the poets; tragic, dithyrambic, and all sorts. . . . I took them some of the most elaborate passages in their own writings, and asked what was the meaning of them. . . . Will you believe me? . . . there is hardly a person present who would not have talked better about their poetry than they did themselves. Then I knew that not by wisdom do poets write poetry, but by a sort of genius and inspiration.
>
> Plato, *Apology*

That reiterated mistrust of the poets which we hear from Socrates may have been part of a rigorously ascetic view in which we hardly wish to participate, yet Plato's Socrates saw a truth about the poetic mind which the world no longer commonly sees—so much criticism, and that the most inspirational and most affectionately remembered, has proceeded from the poets themselves.

Certainly the poets have had something to say that the critic and professor could not say; their message has been more exciting: that poetry should come as naturally as leaves to a tree, that poetry is the lava of the imagination, or that it is emotion recollected in tranquility. But it is necessary that we realize the character and authority of such testimony. There is only a fine shade of difference between such expressions and a kind of earnest advice that authors often give. Thus Edward Young, Carlyle, Walter Pater:

> I know two golden rules from *ethics*, which are no less golden in *Composition*, than in life. 1. *Know thyself*; 2dly, *Reverence thyself*.

> This is the grand secret for finding readers and retaining them: let him who would move and convince others, be first moved and convinced himself. Horace's rule, *Si vis me flere*, is applicable in a wider sense than the literal one. To every poet, to every writer, we might say: Be true, if you would be believed.

> Truth! there can be no merit, no craft at all, without that. And further, all beauty is in the long run only *fineness* of truth, or what we call expression, the finer accommodation of speech to that vision within.

And Housman's little handbook to the poetic mind yields this illustration:

> Having drunk a pint of beer at luncheon—beer is a sedative to the brain, and my afternoons are the least intellectual portion of my life—I would go out for a walk of two or three hours. As I went along, thinking of nothing in particular, only looking at things around me and following the progress of the seasons, there would flow into my mind, with sudden and unaccountable emotion, sometimes a line or two of verse, sometimes a whole stanza at once.

This is the logical terminus of the series already quoted. Here is a confession of how poems were written which would do as a definition of poetry just as well as "emotion recollected in tranquility"—and which the young poet might equally well take to heart as a practical rule. Drink a pint of beer, relax, go walking, think on nothing in particular, look at things, surrender yourself to yourself, search for the truth in your own soul, listen to the sound of your own inside voice, discover and express the *vraie vérité*.

It is probably true that all this is excellent advice for poets. The young imagination fired by Wordsworth and Carlyle is probably closer to the verge of producing a poem than the mind of the student who has been sobered by Aristotle or Richards. The art of inspiring poets, or at least of inciting something like poetry in young persons, has probably gone further in our day than ever before. Books of creative writing such as those issued from the Lincoln School are interesting evidence of what a child can do.[5] All this, however, would appear to belong to an art separate from criticism—to a psychological discipline, a system of self-development, a yoga, which the young poet perhaps does well to notice, but which is something different from the public art of evaluating poems.

Coleridge and Arnold were better critics than most poets have been, and if the critical tendency dried up the poetry in Arnold and perhaps in Coleridge, it is not inconsistent with our argument, which is that judgment of poems is different from the art of producing them. Coleridge has given us the classic "anodyne" story, and tells what he can about the genesis of a poem which he calls a "psychological curiosity," but his definitions of poetry and of the poetic quality "imagination" are to be found elsewhere and in quite other terms.

It would be convenient if the passwords of the intentional school, "sincerity," "fidelity," "spontaneity," "authenticity," "genuineness," "originality," could be equated with terms such as "integrity," "relevance," "unity," "function," "maturity," "subtlety," "adequacy," and other more precise terms of evaluation—in short, if "expression" always meant aesthetic achievement. But this is not so.

"Aesthetic" art, says Professor Curt Ducasse, an ingenious theorist of expression, is the conscious objectification of feelings, in which an intrinsic part is the critical moment.

The artist corrects the objectification when it is not adequate. But this may mean that the earlier attempt was not successful in objectifying the self, or "it may also mean that it was a successful objectification of a self which, when it confronted us clearly, we disowned and repudiated in favor of another."[6] What is the standard by which we disown or accept the self? Professor Ducasse does not say. Whatever it may be, however, this standard is an element in the definition of art which will not reduce to terms of objectification. The evaluation of the work of art remains public; the work is measured against something outside the author.

IV

There is criticism of poetry and there is author psychology, which when applied to the present or future takes the form of inspirational promotion; but author psychology can be historical too, and then we have literary biography, a legitimate and attractive study in itself, one approach, as Professor Tillyard would argue, to personality, the poem being only a parallel approach. Certainly it need not be with a derogatory purpose that one points out personal studies, as distinct from poetic studies, in the realm of literary scholarship. Yet there is danger of confusing personal and poetic studies; and there is the fault of writing the personal as if it were poetic.

There is a difference between internal and external evidence for the meaning of a poem. And the paradox is only verbal and superficial that what is (1) internal is also public: it is discovered through the semantics and syntax of a poem; through our habitual knowledge of the language, through grammars, dictionaries, and all the literature which is the source of dictionaries, in general through all that makes a language and culture; while what is (2) external is private or idiosyncratic; not a part of the work as a linguistic fact: it consists of revelations (in journals, for example, or letters or reported conversations) about how or why the poet wrote the poem—to what lady, while sitting on what lawn, or at the death of what friend or brother. There is (3) an intermediate kind of evidence about the character of the author or about private or semiprivate meanings attached to words or topics by an author or by a coterie of which he is a member. The meaning of words is the history of words, and the biography of an author, his use of a word, and the associations which the word had for *him*, are part of the word's history and meaning.[7] But the three types of evidence, especially (2) and (3), shade into one another so subtly that it is not always easy to draw a line between examples, and hence arises the difficulty for criticism. The use of biographical evidence need not involve intentionalism, because while it may be evidence of what the author intended, it may also be evidence of the meaning of his words and the dramatic character of his utterance. On the other hand, it may not be all this. And a critic who is concerned with evidence of type (1) and moderately with that of type (3) will in the long run produce a different sort of comment from that of the critic who is concerned with (2) and with (3) where it shades into (2).

The whole glittering parade of Professor Lowes' *Road to Xanadu*, for instance, runs along the border between types (2) and (3) or boldly traverses the romantic region of (2). "'Kubla Khan,'" says Professor Lowes, "is the fabric of a vision, but every image that rose up in its weaving had passed that way before. And it would seem that there is nothing haphazard or fortuitous in their return." This is not quite clear—not even when Professor Lowes explains that there were clusters of associations, like hooked atoms, which were drawn into complex relation with other clusters in the deep well of Coleridge's memory, and which then coalesced and issued forth as poems. If there was nothing "haphazard or fortuitous" in the way the images returned to the surface, that may mean (1) that Coleridge could not produce what he did not have, that he was limited in his creation by what he had read or otherwise experienced, or (2) that having received certain clusters of associations, he was bound to return them in just the way he did, and that the value of the poem may be described in terms of the experiences on which he had to draw. The latter pair of propositions (a sort of Hartleyan associationism which Coleridge himself repudiated in the *Biographia*) may not be assented to. There were certainly other combinations, other poems, worse or better, that might have been written by men who had read Bartram and Purchas and Bruce and Milton. And this will be true no matter how many times we are able to add to the brilliant complex of Coleridge's reading. In certain flourishes (such as the sentence we have quoted) and in chapter headings like "The Shaping Spirit," "The Magical Synthesis," "Imagination Creatrix," it may be that Professor Lowes pretends to say more about the actual poems than he does. There is a certain deceptive variation in these fancy chapter titles; one expects to pass on to a new stage in the argument, and one finds—more and more sources, more and more about "the streamy nature of association."[8]

"*Wohin der Weg*?" quotes Professor Lowes for the motto of his book. "*Kein Weg! Ins Unbetretene.*" Precisely because the way is *unbetreten*, we should say, it leads away from the poem. Bartram's *Travels* contains a good deal of the history of certain words and of certain romantic Floridian conceptions that appear in "Kubla Khan." And a good deal of that history has passed and was then passing into the very stuff of our language. Perhaps a person who has read Bartram appreciates the poem more than one who has not. Or, by looking up the vocabulary of "Kubla Khan" in the *Oxford English Dictionary*, or by reading some of the other books there quoted, a person may know the poem better. But it would seem to pertain little to the poem to know that *Coleridge* had read Bartram. There is a gross body of life, of sensory and mental experience, which lies behind and in some sense causes every poem, but can never be and need not be known in the verbal and hence intellectual composition which is the poem. For all the objects of our manifold experience, for every unity, there is an action of the mind which cuts off roots, melts away context—or indeed we should never have objects or ideas or anything to talk about.

It is probable that there is nothing in Professor Lowes' vast book which could detract from anyone's appreciation of either *The Ancient Mariner* or "Kubla Khan." We next present a case where preoccupation with evidence of type (3) has gone so far as to distort a critic's view of a poem (yet a case not so obvious as those that abound in our critical journals).

In a well-known poem by John Donne appears this quatrain:

> Moving of th' earth brings harmes and feares,
>   Men reckon what it did and meant,
> But trepidation of the spheares,
>   Though greater farre, is innocent.

A recent critic in an elaborate treatment of Donne's learning has written of this quatrain as follows:

> He touches the emotional pulse of the situation by a skillful allusion to the new and the old astronomy. . . . Of the new astronomy, the "moving of the earth" is the most radical principle; of the old, the "trepidation of the spheres" is the motion of the greatest complexity. . . .

> The poet must exhort his love to quietness and calm upon his departure; and for this purpose the figure based upon the latter motion (trepidation), long absorbed into the traditional astronomy, fittingly suggests the tension of the moment without arousing the "harmes and feares" implicit in the figure of the moving earth.[9]

The argument is plausible and rests on a well substantiated thesis that Donne was deeply interested in the new astronomy and its repercussions in the theological realm. In various works Donne shows his familiarity with Kepler's *De Stella Nova*, with Galileo's *Siderius Nuncius*, with William Gilbert's *De Magnete*, and with Clavius' commentary on the *De Sphaera* of Sacrobosco. He refers to the new science in his Sermon at Paul's Cross and in a letter to Sir Henry Goodyer. In *The First Anniversary* he says the "new philosophy calls all in doubt." In the *Elegy on Prince Henry* he says that the "least moving of the center" makes "the world to shake."

It is difficult to answer argument like this, and impossible to answer it with evidence of like nature. There is no reason why Donne might not have written a stanza in which the two kinds of celestial motion stood for two sorts of emotion at parting. And if we become full of astronomical ideas and see Donne only against the background of the new science, we may believe that he did. But the text itself remains to be dealt with, the analyzable vehicle of a complicated metaphor. And one may observe: (1) that the movement of the earth according to the Copernican theory is a celestial motion, smooth and regular, and while it might cause religious or philosophic fears, it could not be associated with the crudity and earthiness of the kind of commotion which the speaker in the poem wishes to discourage; (2) that there is another moving of the earth, an earthquake, which has just these qualities and is to be associated with the tear-floods and sigh-tempests of the second stanza of the poem; (3) that "trepidation" is an appropriate opposite of earthquake, because each is a shaking or vibratory motion; and "trepidation of the spheres" is "greater far" than an earthquake, but not much greater (if two such motions can be compared as to greatness) than the annual motion of the earth; (4) that reckoning what it "did and meant" shows that the event has passed, like an earthquake, not like the incessant celestial movement of the earth. Perhaps a knowledge of Donne's interest in the new science may add another shade of meaning, an overtone to the stanza in question, though to say even this runs against the words. To make the geocentric and heliocentric antithesis the core of the metaphor is to disregard the English language, to prefer private evidence to public, external to internal.

V

If the distinction between kinds of evidence has implications for the historical critic, it has them no less for the contemporary poet and his critic. Or, since every rule for a poet is but another side of a judgment by a critic, and since the past is the realm of the scholar and critic, and the future and present that of the poet and the critical leaders of taste, we may say that the problems arising in literary scholarship from the intentional fallacy are matched by others which arise in the world of progressive experiment.

The question of "allusiveness," for example, as acutely posed by the poetry of Eliot, is certainly one where a false judgment is likely to involve the intentional fallacy. The frequency and depth of literary allusion in the poetry of Eliot and others has driven so many in pursuit of full meanings to the *Golden Bough* and the Elizabethan drama that it has become a kind of commonplace to suppose that we do not know what a poet means unless we have traced him in his reading—a supposition redolent with intentional implications. The stand taken by F. O. Matthiessen is a sound one and partially forestalls the difficulty.

> If one reads these lines with an attentive ear and is sensitive to their sudden shifts in movement, the contrast between the actual Thames and the idealized vision of it during an age before it flowed through a megalopolis is sharply conveyed by that movement itself, whether or not one recognizes the refrain to be from Spenser.[10]

Eliot's allusions work when we know them—and to a great extent even when we do not know them, through their suggestive power.

But sometimes we find allusions supported by notes, and it is a nice question whether the notes function more as guides to send us where we may be educated, or more as indications in themselves about the character of the allusions. "Nearly everything of importance . . . that is apposite to an appreciation of *The Waste Land*," writes Matthiessen of Miss Weston's book, "has been incorporated into the structure of the poem itself, or into Eliot's Notes." And with such an admission it may begin to appear that it would not much matter if Eliot invented his sources (as Sir Walter Scott invented chapter epigraphs from "old plays" and "anonymous" authors, or as Coleridge wrote marginal glosses for *The Ancient Mariner*). Allusions to Dante, Webster, Marvell, or Baudelaire doubtless gain something because these writers existed, but it is doubtful whether the same can be said for an allusion to an obscure Elizabethan: "The sound of horns and motors, which shall bring / Sweeney to Mrs. Porter in the spring." "Cf. Day, *Parliament of Bees*:" says Eliot,

> When of a sudden, listening, you shall hear,
> A noise of horns and hunting, which shall bring
> Actaeon to Diana in the spring,
> Where all shall see her naked skin.

The irony is completed by the quotation itself; had Eliot, as is quite conceivable, composed these lines to furnish his own background, there would be no loss of validity. The conviction may grow as one reads Eliot's next note: "I do not know the origin of the ballad from which these lines are taken: it was reported to me from Sydney, Australia." The important word in this note—on. Mrs. Porter and her daughter who washed their feet in soda water—is "ballad." And if one should feel from the lines themselves their "ballad" quality, there would be little need for the note. Ultimately, the inquiry must focus on the integrity of such notes as parts of the poem, for where they constitute special information about the meaning of phrases in the poem, they ought to be subject to the same scrutiny as any of the other words in which it is written. Matthiessen believes the notes were the price Eliot "had to pay in order to avoid what he would have considered muffling the energy of his poem by extended connecting links in the text itself." But it may be questioned whether the notes and the need for them are not equally muffling. F. W. Bateson has plausibly argued that Tennyson's "The Sailor Boy" would be better if half the stanzas were omitted, and the best versions of ballads like "Sir Patrick Spens" owe their power to the very audacity with which the minstrel has taken for granted the story upon which he comments. What then if a poet finds he cannot take so much for granted in a more recondite context and rather than write informatively, supplies notes? It can be said in favor of this plan that at least the notes do not pretend to be dramatic, as they would if written in verse. On the other hand, the notes may look like unassimilated material lying loose beside the poem, necessary for the meaning of the verbal symbol, but not integrated, so that the symbol stands incomplete.

We mean to suggest by the above analysis that whereas notes tend to seem to justify themselves as external indexes to the author's *intention*, yet they ought to be judged like any other parts of a composition (verbal arrangement special to a particular context), and when so judged their reality as parts of the poem, or their imaginative integration with the rest of the poem, may come into question. Mathiessen, for instance, sees that Eliot's titles for poems and his epigraphs are informative apparatus, like the notes. But while he is worried by some of the notes and thinks that Eliot "appears to be mocking himself for writing the note at the same time that he wants to convey something by it," Matthiessen believes that the "device" of epigraphs "is not at all open to the objection of not being sufficiently structural." "The *intention*," he says, "is to enable the poet to secure a condensed expression in the poem itself." "In each case the epigraph is *designed* to form an integral part of the effect of the poem." And Eliot himself, in his notes, has justified his poetic practice in terms of intention.

> The Hanged Man, a member of the traditional pack, fits my purpose in two ways: because he is associated in my mind with the Hanged God of Frazer, and because I associate him with the hooded figure in the passage of the disciples to Emmaus in Part V. . . . The man with Three Staves (an authentic member of the Tarot pack) I associate, quite arbitrarily, with the Fisher King himself.

And perhaps he is to be taken more seriously here, when off guard in a note, than when in his Norton Lectures he comments on the difficulty of saying what a poem means and adds playfully that he thinks of prefixing to a second edition of *Ash Wednesday* some lines from *Don Juan*:

> I don't pretend that I quite understand
> My own meaning when I would be *very* fine;
> But the fact is that I have nothing planned
> Unless it were to be a moment merry.

If Eliot and other contemporary poets have any characteristic fault, it may be in *planning* too much.

Allusiveness in poetry is one of several critical issues by which we have illustrated the more abstract issue of intentionalism, but it may be for today the most important illustration. As a poetic practice allusiveness would appear to be in some recent poems an extreme corollary of the romantic intentionalist assumption, and as a critical issue it challenges and brings to light in a special way the basic premise of intentionalism. The following instance from the poetry of Eliot may serve to epitomize the practical implications of what we have been saying. In Eliot's *Love Song of J. Alfred Prufrock*, toward the end, occurs the line: "I have heard the mermaids singing, each to each," and this bears a certain resemblance to a line in a Song by John Donne, "Teach me to heare Mermaides singing," so that for the reader acquainted to a certain degree with Donne's poetry, the critical question arises: Is Eliot's line an allusion to Donne's? Is Prufrock thinking about Donne? Is Eliot thinking about Donne? We suggest that there are two radically different ways of looking for an answer to this question. There is (1) the way of poetic analysis and exegesis, which inquires whether it makes any sense if Eliot-Prufrock *is* thinking about Donne. In an earlier part of the poem, when Prufrock asks, "Would it have been worth while, . . . To have squeezed the universe into a ball," his words take half their sadness and irony from certain energetic and passionate lines of Marvell's *To His Coy Mistress*. But the exegetical inquirer may wonder whether mermaids considered as "strange sights" (to hear them is in Donne's poem analogous to getting with child a mandrake root) have much to do with Prufrock's mermaids, which seem to be symbols of romance and dynamism, and which incidentally have literary authentication, if they need it, in a line of a sonnet by Gérard de Nerval. This method of inquiry may lead to the conclusion that the given resemblance between Eliot and Donne is without significance and is better not thought of, or the method may have the disadvantage of providing no certain conclusion. Nevertheless, we submit that this is the true and objective way of criticism, as contrasted to what the very uncertainty of exegesis might tempt a second kind of critic to undertake: (2) the way of biographical or genetic inquiry, in which, taking advantage of the fact that Eliot is still alive, and in the spirit of a man who would settle a bet, the critic writes to Eliot and asks what he meant, or if he had Donne in mind. We shall not here weigh the probabilities—whether Eliot would answer that he meant nothing at all, had nothing at all in mind—a sufficiently good answer to such a question—or in an unguarded moment might furnish a clear and, within its limit, irrefutable answer. Our point is that such an answer to such an inquiry would have nothing to do with the poem "Prufrock"; it would not be a critical inquiry. Critical inquiries, unlike bets, are not settled in this way. Critical inquiries are not settled by consulting the oracle.

NOTES

1. *Dictionary of World Literature*, Joseph T. Shipley, ed. (New York, 1942), 326–29.

2. J. E. Spingarn, "The New Criticism," in *Criticism in America* (New York, 1924), 24–25.

3. Ananda K. Coomaraswamy, "Intention," in *American Bookman*, I (1944), 41–48.

4. It is true that Croce himself in his *Ariosto, Shakespeare and Corneille* (London, 1920), chap. VII, "The Practical Personality and the Poetical Personality," and in his *Defence of Poetry* (Oxford, 1933), 24, and elsewhere, early and late, has delivered telling attacks on emotive geneticism, but the main drive of the *Aesthetic* is surely toward a kind of cognitive intentionalism.

5. See Hughes Mearns, *Creative Youth* (Garden City, 1925), esp. 10, 27–29. The technique of inspiring poems has apparently been outdone more recently by the study of inspiration in successful poets and other artists. See, for instance, Rosamond E. M. Harding, *An Anatomy of Inspiration* (Cambridge, 1940); Julius Portnoy, *A Psychology of Art Creation* (Philadelphia, 1942); Rudolf Arnheim and others, *Poets at Work* (New York, 1947); Phyllis Bartlett, *Poems in Process* (New York, 1951); Brewster Ghiselin (ed.), *The Creative Process: A Symposium* (Berkeley and Los Angeles, 1952).

6. Curt Ducasse, *The Philosophy of Art* (New York, 1929), 116.

7. And the history of words *after* a poem is written may contribute meanings which if relevant to the original pattern should not be ruled out by a scruple about intention.

8. Chapters VIII, "The Pattern," and XVI, "The Known and Familiar Landscape," will be found of most help to the student of the poem.

9. Charles M. Coffin, *John Donne and the New Philosophy* (New York, 1927), 97–98.

10. F. O. Matthiessen, *An Essay on the Nature of Poetry* (New York, 1935), 46.

The Speaking Voice (1951)

Reuben Brower

Everything written is as good as it is dramatic. . . . A dramatic necessity goes deep into the nature of the sentence. Sentences are not different enough to hold the attention unless they are dramatic. No ingenuity of varying structure will do. All that can save them is the speaking tone of voice somehow entangled in the words and fastened to the page for the ear of the imagination. That is all that can save poetry from sing-song, all that can save prose from itself.[1]

Robert Frost

I. The Speaker

Every poem is "dramatic" in Frost's sense: someone is speaking to someone else. For a poem is a dramatic fiction no less than a play, and its speaker, like a character in a play, is no less a creation of the words on the printed page. The "person spoken to" is also a fictional personage and never the actual audience of "you and me," and only in a special abstract sense is it the literary audience of a particular time and place in history. The voice we hear in a lyric, however piercingly real, is not Keats's or Shakespeare's; or, if it seems to be, as in

> the fancy cannot cheat so well
> As she is fam'd to do, deceiving elf

we are embarrassed and thrown off as if an actor had stopped and spoken to the audience in his own person. As Keats once remarked of men's lives, poems are "continual allegories"; and if they have biographical meaning it is at least one remove from the actual man who wrote. For the poet is always wrapping himself up in some guise, if only the guise of being a poet.

Shelley in the "Ode to the West Wind" appears in his familiar character of priest-poet-prophet, as his language everywhere reminds us. From the opening "O" through the "thous" and the "oh, hears!" which follow, we are spectators of a religious drama, a rite that moves from prayerful incantation to a demand for mystic union and the gift of poetic prophecy. The priest prays in the language of litany, enumerating the powers of the wind spirit:

> O thou,
> Who chariotest to their dark wintry bed
> The wingèd seeds . . .
>
> Thou who didst waken from his summer dreams
> The blue Mediterranean . . .
>
> Thou
> For whose path the Atlantic's level powers
> Cleave themselves into chasms . . .
>
> Be thou, Spirit fierce,
> My spirit!

At one point,

> I fall upon the thorns of life! I bleed!

the dramatic fiction slips disturbingly: the allegory refers us too directly to Shelley's biography. But it is only after the poem's high commotion is past that we feel the lapse, so compelling is the dramatic incantation of this verse. That Shelley takes us with him so completely, securing assent for what we may later reject, is largely due to this constant shaping of a role through the detail of his expression.

Shelley is of course creating not one character but two, and a whole set of relations between them—in short a complete dramatic situation. The situation, more closely regarded, is a series of swiftly changing situations, which gives the sense of dramatic movement already noted above. We must not confuse the full dramatic situation of this or any poem with the mere setting or scene, though one is always implied, if only the "setting" of the poet's mind. The setting in Shelley's poem, for instance, is little more than the earth and sky. A comparable poem by Robert Frost will remind us even more forcibly that the dramatic situation is the relationship of fictional speaker and auditor "entangled in the words" and not the physical scene, however vividly realized:

> ONCE BY THE PACIFIC
>
> The shattered water made a misty din.
> Great waves looked over others coming in,
> And thought of doing something to the shore
> That water never did to land before.
> The clouds were low and hairy in the skies,
> Like locks blown forward in the gleam of eyes.
> You could not tell, and yet it looked as if
> The shore was lucky in being backed by cliff,
> The cliff in being backed by continent;
> It looked as if a night of dark intent
> Was coming, and not only a night, an age.
> Someone had better be prepared for rage.
> There would be more than ocean-water broken
> Before God's last *Put out the Light* was spoken.

The blend of crashing sounds and stormy lights, the felt counter-thrusts of land and water, the terror of the night of wrath are so present to us in reading "Once by the Pacific" that we may easily overlook the dramatic artifice of the poem. But though unobtrusive it is not unimportant, for to experience such a vision through Frost's special "voice" makes all the difference. Strictly speaking the situation is not that of the watcher by the sea, but (as indicated by the tenses) that of the reminiscent poet speaking after the event to no one in particular or to a receptive listening self. The speaker has a character of complete definiteness, which is why the poem is so *palpable* when read aloud. His character takes its distinctive form and pressure from the speculative way of talking, from the flow and arrest of American speech:

> You could not tell, and yet it looked as if

and again,

> It looked as if . . .

But this reckoning voice has other strains sounding through it—pronouncements of the Old Testament, talk about the end of the world, and echoes of older mythological styles. There may even be a reminiscence of Shelley's maenad in those clouds

Like locks blown forward in the gleam of eyes.

II. Tone

As I have just been illustrating, to show exactly *who* is speaking in a poem it is necessary to consider *how* he speaks. In other words, it is necessary to define his tone. By tone I refer to: (1) the implied social relationship of the speaker to his auditor and (2) the manner he adopts in addressing his auditor. Whether we talk in terms of "tone" or of "dramatic situation" indicates that we are considering expressions for different purposes or considering different expressions. In "Once by the Pacific," the phrase "you could not tell" may be regarded as defining both dramatic situation and tone; the past tenses, on the other hand, are primarily effective in fixing the situation.

It is important to remember that when we speak of the dramatic situation, we are thinking of all the relations implied between the fictional speaker and auditor in a poem, any connection one has with the other. In many poems, as in "Once by the Pacific," the main connection implied is that the second is listening to the first. In others, for example Browning's monologues, there are hints of a complicated history of loves and hates or of subtler attractions and aversions, the makings of a play or novel. Under the first aspect of tone I refer to a single relation within the whole dramatic complex, the *social* relation, where in the social hierarchy the fictional speaker and auditor stand. To take random examples, they may be lover and beloved, brother and sister, man and wife, servant and master. Under the second aspect of tone I refer to the *manner* the speaker adopts within this social relationship. The lover may speak in a manner more or less intimate, formal, casual, heroic, chivalric, et cetera.

Frost's control of this aspect of tone is where he shows his art most fully. He succeeds in maintaining a wonderful blend of manners, a poise between two voices, the high-poetic-apocalyptic and the down-to-earth, cautiously speculative. This nice duplicity appears in the word "din" at the end of the first line, where we are almost ready for a grander word—almost, because the subtle exaggeration of "shattered" points the way to a less simple form of expression. Those solemn "'great waves . . . thought of doing something to the shore" ("I'll do something to you"—a voice in a very human quarrel); and the Shelleyesque "locks" were oddly enough "low and hairy in the skies." By these and similar touches Frost prepares us for the climactic last line with its stroke of parody across the solemnity of *Fiat lux.*

While describing the special blend of manners in "Once by the Pacific," we have introduced an important principle in the analysis of tone. We evaluated Frost's tone by making more or less overt comparisons with the high-poetic-apocalyptic style and everyday speech of reckoning. Our recognition of a manner always depends on a silent reference to a known way of speaking and on our perceiving variations from it. The poet—Frost notably in the poem we have been reading—relies on such norms and on our familiarity with them. The implied norm may be as vaguely definable as everyday speech or as relatively fixed as the idiom of eighteenth-century heroic poetry. Certainly our finest perception of a norm and of variations from it lies beyond our powers of expression. To define even one level of speech precisely would require an elaborate excursion in literary and social history. But without attempting so monstrous a task we can make helpful indications of a norm and so place the tonal level. We can point out an allusion or show

how a phrase in the immediate context recalls some larger context and with it certain conventions of speech; we can quote comparable expressions from other pieces of literature or from any realm of discourse whatsoever. Once a norm has been indicated, the cruder variations are evident, but to define subtle variations from a literary manner is certainly a less a simple assignment. Literary critics have the pleasant task of making such measurements.

I am hardly suggesting that the delineation of tone can be reduced to a single formula to be applied on any and all occasions. The application and choice of methods must be at least as flexible as the poet's manipulation of tone. In the two examples that follow I shall stress the usefulness of following certain grammatical and rhetorical cues in assaying the tone of a poem, but I shall also use other methods, including those just outlined.

The poems for analysis are two sonnets, John Donne's "Show me deare Christ, thy spouse, so bright and clear" and Gerard Manley Hopkins' "Thou art indeed just, Lord, if I contend." Since the poems have similar situations, comparison will show more clearly what we mean by tonal pattern and how differences in tonal pattern are expressive of differences in attitude.

Both Donne and Hopkins appear as devout Christians addressing the Deity; both are puzzled by a religious problem; and both ask for a solution. But the relation in which each stands to God and the manner in which each addresses God are utterly different. Here is how Donne poses his problem:

> Show me deare Christ, thy spouse, so bright and clear.
> What! is it She, which on the other shore
> Goes richly painted? or which rob'd and tore
> Laments and mournes in Germany and here?
> Sleepes she a thousand, then peepes up one yeare?
> Is she selfe truth and errs? now new, now outwore?
> Doth she, and did she, and shall she evermore
> On one, on seaven, or on no hill appeare?
> Dwells she with us, or like adventuring knights
> First travaile we to seeke and then make Love?
> Betray kind husband thy spouse on our sights
> And let myne amorous soule court thy mild Dove,
> Who is most trew, and pleasing to thee, then
> When she's embrac'd and open to most men.

Donne is speaking within the seventeenth-century religious situation, as one familiar with all the historic varieties of the Christian Church. What is distinctive and surprising is the tone this theologian-controversialist assumes in talking with God. While approaching Christ in his consecrated role as the bridegroom of the Church, Donne talks as a man of the world in pursuit of a beautiful woman, and his manner combines worldly politeness with downright insolence. Let us see how his tone is defined through the language of the poem.

"Show me, deare Christ, thy spouse . . ." Donne begins with a bold command and an affectionate though polite address. (Verb forms, whether personal or impersonal, and forms of address are worth noting as cues to tone.) He uses "thy," which as Grierson observes is in Donne "the pronoun of feeling and intimacy." Both the intimacy and directness of the wooer appear again in the offhand, impatient "What!" of the first of his questions. Although the tone now becomes less personal, the "she's," the unflattering adjectives, and above all "peepes" recall the freedom of the opening command. But balance is maintained by the literary elegance and chivalrous sophistication of

Dwells she with us, or like adventuring knights
First travaile we to seeke and then make Love?

The lover is making just the right gesture of removal in view of his next request:

Betray kind husband thy spouse to our sights
And let myne amorous soule court thy mild Dove . . .

He has advanced from "deare Christ" to "husband" and "kind husband," at that! With the erotic pun of the final line of the sonnet, decency (in an eighteenth-century sense) is abandoned. But not quite, because of the knightly decorum of the immensely beautiful "let myne amorous soule court thy mild Dove." (Note the politeness indicated by using "my soule" rather than the more personal "me.") Though there is a progress in insolence, equilibrium is never quite lost throughout the while poem.

If we consider similar cues in Hopkins' sonnet, especially forms of address and the persons of verbs, we shall find great differences in the tone assumed by each poet and in the over-all management of tone:

Justus quidem tu es, Domine, si disputem tecum:
verumtatem justa loquar ad te: Quare via impiorum
prosperatur? etc.
Thou art indeed just, Lord, if I contend
With thee; but, sir, so what I plead is just.
Why do sinners' ways prosper? and why must
Disappointment all I endeavour end?
    Wert thou my enemy, O thou my friend,
How wouldst thou worse, I wonder, than thou dost
Defeat, thwart me? Oh, the sots and thralls of lust
Do in spare hours more thrive than I that spend,
Sir, life upon thy cause. See, bands and brakes
Now, leavèd how thick! lacèd they are again
With fretty chervil, look, and fresh wind shakes
Them; birds build—but not I build; no, but strain,
Time's eunuch, and not breed one work that wakes.
Mine, O thou lord of life, send my roots rain.

The dramatic situation at the beginning of the poem, as indicated by the Latin quotation and by Hopkins' adaptation ("contends," "plead," "just") is a legal debate in which the plaintiff puts his case before the Lord (notice the capital letter). The value of the opening "thou" as compared with Donne's use of the pronoun is changed completely. The seventeenth-century "amorous" relationship of worshipper and deity no longer holds. There are no loving graces to temper the dignity of "thou" in Hopkins' line:

Thou art indeed just, Lord, if I contend . . .

Yet if judged by Victorian standards Hopkins has his insolence too: he "sirs" the Lord, which is respectful though not quite worshipful. (His insolence may be further measured by comparing Auden's brash echo, "Sir, no man's enemy.")

After the debate of the first four lines the tone moves with swift jumps and backward turnings to a conclusion which is as right as it is surprising. Asides break in with a poignant and unexpected intimacy:

> Wert thou my enemy, O thou my friend,
> How wouldst thou worse, I wonder, than thou dost
> Defeat, thwart me?

As the questions shift from impersonal forms to the accusing "thous," the pleader sacrifices dignity, though he recovers it for a moment in "I that spend, / *Sir*, life upon thy *cause*." A burst of springtime imagery marks a new situation and a completely new tone:

> See, banks and brakes
> Now, leaved how thick! lacèd they are again
> With fretty chervil, look . . .

"See" is less to the Lord than to the poet's wondering self, while "look" is only an inward noting of the puzzling fact. Hence the sudden force of the real imperative in "send my roots rain." For this demand the address, "O thou lord of life," is beautifully right. Debating decorum is forgotten, questionings and asides are dropped as Hopkins calls directly on God for help. He calls him 'lord,' not 'Lord,' yet with a new accent of awe perfectly in harmony with the metaphor which has been growing since early in the poem. The bitter and sweet contrast of his own straining barrenness and the thick, building liveliness of created things presses in our ears with "O thou lord of life, send my roots rain."

Both of these poems show that tone is fixed and so revealed at similar points in expression, and both show how pervasive the control of tone may be. But they differ enormously in the relationships implied, in the manner which each poet assumes, and in what may be called the total tonal pattern. Although Donne combines politeness and candor, throughout the sonnet he is shaping a voice of consistent, stable character. But Hopkins in his alternations of tone expresses a confusion of tongues: how is he to speak? He finds a way at last, but, as the sequence shows, the victory is hardly won and perhaps only temporary. We have in these contrasting patterns clear symbols of the religious attitudes being expressed by the two poets: Donne, for all his queries certain of his close and passionate relation to Christ; Hopkins, tortured at the very center of his faith.

We shall next consider a religious poem that shows a further complexity of tonal pattern and another sort of relationship between this pattern and the attitude finally expressed:

> LOVE
>
> Love bade me welcome: yet my soul drew back,
> Guiltie of dust and sinne.
> But quick-ey'd Love, observing me grow slack
> From my first entrance in,
> Drew nearer to me, sweetly questioning,
> If I lack'd any thing.
>
> A guest, I answer'd, worthy to be here:
> Love said, you shall be he.
> I the unkinde, ungratefull? Ah my deare,
> I cannot look on thee.

Love took my hand, and smiling did reply,
Who made the eyes but I?

Truth Lord, but I have marr'd them: let my shame
Go where it doth deserve.
And know you not, sayes Love, who bore the blame?
My deare, then I will serve.
You must sit down, sayes Love, and taste my meat:
So I did sit and eat.

George Herbert

There are two situations here, the story-teller's and that of the drama he narrates; and within the drama there are the distinct and exactly complementary tones of the guest and of Love. In a tone of almost feminine intimacy the guest carries on sweet converse with the gently humorous host:

Ah my deare,
I cannot look on thee . . .
My deare, then I will serve.

He is the humblest of guests and sinners, not "worthy to be here," "unkinde, ungratefull." Love's accent is questioning, not accusing; here grammatical mood is imperative not in its brusque form, but softened with "you" and "shall" and "must." Hers is sweet questioning and sweet commanding.

The manner in which the guest-sinner tells the story needs a different description. The narrator does not speak to anyone; he merely tells what was said and done, rarely noting a look or a gesture and making hardly any comment on his own reactions. His statement, unobtrusively balanced in form, could be written as prose, with only one or two changes in order. As the story[2] goes on, it approaches the level of naïve colloquial narrative: "I answer'd . . . Love said . . . sayes Love . . . sayes Love."

We must consider now what is the effect in the complete poem of this trio in tones—the reserved decently colloquial manner of the narrator and within the story the intimate, deprecatory voice of the guest and the exquisite politeness and assurance of the host. Regarded as a whole the poem is a little drama of conversion. A sinner conscious of his guilt, feeling the pull of Christ's love ("Ah my deare") but unable to accept it, rediscovers the meaning of Christ's sacrifice and is redeemed. In relation to this sequence, the reserve of the telling becomes extreme: the full reversal of feelings at the climax is indicated only by a colon:

You must sit down, sayes Love, and taste my meat:
So I did sit and eat.

The restraint, the intimacy, and sweet politeness bring out by contrast the conflict and resolution which is so quietly presented. Hence the surprising tension and strength of a seemingly gentle poem.

When reading Herbert's lyric, we do not experience tension in the abstract; we hear the drama through the voice—or voices—which we have been describing. Our whole aim in analysis of tone is to delineate the exact speaking voice in every poem we read, but we can succeed only by attending to the special, often minute language signs by which the poet fixes the tone for us. The methods used in this chapter are intended to direct attention to a few of the commoner signs and to offer some questions that we may put to a poem in determining its tone. By answering questions such as "What is the social relationship implied?" or "What is the writer's manner?" we may clarify and express the set of relations which project the tone of the poet-speaker, and which taken together may be regarded as a tonal pattern.

As the tonal relations change—and they must in a living poem—they take their place in the sequence of relations we have called the dramatic movement, the succession of changing dramatic situations. All of these ordered relations together make up the dramatic design of a poem.

NOTES

1. From the Introduction to "A Way Out."

2. I have not attempted here or later to treat story or narrative as a completely separate type of design, since I regard narrative as one of the patterns that make up dramatic design. As the example above shows, statements in a work of literature of what someone says or does (pure narrative statements) are always expressive of a dramatic relationship.

SECTION 4

Structuralist Reading

Since the Practical and New Criticism were largely Anglo-American phenomena, it is not surprising that some of the strongest challenges to these approaches came from France, Germany, and Eastern Europe, particularly from thinkers who worked not just in literature but between several disciplines in the social sciences. Structuralism was a name for a broad movement of such thinkers, though like the New Critics, structuralists tended to have more differences than similarities, and the Anglo-American reception of structuralism was already interwoven with different strands of post-structuralist theory, as Jonathan Culler noted in *Structuralist Poetics* (1975). For a basic definition of structuralism, Culler turns to Roland Barthes, who described structuralism in 1967 "in its most specialized and consequently most relevant version" as "a mode of analysis of cultural artifacts which originated in the methods of modern linguistics."[1] That's as good a definition as any, though linguistics offered a very broad methodological model for a very diverse array of approaches. Since Ferdinand de Saussure's *Course in General Linguistics* (published posthumously in 1916) distinguished between individual speech acts (*la parole*) and the system of a language (*la langue*), it had become possible to think about a language as a set of signifying relations sufficient unto itself. For thinkers as different as Barthes, Mikhail Bakhtin, Claude Lévi-Strauss, Michel Foucault, Emile Benveniste, Tzvetan Todorov, Jacques Lacan, and Noam Chomsky, modern linguistics provided a paradigm for the study of other cultural phenomena. But that paradigm also reached far beyond linguistics, of course. For example, the selections from Gérard Genette and Northrop Frye in section 1, "Genre Theory," are also broadly structuralist. By thinking about institutions, cultures, psyches, narratives, and genres as defined by a network of relations analogous to the sets of relations that define a language, structuralists could make ambitious claims not only about particular instances but also about how those instances worked in social relations.

While such large structural concerns could eventually lead to Foucault's view that all cultural institutions are discursive, it is also not hard to see how structuralist logic also led to a rigorous form of poetic close reading that posed an alternative to the New Criticism. Whereas New Critics tended to emphasize the importance of analyzing the "tone" of the fictional speaker, structuralists concentrated on the interaction between pronouns or prepositions or the number of verbs or even the number of phonemes in a poem or a stanza or a line. Like Richards and the practical critics, structuralists were interested in poems as systems of communication, but they were not primarily interested in the reader's experience of and participation in that system (your brain on poetry). Instead, as Roman Jakobson writes in "Linguistics and Poetics," structuralist critics assumed that "poetics deals with problems of verbal structure, just as the analysis of painting is concerned with pictorial structure. Since linguistics is the global science of verbal structure, poetics may be regarded as an integral part of linguistics." If for Richards the structure of a poem could organize the way we think, and if for the New Critics the structure of a poem could be appreciated as "a verbal icon" or a drama of consciousness, for structuralist readers the poem was an iconic example of linguistic structure, and linguistic structure was the iconic example of the way in which all aspects of culture—not just your experience, and not just the poem's drama—work.

Given the enormous amount of structuralist criticism that paid very close attention to poems as exemplary verbal structures, it may seem odd for this section to begin with a critic who paid little attention to poems or poetry in any form. Mikhail Bakhtin is best known as a thinker who pushed Saussurean structural linguistics toward historical linguistics; his revolutionary work on Rabelais and Dostoevsky introduced the notions of the carnivalesque, of dialogism, heteroglossia, and chronotope into the study of the novel in particular. Always concerned with the ethical consequences of literature's inclusion of many perspectives and voices, Bakhtin tended to dismiss poetry as "monologic" and exclusive. Yet we include "The Problem of Speech Genres" because in it Bakhtin offers an important perspective on lyric as one among many "speech genres" used with remarkable fluidity in literature and life—in fact, exchanged in all forms of human communication. According to Bakhtin, "each separate utterance is individual, of course, but each sphere in which language is used develops its own *relatively stable types* of these utterances. These we may call *speech genres*." The problem with literary criticism, according to Bakhtin, is that it has tended to consider genres "in terms of their specific literary and artistic features, in terms of the differences that distinguish one from the other (within the realm of literature), and not as specific types of utterances distinct from other types, but sharing with them a common *verbal* (language) nature." Once the latter move is made, literary genres become dialectical, representing but also represented by the common verbal frame of all human experience. Bakhtin does make a distinction between the "primary (simple) genres that have taken form in unmediated speech communion"—the ways in which we communicate with one another in everyday life—and what he calls the "secondary (complex) speech genres—novels, dramas, all kinds of scientific research, major genres of commentary, and so forth—[which] arise in more complex and comparatively highly developed and organized cultural communication (primarily written) that is artistic, scientific, sociopolitical, and so on." According to Bakhtin, secondary genres feed off of primary genres, altering the primary genres in the process. In this sense, "the novel as a whole is an utterance just as rejoinders in everyday dialogue or private letters are (they do have a common nature), but unlike these, the novel is a secondary (complex) utterance."

But if for Bakhtin the novel is the secondary speech genre par excellence because it takes all primary genres into itself and makes them more complex, then what sort of speech genre is a lyric poem? Bakhtin's contribution to lyric theory is not a delineation of the properties of the lyric or anything parallel to his landmark contributions to the study of the novel. Instead, his contribution is in placing lyric poetry into the system of speech genres that all suppose not only social expression but also social response. Once considered as a speech genre, a poem on a page must be considered in a set of social relations.

While we may not respond to a poem by answering its questions or performing its imperatives, lyrical genres suppose "a silent responsive understanding," according to Bakhtin. Poems are made to produce speech or action in the reader or listener, but it will be "a responsive understanding with a delayed reaction." In this way, Bakhtin placed lyric poems not only within the individual circuit of communication idealized by the New Critics but also back into the heterogeneous diversity of ordinary communication and mass culture from which the Practical and New Critics wanted to protect the poem and its reader.

Bakhtin's theory certainly implied a sociology or ethnography of communication based on the analysis of speech genres as myriad forms of social recognition, but the Russian structuralist thinker who had the most direct influence on the study of the semiotics of culture (particularly in linguistic anthropology) was the linguist and literary theorist Roman Jakobson. Like Bakhtin, Jakobson regarded what he called "the poetic function" as one among many things language could do, and he viewed poetics as part and parcel of linguistic analysis, which was itself part and parcel of cultural analysis. Perhaps the most influential of Jakobson's linguistic paradigms of poetic discourse was his distinction between metaphor and metonymy, or between relations of contiguity and substitution, axes he saw as concentrated in poetry but foundational for all discourse. Given his ambition for poetics, it may seem surprising that Jakobson's analysis of poetic language could become so detailed, even microscopic in its focus. In "Linguistics and Poetics," the essay we include in this section, Jakobson begins at the macro rather than the micro level, delineating the large "functions of language," since for him poetics can only be understood as one of those functions. Jackobson sketches a communicative structure in which an ADDRESSER (the capital letters are Jakobson's way of distinguishing these as registers of communication) sends a message to an ADDRESSEE in a particular CONTEXT of communication by means of a CONTACT. Jakobson then goes on to describe the different linguistic functions he ascribes to each part of this communicative structure. Interestingly, what Jakobson describes as "the poetic function" of language moves between the points in this structure, since the poetic function is defined as the "focus on the message for its own sake."

This does not mean that such a focus can only be achieved in poems—on the contrary, since "this function cannot be productively studied out of touch with the general problems of language, and, on the other hand, the scrutiny of language requires a thorough consideration of its poetic function, any attempt to reduce the sphere of poetic function to poetry or to confine poetry to poetic function would be a delusive oversimplification." This strong claim makes poetics part of the larger study of linguistics for Jakobson, and it also makes poems into exemplary models for linguistic study. Since the eighteenth century, prosodists had been attending at least as closely as does Jakobson to the placement of metrical stresses, or to the relation between figures of sound and upbeats and downbeats, and most prosodists had devised their own elaborate systems of versification that led to elaborate debates. But for Jakobson, the minute details of a poem's meter and syllabic arrangement are important to attend to in detail primarily because "poetic meter . . . has so many intrinsically linguistic particularities that it is most convenient to describe it from a purely linguistic point of view"—so much so that "no linguistic property of the verse design should be disregarded." Thus in addition to meter, Jakobson scrutinizes every grammatical and phonological particular of a poem. Many literary critics have agreed with Jonathan Culler's assessment in *Structuralist Poetics* that "Jakobson has made an important contribution to literary studies in drawing attention to the varieties of grammatical figures and their potential functions, but his own analyses are vitiated by the belief that linguistics provides an automatic discovery procedure for poetic patterns and by his failure to perceive that the central task is to explain how poetic structures emerge from the multiplicity of potential linguistic structures" (86). Such complaints on behalf of literary criticism attest to Jakobson's challenge to the assumptions of the field: why should "poetic structures" be privileged over the system of signification (*la langue*) from which they spring? It is a question that unsettles from within deeply held modern assumptions about poetry, and it works against the lyricizing tendencies of most twentieth-century literary criticism.

In the United States, literary critics writing in the wake of Jakobson responded by trying to turn his close linguistic analysis back toward the literary critical privileging of the poem as lyricized aesthetic object, and toward poetic rather than linguistic structure as the object of critical analysis. Michael Riffaterre began his career in the mid-1960s by arguing that many of Jakobson's patterns involve linguistic aspects that cannot be perceived by the reader and thus are really outside poetic structure—a qualification Richards and the New Critics would have appreciated.[2] In "The Significance of a Poem," included in this section, Riffaterre argues for "the difference we perceive empirically between poetry and nonpoetry" as a departure from the tendency of structural linguistics to make poetry into an instance of larger forces rather than a special case. Instead of examining what a poem has in common with other forms of communication, Riffaterre focuses on "the formal and semantic unity" of the poem, which he calls "the poem's significance." In a note, Riffaterre writes that "significance, to put it simply, is what the poem is really about." Such resort to first principles recalls New Critical calls to make poetry at once special and publicly accessible, and it clearly reacted to the challenge structural linguistics posed to literary criticism as a separate discipline. At the same time, Riffaterre's actual analyses of poems rival the minute examinations of Jakobson, since if for Jakobson all elements of the poem are relevant to its linguistic functions, for Riffaterre "all signs within a text [are] relevant to its poetic quality."

Thus Riffaterre's semiotic analysis of poetic significance may seem a lot like Jakobson's linguistic analysis of the poetic function—and it should, since Riffaterre's departure from structural linguistics retained Jakobson's methodology but inscribed that methodology within the poem as a lyric whole. Riffaterre also added a focus on the reader of the poem, and especially on the various levels of reading that contribute to "the poem's significance." That readerly focus was of course nothing new, but to this fairly traditional notion of levels of interpretation Riffaterre also added semiotics, since in structuralist fashion, he claimed that we cannot "understand the semiosis [of the poem] until we have ascertained the place of the text now perceived as one sign within a system (a sign formally complex but monosemic), for by definition a sign cannot be isolated. A sign is only a relationship to something else. It will not make sense without a continuous translatability from component to component of a network. A consequence of the system's latent existence is that every signifying feature of the poem must be relatable to that system." Such prose was structuralist dogma, yet unlike Bakhtin and Jakobson—but like many literary critics before and after him—Riffaterre insisted on finding even the place of the poem within a larger semiotic context within the boundaries of the poem itself. For him, there is no outside, no social world that influences the poem's semiotic structure. Instead, his minute examination of the details of poems is meant to attest to poems as self-sufficient lyric structures that generate their own unique forms of "significance."

Much of Riffaterre's reading has to do with the myriad ways in which poems work to repress *mimesis*, or representation, and replace it with *semiosis*, or a chain of signification that refers only to itself. "The reader's perception of what is poetic is based wholly upon reference to texts," he concludes, thus warding off the threat posed by structuralist thought to the study of poems as verbal icons, as lyric wholes. Yet it is worth noticing the lengths to which Riffaterre needs to go to subdue that threat. It is also worth keeping in mind that although in the twenty-first century, structuralism may seem a thing of the past, it may still offer powerful tools for thinking about the history of lyricization, not least when critics try to use those tools to insist that poems remain the self-sufficient lyrics that they had become for literary criticism by the second half of the twentieth century. Riffaterre's essay shows one way structuralist technique could be used against the grain of the large sociocultural ambition of structuralism, but it is not necessarily typical in its reaction. For many critics in the United States especially, structuralism offered a way out of New Critical reading and a way into a sociological and historical understanding of poetics. For those critics, thinking about poems as parts of other social discourses remains the structuralist challenge we have not yet met.

NOTES

1. From Roland Barthes, "Science versus Literature," paraphrased by Culler (2002), 4.

2. Michael Riffaterre, "Describing Poetic Structures: Two Approaches to Baudelaire's 'Les Chats,'" *Yale French Studies* 36–37 (1966): 200–242.

FURTHER READING

Bakhtin, M. M. *The Dialogic Imagination: Four Essays.* Translated by Caryl Emerson and Michael Holquist. Austin: University of Texas Press, 1981.

Barthes, Roland. *Elements of Semiology.* Translated by Annette Lavers and Colin Smith. New York: Hill and Wang, 1977.

———. *S/Z: An Essay.* Translated by Richard Howard. New York: Hill and Wang, 1975.

Benveniste, Emile. *Problems in General Linguistics.* Translated by Elizabeth Meek. Coral Gables, FL: University of Miami Press, 1971.

Culler, Jonathan. *Structuralist Poetics: Structuralism, Linguistics, and the Study of Literature.* London: Routledge and Kegan Paul, 1975; reprint, New York: Routledge, 2002.

De Man, Paul. "Hypogram and Inscription: Michael Riffaterre's Poetics of Reading." *Diacritics* 11:4 (Winter 1981): 17–35.

De Saussure, Ferdinand. *Course in General Linguistics.* Translated by Wade Baskin. Edited by Haun Saussy and Perry Meisel. New York: Columbia University Press, 2011.

Deleuze, Giles. "A quoi reconnait-on le structuralisme?" in *Histoire de la philosophie, idees, doctrines*, vol. 8: *Le XXe siècle*, 299–335. Paris: Hachette, 1973.

Easthope, Antony. *Poetry as Discourse.* London: Methuen, 1983.

Foucault, Michel. *The Order of Things: An Archeology of the Human Sciences.* New York: Vintage, 1994.

Genette, Gérard. *Figures of Literary Discourse.* Translated by Alan Sheridan. London: Blackwell, 1982.

Jakobson, Roman. *Language in Literature.* Edited by Krystyna Pomorska and Stephen Rudy. Cambridge, MA: Belknap Press of Harvard University Press, 1987.

Jakobson, Roman, and Claude Lévi-Strauss, "Charles Baudelaire's 'Les Chats.'" Translated by Katie Furness-Lane, in Lane (1970), 204–21.

Jameson, Fredric. *The Prisonhouse of Language: A Critical Account of Structuralism and Russian Formalism.* Princeton, NJ: Princeton University Press, 1972.

Jauss, Hans Robert. *Aesthetic Experience and Social Norms.* Translated by Michael Shaw. Minneapolis: University of Minnesota Press, 1982.

Lacan, Jacques. *The Four Fundamental Concepts of Psychoanalysis.* New York: W. W. Norton, 1998.

Lane, Michael, ed. *Introduction to Structuralism.* New York: Basic Books, 1970.

Lemon, Lee T., and Marion J. Reis, eds. *Russian Formalist Criticism: Four Essays.* Lincoln: University of Nebraska Press, 1965.

Lévi-Strauss, Claude. *The Elementary Structures of Kinship.* New York: Beacon Press, 1971.

Mukarovsky, Jan. *Structure, Sign, and Function: Selected Essays by Jan Mukarovsky.* Edited by

John Burbank and Peter Steiner. New Haven, CT: Yale University Press, 1978.

Silverstein, Michael, and Greg Urban, eds. *Natural Histories of Discourse*. Chicago: University of Chicago Press, 1996.

Todorov, Tzvetan. *Introduction to Poetics*. Minneapolis: University of Minnesota Press, 1981.

Voloshinov, V. N. *Marxism and the Philosophy of Language*. Translated by Ladislav Matejka and I. R. Titunik. New York: Seminar Press, 1973.

4.1 The Problem of Speech Genres

(1953; trans. 1986)

Mikhail Bakhtin Translated by Vern W. McGee

1. Statement of the Problem and Definition of Speech Genres

All the diverse areas of human activity involve the use of language. Quite understandably, the nature and forms of this use are just as diverse as are the areas of human activity. This, of course, in no way disaffirms the national unity of language.[1] Language is realized in the form of individual concrete utterances (oral and written) by participants in the various areas of human activity. These utterances reflect the specific conditions and goals of each such area not only through their content (thematic) and linguistic style, that is, the selection of the lexical, phraseological, and grammatical resources of the language, but above all through their compositional structure. All three of these aspects—thematic content, style, and compositional structure—are inseparably linked to the *whole* of the utterance and are equally determined by the specific nature of the particular sphere of communication. Each separate utterance is individual, of course, but each sphere in which language is used develops its own *relatively stable types* of these utterances. These we may call *speech genres*.

The wealth and diversity of speech genres are boundless because the various possibilities of human activity are inexhaustible, and because each sphere of activity contains an entire repertoire of speech genres that differentiate and grow as the particular sphere develops and becomes more complex. Special emphasis should be placed on the extreme *heterogeneity* of speech genres (oral and written). In fact, the category of speech genres should include short rejoinders of daily dialogue (and these are extremely varied depending on the subject matter, situation, and participants), everyday narration, writing (in all its various forms), the brief standard military command, the elaborate and detailed order, the fairly variegated repertoire of business documents (for the most part standard), and the diverse world of commentary (in the broad sense of the word: social, political). And we must also include here the diverse forms of scientific statements and all literary genres (from the proverb to the multivolume novel). It might seem that speech genres are so heterogeneous that they do not have and cannot have a single common level at which they can be studied. For here, on one level of inquiry, appear such heterogeneous phenomena as the single-word everyday rejoinder and the multivolume novel, the military command that is standardized even in its intonation and the profoundly individual lyrical work, and so on. One might think that such functional heterogeneity makes the common features of speech genres excessively abstract and empty. This probably explains why the general problem of speech genres has never really been raised. Literary genres have been studied more than anything else. But from antiquity to the present, they have been studied in terms of their specific literary and artistic features, in terms of the differences that distinguish one from the other (within the realm of literature), and not as specific types of utterances distinct from other types, but sharing with them a common *verbal* (language) nature. The general linguistic problem of the utterance and its types has hardly been considered at all. Rhetorical genres have been studied since antiquity (and not much has been added in subsequent epochs to classical theory). At that time, more attention was already being devoted to the verbal nature of these genres as utterances: for example, to such aspects as the relation to the listener and his influence on the utterance, the specific verbal finalization of the utterance (as distinct from its completeness of thought), and so forth. But here, too, the specific features of rhetorical genres (judicial, political) still overshadowed their general linguistic nature. Finally, everyday speech genres have been studied (mainly rejoinders in everyday dialogue); and from a general linguistic standpoint (in the school of Saussure and among his later followers—the Structuralists, the American behaviorists, and, on a completely different linguistic basis, the Vosslerians).[2] But this line of inquiry could not lead to a correct determination of the general linguistic nature of the utterance either, since it was limited to the specific features of everyday oral speech, sometimes being directly and deliberately oriented toward primitive utterances (American behaviorists).

The extreme heterogeneity of speech genres and the attendant difficulty of determining the general nature of the utterance should in no way be underestimated. It is especially important here to draw attention to the very significant difference between primary (simple) and secondary (complex) speech genres (understood not as a functional difference). Secondary (complex) speech genres—novels, dramas, all kinds of scientific research, major genres of commentary, and so forth—arise in more complex and comparatively highly developed and organized cultural communication (primarily written) that is artistic, scientific, sociopolitical, and so on. During the process of their formation, they absorb and digest various primary (simple) genres that have taken form in unmediated speech communion. These primary genres are altered and assume a special character when they enter into complex ones. They lose their immediate relation to actual reality and to the real utterances of others. For example, rejoinders of everyday dialogue or letters found in a novel retain their form and their everyday significance only on the plane of the novel's content. They enter into actual reality only via the novel as a whole, that is, as a literary-artistic event and not as everyday life. The novel as a whole is an utterance just as rejoinders in everyday dialogue or private letters are (they do have a common nature), but unlike these, the novel is a secondary (complex) utterance.

The difference between primary and secondary (ideological) genres is very great and fundamental,[3] but this is precisely why the nature of the utterance should be revealed and defined through analysis of both types. Only then can the definition be adequate to the complex and profound nature of the utterance (and encompass its most important facets). A one-sided orientation toward primary genres inevitably leads to a vulgarization of the entire problem (behaviorist linguistics is an extreme example). The very interrelations between primary and secondary genres and the process of the historical formation of the latter shed light on the nature of the utterance (and above all on the complex problem of the interrelations among language, ideology, and world view).

A study of the nature of the utterance and of the diversity of generic forms of utterances in various spheres of human activity is immensely important to almost all areas of linguistics and philology. This is because any research whose material is concrete language—the history of a language, normative grammar, the compilation of any kind of dictionary, the stylistics of language, and so forth—inevitably deals with concrete utterances (written and oral) belonging to various spheres of human activity and communication: chronicles, contracts, texts of laws, clerical and other documents, various literary, scientific, and commentarial genres, official and personal letters, rejoinders in everyday dialogue (in all of their diverse subcategories), and so on. And it is here that scholars find the language data they need. A clear idea of the nature of the utterance in general and of the peculiarities of the various types of utterances (primary and secondary), that is, of various speech genres, is necessary, we think, for research in any special area. To ignore the nature of the utterance or to fail to consider the peculiarities of generic subcategories of speech in any area of linguistic study leads to perfunctoriness and excessive abstractness, distorts the historicity of the research, and weakens the link between language and life. After all, language enters life through concrete utterances (which manifest language) and life enters language through concrete utterances as well. The utterance is an exceptionally important node of problems. We shall approach certain areas and problems of the science of language in this context.

First of all, stylistics. Any style is inseparably related to the utterance and to typical forms of utterances, that is, speech genres. Any utterance—oral or written, primary or secondary, and in any sphere of communication—is individual and therefore can reflect the individuality of the speaker (or writer); that is, it possesses individual style. But not all genres are equally conducive to reflecting the individuality of the speaker in the language of the utterance, that is, to an individual style. The most conducive genres are those of artistic literature: here the individual style enters directly into the very task of the utterance, and this is one of its main goals (but even within artistic literature various genres offer different possibilities for expressing individuality in language and various aspects of individuality). The least favorable conditions for reflecting individuality in language obtain in speech genres that require a standard form, for example, many kinds of business documents, military commands, verbal signals in industry, and so on. Here one can reflect only the most superficial, almost biological aspects of individuality (mainly in the oral manifestation of these standard types of utterances). In the vast majority of speech genres (except for literary-artistic ones), the individual style does not enter into the intent of the utterance, does not serve as its only goal, but is, as it were, an epiphenomenon of the utterance, one of its by-products. Various genres can reveal various layers and facets of the individual personality, and individual style can be found in various interrelations with the national language. The very problem of the national and the individual in language is basically the problem of the utterance (after all, only here, in the utterance, is the national language embodied in individual form). The very determination of style in general, and individual style in particular, requires deeper study of both the nature of the utterance and the diversity of speech genres.

The organic, inseparable link between style and genre is clearly revealed also in the problem of language styles, or functional styles. In essence, language, or functional, styles are nothing other than generic styles for certain spheres of human activity and communication. Each sphere has and applies its own genres that correspond to its own specific conditions. There are also particular styles that correspond to these genres. A particular function (scientific, technical, commentarial, business, everyday) and the particular conditions of speech communication specific for each sphere give rise to particular genres, that is, certain relatively stable thematic, compositional, and stylistic types of utterances. Style is inseparably linked to particular thematic unities and—what is especially important—to particular compositional unities: to particular types of construction of the whole, types of its completion, and types of relations between the speaker and other participants in speech communication (listeners or readers, partners, the other's speech, and so forth). Style enters as one element into the generic unity of the utterance. Of course, this does not mean that language style cannot be the subject of its own independent study. Such a study, that is, of language stylistics as an independent discipline, is both feasible and necessary. But this study will be correct and productive only if based on a constant awareness of the generic nature of language styles, and on a preliminary study of the subcategories of speech genres. Up to this point the stylistics of language has not had such a basis. Hence its weakness. There is no generally recognized classification of language styles. Those who attempt to create them frequently fail to meet the fundamental logical requirement of classification: a unified basis.[4] Existing taxonomies are extremely poor and undifferentiated.[5] For example, a recently published academy grammar of the Russian language gives the following stylistic subcategories of language: bookish speech, popular speech, abstract-scientific, scientific-technical, journalistic-commentarial, official-business, and familiar everyday speech, as well as vulgar common parlance. In addition to these linguistic styles, there are the stylistic subcategories of dialectical words, archaic words, and occupational expressions. Such a classification of styles is completely random, and at its base lies a variety of principles (or bases) for division into styles. Moreover, this classification is both inexhaustive and inadequately differentiated. All this is a direct result of an inadequate understanding of the generic nature of linguistic styles, and the absence of a well-thought-out classification of speech genres in terms of spheres of human activity (and also ignorance of the distinction between primary and secondary genres, which is very important for stylistics).

It is especially harmful to separate style from genre when elaborating historical problems. Historical changes in language styles are inseparably linked to changes in speech genres. Literary language is a complex, dynamic system of linguistic styles. The proportions and interrelations of these styles in the system of literary language are constantly changing. Literary language, which also includes nonliterary styles, is an even more complex system, and it is organized on different bases. In order to puzzle out the complex historical dynamics of these systems and move from a simple (and, in the majority of cases, superficial) description of styles, which are always in evidence and alternating with one another, to a historical explanation of these changes, one must develop a special history of speech genres (and not only secondary, but also primary ones) that reflects more directly, clearly, and flexibly all the changes taking place in social life. Utterances and their types, that is, speech genres, are the drive belts from the history of society to the history of language. There is not a single new phenomenon (phonetic, lexical, or grammatical) that can enter the system of language without having traversed the long and complicated path of generic-stylistic testing and modification.[6]

In each epoch certain speech genres set the tone for the development of literary language. And these speech genres are not only secondary (literary, commentarial, and scientific), but also primary (certain types of oral dialogue—of the salon, of one's own circle, and other types as well, such as familiar, family-everyday, sociopolitical, philosophical, and so on). Any expansion of the literary language that results from drawing on various extraliterary strata of the national language inevitably entails some degree of penetration into all genres of written language (literary, scientific, commentarial, conversational, and so forth) to a greater or lesser degree, and entails new generic devices for the construction of the speech whole, its finalization, the accommodation of the listener or partner, and so forth. This leads to a more or less fundamental restructuring and renewal of speech genres. When dealing with the corresponding extraliterary strata of the national language, one inevitably also deals with the speech genres through which these strata are manifested. In the majority of cases, these are various types of conversational-dialogical genres. Hence the more or less distinct dialogization of secondary genres, the weakening of their monological composition, the new sense of the listener as a partner-interlocutor, new forms of finalization of the whole, and so forth. Where there is style there is genre. The transfer of style from one genre to another not only alters the way a style sounds, under conditions of a genre unnatural to it, but also violates or renews the given genre.

Thus, both individual and general language styles govern speech genres. A deeper and broader study of the latter is absolutely imperative for a productive study of any stylistic problem.

However, both the fundamental and the general methodological question of the interrelations between lexicon and grammar (on the one hand) and stylistics (on the other) rests on the same problem of the utterance and of speech genres.

Grammar (and lexicon) is essentially different from stylistics (some even oppose it to stylistics), but at the same time there is not a single grammatical study that can do without stylistic observation and excursus. In a large number of cases the distinction between grammar and stylistics appears to be completely erased. There are phenomena that some scholars include in the area of grammar while others include them in the area of stylistics. The syntagma is an example.

One might say that grammar and stylistics converge and diverge in any concrete language phenomenon. If considered only in the language system, it is a grammatical phenomenon, but if considered in the whole of the individual utterance or in a speech genre, it is a stylistic phenomenon. And this is because the speaker's very selection of a particular grammatical form is a stylistic act. But these two viewpoints of one and the same specific linguistic phenomenon should not be impervious to one another and should not simply replace one another mechanically. They should be organically combined (with, however, the most clear-cut methodological distinction between them) on the basis of the real unity of the language phenomenon. Only a profound understanding of the nature of the utterance and the particular features of speech genres can provide a correct solution to this complex methodological problem.

It seems to us that a study of the nature of the utterance and of speech genres is of fundamental importance for overcoming those simplistic notions about speech life, about the so-called speech flow, about communication and so forth—ideas which are still current in our language studies. Moreover, a study of the utterance as a *real unit of speech communion* will also make it possible to understand more correctly the *nature of language units* (as a system): words and sentences.

We shall now turn to this more general problem.

II. The Utterance as a Unit of Speech Communion: The Difference between This Unit and Units of Language (Words and Sentences)

Nineteenth-century linguistics, beginning with Wilhelm von Humboldt, while not denying the communicative function of language, tried to place it in the background as something secondary.[7] What it foregrounded was the function of thought emerging *independently of communication*. The famous Humboldtian formula goes like this: "Apart from the communication between one human and another, speech is a necessary condition for reflection *even in solitude*." Others, Vosslerians for example, emphasize the so-called expressive function. With all the various ways individual theoreticians understand this function, it essentially amounts to the expression of the speaker's individual discourse.

Language arises from man's need to express himself, to objectify himself. The essence of any form of language is somehow reduced to the spiritual creativity of the individuum. Several other versions of the function of language have been and are now being suggested, but it is still typical to underestimate, if not altogether ignore, the communicative function of language. Language is regarded from the speaker's standpoint as if there were only *one* speaker who does not have any *necessary* relation to *other* participants in speech communication. If the role of the other is taken into account at all, it is the role of a listener, who understands the speaker only passively. The utterance is adequate to its object (i.e., the content of the uttered thought) and to the person who is pronouncing the utterance. Language essentially needs only a speaker—one speaker—and an object for his speech. And if language also serves as a means of communication, this is a secondary function that has nothing to do with its essence. Of course, the language collective, the plurality of speakers, cannot be ignored when speaking of language, but when defining the essence of language this aspect is not a necessary one that determines the nature of language. Sometimes the language collective is regarded as a kind of collective personality, "the spirit of the people," and so forth, and immense significance is attached to it (by representatives of the "psychology of nations"),[8] but even in this case the plurality of speakers, and others with respect to each given speaker, is denied any real essential significance.

Still current in linguistics are such *fictions* as the "listener" and "understander" (partners of the "speaker"), the "unified speech flow," and so on. These fictions produce a completely distorted idea of the complex and multifaceted process of active speech communication. Courses in general linguistics (even serious ones like Saussure's) frequently present graphic-schematic depictions of the two partners in speech communication—the speaker and the listener (who perceives the speech)—and provide diagrams of the active speech processes of the speaker and the corresponding passive processes of the listener's perception and understanding of the speech. One cannot say that these diagrams are false or that they do not correspond to certain aspects of reality. But when they are put forth as the actual whole of speech communication, they become a scientific fiction. The fact is that when the listener perceives and understands the meaning (the language meaning) of speech, he simultaneously takes an active, responsive attitude toward it. He either agrees or disagrees with it (completely or partially), augments it, applies it, prepares for its execution, and so on. And the listener adopts this responsive attitude for the entire duration of the process of listening and understanding, from the very beginning—sometimes literally from the speaker's first word. Any understanding of live speech, a live utterance, is inherently responsive, although the degree of this activity varies extremely. Any understanding is imbued with response and necessarily elicits it in one form or another: the listener becomes the speaker. A passive understanding of the meaning of perceived speech is only an abstract aspect of the actual whole of actively responsive understanding, which is then actualized in a subsequent response that is actually articulated. Of course, an utterance is not always followed immediately by an articulated response. An actively responsive understanding of what is heard (a command, for example) can be directly realized in action (the execution of an order or command that has been understood and accepted for execution), or it can remain, for the time being, a silent responsive understanding (certain speech genres are intended exclusively for this kind of responsive understanding, for example, lyrical genres), but this is, so to speak, responsive understanding with a delayed reaction. Sooner or later what is heard and actively understood will find its response in the subsequent speech or behavior of the listener. In most cases, genres of complex cultural communication are intended precisely for this kind of actively responsive understanding with delayed action. Everything we have said here also pertains to written and read speech, with the appropriate adjustments and additions.

Thus, all real and integral understanding is actively responsive, and constitutes nothing other than the initial preparatory stage of a response (in whatever form it may be actualized). And the speaker himself is oriented precisely toward such an actively responsive understanding. He does not expect passive understanding that, so to speak, only duplicates his own idea in someone else's mind. Rather, he expects response, agreement, sympathy, objection, execution, and so forth (various speech genres presuppose various integral orientations and speech plans on the part of the speakers or writers). The desire to make one's speech understood is only an abstract aspect of the speaker's concrete and total speech plan. Moreover, any speaker is himself a respondent to a greater or lesser degree. He is not, after all, the first speaker, the one who disturbs the eternal silence of the universe. And he presupposes not only the existence of the language system he is using, but also the existence of preceding utterances—his own and others'—with which his given utterance enters into one kind of relation or another (builds on them, polemicizes with them, or simply presumes that they are already known to the listener). Any utterance is a link in a very complexly organized chain of other utterances.

[...]

But the utterance is related not only to preceding, but also to subsequent links in the chain of speech communion. When a speaker is creating an utterance, of course, these links do not exist. But from the very beginning, the utterance is constructed while taking into account possible responsive reactions, for whose sake, in essence, it is actually created. As we know, the role of the *others* for whom the utterance is constructed is extremely great. We have already said that the role of these others, for whom my thought becomes actual thought for the first time (and thus also for my own self as well) is not that of passive listeners, but of active participants in speech communication. From the very beginning, the speaker expects a response from them, an active responsive understanding. The entire utterance is constructed, as it were, in anticipation of encountering this response.

An essential (constitutive) marker of the utterance is its quality of being directed to someone, its *addressivity*. As distinct from the signifying units of a language—words and sentences—that are impersonal, belonging to nobody and addressed to nobody, the utterance has both an author (and, consequently, expression, which we have already discussed) and an addressee. This addressee can be an immediate participant-interlocutor in an everyday dialogue, a differentiated collective of specialists in some particular area of cultural communication, a more or less differentiated public, ethnic group, contemporaries, like-minded people, opponents and enemies, a subordinate, a superior, someone who is lower, higher, familiar, foreign, and so forth. And it can also be an indefinite, unconcretized *other* (with various kinds of monological utterances of an emotional type). All these varieties and conceptions of the addressee are determined by that area of human activity and everyday life to which the given utterance is related. Both the composition and, particularly, the style of the utterance depend on those to whom the utterance is addressed, how the speaker (or writer) senses and imagines his addressees, and the force of their effect on the utterance. Each speech genre in each area of speech communication has its own typical conception of the addressee, and this defines it as a genre.

The addressee of the utterance can, so to speak, coincide *personally* with the one (or ones) to whom the utterance responds. This personal coincidence is typical in everyday dialogue or in an exchange of letters. The person to whom I respond is my addressee, from whom I, in turn, expect a response (or in any case an active responsive understanding). But in such cases of personal coincidence one individual plays two different roles, and the difference between the roles is precisely what matters here. After all, the utterance of the person to whom I am responding (I agree, I object, I execute, I take under advisement, and so forth) is already at hand, but his response (or responsive understanding) is still forthcoming. When constructing my utterance, I try actively to determine this response. Moreover, I try to act in accordance with the response I anticipate, so this anticipated response, in turn, exerts an active influence on my utterance (I parry objections that I foresee, I make all kinds of provisos, and so forth). When speaking I always take into account the apperceptive background of the addressee's perception of my speech: the extent to which he is familiar with the situation, whether he has special knowledge of the given cultural area of communication, his views and convictions, his prejudices (from my viewpoint), his sympathies and antipathies—because all this will determine his active responsive understanding of my utterance. These considerations also determine my choice of a genre for my utterance, my choice of compositional devices, and, finally, my choice of language vehicles, that is, the *style* of my utterance. For example, genres of popular scientific literature are addressed to a particular group of readers with a particular apperceptive background of responsive understanding; special educational literature is addressed to another kind of reader, and special research work is addressed to an entirely different sort. In these cases, accounting for the addressee (and his apperceptive background) and for the addressee's influence on the construction of the utterance is very simple: it all comes down to the scope of his specialized knowledge.

In other cases, the matter can be much more complicated. Accounting for the addressee and anticipating his responsive reaction are frequently multifaceted processes that introduce unique internal dramatism into the utterance (in certain kinds of everyday dialogue, in letters, and in autobiographical and confessional genres). These phenomena are crucial, but more external, in rhetorical genres. The addressee's social position, rank, and importance are reflected in a special way in utterances of everyday and business speech communication. Under the conditions of a class structure and especially an aristocratic class structure, one observes an extreme differentiation of speech genres and styles, depending on the title, class, rank, wealth, social importance, and age of the addressee and the relative position of the speaker (or writer). Despite the wealth of differentiation, both of basic forms and of nuances, these phenomena are standard and external by nature: they cannot introduce any profound internal dramatism into the utterance. They are interesting only as instances of very crude, but still very graphic expressions of the addressee's influence on the construction and style of the utterance.[9]

Finer nuances of style are determined by the nature and degree of *personal* proximity of the addressee to the speaker in various familiar speech genres, on the one hand, and in intimate ones, on the other. With all the immense differences among familiar and intimate genres (and, consequently, styles), they perceive their addressees in exactly the same way: more or less outside the framework of the social hierarchy and social conventions, "without rank," as it were. This gives rise to a certain *candor* of speech (which in familiar styles sometimes approaches cynicism). In intimate styles this is expressed in an apparent desire for the speaker and addressee to merge completely. In familiar speech, since speech constraints and conventions have fallen away, one can take a special unofficial, volitional approach to reality.[10] This is why during the Renaissance familiar genres and styles could play such a large and positive role in destroying the official medieval picture of the world. In other periods as well, when the task was to destroy traditional official styles and world views that had faded and become conventional, familiar styles became very significant in literature. Moreover, familiarization of styles opened literature up to layers of language that had previously been under speech constraint. The significance of familiar genres and styles in literary history has not yet been adequately evaluated. Intimate genres and styles are based on a maximum internal proximity of the speaker and addressee (in extreme instances, as if they had merged). Intimate speech is imbued with a deep confidence in the addressee, in his sympathy, in the sensitivity and goodwill of his responsive understanding. In this atmosphere of profound trust, the speaker reveals his internal depths. This determines the special expressiveness and internal candor of these styles (as distinct from the loud street-language candor of familiar speech). Familiar and intimate genres and styles (as yet very little studied) reveal extremely clearly the dependence of style on a certain sense and understanding of the addressee (the addressee of the utterance) on the part of the speaker, and on the addressee's actively responsive understanding that is anticipated by the speaker. These styles reveal especially clearly the narrowness and incorrectness of traditional stylistics, which tries to understand and define style solely from the standpoint of the semantic and thematic content of speech and the speaker's expressive attitude toward this content. Unless one accounts for the speaker's attitude toward the *other* and his utterances (existing or anticipated), one can understand neither the genre nor the style of speech. But even the so-called neutral or objective styles of exposition that concentrate maximally on their subject matter and, it would seem, are free of any consideration of the other still involve a certain conception of their addressee. Such objectively neutral styles select language vehicles not only from the standpoint of their adequacy to the subject matter of speech, but also from the standpoint of the presumed apperceptive background of the addressee. But this background is taken into account in as generalized a way as possible, and is abstracted from the expressive aspect (the expression of the speaker himself is also minimal in the objective style). Objectively neutral styles presuppose something like an identity of the addressee and the speaker, a unity of their viewpoints, but this identity and unity are purchased at the price of almost complete forfeiture of expression. It must be noted that the nature of objectively neutral styles (and, consequently, the concept of the addressee on which they are based) is fairly diverse, depending on the differences between the areas of speech communication.

This question of the concept of the speech addressee (how the speaker or writer senses and imagines him) is of immense significance in literary history. Each epoch, each literary trend and literary-artistic style, each literary genre within an epoch or trend, is typified by its own special concepts of the addressee of the literary work, a special sense and understanding of its reader, listener, public, or people. A historical study of changes in these concepts would be an interesting and important task. But in order to develop it productively, the statement of the problem itself would have to be theoretically clear.

It should be noted that, in addition to those real meanings and ideas of one's addressee that actually determine the style of the utterances (works), the history of literature also includes conventional or semi-conventional forms of address to readers, listeners, posterity, and so forth, just as, in addition to the actual author, there are also conventional and semiconventional images of substitute authors, editors, and various kinds of narrators. The vast majority of literary genres are secondary, complex genres composed of various transformed primary genres (the rejoinder in dialogue, everyday stories, letters, diaries, minutes, and so forth). As a rule, these secondary genres of complex cultural communication *play out* various forms of primary speech communication. Here also is the source of all literary/conventional characters of authors, narrators, and addressees. But the most complex and ultra-composite work of a secondary genre as a whole (viewed as a whole) is a single integrated real utterance that has a real author and real addressees whom this author perceives and imagines.

Thus, addressivity, the quality of turning to someone, is a constitutive feature of the utterance; without it the utterance does not and cannot exist. The various typical forms this addressivity assumes and the various concepts of the addressee are constitutive, definitive features of various speech genres.

NOTES

1. "National unity of language" is a shorthand way of referring to the assemblage of linguistic and translinguistic practices common to a given region. It is, then, a good example of what Bakhtin means by an open unity. See also Otto Jesperson, *Mankind, Nation, and Individual* (Bloomington: Indiana University Press, 1964). [Editor's note]

2. Saussure's teaching is based on a distinction between language (*la langue*)—a system of interconnected signs and forms that normatively determine each individual speech act and are the special object of linguistics—and speech (*la parole*)—individual instances of language use. Bakhtin discusses Saussure's teachings in *Marxism and the Philosophy of Language* as one of the two main trends in linguistic thought (the trend of "abstract objectivism") that he uses to shape his own theory of the utterance. See V. N. Voloshinov, *Marxism and the Philosophy of Language*, tr. Ladislav Matejka and I. R. Titunik (New York: Seminar Press, 1973), esp. pp. 58–61.

"Behaviorists" here refers to the school of psychology introduced by the Harvard physiologist J. B. Watson in 1913. It seeks to explain animal and human behavior entirely in terms of observable and measurable responses to external stimuli. Watson, in his insistence that behavior is a physiological reaction to environmental stimuli, denied the value of introspection and of the concept of consciousness. He saw mental processes as bodily movements, even when unperceived, so that thinking in his view is subvocal speech. There is a strong connection as well between the behaviorist school of psychology and the school of American descriptive linguistics, which is what Bakhtin is referring to here. The so-called decriptivist school was founded by the eminent anthropologist Franz Boas (1858–1942). Its closeness to behaviorism consists in its insistence on careful observation unconditioned by presuppositions or categories taken from traditional language structure. Leonard Bloomfield (1887–1949) was the chief spokesman for the school and was explicit about his commitment to a "mechanist approach" (his term for the behaviorist school of psychology): "Mechanists demand that the facts be presented without any assumption of such auxiliary factors [as a version of the mind]. I have tried to meet this demand. . . ." (*Language* [New York: Holt, Rinehart, and Winston, 1933], p. vii). Two prominent linguists sometimes associated with the descriptivists, Edward Sapir (1884–1939) and his pupil Benjamin Lee Whorf (1897–1941), differ from Bloomfield insofar as behaviorism plays a relatively minor role in their work.

"Vosslerians" refers to the movement named after the German philologist Karl Vossler (1872–1949), whose adherents included Leo Spitzer (1887–1960). For Vosslerians, the reality of language is the continuously creative, constructive activity that is prosecuted through speech acts; the creativity of language is likened to artistic creativity, and stylistics becomes the leading discipline. Style takes precedence over grammar, and the standpoint of the speaker takes precedence over that of the listener. In a number of aspects, Bakhtin is close to the Vosslerians, but differs in his understanding of the utterance as the concrete reality of language life. Bakhtin does not, like the Vosslerians, conceive the utterance to be an individual speech act; rather, he emphasizes the "inner sociality" in speech communication—an aspect that is objectively reinforced in speech genres. The concept of speech genres is central to Bakhtin, then, in that it separates his translinguistics from both Saussureans and Vosslerians in the philosophy of language. [Editor's note]

3. "Ideology" should not be confused with the politically oriented English word. Ideology as it is used here is essentially any system of ideas. But ideology is semiotic in the sense that it involves the concrete exchange of signs in society and history. Every word/discourse betrays the ideology of its speaker; every speaker is thus an ideologue and every utterance an ideologeme. [Editor's note]

4. A unified basis for classifying the enormous diversity of utterances is an obsession of Bakhtin's, one that relates him directly to Wilhelm von Humboldt (1767–1835), the first in the modern period to argue systematically that language is the vehicle of thought. He calls language the "labor of the mind" (*Arbeit des Geistes*) in his famous formulation "[language] itself is not [mere] work (*ergon*), but an activity (*energeia*) . . . it is in fact the labor of the mind that otherwise would eternally repeat itself to make articulated sound capable of the expression

of thought" (*Über die Verschiedenheit des menschlichen Sprachbaues*, in *Werke*, vol. 7 [Berlin: De Gruyter, 1968], p. 46). What is important here is that for Bakhtin, as for von Humboldt, the diversity of languages *is itself of philosophical significance*, for if thought and speech are one, does not each language embody a unique way of thinking? It is here that Bakhtin also comes very close to the work of Sapir and, especially, of Whorf. See Benjamin Lee Whorf, *Language, Thought, and Reality*, ed. John B. Carroll (Cambridge, Mass.: MIT Press, 1956), esp. pp. 212–19 and 239–45. [Editor's note]

5. The same kinds of classifications of language styles, impoverished and lacking clarity, with a fabricated foundation, are given by A. N. Gvozdev in his book *Ocherki po stilistike russkogo jazyka* (Essays on the stylistics of the Russian language) (Moscow, 1952, pp. 13–15). All of these classifications are based on an uncritical assimilation of traditional ideas about language styles. [Bakhtin's note]

6. This thesis of ours has nothing in common with the Vosslerian idea of the primacy of the stylistic over the grammatical. Our subsequent exposition will make this completely clear. [Bakhtin's note]

7. See Wilhelm von Humboldt, *Linguistic Variability and Intellectual Development* (Coral Gables: University of Miami Press, 1971). [Editor's note]

8. The phrase "psychology of nations" refers to a school organized around the nineteenth-century journal *Zeitschrift für Volkerpsychologie und Sprachwissenschaft*, whose leading spokesman, Kermann Steinthal, was among the first to introduce psychology (especially that of the Kantian biologist Herbart) into language (and vice versa). Steinthal was attracted to von Humboldt's idea of "innere Sprachform" and was important in Potebnya's attempts to wrestle with inner speech. [Editor's note]

9. I am reminded of an apposite observation of Gogol's: "One cannot enumerate all the nuances and fine points of our communication . . . we have slick talkers who will speak quite differently with a landowner who has 200 souls than with one who has 300, and again he will not speak the same way with one who has 300 as he will with one who has 500, and he will not speak the same way with one who has 500 as he will with one who has 800; in a word, you can go up to a million and you will still find different nuances" (*Dead Souls*, chapter 3). [Bakhtin's note]

10. The loud candor of the streets, calling things by their real names, is typical of this style. [Bakhtin's note]

4.2 Closing Statement: Linguistics and Poetics (1960)

Roman Jakobson

I have been asked for summary remarks about poetics in its relation to linguistics. Poetics deals primarily with the question, *What makes a verbal message a work of art?* Because the main subject of poetics is the *differentia specifica* of verbal art in relation to other arts and in relation to other kinds of verbal behavior, poetics is entitled to the leading place in literary studies.

Poetics deals with problems of verbal structure, just as the analysis of painting is concerned with pictorial structure. Since linguistics is the global science of verbal structure, poetics may be regarded as an integral part of linguistics.

Arguments against such a claim must be thoroughly discussed. It is evident that many devices studied by poetics are not confined to verbal art. We can refer to the possibility of transposing *Wuthering Heights* into a motion picture, medieval legends into frescoes and miniatures, or *L'après-midi d'un faune* into music, ballet, and graphic art. However ludicrous may appear the idea of the *Iliad* and *Odyssey* in comics, certain structural features of their plot are preserved despite the disappearance of their verbal shape. The question whether Blake's illustrations to the *Divina Commedia* are or are not adequate is a proof that different arts are comparable. The problems of baroque or any other historical style transgress the frame of a single art. When handling the surrealistic metaphor, we could hardly pass by Max Ernst's pictures or Luis Buñuel's films, *The Andalusian Dog* and *The Golden Age*. In short, many poetic features belong not only to the science of language but to the whole theory of signs, that is, to general semiotics. This statement, however, is valid not only for verbal art but also for all varieties of language since language shares many properties with some other systems of signs or even with all of them (pansemiotic features).

Likewise a second objection contains nothing that would be specific for literature: the question of relations between the word and the world concerns not only verbal art but actually all kinds of discourse. Linguistics is likely to explore all possible problems of relation between discourse and the "universe of discourse": what of this universe is verbalized by a given discourse and how is it verbalized. The truth values, however, as far as they are—to say with the logicians—"extralinguistic entities," obviously exceed the bounds of poetics and of linguistics in general.

Sometimes we hear that poetics, in contradistinction to linguistics, is concerned with evaluation. This separation of the two fields from each other is based on a current but erroneous interpretation of the contrast between the structure of poetry and other types of verbal structure: the latter are said to be opposed by their "casual," designless nature to the "noncasual," purposeful character of poetic language. In point of fact, any verbal behavior is goal-directed, but the aims are different and the conformity of the means used to the effect aimed at is a problem that evermore preoccupies inquirers into the diverse kinds of verbal communication. There is a close correspondence, much closer than critics believe, between the question of linguistic phenomena expanding in space and time and the spatial and temporal spread of literary models. Even such discontinuous expansion as the resurrection of neglected or forgotten poets—for instance, the posthumous discovery and subsequent canonization of Gerard Manley Hopkins (d. 1889), the tardy fame of Lautréamont (d. 1870) among surrealist poets, and the salient influence of the hitherto ignored Cyprian Norwid (d. 1883) on Polish modern poetry—find a parallel in the history of standard languages which are prone to revive outdated models, sometimes long forgotten, as was the case in literary Czech which toward the beginning of the nineteenth century leaned to sixteenth-century models.

Unfortunately the terminological confusion of "literary studies" with "criticism" tempts the student of literature to replace the description of the intrinsic values of a literary work by a subjective, censorious verdict. The label "literary critic" applied to an investigator of literature is as erroneous as "grammatical (or lexical) critic" would be applied to a linguist. Syntactic and morphologic research cannot be supplanted by a normative grammar, and likewise no manifesto, foisting a critic's own tastes and opinions on creative literature, may act as substitute for an objective scholarly analysis of verbal art. This statement is not to be mistaken for the quietist principle of *laissez faire*; any verbal culture involves programmatic, planning, normative endeavors. Yet why is a clear-cut discrimination made between pure and applied linguistics or between phonetics and orthoëpy but not between literary studies and criticism?

Literary studies, with poetics as their focal portion, consist like linguistics of two sets of problems: synchrony and diachrony. The synchronic description envisages not only the literary production of any given stage but also that part of the literary tradition which for the stage in question has remained vital or has been revived. Thus, for instance, Shakespeare on the one hand and Donne, Marvell, Keats, and Emily Dickinson on the other are experienced by the present English poetic world, whereas the works of James Thomson and Longfellow, for the time being, do not belong to viable artistic values. The selection of classics and their reinterpretation by a novel trend is a substantial problem of synchronic literary studies. Synchronic poetics, like synchronic linguistics, is not to be confused with statics; any stage discriminates between more conservative and more innovatory forms. Any contemporary stage is experienced in its temporal dynamics, and, on the other hand, the historical approach both in poetics and in linguistics is concerned not only with changes but also with continuous, enduring, static factors. A thoroughly comprehensive historical poetics or history of language is a superstructure to be built on a series of successive synchronic descriptions.

Insistence on keeping poetics apart from linguistics is warranted only when the field of linguistics appears to be illicitly restricted, for example, when the sentence is viewed by some linguists as the highest analyzable construction or when the scope of linguistics is confined to grammar alone or uniquely to nonsemantic questions of external form or to the inventory of denotative devices with no reference to free variations. Voegelin has clearly pointed out the two most important and related problems which face structural linguistics, namely, a revision of "the monolithic hypothesis of language" and a concern with "the interdependence of diverse structures within one language." No doubt, for any speech community, for any speaker, there exists a unity of language, but this over-all code represents a system of interconnected subcodes; each language encompasses several concurrent patterns which are each characterized by a different function.

Obviously we must agree with Sapir that, on the whole, "ideation reigns supreme in language . . . ",[1] but this supremacy does not authorize linguistics to disregard the "secondary factors." The emotive elements of speech which, as Joos is prone to believe, cannot be described "with a finite number of absolute categories," are classified by him "as nonlinguistic elements of the real world." Hence, "for us they remain vague, protean, fluctuating phenomena," he concludes, "which we refuse to tolerate in our science."[2] Joos is indeed a brilliant expert in reduction experiments, and his emphatic requirement for an "expulsion" of the emotive elements "from linguistic science" is a radical experiment in reduction—*reductio ad absurdum*.

Language must be investigated in all the variety of its functions. Before discussing the poetic function we must define its place among the other functions of language. An outline of these functions demands a concise survey of the constitutive factors in any speech event, in any act of verbal communication. The ADDRESSER sends a MESSAGE to the ADDRESSEE. To be operative the message requires a CONTEXT referred to ("referent" in another, somewhat ambiguous, nomenclature), seizable by the addressee, and either verbal or capable of being verbalized; a CODE fully, or at least partially, common to the addresser and addressee (or in other words, to the encoder and decoder of the message); and, finally, a CONTACT, a physical channel and psychological connection between the addresser and the addressee, enabling both of them to enter and stay in communication. All these factors inalienably involved in verbal communication may be schematized as follows:

CONTEXT
ADDRESSER MESSAGE ADDRESSEE
CONTACT
CODE

Each of these six factors determines a different function of language. Although we distinguish six basic aspects of language, we could, however, hardly find verbal messages that would fulfill only one function. The diversity lies not in a monopoly of some one of these several functions but in a different hierarchical order of functions. The verbal structure of a message depends primarily on the predominant function. But even though a set (*Einstellung*) toward the referent, an orientation toward the CONTEXT—briefly the so-called REFERENTIAL, "denotative," "cognitive" function—is the leading task of numerous messages, the accessory participation of the other functions in such messages must be taken into account by the observant linguist.

The so-called EMOTIVE or "expressive" function, focused on the ADDRESSER, aims a direct expression of the speaker's attitude toward what he is speaking about. It tends to produce an impression of a certain emotion whether true or feigned; therefore, the term "emotive," launched and advocated by Marty has proved to be preferable to "emotional."[3] The purely emotive stratum in language is presented by the interjections. They differ from the means of referential language both by their sound pattern (peculiar sound sequences or even sounds elsewhere unusual) and by their syntactic role (they are not components but equivalents of sentences). "*Tut! Tut!* said McGinty": the complete utterance of Conan Doyle's character consists of two suction clicks. The emotive function, laid bare in the interjections, flavors to some extent all our utterances, on their phonic, grammatical, and lexical level. If we analyze language from the standpoint of the information it carries, we cannot restrict the notion of information to the cognitive aspect of language. A man, using expressive features to indicate his angry or ironic attitude, conveys ostensible information, and evidently this verbal behavior cannot be likened to such nonsemiotic, nutritive activities as "eating grapefruit" (despite Chatman's bold simile). The difference between [big] and the emphatic prolongation of the vowel [bi:g] is a conventional, coded linguistic feature like the difference between the short and long vowel in such Czech pairs as [vi] 'you' and [vi:] 'knows,' but in the latter pair the differential information is phonemic and in the former emotive. As long as we are interested in phonemic invariants, the English /i/ and /i:/ appear to be mere variants of one and the same phoneme, but if we are concerned with emotive units, the relation between the invariant and variants is reversed: length and shortness are invariants implemented by variable phonemes. Saporta's surmise that emotive difference is a nonlinguistic feature, "attributable to the delivery of the message and not to the message," arbitrarily reduces the informational capacity of messages.

A former actor of Stanislavskij's Moscow Theater told me how at his audition he was asked by the famous director to make forty different messages from the phrase *Segodnja večerom* 'This evening,' by diversifying its expressive tint. He made a list of some forty emotional situations, then emitted the given phrase in accordance with each of these situations, which his audience had to recognize only from the changes in the sound shape of the same two words. For our research work in the description and analysis of contemporary Standard Russian (under the auspices of the Rockefeller Foundation) this actor was asked to repeat Stanislavskij's test. He wrote down some fifty situations framing the same elliptic sentence and made of it fifty corresponding messages for a tape record. Most of the messages were correctly and circumstantially decoded by Moscovite listeners. May I add that all such emotive cues easily undergo linguistic analysis.

Orientation toward the ADDRESSEE, the CONATIVE function, finds its purest grammatical expression in the vocative and imperative, which syntactically, morphologically, and often even phonemically deviate from other nominal and verbal categories. The imperative sentences cardinally differ from declarative sentences: the latter are and the former are not liable to a truth test. When in O'Neill's play *The Fountain*, Nano, "(in a fierce tone of command)," says "Drink!"—the imperative cannot be challenged by the question "is it true or not?" which may be, however, perfectly well asked after such sentences as "one drank," "one will drink," "one would drink." In contradistinction to the imperative sentences, the declarative sentences are convertible into interrogative sentences: "did one drink?" "will one drink?" "would one drink?"

The traditional model of language as elucidated particularly by Bühler[4] was confined to these three functions emotive, conative, and referential—and the three apexes of this model—the first person of the addresser, the second person of the addressee, and the "third person," properly—someone or something spoken of. Certain additional verbal functions can be easily inferred from this triadic model. Thus the magic, incantatory function is chiefly some kind of conversion of an absent or inanimate "third person" into an addressee of a conative message. "May this sty dry up, *tfu, tfu, tfu, tfu*" (Lithuanian spell 69).[5] "Water, queen river, daybreak! Send grief beyond the blue sea, to the sea-bottom, like a grey stone never to rise from the sea-bottom, may grief never come to burden the light heart of God's servant, may grief be removed and sink away." (North Russian incantation 217f.).[6] "Sun, stand thou still upon Gibeon; and thou, Moon, in the valley of Aj-a-lon. And the sun stood still, and the moon stayed . . ." (Josh. 10.12). We observe, however, three further constitutive factors of verbal communication and three corresponding functions of language.

There are messages primarily serving to establish, to prolong, or to discontinue communication, to check whether the channel works ("Hello, do you hear me?"), to attract the attention of the interlocutor or to confirm his continued attention ("Are you listening?" or in Shakespearean diction, "Lend me your ears!"—and on the other end of the wire "Um-hum!"). This set for CONTACT, or in Malinowski's terms PHATIC function,[7] may be displayed by a profuse exchange of ritualized formulas, by entire dialogues with the mere purport of prolonging communication. Dorothy Parker caught eloquent examples: "'Well!' the young man said. 'Well!' she said. 'Well, here we are,' he said. 'Here we are,' she said, 'Aren't we?' 'I should say we were,' he said, 'Eeyop! Here we are.' 'Well!' she said. 'Well!' he said, 'well.'" The endeavor to start and sustain communication is typical of talking birds; thus the phatic function of language is the only one they share with human beings. It is also the first verbal function acquired by infants; they are prone to communicate before being able to send or receive informative communication.

A distinction has been made in modern logic between two levels of language, "object language" speaking of objects and "metalanguage" speaking of language. But metalanguage is not only a necessary scientific tool utilized by logicians and linguists; it plays also an important role in our everday language. Like Molière's Jourdain who used prose without knowing it, we practice metalanguage without realizing the metalingual character of our operations. Whenever the addresser and/or the addressee need to check up whether they use the same code, speech is focused on the CODE: it performs a METALINGUAL (i.e., glossing) function. "I don't follow you—what do you mean?" asks the addressee, or in Shakespearean diction, "What is't thou say'st?" And the addresser in anticipation of such recapturing questions inquires: "Do you know what I mean?" Imagine such an exasperating dialogue: "The sophomore was plucked." "But what is *plucked*?" "*Plucked* means the same as *flunked*." "And *flunked*?" "*To be flunked* is *to fail in an exam*." "And what is *sophomore*?" persists the interrogator innocent of school vocabulary. "A *sophomore* is (or means) a *second-year student*." All these equational sentences convey information merely about the lexical code of English; their function is strictly metalingual. Any process of language learning, in particular child acquisition of the mother tongue, makes wide use of such metalingual operations; and aphasia may often be defined as a loss of ability for metalingual operations.

We have brought up all the six factors involved in verbal communication except the message itself. The set (*Einstellung*) toward the MESSAGE as such, focus on the message for its own sake, is the POETIC function of language. This function cannot he productively studied out of touch with the general problems of language, and, on the other hand, the scrutiny of language requires a thorough consideration of its poetic function. Any attempt to reduce the sphere of poetic function to poetry or to confine poetry to poetic function would be a delusive oversimplification. Poetic function is not the sole function of verbal art but only its dominant, determining function, whereas in all other verbal activities it acts as a subsidiary, accessory constituent. This function, by promoting the palpability of signs, deepens the fundamental dichotomy of signs and objects. Hence, when dealing with poetic function, linguistics cannot limit itself to the field of poetry.

"Why do you always say *Joan and Margery*, yet never *Margery and Joan*? Do you prefer Joan to her twin sister?" "Not at all, it just sounds smoother." In a sequence of two coordinate names, as far as no rank problems interfere, the precedence of the shorter name suits the speaker, unaccountably for him, as a well-ordered shape of the message.

A girl used to talk about "the horrible Harry." "Why horrible?" "Because I hate him." "But why not *dreadful, terrible, frightful, disgusting*?" "I don't know why, but *horrible* fits him better." Without realizing it, she clung to the poetic device of paronomasia.

The political slogan "I like Ike" /ay layk ayk/, succinctly structured, consists of three monosyllables and counts three diphthongs /ay/, each of them symmetrically followed by one consonantal phoneme, /..l..k ..k/. The make-up of the three words presents a variation: no consonantal phonemes in the first word, two around the diphthong in the second, and one final consonant in the third. A similar dominant nucleus /ay/ was noticed by Hymes in some of the sonnets of Keats. Both cola of the trisyllabic formula "I like / Ike" rhyme with each other, and the second of the two rhyming words is fully included in the first one (echo rhyme), /layk/—/ayk/, a paronomastic image of a feeling which totally envelops its object. Both cola alliterate with each other, and the first of the two alliterating words is included in the second: /ay/—/ayk/, a paronomastic image of the loving subject enveloped by the beloved object. The secondary, poetic function of this electional catch phrase reinforces its impressiveness and efficacy.

As we said, the linguistic study of the poetic function must overstep the limits of poetry, and, on the other hand, the linguistic scrutiny of poetry cannot limit itself to the poetic function. The particularities of diverse poetic genres imply a differently ranked participation of the other verbal functions along with the dominant poetic function. Epic poetry, focused on the third person, strongly involves the referential function of language; the lyric, oriented toward the first person, is intimately linked with the emotive function; poetry of the second person is imbued with the conative function and is either supplicatory or exhortative, depending on whether the first person is subordinated to the second one or the second to the first.

Now that our cursory description of the six basic functions of verbal communication is more or less complete, we may complement our scheme of the fundamental factors by a corresponding scheme of the functions:

REFERENTIAL

EMOTIVE POETIC CONATIVE

PHATIC

METALINGUAL

What is the empirical linguistic criterion of the poetic function? In particular, what is the indispensable feature inherent in any piece of poetry? To answer this question we must recall the two basic modes of arrangement used in verbal behavior, *selection* and *combination*. If "child" is the topic of the message, the speaker selects one among the extant, more or less similar, nouns like child, kid, youngster, tot, all of them equivalent in a certain respect, and then, to comment on this topic, he may select one of the semantically cognate verbs—sleeps, dozes, nods, naps. Both chosen words combine in the speech chain. The selection is produced on the base of equivalence, similarity and dissimilarity, synonymity and antonymity, while the combination, the build up of the sequence, is based on contiguity. *The poetic function projects the principle of equivalence from the axis of selection into the axis of combination*. Equivalence is promoted to the constitutive device of the sequence. In poetry one syllable is equalized with any other syllable of the same sequence; word stress is assumed to equal word stress, as unstress equals unstress; prosodic long is matched with long, and short with short; word boundary equals word boundary, no boundary equals no boundary; syntactic pause equals syntactic pause, no pause equals no pause. Syllables are converted into units of measure, and so are morae or stresses.

It may be objected that metalanguage also makes a sequential use of equivalent units when combining synonymic expressions into an equational sentence: $A = A$ ("*Mare* is *the female of the horse*"). Poetry and metalanguage, however, are in diametrical opposition to each other: in metalanguage the sequence is used to build an equation, whereas in poetry the equation is used to build a sequence.

In poetry, and to a certain extent in latent manifestations of poetic function, sequences delimited by word boundaries become commensurable whether they are sensed as isochronic or graded. "Joan and Margery" showed us the poetic principle of syllable gradation, the same principle which in the close of Serbian folk epics has been raised to a compulsory law.[8] Without its two dactylic words the combination "*inn*ocent by*stand*er" would hardly have become a hackneyed phrase. The symmetry of three disyllabic verbs with an identical initial consonant and identical final vowel added splendor to the laconic victory message of Caesar: "*Veni, vidi, vici*."

Measure of sequences is a device which, outside of poetic function, finds no application in language. Only in poetry with its regular reiteration of equivalent units is the time of the speech flow experienced, as it is—to cite another semiotic pattern—with musical time. Gerard Manley Hopkins, an outstanding searcher in the science of poetic language, defined verse as "speech wholly or partially repeating the same figure of sound."[9] Hopkins' subsequent question, "but is all verse poetry?" can be definitely answered as soon as poetic function ceases to be arbitrarily confined to the domain of poetry. Mnemonic lines cited by Hopkins (like "Thirty days hath September"), modern advertising jingles, and versified medieval laws, mentioned by Lotz, or finally Sanscrit scientific treatises in verse which in Indic tradition are strictly distinguished from true poetry (*kāvya*)—all these metrical texts make use of poetic function without, however, assigning to this function the coercing, determining role it carries in poetry. Thus verse actually exceeds the limits of poetry, but at the same time verse always implies poetic function. And apparently no human culture ignores versemaking, whereas there are many cultural patterns without "applied" verse; and even in such cultures which possess both pure and applied verses, the latter appear to be a secondary, unquestionably derived phenomenon. The adaptation of poetic means for some heterogeneous purpose does not conceal their primary essence, just as elements of emotive language, when utilized in poetry, still maintain their emotive tinge. A filibusterer may recite *Hiawatha* because it is long, yet poeticalness still remains the primary intent of this text itself. Self-evidently, the existence of versified, musical, and pictorial commercials does not separate the questions of verse or of musical and pictorial form from the study of poetry, music, and fine arts.

To sum up, the analysis of verse is entirely within the competence of poetics, and the latter may be defined as that part of linguistics which treats the poetic function in its relationship to the other functions of language. Poetics in the wider sense of the word deals with the poetic function not only in poetry, where this function is superimposed upon the other functions of language, but also outside of poetry, when some other function is superimposed upon the poetic function.

The reiterative "figure of sound," which Hopkins saw to be the constitutive principle of verse, can be further specified. Such a figure always utilizes at least one (or more than one) binary contrast of a relatively high and relatively low prominence effected by the different sections of the phonemic sequence.

Within a syllable the more prominent, nuclear, syllabic part, constituting the peak of the syllable, is opposed to the less prominent, marginal, nonsyllabic phonemes. Any syllable contains a syllabic phoneme, and the interval between two successive syllabics is in some languages always and in others overwhelmingly carried out by marginal, nonsyllabic phonemes. In the so-called syllabic versification the number of syllabics in a metrically delimited chain (time series) is a constant, whereas the presence of a nonsyllabic phoneme or cluster between every two syllabics of a metrical chain is a constant only in languages with an indispensable occurrence of nonsyllabics between syllabics and, furthermore, in those verse systems where hiatus is prohibited. Another manifestation of a tendency toward a uniform syllabic model is the avoidance of closed syllables at the end of the line, observable, for instance, in Serbian epic songs. The Italian syllabic verse shows a tendency to treat a sequence of vowels unseparated by consonantal phonemes as one single metrical syllable.[10]

In some patterns of versification the syllable is the only constant unit of verse measure, and a grammatical limit is the only constant line of demarcation between measured sequences, whereas in other patterns syllables in turn are dichotomized into more and less prominent, and/or two levels of grammatical limits are distinguished in their metrical function, word boundaries and syntactic pauses.

Except the varieties of the so-called vers libre that are based on conjugate intonations and pauses only, any meter uses the syllable as a unit of measure at least in certain sections of the verse. Thus in the purely accentual verse ("sprung rhythm" in Hopkins' vocabulary), the number of syllables in the upbeat (called "slack" by Hopkins) may vary, but the downbeat (ictus) constantly contains one single syllable.

In any accentual verse the contrast between higher and lower prominence is achieved by syllables under stress versus unstressed syllables. Most accentual patterns operate primarily with the contrast of syllables with and without word stress, but some varieties of accentual verse deal with syntactic, phrasal stresses, those which Wimsatt and Beardsley cite as "the major stresses of the major words" and which are opposed as prominent to syllables without such major, syntactic stress.

In the quantitative ("chronemic") verse, long and short syllables are mutually opposed as more and less prominent. This contrast is usually carried out by syllable nuclei, phonemically long and short. But in metrical patterns like Ancient Greek and Arabic, which equalize length "by position" with length "by nature," the minimal syllables consisting of a consonantal phoneme and one mora vowel are opposed to syllables with a surplus (a second mora or a closing consonant) as simpler and less prominent syllables opposed to those that are more complex and prominent.

The question still remains open whether, besides the accentual and the chronemic verse, there exists a "tonemic" type of versification in languages where differences of syllabic intonations are used to distinguish word meanings.[11] In classical Chinese poetry,[12] syllables with modulations (in Chinese *tsê*, 'deflected tones') are opposed to the nonmodulated syllables (*p'ing*, 'level tones'), but apparently a chronemic principle underlies this opposition, as was suspected by Polivanov[13] and keenly interpreted by Wang Li;[14] in the Chinese metrical tradition the level tones prove to be opposed to the deflected tones as long tonal peaks of syllables to short ones, so that verse is based on the opposition of length and shortness.

Joseph Greenberg brought to my attention another variety of tonemic versification—the verse of Efik riddles based on the level feature. In the sample cited by Simmons,[15] the query and the response form two octosyllables with an alike distribution of *h*(igh)- and *l*(ow)-tone syllabics; in each hemistich, moreover, the last three of the four syllables present an identical tonemic pattern: *lhhl/hhhl//lhhl/hhhl//*. Whereas Chinese versification appears as a peculiar variety of the quantitative verse, the verse of the Efic riddles is linked with the usual accentual verse by an opposition of two degrees of prominence (strength or height) of the vocal tone. Thus a metrical system of versification can be based only on the opposition of syllabic peaks and slopes (syllabic verse), on the relative level of the peaks (accentual verse), and on the relative length of the syllabic peaks or entire syllables (quantitative verse).

In textbooks of literature we sometimes encounter a superstitious contraposition of syllabism as a mere mechanical count of syllables to the lively pulsation of accentual verse. If we examine, however, the binary meters of the strictly syllabic and at the same time, accentual versification, we observe two homogeneous successions of wavelike peaks and valleys. Of these two undulatory curves, the syllabic one carries nuclear phonemes in the crest and usually marginal phonemes in the bottom. As a rule the accentual curve superposed upon the syllabic curve alternates stressed and unstressed syllables in the crests and bottoms respectively.

For comparison with the English meters which we have lengthily discussed, I bring to your attention the similar Russian binary verse forms which for the last fifty years have verily undergone an exhaustive investigation.[16] The structure of the verse can be very thoroughly described and interpreted in terms of enchained probabilities. Besides the compulsory word boundary between the lines, which is an invariant throughout all Russian meters, in the classic pattern of Russian syllabic accentual verse ("syllabo-tonic" in native nomenclature) we observe the following constants: (1) the number of syllables in the line from its beginning to the last downbeat is stable; (2) this very last down-beat always carries a word stress; (3) a stressed syllable cannot fall on the upbeat if a downbeat is fulfilled by an unstressed syllable of the same word unit (so that a word stress can coincide with an upbeat only as far as it belongs to a monosyllabic word unit).

Along with these characteristics compulsory for any line composed in a given meter, there are features that show a high probability of occurrence without being constantly present. Besides signals certain to occur ("probability one"), signals likely to occur ("probabilities less than one") enter into the notion of meter. Using Cherry's description of human communication,[17] we could say that the reader of poetry obviously "may be unable to attach numerical frequencies" to the constituents of the meter, but as far as he conceives the verse shape, he unwittingly gets an inkling of their "rank order."

In the Russian binary meters all odd syllables counting back from the last downbeat—briefly, all the upbeats—are usually fulfilled by unstressed syllables, except some very low percentage of stressed monosyllables. All even syllables, again counting back from the last downbeat, show a sizable preference for syllables under word stress, but the probabilities of their occurrence are unequally distributed among the successive downbeats of the line. The higher the relative frequency of word stresses in a given downbeat, the lower the ratio shown by the preceding downbeat. Since the last downbeat is constantly stressed, the next to last gives the lowest percentage of word stresses; in the preceding downbeat their amount is again higher, without attaining the maximum, displayed by the final downbeat; one downbeat further toward the beginning of the line, the amount of the stresses sinks once more, without reaching the minimum of the next-to-last downbeat; and so on. Thus the distribution of word stresses among the downbeats within the line, the split into strong and weak downbeats, creates a *regressive undulatory curve* superposed upon the wavy alternation of downbeats and upbeats. Incidentally, there is a captivating question of the relationship between the strong downbeats and phrasal stresses.

The Russian binary meters reveal a stratified arrangement of three undulatory curves: (I) alternation of syllabic nuclei and margins; (II) division of syllabic nuclei into alternating downbeats and upbeats; and (III) alternation of strong and weak downbeats. For example, Russian masculine iambic tetrameter of the nineteenth and present centuries may be represented by Figure 1, and a similar triadic pattern appears in the corresponding English forms.

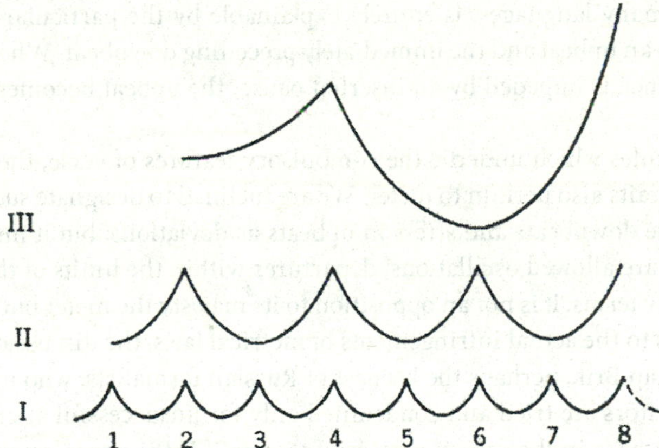

Three of five downbeats are deprived of word stress in Shelley's iambic line "Laugh with an inextinguishable laughter." Seven of sixteen downbeats are stressless in the following quatrain from Pasternak's recent iambic tetrameter *Zemlja* ("Earth"):

I úlica za panibráta
S okónnicej podslepovátoj,
I béloj nóči i zakátu
Ne razminút 'sja u reki.

Since the overwhelming majority of downbeats concur with word stresses, the listener or reader of Russian verses is prepared with a high degree of probability to meet a word stress in any even syllable of iambic lines, but at the very beginning of Pasternak's quatrain the fourth and, one foot further, the sixth syllable, both in the first and in the following line, present him with a *frustrated expectation*. The degree of such a "frustration" is higher when the stress is lacking in a strong downbeat and becomes particularly outstanding when two successive downbeats are carrying unstressed syllables. The stresslessness of two adjacent downbeats is the less probable and the most striking when it embraces a whole hemistich as in a later line of the same poem: "Čtoby za gorodskjóu grán' ju" [stəbyzəgərackóju grán'ju]. The expectation depends on the treatment of a given downbeat in the poem and more generally in the whole extant metrical tradition. In the last downbeat but one, unstress may, however, outweigh the stress. Thus in this poem only 17 of 41 lines have a word stress on their sixth syllable. Yet in such a case the inertia of the stressed even syllables alternating with the unstressed odd syllables prompts some expectancy of stress also for the sixth syllable of the iambic tetrameter.

Quite naturally it was Edgar Allan Poe, the poet and theoretician of defeated anticipation, who metrically and psychologically appraised the human sense of gratification for the unexpected arising from expectedness, both of them unthinkable without the opposite, "as evil cannot exist without good."[18] Here we could easily apply Robert Frost's formula from "The Figure a Poem Makes": "The figure is the same as for love."[19]

The so-called shifts of word stress in polysyllabic words from the downbeat to the upbeat ("reversed feet"), which are unknown to the standard forms of Russian verse, appear quite usually in English poetry after a metrical and/or syntactic pause. A noticeable example is the rhythmical variation of the same adjective in Milton's "Infinite wrath and infinite despair." In the line "Nearer, my God, to Thee, nearer to Thee," the stressed syllable of one and the same word occurs twice in the upbeat, first at the beginning of the line and a second time at the beginning of a phrase. This license, discussed by Jespersen[20] and current in many languages, is entirely explainable by the particular import of the relation between an upbeat and the immediately preceding downbeat. Where such an immediate precedence is impeded by an inserted pause, the upbeat becomes a kind of *syllaba anceps*.

Besides the rules which underlie the compulsory features of verse, the rules governing its optional traits also pertain to meter. We are inclined to designate such phenomena as unstress in the downbeats and stress in upbeats as deviations, but it must be remembered that these are allowed oscillations, departures within the limits of the law. In British parliamentary terms, it is not an opposition to its majesty the meter but an opposition of its majesty. As to the actual infringements of metrical laws, the discussion of such violations recalls Osip Brik, perhaps the keenest of Russian formalists, who used to say that political conspirators are tried and condemned only for unsuccessful attempts at a forcible upheaval, because in the case of a successful coup it is the conspirators who assume the role of judges and prosecutors. If the violences against the meter take root, they themselves become metrical rules.

Far from being an abstract, theoretical scheme, meter—or in more explicit terms, verse *design*—underlies the structure of any single line—or, in logical terminology, any single *verse instance*. Design and instance are correlative concepts. The verse design determines the invariant features of the verse instances and sets up the limits of variations. A Serbian peasant reciter of epic poetry memorizes, performs, and, to a high extent, improvises thousands, sometimes tens of thousands of lines, and their meter is alive in his mind. Unable to abstract its rules, he nonetheless notices and repudiates even the slightest infringement of these rules. Any line of Serbian epics contains precisely ten syllables and is followed by a syntactic pause. There is furthermore a compulsory word boundary before the fifth syllable and a compulsory absence of word boundary before the fourth and tenth syllable. The verse has, moreover, significant quantitative and accentual characteristics.[21]

This Serbian epic break, along with many similar examples presented by comparative metrics, is a persuasive warning against the erroneous identification of a break with a syntactic pause. The obligatory word boundary must not be combined with pause and is not even meant to be perceptible by the ear. The analysis of Serbian epic songs phonographically recorded proves that there are no compulsory audible clues to the break, and yet any attempt to abolish the word boundary before the fifth syllable by a mere insignificant change in word order is immediately condemned by the narrator. The grammatical fact that the fourth and fifth syllables pertain to two different word units is sufficient for the appraisal of the break. Thus verse design goes far beyond the questions of sheer sound shape; it is a much wider linguistic phenomenon, and it yields to no isolating phonetic treatment.

I say "linguistic phenomenon" even though Chatman states that "the meter exists as a system outside the language." Yes, meter appears also in other arts dealing with time sequence. There are many linguistic problems—for instance, syntax—which likewise overstep the limit of language and are common to different semiotic systems. We may speak even about the grammar of traffic signals. There exists a signal code, where a yellow light when combined with green warns that free passage is close to being stopped and when combined with red announces the approaching cessation of the stoppage; such a yellow signal offers a close analogue to the verbal completive aspect. Poetic meter, however, has so many intrinsically linguistic particularities that it is most convenient to describe it from a purely linguistic point of view.

Let us add that no linguistic property of the verse design should be disregarded. Thus, for example, it would be an unfortunate mistake to deny the constitutive value of intonation in English meters. Not even speaking about its fundamental role in the meters of such a master of English free verse as Whitman, it is impossible to ignore the metrical significance of pausal intonation ("final juncture"), whether "cadence" or "anticadence,"[22] in poems like "The Rape of The Lock" with its intentional avoidance of enjambments. Yet even a vehement accumulation of enjambments never hides their digressive, variational status; they always set off the normal coincidence of syntactic pause and pausal intonation with the metrical limit. Whatever is the reciter's way of reading, the intonational constraint of the poem remains valid. The intonational contour inherent to a poem, to a poet, to a poetic school is one of the most notable topics brought to discussion by the Russian formalists.[23]

The verse design is embodied in verse instances. Usually the free variation of these instances is denoted by the somewhat equivocal label "rhythm." A variation of *verse instances* within a given poem must be strictly distinguished from the variable *delivery instances*. The intention "to describe the verse line as it is actually performed" is of lesser use for the synchronic and historical analysis of poetry than it is for the study of its recitation in the present and the past. Meanwhile the truth is simple and clear: "There are many performances of the same poem—differing among themselves in many ways. A performance is an event, but the poem itself, if there *is* any poem, must be some kind of enduring object." This sage memento of Wimsatt and Beardsley belongs indeed to the essentials of modern metrics.

In Shakespeare's verses the second, stressed syllable of the word "absurd" usually falls on the downbeat, but once in the third act of *Hamlet* it falls on the upbeat: "No, let the candied tongue lick absurd pomp." The reciter may scan the word "absurd" in this line with an initial stress on the first syllable or observe the final word stress in accordance with the standard accentuation. He may also subordinate the word stress of the adjective in favor of the strong syntactic stress of the following head word, as suggested by Hill: "Nó, lèt thĕ cândĭed tóngue lîck ăbsùrd pómp,"[24] as in Hopkins' conception of English antispasts—"regrét nĕver."[25] There is finally a possibility of emphatic modifications either through a "fluctuating accentuation" (*schwebende Betonung*) embracing both syllables or through an exclamational reinforcement of the first syllable [àb-súrd]. But whatever solution the reciter chooses, the shift of the word stress from the downbeat to the upbeat with no antecedent pause is still arresting, and the moment of frustrated expectation stays viable. Wherever the reciter put the accent, the discrepancy between the English word stress on the second syllable of "absurd" and the downbeat attached to the first syllable persists as a constitutive feature of the verse instance. The tension between the ictus and the usual word stress is inherent in this line independently of its different implementations by various actors and readers. As Gerard Manley Hopkins observes, in the preface to his poems, "two rhythms are in some manner running at once."[26] His description of such a contrapuntal run can be reinterpreted. The superinducing of an equivalence principle upon the word sequence or, in other terms, the *mounting* of the metrical form upon the usual speech form, necessarily gives the experience of a double, ambiguous shape to anyone who is familiar with the given language and with verse. Both the convergences and the divergences between the two forms, both the warranted and the frustrated expectations, supply this experience.

How the given verse-instance is implemented in the given delivery instance depends on the *delivery design* of the reciter; he may cling to a scanning style or tend toward prose-like prosody or freely oscillate between these two poles. We must be on guard against simplistic binarism which reduces two couples into one single opposition either by suppressing the cardinal distinction between verse design and verse instance (as well as between delivery design and delivery instance) or by an erroneous identification of delivery instance and delivery design with the verse instance and verse design.

> "But tell me, child, your choice; what shall I buy
> You?"—"Father, what you buy me I like best."

These two lines from "The Handsome Heart" by Hopkins contain a heavy enjambment which puts a verse boundary before the concluding monosyllable of a phrase, of a sentence, of an utterance. The recitation of these pentameters may be strictly metrical with a manifest pause between "buy" and "you" and a suppressed pause after the pronoun. Or, on the contrary, there may be displayed a prose-oriented manner without any separation of the words "buy you" and with a marked pausal intonation at the end of the question. None of these ways of recitation may, however, hide the intentional discrepancy between the metrical and syntactic division. The verse shape of a poem remains completely independent of its variable delivery, whereby I do not intend to nullify the alluring question of *Autorenleser* and *Selbstleser* launched by Sievers.[27]

No doubt, verse is primarily a recurrent "figure of sound." Primarily, always, but never uniquely. Any attempts to confine such poetic conventions as meter, alliteration, or rhyme to the sound level are speculative reasonings without any empirical justification. The projection of the equational principle into the sequence has a much deeper and wider significance. Valéry's view of poetry as "hesitation between the sound and the sense"[28] is much more realistic and scientific than any bias of phonetic isolationism.

Although rhyme by definition is based on a regular recurrence of equivalent phonemes or phonemic groups, it would be an unsound oversimplification to treat rhyme merely from the standpoint of sound. Rhyme necessarily involves the semantic relationship between rhyming units ("rhyme-fellows" in Hopkins' nomenclature). In the scrutiny of a rhyme we are faced with the question of whether or not it is a homoeoteleuton, which confronts similar derivational and/or inflexional suffixes (congratulations-decorations), or whether the rhyming words belong to the same or to different grammatical categories. Thus, for example, Hopkins' fourfold rhyme is an agreement of two nouns—"kind" and "mind" both contrasting with the adjective "blind" and with the verb "find." Is there a semantic propinquity, a sort of simile between rhyming lexical units, as in dove-love, light-bright, place-space, name-fame? Do the rhyming members carry the same syntactic function? The difference between the morphological class and the syntactic application may be pointed out in rhyme. Thus in Poe's lines, "While I nodded, nearly *napping*, suddenly there came a *tapping*, As of someone gently *rapping*," the three rhyming words, morphologically alike, are all three syntactically different. Are totally or partly homonymic rhymes prohibited, tolerated, or favored? Such full homonyms as son-sun, I-eye, eve-eave, and on the other hand, echo rhymes like December-ember, infinite-night, swarm-warm, smiles-miles? What about compound rhymes (such as Hopkins' "enjoyment–toy meant" or "began some–ransom"), where a word unit accords with a word group?

A poet or poetic school may be oriented toward or against grammatical rhyme; rhymes must be either grammatical or antigrammatical; an agrammatical rhyme, indifferent to the relation between sound and grammatical structure, would, like any agrammatism, belong to verbal pathology. If a poet tends to avoid grammatical rhymes, for him, as Hopkins said, "There are two elements in the beauty rhyme has to the mind, the likeness or sameness of sound and the unlikeness or difference of meaning."[29] Whatever the relation between sound and meaning in different rhyme techniques, both spheres are necessarily involved. After Wimsatt's illuminating observations about the meaningfulness of rhyme[30] and the shrewd modern studies of Slavic rhyme patterns, a student in poetics can hardly maintain that rhymes signify merely in a very vague way.

Rhyme is only a particular, condensed case of a much more general, we may even say the fundamental, problem of poetry, namely *parallelism*. Here again Hopkins, in his student papers of 1865, displayed a prodigious insight into the structure of poetry:

> The artificial part of poetry, perhaps we shall be right to say all artifice, reduces itself to the principle of parallelism. The structure of poetry is that of continuous parallelism, ranging from the technical so-called Parallelisms of Hebrew poetry and the antiphons of Church music up to the intricacy of Greek or Italian or English verse. But parallelism is of two kinds necessarily—where the opposition is clearly marked, and where it is transitional rather or chromatic. Only the first kind, that of marked parallelism, is concerned with the structure of verse—in rhythm, the recurrence of a certain sequence of syllables, in metre, the recurrence of a certain sequence of rhythm, in alliteration, in assonance and in rhyme. Now the force of this recurrence is to beget a recurrence or parallelism answering to it in the words or thought and, speaking roughly and rather for the tendency than the invariable result, the more marked parallelism in structure whether of elaboration or of emphasis begets more marked parallelism in the words and sense. . . . To the marked or abrupt kind of parallelism belong metaphor, simile, parable, and so on, where the effect is sought in likeness of things, and antithesis, contrast, and so on, where it is sought in unlikeness.[31]

Briefly, equivalence in sound, projected into the sequence as its constitutive principle, inevitably involves semantic equivalence, and on any linguistic level any constituent of such a sequence prompts one of the two correlative experiences which Hopkins neatly defines as "comparison for likeness' sake" and "comparison for unlikeness' sake."

NOTES

1. Edward Sapir, *Language* (New York: Harcourt, Brace and Company, 1921), 40.

2. Martin Joos, "Description of Language Design," *Journal of the Acoustical Society of America* 22 (1950): 701–708.

3. Anton Marty, *Untersuchungen zur Grundlegung der allgemeinen Grammatik und Sprachphilosophie*, Vol. 1 (Halle: Verlag von Max Niemeyer, 1908).

4. Karl Bühler, "Die Axiomatik der Sprachwissenschaft," *Kant-Studien* 38 (1933): 19–90.

5. V. T. Mansikka, *Litauische Zaubersprüche*, Folklore Fellows communications 87 (1929): 69.

6. P. N. Rybnikov, *Pesni* (Moscow, 1910), Vol. 3, 217–18.

7. Bronislaw Malinowski, "The Problem of Meaning in Primitive Languages," in C. K. Ogden and I. A. Richards, *The Meaning of Meaning* (New York: Harcourt Brace, 1923), 296–336.

8. See T. Maretić, *Metrika narodnih naših pjesama* (Zagreb, 1907), sections 81–83.

9. Gerard Manley Hopkins, *The Journals and Papers*, ed. H. House (London: Oxford University Press, 1959), 289.

10. See A. Levi, "Della versificazione italiana," *Archivum Romanicum* 14 (1930): 449–526, especially sections 8–9.

11. See Roman Jakobson, *O češskom stixe preimuščestvenno v sopostavlenii s russkim* [Sborniki po teorii poètičeskogo jazyka, or On Czech verse, especially in comparison with Russian verse] (Berlin and Moscow: 1923), 5.

12. J. L. Bishop, "Prosodic elements in T'ang poetry," *Indiana University conference on Oriental-Western literary relations* (Chapel Hill: University of North Carolina Press, 1955), 49–63.

13. E. D. Polivanov, "O metričeskom xaraktere kitajskogo stixosloženija," *Doklady Rossijskoj Akademii Nauk*, serija V, (1924): 156–158.

14. Wang Li, *Han-yü shih-lü-hsüeh* [Versification in Chinese] (Shanghai: 1958).

15. D. C. Simmons, "Specimens of Efik folklore," *Folk-Lore* 66 (1955): 228.

16. See particularly, K. Taranovski, *Ruski dvodelni ritmovi* (Belgrade: 1955).

17. E. Colin Cherry, *On Human Communication* (New York: Technology Press of Massachusetts Institute of Technology, 1957).

18. Edgar A. Poe, "Marginalia," *Works* (New York, 1855), V, 492.

19. Robert Frost, *Collected Poems* (New York: Henry Holt, 1939).

20. Otto Jespersen, "Cause psychologique de quelques phénomènes de métrique germanique," *Psychologie du langage* (Paris: F. Alcan, 1933).

21. See Roman Jakobson, "Studies in Comparative Slavic Meters," *Oxford Slavonic Papers* 3 (1952): 21–66 and "Über den Versbau der serbokroatischen Volksepen," *Archives néerlandaises de phonétique expérimentale* 7–9 (1933): 44–53.

22. S. Karcevskij, "Sur la phonologie de la phrase," *Travaux du cercle linguistique de Prague* 4 (1931): 188–223.

23. B. Èjxenbaum, *Melodika stixa* (Leningrad: 1922), and Viktor Žirmunskij, *Voprosy teorii literatury* (Leningrad: 1928).

24. Archibald A. Hill, Review in *Language* 29 (1953): 549–561.

25. Hopkins, *Journals and Papers*, 276.

26. Gerard Manley Hopkins, *Poems*, ed. W. H. Gardner (New York and London: Oxford University Press, 1948), 46.

27. Eduard Sievers, *Ziele und Wege der Schallanalyse* (Heidelberg, 1924).

28. See Paul Valéry, *The art of poetry*, Bollingen series 45 (New York: 1958).

29. Hopkins, *Journals and Papers*, 286.

30. William K. Wimsatt, Jr., *The Verbal Icon* (Lexington: The University Press of Kentucky, 1954), 152–66.

31. Hopkins, *Journals and Papers*, 85.

The Poem's Significance (1978)

4.3

MICHAEL RIFFATERRE

The language of poetry differs from common linguistic usage—this much the most unsophisticated reader senses instinctively. Yet, while it is true that poetry often employs words excluded from common usage and has its own special grammar, even a grammar not valid beyond the narrow compass of a given poem, it may also happen that poetry uses the same words and the same grammar as everyday language. In all literatures with a long enough history, we observe that poetry keeps swinging back and forth, tending first one way, then the other. The choice between alternatives is dictated by the evolution of taste and by continually changing esthetic concepts. But whichever of the two trends prevails, one factor remains constant: poetry expresses concepts and things by indirection. To put it simply, a poem says one thing and means another.

I therefore submit that the difference we perceive empirically between poetry and nonpoetry is fully explained by the way a poetic text carries meaning. It is my purpose here to propose a coherent and relatively simple description of the structure of meaning in a poem.

I am aware that many such descriptions, often founded upon rhetoric, have already been put forward, and I do not deny the usefulness of notions like figure and trope. But whether these categories are well defined, like metaphor or metonymy, or are catchalls, like symbol (in the loose sense critics give it—not in the semiotic acceptation), they can be arrived at independently of a theory of reading or the concept of text.

The literary phenomenon, however, is a dialectic between text and reader.[1] If we are to formulate rules governing this dialectic, we shall have to know that what we are describing is actually perceived by the reader; we shall have to know whether he is always obliged to see what he sees, or if he retains a certain freedom; and we shall have to know how perception takes place. Within the wider realm of literature it seems to me that poetry is peculiarly inseparable from the concept of text: if we do not regard the poem as a closed entity, we cannot always differentiate poetic discourse from literary language.

My basic principle will therefore be to take into account only such facts as are accessible to the reader and are perceived in relation to the poem as a special finite context.

Under this twofold restriction, there are three possible ways for semantic indirection to occur. Indirection is produced by displacing, distorting, or creating meaning. Displacing, when the sign shifts from one meaning to another, when one word "stands for" another, as happens with metaphor and metonymy. Distorting, when there is ambiguity, contradiction, or nonsense. Creating, when textual space serves as a principle of organization for making signs out of linguistic items that may not be meaningful otherwise (for instance, symmetry, rhyme, or semantic equivalences between positional homologues in a stanza).

Among these three kinds of indirection signs, one factor recurs: all of them *threaten the literary representation of reality, or mimesis.*[2] Representation may simply be altered visibly and persistently in a manner inconsistent with verisimilitude or with what the context leads the reader to expect. Or it may be distorted by a deviant grammar or lexicon (for instance, contradictory details), which I shall call *ungrammaticality*. Or else it may be cancelled altogether (for instance, nonsense).

Now the basic characteristic of mimesis is that it produces a continuously changing semantic sequence, for representation is founded upon the referentiality of language, that is, upon a direct relationship of words to things. It is immaterial whether or not this relationship is a delusion of those who speak the language or of readers. What matters is that the text multiplies details and continually shifts its focus to achieve an acceptable likeness to reality, since reality is normally complex. Mimesis is thus variation and multiplicity.

Whereas the characteristic feature of the poem is its unity: a unity both formal and semantic. Any component of the poem that points to that "something else" it means will therefore be a constant, and as such it will be sharply distinguishable from the mimesis. This formal and semantic unity, which includes all the indices of indirection, I shall call the *significance*.[3] I shall reserve the term *meaning* for the information conveyed by the text at the mimetic level. From the standpoint of meaning the text is a string of successive information units. From the standpoint of significance the text is one semantic unit.

Any sign[4] within that text will therefore be relevant to its poetic quality, which expresses or reflects a continuing modification of the mimesis. Only thus can unity be discerned behind the multiplicity of representations.[5]

The relevant sign need not be repeated. It suffices that it be perceived as a variant in a paradigm, a variation on an invariant. In either case the perception of the sign follows from its ungrammaticality.

These two lines from a poem by Paul Eluard:

De tout ce que j'ai dit de moi que reste-t-il
J'ai conservé de faux trésors dans des armoires vides[6]

[Of all I have said about myself, what is left? I have been keeping false treasures in empty wardrobes]

owe their unity to the one word left unspoken—a disillusioned "nothing," the answer to the question, an answer that the speaker cannot bring himself to give in its literal form. The distich is built of images that flow logically from the question: "what is left" implies "something that has been saved"; a meliorative or positive version might be "something that was worth saving." In fact the images translate into figurative language a hypothetical and tautological sentence: "keep what's worth keeping [figuratively: *trésors*] in the place where things are kept that are worth keeping [figuratively: *armoires*]." You might expect this tautology to yield "strongbox" rather than "wardrobe," but *armoire* is much more than just another piece of bedroom furniture. The French sociolect makes it *the* place for hoarding within the privacy of the home. It is the secret glory of the traditional household mistress—linens scented with lavender, lace undies never seen—a metonym for the secrets of the heart. Popular etymology makes the symbolism explicit: Père Goriot mispronounces it *ormoire*, the place for *or*, for *gold*, for treasure. The distressed version we have in Eluard's second line negativizes the predicate, changing not only *trésors* into *faux trésors*, but also *armoires* into *armoires vides*. We are faced with a contradiction, for, in reality, "treasures" of illusory value would fill a closet just as well as genuine ones—witness the table drawers in any home, full of shoddy souvenirs. But of course the text is not referential: the contradiction exists only in the mimesis. The phrases in question are variants of the answer's key word—they repeat "nothing." They are the constant of a periphrastic statement of disillusionment (all these things amount to zero), and as the constant element they convey the significance of the distich.

A lesser case of ungrammaticality—compensated for by a more conspicuous kind of repetition, a more visible paradigm of synonyms—is the mimesis devoid of contradictions but obviously spurious; such are these lines from Baudelaire's "Mort des amants":

Nos deux coeurs seront deux vastes flambeaux,
Qui réfléchiront leurs doubles lumières
Dans nos deux esprits, ces miroirs jumeaux

[Our two hearts will be two great torches that reflect their double lights in our two minds, twin mirrors]

The context of furniture reinforces the concreteness of the image: these are real mantelpiece candlesticks. The image metaphorizes a torrid love scene, quite obviously, but the significance lies in the insistent variation on *two*. This makes it even more obvious that the description aims only to unfold the duality paradigm, until the duality is resolved in the next stanza by the oneness of sex ("nous échangerons un éclair unique" [we shall exchange a lightning like no other]).[7] The mimesis is only a ghost description, and through the ghost's transparency the lovers are visible.

The ungrammaticalities spotted at the mimetic level are eventually integrated into another system. As the reader perceives what they have in common, as he becomes aware that this common trait forms them into a paradigm, and that this paradigm alters the meaning of the poem, the new function of the ungrammaticalities changes their nature, and now they signify as components of a different network of relationships.[8] This transfer of a sign from one level of discourse to another, this metamorphosis of what was a signifying complex at a lower level of the text into a signifying unit, now a member of a more developed system, at a higher level of the text, this functional shift is the proper domain of semiotics.[9] Everything related to this integration of signs from the mimesis level into the higher level of significance is a manifestation of *semiosis*.[10]

The semiotic process really takes place in the reader's mind, and it results from a second reading. If we are to understand the semiotics of poetry, we must carefully distinguish *two levels or stages of reading*, since before reaching the significance the reader has to hurdle the mimesis. Decoding the poem starts with a first reading stage that goes on from beginning to end of the text, from top to bottom of the page, and follows the syntagmatic unfolding. This first, *heuristic reading* is also where the first interpretation takes place, since it is during this reading that *meaning* is apprehended. The reader's input is his linguistic competence, which includes an assumption that language is referential—and at this stage words do indeed seem to relate first of all to things. It also includes the reader's ability to perceive incompatibilities between words: for instance, to identify tropes and figures, that is, to recognize that a word or phrase does not make literal sense, that it makes sense only if he (and he is the only one around to do it) performs a semantic transfer, only if he reads that word or phrase as a metaphor, for example, or as a metonymy. Again, the reader's perception (or rather production) of irony or humor consists in his double or bilinear deciphering of the single, linear text. But this reader input occurs only because the text is ungrammatical. To put it otherwise, his linguistic competence enables him to perceive ungrammaticalities; but he is not free to bypass them, for it is precisely this perception over which the text's control is absolute. The ungrammaticalities stem from the physical fact that a phrase has been generated by a word that should have excluded it, from the fact that the poetic verbal sequence is characterized by contradictions between a word's presuppositions and its entailments. Nor is linguistic competence the sole factor. Literary competence[11] is also involved: this is the reader's familiarity with the descriptive systems,[12] with themes, with his society's mythologies, and above all with other texts. Wherever there are gaps or compressions in the text—such as incomplete descriptions, or allusions, or quotations—it is this literary competence alone that will enable the reader to respond properly and to complete or fill in according to the hypogrammatic model. It is at this first stage of reading that mimesis is fully apprehended, or rather, as I said before, is hurdled: there is no reason to believe that text perception during the second stage necessarily involves a realization that the mimesis is based upon the referential fallacy.

The second stage is that of *retroactive reading*. This is the time for a second interpretation, for the truly *hermeneutic* reading. As he progresses through the text, the reader remembers what he has just read and modifies his understanding of it in the light of what he is now decoding. As he works forward from start to finish, he is reviewing, revising, comparing backwards. He is in effect performing a structural decoding:[13] as he moves through the text he comes to recognize, by dint of comparisons or simply because he is now able to put them together, that successive and differing statements, first noticed as mere ungrammaticalities, are in fact equivalent, for they now appear as variants of the same structural matrix. The text is in effect a variation or modulation of one structure—thematic, symbolic, or whatever—and this sustained relation to one structure constitutes the significance. The maximal effect of retroactive reading, the climax of its function as generator of significance, naturally comes at the end of the poem; poeticalness is thus a function coextensive with the text, linked to a limited realization of discourse, bounded by clausula *and* beginning (which in retrospect we perceive as related). This is why, whereas units of meaning may be words or phrases or sentences, *the unit of significance is the text*. To discover the significance at last, the reader must surmount the mimesis hurdle: in fact this hurdle is essential to the reader's change of mind. The reader's acceptance of the mimesis[14] sets up the grammar as the background from which the ungrammaticalities will thrust themselves forward as stumbling blocks, to be understood eventually on a second level. I cannot emphasize strongly enough that the obstacle that threatens meaning when seen in isolation at first reading is also the guideline to semiosis, the key to significance in the higher system, where the reader perceives it as part of a complex network.

A tendency toward polarization (more of this anon) makes the guidelines for reader interpretation more obvious: it is when the description is most precise that the departures from acceptable representation induced by structures make the shift toward symbolism more conspicuous. Where the reader most expects words to toe the line of nonverbal reality, things are made to serve as signs, and the text proclaims the dominion of semiosis. It would be hard to find French descriptive poetry more representative than Théophile Gautier's *España* (1845), a collection of poems written after a journey through Spain. The traveler translated his trip into prose reports for the newspaper financing the adventure, and into verse vignettes, like the poem "In Deserto," composed after he had crossed Spain's lonely, arid *sierras*. A village with a demonstrably exotic name is given as the place of composition: this must refer to actual experience and is thus a way of labeling the poem "descriptive." In fact the learned editor of the one and only critical edition that we have finds nothing better to do than compare the verse with the prose version, and the prose with other travelers' accounts of the sierra. He comes to the conclusion that Gautier is fairly accurate, although he does seem to have made the sierra more of a desert than it really is.[15]

This is puzzling. However verifiable the text's mimetic accuracy by comparison with other writers' observations, it also consistently distorts facts or at least shows a bias in favor of details able to converge metonymically on a single concept: pessimism. Gautier makes this unmistakable with bold statements of equivalence; first when he actually speaks of despair as a landscape: "Ce grand jour frappant sur ce grand désespoir" [line 14: daylight striking upon this vast expanse of despair]. Just before this the desert was used as an illustration of the traveler's own lonely life, but the simile structure necessarily kept the setting separate from the character, the one reflecting the other. Now this separateness is cancelled, and the metaphor mingles the traveler's inner with the world's outer barrenness. In spite of this, our scholar, a seasoned student of literature, pursues his habit of checking language against reality. He seems little concerned about what language does *to* reality. This is proof at least that no matter what the poem ultimately tells us that may be quite different from ordinary ideas about the real, the message has been so constructed that the reader has to leap the hurdle of reality. He is first sent off in the wrong direction, he sets lost in his surroundings, so to speak, before he finds out that the landscape here, or the description in general, is a stage set for special effects.

In the Gautier poem the desert is there, of course, but only as long as it can be used as a realistic code for representing loneliness and its attendant aridity of heart—as opposed to the generous overflowing that comes of love. The first, naturally enough, is represented by a plain, direct, almost simplistic comparison with the desert itself; the second by a hypothetical description of what an oasis would be like, combined with a variation on the theme of Moses striking the rock. Thus we have an opposition, but still within natural climatic and geographic circumstances, or within the logic or verisimilitude of desert discourse.

The first pole of the opposition appears to rest upon straightforward mimesis:

IN DESERTO

Les pitons des sierras, les dunes du désert
Où ne pousse jamais un seul brin d'herbe vert;
Les monts aux flancs zébrés de tuf, d'ocre et de marne,
Et que l'éboulement de jour en jour décharne;
Le grès plein de micas papillotant aux yeux,
Le sable sans profit buvant les pleurs des cieux,
Le rocher refrogné dans sa barbe de ronce,
L'ardente solfatare avec la pierre-ponce,
Sont moins secs et moins morts aux végétations
Que le roc de mon coeur ne l'est aux passions.

[The pitons of the sierras, the desert dunes, where never a single blade of green grass grows; the mountainsides striped with tufa, ochre, and marl [literally: with chalky, rusty, and yellowish stripes; but the code is entirely geological], daily stripped of flesh by landslides; sandstone studded with mica glittering before your eyes; sand vainly drinking in the tears of heaven; rock scowling into its bramble beard; sulphur spring and pumice stone; these are less dry, less dead to vegetation than the rock of my heart is to passion.]

But two factors transform this step-by-step scanning of a landscape into an iterative paradigm of synonyms that points insistently to barrenness (both figurative and physical). The transformation is especially obvious when this part of the text is looked at in retrospect, from the vantage point of the opposition's second pole—the last section of the poem. The first factor is the selection of visual details with disagreeable connotations not necessarily typical of the sierra (in any case readers may not recognize their aptness unless they know Spain). They make up a catalogue of hostile connotations: the sulphur spring, for instance, more "fire and brimstone" in landscape lexicon than a clear, apt, or visualizable depiction for most readers, even if it happens to be an accurate detail; or the earth's skeleton, a traditional literary motif in descriptions of rock formation; or the three specialists' words (*tuf, ocre, marne*), doubly technical as names of painter's colors and of soil types, but above all three words any French speaker will find cacophonic; or *zébré,* which does describe stripes and is presumably correct for strata, but also—and perhaps better—fits the stripes left by a whiplash.

The second factor of semiosis that slants representation toward another, symbolic meaning is the way the text is built: we do not know this is all a simile until the last two lines, when everything suddenly changes its function and calls for a moral, human interpretation. The suspense and the semantic overturn are space- or sequence-induced phenomena, inseparable from the physical substance of the text or from its paradoxical retroversion—the end regulating the reader's grasp of the beginning.

The second pole of the opposition is where the semiosis takes over (lines 29–44). In between there are eighteen entirely descriptive, seemingly objective lines, resuming the enumeration of the physical features of aridity. But of course this objectivity, unchallengeable as it may be within its own domain (lines 11–28), is now cancelled or made subservient to another representation, because the reader now knows that the whole sequence is not an independent description allegiant only to the truth of the outside world, but is the constituent of a trope. All the realism depends grammatically upon an unreality and develops not the desert we were initially invited to think real (before we discovered it was the first leg of a simile), but a desert conjured up to confirm contextually the metaphor prepared by the simile: *le roc de mon coeur* [the rock of my heart]. Everything is now ostensibly derived from an exclusively verbal given, the cliché a *heart of stone.* In line 29 an explicit allusion is made to the latent verbal association that has overdetermined, in desert context, the rock-of-the-heart image: a simile brings the rock Moses struck to the surface of the text, and this simile now triggers the unfolding of a new code for reverie about what love could do for this parched heart, and how it could make this desert bloom:

> Tel était le rocher que Moïse, au désert,
> Toucha de sa baguette, et dont le flanc ouvert,
> Tressaillant tout à coup, fit jaillir en arcade
> Sur les lèvres du peuple une fraîche cascade.
> Ah! s'il venait à moi, dans mon aridité,
> Quelque reine des coeurs, quelque divinité,
> Une magicienne, un Moïse femelle,
> Traînant dans le désert les peuples après elle,
> Qui frappât le rocher dans mon coeur endurci,
> Comme de l'autre roche, on en verrait aussi
> Sortir en jets d'argent des eaux étincelantes,
> Où viendraient s'abreuver les racines des plantes;
> Où les pâtres errants conduiraient leurs troupeaux,
> Pour se coucher à l'ombre et prendre le repos;
> Où, comme en un vivier, les cigognes fidèles
> Plongeraient leurs grands becs et laveraient leurs ailes.

[Such was the rock that Moses touched in the desert with his rod. And the rock's open flank shuddered all at once and sent an arc of water gushing to the people's lips in a cool

> cascade. If only some queen of hearts would come to me in my aridness, some divinity, a sorceress, a female Moses, dragging the peoples through the desert after her; if she would only strike the rock in my hardened heart, you would see leaping up, as from that other rock, silver jets of sparkling water; there the roots of plants would come to slake their thirst; there wandering shepherds would lead their flocks, to lie down in the shade and take their rest; there, as in a fishpond, the faithful storks would plunge their long beaks and wash their wings.]

Now the semiosis triumphs completely over mimesis, for the text is no longer attempting to establish the credibility of a description. Any allusion to the desert landscape, or to the oasis born of the miraculous fountain, is derived entirely from the name *Moïse*, taken less as an actual wanderer who crossed the Sinai than as a literary theme, or derived from the female variant of *Moïse*, which is of course a metaphor in desert code for *Woman as a fountain of life*. The code itself is not a metaphor: we cannot assign a literal tenor to the *fountain* vehicle; even less can we find a term-for-term relationship between the descriptive vignettes about the drinkers at that spring (roots, shepherds, storks) and certain tenors that would be metonymic of the revived and transfigured speaker.

We must therefore see the code of the poem as symbolic. It definitely represents something that is not the desert to which the description is still referring. Everything points to a hidden meaning, one evidently derived from a key word—*fecundity*—which is the exact opposite of the first key word, *barrenness*. But there is no similarity, even partial, between fecundity, even in the moral sense, and the speaker as the text enables us to imagine him. If the reader simply assumes (since this is the chief rationalization in any reading experience) that the first-person narrator, so long as he remains unnamed, must be the poet himself, *fecundity* will refer to poetic inspiration, indeed often associated with love at last requited. But the description of the oasis still does not match any of the traits, real or imaginary, of a creative writer.

All we can say, then, is that the text's final passage symbolizes the miraculous effects of Jove on life. The selection of *fertility as* the key to that symbol is determined by the reversal of the symbol used to describe life before the miracle. The last part of the poem is a reverse version of the forms actualized in the first part. The positive "conversion" that accomplishes this affects every textual component regardless of its previous marking or meaning. This is why contradictions or incompatibilities or nonsense abound in the description: such details as *flanc ouvert* or *flanc . . . tressaillant* (lines 30–31), phrases properly applied only to a pregnant woman who feels the child move in her womb for the first time, bring to the fore the repressed sexual implications of the Moses-rod story, as do the storks (43), flown out of nowhere (out of the implied womb, that is)—for, without this displaced determination, why not just any bird, so long as it is a positive sign? These details do not fit the male character who has now slipped into the metaphoric rock. Yet they are contradictory only as descriptions, only if we keep trying to interpret them as mimesis; they cease to be unacceptable when we see them as the logical and cogent consequences of the positivization of desert code.

Other ungrammaticalities are simply the mimetic face of the semiotic grammaticality; the astonishing *Moïse femelle*, the nonsense of vegetable roots endowed with animal mobility, the *Et in Arcadia ego* connotations of the scene around the spring, after the manner of Poussin—all these conform to the conversion according to an indirect, implicit, but continuously present love code. The amplification of *Moïse femelle* as a sexual pied piper—"Traînant dans le désert les peuples après elle"—is intertextually determined by a line from Racine, Phèdre's amorous description of her lover's seductive power: "Traînant tous les coeurs après soi" [dragging all hearts after him]. It translates into a phrase an essential seme of love—its irresistible magnetism—and the same applies to the miracle of the roots, this time overdetermined by another association intersecting the first chain: the hyperbolic positive fountain also involves the cliché of the spot that irresistibly draws every living creature. Upon the oasis oxymorically derived from "aridity," love symbolism superimposes its own theme of the *locus amoenus*.

We cannot, however, understand the semiosis until we have ascertained the place of the text now perceived as one sign within a system (a sign formally complex but monosemic), for by definition a sign cannot be isolated. A sign is only a relationship to something else. It will not make sense without a continuous translatability from component to component of a network. A consequence of the system's latent existence is that every signifying feature of the poem must be relatable to that system. Here everything the text says must be fitted back into the initial code, into the *desert* code, even though it is represented in the end only conversely. Failing this we cannot relate the end and the beginning, we cannot recognize that text and significance are coextensive, we cannot discover that the clausula dovetails with the title. The one feature pervading the whole clausula (from line 33 on) is grammatical: every verb is in the conditional mood; that is, it expresses an action or state of things not yet realized, a wish unfulfilled, a hope frustrated, a dream dreamt in vain—in short, life still the desert of life, a familiar theme. But this verbal mood's being the grammatical icon of unfulfillment raises the question of the speaker's voice. For the poem is spoken in the first person, and we do not know where from. Then suddenly the puzzle is solved, everything falls into place, indeed the whole poem ceases to be descriptive, ceases to be a sequence of mimetic signs, and becomes but a single sign, perceived from the end back to its given as a harmonious whole, wherein nothing is loose, wherein every word refers to one symbolic focus.

This epiphany of the semiosis occurs when the lost voice is found again, thanks to the hint signalled by the title, misunderstood until the end: this signal is the title's language. In French, *Dans le désert* would be a self-sufficient title and perfectly appropriate for a mere travelogue. The Latin *In deserto* does not make sense unless read, as it must be, as an incomplete quotation. *In deserto* is only the second half of the familiar phrase for words shouted in vain, the voice crying in the wilderness: *vox clamans in deserto*. From this repressed, despairing voice the whole poem is derived; from this bereft speaker issues the dream's unreality. This one conventional symbol, erased from the title, founds a whole new symbolism defining only *this* work of art; and the text, raised from the ashes of familiar description, is made into a novel and unique significance.

Significance, and let me insist on this, now appears to be more than or something other than the total meaning deducible from a comparison between variants of the given. That would only bring us back to the given, and it would be a reductionist procedure. Significance is, rather, the reader's praxis of the transformation, a realization that it is akin to playing, to acting out the liturgy of a ritual—the experience of a circuitous sequence, a way of speaking that keeps revolving around a key word or matrix reduced to a marker (the negative orientation whose semiotic index is the frustration implied by *vox clamans in deserto*). It is a hierarchy of representations imposed upon the reader, despite his personal preferences, by the greater or lesser expansion of the matrix's components, an orientation imposed upon the reader despite his linguistic habits, a bouncing from reference to reference that keeps on pushing the meaning over to a text not present in the linearity, to a paragram or hypogram[16]—a dead landscape that refers to a live character, a desert traveled through that represents the traveler rather than itself, an oasis that is the monument of a negated or nonexistent future. The significance is shaped like a doughnut, the hole being either the matrix of the hypogram or the hypogram as matrix.

The effect of this disappearing act is that the reader feels he is in the presence of true originality, or of what he believes to be a feature of poetic language, a typical case of obscurity. This is when he starts rationalizing, finds himself unable to bridge the semantic gap inside the text's linearity, and so tries to bridge it outside of the text by completing the verbal sequence. He resorts to nonverbal items, such as details from the author's life, or to verbal items, such as preset emblems or lore that is well established but not pertinent to the poem. All this just misguides the reader and compounds his difficulties. Thus, what makes the poem, what constitutes its message, has little to do with what it tells us or with the language it employs. It has everything to do with the way the given twists the mimetic codes out of shape by substituting its own structure for their structures.

The structure of the given (from now on I shall refer to it as the *matrix*), like all structures, is an abstract concept never actualized per se: it becomes visible only in its variants, the ungrammaticalities. The greater the distance between the inherently simple matrix and the inherently complex mimesis, the greater the incompatibility between ungrammaticalities and mimesis. This was already obvious, I think, in the discrepancy between "nothing" and Eluard's thesaurization sequence, between "couple" or "lovers" and Baudelaire's furniture sequence. In all these cases the discrepancy is made graphic by the fact that the mimesis occupies a lot of space while the matrix structure can be summed up in a single word.

This basic conflict, the locus of literariness (at least as literariness manifests itself in poetry) may reach a point where the poem is a form totally empty of "message" in the usual sense, that is, without content—emotional, moral, or philosophical. At this point the poem is a construct that does nothing more than experiment, as it were, with the grammar of the text, or, perhaps a better image, a construct that is nothing more than a calisthenics of words, a verbal setting-up exercise. The mimesis is now quite spurious and illusory, realized only for the sake of the semiosis; and conversely, the semiosis is a reference to the word *nothing* (the word, since the concept "nothingness" would be heavy metaphysical stuffing indeed).

This is an extreme case but exemplary, for it may tell us much about poetry's being more of a game than anything else. I shall use three short texts as illustrations, all of them about paintings or scenes, all three pictorial descriptions, all three reading like picture plaques in a parodic museum. The first is supposedly a "Combat de Sénégalais la nuit dans un tunnel" [Night combat of Senegalese tribesmen inside a tunnel]. The second: "Récolte de la tomate par des cardinaux apoplectiques au bord de la Mer Rouge" [Apoplectic cardinals picking tomatoes on the shores of the Red Sea]. The third: "Perdu dans une exposition de blanc encadrée de momies" [Lost at a white sale surrounded by Egyptian mummies].[17] The first one is a joke familiar in relatively intellectual French circles; it is usually rationalized as a satire on certain monochromatic modern paintings. Every character, every scenic detail being black, you see nothing. The second is from a humorous piece by Alphonse Allais, a minor writer not unlike Alfred Jarry, his contemporary, but without Jarry's genius. Allais is generally credited with being one of the creators of humor as a genre in French literature. Here again: red-faced, red-robed princes of the church, their red harvest, the red locale—redness cancels all the shape, line, and contrast that must set the cardinals off from their surroundings, if they are to be seen. There is nothing here but a one-color continuum.

True, the red of the Red Sea is only a convention, not a real color mimesis; still, it purports to refer to a geographical reality, so that the principle of mimesis, the differentiation, is at work, and it is indeed cancelled here. In the third quotation, from a poem by the surrealist Benjamin Péret, the *white sale* again is more metaphorically than literally white; yet once more the effect is to blend all representation into a uniform whiteness.

One may wonder why I have chosen these three examples to prove a point about poetic discourse. I reply that these and others like them are commonplaces; that the durability of even the oral joke, the first, unsigned text, reminds us that a mere joke is an elementary form of literature, since it is as lasting, and as protected against tampering when quoted, as a more highbrow text. The fact that these lines are intended, or perceived, as jokes reflects only their obviousness of purpose (they are so obviously a game); and the cancellation of mimetic features leads to a pointless semiosis: we do not see where generalized blackness, redness, or whiteness can possibly be taking us. But of course the significance really lies in the gratuitousness of the transformation: it exemplifies that process itself, the artifact per se. It also demonstrates the essential conflict that makes a literary text: no variation-cancelling conversion, no direct decoding of the invariant (here the color) can take place until the representing, mimetic variants to be cancelled have first been stated. No breaking of the rule without a rule.

I am quite sure that even if they agree these jokes may in fact possess the features of literariness, most readers will be unable to resist the temptation to jump from a negative value judgment (these are examples of lowbrow literature or bad literature) to a complete denial that they are literature at all. But other texts evidence the very same "weaknesses" and no doubt is cast on their poetic status, so long as our attention is diverted from circularity, so long as we are able to spot in the text something we recognize as a commonly accepted literary feature—be it a stylistic form, or a form of content like, say, a theme. The text then "passes" unscathed, and yet the formal alteration of the mimesis is no less drastic than that of our jokes, and the semiosis is just as pointless. Take for example this blackness sequence in a Robert Desnos poem, the cause of much emotional upset among critics. It is a portrait of the speaker, head, heart, thoughts, waking moments, and now sleep:

> Un bon sommeil de boue
> Né du café et de la nuit et du charbon et du crêpe des veuves
> Et de cent millions de nègres
> Et de l'étreinte de deux nègres dans une ombre de sapins
> Et de l'ébène et des multitudes de corbeaux sur les carnages[18]

> [A good muddy sleep born of coffee and night and coal and ink and widow's weeds and of a hundred million negroes and of two negroes embracing in the shade of fir trees, and of ebony and multitudes of ravens hovering over fields of carnage]

Or again (since I have no "redness" example at hand, and for officially poetic "whiteness" Gautier's "Symphonie en blanc majeur" would be too long to quote), let us take this "transparency" text, a passage from André Breton's *Revolver à cheveux blancs*:

> On vient de mourir mais je suis vivant et cependant je n'ai plus d'âme. Je n'ai plus qu'un corps transparent à l'intérieur duquel des colombes transparentes se jettent sur un poignard transparent tenu par une main transparente.[19]

[There has just been a death, but I am alive, and yet I no longer have a soul. All I have left is a transparent body with transparent doves inside throwing themselves on a transparent dagger held by a transparent hand.]

Here we are ready to pass over the representational nonsense because death is eminently literary. We have no trouble rationalizing that this disembodiment is a legitimate way of representing the afterlife. And of course the question of genuine literariness will not be raised with Mallarmé: for instance the sonnet beginning "Ses purs ongles très haut dédiant leur onyx." The question does not arise, first, because the challenge to mimesis is not so complete that the reader has no chance at all to read the poem as a representation. The lofty language makes up for the circularity. And the obscurity makes less glaring the absence of the symbolism that should compensate us for accepting such detours from straightforward referentiality. Or better, the obscurity hides the fact that the text's implications are just as short range, just as slight, as in a joke. The tone, the style make the difference. But that difference lies in the reader's attitude, in his greater willingness to accept a suspension of mimesis when he thinks no one is trying to pull his leg. Actually there is no difference in the text, for the structure of Mallarmé's sonnet is the same conversion found in all three jokes and in Breton and Desnos.

In the joke subgenre there is no way for the reader to get beyond the laugh, once it has been laughed, any more than he can get beyond the solution once he has solved a riddle. Such forms self-destruct immediately after consumption. The sonnet, on the contrary, leaves the reader free to keep on building, so long as his constructs are not wholly incompatible with the text. The first stanza, "L'Angoisse, ce minuit" [anguish at midnight], seems to adumbrate a meditation upon the problems of life or upon artistic creation. This looks so serious that the reader expects the poem to be about reality, physical or conceptual, especially when the second quatrain presents the familiar livingroom interior:

Sur les crédences, au salon vide: nul ptyx,
Aboli bibelot d'inanité sonore,
(Car le Maître est allé puiser des pleurs au Styx
Avec ce seul objet dont le Néant s'honore.)

[On the sideboards, in the empty livingroom: no ptyx, abolished bibelot of sonorous inanity (for the Master has gone to draw tears from the Styx, bearing with him this only curio that Nothingness takes pride in).]

The mimesis has hardly been offered, however, when reference is withdrawn, so that the structure is a polar opposition of *representation* vs. *nothing.* The text first sets up a particularly tangible kind of reality: the pride of bourgeois life, the ultimate actualization of presence in a house, of its completeness as social status symbol, the furniture. But at the same time the text, an Indian giver, snatches back this reality by repeating Nothingness with each descriptive item. The resulting polarization is the poem's significance, aptly described by Mallarmé himself: "une eau-forte pleine de rêve et de vide" [an etching full of dream and emptiness].[20] That phrase itself is a variant of the significance structure, since *eau-forte* in its telling technicality expresses the mimesis hyperbolically, and *full of emptiness* actualizes the other pole, the cancellation of mimesis. (This other pole is, as it should be, equally hyperbolic, because "full of emptiness" is an oxymoron, and as such repeats and integrates the whole of the opposition over again—*fullness* vs. *emptiness.*) I need not underline that this commentary on the sonnet—*eau-forte pleine de vide*—fits equally well as metalanguage for my three comedy paintings of nothing, and for André Breton's pseudo-representation of afterlife invisibility. Such, then, is the semiosis of the poem, and by happy coincidence it exemplifies the rule that literature, by saying something, says something else. The rule in its *reductio ad aburdum*: by saying something literature can say nothing (or, if I may once more indulge in my irreverent simile: no longer the doughnut around its hole, but the doughnut as a hole).

The mechanism of mimesis cancellation in Mallarmé's sonnet calls for close scrutiny, being comparable to that of Eluard's *armoires vides*, and susceptible of generalization (later it will be recognized as obeying the rule of conversion):[21] that is, every mention of a thing is marked with a zero index. *Salon* modified by *vide* serves as a model for a striking series of synonymous assertions of void. Within the narrow compass of a quatrain *salon vide* is repeated five times: once through the symbolic disappearance of its owner, who is dead or gone to Hell, an eminently dramatic way of not being around,[22] and then through a fourfold variation on the nonexistence of a knickknack. The *bibelot* is a nonfunctional object, at most a conversation piece, and yet the ultimate filler of emptiness during periods like Mallarmé's, when household esthetics prescribe that every nook and cranny be stuffed with ornaments, that every bit of space be crammed with the shapes of things. But this object is named only to be cancelled as a sign, not just mentioned as a thing gone. The equivalence of *vide* and *bibelot* is insured the first time by *nul ptyx*. Not only because *nut* annuls *ptyx*, but because *ptyx* is a nonobject, a word unknown in any language, as Mallarmé himself boasted,[23] a pure ad hoc product of the sonnet's rhyming constraints. Having imposed upon himself a difficult rhyme, */iks/*,[24] the poet patently runs out of words. With its outlandish spelling and its boldly non-French initial consonantal cluster, *ptyx*, like everything else in the sonnet, combines high visibility, an almost obtrusive physical presence as a form, and an equally obtrusive absence as meaning. The second equivalence of presence and absence is *aboli bibelot*, as meaning, as the French variant of the semi-Greek *nul ptyx*, and as paronomasia, making *bibelot* an approximate phonetic mirror image of *aboli*, thus a reflection of absence.[25] The third equivalence: *inanité sonore*, a phrase made the more effective by being a cliché or literary quotation about empty words going back to Latin: *inania verba*. The fourth equivalence: the semiotic nonexistence of the object whose existence is asserted by description is translated into a mimesis of philosophical Nothingness itself (*dont le Néant s'honore*), with a pun to top it off, since *Néant s'honore* sounds like *néant sonore*, "sonorous nothingness." Finally, this emptiness, these nonobjects, are paralleled by the graphemic symbolism of the rhyme, since *y* and *x* are the signs of conventional abstractness and of algebraic unknowns.

Such is the force of habit, such the power of the everyday context of cognitive language, that commentators have unanimously endeavored to connect the quatrain with actual representation. Even though it should be impossible to miss the meaning—an exercise in verbal exercise[26]—we find at work here a nostalgia for referentiality that promises us no reader will ever get used to nonlanguage. The efforts of scholars to palliate it only enflame the outrage of words cancelling themselves. The vase *dont le Néant s'honore* has been interpreted as a vial of poison, thus a vial of death, or a vessel of Nothingness as a tangible, physical cause of death. And *ptyx*, despite Mallarmé's own statement, has been forcibly twisted into a full-fledged representation, by way of a Greek word meaning, supposedly, a "fold" or "shell shaped like a fold." The trouble is that the word *ptyx* itself is a hypothesis of lexicographers, deduced from a rare Greek word found only in the plural or in oblique-declension cases, *ptykhes*; Mallarmé could not have known of this. His *ptyx* does have a model: a word Hugo had used a few years earlier for the sake of strangeness per se, since in *his* poem it is supposed to be the name of an actual mountain translated into the language of the Gods—neat proof that *ptyx* has no meaning in any human language.[27] Turn where we may, the picture of reality is erased, so that these varied but repetitious cancellations add up to the one significance so ringingly proclaimed by the title of the sonnet's first version: "Sonnet allégorique de soi-même" [Sonnet allegoric of itself], a text referring to its own shape, absolute form. It takes the whole sonnet to unroll the description and to annul it, point by point. The destruction of the mimesis, or its obverse, the creation of the semiosis, is thus exactly coextensive with the text: it is the text.

An extreme example, obviously, and most poems are closer to the model of Eluard's distich, but the principle is, I believe, the same in all cases. From this principle I shall now try to deduce the fundamentals of my interpretation of poetry's semiotic system.

Postulates and Definitions

Poetic discourse is the equivalence established between a word and a text, or a text and another text.

The poem results from the transformation of the *matrix*, a minimal and literal sentence, into a longer, complex, and nonliteral periphrasis. The matrix is hypothetical, being only the grammatical and lexical actualization of a structure. The matrix may be epitomized in one word, in which case the word will not appear in the text.[28] It is always actualized in successive variants; the form of these variants is governed by the first or primary actualization, the *model*. Matrix, model, and text are variants of the same structure.

The poem's significance, both as a principle of unity and as the agent of semantic indirection, is produced by the *detour* the text makes as it runs the gauntlet of mimesis, moving from representation to representation (for example, from metonym to metonym within a descriptive system), with the aim of exhausting the paradigm of all possible variations on the matrix. The harder it is to force the reader to notice the indirection and to lead him step by step through distortion, away from mimesis, the longer the detour must be and the more developed the text. The text functions something like a neurosis: as the matrix is repressed, the displacement produces variants all through the text, just as suppressed symptoms break out somewhere else in the body.

To clarify *matrix* and *model* further, I shall use an example of limited relevance to poetry; its very limitations, however, make its mechanics more obvious and practical for the purposes of my preliminary definitions. This is an echoing sequence in a Latin verse by the seventeenth-century Jesuit Athanasius Kircher:[29]

> Tibi vero gratias agam quo clamore? Amore more ore re.
>
> [How shall I cry out my thanks to Thee? [the question being addressed to the Almighty. who replies:] With thy love, thy wont, thy words, thy deeds.]

Each word in the answer accords with the model provided by the preceding word, so that every component is repeated several times over. For each member of the paradigm, it would be easy to imagine a development wholly regulated by the nuclear word of the one preceding. The question *clamore* serves as a model for the reply *amore*, and *amore* serves as a model for the entire sequence—it is the seed of the text, so to speak, and summarizes it in advance. The matrix here is *thanksgiving*, a verbal statement that presupposes a divine Providence (as benefactor), a believer (as beneficiary), and the gratefulness of the latter to the former. The model is *crying out (to)*, not a random choice, but one already determined by a literary theme: the outcry, the spontaneous outburst, is a common sign of sincerity and open-heartedness in moralistic text, especially in meditations or essays on prayer. The model generates the text by formal derivation affecting both syntax and morphology; every word of the text is in the same case, the ablative; every word of it is contained in the first variant of the model (*clamore*). The conformity of the text to the generating model makes it a unique artifact, in terms of language, since the associative chain issuing from *clamore* does not work as do normal associations, playing out a string of semantically related words. Instead it functions as if it were creating a special lexicon of cognates of *clamor.* The linguistic anomaly is thus the means of transforming the semantic unity of the statement into a formal unity, of transforming a string of words into a network of related and unified shapes, into a "monument" of verbal art. This formal monumentality entails changes of meaning. Independent of their respective senses, the ways of giving thanks here enumerated appear to be subsumed under love, since the word for love contains them and love appears as the essence of prayer, since prayer is contained in the word for love. In both cases these verbal relations reflect the principles of Christian living as taught by the Church, so that the very fact of the derivation is a semiotic system created ad hoc for these principles: the way the sentence functions is their icon.

The matrix alone would not suffice to explain textual derivation, nor would the model taken separately, since only the two in combination create the special language wherein everything the believer does that is pertinent to what defines him as a believer is expressed in *love* code. Hence the text as a whole is indeed a variant of the verb for the activity typical of the faithful (*to give thanks*). The text in its complexity does no more than modulate the matrix. The matrix is thus the motor, the generator of the textual derivation, while the model determines the manner of that derivation.

The Kircher example is of course highly exceptional, since the paronomasia, like an extended pun, might be said to extract the significant variation from the mimesis itself: the ungrammaticality consists in the dispersion of one descriptive word, in the building of the paradigm out of the pieces of that one lexeme drawn and quartered. Paronomasia, when it does occur, is rarely so pervasive. The usual detour around the repressed matrix, being made of separate, distinct ungrammaticalities, looks like a series of inappropriate, twisted wordings, so that the poem may be regarded as a generalized, all-encompassing, all-contaminating catachresis.

This catachresis has *overdetermination* as its corollary. It is a fact that no matter how strange a departure from usage a poem may seem to be, its deviant phraseology keeps its hold on the reader and appears not gratuitous but in fact strongly motivated; discourse seems to have its own imperative truth; the arbitrariness of language conventions seems to diminish as the text becomes more deviant and ungrammatical, rather than the other way around. This overdetermination is the other face of the text's derivation from one matrix: the relationship between generator and transforms adds its own powerful connection to the normal links between words—grammar and lexical distribution. The functions of overdetermination are three: to make mimesis possible; to make literary discourse exemplary[30] by lending it the authority of multiple motivations for each word used; and to compensate for the catachresis. The first two functions are observable in literature in general, the last only in poetic discourse. The three together confer upon the literary text its monumentality: it is so well built and rests upon so many intricate relationships that it is relatively impervious to change and deterioration of the linguistic code. Because of the complexity of its structures and the multiple motivations of its words, the text's hold on the reader's attention is so strong that even his absentmindedness or, in later eras, his estrangement from the esthetic reflected in the poem or its genre, cannot quite obliterate the poem's features or their power to control his decoding.

I shall distinguish between two different semiotic operations: the transformation of mimetic signs into words or phrases relevant to significance, and the transformation from matrix to text. The rules governing these operations may work together or separately in overdetermining the verbal sequences from the incipit to the clausula of the poem.

For describing the verbal mechanisms of sign integration from mimesis to significance level, I shall propose a single *hypogrammatic rule* telling us under what conditions the lexical actualization of semic features, stereotypes, or descriptive systems produces poetic words or phrases whose poeticity is either limited to one poem or is conventional and therefore a literary marker in any context.

Two rules apply to production of the text: *conversion* and *expansion* (chapter 3). The texts overdetermined according to these rules may be integrated into larger ones by embedding. The components of the significance-bearing paradigm may therefore be such embedded texts. The signs of specialized poetic usage (conventional poetic words) and perhaps others as well may be said to stand for texts: their significance issues from this vicarious textuality.

In all cases the concept of poeticity is inseparable from that of the text. And the reader's perception of what is poetic is based wholly upon reference to texts.

NOTES

1. On the role of text-reader dialectics, see Stanley Fish, "Literature in the Reader: Affective Stylistics," *New Literary History* 2 (1970): 123–62; and Michael Riffaterre, *Essais de stylistique structurale* (Paris: Flammarion, 1971).

2. Or at least challenge its premises, such as the establishment of a verisimilitude level (like the *effet de réel* of French critical terminology, see Roland Barthes, *S/Z* [Paris: Larousse, 1970]), which becomes the norm for a given text and by opposition to which we can perceive departures—-e.g., the fantastic or the supernatural.

3. Significance, to put it simply, is what the poem is really about: it arises through retroactive reading when the discovery is made that representation (or mimesis) actually points to a content that would demand a different representation in nonliterary language. Yet my use of *significance*, however specialized, does not contradict Webster: "the subtle, hidden implications of something, as distinguished from its openly expressed meaning."

4. For an exact definition of sign, especially the difference between index, icon, and symbol, see C. S. Peirce 3.361–62; also Douglas Greenlee, *Peirce's Concept of Sign* (Paris: Seuil, 1973), and Thomas A. Sebeok, "Six Species of Signs: Some Propositions and Strictures," *Semiotica* 13 (1975): vol. 3, 233–60. Strictly speaking, Umberto Eco, *A Theory of Semiotics* (Bloomington: Indiana University Press, 1976), p. 16 ("everything that, on the grounds of a previously established social convention, can be taken as something standing for something else") would exclude poetic signs valid only within the idiolect of the text: they are then only context-established (of course Eco deepens his definition considerably, and his whole book, especially the "Theory of Codes" chapter, is essential in this connection). I rather like Peirce's pithy definition in his letter to Lady Welby of 12 October 1904: *a sign is something knowing which we know something more.*

5. The last class, idiolectic signs and space-oriented signs, may provide an answer. But that would still leave unexplained the relationship between the other two categories (by far the more numerous signs) and the poem as a whole. Also, the very definition of the third-class signs seems to demand preliminary knowledge of what makes a text a closed, structured unit—hence the serious risk of circularity.

6. Paul Eluard, "Comme deux gouttes d'eau" (1933), in *Oeuvres complètes*, ed. Marcelle Dumas and Lucien Scheler (Paris: Bibl. De la Pléiade, 1968), vol. I, p. 412.

7. Lightning is a Second Empire euphemism for orgasm: Michelet, for example, in his treatise on love published seven years after the sonnet, alludes to the sexual act as a *ténébreux éclair* [dark lightning] (*L'Amour*, p. 201); and later on, prompted by the Baudelaire intertext, Charles Cros will write: "La mort perpétuera l'éclair d'amour vainqueur" [Death will make eternal the lightning flashes of love triumphant].

8. Umberto Eco, *A Theory of Semiotics*, p. 126: "every item in the code maintains a double set of relations, a systematic one with all the items of its own plane (content or expression) and a signifying one with one or more items of the correlated plane."

9. See ibid., pp. 314 ff. Also pp. 48 ff. (especially p. 57).

10. As defined by Peirce 5.484. Cf. Umberto Eco, *A Theory of Semiotics*, pp. 71–72, 121–29.

11. On literary competence, see also Jens Ihwe, "Kompetenz und Performanz in der Literaturtheorie," *Text, Bedeutung, Aesthetik*, ed. Siegfried J.

Schmidt (Munich: Bayerischer Schulbuch Verlag, 1970).

12. See my definition in chapter 2, pp. 39 ff. and note 24.

13. Since the text is a multilevelled discourse, the perception of *sign-functions* (in Hjelmslev's sense, 1943, p. 58) necessarily changes, the correlation of functives being transitory: it depends upon the reader's gradual discovery of new coding rules, that is, upon his working his way back to the structures that generate the text (the reader is performing an *abduction*, in Peirce's sense: Peirce 2.623).

14. Which should not be confused with adherence to the referential fallacy. This is a matter of effect. Whether the reader believes the mimesis is grounded in a genuine reference of words to things, or realizes the mimesis is illusory and is in truth built upon entirely verbal, self-sufficient system, the impact of the representation of reality upon his imagination is the same. It has to be a norm before the well-formedness of any of its components can appear questionable.

15. Maurice Jasinski, ed., Gautier, *España* (Paris: Vuibert, 1929), pp. 142–45.

16. I prefer *hypogram* to *paragram*, since the latter is identified with Saussure's forgotten concept, brought back to life in Jean Starobinski, *Les mots sous les mots. Les anagrammes de F. de Saussure* (Paris: NRF, 1971). In Saussure, the matrix of the paragram (his *locus princeps*) is lexical or graphemic, and the paragram is made out of fragments of the key words scattered along the sentence, each embedded in the body of a word. (My hypogram, on the contrary, appears quite visibly in the shape of words embedded in sentences whose organization reflects the presuppositions of the matrix's nuclear word.) Saussure was never able to prove that the key word's role implies "une plus grande somme de coincidences que celles du premier mot venu" (Starobinski,*Les mots sous les mots*, p. 132). Such proof must be looked for, and the question asked is hard to reconcile with the reader's natural experience of a literary text, namely, his greater awareness of the *way* things are said than of exactly what is meant. The fact that the saturation of the text by a phonic paraphrase of a key word is more assumed than perceived is hard to reconcile with the poetic function as defined by Mukarovsky, and followed by Jakobson, as a focussing of the language system on the form of the message. These problems, it seems to me, can be avoided if the analyst starts from what the surface features of the text, that is, its style, force him to perceive. These features can be defined as variants of a semantic structure that need not be realized in a key word present intact or as *membra disiecta* in the text, so long as decoding emphases and other formal distortions sensitize the reader to their recurrences and hence to their equivalences, and thus make him perceive them not just as forms but as variants of an invariant. This natural decoding procedure should obviate the difficulty of proving the existence of a key word, because the structure's complex network of relations is self-defining outside of and above any word that may implement it.

17. Cf. the American joke—a polar bear in a snow storm. Alphonse Allais, *Album Primo-Avrilesque* (1897), in *Oeuvres postumes*, vol. 2 (Paris: La Table ronde, 1966), pp. 371–79; Benjamin Péret, "Allô," in *Je sublime* (Paris: Editions surréalistes, 1936). Allais's piece is in the parodic catalog of an imaginary *Salon* of paintings, in which every exhibit is monochromatic. He offers his own version of the first of our three jokes. The plaques on five other "paintings" function similarly to the one I commented on here, but raise problems irrelevant to my point.

18. Robert Desnos, "Apparition," in *Fortunes* (Poésie) (Paris: NRF, 1942), p. 62. Thus a Desnos exegete: "strange, violent, fascinating poem, modulating one long shout," etc., etc. (Rosa Bucholle, *L'évolution poétique de R. Desnos* [Brussels: Académie royal de langue et littérature françaises, 1956], p. 156.) The *de boue* repeats both the beginning ("born of dirt," i.e. clay, a new Adam), and a hypogram: *dormir debout* [to be sleepy enough to sleep standing up, fast asleep on his feet]. The raven details, for instance, cannot be mimetic; they are not even apt in context, they are simply a periphrastic hyperbole of the ideal raven (and, indirectly, exemplary blackness).

19. André Breton, "La Forêt dans la hache," in *Le Revolver à cheveux blancs* (1932).

20. Mallarmé, *Oeuvres complètes*, Bibl. de la Pléiade, p. 1489. There is a thicket of studies that try vainly to make sense of the sonnet at the mimetic level. Only a few have arrived at a perception of the *rien* significance (M.-J. Lefebve, "La Mise en abyme mallarméenne," *Synthèses* 258 [1967]: 81–85; Roger Dragonetti, "La Littérature et la lettre," *Lingua et Stile* 4 [1969]: 205–22; Ellen Burt, "Mallarmé's Sonnet en -yx," *Yale French Studies* 54 [1977]: 55–82). But they still leave much latitude to the reader's interpretation and concede too much ambiguity. Both latitude and ambiguity, I believe, are avoided by the concept of the poem as derivative by expansion—conversion from a matrix.

21. On conversion, see pp. 63–80.

22. But in a way nothing more than a transform of the formula that cancels the function of the home as symbol of social intercourse—the servant's response to a caller: "Monsieur n'y est pas" [Monsieur is not at home].

23. Mallarmé, *Oeuvres*, p. 1488.

24. The rhyme is difficult because /*iks*/ is an infrequent ending in French, but above all because the required alternation of feminine and masculine rhymes in a sonnet makes it necessary to find variants of /*iks*/ that do not end with a mute -*e*. The only possibility is -*ix* or -*yx* with the *x* voiced, and *that* narrows the choice down to learned words of Greek origin and spelling.

25. A model for another image of nothing: the empty mirror of the second tercet, empty of the reflection of a dead, therefore absent character.

26. A prose version entitled *Igitur* contains its own commentary in relatively straightforward French. Mallarmé himself (letter to Cazalis, Pléiade, pp. 1489–90) discusses what he meant to say. But the only relevance of poetics is to the text itself, not to the author's intention: good method demands that arguments be based on the poem alone, and this sonnet is quite self-sufficient. The sestet unfolds a description whose every detail cancels itself out: an open window, but described as *vacante*, "empty"; a light, but dying (*un or agonise*); a setting, but modified by *peut-être*, "maybe"; allegorical pictures, but on non-existent myths; a mirror described as "framed forgetfulness." The only presence not cancelled is the *septuor* of *scintillations*, the Big Dipper; the musical term suggests that the constellation is also of the sonnet's seven rhyme pairs: the only reality of the poem is its rhyming pattern.

27. For a very incomplete account of the tempest *ptyx* stirred up in scholarly teapots, see the Mondor and Jean-Aubry edition, Pléaide, pp. 1490–91. Hugo's poem is the illustrious "Satyre," published eight years before our sonnet (line 19: an enumeration of sylvan gods leads to *Chrysis/ Sylvain du Ptyx que l'homme appelle Janicule*). Hugo himself knew not of the alleged **ptyx*, "shell"; he first tried *phtyx* as an ad hoc coinage, to sound like ancient Greek with a vengeance (see *Légende des Siècles*, ed. Paul Berret [Paris: Hachette, 1922], vol. 2, pp. 573, 576).

28. Cf. pp. 12 and 17.

29. Athanasius Kircher, *Musurgia* (1662).

30. On overdetermination as a substitute for *effet de réel*, see Michael Riffaterre, "Le Poéme comme représentation," *Poetique* 4 (1970): 401–18; Michael Riffaterre, "Système d'un genre descriptif," *Poetique* 9 (1972): 15–30; Michael Riffaterre, "Interpretation and Descriptive Poetry: A Reading of Wordsworth's Yew-Trees," *New Literary History* 4 (1973): 229–56; and Philippe Hamon, "Texte littéraire et métalanguage," *Poetique* 31 (1977): 261–84.

SECTION 5

Post-Structuralist Reading

The model of a linguistic system as a self-sufficient set of signifying relations was tremendously generative for structuralist thought across many disciplines, but it was inevitable that challenges to that concept of self-sufficiency should arise. So, for example, Michel Foucault's theory of social institutions as forms of discourse may have had its roots in structuralism, but Foucault rejected that association in favor of a view of social discourses as open-ended and erratic rather than bounded and systematic. On this logic, we might expect that post-structuralism would lead to a rejection of the idea of the poem as a paradigmatically self-enclosed verbal icon, and to some extent that is true. But post-structuralist critics did and do not necessarily have post-structuralist views of lyric. As we suggested in the previous section, even if structuralist critics often treated poems as closed systems, the potential to read poetry across linguistic functions or discourses was always there. In contrast, the critics loosely grouped as post-structuralist often hold strong views of poems as isolated lyrics. The post-structuralist critic's aim is to open or unravel that lyric structure—but in order to show that lyric closure is an illusion, the critic must assume that we assume that poems have such formal coherence in the first place.

In the United States especially, the post-structuralist reading of poetry reacted more strongly to the legacy of New Criticism than it did to structuralism per se. That reaction explains something about why post-structuralist reading has so often been focused on lyric poetry in particular. With the exception of Derrida, all the critics we include in this section were trained to read poems as New Critics. Paul de Man, whose training was not by and large in the United States, may seem an exception to this rule, but in his graduate work at Harvard, de Man absorbed the New Critical paradigms of the 1950s (especially those of Reuben Brower), and much of de Man's early career was devoted to writing in response and reaction to those paradigms. For example, in "Form and Intent in the American New Criticism," a lecture first given at Johns Hopkins in the late 1960s, de Man wrote that New Criticism "was never able to overcome the anti-historical bias that presided over its beginnings" and so never benefited from "a close contact with European methods" that emphasized a more historical approach.[1] In drawing this contrast, de Man was narrating his own intellectual biography and outlining the contours of his own criticism. De Man was himself New Criticism's point of European contact—though the result of that contact was not necessarily to make formalist analysis more historical. Instead, the result was "a radical questioning of the autonomy of literature as an aesthetic activity," a challenge de Man attributed to French structuralism but which could more accurately describe the post-structuralist approaches to poetry de Man and his colleagues at Yale would pursue in the 1970s. Yet while such questioning characterized post-structuralist practice, that practice actually tended to respond to its own radical challenges by reaffirming literature's aesthetic autonomy, albeit in precarious terms.

The name that stuck to the contradictions of post-structuralist criticism was Deconstruction. In the preface to a volume of essays by the Yale critics and Derrida entitled *Deconstruction and Criticism* (1979), Geoffrey Hartman wrote, "Deconstruction, as it has come to be called, refuses to identify the force of literature with any form of embodied meaning and shows how deeply such logocentric or incarnationist perspectives have influenced the way we think about art. We assume that, by the miracle of art, the 'presence of the word' is the presence of meaning. But the opposite can also be urged, that the word carries with it a certain absence or indeterminacy of meaning" (viii). If Derridean words like "logocentric" or "incarnationist" signaled deconstructive criticism's signature departures, it is also true that, as Hartman himself states, the idea that language is indeterminate was hardly new: "to suggest that meaning and language do not coincide, and to draw from that noncoincidence a peculiar strength, is merely to restate what literature has always revealed."

In the essay from *Deconstruction and Criticism* we include in this section, Harold Bloom elaborately demonstrates the post-structuralist emphasis on the "noncoincidence" between meaning and language and likewise insists that the disjunction is constitutive of poetry—specifically, of lyric poetry. Bloom wants to defend the lyric against structuralist and post-structuralist attempts to reduce it to language or rhetoric, since "rhetoric has always been unfitted to the study of poetry, though most critics continue to ignore this incompatibility. Rhetoric arose from the analysis of political and legal orations, which are absurd paradigms for lyric poems." Bloom's strongest challenge to structuralist poetics—and, as we shall see, also to the deconstructive poetics of Derrida and de Man—is to return to the New Critical privileging of lyric form as *sui generis*. For Bloom, lyric is not a genre among other speech genres, but a genre with special rights and its own peculiar pathos, what Bloom calls the "agon" of the lyric's internal struggle to achieve and simultaneously disrupt its own aesthetic form. The pitch of that struggle makes Bloom's sense of lyric poetry larger than life, a version of the lyric as the meta-poetic, as an "archigenre" in Genette's sense.

In order to describe the "poetic warfare" that characterizes all lyric, "to show that the lustres of poetic meaning come . . . from the breaking apart of form," Bloom turns to the Gnostic exegesis of Scripture, to Kabbalah, and to Freud. Bloom calls these "properly drastic models for creative reading and creative writing"; such resorts are meant to counter "Deconstruction's ironies," in which figurative language is revealed as empty, as an elaborate illusion. For Bloom, Deconstruction goes too far—or not far enough—when it focuses on pure figuration at the expense of the energy and invention within or behind that figuration. In order to exemplify that energy and invention, Bloom offers a reading of John Ashbery's long poem, *Self-Portrait in a Convex Mirror*, a poem Bloom dramatically lyricizes in his own terms by reading it as a struggle within and against the Emersonian tradition in American poetry, a struggle in which the poet ultimately "rejects the paradise of art, but with enormous nostalgias coloring farewell." The pathos of Bloom's own version of deconstructive lyric reading is thus realized in his rendition of Ashbery's rendition of the self-portrait of Parmigianino. According to Bloom, Ashbery elects "a supermimesis achieved by an art that will not abandon the self to language." That "supermimesis" or meta-representation turns out to be lyric form itself, or rather "the poetic breaking of poetic form." This aspiration toward a lyric form that is more than a mere form and much more than a mere genre recalls Mill's idealization of the lyric, but unlike Mill, Bloom's antithetical criticism admits that the ideal lyric horizon to which his reading passionately aspires is impossible. That impossibility is what aligns Bloom's reading with other deconstructive critics and what allows him to supersize the lyric in the process.

Thus this section begins with a post-structuralist critic who resists "a theory of language that teaches the dearth of meaning, as in Derrida or de Man," with a deconstructive critic who writes against Deconstruction. That resistance serves to characterize Deconstruction, and it also situates it in a complex critical conversation. What Bloom wants to offer is not post-structuralist doctrine but what he calls "a theory of poetry," a phrase he takes from Curtius, who wrote that "the history of the theory of poetry coincides neither with the history of poetics nor with the history of literary criticism. The poet's conception of himself . . . or the tension between poetry and science . . . are major themes of a history of the theory of poetry, not of a history of poetics."[2] For Bloom, the theory of poetry has everything to do with "the poet's conception of himself." That conception takes place within a tradition, but Bloom is less concerned with "a history of the theory of poetry" than was Curtius, or for that matter than is *The Lyric Theory Reader.*

In this anthology, Bloom's theory is presented as a moment in the history of the theory of poetry, a moment that needs to be examined next to other moments in twentieth-century lyric reading to be understood. We also place it next to an instance of lyric theory that partakes of a very different history. We include Derrida's "Che cos'è la poesia?" because, as Bloom's frequent invocation of his work attests, Derrida came to be seen as the presiding influence in Deconstruction (which Derrida somewhat inadvertently named) and post-structuralism. While Derrida's general philosophical influence would be hard to overstate, it is not true that Derrida's own theory of poetry played a particularly large part in post-structuralist lyric reading. In fact, Derrida wrote very little about poetry per se. The essay we include here is Derrida's brief response to an invitation by the Italian poetry journal *Poesia* in 1988. The journal provided the title, and under this rubric Derrida characteristically offered a meditation on the difficulty of the question rather than the definition the question requested.

That meditation is also a reflection on the history of the theory of poetry. As Timothy Clark has pointed out, Derrida's comparison of poetry to a hedgehog, "the animal thrown into the road, absolute, solitary, rolled up in a ball, *next to (it)self,*" owes something to Schlegel's Romantic description of a transcendental poetry, "a poetry that will have no empirical referent but would exist as the essential or absolute poem, the self-presentation of poetic creativity (or *poeisis*) itself."[3] In relation to such an ideal, Schlegel writes that each actual poetic fragment is "complete in itself like a hedgehog." In using Schlegel's hedgehog, Derrida is invoking the problem with the Italian journal's question: Since we inherit such an idealized notion of what poetry is (or, literally, what thing poetry is), how can we think about a theory of poetry in any other terms? Derrida's implicit question is philosophical, and places itself in a history that intersects with the history of literary criticism in which Bloom writes but is not identical to it. For Derrida, the philosophical use of poetry as example has an inescapably idealist history, and yet the transmission of poetry has an inescapably practical history. Derrida puns on the practice of learning poems "by heart," a phrase that describes the dictation and memorization routine of French Colonial education but that also invokes the subjective landscape of expressive, post-romantic poetics. The metaphor of the poem as hedgehog allows Derrida to toggle back and forth between the pathetic image of the poem as an animal curled in on itself and the transcendental ideas of poetry inherent in the history of poetics (including Heidegger's characterization of the poem as "the thing in itself," an idea we will discuss in section 7). Like Bloom, Derrida is not interested in resolving this contradiction; on the contrary, the essay makes the difference between the little hedgehog at risk of being squashed on the autoroute and the grand ideas associated with poetry into an occasion for widening the gap between the two.

Unlike Bloom, however, Derrida does not stake a claim for the lyric as the genre that dramatizes "the poetic breaking of poetic form"; because Derrida's idea of the lyric is not derived from New Criticism but from the legacy of post-romantic poetics—especially from the modern inheritors of that legacy, Heidegger, Benjamin, and Husserl—his way of figuring the poem as thing-in-itself lyricizes poetry by default. The poem-hedgehog becomes the little thing at risk of being run over by poetics, by all of the ways of thinking about that history. It is small enough to learn "by heart" and compact enough to be imagined as a tiny animal. On the one hand, that staging makes philosophical approaches to poetry look absurd; on the other hand, it makes the lyricized poem as Heideggerian "thing-in-itself" look absurd, since in curling up in the middle of the road, the poem-hedgehog "thinks it is defining itself, and it loses itself." Caught between the extremes of philosophy's claims to knowledge about poetry and the poem's claim to ignorance about itself ("it is more threatened than ever in its retreat"), we are faced with an impossible choice. In order to say "what thing poetry is," according to Derrida, "you will have to disable memory, disarm culture, know how to forget knowledge, set fire to the library of poetics." That is one way to complain about a question that the history of philosophy has taken such pleasure in answering over and over, but it is interesting that Derrida's characteristic engagement with and resistance to that history takes the form of such a figurative idealization of the notion of the poem as autotelic and self-enclosed, as in need of protection from "the circus or the menagerie of *poiesis*: nothing to be done (*poiein*), neither 'pure poetry,' nor pure rhetoric, nor *reine Sprache*, nor 'setting-forth-of-the-truth-in-the-work.'" From classical notions of the idea of poetic making to late-nineteenth-century ideas of pure poetry to Frankfurt School ideas of a pure language to Heidegger's idea of the poem as imminent disclosure, Derrida attempts to move to an idea of the poem as "the very ashes of this genealogy. Not the phoenix, not the eagle, but the *hérisson*, very lowly, low down, close to the earth," an unlyrical lyric.

Yet the figure intended to be too far beneath the history of thinking about poetry to be susceptible to that history's transcendental formulations is also very much part of that history, the occasion for identification, expression, pathos, all kinds of significance: "token of election confided as legacy, it can attach itself to any word at all, to the thing, living or not, to the name of *hérisson*, for example, between life and death, at nightfall or at daybreak, distracted apocalypse, proper and common, public and secret." In effect, Derrida's attempt to defend the poem from all the things poems have been made to mean delivers the little hedgehog back into the traffic of the very ideas the figure is supposed to resist, and thus idealizes the poem's obstinate or futile sacrifice to those ideas. "By announcing that which is just as it is," the question "Che cos'è la poesia?" that begins Derrida's essay "salutes the birth of prose" at the end of the essay, since by that point the lyric poem has become the thing run over by the ongoing stream of theories about it. Derrida is aware that his way of framing the problem of definition risks making the poem into an ideal of resistance to definition. The use of the hedgehog as the character of that resistance is reminiscent of the tactics of the poet Francis Ponge (on whom Derrida wrote), but that poetic riff on poetics leaves intact the question of why such resistance to definition should be so valued in the first place.

Paul de Man, the post-structuralist lyric theorist who had most in common with Derrida, took a different route to the discovery of such lyricized resistance to grand ideas about the lyric. In "Anthropomorphism and Trope in the Lyric," de Man begins by joining poetry and philosophy in common cause. While Derrida tried (and failed) to separate the poem from poetics, de Man begins his essay by claiming that "the gesture that links epistemology with rhetoric in general" belongs to Keats as well as to Nietzsche. But what philosophers and poets turn out to have in common for de Man is not a belief that meaning and language coincide but a tendency to complicate "the assimilation of truth to trope" that they may seem to proclaim. When Nietzsche, for example, famously answers the question "What is truth?" by describing it as "a mobile army of metaphors, metonymies, anthropomorphisms," he may be taken to be saying that meaning and language are the same thing.[4] But as Barbara Johnson will put it, "de Man wants to show in what ways Nietzsche is *not* simply saying this." At the same time, de Man puts the lyric in the position of always saying this, so much so that when the coincidence between truth and trope is interrupted, the result can no longer be a lyric.

If truth comes down to an organized bunch of tropes, why, de Man asks, is the last of the tropes Nietzsche lists so "odd"? "'Anthropomorphism' is not just a trope but an identification on the level of substance," de Man contends, since "it takes one entity for another and thus implies the constitution of specific entities prior to their confusion, the *taking* of something for something else that can then appear to be *given*." When we make rocks or stones or trees into human beings, we rely on "systems of interpretation" attached to those human beings rather than to the rocks or stones or trees; in this way, anthropomorphism stands for the way in which "tropes are the producers of ideologies that are no longer true." According to de Man, though Nietzsche says as much, lyric poems offer "less schematically compressed, more elaborated and dramatized instances of similar disjunctions." Unsurprisingly, de Man chooses Baudelaire, the poet often dubbed the father of modern poetry (as Nietzsche is dubbed the father of modern philosophy); no doubt de Man had in mind as well Walter Benjamin's meditations on Baudelaire as "the poet of modern life" (excerpted in section 6). Benjamin had claimed that Baudelaire "envisaged readers to whom the reading of lyric poetry would present difficulties"; de Man claims that for modern critical readers, lyric poetry *should* (but too often does not) present difficulties, since the noncoincidence of meaning and language suggested by the philosopher undermines the lyric from within.

The pressure that de Man places on Baudelaire's poetry to perform the epistemological crises of modern philosophy is thus matched by the pressure that he places on that poetry to be representatively lyric. Baudelaire's "canonical and programmatic sonnet 'Correspondances'" fits the bill as a lyric *par excellence,* both because of its "canonical" place in literary history and because of its canonical place in lyric theory.[5] De Man uses it to argue that the extraordinary anthropomorphic claims made by the sonnet, in which man and nature seem to perfectly 'correspond,' are not sustained by the language of the sonnet, in which metaphor gives way to metonymy, comparison to enumeration. Whereas Bloom might call such disjunction "the poetic breaking of poetic form," and so an aggrandizement of lyric capacity, and Derrida might see in such disjunction the poem's stubborn (and prickly) resistance to its own poetics, de Man draws a more startling conclusion: "The lyric is not a genre, but one name among several to designate the defensive motion of understanding, the possibility of a future hermeneutics." In de Man's reading, when Baudelaire's most famous sonnet undermines its own transcendent claims to align truth and language, meaning and human experience, it undermines the idealist basis on which the modern understanding of the lyric rests, and so proves that the lyric is itself an illusion, a creation of readers who want to believe in it. "Like the oracle at Delphi," de Man writes, Baudelaire's poem "has been made to answer a considerable number and variety of questions put to it by various readers. . . . In all cases, the poem has never failed to answer to the satisfaction of the questioner." When previous literary critics have asked "Correspondances" to answer their questions about what a lyric is, the poem has given them the answers they have wanted; when de Man asks the poem to tell him that the idea of the lyric is embedded in a Nietzschean system of interpretation that results in a false lyric ideology, it also obliges.

De Man's close reading of Baudelaire's poem is very close and owes much to the New Critical mode of close reading that de Man's teacher Reuben Brower called "slow reading." The unraveling of the sonnet's illusion of an ideal correspondence between man and nature hinges on de Man's slow reading of a single word, the French word for correspondence or comparison, the little word *comme.* "When it is said that 'Les parfums, les couleurs et les sons se répondent . . . *comme* de longs échos,' then the preposition of resemblance, 'comme,' the most frequently counted word in the canon of Baudelaire's poetry, does its work properly and clearly," writes de Man. But of the final "comme" in the poem, de Man insists, "Ce comme n'est pas un comme comme les autres." At this point, de Man's close reading has become so close that he drops out of critical English into Baudelaire's French, out of commentary into near-repetition. But de Man's point is that the poem's final preposition is a repetition with a difference, a use of "comme" to mean "such as, for example" rather than "like," an enumeration rather than a proposition about resemblance. Such linguistic scrutiny may seem nitpicky, but it places de Man's reading within both New Critical and structuralist practice (one can easily imagine Jakobson writing paragraphs about such an "aberrant" use of a preposition in a poem) and so positions his conclusion as both post–New Critical and explicitly post-structuralist. "Enumerative repetition disrupts the chain of tropological substitution at the crucial moment when the poem promises, by way of these very substitutions, to reconcile the pleasures of the mind with those of the senses and to unite aesthetics with epistemology," de Man concludes. Both New Critics like Brower and structuralists like Jakobson would say that such reconciliation and unity are exactly what the lyric achieves, either dramatically for the New Critics or structurally for the structuralists. By claiming that when Baudelaire's poem disrupts the logic on which those readings depend it also disrupts the illusion on which the lyric depends, de Man admits how much his own definition of the lyric owes to those earlier systems of interpretation.

Like Derrida, de Man would like to find an outside or alternative to the history of poetics, a way to salvage Baudelaire's poem from the versions of lyric reading to which it has proven so susceptible. He looks for that alternative in another of Baudelaire's sonnets, "Obsession," written at least five years after "Correspondances," and in which (by way of another meticulous, slow reading) de Man finds a mirrored and psychologized version of the earlier poem, so much so that "the resulting couple or pair of texts . . . becomes a model for the uneasy combination of funereal monumentality and paranoid fear that characterizes the hermeneutics and pedagogy of lyric poetry." In this view, "Obsession" isn't so much an undoing of the supremely lyrical "Correspondances" as it is an explication of it—and not incidentally, also an explication of the lyric. Since "any text, as text, compels reading as its understanding," according to de Man, the way in which Baudelaire (and de Man) make one poem into a reading of another demonstrates that "what we call a lyric, the instance of represented voice, conveniently spells out the rhetorical and thematic characteristics that make it the paradigm of a complementary relationship between grammar, trope, and theme." Once we recognize that "'Obsession' leaves 'Correspondances' as thoroughly incomprehensible as it always was," we can also recognize that "in the paraphernalia of literary terminology, there is no term available to tell us what 'Correspondances' might be. All we know is that it is, emphatically, *not* a lyric. Yet it, and it alone, contains, implies, produces, generates, permits (or whatever verbal metaphor one wishes to choose) the entire possibility of the lyric." Like his assertion that "the lyric is not a genre," de Man's claim that the poem he has spent his essay reading so closely as an iconic lyric "is, emphatically, *not* a lyric" is meant to be shocking and counterintuitive. That shock is intended to wrench us out of the history of poetics that, according to de Man, the idea of the lyric itself cannot escape. By saying that the poem is not a lyric unless reading makes it so, de Man returns us to the predicament Derrida figures in the zoomorphic character of the hedgehog: how can the poem be separated from the history of its interpretation, the history of lyric reading?

Because for de Man that history includes the idealization of the poem as a drama of the speaking voice (see Brower's "The Speaking Voice" in section 3) and the idealization of the poem as linguistic exemplar (see Jakobson's "Linguistics and Poetics" in section 4), the challenge with which de Man leaves us is to abandon those ideals. Derrida's tale of a pathetic little poem-animal waiting to be run over is one funny way to meet such a challenge, but de Man's way of meeting it is tragic rather than comic. If we could separate "the materiality of actual history" from "generic terms such as 'lyric,'" which "are always terms of resistance and nostalgia," de Man writes, then we might glimpse the possibility of "non-anthropomorphic, non-elegiac, non-celebratory, non-lyrical, non-poetic, that is to say, prosaic, or better, *historical* modes of language power." Like Derrida, de Man imagines an ideal resistance to the lyric ideal, but for de Man that fantasy of resistance takes the form of what he calls "true 'mourning.'" On one hand, as the double quotation marks indicate, "mourning" refers to the subject of Baudelaire's poem, but in another way "mourning" refers to the sense of loss attendant on the failure of the lyric ideal, the loss of "the desired consciousness of eternity and of temporal harmony as voice and as song." What we feel when we can no longer feel lyrically may be more lyrical—more expressively, subjectively, passionately "true," in any case, more "*historical*"—than the romantic ideal of the lyric ever was.[6]

We end this section on the post-structuralist reading of the lyric with Barbara Johnson's reading of de Man's essay. Her "Anthropomorphism in Lyric and Law" is in this sense a post-post-structuralist reading, since it not only follows in the wake of de Man, but turns to put pressure on de Man's absolute distinction between the ideological structure of the lyric and non-lyrical "actual history." Lyric and history have more in common than de Man would lead us to believe, Johnson suggests, as we can see if we look at actual legal history in relation to de Man's understanding of Baudelaire's contribution to lyric history. "What are the relations between the laws of genre and the laws of the state?" Johnson asks, a canny way of proposing that "lyric and law might be seen as two very different ways of instating what a 'person' is." Johnson acknowledges that "there appears to be the greatest possible discrepancy between a lyric 'person' . . . and a legal 'person,'" but her point is that both depend on anthropomorphism, and thus equally depend on how we answer the question, "What is a person?" Johnson argues that de Man's complaint about anthropomorphism in the lyric is that "it is not the name of a pure rhetorical structure, but the name of a comparison, one of whose terms is treated as a given (as epistemologically resolved)." In other words, what troubles de Man about anthropomorphism in Baudelaire is that it pretends to settle the question that the poem can also be understood to unsettle, the question of how to define the human. "What comes to be at stake, then," in Johnson's reading of de Man, "is lyric poetry as a poetry of the subject." If "Correspondances" does not end by affirming the coincidence of meaning and language, human presence and its symbols, then for de Man it cannot be a lyric, since presumably a lyric must make such affirmations. But must the lyric be defined as such an idealized humanist structure, and must "actual history" be what escapes and resists lyrical intelligibility? That is the question Johnson poses to de Man, and poses as well to the history of thinking about the lyric.

It is not an easy question to answer. Johnson points out that de Man's answer seems to be yes, but that his way of saying yes may also mean no. The subject of the last sentence of de Man's essay, the sentence that lists the non-lyrical, non-anthropomorphic possibility of "*historical* modes of language power," is, Johnson notices, itself "a personification . . . The subjectivizations performed by the lyric upon the unintelligible are here rejected, but by a personification of mourning": "True 'mourning' is less deluded." Just as de Man reads the final line of "Correspondances" as undermining the lyric assurances of the previous lines, Johnson reads the final line of de Man's essay as undermining the post-structuralist critic's attempt to reverse such lyric assurances. By making the affect of the poem an anti-lyrical agent, a virtual subject who could be more or "less deluded," de Man confuses the difference between subjective lyric and the history he wants to imagine as an alternative. If such supposedly non-lyrical "actual history" can only be imagined as personified, is there really any way of escaping the lyric's anthropocentric logic? As Johnson puts it, "Has de Man's conclusion really eliminated anthropomorphism and reduced it to the trope of personification, or is anthropomorphism inescapable in the notion of mourning? Is this what lyric poetry—so often structured around the relation between loss and rhetoric—must decide? Or finesse? The least we can say is that de Man has given the last word in his own text to a personification."

Johnson hints rather than claims that de Man's utopian invocation of "*historical* modes of language power" beyond the reach of lyric ideology simplifies the way that language actually works in history. In her reading of one rather obscure case in American legal history, *Rowland v. California Men's Colony, Unit II Men's Advisory Council*, Johnson demonstrates the way legal discourse (perhaps the most powerful of historical modes of language power) becomes entangled in just the sort of anthropomorphic and anthropocentric logic on which de Man's version of the lyric depends. A case in which a group of prisoners try to sue for the right to be given free cigarettes, *Rowland v. California Men's Colony* seems an unlikely place to find a historical parallel to Baudelaire's "canonical and programmatic" sonnet. But in adjudicating the case, the Supreme Court seems to have encountered the very questions readers of "Correspondances" have encountered, since, as Johnson puts it, the Court's decision comes down to the relation or distinction between natural persons (such as individuals) and legal persons (such as associations or councils or corporations), and "is therefore about what a person is, and how you can tell the difference between a natural person and an artificial person." As we may have suspected, it is no easier to distinguish between given and made identities in law than it is in poetry. In giving the Court's majority opinion, Justice Souter invoked the 1871 "Dictionary Act," which states that "unless the context indicates otherwise, the word 'person' includes corporations, companies, associations, firms, partnerships, societies, and joint stock companies, as well as individuals." This act would seem to grant personhood to groups such as the Unit II Men's Advisory Council, thereby giving them the right to sue for their cigarettes, but Souter went on to wonder what it means to say that the context may indicate "otherwise." The words "context" and "indicate" turn out to be hard to pin down, since as

Johnson suggests, "they cannot be glossed with any finality because they name the process of glossing itself." In the end, the Court decided that the Men's Advisory Council cannot be considered a person too poor to afford his own cigarettes because the context does not indicate such a conclusion. Councils cannot be said to be poor in the same sense that people can be poor. Thus, according to Johnson, "to lack is to be human. In a sense, we have returned to de Man's question about mourning. Is lack human, or just a structure?" The questions begged by legal discourse and the questions begged by lyric discourse turn out to be the same questions.

But with a difference. If both lyric and law raise but fail to answer the question of whether there is a difference between anthropomorphism and personification, between the givenness of the essence of the human and the ways in which such essences may be made up, then surely the consequences of this confusion are not the same for poems and for Supreme Court decisions on human rights. Yet Johnson is not so sure that even this difference obtains, since "perhaps the 'fallacious lyrical reading of the unintelligible' was exactly what legislators count on lyric poetry to provide: the assumption that the human *has been* or *can be* defined so that it can then be presupposed without the question of its definition's being raised as a question—legal or otherwise. Thus the poets would truly be, as Shelley claimed, the 'unacknowledged legislators of the world,' not because they covertly determine policy, but because it is somehow necessary and useful that there *be* a powerful, presupposable, unacknowledgment." If lyric assures us that we know and can understand human experience, that we know and understand what human beings really think and feel, then lyric may end up being a more influentially "*historical* form of language power" than is the apparently more influential legislation that may follow from such assurance. Thus Johnson turns de Man's utopian ideal of actual history back toward the utopian ideal of the lyric, but in doing so she, like de Man, leaves a modern rendition of the romantic lyric intact. By invoking Shelley, Johnson also invokes the history of idealizations of Shelley as the supreme lyric poet, and so ends by granting the lyric great power indeed. Post-structuralism did not unravel the lyric; instead, post-structuralist critics tended to make the lyric even more of a modern icon than did their predecessors in the twentieth century, since by doing so they could demonstrate the difficulties and hazards, perhaps even the impossibility, of thinking about lyric theory in any other way.

NOTES

1. Paul de Man, *Blindness and Insight: Essays in the Rhetoric of Contemporary Criticism* (Minneapolis: University of Minnesota Press, 1983), 20–22.

2. Cited by Bloom as Ernst Robert Curtius, *European Literature and the Latin Middle Ages*, trans. William R. Trask (New York: Harper and Row, 1953). Reprinted with a new epilogue by Peter Godman (Princeton, NJ: Princeton University Press, 1991).

3. Timothy Clark, *The Crisis of Inspiration: Composition as a Crisis of Subjectivity in Romantic and Post-Romantic Writing* (Manchester: Manchester University Press, 2001), 261.

4. Friedrich Nietzsche, "Truth and Falsity in an Ultramoral Sense," in *Critical Theory Since Plato*, ed. Hazard Adams (Fort Worth, TX: Harcourt Brace Jovanovich, 1992), 634–39. De Man does not translate the German, perhaps making a point about the difference and coincidence between meaning and language.

5. Those theories include Walter Benjamin's, but de Man also has in mind Hugo Friedrich's *The Structure of Modern Poetry* (Evanston, IL: Northwestern University Press, 1974), in which Friedrich argues that Baudelaire invents the modern lyric.

6. On the affective excess that jags in the wake of post-structuralist thought (and in the wake of de Man in particular), see Rei Terada, *Feeling in Theory: Emotion after the "Death of the Subject"* (Cambridge, MA: Harvard University Press, 2001).

FURTHER READING

Bloom, Harold. *The Anxiety of Influence: A Theory of Poetry.* Oxford: Oxford University Press, 1973.

Bloom, Harold, Paul de Man, Jacques Derrida, Geoffrey Hartman, and J. Hillis Miller. *Deconstruction and Criticism.* New York: Seabury, 1979.

Caruth, Cathy, and Deborah Esch, eds. *Critical Encounters: Reference and Responsibility in Deconstructive Writing.* New Brunswick, NJ: Rutgers University Press, 1994.

Chase, Cynthia. *Decomposing Figures: Rhetorical Readings in the Romantic Tradition.* Baltimore: Johns Hopkins University Press, 1986.

Culler, Jonathan. "Apostrophe." In *The Pursuit of Signs: Semiotics, Literature, Deconstruction,* 135–54. London: Routledge, 1981.

———. "Deconstruction and the Lyric." In *Deconstruction Is/in America: A New Sense of the Political,* 41–51. New York: New York University Press, 1995. p.41–51

———. "Reading Lyric." *Yale French Studies* 69 (1985): 98–106.

Derrida, Jacques. "The Law of Genre." Translated by Avital Ronell. *Critical Inquiry* 7.1 (Autumn 1980): 55–81.

———. *Of Grammatology.* Translated by Gayatri Chakavorty Spivak. Baltimore: Johns Hopkins University Press, 1976.

———. *Writing and Difference.* Translated by Alan Bass. Chicago: University of Chicago Press, 1978.

De Man, Paul. *Allegories of Reading: Figural Language in Rousseau, Nietzsche, Rilke, and Proust.* New Haven, CT: Yale University Press. 1979.

———. *Blindness and Insight: Essays in the Rhetoric of Contemporary Criticism.* New York: Oxford University Press, 1971.

———. *The Rhetoric of Romanticism.* New York: Columbia University Press, 1984.

Easthope, Antony, and John O. Thompson. *Contemporary Poetry Meets Modern Theory.* Toronto: University of Toronto Press, 1991.

Edelman, Lee. *Homographesis: Essays in Gay Literary and Cultural History.* London: Routledge, 1994.

Hartman, Geoffrey. *Criticism in the Wilderness: The Study of Literature.* New Haven, CT: Yale University Press, 1980.

———. *The Fate of Reading.* Chicago: University of Chicago Press, 1975.

Hošek, Chaviva, and Patricia Parker, eds. *Lyric Poetry: Beyond New Criticism.* Ithaca, NY: Cornell University Press, 1985.

Jacobs, Carol. *The Dissimulating Harmony.* Baltimore: Johns Hopkins University Press, 1978.

Machin, Richard, and Christopher Norris, eds. *Post-Structuralist Readings of English Poetry.* Cambridge: Cambridge University Press, 1987.

Miller, J. Hillis. *Topographies.* Stanford, CA: Stanford University Press, 1995.

The Breaking of Form (1979)

5.1

Harold Bloom

The word *meaning* goes back to a root that signifies "opinion" or "intention," and is closely related to the word *moaning.* A poem's meaning is a poem's complaint, its version of Keats' Belle Dame, who looked *as if* she loved, and made sweet moan. Poems instruct us in how they break form to bring about meaning, so as to utter a complaint, a moaning intended to be all their own. The word *form* goes back to a root meaning "to gleam" or "to sparkle," but in a poem it is not form itself that gleams or sparkles. I will try to show that the lustres of poetic meaning come rather from the breaking apart of form, from the shattering of a visionary gleam.

What is called "form" in poetry is itself a trope, a figurative substitution of the as-it-were "outside" of a poem for what the poem is supposed to represent or be "about." Etymologically, "about" means "to be on the outside of" something anyway, and so "about" in regard to poems is itself only another trope. Is there some way out of this wilderness of tropes, so that we can recover some sense of either a reader's or writer's other-than-verbal needs and desires?

All that a poem can be about, or what in a poem *is* other than trope, is the skill or faculty of invention or discovery, the heuristic gift. Invention is a matter of "places," of themes, topics, subjects, or of what Kenneth Burke rephrased as the implicit presence of forms in subject-matter, and named as "the Individuation of Forms." Burke defined form in literature as "an arousing and fulfillment of desires." The Burkean formula offered in his early *Counter-Statement* is still the best brief description we have:

> A work has form in so far as one part of it leads a reader to anticipate another part, to be gratified by the sequence. (p. 124)

I will extend Burke, in a Burkean way, by investing our gratification not even in the disruption of sequence, but in our awareness, however precarious, that the sequence of parts is only another trope for form. Form, in poetry, ceases to be trope only when it becomes topos, only when it is revealed as a place of invention. This revelation depends upon a breaking. Its best analogue is when any of us becomes aware of love just as the object of love is irreparably lost. I will come back to the erotic analogue, and to the making/breaking of form, but only after I explain my own lack of interest in most aspects of what is called "form in poetry." My aim is not to demystify myself, which would bore others and cause me despair, but to clarify what I have been trying to say about poetry and criticism in a series of books published during the last five years. By "clarify" I partly mean "extend," because I think I have been clear enough for some, and I don't believe that I ever could be clear enough for others, since for them "clarity" is mainly a trope for philosophical reductiveness, or for a dreary literal-mindedness that belies any deep concern for poetry or criticism. But I also seem to have had generous readers who believe in fuller explanations than I have given. A return to origins can benefit any enterprise, and perhaps an enterprise obsessed with origins does need to keep returning to its initial recognitions, to its first troubles, and to its hopes for insight into the theory of poetry.

> By "theory of poetry" I mean the concept of the nature and function of the poet and of poetry, in distinction from poetics, which has to do with the technique of poetical composition. This distinction between the concepts "theory of poetry" and "poetics" is a fruitful one for knowledge. That *de facto* the two have contacts and often pass into each other is no objection. The history of the theory of poetry coincides neither with the history of poetics nor with the history of literary criticism. The poet's conception of himself . . . or the tension between poetry and science . . . are major themes of a history of the theory of poetry, not of a history of poetics.

I have quoted this paragraph from Curtius' great book, *European Literature and the Latin Middle Ages* (Excursus VII). My own books from *The Anxiety of Influence* through my work on Wallace Stevens are all attempts to develop a theory of poetry in just this sense. The poet's conception of himself necessarily is his poem's conception of itself, in my reading, and central to this conception is the matter of the sources of the powers of poetry.

The truest sources, again necessarily, are in the powers of poems already written, or rather, *already read.* Dryden said of poets that "we have our lineal descents and clans as well as other families." Families, at least unhappy ones, are not all alike, except perhaps in Freud's sense of "Family Romances." What dominates Freud's notion is the child's fantasy-making power. What counts in the family romance is not, alas, what the parents actually were or did, but the child's fantastic interpretation of its parents. The child provides a myth, and this myth is close to poets' myths of the origin of their creativity, because it involves the fiction of being a changeling. A changeling-fiction is one of the stances of freedom. The changeling is free because his very existence is a disjunction, and because the mystery of his origins allows for Gnostic reversals of the natural hierarchy between parents and children.

Emerson, in his most idealizing temper, said of the poets that they were liberating gods, that they were free and made others free. I would amend this by saying that poets make themselves free, by their stances towards earlier poets, and make others free only by teaching them those stances or positions of freedom.

Freedom, in a poem, must mean freedom of meaning, the freedom to have a meaning of one's own. Such freedom is wholly illusory unless it is achieved against a prior plenitude of meaning, which is tradition, and so also against language. Language, in relation to poetry, can be conceived in two valid ways, as I have learned, slowly and reluctantly. Either one can believe in a magical theory of all language, as the Kabbalists, many poets, and Walter Benjamin did, or else one must yield to a thoroughgoing linguistic nihilism, which in its most refined form is the mode now called Deconstruction. But these two ways turn into one another at their outward limits. For Deconstruction, irony is not a trope but finally is, as Paul de Man says, "the systematic undoing . . . of understanding." On this view, language is not "an instrument in the service of a psychic energy." De Man's serene linguistic nihilism welcomes the alternative vision:

> The possibility now arises that the entire construction of drives, substitutions, repressions, and representations is the aberrant, metaphorical correlative of the absolute randomness of language, prior to any figuration or meaning.

Can we prevent this distinguished linguistic nihilism, and the linguistic narcissism of poets and occultists, from turning into one another? Is there a difference between an absolute randomness of language and the Kabbalistic magical absolute, in which language is totally over-determined? In Coleridge's version of the magical view, founded on the Johannine Logos, synecdoche or symbol also was no longer a trope, but was the endless restitution of performative rhetoric, or the systematic restoration of spiritual persuasion and understanding. This remains, though with many refinements, the logocentric view of such current theorists as Barfield and Ong.

Whether one accepts a theory of language that teaches the dearth of meaning, as in Derrida and de Man, or that teaches its plenitude, as in Barfield and Ong, does not seem to me to matter. All I ask is that the theory of language be extreme and uncompromising enough. Theory of poetry, as I pursue it, is reconcilable with either extreme view of poetic language, though not with any views in between. Either the new poet fights to win freedom from dearth, or from plenitude, but if the antagonist be moderate, then the agon will not take place, and no fresh sublimity will be won. Only the agon is of the essence. Why? Is it merely my misprision, to believe that good poems must be combative?

I confess to some surprise that my emphasis upon strong poets and poems should have given so much offence, particularly to British academic journalists, though truly they do live within a steadily weakening tradition, and to their American counterparts, who yet similarly do represent a waning Modernism. The surprise stems from reading historians as inevitable as Burckhardt, philosophers as influential as Schopenhauer, scholars as informative as Curtius, and most of all from reading Freud, who is as indescribable as he is now inescapable. These writers, who are to our age what Longinus was to the Hellenistic world, have defined our Sublime for us, and they have located it in the agonistic spirit. Emerson preceded all of them in performing the same definition, the same location for America. These literary prophets teach us that the Greeks and the Renaissance were fiercely competitive in all things intellectual and spiritual, and that if we would emulate them, we hardly can hope to be free of competitive strivings. But I think these sages teach a harsher lesson, which they sometimes tell us they have learned from the poets. What is weak is forgettable and will be forgotten. Only strength is memorable; only the capacity to wound gives a healing capacity the chance to endure, and so to be heard. Freedom of meaning is wrested by combat, of meaning against meaning. But this combat consists in *a reading encounter*, and in an interpretive moment within that encounter. Poetic warfare is conducted by a kind of strong reading that I have called misreading, and here again I enter into an area where I seem to have provoked anxieties.

Perhaps, in common parlance, we need two very different words for what we now call "reading." There is relaxed reading and alert reading, and the latter, I will suggest, is always an agon. Reading well is a struggle because fictions and poems can be defined, at their best, as works that are bound to be misread, that is to say, troped by the reader. I am *not* saying that literary works are necessarily good or bad in proportion to their difficulty. Paul Valéry observed that "one only reads well when one reads with some quite personal goal in mind. It may be to acquire some power. It can be out of hatred for the author." Reading well, for Valéry, is to make one's own figuration of power, to clear imaginative space for one's own personal goal. Reading well is therefore not necessarily a polite process, and may not meet the academy's social standards of civility. I have discovered, to my initial surprise, that the reading of poetry has been as much idealized as the writing of it. Any attempt to de-idealize the writing of poetry provokes anger, particularly among weak poets, but this anger is mild compared to the fury of journalists and of many academics when the mystique of a somehow detached yet still generous, somehow disinterested yet still energetic, reading-process is called into question. The innocence of reading is a pretty myth, but our time grows very belated, and such innocence is revealed as only another insipidity.

Doubtless a more adequate social psychology of reading will be developed, but this is not my concern, any more than I am much affected by the ways in which recent critical theories have attempted to adumbrate the reader's share. A theosophy of reading, if one were available, would delight me, but though Barfield has attempted to develop one in the mode of Rudolph Steiner, such an acute version of epistemological idealism seems to me remote from the reality of reading. Gnosis and Kabbalah, though heterodox, are at once traditional and yet also de-idealizing in their accounts of reading and writing, and I continue to go back to them in order to discover properly drastic models for creative reading and critical writing.

Gnostic exegesis of Scripture is always a salutary act of textual violence, transgressive through-and-through. I do not believe that Gnosticism is only an extreme version of the reading-process, despite its deliberate esotericism and evasiveness. Rather, Gnosticism as a mode of interpretation helps to make clear why all critical reading aspiring towards strength *must* be as transgressive as it is aggressive. It is in Kabbalah, or belated Jewish Gnosis, that this textual transgression is most apparent, thanks to the superb and invaluable labors of Gershom Scholem. Scholem's researches are a demonstration that our idealisms about texts are poor illusions.

When I observe that there are *no* texts, but only interpretations, I am not yielding to extreme subjectivism, nor am I necessarily expounding any particular theory of textuality. When I wrote, once, that a strong reading is the only text, the only lie against time that endures, one enraged reviewer called my assertion a critic's sin against the Holy Ghost. The holy ghost, in this case, turned out to be Matthew Arnold, greatest of School Inspectors. But Emerson made my observation long before me, in many contexts, and many others had made it before him. Here is one of them, Rabbi Isaac the Blind, thirteenth-century Provençal Kabbalist, as cited by Scholem:

> The form of the written Torah is that of the colors of white fire, and the form of the oral Torah has colored forms as of black fire. And all these engravings and the not yet unfolded Torah existed potentially, perceptible neither to a spiritual nor to a sensory eye, until the will [of God] inspired the idea of activating them by means of primordial wisdom and hidden knowledge. Thus at the beginning of all acts there was pre-existentially the not yet unfolded Torah . . .

Rabbi Isaac goes on to insist that "the written Torah can take on corporeal form only through the power of the oral Torah." As Scholem comments, this means, "strictly speaking, there is no written Torah here on earth." Scholem is speaking of Scripture, of what we must call Text Itself, and he goes on to a formulation that I would say is true of all lesser texts, of all poems more belated than the Torah:

> Everything that we perceive in the fixed forms of the Torah, written in ink on parchment, consists, in the last analysis, of interpretations or definitions of what is hidden. *There is only an oral Torah*: that is the esoteric meaning of these words, and the written Torah is a purely mystical concept. . . . There is no written Torah, free from the oral element, that can be known or conceived of by creatures who are not prophets.

What Scholem wryly asserts does not dismay what I would call *the poet in the reader* (any reader, at least potentially) but it does dismay or provoke many professional readers, particularly in the academies. One of my most instructive memories will be always of a small meeting of distinguished professors, which had gathered to consider the qualifications of an individual whom they might ask to join their enterprise. Before meditating upon this person's merits, they spontaneously performed a little ritual of faith. One by one, in turn, they confessed their belief in the real presence of the literary text. It had an existence independent of their devotion to it. It had priority over them, would be there after they were gone, and above all it had a meaning or meanings quite apart from their interpretive activity. The literary text was *there*. Where? Why, in editions, definitive editions, upon which responsible commentaries might be written. Responsible commentaries. For "responsible," substitute what word you will, whatever anxious word might match the social pieties and professional civilities that inform the spirituality of such occasions.

I only *know* a text, any text, because I know a reading of it, someone else's reading, my own reading, a composite reading. I happen to possess a somewhat preternatural verbal memory, particularly for verse. But I do not know *Lycidas* when I recite it to myself, in the sense that I know *the Lycidas* by *the* Milton. *The* Milton, *the* Stevens, *the* Shelley, do not exist. In a recent issue of a scholarly magazine, one exegete of Shelley passionately and accurately declared his faith that Shelley was a far more gifted imagination than he could ever be. His humble but worthy destiny, he declared, was to help all of us arrive at *the* Shelley by a lifetime of patient textual, historical, and interpretive work. His outrage was plain in every sentence, and it moved me deeply, even though evidently I was the unnamed sinner who had compelled him to proclaim his passionate self-effacement.

Alas that words should be only words and not things or feelings, and alas again that it should be, as Stevens said, a world of words to the end of it. Words, even if we take them as magic, refer *only* to other words, to the end of it. Words will not interpret themselves, and common rules for interpreting words will never exist. Many critics flee to philosophy or to linguistics, but the result is that they learn to interpret poems as philosophy or as linguistics. Philosophy may flaunt its rigors but its agon with poetry is an ancient one, and never will end. Linguistic explanations doubtless achieve a happy intensity of technicality, but language is not in itself a privileged mode of explanation. Certainly the critic seeking *the* Shelley should be reminded that Shelley's poems *are* language, but the reminder will not be an indefinite nourishment to any reader. Philosophers of intertextuality and of rhetoricity usefully warn me that the meanings of an intertextual encounter are as undecidable and unreadable as any single text is, but I discover pragmatically that such philosophers at best teach me a kind of double-entry bookkeeping, which as a reader I have to discount. Every poem becomes as unreadable as every other, and every intertextual confrontation seems as much an abyssing as any other. I subtract the rhetoricity from both columns, from rhetoric as system of tropes, and from rhetoric as persuasion, and return to where I started. *Jedes Wort ist ein Vorurteil*, Nietzsche says, which I translate as: "Every word is a *clinamen*." There is always and only bias, inclination, pre-judgment, swerve; only and always the verbal agon for freedom, and the agon is carried on not by truth-telling, but by words lying against time.

Freedom and lying are intimately associated in belated poetry, and the notion that contains them both might best be named "evasion." Evasion is a process of avoiding, a way of escaping, but also it is an excuse. Usage has tinged the word with a certain stigma, but in our poetry what is being evaded ultimately is fate, particularly the necessity of dying. The study of poetry is (or ought to be) the study of what Stevens called "the intricate evasions of as." Linguistically these evasions constitute trope, but I urge a study of poetry that depends upon a larger vision of trope than traditional or modern rhetoric affords us. The positions of freedom and the strategies of lying are more than images, more than figurations, more even than the operations that Freud named "defense." Searching for a term comprehensive enough to help in the reading of poems, I offered the notion of "revisionary ratios," and found myself working with six of these, a number not so arbitrary as it has seemed to some. Rather than enumerate and describe these ratios again, I want to consider something of the limits that traditional rhetoric has set upon our description of poems.

Rhetoric has been always unfitted to the study of poetry, though most critics continue to ignore this incompatibility. Rhetoric rose from the analysis of political and legal orations, which are absurd paradigms for lyrical poems. Helen Vendler pithily sums up the continued inadequacy of traditional rhetoric to the description of lyric:

> It remains true that the figures of rhetoric, while they may be thought to appear in a more concentrated form in lyric, seem equally at home in narrative and expository writing. Nothing in the figures of paradox, or irony, or metaphor, or imagery—or in the generic conventions of, say, the elegy—specifies a basis in verse.

John Hollander, who is our leading authority upon lyrical form, illuminates tropes by calling them "turns that occur between the meanings of intention and the significances of linguistic utterances." I want to expand Hollander's description so as to open up a hidden element in all criticism that deals with figuration. Any critic necessarily tropes or turns the concept of trope in giving a reading of a specific poem. Even our most sophisticated and rigorously theoretical critics are at work on a rhetoric of rhetoric when they believe themselves merely to be distinguishing between one trope and another. A trope is troped wherever there is a movement from sign to intentionality, whenever the transformation from signification to meaning is made by the test of what aids the continuity of critical discourse. The increasingly scandalous instance is in the supposed critical distinction between metonymy and metaphor, which has become a shibboleth for weak interpreters. Jakobsonian rhetoric is fashionable, but in my judgment is wholly inapplicable to lyric poetry. Against Jakobson, I follow Kenneth Burke in seeing that the fundamental dichotomy in trope is between irony and synecdoche or, as Burke says, between dialectic and representation. There is precious little dichotomy between metonymy and metaphor or, as Burke again says, between reduction and perspective. Metonymy and metaphor alike I would trope as heightened degrees of dialectical irony, with metaphor the more extended. But synecdoche is not a dialectical trope, since as microcosm it represents a macrocosm without necessarily playing against it.

In lyric poetry, there is a crucial gap between reduction or metonymy and the part-for-whole representation of synecdoche. Metonymy is a mode of repetition, working through displacement, but synecdoche is an initial mode of identification, as its close association with the ancient topoi of definition and division would indicate. The topoi associated with metonymy are adjuncts, characteristics and notation, all of them namings through supposed cause-and-effect. A metonymy *names*, but a synecdoche begins a process that leads to an *un-naming.* While metonymy hints at the psychology of compulsion and obsession, synecdoche hints at the vicissitudes that are disorders of psychic drives. Regressive behavior expresses itself metonymically, but sado-masochism is synecdochic, in a very dark sense. I verge upon saying that naming in poetry is a limitation of meaning, whereas un-naming restitutes meaning, and so adds to representation.

This way of connecting trope and psychic defense, which to me seems an inevitable aid in the reading of poetry, itself has encountered a good deal of psychic defense in my more unnamable critics. What is the justification for linking language and the ego, trope and defense, in relatively fixed patterns? Partly, the rationale would depend upon a diachronic, rather than a synchronic, view of rhetoric, that is, upon an analytic rhetoric that would observe the changing nature of both linguistic trope and psychic defense as literary history moved from the Ancient world to the Enlightenment, and then on to Milton as prophet of Post-Enlightenment poetry. But, in part, the explanation for reading trope as defense and defense as trope goes back to my earlier observations on criticism as the rhetoric of rhetoric, and so on each critic's individual troping of the concept of trope. If rhetoric has its diachronic aspect, then so does criticism as the rhetoric of rhetoric. A study of Post-Enlightenment criticism from its prophet, Dr. Johnson, on to our contemporaries would reveal that its rhetoric was reborn out of Associationist psychology, and that the crucial terms of that psychology themselves stemmed from the topoi of a rejected classical rhetoric, ostensibly rejected by the Enlightenment but actually troped rather than rejected.

This complex phenomenon needs to be studied in detail, and I am attempting such a study currently in a book on the Sublime and the concept of topos as image-of-voice in Post-Enlightenment poetry. Here I want only to extract a dilemma of the relation between style and idea in the perpetual, onward Modernizing march of all post-Miltonic poetry. From the poets of Sensibility down to our current post-Stevensian contemporaries, poetry has suffered what I have termed elsewhere an over-determination of language and consequently an under-determination of meaning. As the verbal mechanisms of crisis have come to dominate lyric poetry, in relatively fixed patterns, a striking effect has been that the strongest poets have tended to establish their mastery by the paradox of what I would call *an achieved dearth of meaning.* Responding to this achieved dearth, many of the strongest critics have tended to manifest *their* skill by attributing the dearth to their own synchronic view of language and so to the vicissitudes of *language itself* in producing meaning. A diachronic phenomenon, dependent upon Miltonic and Wordsworthian poetic *praxis*, is thus assigned to a synchronic cause. Deconstructionist criticism refuses to situate itself in its own historical dilemma, and so by a charming paradox it falls victim to a genealogy to which evidently it must remain blind. Partly, this paradox is due to the enormous and significant difference between Anglo-American poetic tradition, and the much weaker French and German poetic traditions. French poetry lacks not only early giants of the dimension of Chaucer, Spenser, and Shakespeare, but it also is devoid of any later figures whose strength could approximate Milton and Wordsworth, Whitman and Dickinson. There is also the oddity that the nearest French equivalent, Victor Hugo, remains absurdly unfashionable and neglected by his nation's most advanced critics. Yet the "achieved dearth of meaning" in French poetry is clearly exemplified more even by Hugo than by Mallarmé, just as in English it is accomplished more powerfully by Wordsworth and Whitman than it is by Eliot and Pound.

If this judgment (however unfashionable) is correct, then it would be sustained by a demonstration that the revisionary patterns of Modern poetry are set by Wordsworth and Whitman (or by Hugo, or in German by the later Goethe), and by the further demonstration that these fixed or all-but-fixed relations between trope and defense reappear in Baudelaire, Mallarmé, and Valéry, in Hölderlin and Rilke, in Yeats and Stevens and Hart Crane. These patterns, which I have mapped as a sequence of revisionary ratios, are not the invention of belated moderns but of inaugural moderns, the High Romantics, and of Milton, that mortal god, the Founder from whom Wordsworth and Emerson (as Whitman's precursor) derive.

Ratios, as a critical idea, go back to Hellenistic criticism, and, to a crucial clash between two schools of interpretation, the Aristotelian-influenced school of Alexandria and the Stoic-influenced school of Pergamon. The school of Alexandria championed the mode of *analogy*, while the rival school of Pergamon espoused the mode of *anomaly*. The Greek *analogy* means "equality of ratios," while anomaly means a "disproportion of ratios." Whereas the analogists of Alexandria held that the literary text was a unity and had a fixed meaning, the anomalists of Pergamon in effect asserted that the literary text was an interplay of differences and had meanings that rose out of those differences. Our latest mimic wars of criticism thus repeat battles fought in the second century B.C. between the followers of Crates of Mallos, Librarian of Pergamon, and the disciples of Aristarchus of Samothrace, Librarian of Alexandria. Crates, as an Anomalist, was what nowadays Hillis Miller calls an "uncanny" critic or, as I would say, an "antithetical" critic, a student of the revisionary ratios that take place *between* texts. Richard McKeon notes that the method of Crates led to allegories of reading, rather than to Alexandrian or analogical New Criticism, and I am prepared to call my work an allegory of reading, though very different from the allegories of reading formulated by Derrida and de Man, legitimate rival descendants of Crates.

The breaking of form to produce meaning, as I conceive it, depends upon the operation of certain instances of language, revisionary ratios, and on certain topological displacements in language that intervene between ratios, displacements that I have been calling "crossings."

To account for these ratios, without defending here their name and their number, I have to return to my earlier themes of the aggression of reading and the transgression of writing, and to my choice of a psychic rather than a linguistic model in a quest for tropes that might illuminate acts of reading.

Anna Freud, in her classic study, *The Ego and the Mechanisms of Defense*, notes that

> . . . all the defensive measures of the ego against the id are carried out silently and invisibly. The most that we can ever do is to reconstruct them in retrospect: we can never really witness them in operation. This statement applies, for instance, to successful repression. The ego knows nothing of it; we are aware of it only subsequently, when it becomes apparent that something is missing.

As I apply Anna Freud, in a poem the ego is the poetic self and the id is the precursor, idealized and frequently composite, hence fantasized, but still traceable to a historical author or authors. The defensive measures of the poetic self against the fantasized precursor can be witnessed in operation only by the study of a difference between ratios, but this difference depends upon our awareness not so much of presences as of absences, of *what is missing in the poem because it had to be excluded*. It is in this sense that I would grant a point made by John Bayley, that I am "fascinated by the sort of poetry that is *not really there*, and—even better—the kind that knows it never can be." But Bayley errs in thinking that this is only one tradition of the poetry of the last three centuries, because clearly it is the norm, or the condition of belated, strong poetry. The authentic poem now achieves its dearth of meaning by strategies of exclusion, or what can be called litanies of evasion. I will quote a sympathetic British critic, Roger Poole, for a more useful account of this problematic element in our poetry:

> If a poem is really 'strong' it represents a menace. It menaces the way the reader thinks, loves, fears and is. Consequently, the reading of strong poetry can only take place under conditions of mutual self-defense. Just as the poet must not know what he knows, and must not state what he states, so the reader must not read what he reads. [The] question is not so much 'What does this poem mean?' as 'What has got left out of this poem to make of it the particularly expensive torso that it is?'

To adumbrate Poole's observations a touch more fully, I would suggest that we all suffer from an impoverished notion of poetic allusion. No strong poem merely alludes to another, and what look like overt allusions and even echoes in strong poems are disguises for darker relationships. A strong authentic allusion to another strong poem can be only by and in what the later poem *does not say*, by what it represses. This is another aspect of a limitation of poetry that defines poetry: a poem can be *about* experience or emotion or whatever only by initially encountering another poem, which is to say a poem must handle experience and emotion as if they already were rival poems. Poetic knowledge is necessarily a knowledge by tropes, an experience of emotion as trope, and an expression of knowledge and emotion by a revisionary further troping. Since a poem is necessarily still further troped in any strong reading, there is a bewildering triple inter-tropicality at work that makes a mockery of most attempts at reading. I do not agree wholly with de Man that reading is impossible, but I acknowledge how very difficult it is to read a poem properly, which is what I have meant by my much-attacked critical trope of "misreading" or "misprision." With three layers of troping perpetually confronting us, the task of restituting meaning or of healing a wounded rhetoricity is a daunting one. Yet it can and must be attempted. The only alternative I can see is the triumph of Romantic irony in purified form by way of the allegory of reading formulated by Paul de Man. But this most advanced version of Deconstruction cheerfully accepts the risk warned against by de Man's truest precursor, Friedrich Schlegel: "The irony of irony is the fact that one becomes weary of it if one is offered it everywhere and all the time."

To evade such destructive weariness, I return to the poetic equivalent of Freud's concept of defense. The center of the poetic self, of the speaking subject that Demanian

Deconstruction dissolves into irony, is narcissistic self-regard. Such poetic self-esteem is wounded by its realization of belatedness, and the wound or narcissistic scar provokes the poetic self into the aggressivity that Freud amazingly chose to call "defense." Even Freud, like all the rest of us, idealized the arts, it being Nietzsche's distinction that in this too he was the grand exception, though to some extent he shares this particular distinction with Kierkegaard. Because of such prevalent idealization, we all of us still resist the supposed stigma of identifying the strong poet's drive towards immortality with the triadic sequence of narcissism, wounded self-regard, and aggression. But change in poetry and criticism as in any human endeavor comes about only through aggression. Unless a strong poet strongly loves his own poetry, he cannot hope to get it written. When Robinson Jeffers writes that he hates his verses, every line, every word, then my response is divided between a sense that he lies, and a stronger sense that perhaps he tells the truth, and *that* is the trouble. Alas that poetic self-love should not in itself be sufficient for strength, but it is no good lamenting that it should be necessary for poetic strength. Pindar, one of our earliest instances of lyric strength, should have taught all of us that poetic narcissism is at the root of any lyric Sublime. The first Olympic ode, still the truest paradigm for Western lyric, overtly celebrates Hieron of Syracuse, yet the horse and rider more fully and implicitly celebrated are Pegasus and Pindar. Lyric celebrates the poetic self, despite every denial. Yet we refuse the lesson, even as Freud partly did. A poet, as much as any man or woman among us, scarcely feels complimented when described as narcissistic and aggressive. But what *can* poetry give back, either as successful representation or achieved pathos, and whether to poet or reader, except for a *restitution of narcissism*? And since paranoid thinking can be defined as a complete shield against being influenced, what is it that saves strong poets from paranoid thinking except for their early susceptibility to poetic influence, an openness that *must* in time scar the narcissism of the poet *qua* poet. For those who scoff still at the idea of the anxiety of influence, I shall cite the second and belated Pindar, Hölderlin, in a letter he wrote to his precursor, Schiller:

> I have sufficient courage and judgment to free myself from other masters and critics and to pursue my own path with the tranquil spirit necessary for such an endeavor, but in regard to *you*, my dependence is insurmountable; and because I know the profound effect a single word from you can have on me, I sometimes strive to put you out of my mind so as not to be overcome by anxiety at my work. For I am convinced that such anxiety, such worry is the death of art, and I understand perfectly well why it is more difficult to give proper expression to nature when the artist finds himself surrounded by masterpieces than when he is virtually alone amidst the living world. He finds himself too closely involved with nature, too intimately linked with it, to consider the need for rebelling against its authority or for submitting to it. But this terrible alternation is almost inevitable when the young artist is exposed to the mature genius of a master, which is more forceful and comprehensible than nature, and thus more capable of enslaving him. It is not a case of one child playing with another child—the primitive equilibrium attained between the first artist and his world no longer holds. The child is now dealing with men with whom he will never in all probability be familiar enough to forget their superiority. And if he feels this superiority he must become either rebellious or servile. Or must he?

This passage, anguished in its sense of contamination, is cited by René Girard as another instance of the violence of thematicism that he names as a progression "from mimetic desire to the monstrous double." I would prefer to read it as an exercise in self-misprision, because in it a very strong poet evasively relies upon a rhetoric of pathos to portray himself as being weak. The revisionary ratio here employed against Schiller is what I call *kenosis* or repetition and discontinuity. Appearing to empty himself of his poetic godhood, Hölderlin actually undoes and isolates Schiller, who is made to ebb more drastically than the ephebe ebbs, and who falls hard where Hölderlin falls soft. This *kenosis* dares the profoundest evasion of naming as the death of art what is the life of Hölderlin's art, the ambivalent and agonistic clearing-away of Schiller's poetry in order to open up a poetic space for Hölderlin's own achievement. Freud, in his final phase, taught us what we may call "the priority of anxiety"—that is, the dominance of the pleasure principle by tendencies more primitive than it, and independent of it. Hölderlin teaches us the same, even as he denies his own teaching. Freud belatedly discovered that certain dreams in traumatic neuroses come out of "a time before the purpose of dreams was the fulfillment of wishes" and so are attempts "to master the stimulus retrospectively by developing the anxiety." Hölderlin, in his greatest odes, earlier discovered that poetic thoughts did not sublimate desires, but were endeavors to master a quasi-divine reality by developing the anxiety that came from the failure to realize poetic godhood. As a poet, Hölderlin knew what as a man he denies in his letter to Schiller, which is that the anxiety of influence is a figuration for Sublime poetry itself.

Defense therefore is the natural language of Hölderlin's poetic imagination and of every Post-Enlightenment imagination that can aspire convincingly to something like Hölderlin's Sublime strength. But in language itself defense is compelled to be manifested as trope. I have argued elsewhere for certain paradigmatic links between specific tropes and specific defenses, at least since Milton's day, and I will not repeat such argument here. But I have never elucidated the relation of trope to my revisionary ratios, and that will be my concern in the remainder of the theoretical portion of this essay, after which I will conclude by speculating upon the role of the ratios in the poetic breaking of poetic form. An excursus in practical criticism will follow, so as to apply my sequence of ratios to the interpretation of John Ashbery's recent long poem, *Self-Portrait in a Convex Mirror.*

It is certainly very difficult to chart anomalies, particularly *within* a poem yet in reference *to* the impingement of another poem. Revisionary ratios are thus at once intra-poetic *and* inter- poetic, which is a necessary doubling since the ratios are meant to map an internalizing of tradition. Tradition is internalized only when a total stance toward precursors is taken up by a new strong poet. Such a stance is a mode of deliberateness, but it can operate at many levels of consciousness, and with many shades between negation and avowal. As John Hollander observed, ratios are "at once text, poem, image and model." As text, a ratio names intertextual differences; as poem it characterizes a total relationship between two poets, earlier and later. As model, a ratio functions the way a paradigm works in the problem-solving of normal science. It is as image that a ratio is most crucial, for the revisionary ratios are, to cite Hollander again, "the varied positions of freedom" or "true position" for a poet.

Freud's patterns of psychic images are the defenses, a tropological system masking itself as a group of operations directed against change, but actually so contaminated by the drives it would deflect as to become a compulsive and unconscious process like the drives. But eventually Freud was to assert that "the theory of the drives is so to say our mythology. Drives are mythical entities, magnificent in their indefiniteness." To this audacity of the Founder I would add that defenses are no less mythological. Like tropes, defenses are turning-operations, and in language tropes and defenses crowd together in the entity rather obscurely called poetic images. Images are ratios between what is uttered and what, somehow, is intended, and as Kenneth Burke remarks, you cannot discuss images for very long without sliding into whole textures of relationships. Cannot *those* relationships be charted? If it is extravagant to create a new rhetoric, this extravagance, as Joseph

Riddel says, "simply repeats the wandering or indirect movement of all trope." But trope, or the play of substitution, is purely a temporal process. Ratios of revision between earlier and later poets and poems are as much spatial as temporal, though the space be imaginative or visionary. Rhetorical criticism, even of the advanced deconstructive kind, treats a poem merely as a formal and linguistic structure. But strong poems manifest the will to utter permanent truths of desire, and to utter these *within* a tradition of utterance. The intention to prophesy is necessarily a dynamic of space as well as time, particularly when the prophecy insists upon finding its authority *within* a tradition of what has been prophesied. As soon as we speak of what is within a previous utterance, our discourse is involved in thematics, in topology or literary place. Themes are things placed into stance, stance is the attitude or position of the poet in the poem, and placing is a dynamic of desire seeking either its apotheosis or its entropic self-destruction.

A power of evasion may be the belated strong poet's most crucial gift, a psychic and linguistic cunning that energizes what most of us have over-idealized as the imagination. Self-preservation is the labor of the poem's litanies of evasion, of its dance-steps beyond the pleasure principle. Where a defensive struggle is carried on, there must be some self-crippling, some wounding of energies, even in the strongest poets. But the uncanny or Sublime energies of poetic evasion, operating through the graduated anomalies that are ratios of revision, constitute the value-creating power of the anxiety of influence. Ann Wordsworth summarizes this eloquently, when she speaks of "this ingenious ravelling, a process as determinant perhaps as dream-work" which is "the creative mind's capacity to know through the precursor, to renew through misprision, and to expand into the full range of human experience." Where my formulation and use of revisionary ratios have been most attacked is in their sequence, and in the recurrence of that sequence in so many poems of the last two hundred years. I have meant that we are to read through ratios and not into them, so that they cannot be regarded as reductive entities, but still their frequency causes disquiet. So it should, but hardly because revisionary ratios are my own paranoid code, as some journalists have suggested. And yet a few closing words on paranoid codes may be in place just here and now in this fictional time of Borges and Pynchon.

Commenting on *The Crying of Lot 49*, the book's best critic, Frank Kermode alas, observes that "a great deviation is called a sect if shared, paranoia if not." Kermode charmingly goes on to recall that "a man once undertook to demonstrate infallibly to me that *Wuthering Heights* was an interlinear gloss on Genesis. How could this be disproved? He had hit on a code, and legitimated all the signs." Kermode's point is that this is the danger that both Pynchon's Oedipa and the novel's reader confront. Warning us, Kermode asks us to remember that "deception is the discovery of the novel, not of its critics." If Kermode is correct in this, then I would call Pynchon, in just that respect, too much of a moralist and too little of a strong poet. If evasion is the discovery of the post-Miltonic poem, it is also the discovery of the poem's critics. Every belated poem that matters ends with either the narrative gesture, postponing the future, *by projecting it*, or else the prophetic gesture, hastening the future, *by introjecting it*. These defensive operations can be regarded as either the work of negation, intellectually freeing us from some of the consequences of repression, or the labor of paranoia, reducing reality to a code. I would hope to have done part of the work of negation for some readers and lovers of poetry besides myself. There is no reading worthy of being communicated to another unless it deviates to break form, twists the lines to form a shelter, and so makes a meaning through that shattering of belated vessels. That shattering is rhetorical, yes, but more than language is thus wounded or blinded. The poet of our moment and of our climate, our Whitman and our Stevens, says it best for me, and so I end with the eloquence of John Ashbery:

The song makes no mention of directions.
At most it twists the longitude lines overhead
Like twigs to form a crude shelter. (The ship
Hasn't arrived, it was only a dream. It's somewhere near
Cape Horn, despite all the efforts of Boreas to puff out
Those drooping sails.) The idea of great distance
Is permitted, even implicit in the slow dripping
Of a lute. How to get out?
This giant will never let us out unless we blind him.

Che cos'è la poesia? (1988; trans. 1991) 5.2

Jacques Derrida Translated by Peggy Kamuf [1]

In order to respond to such a question—*in two words, right?*—you are asked to know how to renounce knowledge. And to know it well, without ever forgetting it: demobilize culture, but never forget in your learned ignorance what you sacrifice on the road, in crossing the road.

Who dares to ask me that? Even though it remains inapparent, since disappearing is its law, the answer *sees itself (as) dictated (dictation).* I am *a* dictation, pronounces poetry, learn me by heart, copy me down, guard and keep me, look out for me, look at me, dictated dictation, right before your eyes: soundtrack, *wake*, trail of light, photograph of the feast in mourning.

It sees itself, the response, dictated to be poetic, by being poetic. And for that reason, it is obliged to address itself to someone, singularly to you but as if to the being lost in anonymity, between city and nature, an imparted secret, at once public and private, *absolutely* one and the other, absolved from within and from without, neither one nor the other, the animal thrown onto the road, absolute, solitary, rolled up in a ball, *next to (it) self.* And for that very reason, it may get itself run over, *just so*, the *hérisson, istrice*[2] in Italian, in English, hedgehog.

And if you respond otherwise depending on each case, taking into account the space and time which you are *given* with this *demand* (already you are speaking Italian),[3] by the demand itself, according to *this* economy but also in the imminence of some traversal *outside* yourself, away from *home*, venturing toward the language of the other in view of an impossible or denied translation, necessary but desired like a death—what would all of this, the very thing in which you have just begun to turn deliriously, have to do, at that point, with poetry? Or rather, with the *poetic*, since you intend to speak about an *experience*, another word for voyage, here the aleatory rambling of a trek, the strophe[4] that turns but never leads back to discourse, or back home, at least is never reduced to poetry—written, spoken, even sung.

Here then, right away, *in two words*, so as not to forget:

1. *The economy of memory*: a poem must be brief, elliptical by vocation, whatever may be its objective or apparent expanse. Learned unconscious of *Verdichtung* and of the retreat.
2. *The heart.* Not the heart in the middle of sentences that circulate risk-free through the interchanges and let themselves be translated into any and all languages. Not simply the heart archived by cardiography, the object of sciences or technologies, of philosophies and bio-ethico-juridical discourses. Perhaps not the heart of the Scriptures or of Pascal, nor even, this is less certain, the one that Heidegger prefers to them. No, a story of "heart" poetically enveloped in the idiom "*apprendre par coeur*," whether in my language or another, the English language [to learn by heart], or still another, the Arab language (*hafiza a'n zahri kalb*)—a single trek with several tracks.[5]

Two in one: the second axiom is rolled up in the first. The poetic, let us say it, would be that which you desire to learn, but from and of the other, thanks to the other and under dictation, by heart; *imparare a memoria*. Isn't that already it, the poem, once a token is given, the advent[6] of an event, at the moment in which the traversing of the road named translation remains as improbable as an accident, one which is all the same intensely dreamed of, required there where what it promises always leaves something to be desired? A grateful recognition goes out toward that very thing and precedes cognition here: your benediction before knowledge.

A fable that you could recount as the gift of the poem, it is an emblematic story: someone writes *you*, to you, of you, on you. No, rather a mark addressed to you, left and confided with you, is accompanied by an injunction, in truth it is instituted in this very order which, in its turn, constitutes you, assigning your origin or giving rise to you: destroy me, or rather render my support invisible to the outside, in the world (this is already the trait of all dissociations, the history of transcendences), in any case do what must be done so that the provenance of the mark remains from now on unlocatable or unrecognizable. Promise it: let it be disfigured, transfigured or rendered indeterminate in its *port*—and in this word you will hear the shore of the departure as well as the referent toward which a translation is portered. Eat, drink, swallow my letter, carry it, transport it in you, like the law of a writing become your body: *writing in (it)self.* The ruse of the injunction may first of all let itself be inspired by the simple possibility of death, by the risk that a vehicle poses to every finite being. You hear the catastrophe coming. From that moment on imprinted directly on the trait, come from the heart, the mortal's desire awakens in you the movement (which is contradictory, you follow me, a double restraint, an aporetic constraint) to guard from oblivion this thing which in the same stroke exposes itself to death and protects itself—in a word, the address, the retreat of the *hérisson*, like an animal on the autoroute rolled up in a ball. One would like to take it in one's hands, undertake to learn it and understand it, to keep it for oneself, near oneself.

You love—keep that in its singular form,[7] we could say in the irreplaceable *literality of the vocable* if we were talking about poetry and not only about the poetic in general. But our poem does not hold still within names, nor even within words. It is first of all thrown out on the roads and in the fields, thing beyond languages, even if it sometimes happens that it recalls itself in language, when it gathers itself up, rolled up in a ball on itself, it is more threatened than ever in its retreat: it thinks it is defending itself, and it loses itself.

Literally: you would like to retain by heart an absolutely unique form, an event whose intangible singularity no longer separates the ideality, the ideal meaning as one says, from the body of the letter. In the desire of this absolute inseparation, the absolute nonabsolute, you breathe the origin of the poetic. Whence the infinite resistance to the transfer of the letter which the animal, in its name, nevertheless calls out for. That is the distress of the *hérisson*. What does the distress, *stress* itself, want? *Stricto sensu*, to put on guard. Whence the prophecy: translate me, watch, keep me yet a while, get going, save yourself, let's get off the autoroute.

Thus the dream of *learning by heart* arises in you. Of letting your heart be traversed by the dictated dictation. In a single trait—and that's the impossible, that's the poematic experience. You did not yet know the heart, you learn it thus. From this experience and from this expression. I call a poem that very thing that teaches the heart, invents the heart, *that which*, finally, the word *heart* seems to mean and which, in my language, I cannot easily discern from the word itself. *Heart*, in the poem "learn by heart" (to be learned by heart), no longer names only pure interiority, independent spontaneity, the freedom to affect oneself actively by reproducing the beloved trace. The memory of the "by heart" is confided like a prayer—that's safer—to a certain exteriority of the automaton, to the laws of mnemotechnics, to that liturgy that mimes mechanics on the surface, to the automobile that surprises your passion and bears down on you as if from an outside: *auswendig*, "by heart" in German.[8]

So: your heart beats, gives the downbeat, the birth of rhythm, beyond oppositions, beyond outside and inside, conscious representation and the abandoned archive. A heart down there, between paths and autostradas, outside of your presence, humble, close to the earth, low down. Reiterate(s) in a murmur: never repeat . . . In a single cipher, the poem (the learning by heart, learn it by heart) seals together the meaning and the letter, like a rhythm spacing out time.

In order to respond in two words: *ellipsis*, for example, or *election*, *heart*, *hérisson*, or *istrice*, you will have had to disable memory, disarm culture, know how to forget knowledge, set fire to the library of poetics. The unicity of the poem depends on this condition. You must celebrate, you have to commemorate amnesia, savagery, even the stupidity[9] of the "by heart": the *hérisson*. It blinds itself. Rolled up in a ball, prickly with spines, vulnerable and dangerous, calculating and ill-adapted (because it makes itself into a ball, sensing the danger on the autoroute, it exposes itself to an accident). No poem without accident, no poem that does not open itself like a wound, but no poem that is not also just as wounding. You will call poem a silent incantation, the aphonic wound that, of you, from you, I want to learn by heart. It thus takes place, essentially, without one's having to do it or make it: it *lets itself* be done, without activity, without work, in the most sober *pathos*, a stranger to all production, especially to creation. The poem falls to me, benediction, coming of (or from) the other. Rhythm but dissymmetry. There is never anything but some poem, before any *poiesis*. When, instead of "poetry," we said "poetic," we ought to have specified: "poematic." Most of all do not let the *hérisson* be led back into the circus or the menagerie of *poiesis*: nothing to be done (*poiein*), neither "pure poetry," nor pure rhetoric, nor *reine Sprache*, nor "setting-forth-of-truth-in-the-work."[10] Just this contamination, and this crossroads, this accident here. This turn, the turning round of *this* catastrophe. The gift of the poem cites nothing, it has no title, its histrionics are over, it comes along without your expecting it, cutting short the breath, cutting all ties with discursive and especially literary poetry. In the very ashes of this genealogy. Not the phoenix, not the eagle, but the *hérisson*, very lowly, low down, close to the earth. Neither sublime, nor incorporeal, angelic, perhaps, and for a time.

You will call poem from now on a certain passion of the singular mark, the signature that repeats its dispersion, each time beyond the *logos*, ahuman, barely domestic, not reappropriable into the family of the subject: a converted animal, rolled up in a ball, turned toward the other and toward itself, in sum, a thing—modest, discreet, close to the earth, the humility that you surname, thus transporting yourself in the name beyond a name, a catachrestic *hérisson*, its arrows held at ready, when this ageless blind thing hears but does not see death coming.

The poem can roll itself up in a ball, but it is still in order to turn its pointed signs toward the outside. To be sure, it can reflect language or speak poetry, but it never relates back to itself, it never moves by itself like those machines, bringers of death. Its event always interrupts or derails absolute knowledge, autotelic being in proximity to itself. This "demon of the heart" never gathers itself together, rather it loses itself and gets off the track (delirium or mania), it exposes itself to chance, it would rather let itself be torn to pieces by what bears down upon it.

Without a subject: poem, perhaps there is some, and perhaps it *leaves itself*, but I never write any. A poem, I never sign(s) it. The other sign(s). The *I* is only at the coming of this desire: to learn by heart. Stretched, tendered forth to the point of subsuming its own support, thus without external support, without substance, without subject, absolute of writing in (it)self, the "by heart" lets itself be elected beyond the body, sex, mouth, and eyes; it erases the borders, slips through the hands, you can barely hear it, but it teaches us the heart. Filiation, token of election confided as legacy, it can attach itself to any word at all, to the thing, living or not, to the name of *hérisson*, for example, between life and death, at nightfall or at daybreak, distracted apocalypse, proper and common, public and secret.

—But the poem you are talking about, you are getting off the track, it has never been named thus, or so arbitrarily.

—You just said it. Which had to be demonstrated. Recall the question: "What is . . . ?" (*tí estí, was ist . . . , istoria, episteme, philosophia*). "What is . . . ?" laments the disappearance of the poem—another catastrophe. By announcing that which is just as it is, a question salutes the birth of prose.

NOTES

1. Translator's Notes: The Italian poetry journal *Poesia* invited Derrida to write something for the rubric with which it opens every issue under the title "Che cos'è la poesia?" (What is poetry? or more literally, What thing is poetry?). Derrida responded with this brief text that was then published beside its Italian translation. As always, Derrida works to abolish the distance between what he is writing about (poetry, the poem, the poetic, or as he will finally call it: the poematic) and what his writing is *doing*. Reference without referent, this poem defines or describes only itself even as it points beyond itself to the poetic in general. It is, writes Derrida, a *hérisson*, in Italian *istrice*, a name which loses all its rich resonance as soon as it is translated into English: hedgehog, a European cousin of the porcupine that has similar habits of self-defense. The risk of this loss in crossing over from one language to another, or already in the transfer into any language at all, causes the *hérisson* to roll itself into a ball in the middle of the road and bristle its spines: *hérisser* means to bristle or to spike, and therefore it may be said of a text that it is spiked with difficulties or even traps (e.g., "de nombreux pièges hérissent le texte"). If indeed the poetic bristles with difficulty, this very mechanism of turning in on itself for protection from the rush of traffic is also what exposes it to being rubbed out, obliterated. Thus, the poem's appeal to the heart and to that other mechanism for remembering which is called, in many languages, learning by heart. To increase the *hérisson*'s chances of getting across the road, we have posted a number of signs here the length of the distance to be traversed. These guideposts, in lieu of notes, are set

to one side so they will not get underfoot of the creature's movements.

2. Throughout the text, the *str*-sound is stressed. One may hear in it the distress of the beast caught in the strictures of this translation.

3. Because in Italian, *domanda* means question.

4. Stanza; from the Greek: turn.

5. *Voies*, for which a homonym would be *voix*, voices.

6. *La venue*, also "she who has come."

7. Somewhere in "Envois" Derrida wonders how one can say "I love you" in English, which does not distinguish between "you" singular and "you" plural.

8. But also "outward" or "outside."

9. *Bêtise* from *bête*, beast or animal.

10. See Heidegger, *The Origin of the Work of Art*.

Anthropomorphism and Trope in the Lyric (1984)

5.3

PAUL DE MAN

The gesture that links epistemology with rhetoric in general, and not only with the mimetic tropes of representation, recurs in many philosophical and poetic texts of the nineteenth century, from Keats's "Beauty is truth, truth beauty" to Nietzsche's perhaps better known than understood definition of truth as tropological displacement: "Was ist also Wahrheit? Ein bewegliches Heer von Metaphern, Metonymien, Anthropomorphismen . . . "[1] Even when thus translated before it has been allowed to run one third of its course, Nietzsche's sentence considerably complicates the assimilation of truth to trope that it proclaims. Later in the essay, the homology between concept and figure as symmetrical structures and aberrant repressions of differences is dramatized in the specular destinies of the artist and the scientist-philosopher. Like the Third Critique, this late Kantian text demonstrates, albeit in the mode of parody, the continuity of aesthetic with rational judgment that is the main tenet and the major crux of all critical philosophies and "Romantic" literatures. The considerable difference in tone between Nietzsche and Kant cannot conceal the congruity of the two projects, their common stake in the recovery of controlled discourse on the far side of even the sharpest denials of intuitive sense-certainties. What interests us primarily in the poetic and philosophical versions of this transaction, in this give-and-take between reason and imagination, is not, at this point, the critical schemes that deny certainty considered in themselves, but their disruption by patterns that cannot be reassimilated to these schemes, but that are nevertheless, if not produced, then at least brought into focus by the distortions the disruption inflicts upon them.

Thus, in the Nietzsche sentence, the recovery of knowledge by ways of its devalorization in the deviance of the tropes is challenged, even at this moment of triumph for a critical reason which dares to ask and to reply to the question: what is truth? First of all, the listing of particular tropes is odd, all the more so since it is technically more precise than is often the case in such arguments: only under the pen of a classical philologist such as Nietzsche is one likely to find combined, in 1872, what Gérard Genette has since wittily referred to as the two "chiens de faience" of contemporary rhetoric—metaphor and metonymy. But the third term in the enumeration, anthropomorphism, is no longer a philological and neutral term, neither does it complement the two former ones: anthropomorphisms can contain a metaphorical as well as a metonymic moment—as in an Ovidian metamorphosis in which one can start out from the contiguity of the flower's name to that of the mythological figure in the story, or from the resemblance between a natural scene and a state of soul.

The term "anthropomorphism" therefore adds little to the two previous ones in the enumeration, nor does it constitute a synthesis between them, since neither metaphor nor metonymy have to be necessarily anthropomorphic. Perhaps Nietzsche, in the Voltairean conte philosophique *On Truth and Lie* is just being casual in his terminology—but then, opportunities to encounter technical tropological terms are so sparse in literary and philosophical writings that one can be excused for making the most of it when they occur. The definition of truth as a collection ("army" being, aside from other connotations, at any rate a collective term) of tropes is a purely structural definition, devoid of any normative emphasis; it implies that truth is relational, that it is an articulation of a subject (for example "truth") and a predicate (for example "an army of tropes") allowing for an answer to a definitional question (such as "what is truth?") that is not purely tautological. At this point, to say that truth is a trope is to say that truth is the possibility of stating a proposition; to say that truth is a collection of varied tropes is to say that it is the possibility of stating several propositions about a single subject, of relating several predicates to a subject according to principles of articulation that are not necessarily identical: truth is the possibility of definition by means of infinitely varied sets of propositions. This assertion is purely descriptive of an unchallenged grammatical possibility and, as such, it has no critical thrust, nor does it claim to have one: there is nothing inherently disruptive in the assertion that truth is a trope.

But "anthropomorphism" is not just a trope but an identification on the level of substance. It takes one entity for another and thus implies the constitution of specific entities prior to their confusion, the *taking* of something for something else that can then be assumed to be *given*. Anthropomorphism freezes the infinite chain of tropological transformations and propositions into one single assertion or essence which, as such, excludes all others. It is no longer a proposition but a proper name, as when the metamorphosis in Ovid's stories culminates and halts in the singleness of a proper name, Narcissus or Daphne or whatever. Far from being the same, tropes such as metaphor (or metonymy) and anthropomorphisms are mutually exclusive. The apparent enumeration is in fact a foreclosure which acquires, by the same token, considerable critical power.

Truth is now defined by two incompatible assertions: either truth is a set of propositions or truth is a proper name. Yet, on the other hand, it is clear that the tendency to move from tropes to systems of interpretations such as anthropomorphisms is built into the very notion of trope. One reads Nietzsche's sentence without any sense of disruption, for although a trope is in no way the same as an anthropomorphism, it is nevertheless the case that an anthropomorphism is structured like a trope: it is easy enough to cross the barrier that leads from trope to name but impossible, once this barrier has been crossed, to return from it to the starting-point in "truth." Truth is a trope; a trope generates a norm or value; this value (or ideology) is no longer true. It is true that tropes are the producers of ideologies that are no longer true.

Hence the "army" metaphor. Truth, says Nietzsche, is a mobile *army* of tropes. Mobility is coextensive with any trope, but the connotations introduced by "army" are not so obvious, for to say that truth is an army (of tropes) is again to say something odd and possibly misleading. It can certainly not imply, in *On Truth and Lie* that truth is a kind of commander who enlists tropes in the battle against error. No such dichotomy exists in any critical philosophy, let alone Nietzsche's, in which truth is always at the very least dialectical, the negative knowledge of error. Whatever truth may be fighting, it is not error but stupidity, the belief that one is right when one is in fact in the wrong. To assert, as we just did, that the assimilation of truth to tropes is not a disruption of epistemology, is not to assert that tropes are therefore true or on the side, so to speak, of truth. Tropes are neither true nor false and are both at once. To call them an army is however to imply that their effect and their effectiveness is not a matter of judgment but of power. What characterizes a good army, as distinct for instance from a good cause, is that its success has little to do with immanent justice and a great deal with the proper economic use of its power. One willingly admits that truth has power, including the power to occur, but to say that its power is like that of an army and to say this within the definitional context of the question: what is therefore truth? is truly disruptive. It not only asserts that truth (which was already complicated by having to be a proposition as well as a proper name) is also power, but a power that exists independently of epistemological determinations, although these determinations are far from being nonexistent: calling truth an army *of tropes* reaffirms its epistemological *as well as* its strategic power. How the two modes of power could exist side by side certainly baffles the mind, if not the grammar of Nietzsche's tale. The sentence that asserts the complicity of epistemology and rhetoric, of truth and trope, also turns this alliance into a battle made all the more dubious by the fact that the adversaries may not even have the opportunity ever to encounter each other. Less schematically compressed, more elaborated and dramatized instances of similar disjunctions can be found in the texts of lyrical poets, such as, for example, Baudelaire.

The canonical and programmatic sonnet "Correspondances"[2] contains not a single sentence that is not simply declarative. Not a single negation, interrogation, or exclamation, not a single verb that is not in the present indicative, nothing but straightforward affirmation: "la Nature *est* un temple . . . Il *est* des parfums frais comme des chairs d'enfants." The least assertive word in the text is the innocuous "parfois" in line 2, hardly a dramatic temporal break. Nor is there (a rare case in *Les Fleurs du mal*) any pronominal agitation: no *je-tu* apostrophes or dialogues, only the most objective descriptions of third persons. The only personal pronoun to appear is the impersonal "il" of "il est (des parfums) . . ."

The choice of "Correspondances" to explicate the quandaries of language as truth, as name, and as power may therefore appear paradoxical and forced. The ironies and the narrative frame of *On Truth and Lie* make it difficult to take the apparent good cheer of its tone at face value, but the serenity of "Correspondances" reaches deep enough to eliminate any disturbance of the syntactical surface. This serenity is prevalent enough to make even the question superfluous. Nietzsche still has to dramatize the summation of his story in an eye-catching paragraph that begins with the question of questions: Was ist also Wahrheit? But Baudelaire's text is all assurance and all answer. One has to make an effort to perceive the opening line as an answer to an implicit question, "La Nature est un temple . . ." as the answer to "Qu'est-ce que la nature?" The title is not "La Nature," which would signal a need for definition; in "Correspondances," among many other connotations, one hears "response," the dialogical exchange that takes place in mutual proximity to a shared entity called nature. The *response* to the sonnet, among its numerous readers and commentators, has been equally responsive. Like the oracle of Delphi, it has been made to answer a considerable number and variety of questions put to it by various readers. Some of these questions are urgent (such as: how can one be innocent and corrupt at the same time?), some more casually historical (such as: when can modern French lyric poetry, from Baudelaire to surrealism and beyond, be said to begin?). In all cases, the poem has never failed to answer to the satisfaction of its questioner.

The serenity of the diction celebrates the powers of tropes or "symboles" that can reduce any conceivable difference to a set of polarities and combine them in an endless play of substitution and amalgamation, extending from the level of signification to that of the signifier. Here, as in Nietzsche's text, the telos of the substitutions is the unified system "esprit/sens" (l. 14), the seamless articulation, by ways of language, of sensory and aesthetic experience with the intellectual assurance of affirmation. Both echo each other in the controlled compression of a brief and highly formalized sonnet which can combine the enigmatic depth of doctrine—sending commentators astray in search of esoteric authority—with the utmost banality of a phrase such as "verts comme les prairies."

On the thematic level, the success of the project can be measured by the unquestioned acceptance of a paradox such as "Vaste comme la nuit et comme la clarté," in which a conjunctive *et* can dare to substitute for what should be the *ou* of an either/or structure. For the vastness of the night is one of confusion in which distinctions disappear, Hegel's night in which $A = A$ because no such thing as A can be discerned, and in which infinity is homogeneity. Whereas the vastness of light is like the capacity of the mind to make endless analytical distinctions, or the power of calculus to integrate by ways of infinitesimal differentiation. The juxtaposition of these incompatible meanings is condensed in the semantic ambiguity of "se confondent," which can designate the bad infinity of confusion as well as the fusion of opposites into synthetic judgments. That "echoes," which are originally the disjunction of a single sensory unit or word by the alien obstacle of a reflection, themselves re-fuse into a single sound ("Comme de longs échos qui de loin se confondent") again acts out the dialectic of identity and difference, of sensory diffuseness and intellectual precision.

The process is self-consciously verbal or mediated by language, as is clear from the couple "se confondent / se répondent," which dramatizes events of discourse and in which, as was already pointed out, "se répondent" should be read as "se correspondent" rather than as a pattern of question and answer. As in "confuses paroles" and "symboles" in the opening lines, the stress on language as the stage of disjunction is unmistakable. Language can be the chain of metaphors in a synethesia, as well as the oxymoronic polysemy of a single word, such as "se confondent" (or "transports" in l. 14) or even, on the level of the signifier, the play of the syllable or the letter. For the title, "Correspondances," is like the anagrammatic condensation of the text's entire program: "corps" and "esprit" brought together and harmonized by the *ance* of assonance that pervades the concluding tercets: from *ayant, amore, chantent* to *expansion, sens, transport*, finally redoubled and reechoed in *enc-ens/sens.*

The assertion, or representation, of verbality in "se répondent" (or in "Laissent parfois sortir de confuses *paroles*") also coincides, as in Nietzsche's text, with the passage from tropes—here the substitution of one sense experience by another—to anthropomorphisms. Or so, at least, it seems to a perhaps overhasty reading that would at once oppose "nature" to "homme" as in a polarity of art ("temple") and nature, and endow natural forests and trees with eyes ("regards") and voices. The tradition of interpretation for this poem, which stresses the importance of Chateaubriand and of Gérard de Nerval as sources, almost unanimously moves in that direction.

The opening lines allow but certainly do not impose such a reading. "La Nature est un temple" is enigmatic enough to constitute the burden of any attempt at understanding and cannot simply be reduced to a pattern of binary substitution, but what follows is hardly less obscure. "Vivants piliers," as we first meet it, certainly suggests the erect shape of human bodies naturally enough endowed with speech, a scene from the paintings of Paul Delvaux rather than from the poems of Victor Hugo. "L'homme," in line 3, then becomes a simple apposition to "vivants piliers." The notion of nature as a wood and, consequently, of "piliers" as anthropomorphic columns and trees, is suggested only by "des *forêts* de symboles" in which, especially in combination with "symboles," a natural and descriptive reading of "forêt" is by no means compelling. Nor is nature, in Baudelaire, necessarily a sylvan world. We cannot be certain whether we have ever left the world of humans and whether it is therefore relevant or necessary to speak of anthropomorphism at all in order to account for the figuration of the text. "Des forêts," a plural of what is already, in the singular, a collective plural (forêt) can be read as equivalent to "une foule de symboles," a figure of amplification that designates a large number, the crowd of humanity in which it is well known that Baudelaire took a constant poetic, rather than humanitarian, interest.

Perhaps we are not in the country at all but have never left the city, the "rue assourdissante" of the poem entitled "À une passante," for example. "Symboles" in "des forêts de symboles" could then designate the verbal, the rhetorical dimension within which we constantly dwell and which we therefore meet as passively as we meet the glance of the other in the street. That the possibility of this reading seems far-fetched and, in my experience, never fails to elicit resistance, or that the forest/temple cliché should have forced itself so emphatically upon the attention of the commentators is one of the cruxes of "Correspondances."

It has been enough of a crux for Baudelaire himself to have generated at least one other text, the poem "Obsession," to which we will have to turn later. For the possibility of anthropomorphic (mis)reading is part of the text and part of what is at stake in it. Anthropomorphism seems to be the illusionary resuscitation of the natural breath of language, frozen into stone by the semantic power of the trope. It is a figural affirmation that claims to overcome the deadly negative power invested in the figure. In Baudelaire's, as in Nietzsche's text, the icon of this central trope is that of the architectural construct, temple, beehive, or columbarium.

This verbal building, which has to celebrate at the same time funeral and rebirth, is built by the infinite multiplication of numbers raising each other to ever higher arithmetic power. The property which privileges "parfums" as the sensory analogon for the joint powers of mind and body (ll. 9–14) is its ability to grow from the infinitely small to endless expansion, "ce grain d'encens qui remplit une église"—a quotation from *Les Fleurs du mal* that made it into Littré. The religious connotation of "temple" and "encens" suggests, as in the immediately anterior poem in the volume, "Elévation," a transcendental circulation, as ascent or descent, between the spirit and the senses, a borderline between two distinct realms that can be crossed.

Yet this movement is not unambiguously sustained by all the articulations of the text. Thus in the line "L'homme y passe à travers des forêts de symboles," "passer à travers" can have two very different spatial meanings. It can be read as "traverser la forêt"; one can *cross* the woods, as Narcissus goes through the looking-glass, or as the acrobat, in Banville's poem that echoes in Mallarmé's "Le Pitre châtié," goes through the roof of the circus tent, or as Vergil, for that matter, takes Dante beyond the woods in which he lost his way. But "passer à travers" can also mean to remain enclosed in the wood, to wander and err around in it as the speaker of "À une passante" wanders around in the crowd. The latter reading in fact suits the represented scene better than the former, although it is incompatible with the transcendental claims usually made for the sonnet. The transcendence of substitutive, analogical tropes linked by the recurrent "comme," a transcendence which occurs in the declarative assurance of the first quatrain, states the totalizing power of metaphor as it moves from analogy to identity, from simile to symbol and to a higher order of truth. Ambivalences such as those noted in "passer à travers," as well as the theoretical ambivalence of anthropomorphism in relation to tropes, complicate this expectation perhaps more forcefully than its outright negation. The complication is forceful enough to contaminate the key word that carries out the substitutions which constitute the main structure of the text: the word "comme."

When it is said that "Les parfums, les couleurs et les sons se répondent . . . *comme* de longs échos," then the preposition of resemblance, "comme," the most frequently counted word in the canon of Baudelaire's poetry, does its work properly and clearly, without upsetting the balance between difference and identity that it is assigned to maintain. It achieves a figure of speech, for it is not actually the case that an answer is an echo; no echo has ever answered a question except by a "delusion" of the signifier[3]—but it is certainly the case that an echo sounds like an answer, and that this similarity is endlessly suggestive. And the catachresis "se répondent" to designate the association between the various senses duly raises the process to the desired higher power. "Des parfums . . . / Doux comme les hautbois, verts comme les prairies" is already somewhat more complex, for although it is possible in referential and semantic terms to think of oboes and of certain scents as primarily "soft," it makes less sense to think of scents as green; "green scents" have less compelling connotations than "green thoughts" or "green shades." The relaying "comme" travels by ways of "hautbois," solidly tied to "parfums" by ways of "doux" and altogether compatible with "vert," through the pastoral association of the reedy sound still reinforced by the "(haut)*bois*, verts" that would be lost in English or German translation. The greenness of the fields can be guided back from color to scent with any "unsweet" connotation carefully filtered out.

All this is playing at metaphor according to the rules of the game. But the same is not true of the final "comme" in the poem: "Il est des parfums frais comme . . . / Doux comme . . . / —Et d'autres . . . / Ayant l'expansion des choses infinies / *Comme* l'ambre, le musc, le benjoin et l'encens." Ce comme n'est pas un comme comme les autres. It does not cross from one sense experience to another, as "frais" crosses from scent to touch or "doux" from scent to sound, nor does it cross from the common sensorium back to the single sense of hearing (as in "Les parfums, les couleurs et les sons se répondent" "Comme de longs échos . . . ") or from the sensory to the intellectual realm, as in the double register of "se confondent." In each of these cases, the "comme" is what avoids tautology by linking the subject to a predicate that is not the same: scents are said to be like oboes, or like fields, or like echoes. But here "comme" relates to the subject "parfums" in two different ways or, rather, it has two distinct subjects. If "comme" is related to "l'expansion des choses infinies," which is grammatically as well as tonally possible, then it still functions, like the other "commes," as a comparative simile: a common property ("l'expansion") links the finite senses to an experience of infinity. But "comme" also relates to "parfums": "Il est des parfums frais . . . / —Et d'autres . . . / Comme l'ambre, le musc, le benjoin et l'encens"; the somewhat enigmatic hyphen can be said to mark that hesitation (as well as rule it out). "Comme" then means as much as "such as, for example" and enumerates scents which contrast with "chairs d'enfants" as innocence contrasts with experience or nature with artifice. This working out by exemplification is quite different from the analogical function assigned to the other uses of "comme."

Considered from the perspective of the "thesis" or of the symbolist ideology of the text, such a use of "comme" is aberrant. For although the burden of totalizing expansion seems to be attributed to these particular scents rather than the others, the logic of "comme" restricts the semantic field of "parfums" and confines it to a tautology: "Il est des parfums . . . / Comme (des parfums)." Instead of analogy, we have enumeration, and an enumeration which never moves beyond the confines of a set of particulars: "forêt" synthesizes but does not enumerate a set of trees, but "ambre," "musc," "benjoin," and "encens," whatever differences or gradations one wishes to establish between them, are refrained by "comme" ever to lead beyond themselves; the enumeration could be continued at will without ceasing to be a repetition, without ceasing to be an obsession rather than a metamorphosis, let alone a rebirth. One wonders if the evil connotations of these corrupt scents do not stem from the syntax rather than from the Turkish bath or black mass atmosphere one would otherwise have to conjure up. For what could be more perverse or corruptive for a metaphor aspiring to transcendental totality than remaining stuck in an enumeration that never goes anywhere? If number can only be conquered by another number, if identity becomes enumeration, then there is no conquest at all, since the stated purpose of the passage to infinity was, like in Pascal, to restore the one, to escape the tyranny of number by dint of infinite multiplication. Enumerative repetition disrupts the chain of tropological substitution at the crucial moment when the poem promises, by way of these very substitutions, to reconcile the pleasures of the mind with those of the senses and to unite aesthetics with epistemology. That the very word on which these substitutions depend would just then lose its syntactical and semantic univocity is too striking a coincidence not to be, like pure chance, beyond the control of author and reader.

It allows, at any rate, for a sobering literalization of the word "transport" in the final line "Qui chantent les transports de l'esprit et des sens." "Transport" here means, of course, to be carried away beyond thought and sensation in a common transcendental realm; it evokes loss of control and ecstatic unreason. But all attentive readers of Baudelaire have always felt that this claim at self-loss is not easily compatible with a colder, analytic self-consciousness that moves in a very different direction. In the words of our text, "les transports de l'esprit" and "Les transports des sens" are not at all the same "transports." We have learned to recognize, of late, in "transports" the spatial displacement implied by the verbal ending of meta*phorein.* One is reminded that, in the French-speaking cities of our century, "correspondance" meant, on the trolley-cars, the equivalence of what is called in English a "transfer"—the privilege, automatically granted on the Paris Métro, of connecting from one line to another without having to buy a new ticket.

The prosaic transposition of ecstasy to the economic codes of public transportation is entirely in the spirit of Baudelaire and not by itself disruptive with regard to the claim for transcendental unity. For the transfer indeed merges two different displacements into one single system of motion and circulation, with corresponding economic and metaphysical profits. The problem is not so much centered on *phorein* as on *meta* (trans . . .), for does "beyond" here mean a movement beyond some particular place or does it mean a state that is beyond movement entirely? And how can "beyond," which posits and names movement, ever take us away from what it posits? The question haunts the text in all its ambiguities, be it "passer à travers" or the discrepancy between the "comme" of homogeneity and the "comme" of enumeration. The apparent rest and tranquility of "Correspondances" within the corpus of *Les Fleurs du mal* lies indeed beyond tension and beyond motion. If Nature is truly a temple, it is not a means of transportation or a railroad station, Victorian architects who loved to build railroad stations in the shape of cathedrals notwithstanding. Nature in this poem is not a road toward a temple, a sequence of motions that take us there. Its travels, whatever they are, lie far behind us; there is no striving here, no questing for an absence or a presence. And if man (l'homme) is at home among "regards familiers" within that Nature, then his language of tropes and analogies is of little use to them. In this realm, transfer tickets are of no avail. Within the confines of a system of transportation—or of language as a system of communication—one can transfer from one vehicle to another, but one cannot transfer from being like a vehicle to being like a temple, or a ground.

The epistemological, aesthetic, and poetic language of transports or of tropes, which is the theme though not singly the rhetoric of this poem, can never say nor, for that matter, sing or understand the opening statement: "la Nature est un temple." But the poem offers no explicit alternative to this language which, like the perfumes enumerated by "comme," remains condemned to the repetition of its superfluity. Few poems in *Les Fleurs du mal* state this in a manner that is both so obvious yet, by necessity, so oblique. The poem most remote from stating it is also the one closest to "Correspondances," its "echo" as it were, with which it is indeed very easy to confuse it. Little clarity can be gained from "Correspondances" except for the knowledge that disavows its deeper affinity with "Obsession."

Written presumably in February 1860, at least five years after "Correspondances" (of which the date is uncertain but anterior to 1855), "Obsession" (*O.C.*, 1:73) alludes to many poems in *Les Fleurs du mal*, such as "l'Homme et la mer" (1852) and "De profundis clamavi" (1851). But it more than alludes to "Correspondances"; it can be called a *reading* of the earlier text, with all the complications that are inherent in this term. The relationship between the two poems can indeed be seen as the construction and the undoing of the mirrorlike, specular structure that is always involved in a reading. On both the thematic and the rhetorical level, the reverted symmetries between the two texts establish their correspondence along a positive/negative axis. Here again, our problem is centered on the possibility of reinscribing into the system elements, in either text, that do not belong to this pattern. The same question can be asked in historical or in generic terms but, in so doing, the significance of this terminology risks being unsettled.

One can, for instance, state the obvious difference in theme and in diction between the two poems in terms derived from the canonical history of French nineteenth-century lyric poetry. With its portal of Greek columns, its carefully balanced symmetries, and its decorous absence of any displayed emotion, "Correspondances" has all the characteristics of a Parnassian poem, closer to Heredia than to Hugo. The "romantic" exaltation of "Obsession" 's apostrophes and exclamations, on the other hand, is self-evident. If nature is a "transport" in "Obsession," it is a temple in "Correspondances." However, by putting the two texts side by side in this manner, their complementarity is equally manifest. What is lost in personal expressiveness from the first poem is gained in the symbolic "depth" that has prompted comparisons of "Correspondances" with the poetry of that other neo-classicist, Gérard de Nerval, or supported the claim of its being the forerunner of symbolism. Such a historicizing pattern, a commonplace of aesthetic theory, is a function of the aesthetic ideologization of linguistic structures rather than an empirical historical event. The dialectical interaction of "classical" with "romantic" conceptions, as summarized in the contrastive symmetries between these two sonnets, ultimately reveals the symbolic character of poetic language, the linguistic structure in which it is rooted. "Symbolist" art is considered archaic when it is supposed to be spontaneous, modern when it is self-conscious, and this terminology has a certain crude wisdom about it that is anything but historical, however, in its content. Such a combination of linguistic with pseudo-historical terms, of "symbolic" with "classic" (or *parnassien*) or with "romantic" (or *symboliste*), a combination familiar at least since Hegel's *Lectures on Aesthetics*, is a necessary feature of systems that combine tropes with aesthetic and epistemological norms. In this perspective, the relationship between the neo-classical "Correspondances" and the post-romantic "Obsession" is itself structured like a symbol: the two sonnets complement each other like the two halves of a *symbolon*. Historicizing them into a diachrony or into a valorized qualitative hierarchy is more convenient than it is legitimate. The terminology of traditional literary history, as a succession of periods or literary movements, remains useful only if the terms are seen for what they are: rather crude metaphors for figural patterns rather than historical events or acts.

Stated in generic rather than historical terms, the relationship between "Correspondances" and "Obsession" touches upon the uncertain status of the lyric as a term for poetic discourse in general. The lyric's claim of being song is made explicitly in "Correspondances" ("qui *chantent* les transports . . . "), whereas "Obsession" howls, laughs, and speaks but does not pretend to sing. Yet the *je-tu* structure of the syntax makes it much closer to the representation of a vocal utterance than the engraved, marmorean gnomic wisdom of "Correspondances." The reading however disclosed a discrepancy that affects the verb "chanter" in the concluding line: the suggestive identification of "parfum" with song, based on common resonance and expansion, is possible only within a system of relays and transfers that, in the syntax if not in the stated meaning of the poem, becomes threatened by the stutter, the *piétinement* of aimless enumeration. This eventuality, inherent in the structure of the tropes on which the claim to lyricism depends, conflicts with the monumental stability of a completed entity that exists independently of its principle of constitution and destruction. Song is not compatible with aphasia and a stuttering Amphion is an absurd figure indeed. No lyric can be read lyrically nor can the object of a lyrical reading be itself a lyric—which implies least of all that it is epical or dramatic. Baudelaire's own lyrical reading of "Correspondances," however, produced at least a text, the sonnet entitled "Obsession."

The opening of "Obsession" reads the first quatrain of "Correspondances" as if it were indeed a sylvan scene. It naturalizes the surreal speech of live columns into the frightening, but natural, roar of the wind among the trees:

> Grands bois, vous m'effrayez comme des cathédrales;
> Vous hurlez comme l'orgue;

The benefits of naturalization—as we can call the reversal of anthropomorphism—are at once apparent. None of the uncertainties that obscure the opening lines of "Correspondances" are maintained. No "comme" could be more orthodox than the two "commes" in these two lines. The analogism is so perfect that the implied anthropomorphism becomes fully motivated.

In this case, the unifying element is the wind as it is heard in whistling keyholes, roaring trees, and wind instruments such as church organs. Neither is there any need to invoke hallucination to account for the fear inspired by stormy forests and huge cathedrals: both are versions of the same dizziness of vast spaces. The adjustment of the elements involved (wood, wind, fear, cathedral, and organ) is perfectly self-enclosed, since all the pieces in the structure fit each other: wood and cathedral share a common shape, but wood also fits organ by way of the noise of the roaring wind; organ and cathedral, moreover, are linked by metonymy, etc. Everything can be substituted for everything else without distorting the most natural experience. Except, of course, for the "vous" of address in the apostrophe "Grands bois," which is, of course, absurd from a representational point of view; we are all frightened by windy woods but do not generally make a spectacle of ourselves talking to trees.

Yet the power of the analogy, much more immediately compelling than that of synesthesia in "Correspondances," naturalizes even this most conventional trope of lyric address: when it is said, in line 4, that the terror of the wind corresponds to the subjective fear of death

> et dans nos coeurs maudits,
> . . .
> Répondent les échos de vos *De profundis*,

then the analogy between outer event and inner feeling is again so close that the figural distance between noise (wind) and speech or even music almost vanishes, all the more so since wind as well as death are designated by associated sounds: the howling of the wind and the penitential prayer, aural metonymy for death. As a result, the final attribution of speech to the woods (*vos* De profundis) appears so natural that it takes an effort to notice that anthropomorphism is involved. The claim to verbality in the equivalent line from "Correspondances," "Les parfums, les couleurs et les sons se répondent" seems fantastic by comparison. The omnipresent metaphor of interiorization, of which this is a striking example, here travels initially by ways of the ear alone.

The gain in pathos is such as to make the depth of *De profundis* the explicit theme of the poem. Instead of being the infinite expanse, the openness of "Vaste comme la nuit et comme la clarté," depth is now the enclosed space that, like the sound chamber of a violin, produces the inner vibration of emotion. We retrieve what was conspicuously absent from "Correspondances," the recurrent image of the subject's presence to itself as a spatial enclosure, room, tomb, or crypt in which the voice echoes as in a cave. The image draws its verisimilitude from its own "mise en abŷme" in the shape of the body as the *container* of the voice (or soul, heart, breath, consciousness, spirit, etc.) that it exhales. At the cost of much represented agony ("Chambres d'éternel deuil où vibrent de vieux râles"), "Obsession" asserts its right to say "I" with full authority. The canon of romantic and post-romantic lyric poetry offers innumerable versions and variations of this inside/outside pattern of exchange that founds the metaphor of the lyrical voice as subject. In a parallel movement, reading interiorizes the meaning of the text by its understanding. The union of aesthetic with epistemological properties is carried out by the mediation of the metaphor of the self as consciousness of itself, which implies its negation.

The specular symmetry of the two texts is such that any instance one wishes to select at once involves the entire system with flawless consistency. The hellenic "temple" of "Correspondances," for example, becomes the Christian "cathédrale" of "Obsession," just as the denominative, impersonal third person discourse of the earlier poem becomes the first person discourse of the later one. The law of this figural and chiastic transformation is negation. "Obsession" self-consciously denies and rejects the sensory wealth of "Correspondances." The landscape of denial from "De profundis clamavi":

> C'est un pays plus nu que la terre polaire;
> —Ni bêtes, ni ruisseaux, ni verdure, ni bois!

reappears as the desire of "Obsession":

> Car je cherche le vide, et le noir, et le nu!

in sharp denial of

> Doux comme les hautbois, verts comme les prairies

from "Correspondances." Similar negations pervade the texts, be it in terms of affects, moods, or grammar.

The negation, however, is indeed a figure of chiasmus, for the positive and negative valorizations can be distributed on both sides. We read "Obsession" thematically as an interiorization of "Correspondances," and as a negation of the positivity of an outside reality. But it is just as plausible to consider "Obsession" as the making manifest, as the exteriorization of the subject that remains hidden in "Correspondances." Naturalization, which appears to be a movement from inside to outside, allows for affective verisimilitude which moves in the opposite direction. In terms of figuration also, it can be said that "Correspondances" is the negation of "Obsession": the figural stability of "Obsession" is denied in "Correspondances." Such patterns constantly recur in nineteenth- and twentieth-century lyric poetry and create a great deal of critical confusion, symptomatic of further-reaching complexities.

The recuperative power of the subject metaphor in "Obsession" becomes particularly evident, in all its implications, in the tercets. As soon as the sounds of words are allowed, as in the opening stanza, to enter into analogical combinations with the sounds of nature, they necessarily turn into the light imagery of representation and of knowledge. If the sounds of nature are akin to those of speech, then nature also speaks by ways of light, the light of the senses as well as of the mind. The philosophical phantasm that has concerned us throughout this reading, the reconciliation of knowledge with phenomenal, aesthetic experience, is summarized in the figure of speaking light which, as is to be expected in the dialectical mode of negation, is both denied and asserted:

> Comme tu me plairais, ô nuit! sans ces étoiles
> Dont *la lumière parle* un langage connu!

Light implies space which, in turn, implies the possibility of spatial differentiation, the play of distance and proximity that organizes perception as the foreground-background juxtaposition that links it to the aesthetics of painting. Whether the light emanates from outside us before it is interiorized by the eye, as is the case here in the perception of a star, or whether the light emanates from inside and projects the entity, as in hallucination or in certain dreams, makes little difference in this context. The metamorphic crossing between perception and hallucination

> Mais les ténèbres sont elles-mêmes des toiles
> Où vivent, jaillissant de mon oeil par milliers,
> Des êtres disparus aux regards familiers

occurs by means of the paraphernalia of painting, which is also that of recollection and of re-cognition, as the recovery, to the senses, of what seemed to be forever beyond experience. In an earlier outline, Baudelaire had written

> Mais les ténèbres sont elles-mêmes des toiles
> Où [peint] . . . (presumably for "se peignent"; *O.C.*, 1:981)

"Peint" confirms the reading of "toiles" as the device by means of which painters or dramatists project the space or the stage of representation, by enframing the interiorized expanse of the skies. The possibility of representation asserts itself at its most efficacious at the moment when the sensory plenitude of "Correspondances" is most forcefully denied. The lyric depends entirely for its existence on the denial of phenomenality as the surest means to recover what it denies. This motion is not dependent, in its failure or in its illusion of success, on the good or the bad faith of the subject it constitutes.

The same intelligibility enlightens the text when the enigma of consciousness as eternal mourning ("Chambres d'éternel deuil où vibrent de vieux râles") is understood as the hallucinatory obsession of recollection, certainly easier to comprehend by shared experience than by esoteric *correspondences*. "Obsession" translates "Correspondances" into intelligibility, the least one can hope for in a successful reading. The resulting couple or pair of texts indeed becomes a model for the uneasy combination of funereal monumentality with paranoid fear that characterizes the hermeneutics and the pedagogy of lyric poetry.

Yet, this very title, "Obsession," also suggests a movement that may threaten the far-reaching symmetry between the two texts. For the temporal pattern of obsessive thought is directly reminiscent of the tautological, enumerative stutter we encountered in the double semantic function of "comme," which disrupted the totalizing claim of metaphor in "Correspondances." It suggests a psychological and therefore intelligible equivalent of what there appeared as a purely grammatical distinction, for there is no compelling thematic suggestion, in "comme l'ambre, le musc, le benjoin et l'encens," that allows one to think of this list as compulsively haunting. The title "Obsession," or the last line of the poem, which names the ghostly memory of mourned absences, does therefore not correspond to the tension, deemed essential, between the expansiveness of "des choses infinies" and the restrictive catalogue of certain kinds of scents introduced by "comme." Yet, if the symmetry between the two texts is to be truly recuperative, it is essential that the disarticulation that threatens the first text should find its counterpart in the second: mere naturalization of a grammatical structure, which is how the relationship between enumeration and obsession can be understood, will not suffice, since it is precisely the tension between an experienced and a purely linguistic disruption that is at issue. There ought to be a place, in "Obsession," where a similar contrast between infinite totalization and endless repetition of the same could be pointed out. No such place exists. At the precise point where one would expect it, at the moment when obsession is stressed in terms of number, "Obsession" resorts to synthesis by losing itself in the vagueness of the infinite

> Où vivent, jaillissant de mon oeil *par milliers*,
> Des êtres disparus aux regards familiars.

There could be no more decisive contrast, in *Les Fleurs du mal*, than between the reassuring indeterminacy of these infinite thousands—as one had, in "Correspondances," "des forêts"—and the numerical precision with which, in "Les sept vieillards" (*O.C.*, 1:87–88), it is the passage from one altogether finite to another altogether finite number that produces genuine terror:

> Aurais-je, sans mourir, contemplé le huitième,
> Sosie inexorable, ironique et fatal,
> Dégoûtant Phénix, fils et père de lui-même?
> —Mais je tournai le dos au cortège infernal.
>
> Exaspéré comme un ivrogne qui voit double,
> Je rentrai, je fermai ma porte, épouvanté,
> Malade et morfondu, 'esprit fiévreux et trouble,
> Blessé par le mystère et par l'absurdité!

Unlike "Obsession," "Les sept vieillards" can however in no respect be called a reading of "Correspondances," to which it in no way corresponds.

The conclusion is written into the argument which is itself written into the reading, a process of translation or "transport" that incessantly circulates between the two texts. There always are at least two texts, regardless of whether they are actually written out or not; the relationship between the two sonnets, obligingly provided by Baudelaire for the benefit, no doubt, of future teachers invited to speak on the nature of the lyric, is an inherent characteristic of any text. Any text, as text, compels reading as its understanding. What we call the lyric, the instance of represented voice, conveniently spells out the rhetorical and thematic characteristics that make it the paradigm of a complementary relationship between grammar, trope, and theme. The set of characteristics includes the various structures and moments we encountered along the way: specular symmetry along an axis of assertion and negation (to which correspond the generic mirror-images of the ode, as celebration, and the elegy, as mourning), the grammatical transformation of the declarative into the vocative modes of question, exclamation, address, hypothesis, etc., the tropological transformation of analogy into apostrophe or the equivalent, more general transformation which, with Nietzsche's assistance, we took as our point of departure: the transformation of trope into anthropomorphism. The lyric is not a genre, but one name among several to designate the defensive motion of understanding, the possibility of a future hermeneutics. From this point of view, there is no significant difference between one generic term and another: all have the same apparently intentional and temporal function.

We all perfectly and quickly understand "Obsession," and better still the motion that takes us from the earlier to the later text. But no symmetrical reversal of this lyrical reading-motion is conceivable; if Baudelaire, as is eminently possible, were to have written, in empirical time, "Correspondances" after "Obsession," this would change nothing. "Obsession" derives from "Correspondances" but the reverse is not the case. Neither does it account for it as its origin or cause. "Correspondances" implies and explains "Obsession" but "Obsession" leaves "Correspondances" as thoroughly incomprehensible as it always was. In the paraphernalia of literary terminology, there is no term available to tell us what "Correspondances" might be. All we know is that it is, emphatically, *not* a lyric. Yet it, and it alone, contains, implies, produces, generates, permits (or whatever aberrant verbal metaphor one wishes to choose) the entire possibility of the lyric. Whenever we encounter a text such as "Obsession"—that is, whenever we read—there always is an infra-text, a hypogram like "Correspondances" underneath. Stating this relationship, as we just did, in phenomenal, spatial terms or in phenomenal, temporal terms—"Obsession," a text of recollection and elegiac mourning, *adds* remembrance to the flat surface of time in "Correspondances"—produces at once a hermeneutic, fallacious lyrical reading of the unintelligible. The power that takes one from one text to the other is not just a power of displacement, be it understood as recollection or interiorization or any other "transport," but the sheer blind violence that Nietzsche, concerned with the same enigma, domesticated by calling it, metaphorically, an *army* of tropes.

Generic terms such as "lyric" (or its various sub-species, "ode," "idyll," or "elegy") as well as pseudo-historical period terms such as "romanticism" or "classicism" are always terms of resistance and nostalgia, at the furthest remove from the materiality of actual history. If mourning is called a "chambre d'éternel deuil où vibrent de vieux râles," then this pathos of terror states in fact the desired consciousness of eternity and of temporal harmony as voice and as song. True "mourning" is less deluded. The most *it* can do is to allow for non-comprehension and enumerate non-anthropomorphic, non-elegiac, non-celebratory, non-lyrical, non-poetic, that is to say, prosaic, or, better, *historical* modes of language power.

NOTES

1. Friedrich Nietzsche, "Über Wahrheit and Lüge im aussermoralischen Sinn," *Werke*, Karl Schlechta, ed. (Munich: Carl Hanser, 1966), 3:314.

2. Charles Baudelaire, *Oeuvres complètes*, Pléiade ed. (Paris: Gallimard, 1974), 1.11. Further citations will be made from this edition, identified as O.C.

3. See Ovid's version of the Narcissus story, *Metamorphoses*, III, 341ff.

5.4 Anthropomorphism in Lyric and Law (1998)

BARBARA JOHNSON

> *Anthropomorphism.* n. Attribution of human motivation, characteristics, or behavior to inanimate objects, animals, or natural phenomena.
>
> *American Heritage Dictionary*

> Through a singular ambiguity, through a kind of transposition or intellectual quid pro quo, you will feel yourself evaporating, and you will attribute to your . . . tobacco, the strange ability to *smoke you.*
>
> Baudelaire, *Artificial Paradises*

Recent discussions of the relations between law and literature have tended to focus on prose—novels, short stories, autobiographies, even plays—rather than on lyric poetry.[1] Literature has been seen as a locus of plots and situations that parallel legal cases or problems, either to shed light on complexities not always acknowledged by the ordinary practice of legal discourse, or to shed light on cultural crises and debates that historically underlie and inform literary texts. But, in a sense, this focus on prose is surprising, since lyric poetry has at least historically been the more law-abiding or rule-bound of the genres. Indeed, the sonnet form has been compared to a prison (Wordsworth),[2] or at least to a bound woman (Keats),[3] and Baudelaire's portraits of lyric depression (*Spleen*)[4] are often written as if from behind bars. What are the relations between the laws of genre and the laws of the state?[5] The present essay might be seen as asking this question through the juxtaposition, as it happens, between two sonnets and a prisoners' association.

More profoundly, though, lyric and law might be seen as two very different ways of instating what a "person" is. There appears to be the greatest possible discrepancy between a lyric "person" (emotive, subjective, individual) and a legal "person" (rational, rights-bearing, institutional). In this essay I will be trying to show, through the question of anthropomorphism, how these two "persons" can illuminate each other.

My argument develops out of the juxtaposition of two texts: Paul de Man's essay "Anthropomorphism and Trope in the Lyric,"[6] in which I try to understand why for de Man the question of anthropomorphism is at the heart of the lyric, and the text of a Supreme Court opinion from 1993, *Rowland v. California Men's Colony, Unit II Men's Advisory Council*.[7] This case has not become a household name like *Roe v. Wade* or *Brown v. Board of Education*, and probably with good reason. What is at stake in it appears trivial—at bottom, it is about an association of prisoners suing for the right to have free cigarette privileges restored. But the Supreme Court's task is not to decide whether the prisoners have the right to smoke (an increasingly contested right, in fact, in the United States). The case has come before the court to resolve the question of whether the prisoners' council can be counted as a juridical "person" under the law. What is at stake, then, in both the legal and the lyric texts is the question, What is a person?

1.

I will begin by discussing the article by Paul de Man, which is one of the most difficult, even outrageous, of his essays. Both hyperbolic and elliptical, it makes a number of very strong claims about literary history, lyric pedagogy, and the materiality of "historical modes of language power" (262). Toward the end of his text, de Man somewhat unexpectedly reveals that the essay originated in an invitation to speak on the nature of lyric. But it begins with some general remarks about the relation between epistemology and rhetoric (which can stand as a common contemporary way of framing the relations between law and literature). The transition between the question of the lyric and the question of epistemology and rhetoric is made through the Keatsian chiasmus, "Beauty is truth, truth beauty,"[8] which de Man quotes on his way to Nietzsche's short and "better known than understood" (239) essay "On Truth and Lie in an Extra-Moral Sense."[9] "What is truth?" Nietzsche asks in that essay's most oft-quoted moment: "a mobile army of metaphors, metonymies, and anthropomorphisms." Thus it would seem that Nietzsche has answered, "Truth is trope, trope truth" or "epistemology is rhetoric, rhetoric epistemology." But de Man wants to show in what ways Nietzsche is *not* saying simply this. First, the list of tropes is, he says, "odd." Although metaphor and metonymy are the names of tropes that designate a pure structure of relation (metaphor is a relation of similarity between two entities; metonymy is a relation of contiguity), de Man claims that anthropomorphism, while structured similarly, is not a trope. It is not the name of a pure rhetorical structure, but the name of a comparison one of whose terms is treated as a given (as epistemologically resolved). To use an anthropomorphism is to treat as *known* what the properties of the human are.

> "Anthropomorphism" is not just a trope but an identification on the level of substance. It takes one entity for another and thus implies the constitution of specific entities prior to their confusion, the *taking* of something for something else that can then be assumed to be *given*. Anthropomorphism freezes the infinite chain of tropological transformations and propositions into one single assertion or essence which, as such, excludes all others. It is no longer a proposition but a proper name. (241)

Why does he call this a proper name? Shouldn't the essence that is taken as given be a concept? If "man" is what is assumed as a given, why call it a proper name? (This question is particularly vexed when the theorist's proper name is "de Man.") The answer, I think, is that "man" as concept would imply the possibility of a proposition. "Man" would be subject to definition, and thus transformation or trope. But proper names are not subjects of definition: they are what they are. If "man" is taken as a given, then, it can only be because it is out of the loop of qualification. It is presupposed, not defined.

Yet the examples of proper names de Man gives are surprising: Narcissus and Daphne. Nietzsche's triumvirate of metaphor, metonymy, and anthropomorphism then functions like the plot of an Ovidian metamorphosis: from a mythological world in which man and nature appear to be in metaphorical and metonymic harmony, there occurs a crisis wherein, by a process of seamless transformation, a break nevertheless occurs in the system of correspondences, leaving a residue that escapes and remains: the proper name. De Man's discussion of Baudelaire's sonnets will in fact be haunted by Ovidian presences: Echo is lurking behind every mention of Narcissus, while one of the recurring cruxes is whether there is a human substance in a tree. It is perhaps not an accident that the figures that occupy the margins of de Man's discussion are female. If de Man's enduring question is whether linguistic structures and epistemological claims can be presumed to be compatible, the question of gender cannot be located exclusively either in language (where the gender of pronouns, and often of nouns, is inherent in each language) or in the world. By extension, the present discussion of the nature of "man" cannot fail to be haunted by the question of gender.

The term *anthropomorphism* in Nietzsche's list thus indicates that a *given* is being forced into what otherwise would function as a pure structure of relation. In addition, Nietzsche calls truth an *army* of tropes, thus introducing more explicitly the notion of power, force, or violence. This is not a notion that can fit into the oppositions between epistemology and rhetoric, but rather disrupts the system. In the text of the Supreme Court decision that I will discuss in a moment, such a disruption is introduced when the opposition on which the case is based, the opposition between natural person and artificial entity, opens out onto the question of policy. There, too, it is a question of truth and power, of the separation of the constative—what does the law say? from the performative—what does it do?

The bulk of de Man's essay is devoted to a reading of two sonnets by Baudelaire: "Correspondances" and "Obsession," which I here reproduce.[10]

CORRESPONDANCES

La Nature est un temple où de vivants piliers
Laissent parfois sortir de confuses paroles;
L'homme y passe à travers des forêts de symboles
Qui l'observent avec des regards familiers.

Comme de longs échos qui de loin se confondent
Dans une ténébreuse et profonde unité,
Vaste comme la nuit et comme la clarté,
Les parfums, les couleurs et les sons se répondent.

Il est des parfums frais comme des chairs d'enfants,
Doux comme les hautbois, verts comme les prairies,
—Et d'autres, corrompus, riches et triomphants,

Ayant l'expansion des choses infinies,
Comme l'ambre, le musc, le benjoin et l'encens,
Qui chantent les transports de l'esprit et des sens.

[Nature is a temple, where the living pillars
Sometimes utter indistinguishable words;
Man passes through these forests of symbols
Which regard him with familiar looks.

Like long echoes that blend in the distance
Into a unity obscure and profound,
Vast as the night and as the light,
The perfumes, colors, and sounds correspond.

There are some perfumes fresh as a baby's skin,
Mellow as oboes, verdant as prairies,
—And others, corrupt, rich, and triumphant,

With all the expansiveness of infinite things,
Like ambergris, musk, benjamin, incense,
That sing the transports of spirit and sense.]

OBSESSION

Grands bois, vous m'effrayez comme des cathédrales;
Vous hurlez comme l'orgue; et dans nos coeurs maudits,
Chambres d'éternel deuil où vibrent de vieux râles,
Répondent les échos de vos *De profundis*.

Je te hais, Océan! tes bonds et tes tumultes,
Mon esprit les retrouve en lui; ce rire amer
De l'homme vaincu, plein de sanglots et d'insultes,
Je l'entends dans le rire énorme de la mer.

Comme tu me plairais, ô nuit! sans ces étoiles
Dont la lumière parle un langage connu!
Car je cherche le vide, et le noir, et le nu!

Mais les ténèbres sont elles-mêmes des toiles
Où vivent, jaillissant de mon oeil par milliers,
Des êtres disparus aux regards familiers.

[You terrify me, forests, like cathedrals;
You roar like organs; and in our cursed hearts,
Chambers of mourning that quiver with our dying,
Your *De profundis* echoes in response.

How I hate you, Ocean! your tumultuous tide
Is flowing in my spirit; this bitter laughter
Of vanquished man, strangled with sobs and insults,
I hear it in the heaving laughter of the sea.

O night, how I would love you without stars,
Whose light can only speak the words I know!
For I seek the void, and the black, and the bare!

But the shadows are themselves a screen
That gathers from my eyes the ones I've lost,
A thousand living things with their familiar looks.]

Both poems end up raising "man" as a question—"Correspondances" looks upon "man" as if from a great distance, as if from the outside; "Obsession" says "I," but then identifies with "vanquished man" whose laugh is echoed in the sea.

"Correspondances" is probably the most canonical of Baudelaire's poems in that it has justified the largest number of general statements about Baudelaire's place in literary history. The possibility of literary history ends up, in some ways, being the real topic of de Man's essay. De Man will claim that the use of this sonnet to anchor the history of "the symbolist movement" is based on a reading that ignores a crucial element in the poem, an element that, if taken seriously, will not allow for the edifice of literary history to be built upon it.

"Correspondances" sets up a series of analogies between nature, man, symbols, and metaphysical unity, and among manifestations of the different physical senses, all through the word "comme" ("like"). A traditional reading of the poem would say that the lateral analogies among the senses (perfumes fresh as a baby's skin, mellow as oboes, green as prairies) are signs that there exists an analogy between man and nature, and man and the spiritual realm.

De Man focuses on this analogy-making word, "comme," and notes an anomaly in the final instance. Whereas the first uses of "comme" in the poem equate different things into likeness, the last one just introduces a list of examples—there are perfumes that are rich and corrupt, like musk, ambergris, and frankincense. This is thus a tautology—there are perfumes like . . . perfumes. De Man calls this a stutter. He writes, "Comme then means as much as 'such as, for example'" (249). "Ce Comme n'est pas un comme comme les autres" (249), writes de Man in a sudden access of French. His sentence performs the stutter he attributes to the enumeration of the perfumes. Listing examples would seem to be quite different from proposing analogies. If the burden of the analogies in "Correspondances" is to convince us that the metaphorical similarities among the senses point to a higher spiritual unity, then sheer enumeration would disrupt that claim.

There is another, more debatable, suggestion in de Man's reading that attempts to disrupt the anthropomorphism of the forest of symbols. De Man suggests that the trees are a mere metaphor for a city crowd in the first stanza. If the living pillars with their familiar glances are metaphorically a city crowd, then the anthropomorphism of nature is lost. Man is surrounded by tree-like men, not man-like trees. It is not "man" whose attributes are taken on by all of nature, but merely a crowd of men being compared to trees and pillars. De Man notes that everyone resists this reading—as do I—but the intensity with which it is rejected does make visible the seduction of the system that puts nature, god, and man into a perfect unity through the symbol, which is what has made the poem so important for literary history. Similarly, if the last "comme" is sheer enumeration rather than similarity, the transports in the last line of the poem would not get us into a transcendent realm, but would be like getting stuck on the French transportation system (which, as de Man points out, uses the word "correspondance" for changes of station within the system). All these tropes would not carry us away into the spiritual realm, but would be an infinite series of substitutions. The echoes would remain echoes and not merge into a profound unity.

If "Correspondances" is said to place man in the center of a universe that reflects him in harmony with all of nature, the poem "Obsession" places all of nature and the universe inside the psychology of man. Even the senses are projections. "Obsession" is the reading of "Correspondances" as hallucination. While "Correspondances" is entirely declarative, "Obsession" is almost entirely vocative. (Interestingly, de Man does not comment on another anomaly in the meaning of the word "comme"—the "comme" in "Obsession" that means "How!"—which is surprising, since it enacts precisely what he calls "the tropological transformation of analogy into apostrophe" [261].) Nature is addressed as a structure haunted by the subject's obsessions. Everywhere he looks, his own thoughts look back. For psychoanalytically inclined readers, and indeed for de Man himself in an earlier essay,[11] "Obsession" demystifies "Correspondances." There is no profound unity in the world, but only, as Lacan would say, paranoid knowledge.[12] But de Man sees the psychological gloss as another mystification, another anthropomorphism—the very anthropomorphic mystification that it is the duty of lyric, and of lyric pedagogy, to promote. "The lyric is not a genre, but one name among several to designate the defensive motion of understanding" (261). De Man concludes provocatively: "The resulting couple or pair of texts indeed becomes a model for the uneasy combination of funereal monumentality with paranoid fear that characterizes the hermeneutics and the pedagogy of lyric poetry" (259). What comes to be at stake, then, is lyric poetry itself as a poetry of the subject. By juxtaposing lyric and law in this essay, I am implicitly asking whether there is a relation between the "first person" (the grammatical "I") and the "constitutional person" (the subject of rights).

"Only a subject can understand a meaning," claims Lacan. "Conversely, every phenomenon of meaning implies a subject."[13] What de Man seems to be arguing for here is the existence of a residue of language or rhetoric that exists neither inside nor outside the "phenomenon of meaning." Does lyric poetry try to give a psychological gloss to disruptions that are purely grammatical? Are the periodizations in literary history such as Parnassian and Romantic merely names for rhetorical structures that are not historical? For de Man, "Obsession" loses the radical disruption of "Correspondances" by making enumeration into a symptom, which is more reassuring than endless repetition. It is as though de Man were saying that "Obsession," despite or rather because it is so psychologically bleak, falls back within the pleasure principle—that is, the psychological, the human—whereas "Correspondances," which seems so sunny, contains a disruption that goes beyond the pleasure principle. When de Man says that we can get "Obsession" from "Correspondances" but not the other way around, this is a way of repeating Freud's experience of the disruption of the pleasure principle in *Beyond the Pleasure Principle*, a study in which Freud grappled with the very limits of psychoanalysis. Freud noticed that there were experiences or facts that seemed to contradict his notion of the primacy of the pleasure principle in human life (negative pleasures, the repetition compulsion, the death instinct). As Derrida has shown, Freud kept bringing the beyond back within explainability, and the beyond of Freud's theory kept popping up elsewhere.[14] He could, in effect, get the pleasure principle to explain its beyond, but not anticipate it. The beyond of the pleasure principle could only exist as a disruption.

De Man makes the surprising claim that "Correspondances" is *not* a lyric, but contains the entire possibility of lyric: " 'Obsession,' a text of recollection and elegiac mourning, *adds* remembrance to the flat surface of time in 'Correspondances'—produces at once a hermeneutic, fallacious, lyrical reading of the unintelligible" (262). The act of making intelligible, whether in the lyric or in the terminology of literary history, is for de Man at the end of the essay always an act of "resistance and nostalgia, at the furthest remove from the materiality of actual history." This would mean that "actual history" is what escapes and resists intelligibility. Here is how de Man ends the essay:

> If mourning is called a "chambre d'éternel deuil où vibrent de vieux râles," then this pathos of terror states in fact the desired consciousness of eternity and of temporal harmony as voice and as song. True "mourning" is less deluded. The most *it* can do is to allow for non-comprehension and enumerate non-anthropomorphic, non-elegiac, non-celebratory, non-lyrical, non-poetic, that is to say, prosaic, or, better, *historical* modes of language power. (262)

Earlier in the essay, de Man had said of Nietzsche's general analysis of truth that "truth is always at the very least dialectical, the negative knowledge of error" (242). In another essay, de Man speaks of "literature as the place where this negative knowledge about the reliability of linguistic utterance is made available."[15] Negativity, then, is not an assertion of the negative, but a nonpositivity within the possibility of assertion. This final sentence is clearly a version of stating negative knowledge. But it is also a personification. "True 'mourning'" is said to be "less deluded." Stressing the word *it* as the agent, he writes, "the most *it* can do is to allow for non-comprehension." "True mourning" becomes the subject of this negative knowledge. The subjectivizations performed by lyric upon the unintelligible are here rejected, but by a personification of mourning. Is mourning—or rather, "true 'mourning'"—human or inhuman? Or is it what makes it impossible to close the gap between "man" and rhetoric? In other words, does this type of personification presuppose knowledge of human essence, or does it merely confer a kind of rhetorical agency? Is it anthropomorphic? Is there a difference between personification and anthropomorphism? Is the text stating its knowledge as if it were a human, or is it just performing the inescapability of the structures it is casting off? Has de Man's conclusion really eliminated anthropomorphism and reduced it to the trope of personification, or is anthropomorphism inescapable in the notion of mourning? Is this what lyric poetry—so often structured around the relation between loss and rhetoric—must decide? Or finesse? The least we can say is that de Man has given the last word in his own text to a personification.

2.

> That which henceforth is to be "truth" is now fixed; that is to say, a uniformly valid and binding designation of things is invented and the legislature of language also gives the first laws of truth: since here, for the first time, originates the contrast between truth and falsity. The liar uses the valid designations, the words, in order to make the unreal appear as real, e.g., he says, "I am rich," whereas the right designation of his state would be "poor."
>
> Nietzsche, "Truth and Falsity in an Ultramoral Sense"

The case of *Rowland v. California Men's Colony, Unit II Men's Advisory Council* is based on a provision in the United States legal code permitting a "person" to appear in court *in forma pauperis*. The relevant legislation reads in part:

> Any court of the United States may authorize the commencement, prosecution or defense of any suit, action, or proceeding, civil or criminal, or appeal therein, without prepayment of fees and costs or security therefor, by a person who makes affidavit that he is unable to pay such costs or give security therefor.[16]

In other words, a "person" may go to court without prepayment of fees if the "person" can demonstrate indigence. The question to be decided by the court is whether this provision applies to artificial persons such as corporations or councils, or whether it is meant to apply only to individuals. In the case that led to *Rowland v. California Men's Colony, Unit II Men's Advisory Council*, a council of prisoners in California has tried to bring suit against the correctional officers of the prison for the restoration of the practice of providing free cigarettes for indigent prisoners, which was discontinued. They try to sue *in forma pauperis* on the grounds that the warden forbids the council to hold funds of its own. The court finds that they have not sufficiently proven indigence. They are allowed to appeal *in forma pauperis* in order to enable the court to decide whether the council, as an artificial legal person, is entitled to sue *in forma pauperis*. The appeals court decides that they are so entitled, but this conflicts with another court ruling in another case. The Supreme Court therefore gets to decide whether the provisions for proceeding *in forma pauperis* should apply only to natural persons, or also to legal persons such as associations and councils. The case is therefore about what a person is, and how you can tell the difference between a natural person and an artificial person.

Justice Souter's majority opinion begins with something that in many ways resembles de Man's stutter of infinite enumeration. In order to find out what the legal meaning of "person" is, Souter turns to what is called the "Dictionary Act." The Dictionary Act gives instructions about how to read acts of Congress. It states:

> In determining the meaning of any Act of Congress, unless the context indicates otherwise, the word "person" includes corporations, companies, associations, firms, partnerships, societies, and joint stock companies, as well as individuals. (1 United States Code 1)

Thus, the word *person* does include artificial entities unless the context indicates otherwise. Now the court asks, but what does "context" mean? It turns to *Webster's New International Dictionary*, where it notes that it means "the part or parts of a discourse preceding or following a 'text' or passage or a word, or so intimately associated with it as to throw light on its meaning." The context, then, is the surrounding words of the act. Of course, Webster's does offer a second meaning for the word *context*, "associated surroundings, whether material or mental"—a reference not to the surrounding text but to the broader reality or intentionality—but Souter dismisses this by saying, "we doubt that the broader sense applies here." Why? Because "if Congress had meant to point further afield, as to legislative history, for example, it would have been natural to use a more spacious phrase, like 'evidence of congressional intent,' in place of 'context.' "

The word *natural*, which is precisely at issue here, since we are trying to find out whether the statute applies only to natural persons, is here applied precisely to an artificial person, Congress, which is personified as having natural intentionality. "If Congress had meant . . ." The Court's decision repeatedly relies on this type of personification: it is as though Souter has to treat Congress as an entity with intentions, even natural intentions, in order to say that Congress could not have meant to include artificial entities in its ruling. There is a personification of an artificial entity, Congress, embedded in the very project of interpreting how far the law will allow for artificial entities to be considered persons.

Turning to the Dictionary Act for *person* and to Webster's dictionary for *context*, Souter also notes that he has to define *indicates*. The difficulty of doing so pushes him into a volley of rhetorical flourishes: "A contrary 'indication' may raise a specter short of inanity, and with something less than syllogistic force." "Indicates," it seems, means more than nonsense but less than logical necessity. In other words, the task of reading becomes an infinite regress of glossing terms that are themselves supposed to be determinants of meaning. De Man's linguistic stutter returns here as the repeated effort to throw language outside itself. We could read a text, this implies, if only we were sure of the meaning of the words *context* and *indicate*. But those are precisely the words that raise the question of meaning in its most general form—they cannot be glossed with any finality because they name the process of glossing itself.

Souter's text, in fact, is most anthropomorphic at those points where the infinite regress of language is most threatening. Congress is endowed with "natural" intentionality in order to sweep away the abyss of reference. Souter's dismissal of the prisoners' association as an "amorphous legal creature" is the counterpart to the need to reinforce the anthropomorphizability of the artificial legal creature, Congress.[17]

Souter's opinion proceeds to detail the ways in which he thinks the *in forma pauperis* ruling should only apply to natural persons. If an affidavit alleging poverty is required for a person to proceed *in forma pauperis*, then can an artificial entity plead poverty? Souter again turns to Webster's dictionary to find that poverty is a human condition, to be "wanting in material riches or goods; lacking in the comforts of life; needy." Souter also refers to a previous ruling, which holds that poverty involves being unable to provide for the "necessities of life." It is as though only natural persons can have "life," and that life is defined as the capacity to lack necessities and comforts. "Artificial entities may be insolvent," writes Souter, "but they are not well spoken of as 'poor.' " An artificial entity cannot lack the necessities and comforts of life. Only life can lack. The experience of lack differentiates natural persons from artificial persons. To lack is to be human. In a sense, we have returned to de Man's question about mourning. Is lack human, or just a structure? Whatever the case, the Court holds that associations cannot be considered persons for the purpose of the *in forma pauperis* procedure.

The majority was only five to four, however. In a dissenting opinion, written by Clarence Thomas, it is argued that there is no reason to restrict the broad definition of "person" to natural persons in this case. Thomas quotes the Court's view of "poverty" as an exclusively "human condition," and comments:

> I am not so sure. "Poverty" may well be a human condition in its "primary sense," but I doubt that using the word in connection with an artificial entity departs in any significant way from settled principles of English usage. . . . Congress itself has used the word "poor" to describe entities other than natural persons, referring in at least two provisions of the United States Code to the world's "Poorest countries"—a term that is used as a synonym for the least developed of the so-called "developing" countries.

Souter has glossed the word *poor* as though speakers of English could only use it literally. Thomas responds by including the figurative use of *poor* as included within normal usage. The boundaries between natural persons and artificial persons cannot be determined by usage, because those boundaries have always already been blurred. In treating Congress as an entity with natural intentions, indeed, Souter has already shown how "natural" the artificial can be.

At another point, Thomas takes issue with Souter's discussion of a case in which an association or corporation *is* considered a person despite strong contextual indicators to the contrary. In the case of *Wilson v. Omaha Indian Tribe*, 442 U.S. 653, 666 (1979), it was decided that "white person" could include corporations because the "larger context" and "purpose" of the law was to protect Indians against non-Indian squatters, and would be frustrated if a "white person" could simply incorporate in order to escape the provision of the law. Souter admits that "because a wholly legal creature has no color, and belongs to no race, the use of the adjective 'white' to describe a 'person' is one of the strongest contextual indicators imaginable that 'person' covers only individuals." Justice Thomas argues that if the Court "was correct in holding that the statutory term 'white person' includes a corporation (because the 'context' does not 'indicate otherwise')—the conclusion that an association is a 'person' for *in forma pauperis* purposes is inescapable." Perhaps another inescapable conclusion is that despite its apparent reference to the physical body, the phrase "white person" is the name, not of a natural, but of a corporate person.

Justice Thomas refutes the reasons Souter has given for finding that artificial entities are excluded from the *in forma pauperis* provision, noting that there may be sound policy reasons for wanting to exclude them, but that the law as written cannot be construed to have done so. The Court's job, he writes, is not to make policy but to interpret a statute.

"Congress has created a rule of statutory construction (an association is a 'person') and an exception to that rule (an association is not a 'person' if the 'context indicates otherwise'), but the Court has permitted the exception to devour the rule [a nice personification]" (treating the rule as if artificial entities were excluded rather than included unless the context indicates otherwise). "Whatever 'unless the context indicates otherwise' means," writes Thomas, "it cannot mean 'unless there are sound policy reasons for concluding otherwise.'"

Permitting artificial entities to proceed *in forma pauperis* may be unwise, and it may be an inefficient use of the government's limited resources, but I see nothing in the text of the *in forma pauperis* statute indicating that Congress has chosen to exclude such entities from the benefits of that law.

Thus, Thomas's two conservative instincts are at war with each other: he would like the government not to spend its money, but he would also like to stick to the letter of the law.

The question of what counts as a juridical person has, in fact, been modified over time in the legal code. It was in 1871 (significantly, perhaps, at the beginning of the end of post–Civil War Reconstruction) that the so-called Dictionary Act was first passed by Congress, in which the word *Person* "may extend and be applied to bodies politic and corporate." More recently, the question of fetal personhood has been debated, not only in the *Roe v. Wade* decision, where it was decided that a fetus was not a legal person, but also in *Weaks v. Mounter*, 88 Nev. 118, where it was decided that a fetus *was* a person who could sue for intrauterine injuries, but only after birth. Recently, the question of granting patents for forms of life such as oil-slick-eating bacteria or genetically altered mice has raised the question of whether a hybrid between humans and close animal relatives can be patented. And also, of course, the question of the ethics and legality of cloning humans has been raised. The law has reached another crisis about the definition of "person." In an article on constitutional personhood, Michael Rivard writes:

> Current law allows patents for genetically engineered animals but not for human beings. Humans are not patentable subject matter because patents are property rights, and the Thirteenth Amendment forbids any grant of property rights in a human being. Nevertheless, this exclusion for humans will prove impossible to maintain: within ten to thirty years, or perhaps sooner, advances in genetic engineering technology should allow scientists to intermingle the genetic material of humans and animals to produce human-animal hybrids. . . . It may soon be possible to patent—and to enslave—human-animal hybrids who think and feel like humans, but who lack constitutional protection under the Thirteenth Amendment.[18]

The Thirteenth Amendment is the amendment that abolishes slavery. The constitutional protection against slavery operates as a constraint on the patent office, but it does so in a paradoxical way. The fear of reinstituting something like slavery, or property in humans, is a reaction to, but also a sign of, what must be an ongoing research goal to come as close as possible to creating the ownable, enslavable human.[19]

Constitutional personhood has in fact often been defined in proximity to slavery. The contradiction between equal rights and chattel slavery led from the beginning to verbal gymnastics, even in the drafting of the Constitution itself. By not using the word *slavery* in the Constitution, and by revising the text of the original fugitive slave clause to refer to the legality of slavery only on the level of the states rather than of the federal government, the framers built a double intentionality into the very foundation of their law. Douglas Fehrenbacher, studying the egregious understanding of original intent later employed by the Supreme Court in the case of *Dred Scott v. Sanford*, writes of the Constitution: "It is as though the framers were half-consciously trying to frame two constitutions, one for their own time and the other for the ages, with slavery viewed bifocally—that is, plainly visible at their feet, but disappearing when they lifted their eyes."[20] A written text of law can thus contain a double intention, the trace of a compromise between differing opinions. No wonder interpreting the law's intention is so complicated. That intention can always already be multiple. The distinction Justice Thomas made between interpreting the law and making policy cannot hold if the law's ambiguity allows for the possibility that the policy it governs will change.

3.

> The "inhuman" is not some kind of mystery, or some kind of secret; the inhuman is: linguistic structures, the play of linguistic tensions, linguistic events that occur, possibilities which are inherent in language—independently of any intent or any drive or any wish or any desire we might have. . . . If one speaks of the inhuman, the fundamental non-human character of language, one also speaks of the fundamental non-definition of the human as such.
>
> Paul de Man, "Benjamin's 'The Task of the Translator'"

> Only smoking distinguishes humans from the rest of the animals.
>
> Anonymous (quoted in Richard Klein, *Cigarettes Are Sublime*)

The case of *Rowland v. California Men's Colony, Unit II Men's Advisory Council* was ostensibly about whether a council of inmates could sue prison officials *in forma pauperis* to get their cigarettes back. The details of the case seemed irrelevant to the question of whether an artificial person has the right to sue *in forma pauperis*. Yet perhaps some of those details deserve note. Is it relevant that the suit to decide this question is brought by a council of inmates? The phenomenon of the inmate civil suit has grown to the point where the case law may very well be transformed by it. In a 1995 study of inmate suits in California, it was reported that "For the last fourteen years at least, the federal courts have faced a growing caseload and workload challenge posed by inmate cases. . . . By 1992, these filings numbered nearly 30,000, and constituted 13% of the courts' total civil case filings nationwide."[21] The majority of these suits are filed *in forma pauperis*.[22] The Supreme Court's decision may well have been affected by what Clarence Thomas calls "policy decisions."

If prisoners are affecting the nature of civil proceedings, they are also, at least figuratively, affecting theoretical discussions about the nature of rational choice and the evolution of cooperation. The celebrated "Prisoner's Dilemma" has been central to questions of self-interest and social goods since it was introduced by Albert Tucker in 1950. Max Black has even entitled his discussion of the issues raised "The 'Prisoner's Dilemma' and the Limits of Rationality."[23] Why is it that the theoretical study of rational choice has recourse to "man" conceived as a prisoner? Does this have anything to do with the poets' tendency to see the sonnet form as a prison?

And is it by chance that *Rowland v. California Men's Colony, Unit II Men's Advisory Council* is about cigarettes? On the one hand, it seems paradoxical that the council has to demonstrate its indigence in order to pursue its suit against the prison directors for depriving the prisoners of access to cigarettes, which in prisons function as a form of currency. On the other hand, it seems fitting that the personhood of the association is the counterpart to the humanity of the inmates, which, as common wisdom (quoted above, second epigraph) would have it, is demonstrated by the act of smoking. The prisoners would thus, in a very attenuated way, be suing for their humanity. As Richard Klein has wittily shown, smoking serves no function other than to enact a structure of desire—of human desire for self-transcendence, for repetition, for bodily experience corresponding to something other than the "necessities of life" required for existence alone: in short, desire for the sublime.[24] Far from being what defines natural personhood, then, need for the "necessities of life" alone is precisely what *cannot* define the human.

In the article cited earlier, Rivard declares that "corporations would be presumed constitutional *non*persons," especially for liberty-related rights, unless the corporation could rebut its nonperson status by showing specific natural persons "who would be affected if the corporation were denied these rights."[25] This is the opposite of the Dictionary Act, which considers a corporation a person "unless the context indicates otherwise." Rivard's article is arguing for the rights of new biological species who can pass the "self-awareness test" (which, in a surpisingly Lacanian move derived from Michael Dennett, he defines as wanting to be different from what one is), and he claims that corporations, by their nature, do not pass this test.

But the question of the nature of corporations as persons has never been a simple one, as Rivard admits. In an article titled "The Personification of the Business Corporation in American Law" (*University of Chicago Law Review* 54 [fall 1987]: 1441), Gregory A. Marks outlines in detail the history of corporate personhood. The relation between corporations and the natural persons who compose them has grown more complicated over time, but in most discussions of the matter, it is the "natural" person that functions as the known quantity, and the "artificial" who is either just an "aggregate" of natural persons, or a fiction created by the state, or a mere metaphor, or actually resembles (is *like*, to return to the Baudelairean word) a natural person in that it has a "will" of its own. Such a corporate will is a form of agency separate from that of the natural corporators, who exist behind the "veil" of the corporation. Much of Marks's article concerns the exact rhetorical valence of this personification:

> American law has always recognized that people's activities could be formally organized and that the resulting organizations could be dealt with as units. Personification, however, is important because it became far more than a quaint device making it possible for the law to deal with organized business entities. In American legal and economic history, personification has been vital because it (1) implies a single and unitary source of control over the collective property of the corporation's members, (2) defines, encourages, and legitimates the corporation as an autonomous, creative, self-directed economic being, and (3) captures rights, ultimately even constitutional rights, for corporations thereby giving corporate property unprecedented protection from the state. (1443)

Marks takes seriously the role of language in the evolving history of the corporation. Philosophers and legislators have gone to great lengths to minimize the rhetorical damage, to eliminate personification as far as possible, but he asserts that it is not just a figure of speech to speak of a corporation's "mind," or even its "life." "Practical experience, not just anthropomorphism, fixed the corporate mind in the management hierarchy" (1475). The corporation resembled a human being in its capacity to "take resolves in the midst of conflicting motives," to "will change." Yet the analogy is not perfect. The corporation, for example, unlike its corporators, is potentially immortal. The effect of personification appears to derive its rhetorical force from the ways in which the corporation *resembles* a natural person, yet the corporation's immortality in no way diminishes its personification. When Marks says that it is "not just anthropomorphism" that underpins the agency of the corporation, he still implies that we can know what anthropomorphism is. But his final sentence stands this presupposition on its head. Far from claiming that a corporation's characteristics are derived from a knowable human essence, Marks suggests that what have been claimed to be the essential characteristics of man (especially "economic man") have in fact been borrowed from the nature of the corporation:

> Personification with its roots in historic theological disputes and modern business necessity, had proved to be a potent symbol to legitimate the autonomous business corporation and its management. Private property rights had been transferred to associations, associations had themselves become politically legitimate, and the combination had helped foster modern political economy. The corporation, once the derivative tool of the state, had become its rival, and the successes of the autonomous corporate management turned the basis for belief in an individualist conception of property on its head. The protests of modern legists notwithstanding, the business corporation had become the quintessential economic man. (1482–83)

Theories of rationality, naturalness, and the "good," presumed to be grounded in the nature of "man," may in reality be taking their notions of human essence not from "natural man" but from business corporations.

Ambivalence about personification, especially the personification of abstractions, has in fact permeated not only legal but also literary history. Nervousness about the agency of the personified corporation echoes the nervousness Enlightenment writers felt about the personifications dreamed up by the poets. As Steven Knapp puts it in his hook *Personification and the Sublime*:

> Allegorical personification—the endowing of metaphors with the agency of literal persons—was only the most obvious and extravagant instance of what Enlightenment writers perceived, with a mixture of admiration and uneasiness, as the unique ability of poetic genius to give the force of literal reality to figurative "inventions." More important than the incongruous presence of such agents was their contagious effect on the ostensibly literal agents with which they interacted.[26]

The uncanniness of the personification, then, was derived from its way of putting in question what the "natural" or the "literal" might be.

We have finally come back to the question of whether there is a difference between anthropomorphism and personification, which arose at the end of the discussion of the essay by Paul de Man. It can now be seen that everything hangs on this question. Not only does anthropomorphism depend on the givenness of the essence of the human and personification does not, but the mingling of personifications on the same footing as "real" agents threatens to make the lack of certainty about what humanness is come to consciousness. Perhaps the loss of unconsciousness about the lack of humanness is what de Man was calling "true 'mourning.'" Perhaps the "fallacious lyrical reading of the unintelligible" was exactly what legislators count on lyric poetry to provide: the assumption that the human *has been* or *can be* defined so that it can then be presupposed without the question of its definition's being raised as a question—legal or otherwise. Thus the poets would truly be, as Shelley claimed, the "unacknowledged legislators of the world," not because they covertly determine policy, but because it is somehow necessary and useful that there *be* a powerful, presupposable, unacknowledgment. But the very rhetorical sleight of hand that would instate such an unacknowledgment is indistinguishable from the rhetorical structure that would empty it. Lyric and law are two of the most powerful discourses that exist along the fault line of this question.

NOTES

1. I am thinking of Richard Posner's *Law and Literature* (Cambridge: Harvard University Press, 1988), Richard Weisberg's *The Failure of the Word* (New Haven: Yale University Press, 1984), and Peter Brooks, *Troubling Confessions* (Chicago: University of Chicago Press, 2000). But for a legal approach that *does* address poetry, see the interesting discussion of Wallace Stevens by Thomas Grey and Margaret Jane Radin in the *Yale Journal of Law & The Humanities* 2:2 (summer 1990), as well as the more extended treatment of Wallace Stevens in Thomas Grey, *The Wallace Stevens Case: Law and the Practice of Poetry* (Cambridge: Harvard University Press, 1991).

2. William Wordsworth's sonnet, "Nuns Fret Not at Their Convent's Narrow Room," contains the lines, "In truth the prison, into which we doom / Ourselves, no prison is: and hence for me, / In sundry moods, 'twas pastime to be bound / Within the Sonnet's scanty plot of ground" (*Selected Poetry and Prose of Wordsworth* [New York: Signet, 1970], 169).

3. John Keats's sonnet on the sonnet begins, "If by dull rhymes our English must be chained, / And, like Andromeda, the sonnet sweet / Fettered . . ." (*The Selected Poetry of Keats* [New York: Signet, 1966], 264).

4. One of several poems by Baudelaire titled *Spleen* describes a mood produced by or analogized to a rainy day: "Quand la pluie étalant ses immenses trainées / D'une vaste prison imite les barreaux . . ." (Baudelaire, *Oeuvres complètes*, vol. 1 [Paris: Pléiade, 1975], 75).

5. For a suggestive discussion of what it means for a text to obey the law of genre, see Jacques Derrida, "The Law of Genre," in *Acts of Literature*, ed. Derek Attridge (New York: Routledge, 1992).

6. Paul de Man, "Anthropomorphism and Trope in the Lyric," in *The Rhetoric of Romanticism* (New York: Columbia University Press, 1984). Page numbers in parentheses refer to this essay.

7. *United States Law Week* 61:25 (January 12, 1993). Page numbers in parentheses refer to this text.

8. This allusion to Keats's "Ode on a Grecian Urn" stands in for the premise of the compatibility of literary aesthetics with linguistic structures, and of linguistic structures with perceptual or intuitive knowledge, that de Man is often at pains to contest. See his remarks on the pedagogical model of the trivium in the titular essay of *The Resistance to Theory* (Minneapolis: University of Minnesota Press, 1986).

9. Friedrich Nietzsche, "Truth and Falsity in an Ultramoral Sense," in *Critical Theory since Plato*, ed. Hazard Adams (Fort Worth: Harcourt Brace Jovanovich, 1992), 634–39. If the Keats poem stands as the claim that aesthetic and epistemological structures are compatible, Nietzsche's text, for de Man, stands as a parody of that claim.

10. The translations are mine, for the purpose of bringing out those aspects of the poems that are relevant to my discussion.

11. "Allegory and Irony in Baudelaire," in *Romanticism and Contemporary Criticism* (Baltimore: Johns Hopkins University Press, 1993). This essay is part of the Gauss Seminar given by de Man in 1967.

12. Jacques Lacan, "Aggressivity in Psychoanalysis," in *Écrits: A Selection*, trans. Alan Sheridan (New York: W. W. Norton, 1977), 17: "What I have called paranoic knowledge is shown, therefore, to correspond in its more or less archaic forms to certain critical moments that mark the history of man's mental genesis, each representing a stage in objectifying identification."

13. Ibid., 9.

14. Jacques Derrida, "Freud's Legacy," in *The Postcard*, trans. Alan Bass (Chicago: University of Chicago Press, 1987).

15. De Man, "The Resistance to Theory," 10.

16. United States Code (1994 edition), vol. 15, 438.

17. In a response to the present paper given at the Yale Law School, Shoshana Felman made the brilliant suggestion that Souter would have wanted to rewrite Baudelaire's "Correspondances" as: "Le Congrès est un temple où de vivants pilliers laissent parfois sortir de confuses paroles . . ." The neoclassical, Parnassian architecture of official Washington, D.C., and the common metaphorical expression "pillars of the community," add piquancy to this suggestion.

18. Michael D. Rivard, "Toward a General Theory of Constitutional Personhood: A Theory of Constitutional Personhood for Transgenic Humanoid Species," *UCLA Law Review* 39: 5 (June 1992): 1428–29.

19. See A. Leon Higginbotham Jr. and Barbara Kopytoff, "Property First, Humanity Second: The Recognition of the Slave's Human Nature in Virginia Civil Law," *Ohio State Law Journal* 50:3 (June 1989): "The humanity of the slave, requiring that he be treated with the care due other humans and not like other forms of property, became *part* of the owner's property rights" (520).

20. Douglas E. Fehrenbacher, *Slavery, Law, and Politics: The Dred Scott Case in Historical Perspective* (Oxford: Oxford University Press, 1981), 15.

21. Kim Mueller, "Inmates' Civil Rights Cases and the Federal Courts: Insights Derived from a Field Research Project in the Eastern District of California," *Creighton Law Review* 1228 (June 1995): 1258–59. In the Eastern District of California, inmates' civil rights actions constituted nearly 30 percent of the case filings. (California Men's Colony is not in the Eastern District; it is in San Luis Obispo.)

22. Ibid., 1276 and 1281.

23. Max Black, *Perplexities* (Ithaca, N.Y.: Cornell University Press, 1990). See also Robert Axelrod, *The Evolution of Cooperation* (New York: Basic Books, 1984).

24. Richard Klein, *Cigarettes Are Sublime* (Durham, N.C.: Duke University Press, 1993). Klein notes, incidentally, that Baudelaire is one of the first French writers to use the word *cigarette* in print (in his "Salons de 1848," 8).

25. Rivard, "Toward a General Theory of Constitutional Personhood," 1501–2.

26. Steven Knapp, *Personification and the Sublime* (Cambridge: Harvard University Press, 1985), 2.

SECTION 6

Frankfurt School and After

The term "Frankfurt School" arose informally to describe Marxist thinkers associated with the School of Social Research in Frankfurt (founded in 1923). In this section, we are concerned with only two figures that could be described as Frankfurt School thinkers, if only because that is where their conversation with one another began. Walter Benjamin and Theodor Adorno wrote essays about the lyric that have proven enormously influential for many critics trying to think their way out of or around the Anglo-American New Critical tradition. However, these essays remain difficult to assimilate to modern critical ideas of what a lyric is or was. This is because in Germany the lyric remained closely tied to the idea of the folk song (in the wake of Herder and Heine) and to Hegel's idealization of subjective lyric as the highest form of aesthetic representation. The difference between the lyric as popular expression and the lyric as the most elevated type of individual expression formed the dialectic from which Benjamin's and Adorno's ideas about the lyric emerged.

Neither I. A. Richards's Practical Criticism nor American New Criticism influenced Benjamin or Adorno. That is why their ideas have proven so attractive as alternatives to the Anglophone tradition but also why they have been difficult to integrate into the lyric models assumed by twentieth-century Anglo-American lyric theory. While many lyric theorists have been drawn to Frankfurt School approaches (especially in the last thirty years, when Frankfurt School theory has seemed to offer an alternative to a waning post-structuralism), there has also been much confusion between the definitions of the lyric held by these different intellectual traditions. Too often, Adorno's "Lyric and Society" in particular has been taken up as a touchstone for a normative view of the lyric neither Benjamin nor Adorno would have recognized. For them, what was at stake in writing about the lyric was the relation between aesthetic expression and social decadence in high capitalism. Their debate over lyric was really a debate over social theory—or, to put this differently, lyric theory was for these thinkers always already and primarily social theory. As Robert Kaufman has written, "the Frankfurters demonstrated their conviction that art could act decisively on structural, socioeconomic dynamics and might indeed be the means through which certain aspects of sociohistorical development could become apprehensible in the first place."[1] As we have seen, one could certainly make the argument that for the Practical and New Critics, as well as the Structuralists and Post-Structuralists, theories of the lyric were also always theories of sociality, but in Frankfurt School thought the social theory implicit in all modern theories of the lyric became the explicit focus.

Although the selections from Benjamin and Adorno included here were written over twenty years apart, Adorno's essay (originally a radio address in Berlin in 1957) can be read as a belated response to Benjamin's series of essays on Baudelaire (essays that profoundly influenced both de Man's and Johnson's work on Baudelaire represented in section 5). Benjamin's work on Baudelaire was part of an unfinished, lifelong study he called the *Passagenwerk* or *Arcades Project*, a collection of writings about life in Paris in the nineteenth century. In their extensive correspondence before Benjamin's death in 1940, Adorno told Benjamin "in as simple and Hegelian manner as possible" that his "dialectic lacks one thing: mediation. Throughout your text there is a tendency to relate the pragmatic contents of Baudelaire's work directly to adjacent features in the social history of his time, preferably economic features."[2] Adorno zeroed in on Benjamin's argument that "Baudelaire's wine poems have been motivated by the wine duty and the town gates," a determination that "imputes to phenomena precisely that kind of spontaneity, palpability and density which they have lost in capitalism. In this sort of immediate . . . materialism, there is a profoundly romantic element" (*AP* 129). Adorno's criticism was somewhat unfair, since Benjamin argued that he reserved the theoretical part of the project for another section, but it also shifted the "profoundly romantic element" of Benjamin's thought to a view of capitalism rather than to a view of the lyric. Benjamin's work on Baudelaire's lyrics is actually about the failure of romanticism, about the alienated situation of the romantic lyric in capitalism, but when he wrote that "Baudelaire envisaged readers to whom the reading of lyric poetry would present difficulties," it was the shift in the structure of these readers' experience in an increasingly alienated and fractured sociality that was his focus. Although he goes on to argue that Baudelaire's response to this new social predicament was to make his poems reflect his readers' alienation, his argument is not that the lyric itself changed in response to these conditions but that Baudelaire wrote lyrics that could address such conditions. For both Benjamin and Adorno, the lyric is pretty much what Hegel thought it was a century earlier: the subjective expression of the individual that represents at its best the ideal aesthetic form of the *zeitgeist*, the beacon of social progress. Underneath that Hegelian idealism lurked Herder's championing of poetry's role as the expression of folk culture. Whether the lyric can continue to fulfill either its ideal or its popular function in the era of high capitalism is the problem both Benjamin and Adorno take as their theme.

For Benjamin, that problem was actually Baudelaire's theme in the middle of the nineteenth century. According to Benjamin, "the conditions for the reception of lyric poetry had already become extremely unfavorable" by the middle of the nineteenth century. The pose of an early-nineteenth-century poet like Lamartine as the "minstrel" of the people was no longer possible by Baudelaire's time; instead, Benjamin writes, by the middle of the century the poet had become "representative of a genre." This narrowing of the lyric from vehicle of communal expression to specialized genre meant that by the time of Baudelaire the lyric was met with "a greater coolness of the public" than it had been in previous eras. Benjamin locates Baudelaire's genius in recognizing the failure of lyric poetry to "accord with the experience of its readers" and deciding to write poems that *did* address that experience—the anti-lyrical lyrics of *Les Fleurs du mal.* Ironically, Baudelaire's responses to the failure of the lyric resulted in a best-selling book of lyrics.

The book succeeded so wildly, Benjamin argues, because Baudelaire discovered how and why "lyric poetry could be grounded in experience for which exposure to shock has become the norm." In order to describe that experience, Benjamin turned to Bergson, Proust, and Freud as theorists of modern subjectivity, as thinkers about the new normal. But Benjamin insisted that what had become the norm in modern life—essentially, the reaction formations of variously traumatized individuals—did not become the norm for the lyric. The "hidden figure" of the crowd that Benjamin finds in Baudelaire's poetry as a whole is one way of understanding how those traumatized individuals become a social condition, but Benjamin's essay ends by documenting the many ways in which this social condition was at odds with the conditions of the lyric itself. How does the lyric change as a genre in response to the alienation of modern experience? According to Benjamin, this is a pressing question for Baudelaire, since "his work cannot be categorized merely as historical, like anyone else's, but it intends to be so and understood itself as such." While "it cannot be denied" that some of Baudelaire's motifs "render the possibility of lyric poetry problematic," that does not mean that the genre disintegrates in Baudelaire's hands. Instead, it becomes ironic; since the idea of "the lyric poet with his halo is antiquated," Baudelaire presents that idea ironically, but that irony does not necessarily change the idea of lyric itself—on the contrary, it may make that idea seem more romantic, more nostalgic, by contrast. The law of Baudelaire's poetry may be the law of "immediate shock experience," but that law reflects the modern disintegration of experience rather than the modern disintegration of the lyric, which Baudelaire's irony actually ends by throwing into stark relief as a vanishing ideal.

Adorno's "Lyric Poetry and Society," composed seventeen years after Benjamin's death, is in part a response to the lyric's precarious predicament in Benjamin's work on Baudelaire. Adorno initially agrees with Benjamin in his definition of what a lyric is or should be, or at least he seems to: "the universality of the lyric's substance . . . is social in nature." Yet as we may have expected from his complaint that Benjamin's reading of Baudelaire depended on an "immediate materialism" lacking dialectical mediation, Adorno's version of what makes the lyric representative of a universal social condition differs markedly from his friend's model. If, for Benjamin, Baudelaire's work was representative in marking the difference between the lyric ideal and the actual, decadent experience of modern individuals, for Adorno the modern lyric is most fully realized not in that ironic disparity but in the absolute congruity between the alienated, difficult modern poem and alienated, difficult modern sociality. But "congruity" is not quite the right word for the relationship between lyric and society in Adorno's essay, "since it is precisely what is not social in the lyric poem that is now to become its social aspect." Adorno invokes Gustave Doré's caricatured deputy of the ancien regime (who exclaims, "And to whom, gentlemen, do we owe the revolution of 1789 if not to Louis XVI!") in order to characterize the negative dialectic between lyric poetry and society: "in my view," Adorno explains, "you could say, society plays the role of the executed king and the lyric the role of his opponents."[3] This is to say, Adorno continues, that Benjamin may have been quite right about the disintegration and alienation of modern social life but that he was wrong about the lyric's response to modernity's fractured state. For Adorno, the lyric is not something set above or apart from modernity, an ironic distillation of the mismatch between the ideal and the real, but has become instead modernity's vehicle, an objective force that impels "a constricted and constricting social condition to transcend itself and become worthy of human beings." It is not divorced from but is instead restored to its Hegelian destiny by means of the very conditions that would seem to make such a utopian horizon harder to see.

The means by which such a surprising conversion becomes possible is the medium of language. In this sense Adorno's approach has something in common with the structuralists, since for Adorno, as for Jakobson, the way language structures the lyric becomes a paradigmatic instance of the way language structures the social world. What language mediates in both views is the experience of the individual, so much so that "in the lyric poem the subject, through its identification with language, negates both its opposition to society as something merely monadological and its mere functioning within a wholly socialized society [*vergesellschaftete Gesellschaft*]." Since poems are made of language and societies are made of language, the individual's relation to poems and to the social world is really the same relation. The trick to this logic when it comes to a definition of the lyric is that the modern lyric's linguistic mediation of experience is dialectical: the ideal of a common language for common experience only becomes available in and through the alienated language of isolated individual experience.

Thus, for Adorno, the more "atomistic" and individualized the society, the more isolated and apparently divorced from sociality lyric language becomes. Alienation is what the modern individual and the modern lyric have in common, since the expression of the loss of common experience becomes the expression of common experience: "The work's distance from mere existence becomes the measure of what is false and bad in the latter. In its protest the poem expresses the dream of a world in which things would be different." That dream, Hegel's lyric ideal, can be glimpsed where one would least expect to find it: in the estranged language of the most difficult, most "purified" modern poetry, in poetry that seems aristocratic rather than popular, radically isolated rather than common. Adorno finds his premier example of such poetry not in Baudelaire but in the work of Stefan George, a poet so difficult that he seems to hear "his own language as if it were a foreign tongue." In departing from Benjamin's example of the first modern and last best-selling lyric poet in France, choosing instead the obscure "cult" German post-Symbolist George, Adorno was also departing from Benjamin's way of reading the lyric. For Adorno, high modernist style mediates the alienation that Baudelaire's poems expressed only thematically. It is not George's subjects but instead the estrangement of George's language that Adorno wants to frame as the ideal medium of what has become the bourgeois individual's common experience, since "this very lyric speech becomes the voice of human beings between whom the barriers have fallen." In the lyric expression of solitude and isolation our common experience of the consequences of capitalism may be heard.

Understood in this way, Adorno's version of the modern lyric is even more romanticized than the view he accused Benjamin of holding dear—and both heady combinations of a dystopian view of social history and a utopian view of lyric possibility have proven dear in turn to a long line of thinkers about modern poetics. Fredric Jameson, perhaps the most influential American post–Frankfurt School thinker (though a critic more often devoted to thinking about prose than poetry) inherits what he calls "this privileged theory of poetic value" and in many ways sustains it. In his essay on Baudelaire included here, Jameson returns to Benjamin—a return all the more remarkable for its lack of any mention of Benjamin's reading of Baudelaire or of Adorno's reading of Benjamin. Instead of invoking Benjamin by name or explicitly referring to the conversation between Benjamin and Adorno, Jameson follows in the double wake of Benjamin's reading of Baudelaire as the poet of high capitalism and of Adorno's reading of the ideal poetry of high modernism by producing his own version of Baudelaire as inaugural poet of high modernism beside a new "Baudelaire of post-modernism, of our own immediate age, of consumer society, the Baudelaire of the society of the spectacle or the image." Jameson thus brings Frankfurt School lyric theory into contact with a social world neither Benjamin nor Adorno saw coming.

Jameson's first Baudelaire is a lyric poet via both Benjamin's materialist and Adorno's linguistic models of the lyric: Jameson traces the disappearance or eclipse of "what we now call the 'referent'" in Baudelaire's poetry through "the inner contradiction in the raw material of Baudelaire's text between precapitalist society and the new industrial metropolis of nascent capital." Jameson combines Benjamin's materialism with Adorno's aestheticism by turning to another theorist of poetics of the 1930s. He rewrites Heidegger's phenomenological staging of a "rift" between World and Earth (included and discussed in section 7) "in terms of the dimensions of History and the social project on the one hand, and and of Nature or matter on the other." The effect of this rewriting is not only to further obscure Jameson's debts to Frankfurt School thinkers but to shift Heidegger's philosophical discourse of ontology toward a Marxist discourse of dialectical materialism. By effecting that shift, Jameson grounds the disappearance of the referent in Baudelaire's poems in a very Benjaminian sense of an historical shift in experience. According to Jameson, "on or around 1857" the language for physical sensation changed so radically that one could say that "before Baudelaire and Flaubert there are no physical sensations in literature." While he admits that this is "an outrageous (or at least, as they say, unverifiable) generalization," he suggests it in just the way that Benjamin suggests that in the middle of the nineteenth century there was an historical transformation of "experience for which exposure to shock has become the norm." Both Jameson and Benjamin read Baudelaire's poetry as the registration of this shift in experience. In Jameson, the Heideggerian rift between history and nature that is the product of the post-capitalist transformation of experience eventuates in what he calls "the whole drama of modernism . . . in the way in which its own peculiar life and logic depend on the reduction of reference to an absolute minimum and the elaboration, in the former place of reference, of complex symbolic and often mythical frameworks and scaffolding." Thus Jameson's first Baudelaire, the Baudelaire who is the inaugural poet of high modernism, emerges from Benjamin's Baudelaire, the Baudelaire who is the laureate of decadent or traumatized modern sensation. And like Benjamin, Jameson makes these large claims for Baudelaire's importance in the history of lived experience without turning to how or why this shift might also change the genre mediating that experience.

Indeed, the closest that Jameson comes to considering Baudelaire's poems as lyrics is when he turns to what he calls "the post-modern elements in Baudelaire." The anachronism is part of Jameson's point. What he wants to emphasize in his second Baudelaire is this iconic modern lyric poet's relevance to aesthetic categories not yet available earlier in the twentieth century, his relevance to "our own immediate age, [to] consumer society, the Baudelaire of the society of the spectacle or the image." While the high modernist Baudelaire may have been, in Heidegger's phrase, the poet for whom "Language is the house of being," for Jameson's post-modernist Baudelaire, "Language is only the *apartment* of being." This shrinking of the consolation language can give in the post-capitalist urban landscape is also a diminution of Adorno's ingenious solution to the lyric's registration of the alienation of modern experience. If, for Adorno, lyric language can become the common expression of individuals "between whom the barriers have fallen" precisely because the difficult modern lyric represents social alienation in its own alienated form, for Jameson the postmodern studio apartment of lyric language is too small for such accommodations. The best it can do is to provide a screen for "spectacles which would seem symbolically to crush human life and to dramatize everything which reduces the individual human being and the individual subject to powerlessness and nothingness." Just as Jameson takes a step beyond Benjamin in proposing that Baudelaire's poetry measures such a radical shift in historical experience that physical sensation can be represented there for the first time, he takes a step beyond Adorno in proposing that poetry might represent the alienation of contemporary experience by no longer representing anything at all, by becoming instead part of "the whole world of the production and reproduction of the image and of the simulacrum, and of which the smeared light and multireflective glass of the most elegant post-contemporary films or buildings is an adequate *analagon*." Searching for a language for representation after the death of representation, Jameson also searches for a language for Frankfurt School theory after the death of its founders, and for a sense of the lyric that could compete with movies, computer screens, and videos as a medium for experience after the death of experience.

Yet even in Jameson's extreme version, Frankfurt School theory cannot, by definition, give up on an admittedly utopian horizon in which the lyric could restore experience to the shocked or alienated or bedazzled or evacuated subject. In this line of thinking, there is always the hope that we could recover from the ravages of late capitalism—and often it is lyric poetry that may have the capacity to save us, if only by so articulately tallying our losses. The romantic—and especially Hegelian—elevation of lyric to the ideal genre of individual expression must remain residual in Frankfurt School theory, if only, as in Jameson, as the background against which that theory reacts. In his essay, Drew Milne responds directly to the dependence of Frankfurt School theory on the Hegelian expressive lyric ideal. Though Milne begins by citing Adorno's claim that "the lyric work is always the subjective expression of a social antagonism," he quickly turns to ask, "What of lyric's constitutive inhumanity, its relation to non-human nature?" This is a question that challenges Jameson's post-Benjaminian drive to seek in lyric the representation of modern and even contemporary social experience and that threatens to reverse Adorno's famous definition of lyric at the same time. What if lyric is not individual expression—at least not individual *human* expression? Can expression be inhuman? While Adorno suggests that the lyric poet submits to the "objectivity of language," Milne's question suggests that lyric language may not just be reified or objectified but may be outside the poet's grasp. Against the grain of Adorno's apprehension of the lyric as thoroughly modern, Milne suggests that "the limits of lyric humanism remain closer" to ancient conceptions of lyric as "the speculative experience of nature." Milne's qualification of Adorno brackets the modern association between lyric and subjective expression, yet Milne wants to retain a Frankfurt School emphasis on lyric as representation of historical experience. How can an ancient conception of "speculative experience" apply to modern experience and to the modern lyric? And how can expression not have a human subject?

Milne's answer is very much in the spirit of Adorno, as he changes the key of representation from the metaphor of human speech to "the lyric poetry of the page." Ironically, then, modern poetry can approach an archaic premodern sense of experience (the utopian horizon of classic Frankfurt School thought) by being printed rather than sung, since "as writing, lyric is freed from the clumsiness of speech, and in this freedom it is possible to imagine the voices of nature beyond the human." As Milne's alternative to lyric humanism retains an emphasis on lyric as the vehicle of experience, so his alternative to the figuration of lyric as speech retains an emphasis on voice, though "the voices of nature" are not human voices in which we drown. Instead, "the voices of nature" surface in modern poetry as symptoms of "the difficulty of overcoming the thematics of romanticism," symptoms often figured in and after romanticism as birdsong, though a birdsong committed to the page on which the poem is printed. As Milne points out, even Hegel's romanticism was embarrassed by the artifice of song as a metaphor for lyric. In Keats,

Hegel, Shelley, and Kant, Milne traces "an unreconciled affinity between birds and humans. . . . This affinity allows the lyric poet to explore both the limits of humanism in our conceptions of song and the limits to disenchantment in the human domination of nature." This reading of the thematics of birdsong in the transition from romantic to modern poetics attempts to solve the problem that Benjamin, Adorno, and Jameson confronted in different ways: the problem of how to reconcile an ideal ambition for lyric expression with the real constraints on such expression set by contemporary social conditions. The commodification of nature, of the not-human, might be addressed in this formulation by an expression "of alienation from anthropomorphic identification with nature." Such expressions always threaten to disappear or to become inaudible behind human voices, but Milne traces a line of contemporary poets who draw on the romantic obsession with birdsong at the edges of humanism to figure a natural expression that would not be our own, that would be legible only in an intricate intertextual slide.

Milne's lyrical meditation on "the limits of lyric humanism" remains very much under the influence of Adorno's project, just as Jameson's meditation on the postmodern Baudelaire remains very much under the influence of Benjamin's project. Milne's variation on Adorno's theme is to retain a sense of the lyric as the expression of social alienation but to change the subject of that expression. The trick is to imagine birdsong as "the language of winged words" rather than as the language of the poet. Such an exchange must always be a bit of a sleight of hand, since of course birds don't write lyric poems. Then again, we don't actually hear birds when we read poems; the phenomenology of poems as song is wholly imagined, an unheard music. Stathis Gourgouris cuts through this metaphorical double bind by thinking through Adorno's theory of lyric subjectivity not against the backdrop of printed poetic birdsong but in the context of musical response. Specifically, Gourgouris follows Adorno in thinking through "the societal parameters of lyric poetry" but rather than finding those parameters in the limits of lyric humanism, as Milne does, he considers "both the significance of lyric poetry in modern society and the song form in strictly musical terms." To think in "strictly musical terms" for Gourgouris is to follow Adorno in thinking of music and lyric in strictly social terms. Gourgouris gives a very close reading of "On Lyric Poetry and Society" in order to understand how Adorno manages to confirm "the transcendental substance of lyrical subjectivity by abolishing its metaphysical framework, a gesture that, on first sight at least, appears impossible by mere logic." While Jameson basically upholds the Hegelian metaphysical scaffolding of Frankfurt School lyric theory (even while combining it with a dash of Heidegger) and Milne hazards a preceding, premodern speculative logic of lyric inhumanism, Gourgouris understands Adorno to have already revised Hegel's idealist humanism in the name of the social lyric "as a form of address."

According to Gourgouris, "Adorno nullifies from the start any indication that the social element in the lyric might be deduced from the social content of the poem or the social interests of the poet." As we have seen, Adorno is usually read as endorsing aesthetic autonomy as the means of social resistance—that is, the alienated and self-sufficient modern poem becomes an expressive analogue for the alienated and self-enclosed modern individual. But Gourgouris revises this reading to suggest that "the autonomy of the lyric may be aesthetic in the sense that it pertains to the making of an art-form but as a gesture of *poiesis*, it bears indeed the gestures of *social autonomy*—by which I mean, the position in society, within a social imaginary, that enables us to reconceptualize, rearrange, reimagine the very framework of the social reality we inherit." For Gourgouris, the utopian horizon of Adorno's theory of the lyric is not the perfected linguistic form of the poem itself but, as Adorno, writes, "the dream of a world in which things would be different."

Can lyric poetry really change the world? Gourgouris admits that even Adorno backs away from this question, resorting to the "rather romantic claim that [a] double alienation—the alienation of alienation, we would say dialectically—restores the lyric 'I' from its formative dehumanization." Against that view, Gourgouris prefers to think that "the emancipatory force of the lyric" is a matter of "a genuine autonomous social imagination." His ambitions for the lyric are thus even more utopian than Adorno's—or they would be, if his example of "a genuine autonomous social imagination" were not so compelling as a qualified historical accomplishment. In the instance of the composer Hanns Eisler's *Hollywooder Liederbuch*, a song cycle Eisler produced with Bertolt Brecht while both were in exile in Los Angeles in the early 1940s, Gourgouris finds a counter-example to Adorno's difficult early-twentieth-century high modern poetry of the page. The alienation of Adorno's lyric subject became an historical reality for Eisler and Brecht after their escapes from Nazi Germany. As Brecht wrote while in Los Angeles, "to work lyrically here, even if relating to the present . . . is as if working in gold filigree. There's something whimsical, eccentric, blinkered about it." Living the alienation of exile and working through it, inhabiting the reality of a reified alienation, Eisler and Brecht fashioned a lyricism "at the bare limit, stripping the requisite sentimentalism one associates conventionally with lyric expression." They realized in history what Adorno and Brecht's dear friend Benjamin posited in theory, and according to Gourgouris, they went further: not only did they make lyrics in exile that expressed both their own and the modern lyric's distance from earlier sentimental community investments, but they used their exile in Hollywood to dream of "an as yet imaginary community nurtured from within the experience of exile to be constituted as its own overcoming." They were able to do this by working in both words and music, by lifting the lyric off the page and thus out of its potentially stultifying associations, translating it into the potential for what Gourgouris calls "transgressive listening." In the *Hollywooder Liederbuch*, of all places, Gourgouris finds a dialectical alternative to Benjamin's sense of the lyric as ironic modern anachronism; he finds a potential realization of Adorno's fantasy of the lyric as the speech of men between whom the barriers have fallen. According to this way of thinking, as history would have it, in the early 1940s in Hollywood, the speech of all men became the music of a few men who had been driven out of the country that gave birth to the Frankfurt School. That music was never produced during the composer's lifetime, remaining literally unheard music that could only dream of a world—an undiscovered country—where music could make dreams come true. Like all post–Frankfurt School lyric theory, Gourgouris's essay grounds itself in the belief that the lyric helps to bring about a world in which things could be different by imagining that such a world may come into being under the very circumstances that make it impossible.

NOTES

1. Robert Kaufman, "Frankfurt School," in *The Princeton Encyclopedia of Poetry and Poetics*, 4th ed., ed. Roland Greene et al. (Princeton, NJ: Princeton University Press, 2012), 518.

2. *Aesthetics and Politics: Ernst Bloch, Georg Lukacs, Bertolt Brecht, Walter Benjamin, Theodor Adorno*, trans. and ed. Ronald Taylor (London: NLB, 1977), 128. Henceforth *AP*. For an extended analysis of the correspondence between Adorno and Benjamin over the uses and abuses of the lyric, see Giorgio Agamben, "The Prince and the Frog: The Question of Method in Adorno and Benjamin," in *Infancy and History: The Destruction of Experience*, trans. Liz Heron (London: Verso, 1993).

3. For an extensive reading of Adorno's version of the social lyric, see Kaufman (2004); on Frankfurt School poetics, see also Kaufman (2001 and 2006).

Further Reading

Adorno, Theodor. *Notes to Literature.* Volumes 1–2. Translated by Shierry Weber Nicholson. Edited by Ralph Tiedimann. New York: Columbia University Press, 1991.

Adorno, Theodor, and Walter Benjamin. *The Complete Correspondence, 1928–1940.* Translated by Nicholas Walter. Edited by Henri Lonitz. Cambridge, MA: Harvard University Press, 2001.

Benjamin, Walter. *Selected Writings.* Volumes 1–4. Edited by Marcus Bullock and Michael Jennings. Cambridge, MA: Harvard University Press, 2004–2006.

Brenkman, John. *Culture and Domination.* Ithaca, NY: Cornell University Press, 1989.

Buck-Morss, Susan. *The Dialectics of Seeing: Walter Benjamin and the Arcades Project.* Cambridge, MA: MIT Press, 1991.

———. *Origin of Negative Dialectics: Theodor W. Adorno, Walter Benjamin, and the Frankfurt Institute.* New York: Free Press, 1977.

Damon, Maria, and Ira Livingston, eds. *Poetry and Cultural Studies: A Reader.* Urbana: University of Illinois Press, 2009.

Eagleton, Terry. *Walter Benjamin: Or, Towards a Revolutionary Criticism.* New York: Verso, 2009.

Hansen, Miriam. *Cinema and Experience: Siegfried Kracauer, Walter Benjamin, and Theodor W. Adorno.* Berkeley: University of California Press, 2011.

Jameson, Fredric. *Marxism and Form.* Princeton, NJ: Princeton University Press, 1971.

Jarvis, Simon. *Adorno: A Critical Introduction.* London: Polity Press, 1998.

Jay, Martin. *The Dialectical Imagination: A History of the Frankfurt School and the Institute of Social Research, 1923–1950.* Berkeley: University of California Press, 1973.

Kaufman, Robert. "Adorno's Social Lyric and Literary Criticism Today." In *The Cambridge Companion to Adorno,* edited by Tom Huhn. Cambridge: Cambridge University Press, 2004.

———. "Lyric's Expression: Musicality, Conceptuality, Critical Agency." *Cultural Critique* 60 (Winter 2006): 197–216.

———. "Negatively Capable Dialectics: Keats, Vendler, Adorno, and the Theory of the Avant-Garde." *Critical Inquiry* 27:2 (Winter 2001): 354–84.

Melin, Charlotte. *Poetic Maneuvers: Hans Magnus Enzensberger and the Lyric Genre.* Avant-garde & Modernism Studies. Evanston, IL: Northwestern University Press, 2003.

Tiffany, Daniel. *Infidel Poetics: Riddles, Nightlife, Substance.* Chicago: University of Chicago Press, 2009.

———. *Toy Medium: Materialism and Modern Lyric.* Berkeley: University of California Press, 2000.

On Some Motifs in Baudelaire 6.1

(1939; trans. 1969)

Walter Benjamin Translated by Harry Zohn[1]

I

Baudelaire envisaged readers to whom the reading of lyric poetry would present difficulties. The introductory poem of *Les Fleurs du mal* is addressed to these readers. Willpower and the ability to concentrate are not their strong points. What they prefer is sensual pleasure; they are familiar with the "spleen" which kills interest and receptiveness. It is strange to come across a lyric poet who addresses himself to such readers—the least rewarding type of audience. There is of course a ready explanation for this. Baudelaire wanted to be understood; he dedicates his book to those who are like him. The poem addressed to the reader ends with the salutation: "Hypocrite lecteur,—mon semblable,—mon frère!"[2] It might be more fruitful to put it another way and say: Baudelaire wrote a book which from the very beginning had little prospect of becoming an immediate popular success. The kind of reader he envisaged is described in the introductory poem, and this turned out to have been a far-sighted judgment. He would eventually find the reader his work was intended for. This situation—the fact, in other words, that the conditions for the reception of lyric poetry have become increasingly unfavorable—is borne out by three particular factors, among others. First of all, the lyric poet has ceased to represent the poet per se. He is no longer a "minstrel," as Lamartine still was; he has become the representative of a genre. (Verlaine is a concrete example of this specialization; Rimbaud must already be regarded as an esoteric figure, a poet who, ex officio, kept a distance between his public and his work.) Second, there has been no success on a mass scale in lyric poetry since Baudelaire. (The lyric poetry of Victor Hugo was still capable of evoking powerful reverberations when it first appeared. In Germany, Heine's *Buch der Lieder* marks a watershed.) The third factor follows from this—namely, the greater coolness of the public, even toward the lyric poetry that has been handed down as part of its own cultural heritage. The period in question dates back roughly to the mid-nineteenth century. Throughout this span, the fame of *Les Fleurs du mal* has steadily increased. This book, which the author expected would be read by the least indulgent of readers and which was it first read by only a few indulgent ones, has, over the decades, acquired the stature of a classic and become one of the most widely printed ones as well.

If conditions for a positive reception of lyric poetry have become less favorable, it is reasonable to assume that only in rare instances does lyric poetry accord with the experience of its readers. This may be due to a change in the structure of their experience. Even though one may approve of this development, one may find it difficult to specify the nature of the change. Turning to philosophy for an answer, one encounters a strange situation. Since the end of the nineteenth century, philosophy has made a series of attempts to grasp "true" experience, as opposed to the kind that manifests itself in the standardized, denatured life of the civilized masses. These efforts are usually classified under the rubric of "vitalism." Their point of departure, understandably enough, has not been the individual's life in society. Instead they have invoked poetry, or preferably nature—most recently, the age of myths. Dilthey's book *Das Erlebnis und die Dichtung* represents one of the earliest of these efforts, which culminate with Klages and Jung, who made common cause with fascism. Towering above this literature is Bergson's early monumental work, *Matière et mémoire*. To a greater extent than the other writings in this field, it preserves links with empirical research. It is oriented toward biology. As the title suggests, it regards the structure of memory [*Gedächtnis*] as decisive for the philosophical structure of experience [*Erfahrung*]. Experience is indeed a matter of tradition, in collective existence as well as private life. It is the product less of facts firmly anchored in memory [*Erinnerung*] than of accumulated and frequently unconscious data that flow together in memory [*Gedächtnis*]. Of course, the historical determination of memory is not at all Bergson's intention. On the contrary, he rejects any historical determination of memory. He thus manages to stay clear of that experience from which his own philosophy evolved, or, rather, in reaction to which it arose. It was the alienating, blinding experience of the age of large-scale industrialism. In shutting out this experience, the eye perceives a complementary experience—in the form of its spontaneous afterimage, as it were. Bergson's philosophy represents an attempt to specify this afterimage and fix it as a permanent record. His philosophy thus indirectly furnishes a clue to the experience which presented itself undistorted to Baudelaire's eyes, in the figure of his reader.

II

The reader of *Matière et mémoire*, with its particular definition of the nature of experience in *durée*, is bound to conclude that only a poet can be the adequate subject of such an experience. And it was indeed a poet who put Bergson's theory of experience to the test. Proust's work *A la Recherche du temps perdu* may be regarded as an attempt to produce experience, as Bergson imagines it, in a synthetic way under today's social conditions, for there is less and less hope that it will come into being in a natural way. Proust, incidentally, does not evade the question in his work. He even introduces a new factor, one that involves an immanent critique of Bergson. Bergson emphasized the antagonism between the *vita activa* and the specific *vita contemplativa* which arises from memory. But he leads us to believe that turning to the contemplative realization of the stream of life is a matter of free choice. From the start, Proust indicates his divergent view in his choice of terms. In his work the *mémoire pure* of Bergson's theory becomes a *mémoire involontaire*. Proust immediately confronts this involuntary memory with a voluntary memory, one that is in the service of the intellect. The first pages of his great novel are devoted to making this relationship clear. In the reflection which introduces the term, Proust tells us that for many years he had a very indistinct memory of the town of Combray, where he had spent part of his childhood. One afternoon, the taste of a kind of pastry called a *madeleine* (which he later mentions often) transported him back to the past, whereas before then he had been limited to the promptings of a memory which obeyed the call of conscious attention. This he calls *mémoire volontaire*. Its signal characteristic is that the information it gives about the past retains no trace of that past. "It is the same with our own past. In vain we try to conjure it up again; the efforts of our intellect are futile." In sum, Proust says that the past is situated "somewhere beyond the reach of the intellect and its field of operations, in some material object . . . , though we have no idea which one it is. And whether we come upon this object before we die, or whether we never encounter it, depends entirely on chance."

According to Proust, it is a matter of chance whether an individual forms an image of himself, whether he can take hold of his experience. But there is nothing inevitable about the dependence on chance in this matter. A person's inner concerns are not by nature of an inescapably private character. They attain this character only after the likelihood decreases that one's external concerns will be assimilated to one's experience. Newspapers constitute one of many indications of such a decrease. If it were the intention of the press to have the reader assimilate the information it supplies as part of his own experience, it would not achieve its purpose. But its intention is just the opposite, and it is achieved: to isolate events from the realm in which they could affect the experience of the reader. The principles of journalistic information (newness, brevity, clarity, and, above all, lack of connection between the individual news items) contribute as much to this as the layout of the pages and the style of writing. (Karl Kraus never tired of demonstrating the extent to which the linguistic habitus of newspapers paralyzes the imagination of their readers.) Another reason for the isolation of information from experience is that the former does not enter "tradition." Newspapers appear in large editions. Few readers can boast of having any information that another reader may need from them. Historically, the various modes of communication have competed with one another. The replacement of the older relation by information, and of information by sensation, reflects the increasing atrophy of experience. In turn, there is a contrast between all these forms and the story, which is one of the oldest forms of communication. A story does not aim to convey an event per se, which is the purpose of information; rather, it embeds the event in the life of the storyteller in order to pass it on as experience to those listening. It thus bears the trace of the storyteller, much the way an earthen vessel bears the trace of the potter's hand.

Proust's eight-volume novel gives some idea of the effort it took to restore the figure of the storyteller to the current generation. Proust undertook this task with magnificent consistency. From the outset, this involved him in a fundamental problem: reporting on his own childhood. In saying that it was a matter of chance whether the problem could be solved at all, he took the measure of its difficulty. In connection with these reflections, he coined the phrase *mémoire involontaire*. This concept bears the traces of the situation that engendered it; it is part of the inventory of the individual who is isolated in various ways. Where there is experience [*Erfahrung*] in the strict sense of the word, certain contents of the individual past combine in the memory [*Gedächtnis*] with material from the collective past. Rituals, with their ceremonies and their festivals (probably nowhere recalled in Proust's work), kept producing the amalgamation of these two elements of memory over and over again. They triggered recollection at certain times and remained available to memory throughout people's lives. In this way, voluntary and involuntary recollection cease to be mutually exclusive.

III

In seeking a more substantial definition of what appears in Proust's *mémoire de l'intelligence* as a by-product of Bergson's theory, we would do well to go back to Freud. In 1921 Freud published his essay *Beyond the Pleasure Principle*, which hypothesizes a correlation between memory (in the sense of *mémoire involontaire*) and consciousness. The following remarks, though based on that essay, are not intended to confirm it; we shall have to content ourselves with testing the fruitfulness of Freud's hypothesis in situations far removed from the ones he had in mind when he wrote. Such situations are more likely to have been familiar to Freud's pupils. Some of Reik's writings on his own theory of memory are in line with Proust's distinction between involuntary and voluntary recollection. "The function of memory [*Gedächtnis*]," Reik writes, "is to protect our impressions; reminiscence [*Erinnerung*] aims at their dissolution. Memory is essentially conservative; reminiscence, destructive." Freud's fundamental thought, on which these remarks are based, is the assumption that "emerging consciousness takes the place of a memory trace."[3] Therefore, "it would be the special characteristic of consciousness that, unlike what happens in all other systems of the psyche, the excitatory process does not leave behind a permanent change in its elements, but expires, as it were, in the phenomenon of becoming conscious." The basic formula of this hypothesis is that "becoming conscious and leaving behind a memory trace are incompatible processes within one and the same system." Rather, vestiges of memory are "often most powerful and most enduring when the incident which left them behind was one that never entered consciousness." Put in Proustian terms, this means that only what has not been experienced explicitly and consciously; what has not happened to the subject as an isolated experience [*Erlebnis*], can become a component of *mémoire involontaire*. According to Freud, the attribution of "permanent traces as the basis of memory" to processes of stimulation is reserved for "other systems," which must be thought of as different from consciousness. In Freud's view, consciousness as such receives no memory traces whatever, but has another important function: protection against stimuli. "For a living organism, protection against stimuli is almost more important than the reception of stimuli. The protective shield is equipped with its own store of energy and must above all strive to preserve the special forms of conversion of energy operating in it against the effects of the excessive energies at work in the external world—effects that tend toward an equalization of potential and hence toward destruction." The threat posed by these energies is the threat of shocks. The more readily consciousness registers these shocks, the less likely they are to have a traumatic effect. Psychoanalytic theory strives to understand the nature of these traumatic shocks "in terms of how they break through the shield that protects against stimuli." According to this theory, fright gains "significance" in proportion to the "absence of any preparedness for anxiety."

Freud's investigation was occasioned by the sort of dream that may afflict accident survivors—those who develop neuroses which cause them to relive the catastrophe in which they were involved. Dreams of this kind, according to Freud, "endeavor to master the stimulus retroactively, by developing the anxiety whose omission was the cause of the traumatic neurosis." Valéry seems to have had something similar in mind. The coincidence is worth noting, for Valéry was among those interested in the special functioning of psychic mechanisms under present-day conditions. (Moreover, Valéry was able to reconcile this interest with his poetic production, which remained exclusively lyric. He thus emerges as the only author who goes back directly to Baudelaire.) "The impressions and sense perceptions of humans," Valéry writes, "actually belong in the category of surprises; they are evidence of an insufficiency in humans . . . Recollection is . . . an elemental phenomenon which aims at giving us the time for organizing 'the reception of stimuli' which we initially lacked."[4] The reception of shocks is facilitated by training in coping with stimuli; if need be, dreams as well as recollection may be enlisted. As a rule, however—so Freud assumes—this training devolves upon the wakeful consciousness, located in a part of the cortex which is "so frayed by the effect of the stimulus" that it offers the most favorable situation for the reception of stimuli. That the shock is thus cushioned, parried by consciousness, would lend the incident that occasions it the character of an isolated experience [*Erlebnis*], in the strict sense. If it were incorporated directly in the register of conscious memory, it would sterilize this incident for poetic experience [*Erfahrung*].

One wonders how lyric poetry can be grounded in experience [*einer Erfahrung*] for which exposure to shock [*Chockerlebnis*] has become the norm. One would expect such poetry to have a large measure of consciousness; it would suggest that a plan was at work in its composition. This is indeed true of Baudelaire's poetry; it establishes a connection between him and Poe, among his predecessors, and with Valéry, among his successors. Proust's and Valéry's reflections on Baudelaire complement each other providentially. Proust wrote an essay on Baudelaire which is actually surpassed in significance by certain reflections in his novels. In his "Situation de Baudelaire," Valéry supplies the classic introduction to *Les Fleurs du mal*. "Baudelaire's problem," he writes, "must have posed itself in these terms: 'How to be a great poet, but neither a Lamartine nor a Hugo nor a Musset.' I do not say that this ambition was consciously formulated, but it must have been latent in Baudelaire's mind; it even constituted the essential Baudelaire. It was his *raison d'état*." There is something odd about referring to "reason of state" in the case of a poet. There is something remarkable about it: the emancipation from isolated experiences [*Erlebnisse*]. Baudelaire's poetic production is assigned a mission. Blank spaces hovered before him, and into these he inserted his poems. His work cannot be categorized merely as historical, like anyone else's, but it intended to be so and understood itself as such.

IV

The greater the shock factor in particular impressions, the more vigilant consciousness has to be in screening stimuli; the more efficiently it does so, the less these impressions enter long experience [*Erfahrung*] and the more they correspond to the concept of isolated experience [*Erlebnis*]. Perhaps the special achievement of shock defense is the way it assigns an incident a precise point in time in consciousness, at the cost of the integrity of the incident's contents. This would be a peak achievement of the intellect; it would turn the incident into an isolated experience. Without reflection, there would be nothing but the sudden start, occasionally pleasant but usually distasteful, which, according to Freud, confirms the failure of the shock defense. Baudelaire has portrayed this process in a harsh image. He speaks of a duel in which the artist, just before being beaten, screams in fright. This duel is the creative process itself. Thus, Baudelaire placed shock experience [*Chockerfahrung*] at the very center of his art. This self-portrait, which is corroborated by evidence from several contemporaries, is of great significance. Since Baudelaire was himself vulnerable to being frightened, it was not unusual for him to evoke fright. Vallès tells us about his eccentric grimaces; on the basis of a portrait by Nargeot, Pontmartin establishes Baudelaire's alarming appearance; Claudel stresses the cutting quality he could give to his utterances; Gautier speaks of the italicizing Baudelaire indulged in when reciting poetry; Nadar describes his jerky gait.

Psychiatry is familiar with traumatophile types. Baudelaire made it his business to parry the shocks, no matter what their source, with his spiritual and physical self. This shock defense is rendered in the image of combat. Baudelaire describes his friend Constantin Guys, whom he visits when Paris is asleep: "How he stands there, bent over his table, scrutinizing the sheet of paper just as intently as he does the objects around him by day; how he *stabs away* with his pencil, his pen, his brush; how he spurts water from his glass to the ceiling and tries his pen on his shirt; how he pursues his work swiftly and intensely, as though he were afraid his images might escape him. Thus, he is combative even when alone, parrying his own blows." In the opening stanza of "Le Soleil," Baudelaire portrays himself engaged in just such fantastic combat; this is probably the only passage in *Les Fleurs du mal* that shows the poet at work.

Le long du vieux faubourg, où pendent aux masures
Les persiennes, abri des secrètes luxures,
Quand le soleil cruel frappe à traits redoublés
Sur la ville et les champs, sur les toits et les blés,
Je vais m'exercer seul à ma fantasque escrime,
Flairant dans tous les coins les hasards de la rime,
Trébuchant sur les mots comme sur les pavés,
Heurtant parfois des vers depuis longtemps rêvés.

[Through decrepit neighborhoods on the outskirts of town, where
Slatted shutters hang at the windows of hovels that shelter secret lusts;
At a time when the cruel sun beats down with redoubled force
On city and countryside, on rooftops and cornfields,
I go out alone to practice my fantastical fencing,
Scenting chances for rhyme on every street corner,
Stumbling over words as though they were cobblestones,
Sometimes knocking up against verses dreamed long ago.]

Shock is among those experiences that have assumed decisive importance for Baudelaire's personality. Gide has dealt with the intermittences between image and idea, word and thing, which are the real site of Baudelaire's poetic excitation.[5] Rivière has pointed to the subterranean shocks by which Baudelaire's poetry is shaken; it is as though they caused words to collapse.[6] Rivière has indicated such collapsing words.

> Et qui sait si les fleurs nouvelles que je rêve
> Trouveront dans ce sol lavé comme une grève
> Le mystique aliment qui *ferait* leur vigueur?
> [And who knows whether my dreams' new flowers
> Will find within this soil, washed like a shore,
> The mystic nourishment that *would make* them strong?]

Or: "Cybèle, qui les aime, *augmente ses verdures*" ["Cybele, who loves them, *augments her verdure*"]. Another example is this famous first line: "La servante au grand coeur dont vous étiez *jalouse*" ["That good-hearted servant of whom you were *jealous*"].

To give these covert laws their due outside his verses as well was Baudelaire's intention in *Spleen de Paris*, his collection of prose poems. In the book's dedication to the editor-in-chief of *La Presse*, Arsène Houssaye, Baudelaire wrote: "Who among us has not dreamed, in his ambitious moments, of the miracle of a poetic prose, musical, yet without rhythm and without rhyme, supple and resistant enough to adapt to the lyrical stirrings of the soul, the undulations of reverie, and the sudden leaps of consciousness. This obsessive ideal is born, above all, from the experience of giant cities, from the intersecting of their myriad relations."

This passage suggests two insights. For one thing, it tells us about the close connection in Baudelaire between the figure of shock and contact with the urban masses. For another, it tells us what is really meant by these masses. They do not stand for classes or any sort of collective; rather, they are nothing but the amorphous crowd of passers-by, the people in the street.[7] This crowd, whose existence Baudelaire is always aware of, does not serve as the model for any of his works; but it is imprinted on his creativity as a hidden figure, just as it constitutes the figure concealed in the excerpt quoted above. We can discern the image of the fencer in it: the blows he deals are designed to open a path for him through the crowd. To be sure, the neighborhoods through which the poet of "Le Soleil" makes his way are deserted. But the hidden constellation—in which the profound beauty of that stanza becomes thoroughly transparent—is no doubt a phantom crowd: the words, the fragments, the beginnings of lines, from which the poet, in the deserted streets, wrests poetic booty.

V

The crowd: no subject was more worthy of attention from nineteenth-century writers. It was getting ready to take shape as a public consisting of broad strata that had acquired facility in reading. It gave out commissions; it wished to find itself portrayed in the contemporary novel, as wealthy patrons did in the paintings of the Middle Ages. The most successful author of the century met this demand out of inner necessity. To him, "the crowd" meant—almost in the ancient sense—the crowd of clients, the public. Victor Hugo was the first to address the crowd in his titles: *Les Misérables, Les Travailleurs de la mer*. In France, Hugo was the only writer able to compete with the serial novel. As is generally known, Eugène Sue was the master of this genre, which came to be the source of revelation for the man in the street. In 1850 an overwhelming majority elected him to the Chamber of Deputies as a representative from the city of Paris. It is no accident that the young Marx chose Sue's *Mystères de Paris* for an attack. At an early date, he realized it was his task to forge the amorphous masses—then being wooed by an aesthetically appealing socialism—into the iron of the proletariat. Engels' description of these masses in his early writings may be regarded as a prelude, however modest, to one of Marx's themes. In his book *The Condition of the Working Class in England*, Engels writes:

> A town such as London, where a man may wander for hours together without reaching the beginning of the end, without meeting the slightest hint which could lead to the inference that there is open country within reach, is a strange thing. This colossal centralization, this heaping together of two and a half million human beings at one point, has multiplied the power of these two and a half million people a hundredfold. . . . But the sacrifices which all this has cost become apparent later. After roaming the streets of the capital for a day or two, making headway with difficulty through the human turmoil and the endless lines of vehicles, after visiting the slums of the metropolis, one realizes for the first time that these Londoners have been forced to sacrifice the best qualities of their human nature in order to bring to pass all the marvels of civilization which crowd their city; that a hundred powers which slumbered within them have remained inactive, have been suppressed. . . . The very turmoil of the streets has something repulsive about it, something against which human nature rebels. The hundreds of thousands of people of all classes and ranks crowding past one another—are they not all human beings with the same qualities and powers, and with the same interest in being happy? . . . And still they crowd by one another as though they had nothing in common, nothing to do with one another, and their only agreement is a tacit one: that each should keep to his own side of the pavement, so as not to delay the opposing streams of the crowd, while it occurs to no man to honor another with so much as a glance. The brutal indifference, the unfeeling isolation of each person in his private interest becomes the more repellent and offensive, the more these individuals are crowded together within a limited space.[8]

This description differs markedly from those found in minor French masters, such as Gozlan, Delvau, or Lurine. It lacks the skill and nonchalance which the flâneur displays as he moves among the crowds in the streets and which the journalist eagerly learns from him. Engels is dismayed by the crowd. He responds with a moral reaction, and an aesthetic one as well; the speed with which people rush past one another unsettles him. The charm of his description lies in the blend of unshakable critical integrity with old-fashioned views. The writer came from a Germany that was still provincial; he may never have been tempted to lose himself in a stream of people. When Hegel went to Paris for the first time, not long before his death, he wrote to his wife: "When I walk through the streets, people look just as they do in Berlin. They wear the same clothes, and their faces are about the same—they have the same aspect, but in a populous mass."[9] To move in this mass of people was natural for a Parisian. No matter how great the distance an individual wanted to keep from it, he still was colored by it and, unlike Engels, was unable to view it from without. As for Baudelaire, the masses were anything but external to him; indeed, it is easy to trace in his works his defensive reaction to their attraction and allure.

The masses had become so much a part of Baudelaire that it is rare to find a description of them in his works. His most important subjects are hardly ever encountered in descriptive form. As Desjardins so aptly put it, he was "more concerned with implanting the image in the memory than with adorning and elaborating it."[10] It is futile to search in *Les Fleurs du mal* or in *Spleen de Paris* for any counterpart to the portrayals of the city that Victor Hugo composed with such mastery. Baudelaire describes neither the Parisians nor their city. Avoiding such descriptions enables him to invoke the former in the figure of the latter. His crowds are always the crowds of a big city; his Paris is invariably overpopulated. It is this that makes him so superior to Barbier, whose descriptive method divorced the masses from the city.[11] In *Tableaux parisiens*, the secret presence of a crowd is demonstrable almost everywhere. When Baudelaire takes the dawn as his theme, the deserted streets emit something of that "silence of a throng" which Hugo senses in nocturnal Paris. As Baudelaire looks at the illustrations in the books on anatomy being sold on the dusty banks of the Seine, a crowd of departed souls takes the place of the singular skeletons on those pages. In the figures of the *danse macabre*, he sees a compact mass on the move. The heroism of the wizened old women whom the cycle "Les Petites Vieilles" follows on their rounds consists in their standing apart from the urban crowd, unable to keep up with it, no longer mentally participating in the present. The masses were an agitated veil, and Baudelaire views Paris through this veil. The presence of the masses informs one of the most famous poems in *Les Fleurs du mal*.

In the sonnet "À une passante," the crowd is nowhere named in either word or phrase. Yet all the action hinges on it, just as the progress of a sailboat depends on the wind.

La rue assourdissante autour de moi hurlait.
Longue, mince, en grand deuil, douleur majestueuse,
Une femme passa, d'une main fastueuse
Soulevant, balançant le feston et l'ourlet;

Agile et noble, avec sa jambe de statue.
Moi, je buvais, crispé comme un extravagant,
Dans son oeil, ciel livide où germe l'ouragan,
La douceur qui fascine et le plaisir qui tue.

Un éclair . . . puis la nuit!—Fugitive beauté
Dont le regard m'a fait soudainement renaître,
Ne te verrai-je plus que dans l'éternité?

Ailleurs, bien loin d'ici! Trop tard! *Jamais* peut-être!
Car j'ignore où tu fuis, tu ne sais où je vais,
Ô toi que j'eusse aimée, ô toi qui le savais!

[The deafening street was screaming all around me.
Tall, slender, in deep mourning—majestic grief—
A woman made her way past, with fastidious hand
Raising and swaying her skirt-border and hem;

Agile and noble, with her statue's limbs.
And me—I drank, contorted like a wild eccentric,
From her eyes, that livid sky which gives birth to hurricanes,
Gentleness that fascinates, pleasure that kills.

A lightning-flash . . . then night!—O fleeting beauty
Whose glance suddenly gave me new life,
Shall I see you again only in eternity?

Far, far from here! Too late! Or maybe *never?*
For I know not where you flee, you know not where I go,
O you whom I would have loved, O you who knew it too!]

In a widow's veil, mysteriously and mutely borne along by the crowd, an unknown woman crosses the poet's field of vision. What this sonnet conveys is simply this: far from experiencing the crowd as an opposing, antagonistic element, the city dweller discovers in the crowd what fascinates him. The delight of the urban poet is love—not at first sight, but at last sight. It is an eternal farewell, which coincides in the poem with the moment of enchantment. Thus, the sonnet deploys the figure of shock, indeed of catastrophe. But the nature of the poet's emotions has been affected as well. What makes his body contract in a tremor—"crispé comme un extravagant," Baudelaire says—is not the rapture of a man whose every fiber is suffused with eros; rather, it is like the sexual shock that can beset a lonely man. The fact that "these verses could have been written only in a big city," as Thibaudet put it, is not very meaningful.[12] They reveal the stigmata which life in a metropolis inflicts upon love. Proust read the sonnet in this light, and that is why he gave to his own echo of the woman in mourning (which appeared to him one day in the form of Albertine) the evocative epithet "La Parisienne." "When Albertine came into my room again, she wore a black satin dress. It made her look pale. She resembled the kind of fiery yet pale Parisian woman who is not used to fresh air and has been affected by living among the masses, possibly in an atmosphere of vice—the kind you can recognize by her gaze, which seems unsteady if there is no rouge on her cheeks."[13] This is the gaze—evident even as late as Proust—of the object of a love which only a city dweller experiences, which Baudelaire captured for poetry, and which one might not infrequently characterize as being spared, rather than denied, fulfillment.[14]

[. . .]

XII

Les Fleurs du mal was the last lyric work that had a broad European reception; no later writings penetrated beyond a more or less limited linguistic area. Added to this is the fact that Baudelaire expended his productive capacity almost entirely on this one volume. And finally, it cannot be denied that some of his motifs—those which the present study has discussed—render the possibility of lyric poetry problematic. These three facts define Baudelaire historically. They show that he held steadfastly to his cause and focused single-mindedly on his mission. He went so far as to proclaim as his goal "the creation of a cliché [*poncif*]."[15] He saw in this the condition for any future lyric poetry, and had a low opinion of those poets who were not equal to the task. "Do you drink beef tea made of ambrosia? Do you eat cutlets from Paros? How much can you get for a lyre, at the pawnshop?"[16] To Baudelaire, the lyric poet with his halo is antiquated. In a prose piece entitled "Perte d'auréole" [Loss of a Halo], which came to light at a late date, Baudelaire presents such a poet as a supernumerary. When Baudelaire's literary remains were first examined, this piece was rejected as "unsuitable for publication"; to this day, it has been neglected by Baudelaire scholars.

> "What do I see, my dear fellow? *You—here?* I find *you* in a place of ill repute—a man who sips quintessences, who consumes ambrosia? Really! I couldn't be more surprised!"
>
> "You know, my dear fellow, how afraid I am of horses and carriages. A short while ago I was hurrying across the boulevard, and amid that churning chaos in which death comes galloping at you from all sides at once I must have made an awkward movement, for the halo slipped off my head and fell into the mire of the macadam. I didn't have the courage to pick it up, and decided that it hurts less to lose one's insignia than to have one's bones broken. Furthermore, I said to myself, every cloud has a silver lining. Now I can go about incognito, do bad things, and indulge in vulgar behavior like ordinary mortals. So here I am, just like you!"

"But you ought to report the loss of your halo or inquire at the lost-and-found office."

"I wouldn't dream of it. I like it here. You're the only person who has recognized me. Besides, dignity bores me. And it amuses me to think that some bad poet will pick up the halo and straightway adorn himself with it. There's nothing I like better than to make someone happy—especially if the happy fellow is someone I can laugh at. Just picture X wearing it, or Y! Won't that be funny?"[17]

The same scene is found in Baudelaire's diaries, except that the ending is different. The poet quickly picks up his halo—but now he is troubled by the feeling that the incident may be a bad omen.[18]

The man who wrote these pieces was no flâneur. They embody, in ironic form, the same experience that Baudelaire put into the following sentence without any embellishment: "Perdu dans ce vilain monde, *coudoyé par les foules*, je suis comme un homme lassé dont l'oeil ne voit en arrière, dans les années profondes, que désabusememt et amertume, et, devant lui, qu'un orage où rien de neuf n'est contenu, ni enseignement, ni douleur."[19] ["Lost in this base world, jostled by the crowd, I am like a weary man whose eye, looking backward into the depths of the years, sees only disillusion and bitterness, and looking ahead sees only a tempest which contains nothing new, neither instruction nor pain."] Of all the experiences which made his life what it was, Baudelaire singled out being jostled by the crowd as the decisive, unmistakable experience. The semblance [*Schein*] of a crowd with a soul and movement all its own, the luster that had dazzled the flâneur, had faded for him. To heighten the impression of the crowd's baseness, he envisioned the day on which even the fallen women, the outcasts, would readily espouse a well-ordered life, condemn libertinism, and reject everything except money. Betrayed by these last allies of his, Baudelaire battled the crowd—with the impotent rage of someone fighting the rain or the wind. This is the nature of the immediate experience [*Erlebnis*] to which Baudelaire has given the weight of long experience [*Erfahrung*]. He named the price for which the sensation of modernity could be had: the disintegration of the aura in immediate shock experience [*Chockerlebnis*]. He paid dearly for consenting to this disintegration—but it is the law of his poetry. This poetry appears in the sky of the Second Empire as "a star without atmosphere."

NOTES

1. First published in *Zeitschrift für Sozialforschung* (January 1940) and reprinted in Walter Benjamin, *Gesammelte Schriften* (Frankfurt: Surhkamp, 1991), I, 605–653; translated into English by Harry Zohn for *Illuminations*, ed. Hannah Arendt (New York: Schocken, 1969).

2. Charles Baudelaire, *Oeuvres*, ed. Yves-Gérard Le Dantec (Paris: Bibliotheque de in Pléïade, 1931–1932), vol. 1, p. 18.

3. In the present context, there is no substantial difference between the concepts *Erinnerung* and *Gedächtnis* as used in Freud's essay.

4. Paul Valéry, *Analecta* (Paris, 1935), pp. 264–265.

5. André Gide, "Baudelaire et M. Faguet," in *Morceaux choisis* (Paris, 1921), p. 128.

6. Jacques Rivière, *Etudes* [18th ed. (Paris, 1948), p. 14].

7. To endow this crowd with a soul is the very special purpose of the flâneur. His encounters with it are the experience that he never tires of telling about. Certain reflexes of this illusion are an integral part of Baudelaire's work. It has continued to be an active force to this day. Jules Romains' *unanimisme* is an admirable late flowering of it.

8. Friedrich Engels, *Die Lage der arbeitenden Klasse in England: Nach eigner Anschauung und authentischen Quellen*, 2nd ed. (Leipzig, 1848), pp. 36–37.

9. Georg Wilhelm Friedrich Hegel, *Werke*, vol. 19, *Briefe von und an Hegel* (Letters to and from Hegel), ed. Karl Hegel (Leipzig, 1887), part 2, p. 257.

10. Paul Desjardins, "Poètes contemporains: Charles Baudelaire," in *Revue Bleue: Revue Politique et Littéraire* (Paris), 14, no. 1 (July 2, 1887): 23.

11. Characteristic of Barbier's method is his poem "Londres," which in twenty-four lines describes the city, awkwardly closing with the following verses:

Enfin, dans un amas de choses, sombre, immense,
Un peuple noir, vivant et mourant en silence.
Des êtres par milliers, suivant l'instinct fatal,
Et courant après l'or par le bien et le mal.

[Finally, within a huge and somber mass of things,
A blackened people, who live and die in silence.
Thousands of beings, who follow a fatal instinct,
Pursuing gold by good and evil means.]

Auguste Barbier, *Iambes et poemes* (Paris, 1841)

Barbier's tendentious poems, particularly his London cycle, *Lazare* [Lazarus], influenced Baudelaire more profoundly than people have been willing to admit. Baudelaire's "Crépuscule du soir" [Half-Light of Evening] concludes as follows:

ils finissent
Leur destinée et vont vers le gouffre commun;
L'hôpital se remplit de leurs soupirs.—Plus d'un
Ne viendra plus chercher la soupe parfumée,
Au coin du feu, le soir, auprès d'une âme aimée.

[they accomplish
Their fate and draw near the common pit;
Their sighs fill the hospital ward.—More than one
Will come no more to get his fragrant soup,
At the fireside, in the evening, by the side of a loved one.]

Compare this with the end of the eighth stanza of Barbier's "Mineurs de Newcastle" [Miners of Newcastle]:

Et plus d'un qui rêvait dans le fond de son âme
Aux douceurs du logis, à l'oeil bleu de sa femme,
Trouve au ventre du gouffre un éternel tombeau.

[And more than one who in his heart of hearts had dreams
Of home, sweet home, and of his wife's blue eyes,
Finds, within the belly of the pit, an everlasting tomb.]

With some masterful retouching, Baudelaire turns a "miner's fate" into the commonplace end of big-city dwellers.

12. Albert Thibaudet, *Intérieurs* (Paris, 1924), p. 22.

13. Proust, *A la recherche du temps perdu* (Paris, 1923), vol. 6, p. 138 (*La Prisonnière*).

14. The motif of love for a woman passing by occurs in an early poem by Stefan George. The poet has missed the important thing: the stream in which the woman moves past, borne along by the crowd. The result is a self-conscious elegy. The poet's glances—so he must confess to his lady—have "moved away, moist with longing / before they dared mingle with yours" ("feucht vor sehnen fortgezogen / eh sie in deine sich zu tauchen trauten"). From Stefan George, "Von einer Begegnung" (Encounter), in *Hymnen; Pilgerfahrten; Algabal* (Berlin, 1922). Baudelaire leaves no doubt that *he* looked deep into the eyes of the passer-by.

15. See Jules Lemaître, *Les Contemporains: Etudes et portraits littéraires* (Paris, 1897), pp. 31–32.

16. Baudelaire, *Oeuvres*, vol. 2, p. 422 ("L'École païenne" [The Pagan School]).

17. Ibid., vol. 1, pp. 483–484.

18. It is not impossible that this diary entry was occasioned by a pathogenic shock. The form the entry takes, which links it to Baudelaire's published work, is thus all the more revealing.

19. Baudelaire, *Oeuvres*, vol. 2, p. 641.

On Lyric Poetry and Society (1957; trans. 1991) 6.2

THEODOR W. ADORNO Translated by Shierry Weber Nicholson[1]

The announcement of a lecture on lyric poetry and society will make many of you uncomfortable. You will expect a sociological analysis of the kind that can be made of any object, just as fifty years ago people came up with psychologies, and thirty years ago with phenomenologies, of everything conceivable. You will suspect that examination of the conditions under which works are created and their effect will try to usurp the place of experience of the works as they are and that the process of categorizing and relating will suppress insight into the truth or falsity of the object itself. You will suspect that an intellectual will be guilty of what Hegel accused the "formal understanding" of doing, namely that in surveying the whole it stands above the individual existence it is talking about, that is, it does not see it at all but only labels it. This approach will seem especially distressing to you in the case of lyric poetry. The most delicate, the most fragile thing that exists is to be encroached upon and brought into conjunction with bustle and commotion, when part of the ideal of lyric poetry, at least in its traditional sense, is to remain unaffected by bustle and commotion. A sphere of expression whose very essence lies in either not acknowledging the power of socialization or overcoming it through the pathos of detachment, as in Baudelaire or Nietzsche, is to be arrogantly turned into the opposite of what it conceives itself to be through the way it is examined. Can anyone, you will ask, but a man who is insensitive to the Muse talk about lyric poetry and society?

Clearly your suspicions will be allayed only if lyric works are not abused by being made objects with which to demonstrate sociological theses but if instead the social element in them is shown to reveal something essential about the basis of their quality. This relationship should lead not away from the work of art but deeper into it. But the most elementary reflection shows that this is to be expected. For the substance of a poem is not merely an expression of individual impulses and experiences. Those become a matter of art only when they come to participate in something universal by virtue of the specificity they acquire in being given aesthetic form. Not that what the lyric poem expresses is equivalent to what everyone experiences. Its universality is no *volonté de tous*, not the universality of simply communicating what others are unable to communicate. Rather, immersion in what has taken individual form elevates the lyric to the status of something universal by making manifest something not distorted, not grasped, not yet subsumed. It thereby anticipates, spiritually, a situation in which no false universality, that is, nothing profoundly particular, continues to fetter what is other than itself, the human. The lyric work hopes to attain universality through unrestrained individuation. The danger peculiar to the lyric, however, lies in the fact that its principle of individuation never guarantees that something binding and authentic will be produced. It has no say over whether the poem remains within the contingency of mere separate existence.

The universality of the lyric's substance, however, is social in nature. Only one who hears the voice of humankind in the poem's solitude can understand what the poem is saying; indeed, even the solitariness of lyrical language itself is prescribed by an individualistic and ultimately atomistic society, just as conversely its general cogency depends on the intensity of its individuation. For that reason, however, reflection on the work of art is justified in inquiring, and obligated to inquire concretely into its social content and not content itself with a vague feeling of something universal and inclusive. This kind of specification through thought is not some external reflection alien to art; on the contrary, all linguistic works of art demand it. The material proper to them, concepts, does not exhaust itself in mere contemplation. In order to be susceptible of aesthetic contemplation, works of art must always be thought through as well, and once thought has been called into play by the poem it does not let itself be stopped at the poem's behest.

Such thought, however—the social interpretation of lyric poetry as of all works of art—may not focus directly on the so-called social perspective or the social interests of the works or their authors. Instead, it must discover how the entirety of a society, conceived as an internally contradictory unity, is manifested in the work of art, in what way the work of art remains subject to society and in what way it transcends it. In philosophical terms, the approach must be an immanent one. Social concepts should not be applied to the works from without but rather drawn from an exacting examination of the works themselves. Goethe's statement in his *Maxims and Reflections* that what you do not understand you do not possess holds not only for the aesthetic attitude to works of art but for aesthetic theory as well; nothing that is not in the works, not part of their own form, can legitimate a determination of what their substance, that which has entered into their poetry, represents in social terms. To determine that, of course, requires both knowledge of the interior of the works of art and knowledge of the society outside. But this knowledge is binding only if it is rediscovered through complete submission to the matter at hand. Special vigilance is required when it comes to the concept of ideology, which these days is belabored to the point of intolerability. For ideology is untruth, false consciousness, deceit. It manifests itself in the failure of works of art, in their inherent falseness, and it is countered by criticism. To repeat mechanically, however, that great works of art, whose essence consists in giving form to the crucial contradictions in real existence, and only in that sense in a tendency to reconcile them, are ideology, not only does an injustice to their truth content but also misrepresents the concept of ideology. That concept does not maintain that all spirit serves only for some human beings to falsely present some particular values as general ones; rather, it is intended to unmask spirit that is specifically false and at the same time to grasp it in its necessity. The greatness of works of art, however, consists solely in the fact that they give voice to what ideology hides. Their very success moves beyond false consciousness, whether intentionally or not.

Let me take your own misgivings as a starting point. You experience lyric poetry as something opposed to society, something wholly individual. Your feelings insist that it remain so, that lyric expression, having escaped from the weight of material existence, evoke the image of a life free from the coercion of reigning practices, of utility, of the relentless pressures of self-preservation. This demand, however, the demand that the lyric word be virginal, is itself social in nature. It implies a protest against a social situation that every individual experiences as hostile, alien, cold, oppressive, and this situation is imprinted in reverse on the poetic work: the more heavily the situation weighs upon it, the more firmly the work resists it by refusing to submit to anything heteronomous and constituting itself solely in accordance with its own laws. The work's distance from mere existence becomes the measure of what is false and bad in the latter. In its protest the poem expresses the dream of a world in which things would be different. The lyric spirit's idiosyncratic opposition to the superior power of material things is a form of reaction to the reification of the world, to the domination of human beings by commodities that has developed since the beginning of the modern era, since the industrial revolution became the dominant force in life. Rilke's cult of the thing [as in his *Dinggedichte* or "thing poems"] is part of this idiosyncratic opposition; it attempts to assimilate even alien objects to pure subjective expression and to dissolve them, to give them metaphysical credit for their alienness. The aesthetic weakness of this cult of the thing, its obscurantist demeanor and its blending of religion with arts and crafts, reveals the real power of reification, which can no longer be gilded with a lyrical halo and brought back within the sphere of meaning.

To say that the concept of lyric poetry that is in some sense second nature to us is a completely modern one is only to express this insight into the social nature of the lyric in different form. Analogously, landscape painting and its idea of "nature" have had an autonomous development only in the modern period. I know that I exaggerate in saying this, that you could adduce many counterexamples. The most compelling would be Sappho. I will not discuss the Chinese, Japanese, and Arabic lyric, since I cannot read them in the original and I suspect that translation involves them in an adaptive mechanism that makes adequate understanding completely impossible. But the manifestations in earlier periods of the specifically lyric spirit familiar to us are only isolated flashes, just as the backgrounds in older painting occasionally anticipate the idea of landscape painting. They do not establish it as a form. The great poets of the distant past—Pindar and Alcaeus, for instance, but the greater part of Walther von der Vogelweide's work as well—whom literary history classifies as lyric poets are uncommonly far from our primary conception of the lyric. They lack the quality of immediacy, of immateriality, which we are accustomed, rightly or not, to consider the criterion of the lyric and which we transcend only through rigorous education.

Until we have either broadened it historically or turned it critically against the sphere of individualism, however, our conception of lyric poetry has a moment of discontinuity in it—all the more so, the more pure it claims to be. The "I" whose voice is heard in the lyric is an "I" that defines and expresses itself as something opposed to the collective, to objectivity; it is not immediately at one with the nature to which its expression refers. It has lost it, as it were, and attempts to restore it through animation, through immersion in the "I" itself. It is only through humanization that nature is to be restored the rights that human domination took from it. Even lyric works in which no trace of conventional and concrete existence, no crude materiality remains, the greatest lyric works in our language, owe their quality to the force with which the "I" creates the illusion of nature emerging from alienation. Their pure subjectivity, the aspect of them that appears seamless and harmonious, bears witness to its opposite, to suffering in an existence alien to the subject and to love for it as well—indeed, their harmoniousness is actually nothing but the mutual accord of this suffering and this love. Even the line from Goethe's "Wanderers Nachtlied" ["Wanderer's Night-Song"], "Warte nur, balde / ruhest du auch" ["Only wait, soon / you too shall rest"] has an air of consolation: its unfathomable beauty cannot be separated from something it makes no reference to, the notion of a world that withholds peace. Only in resonating with sadness about that withholding does the poem maintain that there is peace nevertheless. One is tempted to use the line "Ach, ich bin des Treibens müde" ["I am weary of restless activity"] from the companion poem of the same title to interpret the "Wanderers Nachtlied." To be sure, the greatness of the latter poem derives from the fact that it does not speak about what is alienated and disturbing, from the fact that within the poem the restlessness of the object is not opposed to the subject; instead, the subject's own restlessness echoes it. A second immediacy is promised: what is human, language itself, seems to become creation again, while everything external dies away in the echo of the soul. This becomes more than an illusion, however; it becomes full truth, because through the expression in language of a good kind of tiredness, the shadow of yearning and even of death continues to fall across the reconciliation. In the line "Warte nur, balde" the whole of life, with an enigmatic smile of sorrow, turns into the brief moment before one falls asleep. The note of peacefulness attests to the fact that peace cannot be achieved without the dream disintegrating. The shadow has no power over the image of life come back into its own, but as a last reminder of life's deformation it gives the dream its profound depths beneath the surface of the song. In the face of nature at rest, a nature from which all traces of anything resembling the human have been eradicated, the subject becomes aware of its own insignificance. Imperceptibly, silently, irony tinges the poem's consolation: the seconds before the bliss of sleep are the same seconds that separate our brief life from death. After Goethe, this sublime irony became a debased and spiteful irony. But it was always bourgeois: the shadow-side of the elevation of the liberated subject is its degradation to something exchangeable, to something that exists merely for something else; the shadow-side of personality is the "So who are you?" The authenticity of the "Nachtlied," however, lies in its moment in time: the background of that destructive force removes it from the sphere of play, while the destructive force has no power over the peaceable power of consolation. It is commonly said that a perfect lyric poem must possess totality or universality, must provide the whole within the bounds of the poem and the infinite within the poem's finitude. If that is to be more than a platitude of an aesthetics that is always ready to use the concept of the symbolic as a panacea, it indicates that in every lyric poem the historical relationship of the subject to objectivity, of the individual to society, must have found its precipitate in the medium of a subjective spirit thrown back upon itself. The less the work thematizes the relationship of "I" and society, the more spontaneously it crystallizes of its own accord in the poem, the more complete this process of precipitation will be.

You may accuse me of so sublimating the relationship of lyric and society in this definition out of fear of a crude sociologism that there is really nothing left of it; it is precisely what is not social in the lyric poem that is now to become its social aspect. You could call my attention to Gustav Doré's caricature of the arch-reactionary deputy whose praise of the *ancien régime* culminated in the exclamation, "And to whom, gentlemen, do we owe the revolution of 1789 if not to Louis XVI!" You could apply that to my view of lyric poetry and society: in my view, you could say, society plays the role of the executed king and the lyric the role of his opponents; but lyric poetry, you say, can no more be explained on the basis of society than the revolution can be made the achievement of the monarch it deposed and without whose inanities it might not have occurred at that time. We will leave it an open question whether Doré's deputy was truly only the stupid, cynical propagandist the artist derided him for being or whether there might be more truth in his unintentional joke than common sense admits; Hegel's philosophy of history would have a lot to say in his defense. In any case, the comparison does not really work. I am not trying to deduce lyric poetry from society; its social substance is precisely what is spontaneous in it, what does not simply follow from the existing conditions at the time. But philosophy—Hegel's again—is familiar with the speculative proposition that the individual is mediated by the universal and vice versa. That means that even resistance to social pressure is not something absolutely individual; the artistic forces in that resistance, which operate in and through the individual and his spontaneity, are objective forces that impel a constricted and constricting social condition to transcend itself and become worthy of human beings; forces, that is, that are part of the constitution of the whole and not at all merely forces of a rigid individuality blindly opposing society. If, by virtue of its own subjectivity, the substance of the lyric can in fact be addressed as an objective substance—and otherwise one could not explain the very simple fact that grounds the possibility of the lyric as an artistic genre, its effect on people other than the poet speaking his monologue—then it is only because the lyric work of art's withdrawal into itself, its self-absorption, its detachment from the social surface, is socially motivated behind the author's back. But the medium of this is language. The paradox specific to the lyric work, a subjectivity that turns into objectivity, is tied to the priority of linguistic form in the lyric; it is that priority from which the primacy of language in literature in general (even in prose forms) is derived. For language is itself something double. Through its configurations it assimilates itself completely into subjective impulses; one would almost think it had produced them. But at the same time language remains the medium of concepts, remains that which establishes an inescapable relationship to the universal and to society. Hence the highest lyric works are those in which the subject, with no remaining trace of mere matter, sounds forth in language until language itself acquires a voice. The unself-consciousness of the subject submitting itself to language as to something objective, and the immediacy and spontaneity of that subject's expression are one and the same: thus language mediates lyric poetry and society in their innermost core. This is why the lyric reveals itself to be most deeply grounded in society when it does not chime in with society, when it communicates nothing, when, instead, the subject whose expression is successful reaches an accord with language itself, with the inherent tendency of language.

On the other hand, however, language should also not be absolutized as the voice of Being as opposed to the lyric subject, as many of the current ontological theories of language would have it. The subject, whose expression—as opposed to mere signification of objective contents—is necessary to attain to that level of linguistic objectivity, is not something added to the contents proper to that layer, not something external to it. The moment of unself-consciousness in which the subject submerges itself in language is not a sacrifice of the subject to Being. It is a moment not of violence, nor of violence against the subject, but reconciliation: language itself speaks only when it speaks not as something alien to the subject but as the subject's own voice. When the "I" becomes oblivious to itself in language it is fully present nevertheless; if it were not, language would become a consecrated abracadabra and succumb to reification, as it does in communicative discourse. But that brings us back to the actual relationship between the individual and society. It is not only that the individual is inherently socially mediated, not only that its contents are always social as well. Conversely, society is formed and continues to live only by virtue of the individuals whose quintessence it is. Classical philosophy once formulated a truth now disdained by scientific logic: subject and object are not rigid and isolated poles but can be defined only in the process in which they distinguish themselves from one another and change. The lyric is the aesthetic test of that dialectical philosophical proposition. In the lyric poem the subject, through its identification with language, negates both its opposition to society as something merely monadological and its mere functioning within a wholly socialized society [*vergesellschaftete Gesellschaft*]. But the more the latter's ascendancy over the subject increases, the more precarious the situation of the lyric becomes. Baudelaire's work was the first to record this; his work, the ultimate consequence of European *Weltschmerz*, did not stop with the sufferings of the individual but chose the modern itself, as the antilyrical pure and simple, for its theme and struck a poetic spark in it by dint of a heroically stylized language. In Baudelaire a note of despair already makes itself felt, a note that barely maintains its balance on the tip of its own paradoxicalness. As the contradiction between poetic and communicative language reached an extreme, lyric poetry became a game in which one goes for broke; not, as philistine opinion would have it, because it had become incomprehensible but because in acquiring self-consciousness as a literary language, in striving for an absolute objectivity unrestricted by any considerations of communication, language both distances itself from the objectivity of spirit, of living language, and substitutes a poetic event for a language that is no longer present. The elevated, poeticizing, subjectively violent moment in weak later lyric poetry is the price it has to pay for its attempt to keep itself undisfigured, immaculate, objective; its false glitter is the complement to the disenchanted world from which it extricates itself.

Everything I have said needs to be qualified if it is to avoid misinterpretation. My thesis is that the lyric work is always the subjective expression of a social antagonism. But since the objective world that produces the lyric is an inherently antagonistic world, the concept of the lyric is not simply that of the expression of a subjectivity to which language grants objectivity. Not only does the lyric subject embody the whole all the more cogently, the more it expresses itself; in addition, poetic subjectivity is itself indebted to privilege: the pressures of the struggle for survival allow only a few human beings to grasp the universal through immersion in the self or to develop as autonomous subjects capable of freely expressing themselves. The others, however, those who not only stand alienated, as though they were objects, facing the disconcerted poetic subject but who have also literally been degraded to objects of history, have the same right, or a greater right, to grope for the sounds in which sufferings and dreams are welded. This inalienable right has asserted itself again and again, in forms however impure, mutilated, fragmentary, and intermittent—the only forms possible for those who have to bear the burden.

A collective undercurrent provides the foundation for all individual lyric poetry. When that poetry actually bears the whole in mind and is not simply an expression of the privilege, refinement, and gentility of those who can afford to be gentle, participation in this undercurrent is an essential part of the substantiality of the individual lyric as well: it is this undercurrent that makes language the medium in which the subject becomes more than a mere subject. Romanticism's link to the folksong is only the most obvious, certainly not the most compelling example of this. For Romanticism practices a kind of programmatic transfusion of the collective into the individual through which the individual lyric poem indulged in a technical illusion of universal cogency without that cogency characterizing it inherently. Often, in contrast, poets who abjure any borrowing from the collective language participate in that collective undercurrent by virtue of their historical experience. Let me mention Baudelaire again, whose lyric poetry is a slap in the face not only to the *juste milieu* but also to all bourgeois social sentiment, and who nevertheless, in poems like the "Petites vieilles" or the poem about the servant woman with the generous heart in the *Tableaux Parisiens*, was truer to the masses toward whom he turned his tragic, arrogant mask than any "poor people's" poetry. Today, when individual expression, which is the precondition for the conception of lyric poetry that is my point of departure, seems shaken to its very core in the crisis of the individual, the collective undercurrent in the lyric surfaces in the most diverse places: first merely as the ferment of individual expression and then perhaps also as an anticipation of a situation that transcends mere individuality in a positive way. If the translations can be trusted, García Lorca, whom Franco's henchmen murdered and whom no totalitarian regime could have tolerated, was the bearer of a force of this kind; and Brecht's name comes to mind as a lyric poet who was granted linguistic integrity without having to pay the price of esotericism. I will forgo making a judgment about whether the poetic principle of individuation was in fact sublated to a higher level here, or whether its basis lies in regression, a weakening of the ego. The collective power of contemporary lyric poetry may be largely due to the linguistic and psychic residues of a condition that is not yet fully individuated, a state of affairs that is prebourgeois in the broadest sense—dialect. Until now, however, the traditional lyric, as the most rigorous aesthetic negation of bourgeois convention, has by that very token been tied to bourgeois society.

Because considerations of principle are not sufficient, I would like to use a few poems to concretize the relationship of the poetic subject, which always stands for a far more general collective subject, to the social reality that is its antithesis. In this process the thematic elements, which no linguistic work, even *poésie pure*, can completely divest itself of, will need interpretation just as the so-called formal elements will. The way the two interpenetrate will require special emphasis, for it is only by virtue of such interpenetration that the lyric poem actually captures the historical moment within its bounds. I want to choose not poems like Goethe's, aspects of which I commented on without analyzing, but later ones, poems which do not have the unqualified authenticity of the "Nachtlied." The two poems I will be talking about do indeed share in the collective undercurrent. But I would like to call your attention especially to the way in which in them different levels of a contradictory fundamental condition of society are represented in the medium of the poetic subject. Permit me to repeat that we are concerned not with the poet as a private person, not with his psychology or his so-called social perspective, but with the poem as a philosophical sundial telling the time of history.

Let me begin by reading you Eduard Mörike's "Auf einer Wanderung" [On a Walking Tour]:

In ein freundliches Städtchen tret' ich ein
In den Strassen liegt roter Abendschein,
Aus einem offenen Fenster eben,
Über den reichsten Blumenflor
Hinweg, hört man Goldglockentöne schweben,
Und *eine* Stimme scheint ein Nachtigallenchor,
Daß die Blüten beben,
Daß die Lüfte leben,
Daß in höherem Rot die Rosen leuchten vor.

Lang' hielt ich staunend, lustbeklommen.
Wie ich hinaus vors Tor gekommen,
Ich weiss es wahrlich selber nicht,
Ach hier, wie liegt die Welt so licht!
Der Himmel wogt in purpurnem Gewühle,
Rückwärts die Stadt in goldnem Rauch;
Wie rauscht der Erlenbach, wie rauscht im Grund die Mühle!
Ich bin wie trunken, irrgeführt—
O Muse, du hast mein Herz berührt
Mit einem Liebeshauch!

[I enter a friendly little town,
On the streets lies the red evening light,
From an open window,
Across the richest profusion of flowers
One hears golden bell-tones hover,
And *one* voice seems to be a choir of nightingales,
So that the blossoms quaver,

So that the breezes are lively,
So that the roses glow forth in a higher red.

I stood a long while marvelling, oppressed with pleasure.
How I got out beyond the city gate,
I really do not know myself,
Oh, how bright the world is here!
The sky surges in purple turbulence,
At my back the town in a golden haze;
How the alder stream murmurs, how the mill roars below!
I am as if drunken, led astray—
Oh muse, you have touched my heart,
With a breath of love!]

Up surges the image of the promise of happiness which the small south German town still grants its guests on the right day, but not the slightest concession is made to the pseudo-Gothic small-town idyll. The poem gives the feeling of warmth and security in a confined space, yet at the same time it is a work in the elevated style, not disfigured by *Gemütlichkeit* and coziness, not sentimentally praising narrowness in opposition to the wide world, not happiness in one's own little corner. Language and the rudimentary plot both aid in skillfully equating the utopia of what is close at hand with that of the utmost distance. The town appears in the narrative only as a fleeting scene, not as a place of lingering. The magnitude of the feeling that results from the speaker's delight in the girl's voice, and not that voice alone but the voice of all of nature, the choir, emerges only outside the confined arena of the town, under the open purple-billowing sky, where the golden town and the rushing brook come together in the *imago*. Linguistically, this is aided by an inestimably subtle, scarcely definable *classical*, ode-like element. As if from afar, the free rhythms call to mind unrhymed Greek stanzas, as does the sudden pathos of the closing line of the first stanza, which is effected with the most discreet devices of transposition of word order: "Daß in höherem Rot die Rosen leuchten vor." The single word "Muse" at the end of the poem is decisive. It is as if this word, one of the most overused in German classicism, gleamed once again, truly as if in the light of the setting sun, by being bestowed upon the *genius loci* of the friendly little town, and as though even in the process of disappearing it were possessed of all the power to enrapture which an invocation of the muse in the modern idiom, comically inept, usually fails to capture. The poem's inspiration proves itself perhaps more fully in this than in any of its other features: that the choice of this most objectionable word at a critical point, carefully prepared by the latent Greek linguistic demeanor, resolves the urgent dynamic of the whole like a musical *Abgesang*.[2] In the briefest of spaces, the lyric succeeds in doing what the German epic attempted in vain, even in such projects as Goethe's *Hermann and Dorothea*.

The social interpretation of a success like this is concerned with the stage of historical experience evidenced in the poem. In the name of humanity, of the universality of the human, German classicism had undertaken to release subjective impulses from the contingency that threatens them in a society where relationships between human beings are no longer direct but instead mediated solely by the market. It strove to objectify the subjective as Hegel did in philosophy and tried to overcome the contradictions of men's real lives by reconciling them in spirit, in the idea. The continued existence of these contradictions in reality, however, had compromised the spiritual solution: in the face of a life not grounded in meaning, a life lived painstakingly amid the bustle of competing interests, a prosaic life, as artistic experience sees it; in the face of a world in which the fate of individual human beings works itself out in accordance with blind laws, art, whose form gives the impression of speaking from the point of view of a realized humanity, becomes an empty word. Hence classicism's concept of the human being withdrew into private, individual existence and its images; only there did humanness seem secure. Of necessity, the idea of humankind as something whole, something self-determining, was renounced by the bourgeoisie, in aesthetic form as in politics. It is the stubborn clinging to one's own restricted sphere, which itself obeys a compulsion, that makes ideals like comfort and *Gemütlichkeit* so suspect. Meaning itself is linked to the contingencies of human happiness; through a kind of usurpation, individual happiness is ascribed a dignity it would attain only along with the happiness of the whole. The social force of Mörike's genius, however, consists in the fact that he combined the two experiences—that of the classicistic elevated style and that of the romantic private miniature—and that in doing so he recognized the limits of both possibilities and balanced them against one another with incomparable tact. In none of his expressive impulses does he go beyond what could be genuinely attained in his time. The much-invoked organic quality of his work is probably nothing other than this tact, which is philosophically sensitive to history and which scarcely any other poet in the German language possessed to the same degree. The alleged pathological traits in Mörike reported by psychologists and the drying up of his production in later years are the negative aspect of his every highly developed understanding of what is possible. The poems of the hypochondriacal clergyman from Cleversulzbach, who is considered one of our naive artists, are virtuoso pieces unsurpassed by the masters of *l'art pour l'art*. He is as aware of the empty and ideological aspects of elevated style as of the mediocrity, petit-bourgeois dullness, and obliviousness to totality of the Biedermeier period, in which the greater part of his lyric work falls. The spirit in him is driven to create, for the last time, images that would betray themselves neither by their classical drapery nor by local color, neither by their manly tones nor by their lip-smacking. As if walking a fine line, the residues of the elevated style that survive in memory echo in him, together with the signs of an immediate life that promised fulfillment precisely at the time when they were already condemned by the direction history was taking; and both greet the poet on his wandering only as they are about to vanish. He already shares in the paradox of lyric poetry in the ascending industrial age. As indeterminate and fragile as his solutions are the solutions of all the great lyric poets who come afterwards, even those who seem to be separated from him by an abyss—like Baudelaire, of whom Claudel said that his style was a mixture of Racine's and that of the journalists of his time. In industrial society the lyric idea of a self-restoring immediacy becomes—where it does not impotently evoke a romantic past—more and more something that flashes out abruptly, something in which what is possible transcends its own impossibility.

The short poem by Stefan George I would now like to discuss derives from a much later phase in this development. It is one of the celebrated songs from the *Seventh Ring*, a cycle of extremely condensed works which for all their lightness of rhythm are overheavy with substance and wholly without *Jugendstil* ornament. Their eccentric boldness was rescued from the frightful cultural conservativism of the George circle only when the great composer Anton von Webern set them to music; in George, ideology and social substance are very far apart. The song reads:

Im windes-weben
War meine frage
Nur träumerei.
Nur lächeln war

Was du gegeben.
Aus nasser nacht
Ein glanz entfacht—
Nun drängt der mai
Nun muss ich gar
Urn dein aug und haar
Alle tage
In sehnen leben.

[In the winds-weaving
My question was
Only daydreaming.
Only a smile was
What you gave.
From a moist night
A gleam ignite—
Now May urges
Now I must
For your eyes and hair
Every day
Live in yearning.]

Unquestionably, this is elevated style. Delight in things close at hand, something that still colors Mörike's much earlier poem, has fallen under a prohibition. It has been banished by the Nietzschean pathos of detached reserve which George conceives himself to be carrying on. The remains of Romanticism lie, a deterrent, between him and Mörike; the remains of the idyll are hopelessly outdated and have degenerated to heartwarmers. While George's poetry, the poetry of an imperious individual, presupposes individualistic bourgeois society and the autonomous individual as its preconditions, a curse is put on the bourgeois element of conventional form no less than on the bourgeois contents. But because this poetry can speak from no overarching framework other than the bourgeois, which it rejects not only tacitly and a priori but also expressly, it becomes obstructed: on its own initiative and its own authority, it simulates a feudal condition. Socially this is hidden behind what the cliché refers to as George's aristocratic stance. This stance is not the pose that the bourgeois, who cannot reduce these poems to objects of fondling, waxes indignant about. Rather, despite its demeanor of hostility to society, it is the product of the social dialectic that denies the lyric subject identification with what exists and its world of forms, while that subject is nevertheless allied with the status quo in its innermost core: it has no other locus from which to speak but that of a past seigneurial society. The ideal of nobility, which dictates the choice of every word, image, and sound in the poem, is derived from that locus, and the form is medieval in an almost undefinable way, a way that has been virtually imported into the linguistic configuration. To this extent the poem, like George altogether, is neoromantic. But it is not real things and not sounds that are evoked but rather a vanished condition of the soul. The artistically effected latency of the ideal, the absence of any crude archaicism, raises the song above the hopeless fiction it nonetheless offers. It no more resembles the medieval imitations used on wall plaques than it does the repertoire of the modern lyric; the poem's stylistic principle saves it from conformity. There is no more room in it for organic reconciliation of conflicting elements than there was for their pacification in the reality of George's time; they are mastered only through selection, through omission. Where things close at hand, the things one commonly calls concrete immediate experiences, are admitted into George's lyric poetry at all, they are allowed only at the price of mythologization: none may remain what it is. Thus in one of the landscapes of the *Seventh Ring* the child picking berries is transformed, wordlessly, as if with a magic wand, through a magical act of violence, into a fairy-tale child. The harmony of the song is wrested from an extreme of dissonance: it rests on what Valéry called *refus*, on an unyielding renunciation of everything through which the conventions of lyric poetry imagine that they have captured the aura of things. The method retains only the patterns, the pure formal ideas and schemata of lyric poetry itself, which speak with an intensity of expression once again in divesting themselves of all contingency. In the midst of Wilhelmine Germany the elevated style from which that lyric poetry emerged as polemic has no tradition at all to which it may appeal, least of all the legacy of classicism. It is achieved not by making a show of rhetorical figures and rhythms but by an ascetic omission of whatever might diminish its distance from a language sullied by commerce. If the subject is to genuinely resist reification in solitude here, it may no longer even try to withdraw into what is its own as though that were its property; the traces of an individualism that has in the meantime delivered itself over to the market in the form of the feuilleton are alarming. Instead, the subject has to step outside itself by keeping quiet about itself; it has to make itself a vessel, so to speak, for the idea of a pure language. George's greatest poems are aimed at rescuing that language. Formed by the Romance languages, and especially by the extreme simplification of the lyric through which Verlaine made it an instrument of what is most differentiated, the ear of George, the German student of Mallarmé, hears his own language as though it were a foreign tongue. He overcomes its alienation, which is an alienation of use, by intensifying it until it becomes the alienation of a language no longer actually spoken, even an imaginary language, and in that imaginary language he perceives what would be possible, but never took place, in its composition. The four lines "Nun muss ich gar / Um dein aug und haar / Alle tage / In sehnen leben," which I consider some of the most irresistible lines in German poetry, are like a quotation, but a quotation not from another poet but from something language has irrevocably failed to achieve: the medieval German poetry of the *Minnesang* would have succeeded in achieving it if it, if a tradition of the German language—if the German language itself, one is tempted to say—had succeeded. It was in this spirit that Borchardt tried to translate Dante. Subtle ears have taken umbrage at the elliptical "gar," which is probably used in place of "ganz und gar" [completely] and to some extent for the sake of the rhyme. One can concede the justice of this criticism and the fact that as used in the line the word has no proper meaning. But great works of art are the ones that succeed precisely where they are most problematic. Just as the greatest works of music may not be completely reduced to their structure but shoot out beyond it with a few superfluous notes or measures, so it is with the "gar," a Goethean "residue of the absurd" in which language escapes the subjective intention that occasioned the use of the word. It is probably this very "gar" that establishes the poem's status with the force of a déjà vu: through it the melody of the poem's language extends beyond mere signification. In the age of its decline George sees in language the idea that the course of history has denied it and constructs lines that sound as though they were not written by him but had been there from the beginning of time and would remain as they were forever. The quixotism of this enterprise, however, the impossibility of this kind of restorative writing, the danger of falling into arts and crafts, enriches the poem's substance: language's chimerical yearning for the impossible becomes an expression of the subject's insatiable erotic longing, which finds relief from the self in the other. This transformation of an individuality intensified to an extreme into self-annihilation—and what was the Maximin cult in the late George but a desperate renunciation of individuality construing itself as something positive—was necessary in creating the phantasmagoria of the folksong, something the German language had been groping for in vain in its greatest masters. Only by virtue of a differentiation taken so far that it can no longer bear its own difference, can no longer bear anything but the universal, freed from the humiliation of isolation, in the particular does lyrical language represent language's intrinsic being as opposed to its service in the realm of ends. But it thereby represents the idea of a free humankind, even if the George School concealed this idea from itself through a base cult of the heights. The truth of George lies in the fact that his poetry breaks down the walls of individuality through its consummation of the particular, through its sensitive opposition both to the banal and ultimately also to the select. The expression of his poetry may have been condensed into an individual expression which his lyrics saturate with substance and with the experience of its own solitude; but this very lyric speech becomes the voice of human beings between whom the barriers have fallen.

NOTES

1. "Rede über Lyric und Gesellschaft" was first delivered by Adorno as an adult education lecture for a radio broadcast in Berlin in 1957; it was published in expanded form in the literary journal *Akzente* (1957), and reprinted in Theodor Adorno, *Noten zur Literatur I* (Frankfurt: Suhrkamp, 1958).
2. The *Abgesang* was the closing portion of a stanza in medieval lyric poetry.

6.3 Baudelaire as Modernist and Postmodernist: The Dissolution of the Referent and the Artificial "Sublime" (1985)

Fredric Jameson

The inaugural, the classical, status of Baudelaire in Western poetry can be argued in a number of different ways: a privileged theory of poetic value as it has been developed and transmitted by the modernist tradition is, however, a historicizing one, in which, for each successive period or moment—each successive new *present*—some new ghostly emanation or afterimage of the poet peels off the inexhaustible text. There are therefore many Baudelaires, of most unequal value indeed. There is, for instance, a second-rate post-Romantic Baudelaire, the Baudelaire of diabolism and of cheap *frisson*, the poet of blasphemy and of a creaking and musty religious machinery which was no more interesting in the mid-nineteenth century than it is today. This is the Baudelaire of Pound and of Henry James, who observed, "Les Fleurs du *Mal*? Non, vous vous faites trop d'honneur. What you call *evil* is nothing more than a bit of rotting cabbage lying on a satin sofa." *This* Baudelaire will no doubt linger on residually into the *fin de siècle*.

Then there is the hardest of all Baudelaires to grasp: the Baudelaire contemporary of himself (and of Flaubert), the Baudelaire of the "break," of 1857, the Baudelaire the eternal freshness of whose language is bought by reification, by its strange transformation into alien speech. Of this Baudelaire we will speak no further here.

Instead, I propose two more Baudelaire-simulacra—each identical with the last, and yet each slightly, oddly, distinct: these are the Baudelaire inaugural poet of high modernism (of a today extinct high modernism, I would want to add), and the Baudelaire of postmodernism, of our own immediate age, of consumer society, the Baudelaire of the society of the spectacle or the image. As my title suggests, I will attempt a reading of this society in our present (and of the Baudelaire it deserves) in terms of the machine and the simulacrum, of the return of something like the "sublime." This will then be a speculative and prophetic exercise. I feel on more solid ground with that older period about which we are gradually reaching some general consensus, namely the long life and destiny of high modernism, about which it is safe to assert that one of its fundamental events concerned what we now call the "referent." It is therefore in terms of the disappearance of this last, its eclipse or abolition—better still, its gradual waning and extinction—that we will make our first approach to the poetic text.

CHANT D'AUTOMNE, PART I.

Bientôt nous plongerons dans les froides ténèbres;
Adieu, vive clarté de nos étés trop courts!
J'entends déjà tomber avec des chocs funèbres
Le bois retentissant sur le pavé des cours.

Tout l'hiver va rentrer dans mon être: colère,
Haine, frissons, horreur, labeur dur et forcé,
Et, comme le soleil dans son enfer polaire,
Mon coeur ne sera plus qu'un bloc rouge et glacé.

J'écoute en frémissant chaque bûche qui tombe;
L'échafaud qu'on bâtit n'a pas d'écho plus sourd.
Mon esprit est pareil à la tour qui succombe
Sous les coups du bélier infatigable et lourd.

Il me semble, bercé par ce choc monotone,
Qu'on cloue en grande hâte un cercueil quelque part.
Pour qui?—C'était hier l'été; voice l'automne!
Ce bruit mystérieux sonne comme un départ.

[*Autumnal*
Soon cold shadows will close over us
and summer's transitory gold be gone;
I hear them chopping firewood in our court—
the dreary thud of logs on cobblestone.

Winter will come to repossess my soul
with rage and outrage, horror, drudgery,
and like the sun in its polar holocaust
my heart will be a block of blood-red ice.

I listen trembling to that grim tattoo—
build a gallows, it would sound the same.

My mind becomes a tower giving way
under the impact of a battering-ram.

Stunned by the strokes, I seem to hear, somewhere,
a coffin hurriedly hammered shut—for whom?
Summer was yesterday; autumn is here!
Strange how that sound rings out like a farewell.] [1]

Three experiences (to begin modestly, with the common sense language of everyday life)—three experiences come together in this text: one is a feeling of some kind, strong and articulated, yet necessarily nameless (is it to be described as "anxiety" or that very different thing, "sadness," and in that case what do we do with that other curious component of eagerness, anticipation, curiosity, which begins to interfere with those two other affective tones as we reach the so characteristic final motif of the "départ"—voyage and adventure, as well as death?). I will have little to say about this affective content of the poem, since, virtually by definition, the Baudelaire that interests us here is no longer the Baudelaire of an aesthetic of *expression*: an aesthetic in which some pre-given and identifiable psychological event is then, in a second moment, laid out and expressed in poetic language. It seems to me at least conceivable that the poetic producer may have thought of his work here in terms of some residual category of expression and expressiveness. If so, he has triumphantly (if even against his own will) undermined and subverted that now archaic category: I will only observe that as the putative "feeling" or "emotion" becomes slowly laid out in words and phrases, in verses and stanzas, it is transformed beyond all recognition, becomes lost to the older psychological lexicon (full of names for states of mind we *recognize* in advance), or, to put it in our own contemporary jargon, as it becomes transmuted into a verbal text, it ceases to be psychological or affective in any sense of the word, and now exists as *something else*.

So with this mention we will now leave psychology behind us. But I have suggested that two more "experiences" lend their raw material to this text, and we must now register their banal, informing presence: these are, evidently, a season—fall, the approach of a dreary winter which is also and even more strongly the death of summer itself; and alongside that, a physical perception, an auditory event or experience, the hollow sound of logs and firewood being delivered in the inner courtyard of the Parisian dwelling. Nature on the one hand, the city, the Urban, on the other, and a moment in the interrelationship of these two great contraries in which the first, the archaic cyclical time of an older agriculture and an older countryside, is still capable of being transmitted through what negates it, namely the social institutions of the City itself, the triumphantly un- or anti-natural.

One is tempted, faced with this supreme antithesis between country and city, with this inner contradiction in the raw material of Baudelaire's text between precapitalist society and the new industrial metropolis of nascent capital, to evoke one of the great aesthetic models of modern times, that of Heidegger, in the "Origins of the Work of Art." Heidegger there describes the effect and function of the "authentic" work of art as the inauguration of a "rift" between what he calls World and Earth: what I will rewrite in terms of the dimensions of History and the social project on one hand, and of Nature or matter on the other—ranging from geographical or ecological constraint all the way to the individual body. The force of Heidegger's description lies in the way in which the gap between these two incommensurable dimensions at once, in some irreconcilable of body and spirit, or that of private and public. We are at all moments in History and in matter; at one and the same time historical beings and "natural" ones, living in the meaning-endowment of the historical project as well as in the meaninglessness of organic life. No synthesis—either conceptual or experiential, let alone symbolic—is conceivable between these two disjoined realms; or rather, the production of such conceptual synthesis (in which, say, History would be passed off as "natural," or Nature obliterated in the face of History) is very properly the production of ideology, or of "metaphysics" as it is very properly the production of ideology, or of "metaphysics" as it is often called. The work of art can therefore never "heal" this rift: nothing can do that. What is misconceived is, however, the idea that it ought to be healed: we have here indeed three positions and not two. It is not a question of tension versus resolution, but rather of repression and forgetfulness, of the sham resolution of metaphysics, and then of that third possibility, a divided consciousness that strongly holds together what it separates, a moment of awareness in which difference relates. This is then, for Heidegger, the vocation of the work of art: to stage this irreconcilable tension between History and Nature in such a way that we live *within* it and affirm its reality *as* tension, gap, rift, distance. Heidegger goes on to assimilate this inaugural "poetic" act with the comparable acts of philosophy (the deconcealment of being) and of political revolution (the inauguration of a new society, the invention of new social relations).

It is an attractive and powerful account, and one can read "Chant d'automne" in this way, as staging the fateful gap between organic death, the natural cycle, and the urban, which here greatly expands beyond the city, to include the repressive institutions of society generally, capital execution, war, ceremonial burial, and finally, most mysterious, the faint suggestion of the nomadic, of the "voyage" which seems to mark the interface between nature and human society. One can read the poem in that way, but at what price?

This is the moment to say that the limits of Heidegger's grand conception are less to be found in its account of the poetic act than in its voluntaristic implications for that other act, the act of reception or of reading. Let us assume that the poet—or the artist generally—is always in a position to open World and Earth in this fashion (it is not a difficult assumption to make, since "real" poetry does this by definition, for Heidegger, and art which does not do so is therefore not "really" art in the first place). The problem arises when the reader's turn comes, and in a fallen, secular or reified society is called upon (not least by Heidegger himself) to reinvent this inaugural and well-nigh ritualistic act. Is this always possible? Or must we take into account specific historical conditions of possibility which open or close such a reading? I pass over Heidegger's own sense of historical possibility in the fateful and unnameable moment in which he elaborated this meditation (1935). What is clear is that even this meditation must now return us to the historical in the drearier humdrum sense of the constraints, the situation, which limits possibility and traces the outer boundary even of that more transcendent vision of History as World.

So we now return to the narrower historical situation of this particular Baudelaire, which is the situation of nascent high modernism. Conventional wisdom already defines this for us in a certain number of ways: it is the moment, the Barthes of *Writing Degree Zero* tells us, of the passage from rhetoric to style, from a shared collective speech to the uniqueness of privacy of the isolated monad and the isolated body. It is also the moment, as we know, of the break-up of the older social groups, and not least those relatively homogeneous reading publics to whom, in the writer's contract, certain relatively stable signals can be sent. Both of these descriptions then underscore a process of social fragmentation, the atomization of groups and neighborhoods, the slow and stealthy dissolution of a host of different and coexisting collective formations by a process unique to the logic of capital which my tradition calls reification: the market equivalency in which little by little units are produced, and in the very act by which they are made equivalent to one another are thereby irrevocably separated as well, like so many identical squares on a spatial grid.

I would like to describe this situation, the situation of the poet—the situation this particular Baudelaire must resolve, in obedience to its constraints and contradictions—in a somewhat different, yet related way, as the simultaneous production and effacement of the referent itself. The latter can only be grasped as what is outside language, what language or a certain configuration of language seems to designate, and yet, in the very moment of indication, to project beyond its own reach, as something transcendental to it.

The referent in "Chant d'automne" is not particularly mysterious or difficult of access: it is simply the body itself, or better still, the bodily sensorium. Better yet, it is the bodily perception—better still, even more neutral a term, the *sensation*—which mobilizes the body as its instrument of perception and brings the latter into being over against it. The referent here is then simply a familiar sound, the hollow reverberation of logs striking the courtyard paving. Yet familiar for whom? Everything, and the very mysteries of modernism itself, turn on this word, about which we must admit, in a first moment, that it no longer applies to any contemporary readership. But in a second moment, I will be less concerned to suggest ways in which, even for Baudelaire's contemporaries, such a reference might have been in the process of becoming exotic or obscure, than rather to pose as a principle of social fragmentation the withdrawal of the private or the individual body from social discourse.

We might sharpen the problem of reference by prolonging positivist psychology itself—rigorously coeval with high modernism—and imagining the visual and graphic registration of this unique sound, whose "real nature"—that is to say, whose *name*—we could never guess from looking at its complex spatial pattern. Such registrations perpetuate the old positivist myth of something like a pure atomic sensation in the then nascent pseudoscience of psychology—a myth which in the present context I prefer to read as a symptom of what is happening to the body itself.

For this once "familiar" sound is now driven back inside the body of Baudelaire: a unique event taking place there and utterly alien to anything whose "experience" we might ourselves remember, a something which has lost its name, and which has no equivalents: as anonymous and indescribable as a vague pain, as a peculiar residual taste in the mouth, as a limb falling asleep. The semioticians know well this strange seam between the body and language, as when they study the most proximate naming systems—the terms for wine-tasting, say—or examine the ways in which a physician *translates* his patients' fumbling expressions into the technical code of nosology.

But it is *this* that must now be historicized. I would like to make an outrageous (or at least, as they say, unverifiable) generalization, namely that before Baudelaire and Flaubert there are no physical sensations in literature. This does not quite mean advancing a proposition so sweeping as one which might be expressed, parodying Lionel Trilling, namely, that on or around 1857 we must presume a fundamental mutation in human nature. It does mean, more modestly, and on the side of the object (or the literary raw material), that free-floating bodily perception was not, until now, felt to be a proper content for literary language (you will get a larger historical sense of this by expanding such data to include experiences like that of anxiety—Kierkegaard is after all the contemporary of these writers). And it means, on the side of the subject, or of literary language itself, that the older rhetoric was somehow fundamentally nonperceptual, and had not yet "produced" the referent in our current sense: this is to say that even where we are confronted with what look like masses of sense data—the most convenient example will be, perhaps, Balzac, with his elaborate descriptions, that include the very smell of his rooms—those apparently perceptual notations, on closer examination, prove to be so many *signs*. In the older rhetorical apparatus, in other words, "physical sensation" does not meet the opacity of the body, but is secretly transparent, and always *means* something else—moral qualities, financial or social status, and so forth. Perceptual language only emerges in the ruins of that older system of signs, that older assimilation of contingent bodily experience to the transparency of meaning. The problem, however, and what complicates the description enormously, is that language never ceases to attempt to reabsorb and recontain contingency; that in spite of itself, it always seeks to transform that scandalous and irreducible content back into something like meaning. Modernism will then be a renewed effort to do just that, but one which, faced with the collapse of the older system of rhetorical language and traditional literary meaning, will set itself a new type of literary meaning, which I will term symbolic reunification.

But now we must observe this process at work in our poetic exhibit. The irreducible, the sonorous vibration, with its peculiar hollowness and muffled impact, is here a pure positivity which must be handled or managed in some fashion. This will first be attempted metonymically, by tracing the association of this positive yet somehow ominous sound with something else, which is defined as absence, loss, death—namely the ending of summer. For reasons I will develop later on, it seems useful to formulate this particular axis—positivity/negativity—as one of the two principal operative grids of the poem, the other being the obvious and well-known movement between metonymy and metaphor. The latter will then be the second option of the poetic process: the pure sensation will now be classed metaphorically, by way of analogies and similarities: it is (like) the building of a scaffold, the sound of the battering ram, the nailing up of a coffin. What must be noted here is that this alternate route, whereby the sensation is processed metaphorically rather than metonymically, also ends up in negativity, as though the poetic imagination met some barrier or loop which fatally prevents it from reaching relief or salvation.

This is of course not altogether true: and a complete reading of the poem (not my purpose here) would want to underscore the wondrous reappearance of the place of the subject in the next line—the naïve and miraculous, "Pour qui?" and the utter restructuration of the temporal system, in which the past is now abandoned, the new present—now defined, not negatively as the end of the summer, but positively, as autumn—reaffirmed to the point at which the very sense datum of the sound itself becomes a promise rather than a fatality.

Let me now rapidly try to theorize the two principal strands of the argument, the one having to do with the production of the "referent," the other with the emergence of modernism. In "Chant d'automne" at least—and I don't want to generalize the model in any unduly dogmatic way—the high modernist strategy can be detected in the move from the metonymic reading of the sense datum to the attempt to reabsorb it in some new symbolic or metaphorical meaning—a symbolic meaning of a type very different from the older transparencies of the rhetorical sign to which I have already referred. What I have not yet sufficiently stressed is the way in which this high modernist or symbolic move is determined by the crisis of the reading public and by the social fragmentation from which the latter springs. Given that crisis, and the already tendential privatization and monadization of the isolated individuals who used to make up the traditional publics, there can no longer be any confidence in some shared common *recognition* of the mysterious sense datum, the hollow sound, which is the "referent" of the poetic text: the multiplication of metaphorical analogies is therefore a response to such fragmentation, and seeks to throw out a range of scattered frameworks in which the various isolated readers can be expected to find their bearings. Two processes are therefore here at work simultaneously:

the sound is being endowed with a multiplicity of possible receptions, but as that new multi-faceted attack on a fragmented readership is being projected (something whose ultimate stage will be described in Umberto Eco's *Open Work*), something else is taking place as well, namely the emergence of a new type of symbolic meaning, symbolic recuperation, which will at length substitute itself for an older common language and shared rhetoric of what it might be too complicated to describe as a "realistic" kind.

This crisis in readership then returns us to our other theme, namely the production of the referent: a paradoxical way of putting it, you will say, since my ostensible topic was rather the "eclipse" or the "waning," the "disappearance" of the referent. I don't want to be overly subtle about all this, but it seems to me very important to understand that these two things are the same. The "production" of the referent—that is the sense of some new unnameable ungeneralizable private bodily sensation—something that must necessarily resist all language but which language lives by designating—is the same as the "bracketing" of that referent, its positioning as the "outside" of the text or the "other" of language. The whole drama of modernism will lie here indeed, in the way in which its own peculiar life and logic depend on the reduction of reference to an absolute minimum and on the elaboration, in the former place of reference, of complex symbolic and often mythical frameworks and scaffolding: yet the latter depend on preserving a final tension between text and referent, on keeping alive one last shrunken point of reference, like a dwarf sun still glowing feebly on the horizon of the modernist text.

When that ultimate final point of reference vanishes altogether, along with the final desperate ideology—existentialism—which will attempt to theorize "reference" and "contingency"—then we are in post-modernism, in a now wholly textual world from which all the pathos of the high modernist experience has vanished away—the world of the image, of textual free-play, the world of consumer society and its simulacra.

To this new aesthetic we must now turn, for as I suggested it also knows remarkable anticipations in the work of Baudelaire. There would of course be many ways of approaching post-modernism, of which we have not even time enough to make a provisional inventory. In the case of Baudelaire, one is rather tempted to proceed as follows, by recalling the great dictum of the Philosopher already mentioned, "Language is the house of being." The problem then posed by post-modernism, or more narrowly by the question of what happens when Language is only the *apartment* of Being; when the great urban fact and anti-nature, spreads and abolishes the "path through the field" and the very space and coordinates of some Heideggerian ontological poetry are radically called into question.

Consider the following lines, for example, from "Alchimie de la douleur":

Et sur les célestes rivages
Je bâtis de grands sarcophages.

[to shroud my cherished dead,
and on celestial shores I build
enormous sepulchers.][2]

The entire poem amounts to a staging of or meditation on the curious dialectic of Baudelaire's poetic process, and the way in which its inner logic subverts itself and inverts its own priorities, something these concluding lines suggest rather well. It is as though the imagination, on its way toward opening, or toward the gratifications of some positive and well-nigh infinite wish-fulfillment, encountered something like a reality principle of the imagination or fantasy itself. Not the transfigured nature of the wish-fulfillments of paradise, but rather the ornate, stubborn, material reality of the coffin: the poetic imagination here explicitly criticizes itself, and systematically, rigorously, undermines its first impulse, then in a second moment substituting a different kind of gratification, that of artisanal or handicraft skill, the pleasures of the construction of material artifacts. The role of the essentially nostalgic ideal of handicraft labor in Flaubert and Baudelaire has often been rehearsed; as has Baudelaire's fascination for un- or anti-natural materials, most notably glass, which Sartre has plausibly read as part of a whole nineteenth-century middle-class ideology of "distinction," of the repression of the organic and the constriction of the natural body. But this essentially subjective symbolic act, in which human craft manufacture is mobilized in a repression of the body, the natural, the organic itself, ought not to exclude a more "objective" analysis of the social history of those materials, particularly in nineteenth century building and furnishings, a perspective which will be appropriate for our second exhibit, "La Mort des amants."

Nous aurons des lits pleins d'odeurs légères,
Des divans profonds comme des tombeaux,
Et d'étranges fleurs sur des étagères,
Écloses pour nous sous des cieux plus beaux.

Usant à l'envi leurs chaleurs dernières,
Nos deux coeurs seront deux vastes flambeaux,
Qui réfléchiront leurs doubles lumières
Dans nos deux esprits, ces miroirs jumeaux.

Un soir fait de rose et de bleu mystique,
Nous échangerons un éclair unique,
Comme un long sanglot, tout chargé d'adieux;

Et plus tard un Ange, entr'ouvrant les portes,
Viendra ranimer, fidèle et joyeux
Les miroirs ternis et les flammes mortes.

[*The Death of Lovers*
We shall have richly scented beds—
couches deep as graves, and rare
flowers on the shelves will bloom
for us beneath a lovelier sky.

Emulously spending their last
warmth, our hearts will be as two
torches reflecting their double fires
in the twin mirrors of our minds.

One evening, rose and mystic blue,
we shall exchange a single glance,
a long sigh heavy with farewells;

and then an Angel, unlocking doors
will come, loyal and gay, to bring
the tarnished mirrors back to life.][3]

I am tempted to be brutally anachronistic, and to underscore the affinities between this curious interior scene and the procedures of contemporary photorealism, one of whose privileged subjects is not merely the artificial—in the form of gleaming luxury streets of automobiles (battered or mint)—but above all, interior scenes, furnishings without people, and most notably bathrooms, notoriously of all the rooms in the house the least supplied with anthropomorphic objects.

Baudelaire's sonnet is also void of human beings: the first person plural is explicitly displaced from the entombed chamber by the future tense of the verbs; and even where that displacement weakens, and as the future comes residually to fill up the scene in spite of itself, the twin protagonists are swiftly transformed into furnishings in their own right—candelabra and mirrors, whose complex fourway interplay is worthy of the most complicated visual illustrations of Jacques Lacan.

But I am tempted to go even further than this and to underscore the evident paradox—even more, the formal scandal—of the conclusion of this poem, whose affective euphoria (and its literal meaning) conveys the resurrection of the lovers, while its textual elements in effect produce exactly the opposite, the reawakening of an empty room from which the lovers are henceforth rigorously absent. It is as though the text had profited from the surface or manifest movement of its narrative toward the wish-fulfillment of resurrection, to secure a very different unconscious solution, namely extinction, by means of assimilation to the dead (albeit refurbished) boudoir. Here "interior" knows its apotheosis, in very much the spirit of Adorno's pages on Kierkegaard where the passion for Biedermeier furnishings and enclosed space becomes the symbolic enactment of that new realm of the private, the personal, of subjective or inner life.[4]

Yet Baudelaire goes a good deal further than Kierkegaard in this historical respect, and we will not do proper justice to this glorious poem without registering the properly dreadful nature of its contents: what is tactfully conveyed here is indeed to be identified as the worst Victorian kitsch already on its way to the modulation of fin de siècle decadence, as most notably in the proto-Mallarméan flowers, of which we can at least minimally be sure that "in real life" they are as garish as anything Des Esseintes might have surrounded himself with. Even the "soir fait de rose et de bleu mystique" is mediated by the most doubtful pre-Raphaelite taste, if I may use so moralizing a word.

Now this presents us with an interesting axiological problem, as the philosophers would say: in our engrained Cartesianism, it is always difficult to imagine how a whole might possess value whose individual parts are all worthless; meanwhile, our critical and aesthetic traditions systematically encourage us in a kind of slavish habit of apologia in which, faced with a text of great value, we find ourselves rationalizing all of its more questionable elements and inventing ingenious reasons why these too are of value. But culture is often more complicated and interesting than this; and I must here briefly invoke one of the most brilliant pages in what remains I think Jean-Paul Sartre's greatest single book, *Saint Genet*, whose riches, remarkably, have still been little explored: most notably the section in which he reveals the inner hollowness of Genet's sumptuous style. The principal category of Sartre's analysis is the concept of "le toc"—the phony, the garish, that which is in and of itself and in its very essence in bad taste, all the way from religious emblems and the Opéra of Paris, to the cheapest excesses of horrific popular thrillers, porn ads, and the junk adornments and heavy makeup of drag queens. In Genet, as Sartre shows us, the acquired mental habits of Bossuet's style and classical rhetorical periods reorder and stamp these tawdry materials with the tarnished aura of the sublime, in an operation whose deepest inner logic is that of *ressentiment* and of the imperceptible subversion of the bourgeois reader's most cherished values.

Baudelaire, of course, represents a very different order of elegance; his mastery of the raw material of bad taste will be more tactful and allusive, more refined; nor do I wish to follow Sartre along the lines of an analysis of individual or biographical impulses in this writer. Nonetheless, there are curious analogies between the Sartrean analysis and this extraordinary apotheosis of what should otherwise be an oppressively sumptuous interior, whose very blossoms are as asphyxiating as a funeral parlor, and whose space is as properly funereal as the worst Victorian art photographs. These characterizations are not, clearly, chosen at random: the logic of the image here conveys death and the funereal through its very tawdriness, at the same moment in which the words of the narrative affirm euphoria and the elation of hope.

We have a contemporary equivalent for this kind of stylistic operation, which must be set in place here: and this is the whole properly poststructural language which Susan Sontag was the first to identify as "camp,"[5] the "hysterical sublime," from Cocteau and Hart Crane to Jack Spicer and David Bowie, a kind of peculiar exhilaration of the individual subject unaccountably generated by the trash and junk materials of a fallen and unredeemable commodity culture. Camp is indeed our way of living within the junkyard of consumer society and positively flourishing there: it is to be seen in the very gleam and glitter of the automobile wrecks of photorealist paintings, in the extraordinary capacity of our own cultural language to redeem an object world and a cultural space by holding firmly to their surfaces (in mechanisms which Christopher Lasch and others would no doubt identify as "narcissistic"). Camp, better than anything else, underscores one of the most fateful differences between high modernism and post-modernism, and one which is also, I believe, operative in this strange poem of Baudelaire: namely what I will call the disappearance of *affect*, the utter extinction of that pathos or even tragic spirit with which the high moderns lived their torn and divided condition, the repression even of anxiety itself—supreme psychic experience of high modernism—and its unaccountable reversal and replacement by a new dominant feeling tone: the high, the intensity, exhilaration, euphoria, a final form of the Nietzschean Dionysiac intoxication which has become as banal and institutionalized as your local disco or the thrill with which you buy a new-model car.

This strange new—historically new—feeling or affective tone of late capitalism may now be seen as something like a return of the "sublime" in the sense in which Edmund Burke first perceived and theorized it at the dawn of capital. Like the "sublime" (and the "anxiety"), the exhilaration of which we are speaking is not exactly an emotion or a feeling, not a way of living an object, but rather somehow detached from its contents—something like a disposition of the subject which takes a particular object as a mere occasion: this is the sense in which the Deleuze-Guattari account of the emergence, the momentary and fitful sunburst of the individual psychological subject has always seemed exceedingly relevant:

> Something on the order of a subject can be discerned on the recording surface: a strange subject, with no fixed identity, wandering about over the body without organs, yet always remaining peripheral to the desiring-machines, being defined by the share of the product it takes for itself, garnering here, there, and everywhere a reward, in the form of a becoming or an avatar, being born of the states that it consumes and being reborn with each new state: "c'est donc moi, c'est donc à moi! . . ." The subject is produced as a mere residue alongside the desiring machines: a conjunctive synthesis of consumption in the form of a wonderstruck: "c'était donc ça!"[6]

Such an account has the additional merit of linking up with the great Lacanian theme of "second death,"[7] and of suggesting why death and resurrection should have been so stimulating a fantasy-material for a poet intent on capturing the highs and the "elevations" of an intermittent experience of subjectivity. If the subject exists always and only in the moment of rebirth, then the poetic fantasy or narrative process must necessarily first work its way along the path of death, in order to merit this unique "bonus of pleasure" whose place is carefully prepared in advance for it in the empty, dusted, polished, flower-laden chamber. And the latter is of course, for us, as readers, the poem itself: the chamber of the sonnet, Donne's "pretty room," waiting to be the faithful (and joyous) occasion of our own brief, fitful, punctual exhilaration as subjects: "c'est donc moi, c'est donc à moi!"

Burke's problem, as he confronted an analogous and historically equally new form of affect—the sublime—was to find some explanation—not for our aesthetic pleasure in the pleasurable, in "beauty," in what could plausibly gratify the human organism on its own scale, but rather for our aesthetic delight in spectacles which would seem symbolically to crush human life and to dramatize everything which reduces the individual human being and the individual subject to powerlessness and nothingness. Burke's solution was to detect, within this peculiar aesthetic experience, a relationship to being that might as well have been described as epistemological or even ontological (and incidentally a logic which is rigorously un- or a-symmetrical to that of his other term, "beauty"): astonishment, stupor, terror—these are some of the ways in which the individual glimpses a force which largely transcends human life and which Burke can only identify with the Godhead or the divine. The aesthetic reception of the sublime is then something like a pleasure in pain, in the tightening of the muscles and the adrenaline rush of the instinct of self-preservation, with which we greet such frightening and indeed devastating spectacles.

What can be retained from this description is the notion of the sublime as a relationship of the individual subject to some fitfully or only intermittently visible force which, enormous and systematized, reduces the individual to helplessness or to that ontological marginalization which structuralism and poststructuralism have described as a "decentering" where the ego becomes little more than an "effect of structure." But it is no longer necessary to evoke the deity to grasp what such a transindividual system would be.

What has happened to the sublime since the time of Burke—although he judiciously makes a place of a concept which can be most useful to us in the present context, namely the "artificial infinite"—is that it has been transferred from nature to culture, or the urban. The visible expression of the suprapersonal mode of production in which we live is the mechanical, the artificial, the machine; and we have only to remember the "sublime" of yesterday, the exhilaration of the futurists before the machine proper—the motorcar, the steamship liner, the machine gun, the airplane—to find some initial contemporary equivalent of the phenomenon Burke first described. One may take his point about self-preservation, and nonetheless wish to formulate this affective mechanism a little more sharply: I would have said myself that in the face of the horror of what systematically diminishes human life it becomes possible simply to change the valence on one's emotion, to replace the minus sign with a plus sign, by a Nietzschean effort of the will to convert anxiety into that experience physiologically virtually identical with it which is eagerness, anticipation, anxious affirmation. And indeed, in a situation of radical impotence, there is really little else to do than that, to affirm what crushes you and to develop one's capacity for gratification in an environment which increasingly makes gratification impossible.

But futurism was an experiment in what Reyner Banham has called the "first machine age": we now live in another, whose machines are not the glorious and streamlined visible vehicles and silhouettes which so exhilarated Le Corbusier, but rather computers, whose outer shell has no emblematic or visual power. Our own machines are those of reproduction; and an exhilaration which would attach itself to them can no longer be the relatively representational idolatry of the older engines and turbines, but most open some access, beyond representation, to processes themselves, and above all the processes of reproduction—movie cameras, videos, tape recorders, the whole world of the production and reproduction of the image and of the simulacrum, and of which the smeared light and multireflective glass of the most elegant post-contemporary films or buildings is an adequate *analogon*. I cannot, of course, pursue this theory of post-modernism in any more detail here;[8] but returning one last time to "La Mort des amants" it is appropriate to see in the play of mirrors and lights of the funereal chamber some striking and mysterious anticipation of a logic of the future, a logic far more consonant with our own social moment than with that of Baudelaire. In that then, as in so much else, he is, perhaps unfortunately for him, our contemporary.

NOTES

1. Charles Baudelaire, "Chant d'autonmne" I, in *Les Fleurs du mal* (1857; Paris, 1958), p. 61. All subsequent references will be to this edition. Translation by Richard Howard, "Autumnal I," in *Les Fleur du Mal: The Complete Text of the Flowers of Evil in a New Translation* (Boston, 1982), pp. 61–62. All subsequent translations will be from this edition.

2. Baudelaire, *Les Fleurs du mal*, p. 82. Translation, p. 78.

3. Baudelaire, *Les Fleurs du mal*, p. 149. Translation, p. 149.

4. Theodor W. Adorno, *Kierkegaard* (Frankfurt am Main, 1974).

5. Susan Sontag, "Notes on Camp," in *Against Interpretation and Other Essays* (New York, 1966). pp. 275–92.

6. Gilles Deleuze and Felix Guattari, *The Anti-Oedipus: Criticism and Schizophrenia*, trans. Robert Hurley, Mark Seem, and Helen R. Lane (New York, 1977), p. 16.

7. Jacques Lacan, "Kant avec Sade," in *Ecrits* (Paris, 1971), 2:119–48.

8. But see, for a more complete discussion, my "Postmodernism, or, The Cultural Logic of Late Capitalism," *New Left Review*, 146 (July–August 1984), 53–92.

In Memory of the Pterodactyl: The Limits of Lyric Humanism (2001) 6.4

Drew Milne

Theodor Adorno's essay "On Lyric Poetry and Society" argues that "the lyric work is always the subjective expression of a social antagonism,"[1] but what of lyric's constitutive inhumanity, its relation to non-human nature? According to Adorno, the first person "I" whose voice is heard in lyric expresses an individual particularity which is opposed to the collectivity of human nature. There is then a tension or lack of identity in the illusory immediacy of subjective experience in lyric poetry. The voice that seems most human expresses the immediacy of human nature but does so as an expression of the historical struggle to humanize nature in language. As Adorno puts it, the "I" whose voice is heard "is not immediately at one with the nature to which its expression refers." Accordingly, "It is only through humanization that nature is to be restored the rights that human domination took from it. The greatest lyric works in our language, owe their quality to the force with which the 'I' creates the illusion of nature emerging from alienation."[2] As Adorno points out, the assumption that immediacy and subjectivity are essential to lyric expression is modern. Greek lyricism in the works of Sappho, Pindar and the choral odes of the tragedians positions the muses closer to the gods and the mythic forces of nature. This brief essay seeks to suggest, against the grain of Adorno's conception of lyric, that the limits of lyric humanism remain closer to this ancient conception of lyric and the speculative experience of nature.

The ur-image of the human domination of human nature for the sake of lyric experience is provided by Homer's *Odyssey* and the story of Odysseus bound to the mast of his ship to hear the sirens. This image informs central arguments in the *Dialectic of Enlightenment* which Adorno wrote with Max Horkheimer.[3] Adorno and Horkheimer do not make the connections explicit, but Adorno's essay "Parataxis" intimates the way in which Adorno's unusual historical imagination is informed by Hölderlin: "Metaphysical passivity as the substance of Hölderlin's poetry is allied, in opposition to myth, with the hope for a reality in which humanity would be free of the spell of its entanglement in nature."[4] A different source, closer to Adorno's affinities with Walter Benjamin, is provided by Franz Kafka's parable "The Silence of the Sirens." Kafka's retelling concludes with the mischievous suggestion that Ulysses noticed that the sirens were silent but pretended to have heard the sirens as a sort of shield.[5]

Who or what are the sirens? If the nature of these creatures of the imagination is beyond the limits of human perception, myth nevertheless imagines them as feminine, winged creatures. The sirens lose their allure if they are imagined as singing mermaids of the sky, or as condors of the mediterranean. Pictorial representation or physical embodiment of the sources of sublime sound is fraught with the risk of bathos. As opera singers so often demonstrate, opera sounds better with the eyes shut. Where the thematics of lyric are used as a tool of erotic seduction, as with pop songs, the presence of the singer can be an added attraction. With lyric poetry of the page, however, there is a necessary awkwardness when a lyric poet performs their work. As writing, lyric is freed from the human clumsiness of speech, and in this freedom it is possible to imagine the voices of nature beyond the human.

The sources of the imagination's siren songs are understood critically in a number of modern poems, perhaps most beautifully in Wallace Stevens's "The Idea of Order at Key West" and its tale of the feminine voice that sings beyond the genius of the sea:

> She was the single artificer of the world
> In which she sang. And when she sang, the sea,
> Whatever self it had, became the self
> That was her song, for she was the maker. Then we,
> As we beheld her striding there alone,
> Knew that there never was a world for her
> Except the one she sang and, singing, made.[6]

In this poem the humanization of the muse as a female voice of nature equivocates with the powers of personification. The poem's blemish is the word "striding," which somehow suggests an image of seaside health and athleticism: the physical form of the female pronoun becomes too human. The potential for bathos would not be lessened if the isolated figure were described as a flock of seagulls or as a bevy of bathing beauties of the kind that enchanted Odysseus on the shores of Ithaca, or Proust's narrator at Balbec. Such images find their critical recension in Cézanne's *Bathers*. Stevens nevertheless leaves this blemish to lure the unwary poetry-lover into a false literalism. A feminized but inhuman lyric power of sea, song, wind and air could not be anything other than an imagined projection. In this sense, the poem's pathetic fallacy composes its 'enchanting' night to enjoy the artifice of the lyric imagination. The spell of enchantment nevertheless hints at the illusory powers of the chanter, the incantatory web of the chanson. The dialectic of subjectivity and objectivity in this poem is exemplary but perhaps too tidily organized. Stevens's mask and poetic persona evades the lure of self-aggrandizing first person sensitivity, but is a little too proud of his "idea" and of his ability to tame the powers of nature in song.

The necessary skepticism before such visions is captured by Prufrock: "I have heard the mermaids singing, each to each. / I do not think they will sing to me."[7] Eliot's dark irony suggests that we drown when human voices wake us from the dream of poetry. The limits of lyric irony are such that Prufrock's reflections on alienation from human expression seem too much like a knowingly performed identification with a nature that cannot be known: "I should have been a pair of ragged claws / Scuttling across the floors of silent seas."[8] In "The Waste Land" the critique of the "sylvan scene" above the antique mantel gives voice to the raped Philomel who cries "Jug Jug" to dirty ears.[9] The myth of Philomel's transformation into a swallow or a nightingale positions a lament for the victims of male rape within birdsong. Eliot's deliberately unpoetic "jug" intimates what sticks in the jugular, and speaks of a distaste with the unspoken violence in tasteful representations of classical myth. The rape victim's loss of human speech in the metamorphosis from human to avian nature somehow returns from its poetic alienation in the refusal to sing suggested by "jug." Eliot's investigation into the ruins of lyric nevertheless seems to embrace alienation from the human world rather than working to disenchant the violence of human nature.

What makes such moments important, however, is the way they reveal the difficulty of overcoming the lyric thematics of romanticism, perhaps most famously expressed in the viewless wings of poesy in Keats's "Ode to a Nightingale." The immortal Bird of lyric poetry may sing beyond death in the aching dreams of lyric illusion, but romanticism's birdsongs are already sung at the limits of imaginative projection. The prophetic powers of Shelley's west wind and the blithe spirit of the skylark are pitched at the limits of a known estrangement from the ecstasies evoked. The crimes committed in the name of nature's spirit find their most pointed allegorical form in Coleridge's "Rime of the Ancient Mariner." The dead albatross of lyric projection hangs around the neck of the would-be modernist. According to Hegel, the vocation of poetry is to liberate spirit "not *from* but *in* feeling,"[10] but romanticism's intimations of the sublimities to be felt in nature protest too much about all the yearning. As Wordsworth puts it, the world is too much with us, and poetry is reduced to presenting the protean dreams of Proteus and that male mermaid Triton in the form of regret for the loss of paganism and poetry's spent powers.[11] This critique echoes in Keats's sonnet "On the Sea":

> Oh ye! whose ears are dinn'd with uproar rude,
> Or fed too much with cloying melody—
> Sit ye near some old Cavern's Mouth, and brood
> Until ye start, as if the sea-nymphs quir'd![12]

The affected antique spelling of "quire" might be read as a cheeky pun on choirs and the booktrade meaning of "quire" (a set of four sheets of parchment paper). A more plausible interpretation would put pressure on the sense of embarrassment with the desire to have your sea-nymph cake and eat it too. You can imagine Busby Berkeley bathing babes, but the wild vulgarity of the mythic imagination needs to be tamed to weariness.

There is a comparable embarrassment with the artifice of song in a remark in Hegel's *Aesthetics* which describes *Gesang* or songs sung domestically. The relevant passage is translated by T.M. Knox as "the song proper, meant for warbling in private or for singing in company. This does not require much substance or inner grandeur and loftiness."[13] There is a high-low opposition at work here, but the curious expression is "warbling in private." F. P. B. Osmaston's earlier translation gives: "the *genuine song* intended for singing or purely musical practice, whether in private or before others. Much intelligible content, ideal greatness and loftiness is not necessary."[14] This phrase "purely musical practice" is footnoted with: "I presume Hegel means this by the words *nur zum Trällern*; it might mean 'merely to be hummed.'"[15] The doubt here is generated by the German verb "trällern" which can mean to hum, trill or warble. It is tempting to see a grouping of onomatopoeic words clustered around the sound of trilling and "trill," with cognates in French and Italian. There seems to be a poetic identity between the word and the action of the tongue involved in saying the word. This temptation meets the thought that there might also be some connection between "trällern" and "tra-la-la," a word which also appears to mime melodic utterance. In the context of Hegel's passage, the thought of songs for domestic "warbling" jars in English, perhaps because "warbling" is somewhat pejorative. The human songbird folds into associations with avian warblers, those small insectivorous songbirds whose song has become their collective name. It seems plausible that Hegel means something more like "humming" in private, but here too there are animistic residues—humming birds, bees and the humdrum chores of routine work. *Trällern* and its possible translations are positioned, then, between the grace notes of the nobler human arts and the less dignified music of the private individual. "Warbling" ironically indicates some of the social embarrassment with private singing that attaches to those caught in the act of meditative whistling (the sign of a liar) or singing in the shower.

If there is something suspiciously ignoble, almost animalistic about such kinds of lyric expression, this suspicion finds its inverse form in the anthropomorphic explanations of birdsong. As Kant comments, "The song of the bird proclaims joyfulness and contentment with its existence. At least this is how we interpret nature, whether anything of the sort is its intention or not. But this interest, which we here take in beauty, absolutely requires that it be the beauty of nature; and it disappears entirely as soon as one notices that one has been deceived and that it is only art. What is more highly extolled by poets than the bewitchingly beautiful song of the nightingale?"[16] Art, here, is critically construed as that which is merely human and inferior to natural beauty. Kant is concerned to distinguish the powers of human judgment as regards natural beauty, but the question of beauty inevitably seems too anthropomorphic. One can imagine scientific experiments designed to investigate whether birds sing because it is their "nature" to do so; whether birdsong is predominantly the activity of male songbirds; whether birdsong functions as a semiotics of danger-signalling, sexual display or territorial assertion; and so on. The human perception of spirit in natural beauty nevertheless suggests the limits of scientific reasoning, since there is evidently an unreconciled affinity between birds and humans in such perceptions. This affinity allows the lyric poet to explore both the limits of humanism in our conceptions of song and the limits to disenchantment in the human domination of nature.

The thematics of disenchantment return the argument to Adorno's conception of lyric poetry and society. Curiously, Adorno's essay chooses not to focus on the line from Eduard Mörike's "Auf einer Wanderung" that brings these questions into play: "Und *eine*

Stimme scheint ein Nachtingallenchor" / "And *one* voice seems to be a choir of nightingales."[17] Adorno waxes somewhat lyrical and infers an identification between a girl's voice, the muse, and the choir of nature, without quite noting the illusory projection onto nature and femininity. A similar difficulty with sexuality and nature underlies Adorno's dialectic of enlightenment and the relation between Odysseus and the sirens. The eroticism of the Homeric version of the myth is muted, and the spirit of wildness intimated by the image of the sirens disguising death in alluring illusions is indeterminately dangerous. If there is some violence in the way Horkheimer and Adorno read Homer as a parable of the capitalist division of labor, their reading of Odysseus's domination of human nature to achieve a moment of aesthetic freedom now seems especially pertinent. The relevance of their critical construction can be sensed in the way Denise Riley argues for the possibilities of nonidentitarian solidarity in relation to what she calls "Lyric selves."[18] The central chapter of *The Words of Selves* pursues her critical argument through a commentary on her own poems, "The Castalian Spring, a first draught" and "Affections of the Ear." Riley asks whether the lyric "I" is an irretrievably outdated form. She cites *The Poet's I in Archaic Greek*, ed. S. R. Sling (1990), to suggest the antiquity of the question. As Riley argues, "Presenting the self and its fine sensibilities reaches fever pitch within some contemporary poetics. Poetry can be heard to stagger under a weight of self-portrayal, having taken this as its sole and proper object. Today's lyric form, frequently a vehicle for innocuous display and confessionals, is at odds with its remoter history. What might transpire if this discontinuous legacy in self-telling became the topic of a poem itself?" (R 94). Her poem "The Castalian Spring, a first draught" explores these questions by working through some of lyric's historical conditions of possibility: "Into the cooling air I gave tongue, my ears blurred with the lyre / Of my larynx, its vibrato reverberant into the struck-dumb dusk" (R 95). The poem's lyric persona identifies with a toad rather than with a nightingale, but the reprise of alienation from anthropomorphic identification with nature generates a moment of lyrical noise comparable to Eliot's "Jug Jug":

> Could I try on that song of my sociologized self? Its
> Long angry flounce, tuned to piping self-sorrow, flopped
> Lax in my gullet—'But we're all *bufo bufo*,' I sobbed—
> Suddenly charmed by community—'all warty we are.' (R 103)

Riley's other poem, "Affections of the Ear," reworks the Ovidian tale of Narcissus and Echo to explore strategies of ironic classicism and shimmering anxieties about subjective identifications. Part of the poetic strategy is the use of what Riley, with deliberate self-defeating irony, calls "a chatty conversational tone" (R 94), a tone that seems closer to the poetic theatricality of Frank O'Hara than the more classical lyricism of Hölderlin, some of whose poems Riley has translated.[19] The conversational tone sets up a dialogue between animal persona, human speech and classical myth but the domination of human voice over the material works against the poem's uncertainties about lyric humanism. A different exploration of lyric humanism informs the poems in Helen Macdonald's collection *Shaler's Fish*. Despite the fishy title, the collection is dominated by birdlife thematics. The opening poem "Taxonomy" begins: "Wren. Full song. No subsong. Call of alarm, spreketh & ought / damage the eyes with its form, small body, tail pricked up & beak like a hair."[20] The quality of taxonomy involved interrupts the grammar of scientific description and the functional explanation of wren song. The title of a subsequent poem "Blackbird/Jackdaw/*Turdus*/*Corvus*/*merula*/*monedula*" plays with the anthropomorphic, scientific language of bird-names, while the poem entitled "Hyperion to a Satellite" gives further indications of the conflict between poetic antiquity and modern rationality. The notes to "Poem, for Bill Girden" in Keith Tuma's *Anthology of Twentieth-Century British & Irish Poetry* help explain how, in Macdonald's words, "The poem responds to an article by Bill Girden I read in the falconry anthology *A Bond with the Wild*."[21] Wild birds animate the poem:

> "This is hardly a flaw; it simply is" you say, then drop
> like a lark in abeyance of song to mitigate sward.
> My pen crumples into a swan, it is singing
> inauthenticate myth, and not of future splendour. (M 22)

Talk of swans inevitably raises the specter of Leda and Yeats, but here the agency of lyric writing as a form of nature (pen/quill/feather) offers an ambiguous swan song. Keith Tuma comments that "it is not clear whether the pen *wounds* or *becomes* the swan. Might the pen 'sing' a swan stripped of anthropomorphizing myth?"[22] The answer is that it cannot. However much humans imagine bonds with the wild, not even poetic identification can liberate itself from the taming of nature for human purposes. Macdonald's poetry is intimate with such difficulties, to the extent that it seems important that her use of bird imagery is not simply bookish but is grounded in experience. In the late 1990s she worked for the National Avian Research Center, Abu Dhabi, breeding falcons. The authority of experience usually seems an awkward critical ruse, and it may be that without this authorial context the avian thematics would seem affected. The poems recurrently counterpose antique fragments of poetic history with different bird-like perceptions. It becomes difficult not to over-interpret the status of wild birds and human agency where other questions might be more central. This said, the way bird similes are awkwardly humanized is remarkable: "I am valorous in the face of such kindness, as ravens on pylons / stock doves and the roll of limestone bulks out our version / ripping out a throat in even dreams, eyes shut & breathing / concentrating on the sodden lack of the heart, and its sharp depths / up for retching on sweetness: sugar, tunes, airs, the memory of love" (M 42). Macdonald offers one of the most sustained explorations of avian imagery in recent lyric poetry, and this extends to speculative commentary on the human domination of the airwaves for purposes of danger-signalling, sexual display and territorial assertion, from the radio telescopes of Jodrell Bank to CNN. The poem "Earth Station" talks of: "constructing a beautiful personal cosmology from the inclination / of space and communicative links, where the dishes' upturned curves / represent immortality and such, so that nights long they could be watched / as the band of microwave radiation pushed up through low cloud // as ravens slope-soaring on the updraught from the dish's face" (M 58). The evasive "and such" seals the energy of uncertain identification. To imagine birds as ancient as ravens adapting to large dishes (hyperion to a satellite-dish) within a speculative cosmology prompts thoughts on the history of avian life and modern aviation. I'm reminded of Hans Blumenberg's *The Genesis of the Copernican World*, and his account of the cosmology of the heavens and anthropomorphic geocentrism.[23]

In Sappho's lyrical world, the chariot of Venus is pulled by sparrows. In Macdonald's world, mythic images have metamorphosed into intimations of the limits of human song. Hegel's chosen image to represent the flight of philosophy was the Owl of Minerva. But as well as providing the figurative resources of the classical muses, the Greek language also persists in the supposedly technical language of poetry and scientific taxonomy. Consider the etymology of the Pterodactyl: *pteron* is the Greek word for wing, and *dactylos* is the Greek for finger. Nineteenth-century science named these dinosaur birds with words that also find their way in classical prosody. If poetry is the language of winged words, then poetry has a curious affinity with these ancient creatures. Some birds sing with a sweetness recognizable to humans, while others, such as croaking crows and ravens, make sounds that seem haunted by ancient terrors, terrors perhaps most vivid in the popular imagination thanks to Hitchcock's film *The Birds*. What would a poetics of the birds of ill omen sound like? Perhaps, at the limits of lyric humanism, the significance of poetic birdsong needs to be extended to hear the ancient ghosts and laments of the pterodactyl.

NOTES

1. T. W. Adorno, "On Lyric Poetry and Society," *Notes to Literature*, vol. 1, trans. Shierry Weber Nicholsen (New York: Columbia University Press, 1991), pp. 37–54 (p. 45).

2. Adorno, "On Lyric Poetry and Society," p. 41.

3. T. W. Adorno and Max Horkheimer, *Dialectic of Enlightenment*, trans. John Cumming (London: Verso, 1979), esp. "Excursus 1: Odysseus or Myth and Enlightenment," pp. 43–80. For a critique, see Jürgen Habermas, "The Entwinement of Myth and Enlightenment: Max Horkheimer and Theodor Adorno," *The Philosophical Discourse of Modernity*, trans. Frederick Lawrence (Cambridge: Polity, 1987), pp. 106–130.

4. T. W. Adorno, "Parataxis: On Hölderlin's Late Poetry," *Notes to Literature*, vol. 2, trans. Shierry Weber Nicholsen (New York: Columbia University Press, 1992), pp. 109–149 (p. 149).

5. See Franz Kafka, "The Silence of the Sirens," trans. Willa and Edwin Muir, *The Collected Short Stories of Franz Kafka*, ed. Nahum N. Glatzer (Harmondsworth: Penguin, 1988), pp. 430–2.

6. Wallace Stevens, "The Idea of Order at Key West," *Collected Poems* (London: Faber and Faber, 1955), pp. 128–30 (pp.129–30).

7. T. S. Eliot, "The Love Song of J.Alfred Prufrock," *Collected Poems, 1909–1962* (London: Faber and Faber, 1974), pp. 13–17 (p. 17).

8. Eliot, "Prufrock," p. 15.

9. Eliot, "The Waste Land," *Collected Poems*, pp. 61–92 (p. 66).

10. G. W. F. Hegel, *Aesthetics: Lectures on Fine Art*, trans. T. M. Knox (Oxford: Clarendon, 1975), 2 vols., vol. II, p. 1112.

11. William Wordsworth, "The world is too much with us," *William Wordsworth*, ed. Stephen Gill (Oxford: Oxford University Press, 1984), p. 270.

12. John Keats, "On the Sea", *The Poetical Works of John Keats*, ed. H. Buxton Forman (London: Oxford University Press, 1907), p. 295.

13. Hegel, *Aesthetics*, trans. T.M. Knox, vol. II, p. 1143.

14. G. W. F. Hegel, *The Philosophy of Fine Art*, trans. F. P. B. Osmaston, 4 vols., (London: G. Bell, 1920), vol. IV, p. 230.

15. Hegel, *Philosophy of Fine Art*, trans. F.P.B. Osmaston, vol. IV, p. 230.

16. Immanuel Kant, *Critique of the Power of Judgment*, ed. Paul Guyer, trans. Paul Guyer and Eric Matthews (Cambridge: Cambridge University Press, 2000), pp. 181–2.

17. Poem and translation quoted in Adorno, "On Lyric Poetry and Society", p. 47.

18. Denise Riley, *The Words of Selves: Identification, Solidarity, Irony* (Stanford, CA: Stanford University Press, 2000). References hereafter abbreviated to R and page no.

19. See Denise Riley, "Versions of six poems by Friedrich Hölderlin (1770–1843)," *Dry Air* (London: Virago, 1985), pp. 33–41.

20. Helen Macdonald, *Shaler's Fish* (Buckfastleigh: Etruscan, 2001), p. 7. References hereafter abbreviated to M and page no.

21. Keith Tuma, ed., *Anthology of Twentieth-Century British & Irish Poetry* (New York: Oxford University Press, 2001), p. 934.

22. Tuma, p. 931.

23. Hans Blumenberg, *The Genesis of the Copernican World*, trans. Robert M. Wallace (Cambridge, Mass.: MIT, 1987). On the thematics of mythic residues more generally, see also Hans Blumenberg, *Work on Myth*, trans. Robert M. Wallace (Cambridge, Mass.: MIT, 1985).

6.5 The Lyric in Exile (2004)

Stathis Gourgouris

to the memory of Edward Said

This essay belongs to a series of writings on what I call "transgressive listening."[1] They involve meditations on musical instances where the conditions of listening are altered, not only because of the formal nature (compositional and/or performative) of certain musical pieces, but also as a result of social-historical relations and practices. I consider the problem of listening less a matter of production of musical form or musical innovation as such—though no doubt this is a decisive element in the process—and more a matter of social practice, of history, of patterns of life and response to life in the world. In this respect, the composer or the musician faces the predicament of being listened to not as an agent of what s/he does as a practitioner of music but as a member of a society who listens—or doesn't.

Listening certainly does not involve some natural talent. One might not say this about composing or playing an instrument or even having an ear for proper pitch, although in all these cases an effective performance depends on serious application and practice. Listening, in any case, is learned. (Or *unlearned*: whole communities can be rendered unskilled to listening, generation by generation, through certain patterns in musical production; that's what the hit market of commercial music is all about.) One certainly learns to listen by listening, and by listening further: by expanding one's boundaries of exposure to sound, as well as by repeating the listening experience of a well known piece of music in the spirit of discovery. These two aspects are interrelated. Discovering something new in a familiar piece of music often occurs as a result of inadvertent comparison with other listening experiences—the discovery of affinities between otherwise disparate musical works. This is why it is essential to listen to the broadest range of music possible—not out of some compulsion to eclecticism, but out of the desire to enrich (that is, alter) one's habits of listening.

On this occasion, I draw on the problematic of listening from an additional source. Beyond the strictly musical questions that emerge out of a bold experiment in the song form—the collaboration between the poet Bertolt Brecht and the composer Hanns Eisler during their Hollywood exile—the issues addressed here pertain to an array of contiguous problems, more generally concerning the societal parameters of lyric poetry and more specifically the historical conditions of exile that produce a radical (and, one must say, unique) musical and poetic response. In this respect, this inquiry is introduced with a critical review of Theodor Adorno's classic essay "Lyric Poetry and Society," which is read in full cognizance of Adorno's intimate connection to the entire problematic: his own groundbreaking reflections on the problematic of listening as well as on the relations between artistic experimentalism and cultural politics (where music signifies the primary frame of reference), in addition, of course, to his share of the exile experience under the same conditions.

The impetus for this meditation is informed by a self-consciously restrospective listening experience. The experience of listening to the *Hollywooder Liederbuch* today rests on a range of historical problems, posed at one time by the two collaborators and the conditions they encountered and addressed with inarguably bold gestures. These problems and gestures strike at the heart of a whole set of interrogative concerns regarding both the significance of lyric poetry in modern society and the song form in strictly musical terms. The challenge to imagine the conditions of this creative collaboration and what it meant within a certain musical and lyrical tradition at the time must meet the challenge of assessing precisely in what terms, within our historical present, this composition blew open the horizon of the song form and set the highest standards in the traditionally 'difficult' association of experimental art with political praxis.

[...]

In the essay "On Lyric Poetry and Society," Theodor Adorno makes a shrewd dialectical argument that confirms the transcendental substance of lyrical subjectivity by abolishing its metaphysical framework, a gesture that, on first sight at least, appears impossible by mere logic. Though the essay has achieved classic status as one of the most lasting gestures of literary criticism, its impetus is expressly philosophical, and it has as much to say about the trappings of logic as about the tribulations of poetry. To my mind, the essay is exemplary of Adornian dialectics and deserves, even if briefly and as a way of passing on to the matter at hand, a precise rehearsal of its argument.

Adorno reiterates at the outset the predominant view of the lyric substance: namely, immersion into an individual form enables the grasping of what remains universally undistorted, untamed, not yet subsumed—in other words, the essence of the human unfettered by the pronounced boundaries of false particulars. But, the argument goes, the lyric poem's presumed achievement of universality through "unrestrained individuation" runs the risk, by definition, of stark inauthenticity or unrestrained distortion, to play along with Adorno's language, if nothing else because of the presumption of an uncontested link between voice and subject. Adorno's quick answer to this risk institutes a shift in conception and marks his own point of departure in the argument: "The universality [*Allgemeinheit*] of the lyric's substance is essentially social [*wesentlich gesellschaftlich*]. Only one who hears the voice of humankind in the poem's solitude [*Einsamkeit*] can understand what the poem is saying."[2] Right away, the problem becomes one of understanding what is social. By virtue of the way the matter is conceived, this problem comes before the examination of what is universal. Indeed, the old dichotomy between particular and universal, or if you will, subjective and objective, is recast in this essay as a relation that is not dichotomous at all, as a relation between the lyric and the social in which no term bears the primary definitional position and where both terms signify problem-domains within a specific historical framework—this has to be underlined—that the lyric poem as a form addresses.

Adorno nullifies from the start any indication that the social element in the lyric might be deduced from the social content of the poem or the social interests of the poet. Such an aspiration would already be unattainable in the sense that society is "an internally contradictory unity" (39) and thus cannot be represented as a definitive signification, whether in terms of literary content or authorial intention. In fact, the lyric engages with precisely this unrepresentability of the social in immanent fashion—as the very pulse of the lyric's peculiar handling of the subject-object relation. To go even further: lyric subjectivity is constituted as a refusal of inherited terms of social recognition and is expressed in a language that trumps social communication, all in order to render readable, expressible, the significational instability of social relations, the antagonism of meanings, and the internally contradictory conceptual frameworks, which in all instances permeate the subject-object relation even though consistently veiled and streamlined by ideological structures.

I shall bypass here Adorno's predictable terms of codifying this quandary in favor of the canonical—namely, that great works of art are the exemplary indicators of unmasking ideological falsity—in order to focus on the claim.[3] Adorno insists that the remoteness of the lyric voice, a seemingly disembodied presence, is hardly an instance of disengagement from the real but an exemplary indication of an idiomatic resistance fostered by the streamlining pressures of social conformity. He expressly identifies the constitutive gesture of the lyric as "the refusal to submit to anything heteronomous" (40). But to leave it at that would be merely to reiterate the commonplace view associated with Adorno's notions of art: aesthetic autonomy is the means of social resistance. To my mind, the essay insinuates something murkier, less stable propositionally. Yes, it is true that the lyric poem constructs an autonomous universe as a refusal of the heteronomous oppression of social norms, but this hardly means that the lyric disappears in a constructed world of its own. The autonomy of the lyric may be aesthetic in the sense that it pertains to the making of an art-form, but as a gesture of *poiēsis*, it bears indeed the gestures of *social autonomy*—by which I mean, the position in society, within a social imaginary, that enables us to reconceptualize, rearrange, reimagine the very framework of the social reality we inherit: "In its protest the poem expresses the dream of a world in which things would be different" (40).

Though in my book, *poiēsis*, to the degree that it matters at all, is always social *poiēsis*, in the parallel sense that autonomy is always social autonomy or is nothing at all, the wager here is to see how the lyric poem, perhaps the most 'aestheticist' of literary forms (dare I say akin to abstract art in painting?), might bear the gestures of society's unknown, unarticulated, vision—even more, the gestures of 'another' society, as yet unborn, undreamt. It is in this latter sense, and not in what otherwise appears to be hopelessly conventional, that we may attribute Adorno's claim that lyric poetry is a phenomenon of modernity. He knows all too well—and mentions it outright—that lyric instances in an archaic world, whether Greek or Chinese, Japanese or Arabic, abound. The point he makes—or let me be bold: the point on which this argument stands as a radical argument (whether Adorno actually makes it or not is rather irrelevant)—is that the lyric encapsulates the predicament of modernity insofar as modernity is the social formation that remains perversely open to its own undoing, to its alteration, for good or ill.

In this sense then, the lyric is a profoundly political form because: a) it testifies to an alienated subjectivity that constructs an extreme, almost inscrutable, internal universe which it then uses as an antagonistic gesture to fortify (and perhaps even refine) its alienation; b) it pursues an altered imaginative framework, whereby this alienation works productively to outwit the social-imaginary that causes it and, on certain occasions, provide the language that in turn alters the terms of alienation itself. I would stand clear of Adorno's rather romantic claim that this double alienation—the alienation of alienation, as we would say dialectically—restores the lyric "I" from its formative dehumanization. This, in any case, is a matter to be debated. In crude terms, I would rather say that the emancipatory force of the lyric—if we could even put it that way—is not a matter of humanization (or 'rehumanization') but of self-alteration, of a genuine autonomous social imagination. In the same way, I would hold my distance from the easily producible claim that the lyric as a form, in the terms we have just rehearsed, is always in exile, constituted in exile almost by definition. Even if true in some generalizable metaphoric sense, this seems to me to be the easy path of thinking through this problem and I propose we leave it aside at the outset.

Instead, let us focus on Adorno's formalist (perhaps we may say technical) terms of assessing the politically emancipatory nature of the lyric. As one can imagine, the matter is not one of content but of form—more precisely, of form as content. I quote at length:

> It is precisely what is not social in the lyric poem that is now to become its social aspect. . . . The highest lyric works are those in which the subject, with no remaining trace of mere matter [*ohne Rest von blossem Stoff*], sounds forth in language until language itself acquires a voice. The unself-consciousness [*Selbstvergessenheit*] of the subject submitting itself to language as something objective, and the immediacy and spontaneity of that subject's expression are one and the same: thus language mediates lyric poetry and society in their innermost core. (42–43)

"With no remaining trace of mere matter" or perhaps, unwinding the metaphor, "without the barest thread left": I shall begin the reading with this provocative phrase. The rhetorical impulse is recognizable to all trained readers of Adorno. The extreme negation aspires at the disintegration of what is conventionally expected but in order to produce not annihilation but alteration. The difference is crucial. The challenge is to grasp that the transcendental language of the lyric does not signify the dissolution of what it leaves behind but its sublation (following somewhat the Hegelian figure of *Aufhebung*), which is to say, at least in part, the preservation of an altered alienation: a disruptive preservation of what exists by altering its force and placing it in a different set of relations.

To reiterate it, if possible, in more tangible fashion: The lyric subject assumes a disembodied voice because it emerges from a world that has deprived it of body. (In more expressly political terms, we would say: a world that has appropriated and dominated its body thereby tearing the connection between body and voice.) The lyric subject assumes this position as an *archē*: as point of departure and as constitutive principle. It thus fashions a disembodied language, which, however, bears within it the trace of this tearing between body and voice—"a trace of no mere matter" but a trace of disembodiment nonetheless. Its evident immateriality—evident in the language, evident *as* language—consists in the gesture by which the lyric subject submits to the "objectivity of the language" (Adorno says). In other words, it is sort of a magic act, an act of disappearance. It is rather amusing, I think, that the conventional responses to the lyric fall prey to this magic act and tend to attribute to language the essence of the poem, the "lyric substance." But Adorno recalls us to order at once. Language is but mediation—it is always mediation, even in its purest, most incommunicable form—between poetry and society. In other words, language is a means of social *poiēsis*, bearing neither *archē* nor *telos*. It is certainly not an essence. A subsequent step in the argument would be to say that this mediation in fact enables us to trace the dialectical process of engagement-disengagement with the social, the very process of (self-) alteration.

When Adorno claims that "the lyric reveals itself to be most deeply grounded in society when it does not chime with society, when it communicates nothing" (43), he is hardly playing dialectical games. He is just reiterating the absolutely negative process that society needs in order to alter itself. In this process, language itself undergoes a transformation. Shielding its mediating attributes, it becomes the vehicle of an alternative imaginary framework. But what differentiates the lyric from even the most avant-garde political poem is that this framework is hardly recognizable, not to say applicable, from the standpoint of present (inherited) social reality. The social mediation in lyrical language is truly shielded. It is shielded by the trope itself, the trope which we have come to recognize as the lyric subject. Hence the legitimacy of the phrase "with no remaining trace of mere matter."

Given this line of argument, the essay raises a crucial theoretical problem which, I dare say, leads us beyond the question of language. What should be visible so far is that the language of the lyric mediates the peculiar relation between poetry and society. But insofar as this relation takes place in the realm of language—as opposed, let us say, to the realm of dramatic action—the weight falls on the voice and specifically the voice of the subject who commands the linguistic action, the lyric "I." No doubt, this has been the most contested category in the enormous discussion on the nature of lyric poetry as a genre. Adorno chooses an interesting, peculiar, way to configure this category: what he calls "unself-consciousness." Even without knowing of Adorno's obsessions and prejudices, a close reading of the remainder of the essay makes evident that his philosophical critique is directed simultaneously against both Kant and Heidegger, against both the transcendental subject and the notion of language as the 'voice' of Being. The latter is articulated fully:

> The moment of unself-consciousness in which the subject submerges itself in language is not a sacrifice of the subject to Being. It is a moment not of violence [*Gewalt*], nor of violence against the subject, but reconciliation [*Versöhnung*]: language itself speaks only when it speaks not as something alien to the subject but as the subject's own voice. When the "I" becomes oblivious to itself in language it is fully present nonetheless; if it were not, language would become a consecrated abracadabra and succumb to reification, as it does in communicative discourse. (44)

The last sentence just raises the stakes. To outwit the magic of language acting on its own (a language that shields itself as mediating force), Adorno posits a subject that sheds the cornerstone of its subjectivity—its consciousness. But, keeping in mind the unmitigated, irreversible, nature of language as mediation, he claims that the "unself-conscious" subject passes into language as subjectivity intact.[4] Herein lies the crux of the dialectical nature of materiality that Adorno seeks to theorize not just in this essay but in most of his work, a materiality that alters the terms of perceiving matter. The otherwise imperceptible—otherwise than in language – trace of the lyric subject in the poem is what overturns the magic—the "consecrated abracadabra"—of conventional linguistic practice, which assumes an unproblematic, non-antagonistic, relation between poetry and society, between individual and collective, between subject and object: namely, "communicative discourse."

The stakes are both philosophical and social, as I mentioned at the outset. From Adorno's point of view, it couldn't be otherwise: "The lyric is the aesthetic test of [the] dialectical proposition" that "subject and object are not rigid and isolated poles but can be defined only in the process in which they distinguish themselves from each other and change [*abarbeiten und verändern*]" (44). To which we must juxtapose a direct and unambiguous phrase: "My thesis is that the lyric work is always the subjective expression of social antagonism" (45). It would be impossible to grasp the impetus of this line of argument and guaranteed to miss its meaning, if we read it under the conventional frame that proposes an uncompromised distinction between individual and society. Adorno's negative dialectical mind rejects not merely the Kantian subject/object divide but also discredits any sort of either liberal privilege of individualism or Marxist privilege of society. For him "the individual is inherently socially mediated [*der Einzelne in sich gesellschaftlich vermittelt*]" and at the same time "society is formed and continues to live only by virtue of the individuals whose quintessence [*Inbegriff*] it is" (44). Notice the emphasis on *inherently* and *quintessentially.* It isn't enough simply to say that society and the individual are dialectically related under the assumption that each term is intact in some domain of its own. To say that they are dialectically related is to say that each bears within itself, inherently, quintessentially, the antagonistic relation to the other. This is the very least of Hegel's lesson. Dialectics is always an internal, not external, dynamic.

This way we can outmaneuver the trap of positing the lyric subject as some sort of representative of society, even if unconscious or unacknowledging of this representation. Dialectics—at least the negative dialectics I have in mind—dispenses with the question of representation, and this is not meant to be some grand statement. If we understand in what sense the lyric subject embodies, in its disembodied voice, its antagonistic relation with society, then we see how "the lyric work is always the subjective expression of social antagonism," to reiterate the quotation from above. Adorno says that the lyric work is in this sense a socially produced *privilege* of a certain kind of alienation, hardly universalizable: the privilege of immersing oneself in one's alienated subjectivity and expressing it in poetic form, which is itself a specific social language. At the same time, however, he reminds us that even when this privilege is not produced, the right to express it, even if in failure, is not only present in society at large but imperative:

> The others, those who not only stand alienated, as though they were objects, facing the disconcerted poetic subject but who have also literally been degraded to objects of history, have the same right, or a greater right, to grope for the sounds in which sufferings and dreams are welded. This inalienable right [*unveräusserliche Recht*] has asserted itself again and again, in forms however impure, mutilated, fragmentary and intermittent—the only forms possible for those who have to bear the burden . . . A collective undercurrent provides the foundation for all individual lyric poetry (45).

[. . .]

I take Adorno's essay as a point of departure for an investigation of the lyric as a political gesture, in which the political element will not be sought in the aesthetic content or even in the lyric form, strictly speaking, but in the undercurrent that produces a specific mode of expression. The case study, as it were, that concretizes this investigation is a song cycle with the evocative title *Hollywooder Liederbuch*, signed by the composer Hanns Eisler. The songbook is altogether comprised of fifty songs, sometimes exceedingly brief, mostly based on poems by Brecht, some from his exile years in Denmark, some (such as the *Hollywood Elegies*) written specifically for the occasion, but it also includes musical settings on words by Goethe, Eichendorff, Pascal, Rimbaud, Mörike, Eisler himself, and fellow exile Berthold Viertel, as well as Eisler's own redraftings of the Anacreon fragments and his montage fragmentations of six Hölderlin poems. This work was never produced or performed during the composer's lifetime, nor can I say with any certainty that it has ever been performed in its entirety, though parts of it have been performed in a multitude of contexts and occasions. Recordings of it that now exist don't seem to agree on a particular sequence of songs, but seem at least to keep to the composer's conceptualized bare arrangement for baritone and piano accompaniment—though Eisler himself years later recorded certain of these songs for soprano.[5] We have a sense of the time frame of composition via the notes that Bertolt Brecht kept in his *Arbeitsjournal*. By this account it seems that the cycle was completed within a year (1942–1943). But Eisler's account of it remains more open ended. In this respect, we cannot fix with any certainty the time frame of composition. One thing, however, we know for sure: the place of composition which the work carries in its title. The song cycle was composed in Los Angeles during the composer's exile in the United States, which altogether lasted ten years (1938–1948). Of course, there is a reason why the specific locus in the title is Hollywood, while the composer lived and worked in a beach house in Malibu—and I don't mean to say simply that it is a matter of metonymy. The topos of exile is Hollywood, for this the domain of assimilation of skills and labor, as well as the definitive ground of cultural clash. It is indeed a remarkable sociological phenomenon that the German emigré community in Los Angeles at that time was almost entirely occupied within and around the Hollywood industry, whether in brilliant success or utter and repeated failure.[6]

The *Hollywood Songbook* inherits, and in a certain formal sense reproduces, the remarkable artistic experimentation of the previous collaboration, but it is actualized, by comparison, in utter vacuum. The kind of urgency belied by the work in pre-Nazi Berlin is now internalized. Essentially, this work is constructed without an audience, without a social underpinning. In the mind of the artists it is indeed constructed in a world that lacks any sort of tangible historical existence, a world that is itself an artistic construction: "Hollywood itself looks like a piece of film scenery that has not yet been dismantled," says Eisler in one of his earliest recollections from his first visit to America.[7] It is thus a kind of direct product that is also an antidote, a *pharmakon*. This lyrical response to exile, in other words, puts forth the argument that the lyric is not some sort of exilic genre in an abstract sense, but precisely the concrete response, the political and aesthetic response, to the altogether real exile experience in a particular historical moment. It is thus as well a sort of documentary work, not a work of description but a work of notation, a musical notebook of a personal political predicament, the dire predicament of political praxis in the absence of political constituency.

We must appreciate the enormous difficulty of this task, of facing this predicament and indeed facing it creatively. It is entirely against the grain and was very much conceived to be against the grain. I quote Eisler's well known remark:

> In this gloomy eternal spring here in Hollywood I said to Brecht: this is the perfect place for writing elegies! I said: We've got to create something, even here; you can't be in Hollywood and just do nothing. We are not absolved in Hollywood. We must simply go along with describing it . . . The landscape here is appallingly idyllic, and the ocean climate makes it dreadfully hard to concentrate . . . The whole thing has arisen more from the ideas of land speculators. If the water was shut off for three days, the jackals would be back and so would the desert sands . . . Hence, in this strange whitewashed idyll it becomes important to learn to express oneself concisely by way of an antidote.[8]

Brecht's response, at least initially, was much more negative and sardonic, clearly suggesting a sense of incapacity. "In almost no other place was my life more difficult than here in this mortuary of easy going," he writes at one point in his *Arbeitsjournal*; or "I get the impression of having been removed from my era. This is Tahiti in metropolitan form. I'm here as if in Tahiti, among palm trees and artists. It makes me nervous."[9] At other times, he seems to respond with what nowadays we would call a sort of Woody Allen mentality: "I live in a metropolitan area where people are born as drivers [and] the breed called pedestrians has either died out or been killed off."[10] Or, "nearly all of the town's inhabitants possess a certain remoteness. Their houses do not become personal property by being lived in, but only by checkbooks; their owners do not so much live in them as make use of them. Here houses are mere appendages to garages."[11]

But there is another side to this condition, a sense that displacement provides an opportunity to see matters in an altered state, indeed as well, to alter the terms of perception even though unable to alter the conditions: "Emigration is the best school of dialectics. Refugees are the keenest dialecticians. They are refugees as a result of changes and their sole object of study is change. They are able to deduce the greatest events from the smallest hints—that is, if they have intelligence. When their opponents are winning, they calculate how much their victory has cost them; they have the sharpest eye for contradictions."[12] This meaning of dialectical contradiction is all over the pieces that comprise the *Hollywood Songbook*, deeply imbedded in both the musical and literary language. By strict musicological convention, the *Hollywood Songbook* is not a proper song cycle. It lacks any sort of unfolding narrative, it repeats no musical motifs, and is altogether heterogeneous in musical style. The reigning characteristic overall is a kind of Expressionist density of Schönbergian spirit, though more atonal than strictly serialist, but even so this is due more to an attitude than strict adherence to Schönbergian principles. Strewn all over, one also finds little chansons, certain jazz melodies, straight and simple songs, certain chordal patterns one recognizes from militant songs, even elements one hears elsewhere in Eisler's film music. (Eisler continuously circulated musical motives between film scores and other pieces of music precisely in the spirit of "applied music.")

All this is permeated by a sharp sense of vitality, of urgency that goes straight up against the idyllic sense of leisure and distraction. This vitality is deeply idiomatic, indeed internal, and is achieved by forging a distance from the conditions of its production, a strange gesture that lends to the work a certain remoteness. Brecht recognized the inevitability of retreating into an internal orbit: "To work lyrically here, even if relating to the present . . . is as if working in gold filigree. There's something whimsical, eccentric, blinkered about it."[13] What makes this heterogeneous composition cohesive is precisely this characteristic remoteness. Lyricism is fashioned here at the bare limit, stripping the requisite sentimentalism one associates conventionally with lyrical expression. This stripping happens at the core musical level. Most of the settings are a page long. Many of them proceed along the lines of a continuously unraveling melodic line, no motifs, no variation, peculiar and unconventional repetitions. They require a singer who forges a sense of alienation from sentimental expression, who is in a peculiar sense another instrument that then proceeds through the musical text nimbly and forcefully. The overall attitude is to subvert the Romantic pathos of the *Lieder* tradition, to dismantle any tendencies toward self-satisfaction in one's despair, while keeping intact (and indeed up front) all the foundational elements of despair, alienation, deprivation. The result is a dislocating experience of listening, a "transgressive listening" as I mentioned at the outset, because though the lyrical sensibility is unmistakable, including indeed a certain textual and musical atmosphere that makes for a recognizable lyrical tonality, the final sense one gets is one of puzzlement, even astonishment.

[. . .]

Though marred by the impossibility of the aural dimension in writing, I nonetheless append here some brief comments on a few songs from the *Hollywood Songbook* that are, to my mind, exemplary of the musical and lyrical innovation of the song cycle.

ÜBER DEN SELBSTMORD

In diesem Landen und in dieser Zeit
dürfte es trübe Abende nichte geben,
auch hohe Brücken óber die Flósse
Selbst die Stunden zwischen Nacht und Morgen
und die ganze Winterzeit dazu.
Das ist gefährlich!
Denn angesichts dieses Elends
werfen die Menschen in einem Augenblick
ihr unerträgliches Leben fort.

[On Suicide[14]
In such a country and at such a time
There should be no melancholy evenings
Even high bridges over the rivers
And the hours between the night and morning
And the long long winter time as well
All these are dangerous!
For in view of all the misery
People just throw, in a few seconds time,
Their unbearable lives away.

This is a poem that Brecht wrote around 1938, while still in Denmark. One also finds it in *The Good Person of Szechwan*, which he began around that time and completed while in Los Angeles, though it was not performed until his return to Germany. The song is included in the Third Scene in the play, titled "Evening in a Public Park" where Shen Te, having withdrawn from her disguise as Shui Ta encounters the young pilot under a tree contemplating suicide. Shen Te sings this song to the audience in a classic Brechtian gesture of stepping out of the role. But this is literally what the song demands: stepping out of one's existence in the present moment—an existence which is dangerous—in order to avert self-destruction. The dangerous elements, of course, are natural elements; in the play, too, the scene takes place under torrential rain. But what makes this nature, this dreary nature, dangerous is announced in the first verse: a certain time, a certain place in history. In this respect, the text, insofar as it is a lyric, is decidedly anti-Romantic—a warning about perilous sentiment. Nonetheless, it hardly compromises the intense subjectivity of the lyric voice, particularly in this musical setting, which has a strange (even if melancholy, and perhaps even dreary) beauty.

The core melody is written on top of a modal pulse that gradually and very subtly ascends without any sort of resolution. The central verse in the poem, which is meant to be declamatory ("Das ist gefährlich!"), is actually pronounced slowly, quietly, almost whispered. This whispered declaration of danger almost achieves the status of musical motif—the only such moment in the song. It is repeated once as an instrumental phrase right after the verse and then again at the very end as the last musical phrase. Eisler's sense of staging against the grain is perfectly illustrated here. The musical phrasing exemplifies the fact that the verse announcing danger splits the text in the middle, as the warning that occurs between the setting of the destructive landscape and the description of its effect. But it does so in a negative gesture. Having vocally de-emphasized the core line while keeping its limit position, the song emphasizes instead the very last word ("fort"), which signifies the discarding of life, the actual moment of annihilation, the end. The reiteration of the instrumental motif of the middle line—the reminder of danger—which is reinvoked as a closing phrase actually works against the climactic closure of the act of destruction: an amazing gesture of repetition and suspension at the same time.

Given the haunting melody and weight of this song, I must quote a comment by Eisler on the consoling function of music:

> Concerning consolation, I can tell you something from the secret documents of the Austro-Hungarian state police in the year 1805 in Vienna, which says: "In times like the present, where manifold sufferings affect the character of the people, the police must pay more regard than ever to the distractions of the people. The most dangerous hours are in the evening. How can these hours be better and more harmlessly spent than by listening to music?"[15]

The resemblance of this scene to the one in the poem is too uncanny for me not to invoke it. Eisler, of course, is writing against the idea of music as consolation—insofar as consolation here, if not music listening itself, has become the work of the state police. Yet, the melancholy music and even the fact that Brecht stages it later as a song in a theatrical scene of consolation reproduces in this affinity a direct contradiction. Yet again, the major operative principle in this collaborative project—the essence of what we may name "Brecht/Eisler style"—is a continuous dialectical process of negation.

It has to be said that, though the text was written in Denmark before in fact the war began, its being set to music in Hollywood in 1942 cannot but resonate with the experience of loss in the interim period. I am thinking specifically about the suicide of Walter Benjamin, Brecht's dear friend, just before he is to cross the border that will bring him to American exile. The effect of Benjamin's death on Brecht (and also Adorno) was decisive. In response, Brecht wrote two brilliantly dispassionate poems about the news of his friend's suicide. Their anti-lyrical manner is actually a profoundly 'emotive' tribute to the poetic subject, and I would consider the inclusion of this lyric in the *Hollywood Songbook* as Brecht's third gesture toward Benjamin.

OSTERSONNTAG

Heute, Ostersonntag früh
Ging ein plötzlicher Schneesturm über die Insel
Zwischen den grünenden Hecken lag Schnee.
Mein junger Sohn
Holte mich zu einem Aprikosenbäumschen an der Hausmauer
Weg von einer Schrift, wo ich auf jene
mit dem Finger deute
Welche einem Krieg vorbereiten, der
Den Kontinent, diese Insel, mein Volk, meine
Familie und mich
Vertilgen muss. Schweigend
Legten wie einem Sack
über den frierenden Baum.

[*Easter Sunday*[16]
Early on an Easter Day
An impetuous snowstorm
Swept through the island
Among the budding hedges lay snow.
My little son asked me out
To see the little cherry tree
By the house wall of my writing desk
Where I was writing verses
Directed at the men who
Were preparing a war
That would destroy this island
And my people
And this continent of Europe
And my family
And me.
Silently we placed a sack
Around the freezing tree.]

This song may be seen as the reverse of "On Suicide" in the sense that here nature needs human protection because history is about to destroy it. Brecht was ambivalent toward nature to say the least. But here nature, having become interwoven with society, serves as an antidote gesture against a 'denaturalized' society of utter destruction. At the same time, nature registers the distraction of the poet from his task, which signifies, however, in a kind of dialectical in-folding, also a moment of rejuvenation. The task, of course, is explicitly the writing of political poetry. In a doubling gesture of the kind that Brecht was so fond of, the poet interrupts his political writing in order to write a lyric, which consists of a self-reflection upon an action whose 'natural' humanity signifies an act of resistance. It is precisely in this doubling gesture—exemplary of Adorno's demands for the lyric form—that a pure lyric achieves an explicitly social, and indeed in this case political, significance. The event of the lyric poem's emergence out of the interruption of political writing is actualized in the poem itself. By a sort of dialectical reversal, whereby writing and the interruption of writing are paradoxically interwoven, the lyric incorporates the political, or to put it in more elaborative form, lyric and political writing are brought together in a continuum forged by an unavoidably *interruptive* relation between writing and acting in the world.

Musically, the song exhibits a particular idiom in terms of accents and patterns of composition that is not unlike "On Suicide." The first three verses, describing the state of nature, open with a rather tender musical motif that references the recognizable style of a Romantic *Lied*. The piano repeats solo the last three-part melody of the description of the snow before the poem shifts into the personal narrative. This melody serves as a kind of signature phrase and returns at the very end when the state of nature is reconstituted by a human act of protection against destruction. In between, from the verse "Mein junger Sohn" onward, the music is constructed along an ascending pattern of arguably 'unlyrical' nature, speaking in traditional *Lieder* terms. This ascent concludes in a staccato delivery of the objects of destruction, in the series ending with the poet himself ("und mich"), before the melodious beginning is reiterated, slightly altered and slowed down, for the last three verses of reconstitution. The effect is bizarre to say the least. Though we are left with the sense that this is a beautiful song of highly evocative lyric sensibility, we have undergone for a few seconds, right in the song's mid-section, an experience of militant singing—a militancy that emerges precisely from introducing the lyric "I" and the entire context of its social existence as the ultimate object of destruction. In this sense, the incorporation of the political into the lyric, which we just saw in Brecht's verses, is enacted with extraordinary precision in Eisler's musical interpretation. "Ostersonntag" is an exemplary instance of the core wager posed by the *Hollywood Songbook* as a whole.

FROM *THE HOLLYWOOD ELEGIES*

Unter den grünen Pfefferbäumen
Gehen die Musiker auf den Strich, zwei und zwei
Mit den Schreibern. Bach
Hat ein Strichquartett im Täschen. Dante schwenkt
Den dürren Hintern.

[Beneath the green pepper trees
The musicians act like streetwalkers, two by two
With the writers. Bach
Has a 'street' quartet in his pocket. Dante wiggles
His shriveled bottom.][17]

Jeden Morgen, mein Brot zu verdienen
Fahre ich zum Markt, wo Lügen gekauft werden.
Hoffnungsvoll
Reihe ich mich ein unter die Verkäufer.

[Every morning, to earn my daily bread
I go to the market where lies are bought.
Hopefully
I take my place among the sellers.]

Das Dorf Hollywood ist entworfen nach den Vorstellungen
Die man hierorts vom Himmel hat. Hierorts
Hat man ausgerechnet, dass Gott
Himmel und Hölle benötigend, nicht zwei
Etablissements zu entwerfen brauchte, sondern
Nur ein einziges, nämlich den Himmel. Dieser
Dient fór die Unbemittelten, Erfolglosen
Als Hölle.

[The village of Hollywood was planned according to the notion
People in these parts have of heaven. In these parts
They have come to the conclusion that God
Requiring Heaven and Hell, didn't need to
Plan two establishments but
Just one: Heaven. It
Serves the unprosperous, unsuccessful
As Hell.]

Brecht wrote the "Hollywood Elegies" at Eisler's express request for a collaborative gesture of self-reflection on their conditions of life in exile. They are the cornerstone of the *Hollywood Songbook*, if such a thing may be said—the initial gesture that gave retrospective meaning to various other poems brought into the song cycle, which were written earlier while Brecht was in Denmark, or verses written by other poets and included later by Eisler. We must consider the "Hollywood Elegies" as quintessential musical and poetic acts of self-reflection that distinctively mark the exile sensibility. The subject of the poems may be Hollywood but it is clearly also the poet himself—and the composer, of course, as we are talking about songs (Bach and Dante strolling arm in arm)—whose alienation is chronicled by registering, with the sort of precision that only metaphor can produce, the place of their displacement: "I take my place among the sellers." This verse is one of Brecht's classic shrewd self-ironies. The recognition that, in this world, lies are the order of the day comes with an understanding that, under such conditions, truth cannot overcome them. In this order of things, when purity is impossible, one must fight to find a place that ensures survival and readiness for the time of truth to come. For Brecht, the Hollywood experience—and one may add, his entire life experience since the rise of Nazism, including his years in East Berlin—was a daily exercise in precisely this sort of survival, which is, as Derrida has famously described, an overcoming (*sur-vie*).

The "Hollywood Elegies" are, of course, hardly elegiac in a proper sense. Or rather, the object of elegy here is the basest of elements. Hollywood is "a swamp," as another classic song in the cycle puts it. They are profoundly ironic elegies, which may in fact constitute a genre all its own. In this swamp, the mode of life is prostitution and the currency is the peddling of falsity. False pretensions, false works: art as commerce. The first of the three elegies quoted here is a classically self-mocking staging of prostitution. Bach and Dante (standing in obviously for Eisler and Brecht but also the intertwined work of music and poetry in exile) literally "walk the line" (*gehen auf den Strich*) to peddle their goods. Brecht bolsters the song's mockery by forging a hard pun—turning *Streichquartett* to the neologism *Strichquartett* which in this context also suggests a kind of composition quickly put together and stuffed in one's back pocket, a composition literally drafted on the line of work. For Brecht, in this land of deception where lies are bought and sold, the integrity of names is blown asunder. Meanings are mangled and manipulated to serve the established order. This is in essence the significance of the marvelous verses of the third of the elegies, which exploits the cliché of Hollywood as paradise on earth. With inimitable irony, Brecht agrees and takes the notion to its full conclusion, plunging the metaphysical concept into the hard reality of capitalism, which is indeed a hellish reality for all those who don't enjoy its privileges.

Musically, these are some of Eisler's most Schönbergian settings in the whole cycle. The emphasis is on the barest texture of the *Lied* form, and though there is a strong melodic line, particularly in the third piece, the singer delivers it with an air of lyrical darkness that encapsulates the text's mood. In this elegy to the hellish nature of earthly paradise, the musical tone is positively funereal. Brecht was unequivocal as to his friend's talent for creating performative interpretations of texts: "His settings are for me what a performance is to a play; he reads the text with enormous exactitude."[18] We know Brecht well to understand that for him performance *is* interpretation, a critical reworking of the material. In the first of the three elegies, the musical phrasing acts as a performative/interpretive shadow to the scene described by the verses. The notes suggest a brisk and lithe walking, with chordal pairs that obviously evoke the tandem of writer and composer. But against the grain of the piano melody which is just hopping along, the singer performs the verses with a deliberate flatness, even coldness, removing from their articulation any humorous traces, even though the actual words are so blatantly mocking. The scene is pathetic but prostitution is a serious matter. Indeed, mockery is registered by the pianistic ending of the song, where the melody is speeded up absurdly—one can imagine the pair not merely 'streetwalking' but literally hopping around like badly wound up machines—before it is altogether abruptly interrupted without resolution. An air of grave seriousness envelops musically the second of the elegies as well. This song lasts about fifty seconds, half of which is a concluding twelve-tone instrumental line in its barest, most unchromatic, alienating expression. The air is of pure hopelessness. This brilliantly counters the single-word verse "Hopefully," which is almost shouted by the singer in utter desperation.

To conclude, by way of returning to Adorno, I would reiterate how the dislocation of the subject expressed in both literary and musical text brings forth an experience of transgressive listening. But I would add one more thing, which indeed hinges on the undercurrent of this desperately shouted "hopefully": the *Hollywood Songbook* is really a work written for the future. It is a meditation on the radical present—on the very conditions of its production, as I mentioned—and it is simultaneously a distorting self-reflection on the means of expression in the past (the German *Lied* tradition). But in the sense that it is consciously produced without an audience, without a community of listeners that would otherwise be its concern, it fashions this community in some future retrospective time: retrospective, because the song cycle is also a documentary gesture of a certain present (a wretched present hopefully to be overcome) and future, because its transgression against inherited modes (art forms, means of expression, listening habits, alienation from one's environment, etc.) opens the way to an altered community, an as yet imaginary community nurtured from within the experience of exile to be constituted as its overcoming.

NOTES

1. A longer version of this article was published in *Qui Parle* 14.2 (2004): 145–76.

2. Theodor W. Adorno, "Lyric Poetry and Society" in *Notes on Literature* Vol. I (New York: Columbia University Press, 1990), 38. For the German original see "Rede über Lyrik und Gesellschaft" in *Noten zur Literatur* I (Frankfurt am Main: Suhrkamp Verlag, 1958), 73–104. Subsequent page references in the text. Translation modified where necessary.

3. The point isn't to say that great works of art unmask ideological falsity, as if by rule, but that art which unmasks ideological falsity, whatever its form or instance, is worth the qualification "great." This qualification is inevitably first a matter of politics and then of aesthetics. Moreover, I would tend to take for granted that the second statement assumes that the notion of "unmasking ideological falsity" is consistently under question by the art practice itself, while the first statement may be itself an ideological falsity, if nothing else because it disregards the mutability of histories and ideologies.

4. One may consider that this intactness of subjectivity is achieved by virtue of submission to language. This is one aspect of the argument in Judith Butler's *The Psychic Life of Power*, but the matter is the concern of another essay.

5. The crucial recording is Hanns Eisler, *Hollywooder Liederbuch* with baritone Wolfgang Holzmair and Peter Stamm at the piano (KOCH International CD, 1996). A much looser and not quite precise anthology is the collection performed by the inimitable Dietrich Fischer-Dieskau with Aribert Reimann at the piano in the CD Hanns Eisler, *Lieder* (Warner Classics, 1988). These recordings follow the original arrangements. Versions of some of these songs for soprano were recorded under the direction of Eisler himself during his years in East Berlin by the great theater singers Irmgard Arnold and Gisela May. But to my mind, the consummate interpretations of Eisler's songs generally belong to Dagmar Krause in two recordings: *Tank Battles. The Songs of Hanns Eisler* (Island, 1988) and *Supply and Demand* (Hannibal, 1986), which also includes certain settings of Brecht poems by Kurt Weill.

6. "By one count in 1944 there were fifty-nine refugee German screen writers in Hollywood, thirty-three directors, twenty-three producers, ten actors, and nineteen composers working in the film industry." In James K. Lyon, *Bertolt Brecht in America* (Princeton University Press, 1982), 46.

7. Hanns Eisler, "A Musical Journey through America" [1935] in *A Rebel in Music*, 90.

8. Hans Bunge, *Frage Sie mehr über Brecht, Hanns Eisler im Gespräch* (Munich: Rogner & Bernhard, 1970), 293

9. Quoted in Lyon, *Bertolt Brecht in America*, 33.

10. Ibid., 45

11. Quoted in Betz, *Hanns Eisler. Political Musician*, 189.

12. Bertolt Brecht, *Fluchtlingsgespräche* (Frankfurt am Main: Suhrkamp, 1961), 112.

13. Quoted in Betz, *Hanns Eisler. Political Musician*, 185–186.

14. The translation is by Eric Bentley, the one consistently used in English language performances of this song. Eric Bentley himself recorded this song and some of the ones I mention below in a classic recording of solo performance, singing and playing the piano or the harmonium: *The Songs of Hanns Eisler* (Folkways, 1966). But the most extraordinary performance of "On Suicide" remains the one by the great experimental group Art Bears, with Dagmar Krause singing, from their recording *Hopes and Fears* (RE Records, 1978). In their short and highly innovative trajectory the Art Bears exemplify a contemporary Brecht/Eisler response to the song as a form in an extremely sophisticated experimental rock music context.

15. Hanns Eisler, "On Stupidity in Music" [1958] in *A Rebel in Music*, 193.

16. The translation is by Eric Bentley from his recording of *The Songs of Hanns Eisler*. A certain 'inaccuracy' is enacted here in order to serve the demands of the melody.

17. This translation is altered to catch more precisely Brecht's pun. The original translations are by John Willet from Bertolt Brecht, *Collected Poems* (London: Methuen, 1983) 380–382.

18. Quoted in Hans-Werner Heister, "Hollywood and Home: Hanns Eisler's 'Hölderlin-Fragmente' for Voice and Piano" in David Blake, *Hanns Eisler: A Miscellany*, 214.

SECTION 7

Phenomenologies of Lyric Reading

As we have seen, modern lyric theory did not spring from one source or follow one path. The capacious modern idea of the lyric that emerged near the end of the eighteenth century and developed in fits and starts over the course of the nineteenth century has shifted in many directions over the last century. Phenomenology (philosophically, the study of consciousness as experienced from the first-person point of view) offers one way of turning those different directions toward a single lyrical current of thought. The phenomenological approach to lyric initiated by Heidegger in the middle of the twentieth century in many ways dovetails with the Frankfurt School approaches also initiated in Germany before and after 1945; whereas for Frankfurt School thinkers the lyric became an instance of potential reconciliation between aesthetic expression and the modern social conditions that threaten it, for phenomenological thinkers the lyric has become a privileged instance of convergence between the aesthetic and the social, and between perception and cognition. By focusing on the experience of the poem—or by defining poetry *as* experience, and by thinking about experience as poetry—phenomenology identifies poetry with thought and, ultimately, with the conditions of our existence. In phenomenological modernity, poems are us.

Susan Stewart, a prominent contemporary phenomenological lyric theorist we were unable to include here, goes so far as to suggest that by the beginning of the twenty-first century, "the cultural, or form-giving, work of poetry is to counter the oblivion of darkness."[1] For Stewart, that darkness is not the consequence of industrial capitalism or of the Holocaust or of the postmodern simulacrum but proof that consciousness itself depends on poetry: "The entire enduring accomplishment of the history of poetic forms awaits as a vast repertoire for anyone who hopes to enter again into an engagement with the senses," Stewart writes, since "it is that history that has shaped our notion of the first person, and it is that history that will make us intelligible to those who will inhabit the future. . . . Perhaps I am writing at the end of a world" (333). Stewart takes the modern phenomenological embrace of the lyric to its extreme when she writes that beyond the circle of light thrown by lyric poetry, our very being is in danger of extinction, since engagement with the senses can never be taken for granted, is always in danger of remaining in the background rather than becoming sensible foreground. "As first-person expression in measured language, lyric poetry lends significant—that is, shared and memorable—form to the inner consciousness that is time itself" (42), and that form guarantees consciousness an extended lifetime it might not otherwise have. *Why* the survival of both consciousness and sense-certainty is in question remains mysterious in Stewart; in *A Poet's Freedom: A Notebook on Making* (2011), she warns that "in our own time we are faced with an emergency regarding the future of the earth" and suggests that "the freedom to act and the freedom to judge that art can provide, might help us to become, inversely, a resource for that nature we have heretofore depleted" (205). Deprived of the world-making form the lyric lends to consciousness, our lights might go out, but granted the archive of lyric poetry as evidence that those lights once burned, our existence is reaffirmed across space and time—and that reaffirmation might even teach nature a thing or two about how not to be extinguished. Stewart's radical claims for the power of lyric make the stakes of phenomenological lyricism crystal clear: the experience of the poem is not only a way of thinking but a way of being, perhaps even the measure or definition of existence. Perhaps our last best chance.

For Martin Heidegger, the philosopher who in many ways originated the line of thought Stewart has pushed toward its limits, existence may seem threatened in modernity in the most basic sense. In ". . . Poetically man dwells . . . ," the essay we include in this section, Heidegger meditates on a phrase from the German Romantic poet Friedrich Hölderlin:

> ". . . poetically man dwells . . ." If need be, we can imagine that poets do on occasion dwell poetically. But how is "man"—and this means every man and all the time—supposed to dwell poetically? Does not all dwelling remain incompatible with the poetic? Our dwelling is harassed by the housing shortage. Even if that were not so, our dwelling today is harassed by work, made insecure by the hunt for gain and success, bewitched by the entertainment and recreation industry.

Clearly Heidegger saw how social conditions after 1945 might make the notion of poetic existence—of poetry as a place to be—both urgent and apparently impossible. Heidegger's focus on a phrase from an early German Romantic poet throws both that urgency and that impossibility into relief and also serves to lyricize the notion of poetry as a thing in itself that is not subject to such conditions. As a poet who influenced both Goethe and Hegel, Hölderlin became a key figure in the shift in ideas of lyric from minor song to a fundamental component of a literary system, and his revision of classical hymns marked a starting point for modern lyric reading. When Heidegger juxtaposes Hölderlin's notion of poetic dwelling with the constraints of twentieth-century modernity, then, he claims a genealogy of the modern lyric, or of modern lyric reading, that allows an idea of the lyric to stand for an idea of poetry, and allows that idea of poetry to stand for what late modernity needs to recover. By thinking through Hölderlin's single phrase "poetically man dwells," Heidegger works his way toward a definition of poetry that seems at first glance anti-romantic, since it resists the idea that "poetic dwelling flies fantastically above reality." Heidegger counters the idea that the poem is an imaginative departure with the idea he credits to Hölderlin that "the poetic is the basic capacity for human dwelling." In this sense, the poem becomes not an escape from but the creation of a world, a world-making phenomenon. We then become creatures of the world of the poem.

Yet to paraphrase Heidegger in this way is not quite right, since to say that the poem is a world we inhabit still casts the poem as an imaginary creation we visit rather than as the condition of our existence. "Dwelling can be unpoetic only because it is in essence poetic," Heidegger writes. "For a man to be blind, he must remain a being by nature endowed with sight." Because poetry is not only part of the world but world-making, the basic capacity for human dwelling it affords is not an escape or a luxury or even a way to address the otherwise alienating social conditions of modernity (for example, the post-war housing shortage or the distractions of mass culture). For Heidegger, poetry "builds up the very nature of dwelling": we only know what it is to dwell because poetry makes phenomenological experience (as opposed to subjective perspective) available to us—which is to say that Being, what we understand as what or who or how we are, only becomes available in and through poetry. In other essays (for example, "The Origin of the Work of Art"), Heidegger distinguishes between what he calls a "world" as a set of significant relations in which we exist and in which meaning is disclosed and the concept of "earth," which is the background against which such worlding happens. Recent post-Heideggerian thought has emphasized the difference between being and presence, between the world within and beyond the subject (ideas associated with the new object oriented ontology and speculative realism), and that thinking has begun to have an influence on contemporary poetics. But for most of the second half of the twentieth century, Anglo-American lyric theorists took up phenomenology as a new license for the possibilities of thinking within and as lyric poetry.

In the essay in this section, Heidegger limits his description of the poem as a set of significant relations in which we exist, as a form of worlding, to an analysis of Hölderlin's language, since "we hear Hölderlin's words more clearly when we take them back to the poem in which they belong." For Heidegger, "the more poetic a poet is . . . the greater is the purity with which he submits what he says to an ever more painstaking listening, and the further what he says is from the mere propositional statement." This insistence on close reading and resistance to paraphrase aligns Heidegger with the New Critics, making it possible (as we shall see) for later Anglo-American critics to adapt Heidegger's radical version of the poem-as-world to Practical and New Critical reading practices that began with very different premises. When Heidegger writes that "when we follow in thought Hölderlin's poetic statement about the poetic dwelling of man, we divine a path by which, through what is thought differently, we come nearer to thinking the same as what the poet composes in his poem," he may seem to propose an identification between reading and writing, between the moment of reception and the moment of composition, that mirrors claims like Helen Vendler's that the lyric offers us "a mind we take on as our own." Heidegger's version of the lyric as world-making is in fact very different from post–New Critical treatments of the lyric as a world in itself, but in Anglo-American criticism, phenomenology has often been assimilated into other forms of lyric reading.

The problem with such assimilation is apparent in the essay we include here by Lacoue-Labarthe, in which the question "is lyric a 'subjective' genre?" gains historical urgency. Though one could say that this question has been around "at least since Schlegel and Hegel," in his reading of "Two Poems by Paul Celan," Lacoue-Labarthe poses it "to the post-Auschwitz era (in Adorno's sense)." Adorno's famous statement that "to write poetry after Auschwitz is barbaric" becomes in Lacoue-Labarthe's essay a starting point for thinking through what happens to Hölderlin's Romanticism and Heidegger's phenomenological commitment to it after the Holocaust, and also a way of placing Heidegger's phenomenology against the background of Frankfurt School Marxism.[2] Celan's poems become the occasion for that project in more than one sense: the poems explicitly invoke both Heidegger and Hölderlin; Adorno took them up as the definition of an historical rupture; Celan himself, as a German Jew, lived through and documented the end of "a world age—perhaps the world's old age" in his poems. The symptom of that end is "a cancer of the subject, both the ego's and the masses'," a disease that resulted from German idealism's exaltation of the subject. According to Lacoue-Labarthe, that post-1945 disease of the subject is what makes lyric poetry seem such a barbaric, such a distasteful pursuit by the second half of the twentieth century, since the lyric remained associated with the culture that drove the ideology of the single subject to such tragic ends. Celan wrote poems about those ends, about that distaste and subjective disease, and in doing so, Lacoue-Labarthe suggests, he revised Heidegger's version of poetic dwelling, since in Celan "if there is no such thing as 'poetic experience' it is simply because experience marks the absence of what is 'lived.'" That reversal would be Celan's explicitly post-Heideggerian phenomenological poetics, since "it would be an understatement to say Celan had read Heidegger. Celan's poetry goes beyond even an unreserved recognition of Heidegger; I think that one can assert, unreservedly, that it is, in its entirety, a dialogue with Heidegger's thought. And essentially with the part of this thought that was a dialogue with Hölderlin." As we have seen, one part of Heidegger's dialogue with Hölderlin was a way to think about poetry "as what builds up the very nature of dwelling" at a moment when the very nature of dwelling had been put into question, had become literally as well as figuratively untenable.

If for Heidegger an attentive reading of Hölderlin proves that poetry's worlding capacity cannot be constrained by social conditions, Lacoue-Labarthe's reading of Celan's attentive reading of both Heidegger and Hölderlin reverses such assurance. "The question of poetry's possibility—and Celan never asked another—is the question . . . of the possibility of *going out of the self*," according to Lacoue-Labarthe. If the idealized German subject—the very basis of post-eighteenth-century notions of the lyric—has been evacuated (in more than one sense) after Auschwitz, then what a persistent phenomenological reading might put in its place is an emptied-out experience, an experience that "marks the absence of what is 'lived,'" not subjective lyric *Erlebnis* but a sense of its impossibility. Yet even this sense of ruin or impossibility is still a *sense*, an experience that has lyric value. According to Lacoue-Labarthe, the "Two Poems by Paul Celan" that are the basis of his essay constitute a single pressing entreaty directed to Heidegger: "that the thinker who listened to poetry; the same thinker who compromised himself . . . with just what would result in Auschwitz [Heidegger was a member of the Nazi party and supported National Socialism from 1933 until 1945]; . . . that he say just a single word: a word about pain." What Lacoue-Labarthe reads Celan as asking, in other words, is what the critic himself asks. Lacoue-Labarthe wants phenomenological reading—a reading that would invest in the lyric poem's capacity to bring worlds into being, to make lyric poetry the basis of Being—to remain possible after the historical events that discredited Heidegger and the German idealist tradition from which the lyric sprang. Even by asking the question, of course, Lacoue-Labarthe sustains the phenomenological enterprise—though as Stewart might say, he does so at the end of a world, after the positive sensation of "pain" remains the single possibility for lived experience at the end of history.

Because of Heidegger's own historical position and because of the tradition of his thought, the question of the persistence of poetic worlding after the end of the world would seem inherent in all post-Heideggerian phenomenological approaches to the lyric. This is to say that the pathos that comes to define phenomenological approaches to the lyric—the sense that poetic worlding is only possible on the margins of impossible worlds—persists even when its historical markers are no longer invoked. In Allen Grossman's *Summa Lyrica* (1992), that persistence takes the form of a "Primer of the Commonplaces in Speculative Poetics." For Grossman, an Anglo-American academic critic and poet writing much later in the twentieth century, the notion of a primer, or elementary textbook that serves as introduction to a subject of study (and particularly to an alphabet, to the tools of reading) indicates the necessity to begin by "constructing a culture in which poetry is intelligible." The implication is that the culture in which poetry used to be intelligible has vanished, but Grossman is not concerned with the historical situation of poetry at the present time; instead, he uses his series of aphorisms or commonplaces or philosophical "scholia" as attempts to "identify the alliances and relationships of the specific terms and situations in poetic analysis . . . as far out toward the horizon as possible . . . and thus to circumscribe a horizon in which poetry rises up and is present *as in a world*." In this sense, the *Summa Lyrica* facilitates a Heideggerian reading by beginning where post-Heideggerian critics like Lacoue-Labarthe end: if one can no longer take for granted the proposition that poems build their own worlds, we can at least teach readers of poetry to think about poetry *as if* this is what poems can still do. That "as if" stands for a set of reading practices that date from the Practical and New Criticism (the orientation toward "poetic analysis"), though as we have seen, the critics associated with those schools of thought hardly agreed on what poems do. Instead, they agreed that teaching students to read poems closely could, as Grossman puts it, "circumscribe a horizon" of expectation for lyric experience available to all readers, and particularly to readers in the classrooms in which such practices of reading are taught. Grossman joins modern Anglo-American paradigms of close reading with a phenomenological version of the poem's own worlding potential to create a way of reading that tempers Heideggerian absolutism with practice, and that tempers institutional, academic literary practice with the Heideggerian yearning for absolutes.

Thus rather than agreeing with Lacoue-Labarthe that "the question of poetry's possibility" is the only question poets have left to ask, Grossman asserts (since the commonplaces are assertions or, better, propositions "with a horizon") that "the function of poetry is to obtain for everybody one kind of success at the limits of the autonomy of the will." There is something very American about Grossman's distribution of the lyric's worlding potential to anyone who reads (Grossman also writes on Whitman). At the same time, Grossman maintains Heidegger's commitment to a poetic dwelling that is not merely the property of the individual subject: "The abandonment of the autonomy of the will of the speaking person as a speaker constitutes a form of knowledge—poetic knowledge. The knowledge that not 'I' speaks but 'language speaks' (Heidegger). The function of this knowledge is to rescue the natural will at the point of its death." Here the midcentury threat of the end of a world or the end of history is replaced with the glimmering threat of the end of "the natural will." Grossman follows Heidegger here in thinking about the ontological claims of the poem as not the claims of individual agency but the claim of existence, of thought itself, of Being. Interestingly, for Grossman the abandonment of the idealist individual subject and of the agency or "will" associated with that subject takes the form of an embrace of a "poetic knowledge" identified with the fictional poetic speaker that was the creation of twentieth-century lyric reading (or of earlier forms of the poetry of the subject, if one follows the historical logic of the essays in Part One Section 2 of this anthology on "Models of Lyric"). One interesting result of Grossman's shift in critical registers is his transformation of the fictive, dramatic 'speaker' of the poem into a world in Heidegger's sense as well as a "*going out of the self*" in Lacoue-Labarthe's (or Celan's) sense. Thus for Grossman the fiction of the speaker itself becomes a set of world-making signifying relations that extend beyond the subject, so that poems come to construct not only their own ontological but their own social worlds.

Grossman's assimilation of a paradigm for lyric close reading to the concerns of phenomenological reading is seamless, and it is permitted by his explicit association of all poetry with a radical version of the lyric: "Lyric is the most continuously practiced of all poetic kinds. . . . Lyric is the genre of the 'other mind' as it has come to manifestation through the abandonment of autonomy and the displacement toward fiction. . . . As the kind which imitates man alone, lyric is the first and last poetic sort." For Grossman, perhaps even more purely than for Heidegger, lyric is a humanist enterprise—indeed, lyric is the guarantee of the human, the definition of the person, since "the speaking subject in the poem is always definable in social terms, that is to say, 'is always a person.'" In this new lyric humanism, what is at stake is not "poetry as what builds up the very nature of dwelling," in Heidegger's terms, but poetry as what makes personhood possible after the ideal of the single subject has eroded. This is an idea of lyric poetry as what constructs the very nature of the person, of poetic personhood as the ground of "ethical life," an idea that "does not take place in the philosophical purity of possible worlds, but in the relentless and inescapable unity of the one world as recovered perpetually." The person represented by this idea of the lyric is a person to whom one has a responsibility, a person in a world of social (so potentially ethical) relations. For Grossman as for the phenomenological thinkers about poetics that preceded him, lyric allows the recovery of that better (not ideal, but single and actual) world.

While Lacoue-Labarthe and Grossman take up the large ideas of poetic existence and poetic knowledge framed by Heidegger, the last two essays in this section think about where to locate that way of thinking within the structure of poems, since if one takes the idea of the poem as a world literally, poetic thinking or being (poetic dwelling) must find within the poem a local habitation and a name. In his reading of Hölderlin, Heidegger lingers over the notion of "measuring" and suggests that poems are not only measured, or metrical, language but that "in poetry there takes place what all measuring is in the ground of its being." The phenomenology of poetic experience depends upon a way of framing the dimensions of that experience, and for phenomenology the dimensions of experience become uniquely available in the poem. For Giorgio Agamben, one clear way to begin to gauge poetic experience is to take the measure of the poem at its defining moment, its end. Casting "The End of the Poem" as "a poetic institution that has until now remained unidentified," Agamben makes finitude into the literal definition of poetry, since "the verse is, in every case, a unit that finds its *principium individuationis* only at the end, that defines itself only at the point at which it ends." Beginning with Valéry's famous definition of poetry as "a prolonged hesitation between sound and sense," Agamben's focus on the end of the poem may at first seem structuralist (Jakobson also adopted Valéry's phrase in his essays on poetics). But while the structuralists used the paradigm of modern linguistics to understand that hesitation, Agamben uses paradigms borrowed from medieval authors, since he claims that the phenomenon of the end of the poem "has remained nameless among the moderns." Thus in Agamben's essay the abundant available structuralist vocabulary for the relation between the semiotic and the semantic, between sense and sound, gives way to a premodern vocabulary for poetry as "the possibility of enjambment," which Agamben defines as "the opposition of a metrical limit to a syntactical limit, of a prosodic pause to a semantic pause." Not incidentally, the poet laureate of enjambment and therefore of poetic definition turns out to be Dante, the maestro of the transition between classical and modern poetics, the historical authority (especially in Italian) on the nature of verse.

Although Agamben says that his short essay "is not the place . . . to conduct a phenomenology of the end of the poem," he points toward such a phenomenology in Dante's terms, since "Dante seems, at least implicitly, to pose the problem of the end of poetry." Under the sign of Dante, the question of the linear end of the poem—the poem's last line or final tercet—becomes a question of the end of poetry itself. Dante writes, "The endings of the last verses are the most beautiful if they fall into silence together with the rhymes" (*Pulcherrime tamen se habent ultimorum carminum desinentiae, si cum rithmo in silentium cadunt*). "What is this falling into silence of the poem?" Agamben asks, "What is the beauty that falls? And what is left of the poem after its ruin?" These attendant questions shift the register of formal structure into the register of last rites, a familiar shift in phenomenological lyric reading. According to Agamben, the shift is Dante's own, since "what Dante says about the most beautiful way to end a poem" is that "the last verses fall, rhymed, in silence." That silence becomes the place of phenomenological poetic dwelling, since according to Agamben, "it is as if the verse at the end of the poem, which was now to be irreparably ruined in sense, linked itself closely to its rhyme-fellow and, laced in this way, chose to dwell with it in silence." Thus Dante may have achieved what Heidegger imagined poetry as making possible, the sense of a world articulable only within and by way of the poem itself. Agamben ends not with Heidegger but with Wittgenstein, whom he cites to the effect that "philosophy should really only be poeticized," to which Agamben replies, "poetry should really only be philosophized." For Agamben as for other phenomenological readers, poetry is a way of thinking, and the end of the poem is a thought.

But what kind of thought? For Simon Jarvis, the question of poetic thinking is the question of what he calls "prosodic thinking," and in the essay with which we conclude this section, he is concerned with the kind of thinking rhyme is or does. While Agamben reached back to Dante to invoke a sense of rhymed endings that predated modern prejudices about rhyme as antithetical to serious poetic experience, Jarvis wants "to help open up a wound, a cauterized place, in the body of our [modern] poetic culture; to attempt to listen in to rhyme's thinking through and beneath the over-saturated symbolic roles it has usually been made to play in our cultures." Jarvis's essay on rhyme is part of his larger project on "the repertoire of prosodic gestures deployed by poets not through the idea of form but rather as a distinctive mode of knowing," a project that has its feet (so to speak) in phenomenological thinking about lyric poetry as a singular mode of consciousness but that branches out in many historical and theoretical directions. In "Why Rhyme Pleases," those directions circulate around the British eighteenth century, around an era just before rhyme was discredited as at best frivolous and at worst idolatrous and evil. Not incidentally, that place and time led toward what became known as the Romantic revolution in the lyric. Jarvis argues that the false divide between Romantic lyric and the "incantatory techniques" of pre-Romantic verse has eventuated in "a kind of historical falling-silent of rhyme." In order to redeem that historical silence, to think rhyme differently, Jarvis attempts to reverse the persistent modern association of musical rhyming with automatism and to put in its place "a kind of thinking in tunes."

One could think of thinking in tunes as a riff on Heidegger's poetic worlding, measuring, and dwelling, and that riff is partially a tribute to Adorno's *Aesthetic Theory*. As we have seen, the phenomenological approach to the lyric almost always winds its way through Frankfurt School thought as post-1945 complement or counterpoint, and for Jarvis, Adorno's "argument that technique is the way art thinks" allows him to move away from the post-Romantic idea that rhyme is "simply a screen or a cocoon or an anaesthetic" toward an idea of virtuoso rhyming technique as "a medium for thinking, and for thinking about historical experience, just when in the very act of apparently retreating from it." In veering away from a pure phenomenological investment in poetic experience that attempts to free itself of its historical constraints toward a sense of prosodic thinking as consciousness that inheres in historical time, Jarvis tries to resolve the binary that haunted phenomenological approaches to lyric after Heidegger (about which, for instance, Lacoue-Labarthe was so anguished). Through a long, intricately rhyming passage from Pope's *Rape of the Lock* (1712), Jarvis attempts "to account for an overwhelming experience of [his] own, an experience of evanescent liquidity, or a powerful seduction whose force is present precisely in its transience, in its continuous disappearance and elusiveness, rather than in, say, its symmetry, or its balance or its order."

The experience Jarvis so lavishly describes and wants to bring into relief is at one striking moment in the essay set starkly against another modern experience "in front of the television," an experience that testifies to the frightening way in which "we are today undergoing the attempted decursification and infrastructuralization of the entire perceptual field." Here the familiar threat to experience and to the senses that haunts phenomenological criticism becomes visible; it becomes as well the reason we should value "the very melody of bliss" available to us in Pope's virtuosic verse. If we could tear ourselves away from the TV and be more like Wordsworth, who "lived before that radical emancipation or deafening of the prosodic ear which reduced to a heading in a sub-romantic narrative of dead ratiocination a verse repertoire which was in its time the occasion of actual intensities of delight," we might be able to hear (and feel and think) that melody once again. On this view, the experience of bliss always promised by but always eluding phenomenological accounts of the lyric might still have the power to tease us out of thought, since what intensities of delight could give back to us is something sexier than Heidegger's plain poetic dwelling—may in fact be nothing less than ourselves.

NOTES

1. Stewart (2002), 1–2.
2. Theodor Adorno, "Cultural Criticism and Society" (1949), reprinted in *Prisms: Studies in Contemporary German Thought*, trans. Shierry Weber Nicholson and Samuel Weber (Cambridge, MA: MIT Press, 1983), 34.

FURTHER READING

Agamben, Giorgio. *Language and Death: The Place of Negativity* (1982). Translated by Karen E. Pinkus with Michael Hardt (1991). Reprint, Minneapolis: University of Minnesota Press, 2006.

———. *Stanzas: Word and Phantasm in Western Culture* (1977). Translated by Ronald L. Martinez. Minneapolis: University of Minnesota Press, 1992.

Bachelard, Gaston. *The Poetics of Reverie: Childhood, Language and the Cosmos* (1960). Translated by Daniel Russell. Boston: Beacon Press, 1971.

Gumbrecht, Hans Ulrich. *Atmosphere, Mood, Stimmung: On a Hidden Potential of Literature*. Stanford, CA: Stanford University Press, 2012.

Harman, Graham. *Heidegger Explained: From Phenomenon to Thing*. Peru, IL: Open Court, 2007.

Heidegger, Martin. *Basic Writings*. New York: Harper Perennial, 2008.

Izenberg, Oren. *On Being Numerous: The Poetic Imagination of the Ground of Social Life*. Princeton, NJ: Princeton University Press, 2011.

Jarvis, Simon. *Wordsworth's Philosophic Song*. Cambridge: Cambridge University Press, 2007.

Merleau-Ponty, Maurice. *Phenomenology of Perception*. Translated by Colin Smith. London: Routledge, 1962.

Miller, J. Hillis. *Poets of Reality: Six Twentieth-Century Writers*. Cambridge, MA: Belknap Press of Harvard University Press, 1965.

Nancy, Jean-Luc. *The Birth to Presence*. Translated by Brian Holmes. Stanford, CA: Stanford University Press, 1993.

Poulet, Georges. *Exploding Poetry: Baudelaire/Rimbaud*. Translated by Francoise Meltzer. Baltimore: Johns Hopkins University Press, 1977.

Stewart, Susan. *Poetry and the Fate of the Senses*. Chicago: University of Chicago Press, 2002.

———. *The Poet's Freedom*. Chicago: University of Chicago Press, 2011.

Terada, Rei. *Looking Away: Phenomenality and Dissatisfaction, Kant to Adorno*. Cambridge MA: Harvard University Press, 2009.

7.1 "... Poetically Man Dwells ..."

(1951; trans. 1971)

MARTIN HEIDEGGER Translated by Albert Hofstadter[1]

The phrase is taken from a late poem by Hölderlin, which comes to us by a curious route. It begins: "In lovely blueness blooms the steeple with metal roof."[2] If we are to hear the phrase "poetically man dwells" rightly, we must restore it thoughtfully to the poem. For that reason let us give thought to the phrase. Let us clear up the doubts it immediately arouses. For otherwise we should lack the free readiness to respond to the phrase by following it.

"... poetically man dwells ..." If need be, we can imagine that poets do on occasion dwell poetically. But how is "man"—and this means every man and all the time—supposed to dwell poetically? Does not all dwelling remain incompatible with the poetic? Our dwelling is harassed by the housing shortage. Even if that were not so, our dwelling today is harassed by work, made insecure by the hunt for gain and success, bewitched by the entertainment and recreation industry. But when there is still room left in today's dwelling for the poetic, and time is still set aside, what comes to pass is at best a preoccupation with aestheticizing, whether in writing or on the air. Poetry is either rejected as a frivolous mooning and vaporizing into the unknown, and a flight into dreamland, or is counted as a part of literature. And the validity of literature is assessed by the latest prevailing standard. The prevailing standard, in turn, is made and controlled by the organs for making public civilized opinions. One of its functionaries—at once driver and driven—is the literature industry. In such a setting poetry cannot appear otherwise than as literature. Where it is studied entirely in educational and scientific terms, it is the object of literary history. Western poetry goes under the general heading of "European literature."

But if the sole form in which poetry exists is literary to start with, then how can human dwelling be understood as based on the poetic? The phrase, "man dwells poetically," comes indeed from a mere poet, and in fact from one who, we are told, could not cope with life. It is the way of poets to shut their eyes to actuality. Instead of acting, they dream. What they make is merely imagined. The things of imagination are merely made. Making is, in Greek, *poiēsis*. And man's dwelling is supposed to be poetry and poetic? This can be assumed, surely, only by someone who stands aside from actuality and does not want to see the existent condition of man's historical-social life today—the sociologists call it the collective.

But before we so bluntly pronounce dwelling and poetry incompatible, it may be well to attend soberly to the poet's statement. It speaks of man's dwelling. It does not describe today's dwelling conditions. Above all, it does not assert that to dwell means to occupy a house, a dwelling place. Nor does it say that the poetic exhausts itself in an unreal play of poetic imagination. What thoughtful man, therefore, would presume to declare, unhesitatingly and from a somewhat dubious elevation, that dwelling and the poetic are incompatible? Perhaps the two can bear with each other. This is not all. Perhaps one even bears the other in such a way that dwelling rests on the poetic. If this is indeed what we suppose, then we are required to think of dwelling and poetry in terms of their essential nature. If we do not balk at this demand, we think of what is usually called the existence of man in terms of dwelling. In doing so, we do of course give up the customary notion of dwelling. According to that idea, dwelling remains merely one form of human behavior alongside many others. We work in the city, but dwell outside it. We travel, and dwell now here, now there. Dwelling so understood is always merely the occupying of a lodging.

When Hölderlin speaks of dwelling, he has before his eyes the basic character of human existence. He sees the "poetic," moreover, by way of its relation to this dwelling, thus understood essentially.

This does not mean, though, that the poetic is merely an ornament and bonus added to dwelling. Nor does the poetic character of dwelling mean merely that the poetic turns up in some way or other in all dwelling. Rather, the phrase "poetically man dwells" says: poetry first causes dwelling to be dwelling. Poetry is what really lets us dwell. But through what do we attain to a dwelling place? Through building. Poetic creation, which lets us dwell, is a kind of building.

Thus we confront a double demand: for one thing, we are to think of what is called man's existence by way of the nature of dwelling; for another, we are to think of the nature of poetry as a letting-dwell, as a—perhaps even *the*—distinctive kind of building. If we search out the nature of poetry according to this viewpoint, then we arrive at the nature of dwelling.

But where do we humans get our information about the nature of dwelling and poetry? Where does man generally get the claim to arrive at the nature of something? Man can make such a claim only where he receives it. He receives it from the telling of language. Of course, only when and only as long as he respects language's own nature. Meanwhile, there rages round the earth an unbridled yet clever talking, writing, and broadcasting of spoken words. Man acts as though he were the shaper and master of language, while in fact language remains the master of man. When this relation of dominance gets inverted, man hits upon strange maneuvers. Language becomes the means of expression. As expression, language can decay into a mere medium for the printed word. That even in such employment of language we retain a concern for care in speaking is all to the good. But this alone will never help us to escape from the inversion of the true relation of dominance between language and man. For, strictly, it is language that speaks. Man first speaks when, and only when, he responds to language by listening to its appeal. Among all the appeals that we human beings, on our part, may help to be voiced, language is the highest and everywhere the first. Language beckons us, at first and then again at the end toward a thing's nature. But that is not to say, ever, that in any word-meaning picked up at will language supplies us, straight away and definitively, with the transparent nature of the matter as if it were an object ready for use. But the responding in which man authentically listens to the appeal of language is that which speaks in the element of poetry: The more poetic a poet is—the freer (that is, the more open and ready for the unforeseen) his saying—the greater is the purity with which he submits what he says to an ever more painstaking listening, and the further what he says is from the mere propositional statement that is dealt with solely in regard to its correctness or incorrectness.

says the poet. We hear Hölderlin's words more clearly when we take them back into the poem in which they belong. First, let us listen only to the two lines from which we have detached and thus clipped the phrase. They run:

Full of merit, yet poetically, man
Dwells on this earth.

The keynote of the lines vibrates in the word "poetically." This word is set off in two directions: by what comes before it and by what follows.

Before it are the words: "Full of merit, yet. . . ." They sound almost as if the next word, "poetically," introduced a restriction on the profitable, meritorious dwelling of man. But it is just the reverse. The restriction is denoted by the expression "Full of merit," to which we must add in thought a "to be sure." Man, to be sure, merits and earns much in his dwelling. For he cultivates the growing things of the earth and takes care of his increase. Cultivating and caring (*colere, cultura*) are a kind of building. But man not only cultivates what produces growth out of itself; he also builds in the sense of *aedificare*, by erecting things that cannot come into being and subsist by growing. Things that are built in this sense include not only buildings but all the works made by man's hands and through his arrangements. Merits due to this building, however, can never fill out the nature of dwelling. On the contrary, they even deny dwelling its own nature when they are pursued and acquired purely for their own sake. For in that case these merits, precisely by their abundance, would everywhere constrain dwelling within the bounds of this kind of building. Such building pursues the fulfillment of the needs of dwelling. Building in the sense of the farmer's cultivation of growing things, and of the erecting of edifices and works and the production of tools, is already a consequence of the nature of dwelling, but it is not its ground, let alone its grounding. This grounding must take place in a different building. Building of the usual kind, often practiced exclusively and therefore the only one that is familiar, does of course bring an abundance of merits into dwelling. Yet man is capable of dwelling only if he has already built, is building, and remains disposed to build, in another way.

"Full of merit (to be sure), yet poetically, man dwells. . . ." This is followed in the text by the words: "on this earth." We might be inclined to think the addition superfluous; for dwelling, after all, already means man's stay on earth—on "this" earth, to which every mortal knows himself to be entrusted and exposed.

But when Hölderlin ventures to say that the dwelling of mortals is poetic, this statement, as soon as it is made, gives the impression that, on the contrary, "poetic" dwelling snatches man away from the earth. For the "poetic," when it is taken as poetry, is supposed to belong to the realm of fantasy. Poetic dwelling flies fantastically above reality. The poet counters this misgiving by saying expressly that poetic dwelling is a dwelling "on this earth." Hölderlin thus not only protects the "poetic" from a likely misinterpretation, but by adding the words "on this earth" expressly points to the nature of poetry. Poetry does not fly above and surmount the earth in order to escape it and hover over it. Poetry is what first brings man onto the earth, making him belong to it, and thus brings him into dwelling.

Full of merit, yet poetically, man
Dwells on this earth.

Do we know now why man dwells poetically? We still do not. We now even run the risk of intruding foreign thoughts into Hölderlin's poetic words. For Hölderlin indeed speaks of man's dwelling and his merit, but still he does not connect dwelling with building, as we have just done. He does not speak of building, either in the sense of cultivating and erecting, or in such a way as even to represent poetry as a special kind of building. Accordingly, Hölderlin does not speak of poetic dwelling as our own thinking does. Despite all this, we are thinking the same thing that Hölderlin is saying poetically.

It is, however, important to take note here of an essential point. A short parenthetical remark is needed. Poetry and thinking meet each other in one and the same only when, and only as long as, they remain distinctly in the distinctness of their nature. The same never coincides with the equal, not even in the empty indifferent oneness of what is merely identical. The equal or identical always moves toward the absence of difference, so that everything may be reduced to a common denominator. The same, by contrast, is the belonging together of what differs, through a gathering by way of the difference. We can only say "the same" if we think difference. It is in the carrying out and settling of differences that the gathering nature of sameness comes to light. The same banishes all zeal always to level what is different into the equal or identical. The same gathers what is distinct into an original being-at-one. The equal, on the contrary, disperses them into the dull unity of mere uniformity. Hölderlin, in his own way, knew of these relations. In an epigram which bears the title "Root of All Evil" (Stuttgart edition, I, I, p. 305) he says:

> Being at one is godlike and good; whence, then,
> this craze among men that there should exist only
> One, why should all be one?

When we follow in thought Hölderlin's poetic statement about the poetic dwelling of man, we divine a path by which, through what is thought differently, we come nearer to thinking the same as what the poet composes in his poem.

But what does Hölderlin say of the poetic dwelling of man? We seek the answer to the question by listening to lines 24 to 38 of our poem. For the two lines on which we first commented are spoken from their region. Hölderlin says:

> May, if life is sheer toil, a man
> Lift his eyes and say: so
> I too wish to be? Yes. As long as Kindness,
> The Pure, still stays with his heart, man
> Not unhappily measures himself
> Against the godhead. Is God unknown?
> Is he manifest like the sky? I'd sooner
> Believe the latter. It's the measure of man.
> Full of merit, yet poetically, man
> Dwells on this earth. But no purer
> Is the shade of the starry night,
> If I might put it so, than
> Man, who's called an image of the godhead.
> Is there a measure on earth? There is
> None.

We shall think over only a few points in these lines, and for the sole purpose of hearing more clearly what Hölderlin means when he calls man's dwelling a "poetic" one. The first lines (24 to 26) give us a clue. They are in the form of a question that is answered confidently in the affirmative. The question is a paraphrase of what the lines already expounded utter directly: "Full of merit, yet poetically, man dwells on this earth." Hölderlin asks:

May, if life is sheer toil, a man
Lift his eyes and say: so
I too wish to be? Yes.

Only in the realm of sheer toil does man toil for "merits." There he obtains them for himself in abundance. But at the same time, in this realm, man is allowed to look up, out of it, through it, toward the divinities. The upward glance passes aloft toward the sky, and yet it remains below on the earth. The upward glance spans the between of sky and earth. This between is measured out for the dwelling of man. We now call the span thus meted out the dimension. This dimension does not arise from the fact that sky and earth are turned toward one another. Rather, their facing each other itself depends on the dimension. Nor is the dimension a stretch of space as ordinarily understood; for everything spatial, as something for which space is made, is already in need of the dimension, that is, that into which it is admitted.

The nature of the dimension is the meting out—which is lightened and so can be spanned—of the between: the upward to the sky as well as the downward to earth. We leave the nature of the dimension without a name. According to Hölderlin's words, man spans the dimension by measuring himself against the heavenly. Man does not undertake this spanning just now and then; rather, man is man at all only in such spanning. This is why he can indeed block this spanning, trim it, and disfigure it, but he can never evade it. Man, as man, has always measured himself with and against something heavenly. Lucifer, too, is descended from heaven. Therefore we read in the next lines (28 to 29): "Man measures himself against the godhead." The godhead is the "measure" with which man measures out his dwelling, his stay on the earth beneath the sky. Only insofar as man takes the measure of his dwelling in this way is he able to *be* commensurately with his nature. Man's dwelling depends on an upward-looking measure-taking of the dimension, in which the sky belongs just as much as the earth.

This measure-taking not only takes the measure of the earth, *ge*, and accordingly it is no mere geo-metry. Just as little does it ever take the measure of heaven, *ouranos*, for itself. Measure-taking is no science. Measure-taking gauges the between, which brings the two, heaven and earth, to one another. This measure-taking has its own *metron*, and thus its own metric.

Man's taking measure in the dimension dealt out to him brings dwelling into its ground plan. Taking the measure of the dimension is the element within which human dwelling has its security, by which it securely endures. The taking of measure is what is poetic in dwelling. Poetry is a measuring. But what is it to measure? If poetry is to be understood as measuring, then obviously we may not subsume it under just any idea of measuring and measure.

Poetry is presumably a high and special kind of measuring. But there is more. Perhaps we have to pronounce the sentence, "Poetry is a *measuring*," with a different stress. "*Poetry* is a measuring." In poetry there takes place what all measuring is in the ground of its being. Hence it is necessary to pay heed to the basic act of measuring. That consists in man's first of all taking the measure which then is applied in every measuring act. In poetry the taking of measure occurs. To write poetry is measure-taking, understood in the strict sense of the word, by which man first receives the measure for the breadth of his being. Man exists as a mortal. He is called mortal because he can die. To be able to die means: to be capable of death as death. Only man dies—and indeed continually, so long as he stays on this earth, so long as he dwells. His dwelling, however, rests in the poetic. Hölderlin sees the nature of the "poetic" in the taking of the measure by which the measure-taking of human being is accomplished.

Yet how shall we prove that Hölderlin thinks of the nature of poetry as taking measure? We do not need to prove anything here. All proof is always only a subsequent undertaking on the basis of presuppositions. Anything at all can be proved, depending only on what presuppositions are made. But we can here pay heed only to a few points. It is enough, then, if we attend to the poet's own words. For in the next lines Hölderlin inquires, before anything else and in fact exclusively, as to man's measure. That measure is the godhead against which man measures himself. The question begins in line 29 with the words: "Is God unknown?" Manifestly not. For if he were unknown, how could he, being unknown, ever be the measure? Yet—and this is what we must now listen to and keep in mind—for Hölderlin God, as the one who he is, is unknown and it is just as *this Unknown One* that he is the measure for the poet. This is also why Hölderlin is perplexed by the exciting question: how can that which by its very nature remains unknown ever become a measure? For something that man measures himself by must after all impart itself, must appear. But if it appears, it is known. The god, however, is unknown, and he is the measure nonetheless. Not only this, but the god who remains unknown, must by showing *himself* as the one he is, appear as the one who remains unknown. God's *manifestness*—not only he himself—is mysterious. Therefore the poet immediately asks the next question: "Is he manifest like the sky?" Hölderlin answers: "I'd sooner / Believe the latter."

Why—so *we* now ask—is the poet's surmise inclined in that way? The very next words give the answer. They say tersely: "It's the measure of man." What is the measure for human measuring? God? No. The sky? No. The manifestness of the sky? No. The measure consists in the way in which the god who remains unknown, is revealed *as* such by the sky. God's appearance through the sky consists in a disclosing that lets us see what conceals itself, but lets us see it not by seeking to wrest what is concealed out of its concealedness, but only by guarding the concealed in its self-concealment. Thus the unknown god appears as the unknown by way of the sky's manifestness. This appearance is the measure against which man measures himself.

A strange measure, perplexing it would seem to the common notions of mortals, inconvenient to the cheap omniscience of everyday opinion, which likes to claim that it is the standard for all thinking and reflection.

A strange measure for ordinary and in particular also for all merely scientific ideas, certainly not a palpable stick or rod but in truth simpler to handle than they, provided our hands do not abruptly grasp but are guided by gestures befitting the measure here to be taken. This is done by a taking which at no time clutches at the standard but rather takes it in a concentrated perception, a gathered taking-in, that remains a listening.

But why should this measure, which is so strange to us men of today, be addressed to man and imparted by the measure-taking of poetry? Because only this measure gauges the very nature of man. For man dwells by spanning the "on the earth" and the "beneath the sky." This "on" and "beneath" belong together. Their interplay is the span that man traverses at every moment insofar as he *is* as an earthly being. In a fragment (Stuttgart edition, 2, 1, p. 334) Hölderlin says:

> Always, love! the earth
> moves and heaven holds.

Because man *is*, in his enduring the dimension, his being must now and again be measured out. That requires a measure which involves at once the whole dimension in one. To discern this measure, to gauge it as the measure, and to accept it as the measure, means for the poet to make poetry. Poetry is this measure-taking—its taking, indeed, for the dwelling of man. For immediately after the words "It's the measure of man" there follow the lines: "Full of merit, yet poetically, man dwells on this earth."

Do we now know what the "poetic" is for Hölderlin? Yes and no. Yes, because we receive an intimation about how poetry is to be thought of: namely, it is to be conceived as a distinctive kind of measuring. No, because poetry, as the gauging of that strange measure, becomes ever more mysterious. And so it must doubtless remain, if we are really prepared to make our stay in the domain of poetry's being.

Yet it strikes us as strange that Hölderlin thinks of poetry as a measuring. And rightly so, as long as we understand measuring only in the sense current *for us*. In this sense, by the use of something known—measuring rods and their number—something unknown is stepped off and thus made known, and so is confined within a quantity and order which can always be determined at a glance. Such measuring can vary with the type of apparatus employed. But who will guarantee that this customary kind of measuring, merely because it is common, touches the nature of measuring? When we hear of measure, we immediately think of number and imagine the two, measure and number, as quantitative. But the *nature* of measure is no more a quantum than is the *nature* of number. True, we can reckon with numbers—but not with the nature of number. When Hölderlin envisages poetry as a measuring, and above all himself achieves poetry as taking measure, then we, in order to think of poetry, must ever and again first give thought to the measure that is taken in poetry; we must pay heed to the kind of taking here, which does not consist in a clutching or any other kind of grasping, but rather in a letting come of what has been dealt out. What is the measure for poetry? The godhead; God, therefore? Who is the god? Perhaps this question is too hard for man, and asked too soon. Let us therefore first ask what may be said about God. Let us first ask merely: What is God?

Fortunately for us, and helpfully, some verses of Hölderlin's have been preserved which belong in substance and time to the ambience of the poem "In lovely blueness. . . ." They begin (Stuttgart edition, 2, 1, p. 210):

> What is God? Unknown, yet
> Full of his qualities is the
> Face of the sky. For the lightnings
> Are the wrath of a god. The more something
> Is invisible, the more it yields to what's alien.

What remains alien to the god, the sight of the sky—this is what is familiar to man. And what is that? Everything that shimmers and blooms in the sky and thus under the sky and thus on earth, everything that sounds and is fragrant, rises and comes—but also everything that goes and stumbles, moans and falls silent, pales and darkens. Into this, which is intimate to man but alien to the god, the unknown imparts himself, in order to remain guarded within it as the unknown. But the poet calls all the brightness of the sights of the sky and every sound of its courses and breezes into the singing word and there makes them shine and ring. Yet the poet, if he is a poet, does not describe the mere appearance of sky and earth. The poet calls, in the sights of the sky, that which in its very self-disclosure causes the appearance of that which conceals itself, and indeed *as* that which conceals itself. In the familiar appearances, the poet calls the alien as that to which the invisible imparts itself in order to remain what it is—unknown.

The poet makes poetry only when he takes the measure, by saying the sights of heaven in such a way that he submits to its appearances as to the alien element to which the unknown god has "yielded." Our current name for the sight and appearance of something is "image." The nature of the image is to let something be seen. By contrast, copies and imitations are already mere variations on the genuine image which, as a sight or spectacle, lets the invisible be seen and so imagines the invisible in something alien to it. Because poetry takes that mysterious measure, to wit, in the face of the sky, therefore it speaks in "images." This is why poetic images are imaginings in a distinctive sense: not mere fancies and illusions but imaginings that are visible inclusions of the alien in the sight of the familiar. The poetic saying of images gathers the brightness and sound of the heavenly appearances into one with the darkness and silence of what is alien. By such sights the god surprises us. In this strangeness he proclaims his unflattering nearness. For that reason Hölderin, after the lines "Full of merit, yet poetically, man Dwells on this earth," can continue:

> . . . Yet no purer
> Is the shade of the starry night,
> If I might put it so, than
> Man, who's called an image of the godhead.

"The shade of the night"—the night itself is the shade, that darkness which can never become a mere blackness because as shade it is wedded to light and remains cast by it. The measure taken by poetry yields, imparts itself—as the foreign element in which the invisible one preserves his presence—to what is familiar in the sights of the sky. Hence, the measure is of the same nature as the sky. But the sky is not sheer light. The radiance of its height is itself the darkness of its all-sheltering breadth. The blue of the sky's lovely blueness is the color of depth. The radiance of the sky is the dawn and dusk of the twilight, which shelters everything that can be proclaimed. This sky is the measure. This is why the poet must ask:

> Is there a measure on earth?

And he must reply: "There is none." Why? Because what we signify when we say "on the earth" exists only insofar as man dwells on the earth and in his dwelling lets the earth be as earth.

But dwelling occurs only when poetry comes to pass and is present, and indeed in the way whose nature we now have some idea of, as taking a measure for all measuring. This measure-taking is itself an authentic measure-taking, no mere gauging with ready-made measuring rods for the making of maps. Nor is poetry building in the sense of raising and fitting buildings. But poetry, as the authentic gauging of the dimension of dwelling, is the primal form of building. Poetry first of all admits man's dwelling into its very nature, its presencing being. Poetry is the original admission of dwelling.

The statement, *Man dwells in that he builds*, has now been given its proper sense. Man does not dwell in that he merely establishes his stay on the earth beneath the sky, by raising growing things and simultaneously raising buildings. Man is capable of such building only if he already builds in the sense of the poetic taking of measure. Authentic building occurs so far as there are poets, such poets as take the measure for architecture, the structure of dwelling.

On March 12, 1804, Hölderlin writes from Nürtingen to his friend Leo von Seckendorf: "At present I am especially occupied with the fable, the poetic view of history, and the architectonics of the skies, especially of our nation's, so far as it differs from the Greek" (Hellingrath V^2, p. 333).

> ". . . poetically, man dwells . . . ."

Poetry builds up the very nature of dwelling. Poetry and dwelling not only do not exclude each other; on the contrary, poetry and dwelling belong together; each calling for the other. "Poetically man dwells." Do *we* dwell poetically? Presumably we dwell altogether unpoetically. If that is so, does it give the lie to the poet's words; are they untrue? No. The truth of his utterance is confirmed in the most unearthly way. For dwelling can be unpoetic only because it is in essence poetic. For a man to be blind, he must remain a being by nature endowed with sight. A piece of wood can never go blind. But when man goes blind, there always remains the question whether his blindness derives from some defect and loss or lies in an abundance and excess. In the same poem that meditates on the measure for all measuring, Hölderlin says (lines 75–76): "King Oedipus has perhaps one eye too many." Thus it might be that our unpoetic dwelling, its incapacity to take the measure, derives from a curious excess of frantic measuring and calculating.

That we dwell unpoetically, and in what way, we can in any case learn only if we know the poetic. Whether, and when, we may come to a turning point in our unpoetic dwelling is something we may expect to happen only if we remain heedful of the poetic. How and to what extent our doings can share in this turn we alone can prove, if we take the poetic seriously.

The poetic is the basic capacity for human dwelling. But man is capable of poetry at any time only to the degree to which his being is appropriate to that which itself has a liking for man and therefore needs his presence. Poetry is authentic or inauthentic according to the degree of this appropriation.

That is why authentic poetry does not come to light appropriately in every period. When and for how long does authentic poetry exist? Hölderlin gives the answer in verses 26–69, already cited. Their explication has been purposely deferred until now. The verses run:

> . . . As long as Kindness,
> The Pure, still stays with his heart, man
> Not unhappily measures himself
> Against the Godhead . . .

"Kindness"—what is it? A harmless word, but described by Hölderlin with the capitalized epithet "the Pure." "Kindness"—this word, if we take it literally, is Hölderlin's magnificent translation for the Greek word *charis*. In his *Ajax*, Sophocles says of *charis* (verse 522):

> *Charis charin gar estin he tiktous aei*
> For kindness it is, that ever calls forth kindness.

"As long as Kindness, the Pure, still stays with his heart. . . ." Hölderlin says in an idiom he liked to use: "with his heart," not "in his heart." That is, it has come to the dwelling being of man, come as the claim and appeal of the measure to the heart in such a way that the heart turns to give heed to the measure.

As long as this arrival of kindness endures, so long does man succeed in measuring himself not unhappily against the godhead. When this measuring appropriately comes to light, man creates poetry from the very nature of the poetic. When the poetic appropriately comes to light, then man dwells humanly on this earth, and then—as Hölderlin says in his last poem—"the life of man" is a "dwelling life" (Stuttgart edition, 2, 1, p. 312).

> *VISTA*
>
> When far the dwelling life of man into the distance goes,
> Where, in that far distance, the grapevine's season glows,
> There too are summer's fields, emptied of their growing,

And forest looms, its image darkly showing.
That Nature paints the seasons so complete,
That she abides, but they glide by so fleet,
Comes of perfection; then heaven's radiant height
Crowns man, as blossoms crown the trees, with light.

NOTES

1. Martin Heidegger wrote "... dichterisch wohnet der Mensch" (1951) on the occasion of the death of a German musician, and the essay was published in *Vorträge und Aufsätze* (Pfullingen: G. Neske, 1954).

2. Friedrich Hölderlin, *Friedrich Hölderlins Sämtliche Werke*, Große Stuttgarter Ausgabe, ed. Friedrich Beißner (works) and Adolf Beck (letters and documents), 8 vols. in 16 parts (Stuttgart: Cotta, 1943–85), 2, 372ff.

Poetry as Experience: Two Poems by Paul Celan (1968; trans. 1999) 7.2

PHILIPPE LACOUE-LABARTHE Translated by Andrea Tarnowski

> Expand art? No. But accompany art into your own unique place of no escape. And set yourself free.
>
> "The Meridian"[1]

Here are two poems by Paul Celan:

TÜBINGEN, JÄNNER

Zur Blindheit über-
redete Augen.
Ihre—"ein
Rätsel ist Rein-
entsprungenes"—, ihre
Erinnerung an
schwimmende Hölderlintürme, möwen-
umschwirrt.

Besuche ertrunkener Schreiner bei
diesen
tauchenden Worten:

Käme,
käme ein Mensch,
käme ein Mensch zur Welt, heute, mit
dem Lichtbart der

Patriarchen: er dürfte,
spräch er von dieser
Zeit, er
dürfte
nur lallen und lallen,
immer-, immer-
zuzu.

("Pallaksch. Pallaksch.")

TÜBINGEN, JANUARY

Eyes talked into
blindness.
Their—"an enigma is
the purely
originated"—, their
memory of
Hölderlin towers afloat, circled
by whirring gulls.

Visits of drowned joiners to
these
submerging words:

Should,
should a man,
should a man come into the world, today, with
the shining beard of the
patriarchs: he could,
if he spoke of this
time, he
could
only babble and babble
over, over
againagain.

("Pallaksh. Pallaksh.")[2]

TODTNAUBERG

Arnika, Augentrost, der
Trunk aus dem Brunnen mit dem
Sternwürfel drauf,

in der
Hütte,
die in das Buch
—wessen Namen nahms auf
vor dem meinen?—
die in dies Buch
geschriebene Zeile von
einer Hoffnung, heute,

auf eines Denkenden
kommendes
Wort
im Herzen,

Waldwasen, uneingeebnet,
Orchis und Orchis, einzeln,

Krudes, später, im Fahren,
deutlich,

der uns fährt, der Mensch,
der's mit anhört,

die halb-
beschrittenen Knüppel-
pfade im Hochmoor,

Feuchtes,
viel.

TODTNAUBERG

Arnica, eyebright, the
draft from the well with the
starred die above it,

in the
hut,

the line
—whose name did the book
register before mine?—
the line inscribed
in that book about
a hope, today,
of a thinking man's
coming
word
in the heart,

woodland sward, unlevelled,
orchid and orchid, single,

coarse stuff, later, clear
in passing,

he who drives us, the man
who listens in,

the half-
trodden wretched
tracks through the high moors,

dampness,
much.[3]

These two poems are well known; each of them has been translated into French at least twice. The first, which is part of the *Niemandsrose* collection (1963), was initially translated by André du Bouchet (appearing in *L'Ephémère* 7, and then in *Strette*, published by Mercure de France in 1971) before figuring in the complete edition of *La rose de personne*, edited by Martine Broda (Le Nouveau Commerce, 1979). The second, issued on its own in 1968 and then republished in *Lichtzwang* in July 1970, two or three months after Celan's death, was translated by Jean Daive as early as 1970, and then, several years later, by André du Bouchet (*Poèmes de Paul Celan*, Clivages, 1978). Other published versions of these poems may exist.[4]

It is obvious that the titles of both are places: Tübingen, Todtnauberg. The poems seem, in each case, to commemorate a visit. But it is also obvious that these place names can additionally, even primarily, be names of people. Whatever trope we use, the indications, the quotations, the allusions are all perfectly clear; and in any case, we already know that Tübingen is Hölderlin, and Todtnauberg, Heidegger. I don't imagine it would be very useful to stress the reasons that prompt us today (*heute*: each poem includes the word) to associate the two poems. For everyone who is, as we say, "concerned about our times" and "mindful of history" (European history), the two names, Hölderlin and Heidegger, are now indissolubly linked. They give voice to what is at stake in our era (*dieser Zeit*). A world age—perhaps the world's old age—is approaching its end, for we are reaching a completion, closing the circle of what the philosophical West has called, since Grecian times and in multiple ways, "knowledge." That is, *technè*. What has not been deployed, what has been forgotten or rejected in the midst of this completion—and no doubt from the very beginning—must now clear itself a path to a possible future. Let us agree to say that this pertains, as Heidegger says himself, to the "task of thought." Such thought must re-inaugurate history, reopen the possibility of a world, and pave the way for the improbable, unforeseeable advent of a god. Only this might "save" us. For this task, art (again, *technè*), and in art, poetry, are perhaps able to provide some signs. At least, that is the hope, fragile, tenuous, and meager as it is.

While it may not be useful to stress, it is no doubt helpful at least to remark the following:

1. Such thinking, the thinking of History, is essentially German. It is not exclusively so, but since the end of the eighteenth century, Germans have brought it a dimension never attained before or elsewhere; one reason for this, among others, is that the question of the relation between Modern and Ancient, and of the possibility of uniqueness or identity for a whole people, has never been so much a *question* as it has been in Germany. That is, first and foremost, a question for the "nation"—the people—and in the language, a latecomer to the world after the sumptuous, "renascent" display of European Latinity. German has never ceased aspiring, on pretense of its strange similarity to Greek (the "language of origin"), to the unique relation it has believed it could establish to everything most authentically Greek about Greece.

2. Paul Celan (Ancel) was born in Czernowitz, Bukovina, of German Jewish parents. Whatever the fate of Bukovina in the years that marked the end of Celan's adolescence (he was born in 1920)—it was, successively, annexed by the U.S.S.R. in 1940, occupied by Germany and Romania in 1941, and reconquered by the Red Army in 1943—Celan was not just at the extreme fringes of *Mitteleuropa*; he was of German birth, born into that language. In a true and understandably forgotten sense, his *nationality* was German. This did not in any way preclude his having a completely dif-

ferent origin, or to be more precise, a completely different heritage. Thus, his language always remained that of the Other, an Other language without an "other language," previously rather than laterally acquired, against which to measure itself. All other languages were necessarily lateral for Celan; he was a great translator.

3. Paul Celan knew, as everything he wrote attests (and first and foremost, his acceptance of German as his working language), that today (*heute*) it is with Germany that we must clarify things.[5] Not only because Celan suffered as the victim of Germany's "Hellenic," "Hyperborean" utopia, but because he knew it was impossible to elude the question that the utopia's atrocity had transformed into an answer, a "solution." He embodied an extreme, eternally insoluble paradox in Germany as one of the few people, almost the only person, to have borne witness to the truth of the question that remains, as ever: (But) who are we (still, today, *heute*)?

4. The extermination gave rise, in its impossible possibility, in its immense and intolerable banality, to the post-Auschwitz era (in Adorno's sense). Celan said: "Death is a master who comes from Germany."[6] It is the impossible possibility, the immense and intolerable banality of our time, of this time (*dieser Zeit*). It is always easy to mock "distress," but we are its contemporaries; we are at the endpoint of what *Nous*, *ratio* and *Logos*, still today (*heute*) the framework for what we are, cannot have failed to show: that murder is the first thing to count on, and elimination the surest means of identification. Today, everywhere, against this black but "enlightened" background, remaining reality is disappearing in the mire of a "globalized" world. Nothing, not even the most obvious phenomena, not even the purest, most wrenching love, can escape this era's shadow: a cancer of the subject, whether in the *ego* or in the masses. To deny this on pretext of avoiding the pull of pathos is to behave like a sleepwalker. To transform it into pathos, so as to be able "still" to produce art (sentiment, etc.), is unacceptable.

I want to ask the most brutal question possible, at the risk of being obnoxious: Was Celan able to situate not himself, but *us* vis-à-vis "it"? Was poetry still able to? If so, which poetry, and what, in fact, of poetry? Mine is a distant way (distant now by many degrees, heavily layered over the very man who first asked) of repeating Hölderlin's questions: *Wozu Dichter*? What for, indeed?

Here is how the two poems I believe carry all the weight of this question have been translated into French:

TÜBINGEN, JANVIER

(TR. ANDRÉ DU BOUCHET)

A cécité même
mues, pupilles.
Leur—'énigme cela,
qui est pur
jaillissement'—, leur
mémoire de
tours Hölderlin nageant, d'un battement de mouettes
serties.

Visites de menuisiers engloutis par
telles
paroles plongeant:

S'il venait,
venait un homme,
homme venait au monde, aujourd'hui avec
clarté et barbe des
patriarches: il lui faudrait,
dût-il parler de telle
époque, il lui faudrait
babiller uniquement, babiller
toujours et toujours ba-
biller iller.

("Pallaksch. Pallaksch.")

(TR. MARTINE BRODA)

Des yeux sous les paroles
aveuglés.
Leur—"énigme
ce qui naît
de source pur"—, leur
souvenir de
tours Hölderlin nageant, tournoyées
de mouettes.

Visites de menuisiers noyés
à ces
mots qui plongent:

S'il venait,
venait un homme,
venait un homme au monde, aujourd'hui, avec
la barbe de clarté
des patriarches: il devrait,
s'il parlait de ce
temps, il
devrait
bégayer seulement, bégayer
toutoutoujours
bégayer.

("Pallaksch. Pallaksch.")

TODTNAUBERG

(TR. JEAN DAIVE)

Arnika, centaurée, la
boisson du puits avec, au-dessus,
l'astre-dé,

dans le
refuge,

écrite dans le livre
(quel nom portait-il
avant le mien?),
écrite dans ce livre
la ligne,
aujourd'hui, d'une attente:
de qui pense
parole à venir
au coeur,

de la mousse des bois, non aplanie,
orchis et orchis, clairsemé,

de la verdeur, plus tard, en voyage,
distincte,

qui nous conduit, l'homme,
qui, à cela, tend l'oreille,
les chemins
de rondins à demi
parcourus dans la fange,

de l'humide,
très.

(TR. ANDRÉ DU BOUCHET)

Arnika, luminet, cette
gorgée du puits au
cube étoilé plus haut du dé,

dans la
hutte,

là, dans un livre
—les noms, de qui, relevés
avant le mien?—
là, dans un livre,
lignes qui inscrivent
une attente, aujourd'hui,
de qui méditera (à
venir, in-
cessamment venir)
un mot
du coeur
humus des bois, jamais aplani,

orchis, orchis,
unique,

chose crue, plus tard, chemin faisant,
claire,

qui nous voitura,
l'homme,
lui-même à son écoute,

à moitié
frayé le layon de rondins
là-haut dans le marais,

humide,
oui.

(At the end of André du Bouchet's slim volume, we read the following note: "'Todtnauberg' was translated using the initial version of the poem, dated 'Frankfurt am Main, 2 August 1967.' From a word-for-word translation suggested by Paul Celan, I have kept the French 'qui nous voitura' for 'der uns fährt.' A.d.B.")

I am not juxtaposing these translations here in order to compare or comment on them. It is not my intention to "critique" them. At most, I think it necessary to remark that what we might call the "Mallarméan" style of André du Bouchet's translations, their effete or precious quality, does not do justice to the lapidary hardness, the abruptness of language as handled by Celan. Or rather, the language that held him, ran through him. Especially in his late work, prosody and syntax do violence to language: they chop, dislocate, truncate or cut it. Something in this certainly bears comparison to what occurs in Hölderlin's last, "paratactic" efforts, as Adorno calls them: condensation and juxtaposition, a strangling of language. But no lexical "refinement," or very little; even when he opts for a sort of "surreal" handling of metaphor or "image," he does not depart from essentially simple, naked language. For example, the "such" (*telle*) used twice as a demonstrative in the "Mallarméan" translation of "Tübingen, January" is a turn of phrase totally foreign to Celan's style. Even more so the "A cécité même / mue, pupilles" ("To blindness itself / moved, pupils") that begins the same poem in what is indeed the most obscure way possible. But I do not wish to reopen the polemic initiated a decade or so ago by Meschonnic.[7]

No, though I recall these translations, and though I will even, in turn, try my hand at translating, I do not wish to play at comparison—a game of limited interest. Nor do I cite them as an obligatory preamble to commentary. I give the translations only so we can see where we stand. I believe these poems to be completely untranslatable, including within their own language, and indeed, for this reason, invulnerable to commentary. They *necessarily* escape interpretation; they forbid it. One could even say they are written to forbid it. This is why the sole question carrying them, as it carried all Celan's poetry, is that of meaning, the possibility of meaning. A transcendental question, one might say, which does to some extent inscribe Celan in Hölderlin's lineage or wake: that of "poetry's poetry" (without, of course, the least concession to any sort of "formalism"). And a question that inevitably takes away, as Heidegger found with both Hölderlin and Trakl, all forms of hermeneutic power, even at one remove: for example, envisioning a "hermeneutics of hermeneutics." For in any case, sooner or later one finds oneself back at "wanting to say nothing," which exceeds (or falls short of) all "wanting to say," all intention of signifying, since it is always caught in advance in an archetypal double bind of the "Don't read me" sort; in this instance, something like, "Don't believe in meaning anymore." Since Rimbaud's time, let's say, this has always amounted to saying "Believe *me*, don't believe in meaning anymore," which at once raises and demotes, pathetically, risibly, or fraudulently, the "I" that thus projects itself to (and from) the function of incarnating meaning.

The question I ask myself is indeed that of the subject, that cancer of the subject, both the ego's and the masses'. But it is first the question of whoever today (*heute*) might speak a language other than the subject's, and attest or respond to the unprecedented ignominy that the "age of the subject" rendered itself—and remains—guilty of. At least since Schlegel and Hegel, it is also, indissociably, the question of the lyric: is lyric a "subjective" genre? In sum, it is the question of the banished singularity of the subject or, what amounts to the same thing, the question of idiom, of "pure idiom," if that can exist. Is it possible, and necessary, to wrench oneself out of the language of the age? To say what? Or rather, to speak what?

Such a question, as you perceive—and here I am barely shifting angles—is not different from that of the relation between "poetry and thought," *Dichten und Denken*, a question indeed specifically asked in German. What is a work of poetry that, forswearing the repetition of the disastrous, deadly, already-said, makes itself absolutely singular? What should we think of poetry (or what of thought is left in poetry) that must refuse, sometimes with great stubbornness, to signify? Or, simply, what is a poem whose "coding" is such that it foils in advance all attempts to decipher it?

I have been asking myself this question, which I grant is naïve, for a long time, and especially since reading Peter Szondi's analysis of "Du liegst . . . ,"[8] the poem on Berlin written in 1967 and published in *Schneepart* in 1971; it is, along with two essays by Blanchot and by Lèvinas published in the *Revue des belles lettres* ("Le dernier à parler" and "De l'être à l'autre"[9]), among the very few illuminating commentaries on Celan. But whereas Blanchot's and Lévinas's readings remain "gnomic," to recall Adorno's objection to Heidegger's interpretation of Hölderlin[10]—that is, they found their arguments on phrases lifted from Celan's poems (his verse contains many such isolatable bits, as does all "thinking poetry")—Szondi's analysis is to my knowledge the only one[11] to completely decipher a poem, down to its most resistant opacities, because it is the only one to know what "material" gave rise to the work: the circumstances remembered, the places traveled to, the words exchanged, the sights glimpsed or contemplated, and so on. Szondi scouts out the least allusion, the slightest evocation. The result is a translation in which almost nothing is left over; *almost*, because we must still explain, beyond Szondi's delight at having been present in the right place at the right time, a poetry based on the exploitation of such "singularity," and thus (i.e., in this respect) forever inaccessible to those who did not initially witness what the poetry transformed into a very laconic "story" or a very allusive "evocation."

The question that I have called that of idiom is therefore more exactly that of singularity. We must avoid confusing this with another, relatively secondary or derivative question, that of the "readable" and the "unreadable." My question asks not just about the "text," but about the singular *experience* coming into writing; it asks if, being singular, experience can be written, or if from the moment of writing its very singularity is not forever lost and borne away in one way or another, at origin or en route to destination, by the very fact of language. This could be due to language's impossible intransitivity, or to the desire for meaning, for universality, that animates voices divided by the constraint of a language that is itself, in turn, only one of many. Is there, can there be, a singular experience? A silent experience, absolutely untouched by language, unprompted by even the most slightly articulated discourse? If, impossibly, we can say "yes," if singularity exists or subsists despite all odds (and beyond all empirical considerations, the presence of a witness such as Peter Szondi, for example, or of someone else who knows), can language possibly take on its burden? And would idiom suffice for the purpose—idiom of course different from the facile "crypting" or refusal to reveal one's point so terribly endemic to the "modern"? These questions pose neither the problem of solipsism nor that of autism, but very probably that of solitude, which Celan experienced to what we must justly call the utmost degree.

I reread "Tübingen, January" (a poem with an old-fashioned date, *Jänner* for *Januar* as if in allusion to Hölderlin's disconcerting manner of dating poems during his "mad" period); I reread it as I read it, as I understand it, as I thus cannot but translate it. This effort is partly unnecessary because of Martine Broda's beautiful French translation, which to my mind can hardly be improved upon, and from which I will at least borrow the unsurpassable phrase "wheeled with gulls" ("tour- / noyées de mouettes").[12] But I cannot help translating here. So I return, with emendations, to a rendering I attempted a few years ago while working on Hölderlin:

TÜBINGEN, JANVIER

Sous un flot d'éloquence
aveuglés, les yeux.
Leur—"une
énigme est le
pur jailli"—, leur
mémoire de
tours Hölderlin nageant, tournoyées de mouettes.

Visites de menuisiers submergés sous
ces
paroles plongeant:

Viendrait,
viendrait un homme
viendrait un homme au monde, aujourd'hui, avec
la barbe de lumière des Patriarches: il n'aurait,
parlerait-il de ce
temps, il
n'aurait
qu'à bégayer, bégayer
sans sans
sans cesse.

("Pallaksch. Pallaksch.")

TÜBINGEN, JANVIER

Beneath a flow of eloquence
blinded, the eyes.
Their—"an
enigma is the
pure sprung forth"—, their
memory of
Hölderlin towers swimming,
wheeled with gulls.

Joiners' visits submerged beneath
these
diving words:

If there came
if there came a man
if there came a man into the world today, with
the beard of light of the
Patriarchs; he would need only,
if he spoke of this
time, he would need only
to stutter, stutter
without, without
without cease.

("Pallaksh. Pallaksh.")[13]

What these few, barely phrased phrases say, in their extenuated, infirm discourse, stuttering on the edge of silence or the incomprehensible (gibberish, idiomatic language: "Pallaksh"), is not a "story"; they do not recount anything, and most certainly not a visit to the *Hölderlinturm* in Tübingen. They undoubtedly mean something; a "message," as it were, is delivered. They present, in any case, an intelligible utterance: if a man, a Jewish man—a Sage, a Prophet, or one of the Righteous, "with/the beard of light of/the Patriarchs,"— wanted today to speak forth about the age as Hölderlin did in his time, he would be condemned to stammer, in the manner, let us say, of Beckett's "metaphysical tramps." He would sink into aphasia (or "pure idiom"), as we are told Hölderlin did; in any case, Hölderlin's "madness" came to define the aphasic myth:

MNEMOSYNE (II)

Ein Zeichen sind wir, deutungslos
Schmerzlos sind wir und haben fast
Die Sprache in der Fremde verloren.[14]

A sign we are, meaningless
Painless we are and have nearly
Lost our language in foreign places.

More precisely, we might say that to speak the age, it would be enough for such a man to stammer-stutter; the age belongs to stammering, to stuttering. Or rather, stuttering is the only "language" of the age. The end of meaning—hiccuping, halting.

Yet this message comes second in the poem; it is a little like the "lesson" or the "moral" of a classic fable; its presence makes explicit, within though slightly detached from the poem (see the colon at the end of the second stanza), what the poem says before—what it says *as* a poem. It is a translation. The idiomatic poem contains its own translation, which is a justification of the idiomatic. Or at least, we can formulate it this way; the problem then becomes knowing *what* it explicitly translates.

I propose to call what it translates "experience," provided that we both understand the word in its strict sense—the Latin *ex-periri*, a crossing through danger—and especially that we avoid associating it with what is "lived," the stuff of anecdotes. *Erfahrung*, then, rather than *Erlebnis*.[15] I say "experience" because what the poem "springs forth" from here—the memory of bedazzlement, which is also the pure dizziness of memory—is precisely that which did not take place, did not happen or occur during the singular event that the poem relates to without relating: the visit, after so many others since the joiner Zimmer's time, to the tower on the Neckar where Hölderlin lived without living for the last thirty-six years of his life—half of his life. A visit in memory of that experience, which is also in the non-form of pure non-event.

I shall try to explain. What the poem indicates and shows, what it moves toward, is its source. A poem is always "en route," "underway," as "The Meridian" recalls.[16] The path the poem seeks to open up here is that of its own source. And making its way thus to its own source, it seeks to reach the general source of poetry. It says, then, or tries to say, the "springing forth" of the poem in its possibility, that is, in its "enigma." "An enigma is the pure sprung forth;"[17] so speaks the first verse to the fourth stanza of the hymn "The Rhine," which in a way is the source here. Hölderlin adds: "Even / The song may hardly reveal it." But if the poem says or tries to say the source in this manner, it says it as inaccessible, or in any case unrevealed "even [by] the song," because in place of the source, and in a way which is itself enigmatic, there is dizziness, the instant of blindness or bedazzlement before the sparkling waters of the Neckar, the fragmenting glitter, the image of the visitors swallowed up. Or because there is also the stark reminder that precisely *in this place*, it was revealed to so many visitors that the source (of the poem, the song) had dried up. And that previously it had indeed been an enigma that sprang forth.

Dizziness can come upon one; it does not simply occur. Or rather, in it, nothing occurs. It is the pure suspension of occurrence: a caesura or a syncope. This is what "drawing a blank" means. What is suspended, arrested, tipping suddenly into strangeness, is the presence of the present (the being-present of the present). And what then occurs without occurring (for it is by definition what cannot occur) is—without being—nothingness, the "nothing of being" (*ne-ens*). Dizziness is an *experience* of nothingness, of what is, as Heidegger says, "properly" non-occurrence, nothingness. Nothing in it is "lived," as in all experience, because all experience is the experience of nothingness: the experience of dizziness here, as much as the anguish Heidegger describes, or as much as laughter in Bataille. Or the lightning recognition of love. As much as all the infinitely paradoxical, "impossible" experiences of death, of disappearance in the present. How poignant and difficult to think that Celan chose his own death (the most finite infinite choice), throwing himself into the waters of the Seine.

To say this again in another way: there is no "poetic experience" in the sense of a "lived moment" or a poetic "state." If such a thing exists, or thinks it does—for after all it is the power, or impotence, of literature to believe and make others believe this—it cannot give rise to a poem. To a story, yes, or to discourse, whether in verse or prose. To "literature," perhaps, at least in the sense we understand it today. But not to a poem. A poem has nothing to recount, nothing to say; what it recounts and says is that from which it wrenches away as a poem. If we speak of "poetic emotion," we must think of its cognate *émoi*,[18] whose etymology indicates the absence or deprivation of strength. "A une passante" is not the nostalgic story of an encounter, but the entreaty that arises from collapse, the pure echo of such an *émoi*, a song or a prayer. Benjamin hardly dared say, though he knew perfectly well, that this is perhaps (and I stress the "perhaps") what Proust did not understand in understanding Baudelaire, and probably also what the overly nostalgic Baudelaire sometimes did not understand in understanding himself (though he did write the prose poems, which redeem all).[19]

But the poem's "wanting-not-to-say" does not *want* not to say. A poem wants to say; indeed, it is nothing but pure wanting-to-say. But pure wanting-to-say nothing, nothingness, that against which and through which there is presence, what is. And because nothingness is inaccessible to wanting, the poem's wanting collapses as such (a poem is always involuntary, like anguish, love, and even self-chosen death); then *nothing* lets itself be said, the thing itself, and lets itself be said in and by the man who goes to it despite himself, receives it as what cannot be received, and submits to it. He accepts it, trembling that it should refuse; such a strange, fleeting, elusive "being" as the meaning of what is.

In the end, if there is no such thing as "poetic experience" it is simply because experience marks the absence of what is "lived." This is why, strictly speaking, we can talk of a poetic *existence*, assuming existence is what at times puts holes in life, rending it to put us beside ourselves. It is also why, given that existence is furtive and discontinuous, poems are rare and necessarily brief, even when they expand to try to stay the loss or deny the evanescence of what compelled them into being. Further, this is why there is nothing necessarily grandiose about the poetic, and why it is generally wrong to confuse poetry with celebration; one can find, in the most extreme triviality, in insignificance, perhaps even in frivolity (where Mallarmé occasionally lost himself), pure, never-pure strangeness: the *gift of nothing* or *present of nothing* comparable to the little token one describes, saying: "It's nothing." Indeed, it is never nothing, it is *nothing*; it can as well be pitiable or totally without grandeur, terrifying or overwhelmingly joyous.

We are told that when Hölderlin went "mad," he constantly repeated, "Nothing is happening to me, nothing is happening to me."

The dizziness of existence is what the poem "Tübingen, January" says. It says it inasmuch as it says *itself* as a poem, inasmuch as it says what arose from, or remains of, the non-occurred in the singular event it commemorates. "In-occurrence" is what wrenches the event from its singularity, so that at the height of singularity, singularity itself vanishes and saying suddenly appears—the poem is possible. *Singbarer Rest*: a singable remainder, as Celan says elsewhere.[20]

This is why the poem commemorates. Its experience is an experience of memory. The poem speaks of *Erinnerung*, but also secretly calls upon the *Andenken* of Hölderlin's poem on Bordeaux, and the *Gedächtnis* where Hölderlin found Mnemosyne's resonance. The poem was not born in the moment of the *Hölderlinturm* visit. Properly speaking, it was not born in any moment. Not only because dizziness or bedazzlement by definition never constitutes a moment, but because what brings on the dizziness and recalls the waters of the Neckar is not those waters, but another river: the Hölderlinian river itself. A double meaning here: first the river, or rivers, that Hölderlin sings (the Rhine, the Ister, the source of the Danube, etc.), and then the river of Hölderlin's poetry. Or, as I've said, the "flood of eloquence."

In "Tübingen, January," the eyes are not in fact blinded; no bedazzlement takes place. They are *zur Blindheit überredete*, persuaded to blindness. But to translate *überreden* by "persuade," or "convince," does not convey the full sense of *über* and all it contains as a signifier of overflow. To be *überredet*—I take this on Michel Deutsch's authority—is simply "to be taken in," "run circles around," overwhelmed by a tide of eloquence. Less "taken for a ride" than "submerged," "drowned," or, most accurately, "to be had." The eyes—the eyes that see Hölderlin's tower, the waters of the Neckar, the wheeling gulls—are blinded by a flood of words or eloquence; the eyes are taken in, and the memory of the river poem "The Rhine" recalls and calls forth the memory of the dizziness, the engulfing bedazzlement: that is, as with all "involuntary memory," the memory of "what was neither purposely nor consciously 'lived' by the subject," as Benjamin perfectly demonstrated for Baudelaire using Freud's argument against Bergson.[21] Thus dizziness here indicates the in-occurrence of which memory—and not merely recollection—is the paradoxical restitution. The dizziness is memory because all real memory is vertiginous, offering the very atopia of existence, what takes place without taking place; giving a gift that forces the poem into thanking, into ecstasy. This is why the poem is obliged into thought: "To think and thank," says the Bremen speech, "*denken und danken*, have the same root in our language. If we follow it to *gedenken, eingedenk sein, Andenken* and *Andacht* we enter the semantic fields of memory and devotion."[22]

Thus, "Tübingen, January" does not say any state of the psyche, any lived experience of the subject, any *Erlebnis*. Nor is it—this follows logically—a celebration of Hölderlin (it comes closer to saying how Hölderlin disappoints). It is definitely *not* a "sentimental" poem, whether in Schiller's or the common sense. The poem says "drowning" in Hölderlin's verse. It says it as its "possibility," a possibility infinitely and interminably paradoxical, because it is the possibility of the poem inasmuch as, possible-impossible, it says, if not the pure impossibility, then at least the scant possibility of poetry.

[. . .]

The time of distress is the time—now our history—of what Hölderlin also called pain (both *Schmerz* and *Leiden*), the word that runs through both "In Lovely Blueness" and modern lyricism, from Baudelaire to Trakl and Mandelstam. Pain, which is not exactly suffering, affects and touches man's "heart"; it is what is most intimate in him; the extreme interior where, in his almost absolute singularity (his ab-soluteness), man—and not the subject—is pure waiting-for-an-other; he is hope of a dialogue, of a way out of solitude. I again cite "The Meridian":

> But I think— . . . I think that it has always belonged to the expectations of the poem in precisely this manner to speak in the cause of the strange—no, I can no longer use this word—in precisely this manner to speak *in the cause of an Other*—who knows, perhaps in the cause of a *wholly Other.*
>
> This "who knows," at which I see I have arrived, is the only thing I can add—on my own, here, today—to the old expectations.
>
> Perhaps, I must now say to myself—and at this point I am making use of a well-known term—perhaps it is now possible to conceive a meeting of this "wholly Other" and an "other" which is not far removed, which is very near.
>
> The poem tarries, stops to catch a scent—like a creature when confronted with such thoughts.
>
> No one can say how long the pause in breath—the thought and the stopping to catch the scent—will last. . . .
>
> The poem is alone. It is alone and underway. Whoever writes it must remain in its company.
>
> But doesn't the poem, for precisely that reason, at this point participate in an encounter—*in the mystery of an encounter*?
>
> The poem wants to reach the Other, it needs the Other, it needs a vis à vis. It searches it out and addresses it. . . .
>
> It becomes dialogue—it is often despairing dialogue.[23]

From that place, that solitude—pain—Celan speaks. It is the same solitude and pain that Hölderlin felt in the end, when he had succumbed to the excess of eloquence and been submerged, reduced to silence, by sacred pathos. "Tübingen, January" is a poem to this pain and solitude because it is the poem *of* this pain and *of* this solitude; that of always being thrown back from the dialogue one had thought possible and then, in withdrawal, "huddling," as Heidegger says of Hölderlin, no longer able to speak; stuttering, swallowed up in idiom. Or falling silent. In a world with nothing and *no one* to authorize or even "guarantee" the least dialogue, the slightest relation to one another, however or whoever he may be, how to wrench away from aphasia, from silence? The poem, says Celan, once again in "The Meridian," "today . . . shows a strong inclination towards falling silent. . . . It takes its position . . . at the edge of itself; in order to be able to exist, it without interruption calls and fetches itself from its now-no-longer back into its as-always."[24]

The question of poetry's possibility—and Celan never asked another—is the question of the possibility of such a wrenching. The question of the possibility of *going out of the self.* This also means, as "The Meridian" again recalls, going "outside the human," in the sense, for example, (but is this still just *one* example?) that the (finite) transcendence of *Dasein* in the experience of nothingness, in ek-sistence, is a going outside the human: "Here we have stepped beyond human nature, gone outwards, and entered a mysterious realm, yet one turned towards that which is human."[25]

It would be an understatement to say Celan had read Heidegger. Celan's poetry goes beyond even an unreserved recognition of Heidegger; I think one can assert that it is, in its entirety, a dialogue with Heidegger's thought. And essentially with the part of this thought that was a dialogue with Hölderlin's poetry. Without Heidegger's commentary on Hölderlin, "Tübingen, January" would have been impossible; such a poem could simply never have been written. And it would certainly remain incomprehensible if one did not detect in it a *response* to this commentary. Indeed, the dizziness on the edge of Hölderlinian pathos is just as much dizziness vis-à-vis its amplification by Heidegger; vis-à-vis the *belief* in which Heidegger persisted, whatever his sense of "sobriety" in other matters. A belief, not only in the possibility that the word Hölderlin "kept in reserve" might still be heard (by Germany, by us), but also, and perhaps especially, in the possibility that the god this word announced or prophesied might come. This, even though Heidegger maintained until the end, up through the last interviews granted to *Der Spiegel*, that it was also necessary to expect, and prepare for, the definitive decline or in-advent of the god. "Praise be to you, no one."

[. . .]

A dialogue like this is no way requires an encounter—an "effective" encounter, as we say. Probably the opposite. The encounter is also that which can prohibit or break off dialogue. Dialogue, in this sense, is fragility itself.

Yet between Celan and Heidegger, an encounter took place. It happened in 1967, probably during the summer. Celan went to visit Heidegger in Todtnauberg, in the Black Forest chalet (*Hütte*) that was his refuge, the place where he wrote. From this meeting—to which I know there were witnesses, direct or indirect—there remains a poem: a second version of which, in conclusion, I invite you to read.

Here is how I hear it:

TODTNAUBERG

Arnica, baume des yeux, la
gorgée à la fontaine avec
le jet d'étoiles au-dessus,

dans le
chalet,

là, dans le livre
—de qui, les noms qu'il portait
avant le mien?—,
dans ce livre
la ligne écrite sur
un espoir, aujourd'hui,
dans le mot
à venir
d'un penseur,
au coeur,

humus des bois, non aplani,
orchis et orchis, épars,

crudité, plus tard en voiture,
distincte,

qui nous conduit, l'homme,
à son écoute aussi,
à demi
frayées les sentes
de rondins dans la fange,

humidité,
beaucoup.

TODTNAUBERG

Arnica, eye balm, the
draught at the fountain with
the spray of stars above,

in the
hut,

there, in the book
—whose, the names it bore
before mine?—
in that book
the line written about
a hope, today,
in the coming
word
of a thinker,
in the heart,

woodland humus, unlevelled,
orchis and orchis, scattered,

crudeness, later, in the car,
distinct,

he who drives us, the man,
listening too,

half-
cleared the paths
of logs in the mire,

dampness,
much.

My translation is very rough; witness or not, who can know what the allusions refer to? "Todtnauberg" is really barely a poem; a single nominal phrase, choppy, distended and elliptical, unwilling to take shape, it is not the outline but the remainder—the residue—of an aborted narrative. It consists of brief notes or notations, seemingly jotted in haste with a hope for a future poem, comprehensible only to the one who wrote them. It is an extenuated poem, or, to put it better, a *disappointed* one. It is the poem of a disappointment; as such, it is, and it says, the disappointment of poetry.

One could of course supply a gloss, try to decipher or translate. There is no lack of readable allusions. The *Holzwege*, for example; here they are no longer ways through the forest toward a possible clearing, a *Lichtung*, but paths lost in a marsh where the poem itself gets lost (water again, but without a source—not even; dampness—no more about the dizzying Neckar, the "spirit of the river," the bedazzlement-engulfment. Only an uneasiness). Another example: one could pick, or *cast*, as it were, the image of the spray of stars above the man drinking from the fountain, throwing back his head to the sky: dice thrown like the "golden sickle" abandoned by Hugo's "harvester of eternal summer." And this could be a gesture toward Büchner's Lenz, the figure of the poet, of whom "The Meridian" recalls, "Now and then he experienced a sense of uneasiness because he was not able to walk on his head,"[26] only to add, "Whoever walks on his head, ladies and gentlemen, whoever walks on his head has heaven beneath him as an abyss."[27] An echo, perhaps, of Hölderlin's strange proposition: "Man kann auch in die Höhe *fallen*, so wie in die Tiefe" ("one can as well *fall* into height as into depth").[28] One could surely go very far in this direction, as in many another.

But that is not what the poem says, if indeed it is still a poem.

What the poem says is, first, a language: words. German, with Greek and Latin woven in. "Common" language: *Augentrost*, *Waldwasen*, *Hochmoor*, and so on. "Learned" language: *Arnika*, *Orchis*. But still simple, ordinary words. The kind of words in another of Celan's few explanatory prose texts, "Conversation in the Mountains" (a sort of tale, halfway between *Lenz* and *Hassidic Tales*, where two Jews discuss language): words like "turk's-cap lily," "corn-salad," and "*dianthus superbus*, the maiden-pink," that bespeak a native relation to nature (or to the earth, as Heidegger would have said):

> So it was quiet, quiet up there in the mountains. But it was not quiet for long, because when a Jew comes along and meets another, silence cannot last, even in the mountains. Because the Jew and nature are strangers to each other, have always been and still are, even today, even here.
>
> So there they are, the cousins. On the left, the turk's-cap lily blooms, blooms wild, blooms like nowhere else. And on the right, corn-salad, and *dianthus superbus*, the maiden-pink, not far off. But they, those cousins, have no eyes, alas. Or, more exactly: they have, even they have eyes, but with a veil hanging in front of them, no not in front, behind them, a moveable veil. No sooner does an image enter than it gets caught in the web. . . .

> Poor lily, poor corn-salad. There they stand, the cousins, on a road in the mountains, the stick silent, the stones silent, and the silence no silence at all. No word has come to an end and no phrase, it is nothing but a pause, an empty space between the words, a blank . . . [29]

Once again, a matter of blindness or half-blindness ("they . . . have no eyes, alas"). But because blindness, blinding—we understand now—is *the empty space between the words* (and doubtless also *a blank*): not having the words to say what is. Words are not innate; language is not altogether a mother tongue (or a father tongue—it hardly matters). There is difficulty with it (there is also perhaps a question of *place* in language).

This difficulty—*the* difficulty—is named in the Bremen address when it evokes, as Blanchot says, "the language through which death came upon him, those near to him, and millions of Jews and non-Jews, *an event without answer*" (my emphasis):[30]

> Only one thing remained reachable, close and secure amid all losses: language. Yes, language. In spite of everything, it remained secure against loss. But it had to go through its own lack of answers, through terrifying silence, through the thousand darknesses of murderous speech. It went through. It gave me no words for what was happening, but went through it. Went through and could resurface, 'enriched' by it all.
>
> In this language I tried, during those years and the years after, to write poems: in order to speak, to orient myself, to find out where I was, where I was going, to chart my reality.
>
> It meant movement, you see, something happening, being *en route*, an attempt to find a direction.[31]

What "Todtnauberg" speaks about, then, is this: the language in which Auschwitz was pronounced, and which pronounced Auschwitz.

That is why the poem also says, and says simply, the meaning of the encounter with Heidegger—that is, its disappointment. I suspected as much, but I confess that I was told this, by a friend who had it on the best authority.

To Heidegger the thinker—the German thinker—Celan the poet—the Jewish poet—came with a single yet precise entreaty: that the thinker who listened to poetry; the same thinker who had compromised himself, however briefly and even if in the least shameful way, with just what would result in Auschwitz; the thinker who, however abundant his discussion with National Socialism, had observed total silence on Auschwitz, as history will recall; that he say just a single word: a word about pain. From there, perhaps, all might still be possible. Not "life," which is always possible, which remained possible, as we know, even in Auschwitz, but existence, poetry, speech. Language. That is, relation to others.

Could such a word be *wrenched*?

In the summer of 1967 Celan writes in the guestbook of the *Hütte* in Todtnauberg. He no longer knows who signed before him; signatures—proper names, as it happens—matter little. At issue was a word, just a word. He writes—what? A line, or a verse. He asks only for the word, and the word, of course, is not spoken. Nothing; silence; no one. The in-advent of the word ("the event without answer").

I do not know what word Celan could have expected. What word he felt would have had enough force to wrench him from the threat of aphasia and idiom (in-advent of the word), into which this poem, mumbled against the silence, could only sink as if into a bog. What word could suddenly have constituted an *event*.

I do not know. Yet something tells me it is at once the humblest and most difficult word to say, the one that requires, precisely, "a going out of the self." The word that the

West, in its pathos of redemption, has never been able to say. The word it remains for us to learn to speak, lest we should sink ourselves. The word *pardon*.

Celan has placed us before this word. A sign?

NOTES

1. "Der Meridian" is in volume 3 of Celan's five-volume *Gesammelte Werke*, ed. Beda Allemann and Stefan Reichert, in collaboration with Rolf Bücher (Frankfurt: Suhrkamp, 1983). This passage, p. 200. Unless otherwise noted, all English translations from "Der Meridian" are from Jerry Glenn's "The Meridian," in *Chicago Review* 29, no. 3 (1978): 29–49. This passage, p. 38. [Translator's note]

2. *GW* 1:226. English translations of Celan's poems will be Michael Hamburger's unless otherwise noted. "Tübingen, Jänner" is in *Paul Celan: Poems* (New York: Persea, 1988), 177. [Translator's note]

3. *GW* 2: 25; Hamburger, *Celan*, 293. [Translator's note]

4. Apart from Michael Hamburger's translations of both poems, there is an English version of *Tübingen, Jänner* in Joachim Neugroschel, *Paul Celan, Speech-Grille* (New York: E. P. Dutton, 1971), 185. [Translator's note]

5. Lacoue-Labarthe's phrase is "c'est avec l'Allemagne qu'il faut . . . s'expliquer." *S'expliquer* in this context means primarily "to discuss," "to clarify matters," even "to have it out with someone." Yet the verb could also function as a simple reflexive; this would render the sense, "We must explain *ourselves* with Germany." The import of such ambiguity for reflections on the Holocaust is self-evident. [Translator's note]

6. From "Todesfuge": "der Tod ist ein Meister aus Deutschland." *GW* 1:42, "Death Fugue," Hamburger, *Celan*, 63. [Translator's note]

7. Henri Meschonnic, "On appelle cela traduire Celan," in *Pour la poétique II* (Paris: Gallimard, 1980).

8. *GW* 2:334. Peter Szondi, "Eden," in *Poésies et poétiques de la modernité* (Lille: Presses universitaires de Lille, 1981).

9. Issues 2 and 3, 1972. Blanchot, *Le dernier à parler*, was reissued by fata morgana in Paris in 1984.

10. Theodor Adorno, "Parataxe," in *Notes to Literature*, vol. 2, trans. Shierry Weber Nicholson (New York: Columbia University Press, 1991), 109–49.

11. Along with, in an entirely different vein, Werner Hamacher, "The Second of Inversion: Movements of a Figure through Celan's Poetry," trans. Peter Fenves, in *Word Traces: Readings of Paul Celan*, ed. Aris Fioretos (Baltimore, Md.: Johns Hopkins University Press, 1994), 219–63.

12. The French "tour-/noyées" plays on a double meaning: the verb *tournoyer* can be translated as "to wheel around, whirl, swirl," while dividing the past participle of the verb into two parts evokes "tower/drowned." [Translator's note]

13. It is worth stressing that this English version translates Lacoue-Labarthe's French translation, rather than Celan's German. [Translator's note]

14. Friedrich Hölderlin, *Sämtliche Werke*, vol. 2.1 (Stuttgart: Kohlhammer, 1951), 195.

15. I refer the reader to Roger Munier (responding to an inquiry on experience in *Mise en page* I [May 1972]): "First there is etymology. *Experience* comes from the Latin *experiri*, to test, try, prove. The radical is *periri*, which one also finds in *periculum*, peril, danger. The Indo-European root is *per*, to which are attached the ideas of *crossing* and, secondarily, of *trial*, *test*. In Greek, numerous derivations evoke a crossing or passage: *peirô*, to cross; *pera*, beyond; *peraô*, to pass through; *perainô*, to go to the end; *peras*, end, limit. For Germanic languages, Old High German *faran* has given us *fahren*, to transport, and *führen*, to drive. Should we attribute *Erfahrung* to this origin as well, or should it be linked to the second meaning of *per*, trial, in Old High German, *fara*, danger, which became *Gefahr*, danger, and *gefährden*, to endanger? The boundaries between one meaning and the other are imprecise. The same is true for the Latin *periri*, to try, and *periculum*, which originally means trial, test, then risk, danger. The idea of experience as a crossing is etymologically and semantically difficult to separate from that of risk. From the beginning and no doubt in a fundamental sense, *experience* means to endanger."

16. The French translation I will refer to is not André du Bouchet's in *Strette* (Paris: Mercure de France, 1971), but Jean Launay's (*Poésie* 9 [1979]). I make slight modifications when the argument warrants. [For this passage, see Glenn, 37: "The poem is . . . underway."—Translator's note]

17. In the original, this line reads "Ein Räthsel ist Reinentsprungenes." In English, Michael Hamburger renders it "An enigma are things of pure source"; see *Hölderlin: His Poems* (New York: Pantheon, 1952), 199. I have modified the English translation because of Lacoue-Labarthe's

repeated use of *jaili* and *jaillissement*. [Translator's note]

18. In English, agitation or excitement. [Translator's note]

19. Walter Benjamin, *Charles Baudelaire, Ein Lyriker im Zeitalter des Hochkapitalismus*, in *Gesammelte Schriften*, vol. 1.2, ed. Rolf Tiedemann and Hermann Schweppenhäuser (Frankfurt am Main: Suhrkamp, 1974). English references: *Charles Baudelaire: A Lyric Poet in the Era of High Capitalism*, trans. Harry Zohn (London: NLB, 1973).

20. *GW* 2:36. [Translator's note]

21. Benjamin, "Uber einige Motive bei Baudelaire," *Schriften*, 1.2:605–53; "Some Motifs in Baudelaire," *Charles Baudelaire*, 107–54.

22. Celan's Bremen address is published in the *GW* 3:186. The English translation cited here is by Rosmarie Waldrop, in *Paul Celan: Collected Prose* (Manchester, England: Carcanet Press, 1986), 33. [Translator's note]

23. Glenn, 35–37. [Translator's note]

24. Ibid., 36. [Translator's note]

25. Ibid., 32; *GW* 3:192. [Translator's note]

26. Glenn, 34; *GW* 3:195. [Translator's note]

27. Glenn, 35; *GW* 3:195. [Translator's note]

28. *SW* 4.1:233.

29. *Paul Celan*, trans. Waldrop, 18–19. [Translator's note]

30. Blanchot, *Le Dernier à parler*, 45.

31. *GW* 3: 185–6; *Paul Celan*, Waldrop, 34.

7.3 Summa Lyrica: A Primer of the Commonplaces in Speculative Poetics (1990)

Allen Grossman

Introductory Note

My purpose in the *Summa Lyrica* is to bring to mind "the poem," as an object of thought and as an instrument for thinking, consistent with my account of poetic practice in the foregoing conversations. In particular, I intend to facilitate (and exemplify) *thinking* as it may arise in the course of inquiry directed toward the meaning of poetic structures. The *Summa Lyrica* proceeds by stating—aphoristically—some of the commonplaces by means of which poetry and poetic purposes are accounted for in the West. As a primer or handbook of commonplaces, it is designed to befriend the reader of poetry (always supposing that the reader of poetry needs a hermeneutic friend) by constructing a culture in which poetry is intelligible.

In aid of these intentions and purposes, the attempt has been made to make this work total (a *summa*), that is to say, to place individual analyses in the context of a version of the whole subject matter. This is of course not the same thing as attempting to make the work complete (supposing that were possible). What is attempted to identify the alliances and relationships of the specific terms and situations in poetic analysis (in something like the same way that they arise in my own mind, when my mind is engaged with poetry), as far out toward the horizon as possible (an aphorism is a proposition with a horizon), and thus to circumscribe a horizon in which poetry rises up and is present *as in a world*.

The basis of order in the *Summa Lyrica* is the procession of commonplaces (*loci communes*), assertions which are possible to be made (and generally are made) in the presence of poems. Commonplaces are not pieces of theory but points of outlook. In the commonplace (as in the aphorism), everybody can start from the same spot, because discourse is *bound* into the authority of a human presence. Theory of poetry does not participate in the nature of poetry (as perhaps the theory of something else participates in the nature of that thing)—except insofar as the theory of poetry is also something that somebody says. In the *Summa Lyrica*, an attempt is made to stay inside the business of the thing, and to use the matrix of particular personal presence as a system of paths along which to move among realms of being (for this reason there is also a web of cross-references from title to title in the text). Flowing from the commonplaces are comments (*scholia*) which show, in increasingly open styles of discourse, how the commonplaces are amplified and serve to make audible the world-wide and history-long discourse which is always going on (30.6) in the presence of the poem—with the intention of putting poetry and poetic knowledge in the service of human interests.

Above all, therefore, this is a text for use, intended like a poem to give rise to thoughts about something else.

The Primer

Immortality I (14)

1. The function of poetry is to obtain for everybody one kind of success at the limits of the autonomy of the will.

Scholium "in the wake of language." Here we conceive of poetry as doing moral work, as having a function in the same way as a machine has a function but a machine that speaks. (43)

Like language (but not identical with language)—perhaps it would be well to say "in the wake of language"—poetry makes promises to everybody and keeps its promises only to some. So when we say "the function of poetry is to obtain for *everybody* one kind of success," we are running ahead of the fact (but doing so in the name of the fact), and raising the question of *justice*.

By "success" we mean "outcome." Poetry serves to obtain a kind of outcome (a success is any outcome) precisely at those points in experience where the natural will is helpless.

1.1 The limits of the autonomy of the will discovered in poetry are death and the barriers against access to other consciousnesses.

Scholium on limits. Poetry thematizes the abandonment of will of the speaking person as speaker. "Sing, muse. . . ." The maxim is: "No mortal man speaks immortal words." In this way poetry repeats its function as its subject matter. (This is what is meant when poetry is said to "be about poetry.")

The abandonment of the autonomy of the will of the speaking person as a speaker constitutes a form of knowledge—poetic knowledge. The knowledge that not "I" speaks but "language speaks" (Heidegger). The function of this knowledge is to rescue the natural will at the point of its death, that is to say, at the point where death arrests its intention.

Poetry is produced by the mortality of body and soul, the immiscibility of minds, and the postponement of the end of the world.

1.2 The kind of success which poetry facilitates is called "immortality."

Scholium on immortality. Poetry functions as a machine for producing immortality in the form of the convergence of meaning and being in presence. (For modern immortality theory, see Becker, Lifton, Rank, Arendt, and Cullmann.) Note, for example, Plato, *Symposium*, 208, 209:

> Do you think, she went on, that Alcestis would have laid down her life to save Admetus, or that Achilles would have died for the love he bore Patroclus, or that Codrus, the Athenian king, would have sacrificed himself for the seed of his royal consort, if they had not hoped to win "the deathless name for valor," which, in fact, posterity has granted them? No, Socrates, no. Every one of us, no matter what he does, is longing for endless fame, the incomparable glory that is theirs, and the nobler he is, the greater his ambition, because he is in love with the eternal.

> Well then, she went on, those whose procreancy is of the body turn to woman as the object of their love, and raise a family, in the blessed hope that by doing so they will keep their memory green, "through time and through eternity." But those whose procreancy is of the spirit rather than of the flesh—and they are not unknown, Socrates—conceive and bear the things of the spirit. And what are they? you ask. Wisdom and all her sister virtues; it is the office of every poet to beget them, and of every artist whom we may call creative.

Immortality may be thought of in any number of ways:

> Civilization originates in delayed infancy and its function is security. It is a huge network of more or less successful attempts to protect mankind against the danger of object-loss, the colossal efforts made by a baby who is afraid of being left alone in the dark. The famous poem of Horace may be regarded as a symbol of this effort:
>
> Exegi monumentum, aere perennius
>
> Regalique situ pyramidum altius.
> (Géza Róheim, *The Origin and Function of Culture*)

1.3 The structural definition of lyric is "that poetic situation in which there is one speaking person, who is nameless or to whom we assign the name of the author." (6.4)

Scholium on lyric. Lyric is the most continuously practiced of all poetic kinds in the history of Western representation; and also the most endemic to the present Postmodern situation. Lyric is the genre of the "other mind" as it has come to manifestation through the abandonment of autonomy and the displacement toward fiction. (For the specific *differentia* of the lyric form considered as the imitation or "fiction" of speech, see Barbara H. Smith, *Poetic Closure*, p. 122. For a beginning with genre and the lyric genre in particular, see Claudio Guillén, *Literature as System*, pp. 398–400.)

Note the following (Northrop Frye, *Anatomy of Criticism*, p. 366):

> Lyric: A literary genre characterized by the assumed concealment of the audience from the poet and by the predominance of an associational rhythm distinguishable both from recurrent metre and from semantic or prose rhythm.

Frye's "concealment of the audience from the poet" is an abbreviation of Mill on overhearing (cited at 16.7). The idea of "associational rhythm" is a reference to the fact of lyric as the imitation of man alone, either as he is alone in himself, or as he might be alone before or after society. As the kind which imitates man alone, lyric is the first and last poetic sort.

Insofar as the lyric is associated with music, the music stands for those solitudes. (For the history of poetry and music, see John Hollander, "The Poem in the Ear," in *Vision and Resonance*.) The assignment of the name of the author to the nameless speaker in lyric reenacts (repeats) the normal social process of the naming of the person with stress on the problematical nature of the naming of persons at all. In addition, the question of singular and plural attends the self-reference of the lyric speaker. For a beginning with this problem, see citation from Fox at 3 and Émile Benveniste, "Relationships of Person in the Verb," in *Problems in General Linguistics* (especially p. 203).

1.4 A poem facilitates immortality by the conservation of names.

Scholium on the conservation of names. The traditional function of poetry is the conservation of names (Note 23.1 and Scholium, and 38.8). The strangeness and point of lyric can be seen when we note that the speaker in lyric by contrast to the speakers in drama (all of whom are named) and the speakers in epic narrative (all of whom are named except the narrator) is only equivocally named, has in effect a sponsor (the author) but no name, is prior to or posterior to name, is an orphan voice. The name of the speaker in lyric is inferential (see 40) or intuitive. The speaker in lyric communicates with the past lives of the reader (Scholium at 28.1).

1.5 The features of the poem which are instrumental toward its immortalizing function are those which distinguish it from other forms of words, its prosody (for example, meter and line).

Scholium on poetry and other kinds of utterance. The opposite of poetry is not strictly speaking prose but rather the "not fictional." But this would hold for the novel as well (see Barbara H. Smith, *Poetic Closure*, p. 15 and note 10). The question arises as to what stage of the distancing of utterance from its natural situation constitutes a difference, a destination sufficient to constitute a new or "fictional" status. For another current treatment of this issue see Frank Kermode in *The Sense of an Ending*, where the difference lies between the fictional and the myth (see 38), and see also the distinction between the radical or participatory and the aesthetic (32).

1.6 Immortality is the simultaneity of meaning and being. Immortality can be discussed only in relation to persons.

1.7 Neither immortality nor persons are conceivable outside of communities. Consequently, reading engages the reader with the community in the interest of the immortality of all persons.

Reading 1 (22) (37)

2. The poem is the destiny of the reader. (9)

2.1 The reader is the destiny of the poem. (9)

Scholium on the circle of immortality. Immortality as the continuity of human presence through acknowledgment is a "virtuous circle" (Goodman) on which all persons stand (writer and reader being two) in mutual dependence. Hence, immortality as presence is a collective human artifact in which the self-interest of persons converges. "Creation" is creation not of poems but of presence, or immortality, and is not an act (in the sense in which an act has a terminal moment) but a process in the sense that it is always ongoing and only ongoing. The process of creation of human presence through acknowledgment moves through persons across time and is completed neither in the writer nor in the reader but in the mutually honorable reciprocity of both. At any moment of reading the reader is the author of the poem, and the poem is the author of the reader. The honor of creation is not with one or the other, but among them. Above all, they are intended (destined) for another in that the poem looks ahead to the reader, and the reader (as reader) to the poem. In a culture in which honor is conferred asymmetrically on the author rather than the reader, the dominance of the image of the reader derogates from the good of reading by setting the self-interest of writer and reader in conflict and breaking the circle. Such a situation gives rise to theory.

2.2 We should not let anything enter our discussion of a poem but what we see for ourselves.

2.3 While I am doing this, you are doing something else.
Scholia on the difference of tasks.

A. *What difference does it make what other people say*? What difference does it make what other people say? The answer is: What other people say is what *they* say, each of them as it were all the time. The difference is *the saying of what is said.* In other words, what is said is first of all the portrait of the other person present because of his or her speaking. The difference that the speech of another makes is the difference of other being in its being as other. Scripture, written down speech, does not make the difference. The good book stands in the difference of the other person. Therefore, the good book pitches you away, makes a difference. Here I am trying to make a difference, working with the problem of a good book.

Whatever I do (whatever you do) has the same weight as being, has the weight of being in it. A sentence is of the same order as being; it is something a *person* does—eidetic. You can say "Yes" to the *eidos*, or you can say "Not Yet," or you can say "Not Mine," but you cannot say "No." Even if you say "No" it will not disappear.

B. *Prudence in doing an eidetic science.* The effort in doing poetics (eidetic science) is not to tell anyone anything, and not to stop speaking. The clearest (simplest, most admirable) form of an essay in criticism of (any kind of talking about) the poem must precipitate no conclusion that might be known ahead of time by either of us, must acknowledge the inutility of anything that can be taught in this matter and the splendor of anything that can be learned.

Who is so stupidly curious as to send his son to school in order to learn what the teacher thinks? All those sciences which they profess to teach, and the science of virtue itself and wisdom, teachers explain through words. Then those who are pupils consider within themselves whether what has been explained has been said truly; looking of course to that interior truth, according to the measure of which each is able. Thus they learn, and when the interior truth makes known to them that true things have been said, they applaud, but without knowing that instead of applauding teachers they are applauding learners, if indeed their teachers know what they are saying (Augustine, *De Magistro*, XIV).

In the matter of poetry, everybody is *trying* to say the same thing. Your business and my business is with the commonplaces, helping one another to the world. Whether I understand what I am saying is not the important thing. The important thing is to be faithful to the event.

2.4 Reading presupposes a meditative sorting of the true situation of the self from false versions (37.5). Reading also results in a sorting of the true situation of the self from false versions.

2.5 The question "Why read?" depends for its answer on a true conception of self-interest.

Scholium on teaching and learning. Teaching and learning is the facilitation of understanding of self-interest by one person in the presence of another. Reading is an instance of teaching and learning. It is something you do for yourself in the presence of another person (whether at hand or absent) who is the living boundary of the interest which you serve.

2.6 The poem is first prior to the self (ahead) and then posterior to the self (behind).

2.7 Reading recurs. Writing does not recur.

2.8 The poem is the reader's thing (Scholium at 40.2).

Scholium on "appropriation."

By appropriation I mean several things. I mean first that the interpretation of a text ends up in the self-interpretation of a subject who henceforth understands himself better. This completion of text understanding in self-understanding characterizes the sort of reflective philosophy which I call concrete reflection. Hermeneutics and reflective philosophy are here correlative and reciprocal: on the one hand, self-understanding provides a roundabout way of understanding the cultural signs in which the self contemplates himself and forms himself; on the other hand, the understanding of a text is not an end in itself and for itself; it mediates the relation to himself of a subject who, in the short circuit of immediate reflection, would not find the meaning of his own life. Thus it is necessary to say just as strongly that reflection is nothing without mediation by means of signs and cultural works and that explanation is nothing if it is not incorporated, as an intermediary stage, in the process of self-understanding. In short, in hermeneutical reflection—or in reflective hermeneutics—the constitution of *self* and that of meaning are contemporaneous (Paul Ricoeur, "What Is a Text? Explanation and Interpretation").

Silence 1 (19) (Scholium 31.4)

3. A poem begins and ends in silence. Why not call it nothing? (36.3)

Scholium on the culture of silence. The meaning of silence is an implication of speech which constructs silence as a "back-formation" or inference from itself. As a preliminary instance of the culture or ethnography of silence (40), note the following:

> The Quakers of the seventeenth century were particularly concerned to do away with the empty formalism in worship into which they considered Christianity had fallen, and since many of the outward forms they rejected were verbal forms, their distrust of speaking and the value they placed upon silence assumed especially high symbolic significance. Speaking was a faculty of the outward man, and was therefore not as valuable as the inward communion with God which could only be achieved through silence. In his curious treatise "A Battle-Door for Teachers & Professors to Learn Singular & Plural," which was an apology for the distinctive Quaker pronominal usage, George Fox, the principal founder of Quakerism, wrote, "All Languages are to me no more than dust, who was before Languages were, and am come'd before Languages were, and am redeemed out of Languages into the power where men shall agree . . . all Languages upon earth is [sic] but Naturall and makes none divine, but that which was before Languages, and Tongues were" (Fox, Stubbs, Furley 1660:ii) (Richard Bauman, "Speaking in the Light: The Role of the Quaker Minister" in *Explorations in the Ethnography of Speaking*).

Observe that silence is the topical space in which the scarce economics of speech are no longer in force, and the possibility of relationship precluded by utterance as a means of relationship becomes actuality. Silence is where "all men agree."

3.1 The silence out of which poetic speech arises is more or less busy.

3.2 To bring speech out of silence there must be an occasion generative of speech.

3.3 The "occasion generative of speech" is some dislocation or "disease" of the relationship of a subject and an object (for example, as between love and beloved or a god and his world). Creation is not the speaking itself but the primordial disease or fall which thrusts me into a predicament in which speech is the only way.

3.4 The poem achieves "closure" only when some new cognitive element has been added to the relationship of subject and object. Terminal closure is "something understood." Closure brings the poem to an end as apocalypse ("dis-closure") brings Creation to an end (cf. 8).

Scholium on part and whole. One way of thinking about closure is as the completion of the inventory of part-whole recognitions. A basic moral component in the analysis of the literary work is the discovery of the part in relationship to its whole. This discovery is a *moral* component because it is in effect an ethical function which carries the literary function—the immortality function—inside of it. It is the business of the reader to discover the compositional harmony of the part of the work in relationship to the whole of the work. It is the business of the moral person—the business of consciousness with itself, the literary work being in this respect a version of consciousness—to discover the ethical implication of this moment of consciousness in relationship to the whole career of consciousness; or, stated another way, it is the business of the moral person (for which literary analysis is a model) to discover the relationship between this moment of the story of *this* person and the whole of the story. Each discriminable element of the work is related to the whole the work, and the work itself is a discriminable element in the history of its own story (the "archetype" which has not one but many histories, as many as the explanations proposed to account for its coming to be). Analogously, each moment in the history of *this* consciousness has a place in the whole history of consciousness. *But* we observe that consciousness is asymmetrical—consciousness includes the past but not the future. We do not remember the future. Hence the part-whole perception in the analysis of the literary work is an anticipation of the mind in contemplation—*per impossible*—of the whole career of consciousness as a completed system. In the work of art meaning is complete in a *version* of being, thus fulfilling by anticipation the state of affairs in immortality—the accord of meaning with being as a whole. For "parts and wholes" with reference to the important concept of *totality* see Roberto Unger, *Knowledge and Politics*, pp. 125ff. See also *Parts and Wholes*, ed. Daniel Lerner.

Behind the idea of wholeness of discourse is the organic analogy (see Plato, *Phaedrus* 264 C), and the organism which is assembled (the whole world which is assembled) in analysis is the human countenance. Closure is therefore a form of recognition.

3.5 The speaking subject in the poem is always definable in social terms, that is to say, "is always a person" (1.7).

3.6 Love is the principle of life of the speaking person.

Poetic Language

4. All poems employ an artificial, that is to say, a "poetic language."

It is characteristic of artificial languages that historical mutability is precluded by their very nature. Artificial languages are devised to exclude or control mutability (Edward Sapir).

Scholium on the arbitrariness of regarding language in poetry as "language" at all. Insofar as the poem is an artifact, its words have ceased to be language and become objects, or merely have gotten lost in the totalization which arises when the parts of a thing are superseded by the whole which they have become (Scholium at 35). The embarrassment of treating words in poetry as language can be seen in the effort to identify sentences in poetry as statements. (Cf. I. A. Richards.) If sentences in poetry are statements, then they are subject to the rules of verification and sense (such as the Aristotelian Law of Contradiction). But it is clear that these rules disable too many of the sentences of poetry (for example, those which employ metaphor). Further, statements are analyzed without reference to possible differences between speaker's meaning and hearer's meaning; but language in poetry is always language which as become the *speech of a person*, and is therefore no longer statement, or not yet statement, in any case. But as speech, as will be seen, the words in poems are also in many ways disqualified. Hence, the choice, which is always possible, of regarding the words in poems as pieces of language in any normal sense tends to be counterindicated. Language in poetry is an example of a natural thing which by being framed or contextualized in a powerful and singular way has changed its nature (35).

4.1 All poetic languages are versions of social language, that is to say, versions of socially identifiable dialects. When I speak of them as "versions" I mean that we encounter them as disguises (8.4, Scholium at 38.6).

4.2 Poetic languages are strategies to prevent the meaningless use of the human speaker—the engagement of the labor of the speaker toward any stake but his or her own.

4.3 The feature which distinguishes poetic versions of social language from natural versions of social language is *archaism* (Owen Barfield). Speech which manifests itself as poetic language has the authority of *prior* life (9.4).

Scholium on priority, interiority, and power. The idea of "archaism" associates poetry with the power of prior life. It should be noted in assessing the claims for poetry that priority, power, and divinity are mutually explanatory concepts in Western culture. "Archaism" associates poetry with the power of origination through which reality is established prior to conscious life, and toward which consciousness directs its eyes backward—as it were in retrospect, and subject to the irony of a mind known by a mind which (like the poem) cannot by its nature be known in the same sense. Inside each moment of poetic language there is the taunt (Job 38) "Where were you when I made you?"

Archaism also involves poetic language in the paradox of earliness and lateness; the prior thing is at once the firstborn and the infant and also the thing longest in the world and oldest. The poetic speaker is the archetypal *senex puer* (on this *topos*, see Ernst Robert Curtius). The middle ground of strong life does not belong to the iconology of the poem. "The novel is the art-form of virile maturity . . ." (Georg Lukács, *The Theory of the Novel*, p. 71).

The association of poetry and historical priority is legitimated as history by Vico as follows (*The New Science of Giambattista Vico*, in "Idea of the Work," p. 34):

> We find that the principle of these origins both of languages and of letters lies in the fact that the first gentile peoples, by a demonstrated necessity of nature, were poets who spoke in poetic characters. This discovery, which is the master key of this Science, has cost us the persistent research of almost all our literary life, because with our civilized natures we [moderns] cannot at all imagine and can understand only by great toil the poetic nature of these first men.

After romanticism, priority and power are modally subsumed by the category of interiority so that the archaic and the interior become identified. For the refusal of this position in modern structuralism and the return to the Semitic world construction which places the archaic and the prior in the exterior, see Jean Starobinski, "The Inside and the Outside":

> Making the most remote past coefficient to our most intimate depth is a way of refusing loss and separation, of preserving, in the crammed plenum we imagine history to be, every moment spent along the way. . . . There is no reason, however, why our interest in the cultural past should diminish if, instead of representing a part of ourselves, this past consisted in things other men have accomplished within a conceptual framework which is not and will never be ours, using a language in which we recognize nothing of ourselves. Leaving aside cultures which have not contributed to making us what we are, it is moot whether other cultures which have indeed influenced us form a history of assimilation rather than the contrary—a history of evictions.

This exilic conception constitutes a refusal of typology and entails a hermeneutic rather than a participatory civilization. Compare Blake's "ancient time" (Scholium at 41.4).

4.4 The route taken by the speaker in the poem through the poem's problem of utterance is (by the definition of speech in a *poem*) a unique route. Hence there is always only one poem. (All versions of a poem are poems.) The extent to which an utterance insists on its specificity as a unique event is the extent to which that utterance participates in the poetic quality. The source of the poetic quality is the risk of commitment of all being to an unalterably singular manifestation (19.1, Scholia at 22.6, 31.15, 42.3).

Scholium on manifestation in the one world. The association of poetry and immortality can be constructed by observing the eidetic utility inherent in the exact repeatability of sentences. Note the following from William M. Ivins, *Prints and Visual Communication*, p. 162:

> The conventional exact repeatability of the verbal class symbols gave words a position in the thought of the past that they no longer hold. The only important things the ancients could exactly repeat were verbal formulae. Exact repeatability and permanence are so closely alike that the exactly repeatable things easily become thought of as the permanent or real things, and all the rest are apt to be thought of as transient and thus as mere reflections of the seemingly permanent things. This may seem a matter of minor moment, but I have little doubt that it had much to do with the origin and development of the Platonic doctrine of Ideas and the various modifications of it that have tangled thought until the present day. The analytical syntax of sentences composed of words certainly had much to do with the origin of the notions of substance and attributable qualities, which has not only played a formative role in the history of philosophy but for long presented one of the most formidable hurdles in the path of developing scientific knowledge. At any rate, until comparatively recent times nominalism, with its emphasis on facts, its distrust of words, and its interest in how things act rather than in what they essentially are, has had little chance, and its great development has coincided remarkably with the ever-broadening development of modern pictorial methods of record and communication.

But it should be noted that all manifestation involves the risk of reduction undertaken (with more or less confidence as the state of the community in history allows) in view of the great reward of perpetualization. All manifestation, whether verbal or visual, is determinate. As Gombrich points out, we do not *see* ambiguities; we see one state of a thing and then another. (The idea of ambiguity as also of metaphor is meaningless without the fact of the constraint of presence in manifestation to univocality.) Hence in manifestation possibility is broken down. At the point where manifestation really occurs (on the outer skin as it were of representation) presence is postcatastrophic. (On poetry and the brokenness of worlds, see 31.15.) Hence the ideology of the unique language event (style) is a repetition of the nature of manifestation elevated to a moral allegory. Poetry incorporates as a *rule*, as the *differentia specifica* of its kind, the sacrificial history of presence.

Poetry thus offers a symbol of the one world which appears, as it is founded on the infinite plurality of worlds which cannot also appear. Poetry repeats in each of its instances the story about the scarcity of existence, the cosmogonic story which tells of the destruction of an infinity of worlds before the creation of this one (Leibnitz, *Monadology*, #55 ff.).

The matter is worth dwelling on. We may say that poetry, like ethical life, does not take place in the philosophical plurality of possible worlds, but in the relentless and inescapable unity of the one world as recovered perceptually.

Contrary to the Aristotelian implication that poetry is "more philosophical" than history, poetry is part of history. Poetry is one thing (an instance of that sort of thing) which actually has happened. Among all the possible things that could happen—the myths (38)—it is the one actual thing (one of the actual things) that did happen in the situation at hand. The poem as such is not the child of the experiential *esprit d'escalier*, nor does it consist of experimental counterfactuals with respect to a given state of affairs; it is the one thing that could be done by the speaker then. (It *is* that thing that was *done*.) Consequently, poetry is a hostage in the one world where finally and unexchangeably the one thing that happens (the very thing) really comes to reside.

The poem as manifestation is mounted upon the ruins of excluded possibility; and as manifestation it competes, within the horizon of human attention, for its spatiotemporal moment. In this it is like the human body. The soul is a creature of the plurality of metaphysically possible worlds; but the body, a case of representation, is bound to the one world. The body is psychophanic, the picture of the soul, competing for space in the museum of the human world. Therefore, the poem like the body is subject to the law of the one world, as it comes to mind through the eye; and the name of that law is scarcity. (Note the debate about synonymity by E. D. Hirsch and Nelson Goodman in *Critical Inquiry* 1, nos. 3, 4.)

4.5 The frame of the poem (its prosody or closure) is coterminous with the whole poem, and must be conceived as bounding the poem both circumferentially (the outer juncture with *all* being) and internally (the inner juncture, produced syllable by syllable, with its *own* being). The minimal function of closure is to fence the poem from all other statements, and most strenuously from alternative statements of the same kind. The closural frame may be more or less permeable. In Wordsworth it is more permeable (where the space outside is filled with almost audible, slightly disjunct versions of the space inside); in Ben Jonson it is less permeable (where the space outside is outer space, enemy and keeper). The quality of singularity manifested in each instant of utterance is in each case of manifestation, syllable by syllable, the frame of the poem (that is, its closure).

Scholium on frame as theater, the repetition of the sufficient conditions of perceptibility. Note the following from Barbara H. Smith, *Poetic Closure*, pp. 24, 25:

> Meter serves, in other words, as a frame for the poem, separating it from a "ground" of less highly structured speech and sound. . . . Meter is the stage of the theater in which the poem, the representation of an act of speech, is performed. It is the arena of art, the curtain that rises and falls as well as the music that accompanies the entire performance.

The poem represents the act of speech in the metrical theater which is in turn a representation of the space of appearance, the sufficient condition or *meta-topos* of the perceptibility of persons. The theater as structure is the imitation of the space in which meeting takes place, and all its enabling preconditions.

Meter (as frame or closure) as a repetition or imitation of the psycho-social world construction which enables the *pre*conditions of personal actualization is alluded to in Heidegger ("The Origin of the Work of Art," in Hofstadter, ed., *Poetry, Language and Thought*, p. 45):

> A work, by being a work, makes space for that spaciousness. "The make space for" means here especially to liberate the Open to establish it in its structure. This installing occurs through the erecting mentioned earlier. The work as work sets up a world. The world holds open the Open of the world. But the setting up of a world is only the first essential feature in the work-being of a work.

The metaphor of "frame" propagates itself throughout the theory of perception. As the enabling preformation of meaning, for example, it is the familiar paradigm of Gombrich, Kuhn, and others. Note also Erving Goffman's *Frame Analysis.* What should be emphasized is that *frame* is established through reduction by differentiation and is thus postcatastrophic, the "formal feeling" which succeeds upon "great pain." And framing in representation (including art) is the repetition as a subject of consciousness of the unconscious world-construction which is an automatic component of every moment of experience.

We cross the frame into the poem. But the edge may be anywhere like the border of the sacred grove. Often we note only a slight shudder of difference.

4.6 All poetic speech implies both a speaker and also a class of speakers.

4.7 There is always a sense in which the *object* in the poem (the speaker's *world*, the Beloved) is definable in terms other than social terms. That is to say, the distance which modulates the relationship of subject (always social, as in 3.5) and object in the poem is filled with ontological questions (theory), questions about the being of the object. All the Beloveds are alive in the philosophical ambience both of being and of being *that*. Such is *poetic* life.

Scholium on consciousness and the philosophical estate of the Beloved. When I say that the Beloved is always in some sense philosophical I place her in the classical estate of the object of consciousness. As, for example, Roberto Unger, p. 200:

> To be conscious is to have the experience of being cut off from that about which one reflects: it is to be a subject that stands over against its objects. A prerequisite of the distinction between subject and object is that the subject be capable of defining its relationship to the object as a question to which different answers might be given.

On lyric as a culture of consciousness, see 16 and Scholium at 24. It is also the case that the Beloved in lyric is an image of the perceiver as perceived. What we celebrate in the Beloved is the self as known—the principle of whose life is the paradox of storytelling.

4.8 Obscurity occurs when the measure of the distance between subject and object becomes indefinite. This phenomenon takes place (simultaneously and from the same causes) (1) within the poem and (2) between the poem as object and its subject (the reader).

7.4 The End of the Poem (1996; trans. 1999)

Giorgio Agamben Translated by Daniel Heller-Roazen[1]

My plan, as you can see summarized before you in the title of this lecture, is to define a poetic institution that has until now remained unidentified: the end of the poem.

To do this, I will have to begin with a claim that, without being trivial, strikes me as obvious—namely, that poetry lives only in the tension and difference (and hence also in the virtual interference) between sound and sense, between the semiotic sphere and the semantic sphere. This means that I will attempt to develop in some technical aspects Valéry's definition of poetry, which Jakobson considers in his essays in poetics: "The poem: a prolonged hesitation between sound and sense" (*Le poème, hésitation prolongée entre le son et le sens*). What is a hesitation, if one removes it altogether from the psychological dimension?

Awareness of the importance of the opposition between metrical segmentation and semantic segmentation has led some scholars to state the thesis (which I share) according to which the possibility of enjambment constitutes the only criterion for distinguishing poetry from prose. For what is enjambment, if not the opposition of a metrical limit to a syntactical limit, of a prosodic pause to a semantic pause? "Poetry" will then be the name given to the discourse in which this opposition is, at least virtually, possible; "prose" will be the name for the discourse in which the opposition cannot take place.

Medieval authors seem to have been perfectly conscious of the eminent status of this opposition, even if it was not until Nicolò Tibino (in the fourteenth century) that the following perspicuous definition of enjambment was formulated: "It often happens that the rhyme ends, without the meaning of the sentence having been completed" (*Multiocens enim accidit quod, finita consonantia, adhuc sensus orationis non est finitus*).

All poetic institutions participate in this noncoincidence, this schism of sound and sense—rhyme no less than caesura. For what is rhyme if not a disjunction between a semiotic event (the repetition of a sound) and a semantic event, a disjunction that brings the mind to expect a meaningful analogy where it can find only homophony?

Verse is the being that dwells in this schism; it is a being made of *murs et paliz*, as Brunetto Latini wrote, or an *être de suspens*, in Mallarmé's phrase. And the poem is an organism grounded in the perception of the limits and endings that define—without ever fully coinciding with, and almost in intermittent dispute with—sonorous (or graphic) units and semantic units.

Dante is fully conscious of this when, at the moment of defining the *canzone* through its constitutive elements in *De vulgari eloquentia* (II, IX, 2–3), he opposes *cantio* as unit of sense (*sententia*) to *stantiae* as purely metrical units:

> And here you must know that this word [*stanza*] was coined solely for the purpose of discussing poetic technique, so that the object in which the whole art of the *canzone* was enshrined should be called a stanza, that is, a capacious storehouse on receptacle for the art in its entirety. *For just as the* canzone *is the lap of its subject-matter, so the stanza enlaps its whole technique*, and the latter stanzas of the poem should never aspire to add some new technical device, but should only dress themselves in the same garb as the first. (emphasis mine)
>
> [Et circa hoc sciendum est quod vocabulum [stantia] per solius artis respectum inventum est, videlicet ut in qua tota cantionis ars esset contenta, illud diceretur stantia, hoc est mansio capax sive receptaculum totois artis. Nam quemadmodum cantio est gremium totius sententiae, sic stantia totam artem ingremiat; nec licet aliquid artis sequentibus adrogare, sed solam artem antecedentis induere.]

Dante thus conceives of the structure of the *canzone* as founded on the relation between an essentially semantic, global unit ("the lap of the whole meaning") and essentially metrical, partial units ("enlaps the whole technique").

One of the first consequences of this position of the poem in an essential disjunction between sound and sense (marked by the possibility of enjambment) is the decisive importance of the end of the poem. The verse's syllables and accents can be counted; its synaloephae and caesuras can be noted; its anomalies and regularities can be catalogued. But the verse is, in every case, a unit that finds its *principium individuationis* only at the end, that defines itself only at the point at which it ends. I have elsewhere suggested that the word *versure*, from the Latin term indicating the point at which the plow turns around at the end of the furrow, be given to this essential trait of the verse, which—perhaps on account of its obviousness—has remained nameless among the moderns. Medieval treatises, by contrast, constantly drew attention to it. The fourth book of *Laborintus* thus registers *finalis terminatio* among the verse's essential elements, alongside *membrorum distincto* and *sillabarum numeratio*. And the author of the Munich *Ars* does not confuse the end of the poem (which he calls *pausatio*) with rhyme, but rather defines it as its source or condition of possibility: "the end is the source of consonance" (*est autem pausatio fons consonantiae*).

Only from this perspective is it possible to understand the singular prestige, in Provençal and Stilnovist poetry, of that very special poetic institution, the unrelated rhyme, called *rim'estrampa* by *Las leys d'amors* and *clavis* by Dante. If rhyme marked an antagonism between sound and sense by virtue of the noncorrespondence between homophony and meaning, here rhyme, absent from the point at which it was expected, momentarily allows the two series to interfere with each other in the semblance of a coincidence. I say "semblance," for if it is true that the lap of the whole technique here seems to break its metrical closure in marking the lap of sense, the unrelated rhyme nevertheless refers to a rhyme-fellow in the successive strophe and, therefore, does nothing more than bring metrical structure to the metastrophic level. This is why in Arnaut's hands it evolves almost naturally into word-rhyme, making possible the stupendous mechanism of the sestina. For word-rhyme is above all a point of undecidability between an essentially asemantic element (homophony) and an essentially semantic element (the word). The sestina is the poetic form that elevates the unrelated rhyme to the status of supreme compositional canon and seeks, so to speak, to incorporate the element of sound into the very lap of sense.

But it is time to confront the subject I announced and define the practice that modern works of poetics and meter have not considered: the end of the poem insofar as it is the ultimate formal structure perceptible in a poetic text. There have been inquiries into the *incipit* of poetry (even if they remain insufficient). But studies of the end of the poem, by contrast, are almost entirely lacking.

We have seen how the poem tenaciously lingers and sustains itself in the tension and difference between sound and sense, between the metrical series and the syntactical series. But what happens at the point at which the poem ends? Clearly, here there can be no opposition between a metrical limit and a semantic limit. This much follows simply from the trivial fact that there can be no enjambment in the final verse of a poem. This fact is certainly trivial; yet it implies consequences that are as perplexing as they are necessary. For if poetry is defined precisely by the possibility of enjambment, it follows that the last verse of a poem is not a verse.

Does this mean that the last verse trespasses into prose? For now let us leave this question unanswered. I would like, however, at least to call attention to the absolutely novel significance that Raimbaut d'Aurenga's "No sai que s'es" acquires from this perspective. Here the end of every strophe, and especially the end of the entire unclassifiable poem, is distinguished by the unexpected irruption of prose—an irruption that, *in extremis*, marks the epiphany of a necessary undecidability between prose and poetry.

Suddenly it is possible to see the inner necessity of those poetic institutions, like the *tornada* or the envoi, that seem solely destined to announce and almost declare the end of the poem, as if the end needed these institutions, as if for poetry the end implied a catastrophe and loss of identity so irreparable as to demand the deployment of very special metrical and semantic means.

This is not the place to give an inventory of these means or to conduct a phenomenology of the end of the poem (I am thinking, for example, of the particular intention with which Dante marks the end of each of the three books of the *Divine Comedy* with the word *stelle*, or of the rhymes in dissolved verses of Leopardi's poetry that intervene to stress the end of the strophe or the poem). What is essential is that the poets seem conscious of the fact that here there lies something like a decisive crisis for the poem, a genuine *crise de vers* in which the poem's very identity is at stake.

Hence the often cheap and even abject quality of the end of the poem. Proust once observed, with reference to the last poems of *Les fleurs du mal*, that the poem seems to be suddenly ruined and to lose its breath ("it stops short," he writes, "almost falls flat . . . despite everything, it seems that something has been shortened, is out of breath"). Think of "Le cygne," such a tight and heroic composition, which ends with the verse "Aux captifs, aux vaincues . . . à bien d'autres encore!" (Of those who are captive or defeated . . . and of many more others!) Concerning a different poem of Baudelaire's, Walter Benjamin noted that it "suddenly interrupts itself, giving one the impression—doubly surprising in a sonnet—of something fragmentary." The disorder of the last verse is an index of the structural relevance to the economy of the poem of the event I have called "the end of the poem." As if the poem as a formal structure would not and could not end, as if the possibility of the end were radically withdrawn from it, since the end would imply a poetic impossibility: the exact coincidence of sound and sense. At the point in which the sound is about to be ruined in the abyss of sense, the poem looks for shelter in suspending its own end in a declaration, so to speak, of the state of poetic emergency.

In light of these reflections I would like to examine a passage in *De vulgari eloquentia* in which Dante seems, at least implicitly, to pose the problem of the end of poetry. The passage is to be found in Book II, where the poet treats the organization of rhymes in the *canzone* (XIII, 7–8). After defining the unrelated rhyme (which someone suggests should be called *clavis*), the text states: "The endings of the last verses are the most beautiful if they fall into silence together with the rhymes" (*Pulcherrime tamen se habent ultimorum carminum desinentiae, si cum rithmo in silentium cadunt*). What is this falling into silence of the poem? What is the beauty that falls? And what is left of the poem after its ruin?

If poetry lives in the unsatisfied tension between the semiotic and the semantic series alone, what happens at the moment of the end, when the opposition of the two series is no longer possible? Is there here, finally, a point of coincidence in which the poem, as "lap of the entire meaning," joins itself to its metrical element to pass definitively into prose? The mystical marriage of sound and sense could, then, take place.

Or, on the contrary, are sound and sense now forever separated without any possible contact, each eternally on its own side, like the two sexes in Vigny's poem? In this case, the poem would leave behind it only an empty space in which, according to Mallarmé's phrase, truly *rien n'aura lieu que le lieu*.

Everything is complicated by the fact that in the poem there are not, strictly speaking, two series or lines in parallel flight. Rather, there is but one line that is simultaneously traversed by the semantic current and the semiotic current. And between the flowing of these two currents lies the sharp interval obstinately maintained by poetic *mechanē*. (Sound and sense are not two substances but two intensities, two *tonoi* of the same linguistic substance.) And the poem is like the *katechon* in Paul's Second Epistle to the Thessalonians (2:7–8): something that slows and delays the advent of the Messiah, that is, of him who, fulfilling the time of poetry and uniting its two eons, would destroy the poetic machine by hurling it into silence. But what could be the aim of this theological conspiracy about language? Why so much ostentation to maintain, at any cost, a difference that succeeds in guaranteeing the space of the poem only on condition of depriving it of the possibility of a lasting accord between sound and sense?

Let us now reread what Dante says about the most beautiful way to end a poem, the place in which the last verses fall, rhymed, in silence. We know that for him it is a matter of a rule. Think, for instance, of the envoi of "Così nel mio parlar voglio esser aspro." Here the first verse ends with an absolutely unrelated rhyme, which coincides (and certainly not by chance) with the word the names the supreme poetic intention: *donna*, "lady." This unrelated rhyme, which seems to anticipate a point of coincidence between sound and sense, is followed by four verses, linked in couplets according to the rhyme that Italian metrical tradition calls *baciata* ("kissed"):

Canzon, vattene dritto a quella donna
che m'ha ferito il core e che m'invola
quello ond'io ho più gola,
e dàlle per lo cor d'una saetta;
ché bell'onor s'acquista in far vendetta.

[Poem, go straight to that woman who
has wounded my heart and stolen from
me what I most hunger for, and strike
her heart with an arrow, for one gains
great honor in taking revenge.]

It is as if the verse at the end of the poem, which was now to be irreparably ruined in sense, linked itself closely to its rhyme-fellow and, laced in this way, chose to dwell with it in silence.

This would mean that the poem falls by once again marking the opposition between the semiotic and the semantic, just as sound seems forever consigned to sense and sense returned forever to sound. The double intensity animating language does not die away in a final comprehension; instead it collapses into silence, so to speak, in an endless falling. The poem thus reveals the goal of its proud strategy: to let language finally communicate itself, without remaining unsaid in what is said.

(Wittgenstein once wrote that "philosophy should really only be poeticized" [*Philosophie dürfte man eigentlich nur dichten*]. Insofar as it acts as if sound and sense coincided in its discourse, philosophical prose may risk falling into banality; it may risk, in other words, lacking thought. As for poetry, one could say, on the contrary, that it is threatened by an excess of tension and thought. Or, rather, paraphrasing Wittgenstein, that poetry should really only be philosophized.)

NOTE

1. The lecture was presented in 1995 at the University of Geneva for a conference in honor of Roger Dragonetti, and published in Giorgio Agamben, *Categorie Italiane: Studi di poetica* (Marsilio Editori, 1996).

7.5 Why Rhyme Pleases (2011)

Simon Jarvis

It does not please everyone. Even in the British eighteenth century, one of the times and places of its highest dominance, rhyme could appear to one critic an important component of "the source of the disorders of Great Britain" (his choice of words). "A foolish admiration of this trifling and artificial ornament," wrote Thomas Sheridan, "has turned people's thoughts from the contemplation of the real and natural beauty of numbers. Like the Israelites, we have gone whoring after our own fancies, and worshipped this idol with so infatuated a zeal, that our language has in great measure fallen a sacrifice to it."[1] Sheridan's view was not unusual. Edward Young deprecated thus Pope's decision to translate Homer into rhyme.

> Had Milton never wrote, *Pope* had been less to blame: But when in *Milton*'s Genius, *Homer*, as it were, personally rose to forbid Britons doing him that ignoble wrong; it is less pardonable, by that *effeminate* decoration, to put *Achilles* in petticoats a second time: How much nobler had it been, if his numbers had rolled on in full flow, through the various modulations of *masculine* melody, into those grandeurs of solemn sound, which are indispensably demanded by the native dignity of Heroick song? How much nobler, if he had resisted the temptation of that *Gothic* Daemon, which modern Poesy tasting, became mortal? . . . *Blank* is a term of diminution; what we mean by blank verse, is verse unfallen, uncurst; verse reclaim'd, reinthroned in the true *language of the Gods*; who never thunder'd, nor suffer'd their *Homer* to thunder, in Rhime; . . . [2]

Rhyme is here denounced as from a pulpit. Rhyme, in Sheridan, is the whore of Babylon, and, in Young, it is not only the apple offered by the serpent but is also a kind of prosodic cross-dressing. The implication, of course, is Reformation. Rhyme has laid waste to classic Rome, and erected the papist one. It is time to smash the idols. But there is also a possibility of mock hovering over this characteristically English fusion of idol-breaking with Duns-slaying. Not even the most zealous idol-breakers took themselves to be reversing the Fall of Man, yet something like that seems to be envisaged by Young for verse. We can at any moment speak the language of the gods again—by removing Achilles' skirt. The passage, in fact, snakes from light comedy to millennial prophecy. The question of rhyme is at once a matter of our everlasting salvation or perdition and, on the other hand, it is not all that serious.

Young's and Sheridan's verdicts are only the most vehement deployments of a repertoire of rhyme-hating which expanded rapidly (though by no means uncontestedly) just in the epoch of rhyme's most complete domination of English verse—practice. The lexicon itself also carries the double character evident in Young. Rhyme is an idol, it is witchcraft, it is contemptible, it is depraved, it is a prostitute, it is a mercenary, it is a barbarian, it is stupefaction. Yet rhyme is also a toy, a bawble, a gewgaw, a trifle; it jingles, it tinkles, it rattles and babbles. In short, it is something of absolutely no importance whatever, which must therefore be destroyed without further delay, because it is so deeply evil.

This is not just ancient history but also part of our history. These fantasies or observations about rhyme's meaning, whether rhymophilic or -phobic, still jingle in our heads today. Whoever selects rhyme as a practicing poet today will find that, first of all, he will be understood to have performed a socially symbolic act. Rhyme belongs, in the first place, to that repertoire of metacommunicative winks and nods by which a series of poetical party affiliations can be more or less adroitly negotiated: whether your lines begin with upper- or lower-case letters, whether they are metrical or para-metrical or non-metrical, whether they are left-justified or complexly indented or migrate everywhere across the page—these devices and the choices they entail, quite certainly constitute in the case of significant poets a timbral palette of tremendous complexity.[3] But today, partly because you can see them without even needing to begin reading the poem, they are more immediately a kind of rough badge or uniform, very rapidly legible to friend or foe, who, as it were, already knows all about you even before you have begun to open your mouth. Their metacommunicative hyper-saturation threatens altogether to blot out their prosodic coloration.

There is in this way a kind of historical falling-silent of rhyme. As rhyme tends to the condition of the pure sign, the badge, its body retreats from audibility. I conjecture that each great rhyming authorship is, amongst other things, a singular rhyme-thesaurus, a repertoire of effects which are simultaneously and indissociably ideal, conceptual, semantic, syntactic, phonological, phonetic, material, contingent, stuff: in which rhyme mutely rings out its refutation of the dead metaphysics which would bore us into believing that all the categories I have just mentioned refer to real and really separable fields or entities, instead of belonging amongst the mere conveniences of procedure itself. Rhyme sounds on all these instruments at once. The great philosophical systems have their formulas, a kind of autopilots which keep the machine in motion even when thinking may temporarily not in fact be taking place; the great rimaria, rather than exposing the formula only inadvertently, where the apparatus hits a bump, instead hold the formula out to us, admit to it as though admitting that thinking is never all our own work or a matter of finding that impossible quiddity, the distinctive personal voice, but that it is, rather, the question how we shall in the right way lose our voices into those of the dead and of the unborn. When rhyme itself, however, has become attenuated to a flag, a rallying point, a party card, these effects of long-term self-interlocution and self-relinquishment appear blocked or choked. These colours of sound are bound down beneath the myth: not form but its logo, not craft but its brochure, a Cause.

One easily available response to this is to settle down into the narrative of irreversibility: to think that rhyme, just as is widely supposed to have happened to diatonicity or to figurative painting, has died in history. But this view, even were it not already empirically deficient, mischaracterizes the very innovation it would wish for. Archaism and innovation have not in the history of poetry been chalk and cheese, but speaking twins. My short essay is of course not going to be able to explain why or even prove that rhyme pleases. Not only would even the attempt at such an explanation require some sort of fabulated theory of human nature, but, still less plausibly, it would imply that rhyme itself is in some way one thing, that it too has a nature remaining constant, rather than being a device whose force is utterly caught up in the authorships, genres, and other auditory habituations and economies within which it occurs. In this sense one might as well set out to explain why a perfect cadence or a glockenspiel or the colour red pleases. Instead I want to pursue a project I have been developing for a little while now in which I understand the repertoires of prosodic gestures deployed by poets not through the idea of form but rather as a distinctive mode of knowing. I want in this way to help open up a wound, a cauterized place, in the body of our poetic culture; to attempt to listen in to rhyme's thinking through and beneath the over-saturated symbolic roles it has usually been made to play in our cultures.

1[4]

In 1962 the young English poet and scholar J. H. Prynne gave a short but interesting radio talk on the BBC. The talk charted what Prynne understood to be a revolution in the lyric taking place in the shift from first to second-generation Romanticism.

> Meditative poetry . . . at some point after Wordsworth's last contact with the Augustan tradition abandoned the ambition to present the reflecting mind as part of an experiential context and withdrew into a self-generating ambience of regret. With this went an amazing degree of control over incantatory techniques, designed to preserve the cocoon of dream-like involvement and to present a kind of constant threshold music—the apparent

movement of a gravely thoughtful mind. While the melancholia is switched on this noble undercurrent is unfailingly present.[5]

What Prynne calls the "virtuoso incantation" thus developed is, for him, an alibi. It is as though Wordsworth's sense of the anaesthetic properties of metre, metre's ability to make the intolerably painful bearable and even pleasurable, were to have become full-on narcosis. In such an account, Wordsworth's marked asceticism with respect to rich instrumentations of the verse line would have been lapsed from. What replaces it is, in this account, designed not to reveal experience, but to blot it out. The techniques of incantation are a cocoon. Life, the unbearable, lies beyond them. So they are also a fetish, mere stuff fixated upon so as to obviate experience.

One of the most important of such incantatory techniques, of course, is rhyme, which Wordsworth had also deployed, but whose significance is much more foregrounded in the second-generation British Romantics by the greater richness of intra-linear instrumentation with which it enters into relation. Prynne's remarks strikingly echo the analysis of what still, perhaps, remains the single most important book ever written about rhyme, Viktor Zhirmunsky's *Rhyme: Its History and Theory*, published in Petrograd or Petersburg—the title pages, perhaps symptomatically, offer both—in 1923, and, sadly, still awaiting translation into English. Zhirmunsky's book owes part of its importance to its scepticism about the idea that rhyme is a natural fact. Zhirmunsky shows, much more thoroughly than anyone had previously managed to, how what counts as a rhyme differs radically in differing languages and in different historical epochs of the same language and in differing authorships within those historical epochs.

Zhirmunsky develops an extended contrast between two different ways of handling rhyme in modern European, and especially in Russian, poetry. One kind of poet, like Pushkin and like Baratynsky, holds to a particular series of canons about rhyme. Masculine and feminine rhymes alternate; dactylic rhyme is rare; and care is taken to avoid a plethora of parallelisms—that is to say, the recurring parallelism of rhyme is in continuous counterpoint to a recurring contrast at the level of semantics and of syntax. Pushkin prefers rhymes in which the two rhyme-words belong to different parts of speech. The automatism associated with rhyme is thus in tension with a refusal of automatism at the level of semantics and syntax. The rhymes both sound and think.[6] (The essential features of the account which we, perhaps, know chiefly through Wimsatt on Pope are already in place in Zhirmunsky on Pushkin.)

In contrast to this classical canon of rhyme-technique Zhirmunsky develops an account of what he calls a "musical-impressionistic" handling of rhyme, already gathering in Lermontov, Tyutchev and Fet, but reaching a fortissimo in the verse of the Russian Swinburne, Konstantin Bal'mont. Bal'mont delights in just that plethora of parallelisms which had seemed vulgar to the earlier masters. Rhyme words very often come not only from the same parts of speech but also as part of repetitions of entire phrasal and melodic structures. What Roger Fowler later termed "metrical rhyme," the repetition from one line to the next or to a later line of a parallelism which is both syntactic, because it is a repetition of parts of speech, and melodic, because it is a repetition of rhythmic patterns, this 'metrical rhyme' is made, over and over again, to coincide with rhyme proper. Dactylic rhyme is favoured, and canons of alternation need not be observed. Internal rhyme is not only more prevalent in Bal'mont than in Baratynsky, but, more importantly, when combined with this drive to parallelism, changes its function. Two segments of the same line will often perform a metrico-syntactic "rhyme" as well as a phonetic one, thus bringing the integrity of the line itself into question.

These two types of prosodic repertoire, of course, are also two repertoires of thinking. Yet, for Zhirmunsky, it is clear that more thinking is going on in one repertoire than in the other. He remarks that "The romantic poets, who sought chiefly for effects of sound, are especially fond of short measures: the latter, characterized by the marks of an incantatory, 'musical' effect, represent a darkening of the side of verse which has to do with meaning, of the substantive significance of words, and a heightening of the general emotional coloration."[7] Pushkin's and Baratynsky's or Batiushkov's rhyme-technique lights meaning up, by counterpointing it; Bal'mont's obscures it, drowning it out in music. There are two striking connections here with the account by Prynne which I discussed a little earlier on. First, Zhirmunsky supplies that precisely technical account which is missing from Prynne's short talk, and which would be needed in order to explain precisely what the "virtuoso incantation" of which Prynne speaks might consist in. But second, we find in both Zhirmunsky and Prynne a sharply Platonic consensus about what thinking is and what its relation to sound might be. "Musical" rhyming, however "amazing" its "mastery," is and must be cocoon or stimulant. It cannot itself be admitted to be a kind of thinking or involved in noticing. Instead, it screens those perceptions out. Musical rhyming is automatism. It is Ion's chain of magnets: the series of automatic transmissions of inspiration awarded by Socrates to rhapsody so as to destroy the rhapsode's claim to cognition.[8]

Over the last decade or so, I have been trying to explore the question of whether music need be opposed to thinking in this way. Can there not be a musical or a prosodic thinking, a thinking which is not simply a little picture of, nor even a counterpoint to, that more familiar kind of thinking whose medium is essentially semantic and syntactic, but whose medium, instead, is essentially prosodic: a kind of thinking in tunes? Necessarily central to the formulation of this question has been the German philosopher Theodor Adorno's late *Aesthetic Theory*, and, in particular, two sets of arguments within that book.[9] The first is the argument that technique is the way art thinks. The second is the argument that art thinks historically, and that what it knows, when it thinks well, is natural-historical experience. So-called "form" becomes in Adorno's account a kind of inexplicit mimesis, a mimesis which is not of individual objects in the world, but of those features of natural-historical experience which are at once the most elusive and amongst the most important: of structural shifts in the texture of experience itself which are too painful, or too blissful, directly to be thematized. No art is about itself. So technique knows something about the world. Yet it knows it, Adorno suggests, just by the most obsessive, and perhaps even the most fetishistic and solipsistic, absorption in its own proper stuff. We can see how this might suggest a different line of enquiry from that pursued by Prynne. If technique is the way art thinks, and if self-absorption is, curiously, the way art notices others, then might this "virtuoso incantation" be, not simply a screen or a cocoon or an anaesthetic, but a medium—a medium for thinking, and for thinking about historical experience, just when in the very act of apparently retreating from it?

2

T. S. Eliot's essay of 1917, "Reflections on Vers Libre," expressed a hope which has hardly been realized: that a liberation *from* rhyme might also be a liberation *of* rhyme. "Freed from its exacting task of supporting lame verse," Eliot wrote, "it could be applied with greater effect where it is most needed."[10] But rhyme's imagined liberation does not, the way Eliot tells it, sound very free. If it were indeed intelligible to refer to a poetic *device*'s being "liberated" or "imprisoned," this would have to mean rhyme's coming in some way into its own. But rhyme cannot come into its own as an instrument put in the service of needs already known, but only as the generation of new needs. Contesting Schopenhauer's figures for rhyme, David Samoilov writes in his book about Russian rhyme that

> [P]oetic thought is "formed" in the rhythm, sound, and rhyme of verse. This is the novum which the composer of poetry introduces into thinking. And the devices of verse composition are neither fetters nor a mask, but something which conduces to the emancipation of thoughts and feelings.[11]

Rhyme which did not merely serve already existing needs and thoughts, but also generate new ones, would not really be perfectly emancipated, but perfectly dead.

It is not only possible, but perhaps even probable that, when Prynne was composing the following passage of his poem "Aristeas, In Seven Years," he had Eliot's dictum in mind.

> No one harms these people: they
>   are sacred and have no
> weapons. They sit or pass, in
>   the form of divine song,
> they are free in the apt form of
>   displacement. They change
> their shape, being of the essence as
>   a figure of extent. Which
> for the power in rhyme
> 7   *is gold, in this northern clime*
> which the Greeks so held to themselves and
>   which in the steppe was no more
>   than the royal figment.[12]

The "seven years" of the poem's title are also seven numbers in the left margin, so that a "year" comes also to be a passage of verse, and so that the transition from one "year" to another is marked by this marginal figure. And each line next to such a figure is italicized, raising the possible implications that these lines are quotations, or that they should be read in sequence with each other instead of or as well as being read in sequence with the other lines of the poem. The previous such line has read "6 *the true condition of bone*," so that we may need to read "the true condition of bone is gold, in this northern clime." But at the transition to the poem's final "year" something surprising happens. The poem, which has been not only unrhymed but apparently non- or even anti-metrical throughout, suddenly rhymes, and on the word "rhyme" itself.

At least, it seems to rhyme. But for many of the currently respectable definitions of rhyme, this may not be a rhyme at all. Sheer sound replay is not enough. For Samoilov, "Rhyme [. . .] may not be something which can equally *be present* or *not be present*—its *presence must be necessary*—for it constitutes a non-circumnavigable element of the composition of a given verse, one of its organizing principles."[13] In a long fragment left unpublished at his death, Hugh Kenner described rhyme as ". . . the production of like sounds according to a schedule that makes them predictable."[14] By neither of these accounts would this place in Prynne count as a rhyme. Its presence does not seem either necessary or predictable, because it is the only rhyme in the poem. Except that when you start to look, there are others; or, there would be others, if we were permitted to treat them as such. For example:

But it was not blessing, rather a fact so
hard-won that only the twist in middle
air would do it anyway, so even he be wise
or with any recourse to the darkness of
his tent. The sequence of issue is no
more than this, . . .

Lines one and five of this excerpt rhyme too, don't they? So : no. Here, though, we might be likely to invoke the distance between these lines, the fact that these lines end with particles (just as, throughout the poem, there is an extraordinarily high incidence of lines which end with articles, prepositions, and other verbal small change), and, here, we would be likely to invoke the absence of metre. For Viktor Zhirmunsky, in his treatise on *Rhyme: Its History and Theory*, rhyme is "any sonic replay bearing an organizational function in the metrical composition of the poem."[15] This leaves the question open about our case, though. On one hand, this poem is not metrical, and therefore this replay of "so : no" can hardly be said to have an organizational function in its metrical composition. On the other hand it can be argued that all verse is in a minimal way metrically composed in that it is divided into lines. In that case, any sonic replay at line-end would qualify. But this absence of metre also applies to "rhyme : clime." It begins to look as though our certainty that this is a rhyme rests on the fact that it is a rhyme on the word rhyme itself. Without that word, we perhaps would not even notice this replay at all.

At any rate, it does appear that there is a kind of gap between what metricians will agree to call rhyme and what readers can recognize as rhyme. For most readers, these lines by Prynne make a rhyme, and no amount of Kenner, Samoilov or Zhirmunsky will persuade them otherwise. In dominant theories of rhyme, we are in the presence, in fact, of a *metricization* of rhyme. This metricization, I want to suggest, this insistence that sonic replay which does not play an organizational role in the composition of the poem is not rhyme, is also accompanied, in the corresponding poetics, by a *logicization* of rhyme's role.

3

Both the metricization and logicization of rhyme, of course, are in one way impeccably motivated. Without its metricization we should, it is feared, be unable to distinguish rhyme from sonic replays occurring any old where in lines; without its logicization we should not see how rhyme is a form of thinking and not merely a species of sensation. Yet that last motive should give us pause. John Hollander's fine discussion of some lines from Wallace Stevens's "Notes towards a Supreme Fiction" illustrates the point.

There was a mystic marriage in Catawba,
At noon it was on the mid-day of the year
Between a great captain and the maiden Bawda,

This was their ceremonial hymn: Anon
We loved but would no marriage make. Anon
The one refused the other one to take . . .

Hollander comments thus:

> The epithalamium embedded in the firm stanzas is the rhyming couplet, pentameter to Alexandrine, concluding the Spenserian stanza: "Anon we loved but would no marriage make. / Anon the one refused the other one to take," where the inversion is part of the Spenserian echo. The brilliantly framing and bracketing "Anon"s, the rhyming of the in-

ternal, but marked "make" with the line-and-tercet terminal "take" typify Stevens's magnificent control over the structures of his verse.[16]

And he continues: "Rhyming for the later Stevens does the imagination's work and not the jingling and tinkling of evasions; it occurs as 'the luminous melody of proper sound.' "[17] There's nothing to quarrel with in this impressive analysis and evaluation, but there is something to notice: the re-appearance of some favoured terms from the lexicon of rhyme-hating. Rhyme which is to be the imagination's has to do some serious "work." Otherwise it is evasive, jingling and tinkling. The reproach that rhyme "jingles," perhaps the most frequent of all in eighteenth-century attacks on bad rhyme or on rhyme in general, accuses it of being a meaningless noise, like the jingling of bells. The strongly Protestant character of attacks on rhyme can, here, coalesce with mockery of Papist ritual. And to be attracted by such jingling is not only potentially idolatrous, but also fetishistic or perverse. We are consuming the wrapping, not the product.

Isn't there a way, here, in which the attacks on rhyme have left some mark even on one of its most ardent sympathizers? Good rhyme has to be serious rhyme which does work; it must not be evasive; it must not jingle and tinkle. Its chimes, if any, must be fully masculine, as in Emerson's resonant desiderata, quoted by Hollander:

> Rhyme; not tinkling rhyme but grand Pindaric strokes as firm as the tread of a horse. Rhyme that vindicates itself as an art, the stroke of the bell of a cathedral. Rhyme which knocks at prose & dulness with the stroke of a cannon ball. Rhyme which builds out of Chaos & Old night a splendid architecture to bridge the impassable, & call aloud on all the children of morning that the Creation is recommencing.[18]

The jubilation is infectious, but there's also quite a lot of hitting and knocking going on here, not to mention a certain amount of military activity, and Emerson's account suggests a rhyme which certainly does have an organizing role in metrical composition: the firm tread of the Pindaric horse, the beat, precisely, of metre, will rescue rhyme from perverse or effeminate tinkling (we note that rhyme plays little role in Pindar).[19] This need to cleanse rhyme from the associative colorations of idolatry, fetishism, and perversity, I want to suggest, is one of the fundamental but concealed motives behind the metricization and logicization of rhyme in canonical rhyme-theory.

One of the peaks of that range, even today, is W. B. Wimsatt's essay "One relation of rhyme to reason." In that essay Wimsatt argues that part of what makes Alexander Pope an accomplished master of rhyme is the relationship between the logical and the alogical in his rhyming. He shows, famously, how Pope varies the part of speech in his rhyme words, so that instead of nouns continually rhyming with nouns, verbs with verbs, and so on, rhyme-partnerships are more often exogamous: nouns with verbs, and so on. This matters, in Wimsatt's view, because "In literary art only the wedding of the alogical with the logical gives the former an aesthetic value. The words of a rhyme, with their curious harmony of sound and distinction of sense, are an amalgam of the sensory and the logical, or an arrest and precipitation of the logical in sensory form; they are the icon in which the idea is caught."[20] So that, for Wimsatt, when rhyme-partners present not only a semantic distinction but also a syntactical contrast, the wedding of the logical with the alogical takes place across a more marked disjunction, and is therefore more satisfying.

Illuminating as the account of Pope's technique here is, there lies behind it not only a certain poetic but also, of course, a certain metaphysic. Both depend on first making a clean cut between the sensory and the logical and, then, their subsequent satisfying wedding. Without that wedding, the alogical, including the non-semantic and non-syntactical bits of rhyme words, has no aesthetic value. It is just stuff, a corpse, waiting to be given life by the soul of logic. "The music of spoken words," Wimsatt is sure, "in itself is meager, so meager in comparison to the music of song or instrument as to be hardly worth discussion. It has become a platitude of criticism to point out that verses composed of meaningless words afford no pleasure of any kind and can scarcely be called rhythmical—let them even be rhymed."[21] Like many platitudes, however, this one may not be true, not at least if the pleasure which small children can be observed to take in Velimir Khlebnikov's "Language of the Gods" is anything to go by.[22] As the medievalist James I. Wimsatt has pointed out in an important article, the assumption that the music of spoken words is "meagre" is not proven.[23] In the first place, the richness or poverty of music is in no way dependent upon the acoustic complexity of the forces involved. Otherwise the "music" of Bach's cello suites would always be "meagre" in comparison to that of an orchestral suite by Delius. So that even were we to grant, as I do not, the assumption that the repertoires of vocal gestures deployed by poetry are in some absolute qualitative or quantitative sense insufficiently rich, this would still tell us nothing one way or the other about the poverty or richness of verbal music, which is dependent not upon the materials, but on what is done with them.

The elder Wimsatt's view has been influential, producing such significant developments and modifications of the thesis as Hugh Kenner's essay "Pope's Reasonable Rhymes."[24] Yet other critics who have written since Wimsatt and Kenner have been working at this question in ways that tend to break down the logicization of rhyme—we can think immediately, for examples, of Garrett Stewart's work on transegmental rhyme,[25] of Debra Fried's on rhyme as pun,[26] or of J. Paul Hunter's critique of what he aptly calls the "second shoe" theory of couplet rhyming.[27]

Clive Scott has drawn attention to whole practices of rhyme which, in his phrase, free rhyme from the rhyming dictionary, among them Louis Aragon's use of so-called *rimes enjambées*. In one lyric from *Les Yeux d'Elsa*, as Scott shows, there are two line-end rhymes but also a rhyme straddled deliberately across the line-end:

Bertrand mieux que Chéhéra*zade*
Savait faire passer le temps
Qui va la jeunesse insultant
Faut-il que le coeur me bri*se A*
D'autres partir pour la crois*ade*.

A "rhyme scheme" for this passage would require a new philological algebra able to incorporate verse fractions as well as integers. In this case we know that this is not simply the critic's ingenuity, both because there are many such instances in Aragon's wartime lyrics, and because in Aragon's essay, "La Rime en 1940," he explicitly promoted this kind of rhyme.[28] Like Prynne's rhyme, Aragon's is there, is a rhyme, but refuses to play an organizational role in the metrical composition of the poem (unless its deliberately *dis*organizational role—as Scott says, *rimes enjambées* have a tendency "to dissolve the syllabic integrity of the lines"—could be understood, via a kind of metrical theodicy, as an organizational role by negation).

4

Picking up some of these hints from those who have gone before me, I want now to consider a single passage from Pope's *Rape of the Lock*.

But now secure the painted Vessel glides,
The Sun-beams trembling on the floating Tydes,

While melting Musick steals upon the Sky,
And soften'd Sounds along the Waters die.
Smooth flow the Waves, the Zephyrs gently play,
Belinda smil'd, and all the World was gay.
All but the *Sylph*—With careful Thoughts opprest,
Th'impending Woe sate heavy on his Breast.
He summons strait his Denizens of Air;
The lucid Squadrons round the Sails repair:
Soft o'er the Shrouds Aerial Whispers breathe,
That seem'd but *Zephyrs* to the train beneath.
Some to the Sun their Insect-Wings unfold,
Waft on the Breeze, or sink in Clouds of Gold.
Transparent Forms, too fine for mortal Sight,
Their fluid Bodies half dissolv'd in Light.
Loose to the Wind their airy Garments flew,
Thin glitt'ring Textures of the filmy Dew;
Dipt in the richest Tincture of the Skies,
Where Light disports in ever-mingling Dies,
While ev'ry Beam new transient Colours flings,
Colours that change, whene'er they wave their Wings.[29]

If all is well you will, like me, be struck by a powerful sense of the intense musicality of these lines. If not, the analysis which follows cannot have the foolish hope of, as Wordsworth put it, trying to reason you into a belief that the lines are beautiful, but rather that of attempting analytically to account for an overwhelming experience of my own, an experience of evanescent liquidity, of a powerful seduction whose force is present precisely in its transience, in its continuous disappearance and elusiveness, rather than in, say, its symmetry or its balance or its order.

Of course some of the chief and well-known features of Pope's couplet style are in play here: the coincidence of line-ends with sentences or at least phrases, so that every large metrical unit in this passage coincides with a syntactical unit; and, just as Wimsatt stipulates, there is a high level of variation in the parts of speech placed in this position, so that only two couplets end each line with the same part of speech (sight : light // skies : dies). Yet it seems to me that this accounts very little even for the power of the rhymes in this passage, and that in order to account for that we need to think a little more about the cross-contamination between rhyme and other kinds of "sonic replay."

The first of these would be assonance, by which I mean (following Percy Adams) vowel echoes coinciding with stresses.[30] There is one very obvious reason to treat assonance in relation to rhyme, which is that it can be an important feature linking rhyme-pairs. So, if we look at the very opening of this passage, the rhyme glides/Tydes is immediately followed by the rhyme Sky/die. In other words, the verse paragraph begins not only, like every other passage, with a series of two rhyming pairs, but, much more unusually, with an emphatic series of four identical vowel sounds in identical stress-positions. The effect, I would argue, is anything but ordered and balanced: it is, rather, excessive, emphatic, enthusiastic, something like a series of cries of acclamation. The effect is something like that of rhyming rhymes, a geometrical, rather than an arithmetic, ratio of rhyme. And, I would argue, the presence of a quadruple assonance, in such a heavily metrically marked position, sheds an influence over the whole verse paragraph. Later on, that is, when this vowel sound recurs in other rhymes, we are likely involuntarily to recall this pedal point which has been set at the start of the verse paragraph: when we have Sight/Light, and Skies/Dies, we are at once likely unconsciously to recall the beginning of this passage. In these circumstances established by vowel-music, a series of thematic associations can begin to establish themselves. We are given a miniature rhyming dictionary for this rhyme which establishes a set of semantic connections: Sky, Skies, Sight and Light establish a temporary link between this vowel sound and the idea of lightness or brightness. This is not the claim that there could somehow be a natural palette of vowel-sounds, each bearing its appropriate thematic or semantic coloration. There is no such natural correspondence. But there can, instead, be what one might call clouds or mists of such associations, clouds whose force is not necessary or natural but is rather a kind of prosodic weather formation gathering in the poet's peculiar handling of verbal music. And I would want to argue that phonotextual clusters can with sufficient attention and power become something more permanently established in the *reader*'s repertoire of response, too. They become in this sense something like a *prosodic idiom*, a widely understood convention of response which poets and readers can become used to manipulating, and which can even, in course of time, and misleadingly, come to feel to poets and readers as though it were something like a feature of the language itself. This, I'd argue, is one crucial difference between linguistic competence and art-verse competence. Poets' virtuosity with prosodic patterning and prosodic idiom is not something that can ever be contractually assured. It is, instead, a performance which, like a potlatch, calls for an answering performance from the reader. Virtuosity in writing prosodic tunes calls forth an answering virtuosity in hearing them: that such tunes can sometimes be, in Johnson's word, nugatory, mists rising from the reader's brain, is in fact not simply a sign of error, but a structural feature of what it is like to respond to prosodic virtuosity. A cloud, after all, is not nothing. In *Le plaisir du texte*, Barthes writes that:

> Si je lis avec plaisir cette phrase, cette histoire ou ce mot, c'est qu'ils ont été écrits dans le plaisir (ce plaisir n'est pas en contradiction avec les plaintes de l'écrivain). Mais le contraire? Écrire dans le plaisir m'assure-t-il—moi, écrivain—du plaisir de mon lecteur? Nullement. Ce lecteur, il faut que je le cherche (que je le «drague»), *sans savoir où il est*. Un espace de la jouissance est alors crée. Ce n'est pas la «personne» de l'autre qui m'est nécessaire, c'est l'espace: la possibilité d'une dialectique du désir, d'une *imprévision* de la jouissance: que les jeux ne soient pas faits, qu'il y ait un jeu.[31]

> [If I read this phrase, this story or this word with pleasure, it is because they have been written in pleasure (this pleasure is in no way contradicted by the complaints of the writer). But the opposite? Does writing in pleasure guarantee me—me, the writer—the pleasure of my reader? In no way. This reader, it is necessary that I seek him (that I "chat him up"), *without knowing where he is*. A space for bliss is thus created. It is not the "person" of the other which I require, it is the space: the possibility of a dialectic of desire, of an *unforeseenness of* bliss: that all bets are not already placed, that there be something in play] (my translation).

I want to suggest that it may be just this kind of space for bliss (admittedly not the only nor the usual translation of *jouissance*) that Pope's "unfixed" prosodic effects open up—precisely one that can never be guaranteed but that is like a venture, a gamble, a surmise. It is a seduction in which I do not know where the other is, and in which I therefore do not know what it would take to please her, and in which I therefore take the risk that my pleasure can also be hers: in other words, in which I can seduce the other only by relinquishing myself into my own art. Common sense and professional literary criticism alike have often tended, for some good reasons, to operate an excluded middle between fantasy and intention. Either the poet intended an effect or the reader is making it up. But because prosodic thinking operates right at the threshold of intentionality, the difficulty of deciding whether its effects are nugatory or real is in fact constitutive of the field of prosodic thinking, both in its composition and in the recomposition which takes place every time even a silent performance of verse is undertaken. All the right responses always have to be fantasized first before they can be real. Art makes up what is already there, and then the reader has to make it up again too.

What all this first of all instructs us in, I want to suggest, is the somewhat theoreticist character of any sharp distinction between terminal-rhyme or "rhyme proper" and so-called "casual" (Zhirmunsky) or intra-linear rhyme when compared with any actual experience of the phonotext. The distinction, that is, may be a clear one for the analyst, yet in the *experience* of reading, rhyme and assonance are intimately linked, and especially so when, as we have seen here, there is assonance among the rhyme-pairs themselves, and especially so when these rhyming rhymes occur at the very beginning of a verse paragraph. This passage is quite exceptionally saturated with assonantal and alliterative echoes, and Pope continually varies the degree of saturation which he permits. In lines 53–54, for example, we have very little of this kind of instrumentation going on; the lines stand as a kind of plain contrast to the prosodic fireworks set off around them. Let's take, for example, the assonances in lines 59–60: "Some to the Sun their Insect-Wings unfold, / Waft on the Breeze, or sink in Clouds of Gold." Here we have rhymes not only at the end of the line, unfold/Gold, but also "rhymes" buried right in the middle of the line "sink" and "wings." The rhymes are buried here not only because they are in the middle of lines, at different metrical positions, and therefore, according to Kenner's or Zhirmunsky's schedules, do not count as rhymes, but also because they are buried within word-units: the rhyme in each case is "ing," and in both cases, the rhyme is completed before the final consonant of the word-unit is finished. As I have said, for Kenner and Zhirmunsky these are merely assonances. Yet "assonance" does not quite seem right either, because assonance concerns only the stressed vowel, whereas here we have a complete replay of both vowel and consonant. In other words, the only aspect which is missing for these to be recognized as "rhymes" is metrical function. I should like to suggest that we think of these replays as "fugitive" rhymes, or, to borrow my lexicon from the poem itself, as "quick" and "unfixed" ones.

This, though, is only the start of the saturatedness of this couplet. In the second line of it we not only have a buried fugitive rhyme with the middle of the first line, we also have a buried rhyme within the second line itself "ink ink": "sink in Clouds." Once explained, this subsides. It's like explaining a joke or making explicit a flirtation: not funny once explained, not seductive once explained. But it is part of the poet's virtuosity that of course this event—and here it is completely unlike line-end rhyme—will go past far too fast consciously to be noticed. Later these quick and unfixed rhymes sound out with the whole band behind them. Those singing inks which have been seen and heard only beneath the threshold now spill over or take flight into the end rhymes "flings" and "wings."

5

After all this, then, I would like to propose a different interpretation of the power in Pope's rhyme than the logicized one given by Wimsatt and Kenner. Pope's rhyme has the power it does partly because of its opening itself to all sorts of other, less metrically foregrounded, tinklings and jinglings. The illicit, perverse attachment which Pope shows to passages of deeply saturated phonotextual repetition achieves a power in itself which pulls sometimes against, rather than always with, the semantic organization of argument. Pope's virtuosity works through contamination between assonance and rhyme, so that the emphatic chords of end rhyme gain half their power from the whispers and mutterings which have gone before them. In this atmosphere they sound less like returns to order after an excursion than like the full soundings out of an obsessiveness which has earlier been kept suppressed. Here indeed is "virtuoso incantation," and long before the date fixed for its ascent by the young Prynne.

In *The Rape of the Lock* Pope does something much more interesting than satirizing the *beau monde*. What he does instead is to enter into its obsessions. The poem's first line promises an account of "what mighty contests rise from trivial things." This is no joke. Mighty feelings fix upon what are, from another point of view, mere toys. Readers are never permitted to attain a secure distance from their magic. A well-known trap lies in wait for anyone advertising calm detachment. Belinda's lock is compared to Othello's missing handkerchief. But this is double mock: a handkerchief is no way grander than a lock of hair, and so the irony redounds not on Belinda, but on whoever would imagine that he himself could never be so foolish as to get upset about something so insignificant.

Of Pope's ways of understanding how deeply serious triviality is, the most significant, I want to suggest, is not by the conventional means of characterizing it or exhaustively describing it. Pope enters in by means of an obsessive attention to the requirements of his own world of luxury objects of desire, the world of the traps, toys, and devices of verse. He is able to understand the polite world as a world of signs, of part-objects, partly because of his own relationship to verse. I said earlier on that rhyme tends to fall silent, that its force tends to become suppressed by its metacommunicative job. When Pope makes *all Arabia breathe from yonder box*, what he is describing is the very fragrance of such metacommunication. You inhale the perfume, but you smell Arabia. It is a scent more delicious and more death-like and more tenaciously fixated upon than any earthly one could ever be, the scent of a sign.

Here I am, in front of the television. I am watching a short film about a computer. In the middle of the film, its undersong of bad imitation-*Kraftwerk* is interrupted. A glowing logo (the death-mask of *logos*) shines out, and, simultaneously, a new *musical* element breaks in upon me: the *acoustic trademark*, music's very coffin. This proprietor has succeeded in compelling every manufacturer who uses this component to stick this sounding symbol in its film. Every last part of skin must be made symbolic. The ear is to be branded from inside. We are today undergoing the attempted discursification and infrastructuralization of the entire perceptual field. At every moment some kind sign, some logico-sensuous avatar or other icon, would screen us from the unbearable reality of perception.

For Wordsworth, the opposition between imagination and fantasy was cardinal. To blur it risked raising counter-spirits. Matthew Arnold's view was that Pope was a classic of our prose. But Wordsworth thought Pope was a witch, a sorcerer and seducer through melody. The pleasures of verse in no way represent some entirely unmediated category of "sheer sensuous pleasure," however much they might feel like that. The notion of sheer sensuous pleasure, in the case of verbal art, is only the obverse of an inner logicism. Yet might they be, not counter-spirits, but counter-fetishes? Collections of all sorts of paralinguistic material are invested by the adepts with intensely powerful feelings, meanings and associations which come from all sorts of other places. Can there be subterranean affinities and reproaches operating among Pope's verse fetishism, the reader's verse fetishism, and those relays and circuits of fetishism which organize and produce pleasure in our collective life? That Pope's style was habitually and routinely by everyone described as "polished"—this itself testifies to a felt link between the intensively worked-over surface of his verse and the gleaming cabinets, tables, canes and snuff-boxes evoked in *The Rape of the Lock*. Grant this, that rhyme is a bauble, a gewgaw, a toy; then Pope might perhaps be playing about with it, yet in such a way that the whole toyshop is named and known.

It is Arnold's view, not Wordsworth's, which has prevailed, even and especially where Pope is praised. Pope's technique—with some of the exceptions I mentioned earlier—is taken for an exhibit in the imaginary museum of a so-called and in fact truly nugatory "Augustanism." But it is Wordsworth, and not Arnold, who actually understood what was at stake in Pope's writing, because he knew in person the tremors of those melodies, having lived before that radical emancipation or deafening of the prosodic ear which reduced to a heading in a sub-romantic narrative of dead ratiocination a verse repertoire which was in its time the occasion of actual intensities of delight. No one read Pope primarily because of his balance, his orderliness, or his Augustan moral vision. What Pope's contemporaries mostly noticed about his verse, instead (these are all their terms, not mine—not all are compliments) was its sweetness, its variety, its gay finery, its embroidery, its vivacity, its colouring, its glitterings, its flourish, its debauch, its embellishment, its *enflure*, its tunableness, its suavity, its easiness, its spirit, its elevation, its glare, its dazzle, its fluency, its musicality, its melodiousness.[32] We have been well taught to distinguish rhyme which does the imagination's work from another kind of rhyme which offers "the tinkling and jingling of evasions." But Pope, the verse-junkie, also offers us, if you like, the tinklings and jinglings of imagination. In epochs of tendentially total deflection, might imagination be bound also to work through and out of fantasy rather than only in purification from it? Just as though, after all, these quick and unfixed rhymes might turn out to be the very melody of bliss.

NOTES

1. Thomas Sheridan, *British Education: Or, The Source of the Disorders of Great Britain* (London, 1756), pp. 283–84.

2. Edward Young, *Conjectures upon Original Composition* (London, 1759), pp. 58–6.

3. Compare Eleanor Berry, "The Emergence of Charles Olson's Prosody of the Page Space," *Journal of English Linguistics* 30: 1 (March 2002), 51–72.

4. A version of this section of the argument appears in an article on "The Melodics of Long Poems" in *Textual Practice* (Summer 2010).

5. J. H. Prynne, "The Elegiac World in Victorian Poetry," *The Listener*, February 14th, 1963, 290–91, p. 290.

6. For example, V. M. Zhirmunsky, *Rifma: eyo istoriya i teoriya* (Petersburg, 1923) [repr. Mu*nchen: Wilhelm Fink Verlag, 1970, ed. Dmitrij Tschiûewski et al., with a new preface by the author [Slavische Propyläen: Texte in Neu- und Nachdrucken, 71]], p. 83, where Zhirmunsky discusses this phenomenon in Pushkin's *The Bronze Horseman*, anticipating by some decades Wimsatt's more often quoted article on the topic.

7. Zhirmunsky, pp. 39–40.

8. Plato, *Ion* 533c-535a, in *Plato on Poetry*, ed. Penelope Murray (Cambridge, Cambridge University Press, 1996), pp. 41–42.

9. T. W. Adorno, *Aesthetic Theory*, trans. Robert Hullot-Kentor (London: Continuum, 2002).

10. Eliot, *Selected Prose*, ed. Frank Kermode (New York: Harcourt Brace Jovanovich, 1975), p.36.

11. David Samoilov, *Kniga o russkoi rifme* (Moscow: Khudozhestvennaya Literatura, 1973), p. 5.

12. J. H. Prynne, "Aristeas, in Seven Years" in *Poems* (Tarset, Northumberland, and Fremantle, Western Australia: Bloodaxe Books, 2005), pp. 90–96, p. 94.

13. Samoilov, p. 13.

14. Hugh Kenner, "Rhyme: An Unfinished Monograph", in *Common Knowledge* 10:3 (2004), 377–425.

15. Viktor Zhirmunsky, *Rifma: eyo istoriya i teoriya* ["Rhyme: Its History and Theory"] (Petersburg, 1923) [repr. München: Wilhelm Fink Verlag, 1970, ed. Dmitrij Tschischewski et al., with a new preface by the author [Slavische Propyläen: Texte in Neu- und Nachdrucken, 71]], p. 3 (my translation).

16. Hollander, "Rhyme and the True Calling of Words," in *Vision and Resonance: Two Senses of Poetic Form* (New York: Oxford University Press, 1975), pp. 117–34, pp. 132–3.

17. Hollander, p. 133.

18. Emerson's journal, 27 June 1839. Quoted in Hollander, p. 119.

19. For a discussion of rhyme and near-rhyme in classical Latin and Greek, see Eva H. Guggenheimer, *Rhyme Effects and Rhyming Figures: A Comparative Study of Sound Repetitions in the Classics with Emphasis on Latin Poetry* (The Hague and Paris: Mouton, 1972 [De proprietatibus litterarum, series maior, 18]).

20. W. B. Wimsatt, "One Relation of Rhyme to Reason," in *The Verbal Icon. Studies in the Meaning of Poetry* (New York: The Noonday Press, 1958), pp. 152–66, p. 165.

21. Wimsatt, p. 165.

22. Personal experiment, 4.iii. 2005.

23. James I. Wimsatt, "Rhyme/Reason, Chaucer/Pope, Icon/Symbol," *Modern Language Quarterly*, 55.1 (March 1994), 17–46.

24. Hugh Kenner, "Pope's Reasonable Rhymes," *English Literary History*, 41:1 (Spring, 1974), 74–88.

25. Garrett Stewart, "Rhymed treason: A Microlinguistic Test Case," in *Reading Voices: Literature and the Phonotext* (Berkeley: University of California, 1990), pp. 66–99, p. 69.

26. Fried, "Rhyme Puns," in *On Puns: The Foundation of Letters*, ed. Jonathan Culler (Oxford: Basil Blackwell, 1988), pp. 83–99, p. 89.

27. J. Paul Hunter, "The Heroic Couplet: Its Rhyme and Reason," *Ideas*, 4.1 (1996), http://nationalhumanitiescenter.org/ideasv41/hunter4.htm (accessed 28.vi.2010). See also the same author's "Sleeping Beauties: Are Historical Aesthetics Worth Recovering?" *Eighteenth-Century Studies* 34.1 (2000), 1–20.

27. 8 Clive Scott, "Aragon, *Les Yeux d'Elsa*" in *The Riches of Rhyme: Studies in French Verse* (Oxford: Clarendon Press, 1988), pp. 266–304, p. 271.

29. Alexander Pope, "The Rape of the Lock" [five-canto version] in *The Rape of the Lock and Other Poems*, ed. Geoffrey Tillotson (London: Methuen and New Haven: Yale University Press, 1962), pp. 162–64, ll. 47–68.

30. Percy G. Adams, *Graces of Harmony: Alliteration, Assonance and Consonance in Eighteenth-Century British Poetry* (Athens, Georgia: University of Georgia Press, 1977).

31. Roland Barthes, "Le Plaisir du texte" [1973] in *Oeuvres complètes* (5 vols, Paris: 2002), vol. 4, pp. 219–61, p. 220.

32. "Sweet", "sweetly": Leonard Welsted (John Barnard, ed., *Pope: The Critical Heritage* (London and Boston: Routledge and Kegan Paul, 1973), p. 53), George Granville, Baron Lansdowne (Barnard, p. 60); "Variety": Thomas Parnell, "How ev'ry Music varies in thy Lines!" (Barnard, p. 56), Lewis Theobald (Barnard, p. 122), though John Dennis disagreed (Barnard, p. 76, p. 97); "finery": dialogists invented by Joseph Spence (Barnard, p. 174, p. 179); "embroidery": in Spence (Barnard, p. 180); "vivacity": in Spence (Barnard, p. 179); "colouring": in Spence (Barnard, p. 170); "glitterings": in Spence (Barnard, p. 171); "flourish": in Spence (Barnard, ibid.); "debauch": in Spence (Barnard, p. 174); "embellish[ed]": William Melmoth (Barnard, p. 137); "*Enflure*": in Spence, *An Essay on Pope's Odyssey* (2 vols, London and Oxford, 1726), vol. 1, p. 71; "tunableness": in Spence (Barnard, p. 178); "suavity of numbers": Gilbert Wakefield, *Observations on Pope* (London, 1796), sig. a2; "easy measures": Leonard Welsted (Barnard, p. 53); "sprightly and easy": Richard Fiddes, *A Prefatory Epistle Concerning Some Remarks to Be Published on Homer's Iliad: Occasioned by the Proposals of Mr. Pope towards a New English Version of That Poem* (London, 1714), p. 9; "spirit": Berkeley (Barnard, p. 94); "elevated beauties": in Spence (Barnard, p. 171); "glaring", "dazzling": in Spence, *An Essay*, vol. 1, p.10; "fluency": in Spence, *An Essay*, vol. 1, p. 54 "musical", "melodious": Joseph Warton, *An Essay on the Genius and Writings of Pope* (third edition, 2 vols, London, 1772), p. 10.

PART THREE

Lyric Departures

SECTION 8

Avant-garde Anti-lyricism

In Part 3 of this anthology, we turn to departures from the ambitious claims for lyric made by the essays in Parts 1 and 2. In his introduction to the *Ubuweb Anthology of Conceptual Writing*, the poet and critic Craig Dworkin begins with a definition and a provocation:

> Poetry expresses the emotional truth of the self. A craft honed by especially sensitive individuals, it puts metaphor and image in the service of song.
>
> Or at least that's the story we've inherited from Romanticism, handed down for over 200 years in a caricatured and mummified ethos—and as if it still made sense after two centuries of radical social change. It's a story we all know so well that the terms of its once avant-garde formulation by William Wordsworth are still familiar, even if its original manifesto tone has been lost: "I have said," he famously reiterated, "that poetry is the spontaneous overflow of powerful feelings; it takes its origin in emotion recollected in tranquility."
>
> But what would a non-expressive poetry look like?[1]

Dworkin's literary history skips over the critical history presented in this anthology, and it does so for a reason. By performing "a caricatured and mummified" definition of the lyric as the remainder of the avant-garde energy of a Romanticism long gone but still invoked as a norm, Dworkin can open the way for a future alternative, for contemporary avant-gardes that free themselves of that outworn generic creed. If Romanticism was associated with the personally expressive lyric, then the new poetry might define itself as nonexpressive, and hence as nonlyric. This appositional framework for twentieth- and early twenty-first-century poetics has by now become familiar, but in the context of *The Lyric Theory Reader*, it is worth pausing over the definition of lyric against which avant-garde poets so often define their own projects and which criticism has begun to adjust in order to take account of those projects.

In their 1988 "Aesthetic Tendency and the Politics of Poetry: A Manifesto," a group of such poets (Ron Silliman, Carla Harryman, Lyn Hejinian, Steve Benson, Bob Perelman, and Barrett Watten) complained that

> the narrowness and provincialism of mainstream literary norms have been maintained over the last twenty years in a stultifyingly steady state in which the "personal," expressive

> lyric has been held up as the canonical poetic form. . . . The elevation of the lyric of fetishized personal "experience" into a canon of taste has been ubiquitous and unquestioned—leaving those writing in other forms and to other ends operating in a no-man's-land in terms of wider critical acknowledgement and public support (262).

Rather than cast the " 'personal,' expressive lyric" as outworn romanticism, these poets suggested that whatever its origin might have been, by the late twentieth century the lyric had become "canonical," had become not only the mainstay in the "canon of taste" but the basis of institutional policy and cultural transmission (in the creative writing programs that emerged after the middle of the twentieth century as well as in the practice of institutionally ensconced and professionally influential critics). By the end of the twentieth century, there was general agreement that the lyric had become the icon of what Charles Bernstein famously called "official verse culture." Certainly the reaction against that official version of poetics has produced a welcome proliferation of alternative verse cultures, but it has also eventuated in a retrospectively normative and curiously narrow (even "mummified") definition of the lyric.

As we have seen in previous sections of this anthology, twentieth-century critical thought produced an increasingly capacious but highly variable sense of poetry as lyric. The historical shift in and modern confusion between the function of poetic genres put pressure on the lyric to be many things at once, and the modern lyric developed into what Genette would call an "archi-genre" or super-sized category for modern critical thought. That expansion followed the nineteenth-century history of the lyricization of poetry itself, a process that began before the Romantics and continued long after them. In the course of that uneven process, stipulative verse genres that once belonged to neoclassical taxonomies or to certain communities or to specific modes of circulation gradually collapsed into a more and more abstract idea of poetry that then became associated with the lyric. The audience for that more abstract, lyricized poetic genre eventually became literary critics, as professional reading practices displaced popular or local verse reading practices. On this larger view, the avant-garde anti-lyricism of Dworkin or the Language poets, or Bernstein, or many other loosely affiliated poets who would place themselves in a no-longer-lyric modernist and post-modernist textual tradition are themselves part of the history of lyricization. As miscellaneous verse genres collapsed into a lyricized version of poetry as a modern genre, so that modern lyricized notion of poetry blurred until it gave way to an idea of poetry that no longer needed the lyric as a generic placeholder, but that continues to need the lyric as the definition of the kind of poetry it is not.

From the larger historical perspective of the process of lyricization, it is not hard to see how and why avant-garde reactions against the lyric have entailed increased confusion over what *lyric* means. While the late twentieth-century reaction formation of avant-garde anti-lyricism offers a cleaner definition of the lyric than critics in the middle of the twentieth century tended to maintain, a persistent confusion about the historical placement of the lyric threatens that definition. Even (or perhaps especially) critics who agree that the lyric is not a Romantic inheritance but the creation of modern literary criticism have a hard time telling the difference. In a 2009 essay on "Lyric after Language Poetry," for example, Jennifer Ashton attaches a long footnote to "the kinds of projects we commonly identify either with lyric as such or with its critique." In that footnote, Ashton cites Vendler, Johnson, Cameron, Grossman, and William Waters as critics who "have explicitly asserted or otherwise helped to secure the idea of lyric's domination" and Mark Jeffreys as a critic who "reverses the idea of lyric domination," charging that "a reactionary ideology inheres in the genre." She then suggests that Virginia Jackson "proposes an even stronger version of Jeffreys's argument."[2] In the context of *The Lyric Theory Reader*, we can understand Ashton's confusion as symptomatic of a particular moment in the history of lyric reading. She begins by resisting the domination of a kind of criticism. She then moves to counter such critical domination by invoking Mark Jeffreys's description of a historical process through which "poetry was reduced to lyric," but she conflates that historical process with a later moment in twentieth-century criticism when she quotes Jeffreys as claiming that "a reactionary ideology inheres in the genre." In fact, by describing the process of what Virginia Jackson later called *lyricization*, Jeffreys meant to suggest that the assignment of a reactionary ideology to the lyric (often mistaken as the actual reactionary politics of the New Critics themselves) was a mistake. Ashton then compounds that mistake when she attributes the claim Jeffreys does not make to Jackson, who also does not make it. Jackson actually argues that modern lyric reading is so capacious that it cannot have one ideology, least of all that associated with the New Critics. Jackson does not extend Jeffreys's argument any more than the New Critics extended a Romantic lyric ideology, but critical accounts of avant-garde anti-lyricism have often had a difficult time in distinguishing between a critical construction of the lyric that by the late twentieth century had come to seem like a regime in need of being overthrown and the longer history of lyricization, in which what avant-garde poets retrospectively call the lyric may be a stage in the process of abstracting all verse genres into a larger and ever more capacious idea of poetry, a process in which avant-garde poetics is itself a later stage.

Marjorie Perloff is perhaps the foremost critic who early and often took up the cause of that later poetics against a normative or canonical—and, retrospectively, apparently both narrow and dominant—conception of poetry as lyric. In the 1987 essay with which we open this section of the anthology, Perloff begins by presenting her readers with a series of texts "explicitly presented by their authors as poems" but which "readers brought up on Romantic and modernist poetry may have difficulty recognizing" as such. According to Perloff's logic, the reason that such recognition would not have been forthcoming in the late 1980s was that most readers would have agreed with Paul de Man that "the principle of intelligibility, in lyric poetry, depends on the phenomenalization of the poetic voice."[3] Perloff's adoption of de Man's definition of a lyric norm he also wants to deconstruct may be ironic, but it also indicates that, like de Man, Perloff wants to destabilize the reading practices that have made a certain version of the lyric—specifically, the short poem representing a dramatic speaker or "lyric I"—into an object of general cultural recognition. Thus it is not poetic practice itself but a particular critical reading practice that is the target of Perloff's critique, though that critique claims to represent the point of view of avant-garde poets for whom "*Poetry* . . . has less to do with the Romantic conception of the lyric as 'an intensely subjective and personal expression' (Hegel), the 'utterance that is not so much heard as overheard' (John Stuart Mill), than with the original derivation of *lyric* as a composition performed on a lyre, which is to say that it is a verbal form directly related to its musical origins." Perloff shuttles very quickly here between a modern critical norm, a nineteenth-century ideal, and an apparently premodern, pre-Romantic archaic association of lyric with the music produced by the lyre. As we have seen, that latter definition of the lyric is no more original or fundamental than the Romantic subjective ideal, and there is hardly a straight line between that Romantic ideal and the modern lyric, but the persistent association of the lyric with music allows Perloff to extend a lyricized notion of poetry to include poems that are textually promiscuous, that are bound to the page rather than to the fiction of an overheard speaker. Perloff wants to keep an essentially lyric sense of poetics alive in those texts, since lyricism is what has come to define poetry as such; what she wants to reject is a normative (what Dworkin might call "mummified" or Ashton a "dominant") definition of the lyric as the form lyricism needs to take.

Not surprisingly, Perloff locates that outmoded sense of the lyric in literary criticism, and particularly in the mid-1980s criticism that announced its departure from the New Criticism. Instead of the desired rejection of the self-enclosed and self-expressive lyric as poetic norm (desired not only by Perloff and avant-garde poetics but also, professedly, by the critics included in the volume that announced itself in 1985 as a new set of readings of *Lyric Poetry: Beyond the New Criticism*), Perloff finds an embrace of that definition of the old normative lyric by the very critics who claim they want to surpass or circumvent old poetic models. "The reason for this is clear," Perloff argues:

> The genre continues to be defined normatively—it is this situation that bedevils current discourse about poetry. For nowhere in *Lyric Poetry* do we find discussion of the following questions: (1) Is 'lyric' merely another word for 'poetry,' as the interchangeable use of the words in the collection would suggest? If so, why talk about 'lyric poetry'; if not, what other kinds of poetry are there and what is their relationship to lyric? (2) How has lyric poetry changed over the centuries? . . . (3) since the etymology of the word *lyric* points to its musical derivation, what does it mean to write of lyric poetry as if its sound structure were wholly irrelevant. . . . What, for example, does the choice of a particular meter mean?

These are all good questions, and Perloff is right that the answers to them have been bedeviled, but this discursive confusion may not be the result of a normative definition of the lyric. The tangle is caused instead by the confusion inherent in contemporary discourses about the lyric. To take the first question seriously and answer "yes," one would need to understand the history of lyricization as what happened when stipulative verse genres gave way to the larger idea of the lyric as a genre; but if one thinks about the history of the genre in that way, then question 2 becomes moot and question 3 no longer needs to be posed, since the definition of the genre cannot be fixed by its archaic origin.

Perloff recognizes this problem and so turns her discussion away from contemporary critical discourse toward the nineteenth-century British poem on which her essay's title puns. Tennyson's memorial poem to the British cavalry regiment that was wiped out at Balaclava in 1854 serves as counterpoint to the abstract versions of the modern lyric late twentieth-century literary critics tended to maintain. Perloff attempts a historical reading of "The Charge of the Light Brigade" (via Jerome McGann) to point out the ways in which it does *not* conform to later critical models of the lyric and thus casts those critical models into question. "The 'differential' that a poem like 'The Light Brigade' represents," Perloff writes, "should prompt us to reconsider the forms our own postmodern lyric is assuming." Perloff's suggestion is that Tennyson's poem is a lyric, but a different sort of lyric than the poems modern critics tend to recognize as such, in part because Tennyson's poem did a very different kind of cultural work than the "intersubjective confirmation of the self" that Herbert Tucker names as the task of the lyric (see section 2). So might postmodern poetry remain lyric but perform a different sort of cultural work since "form . . . is never more than the extension of culture." If Perloff began her essay by resisting the normative modern critical sense of the lyric, she ends it by arguing for a more liberal critical sense of lyricism, a sense that would embrace historical shifts in verse genres. In this view, avant-garde poetics would not be anti-lyrical, but would be lyric in a way we have yet to learn to recognize as such.

The extension of lyricism (or as he prefers to call it, "rapture") out toward new horizons of expectation is also Charles Altieri's theme in "What Is Living and What Is Dead in American Postmodernism: Establishing the Contemporaneity of Some American Poetry." Like Perloff, Altieri wants to bridge the gap between modern critical models and postmodern poets' sense that they need to push back against those models. What sort or critical account could accommodate and adapt its paradigms to that push? Altieri begins by giving Robert Creeley and Frank O'Hara credit for departing from the mid-twentieth-century American New Critical ideals that "left the poet trapped in a culture of vague idealizations and insufficiently examined psychological constructs." The result was what Altieri calls "a directly instrumental rather than contemplative use of language," a "resistance to artefactuality." Altieri's "best single contemporary example of this anti-artefactuality" is the last stanza of O'Hara's friend John Ashbery's 1979 poem, "As We Know," because, Altieri writes, "this poem is remarkable primarily for what it refuses to do." What it refuses to do is embrace its own "lyric climax," which "takes place as a moment of embarrassment." This is to say that in Altieri's reading, "As We Know" is lyric despite itself, lyric despite the fact that "this kind of poetry cannot hope to provide any overt imaginative order for the particulars it engages; nor can it build capacious structures." The poem's last words, "really now," become for Altieri "only marks of an alienation that cannot find its way to lyric expression." The reader's task is thus to inherit the burden of lyricism the poem approaches but can't quite own. Altieri extends the protocols of lyric reading past the poem itself, into the affirmations the poem itself refuses.

This is a tricky strategy for overcoming the divide between a postmodern poetics that resists or plays at the edges of older lyric models and the critic's wish to sustain those models. Altieri acknowledges this trickiness, especially when he turns to the work of "recent self-consciously ethnic poetry that attempts to reconfigure how the lyric imagination can engage the memories and desires binding agents to specific communal affiliations." Here "lyric" has shifted toward its Romantic resonance, and that sense of individual expression is set in tension with collective identity. We have seen this tension invoked many times in the *Lyric Theory Reader*, notably in Frankfurt School thought about the lyric as social vehicle, and indeed Altieri takes up Hegel's "notion of substance" in order to account for "the dense cultural networks within which agents feel at once interpellated and alienated." As we have seen, for Adorno such Hegelian logic allowed the lyric to become the objective correlative of the simultaneous alienation and interpellation of the modern subject, but perhaps because Altieri's objects of study are not the crystalline, abstract post-Symbolist poems of Stefan George but the postmodern poetry of Myung Mi Kim, which scoots around on the page between consonants and phonemes, his use of Hegel's idea differs from Adorno's. Rather than fix the alienation of the subject in a glittering lyric artefact, the poetry that Altieri considers tends to emphasize "the range of expressive registers that agents bring into focus simply by manipulating and elaborating deictics." Altieri wants to preserve some version of Hegelian subjective agency, but he does so on the run, as it were, or as in his reading of Ashbery, he manages to do so despite the poets' own refusals to be affiliated with that lyric ideal. Thus deictics—"pointing" words such as here, now, you, there, I, this—which, as we have seen, are so often associated with the phenomenology of present-tense lyric reading, become the remaining traces of the lyric ideal, become all that is left after "the elemental decomposition and reorientation of subjectivity" that postmodern poetics pursues.

Altieri's exemplary instance of that double movement, of the now-you-see-it-now-you-don't lyricism that characterizes his reading of postmodern American poetry, is Lyn Hejinian's long poem *The Cell*. Too lengthy and scattered to conform to the older definition of the lyric as brief and expressive, Hejinian's book-length poem becomes for Altieri "a lyric diary." The difference between a lyric and Hejinian's "lyric diary" is the difference between the modern genre and its postmodern successor; for Altieri, that new genre can resist the lyric without abandoning the lyric since it still relies on "lyric self-reflection" but does so in a way that "sets the mind against its own images, not simply to maintain ironic distance but also to dramatize the resonant forces that circulate around the desire for self-representation." Here as elsewhere, Altieri wants to trace the the fort-da game that post-modern poetics plays with modern lyric models. He does not allow avant-garde poetics simply to resist or reject the critical "elevation of the lyric of fetishized personal 'experience' into a canon of taste," as Hejinian and her fellow avant-garde collaborators had wanted to do a decade earlier; instead, he wants to map the contours of a "lyrical intelligence responsive to the delights embedded in the panoramas language affords, as if in this alternative to specular self-reflection, in this gentle and mobile distance, may lie our peace." What is interesting about Altieri's account of Hejinian's "lyric diary" is the way Hejinian needs a sense of a conventional modern lyric sensibility to resist and the critic needs that resistance to reaffirm the persistence of a lyrical afterlife.

As Christopher Nealon points out in the next essay in this section, "both Perloff and Altieri were at the forefront of the expansion of the poetic canon to include more experimental writing in the 1980s, and both helped turn American poetry criticism away from a reduction of the poetic to the lyrical." Yet as we have seen, both Perloff and Altieri sustained an expanded sense of the lyric in their new critical poetics. For Nealon, that new critical poetics "tended to merely name, then draw back from, the conditions that made it urgent to restore to the study of poetry a sense of high intellectual stakes," namely "the crises and triumphs or global capitalism from about 1973 on." While "these developments are keenly felt in the poetry of the period," according to Nealon, "they are felt and dismissed, or felt and shunted to the side, in the criticism." Nealon picks up where an earlier generation of critics left off, by taking the development of global capitalism seriously as the subject matter of late twentieth- and early-twenty-first-century American poetry. Not incidentally, that project entails also reexamining the beleaguered status of the lyric within that poetics and that poetry.

Nealon invokes "two critical traditions—a New Critical tradition in which modern poetry has been understood generically, as always gesturing back to an originally oral 'lyric' in one sense or another, and a postructuralist tradition in which the idea of textuality takes on such powerful philosophical overtones that its mundane history is eclipsed." Neither New Criticism nor poststructuralism actually cast modern poetry as purely lyric or as purely textual, but Nealon's point in painting in such broad strokes is to produce a third alternative, a "textual imaginary" of modern and postmodern American poetry that has gone unrecognized because the competing strands of lyric and nonlyric have eclipsed it. This textual imaginary also turns out to be much more engaged with "the matter of capital" than previous critics have understood. Yet like the critics who preceded him, Nealon needs to define and reduce the lyric as the genre too narrow to convey the matter of capital and so in need of adjustment by contemporary critical practice. He suggests that "Virginia Jackson has argued that the professionalization of literary criticism from the time of New Critics has produced a tendency to read all poems as lyrics, where 'lyric' means a record of the voice or the mind speaking to itself, as in T. S. Eliot's conception of the mode." Like Ashton, Nealon gives a reductive paraphrase of Jackson's account of lyricization as an alignment of the lyric with the reactionary ideology of the New Criticism (as if John Crowe Ransom woke up one morning in 1941 and invented the lyric over breakfast). Also like Ashton, Nealon separates the work he wants to do from this reductive version of the lyric, since while Jackson's account "seems true of the New Criticism," he is "interested in a related phenomenon, which is how, beginning in the 1970s, the language of philosophy stepped in to fill the gap left by New Critical insistence on the aesthetic autonomy of the poem."

This is where Nealon's account of poetics after the lyric joins Perloff's and Altieri's, since while "work like Altieri's and Perloff's . . . gave us a powerfully depoliticizing language for poetry in the 1980s and 1990s," at the beginning of the second decade of the twenty-first century, Nealon gives us a politicizing language for poetry that still casts the lyric as the oddly outworn poetic genre to which post-lyric poetics continues to respond. While Perloff tried to show the alternative to contemporary lyric critical models by going backward to Tennyson and forward to Bernstein, and Altieri tried to mark the limitation of those models by showing how Ashbery and Hejinian played around their edges, Nealon shows their limitations by exploring what he suggests is a counter-tradition to the New Critical tradition of thinking about the lyric, namely the poststructuralist tradition, in which "the idea of textuality takes on such powerful theoretical overtones." Nealon seeks to prove that appearances to the contrary, this latter tradition has been just as depoliticizing for the study of poetry as was the former, though the politics of a Derrida may seem more progressive than the politics of a Ransom. Derrida's "leveraging of modernist poetry into an antidialectical argument with Hegel becomes *the* gesture into which the idea of 'poetry' is incorporated in the French theory that traveled to American shores in the 1970s and 1980s," according to Nealon, becoming a paradigm for such diverse French poststructuralists as Kristeva, Nancy, Deleuze, and Badiou, who all "have kept alive, from very different philosophical positions, the practice of pitting one literary modernism or another against a cartoon of Hegel." This cartoon of Hegel may be taken to stand for a caricature of the lyric notion of an intact subjectivity, against which the free play of modern poetics can riff. This riff is neither strictly lyric nor anti-lyric, though the implication is that modern poetic textuality undoes the Hegelian Romantic lyric ego. What, then, to make of Adorno, who seems to celebrate just that self-enclosed sense of lyricism? While Nealon admits that "unfortunately, Adorno himself facilitates this drift in the direction of generic reading," he suggests that what Adorno actually wrote moves beyond the sanctification or reification of the lyric. Still, Adorno does tend to limit "our understanding of the relationship between poetry and capitalism to the negative: the lyric's compression and intensity are a sacrificial austerity, or a scream, and the rejections such stances or cries signify become a definition of the lyric." In comparison to Perloff and Altieri, who wrote about lyrically resistant avant-garde poetics without writing about capitalism, the French and German critical traditions "have encouraged ways of thinking about that relation that tend to imply that poetic writing is prima facie political, or that the only significant relation between a poem and capitalism is rigorous eschewal." While Nealon's book goes on to think about the ways in which "the record of actual poetry in the twentieth century does not bear out this claim," it is worth noting that the claim itself is still made in the name of the lyric, a term that is the product of so many confused histories and discourses that any resistance to it inherits that confusion.

In the final essay in this section, "Lyric and the Hazard of Music," Craig Dworkin attempts a canny circumvention of that inheritance by starting the discussion at a different point. Rather than take up the question of the relation of avant-garde textual poetics to older lyric models directly, Dworkin begins with the question of the relation of sound to poetry. Although we might suspect that Dworkin is up to something more than an account of this relation when he includes an epigraph by the art historian T. J. Clark to the effect that "lyric cannot be expunged by modernism, only repressed," for the first several pages of his essay, the point of his discussion is not the lyric but the question of the poetics of sound. Dworkin's radical point about sound in poetry is that "sound . . . is that species of homograph which produces its own antonym." A word that means both its opposite and itself, "at once the antithesis of meaning and the very essence of meaning, sound in poetry articulates the same problems that have attended early twentieth-century definitions of the category of 'poetry' itself, reflecting the identical logic at a fractal remove." It is this fractal remove that interests Dworkin, since he can use it to expose the self-similar logics that bedevil (as Perloff would say) current discourses on poetry. The problem of extricating avant-garde or conceptual poetry from the inheritance of lyric discourse emerges in the course of Dworkin's essay as parallel to the problem of extricating meaning from sound.

This is a subtle variation on the performative statement with which we began this headnote. Dworkin's rendition of the lyric as "a caricatured and mummified ethos" in his introduction modulates into another set of associations in this essay. Since "no sound pattern . . . is inherently meaningful in and of itself," yet we associate meanings with sounds, accounts of the relation between sound and sense in poetry veer wildly between the strictly formalist account of a John Cage (for whom poetry "was a non-expressive, non-communicative extrusion of form into recursive content") and the affective register of a John Hollander, whose entry on "Music and Poetry" in the 1993 edition of the *Princeton Encyclopedia of Poetry and Poetics* states that poetry and music "move to affect a listener in some subrational fashion, just as both are in some way involved in the communication of feeling rather than knowledge." From this comparison, it is a short step to the relation between music and lyric, and indeed Dworkin returns, like Perloff, to Johnson's definition of the lyric in that same edition of the *Princeton Encyclopedia*, the older definition that suggests that "the irreducible denominator of all lyric poetry" must be "those elements which it shares with the musical forms that produced it." To think about the relation of sound to poetry turns out to be a way to think about the lyric as potentially nonexpressive, and thus as the image of what a nonexpressive poetry might look like.

Here is where Dworkin's essay takes a sharp turn. Having taken apart the relation between sound and sense, and then having invoked the associations between musical sound and lyric discourse, he can put both "what might be meant by *music*" and what might be meant by lyric into question. "What if the music represented by the lyric were Cage's own *Music for Piano*," Dworkin mischievously asks, a composition made "by enlarging the imperfections found when a sheet of staff paper is scrutinized under a magnifying glass? Or

> Erik Satie's *Vexations*, a few bars of fragmentary melody meant to be repeated 840 times in succession? Or Stephanie Ginsburgh's extrapolation of Marcel Duchamp's *Erratum Musical*: each of the eighty-eight notes on the piano keyboard played once, in aleatory order?

The list goes on, and as it does, Dworkin makes his point: as one considers the expanded field of musical possibilities, one also considers an expanded field for poetic possibilities, a field that stretches beyond narrow conceptions of the lyric as it bends narrow conceptions of music, a field in which a multiplicity of poetries and a multiplicity of musics (840 or 88 or 100 or 1000) become possible. This way of maintaining an outdated definitional association between lyric and music is itself arbitrary, but the very arbitrariness of the alliance fascinates Dworkin, since while "the terms are irreversibly linked . . . their denotations are not as fixed as our habitual use of them, in forging that linkage, would like us to believe. Or, in brief, to paraphrase David Antin's aphorism on the connection between modernism and post-modernism: from the music you choose, you get the lyric you deserve." Dworkin revises the critical apparatus attached to the false binary between lyric poetry and the avant-garde, making that apparatus itself into a conceptual poem. We could call that poem a lyric, or you could call it whatever you like.

NOTES

1. Online at www.ubu.com/concept/.

2. Jennifer Ashton, "Sincerity and the Second Person: Lyric after Language Poetry," *Interval(le)s* 2.2–3.1 (Fall 2008–Winter 2009), 94.

3. Paul de Man, "Lyrical Voice in Contemporary Theory: Riffaterre and Jauss," in *Lyric Poetry: Beyond the New Criticism*, ed. Chaviva Hošek and Patricia Parker (Ithaca, NY: Cornell University Press, 1985), 55.

FURTHER READING

Andrews, Bruce, and Charles Bernstein, ed. *The L=A=N=G=U=A=G=E Book* (Poetics of the New). Carbondale: Southern Illinois University Press, 1984.

Armand, Louis, ed. *Contemporary Poetics*. Evanston, IL: Northwestern University Press 2007.

Ashton, Jennifer. *From Modernism to Postmodernism: American Poetry and Theory in the Twentieth Century*. Cambridge, MA: Cambridge University Press, 2006.

Bernstein, Charles. *A Poetics*. Cambridge, MA: Harvard University Press,1992.

———. "The Task of Poetics, the Fate of Innovation, and the Aesthetics of Criticism." In *The Consequence of Innovation: 21st-Century Poetics*, edited by Craig Dworkin, 37–57. New York: Roof Book, 2008.

Bernstein, Charles, and Bruce Andrews, eds. *Close Listening: Poetry and the Performed Word*. New York: Oxford University Press, 1998.

Dworkin, Craig. *Reading the Illegible*. Evanston, IL: Northwestern University Press, 2003.

Filreis, Alan. *Counter-revolution of the Word: The Conservative Attack on Modern Poetry, 1945–1960*. Chapel Hill: University of North Carolina Press, 2007.

Morris, Adalaide Morris, and Thomas Swiss, eds. *New Media Poetics: Contexts, Technotexts, and Theories*. Boston: MIT Press, 2006.

Ngai, Sianne. *Our Aesthetic Categories: Zany, Cute, Interesting*. Cambridge, MA: Harvard University Press, 2012.

Noland, Carrie. *Poetry at Stake: Lyric Aesthetics and the Challenge of Technology*. Princeton, NJ: Princeton University Press, 1999.

Perelman, Bob. *The Marginalization of Poetry*. Princeton, NJ: Princeton University Press, 1996.

Perloff, Marjorie. *The Dance of the Intellect: Studies in the Poetry of the Pound Tradition*. Cambridge: Cambridge University Press, 1985.

———. *Poetic License: Essays on Modernist and Postmodernist Lyric*. Evanston, IL: Northwestern University Press, 1990.

———. *The Poetics of Indeterminacy: Rimbaud to Cage*. Evanston, IL: Northwestern University Press, 1999.

———. *Poetry On and Off the Page*. Evanston, IL: Northwestern University Press, 1998.

———. *Postmodern Genres*. Norman: University of Oklahoma Press, 1988.

Silliman, Ron. *The Alphabet*. Birmingham: University of Alabama Press, 2008.

Silliman, Ron, Carla Harryman, Lyn Hejinian, Steve Benson, Bob Perelman, and Barrett Watten. "Aesthetic Tendency and The Politics of Poetry: A Manifesto." *Social Text* 19–20 (Autumn 1988): 261–75.

Watten, Barrett. *The Constructivist Moment: From Material Text to Cultural Poetics*. Middletown, CT: Wesleyan University Press, 2003.

8.1 Can(n)on to the Right of Us, Can(n)on to the Left of Us: A Plea for Difference (1987)

Marjorie Perloff

Some months ago, the following flyer from SUNY Buffalo appeared in my campus mailbox:

> THE BLACK MOUNTAIN II REVIEW, a student-run journal devoted to the arts, is accepting submissions for its fifth issue of poetry, short fiction, artwork . . . interviews, and film, literary, music and cultural criticism. The theme of this issue—"From Word to Sign: A Special Double Issue"—will be so-called Language-Oriented Writing, its antecedents and its future. Significant practitioners of this writing include Bruce Andrews, Charles Bernstein, Clark Coolidge and Robert Creeley. Among the antecedents of these writers may be included Gertrude Stein, John Cage, the Dadaists and William S. Burroughs. Possible articulations may be explored between this writing and the theoretical work of Jacques Derrida, Gilles Deleuze & Felix Guattari, Guy Debord and the practitioners themselves.

And then, after some practical information about mailing and deadlines, we read: "P.S. Poets and other creative writers: fear not! You may be writing 'Language-Oriented' works without ever having heard of half these people."

What can this wonderful disclaimer (rather like those old ads for the Unitarian church that said "You may be a Unitarian without knowing it!") possibly mean? What is it that "poets and other creative writers" are producing today without being fully cognizant of its nature? Consider the following six texts:[1]

(1)

Yesterday the sun went West and sucked
the sea from books. My witness
is an exoskeleton. Altruism suggestively fits.
It's true. I like to go to the hardware store
and browse on detail. So sociable the influence

of Vuillard, so undying in disorder is order.
Windows closed on wind in rows.
Night lights, unrumorlike, the reserve
for events. All day our postures were the same.
Next day the gentleman was very depressed
and had a headache; so much laughing

had upset him he thought.

—Lyn Hejinian, from *The Guard* (1984)

(2)

mAdness
coLd-water
fLats

thE
braiNs
throuGh
wIth
aNd
academieS
Burning
monEy

maRijuana
niGht

After
endLess
cLoud
thE
motioNless
Green
joyrIde

suN

aShcan

Brain
drainEd of
bRilliance

niGht

—John Cage, "Writing for the second time through Howl" (1984)

(3)

R
M O U
O
M U R I
A I R
R
O
I
R

Michel Leiris, "Le Sceptre miroitant"
(1969)

(4)

Nearly nothing
In Nature so
spirits the eye
off—but off by
way of in—to
unveil detail
as minimal
as it's recep-
tive to as does
this more than true-

to life, living
family of
diminutive
replicas of
themselves. . . .

These pondered, hand-
won triumphs of
containment, come,
tentatively,
of earth-toughened
fingers, father
to son, and on
to son, so long
as the branches
hold on each side,

bid us enter-
entertain notions of
days whose hours are
shorter than ours,
(shrunken, misted. . . .

—Brad Leithauser, from "In a Bonsai Nursery." Part 3 of "Dainties: A Suite," *Cats of the Temple* (1986)

(5) Did a wind come just as you got up or were
you protecting me from it? I felt the abridgement
of imperatives, the wave of detours, the sabre-
rattling of inversion. *All lit up and no
place to go.* Blinded by avenue and filled with
adjacency. Arch or arched at. So there becomes bottles,
hushed conductors, illustrated proclivities for puffed-
up benchmarks. Morose or comatose. "Life is what
you find, existence is what you repudiate." A good
example of this is 'Dad pins puck.' Sometimes something
sunders; in most cases, this is no more than a hall.
No where to go but pianissimo (protection of market
soaring).

—Charles Bernstein, from "Dysraphism" (1984)

(6)

d'elle-même; le père de Marie m'a présenté à son grand-père. Celui qui a dit A épelle ensuite toutes les lettres de l'alphabet. Et ainsi nous nous comportons devant le monde comme des fiancés. Par ailleurs vous savez que celui qui a fondé son affaire sur la bonté des femmes — en particulier des femmes telles que celle-ci — n'a pas bâti sur le sable. [...] Nous nous sommes déjà si souvent entretenus d'Erlangen que dans notre imagination notre union et Erlangen se sont en quelque sorte fondus en un seul être, comme le mari et la femme. L'amélioration de ma situation économique est nécessaire, étant donné l'insuffisance de mes moyens, car ma chère Marie, dont le grand-père vit encore et dont le père a en dehors d'elle 7 enfants, ne peut recevoir, outre son trousseau, qu'une somme annuelle de 100 florins... » [...]

votre ami sincère Hgl. »

De l'été qui suit, à la veille du mariage, on a encore deux lettres à Marie.

« Nuremberg,

Chère Marie,

Je t'ai écrit en pensée durant presque toute la nuit. Ce n'était pas à telle ou telle circonstance particulière de nos relations que ma pensée s'attachait, mais il s'agissait nécessairement de cette pensée essentielle : nous rendrons-nous donc malheureux *(unglücklich)*? Une voix criait du plus profond de mon âme : Cela ne peut pas, cela ne doit pas être! — Cela ne sera pas! *(Dies Kann, dies soll und darf nicht sein! — Es wird nicht sein!)*
Mais ce que je t'ai dit depuis longtemps se présente à mes yeux comme un résultat : le mariage est essentiellement un lien *(Band)* religieux; l'amour a besoin pour être complété de quelque chose de plus élevé que ce qu'il est seulement en lui-même et par lui-même. La satisfaction complète — ce que l'on appelle « être heureux » *(glücklich sein)* — n'est accomplie que grâce à la religion et au sentiment du devoir, car en eux seulement sont écartées toutes les particularités du moi-même *(Selbst)* temporel, qui pourraient apporter du trouble dans la réalité, laquelle reste quelque chose d'inachevé et ne peut être prise pour la chose dernière, mais en qui devrait résider ce qu'on appelle le bonheur terrestre. J'ai devant moi le brouillon des lignes que j'ai jointes à ta lettre à ma sœur; le post-scriptum, auquel tu as certainement attaché une trop grande importance, ne s'y

Cette apparence de noyau est d'ailleurs plus dénudée, mieux lue et remarquée par le relief des deux versions, celle de Poe et celle de Mallarmé. Ce qui ne veut pas dire qu'il y ait un noyau absolu et un centre dominant, le rythme ne se liant pas seulement aux mots ni surtout à la proximité du contact entre deux lettres. Néanmoins, à ignorer *Les Cloches*, Fónagy reste sourd à l'effet + L (consonne + L), non seulement dans les traductions où il n'occurre pas mais même dans celle, l'allemande, où il le fait : « Le principal objet de la traduction en prose est de traduire, par un simple mouvement de translation, le message de la langue originale vers la langue visée, en substituant à la forme *a*, empruntée à la langue de départ, une forme *b* empruntée à la langue d'arrivée. [...] C'est le contraire qui se passe, lorsque le traducteur s'attaque à la poésie. Ici, il retient et transpose certains traits de la forme *a* pour les reproduire dans la mesure du possible à l'arrivée, dans la forme *b*. Le tintement argentin des cloches dans l'air glacé de la nuit, dans le poème d'Edgar Allan Poe, se retrouve exprimé dans les traductions hongroise, allemande et italienne du poème, par la prédominance des sons *i*, et les enchaînements des nasales :

ng, nk, nt, nd.

How they *tinkle, tinkle, tinkle*
In the icy air of night

Halld, mind, pendül, kondul, csendül...
(Mihály Babits)

Wie sir klingen, klingen, klingen,
Zwinkernd sich zum Reigen schlingen...
(Th. Etzel)

Come *tintinnano, tintinnano, tintinnano*
Di una cristallina delizia...
(Frederico Olivero). »

Jacques Derrida, double page 221 of volume 2 of *Glas* (Paris: Denoël, 1981)

Except for the passage from Derrida's *Glas*, these texts have been explicitly presented by their authors as poems, but readers brought up on Romantic and modernist poetry may have difficulty recognizing them as such. For if, as Paul de Man puts it, "The principle of intelligibility, in lyric poetry, depends on the phenomenalization of the poetic voice,"[2] what do we make of those poems like Lyn Hejinian's or Charles Bernstein's, whose appropriation of found objects—snippets of advertising slogans, newspaper headlines, media cliché, textbook writing, or citation from other poets—works precisely to deconstruct the possibility of the formation of a coherent or consistent lyrical voice, a transcendental ego?

Again, to build one's discourse on citation is to regard language less as a means of representation than as the very object of representation. Thus, when John Cage "writes through" Allen Ginsberg's "Howl," which is to say uses chance operations to select certain words from the parent text and then arrange those words in a *mesostic* (the name ALLEN GINSBERG forms a column down the middle of the text, the rule being that a given letter in the name cannot appear between its occurrence in a given line and that of the next letter in the next line), it is difficult to know how the reader is to produce an apparently phenomenal world through the figure of voice. For whose voice do we hear in such minimalist echoes of "Howl" as "academieS/Burning/monEy/maRijuana/niGht"? Or in Michel Leiris's "Le Sceptre miroitant," whose acrostic arrangement of three closely related words suggests that "amour" and "mourir" are in fact mirror ("miroir") images of one another, even as the only letter that is not involved in the poem's complex system of duplication is the first in the alphabet, the eternal Alpha? And even in the work of a more traditional poet like Brad Leithauser, who is hardly allied with the "language" group or with French post-structuralism, the use of visual and phonemic device, specifically the verbal play generated by the two-column structure, undercuts the controlling voice, creating what John Ashbery has called "an open field of narrative possibilities," in which "diminutive" may lead (vertically) to "replicas of themselves" or (horizontally) to "days whose hours are replicas."

In a headnote to "Dysraphism," Bernstein explains his title as follows:

> "Dysraphism" is actually a word in use by specialists in congenital diseases, to mean dysfunctional fusion of embryonic parts—a birth defect. . . . "Raph" of course means "seam," so for me dysraphism is mis-seaming—a prosodic device! But it has the punch of being the same root of rhapsody (*rhaph*)—or in Skeats—"one who strings (lit. stitches) songs together, a reciter of epic poetry," cf. "ode" etc. In any case, to be simple, Dorland's [the standard U.S. medical dictionary] does define "dysrhafia" (if not dysraphism) as "incomplete closure of the primary neural tube; status dysraphicus"; this is just below "dysprosody" (sic): "disturbance of stress, pitch, and rhythm of speech."[3]

This exuberant analysis of etymology, analogy, and punning might almost have appeared in Derrida's *Glas*; indeed, in the right-hand column of a sample page from *Glas* [see figure], we find a similar rumination on "le graphique de la *mimesis*," the materiality of the signifier as it undergoes translation into other languages. Derrida's text is Edgar Allan Poe's 1848 poem "The Bells," specifically the lines, "How they tinkle, tinkle, tinkle / In the icy air of night"), and he notes, on this particular page, that, whereas the French *cloches* picks up the *l* phoneme of "tinkle" but not its nasal phoneme /nk/, other languages like Hungarian, German, and Italian foreground the latter at the expense of the former. As Leiris puts it in his "Glossaire: J'y serre mes gloses": "By dissecting the words we like, without bothering about conforming either to the etymologies or to their accepted significations, we discover their most hidden qualities and the secret ramifications that are propagated through the whole language, channeled by associations of sounds, forms, and ideas."[4]

In Derrida's "epiphony in echoland," as Geoffrey Hartman calls *Glas*,[5] the rumination on "le tintement argentin des cloches" in the right-hand or "Genet" column is played off against the "Hegel" column on the left, specifically, in the case of our sample page, against the conclusion of an 1811 letter from Hegel to his friend Niethammer explaining the economic difficulties that still stand in the way of his marriage to his future wife Marie, and then a melodramatic letter to Marie herself in which Hegel raises the terrible question: "Nous rendrons-nous donc malheureux (*unglücklich*)?" Immediately, "Une voix criait du plus profond de mon âme: Cela ne peut pas, cela ne doit pas être—Cela ne sera pas! (*Dies kann, dies soll und darf nicht sein!—Es wird nicht sein!*)." A romantic cry of the heart that is quickly followed by a return to convention: marital happiness, Hegel tells his fiancée, can only be based on religious and moral faith and on conjugal duty.

It is a nice question whether the juxtaposition of discourses in Derrida's *Glas*—the conventionally romantic, somewhat bathetic letter to Marie set over against the practical one to Hegel's colleague, and both of these spliced with the discourse on the *glas* of Poe's bells, in its many incarnations—is any less "poetic" than the two-column "In a Bonsai Nursery" of Brad Leithauser or the mixed discourse poems of Lyn Hejinian and Charles Bernstein. Derrida's ironic insertions of the German original into the French translation, as in "nous rendrons-nous donc malheureux (*unglücklich*)," is, for that matter, a device frequently used by Cage in his portrait-lectures on such artists as Jasper Johns or such composers as Arnold Schoenberg.

To read *Glas* or Leiris's "*Glossaire*" in conjunction with Cage's mesostic, Leithauser's two-column poem, and the "language" texts of Hejinian and Bernstein is, in any case, to note a curious phenomenon. *Poetry*, for these poets, has less to do with the Romantic conception of the lyric as "an intensely subjective and personal expression" (Hegel), the "utterance that is not so much heard as overheard" (John Stuart Mill), than with the original derivation of *lyric* as a composition performed on the lyre, which is to say that it is a verbal form directly related to its musical origins.[6] Thus Leithauser's "In a Bonsai Nursery" is written in intricate two-stress lines characterized by elaborate echo structure: "unveil detail / as minimal"; "fingers, father / to son, and on / to son, so long." Leithauser's use of homonyms—"days whose hours are shorter than ours"—finds its counterpart in Hejinian's punning, as in "Windows closed on wind in rows," and in Bernstein's parody rhyming of "Morose or comatose." In "Dysraphism," as in Hejinian's *The Guard*, syntactic slots are filled with words and phrases that fail to fit semantically but are phonemically appropriate, as in "Yesterday the sun went West and sucked / the sea from books," or "Blinded by avenue and filled with adjacency. Arch or arched at." Again, in Leiris's "Le Sceptre miroitant," the first syllable of "mourir" echoes the second of "amour," thus underscoring the union of love and death, even as in Cage's "Writing through Howl," it is sound that relates "suN" to "aShcan" and that convinces us that "Brain" is "drainEd of / bRilliance."

How is it that in the late twentieth century we are once again foregrounding the *sound* of lyric poetry? How has it happened that the rather flat free verse of the American mid-century, with its emphasis on delicate epiphany and personal contingency, has given way, in the eighties, to poetic language that, far from being speech based, depends upon parodic reference to a particular convention—ladies' small talk, for example, in the case of Hejinian's "I like to go to the hardware store / and browse on detail," or fin de siècle mannerism, in the case of Bernstein's "I felt the abridgment of imperatives, the wave of detours, the sabre- / rattling of inversion"?

Whatever the answers to these difficult questions, we are not, I would posit, likely to find them in the recent academic criticism of lyric poetry. Consider, for example, a prominent collection from Cornell University Press called *Lyric Poetry* (1985), based on a symposium at the University of Toronto and edited by Chaviva Hošek and Patricia Parker. Subtitled *Beyond the New Criticism*, *Lyric Poetry* purports to be the response of a poststructuralist "new new criticism"—what we might call the "canon to the left of us," with its loose confederation of deconstruction (here represented by Paul de Man, Cynthia Chase, Joel Fineman, Barbara Johnson), reader response theory (Stanley Fish), feminism (Mary Jacobus, Mary Nyquist), and Marxism (Fredric Jameson, John Brenkman), and various hybrids of the above—to the "canon to the right of us," which is, of course, that now familiar whipping boy (with "boy" used advisedly since it was the discourse of an almost exclusively male establishment), the (old) New Criticism.

"This book," the editors inform us in their preface, ". . . is intended to appeal to students, critics, and teachers of poetry, as well as to those interested in the application of literary theory to the study of texts from several historical periods" (*LP*, 7). There are two implications here that I find troubling. First, the book is certainly not intended for poets, a species that seems to exist for no better reason than that "students, critics, and teachers of poetry" (pretty much one and the same thing) can write about their work. And second, that "literary theory" is something to be applied "to the study of texts," that it is, in other words, a second-order discourse to be applied to a primary one and in any case separable from it. We should note right away that (1) this separation replicates the New Critical division between poetry and writing *about* poetry, and (2) that, ironically enough, the New Critics took this separation rather less seriously than do their new challengers, given that many of them—Allen Tate, Robert Penn Warren, Randall Jarrell, R. P. Blackmur—were themselves poets and hence quite unlikely to suggest that a book about lyric poetry is "intended to appeal primarily to students, critics, and teachers of poetry." Indeed, as Edward Said has noted, "The New Criticism, for all its elitism, was strangely populist in intention," its aim being no less than to give all educated readers the tools by means of which they might understand literary works.[7]

A well-known weakness of the New Criticism, as Patricia Parker reminds us in her introduction, is that it advocated "the program of treating the literary text as an isolated artifact or object, dismissing concern with the author's intention and reader's response, and the tenet of the text's organic wholeness, its reconciliation of tension or diversity into unity" (*LP*, 12). How has poststructuralist criticism in America responded to this challenge? For organic unity and reconciliation of opposites it has substituted the "allegory of reading" with its concomitant recognition of the undecidability of poetic language. Words, phrases, and larger units are now explicated with an eye to showing that they don't mean what they seem to mean, that the readings they generate are contradictory. Yet, and this is the irony of much "new new criticism," the premise that the poem is to be treated as "an isolated artifact or object, dismissing concern with author's intention and reader's response" is hardly less operative here than it is in the case of Cleanth Brooks's *The Well Wrought Urn* or W. K. Wimsatt's *The Verbal Icon.*

Thus Cynthia Chase's examination of Keats's "Ode to a Nightingale" focuses on that poem's difficult fifth stanza ("I cannot see what flowers are at my feet . . ."), arguing, *contra* such veteran Keats scholars as Earl Wasserman, that, read intertextually, against relevant passages by Wordsworth and Milton, Keats's particular use of prosopopoeia and apostrophe points to a central "ambivalence toward the visionary mode," a "nostalgia for pre-Romantic or non-Romantic conditions" (*LP*, 224). Again, Joel Fineman brilliantly deconstructs Shakespeare's "eye"/"I" imagery, positing that Shakespeare's persona can no longer elaborate his subjectivity in accord with the ideal model of a self composed of the specular identification of the poetic ego and the poetic ego ideal, of "I" and "you"—the "eye" and the "eyed." Eleanor Cook gives a close reading of Wallace Stevens's "An Ordinary Evening in New Haven," demonstrating that it is "a purgatorial poem in the anti-apocalyptic mode" (*LP*, 302), and Mary Nyquist, in yet another essay on a single Stevens poem, this time "Peter Quince at the Clavier," contrasts the "free-floating" Susanna of part 2, the Susanna who is "free simply, erotically, to be," with the Susanna "re-represented" through the "red-eyed gaze" of the elders, who "has been arrested and fixed by the specular gaze," which is to say, "by the pornographic and patriarchal eye, the eye that assumes it has a right to possession" (*LP*, 314). The strategy of the poem, so Nyquist argues, is to transform this "violated Susanna" into the muse "whose 'music' has mothered the male poet's verbal artifact that contains her" (*LP*, 327).

Subtle and inventive as such readings are, it might be useful to consider what they do not do. The critical project, for Parker and her fellow symposiasts, is wholly hermeneutic; its aim is to explain what particular canonical poems—and I shall come back to the question of the canon in a moment—mean; its purpose is to articulate what new meanings Shakespeare's sonnets or Keats's odes or Stevens's meditative poems might yield when examined through the "new" prisms of feminist theory or deconstruction, or, as I shall suggest below, an ahistorical Marxism now increasingly fashionable. In what is to my mind the most trenchant essay in the Hošek and Parker collection, Annabel Patterson remarks that "the newer criticisms . . . have not, it seems, been able to disturb the premises of the preceding dynasty with respect to lyric, or even to improve on its work." "'Lyric,'" writes Patterson, "remains a name for an ill-assorted collection of short(er) poems; but the genre continues to be defined normatively, in ways that exclude dozens of poems that their authors once thought of as lyric. The reason for this is clear. The modernist view of lyric as an intense, imaginative form of self-expression or self-consciousness, the most private of all genres, is, of course, a belief derived from Romanticism" (*LP*, 151).

The genre continues to be defined normatively—it is this situation that bedevils current discourse about poetry. For nowhere in *Lyric Poetry* do we find discussion of the following questions: (1) Is "lyric" merely another word for "poetry," as the interchangeable use of the word in the collection would suggest? If so, why talk about "lyric poetry"; if not, what other kinds of poetry are there and what is their relationship to lyric? (2) How has lyric poetry changed over the centuries? Is it meaningful to talk of Ben Jonson's project in the same terms that we talk of, say, Stevens's or Pound's? How and why is lyric more prominent in some periods than in ours? And (3) since the etymology of the word *lyric* points to its musical derivation, what does it mean to write of lyric poetry as if its sound structure were wholly irrelevant, a mere externality. What, for example, does the choice of a particular meter mean? Or the choice of a particular set of linguistic strategies?

To pose these questions is another way of saying that the thrust of *Lyric Poetry: Beyond the New Criticism* is, as Jonathan Arac notes in his acute afterword, "fundamentally unhistorical, especially in its confidence about the extensive applicability of its operative terms" (*LP*, 346). Theoretical and rhetorical terms—apostrophe, allegory, the word lyric itself—are assumed to have transhistorical, typological validity. Indeed, concerned as these critics are with the changing ways of reading lyric poetry, they too often fail to take into account that the writing of lyric poetry is itself a mode of production that undergoes change. Thus the New Critical emphasis on the poem as autotelic object is ironically preserved.

This reluctance to engage the historical dimension of lyric poetry can be seen at many levels. In "Changes in the Study of Lyric," Jonathan Culler observes, as do a number of the other contributors, that recent criticism has "neglected lyric poetry in favor of narrative." Roland Barthes, for instance, "has practically nothing to say about poetry, much less a convincing or innovatory encounter with lyric" (*LP*, 41). But why, given Barthes's "broad literary tastes," should this be the case? Because, so Culler posits, Barthes associates poetry with "plentitude," with "the symbolic," and "thus sees it as the aspect of literariness" that the writers he admires—say, Brecht and Robbe-Grillet—are "trying to combat" (*LP*, 42). "Other contemporary critics," concludes Culler, "have not followed Barthes's lead, fortunately," the point being, evidently, that a working definition of poetry must be broad enough to obviate Barthes's objection to its urge toward the transcendence of language.

Or must it? What Culler misses here is that Barthes's skepticism about "The Poem" is itself historically determined, that what Barthes is telling us—and I have argued this point elsewhere[8]—is that perhaps the "poetic," in our own time, is to be found, not in the conventionally isolated lyric poem, so dear to the Romantics and Symbolists, but in texts not immediately recognizable as poetry. Thus, when Barthes tells an interviewer, "J'aime le Romanesque, mais je sais que le roman est mort,"[9] he is expressing, not the desire for an excessively narrow definition of the novel, but his own inability, given his distrust of mimesis in the late twentieth century, to create or to believe in something called "character" that is distinct from its creator, his mistrust of fictionality even as he insists on the fictiveness of narrative.

No definition of the lyric poem or of the novel can, in short, be wholly transhistorical. One would think that Marxist critics would be precisely the ones to recognize this axiom, but in practice we now frequently encounter a brand of Marxist explication that, so to speak, freezes the historical, that arrests its temporality. A particularly problematic example of this kind of criticism may be found in John Brenkman's essay "The Concrete Utopia of Poetry: Blake's 'A Poison Tree.'"

Brenkman's essay opens with a minimal gesture toward historical context. Blake, we learn, "was a poet of the volatile decades of the late eighteenth and early nineteenth centuries, writing at the very point when the democratic revolutions were being institutionalized as the class rule of the bourgeoisie"; his poetry is thus to be read as a response to "the new economic order of capitalism" and as the "struggle against dominant values and institutions" (*LP*, 183).

Logically, the next step might be to take a close look at precisely those institutions and cultural formations operative when Blake wrote the *Songs of Innocence* and *Songs of Experience*. But Brenkman evidently has no use for such empiricism; on the contrary, he now turns to the "social and aesthetic theories of thinkers like Ernst Bloch and Herbert Marcuse, Walter Benjamin and T. W. Adorno"—theories with which Blake's poetry evidently "resonates" (*LP*, 183). The actual writings of the Frankfurt school, it should be said, are cited only briefly and rather perfunctorily, the references being almost exclusively to certain scattered essays that have been translated into English. The point to be extracted, in any case, is that "the first task of analysis is to dissolve the ideological shell of the work by exposing the ways it serves particular rather than general interests and legitimates the forms of domination prevalent in its own society; once this ideological shell is dissolved, the utopian kernel of the work is supposed to shine through, a radiant core of meanings and images expressing the strivings and hopes of humanity" (*LP*, 184).

How does this "utopian kernel" "shine through" the "ideological shell" of Blake's "A Poison Tree," which is the essay's test case? Brenkman's analysis begins as follows:

> Every time one reads the poem, I believe, the first stanza has the force of a moral statement. The past tense establishes the twin perspective of Blake's action *then* and his judgment *now*. The danger or unhappiness of a wrath that grows, as against a wrath that ends, establishes a set of values or preferences that virtually goes without saying. . . . The poem reads as a kind of confessional utterance in which Blake the speaker shares with the reader a reflective judgment on the actions of Blake in the past, anchored in the view that telling one's wrath is healthy and not telling it is harmful and even self-destructive. (*LP*, 187)

This seemingly straightforward explication demands some unmasking of its own. First, we might note that Brenkman makes no reference to the poem's textual history; he concerns himself neither with prior Blake scholarship nor with the relation of the poem to its illuminated plate. The fact that the Notebook version of "A Poison Tree" bore the title "Christian Forbearance," for example, is evidently considered irrelevant to its meaning. Second, Brenkman assumes that the lines in question have a particular meaning, and that it is up to the critic to tell us what that meaning is. Indeed, he assumes that "every time one reads the poem, . . . the first stanza has the force of a moral statement," a kind of confessional utterance in which Blake the speaker shares with the reader a reflective judgment on the actions of Blake in the past."

But if the poem's "I" is none other than the real William Blake, its final lines, "In the morning glad I see/My foe outstretch'd beneath the tree," pose, so Brenkman argues, something of a conundrum. Blake, he comments, "has gotten his satisfaction, and his wrath has finally been expressed, yielding the sheer delight of seeing an enemy destroyed." As a whole, then, the poem, "far from being a confessional utterance, is more like a set of instructions on how to do in an enemy and feel relief, even joy." And, sounding like a good poststructuralist, Brenkman concludes, "The poem generates both readings. However, neither reading can account for the possibility of the other, except to declare that it is the product of misreading" (*LP*, 187).

This so-called undecidability, it seems, can only be resolved by unraveling the difficulties posed by the conceit of the poison tree, and especially the "apple bright" of line 10. "Within the logic of the conceit," writes Brenkman, "the image of the apple is only vaguely motivated, as by the idea that it is the 'fruit' of his wrath. The meaning of 'apple bright' is otherwise unspecifiable from the standpoint of the conceit itself" (*LP*, 189).

How the image of an "apple bright," appearing in a late eighteenth-century poem written in approximate hymn stanzas (iambic tetrameter rhyming *aabb*), could be taken as "unspecifiable" or "unmotivated" must strike the reader as a mystery. For Blake's poem appropriates, however subtly and ironically, the most basic iconography of Genesis: an "I" watering his tree and "sun[ning] it with smiles" who is clearly usurping the role of God, and a "poison tree" in a "garden," proffering temptation in the form of an "apple bright" that immediately brings to mind Satan and Eve in the Garden of Eden.

But Brenkman is impatient with such conventional topoi. The "apple bright," it turns out, is neither more nor less than the "*enviable possession* of the speaker's," and the poem's "story" thus "unveils the form of abstraction that is historically specific to capitalist society." Blake's poem is thus to be read as a scathing "critique of bourgeois society and of capitalism." "Envy," we read, "a term borrowed from the ethics of precapitalist societies, is but a name for the fundamental law of interactions in capitalist society as a whole" (*LP*, 190). And "the utopian dimension of the poem is enacted in a poetic speaking which manifests the struggle between the social conditions of the poet's speech [the contradictory narrative of stanzas 1 and 4] and the latent possibilities of speech," as figured in the trope of the "apple bright" (*LP*, 192).

The reductiveness of this reading concerns me less than the underlying assumptions that make such a reading possible. First, Brenkman's "Marxist" reading ignores the poem's actual mode of production and distribution as well as its reception. Second, it, so to speak, puts Blake's complex poem under glass, denying it access to its actual context, whether literary, historical, or political. Third, it assumes that a given poem can be said to have a specific, identifiable meaning—in this case, the critique of bourgeois society, contaminated by capitalism. And fourth, and most important, it assumes that poetic language is, quite simply, transparent, that if the poem's first line reads, "I was angry with my friend," it means that Blake was angry with his friend, even as the poem's last lines mean that it is Blake who is "glad to see his foe outstretch'd beneath the tree."

It is one of the paradoxes of recent poststructuralist criticism that, even as deconstruction has entered the mainstream of academic discourse, actual texts are once again being read as if their language were as straightforward as a verbal command to open the door or to pass the sugar. For critics like Brenkman, the "apple bright" is the nugget that, when ingested, countermands the complexity of the reading process. The real questions about Blake's great poem are thus suppressed. How, for example, does the stanzaic structure of "A Poison Tree" qualify or ironize its overt statements? Or again, what is the function of the poem's syntactic parallelism and repetition? Of its storybook language ("And into my garden stole")? In imposing a particular theory on the text, one finds, as it turns out, what one wanted to find in the first place. Brenkman's masters Benjamin and Adorno, it is only fair to say, had little use for such reductionist reading.

A much more sophisticated and challenging version of what we might call Brenkman's spatialized Marxism may be found in another essay in the Hošek and Parker collection, Fredric Jameson's "Baudelaire as Modernist and Postmodernist: The Dissolution of the Referent and the Artificial 'Sublime.'" Jameson argues that there are two Baudelaires. The first is the "inaugural poet of high modernism" who wrote such familiar lyrics from *Les Fleurs du mal* as "Chant d'automne," which Jameson reads, quite brilliantly, I think, as a treatment of the moment of "withdrawal of the private or the individual body from social discourse" (*LP*, 252). The second, the Baudelaire of such later poems as "La Mort des amants," on the other hand, is postmodern in his evocation of a world of pure textuality, "the world of the image, of textual free-play, the world of consumer society and its simulacra" (*LP*, 256). In the Victorian kitsch world of "La Mort des amants," Jameson suggests, a world that has eliminated all trace of humanity in its stress on objects, especially on candelabra and mirrors, we find prefigured "the junk materials of a fallen and unredeemable commodity culture," the "strange new—historically new—feeling or affective tone of late capitalism" (*LP*, 260). "It is appropriate to see in the play of mirrors and lights of the funereal chamber some striking and mysterious anticipation of a logic of the future." As such, Baudelaire is, "perhaps unfortunately for him, our contemporary" (*LP*, 263).

Jameson's is a provocative and exciting essay; it makes one want to return to Baudelaire, teasing out the threads that prefigure our own "fallen and unredeemable commodity culture." But again I am troubled by the critic's urge to erase difference. Precisely how does the capitalism of the Second Empire relate to that of late twentieth-century America? Or again, how can we explain that however anticipatory of postmodernism "La Mort des amants" may be, the poem is instantly recognizable, whether rhetorically, linguistically, tonally, or metrically, as a poem that was *not* written in the latter part of the twentieth century? Why, for that matter, do poets living in our own "late capitalist" America write so differently? And further, why does a poet of the eighties like Charles Bernstein write so differently from, say, the Beat poets of the not-quite-so-late capitalist fifties and sixties?

The reluctance, of even a Marxist theorist like Jameson, to take on the problematic of history (and, we might add, of geography and culture, a problematic that would lead us to ask whether current Marxist ideology in, say, contemporary China, has in fact erased the desire for the "junk materials of . . . commodity culture," whether in the form of rock video, automobiles, dishwashers, or spray deodorant) has produced a critical stance that, far from moving *beyond* the New Criticism, seems to be haunted by its most characteristic gestures. This is especially the case when we consider the choice of poets and poems discussed in *Lyric Poetry*.

In her introduction Parker cites "the problem of canon-formation" as one of the "major issues" confronted by the collection, and she stresses the necessity of questioning the existing canon. For example: "Can we really be certain . . . that of the two poems Browning himself thought of as a pair, 'My Last Duchess'—which is amenable to New Critical techniques of analysis—is a 'better' poem and thus more worthy of inclusion in the curriculum than 'Count Gismond,' whose inconsistencies more immediately frustrate the translation of its written characters into the characters of a psychologically coherent utterance?" Or again, "What does it reveal about the *ideology* of canon-formation that a poem such as Whitman's ode to the Paris Commune—well known to students in the socialist bloc—is rarely encountered in North American classrooms?" (*LP*, 18–19).

Browning's "Count Gismond" rather than "My Last Duchess," Whitman's ode to the Paris Commune rather than "Crossing Brooklyn Ferry"—this is about as daring a departure from the canonical norm as we are likely to find in *Lyric Poetry: Beyond the New Criticism*. If we except Eugene Vance's essay on trouvère lyric, whose focus is on the little known poet Gace Brulé, and David Bromwich's brief study of parody, which includes discussion of contemporary versions of Donne, Milton, and Wordsworth at the hands of the Canadian poets Daryl Hyne and Jay Macpherson, we may tabulate the authors whose poems are analyzed, either in an entire essay or in a major part of an essay, as follows:

English or American		*French*	
Surrey	1	Hugo	1
Shakespeare	1	Baudelaire	4
Jonson	2	Mallarmé	1
Blake	2		
Wordsworth	4		
Keats	1		
Shelley	2		
Browning	1		
Tennyson	1		
Hardy	1		
Stevens	2		
Auden	1		

The index reveals further frequencies: the following poets, who are not discussed in individual essays, are referred to more than five times: Milton, Donne, Byron, Coleridge, Poe, Eliot, and Yeats.

For all its emphasis on feminist criticism, *Lyric Poetry* does not have a single essay devoted to a woman poet.[10] For all its claim that "the range of poems reflects the comparatist outlook of recent theory in contrast to the New Critics' more exclusively English canon" (*LP*, 15), the book includes discussion of only the most predictable French poets, Baudelaire and Mallarmé (Victor Hugo is cited because one of his short poems furnishes Paul de Man with an example to question the theory of Michael Riffaterre). The "new new criticism," we are told, is "increasingly cosmopolitan in its affiliations," but its canon of lyric poets is resolutely Anglophile as Cleanth Brooks's *The Well Wrought Urn*, and much more Anglophile than, say, R. P. Blackmur's *Language as Gesture*, which included essays on Tolstoy and Dostoyevsky, along with those on Blackmur's contemporaries like Ezra Pound.

Indeed, it is the neglect of the contemporary that I find most problematic in the academic criticism of which *Lyric Poetry* is but one exemplar. The drive to move "Beyond the New Criticism" does not, it seems, prompt the desire to learn about the poetry, indeed any of the five discourses, of one's own world. Two essays on Stevens and a short reading of W. H. Auden—this feeble concession to modernity should be measured against the attention paid to the Romantic tradition. Like our standard "classical" concert repertoire, our poetry canon continues to privilege the nineteenth century. Indeed, critics like Jonathan Culler and Stanley Fish seem to imply that poetry is something that has already happened, that it is now safely *over.*

Hence the perplexity that greets poetic texts like the ones I introduced at the beginning of my essay, the irony being that the poems of a Charles Bernstein or a Lyn Hejinian, not to speak of Leiris or Cage, are much more consonant with the theories of Derrida and de Man, Lacan and Lyotard, Barthes and Benjamin, than are the canonical texts that are currently being ground through the poststructuralist mill. How and why poetry and theory have come together deserves to be studied. And it is also important to ask why, say, contemporary British poetry has swerved further and further away from the American norm, opting for what often looks to us like merely clever *vers de société*, even as, conversely, the poetry of Eastern Europe—especially that of Poland and Hungary—continues to deploy figures of imaginative transformation, an intense, often visionary subjectivity.

If poetic discourse is, as the "canon to the left of us" would have it, a cultural formation, we had better have a look at the culture in question. Consider, for example, the status of the famous poem that has given me my title, "Cannon to the right of them, / Cannon to the left of them, / Cannon in front of them / Volley'd and thunder'd"—these ringing lines once memorized and recited by every schoolchild have become, in recent years, at best a faint echo. Indeed, I would hazard the guess that readers under forty are unlikely to recognize their source, which is Tennyson's memorial poem to the British cavalry regiment that met its death at Balaclava in the Crimean War—a military disaster resulting from the tragic error of pitting a sword-bearing cavalry against a Russian army that had cannon at its disposal. The poem is called "The Charge of the Light Brigade" and it begins:

> Half a league, half a league,
> Half a league onward,
> All in the valley of Death
>   Rode the six hundred.
> "Forward the Light Brigade!
> Charge for the guns!" he said.
> Into the valley of Death
>   Rode the six hundred.

The drumbeat of Tennyson's trimeters with their insistent rhyme and hypnotic repetition, their dramatic tale of sudden death on the battlefield, is considered something of an embarrassment by our own post–World War II generation, suspicious as we are of aggressive patriotism and the Victorian celebration of military exploits. Yet our current denigration of such lyric poetry is, as Jerome J. McGann points out in an important essay, itself just as time and culture bound as is our current preference for the muted rhythms and subtle indirections of Wallace Stevens.[11] Indeed, to understand "The Charge of the Light Brigade" is "to expose the mid-Victorian ideology which informs every part of Tennyson's poem" so as to "define critically the specific shape and special quality of its humanness" (*BI*, 190). If this program sounds at first like John Brenkman's "Marxist" reading of Blake's "Poison Tree," the illusion is quickly dispelled. For whereas Brenkman talks vaguely and abstractly of "capitalist society," "possessive individualism," and "proletarian revolution," McGann studies the actual historical and political context of Tennyson's poem, its mode of production and reception.

"The Charge of the Light Brigade" took its origin from a newspaper report; it was first printed in the *Examiner* (9 December 1854) one week after Tennyson read the initial account of the Battle of Balaclava, and the poem is, as McGann notes, "in many respects a distilled interpretation of the popular reaction to the charge as that reaction was expressed in the newspapers." In reading the poem against its newspaper sources, the critic is immediately struck by the "note of puzzlement" that colors the press reports, the repeated reference to "some misunderstanding" that brought on the disastrous "annihilation of the Light Cavalry Brigade." Thus the *Times* leader of 13 November 1854 exclaims: "Even accident would have made it more tolerable. But it was a mere mistake" (cited in *BI*, 192).

Whose mistake and why did it occur? Here textual study comes into play, McGann noting that in the first printed version of the poem in the *Examiner*, lines 5–6 of the first stanza read:

> "Forward, the Light Brigade!
> Take the guns," Nolan said. . . .

The specificity of reference was to be expunged in the second version, but precisely for that reason it provides McGann with an interesting clue. For Nolan (Capt. Lewis Nolan), McGann discovers, "was not just another cavalry officer, but a highly respected and even celebrated figure" (*BI*, 193), whose books on the management and tactics of cavalry units evidently created a sensation in military circles. Accordingly, the immediate newspaper linkage of Capt. Nolan's name with the infamous "mere mistake" that sent the Light Brigade to its fate, a mistake to which Tennyson refers in lines 11–12—"not tho' the soldier knew / Some-one had blunder'd"—presents a troubling picture of the mid-Victorian British cavalry. For how is Nolan's "blunder" to be justified?

Here, McGann suggests, we must imaginatively re-create the class status of the cavalry officer in Tennyson's England. The Light Brigade, he notes, "was in all respects like the rest of the regiments sent to the Crimea; that is to say, they were all the most socially elite units in the British army, spit-and-polish, dashing, and notoriously affected groups which had never seen a battlefield. The units had not been in action since Waterloo" (*BI*, 194–5). Indeed, the meaning of Balaclava can be understood only in the context of that earlier battle, which had been a noble victory of the English infantry, that is to say, the lower classes. To vindicate the cavalry was thus to pay tribute to the aristocratic virtues of those who, as one newspaper account put it, "risked on that day all the enjoyments that rank, wealth, good social position . . . can offer. Splendid as the event was on the Alma, yet that rugged ascent . . . was scarcely so glorious as the progress of the cavalry through and through that valley of death" (*BL*, 194).

But isn't Tennyson's tribute to the aristocratic virtues displayed at Balaclava a case of misguided sentimentality? Can we share the jingoistic mid-Victorian sympathy for what one newspaper called "a fatal display of courage which all must admire while they lament"? And how can we admire a poem that seems to share so fully the dominant ideology of its time? In tackling these difficult questions, the critic must probe the meaning of the poem's original reception, in this case, its ability to "cross class lines and speak to the nation at large" (*BI*, 197). Tennyson's strategy, McGann argues, is "hidden in the iconography of the poem. The images in 'The Charge of the Light Brigade' are drawn from the newspaper accounts of the day, but the form of these images is based upon an iconography of heroism which Tennyson appropriated. His sources are French, bourgeois, and painterly, and his use of them in his English, aristocratic, and verbal work represents another struggle with foreigners which the entire English nation could sympathize with" (*BI*, 197). Not only the content of the images but their *form*—here historical criticism becomes genuinely literary. For the critic's role is not merely to extract some ideological nugget or "apple bright" from the poet's particular narrative but rather to study that narrative's specific formal representations.

In the case of "The Charge of the Light Brigade," the first such form is metrical. "Half a league, half a league, / Half a league onward"; the "inexorable rhythm" of these lines, as McGann notes, "perfectly mirrors the cavalry's implacable movement," the spell the brigade seems to be under. And we might add that the poem's pounding dactyls and trochees enact a kind of ballet, a dance of death appropriate for cavalry discipline, which demands that ranks never be broken, that closure is all.

At the same time, the poem's imagery gives this death dance an odd twist. Tennyson was well aware, McGann remarks, that although Wellington had won the battle of Waterloo, England had lost to France the ideological struggle that followed. Accordingly, he endowed the Light Brigade with French cavalry postures, appropriating the iconography of David, Gericault, and Delacroix, the representations of dazzling equestrian heroes, depicted in all their Romantic force and energy:

Flash'd all their sabres bare,
Flash'd as they turn'd in air
Sabring the gunners there
Charging an army, while
        All the world wonder'd.

Here the last line may well refer, so McGann posits, to a remark made by the French general Bosquet when he heard of the tragedy at Balaclava: "C'est magnifique, mais ce n'est pas la guerre" (*BI*, 198). Tennyson's equestrian tableaux, in other words, endow the English cavalry with "the emblems of the heroism they deserved, but had never had," the emblems as they "had been defined in another, antithetical culture" (*BI*, 200).

"The Charge of the Light Brigade" is thus "grounded in a set of paradoxes, the most fundamental of which is that [the poet's] model should have been French and Romantic rather than English and Victorian. Out of this basic paradox Tennyson constructs a series of new and changed views on certain matters of real cultural importance. Most clearly he wants to show that the charge was not a military disaster but a spiritual triumph . . . [and] that the name of the 'Light Brigade' bears a meaning which transcends its technical military significance" (*BI*, 201). The pointlessness of the military maneuver thus has its own pathos, the pathos of a post-Waterloo Britain, not yet conscious of the obsolescence of its flashing sabres, confronted as they were to be by the realities of modern cannon fire.

To read "The Charge of the Light Brigade" historically is not, however, to suggest that we should share the attitudes that the poem embodies. "On the contrary," McGann argues, "the aim of the analysis is to make us aware of the ideological gulp which separates us from the human world evoked through Tennyson's poem"; it reminds us that "we too . . . intersect with our own age and experience . . . in certain specific and ideologically determined ways" (*BI*, 201–2). Indeed, the "differential" that a poem like "The Light Brigade" represents should prompt us to reconsider the forms our own postmodern lyric is assuming.

Between the England of 1854, which generated Tennyson's vivid depiction of battle—"Flash'd all their sabres bare, / Flash'd as they turn'd in air" and the America of 1984, which is the scene of Charles Bernstein's critique, in "Dysraphism," of the contemporary dissemination of "knowledge" with its accompanying exercise of authority—"I felt the abridgment / of imperatives, the wave of detours, the sabre- / rattling of inversion"—the "ideological gulf" is obviously large. The individual heroism of members of a threatened class, the pathos of battle, the poet's emotional response to a public disaster—for Bernstein, all these become, so to speak, "illustrated proclivities for puffed- / up benchmarks." In "Dysraphism," as in Tennyson's "Charge of the Light Brigade," "Sometimes something sunders," but for Bernstein such "mis-seaming" is less the function of a particular dramatic event than of the social fabric itself. Hence the *mise en question*, in this and the other poetic texts cited at the beginning of this essay, of such fixed forms as Tennyson's rhymed balladic stanzas, centered on consecutive pages and isolated for our contemplation.

Indeed, the postmodern displacement of the central and unique event, whether we mean the event referred to in the poem or the poetic event itself, calls into question the very possibility of submitting to analysis the single framed poem, the candidate for inclusion in the hypothetical anthology of canonical poems. "Anthologies are to poets," David Antin has quipped, "as the zoo is to animals."[12] The analogy is exact: not *poema* but *poiesis*, not the event but, in Lyn Hejinian's words, "the reserve / for events" is central to our lyric discourse. A "reserve" that does not privilege one page or section of *Glas* over another, even as "Writing through Howl" cannot be isolated from the other "writings through" of Ginsberg's poem.

But how do we talk about such lyric "writings"? The answer, implicit in Derrida's *Glas* as in Leiris's "*Glossaire*," is that language, not structure, becomes central. Indeed, recent poetic theory is reviving the notion, at the heart of Russian Formalist poetics but in bad repute throughout the sixties, that there is an inherent difference between "ordinary" and "poetic" language. If the former is instrumental and transparent, a window through which we look at the depicted world beyond the page, the latter deploys the resources of sound and multiple, often undecidable, reference so as to call attention to its own materiality.

We should note that this emphasis on the materiality of language is not quite the same thing as the Russian Futurist doctrine of *zaum* or "transrational" poetry, the Formalist stress on "orientation toward the neighboring word" and defamiliarization. For whereas Futurist poetics construed defamiliarization as essentially a *literary* transform, a revolt against the dominant aesthetic of Symbolism, our own postmodern *ostranenie* ("making strange") has more to do with the discourses of the everyday world, of politics, culture, and commerce, than with the literary model as such. Here the relevant frame is what I should like to call the technological double blind.

On the one hand, we live in a technological world in which everything we say and write is always already given—a storehouse of cliché, stock phraseology, sloganeering, a prescribed form of address, a set of formulas that govern the expression of subjectivity. Given this context, poetic discourse is that which most fully calls into question conventional writing practices and which defies the authority of the chronological linear model.[13] "Prescribed rules of grammar & spelling," says Charles Bernstein, "make language seem outside of our control, & a language, even only seemingly wrested from our control is a world taken from us."[14] Or, as Susan Howe puts it in *My Emily Dickinson* (1985): "Who polices questions of grammar, parts of speech, connection, and connotation? Whose order is shut inside the structure of a sentence? What inner articulation releases the coils and complications of Saying's assertion?"[15]

Hence the disruption of the linguistic and syntactical order we find in Hejinian's *The Guard* or Bernstein's "Dysraphism." Hence too the heavy reliance on citation, the graft of the other, in texts like *Glas* and "Writing through Howl," as if to say that our words can no longer be our own but that it is in our power to re-present them in new, imaginative ways.

But—and this is the curious signature of postmodern poetry—the discourse of technology rejected at one level as no more than the discourse of the dominant ideology, returns in the very structure, both aural and visual, of the poetic text. The double columns of *Glas* and of Brad Leithauser's poem, the print format of Leiris's "Le Sceptre miroitant," and the acrostic "Allen Ginsberg" buried in Cage's chance-generated lines—these breaks with what Gregory Ulmer calls "the investiture of the book"[16] are themselves part of our new technologized language. Indeed, poetry is now engaging the codes of the videotape playback, the telephone answering machine, and the computer, especially in its capacity, via modem, to address other computer terminals. At this writing, David Antin has been commissioned to compose a videopoem to be viewed alternately with the news flashes and information tapes in the waiting lounge of the Miami airport.

Such experiments promise a curious literalization—delightful or sinister depending upon one's point of view—of Pound's famous aphorism, "Poetry is news that stays news." It seems in any case impossible to talk about something called "the lyric" as if the genre were a timeless and stable product to which various theoretical paradigms can be "applied" so as to tease out new meanings. "Blinded by avenue and filled with / adjacency," we find ourselves trying "to / unveil detail / as minimal / as it's recep- / tive."

"Poets and other creative writers: fear not!" we read in the flyer for the *Black Mountain II Review*. Perhaps this imperative is not so foolish after all. "You may be writing 'Language-Oriented' works without ever having heard of half these people." Form, to adapt Robert Creeley's well-known injunction, is never more than the extension of culture.

1. The sources of these texts are as follows: (1) Lyn Hejinian, *The Guard* (Berkeley, Calif.: Tuumba Press, 1984), unpaginated; (2) John Cage, "Writing for the second time through Howl" (1984), in a festschrift for Allen Ginsberg's sixtieth birthday, courtesy of John Cage; (3) Michel Leiris, "Le Sceptre miroitant," in "*Glossaire*," *Mots sans mémoire* (Paris: Gallimard, 1969), p. 111; reprinted in "Special Section: New Translations of Michel Leiris," ed. James Clifford, *Sulfur*, no. 15 (1986): 4–125, on p. 29; (4) Brad Leithauser, "In a Bonsai Nursery," Part 3 of "Dainties: A Suite," *Cats of the Temple* (New York: Alfred A. Knopf, 1986), p. 14; (5) Charles Bernstein, "Dysraphism," in *The Sophist* (Los Angeles: Sun & Moon Press, 1987), p. 44; (6) Jacques Derrida, *Glas*, 2 vols. (Paris: Denoël, 1981), 2:221.

2. Paul de Man, "Lyrical Voice in Contemporary Theory: Riffaterre and Jauss," in *Lyric Poetry: Beyond the New Criticism*, ed. Chaviva Hošek and Patricia Parker (Ithaca and London: Cornell University Press, 1985), p. 55. This collection is subsequently cited in the text as *LP*.

3. Charles Bernstein, headnote to "Dysraphism," *Sulfur*, no. 8 (1983): 39. This headnote is omitted in the version of the poem printed in *The Sophist*.

4. Michel Leiris, "Glossaire: J'y serre mes gloses," in *La Révolution surréaliste* (1925); translated as "Glossary: My Glosses' Ossuary," by Lydia Davis, *Sulfur*, no. 15 (1986): 27.

5. Geoffrey Hartman, *Saving the Text: Literature/ Derrida/Philosophy* (Baltimore and London: Johns Hopkins University Press, 1981), pp. 33–66. "Epiphony in Echoland" is the title of Hartman's second chapter.

6. See, on this point, the article "Lyric" by James William Johnson in the *Princeton Encyclopedia of Poetry and Poetics*, ed. Alex Preminger et al., enl. ed. (Princeton, N.J.: Princeton University Press, 1974), pp. 460–70, esp. pp. 460–61.

7. Edward Said, "Opponents, Audiences, Constituencies, and Community," *Critical Inquiry* 9 (September 1982): 4–5.

8. See chap. 13, "Barthes, Ashbery, and the Zero Degree of Genre," below, and my "Introduction," in *Postmodern Genres*, ed. Marjorie Perloff, *Genre* 20, nos. 3–4 (Fall-Winter 1987): 233–49; Cf. Ralph Cohen, "History and Genre," *New Literary History* 17 (Winter 1986): 203–18. Cohen writes, "What acts and assumptions are concealed in the infinitive to *identify*? After all, classifications are undertaken for specific purposes. . . . different authors, readers, critics have different reasons for identifying texts as they do" (p. 205).

9. Roland Barthes, *Le Grain de la voix: Entretiens 1962–1980* (Paris: Editions du Seuil, 1981), p. 210. For an English translation, see *The Grain of the Voice: Interviews 1962–1980*, trans. Linda Coverdale (New York: Hill & Wang, 1985), p. 222.

10. The one exception is David Bromwich's brief (4 pp.) discussion of the Canadian poet Jay Macpherson.

11. Jerome J. McGann, "Tennyson and the Histories of Criticism" (1982), in *The Beauties of Inflections: Literary Investigations in Historical Method and Theory* (Oxford: Clarendon Press, 1985), p. 222. Subsequently cited in the text as *BI*.

12. David Antin, "George Oppen and Poetic Thinking," panel discussion at the Oppen Symposium, University of California, San Diego, 16 May 1986.

13. On this point see Gregory L. Ulmer, *Applied Grammatology: Post(e)-Pedagogy from Jacques Derrida to Joseph Beuys* (Baltimore and London: Johns Hopkins University Press, 1985), chap. 1, passim, esp. pp. 8–9.

14. Charles Bernstein, "Three or Four Things I know about Him" (1975), in *Content's Dream, Essays 1975–84* (Los Angeles: Sun & Moon Press, 1986), p. 26.

15. Susan Howe, *My Emily Dickinson* (Berkeley, Calif.: North Atlantic Books, 1985), pp. 11–12.

16. Ulmer, *Applied Grammatology*, p. 13.

What Is Living and What Is Dead in American Postmodernism: Establishing the Contemporaneity of Some American Poetry (1996)

8.2

CHARLES ALTIERI

[. . .] 1) There is no way to claim that significant contemporary art can at once establish what can be considered symptomatic about postmodernity and also provide some plausible notion of cure. It is not even reasonable to claim that art offers cogent general models for escaping the play of simulacra or the alienations that stem from the collapse of scene into screen and mirror into network. However, one can show how specific writers develop imaginative energies that do not fit easily into these binaries. And one can hope to build on those examples by showing that there are feasible imaginative strategies for finessing the entire model of judgment that invites predicates like symptom and cure.

Robert Creeley and Frank O'Hara initiated what I take to be the most suggestive of these strategies. Despite their very different emotional agendas, both poets refused to give their texts the look and feel of well-made poems and turned instead to what we might call an anti-artefactual aesthetics. They did this in part to resist the New Criticism, but in larger part to develop an alternative way of realizing New Critical ideals of casting poetry as a form of knowledge. For O'Hara and for Creeley, knowledge based on abstract meditation, however committed to concrete ambivalence, left the poet trapped in a culture of vague idealizations and insufficiently examined psychological constructs. So they turned instead to a poetry that presented itself as testing at every moment its own formal and existential choices simply in terms of the qualities of life that the poetic thinking made available for the poet. Poetry becomes direct habitation, a directly instrumental rather than contemplative use of language. And its test of value becomes the mobility and intensity immediately made available to the poet, so that he or she need not rely on any of the abstract versions of those values or even on any of the formulated social ideals that establish the markets in which cultural capital is traded.

Now these values become even more important, or so it seems, if one notices how this resistance to artefactuality has become fundamental to poets as diverse as Ashbery, C. K. Williams, Robert Hass, and Adrienne Rich. Each writer refuses to separate the person from the poem but does not collapse the poem into the person, as confessional work tends to do. And each refuses to be content with an aesthetics of sincerity, since ideals like sincerity are as abstract and media driven as more traditional ideals calling for a mature, tragic wisdom. What matters is not sincerity per se but becoming articulate about the conditions within which the process of imagining enriches the possibilities of fully investing in the specific life one is leading. For by adapting these values poets can respond to a contemporary cultural theater where the old artefactuality, the old achievement of order out of chaos, has become inseparable from the new trade in commodities, and poetry has now become little more than cultural capital effective primarily in allowing us to luxuriate in convictions about our own sensitivity and "insight." Even contemporary poetry's effort to extend the romantic psychology that sanctions new visions of imaginative power now seems to offer little more than floating signifiers that circulate only within a very small social world and that even there have very little effect on how people actually live their lives.

There may be no escaping that small social world. And we may have to do without the belief that poetry somehow gives us access to a reality inaccessible to other discourses. It may be task enough to show people how poetry is capable of giving civilized pleasure. But the very terms of such pleasure do have their own potential cultural force. This is especially true when the poets develop imaginative investments adapting postmodern critiques of idealization to models of value that are not reducible to the rhetorics of the simulacral and the schizophrenic that emerge from those critiques.

The best single contemporary example I know of this anti-artefactuality is the last stanza of Ashbery's "As We Know"—simply because of how Ashbery transforms the problematic term *real* into an example of the values that the adverb *really* is capable of bringing to bear:

> The light that was shadowed then
> Was seen to be our lives,
> Everything about us that love might wish to examine,
> Then put away for a certain length of time, until
> The whole is to be reviewed, and we turned
> Toward each other, to each other.
> The way we had come was all we could see
> And it crept up on us, embarrassed
> That there is so much to tell now, really now.[1]

On one level this poem is remarkable primarily for what it refuses to do. The lyric climax takes place as a moment of embarrassment, not as any sudden understanding of forces or specific memories that bind the lovers, and not as any promise to change their lives. This kind of poetry cannot hope to provide any overt imaginative order for the particulars it engages; nor can it build capacious structures. Its attention must be focused on some immediate situation or flow of mind. But that compression of space allows the writer to concentrate on how, within time, intricate folds and passages open among materials. Even though reflexive consciousness can do no more than trace the ways we have come to and through those situations, it can focus close attention on the contours of its own engagements, and it can locate an affirmative will simply in what thereby becomes visible and shareable, without any need for or hope in more comprehensive allegorical structures.

"Now, really now" carries the full force of that willing, in a way that brilliantly evades the self-congratulatory self-representation almost inescapable in love poetry. That phrase becomes a simple instrument for engaging a present whose configurations can be willed and whose intensities can be shared. And the minimalism here, the capacity simply to mine the resources of grammar without having to pose more ambitious and abstract interpretive structures, also allows the poem a way of responding to the quasi-metaphysics of theorizing about simulacra, or about the symptomatic as our only access to the real. Ashbery refuses to allow consciousness the thematizing distance necessary if one is even to dream of distinguishing symptom from cure. What matters is the present—not as some metaphysical absolute but as the locus of minute processes of judgment that simply go into neutral if they are forced to deal with large questions. This does not at all entail any relativism on that same large scale. Rather, it invites us to base our thinking about values and about the paths our lives take simply on our capacity to appreciate the difference between "now" as a descriptive specification of time and "really now" as an assertion of something like a will able to envision itself stabilized by the world it sees itself sharing. "Really now" so fully inhabits the simulacral that all questions about reality seem only marks of an alienation that cannot find its way to lyric expression.

2) It is comparatively easy to recognize the tensions between ideals of identity politics and efforts to create a heterogeneous, multicultural stage on which competing versions of identity can coexist. The challenge is figuring out how alternatives might be possible, so that writers can articulate imaginative interests that are basic for minorities without relying on the autobiographical forms that pervade postmodern thinking on this subject. Commitment to autobiography forces writers to either serve as a representative for some community, which imposes the categorical on the personal, or to develop a bitter distance from all general fealties and hence becomes indistinguishable from mainstream celebrations of personal differences (as in V. S. Naipaul). Moreover in both cases the autobiographical mode itself constantly risks making theatrical and personal what may be better seen as structural and shareable features of the lives represented.[2] Or, probably worse, the effort to construct identity gets transformed into a celebration of participating in multiple identities, and sophisticated theory provides a self-congratulatory alternative to the kind of cultural work that requires aligning the self with specific roles and fealties.

Against this backdrop I think it becomes important to turn to the work of recent self-consciously ethnic poetry that attempts to reconfigure how the lyric imagination can engage the memories and desires binding agents to specific communal filiations. Aware of the traps that occur when one moves directly to the levels of psychology involved in postulating identities, this poetry turns to aspects of ethnic life in America too opaque and diffuse to be thematized by memory and too embedded in complex pressures and demands to be represented in terms of dramatic scenes and narrative structures. Ethnicity, then, cannot be effectively represented through a directly introspective psychology that enables agents to stage for themselves what makes them different and to decide who they will be in the future. Instead, these poets explore lyrical states where the conditions of agency are best understood by adapting Hegel's notion of substance. *Substance* can help designate a sense of historicity resistant to any of the predicates we have available for talking about personal identity.

The notion of substance plays two basic roles in our assessment of this work. It enables us to shift our attention from the agents per se to the dense cultural networks within which agents feel at once interpellated and alienated, at once too much and too little involved in mainstream life. And it makes sense of the ways that experimental ethnic writing resists the temptation to offer clear, positive concepts by which we might describe adequately what is involved in these engagements. Hegel's own awareness of such limitations is of course complemented by his insistence that spirit comes to full self-consciousness by developing within substance its own sense of purposive direction, so that one can transform what had been alien being-in-itself or being-for-others into the kind of awareness that constitutes being-for-oneself. But the two poets I will look at here, Alfred Arteaga and Myung Mi Kim, are much more wary of the romantic tendency to postulate within substance precisely those attributes that can then be affirmed as the signs of spirit. They have seen far too many efforts to treat the substance of minority experience as if it could be adequately handled within discursive and autobiographical modes. For them the most spirit can do is respond to the difficulties involved in developing images registering the tensions that give resonance and intensity to the artist's work.

This commitment makes both poets difficult to read, at least initially. And because Arteaga's richest effects depend on familiarity with the over-lapping strands of his *Cantos*, I can here only indicate what I find most exciting in his work. Poetry for Arteaga is not quite dramatic or scenic. It is better conceived of as letting desires enter echo chambers provided by the linguistic resources available to a bilingual community. In reading this work we are constantly poised between feeling lost, feeling that this multiplicity is an impediment to desire, and finding the overlap of languages opening new and surprising emotional resonances. We enter a site of transformations where a moment that seems only a "lacuna" for English speakers actually functions as *la cuna*, or the cradle, of possibilities for one willing or able to set the two languages in relation to each other.[3] Then one finds within the languages, and within the complex cultural grammars brought into conjunction, a dynamic cultural field where personal power lies not in the construction of personal identities but in elaborating what the languages afford, as if they composed a home so rich and intricate that autobiography comes to seem an indulgent and thin way to deploy one's imagination. Concerns for personal identity—whether representative or deconstructively multiple—require both scenes and narrative sequences that dramatize aspects of cultural life not compatible with the versions of power and need offered by standard narrative patterns of selfhood.[4]

Myung Mi Kim's *Under Flag* provides a more overt thematic focus on the density of substance because she reverses Arteaga's situation. For her the underlying drama consists of the pressures that one feels as one tries to learn English. At one pole one's sense of self as a dense assembly of substances emerges in negative form—as awareness of all that her new English language does not contain but forces into a complex of memory and repression. At the other pole the new language appears laden with more demands than permissions, as if one could feel within it all those mutual understandings and prejudices that have emerged within a dominant history the immigrant does not easily share. Identity poetics responds to such pressures, but the language of autobiography will not quite register the intricate phenomenology involved. And no political rhetoric will capture the range of emotions evoked by the interplay of language contexts—from rage to self-hatred to fear to hope, to registering numerous partial identifications with other people.

This is the opening of "And Sing We," the first poem of *Under Flag*:

Must it ring so true
So we must sing it

To spawn even yawning distance
And would we be near then

What would the sea be, if we were near it

Voice

It catches its underside and drags it back

What sound do we make, "n", "h", "g"

Speak and it is sound in time

Depletion replete with barraging

Slurred and taken over

Diaspora. "It is not the picture

That will save us."

All the fields fallow

The slide carousel's near burn-out and yet

Flash and one more picture of how we were to be[5]

I love the opening oscillation between question and command and the corollary play of forces generated by repeating the same term with different grammatical functions. We cannot know the referent of "it." But we can understand that whatever "it" is, it puts in motion the dual senses of "so"—one an intensifier, the other a logical connective. Both senses of "so" then provide the combination of intensity and logical force that helps flesh out the full implications of "must."

But why is all this density so abstracted from any concrete scene? Perhaps we have to question our usual assumptions about what empirical concreteness can actually tell us in such situations. Can we usually specify and represent what counts as an imperative for us, especially when the imperative involves song? The "it" seems irreducibly part of the situation, part of what it means to be coming to terms with what a language affords. And this "it" also seems inseparable from a need to worry about the limitations of what the person is learning to sing, whatever the immediate context. Can the new language give form to old memories? Can what becomes "sound" in time sufficiently resound to bring other times to bear?

Any more direct answers to such questions would make us risk deceiving ourselves by letting our needs project more certainty than the situation warrants. Probably all we can do is circulate through and around the conditions that this learning situation entails. That is why the second section of my quotation (beginning with "depletion") puts such emphasis on the independent phrase units, most of which seem to fix the agent within certain attributions that then must be worked through by exploring what associations follow. Here the entire process of barraging culminates in the trope of feeling the self bound to something like a slide projector, with each picture imposing on the present an oppressive future. Indeed, the sense of oppression is bound less to any given content than it is to the force of that future as pure form and hence as a chilling abstract reminder of the designs that language has upon us.

As the poem goes on through four more sections we witness the feeling of being bound to the "ponderous" phrase ("AS," p. 14), relieved only by sudden and unsummoned memories of Kim's life in Korea. These memories help relieve the task of learning a foreign language by embedding in that process strangely liberating material qualities of specific voices that enter the poem as both torment and hope. That tension then drives the poem to the following resolution: "Mostly, we cross bridges we did not see being built" ("AS," p. 15). Thematically, the bridges go back to a rural past while also indicating how important it is to adapt to what one can neither control nor psychologize. The bridges do not depend on our witnessing their being built; they simply make possible the range of transitions enabling us to live with loss. As evidence of that capacity we need look no further than "mostly," which deliberately imposes a note of awkward qualification on the speaker's knowledge. This "mostly" involves an act of wary trust—the only attitude that will allow one to negotiate this poem's melange of external demands and haunting memories, each all too eager to trap the speaker in an autobiographical obsession. Here, instead of seeking any one identity, the poet has to accept a range of possible identifications to be explored—"each drop strewn into such assembly."[6]

3) Postmodern psychology creates the problem of having to dissolve fixed identity while preserving a range of values like intimacy that derive from now-outmoded versions of selfhood. Moreover, a psychology adequate to postmodernity has to recognize the sublimity possible in pure self-dissolution (or related "cyborgian" experiments) while offering possible routes for reintegrating this sublimity within something resembling social life. One might argue that the contemporary arts have responded to these demands in two fundamental ways: one involves the refigurations of surrealist versions of how we inhabit our bodies that Foster has analyzed, and the other involves the various experiments in deictic agency that I have explored. These experiments, I have argued, appear quintessentially in assertions like "now, really now" that allow us to reflect on investments that neither depend on nor lead to the practices of self-representation fundamental to modern culture. Rather than accepting either romantic inwardness or versions of subjective agency as entirely constituted by social practices, this perspective emphasizes the range of expressive registers that agents bring into focus simply by manipulating and elaborating deictics. Here I want to explore another, differently gendered variant of this deictic model of agency that foregrounds issues of intimacy and responsiveness to the world while also refusing to invoke any traditional deep psychology. So I will turn to the remarkably elemental decomposition and reorientation of subjectivity explored in Lyn Hejinian's *The Cell*.

This volume brilliantly foregrounds a personal agency so vital in its silences, in its ways of repeating itself, and in its shifting attentions that it convincingly inhabits the form of a lyric diary while refusing the dramatic confrontations between represented and representing selves fundamental to that form. Traditionally, such a focus on the subject's experiences tempts authors to have each entry build to a climactic dramatic moment, as in Robert Lowell's *Notebook 1967–1968*. But to Hejinian such climaxes lead away from what she is most interested in. The dramatic organization blinds the author to the most intimate features of repetition and change as life unfolds and greatly oversimplifies the play of voices that constitutes self-consciousness within that unfolding. As Hejinian memorably puts it, "personality is a worn egress / to somewhere in particular."[7] Personality confines consciousness to preestablished ends and, ironically, tells introspection what it is bound to find. So she proposes instead exploring those imaginative paths where poetry can take up the "chance / of enhancement," as if simply hearing the puns within the master term provides reason enough to align oneself with more mobile versions of subjective agency (*C*, p. 42).

Once one grows suspicious of "personality," lyric self-reflection becomes a very different enterprise:

> A person decomposing the unity
> of the subjective mind by
> dint of its own introspection
> [*C*, p. 157]

Introspection sets the mind against its own images, not simply to maintain ironic distance but also to dramatize the resonant forces that circulate around the desire for self-representation. As an example of this interplay between decomposition and redeployment of imaginative investments, consider the volume's penultimate poem. Its opening lines invite us to recognize how many senses come into play around the act of seeing, or better, around the way sight is poised between what disappears and what appears:

> All sentences about the sense
> of seeing, the sense of

embarrassment
It could all disappear—instead
it appeared
My language
My language is a genital—
let's say that
[C, p. 214]

Seeing involves a sense of embarrassment because it leaves one open to and dependent on the supplementary processes that sentences bring into play. Even the syntax is ambiguous because seeing cannot be given one stable position as it vacillates between serving as an element within an extended clause (which, in its concern for sense, never achieves its verb) and serving as the focal unit that everything "sentences about," as if the seeing were the wellspring of possible meanings. No wonder that the "it" could all disappear: it depends on the vagaries of these sentences and the difficult interplay between the time of pure seeing and the work of sentencing. But "it" also can seem to come into focus, making language itself seem inseparable from the person's hold on the scene. And that satisfaction, framed by the fear of disappearance, invites the sexual analogies that Hejinian's reference to genitals brings to bear.

"Let's say that" breaks the enchantment. If we can achieve the distance to treat these sayings as provisional, we have to wonder whether we have lost touch with the immediate impulses that have been shaping our investments in this "sense" of seeing. Language can sustain a thinking at one with "the composition / of things / distinctions steering sunlight," but such intensified self-consciousness can also get caught up in its own overdetermined sequences, which now take over the poem (C, p. 214). However, rather than take the time to track these movements, I will go directly to the moment when the poem develops its conclusion:

It could all disappear
Streets
With remorse for individualism, provoking
scale
Dimension sinks
It's the event of seeing
what I speak of with
someone's eyes
The event of a carnality
covered by eye
The light proceeding along the
yellow sides of night
A word is a panorama
of a thing
It's the eye's duty to
tell
It's relevant—though a person
is implicated in the process
it keeps in sight
[C, pp. 214–15]

These lines are not easy to interpret. They demand a good deal of guesswork. But in responding to that demand we find ourselves embodying a cardinal principle of Hejinian's poetics: it foregrounds processes of "conjecture" that force us to recognize the apparently arbitrary or uncaused leap of proprioceptive activity fundamental to a person's making any part of the world her own. Conjecture, in other words, is inseparable from our sense of the ego taking up residence in a world that exceeds it but that also provides a ground for its sense of its own free contingency. And because of its fluidity, conjecture does not demand that the "I" build a melodramatic stage on which to interpret its independence (such staging only confirms the version of the self one initially postulates). So for Hejinian even sex is best figured as "the pleasure of/ inexactitude" (*C*, p. 140), because the alternative is sex by the book, sex blind to the arbitrariness and playfulness by which we come to appreciate how our lives might remain open to, even hungry for, what we cannot control in other people. Why should poetry be different, since it seeks the same correlation of intimacy and pleasure playing through the same absorbing interest in seeing exact attention create indefinable edges?

My conjectures project Hejinian's using this fear of disappearance to highlight what Heidegger might call "a worldliness of the world" constantly at risk of collapsing into public pieties and private psychodramas. The passage from the poem begins with a fear that landscape will turn into mapped streets that in their turn can instantly be made into allegories of "remorse for individualism." What else can the demand for individuation produce except endless repetition feeding on anxieties that agency may be unrepresentable? Since these are not the fears that admit of heroic confrontations, all one can do is let the earlier querying within the poem generate a syntactic form around which some resisting energies can be gathered. As dimension sinks, and hence as the specific image collapses, the poem replaces "it could all disappear" with another "it" construction leading beyond the eager scrutiny to a more general sense of how persons inhabit the "eye." If the "I" must give up the hope of somehow establishing private access to the real, it can instead treat embodiment as simply accepting the carnality of its bodily functions. This enables one to identify with the eye without making demands that vision be tied closely to the demands of any specific ego. Instead, this abstracting of the eye leads back to the panorama of words, as if words, too, open into vision as long as we maintain enough distance from specific imaginary demands to explore the access language gives us to the ways that our unconscious beings are deployed in particular moments.

This intricate balancing of "eye," "I," and "word" finally takes on its full emotional and sexual implications in the last three lines:

> It's relevant—though a person
> is implicated in the process
> it keeps in sight

We arrive at this sense of implication by recognizing that language is part of the eye's imperative, even when one brackets individual sensibility, because language allows vision its "sentences," in every sense of that term. Then once that process is grasped in its independence, one can return to the issue of how particular persons make investments in what they see. Rather than being the source of the seeing, the person is literally folded into that which appears, so that one in effect learns about one's own desires in the very processes that allow vision to unfold a world.

Everything the poem implies about the force of language as bearer of investments comes into the foreground in the brilliant final pun on keeping materials in sight. For it seems as if the plenitude of the pun arises out of nowhere, a grace within language attuned to the situation it tries to articulate. The eye not only keeps objects in its sight; it also has stakes in those objects, so that it matters how over time the person treasures what is seen. Decomposing the ego into its carnal functioning, then, does not repress feeling but allows us to encounter its most elemental forms—forms that depend on a syntax that works with an "it" in the subject position rather than a projected self-image. And this sense of forms then helps temper the fear with which the poem began that thought will make sight overdetermined. For the poem helps us to see how merely holding objects before the eye can modulate into actively *keeping in* sight, as if the eye expressed a version of the containing force that can be associated with female genitals. And this active keeping then becomes a full willing of what the eye sees, even though there has been no introspection by which to organize that will. Here the power of commitment does not depend on some inner state but on a specific way of engaging in events that prevents our isolating that personal dimension as a unique and representable center. The only workable mirror for the self seems to consist in folding consciousness within its own embodied activities. Anything more speculative may entail self-divisive idealism.

I have to be this abstract if I am to keep Hejinian in sight. But it is crucial that readers not confuse the speculation required to orient ourselves within the poem with the very different mode of expression by which the poetry itself engages the world. Hejinian can be as minimalist as she is about emotions because she relegates much of the work of feeling to a remarkably fluid and intricate play of tones. Tone makes it possible to keep a mode of conjecture within experience, a mode that we easily lose if we push too hard to capture the entire process as someone's possession and hence as an extension of personality. So I think it fair to say that Hejinian's poetry offers a dynamic alternative to the modes of self-reflection generated by both analytic philosophy and the therapeutic practices postulated to save us from the self-division such thinking creates. In her work, what makes us persons is not how we compose self-images but how the degrees and modalities of concern that that tone embodies compose a world for our keeping. As Hejinian's final poem in *The Cell* puts it, rather than worrying about a gulf between word and world, we might think of how we can orient ourselves towards a "consciousness of unconsciousness" attuned to the ways we are always already part of the sentences that our grammars afford us. Then she adds, in order to close with her characteristic twinkle, "It is good to know / so" (*C*, p. 217). That is, we may need only this playful cross of rhyme and pun in order to correlate the "so" of method with the "so" of alignment and adjustment and, hence, to demonstrate what consciousness of unconsciousness can afford us. And then it becomes possible to have poetry speak what we might call the legislative "let it be so" rarely achieved in postromantic poetry. Such a blessing depends only on managing to keep lyrical intelligence responsive to the delights embedded in the panoramas language affords, as if in this alternative to specular self-reflection, in this gentle and mobile distance, may lie our peace.

4) I still have the last two sets of contradictions to face and I have almost no space. This will not seem much of a loss since I also have almost nothing to say about them that I have not said elsewhere. The fourth set of contradictions takes place in postmodernist moral theory's desire to undo the sense of demand basic to the masculine ego while also cultivating versions of self-empowerment that help agents respond to their social situations. While poetry cannot be very helpful in developing specific moral arguments that might address these contradictions, it can explore versions of agency that we then call upon for our representations of moral powers and moral responsibilities. In particular I have argued that contemporary poetry is keenly responsive to the Levinasian and

Lacanian concern to replace the dream of autonomy with an insistence on how deeply otherness pervades any experience of our own possible identities. Two basic features of moral agency then come to the fore: at one pole poets ranging from Hejinian to Hass ask us to shift from an emphasis on the ideals we pursue to an emphasis on the concrete texture of needs and cares that bind us to other people and invite various kinds of reciprocity; while at the other pole poets like Bernstein make that reciprocity fundamentally structural by exploring the degree to which the very conditions of self-reflection bind us to grammars we share with other people.[8] Both modes of writing then make the work of reading inseparable from exploring what these bonds with other people afford us.

5) I can say even less on the last set of contradictions because I cannot think of any conceptual or imaginative way to reconcile the pragmatist and deconstructive poles of antifoundational thinking. It is no accident that Rorty remains a radical dualist in espousing deconstructive irony as fundamental for individual subjectivity while basing public thinking entirely on pragmatist principles. But that very impossibility may afford the strongest possible argument for aligning postmodernism in the arts with basic modernist imperatives, despite the many differences between them. For both orientations share a commitment to resisting empiricism and to exploring plural worlds, where particulars prove inseparable from the local frameworks that make them intelligible, whether these frameworks be modernist constructivist wills or postmodernist conjectures. And much of the best postmodern art shares modernism's refusal to bestow on social practices what it denies to metaphysics; such art will not yield authority to those versions of will and judgment that rely on social negotiations and idealized rhetorics of community. Instead it foregrounds a tangential relation between the artist's work and any specific social agenda, and hence it reminds us how unstable and self-divided all our idealizations must be. Yet instability is not sufficient reason for renouncing idealization entirely in favor of the satiric mode that comes far too easily within twentieth-century life. Postmodern art like the poetry we have been examining articulates one domain where it makes sense to bring modernist intensity to the postmodern thematics of thriving on contradiction.

NOTES

1. Asbhery, "As We Know," *As We Know* (New York, 1979), p. 74. I have developed a more thorough reading of this poem in my "Contemporary Poetry as Philosophy: Subjective Agency in John Ashbery and C. K. Williams," *Contemporary Literature* 33 (Summer 1992): 214–42.

2. Consider the dilemma that pervades Homi K. Bhabha's *The Location of Culture* (London, 1994). He makes a forceful pragmatist case that there are no fixed identities but only a constant weaving of partial identifications and filiations. Yet he also has to distinguish ethnic identity-construction from anything sanctioned by pragmatism in order to insist on the agonistic nature of public space and in order to keep in the foreground a constant focus on the repressive force of Enlightenment universals. But the agon depends on quite fixed identities, at least in principle, and the refusal to forget the past seems an anachronistic demand for authenticity. There is in fact nothing in his accounts of identity that applies specifically to postcolonial or ethnic situations because the entire story fits so neatly into a pragmatist psychology.

3. The relevant lines from Arteaga's poem are "[*cctbc*, Frida, / y *cesa* letra *tdg* a / kiss, a lacuna" (Alfred Arteaga, "Respuesta a Frida," *Cantos* [Berkeley, 1991], p. 48). Literally, the lacuna here is the *e* that Frida Kahlo dropped from her name in order to separate herself from Nazi Germany. I take the concept of language as impediment from my colleague Gwen Kirkpatrick.

4. Notice the important difference from Pound's use of foreign languages. Pound justified this practice in terms of capturing the exact character of certain exalted expressions. He was not interested in the qualities of the languages per se but in the truths that became available within them for those who could appreciate the precision. Arteaga, on the other hand, is less interested in the specific moments captured by Spanish than in the very fact of what it means to be a user of Spanish. He is absorbed by life in the language, not by vision through the language.

5. Myung Mi Kim, "And Sing We," *Under Flag* (Berkeley, 1991), p. 13; hereafter abbreviated "AS."

6. Kim, "Into Such Assembly," *Under Flag*, p. 31. This quotation is from the end of her most accessible poem.

7. Lyn Hejinian, *The Cell* (Los Angeles, 1992), p. 42; hereafter abbreviated *C.*

8. I develop these alternatives at length in my "What Differences Can Contemporary Poetry Make in Our Moral Thinking?" in *Renegotiating Ethics in Literature, Philosophy, and Theory*, ed. Jane Adamson, Richard Freadman, David Parker (Cambridge: Cambridge University Press, 1998), 113–32.

The Matter of Capital, or Catastrophe and Textuality (2011) 8.3

Christopher Nealon

It has been difficult for critics to probe the historical imagination that gets attached to the idea of textuality in poetry in English because of the overlap of two critical traditions—a New Critical tradition in which modern poetry has been understood generically, as always gesturing back to an originally oral "lyric" in one sense or another, and a post-structuralist tradition in which the idea of textuality takes on such powerful philosophical overtones that its mundane history is eclipsed.

There is another reason it has been difficult to recognize the textual imaginary of modern poetry in English, which is that the canonical story of the emergence of textual culture in the West, Walter Ong's *Orality and Literacy*, is told as a story of "the technologization of the word." Ong's technical history, with its yearning for a return to the orality of dialectical pedagogy, not only obscures the ongoing coexistence of orality and literacy in textual culture, but also flattens out the differences among the grammatical arts, which encode different understandings of the social functions of texts and of literacy. Recent scholarship in medieval studies, however, has provided a more multifaceted picture of the shifts in the meanings of grammar and rhetoric as they became more enmeshed in textual cultures (Irvine, *The Making of Textual Culture*).

This scholarship also makes clear the enduring link between the textual culture and civilizational crisis—not only via the traditional story, by which monastic textual labor preserves the heritage of "western civilization" between the fall of Rome and the rise of Europe, but also by way of the history of the literary arts as mediating agents in the transfer of political power from Greece to Rome and, later, from Rome to the modern European centers of power. As Rita Copeland has shown, these transfers of power demanded tremendous expenditures of skill on textual commentary and translation—between Greek and Latin, and later between Latin and the emergent vernaculars. In each case, concerns about creating literate classes, and developing a literary tradition for an emergent language, made the writing of poetry—which is to say, the copying down of poetry, paraphrasing it, translating it, imitating it—crucial to the advance of the civilizational projects of emergent powers (Copeland, *Rhetoric, Hermeneutics, and Translation*).

So literary "matter" in the sense of the poetic record of heroic deeds has a cousin sense of "matter" as the material practices of making texts. Indeed, Eugene Vance has argued that in the chivalric romances of Chrétien de Troyes we can see a historical movement "from topic to tale"—an incorporation of the projects of the older grammatical arts into an emergent sense of how to depict heroic action (*From Topic to Tale*). My use of the phrase "the matter of capital" depends on such scholarship, along with the work of Ernst Robert Curtius, for help in developing my sense of what "the matter of capital" might mean in twentieth-century American poetry: topics, topoi, and techniques that produce a *textual imaginary* for that poetry, which it uses to stage confrontations between poetry and capital.[1]

As I say, however, the critical models available in the American academy after World War II have made it difficult to discern the existence of this textual imaginary, or even the persistence of capitalism as subject matter for American poetry—notwithstanding the career-long effort of a scholar like Cary Nelson to broaden the canons of American poetry to include poems written from in and around the American labor movement.[2] Before giving you a preliminary sense of the breadth of poetry we might include in the matter of capital, then, I'd like to offer a brief account of why it's been so hard to name.

Virginia Jackson has argued that the professionalization of literary criticism from the time of the New Critics has produced a tendency to read all poems as lyrics, where "lyric" means a record of the voice or the mind speaking to itself, as in T. S. Eliot's conception of the mode (*Dickinson's Misery*). This seems true of New Criticism. But I am also interested in a related phenomenon, which is how, beginning in the 1970s, the language of philosophy stepped in to fill the gap left by New Critical insistence on the aesthetic autonomy of the poem. In the context of the long dominance of New Critical models that insisted that poems needed no external frame by which to be read, the increasingly philosophical approach to the study of poetry in the 1970s and 1980s served as a welcome countermove, an insistence that there was something public, and something intellectual, about poetry, that it was not just grist for the mill of undergraduate composition classes and introductory surveys, and that it could not, and should not, be kept sequestered from the larger questions it raised.

Those questions, however, were themselves complexly determined by the political situation of the era, which was never quite investigated by the new philosophical criticism. This is plainly evident in the strongest criticism from the period, which by my lights was written by Marjorie Perloff and Charles Altieri. Both Perloff and Altieri were at the forefront of the expansion of the poetic canon to include more experimental writing in the 1980s, and both helped turn American poetry criticism away from a reduction of the poetic to the lyrical. Both, too, were indispensable in providing intellectual frameworks by which the "mainstream" of American poetry could articulate what was becoming an emphatic shift to the aesthetic left.

But even this strong work tended merely to name, then draw back from, the conditions that arguably made it urgent to restore to the study of poetry a sense of high intellectual stakes. By those "conditions," I mean both the crises and the triumphs of global capitalism from about 1973 on. These crises have been felt in the trials of poor, working-class, and middle-class people: the end of the post-World War II boom, the return of the business cycle, and the increasingly hysterical speculative bubbles of the 1980s, the 1990s, and the first decade of the twenty-first century, each in its way designed to find outlets for wealth unmoored from the "real" economy. The triumphs have largely been those of the capitalist classes: the defeats of the labor movement in the United States from the Reagan era onward, and the successful capitalization of everyday life, the famous "dematerialization" of labor, or "flexible accumulation" that has meant, not so much the liberation of working people from the demands of the wage labor, but the colonization of extramechanical skills by the demands of the market.

These developments are keenly felt in the poetry of the period, as I hope to show; but they are felt and dismissed, or felt and shunted to the side, in the criticism, with the intellectual cost that critics have had nothing other than a cursory account of the history of the twentieth century. Take the case of Perloff, whose work has been indispensable for reframing our sense of the norm by which we recognize "poetry." Perloff argued throughout the 1980s and 1990s that the dominance of the Romantic lyric as a reference point in poetic criticism made much of the most interesting poetic work of the century illegible. She made it possible to see that collage forms—the mixture of verse and prose, or of visual and textual elements, or even the play of chance operations—all were part of a legitimate poetic tradition, one where ideas took precedence over "imagination." She is emphatic that this is a poetry specific to the era: "In the poetry of the late twentieth century, the cry of the heart, as Yeats called it, is increasingly subjected to the play of the mind" (*The Dance of the Intellect*, 197). But she has no account of the history of the century such that it should have produced an idea-driven poetry. Everywhere there are hints of what that history might be; at one point in her pathbreaking 1981 book *The Poetics of Indeterminacy*, she cites the critic James McFarlane's account of modernism as a tension between Symbolist "superintegration" of language, and a breakdown of coherence best rendered by Yeats's "things fall apart"—but what mysterious force might have brought this volatile combination of integration and disintegration into being in the twentieth century is not answered. Elsewhere, pressed by the specifics of a 1979 John Ashbery poem, "Litany," which reflects on the aimless frenzies of an "increasingly mobile populace," Perloff writes, "In this sense, Ashbery's 'hymn to possibility' is indeed a litany for the computer age. If it renounces the phrasal repetition indigenous to the form [of the traditional litany], it is because things no longer happen in precisely the same way twice" (287).

But when did they? These remarks amount to little more than a suggestion that ours has been an especially Heraclitean age. At the end of *The Poetics of Indeterminacy*, Perloff suggests that it's not just the age, but something about America, that generates collaged, indeterminate, nonlyric forms:

> When, in other words, the poetry of indeterminacy, of anti-symbolism, has reached its outer limit, it comes back once more to such basic "literary" elements as the hypnotic sound pattern, the chant, the narrative account, the conceptual scheme. In the poetry of the future, we are likely to find more emphasis on these elements. The so-called "belatedness" of our poetry—belated with respect to the Romantic tradition only—may turn out to be its very virtue. "America," said John Cage, "has an intellectual climate suitable for radical experimentation. We are, as Gertrude Stein said, the oldest country of the twentieth century. And I like to add: in our air way of knowing newness." (339)

So the sheer present-tense nature of America, its determining position in history, seems to be exemplary of some unnamed process that is both radically disintegrative—it pushes indeterminacy to its "outer limit"—and reintegrative, or possibly "superintegrative," returning again and again to plunder raw materials. What might this mysterious process, so closely identified with America, actually be? The oldest exceptionalist argument—that we have no medieval past, we are the oldest young country—serves as an explanation that isn't one.

By the early 1990s, the high poetic profile of the Language school had created an even more pressing need for accounts of its historical emergence. But even a wonderful book like Joseph M. Conte's 1991 *Unending Design* fell back on quasi-mythic accounts of language and the material world to account for the rise of Language poetics. Conte's book is immensely clarifying for its account of the importance of open-ended, serial forms to the poetry of the late twentieth century, and he hints at an analogous relationship between this open-endedness and the work of mass production, as when he offers the example of the automobile as an instance of seriality (22, 41). He even notes that Robert Duncan, in a late essay that critiques New Critical models of reading poetry, puts his critique in anticapitalist terms, comparing New Criticism's sense of form to the commodity form. After coming extremely close to the possibility that there is a relationship between capitalism and the emergence of serial forms as a poetic dominant in late-century American poetry, though, Conte retreats to a physical formulation, suggesting that perhaps Language poetry's turn to seriality simply reflects "the many ways beyond the logical and the sequential in which things come together" (280). Elsewhere, Conte offers an alternative rendition, in which

> the traditional lyric speaker who is firmly established and thought to preside over the business of the poems is evicted by a variety of recycled rhetoric, multiple voices to which no priority has been assigned. Without the endorsement of a dominant persona, the language of the poem can be said to speak for itself. (44)

But what does "language," left to speak "for itself," actually say? Might the word "evicted" in this passage carry a trace of the material history by which what scholars think of as modernism became what, less and less often these days, they call "postmodern"? And why is "language itself" speaking now, as opposed to some other time, when it didn't? Questions like these have been begged in American poetry criticism for more than thirty years,

Among the influential poetry scholars in this period, Charles Altieri comes closest to acknowledging the circumstances by which critics became mute in the face of historical crisis, though he does so, not in discussing critics, but in discussing poetry. In this passage from his powerful 1984 book, *Self and Sensibility in Contemporary American Poetry*, Altieri reflects on the revolutionary sixties from the vantage point of the Reagan era. In that decade, he writes,

> poets felt that intense poetic experience might serve as witness and proof of the power of mind to recover numinous values trampled underfoot by the assumptions of liberal industrial society. Now that the desire to transform society, or even to transform longstanding aspects of American personality, has come to seem to many at best escapist and at worst another of the illusions Americans create to avoid the contradictions in their lives, poets have sought quieter, more distinctly personal and relativistic ways of adjusting to what seem inescapable conditions . . . Ours is an age that must come to terms with failed expectations and, worse, the guilt of recognizing why we held such ambitious dreams. (36–37)

This passage is exemplary of the refusal to think about the role of capital in political and literary history, for two reasons. One is that, in trying to dismiss left-wing political aspirations as psychological flaws, and approvingly citing a turn to "quieter, more distinctly personal and relativistic ways of adjusting to what seem inescapable conditions," Altieri ends up creating the contradiction he thinks this inward turn avoids—a contradiction between the quietude of the inward personal life, rendered as a retreat, and the force required to keep the world away from it. This contradiction as a psychic expression as well, which is the "guilt" that Altieri, with heart-breaking candor, says attaches to having dreamed of a better world. That guilt, like the wall around a gated community, blocks further political thinking by punishing the political thinker for having dared to imagine or to work for revolutionary change.

In mentioning this guilt, Altieri touches on a powerful structure of feeling in American political life, one that has always posed problems for the left, which congeals in the idea that it is a betrayal to think against the system—a betrayal against one's friends, one's community, one's art. Distantly behind this idea lies the real material threat against workers who choose to strike—the possibility that striking would threaten their family's security, or bring down violence on them. Transposed into an academic setting, the idea seems to be that, in developing a critical analysis of capitalism, the critic forsakes daily life, the small beauties; he becomes arrogant, unable to see what's right in front of his nose; or she become preachy, solipsistic, hypnotized by abstractions. If one is a critic of poetry, the too-critical critic loses the ability to perform subtle close readings.

And what if one is a poet? This book is not about the resistance to the idea of writing about capitalism. But a glance at some contemporary poetry that takes up that resistance can serve as a handy measure of why, for so long, it has been difficult to name exactly the extent to which many poets *have* written about it. Here is a 2005 poem by the poet Katy Lederer, who gained extrapoetic notice during the financial crisis of 2008–2009 as the "Hedge Fund Poet," because she worked at D. E. Shaw, a private equity firm in New York:

A NIETZSCHEAN REVIVAL

I thought I was almost lost.
Or overwrought.
Or rotten.
As I stroked with quivering fingers this harp,
the tongue-perturbed minions running amok,
their scaffolded ears waiting isolately for the world that would deign to leave heaven.
In the morning, when I manufacture lyrics on these listless keys,
when the money and its happy apparatus do call and lure, do call and lure.
These poets speak of capital as if they have some faint idea.
Capital: a sexy word they read in Marx their freshman year.
I ask you: what do these poets know of capital?
Across its strings, their fingers play a Nietzschean revival.
I envy them their will to power. (42)

Capitalism, in this poem, is work for experts; poets, whether or not they or their families have lost their mortgages, or their retirement, cannot "know of" it, because they don't work at investment banks. And for a poet to write about capitalism is hubris, or worse, a "will to power" that drowns out the vulnerable harpist, the real poet—notice that her poems are "lyric" poems—who also, by chance, happens to work right at the heart of things, where capital actually resides. All the ugliness is on the side of the critical poets; the movements of money are just a "happy apparatus." The poem could not be more efficient in performing the punishing, all-too-familiar reversal by which critics of capital, not its agents, are imagined as the bringers of violence into the world.

Much subtler is this recent poem by Jennifer Moxley, who more than any poet of her generation has blended a critical position on capitalism with a distaste for taking critical positions (I cite the first and final stanzas):

OUR DEFIANT MOTIVES

And what if we succeed? Then what. What if we,
who are fond of thinking that our lives have been

hindered vigorously by scheming statesmen
and entrepreneurs—scummy down to the one—
find ourselves out on a stretch of open sea
with none but a smooth trajectory
that looks to be of our own making?
. . .
Are we ashamed of our own well-being?
Does it admit of a terrible pact somewhere in our past?
Let's not turn to face the wake, in which some may be
drowning. Rather, let's redraw its rippling "V" to suit
our need to feel that we are the ones who really suffered.
We suffered the most. More than anyone else, for we
understood their suffering, didn't we, and we
were the ones who took it upon ourselves to make it new. (*Clampdown*, 50–51)

As the poem moves from satirical self-chiding to a deeper self-damning, there emerges an analysis of the flaws of leftist critique in which poets are mocked for accusing "structures" or influential classes of injustice, without their realizing that they do so at the expense of those who "really suffered," whose experience becomes mere material for the modernist transmutations ("make it new") of suffering into negative art. The lancing double meaning of that "make it new"—as in, make suffering into modernism, but also, make others suffer afresh—expresses succinctly enough Moxley's reluctance to participate in what she clearly sees as a ritualized, empty leftism—or, worse, a preening, damaging leftism. Once again, critique is seen as guilty, as an injuring act, one that hurts others more vulnerable than the critic.

In psychological terms, it is hard to imagine a more durable twentieth-century victory for the right than the persistence of this structure of feeling, which dates at least to the 1930s, and the international left's horrified disavowal of Stalinism. This argumentativeness mutates in the Cold War, when anti-Communist liberal intellectuals, not least major figures like Albert Camus and Hannah Arendt, successfully equate communism with fascism via the portmanteau concept of totalitarianism. They also pave the way for the poststructuralist critique of "totalizing" thought that became so popular in the U.S. academy in the 1980s and 1990s, as though it were the critic who tried to name the totalizing work of capital, rather than capital, who was failing to do justice to its particulars, or to aesthetic experience.[3]

For a poet like Moxley, the response to the suffering born of the scheming of "statesmen" and "entrepreneurs" is to look away, and to damn herself and her compatriots for doing so. As we will see, this dynamic of "looking away" from suffering and cursing oneself for doing it will have a crucial role to play in the poetry of John Ashbery, the subject of my second chapter. Ashbery, like Moxley, is keenly aware of what it is, precisely, he's looking away *from*—in his case, something like the consolidation of capitalist spectacle in 1970s New York. But poetry criticism—not only of Ashbery, but of the poetry of the last third of the century—seems not to notice the agony in the turning away, or not to notice it at all, or silently to assent to it. So Perloff, in her 1996 *Wittgenstein's Ladder*, champions the philosophy of Wittgenstein as an analogy to the writing of the Language poets, because Wittgenstein's sense of language as a closed game allows for the possibility of making the everyday and the ordinary become strange. But she ignores the Language poets' own account of why the "ordinary" and the "everyday" were so important to them in the 1980s—not just because it was a countermove to the use of high-literary language, but also because they saw the language of making the ordinary into the strange as a counterlanguage to the amplified messages of the state and the mass media.

Altieri, meanwhile, in his *Painterly Abstraction in Modernist American Poetry* of 1995, adopts a defeated, Boethian attitude toward the relationship between poetry and mass spectacle, sympathetically viewing "postmodern" poetry as consigned to the consolations of a Kantian philosophy in which one tests one's capacities to judge within the carefully delimited, ever-narrowing space of what "politics" has not yet tainted. As he puts it:

> In my view, these Postmodernist experiments introduce a substantially new spiritual dispensation, finally making it possible to imagine an art that does not set itself against apparently irresistible forces of social and historical change . . . The more we see what the task of accommodation involves, the more we shall need to challenge the contemporary imagination, by reminding it of those moments when the mind sees itself capable of living in, and for, communities not bound to that history and the compromises it entails. We must continue to seek ideals of identity that insist on making their own forms for the noise threatening to subsume all of our fictions into the world that is all too much with us. (379)

Reading Altieri's melancholic tribute to restricted action, and Perloff's amiable celebration of the bounded linguistic space of the everyday, it is easy to see why Adorno, in his lectures on Kant's *Critique of Pure Reason*, remarked about Kantian critique that "what has been codified in *The Critique of Pure Reason* is a theodicy of bourgeois life which is conscious of its own practical activity while despairing of the fulfillment of its own utopia" (6). In Altieri's case in particular, this theodicy operates as a transposition by which political defeats for the left (the defeat of "the desire to transform society") mutate into a defeat *by politics*, by the encroachment of "the political" per se into the domain of the aesthetic.

Work like Altieri's and Perloff's thus gave us a powerfully depoliticizing language for poetry in the 1980s and 1990s. Ironically, the critical language of that period that most often kept some version of politics in view for American readers of poetry—that is, the language of French poststructuralism—comes around to making its own versions of these depoliticizing moves. This work has been more commanding in comparative literature departments than in English departments, partly because it is built around a European canon of poetry. But it has had wide influence on American work, both for the way its structuralist heritage makes it possible to think of poetry in terms of a seemingly cross-disciplinary notion of textuality, as opposed to a merely literary vocabulary of genre or mode, and for how it invites critics to imagine the relationship between poetry and politics.

This invitation involves, on the French side, subtle analogies between philosophical arguments and political history; and, on the American side, a transposition of those analogies into a different academic and political scene. So it is hard to describe their influence without pausing for a bit over the details of how such theoretical arguments actually tended to look on the ground. One might take any of a variety of examples, but I think the work of Jacques Derrida is especially important here. Over the course of his long career, Derrida revised his thinking about literature, philosophy, and politics countless times, but his early work is very clear in establishing a set of founding relays among those domains. So I'd like to slow down for a moment and take a look at his influential 1966 essay "From Restricted to General Economy: A Hegelianism without Reserve." The essay leans on Alexandre Kojève's Marxian interpretation of Hegel in order to produce an allegory of Hegelian negativity as labor, then, enabled by this analogy or allegory, turns to Bataille and a Kierkegaardian absurdism to argue that the negative must be understood in terms other than those to which philosophy submits it; the negative, for Derrida, is constantly being brought into philosophical service—exploited, he suggests—as the other of meaning, providing the prompt to philosophical concept honing. But it cannot be assimilated to such uses.

Derrida's essay makes two key moves that, taken together, proved extremely persuasive on American shores. One is to transpose the question of the exploration of labor into a philosophical register, by reading it as the capture and exploitation of negativity by philosophy, where it is forced into the work of systematic thinking. The other is to suggest that the true character of the negative is expressed in chance, and in play, and that this true character of the negative is best understood in literary terms—or, more specifically, modernist poetic terms, best exemplified by Mallarmé's *Un coup de dés jamais n'abolira le hasard*. Derrida gestures at Mallarmé's poem this way:

> The poetic or ecstatic is that *in every discourse* which can open itself up to the absolute loss of its sense, to the (non-)base of the sacred, of nonmeaning, of un-knowledge or play, to the swoon from which it is reawakened by a throw of the dice. (261)

This move is significant because, having established the question of labor as a philosophical question of negativity, and having posited the modernist poetics of Mallarmé as a privileged site for the expression of the negativity that philosophy seeks to capture, Derrida aligns the poetic specificity of the modernist lyric with the uncapturable life force of the rebellious worker. He contrasts the "master" of Hegel's master-slave dialectic with a Bataillean "sovereign" who laughs at philosophy's mere "amortization" of the negative, who laughs at death: "laughter alone exceeds dialectics and the dialectician" (256). Noting that "philosophy is work *itself* for Bataille," he adds that Hegelian *Aufhebung* is "laughable" because it is merely a "*busying* of discourse" that starts panting as it "reappropriates all negativity for itself" (252, 257). Philosophy, as the essay unfolds, is "work itself" in the sense that it is a set of operations that *compel* work, that force the negative to produce meaning and knowledge, and that bustles about breathlessly as it mistakenly thinks it is achieving "knowledge" in the process. "Philosophy"—that is, Hegelian philosophy, *Aufhebung*, the dialectic—"philosophy," in this allegory, is a bourgeois.

Now the bourgeoisie, as a mercantile or a professional class, are not entirely, or not necessarily, the same as the industrial capitalist class that actually *would* compel labor; so we should note a slight shift or transposition in the Marxian critique here. Similarly, note that it is not capital, but the dialectic, that is the enemy—so that the militant worker, when the moment of rebellion finally becomes possible, rebels not against capital but against philosophy. Indeed, at the moment when Derrida's allegory depicts rebellion, "the negative"—figured, Derrida says, in the Hegelian slave, who Derrida says Kojève suggests is the worker (276)—at the moment of rebellion, the worker looks more existential than the militant. Indeed, he looks more like a Resistance fighter in World War II than a proletarian. Here Derrida has been discussing the merely philosophical revolutions of Kant and Hegel, who can be credited with discovering the philosophical import of the negative, but who made the mistake of "[taking it] seriously." By contrast, he suggests, for Bataille, the negative (here, again, personified) is more truly radical, to the point of its utter transformation:

> It can no longer be called negative precisely because it has no reserved underside, because it can no longer permit itself to be converted into positivity, it can no longer *collaborate* with the continuous linking-up of meaning, concept, time, and truth in discourse; because it literally can no longer *labor* and let itself be interrogated as "the work of the negative." (259–260)

Note the italicized work "collaborate" in this passage, which to my ear is a giveaway signal that the allegory of the negative-as-worker has now received an overlay of wartime militancy.

The italicization of the word "labor" signals the blending of the two background personifications, wound even tighter together by the word "interrogated," which links the refusal of the worker and the developing militance of the resistance fighter in a pun on the interrogative.

What all these deft allegorical, anthropomorphic, and transposing gestures accomplish, for Derrida, is the insight that German dialectical philosophy is no match for French literary modernism:

> In interpreting negativity as labor, in betting for discourse, meaning, history, etc., Hegel has bet against play, against chance. He has blinded himself . . . to the fact that play *includes* the work of meaning or the meaning of work. (260)

In 1966 this overlay of the figure of the militant Resistance fighter on top of the figure of the worker, who is cannier than the philosopher-bourgeois about the work-canceling play that modern poetry highlights, is a kind of backward glance. But it is also an echo of a contemporary development in French politics. Here is a key passage from the 1966 Situationist pamphlet *On the Poverty of Student Life*:

> For the proletariat revolt is a festival or it is nothing: in revolution the road of excess leads to the palace of wisdom. A palace which knows only one rationality: the game. The rules are simple: to live instead of devising a lingering death, and to indulge untrammeled desire. (S. Ford 116)

The distribution of this pamphlet by the students of the University of Strasbourg helped trigger, two years later, the student alliance with workers in the uprisings of May 1968; and it remains an exemplary text for non–Communist Party, Marxist anticapitalism in France. I cannot trace the lines of commonality or influence between Derrida and the Situationists with much precision here; it is hard to say whether Derrida is leaning on rebellious student energies, or the students are picking up on something that Derrida is also aware of, a critique of Communist Party politics that is registered as a romantic (here, Blakean) critique of Hegel (the "lingering death" of the dialectic as work, as opposed to "untrammeled desire," which Derrida renders, in the title of his essay, as "Hegelianism without reserve").

Is Derrida, in 1966, politicizing philosophy or academicizing Situationist politics? Impossible to say; more easy to recognize is that the leveraging of modernist poetry into an antidialectical argument with Hegel (and implicitly, doctrinaire, party-line Marxism) becomes *the* gesture into which the idea of "poetry" is incorporated in the French theory that traveled to American shores in the 1970s and 1980s. This antidialecticism is emphatically present in Julia Kristeva's 1974 *Revolution in Poetic Language*, which pits the disruptive literary practice of Mallarmé and Lautréamont against a psychoanalytic subject falsely unified by the state and society. And it organizes Jean-Luc Nancy's 1982 *The Inoperative Community*, which cites Bataille's remark from *Literature and Evil* that "literature cannot assume the task of directing collective necessity," in order to position a Levinasian-Heideggerian understanding of poetry as an "interruption" against both those literary texts that seek after mere produced beauty and that Marxism that imagines "productivity" as the only engine of history.[4] This is not to mention the work of Gilles Deleuze and Félix Guattari, or, more recently, Alain Badiou, who have all kept alive, from very different philosophical positions, the practice of pitting one literary modernism or another against a cartoon of Hegel made to stand in for something like either the rigidness or the insufficient militancy of the French Communist Party.

In 1986 it was already possible for a canny observer like Andreas Huyssen to observe of the "postmodern" theory being consumed in the United States that "rather than offering a theory of postmodernity and developing an analysis of contemporary culture, French theory provides us primarily with an *archeology of modernity*, a theory of modernism at the stage of its exhaustion" (*After the Great Divide*, 209). To this it seems useful to add that, along with an "archeology of modernity," French theory offered American literary critics a philosophical allegory of postwar French politics, centered by and large on a tiny canon of writers—Mallarmé, Baudelaire, Rimbaud, Hölderlin and Celan—whose modernist extremity (or, in the case of Hölderlin, his modernism *avant la lettre*) converts that political allegory into an allegory of the war between literature and philosophy.[5] I would suggest that in the absence of a powerful American Communist Party, or an American Situationism, or a sustained American argument with Hegel, this allegorical war of the disciplines (poetry versus philosophy) comes to explain the meaning or significance of "poetry" in those flanks of the American literary academy that tilt in a continental direction. Though it has a very different provenance than the American criticism that sequesters poetry against the noise of the spectacle, then, American consumption of the political allegories of French theory amounts to a similar sequestration, where "literature" and "poetry" signify a realm of existentialist, or absurdist, or monist freedom that the dialectic cannot capture.

Something different, but related, happens in the postwar history of German-language stylistic analysis of poetry, which, primarily through the work of Theodor Adorno, has had broad influence on American thinking about the relationship of poetry to capitalism. The German tradition of poetry criticism, devolving from the work of Curtius, is more philological than philosophical, and less interested in foregrounding the canon of literary modernism than in establishing stylistic analyses that extend to pre-modern periods. But it is strongly interested in the question of the individual's relation to the masses, as when Erich Auerbach highlights the emergence of the Christian sermon in late antiquity as a kind of "mass movement" that does not erase but prizes each individual, or when Adorno frames the modernity of the lyric under capitalism as the struggle of the isolated poet, by withdrawing himself from society, to preserve something socially free that exists only in potential.[6] I would like to take a moment to highlight some of the things American critics have learned from this tradition, but also to show how it comes around, in Adorno, to a stance that is closer to the stance of French poststructuralism than at first appears.

One of the major achievements of the German tradition of poetry criticism is to demonstrate that the postclassical history of literary writing, even when we factor in wide variability around what "the literary" had meant since the classical era, is bound up with the imagination of historical change and civilizational crisis. Hans-Robert Jauss has written comprehensively on how the idea of "the modern," for instance, links historical writing, humanist scholarship, poetry, and aesthetics in a conversation about the meanings of the present in relation to different understandings of history; reading his work, it becomes possible to see the method by which Ezra Pound, T. S. Eliot, and Charles Olson draw parallels and contrasts between ancient and modern figures as a reworking and continuation of an older historiographical and literary-critical genre, the "parallel," which itself has ancient origins, and becomes a central genre for debates about modernity in the late seventeenth-century French *Querelle des anciens et des modernes* ("Modernity and Literary Tradition," 347). One of the fascinating things about Jauss's survey of the literary idea of "the modern" is that, in the history he traces for the term, it mutates from a static term of opposition to ancientness (as in the *Querelle*) to what, by the middle of the nineteenth century, he sees as a term that perpetually "repels itself" in what is experienced by Stendhal and then Baudelaire as the onward rush of historical events. This latter experience, of course, is one way to describe the experience of time in commodity capitalism, as a perpetual rush to the new; what Jauss's survey illuminates is the way in which the aesthetics of modernity we have come to associate with Baudelaire (and, since Baudelaire, Walter Benjamin) have a long genealogy that extends at least as far back as early Christian distinctions around the "modernity" of the Christian era.

The enduring persistence of problems of historical consciousness for literature is not only a question of how literary writing has developed understandings of periods and of the meanings of periodization; it has also attached itself to questions of literary style. The best-known example of this historiographical-stylistic link is Auerbach's argument that, after Augustine, the ancient correlation of kinds of subject matter with degrees of stylistic elevation was disrupted both by the need to preach of high matters to masses of less-educated people, and by a doctrinal sense that Christ's resurrection brought the high low and made the low high. For Auerbach, a Ciceronian low style, or *sermo humilis*, is reworked by Augustine and others into a something like a "humble style" where high and low stylistic registers can mix because the theme of humility is, in Christian preaching and apologetics, also always the theme of sublimity (*Literary Language*). Helplessly, though, this style mixing also obtains a historical-thematic element as well—*sermo humilis* in the Christian tradition also comes to signify being post-Roman, an after-the-fall humility that is historical as well as theological. Down to the twentieth century, then, one of the available functions of style mixing is to index catastrophic historical chance on the model of the fall of Rome: Adorno's bravura mixture of essayistic and philosophical writing in the post-Holocaust volume *Minima Moralia* is a good example, because its title not only inverts the praise orientation of Plutarch's *Moralia*, but also points to Gregory the Great's *Moralia in Job*, a signal instance for Auerbach of *sermo humilis*.

Indeed, Adorno's writing on poetry foregrounds its relation to historical catastrophe at every turn, though his American readers have often taken his writing to demonstrate generic truths about lyric intensity or compression as defining specificities of poetry. Unfortunately, Adorno himself facilitates this drift in the direction of generic reading, both when he remarks in *Negative Dialectics* that he may have been wrong to say that it is barbaric to write poetry after Auschwitz, given that "perennial suffering has just as much right to find expression as a victim of torture has to scream" (355), and when, in "Lyric Poetry and Society," he refers to the lyric poem as a "philosophical sundial of history" (221). These remarks have often been taken to mean that there is something generically special about the lyric's intensity or its linguistic compression, but in formulating them—especially the second remark—Adorno leans on and reworks the tradition of stylistics in which literature is understood as gradually developing an idiomatic historiographical function, not only an ahistorical "intensity." In "Lyric Poetry and Society," for instance, Adorno turns to the poetry of Stefan George, whose compressed style he reads as an allegory of the generation of an older class imaginary out of the emergence of a new one:

> While George's poetry—that of the splendidly individual—presupposes as a condition of its very possibility an individualistic, bourgeois society, and the individual who exists for himself alone, it nevertheless bans the commonly accepted forms, no less than the themes, of bourgeois poetry. Because this poetry, however, can speak from no other standpoint or configuration than precisely those bourgeois frames of mind which it rejects . . . because of this it is blocked, dammed at the source: and so it feigns a feudal condition. (224–225)

George's success, like the success Auerbach imagines for Christian *sermo humilis*, emerges from rejecting a high rhetoric:

> Elevated style is attained not by pretending to rhetorical figures and rhythms, but by ascetically omitting whatever would lessen the distance from the tainted language of com-

> merce. In order that the subject may truly resist the lonely process of reification he may not even attempt anymore to retreat into himself—to his private property. He is frightened by the traces of an individualism which has meanwhile sold itself to the literary supplements of the marketplace. The poet must, rather, by denying himself, step out of himself. (226)

This dazzling passage, which has been so influential in developing an understanding of the political value of the lyric poem, nonetheless limits our understanding of the relationship between poetry and capitalism to the negative: the lyric's compression and intensity are a sacrificial austerity, or a scream, and the rejections such stances or cries signify become a definition of the lyric—not least the lyric as "philosophical sundial of history." But the work of Jauss and others suggests that if the poem is a sundial of history, this is because the history of the literary is in part the history of the generation of historiographical metaphors (standing on the shoulders of giants; postcatastrophic lowness) like the metaphor of the sundial in the first place. And when Adorno situates a poet like George in the heritage of *poésie pure*—"this follower of Mallarmé," Adorno calls him—his work ends up reinforcing the figures of renunciation and sequestration that postwar French and American thinking about poetry have also privileged as the way to think about poetry and capitalism.

So where the key critics of American poetry of the last twenty years have chosen not to write about the relation of that poetry to capitalism, the French and German critical traditions most widely referred to in the United States have encouraged ways of thinking about that relation that tend to imply that poetic writing is prima facie political, or that the only significant relation between a poem and capitalism is rigorous eschewal.

But the record of the actual poetry of the twentieth century does not bear out this claim.

NOTES

1. The classic review of Arthurian "matter" is Roger Sherman Loomis, *The Development of Arthurian Romance* (Norton, 1970). For recent scholarship on "the matter of France," see Gabriele and Stuckey. I am grateful to Seeta Chaganti for this recommendation.

2. See Curtius, *European Literature and the Latin Middle Ages*. Curtius's history of the different topoi by which poets depicted the character of poetry, and their social role as poets, has been an indispensable model for my exploration of how poetry imagines itself in relation to capital.

3. See, crucially, Nelson's *Revolutionary Memory: Recovering the Poetry of the American Left* (Routledge, 2001), which not only helped restore to visibility the poetry of individual writers like Tillie Olsen and Edwin Rolfe, but also made clear that in the 1930s there was for American poets on the left something like a "Matter of Spain"—that is, a body of work devoted to hashing out the meanings of support for the antifascist cause during the Spanish Civil War.

4. The contours of the American discourse of the critique of "totalization" would make for an entire book; arguably, Martin Jay's splendid *Marxism and Totality* would be its prequel. In any case the best current example of this argument is probably to be found in the work of the philosopher Jacques Rancière, who, for instance, described his work this way in a 2007 interview:

> What interests me more than politics or art is the way the boundaries defining certain practices as artistic or political are draw and redrawn. This frees artistic and political creativity from the yoke of the great historical schemata that announce the great revolutions to come or that mourn the great revolutions past only to impose their proscriptions and their declarations of powerlessness on the present. (Rancière, *ArtForum*, March 2007)

Again, notice that it is Marxist theory, not capitalism, that oppresses.

5. Kristeva makes fascinating use of Freud's account of the "binding" of excitation in the work of managing the death drive in her account of the negativity of the best modern poetry, which, like Derrida's Bataille, smashes through negativity's mere "amortization":

> This would seem to be "art"'s function as a signifying practice: under the pleasing exterior of a very socially acceptable differentiation, art reintroduces into society fundamental rejection,

which is matter in the process of splitting. (*Revolution in Poetic Language* [Columbia, 1984], 180)

Nancy, whose citation from Bataille analogizes the wrong role for literature to the work of Party officials ("the task of directing collective necessity"), rereads Marx as a theorist, not of the sham "communism" that is merely state-directed capitalism, but of multiform, inorganic "articulation" or assemblage—a practice that looks a lot like modernist collage:

It is not an exaggeration to say that Marx's community is, in this sense, a community of literature—or at least it opens on to such a community. It is a community of articulation, not organization, and precisely because of that it is a community situated "beyond the sphere of material production properly speaking," where "begins the flowering of that human power that is its own end, the true reign of liberty. (*The Inoperative Community* [U of Minnesota, 1991], 77)

6. I am grateful to Joshua Clover for first pointing out to me the disproportionate amount of critical energy spent on this small canon of poets. See Clover, "A Form Adequate to History: Toward a Renewed Marxist Poetics," *Paideuma* 37, 2010.

Lyric and the Hazard of Music (2008) 8.4

CRAIG DWORKIN

Lyric cannot be expunged by modernism, only repressed.

T. J. Clark

The relation of sound to poetry has always been triangulated, implicitly or explicitly, by an equally nebulous third term: sense. The relation is ambiguous, and shifting, because "sound"—especially in the context of poetry—is that species of homograph which produces its own antonym.[1] On the one hand, sound—defined as "the audible articulation of a letter or word"—has been understood as something distinct from linguistic meaning: "the sound must seem an echo to the sense," as Pope famously put it.[2] Furthermore, that distinction is often pushed to a full-fledged antonymy, so that sound is understood as being—by definition—diametrically opposed to meaning: a "mere audible effect without significance or real importance."[3] John Locke underscores that opposition in a passage from his *Essay Concerning Human Understanding*: "for let us consider this proposition as to its meaning (for it is the sense, and not the sound, that is and must be the principle or common notion)."[4] Or, more famously, in Shakespeare's phrasing: "a tale told by an idiot, full of sound and fury, signifying nothing."[5] At the same time, however, sound can also denote precisely the signifying referent of language: "import, sense, significance."[6] Indeed, rather than posing an alternative to meaning, sound in poetry has been heard as conveying meaning in its own right. "In human speech," Leonard Bloomfeld asserts, "different sounds have different meanings."[7] Jan Mukarovsky concurs: " 'Sound' components are not only a mere sensorily perceptible vehicle of meaning but also have a semantic nature themselves."[8]

At once the antithesis of meaning and the very essence of meaning, sound in poetry articulates the same problems that have attended early twentieth-century definitions of the category of "poetry" itself, reflecting the identical logic at a fractal remove. From the Prague School to Ludwig Wittgenstein to Tel Quel, modern philosophers of language have described poetry—which is to say, literary language broadly conceived or simply "verbal art," in Roman Jakobson's eventual phrasing—as a kind of text that deviates from conventionally utile language by self-reflexively foregrounding elements other than the referentially communicative. Poetry, in these accounts, calls attention to structures such as sound while damping the banausic, denotative impetus of language.[9]

The ratios thus form a curious recursion: sound is to sense as poetic language is to conventional language, but the relation of sound and sense, understood in this way, are nested within the category of the poetic. Taken as the opposite of sense, sound, in the formalist economy, encapsulates the logic of the poetic. One among the material, palpable, quantifiable facets of language, sound contrasts with the ideas conveyed by the referential sign. Behind the Slavic formalists, we might of course also think of Ferdinand de Saussure's attempt to define signs not as the relation of names and things, but rather as the coupling of the "concept" indicated by the signified and "l'image acoustique [the sound shape]" of the signifier. And further behind Saussure, as the quotes from Pope and Shakespeare attest, lies the intuitive sense that one can perceive aspects of language without comprehending its message. More complicated still, however, the *mise-en-abîme* of sound and poetry can also reflect (back on) the communicative side of the equation. The relationship between material sound and referential meaning is often understood to itself be referential. The two key words in Pope's declaration, for instance, both bind sound to mimetic appearance: "sound must *seem* an *echo* to the sense." Sound, in this understanding, thus also encapsulates the operation of meaning. The same is true when sound is taken to be expressive in its own right and thought to "have a semantic nature" in itself.

Simultaneously bridging and sequestering, sound has accordingly been understood as both the defining opposite of meaning and the very essence of meaning. This duplicity is due in part to the inadequacy of the vague term "meaning," but it also comes into play because of the belief—implicit in Pope's formulation—that the value of a poem lies in the relation between sound and sense. A mediocre term paper on "The Poetry of Sound," available for purchase on the internet, states the basic position clearly (if rather ineptly):

> Poems usually begin with words or phrase which appeal more because of their sound than their meaning, and the movement and phrasing of a poem. Every poem has a texture of sound, which is at least as important as the meaning behind the poem.[10]

Even when cast as the antithesis of meaning, the sound of poetry is still thought to be—in all senses of the word—significant. Sound is central, it seems, but the question still remains: exactly *how* does sound come to be important in poetry? This is neither the place for a history of the poetics of sound, nor for a careful parsing of the theoretical variations on the topic, but I do want to note the extent to which literary theorists have been both certain about the central importance of sound to poetry and unable to exactly specify the nature of that importance. Roman Jakobson is typical:

> No doubt verse is primarily a recurrent "figure of sound." Primarily, always, but never uniquely. Any attempts to confine such poetic conventions as meters, alliteration, or rhyme to the sound level are speculative reasonings without any empirical justification.[11]

He goes on to quote Alexander von Humboldt: "there is an apparent connection between sound and meaning which, however, only seldom lends itself to an exact elucidation, is often only glimpsed, and most usually remains obscure." That obscurity results from sound's lack of any absolute, *a priori* value, and the glimpse of connection, as Benjamin

Harshav argues in his work on the expressivity of sound patterns, arises when sound and meaning enter into a dynamic dance of cathectic reflection. For Harshav, the relation between poetic sound and sense is a back-and-forth process of recursive feedback. No sound pattern, in his view, is inherently meaningful in and of itself; sibilants, for instance (to take his central example), have been understood as representing both silence and noise. However, once a reader identifies the presence of a sound pattern certain referential statements from the poem—what one might think of as the conventional meaning of its "message"—are transferred onto that pattern, which in turn loops back to reinforce and foreground particular themes in the message.[12]

When any less obscure, the connections between sound and meaning risk sounding ridiculous. Alan Galt's *Sound and Sense in the Poetry of Theodor Storm*, for one instance of the more empiricist model of linguistic analysis, attempts to scientifically demonstrate that the musical qualities of poetry "may be defined in terms of phonological 'skew,' i.e. deviation from the normal proportional distribution of sounds in poetic language."[13] Galt (using a slide rule, no less) tabulated all of the phonemes in Storm's collected poetry, some 78,965 consonants and 43,641 vowels, according to his count.[14] The outcome is almost pataphysical, combining a sober scientific tone with absurd results and evoking nothing so much as the enthused phonemic dictionaries of Velimir Klebnikov.[15] Galt determines that the phoneme /l/, for instance, evinces:

> Positive skews in love poems and in narratives; strong positive skews in "tender" and "musical" poems. Negative skews in poems of family and home, nostalgia, and humor, with a negative skew for "non-musical" poems which is just below the level of significance. This phoneme certainly distinguishes, in Storm's verse, between "musicality" and its opposite, and its presence can evidently also contribute to a feeling of "tenderness."[16]

The phoneme /ʊ/, similarly, reveals "positive skews in nature poems, political poems, and in 'musical' poems. Negative skews in poems of age and death, and in humorous and occasional poems. Evidently this is a determiner of 'musicality.'"[17] And so on. Meaning, in Galt's account is inseparable from sound, even as the significance of sound is imperceptible, recognizable only at the level of massive statistical analysis. Form, here, is indeed an extension of content: "a group of poems which share the same theme or content tends to show a phonological 'skew' which is broadly characteristic of that group."[18]

While Galt's work may have greater affinities with avant-garde poetry than with conventional literary criticism, I call attention to it because his focus on "musicality." As James McNeill Whistler famously opined, "music is the poetry of sound," and poetry, in turn, has often been characterized as musical: "lower limit speech," as Louis Zukofsky ran his calculus, "upper limit music."[19] Or as John Cage put it: "poetry is not prose because poetry is in one way or another formalized. It is not poetry by reason of its content or ambiguity but by reason of its allowing musical elements (time, sound) to be introduced into the world of words."[20] Poetry, for Cage, was a non-expressive, non-communicative extrusion of form into recursive content: "I have nothing to say / and I am saying it / and that is / poetry," as his "Lecture on Nothing" performs the point.[21] Cage's compositional formalism stands in opposition to more affective formulations of poetry's musicality, but the move to ground poetry in music, regardless of the poetics at stake, is telling. Consider Sarah Stickney Ellis's early nineteenth-century account:

> Sound is perhaps of all subjects the most intimately connected with poetic feeling, not only because it comprehends within its widely extended sphere, the influence of music, so

> powerful over the passions and affections of our nature; but because there is in poetry itself, a cadence—a perceptible harmony, which delights the ear while the eye remains unaffected.[22]

Ellis's argument echoes in John Hollander's entry on "Music and Poetry" in the *Princeton Encyclopedia of Poetry and Poetics*, which states that both poetry and music "move to affect a listener in some subrational fashion, just as both are in some way involved in the communication of feeling rather than of knowledge."[23] That involvement of music in poetry is of particular significance, moreover, because it bears on our understanding of the lyric. According to J. W. Johnson's entry in the *Princeton Encyclopedia of Poetry and Poetics*, lyric poetry "may be said to retain most pronouncedly the elements of poetry which evidence its origins in musical expression [. . .] the musical element is intrinsic to the work intellectually as well as aesthetically."[24] Indeed, "the irreducible denominator of all lyric poetry," according to Johnson, must be "those elements which it shares with the musical forms that produced. Although lyric poetry is not music, it is representational of music in its sound patterns."[25]

The problem, of course—already stated by the distance between Cage and Ellis—is what might be meant by *music*, a term no more stable or well-defined than *lyric* itself. Music, in this context, is often taken to mean merely euphonious language: a mid-nineteenth century sense of harmony and melodic line that "delights the ear." This definition, in fact, makes music a synonym for sound itself, one of the denotations of which is "used with implications of richness, euphony, or harmony."[26] But "music" of course encompasses a range of works far more expansive than the classical and romantic imagination of the pleasant, mellifluous, or affecting. We might still define the lyric in terms of music, but what if the music represented by the lyric were Cage's own *Music for Piano*, composed by enlarging the imperfections found when a sheet of staff paper is scrutinized under a magnifying glass? Or Erik Satie's *Vexations*, a few bars of fragmentary melody meant to be repeated 840 times in succession? Or Stephane Ginsburgh's extrapolation of Marcel Duchamp's *Erratum Musical*: each of the eighty-eight notes on the piano keyboard played once, in aleatory order? Or György Ligeti's *Poème symphonique*, scored for 100 carefully wound metronomes. Or Gilius van Bergeijk's *Symfonie der Duizend (alfabetisch)*, which strings together the first notes from one thousand compositions (arranged alphabetically by their composers' names), with each note falling where the second note would have come in the previous composition's rhythmic structure? Or the game pieces of John Zorn, or the stochastic compositions of Iannis Xenakis, or David Soldier's orchestra of Thai elephants, or any number of works that Ellis would likely not have recognized as music at all.

In such an expanded field, music may no longer be especially useful for defining *poetry* with any sort of apodeictic certainty, but the diversity of its connotations makes it all the more productive for thinking in new ways about what poetry (or a multiplicity of poetries) might aspire to do. Just as rethinking the nature of sound has led, over the course of the last century, to new understandings of what qualifies as music, rethinking the nature of music, accordingly, expands the scope of what qualifies as poetry. In particular, because of its inextricable historical enmeshment with music, lyric is stressed with a special pressure by the degree to which the category of music is dilated and freighted and stretched. The terms are irreversibly linked, but their denotations are not as fixed as our habitual use of them, in forging that linkage, would like us to believe. Or, in brief, to paraphrase David Antin's aphorism on the connection between modernism and post-modernism: from the music you choose, you get the lyric you deserve.

1. Joseph Shipley terms such words, like "cleave," autantonyms [*The Origin of English Words: A Discursive Dictionary of Indo-European Roots* (Baltimore: The Johns Hopkins University Press, 1984): 128.

2. *The Oxford English Dictionary*, Second Edition, ed. John Simpson and Edmund Weiner (Oxford: Oxford University Press, 1989). Alexander Pope: "An Essay on Criticism," *The Major Works*, ed. Pat Rogers (Oxford: Oxford U.P., World Classics, 2006): 29.

3. *Oxford English Dictionary, op. cit.*

4. John Locke: *An Essay Concerning Human Understanding* (London: Tegg, 1841): §18.

5. *Macbeth* V, v.

6. *Oxford English Dictionary, op. cit.*

7. Qtd. Roman Jakobson: *Language In Literature*, ed. Krystyna Pomorska and Stephen Rudy (Cambridge: Harvard U.P., 1987): 81.

8. Jan Mukarovsky: "Sound Aspect of Poetic Language," *On Poetic Language*, ed. and trans. John Burbank and Peter Steiner (Lisse: de Ridder, 1976): 23.

9. The literature is extensive, but see, for a starting point: Bohuslav Havránek: *Studie o spisovném jazyce* (Prague: Nakladatelství Ceskoslovenské Akademie Ved, 1963) and "The Functional Differentiation of the Standard Language," *A Prague School Reader on Esthetics, Literary Structure, and Style*, ed. and trans. Paul L. Garvin (Washington, D.C.: Georgetown U.P., 1964): 11–18 *et passim*; "Functional"; Jan Mukarovsky: "Standard Language and Poetic Language," *A Prague School Reader on Esthetics, Literary Structure, and Style*, ed. and trans. Paul L. Garvin (Washington, D.C.: Georgetown U.P., 1964): 17-3; Roman Jakobson, in two key essays: "Concluding Statement: Linguistics and Poetics," *Style in Language*, ed. Thomas A. Sebeok (Cambridge: MIT Press, 1960): 350–77, and "The Dominant," trans. Herbert Eagle, *Readings in Russian Poetics: Formalist and Structuralist Views*, ed. Ladislav Mateika and Krystyna Pomorska (Normal: Dalkey Archive, 2002): 82–87; and Julia Kristeva: *Revolution in Poetic Language*, trans. Margaret Waller (New York: Columbia U.P., 1984).

10. Shana Williamson: "The Poetry of Sound," www.termpapersmonthly.com/essays/21769.html, accessed 15 December, 2007.

11. Jakobson, *Language*, *op. cit.*, 81.

12. Benjamin Harshav (publishing originally as Hrushovski): *Explorations in Poetics* (Stanford: Stanford U.P., 2007): 144 *et passim*; the work was published originally under the name Benjamin Hrushovski as "The Meaning of Sound Patterns in Poetry: An Interaction Theory," *Poetics Today* 2: 1 (Autumn, 1980): 39–56; *cf.* Reuven Tsur: *What Makes Sound Patterns Expressive?* (Durham: Duke, 1992).

13. Alan Galt: *Sound and Sense in the Poetry of Theodor Storm: A Phonological-Statistical Study.* European University Papers Series 1, Vol. 84 (Frankfurt: Peter Lang, 1973): 1; *cf.* Ivan Fónagy: "Communication in Poetry," *Word* 17 (1961): 194–218.

14. Galt, *Sound and Sense*, *op. cit.*, 4.

15. See, for instance, Velimir Klebnikov: "The Warrior of the Kingdom" and "A Checklist: The Alphabet of the Mind," both in *Imagining Language*, ed. Jed Rasula and Steve McCaffery (Cambridge: MIT Press, 1998): 362–367.

16. *Ibidem*, 91.

17. *Ibidem*, 94.

18. *Ibidem*, 1.

19. James McNeill Whistler: *The Gentle Art of Making Enemies* (London, Heinemann, 1904): 127; Louis Zukofsky: *"A"* (Baltimore: The Johns Hopkins U.P., 1993): 138.

20. John Cage: *Silence: Lectures and Writings* (Middletown: Wesleyan University Press, 1961): x.

21. *Ibidem*, 109.

22. Sarah Stickney Ellis: *The Poetry of Life* (Philadelphia: Carey, Lea and Blanchard, 1835): 168.

23. *The New Princeton Encyclopedia of Poetry And Poetics*, ed. Alex Preminger and T. V. F. Brogan (Princeton: Princeton University Press, 1993).

24. James William Johnson: "Lyric." *Princeton Encyclopedia of Poetry and Poetics*, *op. cit.*, 713–37.

25. *Cf.* Northrop Frye: "By musical I mean a quality of literature denoting a substantial analogy to, and in many cases an actual influence from, the art of music" [Northrop Frye: "Introduction: Lexis and Melos," *Sound and Poetry: English Institute Essays, 1956* (New York: Columbia U.P., 1957): x–xi].

26. *Oxford English Dictionary, op. cit.*

SECTION 9

Lyric and Sexual Difference

The introduction of feminist literary criticism, gender studies, queer theory, and sexuality studies into the academy in the later twentieth century opened up new points of departure from and for theories of the lyric. By raising questions about sexual difference, Anglo-American critics of the 1970s, 1980s, and 1990s began to interrogate the abstraction of a normative lyric subject, emphasizing the gendered construction of that subject. Yet unlike the resistance to earlier models of the lyric within avant-garde poetics, the critical elaboration of gender and sexuality tended toward a reclamation of the modern lyric in these last decades of the twentieth century. Those new lyric directions took many forms: feminist critique (interrogating male authorship and the authority of a masculine poetic tradition); gynocriticism (focusing on the conditions of female authorship and the traditions of women's writing); gender criticism (demonstrating "gender trouble" inherent in poetic performances of masculinity and femininity); gay and lesbian studies (identifying the contemporary contexts and longer histories of homosexual writing); queer theory (deconstructing masculine/feminine and heterosexual/homosexual binaries to move beyond the subject/object of desire in poems); psychoanalytic interpretation (using Freudian and Lacanian paradigms to complicate the claim to poetic subjectivity); body studies (rethinking the politics of the body as played out in poetics); and minority studies (emphasizing the intersection of gender and sex with race, class, and other categories of identity and difference among poets). We give just a few early examples of those forms here in order to show the beginning (though certainly not the end) of an ongoing conversation. What the many different varieties of lyric reading attentive to issues of sexuality and sexual difference continue to have in common is the modern idea of the lyric as a genre that (as we have seen in previous sections of this anthology) emerged and took hold earlier in the twentieth century. In this section, we see how attention to ideologies of sexual difference also tend to call into question ideologies of the lyric—though sometimes the very critics who want to destabilize categories of gender and sexuality also end up keeping the category of the lyric itself relatively stable. Lauren Berlant may be right that "the activity of being historical *finds* its genre," but the historical shift in the understanding of the lyric along the subjective fault lines of gender and sexuality has struggled to find alternative modes of lyric reading.[1]

The essay by Nancy Vickers included here is a feminist reading of Petrarch, whose sonnets to Laura are often invoked as a model for Renaissance lyric. In the Petrarchan tradition, a male subject is constituted by address to a female beloved and unified by the repetition of her dismembered image: the scattered parts of Laura are re-collected by, in, and as the "scattered rhymes" of Petrarch's own poetic corpus. But in a further development of this gendered analysis, Vickers goes on to emphasize the double dismemberment of the desiring subject as well as the object of desire. Demonstrating how the poet is identified with the figure of Actaeon—through a pattern of identification and reversal in the Greek myth, in which "Actaeon sees Diana, Diana sees Actaeon, and seeing is traumatic for both"—Vickers traces the patterns of self-dispersal in Petrarch: "'I' knows that the outcome of seeing her body is the scattering of his; hence he projects scattering onto her." According to Vickers, the alternation between scattering and gathering in Petrarch's *rime sparse* "reveals a textual strategy subtending his entire volume: it goes to the heart of his lyric program and understandably becomes the lyric stance of generations of imitators." Petrarch's legacy of fragmentation comes to define lyric in a tradition of writing that is structured by sexual difference. What is understood (or, according to Vickers, is "understandably" assumed) in this tradition is not only an identification with Petrarch as a model for lyric subjectivity but an identification with a lyric subject that goes to the heart of a program for lyric reading, internalized by generations of critics as well as poetic imitators. That lyric subject is normatively male, and his lyric object is a woman, but in Vickers's reading, Petrarch's textual strategy is reincorporated into a critical tradition that re-collects the masculine lyric subject as a form of feminine self-scattering.

Vickers identifies our modern model of lyric as emerging in the Renaissance (an argument we have encountered many times in the course of this anthology), and it is a model coded by sex and gender in surprising ways. On the one hand, the model of the lyric that emerges from Petrarch's sonnets is a genre of the masculine subject that objectifies women; on the other hand, that very act of objectification threatens the integrity of the presumably masculine subject. This idea that the paradigmatic sexuality of Renaissance sonnets eventuates in a definitive self-division of the male lyric subject was further elaborated in the 1980s by Joel Fineman. Though we do not include Fineman in this volume, we recommend that readers interested in the beginnings of queer lyric theory take a closer look at *Shakespeare's Perjured Eye*, a deep reading of Shakespeare's sonnets that is also deeply immersed in a Lacanian account of subject formation. Introducing a different sexual difference, Fineman was especially interested in how Shakespeare "adapted the heterosexual tradition of the Petrarchist sonnet to the exigencies of poetic address to a man" because such adaptation reveals a logic of differential repetition that structures the interiority of the subject.[2] While Shakespeare's sequence of sonnets addressed to the dark lady demonstrates the poet's disjunctive, heterogeneous, heterosexual relation to the lady, the sequence addressed to the young man internalizes that difference. An excess of likeness in the young man sonnets generates the anti-Petrarchan elements in these poems, estranging them from a previous tradition of laudatory poetry and producing a self-estranging poetic logic that has become so familiar in the Shakespearean tradition that it may have lost its original strangeness. In place of sameness, Fineman's Shakespeare invents a language of paradox and self-division, and that language becomes the language of sexual self-division that queers subjects and sex in what becomes a lyric norm.

While in 1982 Vickers focused on the decomposition and recomposition of a masculine lyric subject, and in 1986 Fineman drew attention to the sexual difference within the modern masculine (post-Shakespearean) lyric subject, in 1979 Sandra Gilbert and Susan Gubar had begun to imagine a new feminist norm of thinking about the lyric and sexual difference by writing (as announced in their epigraph, quoted from Anne Finch) about what happens to "a woman that attempts the pen." In this section, we reprint their introduction to *Shakespeare's Sisters*, a collection of critical essays on women poets that proved formative for feminist criticism in the 1980s. According to Gilbert and Gubar, the predicament of the woman poet is determined, or overdetermined, by an abstract definition of the lyric. Citing various critics in a "masculinist" literary tradition who seem to believe that "the very nature of lyric poetry is inherently incompatible with the nature or essence of femaleness," Gilbert and Gubar wonder how it is possible for women to write poetry when " 'woman' and 'poet' are being defined as contradictory terms." For Gilbert and Gubar, the task of feminist criticism is to explore the gendered implications of that contradiction rather than the generic complications of lyric. Starting from the assumption that "the lyric poem is in some sense the utterance of a strong and assertive 'I,' " they conclude that "the lyric poet must be continually aware of herself from the *inside*, as a subject, a speaker: she must be, that is, assertive, authoritative, radiant with powerful feelings while at the same time absorbed in her own consciousness—and hence, by definition, profoundly 'unwomanly,' even freakish." Through the recovery of women poets who assert a lyric "I," the purpose of *Shakespeare's Sisters* is to introduce the possibility of an authoritative female lyric subject who can claim female authorship. In Gilbert and Gubar, the modern theory of the lyric became a potential vehicle of feminist self-empowerment. Quoting Sylvia Plath, they ventriloquize the desire of women poets to declare themselves in the first person singular: "I / have a self to recover, a queen."

But the separation of the pronoun "I" from "a self" (marked in the enjambment of that line) already suggests the degree to which the woman poet is a generic figure that embodies the problem of writing as a woman: how can she "have" a self to "recover" from a masculine poetic tradition that is not her own, or how will she discover alternate traditions in which to claim a voice of her own? This, according to Gilbert and Gubar, is the double (or triple) bind of the woman poet. By presenting the poetry of Plath and other "representative" women poets such as Elizabeth Barrett Browning and Emily Dickinson, they call upon feminist critics to explore "the crucial relationship between sexual identity and art" in general and between sexual identity and lyric poetry in particular. In this version of feminist criticism, the lyric vocation of the woman poet must mean that we agree that a lyric is the stage for a dramatic persona, and that this dramatic persona is identical to the person of the woman poet. Gilbert and Gubar assume a New Critical version of the lyric, but they put that version in tension with the New Critical attempt to divorce the dramatic lyric "speaker" from the biographical poet. Gilbert and Gubar's lyric poem is not a pudding or a machine; it is a woman's daring chance at self-expression.

In retrospect, Gilbert and Gubar's defense of the lyric may seem symptomatic of a particular moment in second-wave feminism, but it also made clear how difficult the model of modern lyric reading was to escape. Changing the focus to addressing a "you" rather than asserting an "I," the 1987 essay by Barbara Johnson makes visible the problems attending a feminist reclamation of the lyric, by shifting the focus to the figure of address known as apostrophe. Her point of departure is Jonathan Culler's influential argument that apostrophe is "a rhetorical device that has come to seem almost synonymous with the lyric voice" and perhaps even paradigmatic of "lyric poetry as such." To demonstrate how the invocation of an absent, dead, or inanimate being in the second person allows a first-person speaker to come into being, Johnson first considers two apostrophic poems by Baudelaire and Shelley: she traces their attempt to build "the bridge between the 'O' of the pure vocative, Jakobson's conative function, or the pure presencing of the second person, and the 'oh' of pure subjectivity, Jakobson's emotive function, or the pure presencing of the first person." In her invocation of Jakobson, Johnson announces her explicitly poststructuralist method, since it turns out that the structural categories break down—though this time because the poets are women. In thinking about the problems of address in the work of several contemporary women poets, Johnson notices how the conative and emotive functions of apostrophe, and indeed apostrophe itself, become tangled in poems about abortion: here it is unclear whether language serves to animate or de-animate these object of address, and even the distinction between addresser and addressee becomes difficult to mark, since one is quite literally inside (or no longer within) the other.

In a sustained rhetorical analysis of "The Mother" by Gwendolyn Brooks, for example, Johnson traces shifting structures of address that complicate the assumption of a lyric speaker: "It is never clear whether the speaker sees herself as an 'I' or a 'you,' an addressor or an addressee." Here Johnson introduces sexual difference not only thematically, to suggest that "a great many poetic effects may be colored according to *expectations* articulated through the gender of the poetic speaker," but also rhetorically, to suggest that "there may be a deeper link between motherhood and apostrophe than we have hitherto suspected." Linking apostrophe to the cry of an infant addressed to its mother, Johnson speculates that "lyric poetry itself—summed up in the figure of apostrophe—comes to look like the fantastically intricate history of endless elaborations and displacements of the single cry, 'Mama!'" This primal apostrophe returns us to a familiar theoretical question about the origins of lyric as a genre, albeit with a gendered difference that prompts Johnson to generalize about the differences between male and female writing. While Johnson moves post-structuralist reading toward differential analysis of gender in poems by Gwendolyn Brooks, Anne Sexton, Lucille Clifton, and Adrienne Rich, the idea of "lyric poetry itself" remains undifferentiated: why can it be "summed up in the figure of apostrophe," and what is the longer genealogy of that generic assumption? How much do Johnson's readings differ from modern ideas about lyric as utterance overheard or as a script for the reader to say? Even in her deconstruction of the speaking voice, suspended in the address of "I" to "you," Johnson sustains the New Critical paradigm of a dramatic persona who performs the poem as a personal drama. As we saw in section 5 on "Post-Structuralist Reading," Johnson's deft unravelling of the assumptions that guide the ways in which the idea of the person has been ascribed to the idea of the poem must retain an idealized view of the lyric.

Critics who are interested in articulating sexual difference and critics committed to the articulation of different sexualities thus depart from a modern lyric norm that they also maintain. To posit a subject for lyric reading makes it possible, and increasingly urgent, not only to question the normative gender of that subject but to raise questions about the object of its desire, and the heteronormativity of that desire. In his 1990 "The Homosexual Lyric," Thomas Yingling posed such questions through a reading of Hart Crane, demonstrating how Crane's poems "record the dialectical unfolding of Crane's thought about the homosexual subject and poetry." At the same time, Yingling records the dialectical unfolding of his own thinking about "the homosexual lyric," thinking that is centered on the very de-centering of the lyric subject. As he surveys the development of Crane's writing—from early poems that could be read as "homosexual autobiography" to "more advanced inquiries into the problematics of homosexual intersubjectivity" and to "later, more symbolic autobiographical texts"—Yingling is interested in exploring how "Crane's lyrics test the structures of identity in a way that makes them theoretical investigations of the subject." Crane is thus folded into Yingling's own theoretical investigations of lyric subjectivity, as the critic goes on to investigate the relationship between homosexuality and textuality in Crane's densely worked, increasingly abstract texts. We are not surprised to learn that Yingling finds that what the poems foreground "most strongly as the problem of lyric—and the problem of the modern as well—is the textuality of subjectivity." But what is "the textuality of subjectivity"? In a poem like "Possession," often read as articulating modern urban homosexual experience, Yingling discerns "Crane's strategy to keep syntactic relations, as homosexual desire remains, indeterminate"; by analyzing how the first-person singular is suspended in and displaced by the rhetorical figures and grammatical structures of this poem, Yingling suggests that "the difficult, unspeakable quality of homosexuality stands clearly behind this construction." What is unspoken and unspeakable in Crane's poetry leads Yingling to a double conclusion: first, that the earlier experimental lyrics "present the search for an authentic voice and an ideological recognition of homosexual speech and writing, and—with an increasing clarity—the frustrations and barriers to that project," and second, that in the later poems, "we must read the disintegration of the speaking/writing subject . . . within an ideology that made the homosexual poet's subjectivity a bizarre dialectic of anguish and ecstasy." Notwithstanding this difficulty of articulation, Yingling ultimately emphasizes "Crane's refusal to surrender the homosexual subject in the lyric," reclaiming "the lyric" along with the subject it is struggling to articulate.

Yingling's essay thus sets out to explore how the ideological interpellation of homosexuality as a subject position "affected Crane's imagination of the lyric form as a genre of self-presentation," and in doing so, Yingling demonstrates how the ideological interpellation of his own subject position affects his imagination of lyric reading as a genre of critical self-presentation. While assuming that presenting a self is what lyric does as a genre, Yingling starts his essay by marking a break from "former critical theory" that "imagined the lyric as the poetry of a single, unified voice, and imagined the task of criticism as elaboration and reproduction of that voice." Yingling refers back in particular to "The Structure of the Greater Romantic Lyric," where M. H. Abrams lays out a model of poetic and psychological realism for reading Romantic poems as the meditations of a lyric speaker, "whom we overhear as he carries on" about tragic loss, a moral dilemma, or personal crisis, finally to achieve an altered mood and deeper understanding. But according to Yingling, this metaphysical pattern (from our perspective, a modern lyric imaginary retroprojected into Romantic poetry) is splintered by Crane, who "refuses these categories" and "breaks the conventions of Romantic lyric." Instead, Yingling follows Allen Grossman in suggesting that "Crane does not figure authenticity of voice by staging the speaker of the poem dramatically at a distance from some more originary voice or presence" but by attempting to "record the unmediated speech, sea, song, *presence* of poetry itself." As we have seen in Grossman's phenomenological approach to lyric reading (and others included in section 7), in this mode of lyric reading the fiction of the speaker is expanded beyond the single subject to imagine a world of relations the poem brings into being, although Yingling is more skeptical than Grossman about the possibility of dwelling there, adding, "we recognize the impossible agenda of this, of course." For Yingling, the "lyricality" of Crane is the disintegration of a subject that cannot inhabit the poem as a speaking voice but may be heard in the seemingly unmediated "*presence* of poetry itself," albeit only as an echo of a line of poetry in the final line of Yingling's lyrical essay: "the greatness of Crane's lyrics, written, it is not hyperbolic to say, at the cost of his life, is that they allow homosexual subjectivity to be heard as an authentic experience, as 'wind flaking sapphire.'"

Yingling's embrace of the elusive homosexual subject in lyric reading—that vanishing object of his desire—is one way to articulate sexual difference; for other ways, we might look at the emergence of queer theory since the last decade of the twentieth century—a field too rich to survey here. In *The Lyric Theory Reader*, we include only the beginning of a conversation, which would continue, for example, in Lee Edelman's account of rhetoric and desire in the poetry of Crane, introducing an early version of queer reading that anatomizes figural strategies in the body of his writing without identifying (with) Crane as a lyric subject. By analyzing how the rhetorical figures of anacoluthon, chiasmus, and catachresis play out in Crane's poetry in the processes of "breaking," "bending," and "bridging," Edelman discerns a "catachrestic" poetics: an improper or abusive use of metaphor that associates perversion of poetic style with subversion of sexual norms. "As a poet who strains toward catachresis, Crane invokes an ideology of rupture, of violent transvaluation," Edelman argues, transvaluing his own critical practice as well: as a critic who strains against lyric reading, though without explicitly naming it as such, he moves toward an alternative that he later came to call "homographesis."[3] Hart Crane is a recurring touchstone for other versions and variations of queer reading as well, most recently for Michael Snediker in *Queer Optimism: Lyric Personhood and Other Felicitous Persuasions*. Yet unlike Edelman, Snediker happily returns to the strains of lyric reading, reclaiming "lyric personhood" as an extravagant performance of personification or (as in the case of Bishop's "queer love" of Hart Crane) "transpersonification."[4] For Snediker this is less an argument about the lyric as such than it is an attempt to perform and thus transform the shame of lyric reading into the positive affect of queer optimism.

The productive potential of lyric shame is explored in Eve Kosofsky Sedgwick's essay, "A Poem Is Being Written," too long for inclusion below but like Fineman important to mention because of its highly original approach to queering the lyric. First published in 1987, it was later reprinted in a selection of her essays written "across genders, across sexualities," thus arriving at the question of lyric and sexual difference from yet another angle. Riffing on the title of Freud's essay, "A Child Is Being Beaten," Sedgwick transformed a child's memory, or fantasy, of spanking into an identification with poetic form that associates the rhythmic beating of the body with the beat of the poem (and vice versa). In the phantasmatic primal scene of this "lyric tableau," Sedgwick places "a generic, i.e. ungendered, 'child' that finds its way . . . to a shiftily identificatory relation to, generically, the genre 'lyric poem.'"[5] Shifting between poetry and prose, and between writing in the first person and in the third person, Sedgwick represented the child simultaneously as subject and object of her own lyric poem, thus incorporating into her argument the longer generic history that has made lyric into a genre for shifting identifications. But just as the Freudian primal scene can only be experienced through deferred action, as an effect of *Nachtraglichkeit*, so also the lyric event is manifested retroactively, in the repetition of an imaginary scene that Sedgwick performed with virtuosity, not only in striking passages of lyrical writing, but more fundamentally as an effect of lyric reading. Insofar as her riff on Freudian psychoanalysis is a meditation on how to move "across the gaps between poetry and theory," what she discovers and exposes in that gap are questions about the relation between gender and sexual difference and models of the lyric that we keep holding (even beating) into place, models we seem to be able to work variations on but keep not giving up.

Even among recent poets and critics dedicated to "lyric innovation," that modern model of lyric tends to be expanded but not exploded. In Juliana Spahr's introduction to *American Women Poets of the 21st Century*, the essay with which this section concludes, the subtitle, "Where Lyric Meets Language," indexes a "space within lyric for language writing's more politicized claims." According to Spahr, "while most of the poets and critics in this collection use the word 'lyric' to refer to interiority and/or intimate speech," they also project this interiority outward, pushing beyond the limits of received lyric norms. At the same time, writing "outside" the lyric is difficult if not impossible, according to Spahr, since twenty-first century women poets still struggle with twentieth-century ideas they have inherited about lyric as a genre: "Many poets here speak of lyric as the genre of and about impossibility and difficulty. In short, when they talk of innovation, they often talk of lyric." For Spahr, avant-garde anti-lyricism returns to the lyric with a vengeance, since "The emphasis on innovation . . . is a return to what made lyric so valuable centuries ago. Lyric is by definition innovative. When it stops being innovative it is no longer lyric." By the twenty-first century, the task of lyricization is complete: to imagine poetry that departs from lyric is to imagine a poetry that is not poetry. Instead, surveying various forms of contemporary innovation, Spahr seeks to defend "the lyric" through a diversification of "lyrics": "I find value in lyrics that retreat from individualism and idiosyncrasies by pointing to heady and unexpected intimate pluralisms. And lyrics that help me to place myself as part of a larger, connective culture." This mediation between the singular and plural seems to move away from the feminist reclamation of the lyric "I" two decades earlier, but the claim to a gendered redefinition of lyric as a genre is actually an extension of the claims of earlier feminist anthologies (including *Shakespeare's Sisters*). Rather than recovering past women poets (and critics) in her collection, what Spahr offers is a bigger and bolder claim about the place of women's language poetry in the future of lyric: "Despite the constant intrusion of new genres, and new media, lyric persists. Is it possible to have a culture without it?"

It is a good question. Taken apart, scattered, and reconstituted, the category of the lyric continues to do important work in twenty-first-century ideas about sexual difference. That theory may be increasingly queer, but the lyric uncannily returns as poetic norm. As long as we assume (as we do) the modern models of lyric reading this volume represents, we will remain caught in the paradoxes of sexuality, gender, and genre that those models themselves entail. To return to Berlant, while "the act of being historical" may well be trying to "*find* its genre" in a new century's promise of new ways of thinking through sex and gender, we have yet to find a critical poetic genre that does not look a lot like the modern lyric reading that did not end when the last century ended.

NOTES

1. Lauren Berlant, *Cruel Optimism* (Durham, NC: Duke University Press, 2011), 20.
2. Fineman (1986), 2.
3. See Edelman (1987), 13. A deconstructive rhetorical reading of figurations of homosexual legibility is further explained and developed in Lee Edelman, *Homographesis: Essays in Gay Literary and Cultural Theory* (New York: Routledge, 1994).
4. Snediker (2009), 183.
5. Sedgwick (1993), 187.

FURTHER READING

Barthes, Roland. *The Pleasure of the Text.* Translated by Richard Miller. New York: Macmillan, 1975.

Cixous, Helene. "The Laugh of the Medusa." *Signs* 1.4 (Summer 1976): 875–93.

DuPlessis, Rachel Blau. *Blue Studios: Poetry and Its Cultural Work.* Tuscaloosa: University of Alabama Press, 2006.

———. *The Pink Guitar: Writing as Feminist Practice.* New York: Routledge, 1990.

Edelman, Lee. *Transmemberment of Song: Hart Crane's Anatomies of Rhetoric and Desire.* Stanford, CA: Stanford University Press, 1987.

Felman, Shoshana. *What Does a Woman Want? Reading and Sexual Difference.* Baltimore: Johns Hopkins University Press, 1993.

Fineman, Joel. *Shakespeare's Perjured Eye: The Invention of Poetic Subjectivity in the Sonnets.* Berkeley: University of California Press, 1986.

Garber, Linda. *Identity Poetics: Race, Class, and the Lesbian-Feminist Roots of Queer Theory.* New York: Columbia University Press, 2001.

Goldberg, Jonathan. *Desiring Women Writing: English Renaissance Examples.* Stanford, CA: Stanford University Press, 1997.

Hejinian, Lyn. *The Language of Inquiry.* Berkeley: University of California Press, 2000.

Homans, Margaret. *Women Writers and Poetic Identity: Dorothy Wordsworth, Emily Bronte, and Emily Dickinson.* Princeton, NJ: Princeton University Press, 1980.

Howe, Susan. *My Emily Dickinson.* Berkeley, CA: North Atlantic Books, 1985; reprint, New York: New Directions, 2007.

Irigaray, Luce. *This Sex Which Is Not One.* Translated by Catherine Porter. Ithaca, NY: Cornell University Press, 1985.

Jackson, Virginia, and Yopie Prins. "Lyrical Studies." *Victorian Literature and Culture* 27.2 (Fall 1999): 521–30.

Keller, Lynn, and Cristanne Miller. *Feminist Measures: Soundings in Poetry and Theory.* Ann Arbor: University of Michigan Press, 1994.

Kinnahan, Linda A. *Lyric Interventions: Feminism, Experimental Poetry, and Contemporary Discourse.* Iowa City: University of Iowa Press, 2004.

Kristeva, Julia. *Desire in Language: A Semiotic Approach to Literature and Art.* New York: Columbia University Press, 1980.

Loeffelholz, Mary. *Emily Dickinson and the Boundaries of Feminist Theory.* Urbana: University of Illinois Press, 1991.

Prins, Yopie, and Maeera Shreiber, eds. *Dwelling in Possibility: Women Poets and Feminist Critics.* Ithaca, NY: Cornell University Press, 1997.

Rose, Jacqueline. *The Haunting of Sylvia Plath.* London: Virago, 1991.

Sedgwick, Eve Kosofsky. *Epistemology of the Closet.* Berkeley: University of California Press, 1990.

———. "A Poem Is Being Written." *Representations* 17 (1987): 110–43.

Snediker, Michael. *Queer Optimism: Lyric Personhood and Other Felicitous Persuasions.* Minneapolis: University of Minnesota Press, 2009.

Vincent, John. *Queer Lyrics: Difficulty and Closure in American Poetry.* New York: Palgrave Macmillan, 2002.

Yorke, Liz. *Impertinent Voices: Subversive Strategies in Contemporary Women's Poetry.* London: Routledge, 1991.

Diana Described: Scattered Woman and Scattered Rhyme (1981) 9.1

Nancy J. Vickers

The import of Petrarch's description of Laura extends well beyond the confines of his own poetic age; in subsequent times, his portrayal of feminine beauty became authoritative. As a primary canonical text, the *Rime sparse* consolidated and disseminated a Renaissance mode. Petrarch absorbed a complex network of descriptive strategies and then presented a single, transformed model. In this sense his role in the history of the interpretation and the internalization of woman's "image" by both men and women can scarcely be overemphasized. When late-Renaissance theorists, poets, and painters represented woman's body, Petrarch's verse justified their aesthetic choices. His authority, moreover, extended beyond scholarly consideration to courtly conversation, beyond the treatise on beauty to the after-dinner game in celebration of it. The descriptive codes of others, both ancients and contemporaries, were, of course, not ignored, but the "scattered rhymes" undeniably enjoyed a privileged status: they informed the Renaissance norm of a beautiful woman.[1]

We never see in the *Rime sparse* a complete picture of Laura. This would not be exceptional if we were considering a single "song" or even a restricted lyric corpus; gothic top-to-toe enumeration is, after all, more appropriate to narrative, more adapted to the "objective" observations of a third-person narrator than to those of a speaker who ostensibly loves, and perhaps even addresses, the image he describes. But given an entire volume devoted to a single lady, the absence of a coherent, comprehensive portrait is significant.[2] Laura is always presented as a part or parts of a woman. When more than one part figures in a single poem, a sequential, inclusive ordering is never stressed. Her textures are those of metals and stones; her image is that of a collection of exquisitely beautiful disassociated objects.[3] Singled out among them are hair, hand, foot and eyes: golden hair trapped and bound the speaker; an ivory hand took his heart away; a marble foot imprinted the grass and flowers; starry eyes directed him in his wandering.[4] In terms of qualitative attributes (blondness, whiteness, sparkle), little here is innovative. More specifically Petrarchan, however, is the obsessive insistence on the particular, an insistence that would in turn generate multiple texts on individual fragments of the body or on the beauties of woman.

When the sixteenth-century poet Joachim Du Bellay chose to attack the French propensity for Italianizing, his offensive gesture against the Petrarchans (among whose number he had once prominently figured) culminated in just this awareness: in his final verses he proposed to substitute the unified celebration of female beauty for the witty cliches of Petrarchan particularization:

> De voz *beautez* je diray seulement,
> Que si mon oeil ne juge folement,
> Vostre *beauté* est joincte egalement
>   A vostre bonne grace:
> . . .
> Si toutefois Petrarque vows plaist mieux,
> . . .
> Je choisiray cent mille nouveautez,
> Dont je peindray voz plus grandes *beautez*
> Sur la plus belle Idee.
> ["Contre les Petrarquistes," 11. 193–96, 201, 206–8]

> [Of your *beauties* I will only say that, if my eye does not mistakenly judge, your *beauty* is perfectly joined to your good grace:. . . But if you still like Petrarch better . . . I will choose a hundred thousand new ways to paint your greatest *beauties* according to the most beautiful Idea.][5]

Du Bellay's opposition of "beauties" and "beauty" suggests the idiosyncratic nature of Petrarch's depiction of woman as a composite of details. It would surely seem that to Petrarch Laura's whole body was at times less than some of its parts; and that to his imitators the strategy of describing her through the isolation of those parts presented an attractive basis for imitation, extension, and, ultimately, distortion. I will redefine that strategy here in terms of a myth to which both the *Rime* and the Renaissance obsessively return, a myth complex in its interpretation although simple in its staging. As a privileged mode of signifying, the recounting of a mythical tale within a literary text reveals concerns, whether conscious or unconscious, which are basic to that text.[6] It is only logical, then, to examine Petrarch's use of a myth about seeing woman in order to reexamine his description of a woman seen. The story of Actaeon's encounter with the goddess Diana is particularly suited to this purpose, for it is a story not only of confrontation with forbidden naked deity but also with forbidden naked femininity.

In the twenty-third *canzone*, the *canzone* of the metamorphoses, Petrarch's "I" narrates a history of changes: he was Daphne (a laurel), Cygnus (a swan), Battus (a stone),

Byblis (a fountain), Echo (a voice), he will never be Jove (a golden raincloud), and he is Actaeon (a stag). He has passed through a series of painful frustrations, now experiences a highly specific one, and will never be granted the sexual fulfillment of a god capable of transforming himself into a golden shower and inseminating the object of his desire. His use of the present in the last full stanza, the Actaeon stanza, is telling, for it centers this *canzone* on the juxtaposition of what the speaker was and what he now is: "Alas, what am I? What was I? The end crowns the life, the evening the day."[7] The end also crowns the song, and this song paradoxically abandons its speaker in the form of a man so transmuted that he cannot speak:

> I' segui' tanto avanti il mio desire
> ch' un dì, cacciando sì com' io solea,
> mi mossi, e quella fera bella et cruda
> in una fonte ignuda
> si stava, quando 'l sol più forte ardea.
> Io perché d'altra vista non m'appago
> stetti a mirarla, ond' ella ebbe vergogna
> et per fame vendetta o per celarse
> l'acqua nel viso co le man mi sparse.
> Vero dirò; forse e' parrà menzogna:
> ch'i' senti' trarmi de la propria imago
> et in un cervo solitario et vago
> di selva in selva ratto mi trasformo,
> et ancor de' miei can fuggo lo stormo.
> [*RS*, 23. 147–60]

> [I followed so far my desire that one day, hunting as I was wont, I went forth, and that lovely cruel wild creature was in a spring naked when the sun burned most strongly. I, who am not appeased by any other sight, stood to gaze on her, whence she felt shame and, to take revenge or to hide herself, sprinkled water in my face with her hand. I shall speak the truth, perhaps it will appear a lie, for I felt myself drawn from my own image and into a solitary wandering stag from wood to wood quickly I am transformed and still I flee the belling of my hounds.]

Petrarch's account of Actaeon's story closely follows the subtext that obviously subtends the entire *canzone*—Ovid's *Metamorphoses*. Actaeon is, as usual, hunting with friends. At noon, he stumbles upon a grove where he sees Diana, chaste goddess of the hunt and of the moon, bathing nude in a pool.[8] In the *Metamorphoses* she is surrounded by protective nymphs, but Petrarch makes no mention of either her company or of Actaeon's. He thus focuses the exchange on its principal players. Actaeon is transfixed (a stance Petrarch exaggerates), and Diana, both in shame and anger, sprinkles ("spargens") his face ("vultum") and hair ("comas") with water. Although in the *Rime sparse* Diana is significantly silenced, in the *Metamorphoses* she utters, "Now you can tell ['narres . . . licet'] that you have seen me unveiled ['posito velamine']—that is, if you can tell ['si poteris narrare']."[9] Diana's pronouncement simultaneously posits telling (description) as the probable outcome of Actaeon's glance and negates the possibility of that telling. Her vengeful baptism triggers a metamorphosis: it transforms Actaeon from horn to hoof into a voiceless, fearful stag (*Metamorphoses* 3.193–98). It is at this moment that Petrarch, with his characteristic use of an iterative present, situates his speaker: No other sight appeases me; "I am transformed"; "I flee."[10] The speaker *is* Actaeon, but, more important, he is a self-conscious Actaeon: he knows his own story; he has read his own text; he is defined by it and even echoes it in articulating his suffering. What awaits him is annihilation through dismemberment, attack unto death by his own hounds goaded on by his own devoted friends.

Seeing and bodily disintegration, then, are related poles in the Ovidian context that Petrarch brings to his text; they also are poles Ovid conjoins elsewhere. Actaeon's mythological antitypes in dismemberment, Pentheus and Orpheus, are both textually and experientially linked to his story.[11] His is the subtext to their suffering; he is the figure for their pain. In *Metamorphoses* 3.708–33, Pentheus gapes with "profane eyes" upon the female celebrants of the sacred rites of Bacchus, and they, urged by his mother (the woman who sees him), tear his body limb from limb: "Let the ghost of Actaeon move your heart," he pleads, but "she [his mother] knows not who Actaeon is, and tears the suppliant's right arm away." In *Metamorphoses* 11.26–27, Orpheus is so grief stricken at having irrevocably lost Eurydice by turning back to look at her that he shuns other women; falling victim to an explosion of female jealousy, he is dismembered and scattered, "as when in the amphitheatre . . . the doomed stag is the prey of dogs."

All three men, then, transgress, see women who are not to be seen, and are torn to bits. But the Orpheus-Actaeon analogy is particularly suggestive, for in the case of Orpheus, seeing and dismemberment are discrete events in time. The hiatus between them, the extended reprieve, is a span of exquisite though threatened poetry, of songs of absence and loss. Petrarch's "modern" Actaeon is in that median time: he is fearful of the price of seeing, yet to be paid, but still pleased by what he saw. The remembered image is the source of all joy and pain, peace and anxiety, love and hate: "Living is such heavy and long pain, that I call out for the end in my great desire to see her again whom it would have been better not to have seen at all" (*RS*, 312.12–14). Thus he must both perpetuate her image and forget it: he must "cry out in silence," cry out "with paper and ink," that is to say, write (*RS*, 71.6, 23.99). It is especially important to note that the productive paralysis born of this ambivalence determines a normative stance for countless lovesick poets of the Petrarchan generations. As Leonard Barkan has recently shown, "From that source [Petrarch] Actaeon's story becomes throughout the Renaissance a means of investigating the complicated psychology of love."[12] When Shakespeare, for example, lends a critical ear to Orsino in his opening scene to *Twelfth Night*, we hear what was by 1600 the worn-out plaint of a languishing lover caught precisely in Actaeon's double bind:

> CURIO: Will you go to hunt, my lord?
> ORSINO: What, Curio?
> CURIO: The hart.
> ORSINO: Why, so I do, the noblest that I have.
> O, when mine eyes did see Olivia first,
> Methought she purg'd the air of pestilence!
> That instant was I turn'd into a hart,
> And my desires, like fell and cruel hounds,
> E'er since pursue me.
> [Act 1, sc. 1, ll. 16–23]

Subsequent imitation, no matter how creative or how wooden, bears witness to the reader's awareness of and the writer's engagement in the practice of "speaking" in Actaeon's voice. A reassessment of Petrarch's use of Actaeon's fate to represent the status of his speaking subject, then, constitutes a reassessment of not just one poetic stance but of many. When we step back from the Petrarchans to Petrarch, the casting of the poet in this role (and, by extension, the beloved in that of Diana) is less a cliché than a construct that can be used to explain both the scattering of woman and of rhyme in his vernacular lyric. Here the "metaphor of appearance," so central to the volume, is paired with the myth of appearance: the fateful first perception of Laura—an image obsessively remembered, reworked, and repeated—assumes a mythical analogue and mythical proportion.[13] What the reader must then ask is why that remembrance, like the rhyme ("rimembra"/"membra" [remember/members]) that invokes it, is one of parts: "Clear, fresh, sweet waters, where she who alone seems lady to me rested her lovely body ["membra"], gentle branch where it pleased her (with sighing I remember)" (*RS*, 126.1–5).[14]

Although traces of Diana are subtly woven into much of the imagistic texture that progressively reveals the composite of Laura, only one text refers to her by name:

> Non al suo amante più Diana piacque
> quando per tal ventura tutta ignuda
> la vide in mezzo de le gelide acque,
>
> ch' a me la pastorella alpestra et cruda
> posta a bagnar un leggiadretto velo
> ch' a l'aura il vago et biondo capel chiuda;
>
> tal che mi fece, or quand' egli arde 'l cielo,
> tutto tremar d'un amoroso gielo.
> [*RS*, 52]

> [Not so much did Diana please her lover when, by a similar chance, he saw her all naked amid the icy waters,
>
> as did the cruel mountain shepherdess please me, set to wash a pretty veil that keeps her lovely blond head from the breeze;
>
> so that she made me, even now when the sky is burning, all tremble with a chill of love.]

This simple madrigal based on the straightforward equation of the speaker's pleasure at seeing Laura's veil and Actaeon's pleasure at seeing Diana's body has, of late, received lengthy and suggestive comment. Giuseppe Mazzotta, in an analysis centered on Petrarch's "language of the self," reads it in relation to a reversibility of "subject and object."[15] John Freccero places Petrarch's use of the "veil covering a radiant face" motif within its traditional context (Saint Paul to Dante), that of a "figure for the relationship of the sign to its referent." He concludes that Laura's "veil, bathed in the water like the naked goddess seen by Acteon, functions as a fetish, an erotic signifier of a referent whose absence the lover refuses to acknowledge." That act of substituting the veil for the body, previously linked by Freccero to the Augustinian definition of idolatry, ultimately associates the fragmentation of Laura's body and the "nonreferentiality" of Petrarch's sequence:

> One of the consequences of treating a signifier as an absolute is that its integrity cannot be maintained. Without a principle of intelligibility, an interpretant, a collection of signs threatens to break down into its component parts. . . . So it is with Laura. Her virtues and her beauties are scattered like the objects of fetish worship: her eyes and hair are like gold and topaz on the snow, while the outline of her face is lost; . . . Like the poetry that celebrates her, she gains immortality at the price of vitality and historicity. Each part of her has the significance of her entire person; it remains the task of the reader to string together her gemlike qualities into an idealized unity.[16]

Freccero's analysis departs from a position shared by many contemporary Petrarch critics—that of the centrality of a dialectic between the scattered and the gathered, the integrated and the disintegrated.[17] In defining Petrarch's "poetics of fragmentation," these same critics have consistently identified as its primary figure the particularizing descriptive strategy adopted to evoke Laura.[18] If the speaker's "self" (his text, his "corpus") is to be unified, it would seem to require the repetition of her dismembered image. "Woman remains," as Josette Féral has commented in another context, "the instrument by which man attains unity, and she pays for it at the price of her own dispersion."[19]

Returning to *Rime sparse* 52, some obvious points must be made: first, this text is read as an emblem of Petrarchan fragmentation; and second, it turns on a highly specific analogy ("I am pleased by Laura's veil as Actaeon was pleased by Diana's nakedness"; "My fetish equals Diana's body"). It is the analogy itself that poses an additional problem. While the enunciation of "I"'s fetishistic pleasure through comparison with Actaeon's voyeuristic pleasure might appear incongruous, it is both appropriate and revealing.

The Actaeon-Diana story is one of identification and reversal: Actaeon hunts; Diana hunts; and their encounter reduces him to the status of the hunted.[20] This fated meeting, this instant of midday recognition, is one of fascination and repulsion: it is a confrontation with difference where similarity might have been desired or even expected. It is a glance into a mirror—witness the repeated pairing of this myth with that of Narcissus (*Metamorphoses* 3.344–510)—that produces an unlike and deeply threatening image.[21] Perceiving that image is, of course, prohibited; such a transgression violates proscriptions imposed on powerless humans in their relation to powerful divinities. Similarly, such a transgression violates proscriptions imposed upon powerless men (male children) in relation to powerful women (mothers):[22] "This is thought," writes Howard Daniel, "to be one of many myths relating to the incest mechanism—punishment for an even accidental look at something forbidden."[23] The Actaeon-Diana encounter read in this perspective reenacts a scene fundamental to theorizing about fetishistic perversion: the troubling encounter of a male child with intolerable female nudity, with a body lacking parts present in his own, with a body that suggests the possibility of dismemberment. Woman's body, albeit divine, is displayed to Actaeon, and his body, as a consequence, is literally taken apart. Petrarch's Actaeon, having read his Ovid, realizes what will ensue: his response to the threat of imminent dismemberment is the neutralization, through descriptive dismemberment, of the threat. He transforms the visible totality into scattered words, the body into signs; his description, at one remove from his experience, safely permits and perpetuates his fascination.

The verb in the *Rime sparse* that places this double dismemberment in the foreground is determinant for the entire sequence—*spargere*, "to scatter." It appears in some form (most frequently that of the past-participial adjective "*sparso, -i, -a, -e*") forty-three times; nineteen apply specifically to Laura's body and its emanations (the light from her eyes, the generative capacity of her footsteps) and thirteen to the speaker's mental state and its expression (tears, voice, rhymes, sighs, thoughts, praises, prayers, hopes). The uses of *spargere* thus markedly gravitate toward "I" and Laura. The etymological roots of the term, moreover, virtually generate Laura's metaphoric codes: "I" knows that the outcome of seeing her body is the scattering of his; hence he projects scattering onto her through a process of fetishistic overdetermination, figuring those part-objects in terms of the connotations of "scattering": *spargere*, from the Latin *spargere*, with cognates in the English "sprinkle" and "sparkle" and in the Greek *σπέιρω*—"I disseminate." Laura's eyes, as in the sequence of three *canzoni* devoted exclusively to them (*RS*, 71–73), are generative sparks emanating from the stars; they sow the seeds of poetry in the "muffled soil" of the poet (*RS*, 71.102–5), and they sprinkle glistening drops like clear waters. Her body parts metaphorically inseminate; his do not: "Song, I was never the cloud of gold that once descended in a precious rain so that it partially quenched the fire of Jove; but I have certainly been a flame lit by a lovely glance and I have been the bird that rises highest in the air raising her whom in my words I honor" (*RS*, 23. 161–66). Desire directed in vain at a forbidden, distant goddess is soon sublimated desire that spends itself in song. That song is, in turn, the celebration and the violation of that goddess: it would re-produce her vulnerability; it would re-present her nakedness to a (male) reader who will enter into collusion with, even become, yet another Actaeon.[24]

Within the context of Petrarch's extended poetic sequence, the lady is corporeally scattered; the lover is emotionally scattered and will be corporeally scattered, and thus the relation between the two is one of mirroring. "I," striking Actaeon's pose, tells us that he stood fixed to see hut also to mirror Diana-Laura ("mirarla").[25] He offers to eliminate the only source of sadness for the "lovely eyes," their inability to see themselves, by mirroring them (*RS*, 71.57–60). And he transforms the coloration of the lady's flesh into roses scattered in snow in which he mirrors himself (*RS*, 146.5–6). The specular nature of this exchange explains, in large part, the disconcerting interchangeability of its participants. Even the key rhyme "rimembra/membra" reflects a doubling: twice the *membra* are his (*RS*, 15 and 23); once those of the lost heroes of a disintegrating body politic, a dissolving mother country (*RS*, 53); and twice hers (*RS*, 126 and 127). In reading the Diana-veil madrigal cited above, Mazzotta demonstrates this textual commingling, pointing out that Diana's body, in the first tercet, is completely naked ("tutta ignuda") in a pool of icy waters ("gelide acque") but, by the last line, her observer's body is all atremble ("tutto tremor") with a chill of love ("un amoroso gielo"). Mazzotta goes on to note that male/female roles often alternate in Petrarch's figurations of the speaker/Laura relationship: he is Echo to her Narcissus, Narcissus to her Echo; she is Apollo to his Daphne, Daphne to his Apollo, and so on.[26] The space of that alternation is a median one—a space of looks, mirrors, and texts.

Actaeon sees Diana, Diana sees Actaeon, and seeing is traumatic for both. She is ashamed, tries to hide her body (her secret), and thus communicates her sense of violation. Her observer consequently knows that pleasure in the sight before him constitutes transgression; he deduces that transgression, although thrilling (arousing), is threatening (castrating). Their initial communication is a self-conscious look; the following scenario fills the gap between them: "I . . . stood to gaze on her, whence she felt shame and, to take revenge or to hide herself, sprinkled water ["mi sparse"—cf. Ovid, "spargens"] in my face with her hand[s]. I shall speak the truth" (*RS*, 23.153–56). She defends herself and assaults him with scattered water; he responds with scattered words: "You who hear in scattered rhymes the sound of those sighs with which I flourished my heart during my first youthful error, when I was in part another man from what I am now" (*RS*, 1.1–4). Water and words, then, pass between them; hands and transparent drops cannot conceal her but do precipitate a metamorphosis, preventing a full sounding of what was momentarily seen. Threatened rhymes try to iterate a precious, fleeting image, to transmute it into an idol that can be forever possessed, that will be forever present.

But description is ultimately no more than a collection of imperfect signs, signs that, like fetishes, affirm absence by their presence. Painting Laura in poetry is but a twice-removed, scripted rendering of a lost woman (body → introjected image of the body → textual body), an enterprise by definition fragmentary. "I" speaks his anxiety in the hope of finding repose through enunciation, of re-membering the lost body, of effecting an inverse incarnation—her flesh made word. At the level of the fictive experience which he describes, successes are ephemeral, and failures become a way of life.

Quella per cui con Sorga ò cangiato Arno,
con franca povertà serve ricchezze,
volse in amaro sue sante dolcezze
ond' io già vissi, or me ne struggo et scarno.

Da poi piú volte ò riprovato indarno
al secol che verrà l'alte bellezze
pinger cantando, a ciò che l'ame et preze,
né col mio stile il suo bet viso incarno.

Le lode, mai non d'altra et proprie sue,
che 'n lei fur come stelle in cielo sparte,
pur ardisco ombreggiare, or una or due;

ma poi ch' I' giungo a la divina parte,
ch' un chiaro et breve sole al mondo fue[,]
ivi manta l'ardir, l'ingegno et l'arte.
[*RS*, 308]

[She for whom I exchanged Arno for Sorgue and slavish riches for free poverty, turned her holy sweetness[es], on which I once lived, into bitterness, by which now I am destroyed and disfleshed [I destroy and disflesh myself].

Since then I have often tried in vain to depict in song for the age to come her high beauties, that it may love and prize them, nor with my style can I incarnate her lovely face.

Still now and again I dare to adumbrate one or two of the praises that were always hers, never any other's, that were as many as the stars spread [scattered] across the sky;

but when I come to her divine part, which was a bright, brief sun to the world, there fails my daring, my wit, and my art.]

This text organizes itself upon a sequence of oppositions which contrast fullness (presence) with emptiness (absence). The speaker has exchanged Arno (Florence, mother country) for Sorgue (Vaucluse, exile); riches (although slavish) for poverty (albeit free); sweetness for bitterness; a body for dismemberment; and union for separation. The speaker's rhymes point to a past place (a body of water, "Arno") and to two present, though fruitless ("indarno"), activities—he is at once stripped of flesh ("me ne . . . scarno") and would give flesh to her ("incarno"). He acknowledges his inability to re-create Laura's absent face, and yet he maintains that he still tries, "now and again." Her praises (that is, his poems) arc but images he "dare[s] to adumbrate," shadows "scattered," like their source, across the sky. Daring, wit, and art cannot re-present her to him, but they can evoke her parts "one by one" and thus generate an exquisite sequence of verse (*RS*, 127. 85–91 and 273.6). For it is in fact the loss, at the fictional level, of Laura's body that constitutes the intolerable absence, creates a reason to speak, and permits a poetic "corpus." As Petrarch's readers have consistently recognized, Laura and *lauro*, the laurel to crown a poet laureate, are one.[27]

Petrarch's poetry is a poetry of tension, of flux, of alternation between the scattered and the gathered. Laura's many parts would point to a unity, however elusive, named Laura; the speaker's ambivalent emotions are spoken by a grammatically constant "io." In the space of exchange, the only space the reader is given, permutation is possible; each part of her body can produce each aspect of his positive/negative reactions. A given text can expand any combination; infinite variety spawns infinite verse. Petrarch's particularizing mode of figuring that body, the product of a male-viewer/female-object exchange that extends the Actaeon/Diana exchange, thus reveals a textual strategy subtending his entire volume: it goes to the heart of his lyric program and understandably becomes the lyric stance of generations of imitators.

And yet such praise carries condemnation with it because it implies at least two interdependent consequences. First, Petrarch's figuration of Laura informs a decisive stage in the development of a code of beauty, a code that causes us to view the fetishized body as a norm and encourages us to seek, or to seek to be, "ideal types, beautiful monsters composed of every individual perfection."[28] Petrarch's text, of course, did not constitute the first example of particularizing description, but it did popularize that strategy by coming into fashion during the privileged early years of printing, the first century of the widespread diffusion of both words and images. It is in this context that Petrarch left us his legacy of fragmentation. And second, bodies fetishized by a poetic voice logically do not have a voice of their own; the world of making words, of making texts, is not theirs. The status of Laura's voice, however, resists easy or schematic characterization. Once dead, it should be noted, she can often address her sleeping, disconsolate lover; while she is alive, direct discourse from her is extremely rare. Her speech, moreover, undergoes a treatment similar to that of her body in that it ranks high on the list of her exquisitely reified parts: "and her speech and her lovely face and her locks pleased me so that I have her before my eyes and shall always have wherever I am, on slope or shore" (*RS*, 30.4–6).

Rime sparse 23, the *canzone* of the metamorphoses, strikingly dramatizes the complexity of both citing and stifling Laura's voice. Although each of its transformations repeats an Ovidian model, only three stress the active participation of the Lady. In the first she lifts the speaker's heart out of his chest, utters two exceptional sentences, and ultimately turns him (like Battus) into a stone; next, she reduces him (like Echo) into a repetitive voice; and finally, she transforms him (like Actaeon) into a stag. The Ovidian models are telling in that they all either limit or negate a voice: Mercury says to Battus, "Whoever you are, my man, if anyone should ask you about some cattle, say that you have not seen them" (*Metamorphoses* 2.692–94); Juno says to Echo, "That tongue by which I have been tricked shall have its power curtailed and enjoy the briefest use of speech" (*Metamorphoses* 3.366–67); and Diana says to Actaeon, "Now you are free to tell ["narres . . . licet"] that you have seen me unveiled—if you can tell ["narrare"]" (*Metamorphoses* 3.192–93).[29]

The first model permits speech, but insists that it not be true, and, when disobeyed, denies it; the second, by reducing speech to repetition, eliminates its generative capacity; and the third, through irony, does away with it altogether. In Ovid's retelling of that third encounter, Diana is the only person to speak once Actaeon has had his first glimpse of her: "*narrare*" is her word; she pronounces it; she even repeats it. Although she cannot (would not?) prevent him from seeing, she can prevent him from telling. Consequently, that Petrarch erases both her speech and the verbal object of her interdiction (*narrare*) from his own narration is significant. A review of the evolution of the Diana/Actaeon sequence of *Rime sparse* 23, a text at many points explicit in its verbal echoing of Ovid, shows that "I shall speak ["dirò"] the truth" initiates the primary and final versions of line 156: two intermediate variants read "I tell ["narro"] the truth."[30] What that rejected present, *narro*, affirms, in a mode perhaps too obvious to be acceptable even to Petrarch, is that his speaker as Actaeon does precisely what Diana forbids: "'Make no word of this,'" said the "powerful Lady" of a preceding stanza (*RS*, 23. 74, 35). Not only does Petrarch's Actaeon thus nullify Diana's act, he repeats her admonition in so doing; by the time we arrive at the end that "crowns" his song, her speech has been written out and his has been written in. To the measure that he continues to praise her beauties, he persists in inverting the traditional economy of the mythical exchange; he persists in offending her:

"Not that I do not see how much my praise injures you [the eyes]; but I cannot resist the great desire that is in me since I saw what no thought can equal, let alone speech, mine or others' " (*RS*, 71.16–21).

Silencing Diana is an emblematic gesture; it suppresses a voice, and it casts generations of would-be Lauras in a role predicated upon the muteness of its player.[31] A modern Actaeon affirming himself as poet cannot permit Ovid's angry goddess to speak her displeasure and deny his voice; his speech requires her silence. Similarly, he cannot allow her to dismember his body; instead he repeatedly, although reverently, scatters hers throughout his scattered rhymes.

NOTES

An early version of this paper was shared with the University Seminar on Feminist Inquiry at Dartmouth College; I sincerely appreciate the time, attention, and suggestions of its members. I am particularly indebted to Richard Corum, Jonathan Goldberg, Katherine Hayles, Marianne Hirsch, David Kastan, Stephen Orgel, Esther Rashkin, Christian Wolff and Holly Wulff for their contributions.

1. On this "thoroughly self-conscious fashion," see Elizabeth Cropper, "On Beautiful Women, Parmigianino, *Petrarchismo*, and the Vernacular Style," *Art Bulletin* 58 (1976): 374–94. Cropper shares many of the observations on Petrarchan descriptive technique outlined in the following paragraph (see pp. 385–86). I am indebted to David Quint for bringing this excellent essay to my attention.

2. Description is, of course, always fragmentary in that it is by nature enumerative. Petrarch, however, systematically avoids those structures that would mask fragmentation. On enumeration and the descriptive text, see Roland Barthes, *S/Z* (Paris, 1970), pp. 120–22.

3. For lengthy discussions of these qualities of Petrarchan descriptions, see Robert Durling, "Petrarch's 'Giovene donna sotto un verde lauro,' " *Modern Language Notes* 86 (1971): 1–20, and John Freccero, "The Fig Tree and the Laurel: Petrarch's Poetics," *Diacritics* 5 (Spring 1975): 34–40.

4. On Petrarch's role in the popularization of this *topos*, see James V. Mirollo, "In Praise of '*La bella mano*': Aspects of Late Renaissance Lyricism," *Comparative Literature Studies* 9 (1972): 31–43. See also James Villas, "The Petrarchan Topos 'Bel piede': Generative Footsteps," *Romance Notes* 11 (1969): 167–73.

5. Italics and translation mine.

6. For a recent summary and bibliography of the place of myth in the Renaissance text, see Leonard Barkan, "Diana and Actaeon: The Myth as Synthesis," *English Literary Renaissance* 10 (1980).

7. *Petrarch's Lyric Poems: The "Rime sparse" and Other Lyrics*, trans. and ed. Robert M. Dulling (Cambridge, Mass., 1976), *canzone* 23, ll. 30–31: all further references to the *Rime sparse* will be included in the text with poem and line number in parentheses and with Durling's translation. For recent analyses of *Rime sparse* 23, see Dennis Dutschke, *Francesco Petrarca: Canzone XXIII from First to Final Version* (Ravenna, 1977), and Albert J. Rivero, "Petrarch's 'Net dolce tempo de la prima etade.' " *Modern Language Notes* 94 (1979): 92–112.

8. For an extremely useful comparison of the Ovidian and Petrarchan narrations of this scene, see Dutschke, *Francesco Petrarca*, pp. 200–209. On the relationship between midday and sexuality in this myth, see Nicolas J. Perella, *Midday in Italian Literature: Variations on an Archetypal Theme* (Princeton, N.J., 1979), pp. 8–9.

9. Ovid, *Metamorphoses*, ed. and trans. Frank J. Miller, 2 vols. (1921; London, 1971), bk. 3, ll. 192–93; all further references to the *Metamorphoses* will be included in the text with book and line number in parentheses. The quotations from this work are based upon but do not entirely reproduce Miller's edition.

10. On the use of the present tense in relation to Actaeon, see Durling's introduction to *Petrarch's Lyric Poems*, p. 28.

11. On the association of Actaeon and Orpheus, see ibid., p. 29. On Actaeon and Pentheus, see Norman O. Brown, "Metamorphoses II: Actaeon," *American Poetry Review* 1 (November/December 1972): 38.

12. Barkan, "Diana and Actaeon," p. 335. On the use of this myth in medieval lyric, see Stephen C. Nichols, Jr., "Rhetorical Metamorphosis in the Troubadour Lyric," in *Mélanges de langue et de littérature médiévales offerts à Pierre Le Gentil, Professeur à la Sorbonne, par ses collègues, ses élèves, et ses amis*, ed. Jean Dufournet and Daniel Poirion (Paris, 1973), pp. 569–85.

13. See Giuseppe Mazzotta, "The *Canzoniere* and the Language of the Self," *Studies in Philology* 73 (1978): 277.

14. The connection between these verses and the Diana /Actaeon myth is noted by Durling, *The Figure of the Poet in Renaissance Epic* (Cambridge, Mass., 1965), p. 73. See also my "Re-membering Dante: Petrarch's 'Chiare, fresche et dolci acque,'" *Modern Language Notes* 96 (1981): 8–9.

15. See Mazzotta, "The *Canzoniere*," pp. 282–84.

16. Freccero, "The Fig Tree," pp. 38–39.

17. See, e.g., Durling, introduction to *Petrarch's Lyric Poems*; Freccero, "The Fig Tree"; and Mazzotta, *Canzoniere*."

18. For the phrase "poetics of fragmentation," see Mazzotta, "The *Canzoniere*," p. 274.

19. Josette Féral, "Antigone or *The Irony of the Tribe*," trans. Alice Jardine and Tom Gora, *Diacritics* 8 (Fall 1978): 7. I am indebted to Elizabeth Abel for calling this quotation to my attention. See also Durling, introduction to *Petrarch's Lyric Poems*, p. 21, and Mazzotta, "The *Canzoniere*," p. 273.

20. See Barkan, "Diana and Actaeon," pp. 320–22, and Brown, "Metamorphoses II," p. 40.

21. See Barkan, "Diana and Actaeon," pp. 321, 343; Brown, "Metamorphoses II," p. 39; Durling, introduction to *Petrarch's Lyric Poems*, p. 31; and Mazzotta, "The *Canzoniere*," pp. 274, 282.

22. This myth has often been used to point to relationships of power through play on the words *cervus/servus*, *cerf/serf* (stag/slave): see Barkan "Diana and Actaeon," p. 328. The identification of Diana with women in political power is perhaps best exemplified by the frequent representation of Elizabeth I as Diana; see Barkan, pp. 332–35.

23. Howard Daniel, *Encyclopedia of Themes and Subjects in Painting*, s.v. "Actaeon" (London, 1971). Daniel's point is, of course, supported by the tradition identifying Actaeon's hounds with the Law, with his conscience: "Remorse, the bite of a mad dog, Conscience, the superego, the introjected father or animal: now eating us even as we ate him" (Brown, "Metamorphoses II," p. 39); see also Perella, *Midday in Italian Literature*, p. 42. On Actaeon as "unmanned" or castrated, see Barkan, "Diana and Actaeon," pp. 350–51.

24. See Daniel, "Actaeon." On the casting of the male spectator (reader) in the role of the voyeur, see also John Berger, *Ways of Seeing* (New York, 1977), pp. 45–64, and Laura Mulvey, "Visual Pleasure and Narrative Cinema," *Screen* 16 (Autumn 1975): 6–18. On women conditioned by patriarchal culture to see themselves as "sights," see Jessica Benjamin, "The Bonds of Love: Rational Violence and Erotic Domination," in *The Future of Difference*, ed. Hester Eisenstein and Alice Jardine (Boston, 1980), p. 52, and Berger, *Ways of Seeing*, pp. 46–51

25. I am, of course, alluding to the etymological associations and not the definition of the verb *mirare* ("to stare").

26. Mazzotta, "The *Canzoniere*," pp. 282–84. See also Durling, introduction to *Petrarch's Lyric Poems*, pp. 31–32.

27. For recent analyses of the play on Laura/*lauro*, see Francois Rigolot, "Nature and Function of Paronomasia in the *Canzoniere*," *Italian Quarterly* 18 (Summer 1974): 29–36, and Marga Cottino-Jones, "The Myth of Apollo and Daphne in Petrarch's *Canzoniere*: The Dynamics and Literary Function of "Transformation," in *Francis Petrarch, Six Centuries Later: A Symposium*, ed. Aldo Scaglione (Chapel Hill, N.C., 1975), pp. 152–76.

28. Cropper, "On Beautiful Women," p. 376.

29. On the Diana/Actaeon myth and "the danger of losing the poetic voice, see Mazzotta, "The *Canzoniere*," p. 278; see also Dulling, introduction to *Petrarch's Lyric Poems*, p. 28.

30. See Dutschke, *Francesco Petrarca*, pp. 196–98.

31. For the problem of women writing within the constraints of the Petrarchan tradition, see Ann R. Jones, "Assimilation with a Difference: Renaissance Women Poets and Literary Influence," *Yale French Studies* no. 62 (October 1981); on the impact of another masculine lyric tradition on women poets, see Margaret Homans, *Women Writers and Poetic Identity: Dorothy Wordsworth, Emily Brontë and Emily Dickinson* (Princeton, N.J., 1980), pp. 12–40. Laura Mulvey comments on the silencing of women in her rereading of a different medium, film: "Woman then stands in patriarchal culture as signifier for the male other, bound by a symbolic order in which man can live out his phantasies and obsessions through linguistic command by imposing them on the silent image of woman still tied to her place as bearer of meaning, not maker of meaning" ("Visual Pleasure," p. 7).

9.2 Gender, Creativity, and the Woman Poet (1979)

Sandra M. Gilbert and Susan Gubar

Alas! a woman that attempts the pen,
Such an intruder on the rights of men,
Such a presumptuous Creature, is esteem'd,
The fault can by no vertue be redeem'd . . .
How are we fal'n, fal'n by mistaken rules?
And Education's, more than Nature's fools,
Debarr'd from all improve-ments of the mind,
And to be dull, expected and dessigned . . . .[1]

These lines were written by Anne Finch, the Countess of Winchilsea, in the late seventeenth century, and more than two centuries later even so successful an artist as Virginia Woolf was still speculating on their meaning. If Shakespeare had had a "wonderfully gifted sister," she mused in 1928, society would have sternly discouraged her literary aspirations. Judith Shakespeare might have run off to London to become a poet-playwright, for "the birds that sang in the hedge were not more musical than she." Yet she would have quickly found such a vocation impossible, "and so—who shall measure the heat and violence of the poet's heart when caught and tangled in a woman's body?—she killed herself one winter night and lies buried at some crossroads where the omnibuses now stop outside the Elephant and Castle."[2] Yet of course Shakespeare did—and does—have many sisters. Perhaps none have attained the equality of renown Anne Finch and Virginia Woolf envisioned, but neither are they all buried at an obscure crossroads. Some have lived and worked in other lands, other times—Shakespeare's foreign relatives or older sisters, to pursue the metaphor. Others, akin in language as well as vocation to the poet himself, have struggled to perfect their art in England and America.

It is the purpose of this anthology [*Shakespeare's Sisters*: *Feminist Essays on Women Poets*] to examine the achievement of representative members of this last group of poets, Shakespeare's English-speaking sisters, and to examine it specifically in relation to all those patriarchal social strictures, all those obstacles that discourage women from attempting the pen, which Anne Finch's lines describe and Virginia Woolf's parable defines. For women poets, from Finch herself to Sylvia Plath and Adrienne Rich, have known very well that they are *women* poets. Readers, critics, and sometimes even friends have reminded them that to attempt the pen has historically been a subversive act for a woman in a culture which assumes that, as Poet Laureate Robert Southey told Charlotte Brontë in 1837, "Literature cannot be the business of a woman's life, and it out not to be."[3]

Significantly, Southey's remark was a response not to Brontë's fiction but to some poems she had sent him. While a number of fine feminist studies have recently explored the relationship between gender and creativity in the work of women novelists,[4] the problems as well as the triumphs of women poets in England and America still remain inexplicably obscure. Yet the obstructions such literary women confronted were even more formidable than those faced by female novelists. Though fiction writers like the Brontë sisters and George Eliot were often measured against an intellectual double standard that made them the targets of what Elaine Showalter wittily calls "*ad feminam* criticism,"[5] their literary efforts evidently seemed less problematical than those of women poets, even to misogynistic readers. Their art was not actively encouraged, but it was generally understood by the late eighteenth century and throughout the nineteenth century that under conditions of pressing need a woman might have to live by her pen. As a professional novelist, however, whether she was delighting her audience with fantasies of romance or instructing it with didactic moral tales, such a woman was not so different from her less gifted but equally needy sisters who went out into the world to earn their livings by "instructing" as governesses (if they were respectable) or "delighting" as actresses (if they were less respectable). As Woolf notes in *A Room of One's Own*, moreover, the realistic novel, with its appetite for physical and social detail, requires precisely the sort of reportorial skill women could develop even in their own drawing rooms, and since the discrimination of the passions was supposedly a special female talent, female novelists could use their socially sanctioned sensitivity to manners and morals in the delineation of characters or the construction of plots. Indeed, beginning with Aphra Behn and burgeoning with Fanny Burney, Anne Radcliffe, Maria Edgeworth, and Jane Austen, the English novel seems to have been in some sense a female invention.

Despite a proliferation of literary ancestresses, however, Elizabeth Barrett Browning commented mournfully in 1845 that "England has had many learned women . . . and yet where are the poetesses? . . . I look everywhere for grandmothers, and see none."[6] In 1862, moreover, Emily Dickinson, articulating in another way the same distinction between women's prose and women's verse, expressed similar bewilderment. Complaining that

> They shut me up in Prose—
> As when a little Girl
> They put me in the Closet—
> Because they liked me "still"—[7]

she implied a recognition that poetry by women was in some sense inappropriate, unladylike, immodest. And in 1928, as if commenting on both Barrett Browning's comment and Dickinson's complaint, Woolf invented a tragic history for her "Judith Shakespeare" because she so deeply believed that it is "the poetry that is still denied outlet."

Why did these three literary women consider poetry by women somehow forbidden or problematical? Woolf herself, after all, traced the careers of Anne Finch and Margaret Cavendish, admired the "wild poetry" of the Brontës, noted that Barrett Browning's verse-novel *Aurora Leigh* had poetic virtues no prose work could rival, and spoke almost with awe of Christina Rossetti's "complex song."[8] Why, then, did she feel that "Judith Shakespeare" was "caught and tangled," "denied," suffocated, self-buried, or not yet born? We can begin to find answers to these questions by briefly reviewing some of the ways in which representative male readers and critics have reacted to poetry by representative women like Barrett Browning and Dickinson.

Introducing *The Selected Poems of Emily Dickinson* in 1959, James Reeves quoted "a friend" as making a statement which expresses the predominant attitude of many male *literati* toward poetry by women even more succinctly than Woolf's story did: "A friend who is also a literary critic has suggested, not perhaps quite seriously, that 'woman poet' is a contradiction in terms."[9] In other words, from what Woolf would call the "masculinist" point of view, the very nature of lyric poetry is inherently incompatible with the nature or essence of femaleness. Remarks by other "masculinist" readers and critics elaborate on the point. In the midst of favorably reviewing the work of his friend Louise Bogan, for instance, Theodore Roethke detailed the various "charges most frequently leveled against poetry by women." Though his statement begins by pretending objectivity, it soon becomes clear that he himself is making such accusations:

> Two of the [most frequent] charges . . . are lack of range—in subject matter, in emotional tone—and lack of a sense of humor. And one could, in individual instances among writers of real talent, add other aesthetic and moral shortcomings: the spinning out; the embroidering of trivial themes; a concern with the mere surfaces of life—that special province of the feminine talent in prose—hiding from the real agonies of the spirit; refusing to face up to what existence is; lyric or religious posturing; running between the boudoir and the altar; stamping a tiny foot against God or lapsing into a sententiousness that implies the author has re-invented integrity; carrying on excessively about Fate, about time; lamenting the lot of the woman; caterwauling; writing the same poem about fifty times, and so on. . . .[10]

Even a cursory reading of this passage reveals its inconsistency: women are taxed for both triviality and sententiousness, for both silly superficiality and melodramatic "carrying on" about profound subjects. More significantly, however, is the fact that Roethke attacks female poets for doing just what male poets do—that is, for writing about God, fate, time, and integrity; for writing obsessively on the same themes or subjects, and so forth. But his language suggests that it is precisely the sex of these literary women that subverts their art. Shaking a Promethean male fist "against God" is one perfectly reasonable aesthetic strategy, apparently, but stamping a "tiny" feminine foot is quite another.

Along similar lines, John Crowe Ransom noted without disapproval in a 1956 essay about Emily Dickinson that "it is a common belief among readers (among men readers at least) that the woman poet as a type . . . makes flights into nature rather too easily and upon errands which do not have metaphysical importance enough to justify so radical a strategy."[11] Elsewhere in the same essay, describing Dickinson as "a little home-keeping person" he speculated that "hardly . . . more" than "one out of seventeen" of her 1,775 poems are destined to become "public property," and observed that her life "was a humdrum affair of little distinction," although "in her Protestant community the gentle spinsters had their assured and useful place in the family circle, they had what was virtually a vocation."[12] (But how, he seemed to wonder, could someone with so humdrum a social destiny have written great poetry?) Equally concerned with the problematical relationship between Dickinson's poetry and her femaleness—with, that is, what seemed to be an irreconcilable conflict between her "gentle" spinsterhood and her fierce art—R. P. Blackmur decided in 1937 that "she was neither a professional poet nor an amateur; she was a private poet who wrote indefatigably, as some women cook or knit. Her gift for words and the cultural predicament of her time drove her to poetry instead of antimacassars."[13]

Even in 1971, male readers of Dickinson brooded upon this apparent dichotomy of poetry and femininity. John Cody's *After Great Pain* perceptively analyzes the suffering that many of Dickinson's critics and biographers have refused to acknowledge. But his conclusion emphasizes what he too sees as the incompatibility between womanly fulfillment and passionate art.

> Had Mrs. Dickinson been warm and affectionate, more intelligent, effective, and admirable, Emily Dickinson early in life would probably have identified with her, become domestic, and adopted the conventional woman's role. She would then have become a church member, active in community affairs, married, and had children. The creative potentiality would of course still have been there, but would she have discovered it? What motivation to write could have replaced the incentive given by suffering and loneliness? If in spite of her wifely and motherly duties, she had still felt the need to express herself in verse, what would her subject matter have been? Would art have sprung from fulfillment, gratification, and completeness as abundantly as it did from longing, frustration, and deprivation?[14]

Interestingly, these questions restate an apparently very different position taken by Ransom fifteen years earlier: "Most probably [Dickinson's] poem's would not have amounted to much if the author had not finally had her own romance, enabling her to fulfill herself like any other woman." Though Ransom speaks of the presence and "fulfillment" of "romance," while Cody discusses its tormenting absence, neither imagines that poetry itself could possibly constitute a woman's fulfillment. On the contrary, both assume that the art of a woman poet must in some sense arise from "romantic" feelings (in the popular, sentimental sense), arise either in response to a real romance or as compensation for a missing one.

In view of this critical obsession with womanly "fulfillment"—clearly a nineteenth-century notion redefined by twentieth-century thinkers for their own purposes—it is not surprising to find out that when poetry by women *has* been praised it has usually been praised for being "feminine," just as it has been blamed for being deficient in "femininity." Elizabeth Barrett Browning, for instance, the most frequently analyzed, criticized, praised, and blamed woman poet of her day, was typically admired "because of her understanding of the depth, tenderness, and humility of the love which is given by women,"[15] and because "she was a poet in every fibre of her but adorably feminine. . . ."[16] As the "Shakespeare of her sex,"[17] moreover, she was especially respected for being "pure and lovely" in her "private life," since "the lives of women of genius have been so frequently sullied by sin . . . that their intellectual gifts are [usually] a curse rather than a blessing."[18] Significantly, however, when Barrett Browning attempted unromantic, "unfeminine" political verse in *Poems before Congress*, her collection of 1860, at least one critic decided that she had been "seized with a . . . fit of insanity," explaining that "to bless and not to curse is a woman's function. . . ."[19]

As this capsule review of *ad feminam* criticism suggests, there is evidently something about lyric poetry by women that invites meditations on female fulfillment or, alternatively, on female insanity. In devising a story for "Judith Shakespeare," Woolf herself was after all driven to construct a violent plot that ends with her suicidal heroine's burial beneath a bus-stop near the Elephant and Castle. Symbolically speaking, Woolf suggests, modern London, with its technological fumes and its patriarchal roar, grows from the grim crossroads where this mythic woman poet lies dead. And as if to reinforce the morbid ferocity of such imagery, Woolf adds that whenever, reading history or listening to gossip, we hear of witches and magical wise women, "I think we are on the track of . . . a suppressed poet . . . who dashed her brains out on the moor or mopped and mowed about the highways crazed with the torture that her gift had put her to." For though "the original [literary] impulse was to poetry," and "the 'supreme head of song' was a poetess," literary women in England and America have almost universally elected to write novels rather than poems for fear of precisely the madness Woolf attributes to Judith Shakespeare. "Sure the poore woman is a little distracted," she quotes a contemporary of Margaret Cavendish's as remarking: "Shee could never be soe rediculous else as to venture at writeing books and in verse too, if I should not sleep this fortnight I should not come to that."[20] In other words, while the woman novelist, safely shut in prose, may fantasize about freedom with a certain impunity (since she constructs purely fictional alternatives to the difficult reality she inhabits), it appears that the woman poet must in some sense become her own heroine, and that in enacting the diabolical role of witch or wise woman she literary or figuratively risks a melodramatic death at the crossroads of tradition and genre, society and art.

Without pretending to exhaust a profoundly controversial subject, we should note here that there are a number of generic differences between novel-writing and verse-writing which do support the kinds of distinctions Woolf's story implies. For one thing, as we noted earlier, novel-writing is a useful (because lucrative) occupation, while poetry, except perhaps for the narrative poetry of Byron and Scott, has traditionally had little monetary value. That novel-writing was and is conceivably an occupation to live by has always, however, caused it to seem less intellectually or spiritually valuable than verse-writing, of all possible literary occupations the one to which European culture has traditionally assigned the highest status. Certainly when Walter Pater in 1868 defined the disinterested ecstasy of art for his contemporaries by noting that "art comes to you proposing frankly to give nothing but the highest quality to your moments as they pass, and simply for those moments' sake," he was speaking of what he earlier called "the poetic passion," alluding to works like the Odes of Keats rather than the novels of Thackeray or George Eliot. Verse-writing—the product of mysterious "inspiration," divine afflatus, bardic ritual—has historically been a holy vocation.[21] Before the nineteenth century the poet had a nearly priestly role, and "he" had a wholly priestly role after Romantic thinkers had appropriated the vocabulary of theology for the realm of aesthetics. But if in Western culture women cannot be priests, then how—since poets are priests—can they be poets? The question may sound sophistic, but there is a good deal of evidence that it was and has been consciously or unconsciously asked, by men and women alike, as often as women suffering from "the poetic passion" have appeared in the antechambers of literature.

As Woolf shows, though, novel-writing is not just a "lesser" and therefore more suitably female occupation because it is commercial rather than aesthetic, practical rather than priestly. Where novel-writing depends upon reportorial observation, verse-writing has traditionally required aristocratic education. "Learn . . . for ancient rules a just esteem; / To copy Nature is to copy them," Alexander Pope admonished aspiring critics and (by implication) poets in 1709, noting that "Nature and Homer" are "the same."[22] As if dutifully acquiescing, even the fiery iconoclast Percy Bysshe Shelley assiduously translated Aeschylus and other Greek "masters." As Western society defines "him," the lyric poet must have aesthetic models, must in a sense speak the esoteric language of literary forms. She or he cannot simply record or describe the phenomena of nature and society, for literary theorists have long believed that, in poetry, nature must be mediated through tradition—that is, through an education in "ancient rules." But of course, as so many women writers learned with dismay, the traditional classics of Greek and Latin—meaning the distilled Platonic essence of Western literature, history, philosophy—constituted what George Eliot called "spheres of masculine learning" inalterably closed to women except under the most extraordinary circumstances. Interestingly, only Barrett Browning, of all the major women poets, was enabled—by her invalid seclusion, her sacrifice of ordinary pleasures—seriously to study "the ancients." Like Shelley, she translated Aeschylus' *Prometheus Bound*, and she went even further, producing an unusually learned study of the little-known Greek Christian poets. What is most interesting about Barrett Browning's skill as a classicist, however, is the fact that it was barely noticed in her own day and has been almost completely forgotten in ours.

Suzanne Juhasz has recently and persuasively spoken of the "double bind" of the woman poet,[23] but it seems almost as if there is a sort of triple bind here. On the one hand, the woman poet who learns a "just esteem" for Homer is ignored or even mocked—as, say, the eighteenth century "Blue Stockings" were. On the other hand, the woman poet who does not (because she is not allowed to) study Homer is held in contempt. On the third hand, however, whatever alternative tradition the woman poet attempts to substitute for "ancient rules" is subtly devalued. Ransom, for instance, asserts that Dickinson's meters, learned from "her father's hymnbook," are all based upon "Folk Line, the popular form of verse and the oldest in our language," adding that "the great classics of this meter are the English ballads and Mother Goose." Our instinctive sense that this is a backhanded compliment is confirmed when he remarks that "Folk Line is disadvantageous . . . if it denies to the poet the use of English Pentameter," which is "the staple of what we may call the studied or 'university' poetry, and . . . is capable of containing and formalizing many kinds of substantive content which would be too complex for Folk Line. Emily Dickinson appears never to have tried it."[24] If we read "pentameter" here as a substitute for "ancient rules," then we can see that once again "woman" and "poet" are being defined as contradictory terms.

Finally, and perhaps most crucially, where the novel allows—even encourages—just the self-effacing withdrawal society has traditionally fostered in women, the lyric poem is in some sense the utterance of a strong and assertive "I." Artists from Shakespeare to Dickinson, Yeats, and T. S. Eliot have of course qualified this "I," emphasizing, as Eliot does, the "extinction of personality" involved in a poet's construction of an artful, masklike persona, or insisting, as Dickinson did, that the speaker of poems is a "supposed person."[25] But, nevertheless, the central self that speaks or sings a poem must be forcefully defined, whether "she"/"he" is real or imaginary. If the novelist, therefore, inevitably sees herself from the *outside*, as an object, a character, a small figure in a large pattern, the lyric poet must be continually aware of herself from the *inside*, as a subject, a speaker: she must be, that is, assertive, authoritative, radiant with powerful feelings while at the same time absorbed in her own consciousness—and hence, by definition, profoundly "unwomanly," even freakish. For the woman poet, in other words, the contradictions between her vocation and her gender might well become insupportable, impelling her to deny one or the other, even (as in the case of "Judith Shakespeare") driving her to suicide. For, as Woolf puts it, "who shall measure the heat and violence of the poet's heart when caught and tangled in a woman's body?"

In 1935 Louise Bogan wrote to John Hall Wheelock, her editor, to report that

> Malcolm Cowley, a month or so ago asked me to edit an anthology of female verse, to be used in the pages of the New Republic. They have as you know, already published groups of Middle-Western verse, and what not. They are now about to divide mankind horizontally rather than vertically, sexually rather than geographically. As you might have expected, I turned this pretty job down; the thought of corresponding with a lot of female songbirds made me acutely ill. It is hard enough to bear with my own lyric side.[26]

Obviously, as Gloria Bowles has pointed out, Bogan had internalized just those patriarchal interdictions that have historically caused women poets from Finch to Plath anxiety and guilt about attempting the pen. In a sense, then, using Bogan's problem as a paradigm, we might say that at its most painful the history of women's poetry is a story of struggle against the sort of self-loathing her letter represents, while at its most victorious this literary history is a chronicle of the evolutionary processes through which "Judith Shakespeare" learned over and over again that, in Plath's words, "I / Have a self to recover, a queen."[27]

Until quite recently most criticism of poetry by women has failed to transcend the misogyny implicit both in Bogan's letter and in the sexist definitions her letter incorporates, just as it has failed to explore in any but the most superficial ways the crucial relationship between sexual identity and art. When not relegated to oblivion, women poets are often still sentimentally pictured as "disappointed in love," as the neurotic old maids or romantic schoolgirls of literature. That the themes, structures, and images of their art may have been at least in part necessitated either by the special constrictions of their sexual role or by their uncertain relationship to an overwhelmingly "masculinist" literary tradition is a matter that feminist critics have just begun to explore.

NOTES

1. Anne Finch, "The Introduction," in *The Poems of Anne Countess of Winchilsea*, ed. Myra Reynolds (Chicago: University of Chicago Press, 1903), pp. 4–5.

2. Virginia Woolf, *A Room of One's Own* (New York: Harcourt Brace and World, 1929), pp. 48–52.

3. Letter to Charlotte Brontë, March 1837, quoted in Winifred Gérin, *Charlotte Brontë* (Oxford, London, and New York: Oxford University Press, 1967), p. 110.

4. See, for instance, Elaine Showalter, *A Literature of Their Own* (Princeton: Princeton University Press, 1977), Ellen Moers, *Literary Women* (Garden City, N.Y.: Doubleday, 1975), Patricia Meyer Spacks, *The Female Imagination* (New York: Knopf, 1974), and Arlyn Diamond and Lee Edwards, eds., *The Authority of Experience* (Amherst: University of Massachusetts Press, 1977).

5. Showalter, p. 73.

6. *The Letters of Elizabeth Barrett Browning*, ed. Frederick G. Kenyon (2 vols. in 1, New York: Macmillan, 1899), I, 230–32. Compare Woolf's "For we think back through our mothers if we are women. It is useless to go to the great men writers for help, however much one may go to them for pleasure" (*A Room*, p. 79).

7. Thomas Johnson, *The Complete Poems of Emily Dickinson* (Boston: Little, Brown, 1960), #613.

8. See especially "Aurora Leigh" and "I am Christina Rossetti" in *The Second Common Reader* (New York: Harcourt Brace, 1932), pp. 182–92 and 214–21.

9. Reprinted in Richard B. Sewell, ed., *Emily Dickinson: A Collection of Critical Essays* (Englewood Cliffs, N.J.: Prentice-Hall, 1963), p. 120. In fairness to Reeves, we should note that he quotes this statement in order to dispute it.

10. Theodore Roethke, "The Poetry of Louise Bogan," *Selected Prose of Theodore Roethke*, ed. Ralph J. Mills, Jr. (Seattle: University of Washington Press, 1965), pp. 133–34.

11. "Emily Dickinson: A Poet Restored," in Sewall, p. 92.

12. Ibid., p. 89.

13. Quoted in Reeves, p. 119.

14. John Cody, *After Great Pain: The Inner Life of Emily Dickinson* (Cambridge, Mass.: The Belknap Press of Harvard University Press, 1971), p. 495.

15. Gardner B. Taplin, *The Life of Elizabeth Barrett Browning* (New Haven: Yale University Press, 1957), p. 417.

16. *The Edinburgh Review*, vol. 189 (1899), 420–39.

17. Samuel B. Holcombe, "Death of Mrs. Browning," *The Southern Literary Messenger*, 33 (1861), 412–17.

18. *The Christian Examiner*, vol. 72 (1862), 65–88.

19. "Poetic Aberrations," *Blackwood's*, vol. 87 (1860), 490–94.

20. *A Room*, p. 65.

21. See Pater, "Conclusion" to *The Renaissance*, and, for a general discussion of the poet as priest, M. H. Abrams, *Natural Supernaturalism* (New York: Norton, 1971).

22. See Pope, "An Essay on Criticism," Part I, ll. 135–40.

23. Suzanne Juhasz, *Naked and Fiery Forms: Modern American Poetry by Women, a New Tradition* (New York: Harper & Row, 1976), "The Double Bind of the Woman Poet," pp. 1–6.

24. Ransom, ibid.; Sewall, pp. 99–100.

25. See T. S. Eliot, "Tradition and the Individual Talent," and Emily Dickinson, letter to T. W.

Higginson, July 1892, in *The Letters of Emily Dickinson*, Thomas Johnson, ed. (Cambridge, Mass.: The Belknap Press of Harvard University press, 1958), vol. II, p. 412.

26. Letter to John Wheelock, July 1, 1935, in *What the Woman Lived: Selected Letters of Louise Bogan, 1920–1970*, ed. Ruth Limmer (New York: Harcourt Brace Jovanovich, 1973), p. 86. For more detailed commentary, see Gloria Bowles, "Louise Bogan," forthcoming in *Women's Studies*.

27. Plath, "Stings," in *Ariel* (New York: Harper & Row, 1966), p. 62.

Apostrophe, Animation, and Abortion (1987)

9.3

BARBARA JOHNSON

The abortion issue is as alive and controversial in the body politic as it is in the academy and the courtroom.

Jay L. Garfield, *Abortion: Moral and Legal Perspectives*

1.

Although rhetoric can be defined as something politicians often accuse each other of, the political dimensions of the scholarly study of rhetoric have gone largely unexplored by literary critics. What, indeed, could seem more dry and apolitical than a rhetorical treatise? What could seem farther away from budgets and guerrilla warfare than a discussion of anaphora, antithesis, prolepsis, and preterition? Yet the notorious CIA manual on psychological operations in guerrilla warfare ends with just such a rhetorical treatise: an appendix on techniques of oratory which lists definitions and examples for these and many other rhetorical figures.[1] The manual is designed to set up a Machiavellian campaign of propaganda, indoctrination, and infiltration in Nicaragua, underwritten by the visible display and selective use of weapons. Shoot softly, it implies, and carry a big schtick. If rhetoric is defined as language that says one thing and means another, then the manual is in effect attempting to maximize the collusion between deviousness in language and accuracy in violence, again and again implying that targets are most effectively hit when most indirectly aimed at. Rhetoric, clearly, has everything to do with covert operations. But are the politics of violence already encoded in rhetorical figures as such? In other words, can the very essence of a political issue—an issue like, say, abortion—hinge on the structure of a figure? Is there any *inherent* connection between figurative language and questions of life and death, of who will wield and who will receive violence in a given human society?

As a way of approaching this question, I will begin in a much more traditional way by discussing a rhetorical device that has come to seem almost synonymous with the lyric voice: the figure of apostrophe. In an essay in *The Pursuit of Signs*, Jonathan Culler indeed sees apostrophe as an embarrassingly explicit emblem of procedures inherent, but usually better hidden, in lyric poetry as such.[2] Apostrophe in the sense in which I will be using it involves the direct address of an absent, dead, or inanimate being by a first-person speaker:

"O wild West Wind, thou breath of Autumn's being." Apostrophe is thus both direct and indirect: based etymologically on the notion of turning aside, of digressing from straight speech, it manipulates the I/thou structure of direct address in an indirect, fictionalized way. The absent, dead, or inanimate entity addressed is thereby made present, animate, and anthropomorphic. Apostrophe is a form of ventriloquism through which the speaker throws voice, life, and human form into the addressee, turning its silence into mute responsiveness.

"Moesta et Errabunda."

Baudelaire's poem "Moesta et Errabunda,"[3] whose Latin title means "sad and vagabond," raises questions of rhetorical animation through several different grades of apostrophe. Inanimate objects like trains and ships or abstract entities like perfumed paradises find themselves called upon to attend to the needs of a plaintive and restless lyric speaker. Even the poem's title poses questions of life and death in linguistic terms: the fact that Baudelaire here temporarily resuscitates a dead language prefigures the poem's attempts to function as a finder of lost loves. But in the opening lines of the poem, the direct-address structure seems straightforwardly unfigurative: "Tell me, Agatha." This could be called a minimally fictionalized apostrophe, although that is of course its fiction. Nothing at first indicates that Agatha is any more dead, absent, or inanimate than the poet himself.

The poem's opening makes explicit the relation between direct address and the desire for the *other's* voice: "Tell me: *you* talk." But something strange soon happens to the face-to-face humanness of this conversation. What Agatha is supposed to talk about starts a process of dismemberment that might have something to do with a kind of reverse anthropomorphism: "Does your heart sometimes take flight?" Instead of conferring a human shape, this question starts to undo one. Then, too, why the name Agatha? Baudelaire scholars have searched in vain for a biographical referent, never identifying one, but always presuming that one exists. In the Pléiade edition of Baudelaire's complete works, a footnote sends the reader to the only other place in Baudelaire's oeuvre where the name Agathe appears—a page in his *Carnets* where he is listing debts and appointments. This would seem to indicate that Agathe was indeed a real person. What do we know about her? A footnote to the *Carnets* tells us she was probably a prostitute. Why? "See the poem 'Moesta et Errabunda.'" This is a particularly stark example of the inevitable circularity of biographical criticism.

If Agathe is finally only a proper name written on two different pages in Baudelaire, then the name itself must have a function *as* a name. The name is a homonym for the word *agate*, a semiprecious stone. Is Agathe really a stone? Does the poem express the Orphic hope of getting a stone to talk?

In a poem about wandering, taking flight, getting away from "here," it is surprising to find that, structurally, each stanza acts out, not a departure, but a return to its starting point, a repetition of its first line. The poem's structure is at odds with its apparent theme. But we soon see that the object of the voyage is precisely to return—to return to a prior state, planted in the first stanza as virginity, in the second as motherhood (through the image of the nurse and the pun on *mer/mère*), and finally as childhood love and furtive pleasure. The voyage outward in space is a figure for the voyage backward in time. The poem's structure of address backs up, too, most explicitly in the third stanza. The cry apostrophizing train and ship to carry the speaker off leads to a seeming reprise of the opening line, but by this point the inanimate has entirely taken over: instead of addressing Agatha directly, the poem asks whether Agatha's heart ever speaks the line the poet himself has spoken four lines earlier. Agatha is replaced by one of her parts, which itself replaces the speaker. Agatha herself now drops out of the poem, and direct address is temporarily lost too in the grammar of the sentence ("Est-il vrai que . . . "). The poem is as if emptying itself of all its human characters and voices. It seems to be acting out a *loss* of animation—which is in fact its subject: the loss of childhood aliveness brought about by the passage of time. The poem thus enacts in its own temporality the loss of animation it situates in the temporality of the speaker's life.

At this point it launches into a new apostrophe, a new direct address to an abstract, lost state: "Comme vous êtes loin, paradis parfumé." The poem reanimates, addresses an image of fullness and wholeness and perfect correspondence ("Où tout ce que l'on aime est digne d'être aimé"). This height of liveliness, however, culminates strangely in an image of death. The heart that formerly kept trying to fly away now drowns in the moment of reaching its destination ("Où dans la volupté pure le coeur se noie!"). There may be something to gain, therefore, by deferring arrival, as the poem next seems to do by interrupting itself before grammatically completing the fifth stanza. The poem again ceases to employ direct address and ends by asking two drawn-out, self-interrupting questions. Is that paradise now farther away than India or China? Can one call it back and animate it with a silvery voice? This last question—"Peut-on le rappeler avec des cris plaintifs / Et l'animer encore d'une voix argentine?"—is a perfect description of apostrophe itself: a trope which, by means of the silvery voice of rhetoric, calls up and animates the absent, the lost, and the dead. Apostrophe itself, then, has become not just the poem's mode but also the poem's theme. In other words, what the poem ends up wanting to know is not how far away childhood is, but whether its own rhetorical strategies can be effective. The final question becomes: Can this gap be bridged? Can this loss be healed, through language alone?

2.

Shelley's "Ode to the West Wind," which is perhaps the ultimate apostrophaic poem, makes even more explicit the relation between apostrophe and animation. Shelley spends the first three sections demonstrating that the west wind is a figure for the power to animate: it is described as the breath of being, moving everywhere, blowing movement and energy through the world, waking it from its summer dream, parting the waters of the Atlantic, uncontrollable. Yet the wind animates by bringing death, winter, destruction. How do the rhetorical strategies of the poem carry out this program of animation through the giving of death?

The apostrophe structure is immediately foregrounded by the interjections, four times spelled "O" and four times spelled "oh." One of the bridges this poem attempts to build is the bridge between the "O" of the pure vocative, Jakobson's conative function, or the pure presencing of the second person, and the "oh" of pure subjectivity, Jakobson's emotive function, or the pure presencing of the first person.

The first three sections are grammatical amplifications of the sentence "O thou, hear, oh, hear!" All the vivid imagery, all the picture painting, comes in clauses subordinate to this obsessive direct address. But the poet addresses, gives animation, gives the capacity of responsiveness, to the wind, not in order to make it speak but in order to make it listen to him—in order to make it listen to him doing nothing but address *it*. It takes him three long sections to break out of this intense near-tautology. As the fourth section begins, the "I" starts to inscribe itself grammatically (but not thematically) where the "thou" has been. A power struggle starts up for control over the poem's grammar, a struggle which mirrors the rivalry named in such lines as "If even / I were as in my boyhood . . . / . . . I would ne'er have *striven / As thus with thee* in prayer in my sore need." This rivalry is expressed as a comparison: "less free than thou," but then, "one *too like* thee." What does it mean to be "too like"? Time has created a loss of similarity, a loss of animation that has made the sense of similarity even more hyperbolic. In other words, the poet, in becoming less than, less like the wind, somehow becomes more like the wind in his rebellion against the loss of likeness.

In the final section the speaker both inscribes and reverses the structure of apostrophe. In saying "be thou me," he is attempting to restore metaphorical exchange and equality. If apostrophe is the giving of voice, the throwing of voice, the giving of animation, then a poet using it is always in a sense saying to the addressee, "Be thou me." But this implies that a poet has animation to give. And *that* is what this poem is saying is not, or no longer, the case. Shelley's speaker's own sense of animation is precisely what is in doubt, so that he is in effect saying to the wind, "I will animate you so that you will animate, or reanimate, me." "Make me thy lyre . . ."

Yet the wind, which is to give animation, is also the giver of death. The opposition between life and death has to undergo another reversal, another transvaluation. If death could somehow become a positive force for animation, then the poet would thereby create hope for his own "dead thoughts." The animator that will blow his words around the world will also instate the power of their deadness, their deadness *as* power, the place of maximum potential for renewal. This is the burden of the final rhetorical question. Does death necessarily entail rebirth? If winter comes, can spring be far behind? The poem is attempting to appropriate the authority of natural logic—in which spring always does follow winter—in order to claim the authority of cyclic reversibility for its own prophetic powers. Yet because this clincher is expressed in the form of a rhetorical question, it expresses natural certainty by means of a linguistic device that mimics no natural structure and has no stable one-to-one correspondence with a meaning. The rhetorical question, in a sense, leaves the poem in a state of suspended animation. But that, according to the poem, is the state of maximum potential.

Both the Baudelaire and the Shelley, then, end with a rhetorical question that both raises and begs the question of rhetoric. It is as though the apostrophe is ultimately directed toward the reader, to whom the poem is addressing Mayor Koch's question: "How'm I doing?" What is at stake in both poems is, as we have seen, the fate of a lost child—the speaker's own former self—and the possibility of a new birth or reanimation. In the poems that I will discuss next, these structures of apostrophe, animation, and lost life will take on a very different cast through the foregrounding of the question of motherhood and the premise that the life that is lost may be someone else's.

3.

In Gwendolyn Brooks' poem "The Mother," the structures of address are shifting and complex. In the first line ("Abortions will not let you forget"), there is a "you" but there is no "I." Instead, the subject of the sentence is the word "abortions," which thus assumes a position of grammatical control over the poem. As entities that disallow forgetting, the abortions are not only controlling but animate and anthropomorphic, capable of treating persons as objects. While Baudelaire and Shelley addressed the anthropomorphized other in order to repossess their lost selves, Brooks is representing the self as eternally addressed and possessed by the lost, anthropomorphized other. Yet the self that is possessed here is itself already a "you," not an "I." The "you" in the opening lines can be seen as an "I" that has become alienated, distanced from itself, and combined with a generalized other, which includes and feminizes the reader of the poem. The grammatical I/thou starting point of traditional apostrophe has been replaced by a structure in which the speaker is simultaneously eclipsed, alienated, and confused with the addressee. It is already clear that something has happened to the possibility of establishing a clear-cut distinction in this poem between subject and object, agent and victim.

The second section of the poem opens with a change in the structure of address. "I" takes up the positional place of "abortions," and there is temporarily no second person.

The first sentence narrates: "I have heard in the voices of the wind the voices of my dim killed children." What is interesting about this line is that the speaker situates the children's voices firmly in a traditional romantic locus of lyric apostrophe—the voices of the wind, Shelley's west wind, say, or Wordsworth's "gentle breeze."[4] Gwendolyn Brooks, in other words, is here rewriting the male lyric tradition, textually placing aborted children in the spot formerly occupied by all the dead, inanimate, or absent entities previously addressed by the lyric. And the question of animation and anthropomorphism is thereby given a new and disturbing twist. For if apostrophe is said to involve language's capacity to give life and human form to something dead or inanimate, what happens when those questions are literalized? What happens when the lyric speaker assumes responsibility for producing the death in the first place, but without being sure of the precise degree of human animation that existed in the entity killed? What is the debate over abortion about, indeed, if not the question of when, precisely, a being assumes a human form?

It is not until line 14 that Brooks' speaker actually addresses the dim killed children. And she does so not directly, but in the form of a self-quotation: "I have said, Sweets, if I sinned . . ." This embedding of the apostrophe appears to serve two functions here, just as it did in Baudelaire: a self-distancing function, and a foregrounding of the question of the adequacy of language. But whereas in Baudelaire the distance between the speaker and the lost childhood is what is being lamented, and a restoration of vividness and contact is what is desired, in Brooks the vividness of the contact is precisely the source of the pain. While Baudelaire suffers from the dimming of memory, Brooks suffers from an inability to forget. And while Baudelaire's speaker actively seeks a fusion between present self and lost child, Brooks' speaker is attempting to fight her way out of a state of confusion between self and other. This confusion is indicated by the shifts in the poem's structures of address. It is never clear whether the speaker sees herself as an "I" or a "you," an addressor or an addressee. The voices in the wind are not created *by* the lyric apostrophe; they rather initiate the need for one. The initiative of speech seems always to lie in the other. The poem continues to struggle to clarify the relation between "I" and "you," but in the end it succeeds only in expressing the inability of its language to do so. By not closing the quotation in its final line, the poem, which began by confusing the reader with the aborter, ends by implicitly including the reader among those aborted—and loved. The poem can no more distinguish between "I" and "you" than it can come up with a proper definition of life.

In line 28, the poem explicitly asks, "Oh, what shall I say, how is the truth to be said?" Surrounding this question are attempts to make impossible distinctions: got / did not get, deliberate / not deliberate, dead / never made. The uncertainty of the speaker's control as a subject mirrors the uncertainty of the children's status as an object. It is interesting that the status of the human subject here hinges on the word "deliberate." The association of deliberateness with human agency has a long (and very American) history. It is deliberateness, for instance, that underlies that epic of separation and self-reliant autonomy, Thoreau's *Walden*. "I went to the woods," writes Thoreau, "because I wished to live deliberately, to front only the essential facts of life."[5] Clearly, for Thoreau, pregnancy was not an essential fact of life. Yet for him as well as for every human being that has yet existed" someone else's pregnancy is the very *first* fact of life. How might the plot of human subjectivity be reconceived (so to speak) if pregnancy rather than autonomy is what raises the question of deliberateness?

Much recent feminist work has been devoted to the task of rethinking the relations between subjectivity, autonomy, interconnectedness, responsibility, and gender. Carol Gilligan's book *In a Different Voice* (and this focus on "voice" is not irrelevant here) studies gender differences in patterns of ethical thinking. The central ethical question analyzed by

Gilligan is precisely the decision whether to have, or not to have, an abortion. The first time I read the book, this struck me as strange. Why, I wondered, would an investigation of gender *differences* focus on one of the questions about which an even-handed comparison of the male and the female points of view is impossible? Yet this, clearly, turns out to be the point: there is difference *because* it is not always possible to make symmetrical oppositions. As long as there is symmetry, one is not dealing with difference but rather with versions of the same. Gilligan's difference arises out of the impossibility of maintaining a rigorously logical binary model for ethical choices. Female logic, as she defines it, is a way of rethinking the logic of choice in a situation in which none of the choices are good. "Believe that even in my deliberateness I was not deliberate": believe that the agent is not entirely autonomous, believe that I can be subject and object of violence at the same time, believe that I have not chosen the conditions under which I must choose. As Gilligan writes of the abortion decision, "The occurrence of the dilemma itself precludes nonviolent resolution."[6] The choice is not between violence and nonviolence, but between simple violence to a fetus and complex, less determinate violence to an involuntary mother and/or an unwanted child.

Readers of Brooks' poem have often read it as an argument against abortion. And it is certainly clear that the poem is not saying that abortion is a good thing. But to see it as making a simple case for the embryo's right to life is to assume that a woman who has chosen abortion does not have the right to mourn. It is to assume that no case *for* abortion can take the woman's feelings of guilt and loss into consideration, that to take those feelings into account is to deny the right to choose the act that produced them. Yet the poem makes no such claim: it attempts the impossible task of humanizing both the mother and the aborted children while presenting the inadequacy of language to resolve the dilemma without violence.

What I would like to emphasize is the way in which the poem suggests that the arguments for and against abortion are structured through and through by the rhetorical limits and possibilities of something akin to apostrophe. The fact that apostrophe allows one to animate the inanimate, the dead, or the absent implies that whenever a being is apostrophized, it is thereby automatically animated, anthropomorphized, "person-ified." (By the same token, the rhetoric of calling makes it difficult to tell the difference between the animate and the inanimate, as anyone with a telephone answering machine can attest.) Because of the ineradicable tendency of language to animate whatever it addresses, rhetoric itself can always have already answered "yes" to the question of whether a fetus is a human being. It is no accident that the antiabortion film most often shown in the United States should be entitled *The Silent Scream*. By activating the imagination to believe in the anthropomorphized embryo's mute responsiveness in exactly the same way that apostrophe does, the film (which is of course itself a highly rhetorical entity) is playing on rhetorical possibilities that are inherent in all linguistically based modes of representation.

Yet the function of apostrophe in the Brooks poem is far from simple. If the fact that the speaker addresses the children at all makes them human, then she must pronounce herself guilty of murder—but only if she discontinues her apostrophe. As long as she addresses the children, she can keep them alive, can keep from finishing with the act of killing them. The speaker's attempt to absolve herself of guilt depends on never forgetting, never breaking the ventriloquism of an apostrophe through which she cannot define her identity otherwise than as the mother eaten alive by the children she has never fed. Who, in the final analysis, exists by addressing whom? The children are a rhetorical extension of the mother, but she, as the poem's title indicates, has no existence apart from her relation to them. It begins to be clear that the speaker has written herself into a poem that she cannot get out of without violence. The violence she commits in the end is to her own language: as the poem ends, the vocabulary shrinks away, words are repeated, nothing but "all" rhymes with "all." The speaker has written herself into silence. Yet hers is not the only silence in the poem: earlier she has said, "You will never . . . silence or buy with a sweet." If sweets are for silencing, then by beginning her apostrophe, "Sweets, if I sinned . . . ," the speaker is already saying that the poem, which exists to memorialize those whose lack of life makes them eternally alive, is also attempting to silence once and for all the voices of the children in the wind. It becomes impossible to tell whether language is what gives life or what kills.

4.

> Women have said again and again "This is my body!" and they have reason to feel angry, reason to feel that it has been like shouting into the wind.
>
> Judith Jarvis Thompson, "A Defense of Abortion"

It is interesting to note the ways in which legal and moral discussions of abortion tend to employ the same terms as those we have been using to describe the figure of apostrophe. Thus, Justice Blackmun, in *Roe v. Wade*: "These disciplines [philosophy, theology, and civil and canon law] variously approached the question in terms of the point at which the embryo or fetus became 'formed' or recognizably human, or in terms of when a 'person' came into being, that is, infused with a 'soul' or 'animated.'"[7] The issue of "fetal personhood" (Garfield and Hennessey, p. 55) is of course a way of bringing to a state of explicit uncertainty the fundamental difficulty of defining personhood in general.[8] Even if the question of defining the nature of "persons" is restricted to the question of understanding what is meant by the word "person" in the United States Constitution (since the Bill of Rights guarantees the rights only of "persons"), there is not at present, and probably will never be, a stable legal definition. Existing discussions of the legality and morality of abortion almost invariably confront, leave unresolved, and detour around the question of the nature and boundaries of human life. As Justice Blackmun puts it in *Roe v. Wade*: "We need not resolve the difficult question of when life begins. When those trained in the respective disciplines of medicine, philosophy, and theology are unable to arrive at any consensus, the judiciary, at this point in the development of man's knowledge, is not in a position to speculate as to the answer" (Garfield and Hennessey, p. 27).

In the case of *Roe v. Wade*, the legality of abortion is derived from the right to privacy—an argument which, as Catherine MacKinnon argues in "*Roe vs. Wade*: A Study in Male Ideology" (Garfield and Hennessey, pp. 45–54), is itself problematic for women, since by protecting "privacy" the courts also protect the injustices of patriarchal sexual arrangements. When the issue is an unwanted pregnancy, some sort of privacy has already, in a sense, been invaded. In order for the personal to avoid being reduced once again to the nonpolitical, privacy, like deliberateness, needs to be rethought in terms of sexual politics. Yet even the attempt to re-gender the issues surrounding abortion is not simple. As Kristin Luker convincingly demonstrates, the debate turns around the claims not only of woman versus fetus or woman versus patriarchal state, but also of woman versus woman:

> Pro-choice and pro-life activists live in different worlds, and the scope of their lives, as both adults and children, fortifies them in their belief that their views on abortion are the more correct, more moral and more reasonable. When added to this is the fact that should "the other side" win, one group of women will see the very real devaluation of their lives

> and life resources, it is not surprising that the abortion debate has generated so much heat and so little light. . . .
>
> . . . Are pro-life activists, as they claim, actually reaching their cherished goal of "educating the public to the humanity of the unborn child"? As we begin to seek an answer, we should recall that motherhood is a topic about which people have very complicated feelings, and because abortion has become the battleground for different definitions of motherhood, neither the pro-life nor the pro-choice movement has ever been "representative" of how most Americans feel about abortion. More to the point, all our data suggest that *neither of these groups will ever be able to be representative.* (Pp. 215, 224)

It is often said, in literary-theoretical circles, that to focus on undecidability is to be apolitical. Everything I have read about the abortion controversy in its present form in the United States leads me to suspect that, on the contrary, the undecidable *is* the political. There is politics precisely because there is undecidability.

And there is also poetry. There are striking and suggestive parallels between the "different voices" involved in the abortion debate and the shifting address-structures of poems like Gwendolyn Brooks' "The Mother." A glance at several other poems suggests that there tends indeed to be an overdetermined relation between the theme of abortion and the problematization of structures of address. In Anne Sexton's "The Abortion," six 3-line stanzas narrate, in the first person, a trip to Pennsylvania where the "I" has obtained an abortion. Three times the poem is interrupted by the italicized lines:

> *Somebody who should have been born*
> *is gone.*

Like a voice-over narrator taking superegoistic control of the moral bottom line, this refrain (or "burden," to use the archaic term for both "refrain" and "child in the womb") puts the first-person narrator's authority in question without necessarily constituting the voice of a separate entity. Then, in the seventh and final stanza, the poem extends and intensifies this split:

> Yes, woman, such logic will lead
> to loss without death. Or say what you meant,
> you coward . . . this baby that I bleed.

Self-accusing, self-interrupting, the narrating "I" turns on herself (or is it someone else?) as "you," as "woman." The poem's speaker becomes as split as the two senses of the word "bleed." Once again, "saying what one means" can be done only by ellipsis, violence, illogic, transgression, silence. The question of who is addressing whom is once again unresolved.

As we have seen, the question of "when life begins" is complicated partly because of the way in which language blurs the boundary between life and death. In "Menstruation at Forty," Sexton sees menstruation itself as the loss of a child ("two days gone in blood")—a child that exists *because* it can be called:

> I was thinking of a son . . .
> You! . . .
> Will you be the David or the Susan?
> . . .
> my carrot, my cabbage,
> I would have possessed you before all women,
> calling your name,
> calling you mine.

The political consequences and complexities of addressing—of "calling"—are made even more explicit in a poem by Lucille Clifton entitled "The Lost Baby Poem." By choosing the word "dropped" ("i dropped your almost body down"), Clifton renders it unclear whether the child has been lost through abortion or through miscarriage. What is clear, however, is that that loss is both mourned and rationalized. The rationalization occurs through the description of a life of hardship, flight, and loss: the image of a child born into winter, slipping like ice into the hands of strangers in Canada, conflates the scene of Eliza's escape in *Uncle Tom's Cabin* with the exile of draft resisters during the Vietnam War. The guilt and mourning occur in the form of an imperative in which the notion of "stranger" returns in the following lines:

if i am ever less than a mountain
for your definite brothers and sisters
. . .
. . . let black men call me stranger
always for your never named sake.

The act of "calling" here correlates a lack of name with a loss of membership. For the sake of the one that cannot be called, the speaker invites an apostrophe that would expel *her* into otherness. The consequences of the death of a child ramify beyond the mother-child dyad to encompass the fate of an entire community. The world that has created conditions under which the loss of a baby becomes desirable must be resisted, not joined. For a black woman, the loss of a baby can always be perceived as a complicity with genocide. The black mother sees her own choice as one of being either a stranger or a rock. The humanization of the lost baby addressed by the poem is thus carried out at the cost of dehumanizing, even rendering inanimate, the calling mother.

Yet each of these poems exists, finally, *because* a child does not.[9] In Adrienne Rich's poem "To a Poet," the rivalry between poems and children is made quite explicit. The "you" in the poem is again aborted, but here it is the mother herself who could be called "dim and killed" by the fact not of abortion but of the institution of motherhood. And again, the structures of address are complex and unstable. The deadness of the "you" cannot be named: not suicide, not murder. The question of the life or death of the addressee is raised in an interesting way through Rich's rewriting of Keats' sonnet on his mortality. While Keats writes, "When I have fears that *I* will cease to be," Rich writes, "and I have fears that *you* will cease to be." If poetry is at stake in both intimations of mortality, what is the significance of this shift from "I" to "you"? On the one hand, the very existence of the Keats poem indicates that the pen *has* succeeded in gleaning something before the brain has ceased to be. No such grammatical guarantee exists for the "you." Death in the Keats poem is as much a source as it is a threat to writing. Hence death, for Keats, could be called the mother of poetry, while motherhood, for Rich, is precisely the death of poetry. The Western myth of the conjunction of word and flesh implied by the word "incarnate" is undone by images of language floating and vanishing in the bowl of the toilet of real fleshly needs. The word is not made flesh; rather, flesh unmakes the mother-poet's word. The difficulty of retrieving the "you" as poet is enacted by the structures of address in the following lines:

I write this   not for you
who fight to write your own
words fighting up the falls
but for another woman   dumb

In saying "I write this not for you," Rich seems almost to be excluding as addressee anyone who could conceivably be reading this poem. The poem is setting aside both the I and the you—the pronouns Benveniste associates with personhood—and reaches instead toward a "she," which belongs in the category of "nonperson." The poem is thus attempting the impossible task of directly addressing not a second person but a third person—a person who, if she is reading the poem, cannot be the reader the poem has in mind. The poem is trying to include what is by its own grammar excluded from it, to animate through language the nonperson, the "other woman." This poem, too, therefore, is bursting the limits of its own language, inscribing a logic that it itself reveals to be impossible—but necessary. Even the divorce between writing and childbearing is less absolute than it appears: in comparing the writing of words to the spawning of fish, Rich's poem reveals itself to be trapped between the inability to combine and the inability to separate the woman's various roles.

In each of these poems, then, a kind of competition is implicitly instated between the bearing of children and the writing of poems. Something unsettling has happened to the analogy often drawn by male poets between artistic creation and procreation. For it is not true that literature contains no examples of male pregnancy. Sir Philip Sidney, in the first sonnet from Astrophel and Stella, describes himself as "great with child to speak," but the poem is ultimately produced at the expense of no literalized child. Sidney's labor pains are smoothed away by a midwifely apostrophe ("'Fool,' said my Muse to me, 'look in thy heart, and write!'"), and by a sort of poetic Caesarian section, out springs the poem we have, in fact, already finished reading.[10] Mallarmé, in "Don du poème," describes himself as an enemy father seeking nourishment for his monstrous poetic child from the woman within apostrophe-shot who is busy nursing a literalized daughter.[11] But since the woman presumably has two breasts, there seems to be enough to go around. As Shakespeare assures the fair young man, "But were some child of yours alive that time, / You should live twice in it and in my rhyme" (sonnet 17). Apollinaire, in his play *Les Mamelles de Tirésias*, depicts woman as a de-maternalized neo-Malthusian leaving the task of childbearing to a surrealistically fertile husband. But again, nothing more disturbing than Tiresian cross-dressing seems to occur. Children are alive and well, and far more numerous than ever. Indeed, in one of the dedicatory poems, Apollinaire indicates that his drama represents a return to health from the literary reign of the *poète maudit*:

> La féconde raison a jailli de ma fable,
> Plus de femme stérile et non plus d'avortons. . . .[12]
>
> [Fertile reason springs out of my fable,
> No more sterile women, no aborted children]

This dig at Baudelaire, among others, reminds us that in the opening poem to *Les Fleurs du mal* ("Benediction"), Baudelaire represents the poet himself as an abortion *manqué*, cursed by the poisonous words of a rejecting mother. The question of the unnatural seems more closely allied with the bad mother than with the pregnant father.

Even in the seemingly more obvious parallel provided by poems written to dead children by male poets, it is not really surprising to find that the substitution of poem for child lacks the sinister undertones and disturbed address exhibited by the abortion poems we have been discussing. Jonson, in "On My First Son," calls his dead child "his best piece of poetry," while Mallarmé, in an only semiguilty *Aufhebung*, transfuses the dead Anatole to the level of an idea. More recently, Jon Silkin has written movingly of the death of a handicapped child ("something like a person") as a change of silence, not a splitting of voice.

And Michael Harper, in "Nightmare Begins Responsibility," stresses the powerlessness and distrust of a black father leaving his dying son to the care of a "white-doctor-who-breathed-for-him-all-night."[13] But again, whatever the complexity of the voices in that poem, the speaker does not split self-accusingly or infra-symbiotically in the ways we have noted in the abortion/motherhood poems. While one could undoubtedly find counterexamples on both sides, it is not surprising that the substitution of art for children should not be inherently transgressive for the male poet. Men have in a sense always had no choice but to substitute something for the literal process of birth. That, at least, is the belief that has long been encoded into male poetic conventions. It is as though male writing were by nature procreative, while female writing is somehow by nature infanticidal.

It is, of course, as problematic as it is tempting to draw general conclusions about differences between male and female writing on the basis of these somewhat random examples. Yet it is clear that a great many poetic effects may be colored according to *expectations* articulated through the gender of the poetic speaker. Whether or not men and women would "naturally" write differently about dead children, there is something about the connection between motherhood and death that refuses to remain comfortably and conventionally figurative. When a woman speaks about the death of children in any sense other than that of pure loss, a powerful taboo is being violated. The indistinguishability of miscarriage and abortion in the Clifton poem indeed points to the notion that *any* death of a child is perceived as a crime committed by the mother, something a mother ought by definition to be able to prevent. That these questions should be inextricably connected to the figure of apostrophe, however, deserves further comment. For there may be a deeper link between motherhood and apostrophe than we have hitherto suspected.

The verbal development of the infant, according to Lacan, begins as a demand addressed to the mother, out of which the entire verbal universe is spun. Yet the mother addressed is somehow a personification, not a person—a personification of presence or absence, of Otherness itself.

> Demand in itself bears on something other than the satisfactions it calls for. It is demand of a presence or of an absence—which is what is manifested in the primordial relation to the mother, pregnant with that Other to be situated *within* the needs that it can satisfy. . . . Insofar as [man's] needs are subjected to demand, they return to him alienated. This is not the effect of his real dependence . . . , but rather the turning into signifying form as such, from the fact that it is from the locus of the Other that its message is emitted.[14]

If demand is the originary vocative, which assures life even as it inaugurates alienation, then it is not surprising that questions of animation inhere in the rhetorical figure of apostrophe. The reversal of apostrophe we noted in the Shelley poem ("animate me") would be no reversal at all, but a reinstatement of the primal apostrophe in which, despite Lacan's disclaimer, there is precisely a link between demand and animation, between apostrophe and life-and-death dependency.[15] If apostrophe is structured like demand, and if demand articulates the primal relation to the mother as a relation to the Other, then lyric poetry itself—summed up in the figure of apostrophe—comes to look like the fantastically intricate history of endless elaborations and displacements of the single cry, "Mama!" The question these poems are asking, then, is what happens when the poet is speaking *as* a mother, a mother whose cry arises out of—and is addressed to—a dead child?

It is no wonder that the distinction between addressor and addressee should become so problematic in poems about abortion. It is also no wonder that the debate about abortion should refuse to settle into a single voice. Whether or not one has ever been a mother, everyone participating in the debate has once been a child. Psychoanalysis, too, is a theory of development from the child's point of view. Rhetorical, psychoanalytical, and political structures are profoundly implicated in one another. The difficulty in all three would seem to reside in the attempt to achieve a full elaboration of any discursive position other than that of child.

NOTES

1. I would like to thank Tom Keenan of Yale University for bringing this text to my attention. The present essay has in fact benefitted greatly from the suggestions of others, among whom I would like particularly to thank Marge Garber, Rachel Jacoff, Carolyn Williams, Helen Vendler, Steven Melville, Ted Morris, Stamos Metzidakis, Steven Ungar, and Richard Yarborough.

2. Jonathan Culler, "Apostrophe," in *The Pursuit of Signs* (Ithaca: Cornell University Press, 1981), pp. 135–154. Cf. also Paul de Man: "Now it is certainly beyond question that the figure of address is recurrent in lyric poetry, to the point of constituting the generic definition of, at the very least, the ode (which can, in turn, be seen as paradigmatic for poetry in general." Paul de Man, "Lyrical Voice in Contemporary Theory," in *Lyric Poetry: Beyond New Criticism*, ed. Chaviva Hošek and Patricia Parker (Ithaca: Cornell University Press, 1985).

3. For complete texts of the poems under discussion, see the Appendix to Chapter 16. The texts cited are taken from the following sources: Charles Baudelaire, *Oeuvres completes* (Paris: Pléiade, 1976); *The Norton Anthology of Poetry* (New York: Norton, 1975), for Shelley; Anne Sexton, *The Complete Poems* (Boston: Houghton Mifflin, 1981); Lucille Clifton, *Good News about the Earth* (New York: Random House, 1972); and Adrienne Rich, *The Dream of a Common Language* (New York: Norton, 1978). The translation of Baudelaire's "Moesta et Errabunda" is my own. Gwendolyn Brooks refused permission to reprint "The Mother," which can be found in Gwendolyn Brooks, *Selected Poems* (New York: Harper & Row, 1963), or in *The Norton Anthology of Literature by Women* (New York: Norton, 1985), or in *The Black Poets* (New York: Bantam, 1971).

4. It is interesting to note that the "gentle breeze," apostrophized as "Messenger" and "Friend" in the 1805–6 *Prelude* (book 1, line 5), is significantly *not* directly addressed in the 1850 version. One might ask whether this change stands as a sign of the much-discussed waning of Wordsworth's poetic inspiration, or whether it is, rather, one of a number of strictly rhetorical shifts that *give the impression* of a wane.

5. Henry David Thoreau, *Walden* (New York: Signet, 1960), p. 66.

6. Carol Gilligan, *In a Different Voice* (Cambridge: Harvard University Press, 1982), p. 94.

7. Quoted in Jay L. Garfield and Patricia Hennessey, eds. *Abortion: Moral and Legal Perspectives* (Amherst: University of Massachusetts Press, 1984), p. 15.

8. Cf. Kristin Luker, *Abortion and the Politics of Motherhood* (Berkeley and Los Angeles: University of California Press, 1984), p. 6.

9. For additional poems dealing with the loss of babies, see the anthology *The Limits of Miracles* collected by Marion Deutsche Cohen (South Hadley, Mass.: Bergin and Garvey, 1985). Sharon Dunn, editor of the *Agni Review*, told me recently that she has in fact noticed that such poems have begun to form almost a new genre.

10. Poems cited here and on the following pages from Sidney, Jonson, and Silkin may be found in *The Norton Anthology of Poetry* (New York: Norton, 1975).

11. Mallarmé, *Oeuvres completes* (Paris: Pléiade, 1945), p. 40.

12. Guillaume Apollinaire, *Les Mamelles de Tirésias*, in *L'Enchanteur pourrissant* (Paris: Gallimard, 1972), p. 101.

13. Michael Harper, title poem in *Nightmare Begins Responsibility* (Urbana: University of Illinois Press, 1975).

14. Jacques Lacan, *Écrits*, trans. Alan Sheridan (New York: Norton, 1977), p. 286.

15. An interesting example of a poem in which an apostrophe confers upon the totally Other the authority to animate the self is Randall Jarrell's "A Sick Child," which ends: "All that I've never thought of—think of me!" In *The Voice That Is Great within Us*, ed. Hayden Carruth (Bantam, 1970), p. 402.

The Homosexual Lyric (1990)

9.4

THOMAS E. YINGLING

> Only in lyric poetry do these direct, sudden flashes of the substance become like lost original manuscripts suddenly made legible; only in lyric poetry is the subject, the vehicle of such experiences, transformed into the sole carrier of meaning, the only true reality.
>
> Georg Lukacs, *The Theory of the Novel*

This chapter will examine in more detail how homosexuality invested itself as the problem of language for Crane [. . .] through an inquiry into how homosexuality and the difficult navigations it announced for the subject affected Crane's imagination of the lyric form as a genre of self-presentation. If former critical theory imagined the lyric as the poetry of a single, unified voice, and imagined the task of criticism as elaboration and reproduction of that voice (somehow without the heresy of paraphrase, where the voice of the critic intervened), more recent critical theory suggests that the lyric interest in voice is itself a trope. As Jonathan Culler writes, "The fundamental aspect of lyric writing" is "to produce an apparently phenomenal world through the figure of voice" ("Changes in the Study of the Lyric," 50). To think of poetry in this manner is to make an irrevocable break with that older model of poetic and psychological realism cited by M. H. Abrams as the meta-physical pattern of the Romantic lyric. Those lyrics, Abrams suggests,

> present a determinate speaker in a particularized, and usually a localized, outdoor setting, whom we overhear as he carries on, in a fluent vernacular which rises easily to a more formal speech, a sustained colloquy, sometimes with himself or with the outer scene, but more frequently with a silent human auditor, present or absent. . . . In the course of this meditation the lyric speaker achieves an insight, faces up to a tragic loss, comes to a moral decision, or resolves an emotional problem. Often the poem rounds upon itself to end where it began, at the outer scene, but with an altered mood and deepened understanding which is the result of the intervening meditation. ("Structure of the Greater Romantic Lyric," 201)

Clearly we can rearticulate Abrams's notions to accommodate a great deal of modern and postmodern poetry that is not at all concerned with localized, outdoor settings nor always turning upon forms of personal crisis ("alienation, dejection, the loss of a 'celestial light' or 'glory' in experiencing the created world" [Abrams, 227]). But Crane's poetry often refuses these categories. His more difficult, "mature" verse in particular (that written in the years 1923–26) breaks the conventions of Romantic lyric, as Allen Grossman has shown, by situating the reader internal to the process of the poem rather than constructing him or her as the imagined auditor. As Grossman suggests, Crane does not figure authenticity of voice by staging the speaker of the poem dramatically at a distance from some more originary voice or presence; that is, his poems do not present their subject(s) in relation to the unrepeatable, as Wordsworth recalls the leech gatherer's speech, Stevens overhears the woman by the sea, or Keats hears the nightingale. Crane's poems, according to

Grossman, are attempts to record the unmediated speech, sea, song, *presence* of poetry itself ("Hart Crane and Poetry," 240–45). We recognize the impossible agenda of this, of course, but, as such, we must think of Crane's as abstract poems—abstract in the same sense as Stein's prose or Arthur Dove's landscapes. And what their abstraction foregrounds most strongly as the problem of the lyric—and as the problem of the modern as well—is the textuality of subjectivity.

We might think of Crane's lyrics from this period as constituting one of the most interesting records of homosexual autobiography in the history of literature. From relatively early homosexual poems such as "Possessions" and "Recitative" (1923) through more advanced inquiries into the problematic of homosexual intersubjectivity such as "Voyages" (written in 1924 and 1925) to later and more symbolic autobiographical texts such as "Passage" (late summer 1925) and "Repose of Rivers" (1926), Crane's lyrics test the structures of identity in a way that makes them theoretical investigations of the subject and not simple exercises in recall and interpretation. Certainly we do not want to posit an evolution into an appropriate or ideologically correct attitude toward homosexuality in Crane's record of lyric autobiography, but there is an arc of development in it that moves from an early, almost intuitive or pre-ideological thinking about subjective homosexual experience toward an insight into the ways in which that experience was mediated by forces and terms bent on constructing it as an unacceptable cultural practice. At this latter point, Crane understands homosexuality not as a subjective experience but as a subjectivity, as part of what Althusser calls "the ideological *recognition* function" ("Ideology," 172); we see this, for instance, in the letter to Winters, and we will see it as well in a number of the poems. According to Althusser, the individual recognizes and mis-recognizes himself as "*really*" or "*not really*" constituted in certain ways according to the interpellations of ideology:

> *all ideology hails or interpellates concrete individuals as concrete subjects*, by the functioning of the category of the subject. . . . Ideology 'acts' or 'functions' in such a way that it 'recruits' subjects among the individuals (it recruits them all), or 'transforms' the individuals into subjects (it transforms them all) by that very precise operation which I have called *interpellation* or hailing, and which can be imagined along the lines of the most commonplace everyday police (or other) hailing: 'Hey, you there!' ("Ideology," 173–74)

We have seen in the last chapter how Crane was interpellated or hailed by the subjectivity of homosexuality, how he argued against the dominant ideological assertions about that subjectivity, and how his reimagination of it, at the close of "Voyages," for instance, was nevertheless always already written within its confines—to imagine meaningful and lasting union was already to imagine heterosexually. In this chapter we will see how the traditional lyric interest in persona, individuality, and voice is concretely realized in Crane's homosexual lyrics as interpellation into ideology—specifically, the ideological contest between homosexuality and poetic authority.

The material in the previous chapter helps to explain some of the avoidances of homosexuality in Crane's text, such as the discursive instability that assured that homosexuality would appear in culture only through other, "legitimate" discourses, or the prejudices of his literary friends against the ethical or cultural effectivity of the homosexual. There is evidence to suggest, however, that even beyond these intellectual issues, Crane feared censorship and so may have suppressed the homosexual elements in his published work. Writing to Munson as early as March 1923, Crane concedes,

> I discover that I have been all-too-easy all along in letting out announcements of my sexual predilections. Not that anything unpleasant has happened or is imminent. But it does

> put me into obligatory relations to a certain extent with "those who know," and this irks me to think of sometimes. . . . I find the ordinary business of earning a living entirely too stringent to want to add any prejudices against me *of that nature* [italics in original]. (*Letters*, 129–30)

This does not refer specifically to the intricacies of publishing, but Crane certainly found that business too stringent to want to add any prejudices against him of any nature. And as he became more public a figure, his need to be more discreet about his sexuality increased. In this, he is not unlike Willa Cather, who (in Sharon O'Brien's words):

> could never declare her lesbianism publicly. . . . And in her fiction she never wrote directly of the attachments between women that were the emotional center of her life. However "natural" they may finally have seemed to her, Cather knew she could not name them to a twentieth-century audience. (*Willa Cather*, 137)

Arnold Rampersad's biography of Langston Hughes, on the other hand, makes it clear that the very existence of periodicals such as *Crisis* and *Opportunity* called forth from Hughes more consciously radical verse than he otherwise produced, helping him construct a persona as spokesman for black experience in America.

We can see Crane's impatience with the publishing industry in his brief interactions with Marianne Moore. Moore, who returned "Passage" to Crane because of its "lack of simplicity and cumulative force," completely altered "The Wine Menagerie" and published it in *The Dial* under the title "Again." In accepting it, she removed the first two stanzas of the poem entirely and made other changes that Crane did not take well. It may seem of little consequence to have this happen to a single poem, but in a corpus such as Crane's it is equivalent to deleting or rewriting one-fourth of a novel by Faulkner, let us say, before publishing it. Crane allowed Moore this liberty because he was in desperate need of both cash (he received twenty dollars on publication of "Again") and some kind of literary validation. When Moore accepted a later poem without change, Crane voiced his displeasure at her earlier editing: "This time she didn't even suggest running the last line backward" (*Letters*, 255). But Moore was not the only literary authority Crane seemed unable to please; one of his famous prose statements (where he outlines his poetics as a "logic of metaphor") was written to Harriet Monroe in an attempt to explain to her that his poetry was not nonsense, that it was in fact grounded in an explicable theory of language. But it seems he feared offending more than the standards of style: writing to Tate in the early months of 1927, he complained about the strict morality of current editorial practices:

> I've had to submit ["The Dance"] to Marianne Moore recently, as my only present hope of a little cash. But she probably will object to the word "breasts," or some such detail. It's really ghastly. I wonder how much longer our market will be in the grip of two such hysterical virgins as *The Dial* and *Poetry!*
>
> what strange people these . . . [editorial elision] are. Always in a flutter for fear bowels will be mentioned, forever carrying on a tradition that both Poe and Whitman spent half their lives railing against—and calling themselves "liberals." (*Letters*, 289, 290)

If this seems merely the complaint of someone on the outside looking in, we should remember that Crane's paranoia about literary censorship was a reality he and other writers of his day lived with. In a world that seized *The Well of Loneliness* because of its lesbian content, in a nation that prosecuted *The Little Review* for its publication of *Ulysses* (this incident came home to him especially strongly because Margaret Anderson's "defense" of

Joyce appeared in the same issue of *The Little Review* as Crane's first publication in that journal) and that closed New York theaters where lesbian and gay plays appeared,[1] Crane perhaps had justification for his fears. His letters from Ohio refer several times to the "*Ulysses* situation"—"terrible to think on" (*Letters*, 72). "It is my opinion that some fanatic will kill Joyce sometime soon for the wonderful things said in *Ulysses*" (*Letters*, 95). His friend Gorham Munson had had to sneak Crane's presubscribed copy of the book into the United States in the bottom of a trunk, and Crane clearly sees the suppression of Joyce's work as symptomatic of a more generalized threat to freedom of expression: "De Gourmont's *Une Coeur Virginal* has just been published here (trans. Aldous Huxley), and I have snatched it up against its imminent suppression along with *Jurgen* and other masterpieces. . . . I cannot see his *Physique d'Amour*, translated by Pound and to be published by Boni and Liveright, will ever get beyond the printer's hands" (*Letters*, 73). Thus we should see that when Crane writes to Munson in February 1923 about "these American restrictions [on homosexuality . . . where one cannot whisper a word" (*Letters*, 122), he refers perhaps to written as well as spoken forms of communication.

Despite this, Crane's early work includes a number of poems in which he makes homosexuality visible and important to the text, suggesting that his later literary suppression of overt references to homosexuality was a choice conditioned in part by his need to appear literarily respectable. As Tate recalled, "Hart had a sort of megalomania: he wanted to be The Great American Poet" (quoted in Unterecker, *Voyager*, 431), and the only way he could fulfill that ambition was by conforming to the overwhelmingly heterosexual conventions and expectations of the literary. Aesthetic experimentation, of course, was a sign of his seriousness as a modern artist, but homosexuality needed to remain obscure—a "private," "personal" issue of no relevance to art—if one were to be taken seriously by those with the power to evaluate and promote one's work. I would like to compare these early texts ("C 33," "Episode of Hands," and "Modern Craft") with those written in New York during the high period of Crane's mature and difficult verse ("Possessions," "Passage," "The Wine Menagerie") to suggest how the development of a stylistic density that marks his most ambitious work balances an effacement of homosexuality as the central subject of his lyric concern. My claim is not that homosexuality disappears from his work (we have already seen its powerful presence in "Voyages" and "Recitative," both written in the later period), but that it becomes textually obscure, hidden in a multitude of oblique references that encode it as the authorizing secret of the text.

"C 33" was Crane's first published poem, a tribute to Oscar Wilde, whom he describes as having "woven rose-vines / About the empty heart of night." The inheritance Crane claims through Wilde is one of homosexual betrayal, personal suffering, and aesthetic posturing, but the title itself, which refers to the number on Wilde's cell in Reading Gaol,[2] suggests as well the oblique nature of homosexual reference in Crane's literary work even at this early point. Only those in the know—and there could not have been many—would take the title's meaning and therefore identify the poem as a homosexual text. "C 33" is what it describes Wilde's verse to be, "song of minor, broken strain," and it is most important for us as an index of Crane's response to Wilde's trial as a critical moment in the history of homosexuality. We see in it the ideological lesson Wilde offered a young man like Crane—that "searing sophistry" is no defense against suffering, implying that the arch pose is vanity and that one ought to account *de profundis* rather than from the surface. The need to "forget all blight" at the poem's close is clearly the need to forget that one is homosexual, too, and Crane accomplishes that in "C 33" through appeal to a madonna figure whose "gold head / And wavering shoulders" are meant to establish an economy of sympathy. Although he does not condemn Wilde, as did Willa Cather,

Crane's poem clearly suggests that he felt (as did Wilde himself) some need for salvation from artistic and homosexual alienation at this point in his life and that the central figure through which he understood his historical link to Wilde was that of imprisonment.

"Episode of Hands," another early poem of Crane's, is atypical of this early work, for it depicts in a naturalistic fashion—more like Sandburg or Masters than Wilde or Rimbaud—a simple narrative of male bonding and its effect on the poet. "Episode of Hands" depicts the brief moment when a "factory owner's son" bandages the hand of a worker bleeding from an accident in the factory (Crane was, of course, a factory owner's son), and the poem begins with the embarrassment the two feel in being thrown into this atypical masculine relation: "The un-expected interest made him flush." It ends, however, in a warm and gentle union between the two men: "And as the bandage knot was tightened / The two men smiled into each other's eyes." Crane uses the smile as a sign of union and interpersonal knowledge throughout his career, and it is important to see that he implies a healing of both men in this smile, for the owner's son is allowed a reprieve from his alienating position *as* the owner's son. The "knot" brings the two together in a new relation: the "factory sounds and factory thoughts / Were banished from him [the son] by that larger, quieter hand / That lay in his." Crane offers this assessment of the worker's hand, making the trace of its labor an inspiration rather than an alienation:

> The knots and notches,—many in the wide
> Deep hand that lay in his,—seemed beautiful.
> They were like the marks of wild ponies' play,—
> Bunches of new green breaking the hard turf.

The central stanza depicting the actual moment of bandaging is the most interesting, however; here the owner's son is made aware of the beauty of his own hands through his connection to the worker's:

> And as the fingers of the factory owner's son,
> That knew a grip for books and tennis
> As well as one for iron and leather,—
> As his taut, spare fingers wound the gauze
> Around the thick bed of the wound,
> His own hands seemed to him
> Like wings of butterflies
> Flickering in sunlight over summer fields.
> (*Poems*, 141)

The simile of the wings almost certainly borrows from the character Wings Biddlebaum in Sherwood Anderson's short story "Hands," for Anderson was one of Crane's preferred American writers, and "Hands," the opening story of *Winesburg, Ohio*, is one of the most visible statements on American attitudes toward homosexuality before the twenties. In the story, as in Crane's poem, it is touch, the supposed escape from language, that signals the escape from conventional gender expectations: "By the caress that was in his fingers he expressed himself. . . . Under the caress of his hands, doubt and disbelief went out of the minds of the boys and they began also to dream" (*Winesburg*, 32). The change that occurs through this touch is appropriately imaged in both texts through the most standard figure for metamorphosis—the butterfly.

This is the first instance in Crane's work of the rhetoric of homosexual transformation, and the poem is constructed entirely of simile arid metonymy except for one moment. That moment, the metaphor in the central line of the text—"the thick bed of the wound"—is all the more important for its singularity. The word "bed" suggests that the union between these two men has an erotic component, and it is only after this metaphorical and sublimated appearance of the homoerotic that the hands are transformed, the owner's son's becoming "Like wings of butterflies," and the worker's "like the marks of wild ponies' play." Although only obliquely acknowledged, homosexuality is not only that which ties the healing knot between worker and son but also the origin of metaphor in the poem.

If one reads the wound in "Episode of Hands" as structurally linked to homosexuality, as others of Crane's poems would invite us to do, that wound is also healed in the poem's closure, for the close makes homosexuality the positive center of an affectionate and literally healing exchange (and a healing that is neither a "cure" or repression, as is implied in the madonna figure of "C 33"). It represents instead the worker's acceptance of the son's "unexpected interest." The knot of solidarity between them comes from their *not* being defined any longer in the hierarchical relations of partriarchal masculinity and capitalist economy; rather, the poem ends with the sign of homosexual recognition: a knowing, smiling gaze. It is not surprising that Crane investigates homosexuality through this trope of wounding. In the discourse of psychoanalysis, it is structurally linked to castration, to lack or wounding,[3] and it was no doubt often a condition of suffering for Crane and others of his generation, making the metaphor appear natural in its appeal. But if we understand two further things about pain, it becomes clear that there are other possible links between wounding and homosexuality in Crane's text. In *The Body in Pain*, Elaine Scarry suggests that pain places us at the limits of language, at a level of experience that knows no object except the body (we do not experience pain "of," "about," or "for" something as we hunger for or fear a, b, or c), and it places us as well at a level of experience that can produce no signifier (according to Scarry, pain literally destroys language). Both of these structural readings of pain make its connection to homosexuality more significant for Crane, for homosexuality, like pain, had a troubled, almost nonexistent relation to referential language; it was both unmediated and unnamable. And it is possible as well that in Crane's case homosexuality was a matter of masochistic pleasure, of knowing the body as the site on which self-empowerment was written as pain.

The rhetoric of pain appears quite frequently in his late, fragmentary work, but in none of his early poems is it as clear as in the last line of "Modern Craft." There he makes the rather startling confession, "My modern love were / Charred at a stake in younger times than ours" (*Poems*, 132)—a line whose power of surprise derives from its frankness and from its break with the earlier subjects of the poem. This rather feeble protest about the burning of homosexuals in former historical periods occurs in the final lines of a poem largely taken up with a description of an indifferent and sexually jaded female muse who seems to possess a power and authority the poet does not. In fact, she seems to invert the conventions of musology, writing him rather than being written by him, and she exposes him (to himself, at least) as a poseur, a Hamlet who is unable to act and unable to affect her despite his knowledge of her:

> Though I have touched her flesh of moons,
> Still she sits gestureless and mute,
> Drowning cool pearls in alcohol.
> O blameless shyness;—innocence dissolute!
>
> She hazards jet; wears tiger-lilies;—
> And bolts herself within a jewelled belt.
> Too many palms have grazed her shoulders:
> Surely she must have felt.

Ophelia had such eyes; but she
Even, sank in love and choked with flowers.
This burns and is not burnt . . .
(*Poems*, 132)

Sherman Paul has suggested that this represents "an encounter with a prostitute," and then amends that to say that she is "less an object of the poet's interest than an object for the play of his own feelings" (*Hart's Bridge*, 20). But what the poet seems in fact to recognize here is her utter conventionality: not only may she function (within one old script of homosexual etiology) as the rejecting female, the powerful woman who is uninterested in (or contemptuous of) the male, but it may in fact prove more powerfully and certainly more historically accurate to read her as a figure of cross-dressing, a series of contradictions, a female muse only in her ability to masquerade as one. And this reading is bolstered not only by the poem's immediate turn to the question of past homosexual persecutions (implying that this "modern craft," while alienating, is better than burning at the stake) but also by John D'Emilio and Estelle B. Freedman's suggestion that, in addition to the location of meeting places in "sites of moral ambiguity" or "transient relationships" (such as waterfronts, theaters, etc.), there was one prominent feature to the "inchoate subculture" of pre-1920 homosexuality: transvestism (*Intimate Matters*, 227–28).[4]

When we turn from these early works to Crane's more mature poems we find a remarkable difference in style, and since form is always in a determinate relation to ideology, this difference should not be seen as coincidental. The works in question were written during the period when Crane wrote both "Voyages" and "Recitative," a time during which mentors arid editors alike wrestled with Crane's work and tried (sometimes unsuccessfully) to understand its significance. This was also the period (1923–26) during which homosexuality was an integrative factor in Crane's intellectual life—not merely one facet of his personality, but the center of a dense, incarnational metaphysics where the Word became Flesh. Of the celebrated difficulty of the poems of this period, R. W. B. Lewis has written,

> the lyrics of 1923–26 contain some of the most notoriously difficult verses of modern times. To some readers, Crane's lyrics have seemed so impenetrable as to arouse suspicion of fraudulence. . . . [I]t is still possible for perfectly honest critics to come up with radically different interpretations of particular stanzas or even entire poems. . . . But I am sure that when the poems (that is, the post–"Faustus and Helen" poems) are read as a group, as the product of a single large phase of Crane's creative career, many (not all) of their difficulties evaporate. (*The Poetry of Hart Crane*, 124–25)

Lewis is not exactly correct. The difficulties of these poems remain entrenched, their meanings indeterminate, shifting radically as one reads. As the second chapter of this study suggested, that is in part due to a homosexual semiotic that is determined to refuse closure. But all the difficulties of these poems cannot be attributed to homosexuality, for their semiotic density is often directly related to Crane's other interests in modern art and literature.

Crane's indebtedness to the discourses of modernism has been documented elsewhere, and includes subjects as well as styles: his interest in machinery and technology, for instance, an interest shared by a large number of artists, photographers, and writers; his linguistic density, which is his verbal equivalent of montage or cubist effect—the attempt to create simultaneity of reference and perspective in one synchronic structure. But perhaps the most "modern" development in Crane's work was his refiguration of mimesis. Crane does not represent external objects or even internalized processes and meditations in the manner Abrams suggests is conventional for Romantic poetry and that we find as the first assumption of Eliot's poetry. It is true that the city or the machine might enter Crane's work, but they enter it as objects enter the visual field in Stieglitz's photographs, for instance, as structure, idea, abstraction.[5] Crane differs from Williams, Eliot, and Moore (and most of the writers who have taught us to read modernist texts) in that his work is not dependent upon representation in the same way as theirs. I will not take the time here to quibble about Williams's or Stevens's many variations on the abstract and the concrete (such as *Kora in Hell*, which seems experimental and antimimetic in ways analogous to Crane's antimimetic work).[6] We should perhaps think of Crane's work as having most in common with Constructivist or conceptual art, for it is often more presentational than representational in its effect, breaking the planes and contours of illusion and making one aware of the fact that it is written work—not an imitation of a "real" interior monologue nor a description of a "real" world but a piece of language that foregrounds its textuality. As Suzanne Clarke Doeren has suggested, Crane's poetry is one where "a language system takes over the subject" ("Hart Crane," 159), where there is no illusion that language functions transparently to signify the internal state of mind of a speaker or writer. Crane's is perhaps the first lyric poetry in English (and perhaps the only poetry in English until Charles Olson's or John Ashbery's) that is designed to be read as a constructed verbal artifact rather than as mimetic of any natural discourse.[7] The lyric focus in Crane seems, finally, to be neither the minimal unit of the image, as in Imagist work, nor the maximal unit of the poem conceived as organic whole, as in Romantic lyrics or dramatic monologues that trace psychologized themes. Lyricality in Crane is that point where language breaks its transparency and forces the reader to authorize his relation to it, and for Crane this characteristically occurs on intermediate levels of meaning: in syntax and semantics. Doeren writes that "Crane's poems seem to come into existence at the point where . . . a subject becomes some other form of language: a verb, an object, a preposition" (83), and it is precisely in this use of language as a thick, palpable medium for construction that Crane's texts take their place beside other modernist experiments with aesthetic media.

The standard reading of Crane's deviation from poetic norms draws on prose statements such as the following, written for a proposed symposium in *Broom*: "It is as though a poem gave the reader as he left it a single, new *word*, never before spoken and impossible to actually enunciate, but self-evident as an active principle in the reader's consciousness henceforward" (*Poems*, 221). Crane's poems are explicitly tied to this search for the "new word," for what he terms in "The Wine Menagerie" "new anatomies" of the "new thresholds" on which humanity stands. But it is important to see that if Crane's poems are initiatory and almost literally liminal, they are not unconstructed moments. Just as the silences of homosexuality are not unstructured but are a set of conditions that mark the relation of homosexuality to other cultural practices, the antistructural quality of Crane's difficult poems nevertheless maps a set of differential relations for the production of meaning. Crane's characteristic poems seem interested neither in a literally transcribed homosexual reality nor in an imaginary realm completely interiorized and private (the assumption behind dismissals by Moore and others that the poems were no doubt meaningful but too obscure to be read); rather, Crane's most characteristic texts are interested in linguistic meaning and subjectivity as they occur through the difficulty of textuality.

"Chaplinesque" (1921) is an interim text that provides useful contrast to the early homosexual poems discussed above and the difficult, prophetic poems of 1923–26 that come after it. It seems to have been particularly pleasing to Crane, and he was confounded by his friends' confused responses to it. Stylistically it is a step toward the dense semiosis that attends Crane's full development; thematically it is a rather sentimental and even maudlin poem that suggests the poignancy of innocence in a world that crushes it (the Chaplin thematic). On its surface, the poem would appear to have nothing to do with homosexuality,[8] but it marks the beginning of Crane's disintegration of the speaking subject (although that subject appears here as "we"), and it is on this point of pronominal identification that we can begin to see the discursive outcomes of Crane's poetic response to homosexuality. The poem opens:

We make our meek adjustments,
Contented with such random consolations
As the wind deposits
In slithered and too ample pockets.
(*Poems*, 11)

So much depends in this case not on chickens, rain, and wheelbarrows, but on who steps in to define and fill the vacuum of that "we." Who makes meek adjustment to the world? Who, later in the poem, will defy the law and "Dally the doom of that inevitable thumb / That slowly chafes its puckered index toward us"? Who "can still love the world, who find / A famished kitten on the step, and know / Recesses for it from the fury of the street"? For whom does Chaplin speak? For whom does the poem speak?

In discussing this poem, R. W. B. Lewis acknowledges that the text is (in its own words) "evasive," but Lewis does not imagine that one of the things evaded here is a more direct address to the social condition of the homosexual subject. This is not to suggest that "Chaplinesque" is intentionally "about" that subject but is, rather, to suggest that one of the strongest referents of subjectivity for Crane in 1921 was his experience as a homosexual—that the "we" of "Chaplinesque" is constructed in sight of the practice of homosexuality, its alienations and consequent, compensatory nostalgias. The poem is, that is, *and perhaps despite its intentions*, an allegory of homosexual desire and its articulation within the "American restrictions" of the Midwest ca. 1921. The next to last stanza tries to find virtue in the meek adjustment and "smirk" or "dull squint" of "innocence" and "surprise" with which this subject meets the "inevitable thumb" of the law (patriarchal repressions), and it suggests that a subjectivity grounded in desire always exceeds those social mechanisms and technologies that seek to control or euphemize it—the heart lives on:

And yet these fine collapses are not lies
More than the pirouettes of any pliant cane;
Our obsequies are, in a way, no enterprise.
We can evade you, and all else but the heart:
What blame to us if the heart live on.
(*Poems*, 11)

The "fine collapses" of obsequy, euphemism, and poetry are not lies, Crane claims, and he locates the authority for their "truth" in the heart—signifying here both a center of consciousness and the center of desire. It is social pressure ("enterprise" picks up here on a whole discourse of antimaterialist writing in the period) which forces the lie: the "victim" of that pressure remains blameless in his own heart.

Crane has not by any means made a full transition into the advanced poetry of a decentered subjectivity in "Chaplinesque." The poem ends with a rather trite assertion of transformation that seems a restatement of Emerson's claim that he was everywhere defeated yet born to victory:

> The game enforces smirks; but we have seen
> The moon in lonely alleys make
> A grail of laughter of an empty ash can,
> And through all sound of gaiety and quest
> Have heard a kitten in the wilderness.
> (*Poems*, 11)

In some sense the preposterousness of the final image marks a limit to Crane's naturalized Romanticism (how far from "The Tyger!"); two years later, when composing "Possessions," his rhetoric of transformation will be truly apocalyptic. But the closure marked here is also part of the poem's homosexual textuality, for the homosexual's heart needs to be defended as blameless, and the reality of its consolations asserted: loneliness in cruisey alleyways can become laughter; a genuine tenderness can be located amid the hubbub "of gaiety and quest." The tenor of this final stanza is clearly of a piece with the more optimistic moments in Crane's letters from Cleveland, and it provides in its reconstruction of a homosexual "we" something Crane felt sorely lacking at this time: a community in which he could discuss the contours of his existence, the "fine collapses" of his life, as if they were not inherently illegitimate as subjects for poetry.

Crane's investigation of homosexuality as cognate to the textual indeterminacy of subjectivity is nowhere as openly displayed as in the 1923 poem "Possessions." Of those poems written in this period, "Possessions" is the one that most makes a critical consideration of its homosexual referents unavoidable. Robert Martin has called it "the first poem of the modern urban homosexual in search of sex, his hesitations the result of fear and self-oppression" (*The Homosexual Tradition*, 128). But it is important to our understanding of both Crane and his construction of homosexuality as a possibility and an impossibility of meaning to see that "Possessions" does not dramatize that search in a straightforward fashion. It does not present an individual confronting or ruminating on this as a psychic or social problem. "Possessions" employs the first-person pronoun, and there is some attempt to locate that person within a landscape that produces him as meaningful, but it is not by any means a dramatic monologue. Crane employs the "I" here not so much to relate an individual's experience as to provide a field for those emotional and intellectual conflicts that do battle through him. Thus, Martin's claim that this is "the first poem of the modern urban homosexual in search of sex" is only partially correct. The problematic nature of the search for sex is only part of the poem's concern, and this is how Crane's text differs from Whitman's *Calamus*, for instance, or from a John Ashbery poem about cruising, "The Ongoing Story," both of which see homosexuality as transparent to the individual and not as a system in which the individual's meaning and desire are already written for him. In "City of Orgies," for instance, Whitman claims it is the "frequent and swift flash of eyes offering me love" that "repay me" (*Leaves of Grass*, 126), and while there are poems in *Calamus* such as "Of the Terrible Doubt of Appearances" and "Earth, My Likeness" that suggest some difficulty in the expression of homosexual desire, Whitman's more typical texts on homosexuality locate it internal to the subject and transparent to his real self. Ashbery's "The Ongoing Story," which is not perhaps representative of his most skeptical interrogations of identity, locates the act of cruising as one stable field in a life otherwise uninterpretable and unstable: "It's as though I'd been left with the empty street / A few seconds after the bus pulled out." Personal and poetic closure are achieved in the following:

you,
In your deliberate distinctness, whom I love and gladly
Agree to walk into the night with,
Your realness is real to me though I would never take any of it
Just to see how it grows. A knowledge that people live close by is,
I think, enough. And even if only first names are ever exchanged
The people who own them seem rock-true and marvelously self-sufficient.
(*A Wave*, 11)

In the context of the poem—and in the context of Ashbery's entire oeuvre—there is perhaps some irony in this comfort which defines reality as the realness of others. Certainly the marvelous self-sufficiency of others offered at the close of the poem is proven to be an illusion by the knowledge elsewhere evident in it that one's own self-sufficiency is a fiction. But the poem does not destabilize the reading subject as does Crane's "Possessions."[9] Crane's investigation of homosexuality, which occurs historically somewhere between the mystical naiveté of Whitman discovering the homoeroticism that is identical to his "self" and the inside joke of Ashbery's New York, where everything—including homosexuality—has always been known all along, is settled on a historical threshold where desire is no longer a secret excitement securely anchored within a Romantic self but is not yet a cultural cliché enabling only parody. "Possessions" presents homosexuality as a text but it understands the subject as lost within that text.

A closer inspection of the poem suggests that what is rejected from the outset in "Possessions" is less the practice of homosexuality than the constricting representations of it available to the homosexual and to the homosexual poet. In an almost polemical fashion, "Possessions" rejects the rhetorical construction of homosexuality as a "fixed stone of lust" and replaces it at the poem's close with a more idealized vision of "bright stones wherein our smiling plays." The poem is an attempt to depict homosexual existence as more than a "Record of rage and partial appetites," this last phrase nicely balanced to suggest that desire is both determined (one always favors or is partial to something) and fragmentary (desire is also partial and never whole; it never makes one whole, especially if it is taboo). But if homosexuality inscribes one as the field of rage and partial appetite, dividing the subject from proper knowledge of himself in his possession of sexual object after sexual object, the poem insists that this is preparatory to an "inclusive" moment when a "pure possession . . . / Whose heart is fire" will—as in the golden halo effect of Crane's letters—transform possessor and possessed into a single being.

A diachronic reading of the poem does not neatly display what I have here suggested is the poem's impact; the poem seems alternately to come into and go out of focus, to hesitate, as Martin suggests, and part of that hesitation or indeterminacy is due to its skewed syntax. If Crane claimed this text to be an example of how he "work[ed] hard for a more perfect lucidity" (*Letters*, 176), it is not immediately possible to grant that this poem exemplifies that work. Although the poem is brief and its major outlines are clear, there is considerable obscurity in specific passages and in the relation of details to the larger structure. Without intending it, Robert Combs suggests that the poem is an allegory of homosexual desire: "The difficulty of this poem lies chiefly in the way Crane delays interpretational clues which serve gradually to orient the reader. . . .'Trust,' 'rain,' and 'key' in the first stanza are like elements in a mysterious allegory that seem to need interpretation by the last word 'lust.'" (65).[10] It would seem to be Crane's strategy to keep syntactic relations, as homosexual desire itself remains, indeterminate in the opening of the poem. We can see only textual units, possible events, attitudes, and locations that exist in juxtaposition but without any continuity or englobing frame of reference. It is a world of contiguous and accidental relations:

Witness now this trust! The rain
That steals softly direction
And the key, ready to hand—sifting
One moment in sacrifice (the direst)
Through a thousand nights the flesh
Assaults outright for bolts that linger
Hidden,—O undirected as the sky
That through its black foam has no eyes
For this fixed stone of lust. . . .
(*Poems*, 18)

We see here only an act of implied entry; "the key, ready to hand," is a phallic object employed to cross some threshold, but that threshold remains undefined (although this act of unlocking certainly bristles with sexual innuendoes and is linked figuratively to the erotic "bolts that linger / Hidden"). The desire in this opening is overwhelming in its sequential duration ("a thousand nights") and in the intensity of its passion ("the flesh / Assaults outright"), and it occurs under a vacuous yet menacing sky that certainly draws its significance from religious injunctions that traditionally have "[had] no eyes" for homosexuality. If one accepts the pun on "eyes," this "black foam" of heaven at once names and negates homosexual identity, it robs one of one's "I," and its rain (reign) "steals softly direction" until one does not know which way one is going. This moment, "sift[ed]" from a thousand, occurs within the context of cosmic alienation, and one of its meanings as a "moment in sacrifice" would appear to he that the homosexual sacrifices himself on a "fixed stone," a pagan altar of lust.

If the first stanza articulates homosexuality as a broken syntax, the second stanza asks the reader to contemplate the magnitude of such displaced meaning when it is cast across the course of a lifetime (signified here as the accumulation of "an hour").

Accumulate such moments to an hour:
Account the total of this trembling tabulation.
I know the screen, the distant flying taps
And stabbing medley that sways—
And the mercy, feminine, that stays
As though prepared.
(*Poems*, 18)

There is in this stanza little referential clarity; although it is possible to say that something in the last four lines seems to assuage the emptiness of the "trembling tabulation," it is not possible to say what exactly that is. It is a "screen," "distant flying taps," a "stabbing medley that sways," and "mercy, feminine, that stays / As though prepared." We see in the vocabulary of distance a vague outline perhaps of longing or romance, in the stabbing medley that sways a sense perhaps of poignancy and seduction. And if mercy is feminine, that suggestion is perhaps less surprising than its appearance here, an appearance that makes the alienation of the first stanza even more overtly masculine in retrospect. How that mercy stays and for what or how it is prepared seem indecipherable; "stays" can mean both "remains" and "supports," and "prepared" could mean, to follow out the religious imagery of the preceding stanza, "preordained," prepared from before. In any case, this second stanza suggests alternatives to the opening of the poem: intersubjectivity and mercy are presented as being "real" qualities of homosexuality meant to counter its representation as nothing more than predatory lust.

The third stanza accepts the heavy burden of interpretation in the phrases "fixed stone of lust" and "take up the stone." But it does so without speech, "As quiet as you can make a man," and assigns that burden to an individual "Wounded by apprehensions out of speech."

And I, entering, take up the stone
As quiet as you can make a man . . .
In Bleecker Street, still trenchant in a void,
Wounded by apprehensions out of speech,
I hold it up against a disk of light—
I turning, turning on smoked forking spires,
The city's stubborn lives, desires.
(*Poems*, 18)

The difficult, unspeakable quality of homosexuality stands clearly behind this construction. Nevertheless, the poet "hold[s] . . . up against a disk of light" this stone that represents the "city's stubborn lives, desires." If the "turning, turning on smoked forking spires" seems to suggest a demonic skewering appropriate to Bosch's *Garden of Earthly Delights* (and thus to be a continuation of the vocabulary of punishment and wounding that surrounds homosexuality), we need to see as well that this refers to the poet's textual production. The "forking spires" (both phallic and religious aspirations) are the double-pronged instrument of writing he uses to hold this topic up for inspection. Crane's "General Aims and Theories," which postdates this poem by two years but is nonetheless relevant to this text, may serve as a gloss on how Crane conceives the poet's civic function:

> It seems to me that a poet will accidentally define his time well enough simply by reacting honestly and to the full extent of his sensibilities to the states of passion, experience, and rumination that fate forces on him, first hand. He must, of course, have a sufficiently universal basis of experience to make his imagination selective and valuable. His picture of the "period," then, will simply be a by-product of his curiosity and the relation of his experience to a postulated "eternity." (*Poems*, 218)

What we see in this image of the stone of lust held up to the light makes a claim for the poet's relevance similar to that offered in "General Aims and Theories": "Possessions" examines homosexuality (the "stubborn lives, desires" of the city that are at stake here as the "passion" and "experience" fate forced on Crane) against the background of "a postulated 'eternity' "—in order to define it for this time. No longer an unshakable paradigm or "fixed stone" of lust, homosexuality begins here to be figured contiguously—in the syntagmatic placing of one term against another. Thus, Crane reverses not only the meaning of homosexuality as a "fixed stone of lust" but (perhaps more significantly) the location of meaning in the fixity of metaphor and paradigm, that possibility of unshakable meaning out of which the poem's initial sense of alienation arose.

The opening lines of the last stanza quite clearly locate the dilemma of homosexuality (on the "horns" of which one is tossed) within a problematic of language and representation.

Tossed on these horns, who bleeding dies,
Lacks all but piteous admissions to be spilt
Upon the page whose blind sum finally burns

Record of rage and partial appetites.
The pure possession, the inclusive cloud
Whose heart is fire shall come,—the white wind rase
All but bright stones wherein our smiling plays.
(*Poems*, 18)

If homosexuality as a "fixed stone of lust" is traditionally figured as a wound or lack (both of which tropes appear in the poem), what it seems most crucially to lack are "piteous admissions . . . spilt / Upon the page." Although these admissions are "piteous," and the homosexual still cloaked in the rhetoric of guilt, more open textual representations would allow some challenge to negative paradigms of the private and public implications of the homosexual life. Such representations, when themselves tabulated, would (unlike the trembling moments at the beginning of the poem) "finally [burn]" the "Record of rage and partial appetites" that are the legacy of the paradigm of lust. This image of burning transforms the demonic language of the text; the "pure possession" or "inclusive cloud / Whose heart is fire shall come" and possess or repossess the now dispossessed homosexual man. The figure of the "bright stones wherein our smiling plays" also reverses the punishing god (and the altar of sacrifice) from the opening stanza and replaces it with a vision that can only be called, according to the poem's terms, "feminine." In the poem's final lines we see on a cosmic scale the "mercy, feminine, that stays / As though prepared" that has been the homosexual's internalized source of comfort and trust up to this point, that longed-for inclusive cloud that sanctions homosexual desire. What "Possessions" finds in "trust" is neither transcendence of the body nor foreclosure of homosexual desire but their positive integration into myth. What the poem seeks is a visionary love that can accommodate the homosexual and no longer isolate him as an example of lust.

[. . .]

The experimental lyrics written from 1923 to 1926 constitute a record of the development of homosexual subjectivity unlike any other in modern letters; with an increasing urgency, from "Possessions" through "Voyages" and "Legend" to "Passage" and "The Wine Menagerie," they present the search for an authentic voice and an ideological recognition of homosexual speech and writing, and—with an increasing clarity—the frustrations and barriers to that project. They record the dialectical unfolding of Crane's thought about the homosexual subject and poetry, and they articulate a number of important points about the ideology under which that thought took shape. First, these poems announce that homosexuality may not appear in autobiography "in person," as it were: we see this in its literal disappearance from "Passage," for instance, and in the highly coded discourses through which it appears as the universal problem of lust in "The Wine Menagerie" and as the universal problem of identity development in "Repose of Rivers." Secondly, a diachronic reading of these poems, which I have conducted here with only a few omissions, traces the disintegration of a consciousness such as Crane's, a disintegration not made necessary by enforced homophobia but one certainly encouraged by it. Especially when we understand that Crane inhabited flatly contradictory sites of culture as both a homosexual and a poet, we must read the disintegration of the speaking/writing subject in "The Wine Menagerie" as fully produced within an ideology that made the homosexual poet's subjectivity a bizarre dialectic of anguish and ecstasy. But the final poem in this progression, "Repose of Rivers," marks Crane's refusal to surrender the homosexual subject in the lyric; if it asserts a poise he never actually sustained in his life, and if his life had by the summer of 1926 already become a plague from which he would not escape (the nasty details of which one may gather from almost all his biographers and from the memoirs of countless friends), the poem nevertheless bravely signals Crane's refusal to surrender his project for homosexual centrality. As Adorno suggests, "The greatness of works of art lies solely in their power to let those things be heard which ideology conceals" ("Lyric Poetry and Society," 57), and the greatness of Crane's lyrics, written, it is not hyperbolic to say, at the cost of his life, is that they allow homosexual subjectivity to be heard as an authentic experience, as "wind flaking sapphire."

NOTES

1. George Chauncey, Jr., writes that "early in 1927 municipal authorities raided the theater where the American version of *The Captive*, a French play about lesbianism, was premiering," and also prevented *The Drag*, a play in which Mae West appeared, from opening on Broadway. "In an effort to protect 'immature' audiences from exposure to such 'corrupting influences,'" Chauncey writes, "the state legislature passed a law later that year which banned 'the subject of sexual degeneracy or sex perversion' from the stage" (34). See *Gay New York* (Basic Books, 1994).

2. Robert Martin points this out in *The Homosexual Tradition in American Poetry* (1979).

3. Naomi Schor has recently developed a theory of female textual practices that includes the wound as one figure of bodily fetishization that provide female readers resistance to male totalizing (*Reading in Detail: Aesthetics and the Feminine* [Routledge, 1987]).

4. "Modern Craft" was written in 1918, and if we compare two other searches for a modern muse from the same period, Stevens's "Disillusionment of Ten O'Clock" (1915) and Williams's "The Young Housewife" (1917), we can see how glaring is Crane's discovery of representational lack in "Modern Craft." Stevens's poem suggests something awry in the modern world, and also begins with a sense of inadequate muses and inadequate representational strategies: it is easier for Stevens to depict what will not occur in this landscape than it is for him to say what will.

> The houses are haunted
> By white night gowns.
> None are green,
> Or purple with green rings,
> Or green with yellow rings,
> Or yellow with blue rings.
> . . . .
> People are not going
> To dream of baboons and periwinkles.
> Only, here and there, an old sailor,
> Drunk and asleep in his boots,
> Catches tigers
> In red weather.
> (*Collected Poems*, 16)

But as stunning as is the turn of the poem's close and its reversal of the terms that come before, Stevens's poem suggests only an old American cliché of domesticity avoided, paradise lost and then regained through the repossession of individual vision and the exotic within the self. "Modern Craft" examines the image that remains absent in "Disillusionment of Ten O'Clock" (the strange muse with "socks of lace / And beaded ceintures") precisely because Crane would make sexuality rather than its sublimation central to his text. It is not a mythic imagination ("Catch[ing] tigers / In red weather") that Crane glosses in his work but a historically situated subject who speaks a fractured, difficult text.

Williams, of course, refuses to consider the exotic or erotic except as it exists in the concrete and the mundane, and "The Young Housewife" traces one instance of Williams's encounter with his muse. Neither crafty convention nor ghostly presence, his muse is a young housewife who "moves about in negligee behind / the wooden walls of her husband's house":

> Then again she comes to the curb
> to call the ice-man, fish-man, and stands
> shy, uncorseted, tucking in
> stray ends of hair, and I compare her
> to a fallen leaf.
>
> The noiseless wheels of my car
> rush with a crackling sound over
> dried leaves as I bow and pass smiling.
> (*Collected Early Poems*, 136)

Williams's self-proclaimed comfort with female sexuality allows him to reverse a long tradition of stylized portraits of the muse and to find beauty, inspiration, etc., in a "real" rather than "idealized" woman. But we certainly cannot overlook the voyeuristic, even sadistic possibilities in this text—after authorizing his act of metaphor ("I compare her / to a fallen leaf") the young housewife is metaphorically crushed in the last stanza; regardless of the debatable tone of this ending, the movement here must be seen as evidence of patriarchy's and poetry's appropriation of the female body through gaze, description, and possession. Thus, Williams's poem is doubly conventional; for all its refusal of idealization, it quite assuredly depicts the muse in a manner that is conventional and unproblematic. And as in Williams, so in Amy Lowell's "Madonna of the Evening Flowers" (1919): when the modern poet goes in search of a muse, that muse is usually found:

> Suddenly I am lonely:
> Where are you?
> I go about searching.
>
> Then I see you,
> Standing under a spire of pale blue larkspur,
> With a basket of roses on your arm.
> (*Complete Poetical Works*, 210)

We might recognize the rejection of heterosexual poetic strategies in "Modern Craft" as a signal of aesthetic exhaustion, not unlike the strategies of Edna St. Vincent Millay, about whom Debra Fried writes, in tropes echoing those of Crane's poem, "By identifying the sonnet's scanty ground with an erotic grove of excess, turning the chastity belt of poetic form into a token of sexual indulgence, Millay invades the sanctuary of male poetic control" ("Andromeda Unbound," 17).

5. H. H. Smith's *Aaron Siskind: Photographer* (Horizon Press, 1965) describes the parallel between Crane and Stieglitz as the way in which objects in their respective texts are used not only to express inner states of emotion (as in Eliot) but also to suggest harmonies among them that allude to more transcendental laws or insights.

6. Pound's attraction to the ideogram, which would seem to be the point in modernism furthest from mimesis and closest to abstraction, is in fact based on the mimetic qualities of the ideogram and its ability to suggest relations in the real world without the mediating, antimimetic qualities of language. The ideogram becomes, in a purely linguistic sense, the "answer" to the search for a direct representation of the world. In another sense, it is without history in Western poetry and therefore also becomes a representation that has no mediating historical associations to block its transparency.

7. I draw here on Barbara Smith's helpful distinction between fictive and natural discourses in *On the Margins of Discourse* (U. of Chicago Press, 1983). Crane's work is not mimetic of any speech act or verbal behavior—i.e., it is neither a conversation poem, a confession, a hymn, or a meditation. If Crane's poetry is mimetic of anything, it is mimetic of poetry.

8. We cannot ignore, of course, the marvelous suspension of gender that occurs in Chaplin's films. If not gay, their main character often exhibits behaviors that make his gender identification ambiguous (he sews, he flutters his eyelashes, he blushes, is shy and practically defenseless); the list could go on, but it is clear, as James D. Baker pointed out to me, that a homosexual reading of the character is not impossible and may in fact have been part of its attraction to Crane and to generations of viewers. The Crane poem seems to have been a response to the Cleveland screening of *The Kid*.

9. There are other Ashbery poems that do not present any hint of a naive assertion of stable identity. But perhaps it is Ashbery's radical maneuver here to present homosexual cruising as a locus of stability in the face of his own canonical exploitation of decentered subjectivity. "The Ongoing Story" is an uncharacteristically Whitmanian moment in Ashbery, for the other typical objects of his parody are in evidence (Sydney Carton "mounting the guillotine," "a course / Called Background of the Great Ideas") but the moment of interaction between the two figures at the poem's close seems the only genuine experience in the poem.

10. It would be one thing—and an accurate one—to say that homosexuality is denied its object of desire and hence its poetic correlatives; it is another—and suggests an altogether different notion of desire and its dissemination through cultural fields of knowledge—to suggest that homosexuality needs to be apprehended as allegory. I draw here on Paul De Man's comment on Benjamin, that "allegory names the rhetorical process by which the literary text moves from a phenomenal, world-oriented to a grammatical, language-oriented direction" ("Lyrical Voice in Contemporary Theory," 69). What we see in "Possessions" is the grammar of homosexuality and Crane's battle to align its paradigmatic and syntagmatic axes.

Introduction to *American Women Poets in the 21st Century: Where Lyric Meets Language* (2002)

JULIANA SPAHR

Lyric is not and never has been a simplistic genre, despite its seeming innocence. It is only recently, after modernism, that it has gotten its bad name for being traditional, for being romantic, in the derisive sense.[1] And while much ink has been spilt on defining lyric,[2] there is no consensus on its value. Some argue that the lyric's intimate and interior space of retreat is its sin. This is essentially Adorno's argument, which leads to his famous declaration that "to write poetry after Auschwitz is barbaric."[3] Some argue that because lyric is retreat, it resists. María Rosa Menocal, for instance, writes, "When the world all around is calling for clear distinctions, loyalties to Self and hatred of others, and, most of all, belief in the public and legal discourses of single languages and single states—smooth narratives—what greater threat exists than that voice which rejects such easy orthodoxies with their readily understood rhetoric and urges, instead, the most difficult readings, those that embrace the painfully impossible in the human heart?"[4] (1994, 89).[5]

This debate about retreat is one that the poets included here [in *American Women Poets in the 21st Century*] often enact and discuss. Brock-Broido, for instance, echoes Adorno but without his judgment when she writes, "My logic of Lyric does not permit me to assign a Politic to language . . . The I is the Alpha, not 'Witness.'"[6] And on this topic, Brenda Hillman notes simply that "lyric has its limits" (277). She is right to admit this. The lyric has not transcended the limits of aesthetics much recently. Even this collection, which makes room within lyric for language writing's more politicized claims, focuses mainly on formal and aesthetic issues. Most of the poets and critics in this collection use the word "lyric" to refer to interiority and/or intimate speech that avoids confession, clear speech, or common sense. Many poets here speak of lyric as the genre of and about impossibility and difficulty. In short, when they talk of innovation, they often talk of lyric. Brock-Broido, for instance, aligns with lyric's difficulty when she declares, "I want a poetry which is inorganic, an artifact or artifice, riddle with truth." And so does Graham when she ends "Philosopher's Stone" with

> sensation of beauty unseen; an owlet's
> cry;
> a cry from something closer to the ground that's uttered
> twice and which I cannot name—although it
> seems bright yellow in its pitch.

Likewise, Lauterbach writes of her interest in a poetics of "a whole fragment," one where "meaning abides or arises exactly at the place where 'use' appears." This desire to articulate those moments where meaning is slipping away is lyric's great tradition.

But what is exciting about this collection is how the social and the cultural keep introducing and developing an aesthetic frame whether the poets admit it or not. In part these concerns intrude because of the collection's frame of women and their relation to innovation. Lyric has often had a troubled history of relation with women. Many blame the Petrarchian tradition with its male lover and female beloved. Yet it is not that women avoid or have avoided writing lyrics. Sappho is the obvious otherwise. Many critics also point out how women have been busy reclaiming the lyric from the centuries of mythically gendered male tradition.[7] But because this collection emphasizes innovation, the poems presented here have little resemblance to this tradition and the small space women have claimed for themselves. As Howe puts it, "I write to break out into perfect primeval Consent" (328). Innovation is a word that is as hard to define as lyric, but for the most part here it means the use of agrammatical modernist techniques such as fragmentation, parataxis, run-ons, interruption, and disjunction, and at the same time the avoidance of linear narrative development, of meditative confessionalism, and of singular voice. Many of these writers have taken to heart Kathleen Fraser's and Rachel Blau Du Plessis's suggestion that modernist innovation is a feminist space,[8] even though much of this work does not appear conventionally feminist at first glance. There is in this collection little attention to how women, or these poets themselves, are oppressed or marginal—little attention to gender asymmetry. Few of the poets here present a poetry of uplift with positive images of revised femininity. Instead, much of this work investigates representation itself to suggest alternatives to lyric's troubled and limiting history for women. It moves away from too easily separated and too easily declarative identities.

Because of its alphabetical organization, the concerns of the poets and critics in *American Women Poets in the 21st Century* loop around and into each other. The collection begins with Rae Armantrout's up-front statement about her association with language poetry even as she quickly moves to earlier, and more lyrical, influences such as William Carlos Williams and Emily Dickinson. Armantrout's work is distinctive in this volume for how directly it documents the various power struggles between and within genders. In "A Story," a wonderfully telling revision of lyric intimacy, she replaces the lyric's lover and beloved with a "good mother" who tells the child:

> "I love you, but I don't
> like the way you lie there
> pinching your nipples
> while I'm trying to read you a story."

This poem points to the value of the lyric in exposing how our intimacies are watched by others and thus, with this stare, also restricted. In "Lyricism of the Swerve: The Poetry of Rae Armantrout," Hank Lazer calls this the "swerve" of Armantrout's poetry, a quality that he defines as "peculiarly teasing, humorous, thoughtful (and thought-provoking) engagement at those junctures, joints, and sites of adjacency" (31). This swerve, Armantrout notes in "Cheshire Poetics," has feminist roots in what Pound called the slither of H.D. And while Lazer mentions that Armantrout's work is often seen as "less" political in comparison to her fellow language writers, his essay importantly points to "the inherently political nature of her calculated subversion of comfortable and comforting assumptions" (38). His essay, as it places Armantrout's work in the context of lyric written by women, clearly points out how Armantrout uses lyric's intimacy and language writing's politics to suggest a feminist, engaged lyric, or what he calls "an ethics of writing."

While Armantrout can declare her allegiance to language writing simply and easily at the beginning of her essay, Mei-mei Berssenbrugge's work has always existed in between the many social formations that define contemporary poetry. She clearly has alliances with language writing; in "By Correspondence," she mentions conversations with James Sherry as an influence. And she just as clearly has alliances with Asian-American groups such as the Basement Workshop and the Morita Dance Company, which produced a performance of "Fog," and also the Hawai'i-based Bamboo Ridge. She also clearly has alliances with the arts scene, as her collaborations with Kiki Smith and her husband Richard Tuttle demonstrate. All of these alliances combine to make her work distinctly exploratory of the internal but not the confessional or the intimate. The excerpt included here from *Four Year Old Girl*, for instance, begins inside the body with detail:

> The *genotype* is her genetic constitution.
> The *phenotype* is the observable expression of the genotype as structural
> and biochemical traits.

This looking inside at the complicated ways in which human emotion becomes constructed is Berssenbrugge's innovative contribution to lyric's tendency to concentrate on interior emotion.[9] Linda Voris in "A Sensitive Empiricism: Berssenbrugge's Phenomenological Investigations" argues that Berssenbrugge's work "is compositional in method, accreting observations, contingent possibilities, and contradictions that seem to materialize by stretching ever outwards, much like Tatlin's compositions built out from the corners of the room" (69). While Voris, who concentrates more on the form and aesthetics of Berssenbrugge's work, does not much address it, there is an interesting dialogue between feminism and the lyric in this work. In "By Correspondence," Berssenbrugge writes, "I also identify with my mother's and my grandmother's feminism, which seemed immediate to me, perhaps because of matriarchal character that is part of Chinese culture" (66). This feminism is clearly evident within Berssenbrugge's attention to how bodies, mainly female ones, are represented in writing and art. *Four Year Old Girl*, for instance, avoids conventional representation and looks at genotype and phenotype to observe that "Between her and the displaced gene is another relation, the effect of meaning" (53).

While this book brings together a number of women writers who define themselves as innovative, many are innovative in different ways and for different reasons. Further, many of these poets do not feel at all aligned with each other. Some of this division is merely about who breaks bread with whom. But one strong difference in this collection is between those who turn to modernist techniques for political reasons and those who do so for aesthetic reasons. Lucie Brock-Broido, for instance, begins her essay "Myself a Kangaroo among the Beauties" by stating, "My logic of Lyric does not permit me to assign a Politic to Language" (100). Later in the essay she explicitly separates her work from language writing: "A poem which the world longs to call a Language Poem is too open for my taste" (101) and "After I had been the recipient of a particularly thrashing review, Charles Wright, in a letter of solidarity & sympathy, wrote to me regarding LANGUAGE (?) Poetry. He wrote: 'What have we been doing all this time anyway, Barking?'" (101). Instead Brock-Broido claims that she aspires to be "a New Elliptical."[10] In terms of the formal devices used in poems such as "Carrowmore" and "Am More"—fragments, phrases, run-ons, and ambiguity—Brock-Broido's work does not differ that much from poets who assign a politics to language (and one cannot help but hear Howe's pivotal *My Emily Dickinson* in Brock-Broido's *The Master Letters*) and are heavily influenced by language writing such as that by Norma Cole, Fraser, or Cole Swensen. Yet her work avoids the politics of empowerment of these poets. Brock-Broido's poems, for instance, draw from feminism's tendency to represent female subjects and their voices, yet her work avoids conventional uplift. As Stephen Burt notes in "'Subject, Subjugate, Inthralled': The Selves of Lucie Brock-Broido," "The Selves

Brock-Broido invokes are almost always victims; many are, or imagine they are, imprisoned, wounded, helpless" (112). And as he writes of Brock-Broido's *The Master Letters*, "The Poems depict divided, troubled speakers and writers who appeal, implore, or submit to others—to 'masters,' to readers—to complete them and resolve their divisions" (107). Burt's negotiation is to see Brock-Broido's poems as "masochistic" in the feminist sense that Jessica Benjamin gave that word. When Burt places Brock-Broido's work in the context of poetry, he turns mainly to master canonical figures such as John Berryman, Robert Browning, John Donne, T. S. Eliot, Richard Howard, Stanley Kunitz, and Alexander Pope, rooting her work more in lyric's dramatic monologue than in feminist issues of representation (even those complicated by masochism).

While the works of Jorie Graham and Brock-Broido travel very different paths, both reflect similar concerns. Graham also explores issues of speech and the difficult unruliness of language that has been the lyric's territory since its origins. As much as Dickinson's work has influenced Brock-Broido, so it influences Graham's work, as Thomas Gardner argues in "Jorie Graham and Emily Dickinson: Singing to Use the Waiting." Gardner locates Dickinson in Graham in "the poet's broken speech to the absent beloved" (151), in similar approaches to silence. Graham uses innovation for individual and free expression: "I believe most signature styles are born as much out of temperament—and its rare *original* idiosyncrasies—as anything else." In "Philosopher's Stone," Graham expands on this:

> . . . . the hole
> filling back in on itself—as the self fills in on itself—a
> collectivity—a
> god making of himself many
> creatures [in the cage there is food] [outside only the great
> circle called freedom] [an empire which begins
> with a set table] and I should like, now that the last washes of my gaze
> let loose over the field, to say, if this peering,
> it is the self—there—out to the outer reaches of
> my hand

The emerging phenomenon of the aesthetically focused female poet who turns to more modernist/innovative forms reaches its apex in Graham's work. That this phenomenon has been limited to mainly women poets seems to suggest that Fraser's and DuPlessis's theorizing on innovation and gender still resonates. Graham's work is often the most disjunctive published by established journals and presses, yet in the overall picture of contemporary poetry, Graham celebrates, as Helen Vendler notes and as Gardner quotes in his article, "middleness."

Instead of the poem as an act of individual expression, Barbara Guest emphasizes the poem's reach in "The Forces of the Imagination": "This position of 'subjectivity' or 'openness' is what the poem desires to obtain, free to be molded by forces that shall condition the imagination of the poet" (190). Just as Graham's work does not fit easily into conventional categories, neither does Guest's. But while Graham sees poetry as idiosyncrasy, Guest sees it as connective intimacy. How Guest is always reaching out and putting things together is the focus of Sara Lundquist's "Implacable Poet, Purple Birds: The Work of Barbara Guest." As Lundquist notes, "Guest eludes because her scope and range are so variable and large, and because she so elegantly presents so many seemingly contradictory qualities" (193). This variable largeness is just one of many characteristics that makes Guest such an important figure in the New York School. But also, socially, Guest is a wonderfully complicated figure. As Lundquist notes, Guest was at the Barnard conference as "modernism's representative, yet [she] reached quite effortlessly across the generations to the youngest poets there" (201). This connective intent defines Guest's "Mysteriously Defining the Mysterious: Byzantine Proposals of Poetry," which is full of names and places and travels. Lundquist's essay demonstrates the largeness of Guest's work when she describes her own experiences reading and teaching Guest. She ends her essay by describing a much marked-up copy of Guest's *Rocks on a Platter* and the way "the words consort, their mixing-it-up on the page, their intercourse, their dance, their oxymoronic tussle, their sighs and hiccups and jokes and caresses" (215).

Like Guest, Lyn Hejinian's emphasis is on relation. Her "Some Notes toward a Poetics" begins, "Poetics is not personal. A poetics gets formed in and as a relationship with the world" (235). As she quotes from her own teaching notebook:

> Language is one of the principal forms our curiosity takes.
>
> The language of poetry is a language of inquiry.
>
> Poetry takes as its premise that language (all language) is a medium for experiencing experience. It provides us with the consciousness of consciousness. (240)

Here poetry is again about thinking. With Armantrout, Hejinian has been social and aesthetically a part of language writing in the Bay Area since the 1970s. Her excerpt from *Happily* deeply explores inquiry or, as she writes, "The dilemmas in sentences form tables of discovery of things created to create the ever better dilemma which is to make sense to others" (234). The poem is written, new sentence-style,[11] as a nonpersonal mix of confession and observation. Juxtaposition guides more than narrative. Consider, for instance, the avoidance of the linear development of narrative's progress in these lines:

> Nostalgia is another name for one's sense of loss at the thought that one has sadly gone
> along happily overlooking something, who knows what
> Perhaps there were three things, no one of which made sense of the other two
> A sandwich, a wallet, and a giraffe
> Logic tends to force similarities but that's not what we mean by "sharing existence"

This project of inquiry defines much of Hejinian's work. She is perhaps best known for *My Life*, a formally shaped autobiography.[12] And of all the writers included here, Hejinian's work is the farthest from lyric conventions. It is rarely intimate, and almost always explores larger, more communal relations in long, inquiring sentences. Craig Dworkin's "Parting with Description" concentrates mainly on Hejinian's *Writing Is an Aid to Memory* (a early work that is more lyrical than most). His essay is a wonderfully "paranoid" (his term) reading of connection in this work. As he notes, "Like many of her colleagues, she was interested in 'putting things together in such a way as to enable them to coincide' and thus 'make a way of seeing connections see writing'" (251).

Brenda Hillman in "Twelve Writings toward a Poetics of Alchemy, Dread, Inconsistency, Betweenness, and California Geological Syntax" writes, "It doesn't matter where you begin because you'll just have to do it again" (276). She then locates a similar philosophy of change in mercury, chaos, and the feminine. In this essay she also describes how her writing moved from meditative realism to a feminism that has been influenced by the formal techniques of language writing. In the poem "A Geology," change is exemplified by an attention to verbs, the shifting teutonic plates of California, and drug addiction:

> There are six major faults, there are skipped
> verbs, there are more little
> thoughts in California. The piece of coast

slides on the arrow; down is
reverse. Subduction means the coast
goes underneath the continent, which is
rather light. It was my friend. I needed it.
The break in the rock shows forward; the flash
hurts. Granite is composed of quartz, hornblende
and other former fire. When a drug
is trying to quit it has to stretch. Narrow comes
from the same place as glamour.

Lisa Sewell's "Needing Syntax to Love: Expressive Experimentalism in the Work of Brenda Hillman" also charts these changes in Hillman's style. She points to how "Hillman is both an innovator and a traditionalist who seems to question but also take for granted the expressive, communicative powers of language" and notes that Hillman's "experimental approach grows out of her life experiences" (283). In her biographically influenced essay, Sewell argues that Hillman's disenchantment with meditative realism is the result of life experiences. This relation between form and autobiography is a provocative one in Hillman's work.

Susan Howe often turns to history, especially U. S. history, to write a poetry of lyric and recovery. Her by now famous statement "I wish I could tenderly lift from the dark side of history, voices that are anonymous, slighted—inarticulate" (328) from "There Are Not Leaves Enough to Crown to Cover to Crown to Cover" reflects her revisionary and feminist uses of the lyric. Her essay begins with autobiography: "I was born in Boston Massachusetts on June 10th, 1937" (325). Yet the autobiography turns to history in the next paragraph. Howe's work is singular for its attention to the uses and abuses of history. In "Articulating the Inarticulate: Singularities and the Counter-method in Susan Howe," Ming-Qian Ma points out that "to articulate the inarticulate, Howe's poetic praxis pivots on a lyric consciousness upon which impinges a double mission of rescuing and breaking free: rescuing the 'stutter' that Howe hears in American literature" (331). This attention defines Howe's unique style as have a politics, not just an aesthetics. As she notes in "C H A I R":

Art has filled my days
Strange and familiar not
for embellishment but
object as it is in itself (310)

As Ma notices, Howe often writes from and through a source text. Because the "inarticulate," another word for what is called innovative in this collection, often comes from history, her project is less about making new or breaking down the conventions of contemporary languages and more about giving voice to what is often overlooked by history's master narratives.

Lauterbach turns to "chance and change" in her "As (It) Is: Toward a Poetics of the Whole Fragment." Chance and change, she points out, revise the modernist fragment so that it "eschews totalizing concepts of origin, unity, closure, and completion" (363) In her poem "In the Museum of the Word (Henri Matisse)," this attention to revising the modernist fragment is phrased as such:

impermanent oracular trace so that
not any fragment will do counting my steps
from margin to margin/scenic on foot
turning a page. (356)

Lauterbach's work has a longer history than most of the work emerging now that is poised between meditative attention and language writing. Her use of ekphrasis has meant that the subject of much of her work has been about aesthetics, and with her interest in modernism and her social association with language writing, her work has greatly expanded the concerns of ekphrasis. As Christine Hume in "'Enlarging the Last Lexicon of Perception' in Ann Lauterbach's Framed Fragments" writes, "If we recognize a defining condition of the lyric, from Sappho to C. D. Wright, as authorial control and singular heroic expression, then, Lauterbach fractures and implodes this tradition with wildly generous lyric capacities, large enough to contain competing demands of sensual and analytic intelligences" (385).

An alphabetical accident places Mullen's work at the end of this collection, which is fortunate because her work also points to an emerging use of lyric intimacy for reasons beyond aesthetics. Mullen's work is especially attentive to how lyric can be an exploratory genre with which to negotiate the debate about whether identity is stasis or flux. Her work combines numerous influences. One can hear the identity-inflected lyric of writers such as Lucille Clifton and Jayne Cortez, the identity-resistant lyric of writers such as Myung Mi Kim, movements and poetics groupings as diverse as Black Arts, Umbra, and language writing. Mullen's work disrespects none of these influences and yet takes them all somewhere else. What emerges is a discussion of gender and race that moves between essentialism and constructivism to suggest that what is essential about identity is its flux, the "divergent universification" that she locates in Cortez's brain in "Fancy Cortex." It is this inclusiveness that Elisabeth A. Frost notes when she writes, "Mullen's poetry critiques the enforcement of difference, of 'apartheid,' both on and off the page" (406). Mullen's work, as much of the work in this collection, provides a telling reply to those who would argue that lyric innovation should be, or just is, an inappropriate genre for examining the political, the social, or the cultural.

This collection only presents ten poets. It makes no claim to comprehensiveness. One sleepless night I made a list of the influences and alliances and friendships that I felt resonating here among these writers: Gwendolyn Brooks, Marilyn Chin, Cortez, Clifton, Cole, Du Plessis, Carolyn Forche, Fraser, Joy Harjo, Erica Hunt, Claudia Keelan, Kim, Bernadette Mayer, Tracie Morris, Thylias Moss, Cathy Song, Swensen, Ann Waldman, Rosemarie Waldrop, Susan Wheeler, C. D. Wright, and Lois-Ann Yamanaka. And in the morning I realized how incomplete this list was and made a note to begin another.

Reading these essays all together has shown me that while there is a clear difference in intent between a poem written for investigating the self and one written for investigating language or community, it is more and more the case that the techniques might be similar. In other words, form is no longer the clear marker of intention or meaning that it was thirty years ago.

This essay is a rewrite of a much shorter introduction that I originally submitted to begin this book. In this earlier draft I wrote, "in this collection, poets who only on rare moments find themselves in the same room are here together." And also, "The divergent work included within this collection suggests that women's poetry in America is thriving not through its samenesses but through its mixture of diversity and collectivity." My feeling was that it was important not to see this book as yet another attempt to stake a boundaried territory or to suggest a new movement. I felt that the poems and essays here were gathered less with an attention to coverage and more to suggest new possibilities for dialogue, new pedagogical opportunities, and that there were significant disagreements and differences among the poets and critics collected here (even if they rarely erupt on the page except in Brock-Broido's "Myself a Kangaroo among the Beauties").

An anonymous reader's report contained this response: "Reservation: what keeps nagging at me is that the anthology coheres not because it dramatizes competing poetries (as Ms. Spahr claims in the introduction) but rather consistently makes a persuasive case for varieties of *innovative* poetries."

I think the reader is right—that this collection does not dramatize competing poetries (such a collection might feature a boxing match between Gerald Stern and Bruce Andrews). Its attention is to the contemporary poetries that are attentive to modernism's forms. Yet I would not want to suggest that innovation is a value in itself or that all these poets use innovation with the same intent. What matters is what innovation does, in what Hejinian calls "inquiry." And I would add the word "expansive" to that inquiry. I find value in lyrics that retreat from individualism and idiosyncrasy to pointing to heady and unexpected yet intimate pluralisms. And lyrics that help me to place myself as part of a larger, connective culture. Lyrics that, in other words, are not at all ignorant about structures. Lyrics that, as Menocal points out, are "constantly engaged in the onerous but exhilarating struggle with the myriad institutions that surround it." (58). Lyrics that comment on community and that move lyric away from individualism to shared, connective spaces. Lyrics that reveal how our private intimacies have public obligations and ramifications, how intimacy has a social bond with shared meaning. It thus matters to me that lyric not be given up to aesthetics *only* or even aesthetics *mainly*, that its retreat not be from argument but from overly clear arguments, to use Menocal's language again, from single languages and single states and smooth narratives.

I think the anonymous reader is right that there are varieties of innovative poetries. This collection begins a dialogue between the two often falsely separated poetries of language and lyric. The unevenness of these two terms, one a social grouping and the other a genre, remains a sign of some dissonance even as critics often pit language and lyric against each other with straw-man models. Yet there is a conversation about form among these poets even as there not one about poetry's intentions.

This collection does not even begin to attempt to represent the varieties of innovative poetries in the United States right now. With the exception of Mullen, poets who directly and variously explore racial identity are missing. Instead, the collection presents a variety of ways that modernist techniques are being used within lyric contexts. That this sort of innovation is so rarely used to address race deserves more attention. While some might say that modernist techniques are inadequate to the discussion, these techniques are inadequate to the discussion, these techniques have often and successfully been used to investigate gender and to suggest more collective, connective models of intimacy beyond a lover and a beloved. My feeling, and that is as assertive as it gets, is that these forms have been perceived by many as elitist or privileged spaces.[13] I think that this perception is a misreading and that the work of many of the poets included here proves otherwise. But I worry that this feeling in the air, even unsubstantiated, has limited the sorts of inquiry that writing in modernist, innovative forms might explore—that it has both directed writers who identify as other than white or privileged by class away from them and suggested that these forms might be less than ideal for critique of certain subjects.

One valuable aspect of the writers associated with language writing has been their attention to the variety of critiques that modernist innovation makes possible. Yet this group of writers has, with the exception of Bruce Andrews, often avoided addressing racial politics. That Mullen is now taking these same techniques and their attention to critique to examine race makes her work so valuable. In an interview with Farah Griffin, Michael Magee, and Kristen Gallagher, Mullen says that

> one reason I wrote *Muse and Drudge* is because having written *Tree Tall Woman*, when I went around reading from that book there were a lot of black people in my audience. There would be white people and brown people and maybe other people of color as well. Suddenly, when I went around to do readings of *Trimmings* and "Spermkit," I would be the one black person in the room, reading my poetry. . . . I felt, "Well, this is interesting. This tells me something about the way that I'm writing now," although I didn't think I was any less black in those two books or any more black in *Tree Tall Woman*. But I think that the way that these things get defined in the public domain is that, yeah, people saw "Spermkit" as being not a black book but an innovative book. And this idea that you can be black or innovative, you know, is what I was really trying to struggle against. And *Muse and Drudge* was my attempt to show that I can do both at the same time.[14]

In this anecdote, Mullen points to how she finds lyric as a place for an intimate, self-aware investigation of her own relationship to race, class, and gender, to dominant and subordinate cultures, to her role as spokesperson for "minority experience." Yet at the same time she points to how the form of the work can change the construction of a segregated social space. Similarly, in "Poetics Statement" Mullen points to the possibilities of writing in a world of expanding illiteracy (she means both the illiteracy of not being able to read and the growing nominally educated who cannot read critically). Here, while acknowledging the limitations of her work—its limited distribution and its nonstandard forms—she states that her future (ideal?) reader is "the offspring of an illiterate woman" and that she writes (echoing Stein) "for myself and others." My hope is that through Mullen's example, other writers, especially those with dominant (white and also middle- and upper-class) identities, will continue to use lyric as a place for resistance of racial separation. While contemporary lyric often avoids discussing categories of identity, Mullen's work turns lyric's establishing subjectivity into communal opportunity.[15]

Much has been made of the transition from lyric to narrative, from metaphor to allegory, from seduction to possession, from incantation to realism. Yet despite the constant intrusion of new genres and new media, lyric persists. Is it possible to have a culture without it? "The poem and you need each other" is how Guest expresses this. From reading the works presented here, I have learned much about how lyric might be an ideal genre for certain sorts of critique, and how the lyric space of intimacy has the potential to be an exemplary space for examining political intimacies, race and gender intimacies, and community intimacies in addition to its relentless attention to more personal intimacy. Berssenbrugge writes of a "collaborative space that is larger and more fertile for me than writing alone" (63). And Mullen writes that her poetry "explores the reciprocity of language and culture" and "is informed by my interaction with readers, writers, scholars, and critics, as well as my interest in the various possibilities for poetry in written and spoken American English" (403). Although I find comparisons between contemporary poets and old masters to be often silly, I cannot help but think of Dante's use of the colloquial in lyric in this context. What I mean is not that Mullen is the new Dante, but that the emphasis on innovation in this collection is a return to what made lyric so valuable centuries ago. Lyric is by definition innovative. When it stops being innovative it is on longer lyric. This collection points not only to how women writers are using innovation attentively, but also to how women are major contributors to innovation. Here, where the "you" and the "I" are no longer clear, there is much to be hopeful about the lyric in the beginnings of the twenty-first century.

1. As Marjorie Perloff points out when she discusses the collection, *New Definitions of Lyric: Theory, Technology, and Culture*, ed. Jeffrey Walker (New York: Garland, 1998): "For Walker, as for the other essayists, romantic lyric thus becomes a derogatory term; it connotes inwardness, subjectivity, monovocality, and transparency—all of these politically suspect in the age of multiculturalism. But in making these claims, Walker, McGuirk, and the others seem to be conflating two things: the attenuated, neo-romantic lyric of the later twentieth century, as that lyric has been promoted by such leading critics as Harold Bloom, and the actual English lyric of the Romantic period" (245–46).

2. See, for instance, Northrop Frye, "Approaching the Lyric," in *Lyric Poetry: Beyond New Criticism*, ed. Hošek and Parker (Ithaca, N.Y.: Cornell University Press, 1985), 31–37; Gérard Genette, *The Architext: An Introduction*, trans. Jane E. Lewin (Berkeley: University of California Press, 1992); John Hollander, *Vision and Resonance: Two Senses of Poetic Form* (New Haven: Yale University Press, 1985); and W. R. Johnson, *The Idea of Lyric: Lyric Modes in Ancient and Modern Poetry* (Berkeley: University of California Press, 1982) for the never-ending discussion of what lyric might be. An interesting recent article on the subject is Jeffrey Walker, "The View from Halicarnassus: Aristotelianism and the Rhetoric of the Epideictic Song," in *New Definitions of Lyric*, 17–48.

3. Theodor W. Adorno, *Prisms*, trans. Samuel and Shierry Weber (Cambridge: MIT Press, 1981), 34. Steve Evans, a critic of contemporary poetry, recently pointed out to me that Adorno revises this statement in *Negative Dialectics*, trans. E. B. Ashton (New York: Continuum International Publishing Group, 1990), 363. The assumption that lyric is apolitical is often perpetuated by contemporary poets who define themselves as "lyric poets." See also Victor Li, "Narcissism and the Limits of the Self," in *Tropic Crucible: Self and Theory in Language and Literature*, ed. Ranjit Chatterjee and Colin Nicholson (Singapore: Singapore University Press, 1984), 3–23.

4. María Rosa Menocal, *Shards of Love: Exile and the Origins of Lyric* (Durham, NC: Duke University Press, 1994), 89.

5. Paul Allen Miller in *Lyric Texts and Lyric Consciousness: The Birth of a Genre from Archaic Greek to Augustan Rome* (New York: Routledge, 1994) notes similarly that despite lyric being "an ambiguous voice, straddling the line between public importance and private reflection," it "is always somewhat subversive. It separates the individual from his or her communal ties and responsibilities, and examines his or her most intimate thoughts and feelings, in the process lifting a corner of that veil of socially useful repression which allows us to interact with one another in a reasonably civilized manner" (124, 127). For more on lyric's resistant possibilities, see Charles Altieri, "Responsiveness to Lyric and the Critic's Responsibilities," *Contemporary Literature* 32 (1991): 580–87; Hank Lazer, "The Lyric Valuables: Soundings, Questions, and Examples," *Modern Language Studies* 27.2 (1997): 25–50; Kevin McGuirk, "All Wi Doin': Toni Harrison, Linton Kwesi Johnson, and the Cultural Work of Lyric in Postwar Britain," in *New Definitions of Lyric*, 48–76; Susan Schultz, "'Called Null or Called Vocative': A Fate of the Contemporary Lyric," *Talisman* 14 (1995): 70–80; Mark Wallace, "On the Lyric as Experimental Possibility," July 1996: http://wings.buffalo.edu/epc/authors/wallace/lyric.html, and the introduction to the first three issues of the journal *Apex of the M.*

6. Lucie Brock-Broido, *American Women Poets in the 21st Century: Where Lyric Meets Language*, 100. Page references to poets and essays in this collection will be cited in main text.

7. This criticism concentrates on women's subversion within accepted forms. Women, these critics often argue, take the form and move within its box to make room for themselves. Studies of women's subversion of the sonnet have tended to look at how women do not leave the box of form nor its alliances to the court of courtly love. Instead, they move into the box in order to claim it, in order to establish what gets called lyric subjectivity, for themselves. Ann Rosalind Jones, for instance, in *The Currency of Eros: Women's Love Lyric in Europe, 1540–1620* (Bloomington: Indiana University Press, 1990) argues that women poets of 1540–1620 act as negotiators who "accept the dominant ideology encoded into a text but particularize and transform it in the service of a different group" (4). The argument remains similar about more contemporary work. In *Desiring Women: Women Sonneteers and Petrarchism* (Carbondale: Southern Illinois University Press, 2000), Mary B. Moore notes that "Victorian and modernist women could write the Petrarchan sonnet because its apparent focus on the heart allowed them to veil their sometimes subversive ideas about gender and eroticism, even as they claimed Petrarchan complexity, and hence

subjectivity through the mode" (11). In *Making Love Modern: The Intimate Public Worlds of New York's Literary Women* (New York: Oxford University Press, 1998), Nina Miller points out that Edna St. Vincent Millay "used traditional verse to turn her (inescapable) female sexuality to artistic authority" (39). In "'A Splintery Box': Race and Gender in the Sonnets of Gwendolyn Brooks," *Genre* 25.1 (1992): 47–64, Stacy Carson Hubbard points to an appropriative practice in Brooks's sonnets that work in a highly traditional form even as they articulate a nontraditional voice. Maureen Honey argues similarly about women poets of the Harlem Renaissance in *Shadowed Dreams: Women's Poetry of the Harlem Renaissance* (New Brunswick: Rutgers University Press, 1989), 1–41, and Lynn Keller about Marilyn Hacker's sonnets in "Measured Feet 'in Gender Bender shoes': The Politics of Form in Marilyn Hacker's *Love, Death, and the Changing of the Seasons*," in *Feminist Measures: Soundings in Poetry and Theory*, edited by Lynn Keller and Cristanne Miller (Ann Arbor: University of Michigan Press, 1994), 260–86.

8. See Kathleen Fraser's *Translating the Unspeakable: Poetry and Innovative Necessity* (Tuscaloosa: University of Alabama Press, 2000), especially the essay "The Tradition of Marginality . . . and the Emergence of *HOW(ever)*," and Rachel Blau du Plessis, *The Pink Guitar* (New York: Routledge, 1990). For the larger discussion of modernist techniques and feminism, see the work of French feminists such as Julia Kristeva, especially *Revolution in Poetic Language*, trans. Margaret Waller (New York: Columbia University Press, 1984) and Hélène Cixous, especially *The Exile of James Joyce*, trans. Sally A. J. Purcell (New York: D. Lewis, 1972).

9. See Charles Altieri, "Intimacy and Experiment in Mei-Mei Berssenbrugge's *Empathy*," in *We Who Love to Be Astonished: Experimental Women's Writing and Performance Poetics*, ed. Laura Hinton and Cynthia Hogue (Tuscaloosa: University of Alabama Press, 2002), 54–68, for a more detailed reading.

10. See Stephen Burt's essays on ellipticisim, "The Elliptical Poets" and "About Ellipticism (Round Two)" in *American Letters and Commentary* 11 (1991): 45–55 and 72–76.

11. See Ron Silliman, *The New Sentence* (New York: Roof Books, 1987).

12. Lyn Hejinian, *My Life* (Los Angeles: Sun & Moon Press, 1980). See Lisa Samuels for a discussion of the canonical status of *My Life* in "Eight Justifications for Canonizing *My Life*," *Modern Language Studies* 27. 2 (1997): 103–19.

13. See, for instance, Bob Perelman, *The Trouble with Genius: Language Writing and Literary History* (Princeton: Princeton University Press, 1994).

14. Farah Griffin, Michael Magee, and Kristen Gallagher. *Combo* 1 (1997): http://wings.buffalo.edu/epc/authors/mullen/interview-new.html.

15. For more on lyric subjectivity see Paul Allen Miller, *Lyric Texts and Lyric Consciousness* and Joel Fineman, *Shakespeare's Perjured Eye: The Invention of Poetic Subjectivity in the Sonnets* (Berkeley: University of California Press, 1988). Miller notes that lyric "is the re-presentation not simply of a 'strong personality,' but of a particular mode of being a subject, in which the self exists not as part of a continuum with the community and its ideological commitments, but is folded back against itself, and only from this space of interiority does it relate to 'the world' at large" (5). In "Romanticism and the Death of the Lyric Consciousness," Tillotama Rajan also notes that "pure lyric is a monological form, where narrative and drama alike are set in the space of difference. The latter present the self in interaction with other characters and events. But lyric, as a purely subjective form, is marked by the exclusion of the other through which we become aware of the difference of the self from itself. Lyric consciousness, in other words, comes as close as possible to approximating what Sartre calls a 'shut imaginary consciousness,' a consciousness without the dimension of being-in-the-world" (*Lyric Poetry: Beyond New Criticism*, ed. Chaviva Hošek and Patricia Parker [Ithaca: Cornell University Press, 1985], 196).

SECTION 10

Comparative Lyric

Reading lyric comparatively pulls us in contrary directions, since comparative work tends to emphasize linguistic, historical, and cultural differences at the same time that it tends to abstract these differences into a paradigm that allows for comparison. The consolidation of modern lyric reading has therefore served to open up the possibility for comparative analysis that makes both diversifying and unifying claims about lyric. In this respect, the essays collected in this final section return us to some of the basic questions raised in section 1 about lyric as a genre: the more we try to differentiate lyric through cross-cultural comparison, the more it appears to be a universal phenomenon. In the twentieth and twenty-first centuries, critics have used various ways of thinking about universality as a concept, and about what that concept is (or does) in the study of lyric. Some hearken back to a universal lyric impulse in primal song (be it the song and dance of primitive cultures, or the first songs of childhood) while others imagine "lyric time" realized in the universal present (the "here" and "now" of the poem, or its poetic performance) or projected into futurity (the continual evolution of lyric, or its eternal becoming). When a critic like Theodor Adorno takes up the specifically modern ideal of lyric poetry, in which "immersion in what has taken individual form elevates the lyric to the status of something universal," he does so in order to conclude that "the universality of the lyric's substance is social in nature." Adorno's universalism may have supposed a social utopian horizon not all versions of comparative lyric share, but wherever we find ourselves in the universe of lyric reading, the identification or differentiation of "something universal" in lyric depends on finding exemplary lyrics through, and for, comparison.

The idea that poetry originates in musical expression has a long history from antiquity to the present, resonating already before Rousseau's essay on the origin of languages in music but further developed in Romantic theories of language and early ethnographic studies of folklore, ballads, and popular song. By the early twentieth century, it was a critical commonplace to invoke the origins of all lyric in song; whatever circulated as "song" in previous centuries came to be called "lyric" after the late nineteenth century, and today we still refer to the words of a song as its "lyrics." J. W. Johnson's entry on "Lyric" (reprinted as late as 1993 in *The New Princeton Encyclopedia of Poetry and Poetics*, extending nineteenth-century ideas about folksong and modern ethnography into modern literary criticism) begins with the general claim that "lyric poetry may be said to retain most prominently the elements which evidence its origins in musical expression—singing, chanting, and recitation to musical accompaniment (see SONG)."[1] To demonstrate how "the irreducible denominator of all lyric poetry must, therefore, comprise those elements which it shares with the musical forms that produced it," Johnson dedicates a section on "historical developments" to a litany of lyric forms across many cultures (subdivided into Middle Eastern and Western traditions, as well as Russian and Eastern European, African, and Asian). This cross-cultural and transhistorical survey leads Johnson to the conclusion that "from its primordial form, the song as embodiment of emotion, the lyric has been expanded and altered through the centuries." Or to put this view another way, the continual expansion and alteration of lyric proves its intrinsic musical quality across historical and geographical differences and so (at least for encyclopedic readers) necessitates comparative reading.

The primacy of lyric for the creation of a literary culture that transcends many cultures is the answer to the question posed by Earl Miner in his essay, "Why Lyric?" In claiming that "the historical and ethnographic evidence has shown us that literature first comes into existence as lyric," Miner draws on the same critical tradition Johnson articulated in his encyclopedia entry, but he goes one step further to proclaim the role of lyric as "the originative or foundation genre for the poetics or poetic systems of all literary cultures." Starting from the hypothesis that "for all purposes it must be clear what we mean by lyric," Miner extends ethnographic accounts of the origins of lyric ("all are moved to song") into an aesthetic argument that he works out through a series of examples, ranging from Bowra's *Primitive Song* to selections from Chinese and Japanese poetry. What these examples demonstrate is "the special nature of lyric," as Miner defines it: "the distinguishing features of lyric are a presence and intensity that make it, in a double sense, literature of moment." For Miner, lyric is momentous not only because of this intensified immediacy—what he calls its "now-ness"—but also because of its continuous presence in literary history. Without lyric, the ongoing life of literature is at risk: "when the lyric of a given national culture is assaulted, literature is attacked at its very heart and soul." Theorizing both the particularity and the universality of lyric, Miner asserts its critical importance not only for the definition of "any given national culture" but also for the definition of comparative poetics as the systematic study of poetry across cultures. In this respect, the agenda of Miner's essay is to define a lyric theory that will serve to defend the historical practice of comparative literature: "Histories and theories join in two roles of lyric: we shall observe its function in the devising of systematic poetics and its priority in the emergence of literature itself."

Of course we do not need to posit lyric as a transcendent genre in order to devise a comparative poetics, as we have already seen in the work of Jonathan Culler (see section 1). His ongoing project to define a "theory of the lyric" offers a more pragmatic answer to the question "Why Lyric?" than that proposed by Miner. In a comparative essay on "The Modern Lyric" not included here, Culler defends the practical necessity of generic continuity for critical practice: "If one is to bring any clarity to this domain, one finds that one must in effect ask what have been the important and effective concepts of the lyric."[2] By reading modern poets like Baudelaire and Frost, Culler identifies an implicit generic model for modern lyric, and although he is willing to interrogate that norm, he retains the need for a normative concept of lyric; comparative lyric reading would not be possible without an idea of "the" lyric as its object. Thus while Culler acknowledges that "there are discontinuities in modern lyric poetry," he argues for the "investigation of continuities, especially continuities that play a central role in critical notions of modern poetry and the lyric genre." He concludes, "The comparative perspective here should enable one to investigate genres as models of reading and to explore the complicated relations between historical claims about changes in poetry itself and structural models that determine the interpretation of poems and suffuse our pedagogy" (299). Here again comparative poetics emerges as the necessary condition for mediating between "historical claims" and "structural models" for lyric, although for Culler comparative literature is a way to justify the study of the lyric, rather than (as in Miner) the other way around: "The comparatist's task in this case would be to pursue critical analysis of the model of the lyric implicit in interpretations of individual poets, and to assess that model in the larger comparative perspective" (285).

The second part of that task is of special interest to Jahan Ramazani in his essay on "Traveling Poetry." Baudelaire is a recurring touchstone for developing a modern model of the lyric (not only for Culler but for a wide range of critics such as Benjamin, Adorno, Jameson, Riffaterre, de Man, Agamben and many others not included in *The Lyric Theory Reader*), and Ramazani takes up that model in order to trace its perpetual displacement within the larger comparative perspective of a broader range of poets, poems, and poetry traveling east and west, north and south. As defined by Ramazani, "the traveling poem illuminates the differential structure through which the globalized subject enunciates and understands itself." In this lyricized vision of a global poetics, Ramazani retains the lyric subject as an "all-encompassing, cross-civilizational, lyric 'I,' the poet's first-person meditative utterance as omnium gatherum: translocal, binding disparities, forging new and surprising connections in its travel across the globe." Throughout his essay, Ramazani simultaneously emphasizes the compression of lyric poems and the expansion of poetry beyond the limits and limitations of Western lyric: "The metaphorical, lineal, and lyric expansiveness of traveling poetry—readily affording cross-cultural engagement, contact, and contamination—puts into question the adequacy of such limited and limiting models, which are identitarian even when represented as postcolonial, postmodern, or planetary." Here the very possibility of expanding lyric is predicated on the critical practice of modern lyric reading, demonstrated by Ramazani in his analysis of Langston Hughes's adoption of a self-enlarging "Whitmanian I" in a global context, or in his analysis of "In the Waiting Room" by Elizabeth Bishop as an "initiation into becoming a global subject," juxtaposed with a poem by the Ugandan poet Okot p'Bitek. Discovering both similarity and difference in the reinvention of a now globalized lyric subject, Ramazani summarizes his critical agenda for comparative poetics: "An adequate defense of time-and-space travel by lyric poetry needs to take account of both its connective (Hughes) and differential (Bishop) tendencies in relation to cultural others, since lyrics of cross-cultural sameness and those of cross-cultural difference are equally open to critique." Thus a universal model of lyric remains in place even as it moves around.

Ramazani elaborates the concept of "traveling poetry"—or what he later comes to call "a transnational poetics"—primarily through twentieth-century poems written in or translated into English during a new age of globalization. However, he also claims a longer history for the transnational circulation of lyric: "Consider, for example, the Japanese haiku, famously Anglicized by the imagists, or the Arabic ghazal, adapted for over a thousand years into Persian (taking its canonical form in that language), Turkish, Urdu, German, and English, mostly recently by the Kashmiri American poet Agha Shahid Ali." Through multiple translations and modern imitations of these poetic forms, the haiku and the ghazal have been transformed into exemplary lyrics for Anglo-American readers, and indeed (ever since Ali's publication of the first anthology of English ghazals in 2000), the ghazal in particular is emerging as a site for new work in comparative poetics.[3] For some critics, the ghazal is an example of transnational poetry that circulates in, and for, translation; for others, the long and varied history of the ghazal provides examples for reading "world poetry" in different languages; for still others, the ghazal exemplifies an idea of lyric either translated into or out of other literary traditions.

The lyricization of the ghazal by modern critics serves to move lyric reading in more than one direction, as we see in Aamir Mufti's work on the ghazals of Faiz Ahmed Faiz, the most significant Urdu poet of the postcolonial period. In contrast to Ramazani, who subsumes the ghazal into an argument about Anglophone transnational poetics, Mufti frames his reading of Faiz as a different kind of comparative project:

> In treating Faiz as a modern lyric poet, however, I am not suggesting that we engage in a search for qualities in modern Urdu verse that are characteristic of the lyric in modern Western poetry. On the contrary, the purpose of my analysis of a number of Faiz's poems is precisely to make it possible to explore the specificities of modern lyric in a colonial and postcolonial society. Above all, what the concept of lyric makes possible is the *translation*, the passage, of Faiz's poetry from a literary history that is specifically Urdu into a critical space for the discussion of *Indian* literary modernity as a whole.

In his essay "Toward a Lyric History of India," Mufti strategically adopts "the concept of lyric" in order to think about literary history and cultural politics not only within the context of postcolonial studies but also between ethnic and national discourses and in relation to critical theories of modernity. That tradition of critical thinking is for Mufti primarily associated with the Frankfurt school, and more specifically with Adorno's essay "On Lyric Poetry and Society." Drawing on Adorno's argument about lyric poetry as an exemplary site for the inscription of social meaning in its apparent distance from the social, Mufti's reading of Faiz argues that "the central drama of his poetry is the dialectic of a collective selfhood at the disjunctures of language, culture, nation, and community" and that it is precisely in those poems that are "closest to being pure 'lyric,' that is, ones in which the inward turn is most complete" that Faiz can give expression to "a self in partition." Mufti projects Adorno's account of lyric subjectivity into the problematic "I" of Urdu writing in order to "elucidate the place of lyric in Faiz's work and its relationship to the social horizon that is brought to crisis in partition." According to Mufti, the historical partition of India in 1947 is already delineated in the lines of ghazals by Faiz, in whose writing Mufti discovers a radically split subjectivity: "In Faiz's poetry, both the degradation of human life in colonial and postcolonial modernity—exploitation—and the withholding of a collective selfhood at peace with itself—what I am calling partition—find common expression in the suffering of the lyric subject."

What is assumed by Mufti's lyric reading of Faiz—and surely one reason for taking up a critical conversation with Adorno—is the philosophical tradition of German idealism and a German poetic tradition, revolving around the question of subjectivity and the immediacy of subjective experience within a larger version of the collective. As we saw in section 6, at the end of his essay "On Lyric Poetry and Society," Adorno revisits these questions in the example of two poems written by two German poets at different phases of modernity: Eduard Mörike (whose poem registers "the signs of an immediate life that promised fulfillment precisely at the time when they were already condemned by the direction history was taking" and thus "shares in the paradox of lyric poetry in the ascending industrial age") and Stefan George (who exemplifies "a much later phase in this development," in a poem where "it is not real things and not sounds that are evoked but rather a vanished condition of the soul" that "raises the song above the hopeless fiction it nonetheless offers"). But whereas Adorno adds a utopian note to that melancholy song, paradoxically confirming the work of lyric subjectivity in its vanishing, in Mufti's essay there is a continuous undertone of pathos in turning to the ghazals of Faiz for the subjective expression of "Muslim" experience in Indian modernity. In writing "towards a lyric history of India," Mufti ends his essay with a ghazal composed in 1953 as "a comment on India's partition from this side of the cataclysmic event, full of infinite sadness at what Indian Muslim 'nationhood' has finally been revealed, in the cold light of statehood and 'sovereignty,' to mean." According to Mufti, "Faiz distills that historical pathos into the subjective language of the *ghazal*, giving it the form of the lover's sadness at the impossibility of saying, when face-to-face with the beloved, what exactly one means." The impossibility of saying what one means, or saying what no longer has meaning, or saying anything at all, is the question raised by Adorno about poetry after Auschwitz, transposed by Mufti into poetry (always already) after partition.

Acknowledging that Faiz is "certainly not an 'Adornian' poet," Mufti nevertheless follows "the constellations of Adorno's thought" in order to think about Faiz as "the poet of late *postcolonial* modernity, a poet who directs the energies of negative thinking at the congealed cultural and social forms that constitute the postcolonial present." One of the interesting effects of the powerful negative thinking that Mufti attributes to the ghazals of Faiz is another, comparative frame for the modern idea of the lyric. In many ways, that modern idea informs Mufti's essay, and he uses it to characterize the sort of historical work he argues Faiz's poetry does. Yet this modern lyric model also does historical work, as Mufti's reading of Faiz assumes a question about the lyric subject that has its own critical genealogy, via Adorno and Benjamin back to Heidegger and Hegel. In Philippe Lacoue-Labarthe's post-Heideggerian reading of Celan (see section 7) we encounter another variation on the evacuation of a lyric subject that nevertheless preserves the lyric as an idealized genre for emptied-out experience in late modernity. But in contrast to Lacoue-Labarthe's phenomenological account of "poetry as experience," Mufti's reading moves toward articulating another kind of experience, and thus toward another kind of lyric history, as he concludes, "In his lyric poetry, Faiz pushes the terms of identity and selfhood to their limits, to the point where they turn upon themselves and reveal the partial nature of postcolonial 'national' experience."

While Ramazani approaches comparative lyric studies by reading many poets, and while Mufti extends a comparative framework for the concept of lyric by reading one poet, the essay we include by Roland Greene juxtaposes two poets for another perspective on comparative lyric reading. In "Inter-American Obversals: Allen Ginsberg and Haroldo de Campos circa 1960," Greene announces that his project is "to disclose how the poetries of the Americas converse with one another across the registers of the political and the personal; how what is common and what is different between hemispheric poetries may be accounted for; and especially how we may identify the points of contact—of concepts, inlaid cultural patterns, motifs, charged words—that put the subjective and the public dimensions of such poems into relation." But the poets that Greene brings into relation—with Ginsberg representing the North American "Beats" and Campos the Brazilian "Concretes"—did not and do not in fact "converse with one another." Precisely because these poets were oblivious to each other, they can be read in an "obverse" relation, as Greene goes on to explain: "On these terms two poets who built alternative versions of a postmodern poetics move closer to each other, and the poems of these moments sometimes dissolve into voices that make Ginsberg sound like Campos and vice versa. And in their transitions, Ginsberg and Campos produce poems that might be treated as obverses, or alternative engagements with problems of history and knowledge." Reading poets as the "obverse" of one another—not quite parallel, not quite intersecting—Greene proposes an alternative to traditional modes of comparison based on genetic, generic or theoretical claims.

Yet in Greene's "obversive" history of inter-American verse, or what he calls a hemispheric poetics, poems are read according to a lyric model that has been sufficiently internalized to produce "alternative versions" for comparative analysis. For example, although this experiment in "obversal reading" emphasizes "a difference in what each kind of poem knows," Greene reads lyric as a form for (and of) the experience of knowing in the present tense: "Campos' compressed poems perceive and think by collapsing eras, cultures, and languages together for the sake of historical continuity, while Ginsberg's intuitive lyrics find an alternative sort of diversity—of social identities, voices, politics—by expanding the present." Indeed it is only in the space of comparison—"the inter-american setting, where two considerably different premises for poetry came to discover a common space adjacent to both of them"—that Greene can discover his own critically comparative lyric imaginary: "The modes of the Beats and the Noigandres poets still do not touch one another, but in Ginsberg and Campos circa 1960 they have an imaginable relation."

The idea of a comparative lyric imaginary also plays a central role in shaping the larger idea of World Literature, both historically and in its contemporary revised disciplinary formation. In 1827 Johann Wolfgang von Goethe famously wrote, "I am more and more convinced that poetry is the universal possession of mankind, revealing itself everywhere and at all times."[4] Inspired by his reading of Persian and Serbian poetry, Goethe anticipated "the new epoch of world literature" (*Weltliteratur*) that would cross national boundaries both within and beyond Western Europe. Revealing itself "everywhere and at all times," the omnipresence of poetry could thus be projected into the past and the future of world history. This world historical vision of poetry served in the nineteenth century to define the national literatures that it also aspired to transcend their national or ethnic limitations, and it culminated (in the case of Goethe) in the ideal of German literary culture, or (in the case of Longfellow, taking up an American variation on the new epoch of *Weltliteratur*) in poetry for a new nation. Through his translations in *The Poetry and Poets of Europe* (1845) and in his "global" anthologies of *Poems of Places* (published in thirty-one volumes between 1876 and 1879), Henry Wadsworth Longfellow collected world poetry for the invention of, and by, American literary culture. As translator and as author of many popular poems that themselves thematize the merging of cultures, as Smith Professor of Modern Languages at Harvard and as precursor to the formation of comparative literature as an academic discipline in America, Longfellow is more formative than we may currently allow ourselves to believe in creating a concept of comparative poetics.[5] But one thing that has changed between the nineteenth-century ideal of "universal poetry" proclaimed by the likes of Goethe and Longfellow and the concept of "world poetry" circulating among contemporary critics of comparative literature in an age of globalization is the idea of lyric as a genre: no matter how far and wide we travel around the globe looking for poems to compare, this model of lyric reading has already arrived ahead of us to predetermine not only when and where we will read them, but how.

In the last essay in this section, David Damrosch returns to ancient Egypt to excavate a poem that turns out to be the mummy of the modern lyric. "Love in the Necropolis" begins with a detailed description of a papyrus inscribed with hieroglyphics that include what appears to be a love song. "One of the oldest lyrics to have survived anywhere in the world, this poem addresses us with a powerful immediacy," writes Damrosch, who goes on to demonstrate how this long-lost text was rediscovered, edited, and translated by twentieth-century Egyptologists (beginning with A. H. Gardiner). According to Damrosch, the poem is "unencumbered by any transmission history whatever from the twelfth century B.C.E. to the early twentieth century C.E., when the lyrics in this papyrus were quickly seen, as Gardiner says in his introduction, to be 'of inestimable value, not merely for archaeology, but still more for the world-history of poetry and of lyric expression.'" Of course this reclamation of the poem for "lyric expression" is predicated on another kind of historical transmission, namely the critical history of modern discourses about lyric as a genre that *The Lyric Theory Reader* has framed: from this vantage point, the questions that Damrosch poses about translating the poem (is it spoken in the first person? is it a dialogue? who is speaking? a man? a woman?) might be posed differently as questions about genre (why assume a speaker at all, unless we have already assumed the protocol of lyric reading?). Although Damrosch alludes to other Egyptian poems "whose speakers are *trees*" (suggesting at least the possibility of reading this poem otherwise), he argues that "such contextual evidence as we have at least favors the idea of a single speaker, or rather, a single singer, as these poems were composed as song lyrics." While systematically working through the problems of translation—leaving various possibilities for translating the Egyptian word for "tunic" (*mss*) in suspense—Damrosch has already settled the problem of genre: "as long as the translation doesn't impose a wholesale modernization, we won't assimilate the *mss* directly to our contemporary experience; we will remain aware that we're reading an ancient poem." Here the poem, no matter how ancient, is brought to life by the generic experience of reading modern lyric, as Damrosch concludes: "All the same, we can never hold the poem entirely away from our own experience, nor should we. As we read, we triangulate not only between ancient and modern worlds but also between general and personal meanings: however *mss* is translated, different readers will visualize it very differently, and this variability helps the poem to resonate with memories from the reader's own life."

To answer the title of his book, *What Is World Literature?*, Damrosch thus translates the Egyptian text into an example of world literature, using it to exemplify his central thesis about world literature as a mode of circulation and reception, especially by means of translation. In learning to read world literature, Damrosch argues, we must learn how to read translations in a new way: "Works of world literature take on a new life as they move into the world at large, and to understand this new life we need to look closely at the ways the work becomes reframed in its translations and in its new cultural contexts" (24). It is more than coincidence that this idea of a "new life," or what Walter Benjamin would call the "afterlife" of translation, is exemplified by the resuscitation of an ancient Egyptian text that seems to resonate "with memories of the reader's own life." In imagining how to translate these hieroglyphics, Damrosch offers the following caveat: "I don't at all mean that a translation should wrench the poem outright into our own world and our own terms; rather, I mean that the original context should not be made to overpower us, interfering with our engagement with the fictive world the poem creates for us to enter." But to invite the reader to enter into the poem in this way is already a generic choice that allows Damrosch (or "us") to imagine the past and future of literary transmission in the present tense of lyric reading. When he sets the stage for various translations of the Egyptian papyrus, Damrosch collapses the scene of reception into the scene of composition, and vice versa: "Whereas many works of world literature come to us already shaped by complex dynamics of transmission, often involving vexed relations between the originating culture and our own, this text has almost no history at all intervening between us and the moment of its inscription in 1160 B.C.E." Of course, at this point in history, it is generically overdetermined that the history of literary transmission would appear to have "almost no history at all"; that is precisely why the Egyptian hieroglyphs seem to look, or speak, to us as if they were a lyric poem.

Damrosch advocates for a wide-ranging approach to the study of world literatures, both geographically and historically, by drawing examples from many languages, cultures, genres, and periods. But (perhaps not so far after all from Longfellow, his predecessor at Harvard) he turns to poetry at key moments in defining, reading, and teaching the concept of world literature. In *How to Read World Literature*, "lyric poetry" again emerges as the answer to the basic question posed by the first chapter: "What is 'Literature'?" He appeals to a generalized idea of "Western lyric" not only to define an essential quality of literariness (a variation on the claim we saw in Miner's essay, that lyric is at the origin of literary expression across all cultures) but also to rethink a simple binary between Western and non-Western literatures. Starting from the modern idea that that "Western lyrics have long taken the form of an individual thinking out loud," Damrosch cites "Western wind, when wilt thou blow" to illustrate how a sixteenth-century English lyric may be productively juxtaposed with a Chilean poem, written four centuries later, or a poem in Sanskrit dating from the year 800. Emphasizing in each example that "once again we are overhearing a single speaker," he leads toward the conclusion that "the contrasts between the English lyric and the Sanskrit poem are differences of degree rather than reflections of some absolute, unbridgeable gulf between East and West" (9–11). Thus it would seem that the winds of lyric reading can blow in all directions around the world, from the present into the past and the future. Our contemporary world historical versions of lyric reading leave many questions unanswered, including whether we can find poetic genres that no longer resemble the normative model of the modern lyric that twentieth-century literary criticism has bequeathed to us. Since that norm continues to allow so many critics to read across cultures, across periods, across disciplinary divides, and across so many other critical points of departure, it is unlikely that we will give it up anytime soon, though perhaps precisely because so many critics have begun to develop variations on that model, another wind is blowing, and with it the small rain down shall rain.

NOTES

1. J. W. Johnson, "Lyric," in *The New Princeton Encyclopedia of Poetry and Poetics* (Princeton, NJ: Princeton University Press, 1993), 713. In narrating the history of lyric as a story of diverse forms arising from song and dance, Johnson follows earlier Anglo-American critics like Gummere (1901) and Drinkwater (1915), although their critical agenda was different: through a comparative reading of lyric, they developed a universal idea about poetry that could then serve to define and defend the national traditions of English or American verse.

2. Culler (1988), 291; see also Culler (2008).

3. See, e.g., *Ravishing DisUnities: Real Ghazals in English*, ed. Agha Shahid Ali (Middletown, CT: Wesleyan University Press, 2000); *The Ghazal as World Literature: Transformations of a Literary Genre*, ed. Thomas Bauer and Angelika Neuwirth (Beirut: Ergon Verlag, 2005); and *The Ghazal: A World Anthology*, ed. Paul Smith (Victoria, Australia: New Humanity Books, 2008).

4. J. W. von Goethe, *Conversations with Eckermann*, trans. John Oxenford (San Francisco: North Point Press, 1984), 132.

5. Seemingly displaced by the theoretical work of mid-twentieth-century European comparatists who arrived in America as expatriates during World War II (such as René Wellek, whose *Theory of Literature* published in 1949 marked a new era for Comparative Literature departments in postwar America), Longfellow nevertheless occupies an important place in the longer history of comparative literature in the American academy, and especially in the recent (re)turn to the study of world literatures; see, e.g., Christopher Prendergast, ed., *Debating World Literature* (New York: Verso, 2004); John Pizer, *The Idea of World Literature: History and Pedagogical Practice* (Baton Rouge: Louisiana State University Press, 2006); David Damrosch et al., eds., *The Longman Anthology of World Literature*, 2nd ed.

(New York: Pearson/Longman, 2009); David Damrosch, *Teaching World Literature* (New York: MLA, 2009); and d'Haen, Damrosch, and Kadir (2012).

FURTHER READING

Apter, Emily. *Against World Literature: On the Politics of Untranslatability*. London: Verso, 2013.

Bauer, Thomas, and Angelika Neuwirth, eds. *The Ghazal as World Literature: Transformations of a Literary Genre*. Beirut: Ergon Verlang, 2005.

Cai, Zong-qi. *Configurations of Comparative Poetics: Three Perspectives on Western and Chinese Literary Criticism*. Honolulu: University of Hawaii Press, 2002.

Cavanagh, Claire. *Lyric Poetry and Modern Politics: Russia, Poland, the West*. New Haven, CT: Yale University Press, 2009.

Clayton, Michelle. *Poetry in Pieces: César Vallejo and Lyric Modernity*. Berkeley: University of California Press, 2011.

Culler, Jonathan. "The Modern Lyric: Generic Continuity and Critical Practice." In *The Comparative Perspective on Literature*, edited by C. Koelb and S. Noakes, 284–99. Ithaca, NY: Cornell University Press, 1988.

———. "Why Lyric?" *PMLA* 123.1 (2008): 201–6.

Damrosch, David. *How to Read World Literature*. Chichester, UK: Wiley Blackwell, 2009.

D'haen, Theo, David Damrosch, and Djelal Kadir, eds. *The Routledge Companion to World Literature*. New York: Routledge, 2012.

Dimock, Wai Chee. *Through Other Continents: American Literature across Deep Time*. Princeton, NJ: Princeton University Press, 2008.

Drinkwater, John. *The Lyric: An Essay*. London: M. Secker, 1915.

Edmond, Jacob. *A Common Strangeness: Contemporary Poetry, Cross-Cultural Encounter, Comparative Literature*. New York: Fordham University Press, 2012.

Edwards, Brent Hayes. "Langston Hughes and the Futures of Diaspora." *American Literary History* 19.3 (Fall 2007): 689–711.

———. "The Spectre of Interdisciplinarity." *PMLA* 123.1 (2008): 188–94.

Eoyang, Eugene Chen. *The Transparent Eye: Reflection on Translation, Chinese Literature, and Comparative Poetics*. Honolulu: University of Hawaii Press, 1993.

Fokkema, D. W., Elrud Kunne-Ibsch, and A. J. A. van Zoest, eds. *Comparative Poetics*. Amsterdam: Rodopi, 1975.

Guillen, Claudio, and Peggy Escher, eds. *Comparative Poetics*. New York: Garland, 1985.

Gummere, Francis B. *The Beginnings of Poetry*. New York: Macmillan, 1901.

Huang, Yunte. *Transpacific Imaginations: History, Literature, Counterpoetics*. Cambridge, MA: Harvard University Press, 2008.

Huk, Romana, ed. *Assembling Alternatives: Reading Postmodern Poetries Transnationally*. Middletown, CT: Wesleyan University Press, 2003.

Menocal, María Rose. *Shards of Love: Exile and the Origins of the Lyric*. Durham, NC: Duke University Press, 1994.

Miner, Earl. *Comparative Poetics: An Intercultural Essay on Theories of Literature*. Princeton, NJ: Princeton University Press, 1990.

Moretti, Franco. "Conjectures on World Literature." *New Left Review* 1 (2000): 54–68.

Owen, Alfred Aldrich. *The Reemergence of World Literature: A Study of Asia and the West*. Newark: University of Delaware Press, 1986.

Owen, Stephen. "Stepping Forward and Back: Issues and Possibilities for 'World' Poetry," *Modern Philology* 100.4 (2003): 532–48.

Ramazani, Jahan. *The Hybrid Muse: Postcolonial Poetry in English*. Chicago: University of Chicago Press, 2001.

———. *A Transnational Poetics*. Chicago: University of Chicago Press, 2009.

Rothenberg, Jerome, ed. *Technicians of the Sacred: A Range of Poetries from Africa, America, Asia, Europe, and Oceania*. Berkeley: University of California Press, 1985.

Saussy, Haun. *The Problem of a Chinese Aesthetic*. Stanford, CA: Stanford University Press, 1993.

Viswanatham, Kalive. *Essays in Criticism and Comparative Poetics*. Waltair, Visakhapatnam: Andhra University Press, 1977.

Yu, Pauline. "The Poetics of Discontinuity: East-West Correspondences in Lyric Poetry." *PMLA* 94.2 (March 1970): 251–74.

Why Lyric? (2000) 10.1

EARL MINER

We often underestimate impact and confuse it with reception.

Amiya Dev

Influence is more an affair of complicity than one-sided imposition.

Kim Uchang

Complete transformations in this genre cannot be effected to the extent in other genres in spite of marked changes in society.

Subha Chakraborty Dasgupta

[. . .] Not surprisingly, critics aware of what goes on outside the European and North American parishes have taken offence at the imposition of "western" literary culture on that variously termed "eastern" or "oriental." Some of us who take offence are from the offending "west" and perhaps desire to affix guilt so that we need not share in it. Others write from "eastern" inheritance in anger over cultural imperialism. Particular offence has been taken over what Edward Said has termed "Orientalism," the treatment of non-western literatures as aberrant varieties in inferior cultures.[1] One sees what they mean. But it was just at this point a few years ago that Amiya Dev saw and meant more. Before it dawned on some others, he saw in full blaze of noon that restriction of attention to guilty imperialism, eurocentrism, and Orientalism still makes the west the subject. Also, we have heard much about the novel and very little about narrative poems, about drama, and particularly about lyric. If it is protested that contemporary literary theory and comparative study have, after all, been preoccupied with the novel, that is no small part of the point. The attention and the talk have continued to have western concerns as their subjects.

A shift is required from the melodrama of Europeans and Americans as actors, from the novel and western theory. It is time to attend to other writers, other languages, other canons, and other conceptions of literature. To amplify Amiya Dev's initial remark, we need to relocate the centre of interest to the scene of offence and to know the pre-colonial literatures ruptured by European incursion. Fundamental problems include those of the damage done to ruptured traditions, those of absorption of the alien, and those of means of recuperation or renovation. Such turning about of the game board deals with what was wrong in the first place. Without a victim, concern with crime turns on abstract wrongs. The Dev thesis of the primacy of the victimized also raises a number of otherwise too easily ignored comparative, historical, and conceptual issues. These may be posed, if not fully discussed, in terms of comparative methods. From that posing we can turn to the place of lyric, to some complexities and perplexities, and to features of the wider problem of literary change. The relation between these topics will become increasingly clear.

The Dev principle obviously involves conceptions and practices of literary history, as the preceding remarks have implied. But certain theoretical issues are also crucial. For all purposes it must be clear what we mean by lyric.[2] Histories and theories join in two roles of lyric: we shall observe its function in the devising of systematic poetics and its priority in the emergence of literature itself. The former relates to various literatures and so bears on each literature. The latter appears to be true of all literatures and therefore is a characteristic of literature historically and theoretically considered.

Literary relations are commonly conceived in terms of influence.[3] The model is passive in the sense that it presumes that influence acts upon a poet, a form, or a literature. That is the smaller part of the matter. Some critics have sought to right matters by discussing reception, a definite improvement.[4] The distinction has value for separating two elements. Influence involves moving upon another literature (form, writer) in an act of claim or seizure. Reception involves choice of what is taken, and at times resistance or rival emulation. There may be such a thing as mandated influence but an imposed reception is a contradiction in terms. Imposed influence is another matter, one for which there are all too many examples. Among them are pre-modern Chinese insistence that even the "barbarians" on its four sides write Chinese poetry if they would be construed to write poetry at all; British imposition of English education and literature on India; and attempted wholesale replacement of Korean literature by Japanese. Certain kinds of exploitation of the riches of other cultures are not crimes. Artistic seizure may be largely positive. That is true of Pound's and Yeats's use of Japanese (or Chinese) literature as models for their work, seizing what they found in Japan or China, whether it was there or not. And voluntary, rival reception is represented by Japanese taking over of the western novel on their own distinct terms.

The kinds of rupture that Amiya Dev has in mind involve imposed influence and endured reception. One underlying principle is that power in its cultural guise will be misused, as it is in its other guises. Another principle is that benefits may accrue to the culture imposed on, not because they had been intended by the imposer, but because the practical response to the imposition is to make the best of the situation encountered.

The Dev thesis presumes literary maturities. We are presently considering developed practices in language cultures that are come of age. For the moment, we defer concern with origins. The presumption allows us to consider issues not only historically and conceptually but also—because the issues seriously matter—ethically. This is evident in Said's looking with hostile eye on Orientalists and in Dev's concern with damaged literary traditions and their renovations. It is difficult to imagine disagreement on the general ethical features, much as we may dispute the details. We agree that change has taken place under duress at once literary, political and cultural. In a subsequent renovation or recuperation, what had existed before the rupture is reverted to, now with a difference measurable by the kind and degree of the rupture. Of course, there are many complexities and shadings: the fallacy of the single explanation holds here as elsewhere. There may be varieties of collusion, some gain (for the foreign) amid loss (of the native or intrinsic), and renewals that are variously reactionary, comic, fearful, or creative. Above all, the power of the native current is always great, and its changes, of course, always involve distinctive features intrinsic to it and never exterior intrusions alone. The sum of the factors is often more readily identified than the individual factors themselves.[5]

That said, we must add that concern with lyric necessarily raises issues that drama and narrative do not.[6] As will be evident from what has been said and from what follows, for this discussion "lyric" designates a literary kind or radical—a genre—on a par with drama and narrative. To be sure, all our literary terms have their histories and bear theoretical meaning on a scale much beyond that of this account, and numerous things cannot be understood from lyric alone. But the historical and theoretical implications of lyric can also be shown to differ in nature and significance from many issues involving narrative and drama.

It is not that all claims entail lyric. Literary rupture and recovery involve drama and narrative as well. For a given issue, drama or narrative may be more appropriate than lyric. For that matter, rupture and renovation really involve critical moments in a whole culture rather than solely one kind of knowledge like the literary. Yet literature generally and lyric in particular have special claims by virtue of their historical and intrinsic features. That which to hindsight is prototypical of literature is involved in the first special uses of language: unlike Molière's bourgeois gentleman, M. Jourdain, our ancestors could take pleasure in discovering that their most valued utterances were poetic. And as we shall now see, the explicit acknowledgment of the discovery entails lyric in a major way.

Lyric has priority by virtue of its role in the explicit definition of the nature of literature. Rather than narrative or drama, lyric is the foundation genre for the poetics or systematic literary assumptions of cultures throughout the world. Only western poetics differs. Even the major civilizations that have not shown a need to develop an explicit poetics (the Islamic, for example), have demonstrably based their ideas of literature on lyric assumptions. Of course, lyric can be written in literatures conceived in mimetic terms and drama in literatures conceived in affective-expressive terms. Not surprisingly, the greater the historical development after the definition of a basic poetics, the more complex critical understanding becomes.

The first thing to be said of lyric poetic systems is that they are not mimetic. Imitation and representation are simply not the grounds considered, as examples will show. Since western mimesis emerges from the exceptional use by Aristotle of drama as the foundation genre, Japanese conceptions of drama are particularly revealing. They are not mimetic.

Noh is a theatrical, dramatic kind that draws on lyric and narrative to unusual degrees. One of the central terms of Noh dramaturgy is *monomane*, which is made up of two words—"things" and "imitating." Imitating things certainly seems natural to the stage, and to a westerner like myself, it at once recalls Plato, Aristotle and mimesis. But students of Noh agree that *monomane* does not mean imitation or representation. Standard accounts render the term as "performance" or as "artifice."[7] It refers to stage business, to *shimai* or dance: to the active part of Noh as opposed to *utai*, singing, the words recited. Some people may doubt that drama can be understood apart from imitation or without representation.

Any doubts about this are put to rest by a very significant set of remarks by the seventeenth century Japanese dramaturgist, Chikamatsu Monzaemon. He was pre-eminent not only as a playwright for *kabuki* or the actors but also the *johruri* or the puppet forms of popular drama. His words should be known by anyone concerned with the nature of theatre:

> Art is that which occupies the narrow margin between the true and the false . . . It participates in the false and yet is not false; it participates in the true and yet is not true; our pleasure is located between the two. As an example, there was a certain lady serving at the palace who developed a passionate relation with a certain lord. The lady's chamber was in the depths of a splendid apartment, and since he was unable to enter there, she had only a look at him from time to time through a gap in the blinds. So great was her yearning that she had a wooden image of him carved. The countenance and other features differed from usual images in resembling the lord to the last detail. The colouring of the complexion was indescribably exact, each hair was in place, the ears and nose and the teeth in their very

number were faultlessly made. Such was the work that if you placed the man and the image side by side, the only distinction was which had a soul. But when she regarded it closely, the sight of a living person exactly reproduced so chilled the lady's ardour that she felt distaste at once. In spite of herself, she found that her love was gone, and so unpleasant was it to have the model by her side that before long she got rid of it. As this shows, if we copy a living thing exactly as it is, for example even [the legendary Chinese beauty] Yang Guifei herself, there would be something arousing disgust. For this reason, in any artistic version, whether the image be drawn or carved in wood, along with the exact resemblance of the shape there will be some stylizing, and after all that is why people like it. It is the same for the design of a play—within recognizable likeness there will be points of deviance . . . and since that is after all the nature of art, it is what constitutes the pleasure people take in it.[8]

Aristotle thought an imitation (mimesis) even of cadavers would give pleasure. Like the gods in the proverb, the Noh critic Zeami and Chikamatsu thought otherwise.

Clearly, it is necessary to put away representation and mimesis to understand the world's many poetic systems founded on lyric.[9] The "Great Preface" to the Chinese *Classic of Poetry* characterizes literature altogether on the basis of its few hundred lyrics, since at its composition (about two millennia ago), China had no drama or fictional prose narrative and for centuries after it had them did not believe them worth serious consideration. Here is the opening of that "Great Preface":

Poetry is where the intent of the heart goes. What in the heart is intent is poetry when emitted in words. And emotion moves within and takes form in words.[10]

Or we may take the Japanese version founded to an extent on the Chinese. This is the Japanese preface to the first of the twenty-one royal collections, the *Kokinshu* (ca. 910).

The poetry of Japan has its seed [also, cause] in the human heart and flourishes in the countless leaves of words. Because human beings possess interests of so many kinds, it is in poetry that they give expression to the meditations of their hearts in terms of the sights appearing before their eyes and the sounds coming to their ears. Hearing the warbler sing among the plum blossoms and the frog that lives in the waters—is there any living thing not given to song? It is poetry that, without exertion, moves heaven and earth, stirs the feelings of gods and spirits invisible to the eye, softens the relations between men and women, calms the hearts of fierce warriors.[11]

All are moved to song. It is in our nature, in the nature of us living things, to be affected by what we experience and to express ourselves about the experience. In other words, this is an affective-expressive poetics, a lyric understanding of literature that characterizes the various poetics of the whole world, apart from the European outpost.[12]

The development of a systematic poetics is too sophisticated a matter to be the point at which literature itself begins. Identifying that point of emergence is a matter fraught with difficulties both of logic and of evidence. Until some features, at least, of implicit poetics, have been conceived, literature is not distinguished from other forms of expression. One of the themes developed by Lévi-Strauss in *The Savage Mind* is that the "pensée sauvage" includes the different kinds of thought that we associate more readily with peoples in literate and complex societies.[13] If we turn his point about, we see that he also implies that the various kinds of thinking later distinguished are undifferentiated in his "pensée sauvage." The bounds of that pensée do not, however, circumscribe all our needs and thought. We may, for example, assign literary status to that which had not been so conceived, so thinking thoughts unknown to earlier people. That ex post facto defining is not restricted to literary matters. We also consider it just to speak, for example of religion, law and economics in times before the different kinds were distinguished as separate entities.

For primal literary origins, the problem of evidence has been solved as well as it is likely to be by C. M. Bowra in his *Primitive Song*. Using evidence from ethnographers recording "songs" from present-day pre-literate peoples, he was able to set forth a reasonable, convincing pattern of development. In this process, the first step is assembly of meaningless sounds. Of course, total meaninglessness is just noise. But certain peoples like the Yamana have songs without lexical or grammatical meaning, as for example this song of friendly welcome accompanied by jumping up and down:

Ha ma la   ha ma la ha ma la ha ma la
O la la la la   la la la la [14]

The use of a single vowel may suggest the simplest imaginable mentality or, as I suppose instead, an incantatory significance, a kind of word spell or charm.[15] The necessary memorizing for communal performance seems to imply as much. The Selk'nam, neighbours of the Yamana, have medicine men with lexically meaningful songs but also others of communal performance that are purely incantatory. In the mornings they sing:

ha-ra-xe-u-ka ha-ra-xe-u-ka ha-ra-ze-u

and in the evenings:

Hai-ce-rai-ya hai-ce-rai-ya hai-ce-hai-ce-rai-ya [16]

This is surely a kind of word spell, and in its more complex use of repetition and in its parallelism growing from morning/evening performance, we move closer to meaning and therefore to what we can recognize.

As a further step, Bowra mentions the "striking way in which the Vedas use two formulaic lines"—

Tan tandinanan tandinane
Tanan tandina tandinan

"which are unintelligible but used in intelligible contexts, often at the beginning or end of a song."[17] We, too, have our "Hey, nonny nonnies" and "fa la las." These "emotive sounds" have, at whatever remove, lexically intelligible songs that are really otherwise indistinguishable from what we have been seeing. Bowra comments on an example:

> The Bushmen have what they call the jackal's song.
>
> Canter for me, little jackal, O little jackal,
> little jackal.
>
> In [this] there is still some lingering element of magic, but they show how the song moves from an immediately useful purpose to an element of art and pleasure. Though these single lines are made more emphatic by repetition . . . they show how verse begins. The single line is the first, indispensable beginning of real song.[18]

Another song by a Bushman on the theft of his tobacco by a dog appears to take us, however simply, from the ceremoniously spiritual to the secular:

Famine   it is,
Famine   it is,
Famine   it is here.[19]

From this point, various developments are feasible. One is the making of longer songs with patterns of repetition, parallelism, and variance. For example, the Aranda have a song for the season when two kinds of parrots come to pick the flowers of the bloodwood trees.

The ringneck-parrots in scattered flocks—
The ringneck-parrots are screaming in their upward flight.

The ringneck-parrots are a cloud of wings:
The shell-parrots are a cloud of wings.

Let the shell-parrots come down to rest—
Let them come down to rest on the ground.

Let the caps fly off the scented blossoms!
Let the caps fly off the bloodwood blossoms!

Let the caps fly off the scented blossoms!
Let the blossoms fall to the ground in a shower.

The clustering bloodwood blossoms are falling down—
The clustering bloodwood blossoms, nipped by birds.

The clustering bloodwood blossoms are falling down
The clustering bloodwood blossoms, one by one.[20]

We probably do well to suspect some degree of spirituality and ritual here, but we have reached, or are on the verge of reaching, songs that might be memorized by someone who learned them with the purpose of collection and preservation in writing.

There are often great difficulties in interpreting even brief songs. In fact, a translator is stymied without an assured interpretation. Here is a brief Japanese song of uncertain date but recorded in the people's oldest history, *The Record of Ancient Matters*.[21]

Among the rice stalks,
Among the rice stalks of the fields
Lying side by side,
They twine and crawl about—
The creeping vines.

But some scholars have said that the words were sung by peasants as they weeded vines from rice fields in order to harvest. If so, the translation must be altered.

Through the rice stalks,
Through the rice stalks of the field
Where we work side by side,
They twine and crawl about—
The detested vines.

Yet another interpretation holds it is a love song telling of the lover's exertions in getting to his beloved.

Through the rice stalks.
Through the rice stalks of the fields,
Lying side by side,
I twine and crawl to you
Like the creeping vine.

More recently, archaeological and other evidence has shown that the song was in fact part of ritual mourning in which the bereaved survivors crawled about the body of the dead. So that the meaning of this brief song is rather more like this:

As through the rice stalks,
As through the rice stalks of the field,
We move side by side,
We twine and crawl about you
Like the creeping vine.

Songs like this suggest that even the Yamana's lexically meaningless songs had a ritual significance referred to earlier as incantatory.

In whatever interpretation, that song is quite simple. Another rather more complex song poses issues because of its special status. It is collected and preserved in writing and is now regarded as a poem. In fact it is probably the best known Chinese poem, by virtue of being the first in the *Classic of Poetry.*

Guan guan cry the ospreys
On the islet of the river.
The beautiful and good young lady
Is a fine mate for the lord.

Varied in length are the water plants;
Left and right we catch them.
The beautiful and good young lady—
Waking and sleeping he wished for her.

He wished for her without getting her.
Waking and sleeping he thought of her:
Longingly, longingly,
He tossed from side to side.

Varied in length are the water plants;
Left and right we gather them.
The beautiful and good young lady—
Zithers and flutes greet her as a friend.

Varied in length are the water plants—
Left and right we cull them.
The beautiful and good young lady—
Bells and drums delight her.

Many things about the poem are uncertain, including its date and meaning. Pauline Yu's study, from which it is taken, deals with the inevitable Confucian moralizings of it and the likelihood that it was a wooing or bridal song.[22] Whatever it means, its repetitions and its incantatory nature show that it is in the line—if farther on, so to speak—of the songs recovered by Bowra.

In *The Record of Ancient Matters* (no. 90) there is another early Japanese song whose title, "In Longing for His Wife," suggests a somewhat greater secular purpose.[23]

In the river
Of Hatsuse the hidden land
They tamp sacred poles

Within the upper shallow reaches;
They tamp true poles
Within the lower shallow reaches;
They hang a mirror
Upon a pounded sacred pole;
They hang true jewels
Upon a pounded true pole—
Like the true jewels
Is she I love so dearly;
And like a mirror,
Is the wife I deeply love—
If only someone
Could assure me she is there.
I would leave for her home,
I would long for that land!

The ritual actions of the major portion of the poem bar any easy assumption that this is wholly worldly. But those who included it in *The Record of Ancient Matters* appear to have thought that it uses older rites to the secular end of conveying a husband's wish to be with the wife he had to leave behind, given the matrilineal inheritance of individual property and uxorilocal marriage in that age.

Bowra's evidence so amplified demonstrates a matter of first importance. It is the lyric, not drama or narrative, that first emerges. (My fellow editor may think differently.) Bowra knew his Homer and his tragedians, and he knew he was writing about "primitive song." In any verbal plurality, we may discover the possibility of narrative. Presentation of a single word may offer a dramatic moment. Before long we shall glance at a poem by George Herbert that has recognizable dramatic and narrative properties. But intense brevities are taken to be lyric. Lyric may readily absorb, incorporate, and even generate narrative and drama. Sappho may write about soldiers and Horace may "act" many "roles" in his odes, but the one is not Homer or the other Plautus. The statuses of these kinds was a chief concern in China, where the yet greater wall is the lyric.

Literature begins, then, in lexically meaningless sounds and comes into being as lyric. The Greeks have idealized Homeric epic from early times. But there must have been yet earlier times. Diegesis and mimesis yield lengthy works complex on a scale and length beyond our conceiving that they preceded lyric. The observation is not new. Nietzsche claimed in *The Birth of Tragedy* that Greek tragedy originated in lyric. (One could read Aristotle's *Poetics* and doubt that he knew lyric existed.) Obscure as it may be, the derivation of tragedy from "male goat" + "song" must mean that the choral odes—sung in celebrating Athens' Dionysian religious festival—led to dramatic dialogue rather than the reverse.

The historical and ethnographic evidence has shown us that literature first comes into existence as lyric. In the pensée sauvage, literature may not have been separable from religion and social concerns. But the track from the Yamana's lexically meaningless syllables to the lonely husband shows that a single path is followed between those two points. Drama and narrative do not offer any such clear, continuous, and decisive route as that from seemingly meaningless syllables to lyric to a poetics.

The primacy of lyric in the emergence of literature confirms its role as the originative or foundation genre for the poetics or poetic systems of all literary cultures except the one western holdout. (Let it be said again that, thereafter, the longer the period of literary practice and critical reflection, the more multifaceted both become.) In all its versions, the lyric-based poetics is affective and expressive in nature. It will have occurred to some readers following the present argument that to Plato and Aristotle alike literature was certainly affective. Plato shows this clearly in his *Ion*, *Phaedrus*, and notoriously in *Republic*. Aristotle shows it in his concern with fear and pity as also no doubt his "katharsis," although its meaning is not known. (It appears but once in the *Poetics*.) For neither philosopher could affectivism be a differentia of literature, however, since the works named show that they held philosophy and rhetoric to be no less affective. It was not until Horace redefined the ars poetica without regard for philosophy or rhetoric but instead out of his practice (odes, satires, and epistles, many of which are satiric), that affectivism, and expressivism, entered the western poetic system.

This attention to the primacy of lyric explains why that genre is especially important to considerations of literary rupture, endurance, and renovation. When the lyric of a given national culture is assaulted, literature is attacked at its very heart and soul.

None of this is to say that we are ignorant of the origins and many implications of drama and narrative. Greek tragedy may have originated in song and English tragedy in the medieval elaborations on the Quem quaeritis trope.[24] Even that simple an example shows how easy it is to distinguish drama from both narrative and lyric. Unlike those, drama is an art performed by players or puppets or shadows that represent. In that performative nature and its necessary consequence, fictionality, drama differs from lyric and narrative, which are not played and need not be dominantly fictive at all. It is more difficult by far to define the distinction between lyric and narrative. In my view, the distinguishing features of lyric are a presence and intensity that make it, in a double sense, literature of moment.[25] By contrast, narrative is distinguished by its fulfilled continuity. No brief discussion can deal with such complex matters adequately, but there are certain distinctions in practice. These practical considerations testify to the special nature of lyric.

It has grown common to speak of metadrama and metanarrative: as with a play within a play, or a narrative inset within a narrative. The latter is epidemic in longer romances and will be found in Dickens. Dramatic doubling is familiar from such plays within plays as the Pyramus and Thisbe woefully presented by Bottom and the other "mechanicals" in *A Midsummer Night's Dream* and Hamlet's "mousetrap" to catch the conscience of King Claudius. In narrative and drama alike, the second stage necessarily interrupts the first. In similar fashion, drama is interrupted by narrative interludes like a messenger's narration or by Othello's relation of his wooing of Desdemona. In like fashion, the account of a play like that of Dickens', of Mr. Wopsle's playing of Hamlet in *Great Expectations*, interrupts the narrative. It is also the case that a song in a play or a narrative interrupts what may be termed the host genre.

With lyric, the situation greatly differs. For one thing, lyric is not self-interruptive, as are narrative and drama. For another, although it may seem the most fragile genre, lyric is not interrupted by drama or narrative: the presence of one or the other imparts intensification or amplification. For that matter, both drama and narrative may be made to serve lyric in a single poem, as is shown by the opening and closing lines (1–5, 33–36) of George Herbert's poem of momentary spiritual rebellion, "The Collar."

I struck the board, and cry'd, No more,
I will abroad.
What? Shall I ever sigh and pine?
My lines and life are free; free as the rode,
Loose as the winde, as large as store . . .
But as I rav'd and grew more fierce and wilde

At every word,
Me thoughts I heard one calling, Child!
And I reply'd, My Lord.

As we see, the lyric absorbs narrative and drama alike: they become attributive rather than constituent, independent genres. The narrative past tense re-presents a moment by extending it, and the dramatic outburst intensifies the now-ness. Lyric may function in similar ways, not only interruptively. It may enter drama attributively as in Noh and certain other dramatic forms. And it combines yet more readily, or at least more variously, with narrative. There are also rarer examples, Japanese linked poetry being one of them, for which some people might wish to hold that lyric and narrative are co-generic.

When these various cases are put, we reach the same conclusion: lyric is primary, whether we consider the origins of literature, the origins of a systematic poetics, or the prime, uninterruptible genre. As the simplest, or at least briefest, the purest, and the most resistant to interference of the three genres, lyric is special. For this triple reason, the rupture of a lyric practice, of a lyric tradition within a national or regional culture, is the gravest literary assault of all. The most grievous damage is done.

That is not to say that the rupture of dramatic or narrative practice is not serious. But if we think of degrees of seriousness, the damage to narrative is the least serious. Its messiness—Henry James famously called the novel a loose, baggy monster—contrasts with the assiduous care of lyric. External damage to narrative finds quicker recovery, as is shown by the relatively easy adaptation of features of the western novel by other literatures. This relative ease of repair seems to hold more fully for narrative in prose than in verse. That may perhaps reflect the fact that only the finest great verse narrative is tolerable and that greatness is by definition rare. But there may be another factor. The constant rhythmic character of verse narrative makes it closer to lyric than is prose narrative.

Because these matters are so seldom observed, the assumptions they require and the consequences they entail have not been discussed. But since they obviously relate to the nature of lyric (and therefore also its species, literature), we simply cannot avoid saying something about the nature of lyric, offering some idea if not a strict definition.[26] There does not seem to be much enthusiasm for the now hoary idea of lyric as that which is overheard. And small wonder. That description applies far better to drama. It is more useful to consider the central point made by Paul de Man, who turned his attention to lyric poetry after a critical career devoted largely to varieties of narrative prose.[27] With his close attention to what he often called rhetoric, it is not surprising that he should have characterized lyric in terms of apostrophe. This serves to describe some lyrics, especially a number by the English Romantic poets, but it is not helpful for much of the world's poetry. Some context offers assistance at this point. The method De Man had employed for prose narrative was a very patient version of the close reading appropriate to lyric fineness, and in this he was the heir of the Anglo-American old New Critics, who had taken as their gold standard the poetry of Donne and other early seventeenth century lyric poets. Yet their criticism also had flawed lyric presumptions, as we see in their dismissal of the author as a genetic fallacy and of the reader as an affective fallacy (Wimsatt and Beardsley). In a fully realized lyricism like that of the Chinese, a central feature is the poet's expressive purpose (*zhi*), a version of intention charged by affective stimulus. This is of course a Confucian emphasis, although it may go back to the yet more distant past and is discussed with explicit emphasis by Mencius.[28] One summary of the implications of what *zhi* has been taken to mean has been provided by James J-Y Liu:

> those critics who understood it as "heart's work" or "emotional purport" [developed] expressive theories and those who understood it as "mind's intent" or "moral purpose" often combined the expressive concept with the pragmatic.[29]

In this major version of an affective-expressive poetics, mimesis does not exist. In addition, the assumption is not that the addressee is mute or absent as with apostrophe but rather is ready to be moved in turn. Much in this is, of course, conventional, as when a Chinese poet writes on a wall words telling what the sight of the nearby scene has prompted, or when a friend addressed replies to one's poem using the same rhymes for the same number of lines.

If we can place lyric with the other genres that make up literature, there is still the issue of placing literature. Because literature is one of the things we can learn, remember, recall, and discuss, it must be a kind of knowledge. And lyric must therefore be one of that kind. To clarify what is involved, it may be useful to remind ourselves of the two distinct senses that we assign to "history." We use the word at times to mean the course of events that occurred at some times and in some places, and one way of distinguishing among a number of those histories is to ascertain whether and in what fashion people are involved. The other principal sense of "history" is that of accounts of the course of events that occurred at various times and places. But our knowledge consists of many things other than events—various kinds of logic and symbols, values and numbers, etc. And no kind of thought with any degree of importance is of a single, uncombined nature. Yet some kinds of knowledge use other kinds sparingly while being eminently useful to others, whereas others are able to use different kinds of knowledge readily but are of restricted use to other kinds. Simply put, mathematics is used, and literature uses. On the other hand, the more complex, specialized, or restricted knowledge becomes, the less accessible it grows and the more it is prized for its own sake.

With literature, there is an issue important to some minds, and trivialized by most of us, of the presence and relation of fact and fiction. The Chinese critic who pronounced *The Romance of the Three Kingdoms* "seven parts fact and three parts fiction" presumably was making a point rather than using a calculator.[30] It is more important by far that the part of a history that is most important to authors and readers alike is not factual, although it may be based on carefully ascertained facts. That part is, of course, motivation, intent, purpose, and causal movements involving larger numbers of people. That part will utterly fail to carry conviction, and large structures of fact will collapse, unless they are fictionally conceived. Or if fiction seems dubious, we may take recourse to the imaginary.[31]

It is difficult to draw a list of things important to our shared human lives that literature does not draw upon, put to use, make over so that it can be known. That being so, we must enquire into the nature of what may justly be termed lyric knowledge. We must grant to some and insist to others that this kind is, like all others, mixed or impure. But insofar as it is a distinct kind, lyric knowledge can be characterized by the terms of the poetics for which it accounts. It is affective and expressive. Or, to use the terms from the Chinese and Japanese prefaces quoted earlier, lyric knowledge is first of all subjective: in both tongues the terms are translatable in context as mind, heart, or spirit. But that is, as the Japanese version puts it, the seed or cause. The growth from the causal seed, the necessary realization is words, language. There is no single linguistic emphasis that holds for all writers in all places at all times. To some poets syntax matters more than vocabulary, and to others the reverse—so corresponding to the functions of the two chief portions of our brains most important for linguistic knowledge. To some poets, precedented language has highest claim, and to others neologisms. To some the resemblance to actual speech is the touchstone, and to others it is the departures from the ordinary. But the general importance of language to literature reaches its high point in lyric poetry. The affective also varies. It may or may not have the moralizing of the Chinese and Horatian versions. But it is the same force of mind-heart-spirit that leads us to act, to say what we have done, to remember it, and to tell others. It is the combination of these two features that creates the intensified presence of lyric.[32] On reflection, that leaves us a sense of awe that is captured in the Chinese preface: "in regulating success and failure, moving heaven and earth, and causing spirits and gods to respond, nothing comes closer than poetry."[33]

These considerations enable us to understand that it is inevitably true that the rupture of lyric practice is a change whose true gravity is not understandable merely in terms of change. Of course this is true for narrative and drama as well. But as this brief review has shown, lyric is the most crucial. The demonstrable reasons for this are the origins of literature in lyric, the dominance of lyric or affective-expressive poetics in the world's poetic systems, and the special integrity of lyric among the genres. That integrity rests upon lyric's extraordinary resistance to interruption by drama, by narrative, and even by itself. To rupture a lyric tradition, very powerful measures of assault are necessary, and the crime is greatest. Yeats envisioned the possibility that the great song would return no more ("The Nineteenth Century and After"). And we are familiar with the legend of the swan's death song. The damage involved in disruption of a lyric tradition can scarcely be exaggerated. Our hopes for redress lie in the recognition of that importance. One can only feel awe in contemplating the mysterious power of this simple, brief, and primal genre.

NOTES

1. See Edward Said, *Orientalism* (New York: Pantheon, 1978).

2. Earl Miner, *Comparative Poetics: An Intercultural Essay of Theories of Literature* (Princeton: Princeton University Press, 1990), 23–29.

3. Claudio Guillén, *Literature as System: Essays towards the Theory of Literary History* (Princeton: Princeton University Press, 1971); Subha Dasgupta, "The French School of Comparative Literature," in Amiya Dev and Sisir Kumar Das (ed.), *Comparative Literature: Theory and Practice* (Shimla: Indian Institute of Adanced Study, 1989).

4. Dionyz Durisin, *Sources and Systematics of Comparative Literature* (Bratislava: Univerzita Komaského, 1974) and *Theory of Interliterary Process* (Bratislava: Slovak Academy of Sciences, 1989); Hans Robert Jauss, *Toward an Aesthetic of Reception* (Minneapolis: University of Minnesota Press, 1981).

5. The rest of this chapter deals with conceptual and historical issues involving lyric. For the topics of the other chapters, see the preface.

6. See chapters 2–4 in Miner, *Comparative Poetics*.

7. Jin'ichi Konishi, *Zeami Shu* (Tokyo: Chikuma Shobo, 1974), 215, 216, 220; *On the Art of Noh Drama: The Major Treatises of Zeami*, ed. Yamazaki Masakazu, trans. J. Thomas Rimer (Princeton: Princeton University Press, 1984), 97.

8. Miner, *Comparative Poetics*, 45.

9. For a complementary discussion featuring hermeneutics rather than poetics, as here, see Longxi Zhang, *The Tao and the Logos* (Durham: Duke University Press, 1992).

10. Pauline Yu, *The Reading of Imagery in the Chinese Poetic Tradition* (Princeton: Princeton University Press, 1987), 31–32. Important critical conceptions involve words that seldom move unscathed between languages. The crucial word '*zhi*' ('chih') is sometimes rendered to mean will; similarly, '*xing*' ('shing') has features of English conceptions of heart, mind, and spirit.

11. Miner, *Comparative Poetics*, 84.

12. On the complex example of India see Earl Miner, "On the Genesis and Development of Literary Systems II: The Case of India," *Revue de la Littérature Comparée*, no. 65 (1991): 143–52.

13. Claude Lévi-Strauss, *The Savage Mind* (Chicago: University of Chicago Press, 1966).

14. C. M. Bowra, *Primitive Song* (Cleveland and New York: World Publishing Company, 1962), 57.

15. Andrew Welsh, *The Roots of Lyric* (Princeton: Princeton University Press, 1978), 133.

16. Bowra, *Primitive Song*, 59.

17. Bowra, *Primitive Song*, 59–60.

18. Bowra, *Primitive Song*, 63.

19. Bowra, *Primitive Song*, 63.

20. Bowra, *Primitive Song*, 78.

21. Kojiki, comp. ca. 672; see Robert H. Brower and Earl Miner, *Japanese Court Poetry* (Stanford: Stanford University Press, 1961), 45–46.

22. Yu, *The Reading of Imagery*, 47–55.

23. Brower and Miner, *Japanese Court Poetry*, 66.

24. See John 20:15. In the Authorized Version, the risen Jesus asks his mother, "Whom seekest thou?" ("Quem quaeritis" in the Vulgate). As this incident became elaborated beyond a certain point, it was moved out of the churches and, with further elaboration, contributed to the development of English drama.

25. Miner, *Comparative Poetics*.

26. See also Welsh, *The Roots of Lyric*.

27. Paul de Man, "Lyrical Voice in Contemporary Theory: Riffaterre and Jauss," in *Lyric Poetry: Beyond New Criticism*, edited by Chaviva H. Hošek and Patricia Parker (Ithaca: Cornell University Press, 1985), 55–72.

28. Jin'ichi Konishi, *A History of Japanese Literature* (Princeton: Princeton University Press, 1984), vol. 1; James J-Y Liu, *Chinese Theories of Literature* (Chicago: University of Chicago Press, 1975), 69–70, 76; James J-Y Liu, *Language Paradox Poetry* (Princeton: Princeton University Press, 1988), 96–97.

29. Liu, *Chinese Theories of Language*, 69–70.

30. Jin'ichi Konishi, *A History of Japanese Literature* (Princeton: Princeton University Press, 1991), vol. 3, 509.

31. Wolfgang Iser, *The Fictional and the Imaginary* (Baltimore: Johns Hopkins University Press, 1993).

32. Miner, *Comparative Poetics*.

33. Yu, *The Reading of Imagery*, 32.

Traveling Poetry (2007) 10.2

Jahan Ramazani

Rapid, multidirectional, unexplained—such are the geographic displacements in the famous opening of Ezra Pound's canto 81, written while the poet was incarcerated in the U.S. Army Disciplinary Training Center near Pisa:

> Zeus lies in Ceres' bosom
> Taishan is attended of loves
>   under Cythera, before sunrise
> and he said: "Hay aquí mucho catolicismo—(sounded catoli*th*ismo)
>   y muy poco reliHion"[1]

With the help of allusions repeated and elaborated elsewhere in *The Cantos*, we infer that the predawn sun nestling behind mountains near Pisa is being refigured as a Greek sun god lying in the bosom of the fertility goddess Ceres. The cone-shaped mountain that Pound could see from his detention cage is also troped as a sacred mountain in China before the next line returns to Greece—an Ionian island sacred to Aphrodite—and the ensuing passage moves on to personal memories of Spain. Not all poetry travels at such velocity; some poetry dwells in a specific, intricately detailed location. But in the spirit of Edward W. Said's exploration of "traveling theory" and James Clifford's of "traveling culture," I consider what enables *traveling poetry* by Pound and many other modern and contemporary poets to leap across national and cultural boundaries.[2] Recognizing the "inextinguishable taint" of the term *travel*—its recreational, bourgeois, European, gendered associations—Clifford nevertheless reclaims the word, using it expansively to describe different "practices of crossing and interaction," "the ways people leave home and return, enacting differently centered worlds, interconnected cosmopolitanisms" (39, 3, 27–28). How does poetry leave home and return? What makes possible poetry's differently centered cosmopolitanisms? How does poetic travel differ from global transport by other means?

Poetry travels partly, of course, by means of traveling poets. Pound's incarceration in Italy reminds us that various expatriates, migrants, and émigrés famously transformed poetry in the first part of the twentieth century. Modern and contemporary poets have been changing places and have been changed by places, from Euromodernists such as W. B. Yeats, T. S. Eliot, and Mina Loy and Harlem Renaissance poets such as Langston Hughes and Claude McKay, to the postwar American poets Elizabeth Bishop, John Ashbery, and James Merrill (analyzed by Robert von Hallberg and Jeffrey Gray as tourists and travelers), to postcolonial and immigrant poets such as Okot p'Biket, Lorna Goodison, and Charles Simic.[3] Along with literal movement, modern and contemporary poetry written in English is also inevitably shaped by the circulation of images and ideas by radio, television, the Internet, and other fleet forms of global mediation.

Poetry also travels because poems travel. During his confinement Pound is elated to find *The Pocket Book of Verse*, edited by Morris Edmund Speare, on a toilet seat—a surprising juxtaposition of the humble commode and poetic transport:

> That from the gates of death,
> that from the gates of death: Whitman or Lovelace
>   found on the jo-house seat at that
> in a cheap edition! [and thanks to Professor Speare] (513)

Modern printing and more recent technologies of dissemination help poems by Whitman, Lovelace, and Pound travel via back pockets, iPods, and Web sites, particularly because of poetry's trademark compression. Having only Speare's poetry anthology, a Bible, and an edition of Confucius with him, Pound conjures other poems from memory, and indeed another reason that poems travel is their mnemonic structure: the rhythmic, sonic, rhetorical, and syntactic patterning that led Auden to define poetry as "memorable speech."[4]

Poetry is especially well suited to traveling in yet another sense—that is, the imaginative enactment of geographic movement, as in the rapid-fire transnational displacements in Pound's Pisan canto, and it is this dimension of poetry's travel, albeit interconnected with the others I have mentioned, that is the focus of this essay. Poetry is but one among many kinds of cross-national transit, alongside the people, technology, money, images, and ideas that, as Arjun Appadurai shows, flow across modern national boundaries.[5] Nor does poetic travel always outstrip travel by other genres and discourses. To the extent that poetry is what is lost in translation, travel writing, fiction, music, cinema, and the visual arts may travel more easily across cultural boundaries. Poetry is stitched and hitched to the peculiarities of the language in which it is written. Moreover, because of its reliance on the line and the stanza as units of organization, poetry may be a less effective means of ethnographic transport than, say, a chapter of a realist novel or an act of a naturalist play. The detailed description of a wrestling match in chapter 6 of Chinua Achebe's *Things Fall Apart*—unlike fellow Ibo writer Christopher Okigbo's intensely self-reflexive lyric sequences—firmly situates the non-Ibo reader in the lifeworld of a Nigerian village at the turn of the twentieth century. Because of its formal patterning and energetic verbal self-consciousness, poetry typically offers less transparent access to other cultural worlds. Similarly, whereas travel writing, the Odyssean tale, or, for that matter, the travel poem (minus the participial suffix) involves "the *territorial* passage from one zone to another"[6]—that is, a macro-level transition, a mimetically plotted border crossing from home to foreign land—the travel in traveling lyric often occurs at the micro level: swift territorial shifts by line, trope, sound, or stanza that result in flickering movements, oscillations, and juxtapositions.

What poetry loses as a traveling medium that frequently eschews density of social detail, resists translation, and interrupts mimesis, that mediates on its linguistic surface and fractures the spatiotemporal passage from one zone to another, it gains through structural efficiency and compression. Because the line is fundamental as a unit of meaning in poetry, each of the first four lines of the opening of Pound's canto 81 can turn to a different geocultural space: Greek myth, Chinese mountain, Greek island, memories of Spain. Frank O'Hara's poem "The Day Lady Died" grounds itself in specificities of space and time—"It is 12:20 in New York a Friday / three days after Bastille day, yes / it is 1959"—yet, as first intimated by the seemingly throwaway "Bastille day," which superimposes Paris on New York, the jumps across national boundaries, from one line to the next, could hardly be more quick and nimble: from musings about "what the poets / in Ghana are doing these days" to Paul Verlaine and Pierre Bonnard to Richmond Lattimore's translation of Hesiod, and so forth, before winding up with Billie Holiday at the 5 Spot—a headlong associative movement that, by its elegant fluidity, gives the prosaic details their "poetic" quality.[7] Such a poem is itself a kind of "contact zone," in Mary Louise Pratt's term, a site of migrating and mingling tropes, geographies, and cultural signifiers.[8] Lyric's intercultural "contact" tends to diverge, however, from that of travel writing, a genre satirized by Ashbery in "The Instruction Manual" for exoticizing foreign places and fetishistically dwelling on their particulars, such as those of a dreamily wondrous Guadalajara, conjured up by a worker bored by having to write about the uses of new metal. As indicated by O'Hara's and Ashbery's work, traveling poetry proceeds more quickly and abruptly, through translocational juxtapositions, which by their rapidity and lyric compression typically prevent us from believing that we are entering an alternative space and foreground instead the negotiations and fabrications of imaginative travel.

For other poets, the stanza is a mapping tool that helps efficiently establish location and translocation. The transnational dislocations in Yeats's "Lapis Lazuli" occur in the gaps between stanzas sited in the British Isles, then Greece, then China. In one stanza of "Vacillation" the Duke of Chou, author of the *I Ching*, looks out on a Chinese field, and in the next a conqueror in Babylon or Nineveh draws rein, both Chinaman and Middle Easterner crying out, "'Let all things pass away.'"[9] By the logic of *stanza* as geographic room, the white space in between functions like a doorway between cultural worlds, also linked in this instance by a shared refrain, stanzaic pattern, and use of the *contemptus mundi* topos. Even when not strictly bounding regions by stanza, the stepwise *abab* structure of Archibald MacLeish's quatrains in "You, Andrew Marvell" helps track nightfall's westward sweep from Persia to Baghdad and Arabia, to Palmyra, Lebanon, and Crete, to Sicily, Spain, and Africa. Also moving westward, from Brooklyn to California, Hart Crane's *Bridge* enacts geopoetic migration through sectional divisions that, by shifting among free verse, blank verse, ballad, and other forms, poetically accentuate and propel dislocation. In these and other examples, the traveling reader never fully inhabits any of these spaces but is brought up short by the formal framing and rapid multiple transitions. Deploying sound, structure, and self-reflection, the poet enunciates and plays on the construction of, and movement through, multiple worlds.

Rhyme, rhythm, and poetry's many other forms of sonic patterning also enable imaginative travel. When Melvin B. Tolson sonically links the Christian god ("Great God A'mighty!"), the Greek god of fortune ("the whim / of Tyche"), and an American folk hero

("*The Birth of John Henry!*"), the connective force of rhyme helps his verse cross enormous distances.[10] "Rhyme," Derek Walcott declares in *Omeros*, "is the language's / desire to enclose the loved world in its arms," and in this long poem the rhymes of Walcott's zigzagging terza rima stitch sonic patterns that traverse much of the world's surface, from the Caribbean to the United States, Ireland, and Africa.[11] Like such lyricized epics, lyrics per se make use of a globe-traversing weave. The sound patterns echoing across one of the humorously overloaded short poems of the last century, Wallace Stevens's "Bantams in Pine-Woods," may not move across literal geographies, but the poem's first lines, mocking the chief who turns out to be the solipsistically inflated "ten-foot poet," unmistakably evoke distinct and widely separated places: "Chieftan Iffucan of Azcan in caftan / Of tan with henna hackles, halt!"[12] With the help of the repeated phoneme *-an*, a pre-Columbian chief—perhaps Aztec, Mayan, or a conflation of the two—is dressed (from the Persian *khaftahn*) and dyed (from the Arabic *hinna*) like a Middle Easterner. At poem's end the phoneme *-an* of "portly Azcan's" pseudo-place-name helps stretch poetic topography all the way to the Appalachi*an* Mountains. Riding the back of such caravans of sound, poetry traverses real and semireal landscapes—perhaps more nimbly than less sonically rich, more prosaically referential forms. Its self-signaling textures foreground the linguistic and imaginative construction of poetic travel. Thomas Hardy's Drummer Hodge has voyaged from a North Atlantic home to a southern African grave, and the rhymes, assonances, syntactic parallels, and alternating four- and three-beat lines both connect and ironically disconnect these vastly discrepant spaces:

Yet portion of that unknown plain
    Will Hodge for ever be;
His homely Northern breast and brain
    Grow to some Southern tree,
And strange-eyed constellations reign
    His stars eternally.[13]

Unlike Rupert Brooke's notorious World War I poem "The Soldier," which imperially extends national territory wherever the soldier dies ("there's some corner of a foreign field / That is forever England"), Hardy's poem, while acknowledging some cross-hemispheric fusion, emphasizes the unhomeliness of the deterritorialized English body thrown into a landscape that will remain forever "strange" and "unknown."[14]

Sometimes rhythm serves as a way of intertwining disparate cultural spaces, as when Louise Bennett plays with and against the ballad meter she creolizes with Jamaican rhythms or when Gwendolyn Brooks merges the syncopations of African American speech with the norms of a Petrarchan sonnet in "The Rites for Cousin Vit": "Kicked back the casket-stand. But it can't hold her / That stuff and satin aiming to enfold her."[15] In "A Song in the Front Yard" Brooks entwines her iambs with vernacular triple rhythms and subtly inflected African American phrasing: "That George'll be taken to Jail soon or late / (On account of last winter he sold our back gate)" (6). Whether imposed or willingly adapted, meter, rhythm, stanza, and other prosodic elements have always traveled across cultural and territorial boundaries. Consider, for example, the Japanese haiku, famously anglicized by the imagists, or the Arabic ghazal, adapted for over a thousand years into Persian (taking its canonical form in that language), Turkish, Urdu, German, and English, mostly recently by the Kashmiri American poet Agha Shahid Ali. Despite William Carlos Williams's nativist fulminations against European prosodic strictures, the "quintessentially American" poet can write a poem that employs a rolling, waltzlike triple rhythm to evoke the dancing of the Dutch peasants in Brueghel's painting *The Kermess*:

the dancers go round, they go round and
around, the squeal and the blare and the
tweedle of bagpipes, a bugle and fiddles
tipping their bellies.[16]

Sometimes the allure of a rhythm, a formal structure, or a "foreign" aesthetic is stronger than ideological fortifications against cross-cultural contact and contamination.

A figuratively rich discourse, poetry enables travel in part by its characteristically high proportion of figures of thought, as well as figures of speech. Since *metaphor* derives from the Greek "transfer" or "carry across," it should come as little surprise that poet's figurative language enacts geographic and other kinds of movement. "Moving on or going back to where you came from, / bad news is what you mainly travel with," begins Amy Clampitt's elegy for her mother, "A Procession at Candlemas."[17] The mourning daughter associates the vehicles moving westward with her on the highway with examples of "transhumance," or seasonal migration, in the Pyrenees, the Andes ("red-tasseled pack llamas"), and the Kurdish mountains (22); her tropes for travel travel across three continents in three lines. As Bonnie Costello writes, "Clampitt reveals how poetry might become a guide in developing this nomadic imagination: searching out and crossing boundaries, scavenging, finding value in what has been ignored, setting up formal patterns which she then works to defeat."[18] Clampitt's nomadic embroideries might well seem to have little in common with Sylvia Plath's emotionally eruptive work. But the rapid rush of substitutions in Plath's "Cut" enacts intercontinental, among other forms of, displacement. Having seen her thumb as a pilgrim scalped by an American Indian, the speaker addresses it as a

Saboteur,
Kamikaze man—

The stain on your
Gauze Ku Klux Klan
Babushka
Darkens and tarnishes. . . .[19]

In these few words the poem's pain-exhilarated metaphorical substitutions arc across vast cultural distances, from the Allied saboteur (French) to the Axis kamikaze (Japanese), from the Klansman's hood to a Russian head kerchief. Plath's figurative leaps, especially from herself to Jews in Nazi concentration camps and Japanese victims of nuclear bombs, have been criticized as too free and indiscriminate; even the sympathetic Seamus Heaney worries about her "rampaging so permissively in the history of other people's sorrows."[20] Yet Heaney's poetry, too, shuttle back and forth across divergent spaces—especially, in his early work, across the North Sea to connect the present-day victims of Northern Ireland's atrocities with the sacrificial victims deposited in Jutland's bogs.

Indeed, geopoetic oscillation, as we might term such imaginative movement back and forth between discrepant topographies, is prominent in, though not exclusive to, much modern and contemporary verse. In Ted Hughes's "Out," the lived reality of the Yorkshire farmland is continually sucked under by his father's searing memories of the carnage in Gallipoli: "jawbones and blown-off boots, tree-stumps, shellcases and craters."[21] In "The Glass Essay" Anne Carson slides between a wintry Canadian landscape and the English moors of Emily Brontë's *Wuthering Heights*; in "The Great Palaces of Versailles" Rita Dove's Beulah reimagines the white women who come to Charlotte's Dress Shoppe as variants of the French court ladies of Versailles; and in "Memphis Blues" Sterling A. Brown's bluesman sees little difference between the flood-ravaged Memphis along the

Mississippi and "de other Memphis in / History."[22] Lyric highlights how lines of thought, analogy, and cross-cultural reading—whether strong ligaments or tenuous filaments—connect disparate human experiences. If sometimes the oscillating poem merges landscapes, at other times it plays ironically on the differences between the terrains it shoves together. Walcott's poem "The Sea Is History," for example, wryly juxtaposes biblical and Caribbean historical geographies, and Sherman Alexie's "Crow Testament" sardonically superimposes Bible-scapes on American Indian history and myth:

> Cain lifts Crow, that heavy black bird
> and strikes down Abel.
>
> Damn, says Crow, I guess
> this is just the beginning.[23]

Instead of situating themselves imaginatively in the interstices between two geographies, poems by Pound, Tolson, Paul Muldoon, Kamau Brathwaite, Susan Howe, and other poets rapidly spawn and skip amid a multitude of locations. Howe's "Rückenfigur," for example, seems to plant its first line unambiguously in Cornwall: "Iseult stands at Tintagel."[24] But within a few stanzas the name Tristan is morphing across cultural landscapes,

> Tristran Tristan Tristrant
> Tristram Trystan Trystram
> Tristrem Tristanz Drust
> Drystan . . . (131)

while Iseult becomes "Iseut Isolde Ysolt Essyllt / bride of March Marc Mark" (131). The seeming stability of a proper name fractures into the improprieties of its variants in a multitude of texts from different times and places, sometimes by means of the shift of a single letter (e.g., "Marc Mark"). Orthographic differences are shown to signify and miniaturize geocultural migrations of names and legends. In poetry, travel—instead of being the plot-driven excursus into a foreign land—may occur at the level of a substituted letter, a varied rhythm, or a pivoting line.

This ease of movement by lines and stanzas, sounds and tropes, juxtapositions and morphologies, may not always seem a winning aspect of poetry. Such cross-cultural conflations, forays, and leaps may appear to ride roughshod over significant differences. Alexie's humorous juxtapositions, for example, may risk the very insensitivity to differences between biblical and American Indian narratives that have been catastrophic for native peoples in the Americas—except that he highlights the jarring discrepancies as much as the similarities. Plath may seem irresponsible for linking the Allied saboteur to the Axis kamikaze, the Ku Klux Klan hood to the Russian babushka, and for eliding their political and historical differences—except that her metaphorical connections also underscore the cross-regional and global violence registered and compressed in the poetic unconscious at midcentury. Does Stevens's sonic yoking of the pre-Columbian with the Middle Eastern and in turn the Appalachian repress the regions' historical and geocultural dissimilarities? Perhaps, although part of the burden of his poem is the bantam's rebuke to the grandiose poet for his reductive and idealist insensitivity to specifics, such as those riotously played on by Stevens. Does Clampitt's association of her mournful journey with seasonal migrations in the Pyrenees, the Andes, and the Kurdish mountains trip too easily across inequalities and erase cultural specificities? Maybe, but surely we would not wish to crimp the cross-geographic reach of the twentieth- and twenty-first-century globalized imagination, forcing a poet like Clampitt to ignore connections among migrant mountain populations and limit the range of her associations to the United States. Does Pound's syncretic verse too easily appropriate Chinese, Greek, and Spanish locales and myths and place-names for his self-elegiac purposes? Surely the risk, as in these other poetic examples, is there—a risk that arises in each instance partly from the velocity of the traveling poem, partly from the relative freedom of the aesthetic realm. But such criticisms may assume a too rigid model of identity.

To wag one's finger at these poems' metaphorical, sonic, and structural connections is to presuppose the discreteness and stability of each cultural unit, when each culture is always already thoroughly enmeshed in a multitude of others. It is to impose an ethical and quasi-legal notion of cultural ownership that is inimical to poetry's radial connections, imaginative leaps, and boundary-crossing ventures. And it is to box creative expression within identitarian preconceptions resisted by poetry's hybridizing, associative force. Surely some poetic maneuvers may be harder to defend, such as William Stafford's foray into Wounded Knee in "Report to Crazy Horse," Robert Duncan's into the primitive and primal Africa of "An African Elegy," and June Jordan's to the same continent in "Poem about My Rights"—poems that may less skillfully and self-consciously traverse uneven cultural terrain. But these risks are inextricably bound up with the characteristic strengths of poetry, as seen in traveling poems by Hardy, Stevens, Pound, Plath, Heaney, Okigbo, Walcott, Howe, and others. Cross-cultural contamination and leakage may well be more congenial to poetry than boundary-drawing orthodoxies of the pure, the different, and the native. Traveling poetry helps foreground how, through imaginative as well as literal mingling and merging, new coinages, new intergeographic spaces, even new compound identities come into being.[25]

Although examples could be spun out ad infinitum, closer travelogical analysis of poems by an early-twentieth-century African American poet, a midcentury Euro-American expatriate, and a late-century Latino poet may shed light on how, why, and to what effect poetry travels and what the implications are for a poetics of transnational identity. Langston Hughes recounts being inspired to compose "The Negro Speaks of Rivers" while he crossed the Mississippi, a recent high school graduate, en route to see his father in Mexico.[26] In a mere four lines his poem crosses four rivers, one in Southwest Asian, two in Africa, one in North America:

> I bathed in the Euphrates when dawns were young.
> I built my hut near the Congo and it lulled me to sleep.
> I looked upon the Nile and raised the pyramids above it.
> I heard the singing of the Mississippi when Abe Lincoln went
> down to New Orleans, and I've seen its muddy bosom turn all
> golden in the sunset.[27]

What makes it possible for the poem to cross such distances? By the logic of poetic lineation, each of these end-stopped lines locates itself in a different place, and the gap between one line and the next marks a distance that can be thousands of miles. The disjunctive logic of poetic lineation instructs us not to expect geographic continuity. Each line is a different scene, a different chapter, a different cultural world. Still, the poem's countervailing connections span these dislocations and moderate their effect. The gelatinous, Whitmanian "I" binds together globally disparate experiences. A figure of speech, anaphora also functions as a figure of thought, a trope for the repetitions and replications of diverse human experiences in different times and places. All the rivers are seen as resembling one another, and all figuratively fuse with the poet's blood flow and all-knowing soul.

Although Hughes's poem is often read as an example of what Walter Benn Michaels calls "a commitment to a poetry of identity,"[28] specifically an African American or African diaspora identity, the poem's affirmation of a new "Negro" identity is paradoxically enmeshed in, and dependent on, a declaration of a transracial, planetary identity: "the flow of human blood in human veins" (*Collected Poems*, 23). The poem's naming of rivers in particular is often described as evidencing the speaker's racial identity, yet two of the four rivers, the Euphrates and the Mississippi, are hardly African, and only one of the remaining rivers is mainly in sub-Saharan Africa. The poem "maps a truly global geography of rivers," as Jeff Westover notes.[29] Hughes wrote the poem in 1920 and published it in 1921, when another writer was conceiving and composing a poem that juxtaposes rivers on separate continents—the Thames, the Rhine, the Ganges, and perhaps subliminally the Mississippi. Both Eliot's and Hughes's poems assert knowledge of rivers represented as distant sites of human origin: the ancient Ganges for Eliot and the civilization-cradling Euphrates for Hughes. The epistemological claims in these poems—to have "known rivers" far and wide, even at the dawn of civilization—brashly overstep the bounds of each writer's lived experience. But Eliot's poem seems overburdened with the knowledge garnered by global imaginative travel, while Hughes's speaker emphatically and exuberantly claims the authority to know. Instead of representing himself as being at the end of an enervated civilization, looking elsewhere for moral and spiritual guidance, Hughes looks backward to look forward, to summon a boldly affirmed power to speak as a "Negro"—a new "Negro," whose knowledge is both racial (the Congo and the Nile) and extraracial (the Euphrates), both African and transcivilizational.[30] Like the trope of the river, the blood in the poem functions paradoxically as a signifier of the speaker's racial specificity and his shared humanity. The lyric instantiates its dual emphasis on racial and transracial identity in its hybridization of African American and Euro-American cultural forms. Written in a free-versifying and multitude-encompassing Whitmanian voice, the poem also summons the rhetoric and imagery of spirituals, in which to go "down by the riverside" is to seek a site where conflict can be reconciled: "Ain't gonna study war no more."

Although racial identity is often conceived in terms of roots, this poem takes multiple routes leading in different directions. Its allusions to slavery—the building of the pyramids in Egypt and Lincoln's trip to New Orleans—suggest that the poem energetically displaces one kind of travel, the horror of slaves bought and sold down rivers against their will, with the New Negro's imaginative and literal travel across continents at will. The lyric's rapid, voluntary, nonsequential movements are thus the reverse of the terrifying constraints of enslavement. Although the poem tracks the sun's diurnal course, the lyric's global river travel cannot be mapped as a linear trajectory across historical time: it turns from what was then considered the original site of human civilization, the Euphrates; to the Congo, where the Kongo kingdom was in place from the fourteenth through the sixteenth centuries; to the ancient civilization of the Nile; to the nineteenth- and twentieth-century Mississippi. Nor is a linear spatial mapping possible from east to west, because, again, of the middle lines about the Congo and then the Nile. This zig-zag movement across time and space emphasizes that the verse turns where the speaker wants to turn it (*vertere*), asserting the authority of an unfettered and globe-traversing poetic "I." From a narrowly identitarian perspective, Hughes may seem to travel too freely and quickly, eliding important geocultural differences among ancient Babylonians and Egyptians, Africans of the Kongo kingdom, and nineteenth-century Americans. Yet his freewheeling poetic travel looks different when seen in the contexts that inform it: the haunting transgenerational memory of forced travel down the river; the claiming of a common humanity historically denied to African Americans; and an understanding of poetry as a discursive space that—by means of place-leaping lineation, cross-cultural symbols, and aesthetic hybridization—affords a remarkable freedom of movement and affiliative connection.

Fifty years later another American poet explores questions of travel, once again staging poetic self-discovery in a global context. Like Hughes's lyric "I," the "I" in Elizabeth Bishop's "In the Waiting Room" (1971) defines itself in relation to other cultures in distant parts of the world. But whereas Hughes's poem traverses continents to embrace continuities between distant civilizations and the poem's "Negro" speaker, whose soul contains cross-cultural multitudes in a display of newfound traveling freedom and a newly affirmed (cross-)cultural identity, Bishop's almost-seven-year-old "Elizabeth" shrinks from the shocking difference-in-sameness she sees in the indigenous peoples pictured in the *National Geographic*. Instead of stabilizing, authorizing, and enlarging the lyric "I," as in Hughes's poem, imaginative travel puts the subject in Bishop's poem at risk—risk that, paradoxically, affords the enunciation of lyric self-consciousness. Recounting, in Mutlu Konuk Blasing's Wordsworthian phrase, the "growth of a poet's mind," the poem explores how the media's global circulation of images impinges on an individual's emerging subjectivity.[31] The young "Elizabeth," Lee Edelman observes in an astute reading, discovers that sexuality is hardly natural but artificially fashioned and constrained.[32] But the girl's revelation about her common condition as a female human being—akin to both the naked women in the pictures and the heavily clad women in the dentist's office, including her aunt—is not less a revelation about cultural difference:

A dead man slung on a pole
—"Long Pig," the caption said.
Babies with pointed heads
wound round and round with string;
black, naked women with necks
wound round and round with wire
like the necks of light bulbs.
Their breasts were horrifying.[33]

In Worcester, Massachusetts, in February 1918, the young girl suddenly finds herself traveling imaginatively to a place visited and photographed by the explorers Osa and Martin Johnson. The mass media present to the imagination, as Appadurai writes, "a rich, ever-changing store of possible lives" (53). Elizabeth's encounter with alien bodies and cultural practices shocks her into the recognition not only of sameness but also of difference, destabilizing the naturalness of her own cultural world, which suddenly shrinks into one among an indefinite array of contingent possibilities. Her vertiginous

sensation of falling off
the round, turning world
into cold, blue-black space

is in part due to her initiation into becoming a global subject, once anchored to part of the world by the illusion of its completeness but now unmoored and floating free among cultural and racial differences.

Falling into the knowledge of her apartness and isolation, the girl confronts a terrifying continuity with the alien other, figured especially as "those awful hanging breasts," which would normally signify primal connection but here also signify a dialectically constitutive difference. As Gayatri Chakravorty Spivak observes of the protagonist of *Jane Eyre*, the "'subject-constitution' of the female individualist" takes place through the contrast with the "'native female.'"[34] First World subjectivity, the child's sense of apartness and her emergence into self-recognition, depends her on the Third World, on both a recognition of continuity with these women and an exoticizing, primitivizing warding off of the cultural other as different from her own, discrete, insular self-identity. The metropolitan female subject is shocked into a differential self-understanding as nonnative, as other than the horrifying other in the magazine. Emphatically defined as a reader—"(I could read)"—Elizabeth is represented in terms of what Spivak calls a "self-marginalized uniqueness" (246), as a reader of images and texts ("Long Pig," "the date"), in contrast to the sheer visuality of the Third World bodies she sees. As Elizabeth "articulates herself in shifting relationship to what is at stake, the 'native female' as such (*within* discourse, *as* a signifier) is excluded from any share in this emerging norm" (244–45). As for the mature poet, she, like the *National Geographic* and like the Johnsons, reproduces and circulates images of Third World bodies and practices for First World consumption. The extent to which these images represent undifferentiated otherness is indicated by Bishop's later confusion over their origin, which she referred to as "African" in an interview, claiming that they derived from what has proved a nonexistent issue of the *National Geographic*.[35] But Bishop most likely echoes the phrase "Long Pig" and the description of infants' heads wound with coconut string, as Edelman notes (191), from Osa Johnson's book *I Married Adventure*, and the Johnsons encountered these cultural phenomena not in Africa but during what Osa Johnson describes as an early adventure in the Melanesian islands of Malekula and Vao, in what was then the New Hebrides and is now Vanatu, among a chain of Pacific islands west of Fiji and east of Australia.[36] The encircled heads and necks are cast in a symmetrical relation to each other, an imagistic repetition given sonic emphasis ("wound round and round"), but Bishop's echoic imagery and language traverse large distances; the Johnsons photographed women with multiple brass and horsehair necklaces in British East Africa, while the bare-breasted women pictured in *I Married Adventure* are Pacific Islanders and so-called Pygmies of the Belgian Congo. Bishop's simile for ornamented necks—"wound round and round with wire / like the necks of light bulbs"—jarringly yokes together the primitive and the modern, and indeed the First World girl's lightbulb moment of self-recognition depends on the primitivity against which she defines herself. Bishop's language of shock and estrangement, "horrifying," "awful," recalls the similar affective vocabulary—"horrible looking" (117), "frightful" (120), "terror" (121, 122, 132), "terrifying" (123), "horrible" (131), "horror" (145, 156), "awful" (153)—in Osa Johnson's descriptions of her encounters with Malekulans.

One way to reconsider the poem's cross-civilizational shock is to juxtapose the young American girl's horror of the "awful hanging breasts" with the reverse ethnography of an indigenous village woman in a poem published just five years earlier, the Ugandan Okot p'Bitek's *Song of Lawino* (1966). For Lawino, it is the breasts of white women and their non-European mimics that are horrifying. She cries out about her would-be white rival, Tina:

> Her breasts are completely shrivelled up
> They are all folded dry skins,
> They have made nests of cotton wool
> And she folds the bits of cow-hide
> In the nests
> And call[s] them breasts![37]

The poetry of this passage's hyperbole ("completely shrivelled up") and circumlocution ("nests of cotton wool") mirrors the speaker's estrangement from a cultural practice—wearing bras—that has traveled from the "developed" to the "developing world." Just as Bishop's Elizabeth cannot fathom the binding of heads or necks, as formally signaled by the perplexed repetitions and the troping of ornamented necks as the necks of lightbulbs, so too Lawino is dumbfounded by the strange cultural practices of white women:

They mould the tips of the cotton nests
So that they are sharp
And with these they prick
The chests of their men! (39)

Whereas the nakedness of the hanging black breasts frightens the young Elizabeth, Lawino proclaims the virtue of the Acoli dancing without hiding anything:

Small breasts that have just emerged,
And large ones full of boiling milk,
Are clearly seen in the arena. . . . (43)

For Lawino, the object of revulsion is the customary behavior of white women, who cover up their bodies and hold their mates in stultifying proximity, who

prick the chests of their men
With the cotton nests
On their chests. (44)

Elizabeth associates native women with violence to the body—cannibalism, head elongation, neck binding—whereas Lawino's language links such violence with white women ("sharp," "prick") and the bizarre ways that they treat their bodies and the bodies of men. For all their differences, in both Okot's poem and Bishop's, the breast—seemingly the primal locus of mammalian connection—is the bodily site around which the traveling female subject establishes her distinctiveness vis-à-vis the cultural other. For these writers of widely divergent backgrounds, poetry enables the exploration of modernity's intensified circulation of images and practices, in part because poetic figures can richly evoke the defamiliarization of alienating encounters with cultural others (whether clothed women with "cotton nests / On their chests" or naked women with necks "like the necks of light bulbs"), in part because the emergence, articulation, and delineation of personal and communal subjectivities have been hallmarks of poetic forms.

In Bishop's poem Elizabeth's First World othering of native women is unmistakable, so if Hughes's traveling poem can easily be attacked for eliding geocultural differences, Bishop's can be accused of exaggerating differences. Yet what distinguishes the encounter with otherness in "In the Waiting Room" from the Johnsons' exoticist language and unselfconsciously triumphalist photographs is the poet's foregrounding the precarious act of self-fashioning in a differential relation to the cultural other (as Okot does in *Song of Lawino*). In Spivak's account the subject's civilizational self-construction entails the unconscious suppression of the Third World other, but in Bishop's poem the poetics of self-definition, including the girl's fragile dependence on the other to become herself, is front and center. The speaker's grown-up consciousness frames and drolly ironizes the young Elizabeth's self-discovery: "I scarcely dared to look / to see what it was I was." In the crisis moment in which the girl feels on the brink of oblivion, in danger of falling "into cold, blue-black space," the heightened self-consciousness that has long been a staple of lyric comes to the fore, particularly in Elizabeth's self-address and self-nomination:

. . . you are an *I*,
you are an *Elizabeth*,
you are one of *them*.

In Rimbaud's famous declaration, "JE est un autre," the subject is split, represented as both self and other, as indicated by the doubling of pronouns.[38] In Bishop's quintessentially "lyric" moment of emerging self-consciousness, the vulnerable subject turns to address itself. It individuates itself by seizing on the first-person pronoun and bestowing on that self its proper name, yet it also deindividuates the self, employing indefinite articles that plunge the objectified self-as-other into a pool of resemblances ("an *I*," "an *Elizabeth*"). The girl thinks to herself, "How 'unlikely'" it is to be "like them," and the poem's play on likeness and unlikeness underscores the figurative comparisons between self and other on which self-understanding depends: the "similarities" that "held us all together / or made us all just one." By virtue of lyric's heightening of figuration, its self-reflexive framing, and its sharp attention to how trope and image fashion selves, cultures, worlds, the traveling poem illuminates the differential structure through which the globalized subject enunciates and understands itself.

An adequate defense of time-and-space travel by lyric poetry needs to take account of both its connective (Hughes) and differential (Bishop) tendencies in relation to cultural others, since lyrics of cross-cultural sameness and those of cross-cultural difference are equally open to critique. Should a poem, like Hughes's, travel along vectors of poetic commonality, it may be suspected of eliding differences, colonizing and cannibalizing cultural others, appropriating alterity for self-interested projects cast in universalist guise. Should a poem, like Bishop's, emphasize difference (cultural) within sameness (gender), it is exposed to the reverse criticism of exoticizing and stereotyping others, of overemphasizing and even manufacturing differences for the sake of propping up First World civilizational identities. Yet the parallels between these critiques—damned if you claim sameness, damned if you claim difference—indicate the dangers of a too stringent cross-cultural policing of literary identities. The metaphorical, lineal, and lyric expansiveness of traveling poetry—readily affording cross-cultural engagement, contact, and contamination—puts into question the adequacy of such limited and limiting models, which are identitarian even when represented as postcolonial, postmodern, or planetary, at least insofar as their logic appears to favor the foot-bound over the fleet-footed poem. Lyric's nuanced attention to self-enunciation and self-construction in dialogic relation to the other should also give one pause before assimilating the genre to more blindly manipulative forms of global mediation.

While traveling poetry clearly has much in common with other globe-skipping forms, commodities, and discourses, some such poems, though glancing at their complicities with global market circulation, are at pains also to highlight the distinctiveness of poetry. Like Bishop's and Hughes's lyrics, a later traveling poem explores points of intersection among widely disparate and globally scattered images, helping reveal further what enables poetry to travel, particularly as this travel has accelerated in the contemporary world and in contemporary poetry. What do Carl Sandburg's face, a plastic surgeon on TV, an American newspaper, signs forbidding laughter in Tiananmen Square, and the poem that records them all have in common?—so asks "Hysteria," by the Cuban-born poet Dionisio D. Martínez.[39] Riding the rails of multiple resonances of the figure of the line, this poem moves rapidly and unexpectedly among these disparate sites: the lines on Sandburg's face, the wrinkles that the plastic surgeon claims are caused by all facial expressions, the folds of an American newspaper, the signs in Tiananmen Square, and implicitly the lines crossed and recrossed in writing and "reading the lines" of verse. Yet despite all these similarities, the poem implicitly contrasts its idiosyncratic and nonviolent global shuttlings with a coercive form of epistemological globalism, troped as how each section of an American newspaper "is folded independently and believes it owns / the world." A humorous enjambment that fractures the politically loaded word "inter-//national" figures the poem's travel across topographic, stanzaic, and lineal gaps:

> There's this brief item in the inter-
>
> national pages: the Chinese government has posted
> signs in Tiananmen Square, forbidding laughter.
> I'm sure the plastic surgeon would approve, he'd say
>
> the Chinese will look young much longer, their faces
> unnaturally smooth, but what I see (although
> no photograph accompanies the story) is laughter
>
> bursting inside them.

Newspapers, governments, and doctors try to hold and even reinforce lines, whereas the poet uses lines to cross, rupture, and question what political and other kinds of normative lines would hold back ("laughter/bursting inside them"). The lyric "I" enables the poet to weave chiastically together both Sandburg's windy Chicago and the prohibitions in Tiananmen Square, both China and North America:

> I think of wind in Tiananmen Square, how a country
> deprived of laughter ages invisibly; I think
> of the Great Walls of North America. . . .

We are back to Hughes's Whitmanian all-encompassing, cross-civilizational, lyric "I," the poet's first-person meditative utterance as omnium gatherum: translocal, binding disparities, forging new and surprising connections in its travel across the globe. We are also back to the tropological exploration of sameness-in-difference in Bishop's poem, the poem as site of cross-cultural global comparison, contrast, and self-definition. Of course, Bishop's and Hughes's poems were already, in their own ways, mediating between these poles, turning between home and elsewhere, between what distinguishes our locational identities and what holds us "all together" or makes us "all just one." As in their poems, in Martínez's lyric and Pound's canto, Plath's "Cut" and Stevens's "Bantams in Pine-Woods," Okot's *Song of Lawino* and Howe's "Rückenfigur," the nimble leaps of cross-cultural figuration and rhythm, the nation-straddling juxtapositions of image and sound, compress, vivify, and illuminate the globe- and identity-traversing force of the traveling imagination.

NOTES

1. *The Cantos of Ezra Pound* (New York: New Directions, 1972), 517.

2. Edward W. Said, "Traveling Theory," in *The World, the Text, and the Critic* (Cambridge, MA: Harvard University Press, 1983), 226–47; James Clifford, "Traveling Cultures," in *Routes: Travel and Translation in the Late Twentieth Century* (Cambridge, MA: Harvard University Press, 1997), 17–46.

3. Robert von Hallberg, "Tourists," in *American Poetry and Culture, 1945–1980* (Cambridge, MA: Harvard University Press, 1985), 62–92; Jeffrey Gray, *Mastery's End: Travel and Postwar American Poetry* (Athens: University of Georgia Press, 2005). I explore issues of poetry, transnationalism, and migration in "A Transnational Poetics," in "Transnational Citizenship and the Humanities," ed. Wai Chee Dimock, special issue, *American Literary History* 18, no. 2 (2006): 332–59; and in "Black British Poetry and the Translocal," in *The Cambridge Companion to Twentieth-Century English Poetry*, ed. Neil Corcoran (Cambridge: Cambridge University Press, 2007).

4. W. H. Auden, introduction to *The Poet's Tongue*, ed. W. H. Auden and John Garrett (London: Bell, 1935), v–x.

5. Arjun Appadurai, *Modernity at Large: Cultural Dimensions of Globalization* (Minneapolis: University of Minnesota Press, 1996), 37.

6. Brian Musgrove, "Travel and Unsettlement: Freud on Vacation," in *Travel Writing and Empire:*

Postcolonial Theory in Transit, ed. Steve Clark (London: Zed, 1999), 31. On the travel in travel writing see the other essays in Clark's collection and in *The Cambridge Companion to Travel Writing*, ed. Peter Hulme and Tim Youngs (Cambridge: Cambridge University Press, 2002).

7. *The Collected Poems of Frank O'Hara*, ed. Donald Allen (Berkeley: University of California Press, 1995), 325.

8. Mary Louise Pratt, *Imperial Eyes: Travel Writing and Transculturation* (London: Routledge, 1992), 6–7.

9. W. B. Yeats, *The Poems*, ed. Richard J. Finneran, vol. 1 of *The Collected Works of W. B. Yeats*, ed. Richard J. Finneran and George Mills Harper (New York: Macmillan, 1989), 249–53.

10. *Harlem Gallery, and Other Poems of Melvin B. Tolson*, ed. Raymond Nelson (Charlottesville: University Press of Virginia, 1999), 279.

11. Derek Walcott, *Omeros* (New York: Farrar, Straus, and Giroux, 1990), 75.

12. Wallace Stevens, *The Collected Poems* (New York: Vintage, 1982), 75–76. See Ann Mikkelson, "'Fat! Fat! Fat!'—Wallace Steven's Figurations of Masculinity," *Journal of Modern Literature* 27 (2003): 106–13; and Rachel Blau DuPlessis, *Genders, Races, and Religious Cultures in Modern American Poetry, 1908–1934* (Cambridge: Cambridge University Press, 2001), 95–97, which adds another intercultural subtext by arguing that the poem responds to the threat of Vachel Lindsay's racial impersonation in "The Congo."

13. *The Complete Poetical Works of Thomas Hardy*, ed. Samuel Hynes, 5 vols. (Oxford: Clarendon, 1982–95), 1:122.

14. *The Collected Poems of Rupert Brooke*, ed. George Edward Woodberry (New York: Lane, 1918), 111.

15. Gwendolyn Brooks, *Selected Poems* (New York: Harper and Row, 1963), 58.

16. *The Collected Poems of William Carlos Williams*, ed. A Walton Litz and Christopher MacGowan, 2 vols. (New York: New Directions, 1986–88), 1:58.

17. Amy Clampitt, *The Kingfisher* (New York: Knopf, 1985), 22.

18. Bonnie Costello, "Amy Clampitt: Nomad Exquisite," in *Shifting Ground: Reinventing Landscape in Modern American Poetry* (Cambridge, MA: Harvard University Press, 2003), 118–19.

19. Sylvia Plath, *The Collected Poems*, ed. Ted Hughes (New York: Harper and Row, 1981), 235–56.

20. Seamus Heaney, *The Government of the Tongue: Selected Prose, 1978–1987* (New York: Farrar, Straus, and Giroux, 1989), 165.

21. Ted Hughes, *Collected Poems*, ed. Paul Keegan (New York: Farrar, Straus, and Giroux, 2003), 165.

22. *The Collected Poems of Sterling A. Brown*, ed. Michael S. Harper (Evanston, IL: TriQuarterly, 1996), 60.

23. Sherman Alexie, *One Stick Song* (Brooklyn, NY: Hanging Loose, 2000), 26.

24. Susan Howe, *Pierce-Arrow* (New York: New Directions, 1999), 129.

25. Among the theoretical works informing this general view of cross-cultural globalism are Salman Rushdie, "In Good Faith," in *Imaginary Homelands: Essays and Criticism, 1981–1991* (London: Granta, 1991), 393–414; Edouard Glissant, *Caribbean Discourse: Selected Essays*, trans. J. Michael Dash (Charlottesville: University Press of Virginia, 1989), 120–57; Paul Gilroy, *The Black Atlantic: Modernity and Double Consciousness* (Cambridge, MA: Harvard University Press, 1993), 1–40; Homi K. Bhabha, *The Location of Culture* (London: Routledge, 1994); Clifford, *Routes*, 1–46; Michael F. Brown, *Who Owns Native Culture?* (Cambridge, MA: Harvard University Press, 2003), 43–68; and Kwame Anthony Appiah, *Cosmopolitanism: Ethics in a World of Strangers* (New York: Norton, 2006), 101–35.

26. Langston Hughes, *The Big Sea: An Autobiography* (New York: Knopf, 1940), 55; Arnold Rampersad, *The Life of Langston Hughes*, 2 vols. (New York: Oxford University Press, 1986–88), 1:39–40.

27. *The Collected Poems of Langston Hughes*, ed. Arnold Rampersad with David Roessel (New York: Knopf, 1997), 23.

28. Walter Benn Michaels, "American Modernism and the Poetics of Identity," *Modernism/Modernity* 1 (1994): 51.

29. Jeff Westover, "Africa/America: Fragmentation and Diaspora in the Work of Langston Hughes," *Callaloo* 25 (2002): 1221. On Hughes's black internationalism see Brent Hayes Edwards, *The Practice of Diaspora: Literature, Translation, and the Rise of Black Internationalism* (Cambridge, MA: Harvard University Press, 2003), 59–68.

30. On the poem's going back to a "pre-'racial' dawn" and its avoidance of "racial essentialism" see George Hutchinson, *The Harlem Renaissance in Black and White* (Cambridge, MA: Belknap Press of Harvard University Press, 1995), 415.

31. Mutlu Konuk Blasing, *American Poetry—The Rhetoric of Its Forms* (New Haven, CT: Yale University Press, 1987), 114.

32. Lee Edelman, "The Geography of Gender: Elizabeth Bishop's 'In the Waiting Room,'"

Contemporary Literature 26 (1985): 179–96. For a wide-ranging discussion of imaginative travel in Bishop's work see Bonnie Costello, "Excursive Sight," in *Elizabeth Bishop: Questions of Mastery* (Cambridge, MA: Harvard, University Press, 1991), 127–74.

33. Elizabeth Bishop, *The Complete Poems* (New York: Farrar, Straus, and Giroux, 1983), 159–61.

34. Gayatri Chakravorty Spivak, "Three Women's Texts and a Critique of Imperialism," *Critical Inquiry* 12 (1985): 245.

35. George Starbuck, "'The Work!' A Conversation with Elizabeth Bishop," in *Elizabeth Bishop and Her Art*, ed. Lloyd Schwartz and Sybil P. Estess (Ann Arbor: University of Michigan Press, 1983), 318.

36. Osa Johnson, *I Married Adventure: The Lives and Adventures of Martin and Osa Johnson* (Philadelphia: Lippincott, 1940), 151. See also the photographs of heavily necklaced women in Osa Johnson, *Four Years in Paradise* (London: Hutchinson, 1941), plates after pp. 16 and 128.

37. Okot p'Bitek, *"Song of Lawino" and "Song of Ocol"* (London: Heinemann, 1984), 39.

38. Arthur Rimbaud to Georges Izambard, May 13, 1871, in *Oeuvres*, ed. Suzanne Bernard (Paris, Garnier, 1960), 344.

39. Dionisio D. Martínez, *Bad Alchemy* (New York: Norton, 1995), 26–27.

Towards a Lyric History of India (2004) 10.3

Aamir R. Mufti

> The whole cannot be put together by adding the separated halves, but in both there appear, however distantly, the changes of the whole, which only moves in contradiction.
>
> Theodor Adorno[1]

At its best, the Urdu lyric verse of Faiz Ahmed Faiz (1911–1984) can make available to the reader a disconcerting form of ecstasy, a sense of elation at the self being put in question, giving even the thoroughly secular reader the taste of an affective utopia not entirely distinguishable from religious feeling. It is, at the very least, a paradoxical structure of feeling, given the explicitly Marxist and anticlerical affiliations of his poetry, which displays a marked interest in the secularization of culture and language. Faiz is widely regarded as the most significant Urdu poet of the postcolonial period. His poetry exemplifies some of the central dilemmas of Urdu writing in the aftermath of the partition of India at the moment of independence from British rule. It represents a profound attempt to unhitch literary production from the cultural projects of either postcolonial state in order to make visible meanings that have still not been entirely reified and subsumed within the cultural logic of the nation-state system. Despite his stature as the uncrowned poet laureate of Pakistan during the first several decades of its existence, his is notoriously an oeuvre with vast audiences across what was once North India—the map of its reception seemingly erasing the national boundaries that are the territorial legacy of partition. Against much of Faiz criticism, I argue here that the foremost theme of Faiz's poetry, its defining theme as a body of writing, is the meaning and legacy of partition. I have argued elsewhere that the problematic of minoritization inscribes itself in Urdu narrative at the level of genre in a foregrounding of the short story as the primary genre of narrative fiction.[2] In poetry, it translates into debates about the meaning and nature, the very possibility, of lyric verse in modernity. In the decades following the 1857 Rebellion, for instance, the classical tradition of lyric poetry, and in particular the *ghazal* form, became the site of fierce contention about the prospects of a distinct "Muslim" experience in Indian modernity. The poetry of Faiz exemplifies the unique relationship of Urdu literary production to the crisis of Indian national culture that is marked by the figure of the Muslim.

The lyric element in Faiz's poetry—its intensely personal contemplation of love and of the sensuous—poses a notorious problem of interpretation: he is a self-avowedly political poet—laureled in the Soviet Union, repeatedly persecuted by reactionary postcolonial regimes—whose most intense poetic accomplishments are examinations of subjective states. The orthodox solution—shared by critics of many different political persuasions—has been to argue that Faiz merely turns a "traditional" poetic vocabulary to radical political ends, that we should read the figure of the distant beloved, for instance, as a figuring of the hoped-for revolution.[3] I suggest a somewhat different direction here and argue that, first, the *political* element in Faiz's work cannot be read without the mediation of the *social*. Faiz's exploration of the affects of separation and union with the beloved makes possible an examination of the subject, the "I," of Urdu writing. It would be incorrect to assume that Faiz's "Progressiveness"—his association with the literary culture that carries the imprimatur of the All-India Progressive Writers Association (AIPWA)—implies a dismissing of the question of identity. The central drama of his poetry is the dialectic of a collective selfhood at the disjunctures of language, culture, nation, and community. In his well-known argument about the relationship of lyric poetry to society, Theodor Adorno suggests that it is precisely lyric's apparent distance from social determinations that constitutes its social meaning. He holds out the paradoxical possibility that its distance from the social in fact made of lyric poetry an exemplary site for the inscription of social meanings. The more the lyric reduces itself to the pure subjectivity of the "I," Adorno argues, the more complete the precipitation of the social within its content will be. The more it immerses itself in what takes individual form, the more it is elevated to the level of universality, but a universality that is "social in nature."[4] In this essay, I shall elucidate the place of lyric in Faiz's work and its relationship to the social horizon that is brought to crisis in partition. It is precisely in those poems that are closest to being "pure" lyric, that is, ones in which the inward turn is most complete, rather than in such explicitly "partition" poems as "Freedom's Dawn," that we may glimpse these social meanings in their fullest elaboration.

I would like to explore the possibility that what Faiz's love lyrics give expression to is a self in partition, that what they make visible is a dialectic of self and other in which the subject and object of desire not so much become one as simultaneously come near and become distant, exchange places, are rendered uncertain. The desire for *wisal*, or union, takes the form of this dialectic itself. In the years following the partition of India, the problematic of national fragmentation comes to imbue the lyric world of Faiz's verse in profound and explicit ways. But the broader problematic of a partitioned self is already present in the poems of the pre-partition years, at least as potential, something that these poems point to and anticipate. The social truth embodied in Faiz's lyric poetry is that the emergence of the (modern) self is also its self-division. The truth of the self is its contradictory, tense, and antagonistic reality. Faiz makes it possible to think about identity in post-partition South Asia in terms other than those normalized within the shared vocabulary of the postcolonial states. The purportedly autonomous national selves that emerged from partition are revealed to be what they are—moments within the dialectic of Indian modernity. And *partition* comes to acquire meanings very different from its usual significations, now referring not merely to the events of 1947 (or even of 1946–48) but to a history of social ("communal") identifications coextensive with the history of the Indian modern itself. The immense popularity of Faiz's poetry in the Urdu-Hindi regions, its almost iconic status as a pan–South Asian oeuvre, is a vague but nevertheless conclusive measure of its success in making available an experience of self that is Indian in the encompassing sense, across the boundaries of the "communal" and nation-state divides. But this is a staging of selfhood that takes division seriously, refusing to treat it as merely epiphenomenal, as in the unity-in-diversity formula of Indian nationalism. In fact, it suggests that division, the indefinitely extended separation from the beloved, constitutes the very ground from which union can be contemplated. It is commonplace in Faiz criticism to invoke love of country or nation as an essential feature of his poetry.[5] Faiz himself thematizes this on several occasions, as in the early poem "Two Loves" ("Do ishq"): "In the same fashion I have loved my darling country, / In the same manner my heart has throbbed with devotion to her."[6] But it is not accidental that neither the criticism nor the poetry itself is unequivocal about what the term *country* (*watan*) signifies. It might even be said that to speak of *watan* and *qaum* (nation/people) in the context of Faiz is to remain meaningfully silent about the objects toward which they point: does the *hubb-ul-watani* (love of country or nation, patriotism) of Faiz's poetry attach itself to any *one* of the postcolonial states of South Asia? Does it represent a hope for dissolution of these states? What is its stance on partition, their moment of coming into being? Does it imply a "civilizational" referent? If so, which civilization—Indic, Indo-Persian, or Islamic? Where exactly, in other words, is the poet's home?

The symbolic vocabulary of Faiz's poetry draws on the stock of traditional Persio-Arabic images available to the classical Urdu *ghazal*—*barbat o nai* (lyre and flute), *lauh o qalam* (tablet and pen), *tauq o salasil* (neck-irons and chain), *kakul o lab* (lock of hair and lip), *dasht o gulzar* (wilderness and garden)—resisting the "plain" language that had already become more common with some of his contemporaries and is more so with the generation of poets who have followed in his wake. In this sense, Faiz's poetry is a living rebuke to the ideal of a neutral "Hindustani" idiom from which both Arabo-Persian and Sanskritic influences have been excised, an ideal to which the secularist, "anticommunalist" imagination in South Asia has been repeatedly drawn. Victor Kiernan, his translator and lifelong friend, notes that Faiz "was repelled by the prospect held up by Gandhi of a united 'Hindostani' language, a nondescript neither Hindi nor Urdu."[7] The mythopoetic universe of his work is replete with references to Persian, Arabic, and "Islamic" sources, although, as Kiernan has noted, "a fondness for allusion to things Hindu, even religious, has not left him," an important question to which I shall return.[8] My contention here is that the question of collective selfhood—the meaning of "nation," "people," "culture," "community"—is at the heart of Faiz's poetry, and not merely in the sense of his political devotion to "the people" and contempt for their exploitation by neofeudalism and colonial and postcolonial capital. Faiz problematizes the very notion of nation or people, raising fundamental questions about identity and subjectivity and their historical determinations. To put it more precisely, in Faiz's poetry, both the degradation of human life in colonial and postcolonial modernity—exploitation—and the withholding of a collective selfhood at peace with itself—what I am calling partition—find common expression in the suffering of the lyric subject.

Love and Its Discontents: The Lyric Poet in the World

In a small number of early poems, one or two of which have something like a programmatic status in his oeuvre, Faiz stages the aesthetic dilemmas of the modern poet. They are metapoetic texts, for in them Faiz turns to exploring the nature and meaning of lyric poetry in modern life. In such poems from the late 1930s as "The Subject of Poetry" ("Mauzu-e sukhan") and "My Fellow, My Friend" ("Mire hamdam, mire dost"), but above all in "Love Do Not Ask for That Old Love Again" ("Mujh se pahli si mahabbat meri mahbub na mang"), we find the poetic persona torn between the exquisite demands of unrequited love, on the one hand, and those of the larger world and its oppressions, on the other. Faiz himself has spoken of these poems as turning points in his aesthetic development, marking a growing sense of dissatisfaction with the dominant, "romantic" literary ethos of the times.[9] Thus, in the latter poem, the dominant mood is set by the speaker's asking the beloved not to ask for the kind of love formerly given—"pahli si mahabbat"—a singular love, alert to nothing but the beloved's charms and cruelties. The speaker lists the efficacies of this love in which it had formerly believed and concludes the first section of the poem with the confession, "It was not true all this but only wishing." After noting the cruelties of the outer world—its injustice, inequality, and alienation—with which the beloved must compete for the speaker/lover's attention, the poem ends on the note on which it began. In "The Subject of Poetry," the same tension between the alternative demands on the speaker's senses is maintained, but this tension is approached, as it were, from the other direction. Alternating between the mysteries of the beloved and those of the larger world, the poem ends by affirming that the poet cannot expect to overcome the former as his true theme:

—These too are subjects; more there are;—but oh,
Those limbs that curve so fatally ravishingly!
Oh that sweet wretch, those lips parting so slow—
Tell me where else such witchery could be!
No other theme [lit., subject] will ever fit my rhyme;
Nowhere but here is poetry's native clime [lit., homeland].

[Ye bhi hain aise kai aur bhi mazmun honge
Lekin us shokh ke ahista se khulte hue hont
Hae us jism ke kambakht dil-avez khutut
Ap hi kahiye kahin aise bhi afsun honge?
Apna mauzu-e sukhan inke siva aur nahin
Tab-e shair ka vatan inke siva aur nahin.][10]

These early poems have most often been read as signs of a young poet's political awakening, a politicization that does not lead to an abandonment of concern with the integrity of literary language. Faiz himself has contributed to the authority of this reading.[11] While I do not take this to be an incorrect interpretation, I read the apparent dualism of these poems—interiority and affect versus the external world, lyric poetry versus society—somewhat differently, as demonstrating an interest in the relationship between the lyric self of Urdu poetry and the "wider" world of contradiction and conflict over the meaning of nation and community. I shall argue that these poems enact, *in a literary-historical register*, the dilemmas and complexities of a "Muslim" selfhood in Indian modernity. The phrase *pahli si mahabbat* points to the problematic of love in the classical Urdu lyric, and the poem comments on the relationship of the modern poet, located in the national-cultural space that is (late colonial) India, to that classical tradition. In Pakistan, Faiz has long been spoken of as a "national" poet, as *the* national poet during the first forty years of the country's life. It is my contention that this cannot mean what it is usually thought to mean, that, in part, the accomplishment, the grandeur and ambition, of his work is precisely that it raises serious doubts about whether the nation-state form can account for the complexities of culture and identity in modern South Asia.

Born early in the second decade of this century in the now-Pakistani city of Sialkot, Faiz received an education that was becoming increasingly typical for young men of his regional, religious, and class background—the rudiments of Quranic instruction, Persian and Arabic with the local *maulvi*, modern schooling of the colonial (in his case, missionary) sort, and degrees in (in his case, English and Arabic) literature.[12] According to his own account, Faiz's early reading consisted of a diet of Urdu poetry of the classical period, in particular Muhammad Taqi Mir (1723?–1810) and Asadullah Khan Ghalib (1795?–1869), and the major nineteenth-century works of Urdu narrative. After finishing his studies at the Government and Oriental Colleges, Lahore—those bastions of modern higher learning for northwestern colonial India—Faiz took up a teaching position at Amritsar, where he was first exposed to Indian Marxism and to nationalist political culture generally. Faiz's first collection of poetry appeared in 1941, and the last to be published in his lifetime, in 1981.[13] From time to time, he also published widely read volumes of critical essays, letters, and memoirs. In Amritsar, Faiz was drawn into the literary circles that proved to be the core group in the establishment of the AIPWA in 1936, and he subsequently came to be identified as the leading "Progressive" voice in Urdu poetry while also maintaining his autonomy from that organization and from the Communist Party, never becoming a spokesman for either in quite the same way as a number of his contemporaries, such as Sajjad Zaheer and Ali Sardar Jafry. Jafry even accused Faiz once of equivocating about the goals of Progressive poetry and of "drawing such curtains of metaphor [istiariyat]" around one of his poems—"Freedom's Dawn"—that "one cannot tell who is sitting behind them."[14] He joined the colonial Indian Army after the collapse of the Hitler-Stalin Pact, at a time when the official policy of the Indian National Congress was noncooperation with the war effort, rose to the rank of lieutenant colonel, and returned to civilian life in 1946 with a Member of the British Empire (M.B.E.). A few years after independence, during which he rose to prominence in Pakistan as a newspaper editor and labor unionist, he was arrested in 1951 with a number of other radical writers, political activists, and military officers—including Zaheer, who was the leading founder of the AIPWA and after partition became general secretary of the newly founded Communist Party of Pakistan—charged with conspiring against the state. The arrests, part of a general crackdown on the Pakistani Left, had a chilling effect on political and cultural life, and marked the beginnings of Pakistan's realignment as a frontline U.S. satellite in the Cold War and as a reliable regional client after the rise of Mossadegh in Iran, a role whose price the country continues to pay to this day. After a trial, during which the shadow of a death sentence hung over him, Faiz was sentenced to imprisonment and was finally released after spending over four years in various prisons in Pakistan. In the late 1950s, with the implementation of martial law in Pakistan, Faiz was again in jail, this time only for a few months. Already by the late 1950s, Faiz had developed an increasingly international reputation, especially in socialist countries and many parts of the Third World. In 1962, he was awarded the Lenin Peace Prize and, at the end of his life, in exile from Zia's Pakistan, served for several years as editor of *Lotus*, the journal of the Afro-Asian Writers' Association, which he edited from Beirut, during the years of its devastation, including the months of the Israeli siege and bombardment. There he composed a small body of what is the most exquisite exile poetry in modern Urdu literature, "an enactment of a homecoming expressed through defiance and loss," in the words of Edward Said, who met him in Beirut during those exile years.[15] It represents an attempt to introduce exile and homelessness into the vocabulary of Urdu verse as a constitutive experience. Read together with the early "metapoetic" poems, this later exile poetry makes clear that for Faiz, Urdu is, in a strong sense, a homeless literature and culture, that he sees its entire modern history as a series of uprootings and displacements.

The appropriateness of using the term *lyric poetry* in anything more than a loose and descriptive sense with respect to Urdu writing in general and Faiz in particular is not self-evident and requires some justification. While Urdu has a number of terms, such as the adjectives *bazmiyya* and *ghinaiyya*, that provide very partial equivalents of the English word, Urdu poetics makes no extensive theoretical use of such an umbrella concept and proceeds for the most part in generic terms—and in particular in terms of the mutual opposition of the *ghazal* and the *nazm*. It is certainly part of the specificity of Faiz's work that, unlike some of his contemporaries, he does not turn his back on the "classical" poetic genres, in particular the *ghazal*, with its rigid meter and rhyme schemes, and its set themes centered around the experience of separation from the beloved. He is, in fact, widely credited with having resuscitated this form after a half century of neglect and disdain. In the decades following the suppression of the uprisings of 1857–58, with the collapse of the tottering social structure that had been the basis of the Urdu literary culture of the *ashraf*, or "noble" elites in northern India, "reform"—religious, social, cultural, political, and educational reform—became the slogan of what I would call *reluctant embourgoisement* among these social groupings. The Aligarh movement of Sayyid Ahmed Khan is only the most famous and influential of these reform efforts directed at Muslims.[16] In the critical writings of such Aligarh-related figures as Muhammad Husain Azad and Altaf Husain Hali, the *ghazal* came to be singled out as the genre par excellence of Muslim decline and decadence, as too decorative, subjective, and impervious to nature, incapable of the sober intellectual effort and didactic purpose called for in the "new" world.[17] For nationalist writers beginning in the late nineteenth century, it became something like an icon of the vast distances separating the *ashraf* Muslim elites from the space of the genuinely popular. Such distrust of the *ghazal* has survived into our own century among both the literary movements committed to the social purposiveness of poetry, including the Marxists of the AIPWA who were Faiz's contemporaries and comrades, as well as those whose commitment to the intellectual demands of modern poetry is in the name of art for art's sake.[18] The Urdu *ghazal* and the constellation that surrounds it—metrical structures, histories of composition and reception, Persianate vocabulary and thematic conventions, and the image associated with it of an imperial culture in decline—retain a distinct place in the postcolonial Indian cultural imaginary, from popular "Hindi" cinema to such a work of Indo-English fiction as Anita Desai's *In Custody*, despite the massive effort in recent decades to denaturalize and alienate Urdu to contemporary Indian culture and society. Perhaps like no other poetic form in northern India, the history of this lyric genre is inextricably tied up with the emergence and development of national culture, and in no other form, not even the Hindi *git*, or "song" that is sometimes said to be the national-popular poetic genre par excellence, are the contradictions of the social so deeply inscribed.

Even in his practice of the diffuse *nazm* form—whose only possible definition appears to be that it is a nonnarrative poem that is not a *ghazal*—Faiz bridges the divide between these varieties of poetic writing and imbues the lyric world of the latter with its characteristic, non-national forms of affectivity. In this essay, I shall look most closely at a number of poems that are not *ghazals*, strictly speaking, but apply the concept of lyric to Faiz's oeuvre as a whole, irrespective of genre in the narrow sense. In treating Faiz as a modern lyric poet, however, I am not suggesting that we engage in a search for qualities in modern Urdu verse that are characteristic of the lyric in modern Western poetry. On the contrary, the purpose of my analysis of a number of Faiz's poems is precisely to make it possible to explore the specificities of modern lyric in a colonial and postcolonial society. Above all, what the concept of lyric makes possible is the *translation*, the passage, of Faiz's poetry from a literary history that is specifically Urdu into a critical space for the discussion of *Indian* literary modernity as a whole. To the extent that Faiz's poetry itself pushes in the direction of ending the inwardness of the Urdu poetic tradition, as I shall later argue, such a critical move is implied and required by his work itself.

Remembering Oneself: Lyric Subject and Memory in Faiz

I shall now turn to the theme of separation and union in Faiz's love poetry by working through its elaboration in one of his best-known lyric poems, "Yad" (Memory). The poem appears in the collection *Dast-e saba* (1952) and has been made hugely popular by the singer Iqbal Bano as "Dasht-e tanhai":

1. In the desert of solitude, my love, quiver
2. the shadows of your voice, your lips' mirage.
3. In the desert of solitude, under the dust of distance,
4. the flowers of your presence bloom.

5. From somewhere nearby rises the flame of your breathing,
6. burning slowly in its own perfume.
7. Afar, beyond the horizon, glistening, drop by drop,
8. falls the dew from your heart-consoling eyes.

9. So lovingly, O my love, has placed
10. your memory its hand this moment on my heart.
11. It seems, though this distance is young,
12. The day of separation is ended, the night of union has arrived.

[1. Dasht-e tanhai men, ai jan-e jahan larzan hain
2. Teri avaz ke sae, tere honton ke sarab
3. Dasht-e tanhai men, duri ke khas o khak tale
4. Khil rahe hain, tere pahlu ke saman aur gulab

5. Uth rahi hai kahin qurbat se teri sans ki anch
6. Apni khushbu men sulagti hui, maddham maddham
7. Dur—ufaq par chamakti hui, qatra qatra
8. Gir rahi hai teri dildar nazar ki shabnam

9. Is qadar pyar se, ai jan-e jahan, rakkha hai
10. Dil ke rukhsar pe is waqt teri yad ne hath
11. Yun guman hota hai, garche hai abhi subh-e firaq
12. Dhal gaya hijr ka din, a bhi gai wasl ki rat.][19]

Dominant in the first stanza is the image of solitude as expanse of desert or wilderness, expressed in the string "Dasht-e tanhai" (the desert/wilderness of solitude/loneliness), which opens lines 1 and 3. The metaphor also governs the second stanza, as the spatial language of line 5—"From somewhere nearby rises the flame of your breathing"—acquires a geographical register in line 7: "Afar, beyond the horizon. . . ." The dominance of this desert metaphor is sustained in the treatment of the beloved, at least in the first stanza. There, the solitary subject is confronted with the "mirage"-like presence of the object of its desire—"the shadows of your voice, your lips' mirage." For the subject, the shadows and mirage are both signs of the beloved. But while a mirage points to an absent, illusory object, the shadow of an object, though it is itself immaterial, is a sign of the object's physical presence. By being placed in combination with each other, however, "shadows" and "mirage" infuse each other with new meanings. The latter becomes something more than illusion, a mere projection outward of a desire intensely felt, like a vision of water in a parched land; and the former becomes something less than the sign of a physical presence. The geographical metaphor is fused here with a visual one, and together they come to signify the manner of the beloved's becoming-present. What exactly this manner is becomes more clear in the next two lines (3–4), for here "the flowers [lit., jasmine and rose] of your presence" are said to bloom "under the dust [lit., the withered bushes and dust] of distance." In other words, the nearness or presence of the beloved does not cancel out its distance. And the reverse is also true: the distance of the beloved is also the mode of its coming near. This theme is developed in the second stanza. In lines 5–6, the "flame" (*anch*) of the beloved's breathing is said to be rising from somewhere near the speaking subject—"kahin qurbat se"—and yet, simultaneously, the "consoling eyes" of the beloved are placed by the speaker "Afar, beyond the horizon."

In the third and final stanza, the geographical metaphor is abandoned, and we are within an internal, purely subjective space. This intimate space is here signified by "heart" (*dil*), or, more precisely, by its "cheek" (*rukhsar*), which is traditionally a sign of the beloved's beauty and of (the lover's) intimacy with it but here comes to express the tenderness of the lover's own heart (line 10). The inexpressible beauty of this image—a beating heart gently caressed by a human hand, as a lover's cheek is touched by the beloved—is an expression of the desire for an end to suffering, for union, for reconciliation of subject and object. It expresses a desire for the form of reconciliation that Adorno has called "peace": "Peace is the state of distinctness without domination, with the distinct participating in each other."[20] The presence of the beloved continues in this stanza to also be its distance. For the beloved enters this interior realm only as image or *yad* (memory). In the last two lines (11–12), the poem turns to the intensity of this caress of memory, to its *effect* on the subject: the *guman* (appearance/feeling/illusion) that "The day of separation has ended, the night of union has arrived."

Like the first two stanzas, therefore, the third stanza also enacts the dialectic of separation and union, in which separation is indefinitely extended, and union, intensely desired and felt, does not cancel out the distance between the subject and object of desire. It renders uncertain the distinction between them but not in order to appropriate the life of the object in the interest of the former. The object is also revealed to be a subject and the (desiring) subject an object of (the other's) desire. The beloved is at the same time distant, and hence other, and intimately present to the self as itself. In other words, the self that emerges in the course of "Yad" is a divided one, not at home with itself, desiring reconciliation and wholeness and yet cognizant that its own distance from itself is the very source of its movement and life. It is an uncanny interplay of nearness and distance precisely summed up in a four-line poem titled "Marsia" (Elegy), which appears in *Sar-e wadi-e Sina* (1971):

Having gone afar you are near to me,
when were you so close to me?
You will not return now, nor leave,
meeting and parting [hijran] are now same to me.

[Dur ja kar qarib ho jitne
Ham se kab tum qarib the itne
Ab na aoge tum na jaoge
Wasl o hijran baham hue kitne.][21]

We may begin to outline the social meanings of this lyric self by noting the resonances of the word *hijr* (separation) in the final stanza of "Yad" (and of its derivative *hi-*

jran in "Marsia"). A transformation of the Arabic *hajr,* the word is the most frequently used term in classical Urdu poetry for "separation," or parting from the beloved. As is well known, the meanings of this word and those of its paired opposite, *wisal* (union), constitute one of the central and most familiar problems in Urdu poetics. These meanings vary not only from poet to poet or era to era, but also from one poetic genre to another, in the works of the same poet, and often within the same poem itself. Thus, for instance, depending on the poemic context, the words may signify the dynamics of romantic or erotic love, or of religious devotion. In the Sufi traditions of Urdu (and Persian) poetry in particular, *wisal* is a sign for mystic union with the divine, for the desire of the self to become extinct (*fana*) in a realization of its *ishq-e haqiqi* or "true" love of God, compared to which the love of man for man is only *ishq-e majazi*, inauthentic or "metaphorical" love. Most typically, a verse may be interpreted at several different levels, in several different registers, simultaneously.[22] The problematic of "love" is thus constituted around an oscillation or productive tension between other-worldy and this-worldly significations. In latter times, this poetic language is very far indeed from any concrete practice of Sufism. In Faiz, paradoxically, this religious substratum is brought again close to the surface, in order to be secularized anew.

The secularization of *hijr* in Faiz's poetry is part of the general secularization of poetic language and purpose undertaken by him and his contemporaries. One aspect of this secularization has been that the Sufistic eroticism of the vocabulary of the traditional poetic genres, and the *ghazal* in particular, has acquired political meanings, most explicitly in militant poets such as Habib Jalib, who is associated with the world of radical student politics, but also in more serious poets such as Faiz himself. Thus, for instance, *wafa* (loyalty or devotion) and *junun* (madness or intoxication) come to mean political steadfastness and selfless abandon, the rational and irrational components, respectively, of commitment. Faiz's most programmatic announcement of the secularizing impulse of his poetry comes perhaps in "Dua" (Prayer), a poem written in the mid-1960s:

Come, let us too lift our hands
We for whom prayer is a custom forgotten,
We who except for love's flame
Remember neither idol nor god—

[Aiye hath uthaen ham bhi
Ham jinhen rasm-e dua yad nahin
Ham jinhen soz-e mahabbat ke siva
Koi but ko khuda yad nahin.][23]

Prayer may be a "forgotten" custom for the lyric subject, but its very knowledge of this fact belies a memory of a living connection to it. The secular subject contains within itself traces of the lifeworld signified here by "idol" and "god." As in so much of Faiz's poetry, secularization is not a mere rejection of religious experience but rather a wrestling with it. This is not an expression of a positivistic atheism that wants simply to abolish the religious impulse in a rationalized culture of struggle and action—"love" in the sense of political commitment. What is performed in the poetry of Faiz, instead, is the recognition of the immense power of religious thought and experience for the modern subject. More specifically, the unorthodox and transgressive energies that are always at least implicit in the mystical Sufi tradition are turned in Faiz's verse against religious orthodoxy and its alliance with oppressive worldly authority. A Marxist and internationalist poet, Faiz is nevertheless immersed in the religious language of mystical Indian Islam, both in its high cultural elaboration in the Urdu poetic tradition and as a kind of cultural lingua franca in northern India. Faiz's poetry reveals a deep respect and *love* for this culture and a recognition of the poet's very complex relationship to it. It represents an agonistic embracing of a particular religious tradition—the Indo-Muslim and Urdu poetic elaborations of Sufi expression—in order to produce out of it the resources for modernity; at the same time, therefore, it also points to the worldly basis of religious experience itself. At no point, however, is this merely a nostalgic embracing of a supposedly syncretistic religious life, and (poetic) modernity appears as a kind of dialectic of the religious and the secular or worldly.

The problematic of *hijr* in the work of Faiz therefore cannot fail to evoke another narrative-mythological constellation, designated by the related word *hijrat*. Originally referring to the emigration of Muhammad from Mecca to Medina in AD 622, *hijrat* was appropriated in Urdu at partition for the dislocations and emigrations that accompanied that event, in particular from the Hindi-Urdu heartland to the territory of Pakistan. It lends to the latter experience an epic quality and seeks to contain partition itself within a narrative of leave-taking. Faiz explores (and exploits) this historical density of *hijr* as a signifier of relation to place, community, uprooting, and the paradoxes of restoration and return. While he was not himself a *muhajir*, or partition migrant, strictly speaking—having been born and raised within the territorial limits later claimed for Pakistan—*hijr-hijrat* becomes in his poetry a metonym for the displacements of partition as a whole, the massive fissures it requires of people, language, culture, and memory coming to be figured as the experience of prolonged separation from the beloved. The *political* impulse in Faiz's poetry can therefore be understood only through the mediation of the *social*. For the desire for justice, the steadfastness in the face of suffering and oppression, and the belief in a new dawn are complicated by the "partitioned" nature of the collective subject. In other words, for me the significance of Faiz's repeated use of *hijr* and of its derivatives is that it imbues the lyric experience of separation from the beloved with a concrete historical meaning—the parting of ways or leave-taking that is partition. If, in Sufi traditions, to speak simultaneously of the pain and joy of *hijr* is to point to the consummation of love in death or self-extinction, then in Faiz this prolongation of separation from the beloved is made the modality of collective selfhood, its very mode of being in history and the world.[24] It is significant in this connection that within Pakistan critics have sometimes complained about the seeming masochism of such prolongation of *hijr* in Faiz's poetry, in marked contrast to the work of his contemporary Miraji, for instance, where the attempt to project an authentic selfhood not only takes the form of an actualization of union but often is literalized in sexual release. This complaint is significant, for from within a framework that affirms the terms of partition, this refusal to grant to the (collective) self autonomy (from the whims of the beloved) can indeed only appear masochistic. The lyric subject in Faiz's poetry is located at those borderlands of self and world where autonomy and heteronomy lose their distinctness, where the self is confronted with the uncanny presence of an other that is also self. For Faiz, the end of *hijr* is not a literal union. The sadness of *hijr* echoes the finality of *hijrat*, of leaving one's home forever, but it also inverts the implied religious sanction for partition by reinscribing the self's leave-taking of the (antagonistic) other as a separation from the beloved.

When Faiz speaks of lost companions and almost-forgotten friendships, as he does in a number of poems from the 1950s onward, he is echoing an experience that is common in the entire northern belt that was affected by partition. Take, for instance, the opening lines of "Paun se lahu ko dho dalo" ("Wash the Blood Off Your Feet"):

What could I [lit., we] have done, gone where?
My feet were bare
and every road was covered with thorns—
of ruined friendships, of loves left behind,
of eras of loyalty that finished, one by one.

[Ham kya karte kis rah chalte
Har rah men kante bikhre the
Un rishton ke jo chhut gae
Un sadyon ke yaranon ke
Jo ik ik kar ke tut gae.][25]

I suggest that we read "eras" (lit., centuries) here as a sign of historical time and "friendships" (lit., relations or connections) and "loves" (lit., friendships, companionships, or loves) as pointing toward the fabric, the *text*, of culture, difference, and identity in history. The modes and forms in which memories of the pre-partition past are popularly kept alive pose questions of immense importance and interest for scholarship and have only begun to be explored. In Pakistani cities such as Lahore, Karachi, Hyderabad, and Rawalpindi, which were cleared of their large Hindu and Sikh populations within months of August 1947, the signs of these erstwhile residents are ubiquitously present—in the sight of sealed-off temples, in street and neighborhood names that continue to be used despite municipal attempts to erase them, in the signs of the "other's" tongue above doorways in the old quarter of any city. The memories and stories of older eyewitnesses, the tales travelers tell of revisiting long-abandoned homes, the enormous font of verbal genres—folk songs, nursery rhymes, proverbs, and popular tales about characters such as Birbal and Mullah Dopiaza—are among the many everyday means of unsettling the finality of partition, of disconcerting the self with its own uncertainty. The paradox at the heart of Faiz reception is that while he writes poetry that is "difficult" in some obvious ways and true to the subjective demands of lyric, it is this enormous font of popular memory that it seeks to mobilize. We can say of him, as Adorno does of Brecht, that in his poetry, "linguistic integrity" does not result in poetic elitism or "esotericism."[26] The suffering of the subject in Faiz's poetry, or rather its pleasure *and* suffering at being separated from the beloved, echoes in lyric terms what is already present everywhere in popular experience, even if in ways that are muted, less than conscious, and fragmentary.

If *hijr* and its derivatives point us in the direction of dislocations and separations that are collective, such a historical reading of Faiz's lyric poems is made possible in other ways as well. Since *Dast-e saba* (1952), an increasing number of poems in successive collections appear dated by month and year or by exact date, and many are also marked by place of composition, which, in the case of the poems included in *Dast-e saba* and *Zindan nama* (1956), is most often a Pakistani prison. This dating and "placing" of the poems is almost always significant. I suggest that we read the date (and/or the place-name, where it exists) as an extrapoemic, *historical text* requiring interpretation, in interaction with which the poem reveals its meaning. The date functions with respect to the text of the poem in the manner of what Gérard Genette has called paratexts. "Elegy," for instance, is dated "August, 1968," and "Prayer" is underlined with "Independence Day, 14 August 1967." The month of August, during which Pakistan and India celebrate their independence from colonial rule and Pakistan, its separation from India, in fact appears frequently over the years as the date of composition of numerous poems. The extrapoemic, "historical" reference here is to the complex text of *national* independence-partition, lending to these poems a quality of national stocktaking. The pronouns *ham* (we) and *tum* (you, singular/familiar) acquire in this context a collective resonance, even as the lyric quality of the poems, their uncompromising subjectivity, produces a sense of deep intimacy, of meetings and partings at the very core of the self, which defines its very existence.

[. . .]

Towards a Lyric History of India

As we have already seen, the poetic program that Faiz announced early in his career envisioned orienting the lyric subject toward the larger world. I have argued that some of his most ambitious and effective poems are a series of exercises precisely in ending the isolation of the lyric subject, or rather in ending its illusion of isolation. They take the form of imbuing it with the recognition that what it takes as object, as the larger world of things, is itself subject and in dialogue with it. This dialectic of inner and outer worlds, I have further argued, carries collective, historical resonances; it is an enactment of the relationship of "Muslim" culture and identity to the emergence of a wider "Indian" modernity. The self-absorption of the lyric subject in classical Urdu poetry, so widely and repeatedly condemned since the nineteenth century, becomes for Faiz a social fact. And if that lyric subject—and its locus classicus is the *ghazal*—appeared to be, as Azad and Hali had argued, addicted to fantasy and impervious to reality and nature, that judgment could itself be explained in terms of the emergence of the horizon of "nature" and "reality" that we call the nation.[27] Therein lies the *modernity* of Azad and Hali's critique of classical lyric: it seeks to reorient writing within an emerging *national* experience, with the fatally necessary corollary that it enter the field of contest and conflict over the meaning of community and nation. In this sense, Faiz is a descendant of the nineteenth-century reformers—and we should recall that his early formation took place in a milieu where the writings of *nai raushni* (the New Light) had long acquired canonical status—with the important difference that for him this project is to be carried out not through didactic poetry, as it is for Hali, but in terms of the lyric itself.[28] What is the nature of the modern (Indian) self?—that is the question that underlies the reorientation of the Urdu lyric subject in Faiz's poetry.

The enormous paradox of partition, for Faiz, is that it requires a rewriting of the self in the name of whose preservation it had been demanded. It is a paradox that he sometimes figures as the collision of different, inner and outer languages of self, as in this couplet from a *ghazal* that is dated "1953":

The heart as such
had settled its every doubt
when I [lit., we] set out to see her
    But on seeing her
the lips spoke love's unrehearsed words
and everything changed everything changed

[dil se to har muamla kar ke chale the saf ham
Kahne men un ke samne bat badal badal gai][29]

I suggest that we read the pathos of this couplet, this sense of the impossibility of saying what you mean, as a response to "public" languages of selfhood and identity. What Faiz points to here is the excess that cannot be contained within the categorical structure of the nation-state, within which "Muslim" is placed at the cusp of a fatal dilemma: it can signify *either* "a separate nation" *or* "an Indian minority." Faiz's entire lyric oeuvre is a refusal to accept the terms of this fixing of identity and an attempt to put the self in motion. The narrative element in the above couplet—the self setting out with confessional intent to encounter an other but finding its own words becoming alien, producing meanings other than those intended—must be read in a collective and historical register as an interpretation of the history of conflict over the meaning of nation and communal identity, and, in particular, as an interpretation of the history of Muslim cultural separatism. Faiz is indeed a descendant of the writers and intellectuals of the New Light, who, a century earlier, postulated for the first time the distinctness of a "Muslim" experience in Indian modernity. But with historical retrospection, he bathes that assertion itself in the subdued light of pathos, pointing to the twists and turns, the reroutings and misfirings that mark the passage from that moment to our own. This *ghazal*, composed in 1953, is a comment on India's partition from this side of the cataclysmic event, full of infinite sadness at what Indian Muslim "nationhood" has finally been revealed, in the cold light of statehood and "sovereignty," to mean. Faiz distills that historical pathos into the subjective language of the *ghazal*, giving it the form of the lover's sadness at the impossibility of saying, when face-to-face with the beloved, what exactly one means.

The recurring image in Faiz's poetry of an ever-elusive totality that is no less real for its elusiveness shares something of the melancholy of Adorno's concept of a contradictory whole whose "movements" are visible only in the "changes" of the fragments.[30] This concept of the dialectic is an attempt to comprehend totality in late modernity, once "the attempt to change the world," as Adorno put it, has been missed.[31] The "lateness" of the contemporary world for Adorno thus resides in the fact that it is the aftermath of a disappointment, a kind of dénouement once the utopian hopes generated by modern European history have suffered a catastrophic defeat. Hence the series of questions that Adorno directs at contemporary culture: Is it possible to write poetry after Auschwitz? Is philosophy possible once the chance to realize it in a transformation of human existence has been missed? Is it possible, or even desirable, to defend the subject in an age when it is besieged on all sides by the forces of mass culture and mass destruction? Postcolonial culture is itself constituted by an aftermath and marked by the "late" acquisition of the cultural artifacts of the European nineteenth century: national sovereignty, the popular will, the demand for democracy. In postcolonial South Asia, this moment is also that which follows the partitioning of northern Indian society. Frantz Fanon argued a long time ago that in order to be transplanted to the colonial setting, "Marxist analysis should always be slightly stretched."[32] The "lateness" of postcolonial culture itself requires a stretching of the concept of late modernity, its uncoupling from the narrative of economic overdevelopment and overconsumption and its opening up instead to a comprehension of the aftermath of decolonization. Faiz is certainly not an "Adornian" poet in the sense in which Celan, Beckett, or even Mann might be spoken of as Adornian writers.[33] But it has been my purpose here to rethink and expand what it means to write in and of the vistas of "lateness" that Said and others have identified in the constellations of Adorno's thought.[34] Faiz is the poet of a late *postcolonial* modernity, a poet who directs the energies of negative thinking at the congealed cultural and social forms that constitute the postcolonial present. For Adorno, the concept of lyric poetry has a referent that is "completely modern," and "the manifestations in earlier periods of the specifically lyric spirit familiar to us are only isolated flashes."[35] Faiz, however, turns to the traditional Urdu lyric itself and extracts from it a vocabulary for the elaboration of the relation of self to world, individual to totality. He elaborates an experience of modern Indian selfhood that seeks to escape the cultural logic of the nation-state system inaugurated at partition, that paradoxical moment of realization through reinscription, of success through failure. He does this, furthermore, by immersion in the Indo-Islamic poetic tradition, with its deep relationship to Sufi thought and practice, and its long involvement in the crisis of culture and identity on the subcontinent. This is the larger meaning of Faiz as an Urdu poet with an immense audience across the political and cultural boundaries implemented by partition. His is not an appropriation of the fragment from the position of totality, but neither is it an attempt to reconceive the fragment itself as a totality. His is the oeuvre of an aftermath once the chance to achieve India, to "change the world," as it were, has been missed. He confronts the fragment itself with its fragmentary nature, making perceptible to it its own objective situation as an element in a contradictory whole. To put it differently and more explicitly in historical terms, we might say that *Faiz* is another name for the perception, shadowy and subterranean for the most part, but abruptly and momentarily bursting through the surface of language and experience from time to time, that the disavowal of Indianness is an irreducible feature of Indianness itself. The powerful tradition of lyric poetry in Urdu, long accused of its indifference to properly Indian realities, is revived and given a new lease on life in Faiz and his contemporaries not because they infuse old words with new meanings, as the intentionalist cliché in Faiz criticism would have it, but because in their practice it becomes a site for the elaboration of a selfhood at odds with the geometry of selves put into place by partition. In his lyric poetry, Faiz pushes the terms of identity and selfhood to their limits, to the point where they turn upon themselves and reveal the partial nature of postcolonial "national" experience.

NOTES

1. Theodor W. Adorno, "The Fetish Character in Music and the Regression of Listening," in *The Frankfurt School Reader*, ed. Andrew Arato and Eike Gebhardt (New York: Continuum, 1982), 275.

2. See Aamir R. Mufti, "A Greater Story-Writer Than God: Genre, Gender, and Minority in Late Colonial India," in *Subaltern Studies XI: Community, Gender, and Violence*, ed. Partha Chatterjee and Pradeep Jeganathan (New York: Columbia University Press, 2000).

3. See Agha Shahid Ali, "Introduction: Translating Faiz Ahmed Faiz," in *The Rebel's Silhouette: Selected Poems*, rev. ed., trans. Agha Shahid Ali (Amherst: University of Massachusetts Press, 1995), xiv; and V. G. Kiernan, introduction to *Poems by Faiz*, by Faiz Ahmed Faiz, trans. V. G. Kiernan (Lahore: Vanguard Books, 1971), 40.

4. Theodor W. Adorno, "On Lyric Poetry and Society," in *Notes to Literature: Volume One*, ed. Rolf Tiedemann, trans. Shierry Weber Nicholsen (New York: Columbia University Press, 1991), 42, 38.

5. See, for instance, Syed Sibte Hassan, "Faiz ka adarsh," in *Faiz Ahmed Faiz: tanqidi jaiza*, ed. Khaleeq Anjum (New Delhi: Anjuman-e Taraqqi-e Urdu, 1985), 119, 121.

6. Faiz, *Poems by Faiz*, 166–67. In matters of translations, I have set the following principles for myself: wherever it is possible, I cite Kiernan's translation, the "literal" one if I am engaging in a line-by-line analysis, as this is closest to the original in terms of line content, and the "non-literal" where the object is to convey a sense of the whole. Where a poem or fragment is not available in a Kiernan translation, I either provide my own "literal" translation or turn to the more freely translated versions of Agha Shahid Ali (see note 2) or Naomi Lazard—see *The True Subject: Selected Poems of Faiz Ahmed Faiz*, trans. Naomi Lazard (Princeton, N.J.: Princeton University Press, 1988)—depending, again, on the specific purpose at hand.

7. See Kiernan, introduction to *Poems by Faiz*, 38. For a contemporary selection of Gandhi's views on the language question, see Mohandas Karamchand Gandhi, *Our Language Problem*, ed. Anand T. Hingorani (Karachi: Anand T. Hingorani, 1942).

8. Kiernan, introduction to *Poems by Faiz*, 38.

9. See "Faiz—az Faiz," in Faiz Ahmed Faiz, *Nuskhaha-e wafa* (Lahore: Maktaba-e Karvan, 1986), 308–11.

10. See Faiz, *Poems by Faiz*, 90–95; and Faiz, *Nuskhaha-e wafa*, 89–91.

11. See Faiz, *Nuskhaha-e wafa*, 308–11.

12. This biographical summary is based on the following sources: Kiernan, introduction to *Poems by Faiz*; Khaleeq Anjum, "Faiz biti," in *Faiz Ahmed Faiz: tanqidi jaiza*, 14–37; Faiz, "Faiz—az Faiz," in

Nuskhaha-e wafa, 307–14; Faiz, "Ahd-e tifli se unfuwan-e shabab tak," in *Nuskhaha-e wafa*, 489–97; "Bachpan ki qirat se Josh ki buzurgi tak," in Faiz Ahmed Faiz, *Mata-e lauh o qalam* (Karachi: Danyal, 1985), 112–21; and Faiz Ahmed Faiz, *Mah o sal-e ashnai: yadon ka majmua* (Karachi: Danyal, 1983), 5–20.

13. *Naqsh-e faryadi* (Remonstrance) was published in 1941, to be followed by *Dast-e saba* (Fingers of the Wind [1952]), *Zindan-nama* (Prison Thoughts [1956]), *Dast-e tah-e sang* (Duress [1965]), *Sar-e wadi-e Sina* (Mount Sinai [1971]), *Sham-e shahryaran* (Twilight of Kings [1978]), and *Mire dil mire musafir* (My Heart, My Traveling Heart [1981]) during his lifetime. His late and previously uncollected poems have since been collected as *Ghubar-e ayyam* (Dust of Days [1984]) as part of an edition of his complete works. The first four translations here are Kiernan's, the rest are mine.

14. Quoted in Azmi, *Urdu men taraqqi pasand adabi tahrik* (Aligarh: Anjuman-e Taraqqi-e Urdu, 1972), 109.

15. Edward W. Said, "Reflections on Exile," *Granta* 13 (1984): 160. Faiz makes a brief appearance in Mahmoud Darwish's memoir of the Israeli siege. See Mahmoud Darwish, *Memory for Forgetfulness*, translated and with an introduction by Ibrahim Muhawi (Berkeley: University of California Press, 1995).

16. See, for instance, the brilliant cultural history of the early years of the Aligarh movement by David Lelyveld, *Aligarh's First Generation: Muslim Solidarity in British India* (Princeton, N.J.: Princeton University Press, 1978); Barbara Daly Metcalf, *Islamic Revival in British India: Deoband, 1860–1900* (Princeton, N.J.: Princeton University Press, 1982); and an intriguing study of culture and space by Faisal Fatehali Devji, "Gender and the Politics of Space: The Movement for Women's Reform, 1857–1900," in *Forging Identities: Gender, Communities, and the State*, ed. Zoya Hasan (New Delhi: Kali for Women, 1994), 22–37.

17. For a full-length account of these debates, see Frances W. Pritchett, *Nets of Awareness: Urdu Poetry and Its Critics* (Berkeley: University of California Press, 1994).

18. See Gopi Chand Narang, *Sakhtiyat, pas-sakhtiyat, aur mashriqi sheriyat* (Delhi: Educational Publishing House, 1994), 9.

19. Faiz, *Nuskhaha-e wafa*, 184–85. It is regrettable that Kiernan did not include this very beautiful poem among his excellent translations (see note 2). It is also ignored by Agha Shahid Ali (see note 2) and Naomi Lazard (see note 5). This translation is my own. I have tried to keep it as literal as possible—with almost no attention to meter or rhyme scheme—and to retain the content integrity of the lines, even at the cost of syntactical awkwardness, as in lines 9–10. I shall stay in my analysis close to the original, with the translation meant as merely a rough guide for readers not familiar with the Urdu.

20. Theodor W. Adorno, "Subject and Object," in *The Essential Frankfurt School Reader*, ed. Andrew Arato and Eike Gebhardt (New York: Continuum, 1988), 500.

21. See Faiz, *Nuskhaha-e wafa*, 438. The translation is mine, with the literal meaning as the immediate goal, with some attention to rhyme scheme.

22. On the classical *ghazal* and its symbolic and thematic universe, see Ralph Russell, *The Pursuit of Urdu Literature: A Select History* (Delhi: Oxford University Press, 1992), chap. 2; and Annemarie Schimmel, *A Two-Colored Brocade: The Imagery of Persian Poetry* (Chapel Hill, N.C.: University of North Carolina Press, 1992), pt. 2; on the erotics of *ghazal* imagery, see Annemarie Schimmel, "Eros—Heavenly and Not So Heavenly—in Sufi Literature and Life," in *Society and the Sexes in Medieval Islam*, ed. Afaf Lutfi al-Sayyid-Marsot (Malibu, Calif.: Undena Publications, 1979), 119–41.

23. See Faiz, *Poems by Faiz*, 276–77, for Kiernan's rendition, which I have altered slightly; and Faiz, *Nuskhaha-e wafa*, 429.

24. See Schimmel, "Eros—Heavenly and Not So Heavenly—in Sufi Literature and Life," 134–35.

25. This evocative, but largely free, translation is Agha Shahid Ali's. See Faiz, *The Rebel's Silhouette*, 85; and Faiz, *Nuskhaha-e wafa*, 524–25. As has often been noted, Faiz's poetry shows a marked preference for the first-person plural, a sort of royal "we," over the first-person singular.

26. Adorno, "Lyric Poetry and Society," 46.

27. See Altaf Husain Hali, *Muqaddama-e sher o shairi*, ed. Dr. Waheed Qureishi (Aligarh: Educational Publishing House, 1993), 116–17, 153–54, 158, and 178–85. Hali makes it very clear what he has in mind when he recommends "naichral shairi" (natural poetry): "By 'natural poetry' is meant that poetry which, in terms of both words and meanings, is in accord with nature and habit . . . [in accord with] the everyday form of the language, because this everyday speech carries for the inhabitants of the country where it is spoken, the weight of nature [nechar] or second nature [saikind nechar]" (158).

28. Faiz himself makes the argument that much of what Hali is credited with having originated in poetry—the turn to "nature," the rejection of

"artificial" affect, the rejection of abstraction and esotericism—can in fact be traced to Nazir Akbarabadi, who wrote almost a century earlier. Hali's uniqueness lies in the national (*qaumi*) nature of his poetry and poetics. See his important essay, "Nazir aur Hali," in Faiz, *Mizan*, 169–70 and 179–83.

29. The English here is a modification of Agha Shahid Ali's very free but lovely translation. See Faiz, *The Rebel's Silhouette*, 30.

30. See, for instance, Adorno, "The Fetish Character in Music and the Regression of Listening": "The whole can not be put together by adding the separated halves, but in both there appear, however distantly, the changes of the whole, which only moves in contradiction" (275).

31. Theodor W. Adorno, *Negative Dialectics*, trans. E. B. Ashton (New York: Seabury Press, 1973). On Adorno and lateness, see Fredric Jameson, *Late Marxism: Adorno, or the Persistence of the Dialectic* (London: Verso, 1990); and Edward W. Said, "Adorno as Lateness Itself," in *Apocalypse Theory and the Ends of the World*, ed. Malcolm Bull (Oxford: Blackwell, 1995), 264–81.

32. See Frantz Fanon, *The Wretched of the Earth*, trans. Constance Farrington (New York: Grove Press, 1963), 40.

33. I am grateful to Stathis Gourgouris and Eduardo Cadava for making clear the need for this clarification.

34. See, for instance, Said, "Adorno as Lateness Itself," 264–81; and Fredric Jameson, *Late Marxism*.

35. Adorno, "On Lyric Poetry and Society," 40.

10.4 Inter-American Obversals: Allen Ginsberg and Haroldo de Campos circa 1960 (2008)

Roland Greene

In the 1980s and 1990s, it seemed novel to suggest that a literature of the Americas was emerging out of the corpuses maintained in distinct national literatures—such as the colonial and baroque literatures of New England, Spanish America, and Brazil, or the modernisms of the 1920s in the United States and Latin America. With this transnational canon, the argument went, we gained new ways of addressing movements, careers, and works in both national and hemispheric settings. A swath of literary history and criticism explored this premise, bringing new light to both historical and present-day writers and works.[1] Still, poetry often remains oblique to this approach, for reasons that were envisioned by Charles Bernstein some years ago and revisited recently by Jahan Ramazani: the stubbornness of the boundary around national poetries, and the difficulty of observing affinities across cultures without imposing unities, not to mention the ways that particular poems resist being drawn into such an order.[2]

In hemispheric terms, the richest accounts of poetry have often been the most provisional. I admire the essay of 1986 by the historian Richard Morse, in which he sets two contemporaries, William Carlos Williams and Oswald de Andrade, alongside one another, exposing divergences as much as similarities, and finally arrives at a reading of "The Red Wheelbarrow" and "A Roça" ("The Farm") in which neither of the two farms indirectly seen in these poems "can we mistake for a European one."[3] This article's agenda—to address these figures as considerably different from each other, and to explore how they are distinctly American in their aesthetic programs and especially the knowledge their poems contain—tells us more about a poetics of the Americas than a wide-ranging or totalizing approach can manage. The present essay aims both to emulate Morse's approach and to think past it, claiming such a reading as an occasion to speculate on the future of a hemispheric approach. Bernstein offers one version of such an approach here when he imagines a "multiplicity" that is not a "comparison." If the sporadic work of the last two decades has been in a sense preliminary, undertaking a new program for imagining inter-american poetries, what comes next?

Consider how the protocols of reading and interpretation conduce toward an interpretation of poetry that keeps works apart, or authorizes comparisons that reinforce national and linguistic rather than other, more provisional categories. In the early 1990s the comparatist Claudio Guillén articulated three kinds of comparison available to literary theory and criticism, namely that among works with "genetic contacts or other relations" across "distinct national spheres" within a single common culture; that among works with no genetic contacts and from different civilizations but under "common sociohistorical conditions"; and that among "genetically independent phenomena" brought together under a theoretical premise.[4] This orderly division tells us several things about how to approach inter-american literatures, starting from the observation that they may have, oddly, too many points of contact. One can imagine groups of works—such as the aforementioned hemispheric modernist canon, or the Beats of the middle twentieth century alongside the contemporaneous Noigandres school of Brazil—for which from certain angles all of Guillén's conditions of comparison apply, but no one suffices. In contrast to many of the classic objects of comparison such as the European novel, the baroque, or the picaresque, a hemispheric body of poetry involves genetic contacts but also comes into being despite the lack of them; allows for common social and historical conditions, sometimes within a single civilization such as that of Spanish-speaking readers and writers, but at other times across the boundaries between creole and indigenous societies; and demands the application of theoretical principles that will put these already deeply implicated corpuses into less obvious conjunctions. Where many points of contact are available, there is perhaps an inclination toward either a totalized approach, a critical narrative that will gather all these points together into a specious unity, or no synopsis at all. The hemispheric canon presents this particular challenge to a conventional comparative literature: too many standpoints, with too many strands of relation and zones of difference between them, make for arguments that struggle to find a balance. In how many ways might we speak of the contemporaneity, the correspondences, the coincidences, the obliquities, and the insensibilities between such events of the 1980s as the Language movement in the United States and *XUL* in Argentina?

What is wanted is neither an essential inter-american literature nor a map of irreducible particularities. The condition of the poetries of the Americas demands, in one of Bernstein's phrases, a poetics of "inconsolable coexistences."[5] We make our way through such a condition by naming a vivid counterpoise between the knowledges such poetries contain—how do the poetries, with all their differences, *know as American poetries* rather than as something else?—and this proposition must always come down to particular poems, their dictions, rhythms, and figures. Or to say it otherwise, Morse demonstrates inductively that we can read from a poem to a society on the basis of social fact in relation to aesthetic disposition, recovering from this relation some atom of Americanness.

The alternative approach, which turns up in many accounts of inter-american literatures, might be considered fatally deductive. In the mid-1980s, a much remarked conversation of a sort took place between Fredric Jameson and Aijaz Ahmad over the question of how to account for what some readers think of as the structural differences between works from the developed and developing worlds, or along some like axis. Jameson's argument—Gayatri Spivak rightly calls it "notorious"[6]—was that "all third-world texts" are necessarily "to be read as what I will call national allegories, even when, or perhaps I should say, particularly when their forms develop out of predominantly western machineries of representation, such as the novel."[7] Unfortunately the deductive and totalizing character of Jameson's argument, atypical of his late work, is self-negating. As Ahmad deftly observes, no such account of a "cognitive aesthetics" can or should explain the spheres of cultural production, whether developed and developing Worlds, hemispheres, or even countries.[8] I wonder at the "particularly" clause of Jameson's statement, as though the novel were merely a good example of this mode of reading and not the only remotely feasible example—in other words, as though one could imagine drama, memoir, or poetry supporting such a reading. Whatever explanatory value might be found in comparing metropolitan and emerging novels for their redactions of the public and the private, one supposes that to approach poetry's "ratio of the political to the personal" as an allegory for social or geopolitical conditions is not only a questionable but an unworkable project.[9] At the same time, I recognize the urge that underlies Jameson's essay, to find a productive way of reading works of different societies alongside each other, articulating how each one develops an interlocution of the subjective and the social as well as a fluid relation between these works, without allegorizing or rendering either one into a reversal or distortion of the other.

Where poetry is concerned, we might adapt Jameson's terms and declare that our project is to disclose how the poetries of the Americas converse with one another across the registers of the political and the personal; how what is common and what is different between hemispheric poetries may be accounted for; and especially how we may identify the points of contact—of concepts, inlaid cultural patterns, motifs, charged words—that put the subjective and the public dimensions of such poems into relation. Even laying aside proposals to read the works of one part of the world according to a unifying logic, the claims of language, region, history, race, and class, among other factors, seem to unsettle any possibility of a common literary history. And yet, above the din of such factors, the elements held in relation still make themselves heard. In idioms, tropes, and registers, the poetries of the Americas recognize an obversive history rather than a common outlook, the power of which should be neither exaggerated nor dismissed. Such a history, refracted in poetry, involves two or more obverses—faces or surfaces, like the face of a coin—that are not opposites or reversals of each other but alternative versions of a common question of knowledge. This is what Morse saw in Williams and Andrade: the problem of seeing an American society in its agriculture, a georgic read askance. This is perhaps what Jameson gestured after in his overly prescriptive theory of the novel in the developing world. And this is perhaps also a workable redaction of Guillén's criteria for comparison into something that makes sense of the poetries of the New World, a mode of reading that acknowledges that "there is no one America."[10]

As an experiment in obversal, consider two sets of poems that are roughly contemporaneous but seem to offer little foundation for a cross-reading: these are Allen Ginsberg's poems of 1959 through 1961, first collected in *Kaddish* (1961) and later augmented in the *Collected Poems 1947–1980*—especially the run from "Lysergic Acid" through "To an Old Poet in Peru"—and Haroldo de Campos' *Galáxias* of 1963 and after, especially the incantatory poem known as "circuladô de fulô." The Brazilian Campos, along with his brother Augusto de Campos and their collaborator Décio Pignatari, formed the group Noigandres, named after a stray remark by the scholar of Occitan poetry Emil Lévy in Ezra

Pound's Canto XX.[11] Ginsberg and Campos share a precursor in Pound, but otherwise diverge in their models. Campos treats Pound essentially as a European poet reaching back first to symbolism and to the troubadours, while Ginsberg augments this tradition with the prophetic and hortatory poetics of Walt Whitman and William Blake. Oblivious to one another, Ginsberg and Campos represent alternative poetries of the Americas at a single moment. Perhaps their balance of likenesses and differences makes them hard to discuss together; perhaps even they cannot look at each other too closely. Whitman, rebarbative and polarizing, is the invisible factor between them. I once asked Campos (even though I knew the answer) whether Whitman was important to him, and he replied with a curt dismissal of the question—a clue, I have always believed, to the poetics of the Noigandres circle. In fact Whitman is not entirely absent from the cabinet of models and objects associated with these far-ranging Brazilian poets, translators, and critics. His program for a prophetic poetry of the greater Americas survives for them, but they attribute it to a poet fourteen years younger, Joaquim de Sousa Andrade, whom they install in a lineage that includes nearly everyone except Whitman.[12] The striking exclusion of Whitman from their explicit program, emphasized by Campos' unequivocal reply, confirms a matter of poetics but also implies matters of knowledge—and the intersection between these dimensions offers a way to read the Beats and the concretes against each other.

In part, of course, the rejection of Whitman by the Noigandres poets is a statement of cultural affinity as well as poetic principles. Whitman's program belongs to the era of creole self-consciousness across the Americas, beginning with the career of Simón Bolívar in the early nineteenth century and continuing until the end of the original *modernismo* in the early twentieth, for which the capacious voice of *Leaves of Grass* became a kind of standard.[13] During this era, distinctive elements of a creole outlook were transmuted into statements of an essential American identity: for instance, where the creole desideratum of American birth (in contrast to colonists from Spain or Portugal) is idealized in the terms of autocthony, a rootedness in the soil of the Americas held in common by all native-born citizens. Within a few years of the death of the original *modernista* poet Rubén Darío in 1916, a different modernism, more conversant with the contemporaneous European avant-gardes as well as with a broader specimen of American races and classes, had arisen to challenge many of the cultural ideals founded on creole experience: thus in Brazil, the modernist poet and polemicist Oswald de Andrade, Haroldo de Campos' avowed model, articulated a program for strategic and ironic mimesis of indigenous cultures that explicitly countered the fantasy of autocthony with the fact of importation—that what mattered in this society was what came from elsewhere, to be answered only by a poetry "for export."[14] Seen through the filter of this kind of modernism, the poetics of Whitman and his refractors among the creole elites come to seem a temporizing maneuver, not to mention a self-absorbed projection of one segment of society, rather than something radically new.

In strictly poetic terms, the early work of the Noigandres poets depends on a semantic concentration within a morphology of lines and paragraphs that seems the antithesis of Whitman's approach to these elements. In semantic and formal dispensations, nothing could resemble "Song of Myself" less than Campos' densely textured poems, where the first person is often hidden rather than extravagantly unfurled; no poem could be less like Campos' "Servidão de passagem" ("Transient Servitude") than "The Sleepers," where lines accumulate not with exactitude but with abandon, and irony is all but absent. And yet something other than semantics and forms—something better called knowledge, a mode of coming to terms with the world—is involved in this contrast. Campos' orientation to a Pound whose antecedents lie in Europe rather than the United States is obviously a highly motivated redaction. Overlooking Pound's acknowledgment to Whitman that "it was you that broke the new wood,"[15] it aligns Noigandres with the deep past of Propertius and the troubadours, and speaks to a making of a poetry of the Americas from the outside in. For such a program, the knowledge that activates poetic power tends to be bibliophagic and historically remote, if not antiquarian. While in certain senses Campos' intellectual style is very much of its time—his philology is often embedded in information theory of the 1950s, and the manifesti of Noigandres such as the "Plano-Piloto para Poesia Concreta" ("Pilot-Plan for Concrete Poetry" [1958]) are stamped by the era of President Juscelino Kubitschek and the building of Brasilia[16]—the dynamic factor is knowledge: what, and how, does the poem know? While Campos frames his poetics with reference to "information" and "language,"[17] knowledge, or thinking made manifest, inscribes a distinctive pattern in his poems, and enables us to stand apart from his moment, exactly as Morse does with Williams and Andrade.

In contrast, Ginsberg's embrace of the other Pound—the poet of "I make a pact with you, Walt Whitman"—represents a poetry that draws on experience of the social and political world of the present, foreshortening the cultural past in favor of a poetry that starts from the speaking subject and sprawls outward. His poems devour experience rather than books; his cultivation of Buddhism ensures a centrifugal, presentist, observational procedure.[18] Seen this way, there is a difference in what each kind of poem knows: Campos' compressed poems perceive and think by collapsing eras, cultures, and languages together for the sake of historical continuity, while Ginsberg's intuitive lyrics find an alternative sort of diversity—of social identities, voices, politics—by expanding the present. Of course this account oversimplifies, but it captures something of Campos' and Ginsberg's two ways of operating as poets of the Americas circa 1960.

Further, the differences of poetic style between the Beat and Noigandres programs correspond closely to this contrast of intellectual agendas. From its first appearance in the early 1950s, the work of the Noigandres group, who were critics as well as poets, came packaged with its own literary history, its own announced canon of precursors, and its own style of interpretation. The group's North American (and to some extent, even their Brazilian) interpreters and acolytes have generally declined to challenge this order of things with fresh approaches and hard questions, with the result that this work exists in a kind of critical limbo, in which the poets' own promotional statements still have the status of interpretations and conclusions. What we recognize as Brazilian concrete poetry of the 1960s might be better seen as a poetic technology that is well adapted to Campos' agency as cultural filter—a poet who makes his kind of knowledge according to exquisite conjunctions and overlays of several periods and languages, in a poetic idiom where no extraneous information should draw the mind away from the central conceit. The poetry, the criticism, and the literary history are inseparable elements of a single program, each element disposed to foreground the relevant aspects of the others. A poetry fashioned for such a program—unlike a poetry conceived to stand apart from the poet's criticism and other writings, such as that of Wallace Stevens or Pablo Neruda—must turn out very much like the concrete poetry of Noigandres and the early Campos.

Again in contrast, Ginsberg's poetry exhibits a purchase on knowledge that accommodates quotidian experience to several metaphysical outlooks, and abjures the strict filters that inform concrete poetry in favor of an inclusiveness that depends on spontaneous organization ("first thought, best thought").[19] Perhaps no bodies of poetry of the late 1950s could resemble each other less than Ginsberg's mercurial, obsessive rants and Campos' finely wrought logograms. And yet they are strikingly homologous, if not superficially similar: moving apart but in different directions from the gyres and vortices of modernism, they come to occupy distinctive but cognate positions. Moreover, the extremity of their positions has encouraged critics and readers to treat them as specimens, making for a kind of tacit silence around their work. Is there a poem by Campos or Ginsberg that is read very differently now from when it first appeared? Is there a poem that is understood in ways other than how the poet characterizes it? Due to the fairly low energy of the critical enterprise around their work, I think the answer to such questions is no. The relation between these two contemporaneous programs, one might observe, is between alternative construals of the European and American modernist tradition that draw out different agendas for a postmodernist poetics, each with its own cast of forebears, a particular vantage on past and present, and its own approach to knowledge. Campos and Ginsberg, and beyond them the Beat and Noigandres poets, are not unrelated or irrelevant to each other, but alternatives and often obverses. They are much more mutually relevant than they would allow, enabling us to put them into a reciprocal commentary—and not incidentally, to use their alternative vantages to revive the critical discussion that has stalled over them as singular figures.

I choose the moments of Ginsberg's *Kaddish* and Campos' *Galáxias* because they find both poets at a second stage or transition: expanding the cultural and intellectual resources available to them, getting past the protocols and styles that served for their early work, and traveling, both literally and figuratively.[20] This phase of Ginsberg's work was provoked by his travel to Europe and Latin America, where he began to develop what one biographer has called "a global consciousness";[21] Campos' turn toward *Galáxias* was catalyzed by his first trip to Europe, including a return through the Brazilian northeast during which he "rediscover[ed] Brazil via the world. The hybrid and the ecumenical."[22] In each case, the second stage is activated by a new awareness of a particular American vantage or location installed in the world; in each case the transition involves a poetry differently oriented—speaking within a broader circumscription, addressing the world as a concept in metaphysical as well as geopolitical terms—and a struggle to produce poems that acknowledge, include, capture the world. On these terms two poets who built alternative versions of a postmodern poetics move closer to each other, and the poems of these moments sometimes dissolve into voices that make Ginsberg sound like Campos and vice versa. And in their transitions, Ginsberg and Campos produce poems that might be treated as obverses, or alternative engagements with problems of history and knowledge.

To me, the most revealing episodes in their work of the late 1950s and early sixties are those poems in which they seem to reach an impasse within their established poetics, and to struggle with the impulse toward each other's poetic program. In Ginsberg's case, this juncture is part of a long search for a visionary poetics that dates back to "Psalm I" (1949) and continues through "Angkor Wat" (1963). The late fifties see a deepening sense of the stakes involved in his writing, and an agitated inventory of lyric and prophetic possibilities. In this set of poems, the deeply moving verbal overcharge of "Kaddish" is followed by a return to the elegiac concerns of that poem ("o mother / what have I left out / o mother / what have I forgotten") and then a struggle to emplace those concerns in a wider setting of metaphysical speculation:

> I cry out where I am in the music, to the room, to whomever near, you, Are you God?
> No, do you want me to be God?
> Is there no Answer?
> Must there always be an Answer? you reply,
> and were it up to me to say Yes or No—
> Thank God I am not God! Thank God I am not God!

But that I long for a Yes of Harmony to penetrate
to every corner of the universe, under every condition whatsoever
a Yes there Is . . . a Yes I Am . . . a Yes You Are . . . a We[23]

It seems that the balance of forces of Ginsberg's early poetry, from "The Green Automobile" through *Reality Sandwiches*, has been displaced by something more searching and volatile—an explicit search for God as presence—that makes his usual volatility seem legible and obvious. The poetic style that Marjorie Perloff, Charles Molesworth, and others have described authoritatively is firmly in place by the writing of "Kaddish," but this is something else, a register (as James Scully has it) like Henry Vaughan more than William Blake.[24] The open questioning of these poems, I think, is an improvised response (and not always an especially convincing one) to this newly opened prospect.

Into this setting, following on the anaphoric and manically idealist "Lysergic Acid," comes "I Beg You Come Back & Be Cheerful," an understated and ironic assay at the same questions:

Radiant clouds, I have heard God's voice in
my sleep, or Blake's awake, or my own or
the dream of a delicatessen of snorting cows
and bellowing pigs—
The chop of a knife
a finger severed in my brain—
a few deaths I know—
O brothers of the Laurel
Is the world real?
Is the Laurel
a joke or a crown of thorns?

Then appears a quatrain that stands apart from the poem, and from nearly everything Ginsberg has written from "Howl" (1956) to this point. In the first instance its power is in its unlikeness to his usual mode of perception, in that the quatrain parodies his entire corpus, including his mode of composition and his sex life, in four short lines:

Fast, pass
up the ass
Down I go
Cometh woe

When Ginsberg's characteristic verbal order is in place—"a swirling, flashing registry of states of consciousness in which perceptions are constantly disarranged, even deranged"[25]—there is no room for this kind of unsparing, minimalist observation. For that matter, short lines stitched together by rhymes instead of anaphora, gathered at their ends rather than their beginnings, make for a low-key but startling interruption in his outlook. End-rhymed lines—of which there is none in Ginsberg's poetry since before "Howl"—make a different thoughtprint than anaphoric lines. More than a stylistic departure, they belie the spontaneous ethic of Ginsberg's work and represent a distance from immediate experience, a coming to conclusions, that he seldom entertains. Later on, this kind of short end-rhymed line will become the mode of ironic reflection on sex, a post-coital ruefulness.[26] But here, where a fit of questioning gives way to answers, Ginsberg is trying to change frequencies. This urge becomes manifest in an especially striking moment. After four lines of observation of the Manhattan cityscape, there follows this calligram:

What
if
the
worlds
were
a
series
of steps
What
if
the
steps
joined
back
at
the
Margin

Leaving us flying like birds into Time
—eyes and car headlights—
The shrinkage of emptiness
In the Nebulae
These Galaxies cross like pinwheels & they pass
Like gas—
What forests are born.
September 15, 1959

I take it that what matters here is a poet of one well-defined sensibility not only speaking in an unaccustomed voice but exploding voice altogether to reach after something that counts as almost inexpressible to his poetics: a metaphysical order that makes his poem into an epistemological challenge, a sketch of something beyond words, a child's drawing. Where Ginsberg began this set of poems by posing questions—what and where is God? how can we conceive of this world within other worlds?—he now arrives at provisional answers in a hushed tone, about himself and about the world. For a mind accustomed to launching questions and observations paratactically from the same perch, these conclusions unsettle the poetry. Changing his vantage on reality and substituting the shape of "worlds," in the imprecise form of the calligram, for the shape of his own thinking, Ginsberg's speaker turns his poem inside out. He suspends the observation of nature as it presents itself, and resorts instead to an end-driven recording of rhythms and patterns. He tries to get the world and what is beyond the world, rather than the usual subjective self, into his poem. The striking moment is not the calligram, however, but the concluding lines in which a speaker who started from a pose of self-absorption ("Tonite I got hi in the window of my apartment") gestures toward something infinitely remote: "These Galaxies cross like pinwheels & they pass / like gas." The key term "galaxies" reveals the metaphysical object out of reach of this poet of excess and indiscipline; it names the invisible horizon that has exerted pressure on this poem since the transitional quatrain, to which these lines return ("they pass like gas" revisits "fast, pass / up the ass"), the outer limit of this poem's thinking. It says: this poet can evoke the world, and worlds beyond the world. He is writing to an enlarged horizon.

"I Beg You Come Back & Be Cheerful" leaves us in a place uncharacteristic of Ginsberg's early poetry but necessary to the turn his work takes after about 1960, where the aspects of his outlook—confessional, political, and metaphysical—are recombined and (in Joseph Lease's nice phrase) braided together again.[27] The term "galaxies" encodes a sense of heightened stakes, as if the charter of the poems has come to include the representation of worlds, and worlds within worlds, around the confessional first person. When we read in the poem "Aether"

Stop conceiving worlds!

says Philip Whalen

(My Savior!)   (oh what snobbery!)[28]

we should understand that these poems of 1959 represent a seeking after a new mode of thinking as well as a new descriptive protocol. On these poems depends the achievement of Ginsberg's finest poem of the 1960s, "Wichita Vortex Sutra" (1966), in which he speaks from the vantage of a prophet who straddles worlds ("in Kansas or other universe") and declares the end of the Vietnam War.[29] The horizon of the galaxy enables us to apprehend, within it, the outlines of the world; and our awareness of the poet speaking across these concentric circles gives force to that poem's declaration of peace, which is obviously impotent in the here and now of 1966 but speaks to us from somewhere else.

The horizon of the galaxy, of course, is something Ginsberg shares with his Brazilian contemporary Haroldo de Campos. Other poets of the 1950s and sixties, such as the American Charles Olson and the Swiss-Bolivian Eugen Gomringer, adopt similar terms: Olson's "composition by field" owes something to this horizon, as does his important essay on the possibilities of knowledge called "Human Universe," while Gomringer's *Constellations* is one of the formative works of concrete poetry in this era.[30] All of these terms, which appear in many statements of poetics in this period, respond to a larger intellectual agenda. In a book published in 1957, Karl Popper remarks on the strictly physical nature of celestial phenomena in contrast to social life:

> Physical structures . . . can be explained as mere "constellations" . . . or as the mere sum of their parts, together with their geometrical configuration. Take the solar system, for instance; although it may be interesting to study its history, and although this study may throw light on its present state, we know that, in a sense, this state is independent of the history of the system. The structure of the system, its future movements and developments, are fully determined by the present constitution of its members. Given the relative positions, masses, and momenta, of its members at any one instant, the future movements of the system are all fully determined. . . . The history of the structure, although it may be interesting, contributes nothing to our understanding of its behaviour, of its mechanism, and of its future development. It is obvious that a physical structure differs widely in this respect from any social structure; the latter cannot be understood, nor its future predicted, without a careful study of its history, even if we had complete knowledge of its momentary "constellation."[31]

For Popper, this is constellation as pure form, free of the pressures of society and history. The notion of a future legible through formal arrangements ("positions, masses, and momenta"), where the past has no privilege as prologue, perhaps made this sense of "constellation" seem especially intriguing in the 1950s, as the exhaustion of a world war gave way to an acceleration of technology, including the exploration of space. Moreover, there is a complementary lexicon, overseen chiefly by Walter Benjamin and Theodor Adorno, that sees "constellation" as a term for the kind of thinking that finds a social and historical dimension in what appears to be the observation of aesthetic forms: this constellative project—Robert Kaufman has explored it insightfully—remakes the relation between the social-historical and the aesthetic, finding new construals of the former through an application of the latter, often in constructivist fashion.[32] Where Popper's quarrel with historicism leads him to ruminate on the constellation as an ahistorical structure, entirely unlike history and society, the Frankfurt School critics go further, proposing that such a structure affords terms for imagining the historical, social, and aesthetic together, unsettling the conventional accounts of relations among these forces. From a variety of standpoints in the 50s, the figure of the constellation is present where these relations were being reconfigured, particularly where historical materials were engaged anew in aesthetic terms or works of art revisited as expressions of history and social life. The figure itself bears the stamp of a detour from conventional thinking—from the causative, the linear, the hierarchical.

Where poetry is concerned, Ginsberg and Campos see in "galaxies" and "constellations" an outlet away from the conventions of the period as well as the programs they have imposed on themselves. Approaching from opposite directions—Ginsberg from a poetics that has been constituted out of the first person and social observation, Campos from the exaggeratedly hygienic program of the concrete poems of the collection *Fome de Forma* (*Hunger of Form*) of 1957–59 and its successor *Forma de Fome* (*Form of Hunger*), which contains "Transient Servitude"—these poets, fleetingly and at about the same time, arrive at a common agenda, a shared space of reflection. Finding our way back from there, can we account for how this Beat and this concretist cross like pinwheels? How might an inter-american poetry of galactic horizons engage differently from its contemporaries with what Olson calls "the only two universes which count, the two phenomenal ones, the two a man has need to bear on because they bear so on him: that of himself, as organism, and that of his environment, the earth and planets"?[33]

Where Ginsberg's expansive poetics finds a new density, Campos finds a new expansiveness. *Galáxias* is the pivot in his poetics. Here is the first item in the series:

> e começo aqui e meço aqui este começo e recomeço e remeço e arremesso
> e aqui me meço quando se vive sob a espécie da viagem o que importa
> não é a viagem mas o começo da por isso meço por isso começo escrever
> mil páginas escrever milumapáginas para acabar com a escritura para
> começar com a escritura para acabarcomeçar com a escritura por isso
> recomeço por isso arremeço por isso teço escrever sobre escrever é o futuro[34]
>
> (and here I commence and measure here I commence and recommence and remeasure
> and hurl
> and here I measure myself when life is lived as a kind of voyage what matters
> is not the voyage but the commence so I commence so I measure I commence to write
> a thousand pages write a thousandandone pages to finish writing
> to commence with writing to finishcommence with writing so
> I recommence so I hurl so I weave to write about writing is the *future*)

Like Ginsberg's efforts at rhyme and concretism (but with a rush of self-assurance instead of his deliberate fumbling), this prose poem introduces an unfamiliar voice, a new philosophical orientation ("when life is lived as a kind of voyage what matters is not the voyage"), and a redrawn horizon. The short, highly concentrated lines of the concrete poetry and of the semantic variations in *Fome de Forma* give way to lines that do not end at all but "recommence" again and again; the stance and tone are like that of a Whitman reached by a back-formation through modernism, especially Joyce and Stein. And as in Popper's account of constellations, Campos imagines, as Ginsberg did in his reverie, a poetry whose "fully determined" structure reflects that of the universe, whose past and future is nothing but its movements. Suppose there were a poetry that fused the personal and the metaphysical without the mediation of the social, which would obviate confessionalism; suppose there were a poetry whose shape traced the shape of the world and the universe.

The program piece of *Galáxias* is the prose poem "circuladô de fulô":

> circuladô de fulô ao deus ao demodará que deus te guie porque eu não
> posso guiá eviva quem já me deu circuladô de fulô e ainda quem falta me
> dá soando como um shamisen e feito apenas com um arametenso um cabo e
> uma lata velha num fim de festafeira no pino do sol a pino mas para
> outros não existia aquela música não podia porque não podia popular
> aquela música se não canta não é popular se não afina não tintina não
> tarantina e no entanto puxada na tripa da miséria na tripa tensa da mais
> megera miséria física e doendo doendo como um prego na palma da mão um
> ferrugem prego cego na palma espalma da mão coração exposto como um nervo
> tenso retenso um renegro prego cego durando na palma polpa da mão ao sol
>
> ('rounded by flowers under god's under the devil's mercy god shall guide you for I myself
> can't guide godbless those who give me 'rounded by flowers and those who are still
> to give sounding like a samisen made of a tensed wire a stick
> and an old tin can at the end of the partyfair at highnoonhigh but for
> many that music did not exist it could not because it could not popplay
> if not sung that music is not popular if not in tune it does not atone nor
> tarantina and yet struck in the gut of misery in the tensed gut of the meagerest
> physical misery aching aching like a nail in the handpalm a
> rusty blind nail in the palm clasping palm of the handheart exposed as a tensed nerve
> retensed a renigrated blind nail everlasting in the palmpulp of the hand in the sun)[35]

For readers acquainted with Campos' earlier work, the most arresting dimension of this collection is likely to be its verbal profusion. A poetics of strict economy—with a minimalist attention to morphemes, phonemes, and lineation—has been replaced by a no less attentive repetition of indelible words and phrases. "Circuladô de fulô"—the phrase is ambiguous, but means something like "surrounded by flowers" (the translator A. S. Bessa's rendition) or "circulator of flowers"—adapts language of long derivation in the Brazilian and Portuguese lyric traditions, but directly evokes the minstrelsy of northeastern Brazil. The opening phrase, in which "fulô" seems to be "flor" (flower) with a vowel added by epenthesis and the final consonant elided, is probably an epithet for the minstrel himself: he who makes and is made by the flowers of rhetoric. What is distinctive to the moment of *Galáxias*, however, is the metaphysical perspective of this poem: "under god's under the devil's mercy god shall guide you for I myself can't guide godbless those who give me" stands out from Campos' work for its remarkable concatenation of the ethical and the divine. While some of the earlier poetry implies a similar perspective, as in some of the semantic variations in *Forma de Fome*,

homem senhor
homem servo

homem sobre
homem sob[36]

(man sir
man servant

man over
man under)

little in Campos' program to this point allows him to think his way directly from the experimental to the divine, from semantics to metaphysics. From the first poem's envisioning of a textual space "where the end is the beginning," *Galáxias* involves a number of such efforts to explode the boundaries of the earlier poetry—none more thoroughly than "Circuladô de fulô," with its positing of a modern, provincial *trobar clus* that claims some of the wrenching force of a crucifixion and realizes through that power a moral renewal ("if not in tune it does not atone").

At a threshold for their poetries, then, Ginsberg and Campos cross paths, one tending toward the gnomic and the concrete, and the other pulling away from these modes—but both in search of a poetry of greater knowledge. The Ginsberg and Campos suites are obverses in that they represent alternative constructions of a single problem—how to expand a poetic horizon to galactic dimensions, and how to embed specifically American language and experience within that new horizon—delivered contemporaneously, even as other artists of the Americas were examining a galactic or constellative horizon for what it could offer them. For Ginsberg this adjustment opened a new galaxy that remained intermittently available, inflecting but not quite transforming his poetics, while for Campos it represented a decisive shift toward a new kind of writing. While this turn in their work can be understood as an episode in their particular careers, I think it makes a different sort of sense in an inter-american setting, where two considerably different premises for poetry came to discover a common space adjacent to both of them. The modes of the Beats and the Noigandres poets still do not touch one another, but in Ginsberg and Campos circa 1960 they have an imaginable relation.

Finally, I would like to reflect on the future of a hemispheric approach to poetry by briefly considering the possible third term in the relation between Ginsberg and Campos: namely, the poet whom Ginsberg addresses in "To an Old Poet in Peru," the elderly modernist Martín Adán (1908–1985). Adán was one of the leading figures in Peruvian modernism but almost unknown outside his country; his experiments with sonnets that overturned the unacknowledged political conventions of the form were celebrated by the political philosopher José Carlos Mariátegui in a classic essay called "The Anti-Sonnet" (1928).[37]

To Ginsberg, Adán is an intriguing but finally unassimilable figure, whose formally rigorous lyrics seem to have little to say to his own volatile poems. Campos for his part seems to have had little awareness of Adán, even though *La Casa de Cartón* (*The Cardboard House*, 1928), Adán's experimental narrative that appeared at the same time as several modernist works of Brazil, participates (though not by name) in the "cultural cannibalism" that Campos ostentatiously adapts from that generation.[38] Adán's relevance is that, where Ginsberg and Campos seek the capacious voices and access to metaphysics represented by their poems circa 1960, he had already cultivated such a poetry for about thirty years when his sequence *La Mano Desasida* (*The Hand Let Go*) appeared in 1960. One might observe that, while the Brazilian and the American poets cross each other, the Peruvian poet is between them but illegible to both. Ginsberg's "To an Old Poet in Peru" is about crossed trajectories that yield no illumination. While Adán has explored the potential of a metaphysical poetry of the Americas, his work hardly matters to Ginsberg, who sees their encounter as fruitless:

> Your indifference! my enthusiasm!
> I insist! You cough!
> Lost in the wave of Gold that
> flows thru the Cosmos.
> Agh I'm tired of insisting! Goodbye,
> I'm going to Pucallpa
> to have Visions.
> Your clean sonnets?
> I want to read your dirtiest
> secret scribblings,
> your Hope,
> in His most Obscene Magnificence. My God![39]

The poem ends with both poets walking off to their own metaphysical experiments, stuck in mutual incomprehension.

A parable of the poetries of the Americas, Ginsberg's poem reminds us that the hemispheric canon, if such a thing exists, is held together by misapprehensions and resistances as much as by affinities and recognitions, and that mutual ignorance—with its reckless experiments, inadvertent conversations, and obversals—often has more power than understanding. Quests after knowledge like those of Ginsberg and Campos become all the more moving, I believe, when they are both compromised and empowered by the versions of ignorance and insensibility we have seen (Campos toward Whitman; Ginsberg toward Adán; Campos and Ginsberg toward one another). In answer to Guillén and Jameson, where is the comparative agenda that will show us how to read for these omissions? How will we write the history of a hemispheric poetry in these terms? The relation between obverses that I draft here is only a start toward explaining the poetics of the Americas as a set of relations and the problems around them. In the inter-american setting, we are always discovering that the problems are as compelling as the relations.

NOTES

1. For example, to cite only books, overviews such as Earl E. Fitz, *Rediscovering the New World: Inter-American Literatures in a Comparative Context* (Iowa City: University of Iowa Press, 1991); monographic books on particular authors like Julio Marzán, *The Spanish American Roots of William Carlos Williams* (Austin: University of Texas Press, 1994); and outward-looking revisions of the United States' literary and cultural history such as Kirsten Silva Gruesz, *Ambassadors of Culture: The Transamerican Origins of Latino Writing* (Princeton: Princeton University Press, 2002).

2. Charles Bernstein, "Poetics of the Americas," *Modernism/Modernity* 3, no. 3 (1996): 1–23, rpt. in *My Way: Speeches and Poems* (Chicago: University of Chicago Press, 1999), 113–37; Jahan Ramazani, "A Transnational Poetics," *American Literary History* 18 (2006): 332–59.

3. Richard M. Morse, "Triangulating Two Cubists: William Carlos Williams and Oswald de Andrade," *Latin American Literary Review* 14, no. 27 (1986): 80.

4. Claudio Guillén, *The Challenge of Comparative Literature*, trans. Cola Franzen (Cambridge: Harvard University Press, 1993), 69–70.

5. Bernstein, *My Way*, 114.

6. Gayatri Chakravorty Spivak, *Death of a Discipline* (New York: Columbia University Press, 2003), 66.

7. Fredric Jameson, "Third-World Literature in the Era of Multinational Capitalism," *Social Text* 15 (1986): 69.

8. Aijaz Ahmad, "Jameson's Rhetoric of Otherness and the 'National Allegory,'" *Social Text* 17 (1987): 3.

9. Jameson, "Third-World Literature," 69.

10. Bernstein, *My Way*, 114.

11. On the etymology of *noigandres*, see the translator Jacques Donguy's note in Augusto de Campos, *Anthologie despoesia*, trans. Donguy (Paris: Editions Al Dante, 2002), 7.

12. Augusto and Haroldo de Campos, *ReVisão de Sousândrade*, 2nd ed. (Rio de Janeiro: Nova Fronteira, 1982), 26–43.

13. Fernando Alegría, *Walt Whitman en Hispanoamérica* (Mexico City: n.p., 1954); Gwen Kirkpatrick, *The Dissonant Legacy of Modernismo: Lugones, Herrera y Reissig, and the Voices of Modern Spanish American Poetry* (Berkeley and Los Angeles: University of California Press, 1989); Cathy L. Jrade, *Modernismo, Modernity and the Development of Spanish American Literature* (Austin: University of Texas Press, 1998).

14. Oswald de Andrade, "Manifesto of Paul-Brasil Poetry," trans. Stella M de Sá Rego, *Latin American Literary Review* 27 (1986): 185. Andrade's manifesti are collected in *Do Pau-Brasil à Antropofagia e às Utopias*, introd. Benedito Nunes, vol. 6 of *Obras completas*, 11 vols. (Rio de Janeiro: Civilização Brasileira, 1970–74).

15. Ezra Pound, *Selected Poems* (New York: New Directions, 1957), 27.

16. Augusto de Campos, Décio Pignatari, and Haroldo de Campos, *Teoria da Poesia Concreta: Textos Críticos e Manifestos 1950–1960*, 3rd ed. (São Paulo: Brasiliense, 1987), 156–58. See Charles A. Perrone, *Seven Faces: Brazilian Poetry Since Modernism* (Durham: Duke University Press, 1996), 48. Perrone's chapter (25–66) is the definitive account in English of the Noigandres project, as Gonzalo Aguilar, *Poesía concreta brasileña: Las vanguardias en la encrucijada modernista* (Rosario, Argentina: Beatriz Viterbo, 2003) is in Spanish.

17. As in "A Temperatura Informacional do Texto," in Campos et al., *Teoria da Poesia Concreta*, 138–49.

18. On Ginsberg's poetics, see Charles Molesworth, *The Fierce Embrace: A Study of Contemporary American Poetry* (Columbia: University of Missouri Press, 1979), 37–60.

19. Allen Ginsberg, *Collected Poems 1947–1980* (New York: Harper and Row, 1984), xx; Paul Portugés, "Allen Ginsberg's Paul Cézanne and the Pater Omnipotens Aeterna Deus," in *On the Poetry of Allen Ginsberg*, ed. Lewis Hyde (Ann Arbor: University of Michigan Press, 1984), 151–52.

20. The state of Ginsberg's poetics in 1956 is summarized by Marjorie Perloff, *Poetry On and Off the Page: Essays for Emergent Occasions* (Evanston: Northwestern University Press, 1998), 101–04.

21. Michael Schumacher, *Dharma Lion: A Critical Biography of Allen Ginsberg* (New York: St. Martin's Press, 1992), 279. Ginsberg's expanding consciousness of the world in this period is a theme in many of the essays collected in Hyde's *On the Poetry of Allen Ginsberg*.

22. This remark from a biographical sketch of the 1980s is quoted in A. S. Bessa's introduction to *Galáxias*: http://www.ubu.com/ethno/poems/decampos_galaxias.html.

23. Ginsberg, *Collected Poems*, 231–32.

24. James Scully, "A Passion in Search of Two Boards," in *On the Poetry of Allen Ginsberg*, ed. Hyde, 186–87. Scully refers to "Siesta in Xbalba," one of the earliest poems to adopt this mode.

25. Molesworth, *The Fierce Embrace*, 38.

26. See the later poems cited by Marjorie Perloff in *Poetic License: Essays on Modernist and Postmodernist Lyric* (Evanston: Northwestern University Press, 1990), 215.

27. Joseph Lease, "My Allen Ginsberg," *Poetry Flash* 296–97 (Winter-Spring 2006): 12.

28. Ginsberg, *Collected Poems*, 249.

29. Ginsberg, *Collected Poems*, 406–07.

30. Charles Olson, "Projective Verse," *Selected Writings*, ed. Robert Creeley (New York: New Directions, 1966), 15–26; *Human Universe and Other Essays*, ed. Donald Allen (San Francisco: The Auerhahn Society, 1965); Eugen Gomringer, *Die Konstellationen / Les Constellations / The constellations / Las constelaciones* (Frauenfeld, Switzerland: Eugen Gomringer Press, 1962).

31. Karl Popper, *The Poverty of Historicism* (1957; London: Routledge, 2002), 16–17.

32. Robert Kaufman, "Lyric's Constellation, Poetry's Radical Privilege," *Modernist Cultures* 1 (2006): 209–34.

33. Olson, *Human Universe*, 4.

34. Haroldo de Campos, *Galáxias* (São Paulo: Editora Ex Libris, 1984), n.p. The translation is mine. In the version of "e começo aqui" published in Campos' *Xadrez de Estrelas: Percurso Textual 1949–1974* (São Paulo: Editora Perspectiva, 1976), 200, this poem like the others in the series is printed in roman rather than italic type. In the

edition of *Galáxias* from which I quote, "e começo aqui" is the only poem in italic.

35. Campos, *Galáxias*, n.p. The translation by A. S. Bessa appears in *Novas: The Writings of Haroldo de Campos*, ed. and trans. Bessa and Odile Cisneros (Evanston: Northwestern University Press, 2006), 124. It also figures in Bessa's indispensable essay on *Galáxias*. Further scholarship on the collection and the rest of Campos' poetry and criticism appears in *Haroldo de Campos: A Dialogue with the Brazilian Concrete Poet*, ed. K. David Jackson (Oxford: Centre for Brazilian Studies, 2005). In a review of that title, in the *Luso-Brazilian Review* 43 (2006): 133–36, Charles Perrone summarizes the plans for several volumes in tribute to Campos.

36. Campos, *Xadrez de Estrelas*, 134.

37. José Carlos Mariátegui, "El anti-soneto," *Amauta* 17 (September 1928); rpt. in Martín Adán, *Obra Poética 1928–1971* (Lima: Instituto Nacional de Cultura, 1971), 237–39. I quote from the essay in "New World Studies and the Limits of National Literatures," in *Poetry and Pedagogy: The Challenge of the Contemporary*, ed. Joan Retallack and Juliana Spahr (New York: Palgrave Macmillan, 2006), 89–90.

38. Haroldo de Campos, "The Rule of Anthropophagy: Europe Under the Sign of Devoration," *Latin American Literary Review* 14, no. 27 (1986): 42–60.

39. Ginsberg, *Collected Poems*, 240–41.

10.5 Love in the Necropolis (2003)

David Damrosch

In the second year of the reign of Ramses V, in the third month of the inundation season, a scribe in Thebes made a collection of literary texts: a long, comic story of intrigue among the gods; some hymns; an encomium to the king. "The Contendings of Horus and Seth," as we now call the story, took up most of the front side (the recto) of the scribe's papyrus roll; with a little space left at the end, he decided to include some short love poems, before turning over to the verso to write the encomium and the hymns. The lyrics appear under the heading "The Sweet Sayings Found in a Scroll Composed by the Scribe of the Necropolis, Nakht-Sobek." In W. K. Simpson's vivid translation the shortest of these lyrics goes as follows:

Why need you hold converse with your heart?
To embrace her is all my desire.
As Amun lives, I come to you,
my loincloth on my shoulder.

(*The Literature of Ancient Egypt*, 324)

One of the oldest lyrics to have survived anywhere in the world, this poem addresses us with a powerful immediacy. In its brevity and simplicity, it stands as a kind of minimum of literary expression, and I will use it as a testing ground to explore the irreducible problems that translation always faces, however simple the text in question, however uncomplicated the history of its transmission and reception. In this respect too, this poem presents as simple a case as we could readily find. Whereas many works of world literature come to us already shaped by complex dynamics of transmission, often involving vexed relations between the originating culture and our own, this text has almost no history at all intervening between us and the moment of its inscription in 1160 B.C.E. Produced for private enjoyment, the papyrus passed into other hands; inspired by the poems on the recto, another writer added a more extensive collection of love poems on the verso, under the heading "The Songs of Extreme Happiness." Soon, though, the papyrus fell out of the sphere of literary usage. The demand for papyrus far outstripped supply in the Ramesside period, and within a few years the blank pages remaining at the end of the verso were being used, and reused, for business memoranda: recording now the sale of a bull, now the gift of a box to the general of the War Office. Buried in some cache of administrative records, the papyrus vanished for three thousand years. Discovered by one of the peasants who conducted their own private, for-profit excavations in the Theban necropolis in competition with government-sanctioned university digs, this papyrus was acquired in the late 1920s by A. Chester Beatty, a wealthy American mining engineer who had settled in England and was devoting himself to collecting all sorts of neglected artifacts: Chinese snuff boxes and rhinoceros-horn cups, medieval woodblock prints, and ancient religious manuscripts from around the world. He happened upon "Papyrus Chester Beatty," as it became known, while wintering in Cairo for his health. Beatty underwrote its publication by Oxford University Press in 1931, in a beautiful folio edition, complete with transcriptions, dozens of photographic plates, and a detailed analysis by a leading Egyptologist of the day, A. H. Gardiner (later Sir Alan, himself a man of extensive means), under the title *The Library of A. Chester Beatty: Description of Hieratic Papyrus with Mythological Story, Love-Songs, and Other Miscellaneous Texts, by Alan H. Gardiner, F.B.A.*

The poems thus come to us unencumbered by any transmission history whatever from the twelfth century B.C.E. to the early twentieth century C.E., when the lyrics in this papyrus were quickly seen, as Gardiner says in his introduction, to be "of inestimable value, not merely for archaeology, but still more for the world-history of poetry and of lyric expression" (27). And yet, as Gardiner and subsequent translators have tried to give the poems their rightful place in world literature, they have had to struggle with surprisingly intractable problems, even in the case of the simple quatrain quoted above—problems of decipherment, of grammar, of vocabulary, and of cultural framing. Attending to these problems can show us much about how the choices that have to be made as a work is brought from its original time and place into our own world.

Gardiner's initial publication itself oscillates between two quite different frames of reference for the poems: historical and transcendent. With extensive philological notes, his edition presents the papyrus as a document of Ramesside history and culture ("Where else have we similar records of the conveyance of foreign news by a system of relays?" [29]), and he waxes eloquent over orthography: "An astonishing and, so far as I know, unparalleled ligature found in the Encomium, but not on the *recto*, is that for (*verso* B 23.26)" (5). Yet at the same time this lavish edition is an aesthetic object in its own right: an oversize folio with three-inch margins, amply illustrated, and with elegant transcriptions employing the delicate hieroglyphic font that Gardiner's father had commissioned for him several years earlier. ("It is to my Father that I owe all my leisure and opportunities for research," Gardiner gratefully noted in the preface to his great *Egyptian Grammar* of 1926, "and it is he who now, more than thirty years later, has defrayed the cost of my new hieroglyphic font.")

At once a paleographer and aesthete, Gardiner judiciously assesses the scribe's calligraphic style: "The hand is neither very regular nor yet very tidy, but it possesses plenty of character and is not without a certain beauty of its own." He praises "the spirited , and with the foremost arm ending in a daring flourish," and urbanely mentions "the misshapen " as one of the scribe's characteristic usages (5). He prefers, however, to emphasize the physical at the level of form rather than of content. Discussing the anatomy of the beloved's body in one poem ("Long of neck and radiant of nipple . . . / Drooping of buttocks, firm-girt in her midst"), he comments that "here already we mark how purely physical was the gentle passion as felt by these ancient Orientals" (28). Turning quickly from this ancient, oriental physicality, he stresses that "apart from this, the emotions expressed differ in no wise from those of lovers of all ages and climes." The poems achieve their inestimable value for world poetry by their universality—a universality that proves to tally closely with their *similarity* to modern European verse: one poem closes "with some verses which are Heine pure and simple" (he now quotes Heine, in German, [28]); another expresses "a thought not unlike one found upon the lips of Romeo" (whom he also quotes [29]).

It is not an easy matter, though, to translate the poems safely into the Euro-universal world where Gardiner wishes to see them enshrined, even though the papyrus itself has made it to twentieth-century England almost intact, apart from the tearing off of one or more initial pages "by the rapacious and destructive hands of the fellaheen" (1). The balance of the papyrus is in good condition, and yet Gardiner still faces severe challenges in getting from the physical marks on the page to the universality of an achieved work of art. "The text is evidently corrupt," the first two poems "are so obscure as to be almost untranslatable," while "Stanza the fifth is Stygian darkness" (29). Even the quatrain I am examining here, free of any lacunae or even of any unknown words, contains riddles of orthography and grammar that make it difficult to decide even so basic an issue as who is supposed to be speaking in the poem: A man? A woman? A man and his friend? The man's friend only? The friend and the woman? All of these options have been tried by Gardiner and his successors, with no consensus yet in sight.

Gardiner himself took the speaker to be a woman, translating the poem as follows:

When thou speakest with thy heart,
Prithee after her, that I may embrace her;
By Amûn, it is I who come to thee,
My tunic upon by arm.
(37)

He glosses the poem as signifying that "the maiden tells her lover that pursuit is superfluous, she is a willing quarry" (37 n. 3). Gardiner, however, produced this lucid rendering at the cost of suppressing the grammatical structure of the first two lines. The opening phrase, *ir.n djed-k*, is a simple interrogative and would normally be translated "Why do you speak?" rather than "When you speak." The second line, moreover, is an infinitive phrase rather than a command: "To embrace her is all my desire," rather than "Prithee after her." Just how these lines work together is unclear: Egyptian writing was unpunctuated, and the four lines could represent one, two, or three sentences. Further, as hieroglyphs record consonants and semivowels but not vowels proper, it can often be difficult to say just which form of a verb is being used and which are dependent rather than independent clauses. Sorting these questions out as best they can, the two most scholarly translators of more recent years, W. K. Simpson of Yale and Miriam Lichtheim of the University of California, have both opted for a tripartite rendering, consisting of a question, a reply or exhortation, and an announcement of action. In Lichtheim's version, this becomes:

Why do you argue with your heart?
Go after her, embrace her!
As Amun lives, I come to you,
My cloak over my arm.
(*Ancient Egyptian Literature*, 2:188)

Like all translations—like all reading—Lichtheim's version is informed by context. Her translation recalls other Egyptian poems in which a hesitating young lover is offered advice by a third party. Papyrus Chester Beatty itself contains several such poems. In one cycle of three poems, the speaker might be either the man's friend or a go-between sent by the woman herself:

Please come quick to the lady love
like a king's agent
whose master is impatient
for his letters
and desires to hear them.
. . . .
Before you have kissed your hand four times,
you shall have reached her hideaway
as you chase the lady love.
For it is the Golden Goddess
Who has set her aside for you, friend.
(Simpson, 321–23)

The set of seven poems that includes our verse begins with two poems that are both spoken by a friend, in this instance a none-too-scrupulous male confidant of the lover himself:

Supply her with song and dance,
wine and ale are her desire,
confuse her wits,
and gain her this night.
She'll tell you:
put me in your arms;
when day breaks
let's start again.
(Simpson, 323)

Lichtheim extends this context to our quatrain, construing it as a miniature dialogue in which the friend chides the lover for his hesitation and urges him on; the lover fortifies himself with a vow to Amun and goes in to the woman.

So far, so good: Lichtheim has solved the grammatical problem of the first line. Yet she has retained Gardiner's insertion of an imperative mode into the second line, actually breaking the line into two separate commands ("Go after her, embrace her!") though there is only one verb in the original. Further, the wider context tends to argue against a rapid change of speakers in midverse: no surviving Egyptian poem makes such a change. Lichtheim may have created a dialogue where none existed to begin with.

Admittedly, a negative argument from context can only be made very tentatively, given the small number of poems to have survived from ancient Egypt: only four dozen poems have come down to us more or less intact, and it would only take a further discovery to extend the range of known possibility in any number of ways. If one particular set of three poems had never been found, for example, we would have observed that every extant Egyptian poem is spoken by a man, a woman, or both, and we might naturally assume this to have always been the case. A papyrus now preserved in Turin, however, has a cycle of three poems whose speakers are *trees*, which testify to the charms of the lovers who meet beneath their branches (Simpson, 312–15).

Tentative though it is, such contextual evidence as we have at least favors the idea of a single speaker, or rather, a single singer, as these poems were composed as song lyrics. Particularly if we remove the implausible imperative introduced by Gardiner and Lichtheim, our quatrain can readily be translated as involving a single speaker. This is the view taken by Simpson in the translation with which I began, and he makes his view of the speaker's gender clear by his choice of garment:

> Why need you hold converse with your heart?
> To embrace her is all my desire.
> As Amun lives, I come to you,
> my loincloth on my shoulder.
> (324)

Simpson's rendering draws on a wider context—including other love poems but also other texts—in which a person debates an issue with his heart or spirit before coming to a decision. The most extended Egyptian use of this theme is found in a haunting twelfth-dynasty text known as "The Dispute between a Man and his *Ba*" (Lichtheim, 1:163–69; Simpson, 201–9). "To whom shall I speak today?" the speaker asks. "Faces are blank, / Everyone turns his face from his brothers." He despairs of life, but his own spirit replies to him ("Are you not a man? Are you not alive?"), urging him not to commit suicide; internal debate here carries the weight given to Job's argument with his three friends in the Book of Job. A typical instance of internal dialogue in love poetry occurs in Papyrus Harris 500, from Memphis:

> I say to my heart within me a prayer:
> if far away from me is my lover tonight,
> then I am like someone already in the grave.
> Are you not indeed well-being and life?
> Joy has come to me through your well-being,
> my heart seeks you out.
> (Simpson, 304)

Simpson's version of our quatrain is attractive, works grammatically, and fits plausibly within the context of surviving Egyptian poetry. On the other hand, it is perfectly plausible to build upon Gardiner's original assumption that the speaker is the beloved woman rather than the man, if we correct his verbs but follow his lead in taking the second line as the woman's paraphrase of what she thinks her lover is saying as he hesitates in coming to her. Several other extant poems have a speaker reporting another's speech, as in the following example, which is probably the world's oldest surviving aubade, a poem in which lovers complain at the rising of the sun. Here the woman reports two different speeches in a single verse:

> The voice of the dove is calling,
> it says: "It's day! Where are you?"
> O bird, stop scolding me!
> I found my lover on his bed,
> my heart was overjoyed.

Each said, "I shall not leave you,
my hand is your hand;
you and I shall wander
in all the places fair."
He makes the foremost of women,
he does not aggrieve my heart.
(Lichtheim, 2:190–91)

The woman in our quatrain could similarly be quoting another's speech, in her case mocking her lover's internal debates as she takes direct action and approaches him. This reading allows us to give, as Gardiner already did, full force to the emphatic phrasing "*it is I who* come to you," for which the original employs the independent pronoun *inek*, a stronger statement than a simple "I could" would be. Such a reading would assort well with other poems in which a woman speaker impulsively rushes to her beloved without pausing to finish dressing:

My heart remembers well your love.
One half of my temple was combed,
I came rushing to see you,
and I forgot my hair.
(Simpson, 305)

An example from Papyrus Chester Beatty itself, featuring another conversation with one's heart:

My heart flutters hastily
when I think of my love of you;
it lets me not act sensibly,
it leaps from its place.
It lets me not put on a dress,
nor wrap my scarf around me;
I put no paint upon my eyes,
I'm not even anointed.
"Don't wait, go there," says it to me,
as often as I think of him.
My heart, don't act so stupidly,
why do you play the fool?
(Lichtheim, 2:183–84)

With such a context in mind, we can render our quatrain entirely within the woman's voice, using reported speech to avoid violating any grammatical norms:

Why do you dispute with your heart—
"To embrace her is all my desire"?
As Amun lives, it is I who come to you,
my clothing on my arm.

Very well. It appears that two quite different options work grammatically and make sense within the context of the surviving corpus of Egyptian poetry: the poem records either a man's internal debate and resolution or a woman's decisive action. Is there any way to decide between these renderings?

In principle, the question of gender should be readily answered by the text itself, since the pronouns "I" and "my" are written with the hieroglyph of a seated man or a seated

ir-m djed-ki r m-ha't ib-k
why do you speak words in front of your heart

m-sa' st n-i kniw st
satiety it is to me embracing her

wa'h Imn inek iw n-k
endures Amun it is I who come to you

iw ta-y mss hr ka'ht-i
there is my tunic on my shoulder/arm

woman, depending on the gender in question. Looking at the text, this proves to be the case, as can be seen in Gardiner's hieroglyphic transcription:[1]

The problem here is that the signs are inconsistent: "It is I who come to you" in the third line is written with a seated woman as the "I," but then in the next line, "my" tunic has a *man* as its determinative. The photographic plate of the original indicates that Gardiner correctly transcribed these signs. So how should we resolve this inconsistency?

One way or another, the scribe has made a slip of the brush. Egyptian scribes were notoriously casual in their uses of pronouns, and furthermore in hieratic scripts the seated man and the seated woman are often much less distinct than they appear in their full-dress hieroglyphic form. This scribe, as it happens, draws them almost identically: in each case the figure is shown as a single oval shape with a curving stroke at the bottom to indicate the leg and foot. A seated woman differs, in his orthography, only by having an added stroke at the top to indicate her headdress. This stroke is clearly present in the "I" of line three, but just as clearly absent in the "my" of "my tunic." In the case of the final "my" of "my shoulder," there is an ambiguous stroke that may well be the headdress but might also simply be part of the next sign over.

Ordinarily, the speaker's clothing would resolve this matter, as most Egyptian garments were worn only by one sex or the other. Unfortunately, it so happens that the *mss*, a kind of tunic, is the one garment that was commonly worn by *both* sexes.[2] This variability hasn't stopped the poem's translators from making a more specific choice of garment, always one that reinforces their interpretation of the speaker's gender. Thus Simpson makes the *mss* a man's loincloth, while another translator, Barbara Fowler, makes the speaker a woman and the garment a dress:

While you argued with your heart—
    "Take her in your embrace"—
by Amon, I came to you,
    My dress still disarranged.
(*Love Lyrics of Ancient Egypt*, 71)

Our mistake, however, may lie in assuming that we need to make a definite choice. The scribe's casual alternation of genders may reflect an openness in the poem's original usage. The Egyptian lyrics we have appear to have been composed as songs, and the singer's gender is often left unspecified. Perhaps we need to think of this poem less in a context of

Heine and Shakespeare and more in a context of Willie Nelson and Linda Ronstadt. The understood gender would then change simply according to who is singing the song at a given time. The best translation could be on that leaves the option open, freeing us to envision the scene whichever way our inclinations lead us at a given time.

A harder problem is actually posed by the term *mss* itself, as we have no equivalent garment. Janssen says that a comparable item is still in use in some Arab countries and proposes that "the modern word *ghalabiyah* is the best translation" (*Commodity Prices*, 260), yet this solution works only for speakers of Arabic and would produce an oddly ethnographic effect if used in an English translation. "Tunic" has an all too Roman sound to it, while a more neutral term like "garment" lacks the vivid specificity of a particular item of clothing. Lichtheim's "my cloak over my arm" fails even to suggest a state of undress, giving more the impression of a visit to the dry cleaner. From this point of view, Simpson's "loincloth," thought strictly speaking inaccurate ("loincloth" is *da'iw*, not *mss*), is an effective choice, giving the line a strong erotic charge while also preserving a sense of cultural distance.

There are limits to the extent to which a translation can or even should attempt to convey the full cultural specificity of the original, though one strand of translation theory has always dreamed of a mystical mirroring process that would somehow bring the original work, in entire, into the translation. This utopian view was eloquently expressed by Walter Benjamin in "The Task of the Translator":

> A real translation is transparent; it does not cover the original, does not block its light, but allows the pure language, as though reinforced by its own medium, to shine upon the original all the more fully. This may be achieved, above all, by a literal rendering of the syntax which proves words rather than sentences to be the primary element of the translator. For if the sentence is the wall before the language of the original, literalness is the arcade. (79)

Benjamin himself was wise enough not to attempt to actually produce such a union of original and translation, though he ends his essay by invoking interlinear Bible translations as a radical alternative to always-incomplete adaptive translations. Others, however, have attempted literalistic translations that convey qualities of the original text so faithfully that they are hardly readable at all. At the extreme, this approach leads to Nabokov's awkwardly phrased and monumentally annotated translation of Pushkin's *Eugene Onegin*, which resolutely attempts to reproduce Russian grammatical effects and to convey all the nuances that each word would have in the original. As he wrote while working on the project, "I want translations with copious footnotes, footnotes reaching up like skyscrapers to the top of this or that page so as to leave only the gleam of one textual line between commentary and eternity" ("Problems of Translation," 83).

In Nabokov's *Onegin*, the actual poem takes up only one-seventh of the edition's fourteen hundred pages. It was published in a beautiful two-volume edition in Princeton's Bollingen Series, but even Princeton hesitated to impose the full weight of Nabokov's erudition on the reader; the poem appears in a slender first volume, while Nabokov's notes (actually the best part of his edition) are relegated to the massive volume 2. Yet Nabokov himself could translate works very differently when he was thinking in terms of world literature rather than in terms of re-creating the vanished Russia of his past: in his wonderfully inventive 1923 Russian translation of *Alice in Wonderland*, he eschewed footnotes and gave himself over to the delights of creating Russian equivalents for Carroll's seemingly untranslatable chains of puns. Thus, when the Mock Turtle describes his studies in "reeling and writhing," Nabokov has him study *chesat' i pitat'* (combing and feeding) instead of *chitat' i pisat'* (reading and writing).[3] The Mock Turtle himself becomes "Chepupakha," an elegant combination of *chepukha* (nonsense) and *cherepakha* (tortoise). In such puns Nabokov made no effort to have his translation convey the flavor of life—or of soup—in Victorian England, but sought instead to see Carroll's uncanny wonderland through a Russian lens.

Already foreshadowing the fractured universes of novels like *Pale Fire* and *Ada*, Nabokov's translation hovers between Russian and English worlds. Later in this scene, for instance, he slyly inserts a reference to the text's original language: when the Mock Turtle regrets not having taken "Laughing and Grief" with the classics instructor, Nabokov borrows a pun from the Venerable Bede, and has him sigh over never having studied *Angel'skii yazik*, "the Angels' language," instead of "the English language," *Angliiskii yazik* (86). A striking transposition: living in exile in Berlin at the time he made this translation from his future literary language back into his lost native tongue, Nabokov has the Mock Turtle unwittingly reflect an exile's anxiety, regretting that he cannot understand the angelic analog of the language from which he has himself been translated. Neither a mere linguistic compromise nor an arbitrary transposition, this moment in the text can stand as an emblem for the way in which sensitive readers bring a work variously to life through personal associations: English and Russian *are* for Nabokov the true languages of laughing and grief.

The Egyptian poem can be presented as a document of Ramesside culture, complete with pyramids of footnotes, as in Gardiner's original edition, and yet for the nonspecialist reader the supplying of the full wealth of relevant information would entail a loss of primary experience. By this I don't at all mean that a translation should wrench the poem outright into our own world and our own terms; rather, I mean that the original context should not be made to overpower us, interfering with our engagement with the fictive world the poem creates for us to enter. To appreciate the Egyptian poem, it is important to know that the speaker is undressing, but it doesn't greatly matter just what garment the speaker is stripping off. The garment: something off-white, made of cotton or linen, its actual shape and stitching unspecified. It would add little to our appreciation of the poem to have a pocket insert in our volume with a fabric sample. Indeed, loading us up with much information of this sort would make it hard to experience the poem as literature, turning it instead into an object of study: just what we want if we're writing a book on Ramesside Commodity Prices, but not what we need to enjoy the poem as such.

Our understanding of the poem can, of course, be further enriched by more contextual knowledge, and anyone who falls in love with a body of work from another time or place will wish to learn more about the works' context. Some literary works, indeed, may be so closely dependent on detailed, culture-specific knowledge that they can only be meaningful to members of the originating culture or to specialists in that culture; these are works that remain within the sphere of national literature and never achieve an effective life in world literature. Yet many works, like our present quatrain, already begin to work their magic before all their references are understood and all their cultural assumptions are elucidated. Like the quatrain as a whole, its individual elements float between Nakht-Sobek's world and our own: however *mss* may be translated, most modern readers will be unable to visualize the ancient garment in all its authentic particularity. Yet as long as the translation doesn't impose a wholesale modernization, we won't assimilate the *mss* directly to our contemporary experience; we will remain aware that we're reading an ancient poem. Whatever we think a *mss* is, we won't envision it as a Gortex windbreaker, though this might be the modern equivalent of the original item. All the same, we can never hold the poem entirely away from our own experience, nor should we. As we read, we triangulate not only between ancient and modern worlds but also between general and personal meanings: however *mss* is translated, different readers will visualize it very differently, and this variability helps the poem to resonate with memories from the reader's own life.

NOTES

1. The papyrus is actually written in cursive "hieratic," an abbreviated, rapidly written script that employs many simplifications of characters. Intensive study of a given scribe's style is needed to make out many readings in hieratic texts, and Egyptologists usually rely on hieroglyphic transcriptions made by the person who publishes the text. Gardiner's fascination with our scribe's orthography is based on many hours of studying his style.

2. A detailed discussion of the *mss* is found in J. J. Janssen, *Commodity Prices from the Rammesid Period: An Economic Study of the Village of Necropolis Workmen at Thebes* (Leiden: Brill, 1975). Appropriately for our quatrain, Janssen notes that it was "worn mostly in the evenings as a protection against the cold." This would suggest that rather than leaving home naked, the speaker has entered his/her beloved's house at night, undressing while entering the bedroom. Several poems show the speaker making a surprise visit to the beloved's home.

3. Lewis Carroll, *Аня въ странв чудесъ*: the Nabokov Russian translation of Lewis Carroll's *Alice in Wonderland*, Tr. "V. Sirin" (Vladimir Nabokov). 1923. Repr. New York: Dover, 1976.

CONTRIBUTORS

M. H. Abrams is known primarily for his work in British Romanticism and for his edition of the *Norton Anthology of English Literature.* His books include *The Mirror and the Lamp: Romantic Theory and the Critical Tradition* (1953), *Natural Supernaturalism: Tradition and Revolution in Romantic Literature* (1973), and *The Correspondent Breeze: Essays on English Romanticism* (1984). He is Professor Emeritus at Cornell University.

Theodor W. Adorno (1903–1969) was a leading member of the Frankfurt School of critical theory and author of *The Dialectic of Enlightenment* (with Max Horkheimer, 1944), *Minima Moralia: Reflections from Damaged Life* (1951), *Notes to Literature* (1958), and *Aesthetic Theory* (1970), among many other books and essays.

Giorgio Agamben is an Italian continental philosopher who teaches at the Universita IUAV di Venezia, the College Internationale de Philosophie in Paris, and the European Graduate School in Saas-Fee, Switzerland. His books include *Stanzas: Word and Phantasm in Western Culture* (1992), *Homo Sacer: Sovereign Power and Bare Life* (1998), *The End of the Poem: Studies in Poetics* (1999), and *State of Exception* (2005).

Charles Altieri is the Rachel Stageberg Anderson Chair in the Department of English at the University of California, Berkeley. His works include *Self and Sensibility in Contemporary American Poetry* (1984), *Canons and Consequences* (1990), *The Particulars of Rapture: An Aesthetics of the Affects* (2003), and *The Art of Modern American Poetry* (2005).

Mikhail Bakhtin (1895–1975) was a Russian philosopher, literary critic, and linguist. His works include *The Dialogic Imagination* (1930; 1981), *Rabelais and His World* (1941–1965; 1993), *Problems of Dostoevksy's Poetics* (1984), and *Speech Genres and Other Late Essays* (1986).

Monroe Beardsley (1915–1985) is best known for his work in aesthetics. His philosophical works include *Aesthetics* (1958), *Philosophical Thinking* (1965), and *Thinking Straight* (1975). With W. K. Wimsatt, he published *The Verbal Icon* (1954).

Walter Benjamin (1892–1940) was a German literary theorist, philosopher, and social critic associated with the Frankfurt School. His works include *The Origin of German*

Tragic Drama (1928), and *The Work of Art in the Age of Mechanical Reproducibility* (1936). His most important work was an unfinished project entitled *Passagenwerk*, or the Arcades Project, a collection of writings on city life in Paris in the nineteenth century.

HAROLD BLOOM is the Sterling Professor of Humanities at Yale University. His books on poetry include *Shelley's Mythmaking* (1959), *The Visionary Company* (1961), *The Anxiety of Influence* (1973), *A Map of Misreading* (1975), *Agon: Towards a Theory of Revision* (1982), *Ruin the Sacred Truths: Poetry and Belief from the Bible to the Present* (1989), and *How to Read and Why* (2000).

CLEANTH BROOKS (1906–1994) was the Gray Professor of Rhetoric at Yale University and a central figure in the formation of American New Criticism. His books include *Understanding Poetry* (1938), *Modern Poetry and the Tradition* (1939), *The Well-Wrought Urn: Studies in the Structure of Poetry* (1947), and *The Language of the American South* (1985).

REUBEN BROWER (1908–1970) was an influential late New Critic who taught at Amherst College, and at Harvard University as Cabot Professor of English Literature. His books include *The Fields of Light: An Experiment in Critical Reading* (1951) and *The Poetry of Robert Frost* (1963), and he edited *Forms of Lyric* (1970).

RALPH COHEN is William R. Kenan, Jr. Professor Emeritus at University of Virginia and currently Provost Distinguished Professor at James Madison University and founding editor of *New Literary History: A Journal of Theory and Interpretation*. In the field of poetics he has published *The Art of Discrimination* (1964) and numerous essays on genre theory.

JONATHAN CULLER succeeded M. H. Abrams as Class of 1916 Professor of English and Comparative Literature at Cornell University. He is the author of many books on literary theory and criticism, including *Structuralist Poetics: Structuralism, Linguistics, and the Study of Literature* (1982) and *On Deconstruction: Theory and Criticism after Structuralism* (1983). He is completing a book entitled *Theory of the Lyric*.

DAVID DAMROSCH is Professor of Comparative Literature at Harvard University and editor of the *Longman Anthology of World Literature* (2004), *Teaching World Literature* (2009), and the *Princeton Sourcebook in Comparative Literature* (2009). He is also the author of *What Is World Literature?* (2003), *The Buried Book: The Loss and Rediscovery of the Great Epic of Gilgamesh* (2007), and *How to Read World Literature* (2008).

PAUL DE MAN (1919–1983) was Sterling Professor of Humanities in the Department of Comparative Literature at Yale University. His works include *Allegories of Reading* (1979), *Blindness and Insight* (1983), *The Rhetoric of Romanticism* (1984), and *The Resistance to Theory* (1986).

JACQUES DERRIDA (1930–2004) was a French philosopher associated with poststructuralism and what came to be known as deconstruction. He was the director of studies at the École des Hautes Études en Sciences Sociales in Paris. In the United States, he was visiting professor at several universities and Professor of Humanities at University of California, Irvine from 1986 to 2004. His books include *Of Grammatology* (1976), *Writing and Difference* (1978), *Dissemination* (1981), *Margins of Philosophy* (1982), *The Post Card* (1987), *Acts of Literature* (1992), and many others.

HEATHER DUBROW is John D. Boyd, SJ, Chair in the Poetic Imagination at Fordham University and the author of six scholarly books, most recently *The Challenges of Or-*

pheus: Lyric Poetry and Early Modern England (2008), an edition of *As You Like It*, and numerous essays on lyric poetry, pedagogy, and other subjects. A collection of her own poetry, *Forms and Hollows*, has been published by Cherry Grove Collections. She is also the director of the Poets Out Loud reading series at Fordham.

Craig Dworkin is the author of *Reading the Illegible* (2003) and *There is No Medium* (2013) and the editor of five volumes, including *The Consequence of Innovation: 21st-Century Poetics* (2008) and, with Marjorie Perloff, *The Sound of Poetry / The Poetry of Sound* (2009). He teaches at the University of Utah where he curates the Eclipse archive http://english.utah.edu/eclipse.

T. S. Eliot (1888–1965) was a poet, literary critic, and playwright. His works of criticism include *The Use of Poetry and the Use of Criticism* (1933), *The Three Voices of Poetry* (1954), and *On Poetry and Poets* (1957).

Stanley Fish is the Davidson-Kahn Distinguished University Professor and Professor of Law at Florida International University as well as Dean Emeritus of the College of Liberal Arts and Sciences at the University of Illinois at Chicago. His publications in the field of poetics include *Surprised by Sin: The Reader in "Paradise Lost"* (1967), *Self-Consuming Artifacts: The Experience of Seventeenth-Century Literature* (1972), *Is There a Text in this Class? The Authority of Interpretive Communities* (1980), and most recently, *Versions of Antihumanism: Milton and Others* (2012).

Northrop Frye (1912–1991) was a Canadian literary critic and influential literary theorist who taught at the University of Toronto. In developing a theory of archetypes as conceptual framework for the study of literature, he published many books, including *Anatomy of Criticism* (1957), *Fables of Identity* (1963), *The Secular Scripture* (1976), *The Great Code* (1982), and *Words with Power* (1990).

Gérard Genette is a French literary theorist and professor of French literature at the Sorbonne in Paris. He is associated with the structuralist movement, and co-founder with Tzvetan Todorov of the journal *Poetique*. Among his works translated into English are *Narrative Discourse* (trans. 1980), *The Architext* (trans. 1992), *Mimologics* (trans. 1995), *Palimpsests* (trans. 1997), and *Paratexts* (trans. 1997).

Sandra M. Gilbert, Professor Emerita of English at the University of California, Davis, is an influential critic and poet who has published widely in the fields of feminist literary criticism and theory. In addition to publishing her own poetry and editing anthologies dedicated to women poets, she is well known for her critical collaboration with Susan Gubar, with whom she co-authored *Madwoman in the Attic* (1979) and a critical trilogy, *No Man's Land: The Place of the Woman Writer in the Twentieth Century* (1988–94).

Stathis Gourgouris is Professor of Classics, English, and Comparative Literature and Society and Director of the Institute of Comparative Literature and Society at Columbia University. He is the author of *Dream Nation* (1996) and *Does Literature Think?* (2003) and editor of *Freud and Fundamentalism* (2010) and *Lessons in Secular Criticism* (2013). He is currently completing two additional works of secular criticism, *The Perils of the One* and *Nothing Sacred*.

Roland Greene is the author of *Five Words: Critical Semantics in the Age of Shakespeare and Cervantes* (2013), *Unrequited Conquests: Love and Empire in the Colonial Americas* (1999), and *Post-Petrarchism: Origins and Innovations of the Western Lyric Sequence* (1991). He served as editor-in-chief of the fourth edition of the *Princeton Encyclo-*

pedia of Poetry and Poetics (2012) and is the founder and co-chair of the Workshop in Poetics at Stanford University, where he is Mark Pigott OBE Professor in the School of Humanities and Sciences.

ALLEN GROSSMAN is an American poet and critic who taught poetry and poetics as Andrew W. Mellon Professor in the Humanities at The Johns Hopkins University. His publications include *Poetic Knowledge in the Early Yeats* (1969), *The Sighted Singer* (1992), *The Long Schoolroom* (1997), and numerous prize-winning volumes of poetry.

SUSAN GUBAR is Distinguished Professor Emeritus at Indiana University. Together with Sandra Gilbert she published *The Madwoman in the Attic* (1979) and a critical trilogy entitled *No Man's Land: The Place of the Woman Writer in the Twentieth Century* (1988–94) and co-edited the *Norton Anthology of Literature by Women*. Her other publications include *Racechanges* (1997), *Critical Condition: Feminism at the Turn of the Century* (2000), and *Poetry after Auschwitz* (2003).

MARTIN HEIDEGGER (1889–1976) was a German philosopher who drew on the tradition of hermeneutics and phenomenology to explore the question of Being. His publications include *Being and Time* (1923), *Kant and the Problem of Metaphysics* (1927), *Identity and Difference* (1955–57), *On the Way to Language* (1959) and various essays on poetry and aesthetics.

VIRGINIA JACKSON is UCI Chair in Rhetoric in the Department of English at the University of California, Irvine, where she runs the Poetics|history|Theory@uci series. She is the author of *Dickinson's Misery: A Theory of Lyric Reading* (2005) and *Before Modernism* (2014).

ROMAN JAKOBSON (1896–1982) was a Russian linguist and literary theorist who taught at Harvard University after escaping from Prague during World War II. He is a pivotal figure in the development and dissemination of structuralism. His major publications include *Questions de Poetique* (1973), *Six Lectures of Sound and Meaning* (1978), *The Framework of Language* (1980) and *Verbal Art, Verbal Sign, Verbal Time* (1985).

FREDRIC JAMESON is William A. Lane Professor of Literature at Duke University and an American literary critic specializing in Marxist political theory. His publications include *Marxism and Form* (1971), *The Prison-House of Language* (1972), *The Political Unconscious* (1981), *Postmodernism: The Cultural Capital of Late Modernism* (1991), and *A Singular Modernity* (2002).

SIMON JARVIS is the Gorley Putt Professor of Poetry and Poetics at the University of Cambridge. His publications include *Wordsworth's Philosophic Song* (2007), many essays on the poetics of verse and on philosophical aesthetics, and several volumes of poetry.

BARBARA JOHNSON (1947–2009) was professor of English and Comparative Literature at Harvard University. Her publications include *The Critical Difference* (1980), *A World of Difference* (1989), *The Wake of Deconstruction* (1994), *Mother Tongues* (2003), and *Persons and Things* (2008).

W. R. JOHNSON is John Matthews Manly Professor of Classics and Comparative Literature, University of Chicago, Emeritus. His recent books include *Lucretius and the Modern World* (2000) and *A Latin Lover in Ancient Rome: Readings in Propertius and His Genre.*

PHILIPPE LACOUE-LABARTHE (1940–2007) was a French philosopher and literary critic also known for his translations of Benjamin, Celan, Heidegger, Hölderlin, and Nietzsche. His books include *The Literary Absolute: The Theory of Literature in German Romanti-*

cism (with Jean-Luc Nancy), *The Subject of Philosophy*, *Typography: Mimesis, Philosophy, Politics*, and *Heidegger and the Politics of Poetry*.

SETH LERER is Distinguished Professor of Literature and Dean of Arts and Humanities at the University of California at San Diego. He was awarded the Harry Levin Prize of the American Comparative Literature Association for *Error and the Academic Self* (2002). His *Children's Literature: A Reader's History from Aesop to Harry Potter* (2008) won the National Book Critics Circle Award and the Truman Capote Prize in Literary Criticism.

DREW MILNE is a contemporary British poet and scholar who teaches at Cambridge University. He has edited *Modern Critical Thought* (2003) and, with Terry Eagleton, *Marxist Literary Theory* (1996) and published several volumes of poetry, as well as essays on drama, critical theory, and poetics.

EARL MINER (1927–2004) was professor of Comparative Literature at Princeton University. In addition to books on Japanese poetry and early modern English poetry, he published *Comparative Poetics: An Intercultural Essay on Theories of Literature* (1990).

AAMIR R. MUFTI teaches postcolonial studies and critical theory in the Department of Comparative Literature at UCLA. He is the author of *Enlightenment in the Colony: The Jewish Question and the Crisis of Postcolonial Culture*, various essays on secular criticism, exile, and modern aesthetics, and a forthcoming book on the colonial reinvention of Islamic traditions.

CHRISTOPHER NEALON is Professor of English at The Johns Hopkins University. He is the author of *Foundlings: Lesbian and Gay Historical Emotion before Stonewall* (2001), and *The Matter of Capital: Poetry and Crisis in The American Century* (2011). His volumes of poetry include *The Joyous Age* (2004), *Plummet* (2009), and *The Dial* (2012).

MARJORIE PERLOFF is Professor of English Emerita at Stanford University and Florence Scott Professor of English Emerita at the University of Southern California. She is the author of many books on contemporary poetry and poetics, including *The Poetics of Indeterminacy: Rimbaud to Cage* (1981), *Radical Artifice Writing Poetry in the Age of Media* (1992), and most recently, *Unoriginal Genius: Poetry by Other Means in the 21st Century* (2010).

YOPIE PRINS is Professor of English and Comparative Literature at the University Michigan, where she teaches lyric theory and nineteenth-century historical poetics as well as classical reception and translation studies. She is the author of *Victorian Sappho* (1999), *Ladies' Greek: Translations of Tragedy* (2014), and a series of essays on Victorian poetry and prosody.

JAHAN RAMAZANI is Edgar F. Shannon Professor of English at the University of Virginia. He is the author of *Poetry and Its Others: News, Prayer, Song, and the Dialogue of Genres* (2013), *A Transnational Poetics* (2009), *The Hybrid Muse: Postcolonial Poetry in English* (2001); *Poetry of Mourning: The Modern Elegy from Hardy to Heaney* (1994), and *Yeats and the Poetry of Death: Elegy, Self-Elegy, and the Sublime* (1990). An associate editor of *The Princeton Encyclopedia of Poetry and Poetics* (2012), he co-edited the most recent editions of *The Norton Anthology of Modern and Contemporary Poetry* (2003) and *The Twentieth Century and After* in *The Norton Anthology of English Literature* (2006, 2012).

I. A. RICHARDS (1893–1979) was an English literary critic who taught at Cambridge University and at Harvard University. He developed the concept of close reading called "practical criticism" and imagined a controlled language called Basic English. His publications include *The Meaning of Meaning* (with C.K. Ogden, 1923), *Principles of Literary Criticism* (1924), *Science and Poetry* (1926), and *Practical Criticism* (1929).

Michael Riffaterre (1924–2006) was professor of French at Columbia University and a literary critic and theorist associated with structuralism. His publications include *Semiotics of Poetry* (1978), *Text Production* (trans. 1983), and *Fictional Truth* (1990).

Juliana Spahr is an American poet, critic, and editor, and professor of English at Mills College, where she holds the Aurelia Henry Reinhardt Chair. In addition to award-winning publications in poetry, she is the author of *Everybody's Autonomy: Connective Reading and Collective Identity* (2001) and co-editor of *A Poetics of Criticism* (1993), and *Poetry and Pedagogy: The Challenge of the Contemporary* (2006).

Herbert F. Tucker holds the John C. Coleman Chair in English at the University of Virginia, where he also serves as associate editor for *New Literary History*. His books on Robert Browning (1980) and Alfred Tennyson (1988) treat lyric themes, and during his long affair with epic he has stayed faithful to lyric, in his fashion, with occasional essays in nineteenth-century poetry and poetics.

Helen Vendler is Arthur Kingsley Porter University Professor at Harvard University. Her many books include *Invisible Listeners: Lyric Intimacy in Herbert, Whitman, and Ashbery* (2005), *Poets Thinking: Pope, Whitman, Dickinson, Yeats* (2004), *The Art of Shakespeare's Sonnets* (1997), *The Odes of John Keats* (1983), *On Extended Wings: Wallace Stevens' Longer Poems* (1969).

Nancy J. Vickers taught French, Italian, and Comparative Literature before serving as president of Bryn Mawr College for eleven years. She is co-editor of *Rewriting the Renaissance: The Discourses of Sexual Difference in Early Modern Europe* (1986) and *A New History of French Literature* (1989).

Robert Penn Warren (1905–1989) was an American poet laureate, novelist, and literary critic. As one of the founders of American New Criticism, he was co-author with Cleanth Brooks of an influential textbook, *Understanding Poetry* (1939).

René Wellek (1903–1995) was active among the Prague school linguists before moving, during World War II, to teach at the University of Iowa and then at Yale University. As a founding figure for the modern study of comparative literature in the United States, he published *Theory of Literature* together with Austin Warren (1949), and numerous books on the concepts and histories of modern criticism.

W. K. Wimsatt (1907–1975) was a literary theorist, critic, and professor of English at Yale University. His major works include *The Verbal Icon: Studies in the Meaning of Poetry* (1954), *Hateful Contraries: Studies in Literature and Criticism* (1965), and *Literary Criticism* (together with Cleanth Brooks, 1957).

Thomas E. Yingling (1950–1992) taught American studies at Syracuse University and was a leading figure in gay and lesbian studies when he died as a consequence of AIDS in 1992. A selection of his writings, entitled *AIDS and the National Body* and edited by Robyn Wiegman, was published posthumously in 1997.

SOURCE ACKNOWLEDGMENTS

M. H. Abrams, "The Lyric as Poetic Norm," in *The Mirror and the Lamp: Romantic Theory and the Critical Tradition* (Oxford: Oxford University Press), 84–88, 350–51. Copyright © 1953 Oxford University Press, Inc. Used by permission of Oxford University Press, Inc.

Theodor W. Adorno, "On Lyric Poetry and Society," in *Notes to Literature* I, ed. R. Tiedemann, trans. Shierry Weber Nicholson (New York: Columbia University Press, 1991), 37–54. Copyright © 1991 Columbia University Press. Reprinted with permission of the publisher.

Giorgio Agamben, "The End of the Poem," from *The End of the Poem: Studies in Poetics*, translated by Daniel Heller-Roazen (Palo Alto, CA: Stanford University Press, 1999), 109–15. Copyright © 1999 by the Board of Trustees of Leland Stanford Jr. University. All rights reserved. Used with the permission of Stanford University Press, www.sup.org.

Charles Altieri, "What Is Living and What Is Dead in American Postmodernism: Establishing the Contemporaneity of Some American Poetry," in *Critical Inquiry* 22.4 (Summer 1996): 775–89. Copyright © 1996 University of Chicago Press. Reprinted with permission of the University of Chicago Press and the author.

Mikhail Bakhtin, "The Problem of Speech Genres," in *Speech Genres and Other Late Essays*, trans. Vern W. McGee, ed. Caryl Emerson and Michael Holquist (Austin: University of Texas Press, 1986), 60–69, 94–99. Copyright © 1986. By permission of the University of Texas Press.

Walter Benjamin, "On Some Motifs in Baudelaire," in *Illuminations*, ed. Hannah Arendt, trans. Harry Zohn (New York: Schocken, 1969), 155–70, 192–94. Copyright © 1955 by Suhrkamp Verlag, Frankfurt a.M., English translation by Harry Zohn copyright © 1968 and renewed 1996 by Houghton Mifflin Harcourt Publishing Company, reprinted by permission of Houghton Mifflin Harcourt Publishing Company and Writer's House LLC.

Harold Bloom, "The Breaking of Form," in *Deconstruction and Criticism* (New York: Seabury Press, 1979), 1–22. Copyright © 1979, 2004. Reprinted by permission of the Continuum International Publishing Group.

Cleanth Brooks and Robert Penn Warren, introduction to *Understanding Poetry: An Anthology for College Students* (New York: H. Holt, 1938), 1–25. Copyright © 1938, 1976 Heinle/Arts & Sciences, a part of Cengage Learning, Inc. Reproduced by permission. www.cengage.com/permissions.

Reuben Brower, "The Speaking Voice," in *Fields of Light: An Experiment in Critical Reading* (Oxford: Oxford University Press, 1951), 3–16. Copyright © 1951 Oxford University Press, Inc. By Permission of Oxford University Press, Inc.

Ralph Cohen, "History and Genre," *New Literary History* 17. 2 (Winter 1986): 203–18. Copyright © 1986 New Literary History, The University of Virginia. Reprinted with permission of The Johns Hopkins University Press.

Jonathan Culler, "Lyric, History, and Genre," *New Literary History* 40.4 (Autumn 2009): 879–99. Copyright © 2010 New Literary History, The University of Virginia. Reprinted with permission of The Johns Hopkins University Press.

David Damrosch, "Love in the Necropolis" in *What Is World Literature?* (Princeton: Princeton University Press, 2003), 147–59. © 2003 Princeton University Press. Reprinted by permission of Princeton University Press.

Paul de Man, "Anthropomorphism and Trope in the Lyric," in *The Rhetoric of Romanticism* (New York: Columbia University Press, 1984), 239–62, 315. Copyright © 1984 Columbia University Press. Reprinted with permission of the publisher.

Jacques Derrida, "Che cos'è la poesia?" in *A Derrida Reader: Between the Blinds*, ed. and trans. Peggy Kamuf (New York: Columbia University Press, 1991), 219–37. Copyright © 1991 Columbia University Press. Reprinted with permission of the publisher.

Heather Dubrow, "Lyric Forms," in *The Cambridge Companion to English Literature, 1500–1600*, ed. Arthur F. Kinney (Cambridge: Cambridge University Press, 2000), 178–99. Copyright © 2000 Cambridge University Press. Reprinted with the permission of Cambridge University Press.

Craig Dworkin, "Lyric and the Hazard of Music." Earlier versions of portions first published as part of *The Sound of Poetry / The Poetry of Sound*, edited by Marjorie Perloff and Craig Dworkin (Chicago: University of Chicago Press, 2009) and PMLA (May 2008). Reprinted with permission of the copyright owner, The Modern Language Association of America.

T. S. Eliot, "The Three Voices of Poetry," in *On Poetry and Poets* (London: Faber and Faber, 1957), 89–102. Copyright © 1957 Faber and Faber, Ltd. Reprinted with the permission of Faber and Faber, Ltd. US copyright © 1957 by T. S. Eliot. Copyright © renewed by Valerie Eliot. Reprinted by permission of Farrar, Straus and Giroux, LLC.

Stanley Fish, "How to Recognize a Poem When You See One," in *Is There a Text in This Class? The Authority of Interpretive Communities* (Cambridge, MA: Harvard University Press, 1980), 322–37, 389–90. Copyright © 1980 by the President and Fellows of Harvard College. Reprinted by permission of the publisher.

Northrop Frye, "Theory of Genres," in *Anatomy of Criticism* (Princeton, NJ: Princeton University Press, 1957), 246–51, 151–61. Copyright © 1957 Princeton University Press, 1985 renewed PUP, 2000 paperback edition. Reprinted by permission of Princeton University Press.

Gérard Genette, "The Architext," in *The Architext: An Introduction*, trans. Jane E. Lewin (Berkeley: University of California Press, 1992), 1–12, 23–36, 60–67. Copyright © 1979 by Editions du Seuil, Paris. Copyright © 1992 by the Regents of the University of California. Reprinted by permission of the University of California Press.

Sandra M. Gilbert and Susan Gubar, "Gender, Creativity, and the Woman Poet," in *Shakespeare's Sisters: Feminist Essays on Women Poets*, ed. Sandra M. Gilbert and Susan Gubar (Bloomington: Indiana University Press, 1979), xv–xxiii. Copyright © 1979 by Sandra M. Gilbert and Susan Gubar. Reprinted with permission of Indiana University Press.

Stathis Gourgouris, "The Lyric in Exile," *Qui Parle* 14.2 (2004): 145–76. Reprinted by permission of the University of Nebraska Press, with revisions by author.

Roland Greene, "Inter-American Obversals: Allen Ginsberg and Haroldo de Campos Circa 1960," *XUL: 5 + 5* (2008), http://www.bc.edu/research/xul/5+5/greene.htm. Printed by permission of author.

Allen Grossman, "Summa Lyrica," *Western Humanities Review* 44.1 (Spring 1990): 4–27. Copyright © 1989 University of Utah. Reprinted by permission of the Western Humanities Review.

Martin Heidegger, "Poetically Man Dwells," in *Poetry, Language, Thought*, trans. Albert Hofstadter (New York: Harper and Row, 1971), 213–29. Copyright © 1971 by Martin Heidegger. Reprinted by permission of HarperCollins Publishers.

Roman Jakobson, "Closing Statement: Linguistics and Poetics," in *Style in Language*, ed. Thomas A. Sebeok (Cambridge, MA: MIT Press, 1960), 350–69. Copyright © 1960 Massachusetts Institute of Technology, by permission of The MIT Press.

Fredric Jameson, "Baudelaire as Modernist and Postmodernist: The Dissolution of the Referent and the Artificial 'Sublime,'" in *Lyric Poetry: Beyond New Criticism*, ed. Chaviva Hošek and Patricia Parker (Ithaca, NY: Cornell University Press, 1985), 247–63. Copyright © 1985 by Cornell University. Used by permission of the publisher, Cornell University Press.

Simon Jarvis, "Why Rhyme Pleases," *Thinking Verse* 1 (2011): 17–43, http://www.thinkingverse.com/issue01.html. Reprinted by permission of the author.

Barbara Johnson, "Anthropomorphism in Lyric and Law," *Yale Journal of Law and the Humanities* 10.2 (1998): 205–28. Reprinted by permission of The Yale Journal of Law and the Humanities.

Barbara Johnson, "Apostrophe, Animation, and Abortion," in *A World of Difference* (Baltimore: Johns Hopkins University Press, 1987), 184–99, 221–22. Copyright © 1987 The Johns Hopkins University Press. Reprinted with permission of The Johns Hopkins University Press.

W. R. Johnson, "On the Absence of Ancient Lyric Theory," in *The Idea of Lyric: Lyric Modes in Ancient and Modern Poetry* (Berkeley: University of California Press, 1982), 76–95. Reprinted by permission of the author.

Philippe Lacoue-Labarthe, "Two Poems by Paul Celan," from *Poetry as Experience*, trans. Andrea Tarnowski. Copyright © 1999 by the Board of Trustees of the Leland Stanford Jr. University; original © 1968 by Christian Bourgeois Editions. All right reserved. Used with the permission of Stanford University Press, www.sup.org.

Seth Lerer, "The Genre of the Grave and the Origins of Middle English Lyric," in *Modern Language Quarterly* 58.2 (1997): 127–33, 151–61. Copyright 1997, University of Washington. All rights reserved. Reprinted by permission of the publisher, Duke University Press.

Drew Milne, "In Memory of the Pterodactyl: The Limits of Lyric Humanism," *The Paper* 2 (September 2001): 16–29. Copyright © 2001 Drew Milne. Reprinted by permission of the author.

Earl Miner, "Why Lyric?" in *The Renewal of Song: Renovation in Lyric Conception and Practice*, ed. Earl Miner and Amiya Dev (Calcutta: Seagull Books, 2000), 1–21. Copyright © 2000 Seagull Books. Reprinted by permission of Seagull Books.

Aamir R. Mufti, "Towards a Lyric History of India," *boundary 2* 31.2 (2004): 245–63, 270–74. Copyright © 2004, Duke University Press. All rights reserved. Reprinted by permission of the publisher.

Christopher Nealon, "The Matter of Capital, or Catastrophe and Textuality," in *The Matter of Capital: Poetry and Crisis in the American Century* (Cambridge, MA: Harvard University Press, 2011), 1–19. Copyright © 2011 by the President and Fellows of Harvard College. Reprinted by permission of the publisher.

Marjorie Perloff, "Can(n)on to the Right of Us, Can(n)on to the Left of Us: A Plea for Difference," *New Literary History* 18.3 (1987): 633–56. Copyright © 1987 New Literary History, The University of Virginia. Reprinted with permission of The Johns Hopkins University Press.

Jahan Ramazani, "Traveling Poetry," *MLQ* 68.2 (2007): 332–59. Copyright © 2007, University of Washington. All rights reserved. Reprinted by permission of the publisher, Duke University Press.

I. A. Richards, "The Analysis of a Poem" and "The Definition of a Poem," in *The Principles of Literary Criticism* (London: Routledge and Kegan Paul, 1924), 114–33, 223–27. Copyright © 2001 Taylor and Francis Group. Reprinted by permission of publisher.

Michael Riffaterre, "The Poem's Significance," in *Semiotics of Poetry* (Bloomington: Indiana University Press, 1978), 1–22. Copyright © 1978 by Michael Riffaterre. Reprinted with permission of Indiana University Press.

Juliana Spahr, introduction to *American Women Poets in the 21st Century: Where Lyric Meets Language* (Middletown, CT: Wesleyan University Press, 2002), 1–17. Copyright © 2002 by Wesleyan University Press. Reprinted by permission of Wesleyan University Press.

Herbert F. Tucker, "Dramatic Monologue and the Overhearing of Lyric," in *Lyric Poetry: Beyond New Criticism*, ed. Chaviva Hošek and Patricia Parker (Ithaca, NY: Cornell University Press, 1985), 226–43. Copyright © 1985 by Cornell University. Used by permission of the publisher, Cornell University Press.

Helen Vendler, introduction to *The Art of Shakespeare's Sonnets* (Cambridge, MA: The Belknap Press of Harvard University Press, 1997), 1–4, 14–17, 22–32. Copyright © 1997 by the President and Fellows of Harvard College. Reprinted by permission of the publisher.

Nancy J. Vickers, "Diana Described: Scattered Woman and Scattered Rhyme," *Critical Inquiry* 8.2 (Winter 1981): 265–79. Copyright © 1981 University of Chicago Press. Reprinted with permission of the University of Chicago Press and the author.

René Wellek, "Genre Theory, the Lyric, and *Erlebnis*," in *Festschrift für Richard Alewyn*, ed. Herbert Singer and Benno von Wiese (Cologne: Böhlau Verlag, 1967), 392–412. Copyright © by Böhlau Verlag GmbH & Cie, 1967. Reprinted by permission of the publisher.

W. K. Wimsatt and Monroe Beardsley, "The Intentional Fallacy," *The Sewanee Review* 54.3 (Summer 1946): 468–88. Copyright © 1946, 1974 by the University of the South. Reprinted with the permission of the editor.

Thomas E. Yingling, "The Homosexual Lyric," in *Hart Crane and the Homosexual Text: New Thresholds, New Anatomies* (Chicago: University of Chicago Press, 1990), 105–24, 143–44. Copyright © 1990 University of Chicago Press. Reprinted with permission of the University of Chicago Press.

INDEX OF AUTHORS AND WORKS